Volatility and Correlation
2nd Edition

Volatility and Correlation
2nd Edition
The Perfect Hedger and the Fox

Riccardo Rebonato

John Wiley & Sons, Ltd

Published 2004   John Wiley & Sons Ltd, The Atrium, Southern Gate, Chichester,
West Sussex PO19 8SQ, England

Telephone (+44) 1243 779777

Email (for orders and customer service enquiries): cs-books@wiley.co.uk
Visit our Home Page on www.wileyeurope.com or www.wiley.com

Reprinted May 2005, April 2006

Other Wiley Editorial Offices

John Wiley & Sons Inc., 111 River Street, Hoboken, NJ 07030, USA

Jossey-Bass, 989 Market Street, San Francisco, CA 94103-1741, USA

Wiley-VCH Verlag GmbH, Boschstr. 12, D-69469 Weinheim, Germany

John Wiley & Sons Australia Ltd, 33 Park Road, Milton, Queensland 4064, Australia

John Wiley & Sons (Asia) Pte Ltd, 2 Clementi Loop #02-01, Jin Xing Distripark, Singapore 129809

John Wiley & Sons Canada Ltd, 22 Worcester Road, Etobicoke, Ontario, Canada M9W 1L1

Wiley also publishes its books in a variety of electronic formats. Some content that appears in print may not be available in electronic books.

Library of Congress Cataloging-in-Publication Data

Rebonato, Riccardo.
Volatility and correlation: the perfect hedger and the fox/Riccardo
Rebonato – 2nd ed.
  p. cm.
  Rev. ed. of: Volatility and correlation in the pricing of equity. 1999.
  Includes bibliographical references and index.
  ISBN 0-470-09139-8 (cloth: alk. paper)
  1. Options (Finance) – Mathematical models. 2. Interest rate
futures – Mathematical models. 3. Securities – Prices – Mathematical models.
I. Rebonato, Riccardo. Volatility and correlation in the pricing of equity.
II. Title.
  HG6024.A3R43 2004
  332.64'53 – dc22

                                        2004004223

British Library Cataloguing in Publication Data

A catalogue record for this book is available from the British Library

ISBN 10: 0-470-09139-8 (HB)   ISBN 13: 978-0470-09139-5 (HB)

Typeset in 10/12 Times by Laserwords Private Limited, Chennai, India
Printed and bound in Great Britain by TJ International, Padstow, Cornwall
This book is printed on acid-free paper responsibly manufactured from sustainable forestry
in which at least two trees are planted for each one used for paper production.

To my parents
To Rosamund

Contents

Preface   **xxi**

  0.1   Why a Second Edition?   xxi

  0.2   What This Book Is *Not* About   xxiii

  0.3   Structure of the Book   xxiv

  0.4   The New Subtitle   xxiv

Acknowledgements   **xxvii**

I   Foundations   **1**

1   Theory and Practice of Option Modelling   **3**

  1.1   The Role of Models in Derivatives Pricing   3

      1.1.1   What Are Models For?   3

      1.1.2   The Fundamental Approach   5

      1.1.3   The Instrumental Approach   7

      1.1.4   A Conundrum (or, 'What is Vega Hedging For?')   8

  1.2   The Efficient Market Hypothesis and Why It Matters for Option Pricing   9

      1.2.1   The Three Forms of the EMH   9

      1.2.2   Pseudo-Arbitrageurs in Crisis   10

      1.2.3   Model Risk for Traders and Risk Managers   11

      1.2.4   The Parable of the Two Volatility Traders   12

  1.3   Market Practice   14

      1.3.1   Different Users of Derivatives Models   14

      1.3.2   In-Model and Out-of-Model Hedging   15

  1.4   The Calibration Debate   17

      1.4.1   Historical vs Implied Calibration   18

      1.4.2   The Logical Underpinning of the Implied Approach   19

      1.4.3   Are Derivatives Markets Informationally Efficient?   21

      1.4.4   Back to Calibration   26

      1.4.5   A Practical Recommendation   27

viii CONTENTS

1.5 Across-Markets Comparison of Pricing and Modelling Practices 27
1.6 Using Models 30

2 Option Replication **31**
2.1 The Bedrock of Option Pricing 31
2.2 The Analytic (PDE) Approach 32
   2.2.1 The Assumptions 32
   2.2.2 The Portfolio-Replication Argument (Deterministic Volatility) 32
   2.2.3 The Market Price of Risk with Deterministic Volatility 34
   2.2.4 Link with Expectations – the Feynman–Kac Theorem 36
2.3 Binomial Replication 38
   2.3.1 First Approach – Replication Strategy 39
   2.3.2 Second Approach – 'Naïve Expectation' 41
   2.3.3 Third Approach – 'Market Price of Risk' 42
   2.3.4 A Worked-Out Example 45
   2.3.5 Fourth Approach – Risk-Neutral Valuation 46
   2.3.6 Pseudo-Probabilities 48
   2.3.7 Are the Quantities π_1 and π_2 Really Probabilities? 49
   2.3.8 Introducing Relative Prices 51
   2.3.9 Moving to a Multi-Period Setting 53
   2.3.10 Fair Prices as Expectations 56
   2.3.11 Switching Numeraires and Relating Expectations Under Different Measures 58
   2.3.12 Another Worked-Out Example 61
   2.3.13 Relevance of the Results 64
2.4 Justifying the Two-State Branching Procedure 65
   2.4.1 How To Recognize a Jump When You See One 65
2.5 The Nature of the Transformation between Measures: Girsanov's Theorem 69
   2.5.1 An Intuitive Argument 69
   2.5.2 A Worked-Out Example 70
2.6 Switching Between the PDE, the Expectation and the Binomial Replication Approaches 73

3 The Building Blocks **75**
3.1 Introduction and Plan of the Chapter 75
3.2 Definition of Market Terms 75
3.3 Hedging Forward Contracts Using Spot Quantities 77
   3.3.1 Hedging Equity Forward Contracts 78
   3.3.2 Hedging Interest-Rate Forward Contracts 79
3.4 Hedging Options: Volatility of Spot and Forward Processes 80

3.5 The Link Between Root-Mean-Squared Volatilities and the Time-Dependence of Volatility 84

3.6 Admissibility of a Series of Root-Mean-Squared Volatilities 85

    3.6.1 The Equity/FX Case 85

    3.6.2 The Interest-Rate Case 86

3.7 Summary of the Definitions So Far 87

3.8 Hedging an Option with a Forward-Setting Strike 89

    3.8.1 Why Is This Option Important? (And Why Is it Difficult to Hedge?) 90

    3.8.2 Valuing a Forward-Setting Option 91

3.9 Quadratic Variation: First Approach 95

    3.9.1 Definition 95

    3.9.2 Properties of Variations 96

    3.9.3 First and Second Variation of a Brownian Process 97

    3.9.4 Links between Quadratic Variation and $\int_t^T \sigma(u)^2 \, \mathrm{d}u$ 97

    3.9.5 Why Quadratic Variation Is So Important (Take 1) 98

4 Variance and Mean Reversion in the Real and the Risk-Adjusted Worlds 101

4.1 Introduction and Plan of the Chapter 101

4.2 Hedging a Plain-Vanilla Option: General Framework 102

    4.2.1 Trading Restrictions and Model Uncertainty: Theoretical Results 103

    4.2.2 The Setting 104

    4.2.3 The Methodology 104

    4.2.4 Criterion for Success 106

4.3 Hedging Plain-Vanilla Options: Constant Volatility 106

    4.3.1 Trading the Gamma: One Step and Constant Volatility 108

    4.3.2 Trading the Gamma: Several Steps and Constant Volatility 114

4.4 Hedging Plain-Vanilla Options: Time-Dependent Volatility 116

    4.4.1 Views on Gamma Trading When the Volatility is Time Dependent 116

    4.4.2 Which View Is the Correct One? (and the Feynman–Kac Theorem Again) 119

4.5 Hedging Behaviour In Practice 121

    4.5.1 Analysing the Replicating Portfolio 121

    4.5.2 Hedging Results: the Time-Dependent Volatility Case 122

    4.5.3 Hedging with the Wrong Volatility 125

4.6 Robustness of the Black-and-Scholes Model 127

4.7 Is the Total Variance All That Matters? 130

4.8 Hedging Plain-Vanilla Options: Mean-Reverting Real-World Drift 131

4.9		Hedging Plain-Vanilla Options: Finite Re-Hedging Intervals Again	135
	4.9.1	The Crouhy–Galai Set-Up	135

5 Instantaneous and Terminal Correlation   **141**

5.1		Correlation, Co-Integration and Multi-Factor Models	141
	5.1.1	The Multi-Factor Debate	144
5.2		The Stochastic Evolution of Imperfectly Correlated Variables	146
5.3		The Role of Terminal Correlation in the Joint Evolution of Stochastic Variables	151
	5.3.1	Defining Stochastic Integrals	151
	5.3.2	Case 1: European Option, One Underlying Asset	153
	5.3.3	Case 2: Path-Dependent Option, One Asset	155
	5.3.4	Case 3: Path-Dependent Option, Two Assets	156
5.4		Generalizing the Results	162
5.5		Moving Ahead	164

II Smiles – Equity and FX   **165**

6 Pricing Options in the Presence of Smiles   **167**

6.1		Plan of the Chapter	167
6.2		Background and Definition of the Smile	168
6.3		Hedging with a Compensated Process: Plain-Vanilla and Binary Options	169
	6.3.1	Delta- and Vega-Hedging a Plain-Vanilla Option	169
	6.3.2	Pricing a European Digital Option	172
6.4		Hedge Ratios for Plain-Vanilla Options in the Presence of Smiles	173
	6.4.1	The Relationship Between the True Call Price Functional and the Black Formula	174
	6.4.2	Calculating the Delta Using the Black Formula and the Implied Volatility	175
	6.4.3	Dependence of Implied Volatilities on the Strike and the Underlying	176
	6.4.4	Floating and Sticky Smiles and What They Imply about Changes in Option Prices	178
6.5		Smile Tale 1: 'Sticky' Smiles	180
6.6		Smile Tale 2: 'Floating' Smiles	182
	6.6.1	Relevance of the Smile Story for Floating Smiles	183
6.7		When Does Risk Aversion Make a Difference?	184
	6.7.1	Motivation	184
	6.7.2	The Importance of an Assessment of Risk Aversion for Model Building	185
	6.7.3	The Principle of Absolute Continuity	186

		6.7.4	The Effect of Supply and Demand	187
		6.7.5	A Stylized Example: First Version	187
		6.7.6	A Stylized Example: Second Version	194
		6.7.7	A Stylized Example: Third Version	196
		6.7.8	Overall Conclusions	196
		6.7.9	The EMH Again	199

7 Empirical Facts About Smiles   **201**

	7.1	What is this Chapter About?		201
		7.1.1	'Fundamental' and 'Derived' Analyses	201
		7.1.2	A Methodological Caveat	202
	7.2	Market Information About Smiles		203
		7.2.1	Direct Static Information	203
		7.2.2	Semi-Static Information	204
		7.2.3	Direct Dynamic Information	204
		7.2.4	Indirect Information	205
	7.3	Equities		206
		7.3.1	Basic Facts	206
		7.3.2	Subtler Effects	206
	7.4	Interest Rates		222
		7.4.1	Basic Facts	222
		7.4.2	Subtler Effects	224
	7.5	FX Rates		227
		7.5.1	Basic Facts	227
		7.5.2	Subtler Effects	227
	7.6	Conclusions		235

8 General Features of Smile-Modelling Approaches   **237**

	8.1	Fully-Stochastic-Volatility Models		237
	8.2	Local-Volatility (Restricted-Stochastic-Volatility) Models		239
	8.3	Jump–Diffusion Models		241
		8.3.1	Discrete Amplitude	241
		8.3.2	Continuum of Jump Amplitudes	242
	8.4	Variance–Gamma Models		243
	8.5	Mixing Processes		243
		8.5.1	A Pragmatic Approach to Mixing Models	244
	8.6	Other Approaches		245
		8.6.1	Tight Bounds with Known Quadratic Variation	245
		8.6.2	Assigning Directly the Evolution of the Smile Surface	246
	8.7	The Importance of the Quadratic Variation (Take 2)		246

9 The Input Data: Fitting an Exogenous Smile Surface   **249**

  9.1   What is This Chapter About?   249

  9.2   Analytic Expressions for Calls vs Process Specification   249

  9.3   Direct Use of Market Prices: Pros and Cons   250

  9.4   Statement of the Problem   251

  9.5   Fitting Prices   252

  9.6   Fitting Transformed Prices   254

  9.7   Fitting the Implied Volatilities   255

       9.7.1   The Problem with Fitting the Implied Volatilities   255

  9.8   Fitting the Risk-Neutral Density Function – General   256

       9.8.1   Does It Matter if the Price Density Is Not Smooth?   257

       9.8.2   Using Prior Information (Minimum Entropy)   258

  9.9   Fitting the Risk-Neutral Density Function: Mixture of Normals   259

       9.9.1   Ensuring the Normalization and Forward Constraints   261

       9.9.2   The Fitting Procedure   264

  9.10 Numerical Results   265

       9.10.1 Description of the Numerical Tests   265

       9.10.2 Fitting to Theoretical Prices: Stochastic-Volatility Density   265

       9.10.3 Fitting to Theoretical Prices: Variance–Gamma Density   268

       9.10.4 Fitting to Theoretical Prices: Jump–Diffusion Density   270

       9.10.5 Fitting to Market Prices   272

  9.11 Is the Term $\frac{\partial C}{\partial S}$ Really a Delta?   275

  9.12 Fitting the Risk-Neutral Density Function:
       The Generalized-Beta Approach   277

       9.12.1 Derivation of Analytic Formulae   280

       9.12.2 Results and Applications   287

       9.12.3 What Does This Approach Offer?   291

10 Quadratic Variation and Smiles   **293**

  10.1 Why This Approach Is Interesting   293

  10.2 The BJN Framework for Bounding Option Prices   293

  10.3 The BJN Approach – Theoretical Development   294

       10.3.1 Assumptions and Definitions   294

       10.3.2 Establishing Bounds   297

       10.3.3 Recasting the Problem   298

       10.3.4 Finding the Optimal Hedge   299

  10.4 The BJN Approach: Numerical Implementation   300

       10.4.1 Building a 'Traditional' Tree   301

       10.4.2 Building a BJN Tree for a Deterministic Diffusion   301

       10.4.3 Building a BJN Tree for a General Process   304

       10.4.4 Computational Results   307

      10.4.5 Creating Asymmetric Smiles   309

      10.4.6 Summary of the Results   311

  10.5 Discussion of the Results   312

      10.5.1 Resolution of the Crouhy–Galai Paradox   312

      10.5.2 The Difference Between Diffusions and Jump–Diffusion Processes: the Sample Quadratic Variation   312

      10.5.3 How Can One Make the Approach More Realistic?   314

      10.5.4 The Link with Stochastic-Volatility Models   314

      10.5.5 The Link with Local-Volatility Models   315

      10.5.6 The Link with Jump–Diffusion Models   315

  10.6 Conclusions (or, Limitations of Quadratic Variation)   316

11 Local-Volatility Models: the Derman-and-Kani Approach   319

  11.1 General Considerations on Stochastic-Volatility Models   319

  11.2 Special Cases of Restricted-Stochastic-Volatility Models   321

  11.3 The Dupire, Rubinstein and Derman-and-Kani Approaches   321

  11.4 Green's Functions (Arrow–Debreu Prices) in the DK Construction   322

      11.4.1 Definition and Main Properties of Arrow–Debreu Prices   322

      11.4.2 Efficient Computation of Arrow–Debreu Prices   324

  11.5 The Derman-and-Kani Tree Construction   326

      11.5.1 Building the First Step   327

      11.5.2 Adding Further Steps   329

  11.6 Numerical Aspects of the Implementation of the DK Construction   331

      11.6.1 Problem 1: Forward Price Greater Than $S(\text{up})$ or Smaller Than $S(\text{down})$ 331

      11.6.2 Problem 2: Local Volatility Greater Than $\frac{1}{2}|S(\text{up}) - S(\text{down})|$ 332

      11.6.3 Problem 3: Arbitrariness of the Choice of the Strike   332

  11.7 Implementation Results   334

      11.7.1 Benchmarking 1: The No-Smile Case   334

      11.7.2 Benchmarking 2: The Time-Dependent-Volatility Case   335

      11.7.3 Benchmarking 3: Purely Strike-Dependent Implied Volatility   336

      11.7.4 Benchmarking 4: Strike-and-Maturity-Dependent Implied Volatility   337

      11.7.5 Conclusions   338

  11.8 Estimating Instantaneous Volatilities from Prices as an Inverse Problem   343

12 Extracting the Local Volatility from Option Prices   345

  12.1 Introduction   345

      12.1.1 A Possible Regularization Strategy   346

      12.1.2 Shortcomings   346

  12.2 The Modelling Framework   347

  12.3 A Computational Method   349

12.3.1   Backward Induction   349
12.3.2   Forward Equations   350
12.3.3   Why Are We Doing Things This Way?   352
12.3.4   Related Approaches   354
12.4   Computational Results   355
12.4.1   Are We Looking at the Same Problem?   356
12.5   The Link Between Implied and Local-Volatility Surfaces   357
12.5.1   Symmetric ('FX') Smiles   358
12.5.2   Asymmetric ('Equity') Smiles   361
12.5.3   Monotonic ('Interest-Rate') Smile Surface   368
12.6   Gaining an Intuitive Understanding   368
12.6.1   Symmetric Smiles   369
12.6.2   Asymmetric Smiles: One-Sided Parabola   370
12.6.3   Asymmetric Smiles: Monotonically Decaying   372
12.7   What Local-Volatility Models Imply about Sticky and Floating Smiles   373
12.8   No-Arbitrage Conditions on the Current Implied Volatility Smile Surface 375
12.8.1   Constraints on the Implied Volatility Surface   375
12.8.2   Consequences for Local Volatilities   381
12.9   Empirical Performance   385
12.10 Appendix I: Proof that $\frac{\partial^2 Call(S_t, K, T, t)}{\partial K^2} = \phi(S_T)|_K$ 386

13 Stochastic-Volatility Processes   **389**
13.1   Plan of the Chapter   389
13.2   Portfolio Replication in the Presence of Stochastic Volatility   389
13.2.1   Attempting to Extend the Portfolio Replication Argument   389
13.2.2   The Market Price of Volatility Risk   396
13.2.3   Assessing the Financial Plausibility of λ_σ 398
13.3   Mean-Reverting Stochastic Volatility   401
13.3.1   The Ornstein–Uhlenbeck Process   402
13.3.2   The Functional Form Chosen in This Chapter   403
13.3.3   The High-Reversion-Speed, High-Volatility Regime   404
13.4   Qualitative Features of Stochastic-Volatility Smiles   405
13.4.1   The Smile as a Function of the Risk-Neutral Parameters   406
13.5   The Relation Between Future Smiles and Future Stock Price Levels   416
13.5.1   An Intuitive Explanation   417
13.6   Portfolio Replication in Practice: The Stochastic-Volatility Case   418
13.6.1   The Hedging Methodology   418
13.6.2   A Numerical Example   420
13.7   Actual Fitting to Market Data   427
13.8   Conclusions   436

14 Jump–Diffusion Processes   **439**

  14.1 Introduction   439

  14.2 The Financial Model: Smile Tale 2 Revisited   441

  14.3 Hedging and Replicability in the Presence of Jumps: First
Considerations   444

      14.3.1 What Is Really Required To Complete the Market?   445

  14.4 Analytic Description of Jump–Diffusions   449

      14.4.1 The Stock Price Dynamics   449

  14.5 Hedging with Jump–Diffusion Processes   455

      14.5.1 Hedging with a Bond and the Underlying Only   455

      14.5.2 Hedging with a Bond, a Second Option and the Underlying   457

      14.5.3 The Case of a Single Possible Jump Amplitude   460

      14.5.4 Moving to a Continuum of Jump Amplitudes   465

      14.5.5 Determining the Function g Using the Implied Approach   465

      14.5.6 Comparison with the Stochastic-Volatility Case (Again)   470

  14.6 The Pricing Formula for Log-Normal Amplitude Ratios   470

  14.7 The Pricing Formula in the Finite-Amplitude-Ratio Case   472

      14.7.1 The Structure of the Pricing Formula for Discrete Jump
Amplitude Ratios   474

      14.7.2 Matching the Moments   475

      14.7.3 Numerical Results   476

  14.8 The Link Between the Price Density and the Smile Shape   485

      14.8.1 A Qualitative Explanation   491

  14.9 Qualitative Features of Jump–Diffusion Smiles   494

      14.9.1 The Smile as a Function of the Risk-Neutral Parameters   494

      14.9.2 Comparison with Stochastic-Volatility Smiles   499

  14.10 Jump–Diffusion Processes and Market Completeness Revisited   500

  14.11 Portfolio Replication in Practice: The Jump–Diffusion Case   502

      14.11.1 A Numerical Example   503

      14.11.2 Results   504

      14.11.3 Conclusions   509

15 Variance–Gamma   **511**

  15.1 Who Can Make Best Use of the Variance–Gamma Approach?   511

  15.2 The Variance–Gamma Process   513

      15.2.1 Definition   513

      15.2.2 Properties of the Gamma Process   514

      15.2.3 Properties of the Variance–Gamma Process   514

      15.2.4 Motivation for Variance–Gamma Modelling   517

      15.2.5 Properties of the Stock Process   518

      15.2.6 Option Pricing   519

15.3   Statistical Properties of the Price Distribution   522
        15.3.1   The Real-World (Statistical) Distribution   522
        15.3.2   The Risk-Neutral Distribution   522
15.4   Features of the Smile   523
15.5   Conclusions   527

16 Displaced Diffusions and Generalizations   **529**
16.1   Introduction   529
16.2   Gaining Intuition   530
        16.2.1   First Formulation   530
        16.2.2   Second Formulation   531
16.3   Evolving the Underlying with Displaced Diffusions   531
16.4   Option Prices with Displaced Diffusions   532
16.5   Matching At-The-Money Prices with Displaced Diffusions   533
        16.5.1   A First Approximation   533
        16.5.2   Numerical Results with the Simple Approximation   534
        16.5.3   Refining the Approximation   534
        16.5.4   Numerical Results with the Refined Approximation   544
16.6   The Smile Produced by Displaced Diffusions   553
        16.6.1   How Quickly is the Normal-Diffusion Limit Approached? 553
16.7   Extension to Other Processes   560

17 No-Arbitrage Restrictions on the Dynamics of Smile Surfaces   **563**
17.1   A Worked-Out Example: Pricing Continuous Double Barriers   564
        17.1.1   Money For Nothing: A Degenerate Hedging Strategy
                  for a Call Option   564
        17.1.2   Static Replication of a Continuous Double Barrier   566
17.2   Analysis of the Cost of Unwinding   571
17.3   The Trader's Dream   575
17.4   Plan of the Remainder of the Chapter   581
17.5   Conditions of No-Arbitrage for the Stochastic Evolution of Future Smile
        Surfaces   582
        17.5.1   Description of the Market   582
        17.5.2   The Building Blocks   584
17.6   Deterministic Smile Surfaces   585
        17.6.1   Equivalent Descriptions of a State of the World   585
        17.6.2   Consequences of Deterministic Smile Surfaces   587
        17.6.3   Kolmogorov-Compatible Deterministic Smile Surfaces   588
        17.6.4   Conditions for the Uniqueness of Kolmogorov-Compatible
                  Densities   589

	17.6.5	Floating Smiles	591
17.7	Stochastic Smiles		593
	17.7.1	Stochastic Floating Smiles	594
	17.7.2	Introducing Equivalent Deterministic Smile Surfaces	595
	17.7.3	Implications of the Existence of an Equivalent Deterministic Smile Surface	596
	17.7.4	Extension to Displaced Diffusions	597
17.8	The Strength of the Assumptions		597
17.9	Limitations and Conclusions		598

III   Interest Rates – Deterministic Volatilities   601

18 Mean Reversion in Interest-Rate Models   603
18.1	Introduction and Plan of the Chapter		603
18.2	Why Mean Reversion Matters in the Case of Interest-Rate Models		604
	18.2.1	What Does This Mean for Forward-Rate Volatilities?	606
18.3	A Common Fallacy Regarding Mean Reversion		608
	18.3.1	The Grain of Truth in the Fallacy	609
18.4	The BDT Mean-Reversion Paradox		610
18.5	The Unconditional Variance of the Short Rate in BDT – the Discrete Case		612
18.6	The Unconditional Variance of the Short Rate in BDT–the Continuous-Time Equivalent		616
18.7	Mean Reversion in Short-Rate Lattices: Recombining vs Bushy Trees		617
18.8	Extension to More General Interest-Rate Models		620
18.9	Appendix I: Evaluation of the Variance of the Logarithm of the Instantaneous Short Rate		622

19 Volatility and Correlation in the LIBOR Market Model   625
19.1	Introduction		625
19.2	Specifying the Forward-Rate Dynamics in the LIBOR Market Model		626
	19.2.1	First Formulation: Each Forward Rate in Isolation	626
	19.2.2	Second Formulation: The Covariance Matrix	628
	19.2.3	Third Formulation: Separating the Correlation from the Volatility Term	630
19.3	Link with the Principal Component Analysis		631
19.4	Worked-Out Example 1: Caplets and a Two-Period Swaption		632
19.5	Worked-Out Example 2: Serial Options		635
19.6	Plan of the Work Ahead		636

20 Calibration Strategies for the LIBOR Market Model **639**

20.1   Plan of the Chapter   639

20.2   The Setting   639

    20.2.1   A Geometric Construction: The Two-Factor Case   640

    20.2.2   Generalization to Many Factors   642

    20.2.3   Re-Introducing the Covariance Matrix   642

20.3   Fitting an Exogenous Correlation Function   643

20.4   Numerical Results   646

    20.4.1   Fitting the Correlation Surface with a Three-Factor Model   646

    20.4.2   Fitting the Correlation Surface with a Four-Factor Model   650

    20.4.3   Fitting Portions of the Target Correlation Matrix   654

20.5   Analytic Expressions to Link Swaption and Caplet Volatilities 659

    20.5.1   What Are We Trying to Achieve?   659

    20.5.2   The Set-Up   659

20.6   Optimal Calibration to Co-Terminal Swaptions   662

    20.6.1   The Strategy   662

21 Specifying the Instantaneous Volatility of Forward Rates **667**

21.1   Introduction and Motivation   667

21.2   The Link between Instantaneous Volatilities and the Future Term Structure of Volatilities   668

21.3   A Functional Form for the Instantaneous Volatility Function   671

    21.3.1   Financial Justification for a Humped Volatility   672

21.4   Ensuring Correct Caplet Pricing   673

21.5   Fitting the Instantaneous Volatility Function: Imposing Time Homogeneity of the Term Structure of Volatilities   677

21.6   Is a Time-Homogeneous Solution Always Possible?   679

21.7   Fitting the Instantaneous Volatility Function: The Information from the Swaption Market   680

21.8   Conclusions   686

22 Specifying the Instantaneous Correlation Among Forward Rates **687**

22.1   Why Is Estimating Correlation So Difficult?   687

22.2   What Shape Should We Expect for the Correlation Surface?   688

22.3   Features of the Simple Exponential Correlation Function   689

22.4   Features of the Modified Exponential Correlation Function   691

22.5   Features of the Square-Root Exponential Correlation Function   694

22.6   Further Comparisons of Correlation Models   697

22.7   Features of the Schonmakers–Coffey Approach   697

22.8   Does It Make a Difference (and When)?   698

IV Interest Rates – Smiles   701

23 How to Model Interest-Rate Smiles   703
23.1 What Do We Want to Capture? A Hierarchy of Smile-Producing
      Mechanisms   703
23.2 Are Log-Normal Co-Ordinates the Most Appropriate?   704
    23.2.1 Defining Appropriate Co-ordinates   705
23.3 Description of the Market Data   706
23.4 Empirical Study I: Transforming the Log-Normal Co-ordinates   715
23.5 The Computational Experiments   718
23.6 The Computational Results   719
23.7 Empirical Study II: The Log-Linear Exponent   721
23.8 Combining the Theoretical and Experimental Results   725
23.9 Where Do We Go From Here?   725

24 (CEV) Processes in the Context of the LMM   729
24.1 Introduction and Financial Motivation   729
24.2 Analytical Characterization of CEV Processes   730
24.3 Financial Desirability of CEV Processes   732
24.4 Numerical Problems with CEV Processes   734
24.5 Approximate Numerical Solutions   735
    24.5.1 Approximate Solutions: Mapping to Displaced Diffusions   735
    24.5.2 Approximate Solutions: Transformation of Variables 735
    24.5.3 Approximate Solutions: the Predictor–Corrector Method 736
24.6 Problems with the Predictor–Corrector Approximation for the LMM   747

25 Stochastic-Volatility Extensions of the LMM   751
25.1 Plan of the Chapter   751
25.2 What is the Dog and What is the Tail?   753
25.3 Displaced Diffusion vs CEV   754
25.4 The Approach   754
25.5 Implementing and Calibrating the Stochastic-Volatility LMM   756
    25.5.1 Evolving the Forward Rates   759
    25.5.2 Calibrating to Caplet Prices   759
25.6 Suggestions and Plan of the Work Ahead   764

26 The Dynamics of the Swaption Matrix   765
26.1 Plan of the Chapter   765
26.2 Assessing the Quality of a Model   766
26.3 The Empirical Analysis   767
    26.3.1 Description of the Data   767
    26.3.2 Results   768

26.4 Extracting the Model-Implied Principal Components   776
      26.4.1 Results   778
26.5 Discussion, Conclusions and Suggestions for Future Work   781

**27 Stochastic-Volatility Extension
    of the LMM: Two-Regime Instantaneous Volatility   783**
27.1 The Relevance of the Proposed Approach   783
27.2 The Proposed Extension   783
27.3 An Aside: Some Simple Properties of Markov Chains   785
      27.3.1 The Case of Two-State Markov Chains   787
27.4 Empirical Tests   788
      27.4.1 Description of the Test Methodology   788
      27.4.2 Results   790
27.5 How Important Is the Two-Regime Feature?   798
27.6 Conclusions   801

Bibliography   805

Index   813

Preface

0.1   Why a Second Edition?

This second edition is, in reality, virtually a whole new book. Approximately 80% of the material has been added, fully reworked or changed. Let me explain why I have felt that undertaking such a task was needed.

Some of the messages of the first edition have, to a large extent, become accepted in the trading community (and perhaps the first edition of this book played a small role in this process). Let me mention a few. It is now more widely understood, for instance, that just recovering today's market prices of plain-vanilla options is a necessary but by no means sufficient criterion for choosing a good model. As a consequence, the modelling emphasis has gradually shifted away from the ability of a model to take an accurate snapshot of today's plain-vanilla option market, towards predicting in a reasonably accurate way the future smile.

To give another example, it is now generally recognized that what matters for pricing is the *terminal* and not just the *instantaneous* correlation among the state variables. Therefore traders now readily acknowledge that time-dependent instantaneous volatilities can be very effective in creating de-correlation among interest rates. As a corollary, the once commonly held view that one needs very-high-dimensional models to price complex interest-rate instruments has been challenged and proven to be, if not wrong, certainly an overstatement of the truth.

Moving to more general pricing considerations, it is now acknowledged that the market-completeness assumption should be invoked to obtain the powerful results it allows (e.g. the uniqueness of the 'fair' price and of the hedging strategy or the replicability of an arbitrary terminal payoff) only if financially justifiable, not just because it makes the modelling easy. So, most traders now recognize that claiming that, say, local-volatility models are desirable *because* they allow a complete-market framework to be retained squarely puts the cart before the horse. The relevant question is whether a given market is truly complete (or completable), not whether a given model assumes it to be so.

As these ideas have become part of the received wisdom as to how models should be used, I have felt that other issues, perhaps not so relevant when the first edition appeared, now need to be looked at more carefully. For instance, I think that the distinction between what I call in my book the fundamental and the instrumental approaches to option pricing has not received the attention it deserves. Different types of traders use models in different ways, and for different purposes. The question should therefore at least be asked whether the same class of models can really simultaneously serve the needs of both types of trader. Is there any such thing as the 'best' model for the plain-vanilla trader and for the exotic trader? Are those features that make a model desirable for the former necessarily appealing to the latter?

Linked to this is the practical and theoretical importance for option pricing of the joint practices of vega hedging and daily model re-calibration. I believe that these two near-universal practices have not been analysed as carefully as they should be. Yet I think that they lie at the heart of option pricing, and that they should influence at a very deep level the choice of a pricing model.

Another reason for updating the original work is that interest-rate smiles were an interesting second-order effect when I was writing the first edition. They have now become an essential ingredient of term structure modelling, and the consensus of the trading community is beginning to crystallize around a sufficiently well-established methodology, that it makes sense to present a coherent picture of the field.

More generally, outside the interest-rate arena traders have encountered great difficulties in fitting market smiles in a financially-convincing and numerically-robust manner starting from a specification of the process for the underlying. As a consequence they have become increasingly interested in trying to model directly the evolution of the smile surface. Is this a sound practice? Can it be theoretically justified, or is it just a practitioner's legerdemain? I had only hinted at these issues in the first edition, but they are given a much fuller treatment in the present work.

Apart from the immediate applications, these developments have given rise to some important questions, such as: What is more important to model, the dynamics of the underlying, or the evolution of the smile surface (i.e. of the associated options)?; Can we (should we) always assume that the changes in option prices can be derived from a stochastic process that can simultaneously account for the evolution of the underlying?; If this were not the case, is it really possible (and practicable) to set up arbitrage strategies to exploit this lack of coherence?

The last question brings me naturally to another aspect of option pricing that I question more explicitly in this second edition, namely the reliance on the informational efficiency of markets implicit in the commonly used calibration and hedging practices. This topic is linked to the popular and, these days, 'trendy' topic of behavioural finance. I discuss at several points in this second edition why I think that one should at least question the classical rational-investor, efficient-market paradigm when it comes to option pricing.

Another topic that I emphasize more strongly in this second edition is the following. In the post Black-and-Scholes era the perfect-replication idea has become the bedrock of option pricing. In a nutshell: 'If we can replicate perfectly, we don't have to worry about aversion to risk.' All models, of course, are wrong, and the real question is not whether they are 'true' in some metaphysical sense but whether they are useful. Looked at in this light, the perfect-replication model has been immensely useful for the first-generation of option products. I feel, however, that, when it comes to some of the products that are traded today, the dichotomous distinction between complete markets, where payoff replication should always be possible, and incomplete markets, where no self-financing hedging strategy can recover with certainty a derivatives payoff, might be fast approaching its 'best-before date'. I make an argument as to why this is the case throughout this new edition, but especially in Part II.

The more one looks into a certain subject, the simpler the overarching structure begins to appear. I think that, by working with pricing models for close to 15 years, I have come to see certain underlying principles and regularities that can greatly help in understanding what different modelling approaches offer. So, simplifying greatly, much of my understanding of the impact of correlation and volatility on option pricing can be condensed as follows. One insight is that different 'complex' (i.e. smile-producing) models can be looked at as machines that produce different types of stochasticity for the quadratic variation of the (logarithmic) price changes, and that the nature of the stochasticity of this quantity is a crucial quantity in understanding the pricing and the degree of replicability of complex options. The second insight is that, for all their apparent complexity and diversity of forms, what stochastic-parameter models 'really' provide is just a mechanism for correlating the future stochastic quadratic variations with the future realizations of the underlying(s). If we focus on this aspect we can quickly recover sight of the pricing wood without our view being obscured by the modelling trees (or bushes). The third insight is that, much as traders, for the reasons hinted at above, would like to prescribe directly the evolution of smile surfaces, process-based approaches give the safest guarantee that they will be able do so avoiding arbitrage. In a way, there is not much more to my book than this. I do not expect these rather Delphic statements to be clear at this stage, but they will hopefully become so as the book unfolds.

0.2 What This Book Is *Not* About

One review by a reader of an earlier book of mine complained that he found the book too narrowly focused on the modelling of interest-rate derivatives. Given that the title of the book in question was *Interest-Rate Models*, my first reaction had been to think that, at least, I should have been absolved from the sins of deception and ambiguity. I have realized, however, that the writer should not assume that a title is always self-explanatory. So, to avoid future complaints, here are a few indications of what this second edition is *not* about.

First of all, I do not deal with the statistical estimation of volatility and correlation using market data. Often, but not always, I will assume that the implied route has been followed, whereby a volatility or correlation input is derived from the prices of plain-vanilla derivatives. However, I do not accept this practice uncritically, and discuss at length its limitations. Also, much as this book is not about statistical techniques to estimate volatility and correlations, I *do* give a lot of importance to the congruence between the outputs of a model and the available empirical evidence. I therefore present in some detail market information about the behaviour of smile surfaces.

I do not cover in this second edition the issues of jumps, volatility and correlation in the context of credit derivatives. The topic is important, the interest in the field is growing rapidly and there is a lot of exciting research activity. I think, however, that the area is still too 'fluid' to allow for a synthesis with reasonable chances of still being useful by the time this second edition reaches the shelves. Also, in the case of credit derivatives I am beginning to doubt more and more the applicability of the possibly-imperfect-but-still-very-good payoff-replication paradigm that is at the basis of current derivatives pricing. Perhaps when replication is so imperfect we should be embracing different ways of pricing options, possibly along the lines of the no-too-good-deal approach (see, for example, Cochrane, 2001), which weakens the requirement of no arbitrage.

Having chosen not to deal with credit derivatives, I have decided not to treat measures of dependence more sophisticated than pairwise correlation. Copula techniques are therefore not covered. This is a pity, but, with the current draft running at over 800 pages, I had to draw the line somewhere. For similar reasons, co-integration techniques, which can be particularly relevant in the case of interest-rate derivatives, are treated in this book only in passing.

0.3 Structure of the Book

Despite the extensive reworkings and extensions, the structure of the second edition has not changed radically. There are now four parts. The first deals with a Black world without smiles. (Things do get more cheerful later on.) The first chapter is important, because it highlights my 'philosophical' approach to option pricing, and justifies why I give a lot of importance to certain aspects (such as the future dynamics of smile surfaces) and relatively little to others (such as what the 'true' process for the underlying is). With the foundations firmly established, I place myself in a diffusive setting with deterministic volatility, and explore in detail the role of volatility in arriving at perfect payoff replication. I stress the difference between volatility and variance, and discuss the role of mean reversion. The interplay between time-dependent volatility and terminal de-correlation is the topic of the last chapter in Part I.

Part II deals with smiles in the equity and FX worlds. First I review relevant empirical information about smiles, and I show how one can go from noisy market quotes of plain-vanilla option prices to a nice and smooth smile volatility surface. I then revisit the concept of quadratic variation, which serves as a *fil rouge* to link the following chapters. These are devoted to local stochastic-volatility, general stochastic-volatility, jump–diffusion and variance-gamma processes. Part II is concluded by an important chapter that discusses if and to what extent one can dispense with an explicit specification of a model, and can directly prescribe the dynamics of the smile surface.

In Part III I revert to a world without smiles, but I focus on interest rates. Since the LIBOR market model is simply a set of no-arbitrage conditions given a volatility and correlation structure, it has pride of place in this part of the book.

Part IV extends the setting used for the deterministic-volatility LIBOR market model in order to account for smiles in a financially motivated and computationally tractable manner. In order of increasing complexity I deal with CEV processes, with diffusive stochastic volatility and with Markov-chain processes. The three approaches are nested within each other and afford an increasingly convincing picture of the empirically observable interest-rate dynamics.

0.4 The New Subtitle

Finally, a brief comment about the new subtitle. It is clearly a pun on the title of a book by Isaiah Berlin (*The Hedgehog and the Fox*), who, in turn, borrowed it from a Russian proverb: 'The fox knows many tricks, but the hedgehog knows one big trick'. As I understand the proverb, it means that, much as the fox might be cunning and have a rich bag of tricks, knowing one simple but powerful 'trick' can be just as effective. In the case of the hedgehog the trick is rolling itself up in a ball of quills. For the perfect hedger, the big trick is perfect payoff replication, and, simple as the trick might be, it has proven extremely powerful and versatile. As mentioned above, one of the points I will try to make in my book is that we might be getting close to the point where we have squeezed all the possible mileage out of the perfect-payoff-replication trick, and we might soon have to begin to behave more like foxes (and introduce new, non-perfect-replication-based tricks into the game).

Acknowledgements

It is a pleasure to thank Lorenzo Liesch for careful reading of an earlier version of the manuscript, and for useful comments. I have greatly benefited from discussions with Dr Mark Joshi, Dr Dherminder Kainth, Dr Sukhdeep Mahal and Dr Jan Kwiatkowski. I would like to thank them all for their suggestions, and for pointing out several ways in which this second edition could be improved. I remain indebted to Dr Emanuele Amerio for discussions relating to the first edition of this book. All remaining errors are mine.

Part I

Foundations

Chapter 1

Theory and Practice of Option Modelling

1.1 The Role of Models in Derivatives Pricing

1.1.1 What Are Models For?

The idea that the price of a financial instrument might be arrived at using a complex mathematical formula is relatively new, and can be traced back to the Black-and-Scholes (1973) formula.[1] Of course, formulae were used before then for pricing purposes, for instance in order to convert the price of a bond into its gross redemption yield. However, these early (pre Black-and-Scholes) formulae by and large provided a very transparent transformation from one set of variables to another, and did not carry along a heavy baggage of model assumptions. The Black-and-Scholes formula changed all that, and we now live in a world where it is accepted that the value of certain illiquid derivative securities can be arrived at on the basis of a model (the acceptance of this is the basis of the practice of marking-to-model).

The models that developed from the family tree that has Black-and-Scholes at its roots shared the common assumptions that the estimation of the drift (growth rate, trend) component of the dynamics of the relevant financial driver was not relevant to arrive at the price of the derivative product. This insight directly follows from the concept of payoff replication, and is discussed in detail in this book in Chapter 2.

In order to implement these models practitioners paid more and more attention to, and began to collect, direct empirical market data at a very 'atomistic' (often transactional) level. This was done for several reasons: for instance, for assessing the reasonableness of a model's assumptions, or for seeking guidance in the development of new models, or for estimating the inputs of existing models. The very availability of this wealth of information, however, suggested new opportunities. Perhaps, embedded in these data, there could be information about the market microstructure that could provide information not only about the 'volatility' of a price series, but also about its short-term direction.

---

[1]Parts of this chapter have been adapted from Rebonato (2004) and from Rebonato (2003b)

Again, the practice was not strictly new, since the idea of predicting future price movements from their past history ('chartism' in a generalized sense) pre-dated Black-and-Scholes probably by decades. Yet these earlier approaches (which, incidentally, never won academic respectability), were typically based on, at most, daily observations, and purported to make predictions over time-scales of weeks and months. The new, transactional-level data, on the other hand, were made up of millions of observations, sometimes collected (as in the case of FX trades) minutes or seconds apart. The availability of these data made possible the calibration of *predictive* models, which try to anticipate stock price movements over time-scales sometimes as short as a few minutes.

This was just the type of data and models that many of the new, and, in the early 2000s, immensely popular, hedge funds required in order to try to 'get an edge' over an ever-growing competition (in 2001 one new hedge fund was being launched every week in continental Europe alone). These hedge funds and the proprietary trading desks of internationally active banks therefore become the users and developers of a second breed of models, which differed from the members of the Black-and-Scholes family because they were explicitly trying to have a predictive directional power. Unlike the early rather crude chartist approaches, these new models employed very complex and sophisticated mathematical techniques, and, if they were not being routinely published in academic journals, it had more to do with the secretive nature of the associated research than with any lack of intellectual rigour.

Two types of model had therefore developed and coexisted by the end of the 1990s: models as predictors (the 'hedge-fund models') and models as payoff-replication engines (the 'derivatives models'). With some caveats, the distinction was clear, valid and unambiguous. It is the derivatives models that are the subject of this book.

Having said that, recent developments in the derivatives industry have increasingly blurred this once-clear-cut distinction. Products have appeared whose payoff depends to first order on, say, the correlation between different equity indices (e.g. basket options), or on the correlation between FX rates and/or between different-currency yield curves (e.g. power-reverse-dual swaps), or on possibly discontinuous moves in credit spreads and default correlations (e.g. tranched credit derivatives). The Black-and-Scholes-inspired replication paradigm remains the prevalent approach when trying to price these new-breed models. Yet their value depends to first order on quantities poorly hedgeable and no easier to predict than directional market trends. The underlying model might well assume that these input quantities are deterministic (as is normally the case for correlations), but this does not take away the fact that they are difficult to estimate, that they render payoff replication very complex, if not impossible, and that their real-world realizations influence to a very large extent the variability of the option-plus-hedge portfolio. The result of this state of affairs is that, once the best hedging portfolio has been put in place, there remains an unavoidable variance of return at expiry from the complex option and its hedges.

Sure enough, *perfect* replication cannot be expected even for the simplest options: markets are not frictionless, trading cannot be continuous, bid–offer spreads do exist, etc. Yet the robustness of the Black-and-Scholes formula (discussed at several points in this book) ensures that the terminal variability of the overall total portfolio is relatively limited. The difference, however, between the early, relatively simple option payoffs and the new, more complex products, while in theory only a matter of degrees, is in practice large enough to question the validity of prices obtained on the basis of the replication approach (i.e. assuming that one can effectively hedge all the sources of uncertainty).

So, in making the price for a complex derivative product, the trader will often have to take a directional market view on the realization of quantities such as correlations between FX rates and yield curves, default frequencies or correlations among forward rates in different currencies and/or equity indices, or sub-sectors thereof. As a consequence, the distinction between predictive models (that explicitly require the ability to predict future market quantities), and models as payoff replication machines (that are supposed to work whatever the future realizations of the market quantities will be) has recently become progressively blurred. This topic is revisited in the final section of this chapter, where I argue that one could make a case for re-thinking current derivatives pricing philosophy, which still implicitly heavily relies on the existence of a replication strategy.

1.1.2 The Fundamental Approach

In option pricing there are at least two prevalent approaches (which I call in what follows the 'fundamental' and 'instrumental') to dealing with models. The general philosophy that underlies the first can be described as follows. We begin by observing certain market prices for plain-vanilla options. We assume that these prices are correct, in the sense that they embody in the best and most complete possible way all the relevant information available about the stochastic process that drives the underlying (and possibly, other variables, such as the stochastic volatility; for simplicity I will confine the discussion to the underlying, which I will also call 'the stock'). We begin by positing that this true process is of a particular form (say, a jump–diffusion). We calculate what the prices should be if indeed our guess was correct. If the call prices derived using the model are not correct, we conclude that we have not discovered the true process for the underlying. If they are better than the prices produced by another model (say, a pure diffusion) we say that we have reason to believe that the new process (the jump–diffusion) could be a more accurate description of the real process for the underlying than the old one (the pure diffusion).

Alternatively, if the model has a large number of 'free parameters' and we believe that the underlying process is correctly specified, we use all of the parameters describing the dynamics of the underlying to recover the market prices of the options. This is what is implicitly done, for instance, with some implementations of the local volatility models (see Chapters 11 and 12).

Or again, if two models give a fit of similar quality to market prices of plain-vanilla options, the conclusion is often drawn that the model that implies the process for the underlying more similar to what is statistically observed in reality is the 'better' one. The relevance of this distinction is that, despite the similarity of the two models in reproducing the *plain-vanilla* prices, better prices for *complex* options (i.e. prices in better agreement with the market practice) would be obtained if the superior process were used.

The fundamental approach sounds very sensible. It is, however, underpinned by one very strong assumption: the trader who chooses and calibrates models this way is subscribing to the view that the market-created option prices must be fully consistent with the true, but a priori unknown, process for the underlying. The market, in other words, must be a perfect information-processing machine, which absorbs all the relevant information about the unknown process followed by the 'stock', and produces prices consistent with each other (no arbitrage) and with this information set (informational efficiency).

This implicit assumption is very widespread: take, for instance, the practice of recovering all the observable option prices using a local-volatility model, discussed in Chapter 11. Even if we knew the true process *of the underlying* to be exactly a diffusion with state-dependent (local) volatility, it would only make sense to determine the shape of the local volatility from the traded option prices if we also believed that these had been correctly created in the first place on the basis of this model. We will see, however (see Chapter 11), that the local-volatility modelling approach will recover by construction any exogenous set of market prices. Therefore, in carrying out the calibration we are implicitly making two assumptions:

1. that we know, from our knowledge of financial markets (as opposed to just from the market prices of options) that the true process *for the underlying* is indeed a local-volatility diffusion; and

2. that the market has fully incorporated this information in the price-making *of plain-vanilla options*.

In other words, by following this procedure we do not allow the possibility that the true process was a local-volatility diffusion, but that the market failed to incorporate this information in the prices of plain-vanilla options.

In reality option prices are not exogenous natural phenomena, nor are they made by omniscient demi-gods with supernatural knowledge of the 'true' processes for the stochastic state variables. Option prices are made by traders who, individually, might have little or no idea about the true stochastic process for the underlying; who might be using the popular 'model of the month'; who, for a variety of institutional constraints, might be afraid to use a model at odds with the current market practice (see Section 1.2.2); or who might be prevented from doing so by the limit structures in place at their trading houses.

A strong believer in market efficiency would counter that the errors of the individual uninformed traders do not matter, in that they will either cancel each other out (if uncorrelated), or will be eliminated (arbitraged away) by a superior and more unfettered trader with the best knowledge about the true process. I discuss the implications for option pricing of this strong form of market efficiency in the next sections, but this position must be squared with several empirical observations such as, for instance, the fact that steep equity smiles suddenly appeared after the equity market crash of 1987 – did traders not know before the event that the true process had a jump component? Another 'puzzling' fact for the believer of the fundamental view is that a close-to-perfect fit to the S&P500 smile in 2001 can be obtained with a cubic polynomial (see Ait-Sahalia (2002)): do we find it easier to believe that the market 'knows' about the true process for the index, prices options accordingly and when the prices obtained by using this procedure are converted into implied volatilities they magically lie on a cubic line? Or is it not simpler to speculate that traders quote prices of plain-vanilla options with a mixture of model use, trading views about the future volatility and cubic interpolation across strikes?

The matter cannot be settled with a couple of examples. For the moment I simply stress that the common and, prima facie, very sensible ('fundamental') approach to choosing and calibrating a model that I have just described can only be justified if one assumes that the observed prices of options reflect in an informationally efficient way everything that can be known about the true process. I will return to this topic in Section 1.4, which deals with the topic of calibration.

1.1.3 The Instrumental Approach

An alternative ('instrumental') way to look at the choice of process for the underlying is to regard a given process specification as a tool not so much for driving the underlying, but for creating present and future prices *of options*. In this approach it is therefore natural to compare how the prices of *options* (not of the underlying) move in reality and in the model. Typically this comparison will not be made in dollar terms, but using the 'implied volatility' language. Since, however, there is a one-to-one correspondence between implied volatilities and option prices (for a given value of the underlying) we can indifferently use either language.

So, traders, who might have no idea about the true process for the underlying, might none the less form ideas about how option prices (or, more likely, the associated implied volatilities) behave over time and in different market conditions: do term structure of volatilities remain roughly similar, or do they change shape in totally unpredictable ways? Do smiles for same-expiry options suddenly appear and then permanently flatten out as calendar time goes by, or do they approximately retain their relative steepness? Do swaption matrices always retain the same shape, or do they display a few fundamental 'modes' of deformation, among which they oscillate? How will the smile surface migrate as the underlying moves? Is it 'sticky' or 'floating'?

These traders, who observe regularities in the implied volatilities (i.e. in the prices of options) rather than in the underlying, tend to have relatively little interest in determining the true process for the 'stock price', and will instead prefer a process capable of producing the desired features in the implied volatilities. The process for the underlying now becomes more instrumental than fundamental: it is simply seen as a tool to obtain something else (i.e. the correct dynamics for the implied volatilities). Indeed, some of the most recent pricing approaches have tried to dispense with the specification of the process for the underlying altogether, and have directly prescribed the dynamics of the implied volatility surface. (See, for example, Schoenbucher (2000) and Samuel (2002).)[2]

Could the process for the underlying be chosen with total disregard of the true process for the underlying, as long as it reproduces the correct behaviour for the implied volatilities? This is unfortunately not the case, because, ultimately, the option trader will want, at the very least, to delta hedge her positions, and the success of the associated trading strategy will depend on the correct specification for the dynamics of the underlying. However, there is a considerable degree of 'robustness' in the hedging process, at least as long as certain important but rather broad features of the stock price process are captured correctly. See the discussions in Sections 4.6, 13.6 and 14.11. Furthermore, if the option prices and the process for the underlying were seriously incompatible, there would lie an obvious arbitrage somewhere, and the trader who totally disregarded the plausibility of the stock dynamics would theoretically expose herself to the risk of becoming a money machine for her fellow traders. In reality, however, real arbitrages are rather complex to put in place in practice, and the threat of being at the receiving end of an arbitrage strategy is often more theoretical than real. I discuss this topic further in Chapter 17 (see, in particular, Section 17.3, 'The Trader's Dream').

---

[2]The difficulties and dangers in doing so are discussed in Chapter 17.

Therefore the second (instrumental) approach is more popular, and, explicitly or implicitly, more widely followed in the market. It is also the conceptual framework that I prefer, and that I will predominantly follow in this book. I will try to justify this choice in this chapter, and, as concrete situations and examples arise, in the course of the book. It is important to keep in mind, however, that neither approach is without conceptual blemishes: the first requires an extreme faith in market efficiency that I consider unwarranted; for the second to work one has to rely on a rather difficult-to-quantify 'robustness' of the hedging process *vis-à-vis* trading restrictions and mis-specifications of the process for the underlying.

The discussion of what I mean by robustness constitutes one of the recurrent themes of this book. At this stage I can give a brief account as follows. I will show (Sections 4.5 and 4.6) that, as long as a certain quantity (the quadratic variation) is deterministic and known, it makes relatively little difference for the success of the hedging programme how the exact 'partitioning' of this quantity actually occurs during the life of the option. I will then go on to argue (Sections 13.6 and 14.11) that, if the quadratic variation is instead either unknown or stochastic, the success of the hedging strategy will rely to a large extent on finding a portfolio whose dependence on the (imperfectly known) realization of the quadratic variation is similar to that of the complex product that has to be hedged. This observation brings us naturally to the topic of vega hedging.

1.1.4   A Conundrum (or, 'What is Vega Hedging For?')

Suppose that a trader has a pricing model that describes the empirical statistical properties of the process of the underlying extremely well, but that recovers the prices of traded options poorly. (By the way, according to the Efficient Market Hypothesis this could not happen, but I postpone the discussion of this point until later sections.) The trader is also aware of another model, which implies a much less realistic process for the underlying, but which reproduces the present and expected future implied volatility surfaces very well. What should the trader do? Which model should she use?

The answer, I believe, is: 'It depends'.

If the trader is a plain-vanilla option trader, she should make use of her superior knowledge, and trade and set up dynamic delta-hedging strategies based on this knowledge of the process for the underlying. She might find it difficult to do so, because her true model will prescribe different amounts of stock to be delta-neutral than the model adopted by the market consensus. Therefore her positions will probably not appear delta-neutral to the risk management function of her institution (unless she can exercise an unhealthy influence on her middle office), and she might run against VaR or other limits. Also, since her back office will presumably use, for something as relatively liquid as plain-vanilla options, mark-to-market (rather than mark-to-model), she will be able to recognize little or no profit as soon as she puts on the advantageous trade, and will have to rely on the difference between the true and wrong option values to 'trickle in' during the life of the option, as her trading strategy unfolds. (See the discussion in Section 1.2.4.) Despite these constraints, however, a plain-vanilla trader will forfeit her competitive advantage if she slavishly follows the market in every price.

If, on the other hand, she is a complex-derivatives trader, vega hedging will be for her at least as important as delta hedging (see the discussion in Section 1.3.2 as to why delta hedging becomes relatively less important for complex-derivative traders – in a nutshell, this is because of the high correlation between the errors in the delta of the complex product, and the errors in the delta of a well-chosen vega-hedging portfolio). It is therefore crucial for her that the future vega re-hedging costs predicted by the model should be as similar as possible to the actual costs encountered during the life of the option. These costs, in turn, will be linked to the future prices of plain-vanilla calls (the future smile surface) that the 'wrong' model recovers well by definition.

Why doesn't the complex-derivatives trader, who knows the true process for the stock price, dispense with vega hedging altogether, and simply engage in a correct delta-hedging strategy? She could only do this if the true process were such as to allow for market completeness by trading just in the underlying, i.e. if any payoff could be exactly reproduced by trading dynamically in the underlying. But this is a very special, and most unlikely, case. In general, market incompleteness is the rule, not the exception, and a trader, even armed with the knowledge of the true process, cannot hope that the future vega of the complex product *will only be a function of the future realization of the stock price*.

A final observation: successful option products, whether plain-vanilla or complex, thrive if there is a strong customer demand for them (customer, in this sense, means counterparties from outside the community of professional traders). Therefore option traders do not routinely make money by pitting their intellects against each other in a (zero-sum) war-game of pricing models. It is for them much more reliable and profitable to deal with the non-trading community, by providing the end users with the financial payoff they want (e.g. interest-rate protection, principal-protected products, yield 'enhancement', cheaper funding costs), and by exacting a compensation for the technological, intellectual and risk-management costs involved in providing this service. Given this trading reality, there are greater benefits in 'being on the market smile', even when it is felt that a more realistic model would not recover these market prices, than in standing alone at odds with the market.

1.2 The Efficient Market Hypothesis and Why It Matters for Option Pricing

I mentioned in the previous section that the Efficient Market Hypothesis (EMH) has a direct bearing on option pricing. In this section I discuss why this is the case. In order to do so it is important to clarify what is meant by market efficiency, and what conditions must be met for it to prevail. In particular, I will stress that rationality of each market player is *not* required for the EMH to hold true, and therefore criticisms of its validity must take a different, and subtler, route.

1.2.1 The Three Forms of the EMH

The EMH can be formulated in forms of wider and wider applicability (see, for example, the treatment in Shleifer (2000), on which this section draws extensively). The most radical form requires that all economic agents are fully informed and perfectly rational. If they can all observe the same history (of prices, economic variables, political events, etc.), then they will all arrive at the same statistical conclusions about the real world, and will form prices by discounting the expected future cash flows from a security at a discount rate dependent on the undiversifiable uncertainty of the security and on their risk aversion.

In this sense the value of the security is said to embed all the information available in the market, its value to be linked to 'fundamentals', and markets to be informationally efficient. All securities are fairly priced, excess returns over the riskless rate simply reflect 'fair' compensation for excess risk, and five-dollar banknotes cannot be found lying on the pavement.

A weaker form of market efficiency (but one that arrives at the same conclusions) does not require all economic agents to be rational, but allows for a set of investors who price securities on sentiment or with imperfect information. Will this affect the market price? Actually, one can show that as long as the actions of the uninformed, irrational investors are random ('uncorrelated'), their actions will cancel out and the market will clear at the same prices that would obtain if all the agents were perfectly rational.

Surely, however, the zero-correlation assumption is far too strong to be swallowed by anybody who has witnessed the recent dotcom mania. The very essence of bubbles, after all, is that the actions of uninformed, or sentiment-driven, investors are just the opposite of uncorrelated. If this is the case, then supply and demand, rather than fundamentals, will determine the price of a security. Is this the end of the efficient market hypothesis? Not quite. Let there be irrational and co-ordinated investors. As long as there also exist rational, well-informed agents who can value securities on the basis of fundamentals *and freely trade accordingly*, price anomalies will not persist. These pseudo-arbitrageurs will in fact buy the 'irrationally cheap' securities and sell the 'sentimentally expensive' ones, and by so doing will drive the price back to the fundamentals. Whether it is due to irrationality and sentiment or to any other cause, in this framework excess demand automatically creates extra supply, and vice versa. Therefore, as long as these pseudo-arbitrageurs can freely take their positions, supply and demand will not affect equilibrium prices, these will again be based on the suitably discounted expectation of their future cash flows (the 'fundamentals') and the EMH still rules.

It is important to stress that the EMH is not only intellectually pleasing, but has also been extensively tested and has emerged, by and large, vindicated. The 'by-and-large' qualifier, however, is crucial for my argument. In the multi-trillion market of all the traded securities, a theory that accounts for the prices of 99.9% of observed instruments can at the same time be splendidly successful, and yet leave up for grabs on the pavement enough five-dollar notes to make a meaningful difference to the year-end accounts and the share prices of many a financial institution. This is more likely to be so if the instruments in question are particularly opaque. The possibility that the pseudo-arbitrageurs might not always be able to bring prices in line with fundamentals should therefore be given serious consideration.

1.2.2 Pseudo-Arbitrageurs in Crisis

What can prevent pseudo-arbitrageurs from carrying out their task of bringing prices in line with fundamentals?

To begin with, these pseudo-arbitrageurs (hedge funds, relative-value traders, etc.) often take positions not with their own money, but as agents of investors or shareholders (Shleifer (2000)). If the product is complex, and thus so is the model necessary to arrive at its price, the ultimate owners of the funds at risk might lack the knowledge, expertise or inclination to assess the fair value, and will have to rely on their agent's judgement. This trust, however, will not be extended for too long a period of time, and certainly not for many years. Therefore, the time-span over which securities are to revert to their fundamental value must be relatively short (and almost certainly will not extend beyond the next bonus date). If the supply-and-demand dynamics were such that the mis-priced instrument might move even more violently out of line with fundamentals, the position of the pseudo-arbitrageur will swing into the red, and the 'trust-me-I-am-a-pseudo-arbitrageur' line might rapidly lose its appeal with the investors and shareholders.

Another source of danger for relative-value traders is the existence of institutional and regulatory constraints that might force the liquidation of positions before they can be shown to be 'right': the EMH does not know about the existence of stop-loss limits, VaR limits, concentration limits, etc.

Poor liquidity, often compounded with the ability of the market to guess the position of a large relative-value player, also contributes to the difficulties of pseudo-arbitrageurs. Consider for instance the case of a pseudo-arbitrageur who, on the basis of a perfectly sound model, concluded that traded equity implied volatilities are implausibly high, and entered large short-volatility trades to exploit this anomaly. If the market became aware of these positions, and if, perhaps because of the institutional constraints mentioned above, the pseudo-arbitrageur had to try to unwind these short positions before they had come in the money, the latter could experience a very painful short squeeze.

Finally, very high information costs might act as a barrier to entry, or limit the number of pseudo-arbitrageurs. Reliable models require teams of quants to devise them, scores of programmers to implement them, powerful computers to run them and expensive data sources to validate them.[3] The perceived market inefficiency must therefore be sufficiently large not only to allow risk-adjusted exceptional profits after bid–offer spreads, but also to justify the initial investment.

In short, because of all of the above the life of the pseudo-arbitrageur can be, if not nasty, brutish and short, at least unpleasant, difficult and fraught with danger. As a result, even in the presence of a severe imbalance of supply or demand, relative-value traders might be more reluctant to step in and bring prices in line with fundamentals than the EMH assumes.

1.2.3 Model Risk for Traders and Risk Managers

I have mentioned the impact of risk management on trading practice and on price formation. It is useful to explore this angle further.[4]

Within the EMH framework the goals of traders and risk managers are aligned: a superior model will bring the trader a competitive advantage, and will be recognized as such by the market with very little time lag. From this point of view, an accurate mark-to-market is purely a reflection of the best information available, and 'true' (fundamental) value, market price and model price all coincide. It therefore makes perfect sense to have a single research centre, devoted to the study and implementation of the best model, which will serve the needs of the front-office trader, of the risk manager and of the product controller just as well. Looked at from this angle, model risk is simply the risk that our current model might not be good enough, and can be reduced by creating better and

---

[3]When I was heading an interest-rate-derivatives trading desk I was half puzzled and half embarrassed when I discovered that the harnessed power of the farm of parallel super-mini-computers in my small trading group ranked immediately after Los Alamos National Laboratory in computing power.

[4]The following two sections have been adapted from Rebonato (2003b).

better models that will track the monotonic, if not linear, improvement of the markets' informational efficiency.

If we believe, however, that pseudo-arbitrageurs might in practice be seriously hindered in bringing all prices in line with fundamentals the interplay between true value, market value and model value can be very different. Across both sides of the EMH divide there is little doubt that, when it comes to trading-book instruments, what should be recorded for books-and-records purposes should be the best guess for the price that a given product would fetch in the market. For the EMH sceptic, however, there is no guarantee that the 'best' available model (i.e. the model that most closely prices the instrument in line with fundamentals) should produce this price. Furthermore, there is no guarantee that the market, instead of swiftly recognizing the error of its ways, might not stray even more seriously away from fundamentals.

Ultimately, whenever a trader enters a position, he must believe that, in some sense, the market is 'wrong'. For the risk manager concerned about marking an option position to model appropriately, on the other hand, the market must be right by definition. For the EMH believer the market can only be wrong for a short period of time (if at all), so there is no real disconnect between the risk manager's price, and the trader's best price. For the EMH sceptic, on the other hand, there is an irreconcilable tension between front-office pricing and the risk-management model price.

1.2.4   The Parable of the Two Volatility Traders

To illustrate further the origin of this tension, let us analyse a stylized but instructive example. Two plain-vanilla option traders (one working for Efficient Bank, and the second for Sceptical Bank) have carefully analysed the volatility behaviour of a certain stock, and both concluded that its level should be centred around 20%. The stock is not particularly liquid, and the brokers' quotes, obtained with irregular frequency, do not deviate sufficiently from this estimate to warrant entering a trade. One day, however, without anything noticeable having happened in the market, an implied volatility quote of 10% appears. Two huge five-dollar notes are now lying on the floor, and both traders swiftly pick them up. Both traders intend to crystallize the value of the mis-priced option by engaging in gamma trading, i.e. by buying the 'cheap' option they will both end up long gamma and will dynamically hold a delta-neutralizing amount of stock, as dictated by their model calibrated to 20% volatility. (See Section 4.3 for a discussion of gamma trading.)

Life is easy for the Efficient Bank trader. She will go to her risk manager, convince him that the model used to estimate volatility is correct and argue that the informationally efficient market will soon adjust the implied volatility quote back to 20%. This has important implications. First of all, the profit from the trade can be booked immediately: the front office and risk management share the same state-of-the-art model, and both concur that the price for the option in line with fundamentals should be obtained with a 20% volatility. Furthermore, should another five-dollar bill appear on the pavement, the trader at Efficient Bank will have every reason and incentive to pick it up again.

The coincidence of the front-office and middle-office models has yet another consequence. The trader works on a 'volatility-arbitrage' desk, and her managers are happy for her to take a view on volatility, but not to take a substantial position in the underlying. They have therefore granted her very tight delta limits. This, however, creates no problem, because her strategy is to be delta-neutral at every point in time and to enjoy the fact that she has bought (at 10%) 'cheap convexity' (see Chapter 4). Crucially, in order to crystallize the model profits from trade, she will engage in a dynamic hedging strategy based on the superior model (calibrated with a 20% volatility), not on the temporarily erroneous market model. Since middle office again shares the same model, the risk manager calculates the delta of the position exactly in the same way as the trader, and therefore sees the whole portfolio perfectly within the desk's delta limits (actually, fully delta neutral).

Life is much harder for the trader at Sceptical Bank. She also works on a volatility-arbitrage desk with tight delta limits, and her middle-office function also recognizes that the model she uses is sound and plausible and concurs that the market must be going through a phase of summer madness. The similarities, however, virtually end here. Her risk-management function does not believe that a superior model must be endorsed by the market with effectively no delay, and therefore is not prepared to recognize the model value implied by the 10% trade as an immediate profit. A model provision will be set aside. Since the trader will not be able to book (all) the model profit upfront, she will have to rely on the profit dripping into the position over the life of the option as a result of trading the gamma. This process will be relatively slow, the more so the longer the maturity of the option. During this period the trader is exposed to the risk that another 'rogue' volatility quote, say at 5%, might even create a negative mark-to-market for her position. Her reaction to a second five-dollar bill will therefore be considerably different from that of her colleague at Efficient Bank. Furthermore, in order to carry out her gamma-trading programme she would like to buy and sell delta amounts of stock based on her best estimate of the 'true' volatility (20%). Middle office, however, who have observed the 10% trade, uses the model calibrated with the lower volatility to calculate the delta exposure of the trade, and therefore does not regard her position as delta-neutral at all. She utilizes more VaR than her colleague, might soon hit against her delta limit, and, if her trading performance is measured on the basis of VaR utilization, she will be deemed to be doing, on a risk-adjusted basis, more poorly than her colleague.

This parable could be expanded further, but the central message is clear: different views about market efficiency can generate very different behaviours and incentives for otherwise identical traders. In the real world, however, financial institutions are organized much more along the lines of Sceptical Bank than of Efficient Bank, and this creates a strong disincentive for a trader to stray too much from the path of the commonly accepted pricing model.

The strength of this disincentive should not be underestimated. The story about Efficient Bank and Sceptical Bank might have been contrived and over-stylized, but a real-life example can bring home the same point with greater force and clarity. As a trader enters a complex derivative transaction for which no transparent market prices are available, the product control function of her institution faces the problem of how to ascribe a value to the trade. Commercial data providers exist to fulfil this need. One such major provider active in the United Kingdom and in the United States acts as follows: the prices of non-visible trades are collected *from the product control functions* of several participating institutions; the outliers are excluded and an average price is created from the remaining quotes; information is then fed back to the contributing banks about the average price and about how many standard deviations away from the consensus their original quote was. If the quotes submitted by an institution are consistently away from the consensus, *the institution is expelled from the contributing group, and will no longer see the consensus prices.* When this happens, the product control function of that bank will no longer be able to discover the price of the opaque derivative, but simply knows that the bank's pricing model (even if it might be, perhaps, a 'better' one) is away from the industry consensus. A model reserve will have to be applied that will typically negate the extra value ascribed by the trader's model to the exotic product. Furthermore, since there is prima facie evidence that where the trader would like to mark her trades is away from the market consensus, a limit on the maximum notional size of the 'offending' positions is likely to be imposed.

Therefore, while today's models are indubitably more effective (at least in certain respects) than the early ones, I do not believe that the 'linear evolution' paradigm, possibly applicable to some areas of physics,[5] and according to which later models are 'better' in the sense of being closer to the 'phenomenon', is necessarily suited to describing the evolution of derivatives models. This real-life example shows that the disincentives against straying away from market consensus (ultimately, the withdrawal of market information) can be even more powerful in practice than in the parable of the two traders. Models can, and do, evolve, but in a less unfettered manner than traditional 'linear' accounts (and the EMH) assume.

Model inertia is therefore certainly a very significant feature to take into account when analysing models. There are however other aspects of market practice that have a profound influence on how models are developed, tested and used. Given their importance, some of these are discussed below.

1.3   Market Practice

1.3.1   Different Users of Derivatives Models

To understand derivatives models it is essential to grasp how they are put to use. In general, a pricing model can be of interest to plain-vanilla-option traders, to relative-value traders and to complex-derivatives traders. Relative-value and plain-vanilla traders are interested in models because of their ability to predict how option prices should move relative to the underlying, and relative to each other, given a certain move in the underlying. For both these classes of user, models should therefore have not just a *descriptive*, but also a *prescriptive* dimension.

The situation is different for complex-derivative traders, who do not have access to readily visible market prices for the structured products they trade in, and therefore require the models to 'create' these price, given the observable market inputs for the underlying and the plain-vanilla implied volatilities. Since complex traders will, in general, vega hedge their positions, exact recovery of the plain-vanilla hedging instruments – the descriptive aspect of a model – becomes paramount. The recovery of present and future option prices is linked to the current and future vega hedging and to model calibration. These very important practices are discussed in the next section.

---

[5]I realize that, with this statement, I am walking into a philosophical thicket, and that some philosophers of science would deny even models in fundamental physics any claim of being 'true' in an absolute sense. I stay clear of this controversy, and the more mundane points I make about the evolution of derivatives models remain valid irrespective of whether an absolute or a 'social' view of scientific progress is more valid.

1.3.2 In-Model and Out-of-Model Hedging

Possibly no aspect of derivatives trading has a deeper-reaching impact on pricing than the joint practices of out-of-model hedging and model recalibration. In-model hedging refers to the practice of hedging a complex option by taking positions in 'delta' amounts of traded instruments to neutralize the uncertainty from the *stochastic* drivers of the process for the underlying. In a Black-and-Scholes world, neutralizing the movements in an option price by buying a delta amount of stock is a classical example of in-model hedging.

Out-of-model hedging is the taking of positions to neutralize the sensitivity of a complex product to variations in input quantities *that the model assumes deterministic* (e.g. volatility). In a Black-and-Scholes world, vega hedging is a prime example of out-of-model hedging.

Needless to say, out-of-model hedging is on conceptually rather shaky ground: if the volatility is deterministic and perfectly known, as many models used to arrive at the price assume it to be, there would be no need to undertake vega hedging. Furthermore, calculating the vega statistics means estimating the dependence on changes in volatility of a price that has been arrived at assuming the self-same volatility to be both deterministic and perfectly known. Despite these logical problems, the adoption of out-of-model hedging in general, and of vega hedging in particular, is universal in the complex-derivatives trading community. The trader who engages in this logically dubious vega hedging *at inception of a trade* can at least console herself as follows. If her model has been correctly calibrated to the current market prices of the vega-hedging instruments, she will be adding to the original delta-neutral portfolio another self-financing, delta-neutral and fairly-valued portfolio of options. By so doing she will simply have exchanged part of her wealth from cash into stock and fairly-priced options, and this can have no impact on the value of the complex trade (because her model was correctly calibrated to the current market prices of the hedging instruments). But what about *future* vega re-hedging transactions? If, conditional on a future level for the underlying, these vega trades will be carried out in the real world at the same future prices that the model ascribes to them today, once again the trader has notionally just added lots of self-financing, delta-neutral and fairly-valued portfolios of forward-starting options. The economic effect of this is zero. This is no longer true, however, if the model predicts today future re-hedging costs different from what will be encountered in reality. If systematic, this difference between the real and theoretical level of future re-hedging transactions can make the whole strategy non-self-financing, and cause money to bleed in or (most likely) out of the trader's account.

Similarly important, universal and difficult to justify theoretically is the practice of re-calibrating a model to the current market plain-vanilla prices throughout the life of the complex trade. Let us look at this practice in some detail. Because of the need to vega hedge at the start of the life of a complex transaction, a trader will begin by calibrating her model in such a way as to recover the current (day-0) prices of all the options needed for hedging. Once the model has been calibrated in this manner, the price of a complex derivative will be calculated, and the trader will begin the dynamic hedging strategy to be carried out until the option expiry. Let us now move a few days into the trade. On day 2, the same model calibration used on day 0 will not in general produce spot (i.e. day-2) plain-vanilla option prices in line with the market. Therefore if the future re-hedging transactions were carried out with the model's parameter as per day-0's calibration, their model prices would not coincide with the market prices. To avoid this, the trader will re-calibrate the model on the basis of these new benchmark option prices, and re-calculate the price of the complex instrument on the basis of the new calibration, *assumed again to be valid until the option expiry*. As an unrepentant sinner, therefore, every morning the trader who re-calibrates a model admits that yesterday's calibration (and price) had been wrong, yet makes a price today (with the new parameters) that rests on the assumption that the new calibration will be valid until the product's expiry.

These two practices are closely linked. In a friction-less market, if a model did not have to be re-calibrated during its life, future vega transactions would have no economic impact. If a model only needed to be calibrated once and for all, it would always imply the same future prices for plain-vanilla options in the same future attainable states of the world. Therefore, contingent on a particular realization of the stock price or rate, these trades would be transacted at the future conditional prices for the plain-vanilla hedging instruments implicit in the day-0 calibration. Exchanging in the future an amount of money equal to the fair value (according to the model) of the future plain-vanilla options required for re-hedging has no economic effect today, and, as a consequence, would not affect today's model price of the complex derivative. This is no longer true, however, if, in order to recover the future spot plain-vanilla prices, the model has to be re-calibrated day after day.

Clearly, no model will be able to predict exactly what the future re-hedging costs will be (even if the Black-and-Scholes approach assumes this to be possible). It is however important to use a model that, as much as possible, 'knows' about possible future re-hedging costs and assigns to them the correct (risk-adjusted) probabilities. Since the true cost of an option is linked (in a complete market, is equal) to the cost of the replicating portfolio, the trader will therefore have to keep two possible sources of cost in mind: the hedging costs incurred at inception, and those encountered during the life of the option. As for the initial costs, these come from in-model hedging (e.g. the cost of the delta amount of stock), and from out-of-model hedging. I have argued that the latter have, in theory and in the absence of bid–offer spreads, no economic effect today, since the trader who has correctly calibrated her model is simply buying at fair value a series of fairly priced options. Indeed, neglecting again bid–offer spreads, after booking these out-of-model hedging initial trades, the P&L account of the trader will display no change. For a small number of products (such as, for instance, European digital options) an initial portfolio is all that is needed to hedge exactly the 'complex' trade until expiry. See, for instance, the discussion in Chapter 17. For this type of trade recovery of today's plain-vanilla prices is all that matters, and the trader does not have to worry whether the future conditional option prices predicted by the model will be in line with reality or not. These pseudo-complex trades, however, are few, and, by and large, uninteresting variations on the plain-vanilla theme. For all bona fide complex trades some degree of in- and out-of-model vega *re*-hedging will always have to be undertaken. The more the future vega trades will be important, the more the trader will be sensitive to the correct prediction by the model of the future conditional plain-vanilla option prices, and the less exact recovery of today's prices becomes the only relevant criterion in assessing the quality of a model.

Choosing good inputs to a model therefore means recovering today's prices in such a way that tomorrow's volatilities and correlations, as predicted by the model, will produce future plain-vanilla option prices as similar as possible to what will be encountered in the market. Given the joint practices of vega re-hedging and model re-calibration, the 'best' calibration methodology is therefore the one that will require as little future re-estimation of the model parameters as possible.

Looking at the problem in this light, one of the most important questions is: How should the model inputs that will give rise to the more stable calibration and to the smallest re-hedging 'surprises' be estimated?[6] Answering this fundamental question requires choosing the source of information (statistical analysis or market 'implication') that can best serve the trading practice. This is therefore the topic of the next section.

1.4 The Calibration Debate

In principle, to calibrate a model in order to price complex derivatives, one could follow two distinct routes: one could prescribe the whole real-world dynamics for the driving factor(s) (e.g. the stock price or the short rate) and for the associated risk premia. Given these inputs, the equilibrium prices for *all* assets (the underlying *and* the derivatives) can be obtained. This approach is called 'absolute pricing'. Alternatively, one could assign the volatility and correlation functions (the covariance structure, for short) of the stochastic state variables. On the basis of this much more limited information, the prices of options *given the price of the underlying* can be obtained. This approach is called 'relative pricing'. Readers familiar with the Black-and-Scholes approach might find that the first (absolute) approach 'goes against the grain', since it fails to take advantage of the greatest strength of relative pricing, i.e. the irrelevance of the difficult-to-estimate real-world drift. Yet, in the interest-rate arena, estimation of the real-world dynamics of the driving factor (typically, the short rate) and a separate specification of the associated risk premium was the approach of choice for the first term-structure models. I discuss the evolution of these models in detail in Rebonato (2004), where I explain why this practice was abandoned in favour of working directly in the risk-neutral measure.

While both routes are in principle possible, these days for practical pricing purposes the relative-pricing route is almost universally adopted for derivatives. Therefore, the specification of a relative-pricing, arbitrage-free model in a complete-market setting has in current trading practice become tantamount to assigning the covariance structure among the state variables (or just the volatility, if only one stochastic variable describes the financial universe).

When this is combined with the market practices of out-of-model hedging and model re-calibration discussed in the previous section, it produces some important consequences, which have a direct bearing on calibration. This is because any choice of volatilities and correlations will determine the model-implied future conditional prices of the plain-vanilla options required to carry out the future re-hedging trades. As a consequence, the universal practices of re-calibrating the model and of re-balancing the vega hedges during the life of the complex trade require that the model should recover to a satisfactory degree the future conditional prices of the hedging instruments. The fundamental calibration question therefore becomes: 'What sources of information can most reliably provide an estimate of the covariance structure capable of producing these desirable future prices?' The answer to this question is as, if not more, important than choosing the 'best' model.

---

[6]Strictly speaking, this statement does not tell the full story. If markets were complete, then it would be possible to set up at inception strategies that would produce gains or losses that exactly offset the 'surprises' coming from the real-world realizations. This possibility is discussed in Section 1.4, where I argue that the complete-market hypothesis is a conceptually useful but often unrealistic idealization.

The question that we have posed is important and it is worthwhile pausing and sketching the logical itinerary followed to formulate it. The starting point is the predominance in current complex-derivatives pricing of the relative-pricing approach. In this approach the real-world drifts and risk premia become irrelevant (this is obvious for the Black-and-Scholes approach, but it is also true for interest-rate modelling). Therefore only the specification of volatility and correlation is required for no-arbitrage pricing (again, obviously for 'stock-like' problems, but, given the Heath-Jarrow-and-Morton (1987, 1989) insight discussed in Chapter 19, also true in a more complex form for interest rates). At the same time, volatilities and correlations determine the present and future smile surfaces. In turn, the future smile surfaces determine future re-hedging costs (this is because of the joint practices of model re-calibration and of vega re-hedging). Therefore the choice of volatilities and correlations will both give concrete form to the no-arbitrage pricing condition and 'predict' the future conditional re-hedging costs. I have also argued that the first desideratum of a model used for the relative pricing of complex products is that it should 'know' not only about the present, but also about the future (re)-hedging costs. Putting all the pieces together it therefore follows that the calibration procedure (i.e. choosing the volatilities and correlations that enter the model) should be carried out in such a way as to ensure that the chosen model will produce the future properties for the hedging options that we desire. This, incidentally, is the reason why this book is called *Volatility and Correlation*. In option pricing no decision is more important than how to choose these two quantities. Yet there is no universal agreement among practitioners or academics as to how volatilities and correlations should be estimated. The next section explains why this is the case.

1.4.1 Historical vs Implied Calibration

The estimation of volatilities and correlations can be arrived at either using historical estimation or via the implied route. With the historical approach the model inputs are determined on the basis of a statistical analysis of the time series of the relevant market quantities. With the implied approach, the input quantities are determined so as to recover the observed market prices of plain-vanilla options. When, for a given set of market prices, there is only one input function to determine, the 'implied' solution is unambiguous. This is the classic case of the Black-and-Scholes implied volatility. But, once this volatility has been estimated from the price of an option, can one use this implied quantity to price something else (e.g. a different-strike option, or an option with a different payoff)? And, what should one do when different combinations of input quantities can give rise to the same set of observable market prices? This is the case, for instance, of market swaption prices, which can be recovered with a variety of possible combinations of correlation and instantaneous volatility functions, as discussed in Chapters 19 and 20. If we are pricing a forward-rate-dependent complex product, should we use the forward-rate correlation 'implied' by the swaption prices, or the one estimated on the basis of statistical analysis? Should we rely on the FX/interest-rate correlation implied by the price of a quanto swap to price a power reverse dual swap, or should we use the available historical information? What use should we make of the information about the implied equity correlation that one can extract from the price of an equity index basket option?

In the context of derivatives pricing, both academics and practitioners have tended to embrace the implied route with far more enthusiasm than the statistical approach. It is common to find in the literature statements such as the following by Alexander (2003):

> ...correlation forecasts [are] difficult to obtain, particularly for short maturity forward rates. The forecasts have a great deal of uncertainty. This is one of the many reasons why we should seek to use market data rather than historical data for calibrating correlations....

Furthermore, the ability of a model to recover simultaneously as many 'market-implied' features as possible (e.g. implied instantaneous volatilities *and* correlations from the prices of caplets *and* swaptions), has generally been regarded as highly desirable. See, for instance, Schoenmakers and Coffey (2000), Brace and Womersley (2000), De Jong *et al.* (1999) and Marris and Lane (2002).[7]

What are the reasons for this preference? Under what assumptions can it be justified? Much as the implied route might appear 'natural' to a trading community trained in the footsteps of the Black-and-Scholes approach, it should not be taken as self-evident. This is the topic explored in the next section.

1.4.2 The Logical Underpinning of the Implied Approach

I will show in Chapter 3 that, in a classic Black-and-Scholes world, once the volatilities have been determined for two options with expiries T_1 and T_2 on the same underlying, for any other option whose payoff depends on the realization of the same volatility from time T_1 to time T_2, one can safely assume that this *future* volatility will be exactly as implied by the two spot volatilities estimated *today*. The precise value of this future volatility prevailing from time T_1 to time T_2 will be obtained in Chapter 3, but, for the purpose of the present discussion the relevant point is that, if unrestricted trading in two options with expiries T_1 and T_2 is possible, the trader does not have to rely on this market-implied guess to be correct, or even plausible. As long as she can trade in the two spot options freely, she can 'lock-in' this future value of the volatility. This practice is very similar to the ability to lock-in a future borrowing rate by trading in two pure discount bonds, and is reflected in the fact that the equilibrium value of a forward rate does not reflect an expectation of future rates, but is obtained from arbitrage considerations. See Rebonato (2002) for a careful discussion of this point.

The justification for this practice is to be found in the completeness of the relevant markets, which in turn stems from the assumed deterministic nature of the volatility function in the Black-and-Scholes world: even if the future volatility were to turn out to be different from what is implied by today's spot prices, by trading in the options available today we will be able to make enough money in each possible future state of the world to compensate us for any discrepancy between the implied and the actually realized value.

In the case of the same-currency correlation function mentioned above, I discuss in Sections 19.5 and 19.6 (see also Rebonato (2002)) that, if caplets, swaptions *and serial options* were liquidly traded, one would indeed find oneself in a situation of market

---

[7]Incidentally, this practice might have been partly motivated or encouraged by the fact that the LIBOR market model has just enough degrees of freedom to fit exactly, if one so wanted, all the caplet and European swaption prices.

completeness,[8] and one would be able to put in place strategies able to 'lock-in' any value of the correlation function implied by these joint prices, no matter how econometrically implausible. This is conceptually equivalent to the statement that, if two discount bonds, P_1 and P_2, maturing in one and two years' time trade in the market at prices $\exp[-y_1 T_1]$ and $\exp[-y_2 T_2]$, I will be able to synthetically borrow money for one year in one year's time at the rate $\exp[-(y_1 - 2y_2)] - 1$. In the interest-rate case, however, serial options are *not* liquidly traded, the market is *not* complete, and the future correlation *cannot* be locked-in with certainty by means of any strategy initiated at time 0. More generally, market incompleteness is the rule and not the exception, and arises when the volatility is stochastic,[9] when jumps are present, and, in general, when the payoffs from the available hedging instruments do not span all the possible future states of the world.

Does this mean that the implied approach is in general useless, and should be abandoned? Not necessarily. While market incompleteness might prevent the trader from locking-in the quantities of interest, yet, under certain conditions, the market-implied estimates might still convey useful information, namely the best collective guess produced by the market as to their value.

This statement must be treated with great care. In general, a market-implied quantity (say, the implied jump frequency in a jump–diffusion model) cannot be directly related to the corresponding real-world quantity, because of risk aversion: assume, for instance, that a set of market players are afraid of equity market crashes and cannot perfectly hedge against them. A different set of market players might provide 'insurance' to them by selling put options that would be priced assuming more frequent and more severe down jumps than observed in reality. This is discussed in detail in Smile Tale 1 in Section 6.4.

Yet, even if investors are risk averse, the market-implied quantity might still clear at the econometric level. This might happen if there is no net imbalance of supply and demand for an option from individually risk-averse investors. As I discuss in Section 6.6, in this case if a trade does take place it will do so at a level that does not incorporate risk aversion and simply reflects the unadjusted views 'of the market'.

Unfortunately, this state of 'natural' balance of demand and supply is in reality rather rare. Another condition can, however, apply, and has been alluded to before: the existence of pseudo-arbitrageurs who do not have a preferred trading habitat and who can take positions judging each trade on the basis of an appropriately discounted expectation of its future payoffs. If pseudo-arbitrageurs exist and can carry out their trades in as large a size as desired, excess demand creates its own supply, and vice versa. If this is the case, again supply and demand ultimately have no direct effect on price formation. In this setting prices do contain useful and direct (i.e. unpolluted-by-risk-aversion) information about the real world.

So far we have reached the conclusion that implying the values of financial quantities from market prices can be justified either if markets are complete, or if they are informationally efficient. Since we can safely rule out the first possibility, we should look carefully at the second.

---

[8]For market completeness to hold, one must also assume, of course, that the deterministic-volatility and deterministic-correlation assumptions hold exactly, that these quantities are perfectly known, and that the process for the forward rates has no jumps.

[9]It is often claimed that the market incompleteness arising from stochastic volatility can be easily exorcised by trading in another plain-vanilla option. While theoretically correct, I discuss the limitations of this solution in Chapter 13.

1.4.3 Are Derivatives Markets Informationally Efficient?

A large body of literature has appeared in the last 15 years or so, which challenges one of the pillars of the classical financial asset pricing, namely the EMH. The name generically applied to these rather disparate studies is that of 'behavioural finance'. In short, two joint claims are implicitly made (although not always explicitly articulated) by the proponents of this school, namely that (i) at least some investors arrive at decisions that are not informationally efficient and (ii) mechanisms that would allow better-informed traders to exploit and eliminate the results of these 'irrationalities' are not always effective. Since the prime mechanism to enforce efficiency is the ability to carry out (pseudo-)arbitrage, an important line of critique of the EMH has been developed (see, for example, Shleifer and Vishny (1997)) which shows that pseudo-arbitrage can in reality be very risky, and that, therefore, the pricing results of irrational decisions made on the basis of psychological features such as, say, over-confidence might persist over long periods of time.

In order to account for the *origin* of the pricing inefficiencies, the original emphasis was put on the psychological features of investors, such as, for instance, over-confidence, anchoring, framing effects, etc. (see, for example, Shefrin (2000) and Shiller (2000)), whence the name *behavioural* finance. Simplifying greatly, behavioural finance questions the assumption that market participants process new information as Bayesian agents, and claims that they maximize their utility function not over total wealth, but over gains and losses from a given reference point. The argument, based on the difficulty and riskiness of pseudo-arbitrage, can, however, still be applied if the price of an asset (and, in our case, of a derivative) is disconnected from 'fundamentals' for any (i.e. not necessarily for psychological) reasons: agency relationships, for instance, can give rise to discrepancies between the observed prices and those predicted by the EMH even if (and, actually, especially when) all the players are fully rational. This is important, because in the derivatives area (largely the arena of professional and sophisticated traders), it is more likely that institutional set-ups, rather than psychological biases, might be at the root of possible price deviations from fundamentals.

The relevance of these possible informational inefficiencies for derivatives pricing can be seen as follows. First, according to the EMH, prices are arrived at by discounting future expected payoffs using an appropriate discount factor.[10] The second step in the argument is that new information (a change in 'fundamentals') can lead an informed trader to reassess the current price for a derivative (a new expectation is produced by the new information), but supply and demand pressures *per se* cannot: if the 'fundamentals' have not changed, a demand-driven increase in the price of a substitutable security will immediately entice pseudo-arbitrageurs to short the 'irrationally expensive' security, and bring it back in line with fundamentals. The more two securities (or bundles of securities) are similar, the less undiversifiable risk will remain, and the more pseudo-arbitrageurs will be enticed to enter 'correcting' trades.

So, answering the question, 'To what extent should one make use of market-implied quantities as input to a model?' means addressing the two joint questions: 'Are there reasons to believe that a systematic imbalance of supply or demand might be present in

---

[10]'Appropriate' in this context means, on the one hand, that it takes the riskiness of the cash flows into account, but, on the other, that it is only affected by non-diversifiable risk. So, if a security (an option) can be replicated by another (the hedging portfolio), then no idiosyncratic risk will be left and the appropriate discount factor is derived from riskless bonds.

the interest-rate plain-vanilla market?' and, if so, 'Are there reasons to believe that the activity of pseudo-arbitrageurs might entail substantial risks?'

Possible Mechanisms to Create a Supply/Demand Imbalance

The dynamics of the supply of and demand for interest-rate derivatives products are very complex, especially in US$, where the mortgage-backed securities market creates a large demand for a variety of derivatives products. If, to begin with, one focuses attention on the non-USD market, in broad terms some relatively simple patterns can be identified. On the one hand there are investors looking for 'yield enhancement' and issuers in search of 'advantageous' funding rates; on the other hand there are floating-rate borrowers who want to reduce their risk by purchasing interest-rate protection. In order to obtain the advantageous yields or funding rates, investors or issuers, respectively, tend to sell the right to call or put a bond, i.e. swaption-type optionality, which is typically 'sold-on' to investment houses. See Rebonato (1998a) for a more detailed description of these structures. Professional traders will therefore find themselves systematically *long* swaption optionality.

At the same time, floating-rate corporate borrowers will seek to limit their exposure to rising rates by purchasing caps from the same trading desks. In the non-USD markets, the latter will therefore find themselves systematically *long* swaption optionality and *short* caplet optionality.

In the USD market the picture is made much more complex by the presence of the Government-sponsored mortgage Agencies, who retain in their investment portfolios very large amounts of mortgage collateral. These mortgages expose the Agencies to pre-payment risk, and make them aggressive bidders of swaption volatility with expiries and underlying maturities dictated by the pre-payment speeds. The demand for swaption volatility is so high that the Agencies choose, or – some commentators claim – are forced, to complement their purchases of over-the-counter European and Bermudan swaptions with a funding programme largely based on callable debt (callable Agency debentures). It is important to point out that the demand for swaption optionality by the Agencies is localized in particular expiries and maturities, which do not necessarily coincide with the expiries and maturities of the swaption optionality that banks receive from investors and non-Agency issuers. As a result of this market dynamics significant supply/demand imbalances of different types of volatility persist, the complex-derivatives trader cannot act as a pure 'volatility broker' and has to warehouse and manage a substantial amount of 'volatility basis risk'.

Moving to the FX area, let us look at Figure 1.1, which shows time series of the implied volatilities for USD/JPY FX options of different expiries. Ignoring smile effects, which should anyway be rather limited for expiries of five or more years, we shall see in Chapter 3 that an increasing series of at-the-money implied volatilities requires that the future instantaneous (spot) volatility should also increase, and even more dramatically so, over time. Looking again at Figure 1.1, do we really believe that an information-ally efficient market is conveying, via the implied volatility quotes, information about the expected future spot volatility? Today's implied volatility for options expiring in 10 years' time can be read from the graph to be around 15%. Yet the future 10-year average volatility embedded in today's 20- and 30-year option prices is approximately twice as large (and three times as large as today's spot volatility). Even a cursory examination

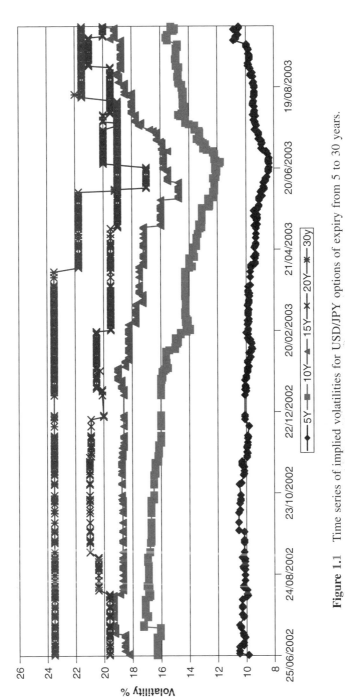

Figure 1.1 Time series of implied volatilities for USD/JPY options of expiry from 5 to 30 years.

of this figure appears to cast serious doubts over the proposition that the implied estimation of volatilities provides a reliable estimate of market expectations. Is there a more convincing explanation?

In order to understand the USD/JPY option-volatility case one should recall that in the first years of the twenty-first century very large volumes of yield-enhancing notes were marketed to JPY investors. (See Jeffrey (2003) for a story of the fortunes of this product.) Embedded in these notes were derivatives called power-reverse-dual swaps, which effectively conferred to the investor a series of very-long-dated callable FX options. The banks that provided these products therefore found themselves short of long-dated FX option volatility, and bid up the prices of the long-dated FX options required to hedge their exposure. These very-long-dated derivatives were virtually unheard of before the appearance of power reverse duals, which *de facto* created the market for this 'underlying'. No other economically motivated market flows were therefore in place to redress the demand imbalance. In my opinion, therefore, it is much simpler to explain the observed pattern in terms of a supply-and-demand effect, than of expectations of future behaviour of the spot volatility of the USD/JPY rate. But if this is correct, the implied at-the-money values do not provide any indication about future realization of the quantity of interest. In particular, unless we are dealing with a complete-market situation and the trader can 'lock-in' these values via static hedging strategies, these implied values are of no assistance in estimating the volatility levels at which future re-hedging trades will have to be carried out.

A different dynamics of supply and demand applies in the equity derivatives market. This market is largely driven by two sets of players: on the one hand, fund managers seeking to protect the value of their equity-invested portfolios; and on the other, especially in the United Kingdom and in continental Europe, retail investors receiving a deleveraged equity return in exchange for capital protection. Both sets of players are therefore net *buyers* of optionality, supplied by the derivatives desks of trading houses. Once again, the market dynamics appear to give rise to a net supply/demand imbalance.

A case can therefore be made as to why there might be systematic imbalances in the derivatives market: in the equity arena ultimately because of a desire for downside protection. In the FX case (at least in the example described above) because of the need to hedge the exposure created by large volumes of investor products. In the interest-rate area because of a more complex dynamics: issuers, investors and the Agencies create a systematic excess demand of cap volatility and excess supply or demand (depending on the exact location in the swaption matrix) of swaption volatility. Clearly, however, both caps and swaptions share the same underlyings (ultimately, forward rates) and should therefore in principle be 'cross-arbitrageable'.

Because of this state of affairs, pseudo-arbitrageurs should be enticed to take advantage of whatever move away from 'fundamentals' the supply/demand imbalance might create in the relative prices of caps and swaptions. Similarly, they should be tempted to sell the expensive put equity volatility and hedge their positions either with the underlying or with cheaper at-the-money options. Are there reasons to believe that the effectiveness of the pseudo-arbitrageurs to carry out these trades might in practice by hampered?

Possible Limitations to Pseudo-Arbitrageur Activity

What can prevent pseudo-arbitrageurs from carrying out their task of bringing prices in line with fundamentals? Without repeating the arguments presented earlier in this chapter (see Section 1.2.2) I will recall the existence of agency relationships (hedge funds, relative-value traders, etc. often take positions not with their own money, but as agents of investors or shareholders); and the existence of institutional and regulatory constraints (stop-loss limits, VaR limits, size constraints, concentration limits, etc.) that might force the liquidation of positions before they can be shown to be 'right'. Furthermore, poor liquidity, often compounded with the ability of the market to guess the position of a large relative-value player, also contributes to the difficulties of pseudo-arbitrageurs. In this context, the role played by pseudo-arbitrageurs as ultimate providers of liquidity has been discussed by Shleifer (2000). Finally, very high information costs might act as a barrier to entry, or limit the number, of pseudo-arbitrageurs.

In short, because of all of the above, even in the presence of a significant imbalance of supply or demand, relative-value traders might be more reluctant to step in and bring prices in line with fundamentals than the EMH assumes.

Empirical Evidence

The literature covering empirical tests of market efficiency is far too large to survey even in a cursory manner (a recent count of papers in behavioural finance aimed at displaying failures of the EMH exceeded 2000), and, beyond the statement that markets are 'by and large' efficient, there has been a strong, and unfortunate, polarization of academic opinion. However, questions of more limited scope can be posed, such as: 'Is there any evidence that the mechanisms discussed above do hamper the activity of pseudo-arbitrageurs?', or 'Does the relative price of caplets and swaptions provide any indication of price deviations from fundamentals compatible with the supply/demand dynamics discussed in Section 1.2.1?'. Both questions are difficult to answer, the first because of the clearly secretive nature of the activities of pseudo-arbitrageurs (hedge funds and proprietary traders); the second, because showing that some prices are 'incorrect' always requires working under a joint hypothesis: what it tested is the deviation from a pricing model, given that the pricing model itself is correct. None the less, some pertinent observations *can* be made.

Starting from the question regarding the actual impact of the factors discussed above on the effectiveness of the pseudo-arbitrageurs, some indirect evidence can be obtained from reconstructions of the market events that surrounded the near-collapse of the LTCM hedge fund in 1998. (See Jorion (2000) and Das (2002) for a description of the events from a risk-management perspective.) Both Dunbar (2000) and Scholes (2000), although from different perspectives and drawing different conclusions, describe a situation where, for instance, the long-dated (5-year) equity implied volatility had reached in the autumn of 1998 levels that would imply for the next several years a realized volatility much higher than what had ever been observed in the past over similar periods. Yet traders (LTCM *in primis*) who attempted to short volatility found their positions moving farther into the red before the volatility finally declined. Many traders/arbitrageurs, including LTCM, faced with margin calls and with their request for additional 'arbitrage' capital from the (technically uninformed) investors turned down, had to cut the positions at a loss before the 'correctness' of their views could be proven. Similarly, swap spreads, which are but tenuously linked to the default risk of banks, reached during the same period levels difficult to reconcile with any plausibly risk-adjusted probability of bank default.[11]

---

[11]Given the role of pseudo-arbitrageurs as providers of liquidity alluded to above, Scholes (2000) argues that, in order to assess the 'fair' level of the swap spread, one should factor in the (time-varying) price for liquidity.

Finally, and most relevantly for the topic of this chapter, a reconstruction of events from market participants suggests that a major international investment house observed during the same period swaptions and caplet volatilities to move away from levels that most models could explain. In particular, for most plausible instantaneous volatility functions that recovered caplet prices, the 'implied correlation' was very different from correlations estimated statistically. The same house is widely thought to have put large (and 'correct'), swaption–caplet 'arbitrage' trades in place, only to have to unwind them at a loss as the positions temporarily moved even more strongly away from 'fundamentals'.

If the account given above is correct, and if therefore supply and demand cannot always be arbitraged away efficiently by proprietary traders, one would expect to observe some systematic effects. For instance, recall that investment houses tend to be long swaption optionality, and short caplet optionality. If this is the case, the market-implied forward-rate instantaneous volatilities estimated from swaption prices would be systematically lower than the same quantities estimated from caplet prices. Similarly, but less directly, the implied jump frequency required to recover the equity smile would have to be substantially higher than the corresponding statistically estimated quantity.

For reasons explained in Chapter 14, the equity 'evidence' is too indirect to lend itself to an unambiguous analysis, but we *can* say something about the caplet–swaption case. Rebonato (2002) displays graphs of the instantaneous volatilities of forward rates for several currencies estimated from the caplet and from the swaption markets.[12] The instantaneous volatility functions thus estimated turned out to have a very similar qualitative shape irrespective of the instruments (caplets or swaptions) used for their estimation, but to be systematically lower in all currencies when estimated from swaption data. This would be consistent with the supply-and-demand story for caplet and swaption optionality outlined above. Similarly, using different market data, Rebonato (2002) finds that the implied correlation required to price a set of co-terminal swaptions given the market prices of the caplets is much lower than what is historically observed. Again, swaptions would appear too 'cheap' relative to caplets, providing further indirect corroboration for the same 'story'.

It should be stressed that these results must be interpreted with care, because what is tested is the joint assumption that supply and demand skew the prices of a theoretically replicable set of securities *and* that the model used for the pricing (with the chosen parametric forms for the volatility and the correlation) is correct. Even with these caveats, however, the results appear to provide some corroboration for the hypothesis that supply/demand imbalances do affect the relative prices of caplets and swaptions.

1.4.4   Back to Calibration

This discussion brings us back to the calibration issue. The prevalent market practice, as evidenced by the references quoted above, seems to favour the 'implied' estimation approach. This would only make sense, however, if complex derivatives markets were

---

If this view is correct, there would be no market inefficiency at play. From the point of view of the calibration of a model, however, the existence of an important, and unhedgeable, risk factor (in this case liquidity) neglected in the pricing would raise similar concerns as to the appropriateness of using the market-implied estimate.

[12]A variety of correlation functions were used in the calibration to swaption prices. For econometrically plausible correlations the results displayed weak dependence on the level and details of the correlation functions. See also De Jong *et al.* (1999) on this point.

either complete or informationally efficient. The traded assets, however, certainly do not span all the possible states of the world (see, for example, the discussion in Section 19.5). And I have argued that there appear to be sufficient reasons to doubt the informational efficiency of the plain-vanilla instruments used for model calibration.

If these conditions are not met, then 'implying' values of financial quantities from option prices might indeed convey information, but probably more about the supply-and-demand dynamics than about intrinsic features of the underlying process. Therefore the generally accepted practice of fitting the free parameters of a model so as to recover the prices of as many plain-vanilla instruments as possible should be carefully questioned in each application. I have argued in this first chapter, and I will do so again at several points in this book, that a more relevant criterion for choosing these input functions should be their ability to recover in a plausible way current *and future* prices of the relevant re-hedging instruments.

1.4.5 A Practical Recommendation

I would like to offer a final recommendation to the trader who is tempted to 'imply' from market prices financial quantities (e.g. statistical properties of the process of the under-lying from prices of the associated options). Whenever such a process of 'implication' is considered, the trader should ask the question: 'If the prices failed to reflect the best estimate of the quantity to be estimated, how easy would it be for a clever trader to exploit this error?' If the answer is that the pseudo-arbitrage is simple and relatively riskless, it is reasonable to expect that the market prices do convey useful information. If, instead, the 'correcting trades' are, for any reason, difficult to put in place or to exploit, then the trader should be much more cautious before relying on the 'best market estimate'.

Let me give a concrete example, related to the quote by Alexander (2000) reported above. Let us suppose that, perhaps for reasons of supply and demand, the correlation among forward rates implied by caplet and swaption prices was found to be out of line with what statistical analysis suggests plausible. How easy would it be to exploit this 'market error'? How can the trader put in place close-to-riskless pseudo-arbitrage strategies? More concretely: how would a trader deal with the gamma mismatch of a vega-neutral portfolio of swaptions and caplets? How can a trader hedge a product (the swaption) sensitive to most of the important modes of deformation of the swaption matrix (see Chapter 26) with products (caplets) which are only affected by a much more restricted set of eigenmodes? If the trader can find a satisfactory answer to these questions (I cannot), she can be reasonably confident that the market-implied correlation will convey useful information, *usable for trades other than caplet–swaption strategies.* If not, I believe that relying on the efficiency of the market as an information-processing machine is unwarranted.

1.5 Across-Markets Comparison of Pricing and Modelling Practices

In the mortgage-backed-securities (MBS) area pre-payment models are coupled with interest-rate models in order to produce the present value of the expected cash flows arising from a pool of mortgages (see, for example, Fabozzi (2001) or Hayre (2001) for a description of the market and of the prevalent pricing approaches). As a first stage in arriving at the price for, say, a pass-through, the cash flows (including pre-payments) are discounted at the riskless (LIBOR) rate. The implicit assumption in doing so is that the hedge ratios suggested not only by the interest-rate model, but also by the pre-payment model, should provide a perfect hedge for the cash-flow uncertainty. From the modelling point of view, this is perfectly justifiable, because the vast majority of pre-payment models use only interest rates as state variables, and therefore allow for theoretically perfect hedging of the pre-payment risk by trading in the interest-rate-sensitive underlying products (swaps, caps, swaptions, indexed-principal swaps, spread locks, etc.). However, it has always been recognized in the MBS market that other variables (such as unemployment, GDP growth, etc.) strongly affect pre-payments, and that these variables are very imperfectly correlated with the interest-rate state variables. Whatever the models might claim, it has therefore always been very clear that hedging against these sources of uncertainty is in practice very difficult.

Because of this, the concept of the option-adjusted spread (OAS) has been introduced. The OAS is defined to be the spread to be added to the risk-less (LIBOR-derived) forward rates in order to obtain the discount factors to present-value the expected cash flows. A non-zero OAS therefore explicitly adjusts the price for all the undiversifiable (unhedgeable) sources of risk, for model uncertainty, for liquidity effects, etc. It is by no means a second-order effect, since, especially in periods of great pre-payment uncertainty (e.g. during the unprecedented wave of mortgage refinancing of 2002, when pre-payment models were constantly 're-calibrated' by trading houses, and the coupon on every outstanding issue was higher than the current par coupon) it reached values well over 100 basis points.

The introduction of the OAS links in an interesting way derivatives pricing when perfect replication is possible with more classic asset-pricing techniques. When pricing is absolute and not relative, i.e. when we are pricing primitive and not derivatives securities, the standard prescription, in fact, is to discount future uncertain cash flows using a rate 'appropriate to the riskiness of the cash flows'. Adding an OAS to the riskless forward rates used to discount the cash flows that the pricing model assumes to be riskless (because replicable) directly introduces an explicit recognition of the real uncertainty associated even with the best hedging strategy.

Why has the equivalent of an OAS not been developed in the derivatives area? Apart from issues of product homogeneity, liquidity and standardization, I believe that an important reason has been the different 'starting points' for the two markets. Even the first MBSs (pass-throughs) have always been perceived as being patently complex. This was due both to the difficulty in estimating the dependence of pre-payments on interest rates (the theoretically perfectly hedgeable part), and because of the inherent difficulty in hedging the non-interest-rate-related risk factors ('media effect', housing mobility, etc.). The appearance of more complex products (IOs, POs, sequentials, PACs, etc.) therefore simply added to an existing substantial modelling complexity, and stressed the relatively poor ability to hedge. Assuming perfect replication, in other terms, was never a realistic working hypothesis.

First-generation derivatives products (such as caplets, simple stock options, etc.), on the other hand, were relatively simple to hedge effectively, and, given the well-known robustness of the Black-and-Scholes model *vis-à-vis* reasonable mis-specification of the input volatility, payoff replicability (which ultimately justifies the risk-less discounting) was a very reasonable working assumption. As new products have been introduced, each incremental increase in complexity has not been so big as to require a totally new and fresh pricing approach. The cumulative effect of this process, however, has been to give rise to products of considerable complexity: some of the instruments that received quite a lot of (unwanted) attention from Warren Buffet in 2002 (such as power-reverse-dual swaps) require the simultaneous modelling of compound optionality arising from the evolution over 30 years or more of two yield curves, of their volatilities and correlations, of the correlations among the forward rates of the two currencies, of the spot FX rate, and of its correlation with the interest forward rates. Most remarkably, one of the 'underlying' instruments behind power-reverse-dual swaps (extremely long-dated FX options) was literally created because of the introduction of the more complex product. At the same time, parallel pricing developments in related areas (credit derivatives, and *n*th-to-default swaps in particular) have brought about similarly difficult modelling challenges. One can therefore argue that these products have become no simpler, and their payoff replication not any easier, than the first mortgage-backed pass-throughs. None the less, due to the *incremental* process of adding relatively small elements of added complexity, no equivalent of the OAS has been introduced in the pricing of these assets, and the paradigm of risk-neutral valuation still reigns supreme. Model reserves are sometimes applied when recognizing the book value of these products, but this has not affected the 'mid' marking to model. The reasons for this, I believe, can be traced to the power of a robust and elegant conceptual framework (the Black-and-Scholes replication insight) and the self-sustaining nature of the 'inertial momentum' that a successful modelling framework generates.

If this analysis is correct the implications for derivatives pricing are not that the approaches described in the rest of this book are of little use: even in the MBS arena state-of-the-art models are continuously refined and developed for the diversifiable risk factors, and the interest-rate models of choice have closely followed the evolution of the (perfect-replication-based) LIBOR market model. What is required, I believe, is a re-assessment of the limitations of the pure-replication-based pricing philosophy, and the introduction in the price-making process of explicit recognition of the existence of substantial unhedgeable components. Because of the unavoidable presence of market imperfections, I will argue in this book that the *qualitative*, 'digital' distinction between complete and incomplete markets, or between replicable or non-replicable payoffs is not the most important characterization of a market or of a set of products. The *quantitative* differences in degrees of replicability are, in my opinion, more important and more relevant to the practice and to the theory of pricing.

Perhaps the equivalent of a 'LIBOR-OAS' could be arrived at in a coherent and theoretically robust manner by following one of the approaches (see, for example the 'no-to-good-deal' approach by Cochrane and Saa-Requejo (2000)) recently introduced in the literature to account for this very state of affairs. I can appropriately close this section by quoting Cochrane (2001):

> Holding [an] option entails some risk, and the value of that option depends on the 'market price' of that risk – the covariance of the risk with an appropriate discount factor. Nonetheless we would like not to [...] go back to 'absolute' methods that try to price all assets. We can [...] still form an approximate hedge based on [...] a portfolio of basis assets 'closest to' the focus payoff. [...]. Then the uncertainty about the option value is reduced only to figuring out the price of the residual.

1.6   Using Models

A few more comments about the use of models are in order before closing this 'foundation' chapter. I will be spending a lot of time discussing models whose conceptual foundation rests on the idea of perfect payoff replicability. At the same time I will argue that the conditions for applicability of these results are never met in practice, and that noticeable 'violations' appear even in very 'benign' settings. Am I being inconsistent, or, worse, am I wasting the reader's time?

I don't think so. Models, *qua* models, are always 'wrong' in the sense that they must leave out some features of the phenomenon they attempt to explain. Recognizing that market frictions 'spoil', to some extent, the Black-and-Scholes results is no different than observing that mechanical friction spoils the Newtonian result that a free ball will roll forever on an ideally smooth surface at constant velocity. Aristotelian physics, by the way, seems to produce, in this case, an answer more similar to 'reality', in that it postulates the need for an engine to keep the ball rolling at constant speed. Yet we find Newtonian mechanics more useful than Aristotelian mechanics for most problems. If we begin to consider objects moving at very high speed, special relativity gives better predictions. If we are in a rapidly varying gravitational field we will have to invoke general relativity. Every 'model' has a domain of applicability beyond which it ceases to be useful. The skill of the researcher is to gauge up to what point a certain modelling framework can be used, and to search for a more complex explanation as soon as, but no sooner than, it ceases to produce useful outputs.

So, yes, we will spend a lot of time looking at models based on perfect replication, and, yes, perfect replication is never possible in practice. There is however no contradiction in the approach, and it would be foolish to discard completely the insight and the power of the replication approach. Much as Newtonian dynamics is contained as a limiting case in special relativity, unique pricing by no-arbitrage can be seen as a limiting case (of vanishing variance for the stochastic discount factor) of Cochrane's no-good-deal approach.

Chapter 2

Option Replication

2.1 The Bedrock of Option Pricing

The replication of an option payoff by trading in the underlying is the theoretical bedrock of unique pricing by no-arbitrage. Exact option-payoff replication is not necessary in order to price options without allowing arbitrage. It is however necessary if we want to associate a *unique* price to an option simply by invoking absence of arbitrage.

As I mentioned at the end of Chapter 1, the conditions under which perfect replication can be achieved are never met in practice: first of all, markets are not frictionless and trading is not continuous. Even if they were, perfect payoff replication by hedging purely with the 'stock' can only be achieved if the process for the underlying satisfies some very strong conditions: it must be a diffusion, and this diffusion must have a volatility either deterministic or, if stochastic, perfectly functionally dependent on the underlying itself (i.e. roughly speaking, of the form $\sigma = \sigma(S_t, t)$). Furthermore, this volatility function must be perfectly known.

Since the financial conditions are certainly violated, and the mathematical ones have been strongly rejected by empirical tests, one might ask: What is the point of taking payoff replication as the starting point of option pricing at all? I have already presented my views about the role of models in Chapter 1, and I will not repeat them here. In this context, I will only point out that the pricing edifice built on the joint pillars of frictionless markets and diffusive processes is very robust and often provides useful answers even when the underlying assumptions are violated. This is particularly so if the *realized* quadratic variation turns out to be not too different from the theoretical quadratic variation used in the pricing. This is one of the reasons why the concept of quadratic variation is central to the treatment I present in this book.

More generally, I am not blind to the fact that perfect replication is always an idealization (as frictionless surfaces, inertial frames or point particles are). Indeed, I will discuss carefully in this book that it is often more fruitful to compare the *degrees* of replicability obtainable if the underlying process is, say, a deterministic–volatility diffusion, a jump–diffusion process or a stochastic–volatility process. Yet, a clear theoretical framework provides secure conceptual guidance also, and perhaps especially, when its strict

31

conditions of applicability are no longer met. Therefore in Part I, I will take payoff replicability very 'seriously', and will embed my treatment in a pure Black-and-Scholes world.

Given the importance of the perfect-replication argument, I present it in the following
from two different angles: analytically (i.e. following the partial differential equation
(PDE) approach) and using a tree construction. Both approaches will be used extensively
in later chapters.

2.2   The Analytic (PDE) Approach

2.2.1   The Assumptions

Let us look in more detail at the requirements for perfect payoff replication. These are

- financial – the market in which the instruments trade must have no bid–offer spreads,
  long and short positions of arbitrarily large size must be allowed, no trading or regulatory limits can exist which might force the unwinding of positions, no taxes are
  levied, and trading is continuous;

- mathematical – the process for the underlying is required to be a diffusion with a
  volatility whose value at time t can be determined from properties of the stock
  process that have been fully revealed by time t. So, it could in principle depend
  on the past history of the stock price. To keep the notation simple, however, it will
  simply be denoted as $\sigma = \sigma(S_t, t)$.

Requiring that the process should be a diffusion is, at the same time, very 'generous'
and very restrictive: it is 'generous' because any continuous semi-martingale can be
represented as a diffusion (albeit, possibly, after undergoing a time change). But it is
also very restrictive because it implies that the path traced by the underlying must be
continuous everywhere: no jumps are allowed.

Requiring the volatility to be at most a deterministic function of time and of the stock
price itself rules out the possibility that another source of randomness, be it diffusive or
discontinuous in nature, might change the volatility over time.[1]

2.2.2   The Portfolio-Replication Argument (Deterministic Volatility)

The argument is familiar and it is only repeated in order to introduce the notation, to
clarify some fundamental concepts regarding the market price of risk, and to provide a
springboard for more complex settings (stochastic volatility, jump–diffusions).

Let us consider a stock, S_t, a (deterministic) riskless bond, B_t, instantaneously earning
the riskless rate, r_t, and an option C_t. Let us assume that

1. the stock follows a Brownian diffusion with deterministic volatility;

---

[1]If the number of possible jump magnitudes is finite, and if these jump amplitudes are known, then perfect
replication is still possible by adding more assets to the basket of hedging instruments. Similarly, if the volatility
is stochastic and its process is also a diffusion, then perfect payoff replication is still possible by adding an option
to the basket of hedging assets. Both cases, however, are only superficially similar to the replication discussed
in this chapter, since knowledge of the full process, and not just of the price, of the hedging instruments is
required. See the discussion in Chapters 13 and 14.

2. arbitrage opportunities should not be allowed; and

3. the time-t price of the option depends on the stock, S_t, and time t: $C_t = C_t(S_t, t)$.

Note that Assumption 3 is not trivial. Therefore:

$$dS_t = \mu_S S_t \, dt + \sigma_t S_t \, dz_t \tag{2.1}$$

$$dB_t = B_t r_t \, dt \tag{2.2}$$

$$C_t = C(S_t, t) \tag{2.3}$$

Because of Assumptions 1 and 2 (and thanks to Ito's lemma) one can write for dC_t:

$$dC_t = C_t \mu_C \, dt + C_t \sigma_C \, dz_t \tag{2.4}$$

with

$$C_t \mu_C = \frac{\partial C}{\partial t} + \frac{\partial C}{\partial S} \mu_S S_t + \frac{1}{2} \frac{\partial^2 C}{\partial S^2} \sigma_t^2 S_t^2 \tag{2.5}$$

$$C_t \sigma_C = \frac{\partial C}{\partial S} \sigma_t S_t \tag{2.6}$$

Note in passing that by writing the stochastic differential equation (SDE) for the option price as in Equation (2.4) we are not making the assumption that it should be log-normally distributed. Indeed, even if σ_t is purely deterministic (and therefore even if S is log-normally distributed), σ_C in general will not be (see Equation (2.6)). The only requirement for the validity of Equation (2.4) is that the option price should be a strictly positive semi-martingale. See, for example, Rebonato (2002), and references therein.

Now construct a portfolio, Π_t, made up of α units of the stock, S, β units of the riskless bond, B, and one unit of the option, C:

$$\Pi_t = \alpha S_t + \beta B_t + C \tag{2.7}$$

The evolution of Π will be:

$$
\begin{aligned}
d\Pi_t &= \alpha \, dS_t + \beta B_t r_t \, dt + dC_t \\
&= \alpha \{\mu_S S_t \, dt + \sigma_t S_t \, dz_t\} + \beta B_t r_t \, dt + C_t \mu_C \, dt + C_t \sigma_C \, dz_t \\
&= \alpha \{\mu_S S_t \, dt + \sigma_t S_t \, dz_t\} + \beta B_t r_t \, dt \\
&\quad + \left[\frac{\partial C}{\partial t} + \frac{\partial C}{\partial S} \mu_S S_t + \frac{1}{2} \frac{\partial^2 C}{\partial S^2} \sigma_t^2 S_t^2 \right] dt + \left[\frac{\partial C}{\partial S} \sigma_t S_t \right] dz_t
\end{aligned} \tag{2.8}
$$

Regrouping terms gives:

$$
\begin{aligned}
d\Pi_t &= \left[\alpha \mu_S S_t + \beta B_t r_t + \frac{\partial C}{\partial t} + \frac{\partial C}{\partial S} \mu_S S_t + \frac{1}{2} \frac{\partial^2 C}{\partial S^2} \sigma_t^2 S_t^2 \right] dt \\
&\quad + \left[\alpha \sigma_t S_t + \frac{\partial C}{\partial S} \sigma_t S_t \right] dz_t
\end{aligned} \tag{2.9}
$$

Let us now impose the following constraints on the portfolio:

1. it should be riskless; and

2. it should be worth zero today.

If the portfolio is riskless and worth zero, then it will be worth zero over the next infinitesimal time step.

Because of constraint 1 we require that the coefficient of the term in dz_t (i.e. the term in square brackets in the last line of Equation (2.9)) should be zero:

$$\alpha = -\frac{\partial C}{\partial S} \tag{2.10}$$

If we also want the portfolio to be worth zero (constraint 2) simple algebra shows that the amount, β, of the bond, B, must be given by

$$\beta = \frac{\frac{\partial C}{\partial S} S - C}{B} \tag{2.11}$$

Exercise 1 *Using equations up to (2.9) derive the amounts α and β, of the bond and the stock, respectively, required to give zero value to the portfolio today and to immunize it against the uncertainty dz_t.*

So, if we hold α amount of stock and β amount of bond, our portfolio will be worth zero, will be purely deterministic, and, by absence of arbitrage, will be worth zero over the next time step. Direct substitution of these two quantities in Equation (2.9) gives

$$\frac{\partial C}{\partial t} + \left(\frac{\partial C}{\partial S} S_t - C_t\right) r_t + \frac{1}{2}\frac{\partial^2 C}{\partial S^2}\sigma_t^2 S_t^2 = 0$$

Note that the drift of the stock, μ_S, has disappeared. This is a PDE to be solved with the appropriate boundary conditions.

2.2.3   The Market Price of Risk with Deterministic Volatility

A simple rearrangement of the equations above can provide some useful insight. Given the choices for α and β (dictated by constraints 1 and 2), one can write under penalty of arbitrage:

$$d\Pi_t = 0 = dC_t + \alpha\, dS_t + \beta\, dB_t \tag{2.12}$$

After substituting Equations (2.4), (2.10) and (2.11) into the drift term of (2.12) one obtains

$$\mu_C C_t + \alpha\mu_S S_t = (\alpha S_t + C_t) r_t \tag{2.13}$$

or, after rearranging,

$$C(\mu_C - r) = -\alpha S(\mu_S - r) \tag{2.14}$$

$$C(\mu_C - r) = \frac{\partial C}{\partial S} S(\mu_S - r) \tag{2.15}$$

Dividing both terms by $C\sigma_C$ gives

$$\frac{C(\mu_C - r)}{C\sigma_C} = \frac{\frac{\partial C}{\partial S} S(\mu_S - r)}{C\sigma_C} \tag{2.16}$$

But we know from (2.6) that $C_t\sigma_C = \frac{\partial C}{\partial S}\sigma_t S_t$ and Equation (2.16) therefore becomes

$$\frac{(\mu_C - r)}{\sigma_C} = \frac{(\mu_S - r)}{\sigma} \tag{2.17}$$

In order to create the hedging portfolio I need not have chosen the stock S: any other derivative instrument, say, C', with a payoff dependent on S would have done.[2] The treatment would have carried through with no changes, and Equation (2.17) could have been rewritten more generally as

$$\frac{(\mu_C - r)}{\sigma_C} = \frac{(\mu_{C'} - r)}{\sigma_{C'}} \tag{2.18}$$

The quantities on both sides of Equation (2.18) are the excess real-world percentage return (over the riskless rate) normalized by the standard deviation. How did we get to this equation? By imposing a diffusive behaviour with deterministic volatility for the stock, by constructing (*thanks to this property*) a riskless portfolio and by requiring that no arbitrage should be allowed.

What does Equation (2.18) tell us? That, under the diffusive assumption, and in the absence of arbitrage opportunities, the ratio of the normalized excess *real-world* returns of any two options (or, for that matter, of any option and the stock) should be independent of the strike, maturity or any other idiosyncratic characteristic of either option. At any point in time, the excess return one can expect from any derivative whose payoff only depends on S, once it is normalized by the volatility, is the same across all such derivatives. In principle, this ratio need not be a constant: it can depend on time, it can depend on the state variable, S_t, itself, and it can even be stochastic. However, it must be 'universal' for all products whose price is given by an expression of the form $C = C(S, t)$:

$$\frac{(\mu_C - r)}{\sigma_C} = \lambda(S_t, t) \tag{2.19}$$

This can be equivalently re-written as

$$\mu_C = r + \lambda(S_t, t)\sigma_C \tag{2.20}$$

---

[2]In other words, any other option whose value is given by a function $C' = C'(S_t, t)$.

Equations (2.18)–(2.20) are financially very suggestive: if one identifies 'risk' with 'standard deviation', these relationships taken together imply that the excess return, $(\mu_C - r)$, should be exactly proportional to 'risk' (σ_C). The proportionality constant, $\lambda(S_t, t)$, can therefore be aptly called the 'market price of risk'. Within the (deterministic–volatility diffusive) universe of securities of the form $C = C(S, t)$, the real-world rate of growth is such as to exactly 'compensate' the investor for the risk (in the sense above) of each security. Thanks to the ability to construct a replicating portfolio, any different degree of compensation would allow an arbitrage.

Despite the similarities between this result and analogous results obtained in other areas of asset pricing, it is important to point out that, in order to arrive at Equations (2.18) and (2.19), I have not required any particular utility function, I have not assumed to be dealing with mean–variance investors, nor have I assumed that the CAPM or any other pricing model holds true. Again, the only financial inputs that have been injected in the treatment have been the requirements that

- no arbitrage should be allowed;
- the process for the stock should be a diffusion; and
- the volatility coefficient in the diffusion should be deterministic.

I am belabouring the point because the intuitional appeal of Equation (2.20) often makes it tempting to use it as a starting point for, rather than the conclusion of, an argument. This is not always correct. If, *for any possible process of the stock price*, we required that the securities in the (one-factor) economy were priced consistently with Equation (2.20), *then* we would be saying something strong about the nature of the risk aversion of the investors (for instance, that when they appraise risk they only care about the variance of returns). The result (2.20) that we have obtained holds true for any pattern of risk aversion, and derives its validity from the type of the posited process for the underlying (or, equivalently, from the Gaussian nature of the conditional and unconditional distributions of prices). These observations and conclusions should be revisited towards the end of the following section and in Chapter 13. It is important to stress again, however, that the function $\lambda(S_t, t)$ need not be deterministic.[3] See the discussion later in this chapter.

2.2.4   Link with Expectations – the Feynman–Kac Theorem

We have tackled the problem of determining the value of a derivative via replication of its payoff. By so doing we have obtained a partial differential equation. The rest of the chapter will solve the same problem following a different route, i.e. by evaluating a

---

[3]If the market price of risk is not deterministic we are allowing for the possibility of an unpredictable change in risk aversion. This approach, despite being intuitively appealing, has not been very popular in asset pricing, because of the observational equivalence of changes in prices due to a change in the riskiness of the asset or due to a change in the risk aversion. See, for example, Misina (2003). Recently, however, explanations based on changing risk aversion have gained attention to explain the financial crises of the late 1990s. See, for example, Kumar and Persaud (2002) and references therein.

suitable discounted expectation of the terminal payoff. Prima facie these two approaches are so different that they might seem to have little in common. In reality there is a deep link between the two, provided by the Feynman–Kac theorem.

Sweeping all the regularity conditions under the carpet, what this theorem says (see, for example, Oksendal (1995)) is the following. Consider a diffusion with time- and/or state-dependent coefficients

$$dx_t = \mu(x_t, t)\, dt + \sigma(x_t, t)\, dz_t \qquad (2.21)$$

and a PDE for some function f of x (and time) of the form

$$\frac{\partial f(t, x)}{\partial t} + \frac{\partial f(t, x)}{\partial x}\mu_t + \frac{1}{2}\frac{\partial^2 f(t, x)}{\partial x^2}\sigma_t^2 = r_t f(t, x) \qquad (2.22)$$

with final[4] condition

$$f(T, x) = \phi(x) \qquad (2.23)$$

Given this final (time-T) condition, and given that the process, x, starts at x_0 at time t_0, the Feynman–Kac theorem states that the solution, $f(t_0, x_0)$, of the PDE (2.22) is given by the expectation

$$f(t_0, x_0) = \exp\left[-\int_{t_0}^{T} r_s\, ds\right] E\left[\phi(x_T)|x_{t_0} = x_0\right] \qquad (2.24)$$

where the expectation is taken under the measure in which the dz_t is the increment of a *standard* (i.e. zero-drift) Brownian motion.

The reader should pause to note the subtle interplay among the various quantities that appear in this equation: the terminal condition (2.23) of the PDE (2.22) appears under the expectation sign in Equation (2.24); the functions that multiply the derivatives of the PDE are the drift and volatility coefficients of the diffusion (2.21); the starting point of the diffusion conditions the expectation (2.24); the function r on the RHS of the PDE (2.22) appears as the 'discounting' term $\exp[-\int_{t_0}^{T} r_s\, ds]$ in Equation (2.24); finally the increment of the Brownian motion in the diffusion (2.21) implicitly defines the measure under which the expectation must be taken.

Indeed, the Feynman–Kac theorem provides the justification for the practice of evaluating today's value of an option ($f(t_0, x_0)$) as the discounted ($\exp[-\int_{t_0}^{T} r_s\, ds]$) expectation ($E[\phi(X_T)|X_{t_0} = x_0]$) of its terminal payoff ($f(T, x) = \phi(x)$). The expectation route to option pricing is explored below in a discrete setting.

---

[4]In PDE language, this condition would often be referred to as an 'initial condition'. Since, however, it refers to the value of the option at expiry, I prefer the more 'physical' term 'final'.

2.3   Binomial Replication

The treatment presented in the previous section shows how to derive the PDE that governs the price of a derivatives contract if the underlying process is a deterministic–volatility diffusion and markets are 'perfect'. Sure enough, there are many additional important and useful results regarding option pricing that can be obtained using an analytic approach in the continuous-time setting. For instance, I have in mind the nature of the transformation brought about by Girsanov's theorem, which leaves the (deterministic) volatilities unchanged, but scrambles the drift terms. Since this book is about volatility and correlation, understanding this result (and being able to answer such questions as: 'What matters for option pricing, the variance or the volatility of a process?') is clearly important. However, obtaining these results in continuous time along analytical routes requires relatively sophisticated mathematical knowledge. I will therefore obtain some results, and simply present plausibility arguments for others, working in a discrete-time setting. This approach also has the advantage of helping the intuition of the reader.[5]

Let us tackle[6] the problem of evaluating the simplest possible contingent claim in a discrete setting. We start from the knowledge of the state of the world prevailing today, ω_0, and we assume to know that this state of the world will evolve, over one time interval, to either of two possible states: ω_1 or ω_2. More precisely, we know that a security S, of price today S_0, will have values S_1 or S_2 according to whether states of the world ω_1 or ω_2 will prevail after the time interval. The possible values S_1 and S_2 are known before the move, but we do *not* assume to know the probability of reaching ω_1 or ω_2 from ω_0. In addition, a default-free discount bond, P, is also available, which pays \$1 with certainty in both states of the world, and which trades in the market today for \$$P_0$. The price of this bond implicitly defines the riskless rate of return over the time period: if continuous compounding is chosen, this riskless rate can be expressed as

$$P_0 = \exp[-r\,\Delta t] \rightarrow r = -\frac{\ln P_0}{\Delta t} \tag{2.25}$$

Finally, a contingent claim C which matures after the time interval Δt has elapsed trades in the economy. Therefore we know with certainty that the contingent claim will be worth \$$C_1$ or \$$C_2$ if state ω_1 or ω_2 prevails, respectively. We want to determine the fair price today, C_0, of the contingent claim. By 'fair' we mean that, were the claim to trade at any other price, an arbitrage profit could be made by entering a suitable strategy in S, P and C. Note that, by the way the problem has been set up, the value of C after one time interval is deemed to depend directly on the states of the world, rather than on the security S. Since ω_1 and ω_2, however, are uniquely associated with the values S_1 and S_2, one could have equivalently required C to be a function of S. If this had been the case, the common description of S and C as the 'underlying' and the 'derivative' security, respectively, would have been obviously justified.

We shall approach the evaluation of the fair price of this contingent claim in four distinct ways: the first, third and fourth approaches will provide the same (correct) answer, whilst the second, despite being perhaps the most intuitively 'plausible' one, will be shown to give a wrong value.

---

[5]For a very good general approach to derivatives pricing in a discrete setting, see Pliska (1997).

[6]Parts of the remainder of this chapter have been adapted from Chapter 5 of Rebonato (1998a).

2.3.1 First Approach – Replication Strategy

Let us form a portfolio Π made up of α units of the stock, S, and β units of the bond, P. Therefore, at time 0,

$$\Pi_0 = \alpha S_0 + \beta P_0 \tag{2.26}$$

If at time 1 state ω_1 prevails, the portfolio will be worth

$$\Pi_1 = \alpha S_1 + \beta P_1 \tag{2.27}$$

and, similarly, if state ω_2 occurs,

$$\Pi_2 = \alpha S_2 + \beta P_2 \tag{2.28}$$

Let us now impose the condition that this portfolio should have the same value as the contingent claim C after one time interval, irrespective of which state of the world might prevail, i.e.

$$C_i = \Pi_i = \alpha S_i + \beta P_i, \quad i = 1, 2 \tag{2.29}$$

For the special case considered here, i.e. for the case where the riskless security is a bond maturing after the time step, $P_1 = P_2 = 1$ with certainty, and therefore Equation (2.29) simplifies to

$$C_i = \Pi_i = \alpha S_i + \beta, \quad i = 1, 2 \tag{2.30}$$

For this particularly simple case the solution is

$$\alpha = \frac{C_1 - C_2}{S_1 - S_2} \tag{2.31}$$

$$\beta = \frac{C_2 S_1 - C_1 S_2}{S_1 - S_2} \tag{2.32}$$

Note in passing the similarity between Equation (2.31) and Equation (2.10). Irrespective of the values of the portfolio in the states ω_1 and ω_2, C_1, C_2, S_1, S_2, P_1 and P_2 are all known quantities, and the system (2.29) of two linear equations in two unknowns will always admit a unique solution as long as the determinant of the associated matrix is not equal to 0, i.e. as long as

$$\det \begin{bmatrix} S_1 & P_1 \\ S_2 & P_2 \end{bmatrix} \neq 0 \tag{2.33}$$

Since certainly P_1 and P_2 cannot both be equal to zero, the determinant requirement simply translates into the condition that

$$S_1 P_2 - S_2 P_1 \neq 0 \rightarrow S_1 \neq S_2 \tag{2.34}$$

What does this condition mean? If S_1 were equal to S_2, the security S would simply be a multiple of the riskless bond, P. Equation (2.34) simply tells us that we cannot hedge a contingent claim, C, dependent in a non-trivial way on ω_1 and ω_2 simply by dealing in riskless bonds.

In matrix form the problem we have looked at so far can be written as

$$A \; b = C \tag{2.35}$$

with

$$A = \begin{bmatrix} S_1 & P_1 \\ S_2 & P_2 \end{bmatrix} \tag{2.36}$$

$$b = \begin{bmatrix} \alpha \\ \beta \end{bmatrix} \tag{2.37}$$

and

$$C = \begin{bmatrix} C_1 \\ C_2 \end{bmatrix} \tag{2.38}$$

The solution vector b, obtainable as

$$b = A^{-1} C \tag{2.39}$$

(where A^{-1} denotes the inverse of matrix A) contains the holdings α and β of the security S and of the bond P, respectively, needed to ensure that the portfolio Π will assume exactly the same values as the contingent claim in each of the two possible states of the world. For future reference, it is important to point out that, if it exists (and it always will, as long as $\det A \neq 0$) the solution is unique. Therefore there is one and only one 'hedging strategy', and no other combination, α', β', of stock and bonds could provide an exact replication of the contingent claim payoff.

Given the way the portfolio has been constructed, it must be worth today no more and no less than the contingent claim itself, i.e.

$$C_0 = \Pi_0 = \alpha S_0 + \beta P_0 \tag{2.40}$$

Substituting the values for α and β derived above, we obtain

$$C_0 = \frac{C_1 - C_2}{S_1 - S_2} S_0 + \frac{C_2 S_1 - C_1 S_2}{S_1 - S_2} P_0 \tag{2.41}$$

This value for the claim is 'fair' in the sense that, if C traded at any other price, unlimited profits could be made by buying (selling) the claim and entering at the same time a short (long) position in the portfolio (which, by construction, replicates all the possible C-payoffs at time 1). In the stylized world we are analysing, the solution that we have found therefore gives a unique and certainly correct value for C_0, against which all other pricing methodologies can be benchmarked.

Finally, before leaving this evaluation procedure, it is just as important to highlight on which quantities the solution *does* depend ($S_0, S_1, S_2, P_0, P_1, P_2, C_1$ and C_2), as to stress on what quantities it does *not* depend. Note, in fact, that no mention was made of the probability of occurrence of ω_1 or ω_2, apart from implicitly requiring that both these probabilities, $\pi(\omega_1)$ and $\pi(\omega_2)$, were non-zero. Therefore, perhaps surprisingly, knowledge of these probabilities turns out not to be necessary for the evaluation of the fair price of the contingent claim. This important observation will be revisited at the end of the next section.

2.3.2 Second Approach – 'Naïve Expectation'

Let us now make the important additional assumption that we can avail ourselves of the extra piece of information that the probability of occurrence of state ω_1, $\pi(\omega_1)$, is, say, $\frac{1}{2}$ (and, therefore, also $\pi(\omega_2) = \frac{1}{2}$). Note that this extra information drastically changes our knowledge with respect to the 'replicating-portfolio' scenario, since we can now evaluate the expected return from the security S. Plausibly, knowledge of this additional important piece of information should allow us to obtain the value of the contingent claim today more directly and easily than we managed to do with the replicating strategy.

One could be tempted to speculate, on the basis of the extra piece of information we now have, that the 'fair' price of the contingent claim today should be equal to the weighted average of the two possible outcomes, C_1 and C_2, appropriately discounted by the rate implied by the riskless bond. After all, one might argue, this 'naïve expectation' would indeed be the average discounted payoff from the contingent claim one would obtain if one were to trade in the same contingent claim (i.e. in a contingent claim with the same possible outcomes and the same known probabilities of occurrence) over and over again. This is, incidentally, what I call 'actuarial pricing'.

A moment's reflection, however, shows that the expectation calculated on the basis of the probabilities we know to apply in the real world to events ω_1 and ω_2 must in general produce a value different from the fair price obtained using the replication strategy. Since, in fact, the exogenous probabilities $\pi(\omega_1)$ and $\pi(\omega_2)$ do not depend in any way on the replication strategy set up in Section 2.3.1, it would be an incredible coincidence if the 'real-world' expectation and the value today of the replicating portfolio turned out to have the same value.

To look at the matter from a different angle, if, because perhaps of the arrival of new information, the probabilities $\pi(\omega_1)$ and $\pi(\omega_2)$ were to change, the expectation of the two possible payoffs would also change, but the replication-strategy results would remain exactly the same. On the other hand, we know from the previous discussion that, if the replication price were not enforced, arbitrage profits could be made by simultaneous trading in the replicating portfolio and the contingent claim. Therefore the 'naïve expectation' price must be not simply different, but unquestionably wrong.

What went wrong in the reasoning that led to the free lunch? To answer the question, notice that, even if *on average* the payoff from the contingent claim might well be given by a precise and certain number (that can be evaluated on the basis of the real-world probabilities), the holder of the claim (unlike the holder of the bond P) will experience *for any given outcome* a return that is not certain, but displays a certain variance. The bedrock of asset pricing is that the return that an investor will demand from a security should be a function not only of its expected return, but also of the uncertainty connected with it. The precise extra return will depend on the investor's appetite for risk: if she is risk-avoiding, then she will demand an extra 'compensation' from a risky security, on top of the return that she would earn holding the riskless bond P; if she is risk-seeking, she will be happy with a lower return than the riskless rate; if she is risk-neutral, she will accept a return exactly identical to the one obtainable from the bond.

If, in addition, one were prepared to assume that the uncertainty in returns can be satisfactorily described by the percentage standard deviation of the returns themselves, then the behavioural attitude towards risk of the 'representative investor' could be expressed by a simple linear relationship of the type

$$\mu_x = r + \lambda \sigma_x \tag{2.42}$$

where μ_x is the required expected return from x, r is the riskless rate, σ_x is the percentage standard deviation per unit time (volatility) of security x, and λ is the (security-independent) compensation per unit risk above the riskless rate. Of course, we have already seen this result in Equation (2.20). But there we *obtained* the result *given* the replication argument (in continuous time). Here, we have not obtained the unique call price by no-arbitrage yet, so we must use Equation (2.42) as our starting point, rather than as our conclusion.

Note also that, much as the various assumptions implicit in Equation (2.42) (about, for instance, the linearity of the dependence of the extra return on the unit risk) might seem reasonable, they are at this stage no more and no less than hypotheses, and that any result derived from them will enjoy no greater validity than the assumptions themselves. This was not the case for the discrete-time replicating strategy presented earlier, which required us to make no assumptions at all beside imposing that arbitrage should not be allowed. With this caveat in mind, we shall attempt a third line of attack towards the evaluation of the contingent claim.

2.3.3   Third Approach – 'Market Price of Risk'

We retain in the third approach the knowledge about the real-world probabilities, $\pi(\omega_1)$ and $\pi(\omega_2)$, and we therefore know both the values attained by S in the two states of the world and the probabilities of reaching these states. In other words, from the values S_1 and S_2 we can now compute both the percentage standard deviation of S (the 'volatility' of S) and the expected percentage return. These quantities could be used together with the market price of risk introduced in the previous section in order to price the option in a way consistent with risk aversion. The problem however arises of how the market risk can be estimated.

One approach is to start from a 'desirable' utility function, i.e. to posit a priori a certain pattern of risk aversion. From this the market price of risk can be obtained (see, for example, Cochrane, 2001), and the option priced accordingly. The approach is theoretically appealing because it allows a consistent description of a whole economy, within which all the asset prices are truly 'explained' and not simply 'accounted for' or 'described'. The drawback, however, is that by following this route we will, in general, not be able to recover the observed market prices (see also the detailed discussion in Rebonato (2004)).

The alternative route is to make the joint assumptions that the market is efficient; that a utility-based description of the investors' attitude to risk is correct; that we know the correct dependence of the market price of risk on the state variables; and that we know the real-world return from the stock (i.e. that we know S_0, S_1, S_2, $\pi(\omega_1)$ and $\pi(\omega_2)$). Then the market price of risk can be extracted ('implied') from the market prices. This is the route followed in this section. Let us see how this can be done.

Armed with the knowledge of the percentage standard deviation of the stock, of the of the riskless rate r and of the return expected from security S (obtainable from its expectation), we are in a position to estimate the market price of risk, λ:

$$E_{t_0}[S] = (\pi_1 S_1 + \pi_2 S_2) = S_0 + \mu_S \Delta t \tag{2.43}$$

$$\sigma_S^2 \Delta t = \pi_1 (S_1 - E[S])^2 + \pi_2 (S_2 - E[S])^2 \tag{2.44}$$

$$\lambda = \frac{\mu_S - r}{\sigma_S} \tag{2.45}$$

We have estimated the market price of risk from the properties of the security, S. By the way the market price of risk is defined, however, it must be security-independent. As such it must apply to the contingent claim as well, which, in turn, must also be priced in a 'fair' market so as to yield a return

$$\mu_C = r + \lambda \sigma_C \tag{2.46}$$

The only quantity that remains to be evaluated is therefore σ_C. We can estimate this quantity using expressions (2.43) and (2.44) above, with C now replacing S.

Given the knowledge of σ_C, we can now value the contingent claim today by averaging the two possible claim values after the time-step and discounting them by the factor $\exp(-\mu_C \Delta t)$ (rather than $\exp(-r \Delta t)$). By so doing we do obtain a value which is, in general, different from the naïve-expectation result, but very similar (indeed, almost identical) to the value obtained with the replication approach, which we know must give the right answer. (A numerical example that clarifies the procedure is presented at the end of this section.)

Therefore, we can indeed recover the fair price of the contingent claim also by making use of the real-world probabilities, but only if these are used in conjunction with the market price of risk. Arriving at the answer following this route will, in general, be more complex: there will be, in fact, as many market prices of risk as there are independent sources of shocks to the economy, and all these risk prices will be 'hidden' in the prices of traded securities. If we manage, however, to give a convincing, albeit perhaps simplified, description of the behavioural attitudes towards different types of risk of the 'representative investor', then we have indeed achieved something richer and more informative than what we managed to accomplish using the replication argument. In a nutshell, this is the difference between equilibrium models and purely no-arbitrage models.

Why is it not a good idea to price derivatives using the market price of risk? Fundamentally, because several rather opaque assumptions have to be introduced in the course of the derivation presented above. Recall, first of all, that we estimated the market price of risk using one security (S), invoked its security-independence and then applied it to another security (C) by using Equation (2.46). Before that, however, we had to make some assumptions about the quantities the market price of risk *can* depend on. In particular, we required that it should be non-stochastic, and actually a constant. In reality, in principle the market price of risk might depend in complex ways on the state of the world, on history, or, as in the case of the Vasicek or CIR interest-rate models, on non-traded state variables, such as the short rate. It might even be stochastic. Furthermore, we have implicitly assumed in the derivation that investors see 'risk' in terms of standard deviation of returns, i.e. that we are dealing with a mean–variance investor. Therefore, our estimation of the market price of risk relied on the assumption that either the returns were drawn from a normal distribution, or that investors only cared about the variance of their portfolios, or that they had a quadratic utility function. Finally, we have assumed that investors are discounted-expected-utility-function maximizers. While this has been a reigning paradigm in asset pricing, it is not without its critics: behavioural finance, for instance, claims that investors are more sensitive to gains and losses than to the level of their utility, and that the risk aversion function (now with gains and losses instead of wealth or consumption on the x-axis) changes convexity in moving from the upper right to the bottom left quadrant. See, for example, Chapter 1 of Kahneman and Tversky (2000). I do not want to take sides on this topic at this point, but it is important to stress that, *when taken as a starting point*, an apparently 'innocuous' statement such as

$$\lambda = \frac{\mu_S - r}{\sigma_S} \tag{2.47}$$

carries along a heavy, and questionable, conceptual baggage that was conspicuously absent in the first (no-arbitrage) approach.

A last but important remark: since we have 'implied' the market price of risk from the observed market prices for the stock, we would have obtained an (almost) identical result for the fair option price even if our exogenous probabilities, $\pi(\omega_1)$ and $\pi(\omega_2)$, had been different. These different probabilities would, in fact, have given rise to a different market price of risk, but the latter would then have been consistently used for both S and C. We have therefore reached an interesting conclusion: on the one hand, in fact, the market price of risk has been shown to be necessary in order to estimate the fair value C_0, if use is to be made of the real-world probabilities. On the other hand, it turns out that, since we chose to estimate the market price of risk from the market prices of traded securities and their statistical properties, even if these probabilities had been different, a new market price of risk would have resulted, but (almost) the same price for C_0 would have been obtained.[7] Within the estimation caveats outlined above, the price for the contingent claim is therefore truly independent of the market price of risk! Once again, estimating the 'true' rate of return from asset S in not really necessary if we 'just' want to establish a fair value for C. If anything, it seems to make things more complicated. This conclusion, after all, should be only mildly surprising, since in the exact replication result no mention was made of the probabilities of occurrence of ω_1 and ω_2, and therefore no expectations could be computed. This important observation can lead to the fourth, and final, line of attack towards the evaluation of the fair value of C_0. Before presenting it, however, a worked-out example can illustrate the reasoning so far.

---

[7]Clearly, this would not happen if we estimated the market price of risk from a utility function. If we did so, however, it is very unlikely that the market prices would be correctly recovered.

2.3.4 A Worked-Out Example

We want to price an option using the market-price-of-risk approach. We intend to estimate the latter using the implied route. Let the stock, the bond and the contingent claim have the values shown in Figure 2.1.

The time-step Δt is 0.1 (in years). The price of the bond implies a continuously compounded riskless rate of return of 10.00%. We know that the real-world probabilities of transition from ω_0 to ω_1 and ω_2 are $\frac{1}{2}$. From the values of the contingent claim in the two states we can estimate a percentage volatility for the contingent claim, σ_C, of 97.821%, and for the security, σ_S, of 20.00%. The expression for the standard deviation of S as a function of the values S_1 and S_2, valid for $\pi_1 = \pi_2 = \frac{1}{2}$, is

$$\sigma_S \sqrt{\Delta t} = \frac{\ln S_2 - \ln S_1}{2} \tag{2.48}$$

Let us use a similar expression for σ_C:

$$\sigma_C \sqrt{\Delta t} = \frac{\ln C_2 - \ln C_1}{2} \tag{2.49}$$

Note that we can only use Equation (2.49) if both $C_2 > 0$ and $C_1 > 0$. More generally, when we have many possible states of the world, the standard deviation σ_C will depend on the level of the contingent claim: $\sigma_C = \sigma_C(C)$. I neglect this for the moment.

From the knowledge of the values S_0, S_1 and S_2 we can obtain the expected return from S. Since the total expected return should be equal to the sum of the riskless rate (10.00%) and a compensation per unit risk times the percentage volatility of the stock (see Equation (2.46)), we can estimate the market price of risk to be $\lambda = 24.00\%$. This value can now be used in conjunction with the estimated percentage volatility of the claim, σ_C, in order to determine (Equation (2.46)) the expected percentage return from the claim. This turns out to be given by $\mu_C = 33.35\%$. Using this value for discounting gives for C_0 the value of 20.786, which compares favourably with the replicating-portfolio value of 20.796.

For the case when the payoff of the contingent claim is given by the function

$$f(S) = \max(S - K, 0) \tag{2.50}$$

Table 2.1 shows the 'true' (REPLICATION) and 'market-price-of-risk' (MPR) result for several values of the strike K.

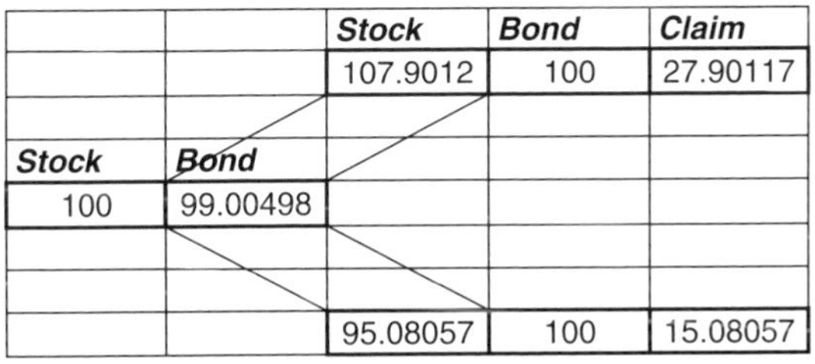

		Stock	Bond	Claim
		107.9012	100	27.90117
Stock	Bond			
100	99.00498			
		95.08057	100	15.08057

Figure 2.1 The values after one time step of the stock, the bond and the contingent claim, and the values today of the bond and the stock.

Table 2.1   Values of the contingent claim C_0 obtained as indicated in the worked-out example. The column labelled MPR gives the value for the contingent claim obtained following the market-price-of-risk route, while the column REPLICATION gives the same quantity evaluated using the replicating-portfolio approach.

Strike	MPR	Replication
94	6.7312	6.9352
92	8.8291	8.9153
90	10.8456	10.8954
88	12.8430	12.8755
86	14.8328	14.8556
84	16.8190	16.8357
82	18.8031	18.8158
80	20.7860	20.7959
78	22.7682	22.7760
76	24.7498	24.7561
74	26.7310	26.7362
72	28.7120	28.7163
70	30.6928	30.6964
68	32.6735	32.6765
66	34.6541	34.6566
64	36.6346	36.6367
62	38.6150	38.6168
60	40.5953	40.5969
58	42.5757	42.5770
56	44.5559	44.5571
54	46.5362	46.5372
52	48.5164	48.5173
50	50.4966	50.4974
48	52.4768	52.4775
46	54.4570	54.4576

Note that the more the option is in the money, the more the claim resembles a stock, and the better the joint log-normal assumption for stock and claim holds. This produces a better estimate of σ_C, and, consequently, a closer agreement between the MPR result and the correct replicating-portfolio result. Conversely, the higher the strike the greater the discrepancy between the two results. In particular, if the strike were higher than S_1, giving a value of $C_1 = 0$, then the estimate of the percentage volatility of the claim would quickly become progressively unsatisfactory, producing significantly different values for the estimated fair value of the contingent claim.

2.3.5   Fourth Approach – Risk-Neutral Valuation

We saw earlier that there are several possible sources of difficulty in estimating the fair value of an option using the MPR route, such as, for instance, the possible mis-specification of the behavioural relationship between risk and expected reward. Because of these difficulties, we want to explore a different avenue.

We saw that, as long as the market price of risk is estimated from prices and from real-world drifts of assets, if we are only interested in relative pricing, its actual value ultimately 'washes out': if we had started from different probabilities, we would have estimated different growth rates and a different market price of risk, but ultimately the same price for the contingent claim. We can express this in an equivalent way by saying that in the implied approach there is a one-to-one correspondence between the real-world probabilities and the implied market prices of risk. As long as the latter quantities are consistently estimated as a function of the former, there is no residual impact on the price of the derivative security. But, if this is the case, why not choose the probabilities in such a way that the market price of risk is exactly zero? Why not make use of the independence from the market price of risk of the fair value of C_0, and choose a market price of risk that corresponds to indifference on the part of the investor towards risk?

This would obviously be inadequate if we wanted to provide a 'true' description of the economy (as an equilibrium approach attempts to achieve), but would serve our purposes perfectly well if we were 'just' interested in pricing a contingent claim given the process for the underlying (as relative-pricing approaches are designed to do). If indeed we were to choose a market price of risk equal to zero, we would neither encounter the problems linked with 'distilling' the 'true' market price of risk from the known values of S_1, S_2, and from the probabilities $\pi(\omega_1)$ and $\pi(\omega_2)$, nor would we meet the difficulties connected with the estimation of σ_C. For the purpose of the evaluation of the fair value of C_0 we will therefore assume that the returns from S, C, P, or, for that matter, from any security are simply equal to the riskless rate (thereby implying a market price of risk equal to zero). We will then obtain the probabilities $\pi(\omega_1)$ and $\pi(\omega_2)$ implied by this choice. To be precise, one should write $\pi_\lambda(\omega_1)$ and $\pi_\lambda(\omega_2)$, to emphasize the dependence of the probabilities on the chosen market price of risk, but, to keep the notation lighter, the subscript will be omitted in what follows.

Note, however, that since we have chosen risk neutrality purely for reasons of computational expedience, the implied probabilities $\pi(\omega_1)$ and $\pi(\omega_2)$ are also purely a computational device, and bear no relationship to the true ('real-world') probabilities. If one performs the calculation with this value of λ, the risk-neutral price of C_0 is, within numerical noise, indeed identical to the replication-portfolio value (which we know must be exact).

That the risk-neutral valuation should bring about the same result as the replicating-portfolio approach should, upon reflection, come as little surprise: the replication strategies taught us how to build a portfolio giving exactly the same payoffs as the contingent claim we wanted to value. Therefore, by combining the portfolio and the contingent claim itself (with long and short positions, respectively) one is creating a new portfolio with identical and known payoffs in all states of the world; but this, apart from a scaling factor, is simply a pure discount bond, which by definition must earn the riskless return.

We have, in a way, come full circle:

- we started from an exact valuation procedure that made no use of probabilities;

- we then introduced real-world probabilities and the accompanying expectations, and showed that a 'naïve', albeit plausible, use of these quantities actually yielded a wrong result;

- we identified the missing ingredient in the expectation approach to be the market price of risk; i.e. we recognized that, since the returns from the non-bond traded securities are uncertain, risk-averse, risk-neutral or risk-seeking investors will demand from them different expected returns;

- we attempted to impute the market price of risk from the price, the standard deviation and the growth rate of the stock;

- we showed that, when one follows this implied route, there is a one-to-one correspondence between the real-world probabilities and the estimated market price of risk;

- finally, we showed how this difficult-to-estimate quantity, the market price of risk, could actually be dispensed with by using a risk-neutral valuation.

The purpose of the exercise was not to repeat a procedure that is, after all, very similar to the well-known Black-and-Scholes original reasoning, but to show both the strengths and the shortcomings of the different approaches (the replicating strategy and the risk-neutral valuation, on the one hand, and the MPR line of approach on the other).

2.3.6   Pseudo-Probabilities

From the discussion above we know that, in the case when P_1 and P_2 are both equal to 1, the holdings of stock and riskless bonds needed to replicate the payoffs of the contingent claim are

$$\alpha = \frac{C_1 - C_2}{S_1 - S_2} \tag{2.51}$$

$$\beta = \frac{C_2 S_1 - C_1 S_2}{S_1 - S_2} \tag{2.52}$$

Therefore, as we showed earlier,

$$C_0 = \frac{C_1 - C_2}{S_1 - S_2} S_0 + \frac{C_2 S_1 - C_1 S_2}{S_1 - S_2} P_0 \tag{2.53}$$

Solving for C_1 and C_2 the expression above can be rearranged to give

$$C_0 = C_1 \left[\frac{S_0}{S_1 - S_2} - \frac{S_2 P_0}{S_1 - S_2} \right] + C_2 \left[\frac{S_1 P_0}{S_1 - S_2} - \frac{S_0}{S_1 - S_2} \right] \tag{2.54}$$

If we now define

$$\pi_1 = \frac{S_0 / P_0 - S_2}{S_1 - S_2} \tag{2.55}$$

$$\pi_2 = \frac{S_1 - S_0 / P_0}{S_1 - S_2} \tag{2.56}$$

we can write

$$C_0 = [C_1 \pi_1 + C_2 \pi_2] P_0 \tag{2.57}$$

Formally, looking at Equation (2.57), one might be tempted to 'interpret' the value today of the contingent claim as if it were given by a discounted expectation of the two possible terminal values, taken with weights or 'probabilities' π_1 and π_2. But, in order to see whether this probabilistic interpretation can be warranted, the two quantities π_1 and π_2 must be examined more closely.

2.3.7 Are the Quantities π_1 and π_2 Really Probabilities?

The first encouraging observation is that both these weights do not depend on the initial or terminal values of the contingent claim itself, and that they are therefore truly state-dependent, rather than security-dependent, as state probabilities should be. Furthermore, as one can directly check from Equations (2.55) and (2.56), their sum always adds up to one:

$$\pi_1 + \pi_2 = 1 \tag{2.58}$$

As for their signs and magnitudes (required to be positive and smaller than 1, respectively, for the probabilistic interpretation to hold), let us begin by considering the case where $S_2 > S_1$. (The opposite case can be dealt with by following exactly the same reasoning.) As long as $S_2 > S_0/P_0$, or, conversely, $S_1 < S_0/P_0$, then it is clear from (2.55) and (2.56) that both π_1 and π_2 are guaranteed to be positive. But these requirements are not as arbitrary as they might at first appear: let us assume, for instance, that

$$S_2 < S_0/P_0 = S_0 \exp[r \, \Delta t] \tag{2.59}$$

If that were the case, then the risky security S would earn, even in the most favourable case, a return $(S_2 - S_0)/S_0$ *below* the return r obtainable by holding the riskless bond P (remember that $S_2 > S_1$). But this would entail an arbitrage: one could enter a strategy consisting of selling one unit of S at time 0, receiving $\$S_0$, and investing the proceeds from the sale in S_0/P_0 units of the bond P. At time 0 the strategy, Σ, would be worth

$$\Sigma_0 = (-1)S_0 + \frac{S_0}{P_0} P_0 = 0 \tag{2.60}$$

After the price move the strategy would be worth

$$\Sigma_1 = (-1)S_1 + \frac{S_0}{P_0} \tag{2.61}$$

$$\Sigma_2 = (-1)S_2 + \frac{S_0}{P_0} \tag{2.62}$$

(since $P_2 = P_1 = 1$) according to whether state 1 or 2 prevails, respectively. But, given our assumptions about the relative magnitudes of S_1, S_2 and S_0/P_0, if S_2 is smaller than

S_0/P_0 (as we assumed), so *a fortiori* is S_1 (which is smaller than S_2). In both states of the world we would therefore have obtained a strictly positive payoff, i.e. we would have devised a strategy that has cost us nothing to put together (Equation (2.60)), and that certainly pays a positive amount. This is even stronger than an arbitrage.[8]

A similar reasoning applies to the case when $S_1 > S_0/P_0$: the strategy, this time, would be to go long the stock and short the bond. Putting the two constraints together, one can see that, to prevent free lunches, the return from the riskless bond must be 'in between' the two possible uncertain returns from the stock. But, if this is the case, looking back at Equations (2.55) and (2.56), one can establish that the following relationships must hold true:

$$\pi_1 > 0 \tag{2.63}$$

$$\pi_2 > 0 \tag{2.64}$$

$$\pi_1 < 1 \tag{2.65}$$

$$\pi_2 < 1 \tag{2.66}$$

$$\pi_1 + \pi_2 = 1 \tag{2.67}$$

If we couple these equations with the contingent claim independence of π_1 and π_2, no further conditions are needed to warrant these two quantities the interpretation of probabilities. Given the generality of the treatment (recall that we have said nothing specific about the payoffs C_1, C_2, S_1 or S_2, and that we found the two quantities π_1 and π_2 to be state-dependent but claim-independent), this result must be true for any contingent claim. This finding can therefore be formalized as follows: given the one-step, two-state universe described above, the fair value at time 0 of any contingent claim can always be evaluated as a discounted expectation of the possible values of the contingent claim at time 1,

$$C_0 = [C_1\pi_1 + C_2\pi_2]\, P_0 \tag{2.68}$$

with probabilities defined by Equations (2.55) and (2.56). Alternatively, and just as importantly, the reasoning outlined above shows that (for the simple universe examined here) one can always find a couple of numbers that have all the properties of probabilities, and such that, if used as prescribed by Equation (2.57) to calculate the value of a contingent claim, no free lunches can take place.

I should stress again that these probabilities have nothing to do with the 'real-world' probabilities that we had assumed to know in the 'naïve-expectation' section (and that proved useless or, at best, cumbersome and imprecise in determining the fair value of the contingent claim). The couple of numbers π_1 and π_2 can therefore be aptly described as 'pseudo-probabilities'. These pseudo-probabilities are a computational construct underpinned by the requirement that no free-lunch strategies should be allowed. Therefore, even if the naïve expectation has been shown to be of no use in computing a fair value for C_0, an 'expectation' of sorts has reappeared from the back door: the securities market (S and P)

---

[8]This strategy is more desirable than an arbitrage because the latter only requires that we never lose money, and we make a profit in *some* states of the world. Here we are guaranteed to make money in *all* states of the world.

described above completely defines a contingent-claim-independent pseudo-probability distribution (as described by π_1 and π_2) in terms of which the fair value of any claim can be obtained as a simple discounted expectation.

2.3.8 Introducing Relative Prices

More insight can be obtained by introducing the concept of relative prices. Let us consider a quantity, Z, defined, at all times and in each state of the world, as the ratio of the price of the contingent claim to the price of the riskless bond:

$$Z = \frac{S}{P} \tag{2.69}$$

Formally, since the pseudo-probabilities are security-independent, after dividing through by P_0 one can rewrite Equation (2.57) as

$$\frac{C_0}{P_0} = [C_1 \pi_1 + C_2 \pi_2] \tag{2.70}$$

or, recalling that $P_1 = P_2 = 1$,

$$\frac{C_0}{P_0} = \frac{C_1}{P_1}\pi_1 + \frac{C_2}{P_2}\pi_2 \rightarrow Z_0 = Z_1\pi_1 + Z_2\pi_2 \tag{2.71}$$

Therefore the value today of the ratio Z is given by the simple (i.e. *undiscounted*) expectation of the values of Z at time 1 obtainable with the same probabilities derived in the previous discussion. The same result would have been obtained if we had defined Z to be the ratio of the security S (which is, after all, a special case of a contingent claim) to the riskless bond. But, since the contingent claim payoffs C_1 and C_2 are completely general, the same result applies to the stock, to the bond (trivially), and to any contingent claim. Therefore, for $Z = X/P$ (with $X = S, C$ or P) it is always true that

$$Z_0 = Z_1\pi_1 + Z_2\pi_2 = E[Z^1/P_1] = E[Z(1)] = X_0/P_0 \tag{2.72}$$

(the notation Z^1 indicates the possible values of Z at time 1, and E[.] is the expectation operator for the pseudo-probabilities π_1 and π_2).

This result is particularly interesting when one recognizes that the dimension-less ratio Z expresses the price of a given security as the price of S in terms of (in units of) security P, or, more precisely, as the number of units of P that correspond to a given price of X. Therefore, if we are prepared to work with this 'normalized' price Z, we can dispense with discounting altogether. More importantly, by simply invoking the absence of free lunches, we can say that there must always exist a set of probabilities π_1 and π_2, determined as above, such that the π-expectation of future realizations of the normalized price of any security is simply equal to the value of the normalized security today. Therefore, in the absence of arbitrage, no return should be expected from this normalized security.

One might fear that the result that we obtained hinged on the security P having a certain value of 1 in all states of the world at time 1, i.e. on its being a riskless asset. As we noted before, however, the choice of $P_1 = P_2 = 1$ was expedient, but not necessary:

the same reasoning would have followed for any security P. The 2×2 system (2.36) would have been replaced by

$$C_1 = \Pi_1 = \alpha S_1 + \beta P_1 \tag{2.73}$$

$$C_2 = \Pi_2 = \alpha S_2 + \beta P_2 \tag{2.74}$$

giving as a solution for α and β:

$$\alpha = \frac{P_2 C_1 - P_1 C_2}{P_2 S_1 - P_1 S_2} \tag{2.75}$$

$$\beta = \frac{C_1}{P_1} + \frac{S_1}{P_1} \frac{P_2 C_1 - P_1 C_2}{P_2 S_1 - P_1 S_2}$$

$$= \frac{C_1 - S_1 \alpha}{P_1} \tag{2.76}$$

It is then easy to show that, following exactly the same reasoning as before, for any security P with strictly positive payoffs P_1 and P_2 at time 1,

- new but similar contingent-claim-independent pseudo-probabilities would have been derived;

- the prices today of contingent claims can be obtained as a discounted expectation taken over these pseudo-probabilities;

- the expectation of relative prices Z (now normalized by the new asset P) are again simply equal to the value of the ratio today Z_0;

- exactly zero return should be expected (in the π-measure world) from the normalized assets Z.

In other words, the choice of a different instrument (not necessarily a riskless bond) not only still allows a replication strategy, but also gives rise to pseudo-probabilities $\{\pi\}$ (different for each choice of P) in terms of which contingent claims can be valued as discounted expectations.

It is important to point out that the result just obtained gives us an alternative and equivalent route to finding the pseudo-probabilities. Rather than solving the system of equations presented above, one can simply choose an arbitrary security P, construct the relative price $Z = S/P$, and work out the probability π_1 that ensures that Z should display no expected growth over the time-step. Since Z_0 is simply given by

$$Z_0 = Z_1 \pi_1 + Z_2 \pi_2 = Z_1 \pi_1 + Z_2 (1 - \pi_1) \tag{2.77}$$

and $\pi_2 = 1 - \pi_1$, the probability π_1 can be found as

$$\pi_1 = \frac{Z_0 - Z_2}{Z_1 - Z_2} \tag{2.78}$$

When this result is extended to multi-step trees, it constitutes the standard procedure in order to ensure that the prices produced by a given model are consistent with the absence of arbitrage. In practice, pseudo-probabilities are only rarely, if ever, calculated directly, and the route followed is actually more similar to the reasoning that leads to Equation (2.77). In the meantime, Equation (2.78), together with the definition of the normalized price Z, clearly shows that changing the security P changes the pseudo-probabilities that ensure the absence of arbitrage.

2.3.9 Moving to a Multi-Period Setting

We would now like to assign a fair price in the sense discussed above to a contingent claim whose terminal payoff depends on the states of the world prevailing after many (rather than just one) steps. We want to allow for as many finite steps as we may wish between today and the terminal date in the trading horizon, i.e. in this context, the expiry of the contingent claim. The evolution of the stock, bond and option prices can therefore be aptly represented by a multi-branch tree. As for its geometry, we choose a non-recombining ('bushy') binomial tree, of the type depicted in Figure 2.2. In practice, recombining trees are by far preferable for computational purposes, but 'bushy' trees are much handier for expositional purposes, since to each node there corresponds one and only one path. As in the one-period case, we do not assume to know a priori the probabilities of moving from one parent node to the two connected arrival nodes.

The winning strategy in the case of the one-period, two-state contingent claim consisted of

- replicating exactly over one time step the payoffs of the claim with a stock-and-bond portfolio; and

- arguing that the set-up cost of this trading strategy had to be equal, under penalty of arbitrage, to the fair value of the contingent claim.

We want to employ a similar procedure in the multi-period case, but one problem stands in our way: we could be tempted to argue that, since each intermediate node 'looks' exactly like the original (time-0) node in the one-period case, we should be able to repeat

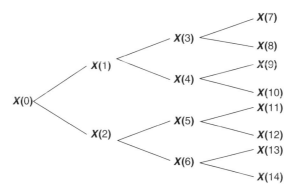

Figure 2.2 The geometry of a non-recombining ('bushy') tree over three time steps, showing the evolution of a generic quantity X (which could be the 'asset' S, the 'bond' P, the contingent claim C, or any relative price, Z). Note that a single path can be associated to any node: for instance, the path $X(0) \rightarrow X(1) \rightarrow X(4) \rightarrow X(10)$ is the only path associated with node $X(10)$.

the reasoning presented above on a node-by-node basis. The crux of the argument in the one-period case, however, was that, after *the* time-step, all the uncertainty in the economy was resolved, and the final value of the contingent claim was known with certainty. In the multi-step case the root of the tree is linked not to terminal option payoff values (about which we must all agree, since they only depend on the values at option expiry of S, which belong to our information set), but also to the a priori unknown value of the contingent claim at time 1.

The classic way to tackle this problem is via backward induction. To see how this works, let us consider the last two steps of a multi-period problem. Let us label by the index n the last time-step. At the time of the last time-step (the expiry time of the contingent claim), we know without doubt what the contingent claim is worth in any of the 2^n states. Let us move backwards in time to time-step $(n-1)$, and consider any of the 2^{n-1} states, say, the jth. This state, by our construction, is 'connected' with two and only two states at time-step n, which we can label as $(n, j+1)$ and $(n, j-1)$. We do not know, at this stage, what transactions and what cash flows might have occurred to get to state j after $(n-1)$ steps. We do know, however, that, given the fact that we are at node $(n-1, j)$, and that at time-step n we reach the expiry time, this problem now *does* look exactly like the simple one-period problem of the previous sections. This is because time-step n corresponds to option expiry, when we must all agree on the value of the option. Ignoring earlier transactions (i.e. how we have got to this node), all the results we have obtained in Sections 2.3.1–2.3.5 therefore still apply. In particular, we can set up a local (conditional) replicating portfolio that will certainly pay at expiry either $C(n, j+1)$ or $C(n, j-1)$, i.e. either of the values of the claim in the two states of the world attainable from node $(n-1, j)$.

Since we can unambiguously speak of how much one should be prepared to pay in the $(n-1, j)$ state of the world in order to obtain an entitlement to $C(n, j-1)$ or $C(n, j+1)$ at time n, we can meaningfully speak of the fair value of the option *contingent upon our being at node* $(n-1, j)$. And, since there was nothing special about state j, one can repeat exactly the same reasoning for all the states at time-step $n-1$. Therefore we have succeeded in bringing back the whole contingent claim by one time slice, with the simple proviso of adding to the expression 'fair value of the contingent claim' the clause 'contingent upon state $(n-1, j)$ having been reached'.

If one looks at the problem in this light, the terminal step looks less 'special': also the terminal (time-n) values of the contingent claim are, in fact, trivially, 'fair' values,[9] and they also are, in a sense, conditional, since they only apply if a particular state obtains. Therefore, even if it would have appeared somewhat pedantic, the terminal values of the contingent claim could have been described as 'fair values of the claim contingent upon a particular state at time n having been reached'. Seen from this perspective, the situation at time slice $n-1$ is exactly identical to the situation at time n. By backward induction, i.e. working with the conditional values of the claim and by repeating the same procedure backwards $n-1$ times, we can work our way back to the root of the tree (where conditional and unconditional expectations are the same). Let us examine carefully what this 'brought-back' contingent claim 'means' at state $(0,0)$ for the simple case of a two-state tree (see Figure 2.3).

By paying $C(0)$ today one can set up a portfolio made up of $\alpha(0)$ and $\beta(0)$ units of S and P that will certainly produce $C(1)$ or $C(2)$ irrespective of which state of the world

---

[9]If standing at time T, would you pay anything but $(S_T - K)^+$ for an instrument that pays $(S_T - K)^+$?

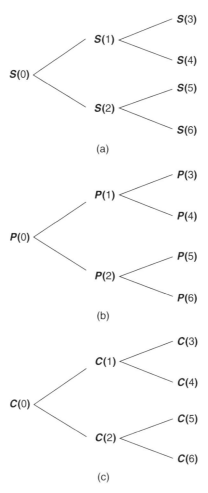

Figure 2.3 The values of (a) the 'asset' S, (b) the 'bond' P, and (c) the contingent claim C, after two steps; geometrically equivalent nodes on the three non-recombining trees, i.e. nodes labelled by the same number, correspond to the same state of the world.

will prevail. But $C(1)$ can be chosen to be the amount of money needed to construct (with obvious notation) the portfolio of $\alpha(1)$ and $\beta(1)$ units of S and P that certainly replicates the payoffs $C(3)$ and $C(4)$. Similarly $C(2)$ can be chosen to be the amount of money required to purchase holdings $\alpha(2)$ and $\beta(2)$ needed to produce $C(5)$ and $C(6)$ with certainty. Therefore, as long as one is prepared to alter, at no extra cost, the composition of the portfolio after the first time-step, one can certainly replicate the payoffs of the contingent claim at the second time step by paying $C(0)$ today!

I want to stress the importance of the 'at no extra cost' qualifier: $C(1)$ and $C(2)$ are needed to replicate $[C(3)$ or $C(4)]$ and $[C(5)$ or $C(6)]$, respectively, but $C(0)$ is all that is required to provide $C(1)$ or $C(2)$, as needed. Note also that it is not necessary to 'peek ahead': one starts with an allocation $\alpha(0)$ and $\beta(0)$ which will not, in general, be the one that will be needed at time-step $n - 1$, i.e. at the time-step before the expiry of the contingent claim. Therefore the hedging strategy is dynamic and not static. We can rest assured, however, that, by transferring wealth in the portfolio between the stock and the bond as and when needed, the contingent claim's payoff at expiry will be replicated. Therefore, the price we have to pay in order to set up the replicating portfolio over the *first* time-step must equal the fair (no-arbitrage) price of the *two*-period contingent claim. By this reasoning we have shown that, also in the multi-period case, the fair price of a contingent claim giving rise to a random payoff after n time-steps is equal to the set-up cost of the replicating portfolio over the first time-step.

2.3.10   Fair Prices as Expectations

Dealing with Nested Expectations

The results of this section are closely linked with the Feynman–Kac theorem, briefly introduced in Section 2.2.4 (and discussed again in Section 4.4.2). It might be useful to re-read that material at this point. In a one-period case we have already found that the fair value of a contingent claim can be expressed as an expectation over the possible terminal payoffs calculated using pseudo-probabilities. These probabilities turned out to have nothing to do with real-world probabilities, but depended on the values of S and on the type of instrument, P, chosen as the 'bond'. If technical conditions are met, the law associating to each possible state of the world a pseudo-probability is referred to as a measure. Therefore, whenever one speaks of expectations, it is essential to specify under what probability distribution (measure) these expectations are taken: as we have seen, each different type of instrument P chosen as numeraire will give rise to a different set of pseudo-probabilities; hence to different measures; hence to different expectations. If, for instance, the instrument P is chosen to be the discount bond maturing at the payoff time of the contingent claim, then the corresponding measure is normally called the 'forward-neutral measure'; if the instrument P had been chosen to be a money-market account, rolled over at each time-step at the then prevailing short rate, then the associated measure would be called the 'risk-neutral measure'. Conceptually, however, there is nothing special about these two choices of numeraire.

We have seen in the previous section that in the multi-period setting we can repeat the one-step reasoning for each node taken with its own two branching states. We can therefore also say that, for the example above, the value of the contingent claim is equal to the expectation in the appropriate measure of the two values C_1 and C_2. Also C_1 and C_2, however, can be seen as expectations, over [C_3 and C_4] and [C_5 and C_6], respectively. Therefore C_0 is an expectation of an expectation. Extending the reasoning, in the case of n steps the fair value C_0 will turn out to be given by n nested conditional expectations.

Since, in general, the evaluation of an expectation can be reduced to performing (analytically or numerically) an integral, it would seem that evaluating a contingent claim should be equivalent to performing an n-dimensional integral, with n potentially very large. This is indeed the route implicitly taken when using computational lattices or trees. Computationally, this route only works because in a binomial tree each expectation is computed in an extremely crude fashion, i.e. by employing just two points.

If, however, the contingent claim is truly European, i.e. if it only depends on the states of the world at one point in time, then a useful result, known as the tower law, can be used to reduce drastically the dimensionality of the underlying integral from n to one. More precisely, the tower law states that the expectation at time i of conditional expectations taken at a later time j is simply equal to the expectation taken at the earlier time i. This result can help us by freeing us from the need to think always in terms of locally replicating portfolios. The reasoning goes as follows. The fair price C_0 can be equivalently regarded as either the set-up cost of the first locally replicating portfolio (which will furnish us with sufficient holdings of instruments and cash to build on the way $n - 1$ further portfolios); or as the (discounted) expectation taken under the appropriate measure of a discounted expectation of a discounted expectation ... of a discounted expectation. But, by the tower law, this is simply the discounted expectation at time 0 over the terminal distribution. Furthermore we know that, if we work in terms of the normalized (relative) prices Z we can dispense with discounting altogether. Therefore, under the appropriate measure, the fair value $Z_0 = C_0/P_0$ can be evaluated as the simple expectation over the terminal distribution of the relative prices Z_T. Needless to say, since P_0 is a known market price today, from the knowledge of Z_0 we can immediately extract the fair value of the un-normalized (i.e. cash) contingent claim.

Finding the Pricing Measure

The only piece of information we still seem to be lacking is how to find this 'appropriate measure'. In order to tackle this task, let us start again from what we know how to do, i.e. from the strung-together replicating portfolios, and let us look again at the results previously obtained immediately after Equation (2.76). We there established that

1. there must always exist a set of probabilities π_1 and π_2, determined as shown in Section 2.3.6, such that the π-expectation of future realizations of the normalized price of any security is simply equal to the value of the normalized security today;

2. no return should be expected from this normalized security.

The second result implies that, over a single time-step, the relative price Z should display no expected growth. The tower law comes in handy again: the property of the process Z of displaying no drift embodies an expectation condition and, by the tower law, this property must apply both locally and globally. Thinking globally, we can require that the expectation of a given relative price at time-step n must be equal to the relative price today. This requirement gives us a tool to determine the 'appropriate' measure: the set of pseudo-probabilities that makes relative prices martingales (i.e. driftless) will certainly produce the 'appropriate' measure under which the expectations have to be taken. This is a generalization of the result obtained in the one-period case.

The important thing to remember is that the martingale condition should apply both *locally* and *globally*: the tower law does provide us with a powerful tool, but does not dispense us from the need to ensure that, under the evaluation measure, relative prices should be martingales at each individual node.

2.3.11   Switching Numeraires and Relating Expectations Under Different Measures

Let me summarize the results so far.[10] We have established:

1. that the replicating-strategy argument still holds on a node-by-node basis, with the proviso that the replicating portfolios have now become conditional;

2. that the cost of setting up the replicating portfolio at node (0,0) is all we have to pay in order to be able to construct, by means of a self-financing trading strategy, the conditional replicating portfolios and hence the terminal payoff of the claim;

3. that this initial set-up cost can be expressed in terms of n nested conditional expectations in an appropriate measure;

4. that one such measure must always exist if market prices are consistent with absence of arbitrage;

5. that, via the tower law, the nested conditional expectations above can all be evaluated as a simple expectation taken at the origin over the terminal values of the relative prices Z;

6. that the pricing measure can be implicitly determined by imposing that, globally and locally, relative prices should be martingales.

Building on these results, we want to explore another important aspect. We have seen that changing the instrument P used as numeraire changes the no-arbitrage pseudo-probabilities on a node-by-node basis. See, for example, Equations (2.77) and (2.78). Switching numeraire induces the change in the measure (see Equation (2.78)) required to turn the new relative prices into martingales. (By the way, it is for this reason that changing instrument P is referred to as 'switching of numeraires'.) Let us examine more closely the nature of this change.

I will follow closely in the rest of this section the treatment presented in Baxter and Rennie (1996). We still work in discrete time and use a bushy tree. Let us assume that we have already found a measure, Q, associated with numeraire, P, under which relative prices are martingales. In concrete terms, the measure Q can be thought of as the full set of pseudo-probabilities $\{\pi(i, j)\}$ that 'price the market'. Let us now choose a different numeraire, P', which will induce a new no-arbitrage measure Q', with associated pseudo-probabilities $\pi'(i, j)$.

Recall that a pseudo-probability connects a parent (starting) and an arrival point. To fix notation, we can therefore assign this pseudo-probability to the 'arrival' node. So, $\pi(1, 1)$ and $\pi(1, -1)$ are the pseudo-probabilities connected with measure Q to go from the root of the tree to nodes $(1, 1)$ and $(1, -1)$, respectively, at time 1. Similarly, $\pi'(1, 1)$ and $\pi'(1, -1)$ are the pseudo-probabilities connected with measure Q' to go from the root of the tree to nodes $(1, 1)$ and $(1, -1)$.

In the two measures the same states of the world are deemed possible, but different probabilities are assigned to them. At each node we can create the ratio of $\pi(i, j)$ to

---

[10]The material covered in the remainder of Section 2.3 (i.e subsections 2.3.11–2.3.13) can be skipped on a first reading.

$\pi'(i, j)$, and call this ratio $y(i, j)$:

$$y(i, j) \equiv \frac{\pi(i, j)}{\pi'(i, j)} \tag{2.79}$$

We can then associate the value

$$y(1, 1) = \frac{\pi(1, 1)}{\pi'(1, 1)} \tag{2.80}$$

to node $(1, 1)$, and

$$y(1, -1) = \frac{\pi(1, -1)}{\pi'(1, -1)} \tag{2.81}$$

to node $(1, -1)$. This leaves undetermined what value of y to assign to the node $(0, 0)$. Let us make the choice $y(0, 0) = 1$.

Given a node (r, s) we can easily evaluate the total probability of reaching it from the root after r steps under measure Q or Q'. This probability will simply be given by the product of the probabilities $\pi(i, j)$ or $\pi'(i, j)$ encountered along the path connecting the root with node (r, s). Since this product is very important, let us define a new quantity, namely the product, for a given path, of the ratios $y(i, j)$ out to node (r, s), and denote it by the symbol $Y(r, s)$.[11]

There is a certain arbitrariness in defining $y(i, j) \equiv \frac{\pi(i,j)}{\pi'(i,j)}$. We could just as well have chosen to work with the ratio $\frac{\pi'(i,j)}{\pi(i,j)}$. Let us do so, and define $f(i, j)$ as the ratio

$$f(i, j) = \frac{\pi'(i, j)}{\pi(i, j)} \tag{2.82}$$

Similarly, let $F(r, s)$ be the product of the terms $f(i, j)$ out to node (r, s). So, symbolically:

$$Y(r, s) = \prod y(i, j) \tag{2.83}$$

$$F(r, s) = \prod f(i, j)$$

For us to be able to switch at will between these two representations, however, all the $\pi(i, j)$ and all the $\pi'(i, j)$ must be different from zero, or either ratio will not be defined. But we saw before, when we discussed the determinant condition (see Equation (2.33) in Section 2.3.1), that indeed both pseudo-probabilities propagating from a given node had to be different from zero for the replicating strategy to be feasible. Therefore, despite the fact that switching numeraires can affect measures in a way that we have not discussed yet, we can already say that this transformation must be such that events impossible under one measure (zero-probability events) will also be impossible under the new measure. This property of two measures is referred to as the *equivalence* of measures Q and Q', or as

---

[11] Note again that, since our tree does not recombine, speaking of a terminal node, such as (r, s), is tantamount to speaking of the specific path leading to it.

the fact that Q and Q' share the same null set. Therefore, as long as we switch between equivalent measures, we can rest assured that the quantities y, f, Y and F will all be well defined.

What use can be made of the products of ratios Y and F?[12] To begin with, the new quantities Y can immediately tell us how to convert an expectation taken under one measure into an expectation taken under the other measure. This is all we need, because, ultimately, we are always interested in expectations taken under given measures, not in the measures themselves. To see how this 'switch of expectations' can be accomplished, let us begin by considering the simplest expectation, i.e. the one taken over the nodes $(1, 1)$ and $(1, -1)$ of the first time-step. In keeping with the notation above, $\pi(1, 1)$, $\pi'(1, 1)$, $\pi(1, -1)$ and $\pi'(1, -1)$ are the pseudo-probabilities, and

$$Y(1, 1) = y(1, 1) = \frac{\pi(1, 1)}{\pi'(1, 1)} \tag{2.84}$$

$$Y(1, -1) = y(1, -1) = \frac{\pi(1, -1)}{\pi'(1, -1)} \tag{2.85}$$

The expectation under Q of any quantity X over the two values occurring at time 1 is simply given by

$$E_0^Q[X_1] = \pi(1, 1)X(1, 1) + \pi(1, -1)X(1, -1) = \sum_i \pi(1, i)X(1, i) \tag{2.86}$$

with $i = -1, 1$. But, for this particularly simple case, $\pi(1, i)$ can be rewritten as $\pi'(1, i)Y(1, i)$ and therefore

$$E_0^Q[X_1] = \sum_i \pi(1, i)X(1, i)$$

$$= \sum_i \pi'(1, i)Y(1, i)X(1, i) = E_0^{Q'}[XY] \tag{2.87}$$

Therefore, for the one-step case, the expectation under Q (i.e. with pseudo-probabilities $\pi(i, j)$) can be replaced by an expectation under Q' (i.e. using pseudo-probabilities $\pi'(i, j)$) simply by multiplying each quantity $X(i, j)$ by the ratio $Y(i, j)$, i.e. by taking the Q'-expectation not of X, but of the product XY:

$$E_0^Q[X_1] = E_0^{Q'}[X_1 Y_1] \tag{2.88}$$

A moment's thought will show that this is true not only for the first time-step, but after an arbitrary number of moves. Indeed, the expectation under Q of a quantity X at time-step s is given by

$$E_0^Q[X_1] = \sum_{i=1,2^s} \left[\prod_{k=1,s} \pi_{ki} \right] X(s, i) \tag{2.89}$$

---

[12]The treatment again closely follows Baxter and Rennie (1996).

where the i sum runs over all the possible paths from the tree root $(0,0)$ to each of the 2^s nodes at time s, and the new notation π_{ki} has been introduced to denote the probability of transition from time $k-1$ to time k for the path originating at the tree root $(0,0)$ and ending at node i at time s. (Recall that there is one and only one path to any such node in a non-recombining tree.) Given the definitions above, each π_{ki} can in fact be re-written as $\pi'_{ki} \, y_{ki}$ and therefore

$$
\begin{aligned}
E_0^Q[X_s] &= \sum_{i=1,2^s} [\Pi_{k=1,s}\pi'_{ki} y_{ki}] X(s,i) \\
&= \sum_{i=1,2^s} [\Pi_{k=1,s}\pi'_{ki} \Pi_{k=1,s} y_{ki}] X(s,i) = \sum_{i=1,2^s} \Pi_{k=1,s}\pi'_{ki} Y_{si} X(s,i) \\
&= E_0^{Q'}[Y_s X_s]
\end{aligned}
\tag{2.90}
$$

where the subscript notation used for the quantities y_{ki} has the same meaning as the subscripts for π_{ki}.

This result is important enough to warrant the quantity Y the special name of the Radon–Nikodým derivative, often symbolically denoted by dQ/dQ'. A worked-out example, reported below, should make these concepts clearer.

2.3.12 Another Worked-Out Example

Let us start from the case of a security S displaying the values shown in Figure 2.4 over the first two steps. Over the same time-step, the first numeraire, P, can assume the values shown in Figure 2.5. With this numeraire, Figure 2.6 shows the relative prices Z (in bold) and the pseudo-probabilities π that are obtained.

As mentioned earlier, the pseudo-probabilities are determined by enforcing the requirement that the relative prices should be martingales. See Equation (2.78). For the bottom corner of the bushy tree after the first step, for instance, this gives the condition that $1.021103 = (0.973913 \times 0.812058) + (1.225000 \times 0.187942)$.

A second numeraire, P', and the accompanying relative prices, Z', and pseudo-probabilities, π', are then shown in Figures 2.7 and 2.8. Once again, the pseudo-probabilities π' are obtained by imposing that the Z' should be martingales. With this information we can obtain the ratios $y = \pi/\pi'$ (see Figure 2.9).

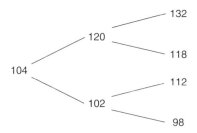

Figure 2.4 Values of the stock price, S, over the first two time-steps.

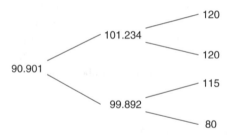

Figure 2.5   Values of the bond price, P, over the first two time-steps.

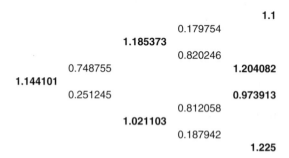

Figure 2.6   Values of the relative prices, Z (in bold), and pseudo-probabilities π over the first two time-steps.

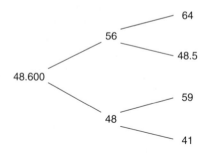

Figure 2.7   Values of a second numeraire, P', over the first two time-steps.

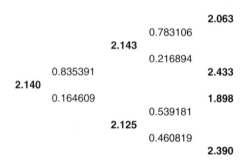

Figure 2.8   Values of the relative prices, Z', associated with the second numeraire (in bold), and pseudo-probabilities, π', over the first two time-steps.

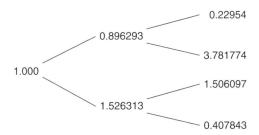

Figure 2.9   Values of $y = \pi/\pi'$ over the first two time-steps.

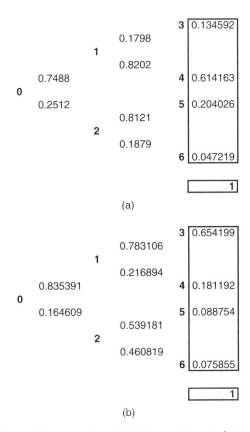

Figure 2.10   Products of the pseudo-probabilities π (a) and π' (b), along paths 1 to 6.

Figures 2.10(a) and 2.10(b) then show the products of the pseudo-probabilities π and π', respectively, along the different possible paths (the integers 0 to 6 label the paths, or, equivalently, the states of the world after two time-steps).

For both trees, one can check that the sum over all the paths of the products of the pseudo-probabilities does add up to one (bottom cell). We can now build the tree for the Radon–Nikodým derivative Y (Figure 2.11).

0.205735

0.896293

3.389577

1

2.298775

1.526313

0.622496

Figure 2.11   Values of the Radon–Nikodým derivative Y.

Table 2.2   Values corresponding to paths 1–6 after two time-steps. The first column reports the terminal state, the second the quantity $\Pi_i \pi_i$, the third the values of stock price, S, in these states, the fourth the quantities SY, and the last the products $\Pi_i \pi_i'$.

3	0.134592	132	27.15708	0.654199
4	0.614163	118	399.9701	0.181192
5	0.204026	112	257.4628	0.088754
6	0.047219	98	61.00459	0.075855
Expectation	117.7157		117.7157	

I have shown above that we can equivalently calculate the expectation of, say, S after two steps either using the pseudo-probabilities π, or by using the pseudo-probabilities π' and the new quantity SY. The resulting arrays of quantities S, SY, $\Pi_i \pi_i$ and $\Pi_i \pi_i'$ corresponding to the various paths (states of the world) after two steps are shown in Table 2.2. The two cells on the bottom line show that indeed the same expectation is obtained for S, in the measure Q associated with numeraire P, either by using the probabilities π, or by using the probabilities π' associated with the measure Q' induced by numeraire P' and by taking the expectation of the product of the variable S and the Radon–Nikodým derivative.

2.3.13   Relevance of the Results

The topic of this book is volatility and correlation. Why have we taken such a long detour to talk about changes of measures and Radon–Nikodým derivatives?

What we have seen so far is that, by changing numeraire, the pricing measure changes, in a possibly very complex way. The Radon–Nikodým derivative 'contains' all the information about this measure change. This information is, however, rather opaque. Indeed, apart from establishing that events possible in the measure implied by a numeraire must be possible also in the measure induced by a different numeraire (i.e. apart from the equivalence of the two measures), we have not been able to establish anything more precise about the nature of the transformation of measure. In particular, we do not know which properties of a process are affected, and which remain unaltered, in moving between measures. Unfortunately, as long as we keep the time intervals fixed and simply work in a discrete-time, discrete-space setting, it is difficult to answer these questions in a general way. What we would like to do is

- to relate the discrete changes in prices to some quantities (e.g. jump sizes, drifts, volatilities) that can be used without explicit reference to a particular and fixed time-step;

- to explore which of these quantities are unaffected by the change of measure, and can therefore be estimated in the real-world measure.

In order to accomplish these tasks, we must address the issue of the justifiability of the two-state branching procedure employed so far. The following sections will deal with this topic.

2.4 Justifying the Two-State Branching Procedure

Up to this point we have kept the length of the time interval fixed. Therefore we have no way of telling whether the price move over the time-step was meant to give a discretized representation of a continuous process, or whether it represented a discontinuous jump. Furthermore, the replication strategy relied heavily on only two states being reachable from each node. Is there a justification for this, apart from computational convenience? A priori, imposing that three, or seven, states should be reachable from a given node appears to be financially just as (in-)plausible. Yet, we would not have had enough 'underlying' instruments to replicate the payoffs even in a three-state setting. Has our analysis been so stylized as to be useless in practice?

In order to answer these questions we will have to investigate how the price move changes as the size of the time-step decreases. In order to explore this I will make use in the following section of the argument originally presented in Merton (1983, 1990) and repeated in Neftci (1996).

2.4.1 How To Recognize a Jump When You See One

Let us slightly generalize the setting presented so far by allowing that, over the next time-step, of length Δt, m realizations of the stock price are possible. We might prefer to work in log space, but this does not change the argument. Also, for the sake of simplicity, let us assume that the expectation of the change in the (log of) the stock price is zero. This will simplify the formulae to follow without changing the gist of the argument. Finally, let us assume that to each realization we can assign a real-world probability, $\pi_i, i = 1, 2, \ldots, m$. With these assumptions the variance of the (log of) the stock price over time-step k, var(S^k) is given by

$$\text{var}(S^k) = \sum \pi_i \left(\Delta S_i^k \right)^2 \tag{2.91}$$

where ΔS_i denotes either an absolute or percentage price change, according to whether we have chosen to work in log space or not.

Let us now consider several, say, n, time-steps in succession. Along any of the possible n^m paths, the variance of the (log) stock price, $\text{var}_n(S)$, will be given by

$$\text{var}_n(S) = \text{E}_0 \left[\sum_{j=1,n} \Delta S_j^2 \right] \tag{2.92}$$

The variance of the (log) price changes is clearly linked in a very fundamental way to the nature of the uncertainty in the stock price dynamics. How might we want to model the uncertainty in the evolution of the stock price? And how might we want to link these desiderata to properties of the variance?

As far as the first question is concerned, it is reasonable to impose the following requirements (see Merton (1990)).

Condition 1 *Consider a finite horizon* $[0\ T]$*, and a number n of trading intervals. We must be able to find a number* $A_1 > 0$*, arbitrarily small but strictly positive and independent of the number of trading intervals, such that* $\text{var}_n(S) > A_1$*.*

Condition 2 *Over any finite interval the variance should be finite. This means that for any finite interval subdivided into n subintervals we should be able to determine a number* $0 < A_2 < \infty$*, such that* $\text{var}_n(S) \leq A_2$*.*

Condition 3 *Consider a finite horizon, subdivided in n trading intervals as above, and denote by VarMax the maximum value of* $\text{var}_n(S)$ *over this interval. Then we want to be able to find a number* $A_3, 0 < A_3 \leq 1$*, such that, for any of the intervals,*

$$\frac{\text{var}_n(S)}{VarMax} \geq A_3 \tag{2.93}$$

What do these conditions mean? By Condition 2 we are excluding, for instance, the possibility that the underlying distribution might have infinite variance (such as a Pareto–Levy distribution).[13] Condition 3 requires that the uncertainty is not 'concentrated' in any subinterval (as might be case, for instance, if the price uncertainty were fully resolved by the outcome of a single event taking place at some time $\tau, 0 < \tau \leq T$). As for Condition 1, we require that the uncertainty should not become so small as we reduce the time-step as to make the *total* uncertainty vanish. In other words, as we 'shrink' the length of the trading subinterval, the variance *will* become smaller, but not 'too quickly'. Therefore we cannot resolve the uncertainty simply by trading more and more frequently.

In short, the variance is not too big, is not too small, and is not too concentrated. These assumptions are reasonable enough. Building on such slender pillars, Merton shows that if these conditions are satisfied, then the variance is asymptotically proportional[14] to the length of the time-step, Δt:

$$\text{var}(S) = O(\Delta t) \tag{2.94}$$

---

[13] See, however, the results by Carr and Wu (2003a) in Chapter 7.

[14] The proof hinges on the concept of asymptotic proportionality, discussed and precisely defined in Merton (1990, p. 63).

The result might seem unsurprising to readers who are familiar with Brownian processes (indeed the proportionality to the time of the variance of a Brownian process is at the root of Ito's calculus). The result obtained here, however, is much more general, since we have not required the discretized process to be a diffusion. Actually, it is the fact that property (2.94) holds true irrespective of the nature of the underlying process, as long as Conditions 1–3 are satisfied, that makes the result interesting and useful. Let us see, in fact, what consequences can be drawn from Equation (2.94).

Let us go back to the analysis of any of the n trading subintervals Δt, say the kth. By Condition 3 we know that this subinterval will not be essentially different from any other interval. Putting together Equation (2.94) with Equation (2.91), we can write

$$\sum \pi_i \left(\Delta S_i^k \right)^2 = O(\Delta t) = c_k \Delta t \qquad (2.95)$$

for some constant c_k. What happens when the time-step is reduced in size? In general, both the probabilities, π_i, and the (log) price increment will change, possibly in a complex way. We now make the assumption that this dependence should be continuous and sufficiently well-behaved to be expressed as a power function of the time step Δt:

Condition 4 *For all the possible states reached over the time-steps the associated probabilities and (log) price changes must satisfy*

$$\pi_i \sim \Delta t^{q_i} \qquad (2.96)$$

$$\Delta S_i^k \sim \Delta t^{r_i} \qquad (2.97)$$

where the symbol '~' denotes proportionality.

If we accept Condition 3, Equation (2.95) requires that

$$\Delta t \sim \pi_i \left(\Delta S_i^k \right)^2 \sim \Delta t^{q_i} \Delta t^{2r_i} \qquad (2.98)$$

or, after taking logarithms, and as Δt goes to zero,

$$q_i + 2r_i = 1 \qquad (2.99)$$

Exercise 2 *Derive Equation (2.99) and show that both q_i and r_i must be positive. (Hint: make use of the positivity of probabilities, and the boundedness of the variance.)*

Given the result of the exercise, it follows that, for any i, $0 \le q_i \le 1$ and $0 \le r_i \le \frac{1}{2}$. What is Equation (2.99) telling us? That if we accept the financial requirements (Conditions 1–3), and the regularity requirement (Condition 4), the way the size of the (log) price move and of its associated probability change as the time-step is reduced cannot be chosen independently, and that there is an important link between the two: the larger the (log) price change, the smaller the probability of its occurrence must be. Let us explore this link in more detail.

Let us distinguish three possible ranges for r_i, and associate a process type to each:

$$r_i = \tfrac{1}{2} \quad \text{Type I} \tag{2.100}$$

$$0 < r_i < \tfrac{1}{2} \quad \text{Type II} \tag{2.101}$$

$$r_i = 0 \quad \text{Type III} \tag{2.102}$$

For a Type-I process (a 'normal' process), we know from (2.99) that $q_i = 0$. This implies that, as the time-step Δt goes to zero, the probabilities ($\pi_i \sim \Delta t^{q_i} = \Delta t^0$) do not decrease in size, but the size of the move decreases as the square root of time ($\Delta S_i^k \sim \Delta t^{r_i} = \Delta t^{1/2}$). These are the properties that we associated with a discretization of a Brownian motion, and we are therefore not surprised to learn, for instance, that the paths generated by a Type-I process are continuous, but lack 'smoothness' (i.e. are nowhere differentiable). See, for example, Neftci (1996).

Consider now Type-III events ('pure jumps'). If, for at least some events i, $r_i = 0$, then q_i must be equal to 1. This means that the probability π_i of that event scales exactly with the size of the time-step ($\pi_i \sim \Delta t^{q_i} = \Delta t$), but that the size of the (log) price moves is unaffected by the reduction in time-step. These are the properties we associate, for instance, with Poisson events (see Chapter 14), where the probability of arrival is given by $\lambda \Delta t$ (for a process with constant intensity λ), but the jump is totally instantaneous.

Not surprisingly, Type-II events present an intermediate behaviour.

This brings us back to the discussion at the end of the previous section. It is now clear that the two-state construction used up to this point is not as arbitrary as it might have appeared when first introduced, but it is both necessary and sufficient for the shocks to the economy to be generated by a non-symmetric random walk, i.e. by the discretized version of a diffusion. That the latter should be the case is, of course, an assumption rather than a 'provable truth', and its virtual ubiquity in option pricing should not make one think otherwise. If we are happy, however, with the Brownian assumption, i.e. if we believe that an equation of the type

$$\Delta S = \mu \Delta t + \sigma \epsilon \sqrt{\Delta t} \tag{2.103}$$

(with ϵ a draw from a standardized normal distribution), can adequately describe the evolution of the price of securities, then we can rest assured that the arguments presented so far all apply. In particular, we know, for instance, that a three-state evolution is unnecessary and that, therefore, the financially unappealing introduction of a third security (needed to solve the 3×3 system) is not required.

Summarizing: this section has clarified the issues connected with the size of the time-step, and more precisely, with the scaling properties of the price moves with the size of the step. The results we have obtained were not only important in their own right, but also necessary for the next section, where, in order to obtain the required results, we will have to let Δt go to zero.

2.5 The Nature of the Transformation between Measures: Girsanov's Theorem

There is still an important conceptual step to make: we know that, in the absence of arbitrage, the choice of a numeraire induces a set of probabilities (a measure Q') such that normalized prices are martingales. We can think of this new measure as the result of a change from the (unknown) real-world probabilities to a new set of pseudo-probabilities. In the previous section we discovered that, if the shocks to the economy are produced by a discretized Brownian motion of known variance, then, in the measure Q', the two-state branching procedure is all that is needed to give an adequate description of the process. However, we can at best have access to the variance of this Brownian motion in the real world. How do we know that, when we work with the 'scrambled' probabilities of the measure Q', the resulting process variance will be the same as the variance that we have estimated statistically in the real world? Indeed, how do we know that, under Q', a Brownian motion is still a Brownian motion at all? More generally, what is the nature of the transformation of a given Brownian motion when we move from the real-world measure Q to the new measure Q'?

I will not attempt to answer this question by providing a proof. I shall, instead, provide an intuitive argument, and work through a specific example that should clarify the ideas behind the proof (Girsanov's theorem).

2.5.1 An Intuitive Argument

Let us start from the intuitive argument. The first step is to recognize that, if we change the drift of a diffusion, we do not change its volatility. Proving this requires little more work than proving that shifting all the (numerical) outcomes of an experiment by a fixed amount changes their expectation but not their variance.

Let us then go back to the discussion we had about the market price of risk. We assumed that all the investors agreed on the real-world properties of the processes of the traded assets. Given their risk-averse nature, they also all agreed that a risk correction should be applied to the real-world return from each uncertain asset in order to make it 'comparable' to a riskless asset. This correction should reflect the aversion to risk of the investors, and the riskiness of each asset. To avoid inconsistencies in the prices, however, this correction should depend on no specific feature of an asset other than its riskiness.

Also these results should be acceptable without too much trouble. They basically say that, if we are risk-neutral, we are not willing to enter 'for free' a 50-50 bet of losing or gaining one million dollars, and we want the *expectation* of the bet to be tilted in our favour before entering it. By how much depends on our risk aversion. And, if different bets were 'inconsistently tilted', we should not be too surprised if we managed to engineer some amazingly good deals simply by entering the gambler's side on some bets and the house's side on others.

This is where the more hand-waving bit comes in: different degrees of risk aversion require a different inducement to enter the bet. Different inducements mean different degrees of tilting of the outcome: say, the bet may be entered for free if the outcomes were a loss of $100 000 or a gain of $1 900 000, corresponding to an upward tilting of the outcomes to compensate for risk aversion by $900 000. Such tilting has changed the real-world expectation of the bet. Alternatively, we can find new (pseudo)-probabilities such that the tilted bet is now fair (i.e. it still has zero expectation). However, we have accepted at the start that such a rigid tilting does not affect the variance. Therefore the logical chain is:

- because of risk aversion we do not accept actuarially fair gambles;
- to be enticed to enter such gambles, we require a rigid tilting in our favour;
- such a tilting can be expressed as a change of measure;
- such a titling changes the expectation of the outcome, but not the variance;
- therefore the change of measure alters the expectation, but does not change the variance.

The argument can be looked at from a more directly financial angle as follows. If we say that the price of a security is $100 today, and that several states are possible tomorrow, it must be the case *under any measure* (i.e. for *any* pattern of risk aversion) that in at least one state of the world the security will be worth strictly less than $100. If this were not the case, buying it for the current market price would be an arbitrage under any (equivalent) measure, i.e. again, for *any* pattern of risk aversion.

For the purpose of this argument it does not matter if the worst possible outcome were $99.9999, or if the probability of such an occurrence were one in a million. There still exists some patterns of risk aversion that would reject this bet. So the price system in Figure 2.12 is compatible with no arbitrage (although it implies a rather pathological aversion to risk), but the apparently more plausible price system in Figure 2.13 is not. This, in a nutshell, is the meaning of Girsanov's theorem applied to asset pricing.

Let us see this in practice with an example.

2.5.2 A Worked-Out Example

Let us consider again the by-now-familiar case of a stock, S, a claim, C, and a bond, P, which move from an initial parent state to two possible states after a time-step Δt.

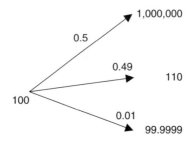

Figure 2.12 The price today ($100) and the prices attainable 'tomorrow', with the real-world probabilities of occurrence. No arbitrage is possible.

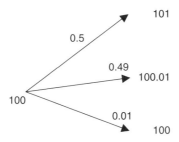

Figure 2.13 The price today ($100) and the prices attainable 'tomorrow', with the real-world probabilities of occurrence. Arbitrage is now possible.

Using P as numeraire, let us determine the pseudo-probabilities π_1 and π_2 that make the relative price $Z' = S/P$, a martingale. From Equations (2.55) and (2.56) of Section 2.3.6 we know that these pseudo-probabilities are given by

$$\pi_1 = \frac{S_0/P_0 - S_2}{S_1 - S_2} \tag{2.104}$$

$$\pi_2 = \frac{S_1 - S_0/P_0}{S_1 - S_2} \tag{2.105}$$

Let us now consider a different asset, T, which we can choose as a second numeraire. This new unit of account will give rise to new relative prices $Z'' = S/T$ and new probabilities π_1' and π_2' under which the relative prices Z'' are driftless. We want to ask the following question: What happens to the variance and drift of S as the interval Δt approaches zero when we move from the probabilities $\{\pi\}$ to the probabilities $\{\pi'\}$ – i.e. when we switch numeraire?

To answer this question, let us begin with a time-step Δt of 0.25 years, and consider the prices in the two possible states for the stock and the bond obtainable using real-world drifts of 10% S and 12% P, and volatilities of 20% S and 16% P, respectively. The resulting values are shown in Figure 2.14, obtained with $\Delta t = 0.25$

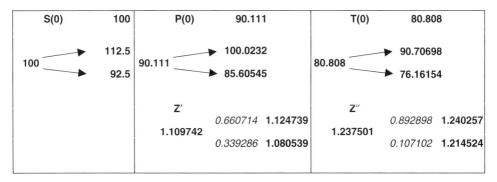

Figure 2.14 Prices of the stock and of the two numeraires after one time-step ($\Delta t = 0.25$).

With these values one can then obtain the relative price of S using numeraire P or T, denoted by Z' and Z'', respectively. Imposing that these relative prices should be martingales then determines the two sets of equivalent pseudo-probabilities, by means of which the expectation and variance of S in the two measures can be calculated. The values are shown in italics in Figure 2.14. For the chosen time-step both the variance and the expectation differ in moving from one measure to the other: the expectation, for instance, is 105.71 and 110.358 in the measures Q and Q', respectively.

If one wanted to reduce the time-step, more significant than the expectations and variances would be the drift (i.e. the expectation divided by the time-step) and the volatility (i.e. the standard deviation per unit time). These quantities are reported for the two numeraires in Table 2.3.

When this scaling is carried out, a very interesting feature becomes apparent: if the time-step becomes smaller and smaller the drifts converge in the two measures to different values; the variance per unit time, however, becomes the same irrespective of whether we are working in the measure Q or in the measure Q'. Therefore the transformation of the probabilities induced by a change of numeraire is such that the 'new' drifts are measure-dependent, but the variances are not, and can therefore be estimated (and will apply with equal validity) in any measure (in particular, the real-world one).

Saying that the drifts are measure-dependent means that, in moving between measures, the return required by the holder of a security will vary. An infinity of real-world measures is in general compatible with the particular pricing measure implied by the traded prices. These real-world measures might well be infinite, but this does not mean that they can be arbitrary. Since they are all related by a *drift* transformation, the volatility will remain unchanged. If we inhabit a world with no redundant securities, there is little more that we can say. If perfect replication is possible, however, there will be a *unique* pricing measure. In order to find it, we do not need to find the real-world (statistical) measure and apply the Radon–Nikodým transformation, because we can simply and directly work with the pseudo-probabilities implied by the price system.

Looking at the problem from a different angle, the measure transformations are both very general and very restrictive. They are very general because they can be very complex (they can be, for instance, both time- and state-dependent). They are, however, also very restrictive because they can only reflect different attitudes to risk compatible with the

Table 2.3 The standard deviations per unit time in measures Q' and Q'' (STD$'[S]$ and STD$''[S]$), respectively, and the expectations per unit time, (E$'[S]$ and E$''[S]$), also in measures Q' and Q'', with the percentage difference (Diff) between the two.

Δt	STD$'[S]$	STD$''[S]$	Diff	E$'[S]$	E$''[S]$	Diff
0.25	18.938%	12.369%	34.69%	22.857	41.432	44.83%
0.125	19.462%	16.378%	15.85%	23.024	42.464	45.78%
0.0625	19.729%	18.217%	7.67%	23.111	43.018	46.28%
0.03125	19.846%	19.113%	3.78%	23.155	43.305	46.53%
0.015625	19.932%	19.558%	1.88%	23.177	43.452	46.66%
0.007813	19.966%	19.779%	0.94%	23.188	43.525	46.72%
0.003906	19.983%	19.889%	0.47%	23.194	43.562	46.76%

absence of arbitrage opportunities in the market prices (see, for instance, the discussion in Section 6.7.3).

These observations about the measure-invariance of the volatility have a direct practical bearing. On the basis of real-world statistical information we can make estimates or predictions about the volatility that will be experienced by an underlying asset during the life of the option. If we want to make use of such estimates for option pricing, then we must have confidence that the volatility will remain unchanged when switching between measures. Girsanov's theorem assures us that this is indeed the case. If it all seems very obvious, recall that the deceptively similar estimation of drift-related properties (such as levels or speeds of mean reversions) is of no relevance to option pricing when replication is possible.

2.6 Switching Between the PDE, the Expectation and the Binomial Replication Approaches

The Feynman–Kac theorem discussed above showed the link between a diffusion, a partial differential equation and an expectation over a terminal payoff. The binomial replication strategy has reduced the problem of evaluating the fair price of a contingent claim to a series of nested expectations. The tower law has allowed us to work with a simple expectation over the terminal payoff, rather than having to work with the nested ones. This result then establishes a link back with the Feynman–Kac theorem, the underlying diffusion and the associated PDE. As usual, crossing the mathematical *t*s and dotting the probabilistic *i*s is not quite as straightforward, but for our purposes we can safely use any of these results in an opportunistic manner, to suit the problem at hand. Therefore in the remainder of this book I will freely move from one approach to the other, to suit the circumstances.

Chapter 3

The Building Blocks

3.1 Introduction and Plan of the Chapter

The purpose of this chapter is threefold. First, I intend to define precisely the quantities (implied, spot, instantaneous, forward, future volatility, etc.) used in the rest of the book. Then, by placing myself in a Black-and-Scholes world, I show that the 'implied' volatility can be linked to a function(al) of the instantaneous (spot) volatility of the underlying, and that, for a given maturity, no smiles are observed. I also explain the fundamental difference between the concepts of volatilities and correlations in the case of equities and FX on the one hand, and of interest rates on the other.

Second, I intend to show the link between the set of *current* implied volatilities and the *future* (spot) volatility of the underlying. In order to do so I will discuss in some detail the case of 'forward-starting' options. I will also explain why, in most cases, working in a forward-based (Black) framework is both simpler and conceptually more satisfactory than working in a spot-based (Black-and-Scholes) setting.

Lastly, I will give a first introduction of the concept of quadratic variation. This quantity is central to the treatment presented in the whole book, and will be revisited in the context of smile-producing models.

3.2 Definition of Market Terms

The analysis of those aspects of option pricing and risk management that are connected with the stochastic behaviour of financial quantities is plagued by imprecise, confusing and often contradictory terminology. The terms 'forward volatility', 'future volatility', 'forward-forward volatility', 'term structure of volatility', 'volatility of a forward', 'instantaneous volatility', to name just a few, often mean different things to different practitioners (and, sometimes, mean very little *tout court*). Even the apparently uncontroversial term 'correlation' can give rise of ambiguity, since the fundamental distinction between *instantaneous* and *terminal* correlation is often overlooked.

This confusion is of more-than-academic relevance: it sometimes prompts some practitioners to claim, for instance, that multi-factor models *must* be employed in order to

account at the same time for the observed prices of caps and swaptions; or, more generally, to argue that, for a model to capture imperfect correlation between rates, it *cannot*
be single-factor. In reality, imperfect instantaneous correlation is but one of the mechanisms that can produce terminal de-correlation amongst rates or prices, and the relative
merits and shortcomings of using multi-factor models against employing time-dependent
volatilities must be carefully weighed and compared. Similarly, confusion often exists
about the *current* volatility of a *forward* quantity, the *future* volatility of a *spot* price or
rate and the *future* volatility of a *forward* quantity.

One reason for this rather confused state of affairs is that the underlying traded quantities in the equity and FX markets on the one hand, and in the interest-rate market on
the other are fundamentally different. Not surprisingly, this gives rise to different links
between the volatilities of the corresponding spot or forward quantities. In order to clarify
these issues is it necessary to define the 'tools of the trade' as precisely as possible. We
shall therefore start by defining:

1. the current volatility of a forward rate or price;

2. the future volatility of a spot rate or price; and

3. the future volatility of a forward rate or price.

In order to define their meaning, one must, in turn, define the concept of forward (rate
or price). This is done as follows:

Definition 1 *The T-maturity forward price today in a given currency of a given security
is the strike that gives zero value to a forward contract for delivery at time T of the same
security in exchange for strike units of the same currency.*

Definition 2 *The T-maturity forward exchange rate (expressed as units of currency A per
unit of currency B) is the strike that gives zero value today to the forward contract for
delivery at time T of strike units of currency A against one unit of currency B.*

Definition 3 *The T-expiry–(T + τ)-maturity forward rate today is the strike that gives
zero value to a forward contract paying at time T + τ the difference between the reset at
time T of the rate spanning the period [T T + τ] and the strike itself.*

Note that in the definitions there is no mention of expectations (either in a mathematical
or subjective sense) about the underlying. As a consequence, distributional assumptions
about the underlying in general, and volatilities and correlations in particular, do not
enter the definition of a forward. When it is possible to take long and short positions in
the underlying without frictions and/or restrictions, forward prices and rates are uniquely
determined by no-arbitrage considerations. (See Hull (1993) or Rebonato (1998a) for an
example in the interest-rate case.) Any introductory text (see, for example, Hull (1993))
shows that, by no-arbitrage, the forward rates and prices are related to the spot quantities
by

$$FS(t, T) = S(t) \exp[(r_{t,T} - d)(T - t)] \qquad \text{Equity case} \qquad (3.1)$$

$$FFX(t, T) = FX(t) \exp\left[(r_{t,T}^{\mathrm{d}} - r_{t,T}^{\mathrm{f}})(T - t)\right] \qquad \text{FX case} \qquad (3.2)$$

$$FR(t, T_1, T_2) = \left[\frac{P(t, T_1)}{P(t, T_2)} - 1\right] \frac{1}{T_2 - T_1} \qquad \text{Interest-rate case} \qquad (3.3)$$

where

- $S(t)$ is the spot price of the equity stock at time t

- $FS(t, T)$ is the time-t forward price of the equity stock for delivery at time T

- $r_{t,T}$ is the $(T - t)$-period spot interest rate from time t to time T

- d is the (constant) dividend yield

- $r_{t,T}^{d}$ ($r_{t,T}^{f}$) is the $(T - t)$-period spot domestic (foreign) interest rate from time t to time T

- $FX(t)$ is the spot FX rate expressed in units of domestic currency per units of foreign currency at time t

- $FFX(t, T)$ is the time-t forward FX rate expressed in units of domestic currency per units of foreign currency for delivery at time T

- $FR(t, T_1, T_2)$ is the time-t value of a forward rate expiring at time T_1 and spanning the period $[T_1\ T_2]$

- $P(t, T)$ is the time-t value of a discount bond maturing at time T.

Note that, in the definitions above, $r_{t,T}$ is not the short rate, but the yield of the T-maturity bond, i.e.

$$\exp[-r_{t,T}(T - t)] \equiv P(t, T) \tag{3.4}$$

Definitions 1 and 2 are basically identical in the equity and in the FX cases (as one can readily see by thinking of one unit of currency B in Definition 2 as 'the security' in Definition 1). Definition 3, however, describes a type of contract that is fundamentally different. In order to appreciate the nature of this difference, in the next section we shall contrast the case of spot hedging forward contracts in equities with the case of hedging forward contracts with spot quantities in the interest-rate case. The analysis will provide a useful framework to treat options in the following section, and to explore the added complexity in the specification of the volatility structure as one moves from equities/FX to interest-rate products.

3.3 Hedging Forward Contracts Using Spot Quantities

Let us begin by considering how to hedge with spot transactions[1] a series of equity forward contracts on the one hand, and a series of interest-rate forward contracts on the other. My goal is to show that solving these two apparently similar hedging tasks requires approaches of an intrinsically different nature. In the equity case a single net position in the spot underlying asset is sufficient. In the interest-rate case delta hedging will require taking a position in a number of *different* assets. The implications of this will become apparent when we deal with options rather than forward contracts.

---

[1] A spot transaction is buying or selling a non-derivative security today at the current market price.

3.3.1   Hedging Equity Forward Contracts

Let us begin with the first case, and assume that we have entered at time t_0 N forward contracts, struck at $X_1, X_2, \ldots, X_N$, for delivery at times $T_1, T_2, \ldots, T_N$ of $A_1, A_2, \ldots, A_n$ amounts of the same given stock. To lighten the notation I will set the dividend yield to zero. The present value of the ith contract, PV_i, is given by

$$
\begin{aligned}
PV_i &= A_i[FS(t_0, T_i) - X_i]P(t_0, T_i) \\
&= A_i[S(t_0)\exp[r_{t_0, T_i}(T_i - t_0)] - X_i]P(t_0, T_i) \\
&= A_i\left[\frac{S(t_0)}{P(t_0, T_i)} - X_i\right]P(t_0, T_i) \\
&= A_i[S(t_0) - X_i P(t_0, T_i)]
\end{aligned}
\tag{3.5}
$$

In going from the second to the third line, use has been made of Equation (3.4). In order to spot hedge this series of positions one can work out the net sensitivity of the forward contracts to the spot price and to the discount bonds. For each contract one can in fact write

$$
\frac{\partial PV_i}{\partial S(t_0)} = A_i
\tag{3.6}
$$

and

$$
\frac{\partial PV_i}{\partial P(t_0, T_i)} = A_i X_i
\tag{3.7}
$$

Therefore the net position, A_{hedge}, to spot hedge the exposure to the stock price of all the forward contracts is simply given by

$$
A_{\text{hedge}} = \sum_{i=1,N} A_i
\tag{3.8}
$$

This is not surprising, since, in the equity stock case, different equity forward prices are the strikes that give zero value to a series of contracts for delivery of the *same* underlying at different points in time. Therefore, holding the amount of stock A_i will certainly allow the trader to fulfil her delivery obligation for the ith forward contract, and the net quantity of stock A_{hedge} will simultaneously perfectly hedge all her forward contracts. Since an FX rate can be thought of as the price of a unit of foreign currency in terms of domestic currency, the same reasoning also applies with little change to the FX case.[2]

Summarizing: if one enters a simultaneous position in a series of equity- (or FX-) based forward contracts, in order to execute a spot hedge (i.e. in order to hedge against movements in the underlying by dealing in the stock today) one simply has to take a

---

[2]In the 'equity-stock example' just presented we assumed that we were dealing with a non-dividend paying stock. For non-zero dividend, d, the 'growth rate' of the stock becomes $r - d$. In the FX case the no-arbitrage growth rate of the domestic currency is given by the difference between the domestic rate, r_d, and the foreign rate, r_f.

suitable single net position in the *same* spot underlying. If one wanted to be fully hedged, one would also have to carry out the hedging transactions required to neutralize the uncertainty from the discounting. This would entail taking positions in different discount bonds. For the moment, however, we are just focusing on hedging the exposure to the underlying ('delta' hedging).

3.3.2   Hedging Interest-Rate Forward Contracts

Let us now consider the apparently similar situation where N forward contracts, struck at $X_1, X_2, \ldots, X_N$, and with notional amounts $A_1, A_2, \ldots, A_N$, are entered at time t_0 on a series of forward rates spanning the periods $[T_1, T_1 + \tau_1], [T_2, T_2 + \tau_2], \ldots, [T_N, T_N + \tau_N]$. (Note that we are not assuming that $T_i + \tau_i = T_{i+1}$, i.e. the payment time of the ith forward contract does not necessarily coincide with the expiry of the $(i + 1)$th; in other words, the forward rates are not necessarily 'spanning' in the sense of Rebonato (1998a, 2002).) The present value of each contract, PV_i, is then given by

$$PV_i = A_i[FR(t_0, T_i, T_i + \tau_i) - X_i]\tau_i P(t_0, T_i + \tau_i)$$

$$= A_i \left\{ \left[\frac{P(t_0, T_i)}{P(t_0, T_i + \tau_i)} - 1 \right] \frac{1}{\tau_i} - X_i \right\} \tau_i P(t_0, T_i + \tau_i)$$

$$= A_i[P(t_0, T_i) - P(t_0, T_i + \tau_i) - X_i \tau_i P(t_0, T_i + \tau_i)]$$

$$= A_i[P(t_0, T_i) - P(t_0, T_i + \tau_i)(1 + X_i \tau_i)] \qquad (3.9)$$

In working out the spot hedges for each of the contracts in the series, one therefore finds

$$\frac{\partial PV_i}{\partial P(t_0, T_i)} = A_i \qquad (3.10)$$

and

$$\frac{\partial PV_i}{\partial P(t_0, T_i + \tau_i)} = -A_i(1 + X_i \tau_i) \qquad (3.11)$$

Despite the superficial similarity between Equation (3.10) and Equation (3.6), note that, unlike the equity/FX case, the partial derivatives are now taken with respect to *different* spot discount bond prices, and the quantity A_i denotes the required amount of the ith bond. Therefore, the netting of the quantities A_i as in Equation (3.8) is no longer possible, and, in order to spot hedge the whole series of N forward contracts, the trader must in general take a spot position in $2N$ assets (discount bonds): *different* interest-rate forwards are the strikes that give zero value to a series of contracts for delivery of *different* underlying instruments at *different* points in time. Even neglecting the hedging of the uncertainty due to discounting (i.e. even if we concentrate on delta hedging), in order to hedge a simultaneous position in N interest-rate forwards contracts one must in general take positions in $2N$ underlying spot assets (bonds).[3]

---

[3]If the forward rates underlying the different forward contracts were spanning (i.e. if the pay-time of one coincided with the expiry time of the next), the number of underlying bonds would be less than $2N$.

The message from the analysis carried out in this section is that, in order to spot hedge forward contracts, the trader has to take positions in one, or several spot underlying assets. Whether the hedging position is in one or many assets depends on the nature of the underlying. The statement appears (and is) rather obvious. However, when one moves from the hedging of forward contracts to the hedging of non-linear derivatives (e.g. options), the choice of hedging instrument is no longer so obvious. One can carry out, in fact, two very similar treatments that give as a result the notionals either of the spot transactions or of the forward contracts that the trader has to enter in order to be delta-hedged. I will argue below that, while mathematically equivalent, the two approaches are financially very different, and that, whenever possible, hedging of options should always be carried out using forward contracts rather than spot transactions. This way of looking at the hedging problem will also clarify my view that it is more fruitful to regard options as being written on forwards rather than on future spot quantities (in other words, the Black, rather than the Black-and-Scholes, framework is, in my opinion, more useful and conceptually more satisfying).

3.4   Hedging Options: Volatility of Spot and Forward Processes

So far we have considered simple forward contracts, for the pricing of which volatilities and correlations are irrelevant. In moving from a series of forward contracts to a series of options on equity or FX forwards, volatilities and correlation do matter, but the reasoning remains otherwise similar. The main change, as far as the argument above is concerned, will be that the notional of the spot hedge will become a volatility-dependent delta amount of the underlying. The exact amount of delta hedge will in turn depend on the model used to price the option, but, at least as long as the discounting is deterministic, only the volatility of the same spot process should matter for equities or FX rates.

Another important result that we obtain in this section is the following. Let us accept for the moment that, in a Black world, given a series of options on forwards with different expiries, the average (root-mean-squared) volatilities out to different horizons will determine the correct hedges (this will be shown to be the case in the next chapter). As the spacing between the maturities for which prices can be observed becomes finer and finer, these root-mean-squared volatilities will in turn be shown to give information about the future instantaneous volatility of the underlying process. Therefore, in order to price and hedge, in a deterministic-discounting regime, N options on equity stock or FX rates all that matters is the time-dependent volatility of the spot process.

The situation is different in the case of interest rates. If the task before us is the pricing and hedging of N interest-rate derivatives, it is the volatilities of (and, possibly, depending on the type of option, the correlations among) $2N$ processes that determine the required delta amounts of spot discount bonds. Specifying volatilities for interest-rate problems is therefore intrinsically more complex, and I will show that, in general, it involves specification of the time dependence of the covariance matrix.

With the definitions and observations above clearly in mind, let us extend the analysis presented above to the simplest possible setting required for option pricing. To do so, let us consider first an (equity or FX) spot process, with time-dependent volatility (no smiles) and deterministic rates. We shall assume that we are given a series of plain-vanilla European options prices, $Opt_1, Opt_2, \ldots, Opt_n$, on the same underlying for different strikes and maturities. In a Black-and-Scholes framework, the stochastic evolution of the underlying spot process in the real world is given by a stochastic differential equation of the form

$$\frac{\mathrm{d}S(t)}{S(t)} = \mu(S, t)\,\mathrm{d}t + \sigma(t)\,\mathrm{d}z(t) \tag{3.12}$$

where $S(t)$ denotes the stock price at time t, μ its real-world drift, σ the instantaneous percentage volatility of the spot process, and $\mathrm{d}z(t)$ is the increment of a standard Brownian motion. In moving from the real-world to the pricing (risk-neutral) measure, Equation (3.12) becomes

$$\frac{\mathrm{d}S(t)}{S(t)} = r(t)\,\mathrm{d}t + \sigma(t)\,\mathrm{d}z(t) \tag{3.13}$$

where all the symbols have the same meaning as in Equation (3.12), and $r(t)$ is the short (riskless) rate at time t. The solution to this stochastic differential equation is given by

$$S(T, \epsilon) = S(0) \exp[\widehat{r}T - \tfrac{1}{2}\widehat{\sigma}^2 T + \widehat{\sigma}\sqrt{T}\epsilon] \tag{3.14}$$

with

$$\widehat{\sigma}^2 T = \int_0^T \sigma(u)^2 \,\mathrm{d}u \tag{3.15}$$

$$\widehat{r}T = \int_0^T r(u)\,\mathrm{d}u \tag{3.16}$$

and $\epsilon \in \mathcal{N}(0, 1)$. The quantity $\widehat{\sigma}$, which is the root-mean-square of the instantaneous volatility, $\sigma(t)$, will be shown to play a central role in option pricing when the underlying process follows a diffusion.

Since we are for simplicity working with deterministic interest rates, we can write

$$\exp\left[-\int_0^T r(u)\,\mathrm{d}u\right] = \exp[-\widehat{r}T] = \exp[-r_{0,T}T] \equiv P(0, T) \tag{3.17}$$

Using the definitions introduced above, Equation (3.14) can therefore be re-written as

$$S(T, \epsilon) = FS(0, T)\exp[-\tfrac{1}{2}\widehat{\sigma}^2 T + \widehat{\sigma}\sqrt{T}\epsilon] \tag{3.18}$$

and, since at expiry $F(T, T) = S(T)$, we can write

$$FS(T, T, \epsilon) = FS(0, T)\exp[-\tfrac{1}{2}\widehat{\sigma}^2 T + \widehat{\sigma}\sqrt{T}\epsilon] \tag{3.19}$$

Comparing Equation (3.19) with Equation (3.14) we can recognize that it implies that the stochastic differential equation for the forward price displays no drift, i.e. that it can be written as

$$\frac{\mathrm{d}FS}{FS} = \sigma_{FS}(t)\,\mathrm{d}z(t) \tag{3.20}$$

where $\sigma_{FS}(t)$ is now the volatility of the forward price. This observation will become important in what follows when we discuss under what circumstances it is possible to move freely from variance to volatility and vice versa. In the meantime one should notice that, *given the assumption of deterministic discounting that we are enforcing so far,* the percentage volatility of the forward rate is the same as the volatility of the spot process. (This can be immediately seen by applying Ito's lemma to $FS = f(S) = S/P$, and treating P as a deterministic function of time.) Therefore, if we denote by $\sigma_{FS}(t)$ the volatility at time t of the forward price, in a deterministic-discounting setting we can put $\sigma_{FS}(t) = \sigma(t)$.

We can draw on these observations to say that the present value of the ith options in our basket can equivalently be written in either of the following equivalent ways:

$$PV(Opt_i) = E[S(T) - X_i]^+ P(t_0, T_i)$$

$$= E\left[\left(S(0)\exp[rT - \tfrac{1}{2}\widehat{\sigma}^2 T + \widehat{\sigma}\sqrt{T}\epsilon] - X_i\right)^+\right]P(t_0, T_i) \qquad (3.21)$$

or

$$PV(Opt_i) = E[(S_T - X_i)^+]P(t_0, T_i)$$

$$= E\left[(FS(T,T) - X_i)^+\right]P(t_0, T_i)$$

$$= E\left[\left(FS(0,T)\exp[-\tfrac{1}{2}\widehat{\sigma}^2_{FS}T + \widehat{\sigma}_{FS}\sqrt{T}\epsilon] - X_i\right)^+\right]P(t_0, T_i)$$

$$= FS(0,T)E\left[\left(\exp[-\tfrac{1}{2}\widehat{\sigma}T + \widehat{\sigma}\sqrt{T}\epsilon] - \tfrac{X_i}{FS(0,T)}\right)^+\right]P(t_0, T_i) \qquad (3.22)$$

where the symbol E denotes the expectation operator, the notation $[a-b]^+$ means max$[a-b, 0]$, the root-mean-squared quantity $\widehat{\sigma}_{FS}$ is defined analogously to the quantity $\widehat{\sigma}$ in Equation (3.15) and the definitions introduced at the beginning of this section have been made use of.

Looking at the expressions (3.21) and (3.4) above one can see that the present value of the option can be expressed as an expectation over the terminal values either of the forward or of the spot price. By the way it has been presented, a treatment in terms of the spot or in terms of the forward process appears to be perfectly equivalent. But is it also equivalent from a financial point of view? Is there a 'preferred set of co-ordinates'?

We have only been able to arrive at the volatility of the forward price, σ_{FS}, using no other information than our assumed knowledge of the volatility of the spot process for the stock, σ, because we made the assumption that the discount factor was deterministic (in which case, as pointed out, the volatility of the forward price is identical to the volatility of the spot price: $\sigma_{FS} = \sigma$). This way of looking at the pricing of options, although common and 'pedagogically' more straightforward, can however be somewhat lopsided, in that it assumes that we start from the knowledge of the volatility of the spot process for the stock and we *derive* from this the volatility of the forward price. In reality, if interest rates were not deterministic, the volatility of the forward price would include a component arising from the volatility of the discount bond that connects the spot and the forward price: $FS = S/P$. If we assume that the dynamics of the (strictly positive) bond price is also of a diffusive nature, its stochastic differential equation can be written in the form

$$\frac{dP}{P} = r\,dt + v(t, T)\,dw \tag{3.23}$$

(with $v(t, T)$ denoting the percentage volatility at time t of a T-maturity bond, and $E[dz_t\,dw_t] = \rho$). A straightforward application of the two-dimensional Ito's lemma applied to the function $FS(t, T) = f(S(t), P(t, T))$ gives for the volatility of the forward price, σ_{FS},

$$\sigma_{FS} = \sqrt{\sigma^2 + v^2 - 2\rho\sigma v} \tag{3.24}$$

where ρ is the correlation between the discount bond and the spot process.[4] From Equation (3.24) we can see that in the case of stochastic interest rates the volatility of the forward price no longer coincides with the volatility of the spot process. So, we should prefer the spot (Black-and-Scholes) formulation if we derive our information about the volatility from a price history of the spot underlying and of the bond (in which case the spot co-ordinates are most appropriate); we should prefer the forward (Black) formulation if we impute the volatility from the traded prices of plain-vanilla options (in which case we should work directly in the forward co-ordinates). Since, in this book, I am mainly looking at volatility and correlation from the perspective of a trader of complex derivatives (as opposed to a plain-vanilla option trader) I will in general favour the forward-price perspective.

Summarizing: from a quoted option price one can extract, by inverting the implied volatility, a single number, i.e. the combination of the spot price volatility, of the discount bond volatility and of the correlation between the two processes that gives Expression (3.24). In other words, the practice of 'implying' a volatility from an option price gives access to the volatility of the forward price (that enters the Black formula), but not of the spot price (that enters the Black-*and-Scholes* formula).

Exercise 1 *Estimate the volatility of the bond price and gauge the relative importance of the discount bond volatility to the volatility of a 3-month, 1-year, and 10-year forward price.*

Because of this, Black's formula has a much wider applicability than the deterministic-discounting case, and still applies even if the discount bond is stochastic. (See, in this respect, Merton's fundamental paper (1973) for a 'traditional' PDE treatment, or, for instance, Baxter and Rennie (1996) for a 'modern' numeraire approach.)

Traders in the market are obviously aware of the stochastic nature of discounting and embed this knowledge in their quotes of the vanilla option prices (from which the implied volatility is obtained). If, however, a naïve trader erroneously believed that these quotes had been made assuming deterministic discounting, she would be implying from each option price a volatility that she would identify with the volatility of the spot process. If, therefore, this trader delta-hedged herself using a spot position in the underlying, she would be buying or selling the wrong delta amount of the *spot* underlying, since she would

---

[4] Note that if ρ denotes the correlation between the underlying and the bond price, the correlation between the underlying and forward rates will be $-\rho$.

be 'misinterpreting' the component of the volatility arising from the discount factor. If the same trader, on the other hand, recognized that the option quote is made in the market taking the stochastic nature of discounting into account, she would correctly interpret the implied volatility as the volatility of the forward price. She would therefore put in place a delta hedge in a forward contract with the same strike and expiry date. This strategy would automatically take the stochastic nature of the discounting bond into account, and would therefore provide not only a more practical, but also a theoretically more satisfactory hedging strategy. Alternatively, if she wanted to, she could still carry out *spot* hedging transactions, but she would have to do so both in the underlying and in the discount bond maturing at the option expiry. In either case the correct hedge ratios would have to be determined using the difficult-to-estimate correlation between the underlying and the discount bond. See Equation (3.24). Needless to say, for short maturities the two volatilities virtually coincide, but the difference becomes far from trivial for long-dated equity and FX options.

For this reason, if one follows an 'implied' rather than a statistical approach to estimating volatility, it is intellectually more satisfactory and more effective in practice to regard all plain-vanilla options as calls or puts on a *forward* price. A quoted market price gives direct information on the root-mean-squared volatility of the associated forward price, not on the root-mean-squared volatility of the spot process.

3.5   The Link Between Root-Mean-Squared Volatilities and the Time-Dependence of Volatility

We go back to the case of purely deterministic discounting to explore the link between the quoted prices of plain-vanilla options and the time dependence of the instantaneous volatility of the underlying. We know that, for equities, all the forwards are a function of the same underlying. Therefore, if discounting is deterministic, a series of option prices can give direct information about the future volatility of the (same!) spot process. This can be seen more precisely as follows. From Equation (3.20) and from the definition of root-mean-squared volatility we can see that each option in our portfolio can be written as some function, f, of the time integral of the square of the (a priori unknown) time-dependent volatility of the spot price:

$$Opt_1 = f\left(\int_0^{t_1} \sigma^2 \, du\right) = f\left(\widehat{\sigma}_{0\to 1}^2\right) \tag{3.25}$$

$$Opt_2 = f\left(\int_0^{t_2} \sigma^2 \, du\right) = f\left(\widehat{\sigma}_{0\to 2}^2\right) \tag{3.26}$$

$$\cdots$$

$$Opt_2 = f\left(\int_0^{t_n} \sigma^2 \, du\right) = f\left(\widehat{\sigma}_{0\to n}^2\right) \tag{3.27}$$

(The quantity $\widehat{\sigma}_{0\to k}$ is proportional to the root-mean-squared volatility from time 0 to time t_k.) Since we know that the solution to the Black pricing formula is a function of the root-mean-squared volatility of the forward rate, we can impute (imply) from the market price of the option the implied Black volatility of the forward rate. By so doing we can therefore construct

$$\hat{\sigma}_{1\to2}^2 = \hat{\sigma}_{0\to2}^2 - \hat{\sigma}_{0\to1}^2$$
$$= \int_{t_1}^{t_2} \sigma^2 \, du = \int_0^{t_2} \sigma^2 \, du - \int_0^{t_1} \sigma^2 \, du \tag{3.28}$$

In the limit as time t_2 becomes closer and closer to time t_1 ($t_2 = t_1 + \epsilon$) we can write

$$\sigma^2(t_1) = \lim_{\epsilon \to 0} \frac{\int_0^{t_1+\epsilon} \sigma^2 \, du - \int_0^{t_1} \sigma^2 \, du}{\epsilon} \tag{3.29}$$

But, if we have access to a *continuum* of option prices,[5] the RHS can be written as a function of market-related quantities:

$$\sigma^2(t_1) = \lim_{\epsilon \to 0} \frac{\hat{\sigma}_{0\to1+\epsilon}^2 - \hat{\sigma}_{0\to1}^2}{\epsilon} \tag{3.30}$$

Under our working assumptions (a Black world without smiles and deterministic discounting) this equation links the not-directly-observable future instantaneous volatility of the spot process from time t_1 to time $t_2 = t_1 + \epsilon$ with the market-observable option prices for the corresponding expiries. The relationship in Equation (3.30) expresses an important relationship between a set of *current* quantities (the root-mean-squared volatilities for different expiries) and the *future* instantaneous volatility. This relationship is often referred to as the 'balance-of-variance condition'.

3.6 Admissibility of a Series of Root-Mean-Squared Volatilities

3.6.1 The Equity/FX Case

From the results above we can immediately deduce that, if we live in a deterministic-discounting Black world and the quantity $\hat{\sigma}_{0\to T}^2 \, T$ is not a strictly increasing function of the equity or FX option expiry, T, there is an arbitrage. (To simplify notation, in what follows I will write $\hat{\sigma}_{0\to T} = \hat{\sigma}_T$.) Finding the arbitrage is very easy, and only requires recalling that the Black option price is a monotonically increasing function of the root-mean-squared volatility: if the quantity $\hat{\sigma}_{T_2}^2 \, T_2$ is smaller than $\hat{\sigma}_{T_1}^2 \, T_1$, it would mean that the uncertainty about the underlying out to time T_2 is *less* than the uncertainty out to time T_1 ($T_1 < T_2$). It is not difficult to set up a model-independent arbitrage to exploit this state of affairs. Therefore, in a Black world, a series of option prices whose associated

---

[5]This assumption might appear unrealistic, but, in reality, an interpolation procedure between actually quoted prices can often be employed (see Chapter 9), and a continuum of 'synthetic' market prices can therefore be assumed to be available without making too drastic an assumption.

root-mean-squared volatilities do not satisfy the relationship

$$\frac{\partial[\widehat{\sigma}_T^2 T]}{\partial T} > 0 \tag{3.31}$$

lend themselves to model-independent arbitrage. Such a collection of option prices, and the associated implied volatilities, therefore constitutes a first example of non-admissible prices (volatilities). The concept of admissibility will be revisited at length in Chapter 17.

In closing this section, I should point out that the reasoning just presented does not apply to the case of interest rates: caplet-implied volatilities, for instance, need not be such that $\sigma_{T_2}^2 T_2 > \sigma_{T_1}^2 T_1$. I discuss this point immediately below.

3.6.2   The Interest-Rate Case

Let us now compare the situation just described with the case of interest rates. We shall do so by looking in some detail at options on a closely-related set of futures contracts. Because of margin calls, futures contracts pay out in a different way than forward-rate agreements (FRAs). These differences give rise to an adjustment to the equilibrium forward rate. For the purpose of the following discussion, however, the distinction between a futures rate and an equilibrium forward rate is immaterial, and I shall 'pretend' that futures contracts are simply standardized FRAs.

Let us begin by considering the following series of futures contracts:

MAR2008

JUN2008

SEP2008

(At the time of writing, the dates above are well into the future. If this book is still in print – and read – close to the expiry dates of these contracts, the reader should mentally substitute some expiry dates a few years in the future.) If we observe the behaviour of the forward rates implied by these futures prices over time, we expect them to move roughly 'in step', i.e. to display a high degree of correlation and a similar volatility. Let us suppose, however, that we observe today that the market volatility of, say, the JUN2008 caplet trades significantly below the volatility of the MAR2008 and SEP2008 caplets. In particular, if T_1, T_2 and T_3 denote expiry times MAR2008, JUN2008 and SEP2008, respectively, the market-implied volatilities are such that

$$\sigma_{T_2}^2 T_2 \ll \sigma_{T_1}^2 T_1 \tag{3.32}$$

$$\sigma_{T_2}^2 T_2 \ll \sigma_{T_3}^2 T_3 \tag{3.33}$$

A trader therefore would be very tempted to sell options on the MAR2008 and SEP2008 contracts (trading at a 'high' implied volatility) and buy options on the JUN2008 contract (trading at a relatively low implied volatility). However, much as the trade might seem common-sensically attractive, the market-observed relationships (3.32) and (3.33) do not imply any violation of arbitrage. Since the different futures contracts refer to different assets, there is no logically compelling reason why the JUN2008 contract should not 'vibrate' throughout its life by much less than its MAR2008 and SEP2008 cousins. Therefore it might well be reasonable to expect that we shall make money from the sell–buy–sell strategy, and the more so the greater the discrepancy between the JUN volatility on the one hand and the MAR and SEP volatilities on the other. However, in the case of interest rates the violation of the condition

$$\hat{\sigma}_{T_1}^2 T_1 < \hat{\sigma}_{T_2}^2 T_2, \quad T_1 < T_2 \tag{3.34}$$

no longer gives rise to an arbitrage, even in a purely Black world. The implications for the joint evolution of interest rates reflected by these market prices might be deemed to be extremely unlikely, but it cannot be ruled out as an impossibility in an arbitrage-free world in the same way as the situation discussed in the previous section could. This conclusion should be contrasted with the arbitrage strategy presented above in the case of equities or FX, where, even in the most far-fetched scenarios, we would make money if the total variance from today to option expiry were not a strictly increasing function of expiry. We shall explore later (see Chapter 19) what the violation of condition (3.34) implies about the evolution of the term structure of volatilities.

From this discussion one can reinforce the conclusion already drawn above: N forward contracts truly represent positions in $2N$ different underlying spot assets. Therefore one must specify the volatility of each of these assets. In addition, each of these assets can have a time-dependent volatility. The problem is no longer how to specify a one-variable function (the volatility of the underlying spot process as a function of calendar time), but how to specify a surface (the volatilities of different forward rates – which cannot be obtained from each other – at different points in time). In addition one also has to specify the (possibly time-dependent) correlation amongst the forward rates. In moving from the equity/FX to the interest-rate world the problem therefore explodes in complexity: the user effectively has to supply a full time-dependent covariance matrix. We shall see in Chapter 5 that for a discrete-look option problem, where the payoff is determined by N realizations of different forward rates (i.e. of different assets), $O(N^3)$ covariances must be supplied: $O(N^2)$ covariances for each of the N price-sensitive times. This is, ultimately, the reason why low-dimensionality (where 'low' sometimes means 'one' or 'two') term-structure models have often been employed in trading practice.

3.7 Summary of the Definitions So Far

For future reference, it is useful to collect the definitions introduced so far, with some further comments where appropriate.

1. When, at time t, we speak about a price process (typically, for equities or FX) described by a diffusive equation of the form

$$\frac{dS(t)}{S(t)} = \mu(S, t)\, dt + \sigma(S, t)\, dz(t) \tag{3.35}$$

the volatility that appears in the equation above is called the present (if $t = t_0$) or future (if $t > t_0$) volatility of the spot process. Therefore:

Definition 4 *The future or present volatility of a spot price* $= \sigma(S, t)$.

In the equities and FX cases, when the future or present volatility of the spot price depends on the future value of the underlying, it is often referred to in the literature as the 'local volatility'. We shall make frequent use of this term when dealing with smiles. The term 'instantaneous volatility' can also be used, but, in this book, it will mainly be used in the context of interest rates. See the definition in point 5 below.

2. When, at time t, we consider a forward-price process (typically, for equities or FX) described by a diffusive equation of the form

$$\frac{\mathrm{d}FS(t, T)}{FS(t, T)} = \mu(FS, t, T)\, \mathrm{d}t + \sigma(FS, t, T)\, \mathrm{d}z(t) \tag{3.36}$$

the volatility that appears in the equation above is called the present (if $t = t_0$) or future (if $t > t_0$) volatility of the forward-price process. Note that we are not using the (meaningless and confusing, but none the less common) expression 'forward volatility': a volatility is not a traded asset, and therefore can be either present or future, but not forward; nor shall we ever use the term 'forward-forward volatility', which probably is used to mean, if anything, the future volatility of a forward quantity. Note also that an additional argument, T, enters the definition of the volatility of a forward price in order to emphasize that forwards of different maturities will not, in general, have the same volatility at time t. Therefore:

Definition 5 *The future or present volatility of a forward price = $\sigma(FS, t, T)$.*

3. Just as in the case of spot processes, another term that is sometimes used in the context of forward price processes is 'instantaneous volatility': it is simply another way to denote the time-dependent volatilities in Equation (3.36). See point 5 below for its more common usage.

4. If the volatility is at most time-dependent, then the time integral of the square of the volatility of a forward or spot price between time T_1 and time T_2 is often called the total variance, var(T_1, T_2), of that forward or spot price:

$$\mathrm{var}(T_1, T_2) = \int_{T_1}^{T_2} \sigma(u)^2 \, \mathrm{d}u \tag{3.37}$$

The term 'total variance' is common, but only appropriate if the drift of the spot or forward price process is at most dependent on time. For most choices of numeraires, this is indeed the case for price processes, but it is not automatically true for interest rates. See Chapters 4 and 19.

5. The square root of the total variance from time 0 to time T of a forward price or rate of expiration T divided by T is the *root-mean-squared volatility, $\widehat{\sigma}(T)$*, of the forward price or rate itself:

$$\widehat{\sigma}(T) = \sqrt{\frac{1}{T} \int_{0}^{T} \sigma(u)^2 \, \mathrm{d}u} \tag{3.38}$$

This quantity is also called the implied volatility or the Black volatility. Note, however, that the term 'implied volatility' can be used in a wider context (i.e. even when the volatility is not deterministic, or the underlying process is not a diffusion), and simply indicates the number that must be input in the Black formula to obtain the correct price. Implied volatilities are discussed at length in Part II, which deals with smiles.

Finally, note carefully that the term 'average volatility' is often used in the literature or in traders' jargon. It is somewhat misleading, since the quantity defined above does not in general coincide with the value $\frac{1}{T}\int_0^T \sigma(u)\,du$, as one would expect from the name. Despite being imprecise, this usage is very common. This leads us to:

Definition 6 *The root-mean-squared volatility to maturity $T = \widehat{\sigma}(T)$.*

6. Whenever, in what follows, we deal with a forward rate, described by a stochastic differential equation of the form

$$\frac{dFR(t, T, T+\tau)}{FR(t, T, T+\tau)} = \mu(FR, t)\,dt + \sigma(FR, t)\,dz_t \qquad (3.39)$$

the volatility experienced at time t by this forward rate of expiry T is always referred to as the present (if $t = 0$) or future (if $t > 0$) *instantaneous volatility* of the forward rate. In the market the term serial volatility is sometimes encountered, because of the importance of the instantaneous volatility in the pricing of serial options. I shall not use this terminology. Therefore:

Definition 7 *The time-t instantaneous volatility of a forward rate, FR $\sigma(FR, t)$.*

7. The function that associates to a forward rate of a given maturity its own Black market-implied volatility is called the *term structure of volatilities*. Notice that the term sometimes has a different meaning in the equity and FX world, where it is used to indicate the time dependence of the volatility of the spot or forward price process. This usage is widespread, but, to avoid confusion, I will never use the term 'term structure of volatilities' in this second meaning. For equities (and spot processes in general) I will talk instead about 'time dependence of volatility' or 'implied volatility as a function of expiry', as appropriate.

Having clarified these concepts, the next two sections will present in detail a couple of case studies that illustrate some of the more subtle points in the definitions just presented.

3.8 Hedging an Option with a Forward-Setting Strike

Let us place ourselves again in a perfect Black world, and let us consider an option with a forward-setting strike (often referred to as a 'forward option'). To be more specific, the contract specification is such that the reset of the stock price at time T_1 will determine the strike for the remaining life of the option from T_1 to T_2. At time T_2 the value of the stock price will then be compared with the strike determined at time T_1, and the payoff of the option at time T_2 will be given by

$$PAYOFF(T_2) = \max \left[\frac{S(T_2) - S(T_1)}{S(T_1)}, 0 \right] \tag{3.40}$$

3.8.1   Why Is This Option Important? (And Why Is it Difficult to Hedge?)

Forward-starting options of the type (3.40) are important because they guarantee the holder the percentage increase in an index, S, if positive. Therefore they have had great appeal with retail investors, who would like to receive a principal-protected equity return. When, in the mid-1990s, interest rates were relatively high and equity volatility relatively low it was easy to offer the product in a very plain-vanilla form: the investor would invest \$100 for, say, five years. $P(0, 5) \times 100$ would be invested in a zero-coupon bond expiring in five years' time, thereby guaranteeing the principal at maturity. The rest, $100 \times [1 - P(0, 5)]$, would be used to buy five forward-setting calls on the yearly percentage increase of an equity index over years 1, 2,....,5. Low volatilities made the 'forward-starting' options 'cheap', and, because of the relatively high rates, the discount to par of the bond would provide enough upfront cash to buy all the 'cheap' options. With the fall in interest rates and the increase in equity volatility in the years between 1998 and 2002, this simple strategy has become more complex, because the discount to par of the five-year bond does not provide enough upfront cash to purchase the now-expensive set of forward-setting options. As a response, variations such as limited-equity-upside structures have been introduced. Therefore, the first plain-vanilla products produced for the selling banks an exposure to the future realization of the at-the-money volatility, while the later call–spread-like structures gave an exposure to the relative volatility level of an at-the-money and an out-of-the-money option (i.e. a forward risk reversal). Since in Part I we do not deal with smiles, in this chapter I will only consider the plain-vanilla structure.

It is easy to see why the option is difficult to hedge. In the simple case of constant volatility, σ, the present value of the forward-setting option, can be written as

$$PV(T_0) = E\left[\left(\frac{S(T_2) - S(T_1)}{S(T_1)} \right)^+ \right] P(0, T_2) = E\left[\left(\frac{S(T_2)}{S(T_1)} - 1 \right)^+ \right] P(0, T_2)$$

$$= E\left[\left(\frac{S_0 \exp[rT_2 - \frac{1}{2}\sigma^2 T_2 + \sigma\sqrt{T_2}\epsilon_2]}{S_0 \exp[rT_1 - \frac{1}{2}\sigma^2 T_1 + \sigma\sqrt{T_1}\epsilon_1]} - 1 \right)^+ \right] P(0, T_2)$$

$$= E\left[\left(\frac{\exp[rT_2 - \frac{1}{2}\sigma^2 T_2 + \sigma\sqrt{T_2}\epsilon_2]}{\exp[rT_1 - \frac{1}{2}\sigma^2 T_1 + \sigma\sqrt{T_1}\epsilon_1]} - 1 \right)^+ \right] P(0, T_2) \tag{3.41}$$

(The expression $(a)^+$ means $\max(a, 0)$.) Note how the dependence on S_0 has disappeared: as the spot moves, the future strike moves as well, and therefore the option will always be at-the-money spot when it comes to life. Therefore the option has zero delta, and zero gamma. However, it does have a vega exposure (see the discussion below). As a consequence, in order to hedge it, we must find a combination of plain-vanilla options with zero delta, zero gamma and positive vega. To do so exactly is clearly impossible, but a (locally) approximating portfolio *can* be built. Note also that ϵ_1 and ϵ_2 are not *independent* standard Gaussian draws. I discuss this point in Chapter 5.

3.8.2 Valuing a Forward-Setting Option

How can we value such an option? A rather wasteful and 'brute-force' approach (useful, however, to appreciate the mechanics of the product) is to do a Monte Carlo simulation of the spot process, $S(t)$. One can first evolve the price from time T_0 to time T_1 in one single move (see Chapter 5 for a discussion and justification of the procedure) using the formula:

$$S(T_1, z_1) = S(0) \exp[rT_1 - \tfrac{1}{2}\widehat{\sigma}^2_{0 \to T_1} T_1 + \widehat{\sigma}_{0 \to T_1} \sqrt{T_1} z_1] \tag{3.42}$$

where $\widehat{\sigma}_{0 \to T_1}$ is the root-mean-squared volatility of S from time T_0 to time T_1. This is obtainable from the price of the option expiring at time T_1. Given this realization one can then evolve the stock price from time T_1 to time T_2. In order to do this the simulation will need the root-mean-squared volatility of the spot price from time T_1 to time T_2, $\widehat{\sigma}^2_{T_1 \to T_2}$:

$$\widehat{\sigma}^2_{T_1 \to T_2} = \frac{1}{T_2 - T_1} \int_{T_1}^{T_2} \sigma(u)^2 \, \mathrm{d}u \tag{3.43}$$

Since we have assumed a perfect Black world and deterministic discounting, we can obtain this future volatility from the quoted prices of plain-vanilla options expiring at the two times, as shown in Section 3.5. Armed with the knowledge of this quantity, and making use of the same formula employed above, one can then obtain for the realization of the stock price at time T_2:

$$S(T_2, z_1, z_2) = S(T_1) \exp[r\tau - \tfrac{1}{2}\widehat{\sigma}^2_{T_1 \to T_2} \tau + \widehat{\sigma}_{T_1 \to T_2} \sqrt{\tau} z_2] \tag{3.44}$$

with $\tau = T_2 - T_1$. Note that the Brownian shocks z_2 and z_1 used in the simulations have been obtained from independent draws, since the increments of a Brownian motion should display no serial correlation.

Having reached time T_2, and having kept track of the realization of the stock price at time T_1, one can easily construct the option payoff, discount and average as usual. By the way it has been presented, one can easily see that the simulation effectively carries out a two-dimensional integration.

While correct, the approach can be made much simpler (and more elegant) as follows. Looking at the payoff formula one can rewrite it as

$$PAYOFF(T_2) = \max\left[\frac{S(T_2) - S(T_1)}{S(T_1)}, 0\right] = \max\left[\frac{S(T_2)}{S(T_1)} - 1, 0\right]$$

$$= \max\left[\frac{FS(T_2, T_2)}{FS(T_1, T_1)} - 1, 0\right] = \max\left[\frac{FS(T_2, T_2)}{FS(T_2, T_1)} - 1, 0\right] \tag{3.45}$$

In obtaining the last two lines use has been made of the fact that $FS(T, T) = S(T)$, and, more subtly, we have extended the definition of the time-t, expiry-T_1 forward price

$F(t, T_1)$ beyond its expiry (i.e. for $t > T_1$) by changing its volatility after T_1 to zero. Formally, we have implicitly defined another quantity, FS', which coincides with FS up until its reset, i.e. until time T_1, and then remains forever constant at this level thereafter. Therefore

$$\frac{dFS'}{FS'} = \sigma'_{FS}(t)\,dz(t), \qquad T_0 \le t \le T_2 \tag{3.46}$$

with

$$\sigma'_{FS_T}(t) = \sigma_{FS_T}(t), \qquad T_0 \le t \le T_1 \tag{3.47}$$

$$\sigma'_{FS_T}(t) = 0, \qquad T_1 < t \le T_2 \tag{3.48}$$

where $\sigma_{FS_T}(t)$ is the time-t volatility of the T-expiry forward. By introducing this 'shadow' variable we can still speak of a forward price after its reset by imposing that it does not change its value after its expiry. We shall drop the prime in what follows to lighten notation.

Expression (3.45) makes it obvious that the payoff is just a call on the ratio $R(T_2) \equiv \frac{FS(T_2, T_2)}{FS(T_2, T_1)}$. Since in a Black world both numerator and denominator are log-normally distributed, so will be their ratio. One therefore simply has to find the volatility of the (log-normal) quantity R and the Black formula will provide the solution. More precisely, what has to be evaluated is the quantity

$$\hat{\sigma}_R^2 T_2 = \int_{T_0}^{T_2} \sigma_R(u)^2\,du \tag{3.49}$$

where $\sigma_R(u)$ is the instantaneous volatility of the ratio, and $\hat{\sigma}_R$ its root-mean-square. Since, by placing ourselves in a perfect Black world, we have implicitly assumed that both forward prices are log-normally distributed, the instantaneous volatility of the ratio is simply given by

$$\sigma_R(u)^2 = \sigma_{FS_{T_1}}^2(u) + \sigma_{FS_{T_2}}^2(u) - 2\rho\sigma_{FS_{T_1}}\sigma_{FS_{T_2}}(u) \tag{3.50}$$

But, for any time u up to time T_1, $\sigma_{FS_{T_1}} = \sigma_{FS_{T_2}}$, and therefore $\sigma_R(u) = 0$ for $0 \le u \le T_1$. For time u between the setting of the strike and option expiry, i.e. for $T_1 < u \le T_2$, we have that $\sigma_{FS_{T_1}} = 0$, by Equation (3.48) above (and, of course, since the first forward price has stopped 'vibrating', $\rho = 0$). Putting the two segments together we therefore have

$$\sigma_R(u) = 0, \qquad T_0 \le u \le T_1 \tag{3.51}$$

$$\sigma_R(u) = \sigma_{FS_{T_2}}(u), \qquad T_1 \le u \le T_2 \tag{3.52}$$

Before time T_1 the ratio does not change in value, and only begins to display a stochastic behaviour after time T_1. As a consequence, the integral in Equation (3.49) simply becomes

$$\hat{\sigma}_R^2 T_2 = \int_{T_0}^{T_2} \sigma_R(u)^2\,du = \int_{T_1}^{T_2} \sigma_R(u)^2\,du = \int_{T_1}^{T_2} \sigma_{FS_{T_2}}^2(u)\,du \tag{3.53}$$

We can see from this expression that the value of the forward-setting option only depends on the volatility of the forward price from time T_1 to time T_2. This is the reason why the two-dimensional Monte Carlo integration was particularly wasteful (and counter-productive). To begin with, it required carrying out a numerical integration of higher dimension than truly needed. More fundamentally, by carrying out the evolution of the underlying from time T_0 to time T_1 using the volatility $\widehat{\sigma}_{0 \to T_1}$, we were blind to the fact that the value of the option actually does not depend on the volatility of the underlying between time T_0 and time T_1.

From this discussion it is clear that the buyer of the option really only has to hedge the portion of the volatility of the forward stock price from time T_1 to time T_2. If the trader only has at his disposal plain-vanilla options it is tempting to hedge the forward vega exposure arising from the position in the forward-starting option by selling volatility out to T_2 (i.e. by selling a plain-vanilla option expiring at time T_2) and buying volatility out to T_1 (i.e. by buying a plain-vanilla option expiring at time T_1). There is a problem, though, with this strategy. We might have been successful in matching the vega of the forward-starting option; the long-and-short plain-vanilla option strategy, however, gives rise to a delta and gamma exposure, which the forward starting option does not have. As we have seen above, in fact, before the strike resets, the value of an option with a forward-setting strike does not change at all with spot, because the (relative) strike moves up and down with the underlying. Therefore, before reset one is always dealing with a future at-the-money option with the same residual maturity. One would need a hedging strategy that gave rise to a vega exposure, but no delta and negligible (or, if possible, zero) gamma. How can we get around this?

An approximate solution to be problem could be to sell and buy wide strangles with maturities T_1 and T_2, and with strikes positioned sufficiently widely around the time-T_1-at-the-money forward level. We could, that is, sell an out-of-the-money put and an out-of-the-money call (a strangle) expiring at time T_2 and buy a similar strangle expiring at time T_1. Since the present value profile of a strangle as a function of spot around

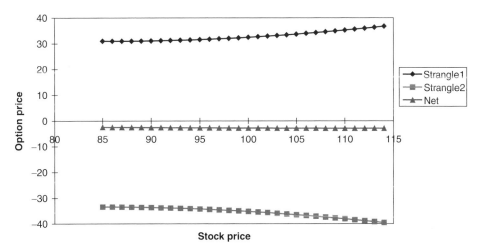

Figure 3.1 The profiles of the two strangles, and of their sum, after 2 years (option details as in the text).

the at-the-money level is very flat, its delta and gamma are indeed close to zero, but the structure still retains an appreciable vega exposure. Furthermore, the residual vega exposure is indeed over the desired time interval (from T_1 to T_2). It is therefore reasonable to hope that the strategy might fulfil the trader's hedging needs.

Let us see how this works in practice with a concrete example. Let us assume a spot price of $100, zero interest rates, strikes for both strangles at $90 and $110, a flat volatility of 20.00%, a reset time for the strike of 9 years and a final maturity of 10 years. Figures 3.1–3.3 show what the strategy, put in place at time t_0, looks like after 2, 8 and 8.9999 years.

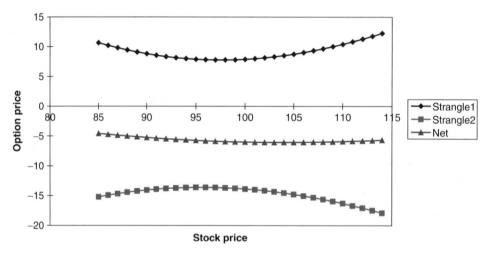

Figure 3.2 The profiles of the two strangles, and of their sum, after 8 years (option details as in the text).

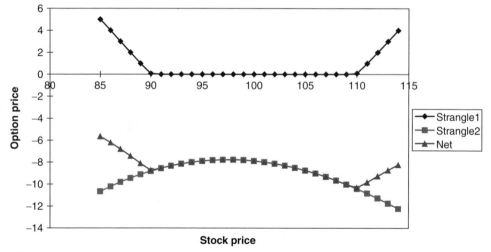

Figure 3.3 The profiles of the two strangles, and of their sum, after 8.999 years (option details as in the text).

As one can see from these figures, during the initial part of the life of the option the net profile is really very flat, even if the spot moves significantly away from the initial value of 100. As time goes on, however, the (approximately) zero-delta and zero-gamma conditions become violated for smaller and smaller deviations of the spot price from the middle point. As the expiry of the forward-setting option approaches, the likelihood of the spot price remaining in the 'flat' region becomes smaller and smaller. In practice, therefore, re-hedges will be necessary over the life of the option, but the trader does not know a priori at which levels of the underlying these re-hedging transactions will take place. In other words, the trader is directly exposed to future realizations of the smile surface. These issues are treated in detail in Chapter 17.

If, in reality, the volatility was not just time-dependent but also state-dependent, thus giving rise to a smile surface, the trader's re-hedging costs will be even more unknown at the beginning. This brings us straight into the problem of smiles, which will be the topic of Part II. The problem of the pricing of an option with a forward-setting strike will be re-examined there in this more complex setting.

3.9 Quadratic Variation: First Approach

In closing this chapter it is useful to present a first introduction to the concept of quadratic variation. This quantity plays a particularly important role in option pricing. When the underlying process is a diffusion, and its volatility at most a deterministic function of time, it provides no more information than the concept of root-mean-squared volatility. However, for more general processes (e.g. jump processes, variance–gamma processes, stochastic-volatility diffusions) it allows a very useful characterization of some of the most important features of a stochastic process in so far as option pricing is concerned. Indeed, I shall show (Chapter 10) that exact knowledge of the quadratic variation of the price process along each path can allow the establishment of very tight bounds on option pricing even in the presence of transaction costs or if we do not know the true nature of the underlying process. Furthermore, if the true process is indeed a Brownian diffusion, knowledge of this quantity is all that is needed to recover the Black price.

In Chapter 10 a classification of models on the basis of the nature (deterministic or stochastic) of the associated quadratic variation on a finite interval will be given. I will argue that, when smiles are present, this classification can provide a useful way to understand how different types of model produce deviations of the implied volatility from the Black flat-across-strikes solution. In the meantime, I present in the rest of this chapter the definition of quadratic variation in the deterministic-volatility setting, and show its equivalence to the root-mean-squared volatility.

3.9.1 Definition

Consider a real-valued function $f(t)$ on an interval $[0\ T]$, and a finite positive number p. For concreteness, we can think of the variable t as time. Divide the interval $[0\ T]$ into n subintervals by means of $n + 1$ points, $\{t_i, i = 0, 1, \ldots, n\}$, the first and last of which coincide with the beginning and end of the interval:

$$0 = t_0 < t_1 < \cdots < t_n = T \tag{3.54}$$

The set of points $\{t_i, i = 0, 1, \ldots, n\}$ is said to be a *partition*, κ_n, of the interval $[0\ T]$. Consider the differences between the values of the function f evaluated at any two consecutive points in the partition: $f(t_i) - f(t_{i-1})$. Construct the sum of the absolute values of these differences raised to the power p, and call this sum $s_p\{f, \kappa\}$:

$$s_p(f, \kappa_n) = \sum_{i=1,n} |f(t_i) - f(t_{i-1})|^p \tag{3.55}$$

Note that the sum we have defined depends on the function, f, on the exponent, p, *and on the particular partition that we have chosen*, κ_n. Consider the case when the function f describes a stochastic process. When this is the case the quantity $s_p(f, \kappa_n)$ evaluated along a particular path partitioned according to the partition κ_n does not have a definite value for any path or partition, but is in general a random variable.

Let us now make this partition finer and finer (subject to the requirements above).[6] Call the value of the sum $s_p(f, \kappa_n)$, corresponding to the limit as the partition becomes finer and finer, the *p*-variation of f, $v_p(f)$:

$$v_p(f) = \lim_{n \to \infty} \{s_p(f, \kappa_n)\} = \lim_{n \to \infty} \sum_{i=1,n} |f(t_i) - f(t_{i-1})|^p \tag{3.56}$$

This new quantity no longer depends on the partition κ, and, in general, it could be zero, finite or infinite. If the limit exists, for $p = 1$ we have the first variation of f; for $p = 2$ we have the second, or quadratic, variation of f; etc.

3.9.2   Properties of Variations

By the way all variations have been defined, they are clearly suited to capturing the degree of stochastic variability of a function. It is for this reason that we are interested in the *absolute* values of the changes, possibly raised to some power. A priori, it is not obvious whether for a given process the limit should be zero, finite or infinite: as the partition becomes finer, we are adding more and more terms, but, if the process is continuous, these will be closer and closer together, and give smaller and smaller contributions. Alternatively, the process could be discontinuous, but the probability of small jumps could increase as their size decreases (as occurs in the variance–gamma process, see Chapter 15). In general, the value of the limit will therefore depend in a subtle way on the interplay between the increase in the number of terms in the sum and the decrease in their magnitude.

Finally, note that variations convey useful summary information about stochastic processes, but are not very descriptive for well-behaved deterministic functions, no matter how rapidly varying these might be. This can be seen as follows. Consider the case of the second variation of a well-behaved, continuous, twice-differentiable function. Write

$$f(t_i) \simeq f(t_{i-1}) + \frac{df}{dt}\Delta t_i + \frac{1}{2}\frac{d^2 f}{dt^2}\Delta t_i^2 + \cdots \tag{3.57}$$

---

[6]As usual, we cannot make the partition finer and finer in a 'silly' way, e.g. by keeping some subinterval of fixed length, and subdividing the others more and more. The partition must become uniformly finer.

The term $|f(t_i) - f(t_{i-1})|^2$ becomes

$$|f(t_i) - f(t_{i-1})|^2 = \left| \frac{\mathrm{d}f}{\mathrm{d}t} \Delta t_i + \frac{1}{2} \frac{\mathrm{d}^2 f}{\mathrm{d}t^2} \Delta t_i^2 + \cdots \right|^2 \tag{3.58}$$

As Δt goes to zero the sum is made up of terms in Δt^2 and therefore the second variation always goes to zero, irrespective of how variable the differentiable function is.

3.9.3 First and Second Variation of a Brownian Process

When the underlying function is a stochastic process, we know that, given any path and any finite partition of this path, the *sample* quadratic variation is a path-and-partition-dependent random variable. We would like to see if, and under what conditions, the quantity $v_2(f) = \lim_{n \to \infty} \{s_2(f, \kappa_n)\}$ no longer depends on the path, and always assumes exactly the same value.

Let us consider the case when the function f is a Brownian process, i.e. a diffusion with deterministic volatility. If this is the case, there are four important results:

- over any finite interval the first variation is infinite;

- over any finite interval the quadratic variation is finite;

- the quadratic variation is exactly proportional to the length of the interval for any finite interval (no matter how small);

- given a fixed time interval $[0 \ T]$, the quadratic variation (which we know to be finite) is exactly the same along every path.

The last property is simply a restatement of the fact that, when we are dealing with diffusions, 'lucky paths' do not matter. I will discuss this feature in Chapter 4, and in Sections 4.3 and 4.4 in particular. Proving the first two properties rigorously would entail a long detour. One can give, however, a 'physicist's proof' as follows.

3.9.4 Links between Quadratic Variation and $\int_t^T \sigma(u)^2 \, \mathrm{d}u$

Suppose that the logarithm, y, of a quantity, f, follows a diffusion with deterministic volatility. The process for y therefore has the form

$$\mathrm{d}y = \mu_y \, \mathrm{d}t + \sigma_y \, \mathrm{d}z \tag{3.59}$$

The quadratic variation of $y = \ln f$ is given by

$$v_2(y) = \lim_{n \to \infty} \sum_{i=1,n} |y(t_i) - y(t_{i-1})|^2 = \lim_{n \to \infty} \sum_{i=1,n} |\Delta y_i|^2$$

$$= \lim_{n \to \infty} \sum_{i=1,n} \sigma_i^2 \Delta t = \int_0^T \sigma(u)^2 \, \mathrm{d}u = \hat{\sigma}^2 T \tag{3.60}$$

The middle terms of the 'derivation' contain enough 'short-cuts' to make strong mathematicians weep,[7] but use has been made of the fact that, from Ito's calculus rules, $dz\, dz = dt$, terms in dt^2 and $dz\, dt$ go to zero with the time interval and that increments of the function df/f and of the logarithm $\ln f$ have the same volatility. So, if the underlying process is a diffusion with deterministic volatility, the quadratic variation is directly linked to its root-mean-squared volatility.[8] We shall see in the next chapter that this is *the* central quantity for option pricing in a Black world. When dealing with deterministic-volatility diffusions I will therefore use the terms 'quadratic variation' and 'root-mean-squared volatility' almost interchangeably (although, of course, they are not even dimensionally identical).

3.9.5   Why Quadratic Variation Is So Important (Take 1)

There are several reasons why the concept of quadratic variation is so important. The first is that I will show in the following chapters that there is a close link between the degree of effectiveness in replicating a payoff and the degree of variability in the realizations of the sample quadratic variation. Strictly speaking, perfect replication does *not* require a perfectly deterministic quadratic variation at the end of a given trading horizon for any path. There is only one case, however, when replication is possible, but the quadratic variation is not deterministic (namely, local-volatility diffusions with the volatility coefficient of the form $\sigma(S_t, t)$, discussed in Chapters 11 and 12). Apart from this 'exception', replicability, and therefore the Black-and-Scholes edifice, begin to shake when, for *any* reason (infrequency of re-hedging, presence of jumps, stochasticity of the volatility, lack of knowledge of the true volatility, etc.), the sample quadratic variation displays large variability. In the language that I employ in Chapter 4, 'lucky' and 'unlucky' paths, which cannot exist in a perfect Black-and-Scholes universe, are the norm in all other 'sub-lunar' worlds.

More generally, the concept of quadratic variation is central to derivatives pricing because

1. The finiteness of quadratic variation is ultimately the key to the Ito formula.

2. Every continuous-time martingale with continuous paths and finite quadratic variation is a (possibly time-changed) Brownian motion (Levy theorem; see, for example, Karatzas and Shreve (1991, Chapter 2)).

3. By and large, models that posit continuous processes for the underlying and produce a finite and deterministic quadratic variation give rise to flat (across strikes) smile surfaces. Therefore, all models that produce non-flat smile surfaces either are diffusions that introduce stochasticity in the quadratic variation (e.g. local-volatility, general-stochastic-volatility, volatility-regime-switching models), or dispense with the requirement that the path should be continuous.

In point 2, a time change is simply a function that transforms time, t, into a function of time, $g(t)$. If the volatility is time-dependent but deterministic the result is really not

---

[7]A mathematically precise but still sufficiently simple treatment can be found in Shreve *et al.* (1997).

[8]Incidentally, since we have 'proven' that a Brownian motion has a finite, non-zero quadratic variation, and that a differentiable function has zero quadratic variation, it follows that a Brownian motion is non-differentiable.

surprising, and, intuitively, it can be understood as a quickening or slowing down of the rate of flow of time, depending on the value of the instantaneous volatility, $\sigma(t)$, in a deterministic manner. It is important to point out, however, that the change in time referred to in the theorem need not be deterministic and the theorem also applies to situations when the quadratic variation over a finite interval is stochastic (as long as it is bounded).

As for point 3, the first part of the statement (that a stochastic quadratic variation implies a non-flat smile surface) is intuitively understandable. Think for instance of a jump–diffusion process: over any given finite interval one or more jumps might or might not have occurred. No matter how fine we might want to make our partition, a discontinuous jump will certainly introduce a contribution to the quadratic variation. The number of jumps along any path of finite length (and, in general, their amplitudes) is, however, random. The second variation will therefore be affected by the possible occurrence of one, two, several or no jumps. In other words, in the presence of jumps, 'lucky paths' do exist. Similarly, if the volatility, instead of being a deterministic function of time, is stochastic, so will be the quadratic variation. As for the variance–gamma process, it is explicitly constructed to make the variance of the process stochastic (and gamma-distributed). Therefore, once again it should come to no surprise that the quadratic variation will be finite but random (realization-dependent).

What is more surprising is that it is possible to have a finite and deterministic quadratic variation, and still obtain a 'smiley' implied volatility surface. This can be achieved by relinquishing the requirement of continuity in the path, but under the constraint that the realized quadratic variation should be exactly a non-zero constant over each and every path. This approach, introduced by Britten-Jones and Neuberger and discussed in Chapter 10, therefore constitutes a nice conceptual bridge between the deterministic-quadratic-variation modelling with flat smiles, and the more general stochastic-quadratic-variation approaches that produce non-flat smile surfaces.

Summarizing: looking at what different processes imply about the quadratic variation constitutes a useful and important classification of the associated pricing models. For this reason the quadratic-variation aspect of the processes presented in Part II will be central to my treatment.

Exercise 2 *Consider (a) a time-dependent, deterministic-volatility process; (b) a stochastic-volatility (with mean reversion) process; (c) a jump–diffusion process, where the jump amplitudes can only assume a finite number of possible values; and (d) a process where the volatility jumps at random times between two levels. For (a), (b) and (c) guess and draw a sketch of the distribution of quadratic variations over a given time interval. For (a), (b), (c) and (d), consider the quadratic variation, $v_2(t)$, as a function of the length of the interval, t. Is $v_2(t)$ a continuous function of time?*

Chapter 4

Variance and Mean Reversion in the Real and the Risk-Adjusted Worlds

4.1 Introduction and Plan of the Chapter

This chapter is not elegant, but extremely important. It is inelegant because the same results can be obtained in a much more concise and mathematically elegant manner. Indeed, a (very) careful reading of Chapter 2 could provide almost all the answers to the questions raised in this chapter. It is important because widespread misconceptions abound regarding the nature of the hedging strategy in a Black-and-Scholes world, especially in the case of time-dependent volatility. This makes me believe that, for all their elegance, the terse proofs presented in most texts sometimes fail to convey an understanding of why, when, how and to what extent hedging really works. In this chapter I will therefore look in detail at several related topics:

1. I will analyse the hedging of options in the presence of constant and time-dependent volatility.

2. I will discuss when it is necessary to distinguish carefully between the real-world variance of a process and (the square of) its volatility.

3. I will provide a first treatment of the topic of mean reversion, both in the real and in the risk-adjusted world.[1] I will highlight that the concept of mean reversion requires particularly careful handling even in the simpler case of options on equity stock or FX. This will provide a backdrop to the fundamental discussion of time-dependent volatility and mean reversion in the risk-neutral world in the case of interest-rate options (see Chapter 18). The conclusions drawn in the discussion of this latter

---

[1]The topic of mean reversion will be explored at greater depth in later chapters in the context of interest-rate models – see, in particular, Chapter 18.

topic will actually constitute one of the important 'messages' that this book tries to convey.

4. I will show which of the quantities observable in the 'real world' are of relevance for option pricing and which are of relevance for risk management. This will have a direct bearing on the statistical methods needed for the estimation of volatility in the different contexts of option pricing and risk management.

5. I will discuss a hedging paradox reported in the literature (Crouhy and Galai (1995)) regarding the interplay between instantaneous and average volatilities in the hedging of options. A further discussion of this paradox will be presented in Chapter 10, after introducing the Britten-Jones–Neuberger approach.

6. By analysing in detail the profit or losses that a trader can expect to make when engaging in gamma trading, I will draw important conclusions about the special nature of diffusion processes.

7. I will revisit the concept of quadratic variation, and show again why it is so important in option pricing.

4.2   Hedging a Plain-Vanilla Option: General Framework

After the treatment in Chapter 2, why do we need to look at hedging again? The reason is twofold. First of all, in this chapter I will take a more 'practical' approach. For instance, despite still neglecting bid–offer spreads and transaction costs in general, I will address such questions as: 'How "small" must the time step be for the approximation to the continuous limit to be acceptable: weeks, days or minutes?'; 'What happens if we do not know exactly the true volatility, and hedge with a wrong one?'; 'If perfect replication cannot be achieved, what variables best explain the experienced slippage between the terminal option value and the value of the hedging portfolio?'; etc.

Interesting as these questions are in their own rights, their answers will raise deeper issues. They will highlight, in fact, that the imperfection of our real-life replication results can be due to a variety of reasons: it might have to do with trading restrictions (finite re-hedging frequency), with market micro-structural features (tick-size moves), or with intrinsic properties of the process of the underlying (e.g. the presence of jumps). The origin of these 'imperfections' can therefore be very diverse. None the less all these different 'blemishes' will reveal themselves by producing an imperfectly predictable (*stochastic*) realized sample quadratic variation. The degree of dispersion of this quantity will be shown to have a strong explanatory power in accounting for the imperfect success of our hedging programme. Our inability to replicate exactly a payoff, and the *degree* of our partial success, will be explained in terms of the *degree* of our ignorance about, or of our ability to 'capture' exactly, the quadratic variation of the underlying process.[2]

---

[2] As presented here, these statements are too strong. The quadratic variation can be stochastic, and yet perfect replication can, in theory, be possible. This happens if the process for the underlying is of the local-volatility type (i.e. a diffusion with volatility of the form $\sigma(S_t, t)$). In this case the stochasticity in the quadratic variation is fully explained by the dynamics of the *traded* underlying, which can therefore be used to remove most uncertainty. See Chapters 11 and 12. Slippages due to finite trading intervals and other market frictions still remain.

Answering these 'practical' questions will therefore greatly enhance the understanding of the workings of the Black-and-Scholes replication programme, and of more complex models.

4.2.1 Trading Restrictions and Model Uncertainty: Theoretical Results

Before analysing some empirical results it is important to have clearly in mind what the theory says about the ability to reproduce a terminal payoff when the underlying process is a deterministic-volatility diffusion, but either there are trading restrictions, or we do not know the correct volatility, or both. The trading restrictions which are normally considered in this type of analysis refer to the inability to trade continuously (while the underlying process is still assumed to be continuous). The analysis of the effect of bid–offer spreads is also important, but is not touched upon in this chapter (see, however, Chapter 10).

The topic of the hedging error incurred when we have imperfect knowledge about the Black-and-Scholes process, or we cannot trade continuously, has been treated in Mahayni (2003), Avellaneda *et al.* (1995), Dudenhausen *et al.* (1998), Lyons (1995), El Karoui *et al.* (1998) and others. In order to understand their results it is necessary to distinguish between binomial hedging strategies directly constructed in discrete time (such as the strategies described in the second part of Chapter 2); and hedging strategies obtained from a discretization of a continuous-time model (such as the Black-and-Scholes). In the limit, the two hedging strategies coincide, but, when the trading intervals are finite, they are in general different. With this distinction in mind, the main results obtained in the works above are:

1. If the true volatility is (locally) bounded and trading is continuous, the hedging strategy implied by the Black-and-Scholes formula using the upper volatility bound is robust for convex payoff functions.

2. If the true process has deterministic (but unknown) volatility, and trading is continuous there always exists a self-financing strategy ensuring that the payoff can be replicated.

3. If a self-financing continuous-time strategy (such as, for instance, the strategy suggested by the Black-and-Scholes formulae) is discretized, the resulting discrete strategy will, in general, not be self-financing (i.e. there will be a non-vanishing cost by the end of the strategy). The discretized strategy will in general not be self-financing *even on average*.

4. If the market is incomplete because of uncertainty in the model and of trading discretization, the discretization of a continuous-time strategy does not produce a superhedge even if the true volatility is bounded.

5. Binomial hedging strategies (such as the ones discussed in Chapter 2), i.e. strategies based in discrete time on the direct replication of payoffs on a node-by-node basis, are robust in the same sense as the Black-and-Scholes hedges are in continuous trading. In particular, super-hedges are possible (although possibly expensive) as long as the 'real' price moves are always smaller than the moves allowed by the binomial branching model.

In what follows I will use a discretization of the continuous-time Black-and-Scholes hedging strategy. On the basis of point 3 above, one should therefore not even expect that the average of the difference between the replicating portfolio and the option to hedge should be centred around zero. Furthermore, the sign of the deviation can be shown to depend (see, for example, Mahayni (2003)) on the sign of the (difficult-to-predict) real-world drift of the underlying. This is all true, but how significant is the effect in practice? If the effect were strong for, say, daily re-hedging frequencies the implications for the practice of hedging would be far-reaching. Looking at the study by Mahayni (2003), however, one begins to notice that, for clarity of exposition, the hedging portfolio analysed in their study was rebalanced only once a month. Perhaps the bias effect becomes much smaller with more realistic re-hedging frequencies. Also, we can ask: Should we worry more about the uncertainty in the 'true' volatility or about the finite re-hedging frequency? Should we be more concerned if we can only re-hedge once a week, or if we mis-estimate the volatility by two vegas? These are some of the questions addressed in the rest of this chapter.

4.2.2   The Setting

This section establishes the framework for the analysis presented in the remainder of the chapter. I will consider a diffusive real-world process for a stock price of the form

$$\frac{\mathrm{d}S_t}{S_t} = \mu(S_t, t) + \sigma(t)\,\mathrm{d}z_t \tag{4.1}$$

As in Chapter 2, $\mu(S_t, t)$ is the real-world drift for the asset price, S, and $\sigma(t)$ its percentage volatility. With Equation (4.1) I have allowed the volatility to depend at most on time. In the first part of the chapter I will actually deal with an even-simpler case, i.e. $\sigma(t) = \sigma_0$, with σ_0 a constant.

As for the drift, we could have made it more complex by allowing, for instance, for a dependence on the history of the stock price up to time t. The form $\mu = \mu(S_t, t)$, however, is sufficiently general for the purposes of the discussion in this chapter.

4.2.3   The Methodology

We will attempt to hedge a plain-vanilla option (a call) of expiry T on a non-dividend-paying stock, S. Since we are in the diffusive framework described in Chapter 2, perfect replication of a terminal payoff is possible, and a unique price for an option can be arrived at purely by invoking absence of arbitrage.[3] The tool that allows replication of an arbitrary terminal payoff is the delta-hedging self-financing hedging strategy, which has also been described in detail in Chapter 2. Both the analytical treatment, and the binomial construction provide us not only with the proof that replication is possible, but also with a prescription (the hedging strategy) on how to achieve it.

We want to look in detail at the effectiveness of the hedging strategy under several circumstances. In order to do so, we shall simulate the evolution of the stock price in the 'real' (as opposed to the risk-neutral) world. This is achieved by dividing the time period

---

[3]The perfect replication will be achieved using a Black-and-Scholes strategy if trading is continuous, or using a payoff-replication technique as discussed in Chapter 2 if trading is discrete.

[0 T] into a large but finite number of time-steps, and by carrying out a Monte Carlo simulation of the *real-world* stock price process using Equation (4.1).

The procedure I follow in this chapter is very different from the conventional approach to price options using Monte Carlo simulations (as pioneered by Boyle (1977)). The standard procedure, in fact, implicitly makes use of the replicability of the option payoff, invokes absence of arbitrage and the law of one price, and directly evolves the stock price in the risk-adjusted world. In calculating the price of an option as the discounted expectation of the terminal payoff, the traditional (i.e. Boyle's) approach therefore implicitly makes use of the Feynman–Kac theorem discussed in Chapter 2.

I will follow a different approach. When evolving the stock price I will not assume that the deterministic part of the price dynamics is described by a risk-neutral drift. I am instead going to assign an arbitrary time- and/or state-dependent drift to the stock price evolution, $\mu(S, t)$, and rebalance, at each time-step, a delta-neutral portfolio made up of

- a (Black) delta amount of stock and

- the required cash (borrowed or lent) to give zero value to the option, the delta amount of stock and the bond itself.

I call a position in a Black–delta amount of stock plus the borrowing or lending 'the hedging portfolio'. The rule to hold a Black–delta amount of stock (plus the invested cash)[4] characterizes our trading strategy. We require this strategy to be self-financing, and therefore we cannot inject or subtract money from our portfolio during the life of the option. As we know, if such a self-financing strategy manages to reproduce the payoff of the option, the set-up cost of this portfolio must be exactly equal to the cost of the option itself. Our strategy will be successful if, by option expiry, the hedging portfolio and the option payoff will be the same along each path. If we succeed in achieving this, we will say that we have obtained perfect replication.

Let me stress again the differences between the usual Monte Carlo evaluation of the option price as described, for instance, in Boyle (1977) and what we are doing here. In the 'direct' (Boyle) approach one evaluates the price of the option as the discounted expectation, *in the pricing measure* (i.e. in the risk-neutral world), of the terminal payoff. In the approach presented below, on the other hand, we are going to simulate (one of the infinitely many possible versions of) the real world, and therefore we are not imposing a risk-neutral evolution to the stock price. We shall none the less still arrive at the same price for the option, but following a less direct route. For each path in the Monte Carlo simulation we shall

- evolve the stock price with the real-world time-dependent drift $\mu(t)$ and the constant volatility σ;

- calculate the required hedges using the Black formula in each state of the world reached along the path;

- rebalance the holdings of stock and bond as required;

- compare the portfolio and the option payoff at expiry time T;

---

[4]Both the amount of stock and the borrowed or lent cash are calculated at the *beginning* of the step – this is the discretization of the continuous-time strategy alluded to above.

- argue that, if the initial portfolio can be readjusted to replicate the final payoff without further injections of cash, its initial set-up cost must equal the price of the option.

4.2.4   Criterion for Success

Since our simulations will obviously take place in discrete time, i.e. by evolving the process (4.2) over a small but finite number of time-steps, we cannot expect the *exact* coincidence of the terminal option payoff and of the portfolio value. In order to obtain useful information about the correctness of the hedging strategy we shall therefore focus attention on a particular stochastic quantity, x, defined as the difference at option expiry between the (imperfectly) replicating portfolio and the option payoff. I shall refer to this quantity as the 'slippage'. The first moment of this variable, i.e. its expectation, will tell us whether we are achieving a match between the option payoff and the terminal value of the portfolio at least on average. By examining, however, how the variance and higher moments of x behave as a function of the time-step size we shall be able to ascertain to what extent, as the continuous limit is approached, the portfolio replicates the payoff on a path-by-path basis.

4.3   Hedging Plain-Vanilla Options: Constant Volatility

We begin our discussion by restricting the setting to the simplest possible case, and progressively adding complexity and generality. The first situation we analyse is therefore the case when both the drift and the percentage volatility are constant. In this case Equation (4.1) specializes to

$$\frac{\mathrm{d}S_t}{S_t} = \mu \, \mathrm{d}t + \sigma \, \mathrm{d}z_t \tag{4.2}$$

For the numerical experiments presented in this chapter, I have chosen an initial stock price of 40, a strike of 40, an expiry time of 0.33 years, a constant interest rate, r, of 12%, a real-world drift, μ, of 0.00% and a volatility of 30.00%. The particular value chosen for μ is, of course, irrelevant. Table 4.1 reports the results obtained with different initial speeds for otherwise identical runs of 2000 simulations of 80 time-steps each.

Several features of the results are worthwhile commenting upon. To begin with, neither the average value of the portfolio nor the average value of the option payoff coincide with the Black-and-Scholes future (expiry) value of the option (nor should they). This observation should come as no surprise, since we are not arriving at the price of the option by carrying out a risk-neutral evolution of the stock price. What matters is that the portfolio does indeed replicate (to within numerical error) the option payoff at expiry. As discussed above, once we have set up the correct replicating portfolio, we become indifferent not only to the real-world average payoff, but also to the outcome of any individual realization. The only quantity that is of interest is therefore the cost of setting up the portfolio that will replicate the option. This is how we 'price' the contingent claim.

Table 4.1 The results of several runs for the constant-volatility case obtained as described in the text. The columns labelled *NumSim*, *Port*, *Option*, *VolLogSt*, *VarStock*, *RevSpd*, *Stock*$_0$, *VolHedge*, *RevLev*, *Vol*, *Nu*, *NumSteps*, *VarPort* and *SetUpCost* display the number of simulations, the average value of the portfolio at expiry, the average value of the option at expiry, the volatility of the logarithm of the stock at expiry, the variance of the stock at expiry, the reversion speed in the real-world dynamics for the stock, the initial value for the stock, the value σ_0 in the expression $\sigma_0 \exp[-vt]$, the value v in the expression $\sigma_0 \exp[-vt]$, the number of steps in each simulation, the variance of the overall portfolio and the set-up cost of the strategy, respectively.

NumSim	Port	Option	VolLogSt	VarStock	RevSpd	Stock$_0$	VolHedge	RevLev	Vol	Nu	NumSteps	VarPort	SetUpCost
2000	2.685305	2.693255	29.898%	47.4393	0	40	30.00%	44	30.00%	0	80	0.074084	3.540505
2000	2.847618	2.856616	30.510%	50.7504	0	40	30.00%	44	30.00%	0	80	0.071871	3.540505
2000	2.916166	2.921015	29.916%	48.3210	0	40	30.00%	44	30.00%	0	80	0.074563	3.540505
2000	2.730329	2.727861	29.807%	47.6642	0	40	30.00%	44	30.00%	0	80	0.071504	3.540505

Note also that the realized unconditional variance of the (log) of the stock price (column *VolLogSt*) is given by

$$\text{var}[\ln(S_T)] = \sigma^2 T \tag{4.3}$$

Taking the square root of the variance divided by T gives the volatility that one must use in the Black formula in order to obtain the correct delta (and price).

Let us also observe that, for the time-step size used, the standard deviation of the terminal payoffs of hedging the portfolio is one order of magnitude smaller than the option price. This quantity could have been reduced further if we had taken more time-steps (as we will show later on), and it is the most important quantity to monitor in these simulations. This is because we want to be indifferent between holding the option or the replicating portfolio *at the end every single path*, and not just on average. Only if this path-by-path condition is fulfilled will the overall portfolio variance go to zero with the number of time-steps.

Finally, the column labelled *SetUpCost* shows (not surprisingly) the set-up cost of the portfolio. As one can readily check, this is indeed exactly equal to the Black-and-Scholes value for the option.

The case considered above showed little more than that our simulation is working properly, and the results should come as no surprise. Understanding exactly how this replication property works its magic even in this simplest of cases, however, can give an understanding about option pricing that can be used in more complex (and realistic) situations. In order to enhance this understanding we shall consider the hedging strategy in detail below. For reasons that will become apparent in the following sections, the strategy is often called 'trading the gamma'.

4.3.1   Trading the Gamma: One Step and Constant Volatility

Break-Even Points

Let us place ourselves in the setting described above. The strategy whereby a trader who has bought an option delta-neutralizes her position and expects to recover the money paid for the premium (or, if the option had been bought at a 'cheap' volatility, to make her profit) by re-hedging dynamically over the life of the option is called 'trading the gamma'. Let us consider the gamma profit from trading the resulting delta-neutral portfolio. For concreteness, we place ourselves in the situation where the trader has *bought* the option and has delta-hedged it. As a consequence of this the trader is long gamma, and would therefore like the stock price to 'vibrate' as much as possible. This is because, in order to remain delta neutral, the trader will be (continuously) buying more stock whenever its price falls and selling it when its price rises. The more frequently the stock price undergoes these 'oscillations' between higher and lower values, the more frequently the trader will be able to adopt this 'buy-low-sell-high' strategy and the more money she will make. Volatility is exactly a measure of these 'vibrational properties' of the stock price, and therefore implicitly it is also a measure of the money the trader should be able to make by following this trading strategy.

Exercise 1 *A trader has bought a call. What if the price moves a lot between trade inception and option expiry, but does so in a straight line? Will the trader be able to 'earn her gamma profit'?*

For the trader who has bought the option, if everything else (e.g. the stock price) remains constant, as time goes by the value of her option will, in general, decline. If, therefore, the stock moves over the time interval Δt by less than a certain critical amount (the break-even point, precisely defined below) she will lose in time decay (theta) more than she can gain thanks to its movement by using the trading strategy. See Figure 4.1.

In order to understand at a more quantitative level the shape of this curve, and to express the break-even points as a function of the stock volatility, let us assume that we discretize the time to the expiry of an option into n time-steps of length Δt. In our perfect Black world the dynamics of the stock price is given by Equation (4.2). We therefore set up a delta-neutral portfolio, Π, made up of a long position in the call, C, a short position in the delta amount of stock, S, plus a balancing position, β, in a bond, B, to give zero value to the portfolio:

$$\Pi = C - \Delta S + \beta B \qquad (4.4)$$

If, for simplicity, we assume zero interest rates, the price of the bond will always be 1. Therefore

$$d\Pi = dC - \Delta \, dS \qquad (4.5)$$

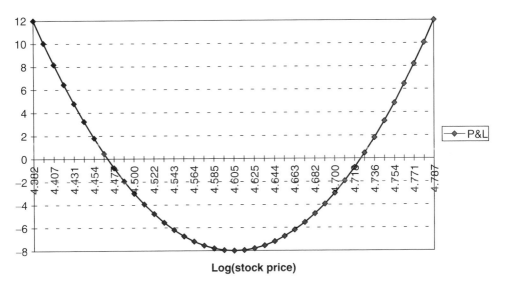

Figure 4.1 The P&L profile of a delta-hedged long option position. If the logarithm of the stock price moves by more than $\sigma\sqrt{\Delta t}$ (i.e. below 4.47 or above 4.70) the strategy will yield a positive profit. The stock values $S_1 = \exp[4.47]$ and $S_2 = \exp[4.70]$ are called the break-even points. See the discussion in the text. If there is no price move at all over the time-step Δt, $\sigma_{\exp} = 0$ and the option will lose the maximum amount ($8 in the figure) in time value (the 'theta decay').

with $\Delta = \frac{\partial C}{\partial S}$. Using Ito's lemma we can write the change in the call price, dC, as

$$dC = \frac{\partial C}{\partial t}\, dt + \frac{\partial C}{\partial S}\, dS + \frac{1}{2}\frac{\partial^2 C}{\partial S^2}\, dS^2 \tag{4.6}$$

Combining Equations (4.6) and (4.5) we obtain:

$$d\Pi = \frac{\partial C}{\partial t}\, dt + \frac{1}{2}\frac{\partial^2 C}{\partial S^2}\, dS^2 \tag{4.7}$$

To simplify notation, we follow the usual practice of defining the theta and gamma terms:

$$\frac{\partial C}{\partial t} = \Theta \quad \text{theta} \tag{4.8}$$

and

$$\frac{\partial^2 C}{\partial S^2} = \Gamma \quad \text{gamma} \tag{4.9}$$

In terms of these quantities Equation (4.7) can be rewritten as

$$d\Pi = \Theta\, dt + \tfrac{1}{2}\Gamma\, dS^2 \tag{4.10}$$

Since the portfolio was constructed to be riskless, and has zero value today (thanks to the 'balancing item' βB), its increment $d\Pi$ must be equal to zero. This implies:

$$\Theta dt + \tfrac{1}{2}\Gamma\, dS^2 = 0 \tag{4.11}$$

Note that we have calculated the Θ and Γ terms using the correct volatility, σ, that, for the moment, we assume to know exactly: $\Theta = \Theta(\sigma)$ and $\Gamma = \Gamma(\sigma)$.

Equation (4.11) establishes a link between the time-step, dt, and the *square of* the price move, dS^2. In the Brownian diffusive setting in which we have placed ourselves, these two quantities are not independent, because the application of Ito's lemma to Equation (4.2) gives, in the limit when dt goes to zero:

$$dS^2 = S^2\sigma^2\, dt \tag{4.12}$$

So, if the absolute size of the price move is exactly equal to $S\sigma\sqrt{dt}$, what the option loses in time decay (the theta term $\Theta\, dt$) the trader will gain from the combined changes in values of the option and of the delta amount of stock. This is because, after the delta terms cancel out, what is left is just the second-order gamma term $\tfrac{1}{2}\Gamma\, dS^2$. When the time-step is finite, but not so big that higher order terms provide a significant contribution, the break-even points in Figure 4.1 are therefore given by $\pm S\sigma\sqrt{\Delta t}$. If the price move has been of this size, the change in value of the portfolio is given by

$$\Delta\Pi = \Theta\Delta t + \tfrac{1}{2}\Gamma S^2\sigma^2\Delta t \simeq 0 \tag{4.13}$$

Table 4.2 Performance of the gamma trading strategy when the stock price moves by the 'correct' amount. See the text for details.

Time-step	Option change	Portfolio change	Price move	Experienced
0.5	8.48799	0.28747	15.19099	0.28747
0.25	5.73113	0.05371	10.51709	0.05371
0.125	3.96713	0.01178	7.32707	0.01178
0.0625	2.77050	0.00274	5.12711	0.00274
0.03125	1.94336	0.00064	3.59878	0.00064
0.015625	1.36672	0.00014	2.53151	0.00014
0.0078125	0.96280	0.00003	1.78348	0.00003
0.00390625	0.67903	0.00001	1.25785	0.00001
0.001953125	0.47926	0.00000	0.88780	0.00000

Of course, the P&L over one time-step is given exactly by the middle term on the RHS of Equation (4.13) only in the limit as Δt goes to zero. In order to appreciate the accuracy of Equation (4.13) when the time-step is finite, let us consider the simple case of a call with the stock price today at 100, the strike also at 100, one year to maturity, zero interest rates and a volatility of 20.00%. If we assume, to begin with, that the stock price moves (say, up) exactly by the break-even amount, Table 4.2 shows the relative value of the change in option price and in the value of the replicating portfolio as the time-step decreases. More precisely, the first column shows the length of the time-step, and the three columns next to it display the changes in the option price, the predicted changes in the portfolio (Equation (4.13)) and the changes in the stock price. The last column shows the changes in the portfolio actually experienced. These results should be compared with the findings in Table 4.2 which refer to the case when the stock does not move by the 'right' (break-even) amount. This case is discussed below.

'Exceptional' Moves

A complementary question is the following: If the price move is not exactly equal to the break-even point, can one use Equation (4.13) to predict the experienced 'slippage', i.e. the difference between the change in value of the option and of the hedging portfolio?

In order to answer this question let us assume that, over a given time-step, the realized price move is, say, greater than the break-even point. See Equation (4.13). In other words, over the time-step Δt we might have experienced a particularly high ('lucky') draw of the stock price move: say, a positive two-standard-deviation move. In order for this degree of 'luck' to be correctly reflected in the size of the associated change in the stock price as a function of Δt, it is useful to express the size of any price move ('normal' or 'lucky') in terms of their 'equivalent volatility'. This can be accomplished as follows. We have seen that a 'normal-size' up price move associated with the break-even points is implicitly defined by[5]

$$\ln S_{t+\Delta t} = \ln S_t + \sigma \sqrt{\Delta t} \qquad (4.14)$$

---

[5]I am ignoring terms in Δt, which become much smaller than terms in $\sqrt{\Delta t}$ as Δt approaches zero.

Similarly, a larger- or smaller-than-normal up move in price is described by

$$\ln S_{t+\Delta t} = \ln S_t + (\sigma + \Delta\sigma)\sqrt{\Delta t} \tag{4.15}$$

with $\Delta\sigma$ positive or negative, respectively. Let us consider the case when $\Delta\sigma > 0$. In this instance the 'lucky' price move can be explicitly written as

$$\Delta S = S(\exp[(\sigma + \Delta\sigma)\sqrt{\Delta t}] - 1) \tag{4.16}$$

The term ΔS^2 is therefore given by

$$\Delta S^2 \simeq S^2\{\exp[2(\sigma + \Delta\sigma)\sqrt{\Delta t}] + 1 - 2(\exp[(\sigma + \Delta\sigma)\sqrt{\Delta t}])\} \tag{4.17}$$

After cancelling terms and expanding the exponential (keeping the quadratic terms) we obtain

$$\Delta S^2 \simeq S^2(\sigma + \Delta\sigma)^2 \Delta t \tag{4.18}$$

Equation (4.10) can therefore be rewritten as

$$d\Pi = \Theta \, dt + \tfrac{1}{2}\Gamma \, dS^2 \simeq \Theta\Delta t + \tfrac{1}{2}\Gamma S^2(\sigma + \Delta\sigma)^2\Delta t \tag{4.19}$$

which can again be expanded to give

$$d\Pi \simeq \Theta\Delta t + \tfrac{1}{2}\Gamma S^2\sigma^2\Delta t + \tfrac{1}{2}\Gamma S^2\Delta\sigma^2\Delta t + \Gamma S^2\sigma\Delta\sigma\Delta t \tag{4.20}$$

We know, however, that the first line in Equation (4.20) is equal to zero because it corresponds to the portfolio changes associated with the 'normal' size move (see Equation (4.11)). Therefore, after a simple algebraic manipulation, we obtain

$$d\Pi = \Theta \, dt + \tfrac{1}{2}\Gamma \, dS^2 \simeq \tfrac{1}{2}\Gamma S^2[(\sigma + \Delta\sigma)^2 - \sigma^2]\Delta t \tag{4.21}$$

Equation (4.21) lends itself to a very simple interpretation (see also Figures 4.2 and 4.3). Recall that the volatility term $\sigma + \Delta\sigma$ has a one-to-one correspondence with the size of the price move. Therefore, if we experienced an 'exceptional' price move (and we are long gamma) we shall make a profit (or a loss) proportional to the difference between the squares of the experienced and 'normal' volatility (where the experienced volatility is implicitly defined by Equation (4.15)). Once again, the relationship becomes exact only as Δt approaches zero. The speed of convergence with the size of the time-step is shown in Table 4.3. In this table the last two columns display the theoretical and experienced price move.

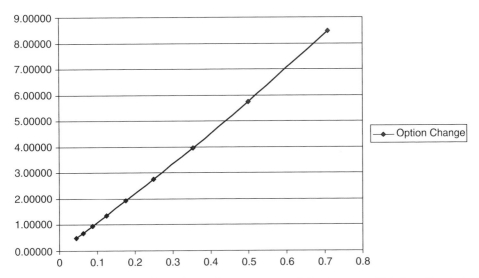

Figure 4.2 Change in the option price vs the square root of the time-step. Note how the straight line goes through the origin: we are dealing with a *continuous* process.

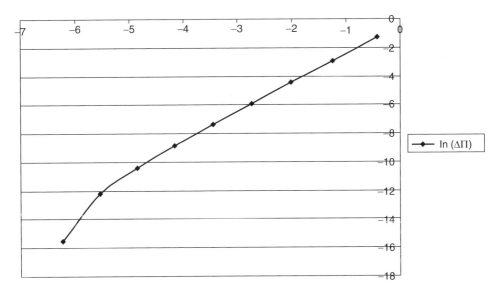

Figure 4.3 The quantity $\ln\left[\exp\left(\Delta t - 1\right)\right]$ vs $\ln(\Delta\Pi)$. Note how the line goes through the origin.

Do 'Lucky Paths' Exist?

The discussion above brings to light an interesting point. If the process for the underlying is truly a diffusion with deterministic and constant volatility, as the time-step Δt approaches zero, is there a non-zero probability for the price move to be anything but

Table 4.3 Performance of the gamma trading strategy when the stock price does not move by the 'correct' amount. See the text for details.

Time-step	Predicted	Experienced	Difference	Price move (theoretical)	Price move
0.5	1.104728296	1.407793057	−0.30306	115.19099	118.49560
0.25	0.515494998	0.555732517	−0.04024	110.51709	112.74969
0.125	0.245487686	0.248550763	−0.00306	107.32707	108.85568
0.0625	0.118592865	0.117397735	0.00120	105.12711	106.18365
0.03125	0.057872981	0.056924442	0.00095	103.59878	104.33393
0.015625	0.028443963	0.027973349	0.00047	102.53151	103.04545
0.0078125	0.01405048	0.013847571	0.00020	101.78348	102.14398
0.00390625	0.006965255	0.006884806	0.00008	101.25785	101.51131
0.001953125	0.00346158	0.003430535	0.00003	100.88780	101.06631
0.0009765625	0.0017233887	0.0017115300	0.00001	100.62696	100.75282

$\pm S\sigma\sqrt{\Delta t}$?[6] After all, the symmetric Brownian motion can be constructed as the limiting process of the *equal-step* random walk. If this construction is used, it is only when several steps are considered together that the price move can have a *distribution* of possible values, but each individual step has by construction always the right 'size'. If the Brownian motion is built as the limit of the equal-step random walk, this distribution is binomial, and approaches the normal one as the number of time-steps increase.

While the construction of the Brownian motion can be arrived at in other ways, this observation is linked to an important general property of diffusion processes: given any finite interval Δt, the realized variance of the *continuous* Brownian process is always and exactly given by $\sigma^2 \Delta t$. Therefore, one can in principle estimate *exactly* the volatility of a diffusion by using no matter how short an observation sample of the *continuous* process, simply by sampling finely enough. Conversely, if the generating process were truly a diffusion, 'lucky' or 'unlucky' paths do not exist: as long as we can sample the process with arbitrary resolution, the discrepancy between the sample and the theoretical variance can be made as small as one wishes. Ultimately this is the reason why, in the absence of market frictions, perfect replication is possible in a Black-and-Scholes world along each and every path (and not just on average).

4.3.2   Trading the Gamma: Several Steps and Constant Volatility

Over a single time-step and with constant volatility the analysis of the profits and losses made in gamma trading is simple enough. Should we worry at all when we extend the analysis to several steps? It is plausible to surmise that, if we traded at the correct volatility and scrupulously carried out the delta hedge using in the discretized Black−delta formula

---

[6]Clearly, this question is not the same as asking whether the real-world price moves really always have the same magnitude as Δt goes to zero. The first question has to do with the properties of a model. The second with the empirical properties of a financial phenomenon. As discussed in Chapter 1, it is up to the trader to judge whether a particular model is a useful tool to describe the financial problem at hand. Understanding the analytical properties of the model is an important part of this process.

the same volatility, we might achieve again perfect replication. Over each time-step, after all, one is exactly in the same situation as in the section above.

When we string several steps together, however, we can ask some more interesting questions. For instance, let us suppose that we know exactly the true (constant) volatility of a stock price process. Let us also suppose that, by virtue of our superior knowledge, we have managed to buy the option for a lower implied volatility (i.e. at a price that can be obtained from the Black-and-Scholes formula with a lower volatility). If we traded at the cheap volatility and hedged on the basis of the true volatility we know a priori what our profit will be. More precisely, we can rest assured that, if we bought a call with implied volatility σ_{trad}, but we (correctly) believe that the true volatility will be $\widehat{\sigma}$ and hedge on the basis of this knowledge, we can certainly lock in a profit equal to the difference in the Black option prices evaluated with $\widehat{\sigma}$ and σ_{trad}.

Exercise 2 *Prove the statement above.*

However, what would happen if we hedged on the basis of the wrong volatility? Can we still quantify the profit? Can we even know for sure that we *will* make a profit? This is in practice very relevant: in reality we never know exactly the 'true' volatility. We can, however, form a trading opinion that a certain quoted volatility is, say, certainly too low. Can we rest assured that, if we hedge on the basis not of the true (and unknown volatility) but of the wrong volatility, we shall still bring home some profit with certainty?

One reason for fearing that the answer to this question might be rather complex when one considers several time-steps is the following. If we consider several time-steps in succession, the overall P&L, *TOTP&L*, will be given by the sum of the many (in the limit, infinite) terms of the same form as above:

$$TOTP\&L = \frac{1}{2} \sum \Gamma S^2 [\sigma_{\text{exp}}^2 - \sigma_{\text{trad}}^2] \Delta t \tag{4.22}$$

If, for a moment, one could assume that the quantity ΓS^2 were a constant, one would immediately conclude that the trade will have been struck at a 'fair' price if the two quantities

$$\sigma_{\text{trad}}^2 T = \sum \sigma_{\text{exp}}^2(i) \Delta t_i \tag{4.23}$$

are equal. The assumption that ΓS^2 is a constant is, however, clearly wrong: as the stock price 'vibrates' stochastically, the option will move in and out of the money, and its gamma will vary accordingly. Therefore, the quantity ΓS^2, depending as it does on the path of the stock, is not only time-dependent, but also stochastic. The profit that we can make over each time-step because the realized volatility is different from the traded (implied) volatility is proportional to the path-dependent quantity ΓS^2. This being the case, what can we say about the *cumulative* profit? Perhaps we can only know for sure that the profit will be strictly positive. Perhaps we cannot even be sure of this.

In order to show that we can be sure to make a profit, recall that we know for sure that we bought the option for an implied volatility lower than the 'true' one. Let us then enter the strategy whereby we hedge and record the value of the option according to the 'wrong' volatility. So, on the day of trade, we record zero value. On day 1, and every following day, we have the wrong amount of delta, but we also record the value of the option wrongly. So, according to our faulty book-keeping, every day we are delta-hedged. At the last step (i.e. at option expiry), the payoff is independent of the assumed volatility, so we will certainly record the true value of the option at expiry (i.e. our book-keeping ceases to be faulty, and becomes correct). Before that, however, at each point in time we have a good surprise (a positive gamma shock, a move greater than the break-even points implied by the low volatility). Therefore, in the limit as Δt becomes vanishingly small, we are guaranteed to make a small profit over each time-step. Perhaps we could have made more money using a cleverer strategy, but we have at least found one strategy that will certainly make us *some* money.

4.4   Hedging Plain-Vanilla Options: Time-Dependent Volatility

Let us now consider the case where the process is a pure random walk with no drift, but the volatility is time dependent:

$$\frac{dS_t}{S_t} = \mu_t \, dt + \sigma_t \, dz_t \tag{4.24}$$

$$\mu_t = 0 \tag{4.25}$$

$$\sigma(t) = \sigma_0 \exp[-\nu t] \tag{4.26}$$

The exponential functional form for the instantaneous volatility has been chosen for its simplicity and analytic tractability. As far as hedging is concerned, the obvious question is: With what volatility should one construct the delta hedge? Unlike the constant-volatility case there are now several plausible candidates: shall we use σ_0? $\sigma_0 \exp[-\nu t]$? The average volatility? The root-mean-squared volatility? More generally, should one make use of a *local* property of the volatility (i.e. its value at the time of hedging), or of some *global* property (such as, say, its average or its root-mean-squared value), or, perhaps, of a combination of local and global information (see Section 4.9)?

   In order to answer these questions, we shall assume again that the chosen volatility will be exactly realized during the life of the option (i.e. during the simulation) and that we are going to delta-hedge dynamically the option position before each time-step. Clearly, delta-hedging correctly implies knowing what the right volatility to put in the Black formula should be. But let us sidestep this issue for the moment, and assume that we know the correct delta amount of stock. A lot can be learned by looking again at the interplay between time decay and the time value of money of an option.

4.4.1   Views on Gamma Trading When the Volatility is Time Dependent

Let us consider again a trader engaged in gamma trading. The trader will sell the option if she believes that the future realized volatility will be lower than the implied volatility at which the option trades, and vice versa. If the trader believed the volatility to be constant, the strategy would be totally unambiguous: at the beginning of the strategy, and at any point during the life of the option there is one and only one volatility that, input into the Black formula for the delta, will provide the required hedge. In the presence of time-dependent volatility, however, which volatility should the trader use in order to achieve a delta-neutral portfolio? And, how should the cheapness of the option be assessed?

The observation that the quantity ΓS^2, crucial to the strategy of trading the gamma, depends on the particular path has given rise to several different 'views' about the nature, and the very existence, of an exact delta-hedging strategy in the presence of time-dependent volatility, even when continuous, frictionless trading is allowed. Since these views are frequently put forth by practitioners, an attempt is made in what follows first to present them as 'sympathetically' as possible, and then to show the arguments and the results of the tests that will indicate which view is correct.

First View: 'Perfect Replication Only Works if the Volatility is Constant'

The typical example put forth by the proponents of this view is that of a simple call priced in the presence of a strongly increasing time-dependent volatility. In this scenario one can then consider a path that, during the first part of the option's life, i.e. when the volatility should be low, brings the stock price deeply out-of-the-money. This path might well be unlikely, but it is still possible, and we are trying to see whether perfect replication can be achieved along each and every path. Then, during the second, high-volatility portion of the option life, the random draws are such that the stock price approximately remains in the same out-of-the-money region. Such a path is also unlikely, but still possible, and the replication strategy requires success along *any* path.

By the time we are in the high-volatility period of the option's life, the argument continues, the option is so out-of-the-money, and the gamma therefore is now so low, that we shall not be able to make enough profit by trading the gamma (i.e. by selling the stock when its price is rising and buying it when the price is falling) to compensate us for the premium we paid to purchase the option. In other words, if this way of looking at the problem of hedging options in the presence of time-dependent volatility were correct, it would seem that 'lucky' and 'unlucky' paths do matter when the volatility is time-dependent. If 'lucky' paths existed, one would presumably obtain a match between the terminal payoff of the option and of the portfolio at best on average, but not on a path-by-path basis (where the average in question is over different paths, not along a single path). Since, in reality, however, we 'live only once', this average payoff-matching would not be enough to eliminate the fears of a risk-averse trader, who along any given path would see a discrepancy between the values of the final replicating portfolio and of the option. It would therefore seem that, in the presence of time-dependent volatility, if we based our hedging strategy on the root-mean-squared volatility, we could not invoke unique pricing by risk-neutral valuation.

Second View: Instantaneous-Volatility Hedging

Another possible way of looking at the problem is to recognize that, as long as the length of each trading interval can be made arbitrarily small, over each of these intervals the volatility can be assumed to be constant. The analysis presented in the constant-volatility case would then appear to apply again, with the volatility to be input into the Black formula in order to determine the delta amount of stock equal to the instantaneous volatility. If the length of the trading intervals were sufficiently small, one could hope that, by following this strategy based on the instantaneous-volatility hedging, the discrepancy between the experienced and average volatility could be made as small as one wished *along each individual path*. A consequence of this view, if correct, would be that only a local property of the volatility (i.e. its current instantaneous value), as opposed to a global property (such as its average or root-mean-squared value) is of relevance in determining the required hedges.

Third View: Initial-Root-Mean-Squared-Volatility Hedging

A third party looks at the problem in yet a different light. To the above-mentioned example of the stock ending deeply out of the money because of the 'unlucky' path (First View), this third camp would reply by noting that, if the stock has ended so far out of the money in the first part of its life, in order to get there in the first place the trader must have had such a 'lucky' (high volatility) path when the volatility was supposed to be low, that she can afford not to make as much money in the high-volatility, but low-gamma, part of the option life. The important quantity, according to this view, is therefore linked to some average property of the volatility over its life *as seen from option inception*, and the trader will be 'OK in the end' because excess profits or losses incurred during different ('lucky' and 'unlucky') parts of the option life will cancel out by option expiry. Therefore, provided again that one can trade frequently enough, 'lucky' or 'unlucky' paths will not matter, and replication will still take place on a path-by-path basis as long as the same *initial* correct value of the root-mean-squared volatility (a *global* property which can be determined once and for all at option inception) is always input into the Black formula throughout the life of the option.

Fourth View: Current-Root-Mean-Squared-Volatility Hedging

The fourth and final view is the following. Let us start from the observation that, if replication is at all possible, the cost of the option must equal the cost of the hedging portfolio. If the correct hedge only depends on the local properties of the volatility (as the second view maintains), two different volatilities (say, one increasing and one decreasing) that have the same value today would give rise to the same 'replicating' portfolio, the same set-up cost, and, therefore, by absence of arbitrage, to the same option price. It is easy to think of 'extreme' behaviours for the time-dependent volatility that lead to implausible or absurd conclusions.[7] Therefore, the fourth view says that if perfect replication is at all possible, it must be based on a global property of the volatility (such as its average or root-mean-squared value) and not on its current value.

As for the initial-root-mean-squared-volatility hedging strategy, if this were correct, this could lock the trader into a situation where she has to hold on to the option until expiry, under penalty of losing money. Suppose, in fact, that the trader has made 'too little money' by gamma trading during the first part of the option life, but expects to be compensated by making 'too much money' during the second part. 'Too much money', in this context, means more money than the residual volatility half-way through the option

---

[7]Think, for instance, of two deterministic time-dependent volatilities that have the same value of, say, 20% for the next micro-second; for the rest of the life of the option one volatility then drops to 0.0001%, and the other rises to 1000%. Could the option price be the same?

life would justify, and just enough to compensate for the deficit of gamma-trading profit during the first part of the option life. A second trader, who does not know or care about whether the original trader has lost to date more in time-decay than she was able to make up for by gamma trading, will certainly not subsidize the losses incurred so far, and would simply look at the volatility ahead. So, if the original trader wanted to be able to make her money back, she could no longer sell the option in the market.

Therefore, the proponents of the fourth view maintain that if replication is at all possible, not only must the correct hedging amount be based on a global property, but, more specifically, on a global property that can only 'know about' the *residual* life of the option (such as the *current* root-mean-squared volatility to expiry).

4.4.2 Which View Is the Correct One? (and the Feynman–Kac Theorem Again)

I shall prove which of the above views is correct in several steps.

If the process is a diffusion and the volatility is deterministic, we know from the algorithmic construction in Chapter 2, Section 2.3, that at least one replicating strategy *must* exist. Actually, the reasoning showed that there was nothing to prevent the volatility from even being stochastic, as long as of the form $\sigma = \sigma(S_t, t)$.

In the same chapter I pointed out that, if replication is possible, the amount of bond and stock to hold must be unique. This simply followed from the uniqueness of the solution of the 2×2 systems associated at each node with the payoffs of the stock, the bond, and the contingent claim.[8]

Given that we know that a hedging strategy exists and is unique, at most one of the views above is correct, and all the others certainly wrong. What we have not established yet is to which of these 'views', if any, the certainly-correct algorithmic construction described in Chapter 2 corresponds.

Since, at each step of the replication argument, we appear to use *local* properties of the stock and bond prices (i.e. their values one step ahead) one might be tempted to argue that a local quantity (perhaps the instantaneous volatility) should be used in the Black formula to obtain the delta amount of stock. This, however, is not correct. Consider the replication construction in the two-time-step situation examined in detail in Section 2.3.9. It is true that the value of the call at the root of the two-step tree depends on the values of the stock and the bond just one step ahead. However, it also depends on the value of the call itself in the up and down states at time 1. These future conditional option values, in turn, were obtained from the values of the stock, the bond and the call at expiry (time 2). Therefore, the value of the call at the root of the tree depends on the call values at time 1, and these, in turn, depend on the tree 'geometry' from time 1 to time 2. Despite the apparently local procedure, the value of the call at the root must therefore contain *global*, and not just *local* information. However, might the right (delta) amount of stock depend both on global *and* local properties (perhaps on some combination of the root-mean-squared and the local volatilities)?

---

[8]Strictly speaking, the construction in the second part of Chapter 2 was based on a *discrete* (as opposed to *discretized*) hedging strategy that is not identical to a Black-and-Scholes delta strategy implemented in discrete time. I show below, however, that for sufficiently small time-steps the difference between the two strategies can be made to approach zero as closely as desired, and therefore I can afford to be imprecise here.

We established in Chapter 2 that, in the limit as the time-step goes to zero, the replication argument and the continuous-time valuation must give the same result. Therefore the same dependence of the option price on the volatility must be asymptotically obtained with the two approaches. For convenience, I now therefore switch to the continuous setting (see the comments in Section 2.5).

When it comes to diffusions, the interplay between local and global quantities is both subtle and profound, and is underpinned by the Feynman–Kac theorem that we first discussed in Section 2.2.4. Recall that the theorem established a relationship between a diffusion, a partial differential equation and an expectation. What is of relevance here is the fact that the expectation was taken simply over the *terminal* distribution of the stock price. This terminal distribution will not depend on the local information embedded in the function $\sigma(t)$, but only on the 'total variance',[9] $\int_t^T \sigma(u)^2 \, du$. In the context of the present discussion, however, the relevance of the Feynman–Kac theorem is that today's value of the option (and of its derivatives) must therefore depend on a global quantity (an expectation taken over the *final*-maturity payoff). This is despite the fact that both the diffusive Equation (2.21) and the PDE (2.22) locally display a dependence on the value assumed by the volatility at each point in time between t and T. Furthermore, this quantity must be $\int_t^T \sigma(u)^2 \, du$, which is directly linked to the *residual* root-mean-squared volatility. The upshot of the local-replication argument combined with the Feynman–Kac theorem is therefore

- that we can value a T-maturity option at time t as if the stock price followed a geometric Brownian process with drift equal to the riskless rate, and instantaneous volatility $\sigma(\tau), t \leq \tau \leq T$; and

- that the call price will be obtained by integrating the terminal payoff over the lognormal density, ϕ:

$$\phi(\ln S_{t,T}) = \mathcal{N}((r - \tfrac{1}{2}\widehat{\sigma}^2)(T - t), \widehat{\sigma}^2(T - t)) \tag{4.27}$$

with

$$\widehat{\sigma}^2(T - t) = \int_t^T \sigma(u)^2 \, du \tag{4.28}$$

The crucial point is that the 'total variance' (4.28) does not depend on how the instantaneous volatility is apportioned between time t_0 and time T (a *local* property), but only on a *global* quantity, i.e. its total value (recall that we are dealing with a European contingent claim). Therefore, in the limit as dt goes to zero, the correct amount of stock must only depend on the *global* quantity $\widehat{\sigma}$, the *residual* root-mean-squared volatility. The conclusion is therefore that, in the presence of time-dependent volatility, one must hedge at each point in time with the root-mean-squared volatility for the residual maturity.

In the final section of this chapter I will discuss an interesting argument by Crouhy and Galai that seems to indicate that this is not always the case. I will show, however, that a dependence of the hedging ratios on the local volatility only appears when we do

---

[9] Speaking of total variance is not strictly correct. See the discussion at the end of this chapter.

not allow time-steps to become smaller and smaller. The discussion, in addition to its intrinsic interest, will therefore alert us again to the fact that discrete-time constructions are useful and intuitively appealing, but that we can easily get ourselves in trouble as soon as we begin to play 'fast and loose' with the discretization. As a rule of thumb, if an interesting result appears to depend crucially on the step-size, on a particular number of steps, or on the tree being exactly bi-, tri- or hepta-nomial, we might indeed be looking at an interesting result, but, more likely, we have simply constructed a numerical artifact.

4.5   Hedging Behaviour in Practice

The arguments presented in the previous section have provided us with a theoretical answer to the question of how one should hedge in the presence of time-dependent volatility in order to obtain perfect replication, at least in the case of frictionless markets. It is important to examine this predicted behaviour in practice by considering, for instance, to what extent 'lucky paths' truly become irrelevant as the time-step goes towards zero. We know, in fact, that the path irrelevance holds exactly true in the continuous limit, but we do not know how far this limit is in practice.

Furthermore, the theoretical answer that one should hedge using the Black formula with the residual root-mean-squared volatility is intellectually satisfying, but appears to be of little use in reality, given the fact that the trader will not know exactly the volatility function. Therefore, the following questions naturally arise. To begin with, how 'wrong' can the wrong strategies be (i.e. in this context, the strategies put in place on the basis of a wrong volatility input), and still produce an acceptable replication? What is more important in practice, choosing the correct (residual as opposed to current) root-mean-squared volatility, or re-hedging with very high frequency? What 'explains' the slippage?

The answers to all these questions go to the heart of the 'robustness' of the Black-and-Scholes approach. This property is possibly the most important feature of the Black-and-Scholes pricing framework, and is fundamental to understanding its widespread use and acceptance, even when it is well known that the underlying assumptions are poorly met in practice. The theoretical answers to some of these questions have been presented in Section 4.2.1. The practical aspects are dealt with in the following section. Recall, however, the link between the theoretical and the 'practical' dimension discussed at the beginning of Section 4.2.

4.5.1   Analysing the Replicating Portfolio

Recall that I have called 'replicating portfolio' the combination of the correct amount of stock and of cash that should reproduce the payoff of the option at expiry, and 'total portfolio' the combination of the replicating portfolio and of the option to be replicated. The total portfolio will be built to have zero value at the beginning of the strategy, and we will try to make it riskless. If we succeeded, it would therefore have zero value at any later time. 'Slippage' is then any non-zero value for the total portfolio by option expiry, i.e. the difference at expiry between the value of the replicating portfolio and the option itself. In what follows I will analyse the statistical properties of the whole distribution of the slippages. This type of analysis is very important not only when the volatility is deterministic, or when the process is a diffusion, but generally for all the models we analyse in Parts II and IV of the book.

Another quantity that I will examine and track during the course of the simulation is the sample variance of the log-price. More precisely, I will study the behaviour as a function of the hedging strategy of the path-dependent quantity, Y^k, defined as

$$Y^k = \sum_{j=1,n} \left(\ln S^k_{j+1} - \ln S^k_j \right)^2 = \sum_{j=1,n} \left(\ln \frac{S^k_{j+1}}{S^k_j} \right)^2 \equiv \sum_{j=1,n} (y^k_j)^2 \qquad (4.29)$$

where n is the number of steps used to reach the maturity of the option, and the superscript k identifies the path. It is easy to recognize that this quantity is the sample counterpart of the quadratic variation of the stock price process along a particular path, introduced in Chapter 3. Therefore it will be referred to as the sample quadratic variation.

4.5.2   Hedging Results: the Time-Dependent Volatility Case

When the volatility is time-dependent, the hedging strategy is based on the correct residual root-mean-squared volatility and the re-hedging frequency is weekly.[10] The first observation (see Figs 4.4 and 4.5) is that the distribution of the slippages appears to be centred around zero, showing that, at least on average, the replicating strategy is in this respect indeed successful. More precisely, one can say that, with the chosen re-hedging frequency the hypothesis that the mean is zero cannot be statistically rejected at a high confidence level (e.g. 95%).

Even more important is to point out that the strategy works not just in a global sense, but also path by path. This is shown by the fact that the standard deviation of the differences between the option and the portfolio goes to zero as the time-step becomes smaller and smaller. Indeed, if one plots the variance of the differences against the time-step one can see clearly a straight line through the origin. Therefore, as long as the re-hedging frequency is sufficiently high, even a highly risk-averse trader who knew the 'true' volatility would have no reason to price the option in any other way.

Table 4.1 above displays the standard deviation of the slippages as a function of the number of time-steps, and also shows the standard deviation of the returns that the trader would experience if she were to leave the option totally unhedged. In this case it is not particularly meaningful to take the ratio between the two quantities because the result retains a dependence on the size of the time-step Δt. In other situations, however, namely when perfect hedging is not possible, this ratio becomes a useful indicator, because we shall see that it does convergence to a non-zero quantity, and that, for step sizes small enough, the ratio becomes independent of the step size itself.

The full distributions of the differences are shown as a function of the step size in Figures 4.4 and 4.5. These should be compared with the distributions discussed in the next sub-section.

For each time-step size I have also collected the realized value of Y^k(the sample quadratic variation) and I display the distribution of this quantity as a function of the step size in Figures 4.6 and 4.7. In Figure 4.8 I also display as a scatter plot the co-dependence between the same quantity and the difference between the option and the

---

[10]For diffusive processes, the re-hedging frequency should always be seen in conjunction with the magnitude of the volatility, in this case of the order of 20%.

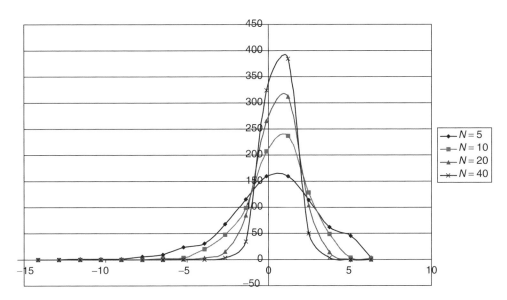

Figure 4.4   The distribution of the slippages as a function of the number of steps to the same final maturity.

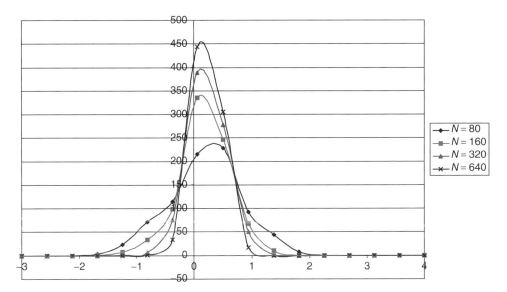

Figure 4.5   The distribution of the slippages as a function of the number of steps to the same final maturity. Note the different scale on the x-axis.

replicating portfolio. As one can appreciate from the scatter plot in Figure 4.8, the degree of dependence is very high, and the quantity Y has a high explanatory power in accounting for the deviations from zero of the slippages.

What is the origin of this strong dependence? What is happening is the following: we know that in the continuous limit lucky and unlucky paths do not exist, and if we

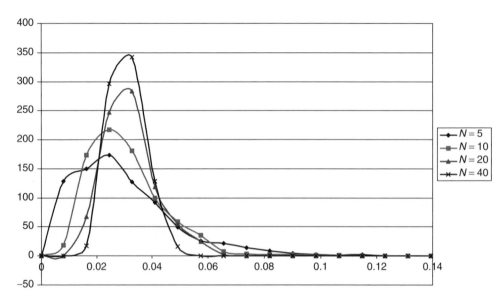

Figure 4.6   The distribution of the sample quadratic variations as a function of the number of steps to the same final maturity.

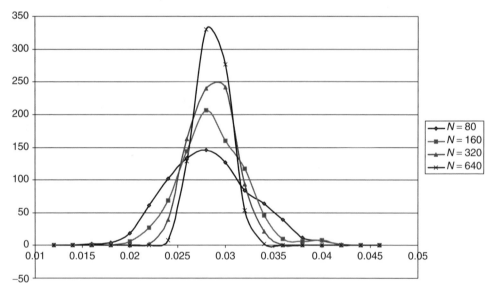

Figure 4.7   The distribution of the sample quadratic variations as a function of the number of steps to the same final maturity. Note the different scale on the *x*-axis.

were truly simulating a continuous-time diffusion, the root-mean-squared volatility of the process should always be exactly the same over a finite interval of any length. However, when we sample the process discretely (and when we can only hedge discretely) the realized value of the quadratic variation is not exactly the same over any particular path. We also know that the portfolio replication does not work perfectly along every path.

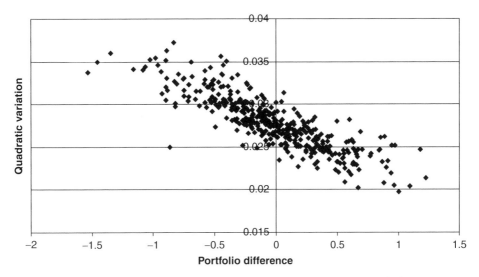

Figure 4.8 Scatter plot of the slippages and sample quadratic variations.

But these two 'imperfections' are not independent. As the figures show, they are strongly correlated: whenever the option replication did not work very well we can expect that the quadratic variation was either too large or too small.

Why is the dependence not perfect? Because I am only looking at the *terminal value* of the quadratic variation. Perhaps there was too high a sample quadratic variation in the first half of the path, and too little in the second, but, by the end, the sample quadratic variation turned out to be about right. However, this, in general, will not bring about a perfect cancellation of differences. Sins, at least in option pricing, are not washed away by virtuous deeds.

It is interesting to observe how the standard deviation of the distribution of the realized quadratic variations decays as a function of the step size. See Figure 4.9. Again, as the time-step goes to zero, lucky paths do not exist.

Even when the hedging frequency is rather low the reduction in variance with respect to the totally unhedged case is substantial. However, with the typical market-like level of volatility used for this example, in order to reduce significantly the ratio of the standard deviations one really has to hedge at least weekly. A daily re-hedging frequency gives a standard deviation of the order of a few percent of the option price. Clearly, in the presence of re-hedging costs, there would be an optimal re-hedging frequency above which the performance of the strategy quickly deteriorates.

These observations may seem rather banal in this context, but will be revisited later in the book in more complex and interesting cases (e.g. in the presence of smiles).

4.5.3 Hedging with the Wrong Volatility

The question we want to answer in this section is the following: How much poorer would the strategy have been if we had hedged our option using a wrong volatility? This question should be seen in the light of the slippages that we know will occur even in the absence of transaction costs because of the finite re-hedging frequency.

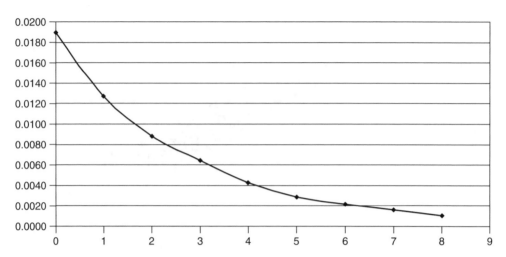

Figure 4.9   The standard deviation of the distribution of the realized quadratic variations decays as a function of the step size.

Table 4.4   Hedging with the wrong volatility. The various columns display the number of steps to the final maturity, the average value of the portfolio minus the option to be replicated, the standard deviation of the portfolio minus the option to be replicated, the average value of the option payoff, its standard deviation, the average root-mean-squared volatility experienced along the paths, the standard deviation of the distribution of the sample quadratic variations, and the correlation between the realized quadratic variations and the terminal values of the slippages.

Nsteps	Avg(P-O)	StDev(P-O)	Avg(O)	StDev(O)	Avg(rms)	StDev (QuadV)	Correlation
5	−0.50090	2.70359	6.58831	10.55644	0.16708	0.02192	−0.857
10	−0.01895	1.78371	5.92662	9.32739	0.16123	0.01329	−0.843
20	−0.09936	1.34303	5.93473	9.10734	0.16578	0.00965	−0.844
40	−0.09436	0.89565	6.28626	9.74451	0.16624	0.00671	−0.818
80	0.04469	0.65925	6.08570	9.77922	0.16527	0.00450	−0.760
160	−0.00852	0.43163	5.97867	9.37252	0.16634	0.00321	−0.687
320	0.04105	0.44749	5.60763	9.03209	0.16596	0.00225	−0.622
640	0.00328	0.35145	5.86355	9.45489	0.16632	0.00159	−0.564
1280	0.04593	0.32532	5.87182	9.57372	0.16594	0.00107	−0.327
2560	0.02847	0.29809	5.95465	9.39027	0.16578	0.00078	−0.293

The true volatility is assumed to have the same time-dependence as in the section above, but I now use a single volatility to re-hedge. Furthermore, I use the root-mean-squared volatility that prevails *at the beginning* of the simulation. Since the instantaneous volatility is decaying, we know for sure that this volatility is not only wrong, but also biased (i.e. it does not even correspond to the average correct volatility that should be used during the simulation). The results are displayed in Table 4.4.

Several features are worth noting. First of all, the slippages now no longer average zero, and there is a definite bias. Also, the variance of the slippages as a function of the

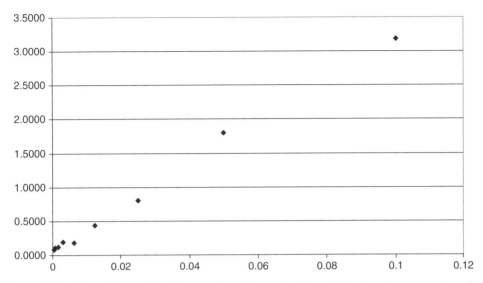

Figure 4.10 The variance of the slippages (y-axis) as a function of the step size in years (x-axis). Note that the curve does not go through the origin.

time-step is no longer a straight line through the origin, but intersects the axis of the ordinates away from the origin. See Figure 4.10.

The explanatory power of the quadratic variation in accounting for the slippage of the replicating portfolio is still very high when the re-hedging frequency is low, but drops dramatically as the time-step approaches zero: this suggests that for very small intervals Δt the main source of error does not come from the finite-sampling effects, but from the fact that we are using the wrong volatility. In other words, as the time-step goes to zero, we simply become more and more 'precisely wrong'. See again Figure 4.10.

The same message is conveyed by looking at the full distribution of the portfolio slippages. See Figure 4.11. Note how, unlike the correct-volatility case, the distributions begin to become more localized when we are in the very-large-time-step regime, but ultimately fail to become progressively narrower as the time-step size approaches zero. The same message is conveyed by the scatter plot between the sample quadratic variations and the slippages, displayed in Figure 4.12. Compare with Figure 4.8.

It is also important to point out that, up to approximately 80 time-steps, the portfolio slippage is still dominated by the finite-time-step-size effect, rather than by the mis-specification of the volatility used for hedging.

Despite these shortcomings, the results are reassuring, since they indicate that it is not necessary, at least in a Black-and-Scholes world, to know the volatility exactly to achieve a dramatic reduction in the dispersion of returns. This brings us directly to the topic of the robustness of the Black-and-Scholes model, discussed in the next section.

4.6 Robustness of the Black-and-Scholes Model

The results discussed in the previous section are very important, and they display one of the reasons why the Black-and-Scholes approach is so successful and so widely used.

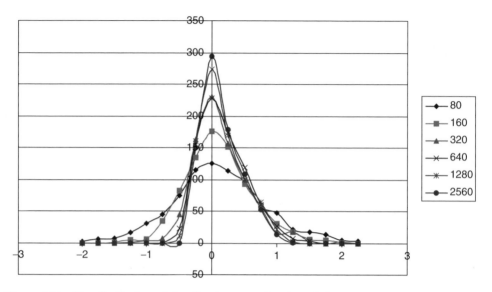

Figure 4.11   The distribution of the slippages as a function of the number of steps to the same final maturity when we hedge with the wrong volatility.

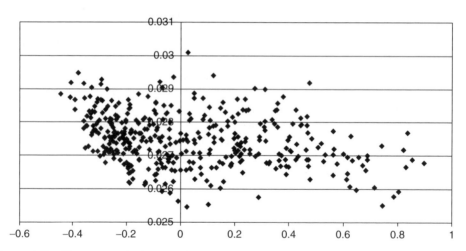

Figure 4.12   The scatter plot between the sample quadratic variations and the slippages when we hedge with the wrong volatility.

For conceptual clarity, it is important to understand on what input quantity the 'correct' hedging should depend, i.e. the residual root-mean-squared volatility. Getting this point right was the purpose of the lengthy discussion in Section 4.4. But, in reality, we can never expect to know the volatility exactly, nor do we expect it to be deterministic. Have we therefore wasted our time in establishing these correct results? No, because the computational findings presented in the previous section indicate that, even if we mis-specify the volatility, our hedging error is relatively small. Actually, up to a point the re-hedging frequency appears to be much more important in ensuring a satisfactory (albeit not perfect) replication of the option payoff. Since, in reality, transaction costs are non-zero, it is clear that the ability to transact the delta-hedging trades close to mid can matter more, for the purpose of hedging a plain-vanilla option, than making a small mistake in guessing the volatility.

The result is actually more general than these initial comments might suggest. Recall that we have concluded that what matters for a good option payoff replication is that we should hedge on the basis of the quadratic variation that is actually realized in practice. With some qualifications, it matters relatively little whether the difference between the quadratic variation assumed in our hedging and the one realized in practice arises because we used a coarse re-hedging interval, because we guessed the volatility incorrectly, or, perhaps, because the volatility was intrinsically stochastic. To some extent, even the presence of jumps would produce slippages related to the difference between the realized and the assumed quadratic variation. See Britten-Jones and Neuberger (1996) and Chapters 10, 13 and 14.

Indeed, in later chapters I will show the following interesting and surprising result. Suppose that we live in a 'complex' and incomplete world (with jumps, stochastic volatility, etc.), but that we hedge pretending that we live in a Black-and-Scholes world. If we do so, the magnitude and distribution of the slippages will be explained to a surprising extent by the distribution of the deviations of the realized quadratic variations from the constant (Black-and-Scholes) value used for hedging.

This observation provides a useful way of looking at different models: one important characterizing feature of their behaviour is the precise nature of the distribution of quadratic variations they produce. I will show in Chapter 17 that another important feature is how future smiles are correlated with future realizations of the underlying. Therefore, in a nutshell, I intend to show in the rest of this book that one key to understanding how complex models work is to analyse what distribution of quadratic variations they produce, and the other is to look at how these distributions are linked to the distribution of future values for the underlying.

For the moment, it is enough to stress that, in a diffusive setting, it is an empirical fact that the dependence of the slippages on the fine features of the distribution of quadratic variations (i.e. on features other than the terminal value) is rather mild. This constitutes the robustness of the Black-and-Scholes approach, and provides a starting point for a hedging strategy in the more complex situations when perfect replication is not possible (i.e. when we are faced with market incompleteness). It is only a mild exaggeration to say that, if the Black-and-Scholes model had not turned out to be robust in the sense above, the current prevailing pricing practice would probably be very different (see, in this context, the comments in Section 1.5).

In closing this section it is important to stress that a deterministic quadratic variation is neither necessary nor sufficient for perfect replication. Processes of the local-volatility type, for instance, produce a quadratic variation that depends on the path, yet exact perfect replication is still possible. What we cannot do in this case is simply determine the delta amount of stock by using the Black-and-Scholes formula with some appropriate value for the input volatility. This topic will be revisited in Chapter 11. Conversely, Chapter 10 will show that even if we know exactly the (deterministic) quadratic variation it might not be possible to ensure perfect replication. At this stage these comments are simply made so as not to convey a wrong impression, and their full implications will be discussed later in the book.

4.7   Is the Total Variance All That Matters?

Looking at Equation (4.29) for the quadratic variation one cannot help noticing that it coincides with the expression for the variance of the log-price in the zero-mean case. Is all this talking about quadratic variation a bit fastidious? Could we not just talk about variance? Did we really have to introduce the qualifications we did when we spoke about 'total variance'? The reason for asking these questions is that we seem to have reached the conclusion that all that matters for pricing a European option is the total variance of the price process out to expiry. We might therefore be tempted to conclude that the more familiar total variance, rather than the quadratic variation, is the all-important quantity for hedging. In reality, we have to be a bit more careful: since the drift for the stock has been chosen to be independent of the stock itself (and actually, in the simulations carried out above, for simplicity, zero), the quadratic variation ($\int_0^T \sigma_u^2 \, du$) happened to coincide with the total variance of the (logarithm of the) stock. This would no longer be true, however, if the stock price drift contained the stock price itself. This would be the case, for instance, if the process were mean reverting. Let us look at this case more carefully.

Suppose that we have a very long time series, generated by the sampling at very high frequency of a diffusion. To be more precise, we have m regularly spaced observations per day, and n days in the sample. So, the sampling interval is δt and we have $n \times m$ points altogether. Suppose now that we are interested in pricing a one-month option. We would like to estimate the volatility to use in the Black-and-Scholes formula. With the data that we have collected we can do several things. We can, for instance, calculate the variance of the percentage changes of the 'stock' price over $\frac{n}{30}$ non-overlapping 30-day periods ($n \gg 30$).[11] Let us call the quantity so estimated $\widetilde{Var}_{30}$. Alternatively, we could estimate the volatility of the quantity x, with

$$x_j \equiv \ln \frac{S_{j+1}}{S_j} \tag{4.30}$$

using $n \times m$ data points. Let us call this quantity $\widetilde{\sigma}\sqrt{\delta t}$ (with $\delta t = \frac{1}{n \times m}$). Both these quantities are meaningful and interesting, and can be estimated with the data at our disposal. However, in general they convey different information. If the process that generated the time series had been a deterministic-volatility diffusion with an at-most time-dependent drift, the sample estimates of σ and Var_{30}, $\widetilde{\sigma}$ and are $\widetilde{Var}_{30}$, respectively, would be linked by

$$Var_{30} = \int_0^T \sigma(u)^2 \, du \tag{4.31}$$

with $T = 30$ days. But if the process had been, say, a mean-reverting diffusion, this relationship would no longer be true, and

$$Var_{30} \neq \int_0^T \sigma(u)^2 \, du \tag{4.32}$$

---

[11]We actually have 30 such estimators, each associated with a different 'starting point'. However, their estimates will be strongly correlated.

This is because if the stock price follows a mean-reverting evolution, then 'high' or 'low' realizations will be pulled towards the long-term mean, and one would therefore expect the spread of the price distribution (i.e. its total variance) to be reduced with respect to the no-drift case after a finite time. So, quadratic variation and total variance do not coincide in this case and tell a different story: the quadratic variation refers to the local 'vibrational' properties of a diffusion, and the total variance refers to its overall spread after a finite time. This naturally raises the following question. Using real-world data we can estimate econometrically two quantities, the unconditional variance per unit time, or the quadratic variation. Which one is the relevant input for option pricing? This is the question addressed in the next section (and, in the case of interest rates, in Chapter 18).

4.8 Hedging Plain-Vanilla Options: Mean-Reverting Real-World Drift

In order to answer the question posed at the end of the previous section, let us now assume that in the real world the stock follows a mean-reverting process:

$$dS_t = RevSpd(RevLev - S_t)\,dt + \sigma S_t\,dz_t \tag{4.33}$$

where *RevSpd* and *RevLev* indicate the reversion speed and level of the process, and all the other symbols have the usual meaning. By Equation (4.33) the stock price will experience a deterministic pull towards the reversion level whenever it is above or below it, with a force proportional to the (positive) reversion speed. Since we have already analysed in detail the case of time-dependent volatility in the previous section, we shall hold the volatility constant in this set of simulations.

Note that the total unconditional variance of the stock process is now smaller than it would have been if the drift had been purely time-dependent (see Figure 4.13). What is the correct volatility to use in order to price the option? Is it still the total variance that matters? Or is it the instantaneous volatility (which, in this particular example, is also equal to the root-mean-squared volatility)?

In order to answer these questions let us set up the hedging portfolio neglecting the total variance, and simply using the (constant) volatility σ as the implied volatility to derive the delta amount of stock. Since we have already ascertained that in the zero-drift case the portfolio variance does go to zero with the number of time-steps in each simulation, for this exercise we will keep the number of steps constant at a value that we already know allows for a 'good' replication.

The results are shown in Tables 4.5 and 4.6. The interesting result is that the correct replication is obtained when the volatility, rather than the square root of the variance, is used to determine the delta amount of stock. Since the difference between the integral of the square of the volatility and the unconditional variance can only be due to the presence of the state variable in the drift term, we can conclude that the existence of mean reversion (in the real world!) of a stock price process does not affect the value of an option on the stock.

This result can be somewhat counterintuitive, and many practitioners find it difficult to accept. The matter is made even more confusing by the fact that mean reversion (in the risk-adjusted world!) of the short-rate process *does* affect the value of an interest-rate

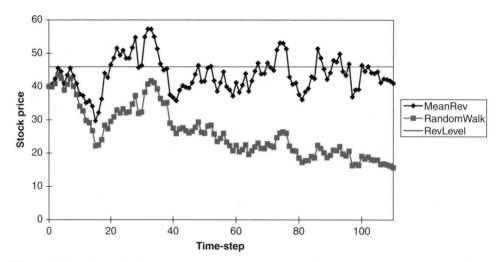

Figure 4.13   The realization of a random walk ($\mathrm{d}S/S = \sigma(t)\,\mathrm{d}z(t)$) and of a mean-reverting process ($\mathrm{d}S_t = RevSpd(RevLev - S_t)\,\mathrm{d}t + \sigma S_t\,\mathrm{d}z_t$) for the same draws of random numbers. Note how the dispersion of the stock price is more limited for the mean-reverting path. The unconditional variance out to a finite time horizon is correspondingly smaller.

option. The topic is addressed in detail in Chapter 18 (see Section 18.3 in particular), but, in the meantime, one can begin to notice that the short rate, unlike the stock price, is not a traded asset, and that, even in the interest-rate case, it is only mean reversion in the *risk-adjusted* world that matters.

Without getting ahead of ourselves, we can already conclude from the discussion in this section that the real-world unconditional variance of a financial quantity does not necessarily have any bearing on the price of an option. If it so happened that, in the real world, the drift of the underlying quantity were constant, or purely time-dependent, the statistical estimation of the finite variance of the volatility would provide equivalent information. In reality, however, very little is known about real-world drifts, and, as far as option pricing is concerned, the safe option is always to estimate volatilities, not variances.

A subtler point is worth making. For the Black-and-Scholes formula to be valid the increments of the Brownian motion must be independently distributed. However, the observation that, in the real world, the *price* increments display a non-zero serial autocorrelation does not automatically mean that the Black-and-Scholes setting is inappropriate. As long as the autocorrelation in the price time series stems from the presence of the state variable in the drift (as is the case with mean-reverting processes) the Black-and-Scholes formula can still apply. This is because the drift is 'removed' for pricing purposes, and only a lack of independence in the stochastic increments would be of concern.

Needless to say, if the estimation were carried out for risk-management, rather than option-pricing, purposes, the full real-world dynamics (drift plus volatility) become of relevance, but this is not the topic addressed here. Finally, given the results presented in Section 2.4.2, one can rest assured that the estimation of the volatility (which can only be carried out in the real world) will not be altered by the transformation to the pricing measure.

Table 4.5 This is the same as Table 4.1, with a mean reverting process for the stock price. The stock price starts above the reversion level. The volatility, rather than the variance, is used to determine the delta amount of stock using the Black-and-Scholes formula.

NumSim	Port	Option	VolLogSt	VarStock	RevSpd	Stock$_0$	VolHedge	RevLev	Vol	Nu	NumSteps	VarPort	SetUpCost
2000	2.411892	2.462435	25.762%	35.5052	0	40	24.65%	44	30.00%	1.28	20	0.189061	3.076328
2000	2.255249	2.262543	25.025%	33.4682	0	40	24.65%	44	30.00%	1.28	40	0.099507	3.076328
2000	2.307111	2.307027	24.920%	33.5025	0	40	24.65%	44	30.00%	1.28	80	0.058878	3.076328
2000	2.270595	2.271829	24.493%	32.0038	0	40	24.65%	44	30.00%	1.28	160	0.030873	3.076328
2000	2.211371	2.212849	24.742%	32.2898	0	40	24.65%	44	30.00%	1.28	320	0.020819	3.076328
2000	2.376446	2.378779	25.164%	34.1875	0	40	24.65%	44	30.00%	1.28	640	0.015308	3.076328
2000	2.328895	2.328684	24.859%	33.3366	0	40	24.65%	44	30.00%	1.28	1280	0.013299	3.076328

Table 4.6 This is the same as Table 4.5, but with a higher stock volatility.

NumSim	Port	Option	VolLogSt	VarStock	RevSpd	Stock$_0$	VolHedge	RevLev	Vol	Nu	NumSteps	VarPort	SetUpCost
2000	4.720868	4.761855	50.366%	141.6323	0	40	49.30%	44	60.00%	1.28	20	0.785646	5.23617
2000	4.342934	4.392445	48.803%	130.4295	0	40	49.30%	44	60.00%	1.28	40	0.412217	5.23617
2000	4.586365	4.610944	50.531%	139.2697	0	40	49.30%	44	60.00%	1.28	80	0.230731	5.23617
2000	4.561978	4.574208	50.625%	144.0375	0	40	49.30%	44	60.00%	1.28	160	0.129780	5.23617
2000	4.530877	4.536652	49.089%	134.6613	0	40	49.30%	44	60.00%	1.28	320	0.086335	5.23617
2000	4.54987	4.551642	48.472%	128.3429	0	40	49.30%	44	60.00%	1.28	640	0.063751	5.23617
2000	4.507015	4.507239	49.865%	132.8913	0	40	49.30%	44	60.00%	1.28	1280	0.049711	5.23617

4.9   Hedging Plain-Vanilla Options: Finite Re-Hedging Intervals Again

When hedging can be carried out as frequently as one wants without incurring any transaction costs, we have obtained in this chapter the important result that the relevant quantity to determine the appropriate hedge ratio is a global function(al) of the residual volatility $\left(\int_t^T \sigma(u)^2\,\mathrm{d}u\right)$, and not a function of the local volatility, σ_t.

We have seen that, if the hedging intervals are finite, then the trader will in general experience a non-zero variance of portfolio returns. In carrying out these tests we have implicitly assumed that, irrespective of whether the volatility is constant or time-dependent, the optimal hedging strategy would still depend on the same quantity, i.e. would be based only on the value of the quantity $\int_t^T \sigma(u)^2\,\mathrm{d}u$. In the light of the discussion in the previous section we should refrain from calling this integral the variance *tout court*, but, if we restrict our attention to the risk-neutral world (where the drift is purely $r(t)$), the total variance does indeed coincide with the time integral of the square of the volatility. In this section, therefore, and with this proviso clearly in mind, we will use the term 'total variance' interchangeably with the expression 'the time integral of the square of the volatility'.

Crouhy and Galai (1995) present an interesting argument that appears to question this assumption. If the re-hedging interval is fixed, they show that the optimal hedge depends neither only on the total variance nor purely on the instantaneous volatility, but on a combination of the two. In order to understand this result more clearly, the Crouhy-and-Galai construction is presented below, both because of its intrinsic interest, and because it is often claimed that the conclusions they reach can be of practical relevance for the choice of volatility with which to compute the optimal hedge.

4.9.1   The Crouhy–Galai Set-Up

Let us consider a two-period problem in two separate universes. In the first, the instantaneous volatility is 10% over the first period, and 20% over the second; in the second universe the volatilities are reversed. The two periods are of equal length. The total variance in both universes is therefore the same. If we could trade (and therefore re-hedge) continuously, we know that the optimal hedge would simply depend on the quantity

$$TotVar = (0.10^2 + 0.20^2)\Delta t \tag{4.34}$$

where Δt is the length of each time period. Let us impose, however, that we can only trade once in each time period (at the beginning), and that the length of each time period cannot be altered. Let us then construct a 'bushy' (i.e. non-recombining) tree that locally matches the two moments of the distribution of the underlying. For simplicity, we will assume zero interest rates. See Figures 4.14–4.17.

Figures 4.14 and 4.15 show the stock prices in the two universes, and Figures 4.16 and 4.17 the option values and the delta amount of stock calculated as

$$\frac{Opt_{\text{up}} - Opt_{\text{down}}}{S_{\text{up}} - S_{\text{down}}} \tag{4.35}$$

Factor	1.10517	1.2214
p(up)	0.47502	0.4502
p(down)	0.52498	0.5498
d	0.90484	0.8187
u	1.10517	1.2214
Vol	10%	20%

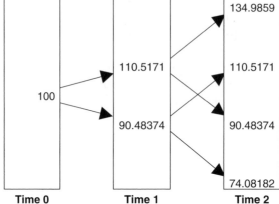

Figure 4.14 The stock price in universe *a*, where the volatility is equal to 10% over the first period, and 20% over the second. The stock moves up to S_u and down to S_d, with $u = Factor$, $d = 1/u$, $Factor = \exp(\sigma\sqrt{\Delta t})$, $p(\text{up}) = (1 - d)/(u - d)$, $p(\text{down}) = 1 - p(\text{up})$.

Factor	1.22140	1.10517
p(up)	0.45017	0.47502
p(down)	0.54983	0.5250
d	0.81873	0.9048
u	1.22140	1.1052
Vol	20%	10%

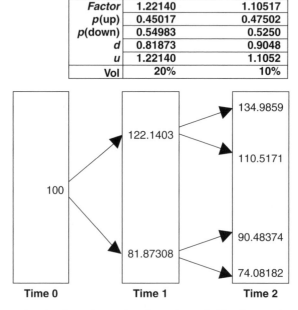

Figure 4.15 The stock price in universe *b*, where the volatility is equal to 20% over the first period, and 10% over the second. All the symbols have the same meaning as in Figure 4.14.

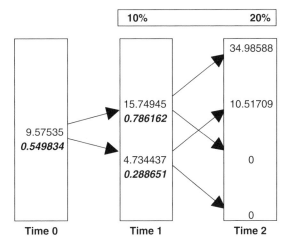

Figure 4.16 The call option value for strike 100 in universe a and the delta amount $\frac{Opt_{up}-Opt_{down}}{S_{up}-S_{down}}$ shown in bold italics.

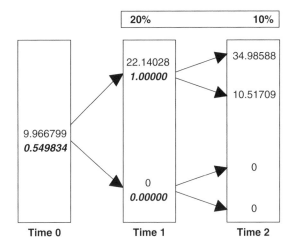

Figure 4.17 The call option value for strike 100 in universe b and the delta amount $\frac{Opt_{up}-Opt_{down}}{S_{up}-S_{down}}$ shown in bold italics.

Note that the delta amounts do not depend on the probabilities for the up and down jumps (see the discussion in Chapter 2), and that they are vastly different in the two universes. For the particular value of the strike chosen, the delta amount at the origin happens to be exactly the same, but, as Crouhy and Galai (CG in what follows) point out, for any other value of the strike it is in general different. (The actual numerical values I obtain are somewhat different from CG's paper because I have chosen zero interest rates, and a different discretization scheme.)

A few comments are in order. To begin with, when one lets the time-step approach zero, as in most applications one would certainly want to do, the actual discretization scheme becomes conceptually irrelevant, and only affects the speed of convergence. Therefore, as Δt goes to zero, the up state can be equivalently modelled as $S_{\text{up}} = S_{\text{old}}(1 + \sigma \sqrt{\Delta t})$, $S_{\text{up}} = S_{\text{old}} \exp(\sigma \sqrt{\Delta t})$, $S_{\text{up}} = S_{\text{old}}(1 + \sigma \sqrt{\Delta t} + \frac{1}{2}\sigma^2 \Delta t)$, or in a variety of other asymptotically equivalent ways. In CG's approach, however, the time-step cannot be allowed to be reduced at will. Different values will therefore be obtained for the state variable, the option price, and its delta, depending on which of the (only asymptotically equivalent) discretization schemes is chosen. Given that CG impose a fixed re-hedging interval, these differences cannot be ignored.

Note that the fixed re-hedging assumption is crucial and is justified by CG (1995) as follows:

> ... because of transaction costs and other execution problems, hedges are re-adjusted discretely, often once a day, or even once a week. The issue of the appropriate volatility measure becomes important in such a trading environment.

With this observation in mind, we plot in Figure 4.18 the delta in the two universes for a variety of strikes between the values where the deltas are exactly equal to one or zero for both volatility regimes. Notice that, in this figure, there are three distinct linear segments for the delta amount, with different slopes and three intersection points: the two 'degenerate' levels at which all the nodes in the tree are in or out of the money, giving a delta of one or zero, and the at-the-money level. If we had subdivided the same trading interval into more and more steps the two different delta curves would have crossed at correspondingly more and more points, and would have progressively begun to merge into each other. Note again, however, that, given the constant-re-hedging-interval assumption, this limiting process cannot be undertaken. Therefore, as a first observation, one can say that, for the CG effect to be significant, the length of each time-step must be of the same order of magnitude as the residual time to expiry.

The second necessary condition for the CG effect to be 'strong' is that the volatility should be significantly non-constant in both universes over the (short) residual life. In the examples above, it either doubled or halved, depending on the universe, in going from the

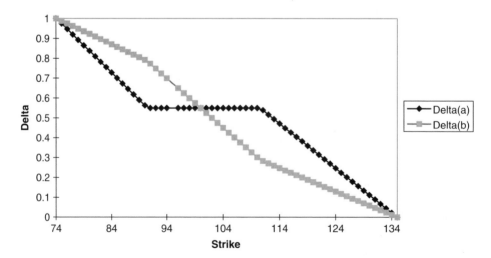

Figure 4.18   The delta amount of stock to hold at the origin (today) in the two universes.

first to the second and last step. This, however, is hardly realistic if the residual maturity is short. If coupled with the first necessary condition ('few' steps), the second requires for the effect to be important that the trading environment should be one of strongly non-constant volatility, the option-maturity-to-time-step ratio small, and the re-hedging periods few.

This observation gives a first indication that the effect presented by CG, while conceptually interesting, is perhaps not very relevant for practical hedging purposes. To use CG's numbers, if one considers the case of only two subdivision periods the deltas for the two universes are indeed significantly different: 0.90 and 0.68 for a K/S ratio of 0.90, and 0.43 and 0.67 for a K/S ratio of 1.1. Simply adding two more steps, however, already makes the deltas very similar (0.85 vs 0.84 for $K/S = 0.90$, and 0.65 vs 0.63 for $K/S = 1.1$).

To look at the problem in a different light, one could ask two related questions: Would a trader really keep her re-hedging interval constant if she were within a day or two of option expiry, and the spot level were roughly at the money? and Would the same trader really expect the volatility to be not only time-dependent, but predictably so, over such a short trading period?

There is, however, a second, and, in my opinion, fundamental rather than practical objection to the CG reasoning. One of the apparent strengths of the CG approach is that the construction of their deltas does not rely on the discretization of a limiting process, or on an asymptotically correct matching of moments. The delta amounts they obtain in the two universes are exactly the amounts needed to replicate in discrete time the final and intermediate option payoffs at the various nodes, given the knowledge of the possible realizations of the underlying in the different 'up' and 'down' states. In Chapter 2 I gave a thorough discussion of this construction, and, in particular, of its limiting properties. CG's observations are certainly correct. The real interest of the two-state, discrete-time dynamics, however, does not lie in the fact that we truly believe that over each time-step only two realizations will be possible for the stock price. After all, if three, instead of two, states were reachable, a possibility that makes as much, or as little, financial sense as the binomial-branching assumption, one would obtain the financially very 'ugly' result that another asset would have to be added in order to replicate the payoff with certainty. The real appeal of the binomial construction lies therefore not in its descriptive realism, but in the fact that, in the limit as Δt goes to zero, two suitably chosen states are all that is needed in order to discretize a continuous Gaussian process. This justification, however, cannot be invoked in CG's setting, since it is crucial to their argument that the trading interval should remain of fixed length as the option maturity approaches. This being the case, no special meaning can be attached to the requirement that each move in the bushy tree should only lead to an 'up' or a 'down' state. Needless to say, if three, or more, states had been allowed, one would have had to introduce correspondingly more securities depending on the same underlying (presumably other options) to replicate exactly all the payoffs, and the resulting delta amounts of stock would have been different.

Given the arbitrariness, for a fixed time-step size, of the choice of two as the number of states to which the stock price can migrate, and the considerations about the actual trading frequency close to expiry put forth in the previous paragraph, it seems fair to say that the effect presented by CG, while interesting, should not be of serious concern to traders in their hedging practice. More generally, this example shows that discretizations must be handled with care, and that results that are not robust to letting the time-step go to zero, or that rely on the computational details of the construction (e.g. number of branches, recombination, etc.), should in general be regarded with suspicion.

Chapter 5

Instantaneous and Terminal Correlation

5.1 Correlation, Co-Integration and Multi-Factor Models

The importance of correlation has often been emphasized, both in the academic literature and by practitioners, in the context of the pricing of derivatives instruments whose payoffs depend on the joint realizations of several prices or rates. Examples of derivative products for which correlation is important are:

1. basket options: often calls or puts on some linear combinations of equity indices or of individual stocks;

2. swaptions: calls or puts on a swap rate, where the latter is seen as a linear combination of imperfectly-correlated forward rates;

3. spread options: calls or puts on the difference between two reference assets (e.g. equity indices) or rates (typical examples could be the spread between, say, the 2- and 10-year swap rates in currency A, or the spread between the 10-year swap rate in currency A and the 10-year swap rates in currency B);

4. tranched credit derivatives: their price will depend on the correlation among the credit spreads of (or, in certain models, on the default correlation among) a certain number of reference assets.

The observation that 'correlation is important' in the pricing of these types of option is not controversial. It is important, however, to understand precisely what correlation can and cannot achieve. To this effect, consider the SDEs of two diffusive variables, say x_1 and x_2:

$$dx_1 = \mu_1 \, dt + \sigma_{11} \, dz_1 \tag{5.1}$$

$$dx_2 = \mu_2 \, dt + \sigma_{21} \, dz_1 + \sigma_{22} \, dz_2 \tag{5.2}$$

with orthogonal increments dz_1 and dz_2. The coefficient of linear correlation between x_1 and x_2, ρ_{12}, is

$$\rho_{12} = \frac{E[dx_1\,dx_2]}{\sqrt{E[dx_1^2]E[dx_2^2]}} = \frac{\sigma_{11}\sigma_{21}}{\sqrt{(\sigma_{11}\sigma_{21})^2 + (\sigma_{11}\sigma_{22})^2}}$$

For simplicity set the drift terms to zero, and consider the new variable $y = x_1 + \lambda x_2$:

$$dy = \sigma_{11}\,dz_1 + \lambda\,(\sigma_{21}\,dz_1 + \sigma_{22}\,dz_2)$$
$$= (\sigma_{11} + \lambda\sigma_{21})\,dz_1 + \lambda\sigma_{22}\,dz_2 \tag{5.3}$$

In general the variable y will be normally distributed, with zero mean and instantaneous variance $\mathrm{var}(y) = \left[(\sigma_{11} + \lambda\sigma_{21})^2 + (\lambda\sigma_{22})^2\right] dt$. After a finite time t, its distribution will be

$$y \sim \mathcal{N}(0, [(\sigma_{11} + \lambda\sigma_{21})^2 + (\lambda\sigma_{22})^2]t) \tag{5.4}$$

Now choose λ such that the coefficient in dz_1 for the increment dy is zero:

$$\lambda = -\frac{\sigma_{11}}{\sigma_{21}} \tag{5.5}$$

It is easy to see that this value of λ gives the lowest possible variance (dispersion) to the variable y:

$$y \sim \mathcal{N}(0, \lambda^2\sigma_{22}^2 t), \quad \lambda = -\frac{\sigma_{11}}{\sigma_{21}} \tag{5.6}$$

If λ were equal to -1 the variable y would simply give the spread between x_1 and x_2, and in this case

$$y \sim \mathcal{N}(0, [(\sigma_{11} - \sigma_{21})^2 + (\sigma_{22})^2]t), \quad \lambda = -1 \tag{5.7}$$

Equation (5.7) tells us that, no matter how strong the correlation between the two variables might be, as long as it is not 1, the variance of their spread, or, for that matter, of any linear combination between them, will grow indefinitely over time. Therefore, a linear correlation coefficient does not provide a mechanism capable of producing long-term 'cohesion' between diffusive state variables.

Sometimes this is perfectly appropriate. At other times, however, we might believe that, as two stochastic variables move away from each other, there should be 'physical' (financial) mechanisms capable of pulling them together. This might be true, for instance, for yields or forward rates. Conditional on our knowing that, say, the 9.5-year yield in 10 years' time is at 5.00%, we would expect the 10-year yield to be 'not too far apart', say, somewhere between 4.50% and 5.50%. In order to achieve this long-term effect by means of a correlation coefficient we might be forced to impose too strong a correlation between the two yields for the short-term dynamics between the two variables to be correct. Or, conversely, a correlation coefficient calibrated to the short-term changes in the two yields is likely to predict a variance for the difference between the two yields considerably higher than what we might consider reasonable.

In order to describe a long-term link between two variables (or, indeed, a collection of variables) we require a different concept, namely co-integration. In general, co-integration occurs when two time series are each integrated of order b, but some linear combination of them is integrated of order $a < b$. Typically, for finance applications, $b = 1$ and $a = 0$. (For a discussion of co-integration see Alexander (2001) for a simple introduction, or Hamilton (1994) for a more thorough treatment.) In a diffusive context, this means that the spread(s) between the co-integrated variables is of the mean-reverting type. More generally, Granger (1986) and Engle and Granger (1987) have shown that if a set of variables is co-integrated an error-correction model, i.e. a process capable of pulling them together, must be present among them.

Why is this relevant in the context of our discussion? Let us lay down the 'facts' in order.

1. Several studies suggest that forward rates of a given yield curve should be co-integrated. See, for example, Alexander (2001). Let us accept this as a fact.

2. In the real world, if these forward rates are co-integrated, they will not disperse 'too much' relative to each other, even after very long time periods.

3. Just positing a correlation structure among the forward rates is not capable of providing the necessary long-term cohesion mechanism among forward rates *in a manner consistent with their short-term dynamics.*

4. In a diffusive setting, in order to describe simultaneously the short-term correlation and the long-term co-integration among forward rates one must introduce error-correction (mean-reverting) terms.

These statements are all true in the real world. They would seem to suggest that, even if *individually* the forward rates followed exactly a diffusive process, in order to price a long-dated option it would be inadequate to describe the nature of their co-dependence simply by means of a correlation matrix. This statement however is not necessarily correct. Even if the underlying forward rates are indeed co-integrated, and even if a correlated diffusion disperses them far too much when compared with the real world, this does not matter for option pricing because, in the diffusive setting, the error-correction (mean-reverting) term appears in the *drift* of the state variables. And we have seen in Chapter 4, the real-world drift does not matter (in a perfect Black-and-Scholes world) for option pricing.[1]

This important caveat is the exact counterpart of the statement proved in Section 4.7 that quadratic variation, and not variance, is what matters for single-asset Black-and-Scholes option pricing. In a single-asset case, what matters are the local 'vibrational' properties of the underlying, not how much it will disperse after a finite period of time. Similarly, in a multi-factor setting, it is guessing the relationship between the *local* vibrations of the underlying assets relative to each other that will allow the trader to set up a successful hedging strategy, not estimating their long-term relative dispersion. In a Black-and-Scholes world, option traders do not engage in actuarial pricing (for which variance and long-term relative dispersion *do* matter), but do engage in local riskless replication.

---

[1] See also the discussion in Sections 18.2 and 18.3.

Therefore in what follows I will focus on the correlation matrix as the only mechanism necessary to describe the link between a set of underlying variables, even if we know that in the real world this might not be appropriate. In particular, we will consider time-dependent volatilities and an imperfect correlation as the only mechanisms relevant for derivatives pricing to produce changes in the shape of a given yield curve. This topic is addressed in the next section.

5.1.1   The Multi-Factor Debate

Historically, the early response to the need of creating mechanisms capable of producing changes in the shape of the yield curve was to invoke multi-factor models. Taking inspiration from the results of principal component analysis (PCA), the early (one-factor) models were seen as capable of moving the first eigenvector (the level of the curve), but ineffectual in achieving a change in slope, curvature, etc. At least two or three independent modes of deformation were therefore seen as necessary to produce the required degree of shape change in the yield curve.

The PCA eigenmodes are orthogonal by construction. When the 'reference axes' of the eigenvectors are translated from the principal components back to the forward rates, however, the latter become imperfectly instantaneously correlated. Therefore the need to produce a change in shape in the yield curve made early modellers believe that the introduction of several, imperfectly correlated, Brownian shocks would be the solution to the problem. Furthermore, Rebonato and Cooper (1995) showed that, in order to model a financially convincing instantaneous correlation matrix, a surprisingly large number of factors was required. Therefore, the reasoning went, to produce what we want (changes in the shape of the yield curve) we require a sufficiently rich and realistic instantaneous correlation matrix, and this, in turn, requires many Brownian factors. In the early-to-mid-1990s high-dimension yield-curve models became, in the eyes of traders and researchers, the answer and the panacea to the pricing problems of the day.

To some extent this is correct. Let us not lose sight, however, of what we are trying to achieve, and let us not confuse our goals with (some of) the means to achieve them. The logical structure of the problem is schematically as follows.

- The introduction of complex derivatives payoffs highlights the need for models that allow the yield curves to change shape. This is a true statement, and a model that allows changes in shape in the yield curve is our goal.

- If one works with instantaneously imperfectly correlated forward rates, the yield curve will change shape over time. This is also a true statement.

- If we want to recover a financially convincing instantaneous correlation structure, many factors are needed. This, too, is a true statement.

- Therefore the imperfect correlation among rates created by a many-factor model is what we require in order to obtain our goal. *This does not necessarily follow.*

The last step, in fact, implies that an imperfect degree of instantaneous correlation is the *only* mechanism capable of producing significant relative moves among rates. But this is not true. Imposing an instantaneous correlation coefficient less than one can certainly produce some degree of independent movement in a set of variables that follows a diffusion. But this is neither the only, nor, very often, the most financially desirable tool by means of which a change in the shape of the yield curve can be achieved. What else can produce our goal (the change in shape in the yield curve)? I show below that introducing time-dependent volatilities can constitute a powerful, and often financially more desirable, alternative mechanism in order to produce the same effect.

If this is the case, in the absence of independent financial information it is not clear which mechanism one should prefer. Indeed, the debate about the number of factors 'really' needed for yield-curve modelling was still raging as late as 2002: Longstaff *et al.* (2000a) argue that a billion dollars are being thrown away in the swaption market by using low-dimensionality models; Andersen and Andreasen (2001) rebut that even a one-factor model, as long as well implemented, is perfectly adequate; Joshi and Theis (2002) provide an alternative perspective on the topic. Without entering this debate (I express my views on the matter in Rebonato (2002)), in the context of the present discussion one can say that the relative effectiveness and the financial realism of the two mechanisms that can give rise to changes in the shape of the yield curve must be carefully weighed in each individual application.

It therefore appears that our goal (i.e. the ability to produce a change in the shape of the yield curve) can be produced by different combinations of the two mechanisms mentioned so far. If this is the case, perhaps different 'amounts' of de-correlation and of time variation of the volatility can produce similar effects, in so far as changes in the shape of the yield curve are concerned. Is there a quantitative measure of how successful we have been in creating the desired effect, *whatever means we have employed*? Surely, this indicator cannot be the coefficient of instantaneous correlation, because, as stated above and proved later in this chapter, a substantial de-coupling between different portions of the yield curve can occur even when we use a one-factor model. The answer is positive, and the quantity that takes into account the combined effects of time-dependent volatilities and of imperfect correlations is the *terminal* correlation, which I define and discuss in Section 5.3. In the following sections I will therefore tackle the following topics:

- I will draw a distinction between *instantaneous* and *terminal* correlation.

- I will show that it is the terminal and not the instantaneous correlation that matters for derivatives pricing.

- I will then proceed to show how a non-constant instantaneous volatility can give rise to substantial *terminal* de-correlation among the underlying variables even when the instantaneous correlation is very high (or, indeed, perfect).

- Having explained why we need a judicious combination of time-dependent volatilities and imperfect instantaneous correlation, I will discuss how a 'naïve' Monte Carlo simulation can be carried out in this setting.

- Finally, I will show how a conceptually more satisfactory and computationally more efficient Monte Carlo valuation can be carried out in this time-dependent environment.

The last point has an intrinsic (i.e. computational) interest. It is even more important, however, for its conceptual relevance. Since this book deals only in passing with numerical techniques, the main reason for discussing it in this chapter is that it shows with great clarity how terminal correlation enters the pricing of derivatives products, and how the role of instantaneous correlation is, in a way, secondary. Again, *instantaneous* correlation is just one of the mechanisms available to produce what we really want (namely, *terminal* correlation).

5.2   The Stochastic Evolution of Imperfectly Correlated Variables

In order to get a qualitative feel for the problem, let us begin by considering the evolution of two log-normally distributed quantities (rates or prices), that we shall denote by x_1 and x_2, respectively:

$$\frac{dx_1}{x_1} = \mu_1 \, dt + \sigma_1(t) \, dw_1 \tag{5.8}$$

$$\frac{dx_2}{x_2} = \mu_2 \, dt + \sigma_2(t) \, dw_2 \tag{5.9}$$

The two Brownian increments, dw_1 and dw_2, are assumed to be imperfectly correlated, and we will therefore write

$$\mathrm{E}[dw_1 \, dw_2] = \rho \, dt \tag{5.10}$$

Note that we have explicitly allowed for the possibility of time dependence in the two volatilities. Also, we have appended an index (1 or 2) to the volatility symbol to emphasize that by $\sigma_1(t)$ and $\sigma_2(t)$ we denote the volatility of different prices or rates at the same time, t (and not the volatility of the same spot process at different times). Let us then choose a final time horizon, T, and let us impose that the unconditional variance of each variable over this time horizon should be exactly the same:

$$\int_0^T \sigma_1(u)^2 \, du = \int_0^T \sigma_2(u)^2 \, du = \widehat{\sigma}^2 T \tag{5.11}$$

For the sake of simplicity, let us finally assume that both variables start at time zero from the same value:

$$x_1(0) = x_2(0) = x_0 \tag{5.12}$$

Let us now run two Monte Carlo simulations of the stock price processes out to time T. For the first simulation, we will use constant volatilities for σ_1 and σ_2 (and therefore, given requirement (5.11), the volatility is the same for x_1 and x_2 and equal to $\widehat{\sigma}$ for both variables), but a coefficient of instantaneous correlation less than one. When running the second simulation, we will instead use two time-dependent instantaneous volatilities as in Equations (5.8) and (5.9) (albeit constrained by Equation (5.11)), but perfect correlation. To be more specific, for the first variable, x_1, we will assign the instantaneous volatility

$$\sigma_1(t) = \sigma_0 \exp(-\nu t), \quad 0 \le t \le T \tag{5.13}$$

with $\sigma_0 = 20\%$, $\nu = 0.64$ and $T = 4$ years. The second variable, x_2, will have an instantaneous volatility given by

$$\sigma_2(t) = \sigma_0 \exp[-\nu(T - t)], \quad 0 \le t \le T \tag{5.14}$$

The reader can check that the variance Equation (5.11) is indeed satisfied.

Having set up the problem in this manner, we can simulate the joint processes for x_1 and x_2 in the two different universes. In the time-dependent case the two variables were subjected to the same Brownian shocks. In the constant-volatility case two different Brownian shocks, correlated as per Equation (5.10), were allowed to shock the two variables. After running a large number of simulations, we ignored our knowledge of the volatility of the two processes and evaluated the correlation between the changes in the logarithms of the two variables in the two simulations using the expression

$$\rho_{1,2} = \frac{\sum_i \left(\ln x_1^i - \overline{\ln x_1}\right)\left(\ln x_2^i - \overline{\ln x_2}\right)}{\sqrt{\sum_i \left(\ln x_1^i - \overline{\ln x_1}\right)^2 \sum_i \left(\ln x_2^i - \overline{\ln x_2}\right)^2}} \tag{5.15}$$

The results of these trials are shown in Figures 5.1 and 5.2.

Looking at these two figures, it is not surprising to discover that the same sample correlation (in this case $\rho_{1,2} = 34.89\%$) was obtained despite the fact that the two de-correlation-generating mechanisms were very different.

For clarity of exposition, in this stylized case a very strongly time-varying volatility was assigned to the two variables. It is therefore easy to tell which figure is produced by which mechanism: note how in Figure 5.1 the changes for Series 1 are large

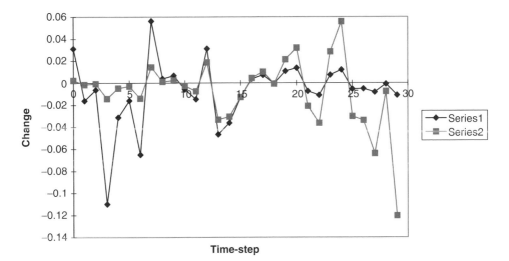

Figure 5.1 Changes in the variables x_1 and x_2. The two variables were subjected to the same random shocks (instantaneous correlation = 1). The first variable (Series 1) had an instantaneous volatility given by $\sigma_1(t) = \sigma_0 \exp(-\nu t)$, $0 \le t \le T$, with $\sigma_0 = 20\%$, $\nu = 0.64$ and $T = 4$ years. The second variable (Series 2) had an instantaneous volatility given by $\sigma_2(t) = \sigma_0 \exp[-\nu(T - t)]$, $0 \le t \le T$. The empirical sample correlation turned out to be 34.89%.

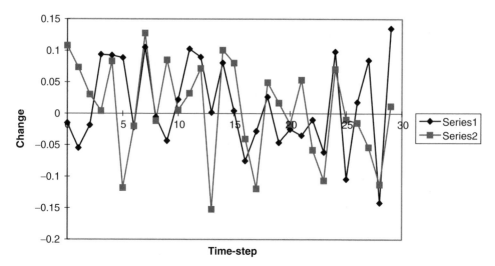

Figure 5.2   Changes in the variables x_1 and x_2. The two variables were subjected to different random shocks (instantaneous correlation = 35.00%). Both variables had the same constant instantaneous volatility of $\sigma_0 = 20\%$. The empirical sample correlation turned out to be 34.89%.

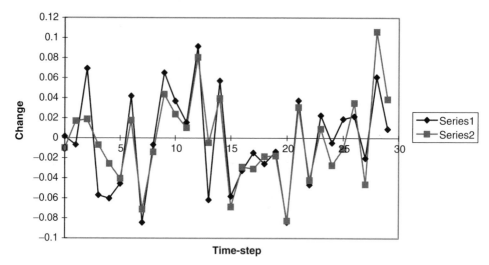

Figure 5.3   Can the reader guess, before looking below, whether this realization was obtained with constant volatility and a correlation of 85%, or with a correlation of 90% and a decay constant v of 0.2? The sample correlation turned out to be 85%.

at the beginning and small at the end (and vice versa for Series 2), while they have roughly the same magnitude for the two series in Figure 5.2. In a more realistic case, however, where the correlation is high but not perfect and the decay factor v not as pronounced, it can become very difficult to distinguish the two cases 'by inspection'. See Figure 5.3.

Table 5.1 The data used to produce Figure 5.4. Note the greater decrease in sample correlation produced by the non-constant volatility when the instantaneous correlation is high.

Instantaneous correlation	Decay constant			
	0.2	0.4	0.6	0.8
1	0.973944	0.90183	0.837356	0.720101
0.8	0.80604	0.705876	0.675758	0.573349
0.6	0.626561	0.470971	0.475828	0.338425
0.4	0.334509	0.330294	0.332757	0.285563
0.2	0.25877	0.172208	0.173178	0.129632
0	0.062323	−0.12066	−0.09665	0.091779

In principle, it is of course possible to analyse the two time series separately beforehand in order to establish the possible existence of time dependence in the volatility function. Armed with this information, the trader could, again in principle, analyse the joint dynamics of the two variables, and estimate an instantaneous correlation coefficient. In practice, however, these statistical studies are fraught with difficulties, and, especially if the instantaneous volatility is mildly time dependent and the correlation relatively high, the task of disentangling the two effects can be extremely difficult. See Figure 5.3.

Unfortunately, the case of mildly-varying instantaneous volatilities and of relatively high instantaneous correlations is the norm rather than the exception when one deals with the dynamics of forward rates belonging to the same yield curve. The combined effects of the two de-correlating mechanisms are priced in the relative implied volatilities of caps and swaptions (see the discussion in Section 10.3), and even relatively 'stressed' but still realistic assumptions for the correlation and volatility produce rather fine differences in the relative prices (of the order of one to three percentage points – vegas – in implied volatility).

In order to study the relative importance of the two possible mechanisms to produce de-correlation, Table 5.1 and Figure 5.4 show the sample correlation between log-changes in the two time series obtained by running many times the simulation experiment described in the captions to Figures 5.1 and 5.2, with the volatility decay constant (v) and the instantaneous correlation shown in the table. More precisely, the first row displays the sample correlation obtained for a series of simulations conducted using perfect instantaneous correlation and more and more strongly time-dependent volatilities (decay constants v of 0.2, 0.4, 0.6 and 0.8); the second row displays the sample correlation obtained with the same time-dependent volatilities and an instantaneous correlation of 0.8; and so on.

The important conclusion that one can draw from these data is that a non-constant instantaneous volatility brings about a relatively more pronounced de-correlation when the instantaneous correlation is high. In particular, when this latter quantity is zero, a non-constant instantaneous volatility does not bring about any further reduction in the sample correlation (apart from adding some noise). From these observations one can therefore conclude that the volatility-based de-correlation mechanism should be of greater relevance in the case of same-currency forward rates, than in the case of equities or FX rates.

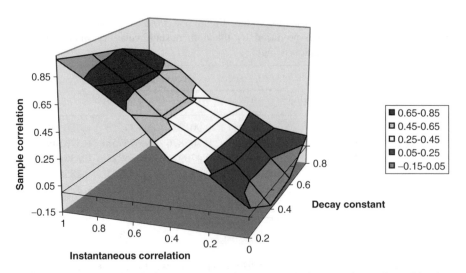

Figure 5.4   The sample correlation evaluated along the path for a variety of combinations of the instantaneous correlation (from 1 to 0) and of the decay constant v (from 0.2 to 0.8). Note how the decrease in sample correlation introduced by the time dependence of volatility is more pronounced the higher the instantaneous correlation. Regimes of high instantaneous correlations are more commonly found in the same-currency interest-rate case, than for equities or FX.

In this section I have tried to give a qualitative feel for the impact on the sample correlation of a time-dependent instantaneous volatility, and of a less-than-perfect instantaneous correlation. At this stage I have kept the discussion at a very qualitative level. In particular, it is not obvious at this point why the terminal, rather then the instantaneous, correlation should be of relevance for option pricing. The discussions in Chapters 2 and 4 about volatilities and variances should make us rather cautious before deciding on the basis of 'intuition' which quantities matter when it comes to pricing an option. The purpose of the next section is therefore to identify in a more precise manner the quantities that affect the joint stochastic evolution of correlated financial variables, in so far as option pricing is concerned.

The analysis will be carried out by considering a 'thought Monte Carlo experiment', but the main focus is more on the conceptual part, rather than on the description of a numerical technique. In order to carry out and analyse these Monte Carlo experiments we will have to discretize Ito integrals, and to make use of some basic results in stochastic integration. These topics are therefore briefly introduced, but in a very non-technical manner. I have reported some results without proof, and provided very sketchy and hand-waving proofs for others. For the reader who would like to study the matter more deeply, the references provided below can be of assistance. For a clear treatment intermediate in length between an article and a slim book, I can recommend the course notes by Shreve (1997). Standard, book-length, references are then Oksendal (1995), Lamberton and Lapeyre (1991), Neftci (1996) and Baxter and Rennie (1996). If the reader were to fall in love with stochastic calculus, Karatzas and Shreve (1991) is properly the bible, but the amount of work required is substantial. Finally, good and simple treatments of selected topics can be found in Bjork (1998) (e.g. for stochastic integrals) and Pliska (1997) (e.g. for filtrations).

5.3 The Role of Terminal Correlation in the Joint Evolution of Stochastic Variables

In what follows we will place ourselves in a perfect Black(-and-Scholes) world. In particular, in addition to the usual assumptions about the market structure, we will require that the spot or forward underlying variables should be log-normally distributed. As a consequence, we will ignore at this stage the possibility of any smiles in the implied volatility. Smile effects are discussed in Part II. Our purpose is to identify what quantities are essential in order to carry out the stochastic part of the evolution of the underlying variables. We will obtain the fundamental result that, in addition to volatilities, a quantity that we will call 'terminal correlation' will play a crucial role. This quantity will be shown to be in general distinct from the instantaneous correlation; in particular, it can assume very small values even if the instantaneous correlation is perfect. In this sense, the treatment to be found in this section formalizes and justifies the discussion in the previous sections of this chapter, and in Chapter 2. *En route* to obtaining these results we will also indicate how efficient Monte Carlo simulations can be carried out.

In order to obtain these results it is important to recall some definitions regarding stochastic integrals. This is undertaken in the next section.

5.3.1 Defining Stochastic Integrals

Let us consider a stochastic process, σ, and a standard Wiener process, Z, defined over an interval $[a\ b]$.[2] Since σ can be a stochastic process, and not just a deterministic function of time, one cannot simply require that it should be square integrable. A more appropriate condition is that the *expectation* of its square should be integrable over the interval $[a\ b]$:

$$\int_a^b E[\sigma^2(u)]\,\mathrm{d}u < \infty \qquad (5.16)$$

The second requirement that should be imposed on the process σ is that it should be adapted to the filtration generated by the Wiener process, Z.[3] Our goal is to give a meaning to the expression

$$\int_a^b \sigma(u)\,\mathrm{d}Z(u) \qquad (5.17)$$

for all functions σ satisfying the two conditions above. The task is accomplished in two steps.

Step 1: Let us divide the interval $[a\ b]$ into n subintervals, with $t_0 = a, \ldots, t_{n-1} = b$. Given this partition of the interval $[a\ b]$ we can associate to σ a new function, σ', defined

---

[2]The treatment in this sub-section follows closely Bjork (1998).

[3]An intuitive definition of adaptness is the following. Let S and σ be stochastic processes. If the value of σ at time t, σ_t, can be fully determined by the realization of the process S up to time t, then the process σ is said to be adapted to S. For instance, let S be a stock price process and σ be a volatility function of the form $\sigma(S_t, t)$. Then the value of the volatility σ at time t is completely known if the realization of the stock price, S, is known, and the volatility process is said to be *adapted* to the stock price process.

to be equal to σ on the initial point of each subinterval:

$$\sigma'(t) = \sigma(t) \quad \text{for } t = t_0, t_1, \ldots, t_{n-1} \tag{5.18}$$

and to be piecewise constant over each interval, $[t_k\ t_{k+1}]$, with $k = 0, 1, \ldots, n-1$. If this is the case, the function σ' can be more simply indexed by k, rather than by a continuous time argument, and can be denoted by the symbol σ'_k: $\sigma'(t) = \sigma_k(t) = \sigma_k$ for $t \in [t_k\ t_{k+1}]$, with $k = 0, 1, \ldots, n-1$.

The *elementary Ito integral* between a and b, $I_n(a, b)$, of the function $\sigma'_n(t)$ is then defined by the expression

$$I_n(a, b) = \int_a^b \sigma'_n(u)\,\mathrm{d}z(u) = \sum_{k=0,n-1} \sigma'_k[Z(t_{k+1}) - Z(t_k)] \tag{5.19}$$

A comment is in order. In defining non-stochastic (e.g. Riemann) integrals, in the limit it does not matter whether the point in the interval where the function is evaluated is chosen to be at the beginning, at the end or anywhere else. When dealing with stochastic integrals, however, the choice of the evaluation point for the function does make a difference, and the limiting process leads to different results depending on its location. In order to ensure that a sound financial ('physical') interpretation can be given to the integral, it is important that the evaluation point should be made to coincide with the left-most point in the interval.

Step 2: Equation (5.19) defines a series of elementary integrals, each one associated with a different index n, i.e. with the number of subintervals $[t_k\ t_{k+1}]$ into which we have subdivided the interval $[a\ b]$. If there exists a limit for the sequence of functions $I_n(a, b)$ as the integer n tends to infinity, then the Ito integral over the integral $[a\ b]$, $I(t; a, b)$, is defined as

$$I(t; a, b) \equiv \int_a^b \sigma(u)\,\mathrm{d}z(u) = \lim_{n\to\infty} I_n(a, b) = \lim_{n\to\infty} \int_a^b \sigma'_n(u)\,\mathrm{d}z(u)$$

$$= \lim_{n\to\infty} \sum_{k=0,n-1} \sigma'_k[Z(t_{k+1}) - Z(t_k)] \tag{5.20}$$

As defined, the Ito integral itself can be regarded as stochastic variable, I. It is therefore pertinent to ask questions about it such as its expectation or its variance. One can prove the following:

- The expectation taken at time a of the Ito integral $I(t; a, b)$ is zero:

$$\mathrm{E}_a\left[\int_a^b \sigma(u)\,\mathrm{d}z(u)\right] = 0 \tag{5.21}$$

- The variance of the Ito integral is linked to the *time* integral of the expectation of the square of σ by the following relationship:

$$\mathrm{var}\left[\int_a^b \sigma(u)\,\mathrm{d}z(u)\right] = \mathrm{E}_a\left[\left(\int_a^b \sigma(u)\,\mathrm{d}z(u)\right)^2\right] = \int_a^b \mathrm{E}_a[\sigma(u)^2]\,\mathrm{d}u \tag{5.22}$$

- If the function σ is a deterministic function of time (instead of a stochastic process), Equation (5.22) simply becomes

$$\text{var}\left[\int_a^b \sigma(u)\,dz(u)\right] = \int_a^b \sigma(u)^2\,du \qquad (5.23)$$

- For deterministic σ, the distribution of the Ito integral is normal with mean zero and variance $\int_a^b \sigma(u)^2\,du$.

5.3.2 Case 1: European Option, One Underlying Asset

Let us see how we can make use of these properties. Let

$$dx(t) = \sigma(t)\,dz(t) \qquad (5.24)$$

with σ a deterministic function of time. Integrating both sides, we obtain

$$x(T) = x(0) + \int_0^T \sigma(u)\,dz(u) \qquad (5.25)$$

The second term on the RHS is an instance of the Ito integral we have just defined. Therefore, we know that the distribution of the Ito integral in Equation (5.25) is normal with zero mean and variance $\int_a^b \sigma(u)^2\,du$, and it follows that $x(T)$ is normally distributed with mean $x(0)$ and variance $\int_a^b \sigma(u)^2\,du$.

Step 3: Let us consider a process of the form

$$\frac{df}{f} = \mu_f\,dt + \sigma_f\,dz \qquad (5.26)$$

Applying Ito's lemma to the function $\ln(f)$ one readily obtains:

$$d\ln[f] = \left[\mu_f - \frac{1}{2}\sigma_f^2\right]dt + \sigma_f\,dz \qquad (5.27)$$

Integrating Equation (5.27) from time 0 to time T one obtains:

$$f(T) = f(0)\exp\left[\int_0^T \left[\mu_f(u) - \frac{1}{2}\sigma(u)^2\right]du + \int_0^T \sigma_f(u)\,dz(u)\right] \qquad (5.28)$$

Let us assume that one were interested, perhaps in order to price a European option, in the value of the process f at time T. Clearly, one could produce a simulation of the process $\ln[f]$ by subdividing the interval $[0\ T]$ in small subintervals, and evolving the quantity $\ln(f)$ according to Equation (5.27) and subject to the initial condition $\ln(f)|_0 = \ln[f(0)]$. The procedure is obviously quite laborious (after evolving the process over n steps we have simply obtained a single realization of the process at the only time, T, where we actually need the stock price). One would therefore be very tempted to make use of Equation (5.28) in order to be able to obtain directly the value of f at the only time

(T) we are interested in. Unfortunately, by looking at Equation (5.28) one can see that, even if the time integral of the drift could be evaluated, one would still have to deal with a stochastic integral as one of the arguments of the exponents. The brute-force solution of evaluating this integral by means of a step-by-step Monte Carlo simulation, whilst obviously correct, would bring no computational improvement over the direct simulation of Equation (5.27). However, we shall show below that this laborious approach is not necessary, and that we can make use of the results presented in the previous section to carry out a single long jump.

Step 4: Identify the terms in Equation (5.25) with the corresponding terms in Equation (5.27) as

$$x(T) = \ln[f(T)] - \int_0^T \left[\mu_f(u) - \frac{1}{2}\sigma(u)^2 \right] du \qquad (5.29)$$

$$x(0) = \ln[f(0)] \qquad (5.30)$$

$$\int_0^T \sigma(u)\, dz(u) = \int_0^T \sigma_f(u)\, dz(u) \qquad (5.31)$$

Then, after noting that the integral $\int_0^T \left[\mu_f(u) - \frac{1}{2}\sigma(u)^2 \right] du$ is purely a function of time and after making use of the results in Steps 1–3, we can conclude that the quantity $\ln[f(T)]$ is normally distributed with variance equal to $\int_0^T \sigma_f(u)^2\, du$. If we call this latter quantity $\widehat{\sigma}^2 T$ (i.e. $\widehat{\sigma}^2 T = \int_0^T \sigma_f(u)^2\, du$), it therefore follows that

$$\ln[f(T)] = \ln[f(0)] + \int_0^T \left[\mu_f(u) - \frac{1}{2}\sigma(u)^2 \right] du + \int_0^T \sigma_f(u)\, dz(u) \qquad (5.32)$$

$$f(T) = f(0) \exp\left[\int_0^T \left\{ \mu_f(u) - \frac{1}{2}\sigma(u)^2 \right\} du + \widehat{\sigma}\sqrt{T}Z \right] \qquad (5.33)$$

with $Z \in \mathcal{N}(0, 1)$

Equation (5.33) tells us that we can simulate a realization of the variable f all the way to time T simply by drawing a single normally distributed standard variable, Z. By means of Equation (5.33) we have therefore succeeded in evolving the process $f(t)$ out to time T in one single step, with an obvious reduction in the computational burden, and in the dimensionality of the integral which is implicitly solved by the Monte Carlo simulation.[4]

As mentioned above, we are using the Monte Carlo framework in this discussion more as a conceptual device, rather than as a practical computational tool. In practice, it might very well be the case that, for certain payoffs, one does not have to solve the option problem numerically, or that other methods (finite differences, computational lattices, trees, etc.) might provide a more efficient computational route. The reasoning has however been cast in the simulation context, because I think that it provides the clearest way to gain an appreciation of the quantities that really affect the value of an option. In particular, we have established, again with the example above, that the only quantity that matters in so far as the stochastic part of this European option problem

---

[4]If one reaches the terminal time T along a single path by evolving the state variable over n steps, one is effectively carrying out an n-dimensional integral.

is concerned is $\int_0^t \sigma(u)^2 \, du$. We have already seen this result in a more imprecise way in Chapters 2 and 4, but the approach followed here will allow us to generalize this conclusion to a multi-look setting, and, most importantly, to the case of several underlying variables.

5.3.3 Case 2: Path-Dependent Option, One Asset

The second case we want to analyse is that of an option, still with a single price or rate as underlying, but whose final payoff will depend on the realization of the state variable at several discrete points in time. For simplicity we will consider a 'two-look' case, the generalization to more price-sensitive events being straightforward.

Let us call the two 'look' times T_1 and T_2. For the sake of concreteness, let us assume that the payoff is a call struck at K on the average of $f(T_1)$ and $f(T_2)$ taken at time T_2. Once again, we could carry out a brute-force Monte Carlo evolution of the process for the underlying in many small steps from time 0 to time T_1. Once time T_1 has been reached, we could 'store in memory' the payoff-sensitive condition encountered at time T_1, and then continue with a short-stepped evolution to T_2. We already know, however, how to evolve the process f from time 0 to time T_1:

$$f(T_1) = f(0) \exp \left[\int_0^{T_1} \left[\mu_f(u) - \frac{1}{2}\sigma(u)^2 \right] dt + \widehat{\sigma_{0,1}}\sqrt{T_1} Z_1 \right] \tag{5.34}$$

and, therefore, we certainly want to make use at least of this equation to carry out a single long jump out to time T_1, where the price-sensitive condition can be observed and 'remembered'. (In the expression above $\widehat{\sigma_{0,1}}$ denotes the root-mean-squared volatility between time 0 and time T_1. A similar notation is used for the second time-step.) The remaining question, since we are not interested in events (price realizations) occurring at any intermediate time between T_1 and T_2, is whether we can carry out a second 'long jump' between the times of the two price-sensitive events. Going back to the reasoning we followed earlier, it is clear that the answer is 'yes', provided that the draw for the second jump is independent of the draw for the first:

$$f(T_2) = f(T_1) \exp \left[\int_{T_1}^{T_2} \left\{ \mu_f(u) - \frac{1}{2}\sigma(u)^2 \right\} du + \widehat{\sigma_{1,2}}\sqrt{T_2 - T_1} Z_2 \right]$$

$$= f(0) \exp \left[\int_{T_0}^{T_2} \left\{ \mu_f(u) - \frac{1}{2}\sigma(u)^2 \right\} du + \widehat{\sigma_{0,1}}\sqrt{T_1} Z_1 + \widehat{\sigma_{1,2}}\sqrt{T_2 - T_1} Z_2 \right]$$

$$\tag{5.35}$$

Therefore, in order to value the two-look path-dependent option on a single underlying asset, we simply have to draw two independent random variates, normally distributed with zero mean and variances $\widehat{\sigma_{0,1}}^2 T_1$ and $\widehat{\sigma_{1,2}}^2 (T_2 - T_1)$.

Note that if the underlying process is a spot price process, we can obtain the market-implied values for the two variances from the traded prices of plain-vanilla options expiring at time T_1 and T_2, as described in Chapter 3. If $f(t)$, however, represented a forward-rate process, the only plain-vanilla option that gives direct information about one of the variances above would be the caplet expiring at time T_2 (assuming, that is, that the option expiry, T_2, coincides with the expiry of the forward rate). No liquid instrument exists to provide information about the variance of the T_2-expiry forward rate at time T_1. Could we not use information from the caplet expiring at time T_1? No. As discussed in Chapter 3, the price of the caplet expiring at time T_1 provides information about the variance of a *different* forward rate (the T_1-expiry forward). This quantity does not provide any direct information about the variance of the T_2-expiry forward rate from time T_0 to time T_1. When dealing with the processes for forward rates, the trader must therefore make some assumptions about the time behaviour of the volatility. A discussion of this topic is presented in the final section of this chapter and, more thoroughly, in Chapter 19.

5.3.4   Case 3: Path-Dependent Option, Two Assets

We now move to the more complex case of a path-dependent option whose final payoff is a function of the joint realizations of two state variables at two different price-sensitive look times. If changes in the two prices or rates were totally independent of each other, clearly the problem could be trivially solved applying twice the approach shown in Case 2 above. We shall instead require in what follows that the increments of the two processes should be instantaneously correlated. The processes of the two underlying variables are therefore given by

$$\frac{dx_1}{x_1} = \mu_1 \, dt + \sigma_1(t) \, dz_1 \tag{5.36}$$

and

$$\frac{dx_2}{x_2} = \mu_2 \, dt + \sigma_2(t) \, dz_2 \tag{5.37}$$

with

$$E[dz_1(t) \, dz_2(t)] = \rho(t) \, dt \tag{5.38}$$

Once again, the brute-force approach, by means of which the two processes are evolved over many small steps from time 0 to time T_1 (where the price-sensitive condition is recorded) and then to time T_2, is still possible. If one wanted to proceed in this manner, one would simply have to carry out the simulation by drawing, for each small step, a first draw, $Z_1 \in \mathcal{N}(0, \delta t)$, used to shock the first variable; and then to make sure that, for each time-step δt, the second draw, Z_2, is given by

$$Z_2 = \rho Z_1 + \sqrt{1 - \rho^2} W \tag{5.39}$$

with W an $\mathcal{N}(0, \delta t)$-distributed variable drawn independently of Z_1. We want to explore, however, whether the long jump procedure is still applicable. More precisely, in light of what we obtained above, we would be very tempted to make an identification similar to the one made above, and write

$$f_1(T_1) = f_1(0) \exp\left[\int_{T_0}^{T_1} \left\{ \mu_{f_1}(u) - \frac{1}{2}\sigma_1(u)^2 \right\} du + \widehat{\sigma_{0,1}^1} \sqrt{T_1} Z_1 \right] \tag{5.40}$$

and

$$f_2(T_1) = f_2(0) \exp\left[\int_{T_0}^{T_1} \left\{\mu_{f_2}(u) - \frac{1}{2}\sigma_2(u)^2\right\} du + \widehat{\sigma_{0,1}^2}\sqrt{T_1}Z_2\right] \quad (5.41)$$

with

$$Z_2 = \widetilde{\rho}Z_1 + \sqrt{1 - \widetilde{\rho}^2}W \quad (5.42)$$

and W independently drawn from a $\mathcal{N}(0, 1)$ normal distribution. What is not obvious, however, is what the quantity $\widetilde{\rho}$ should be equal to: the time average of the instantaneous correlation defined by (5.38)? The value $\rho(T_1)$? The value $\rho(T_0)$? It will actually turn out that, in general, none of these answers is correct. To obtain the correct answer, let us pursue the following reasoning.

Step 1: Let us rewrite Equations (5.36) and (5.37) in such a way that the same correlation structure between the variables x_1 and x_2 is retained, but the equations are expressed in terms of two independent Brownian motions, dz_1 and dw. This can be easily accomplished by writing:

$$dx_1 = \sigma_1 \, dz_1(t) \quad (5.43)$$

$$dx_2 = \rho\sigma_2 \, dz_1(t) + \sqrt{1 - \rho^2}\sigma_2 \, dw(t) \quad (5.44)$$

with

$$E[dz(t) \, dw(t)] = 0 \quad (5.45)$$

It is straightforward to verify that, indeed, corr$[dx_1, dx_2] = \rho$.

Exercise 1 *Check that* corr$[dx_1, dx_2] = \rho$.

Step 2: Integrate Equations (5.43) and (5.44) to obtain:

$$x_1(T_1) = x_1(0) + \int_{T_0}^{T_1} \sigma_1(u) \, dz_1(u) \quad (5.46)$$

$$x_2(T_1) = x_2(0) + \int_{T_0}^{T_1} \sigma_2(u)\rho(u) \, dz_1(u) + \int_{T_0}^{T_1} \sigma_2(u)\sqrt{1 - \rho(u)^2} \, dw(u) \quad (5.47)$$

From the discussion above, we already know that the stochastic integrals $\int_{T_0}^{T_1} \sigma_1(u) \, dz_1(u)$, $\int_{T_0}^{T_1} \sigma_2(u)\rho(u) \, dz_1(u)$ and $\int_{T_0}^{T_1} \sigma_2(u)\sqrt{1 - \rho(u)^2} \, dw(u)$ are three stochastic variables with means and variances given by

$$\text{mean}\left[\int_{T_0}^{T_1} \sigma_1(u) \, dz_1(u)\right] = 0 \quad (5.48)$$

$$\text{mean}\left[\int_{T_0}^{T_1} \sigma_2(u)\rho(u) \, dz_1(u)\right] = 0 \quad (5.49)$$

$$\text{mean}\left[\int_{T_0}^{T_1} \sigma_2(u)\sqrt{1 - \rho(u)^2}\, dw(u)\right] = 0 \tag{5.50}$$

$$\text{var}\left[\int_{T_0}^{T_1} \sigma_1(u)\, dz_1(u)\right] = \int_{T_0}^{T_1} \sigma_1(u)^2\, du \tag{5.51}$$

$$\text{var}\left[\int_{T_0}^{T_1} \sigma_2(u)\rho(u)\, dz_1(u)\right] = \int_{T_0}^{T_1} [\sigma_2(u)\rho(u)]^2\, du \tag{5.52}$$

$$\text{var}\left[\int_{T_0}^{T_1} \sigma_2(u)\sqrt{1 - \rho(u)^2}\, dw(u)\right] = \int_{T_0}^{T_1} \sigma_2(u)^2(1 - \rho_u^2)\, du \tag{5.53}$$

Given the independence of $dw(t)$ and $dz_1(t)$ it also follows that

$$\text{mean}[x_1(T_1)] = x_1(0) \tag{5.54}$$

$$\text{mean}[x_2(T_1)] = x_2(0) \tag{5.55}$$

$$\text{var}[x_1(T_1)] = \int_{T_0}^{T_1} \sigma_1(u)^2\, du \tag{5.56}$$

$$\text{var}[x_2(T_1)] = \int_{T_0}^{T_1} \sigma_2(u)^2\, du \tag{5.57}$$

Therefore the variables $x_1(T_1)$ and $x_2(T_1)$ are jointly normally distributed with means and variances as above. What remains to be evaluated is the correlation between the two variables

Step 3: The correlation we seek to evaluate is given by

$$\text{corr}[x_1(T_1), x_2(T_1)] = \frac{\text{covar}[x_1(T_1), x_2(T_1)]}{\sqrt{\text{var}[x_1(T_1)]\,\text{var}[x_2(T_1)]}} \tag{5.58}$$

From the definition of covariance one can write

$$\text{covar}[x_1(T_1), x_2(T_1)] = E[(x_1(T_1) - x_1(0))(x_2(T_1) - x_2(0))]$$

$$= E\left[\left(\int_0^{T_1} \sigma_1(u)\, dz_1(u)\right)\left(\int_0^{T_1} \sigma_2(u)\rho_u\, dz_1(u) + \int_0^{T_1} \sigma_2(u)\sqrt{1 - \rho_u^2}\, dw(u)\right)\right] \tag{5.59}$$

where, in the last line, use has been made of Equations (5.46), (5.47), (5.48) and (5.49). One can now

- go back to the definition of the Ito integral in Step 1 of Case 1;

- write each integral as the limit of a discrete sum;

- remember that dz and dw are independent, and therefore $E[dz\, dw] = 0$;

- remember the formal rules of stochastic calculus, namely $E[dz\, dt] = 0$ and $E[dz\, dz] = dt$;

- go back to the limit as the partition becomes infinitely fine.

When all the algebra is done (Rebonato (1998a) provides a slightly less sketchy formal derivation), and the identifications analogous to those in Step 5 of Case 1 are carried out, one finally obtains the result we have been looking for:

$$\text{corr}[\ln f_1(T_1), \ln f_2(T_1)] = \widehat{\rho}(T_1) = \frac{\int_{T_0}^{T_1} \sigma_1(u)\sigma_2(u)\rho(u)\, du}{\sqrt{\text{var}[f_1(T_1)]\, \text{var}[f_2(T_1)]}} \qquad (5.60)$$

with

$$\text{var}[\ln f_1(T_1)] = \int_{T_0}^{T_1} \sigma_1(u)^2\, du \qquad (5.61)$$

$$\text{var}[\ln f_2(T_1)] = \int_{T_0}^{T_1} \sigma_2(u)^2\, du \qquad (5.62)$$

Equation (5.60) is all we need to carry out the simulation by using two long jumps per variable. The prescription for the evolution of the two variables is therefore as follows:

1. Sample two independent mean-zero, unit-variance normal random variables, Z_1 and W.

2. Calculate $\widehat{\rho}(T_1)$ as

$$\widehat{\rho}(T_1) = \frac{\int_{T_0}^{T_1} \sigma_1(u)\sigma_2(u)\rho(u)\, du}{\sqrt{\text{var}[f_1(T_1)]\, \text{var}[f_2(T_1)]}} \qquad (5.63)$$

3. Construct Z_2 as $Z_2 = \widehat{\rho} Z_1 + \sqrt{(1 - \widehat{\rho}^2)}\, W$.

4. Evolve f_1 and f_2 out to time T_1 using

$$
\begin{aligned}
f_1(T_1) &= f_1(0)\exp\left[\int_{T_0}^{T_1}\left\{\mu_{f_1}(u) - \frac{1}{2}\sigma_1(u)^2\right\} du + \widehat{\sigma}_1\sqrt{T_1}\, Z_1\right] \\
f_2(T_1) &= f_2(0)\exp\left[\int_{T_0}^{T_1}\left\{\mu_{f_2}(u) - \frac{1}{2}\sigma_2(u)^2\right\} du + \widehat{\sigma}_2\sqrt{T_1}\, Z_2\right]
\end{aligned}
\qquad (5.64)
$$

with $\widehat{\sigma}_1$ and $\widehat{\sigma}_2$ equal to the root-mean-squared volatilities from time T_0 to time T_1 for forward rates 1 and 2, respectively. At this point the outcome of the price-sensitive event at time T_1 can be recorded and the two variables can be further evolved to time T_2 using an identical procedure.

The quantity $\widehat{\rho}(T_1)$ to be used to produce the joint evolution of the variables is therefore neither the instantaneous correlation at time T_1, nor the simple average of the instantaneous correlation out to time T_1, but a weighted average of the instantaneous correlation,

$$\widehat{\rho}(T_1) = \int_{T_0}^{T_1} h(u)\rho(u)\, du \qquad (5.65)$$

with the time-dependent weight, $h(t)$, given by

$$h(t) = \frac{\sigma_1(t)\sigma_2(t)}{\sqrt{\text{var}[f_1(T_1)]\,\text{var}[f_2(T_1)]}} \tag{5.66}$$

This fundamental quantity, $\widehat{\rho}(t)$, is important enough to be given a name of its own, i.e. *terminal correlation*.

We have reached this conclusion using a Monte Carlo evolution of the relevant stochastic variables. The procedure might not have been very elegant, but some of the results obtained were procedure-independent: in particular, whatever quantities (such as the terminal correlation) we have found to determine the value of the derivative product using this numerical construction will also enter any analytic formula that we might be able to find. Reaching this conclusion was the main reason behind presenting the somewhat cumbersome Gedanken Monte Carlo experiment presented above.

Summarizing: in order to evolve the two stochastic variables from time T_0 to time T_1 all that is needed, in so far as the stochastic part of the evolution is concerned, is knowledge of the quantities

$$\int_{T_0}^{T_1} \sigma_1(u)^2 \, du \tag{5.67}$$

$$\int_{T_0}^{T_1} \sigma_2(u)^2 \, du \tag{5.68}$$

and

$$\int_{T_0}^{T_1} \sigma_1(u)\sigma_2(u)\rho(u) \, du \tag{5.69}$$

These are the elements of a (real, symmetric) 2×2 covariance matrix.

Over the following computational step, two cases are then to be distinguished: if the underlying variables were the spot prices of two distinct assets, then the extension is obvious, and the quantities above clearly become

$$\int_{T_1}^{T_2} \sigma_1(u)^2 \, du \tag{5.70}$$

$$\int_{T_1}^{T_2} \sigma_2(u)^2 \, du \tag{5.71}$$

and

$$\int_{T_1}^{T_2} \sigma_1(u)\sigma_2(u)\rho(u) \, du \tag{5.72}$$

The four prices of plain-vanilla options on the two underlyings expiring at times T_1 and T_2 allow the recovery of the market-implied values for the time integrals of the (squares of the) individual volatilities. The trader would 'only' have to provide a 'guess' for the instantaneous correlation $\rho(t)$.

If the variables f_1 and f_2 described forward rates, however, the problem is more subtle, and two further distinctions must be made: if T_1 happens to be the expiry time for forward rate f_1, then this forward rate would reset at time T_1; over the next step the covariance matrix will be degenerate (1×1) and the only residual quantity of relevance will be $\int_{T_1}^{T_2} \sigma_2(u)^2 \, du$. If, on the other hand, T_1 is not the expiry time for either forward rate, they will both have to be evolved over the next time-step, and all the above quantities in the second (2×2) covariance matrix will be relevant.

It is also important to point out that in the interest-rate case no liquid market instrument will give direct information about $\int_{T_0}^{T_1} \sigma_2(u)^2 \, du$ or about $\int_{T_1}^{T_2} \sigma_2(u)^2 \, du$ (the price of a T_2-maturity caplet will provide information about $\int_{T_0}^{T_2} \sigma_2(u)^2 \, du$); if T_1 is the expiry of the T_1-maturity forward rate, then the price of the T_1-maturity caplet will give direct information about $\int_{T_0}^{T_1} \sigma_1(u)^2 \, du$. Otherwise, no liquid market instrument will give any information about the value of this integral either. The trader, much as in the one-forward-rate, path-dependent case, will have to make some assumptions about the time behaviour of the instantaneous volatility. These are discussed in Chapter 19.

Before discussing and generalizing these findings, it is useful to say a few more words on the properties of the terminal correlation. The following obvious limiting cases should be noted:

1. If the volatilities are constant, then the terminal correlation simply coincides with the average correlation over the period.

2. If the correlation is constant, then the terminal correlation is equal to this constant value.

3. If the first volatility is exactly zero whenever the second volatility is non-zero, and vice versa, then and only then can the terminal correlation be zero with a strictly positive instantaneous correlation.[5]

4. If the instantaneous correlation is positive over the integration interval, the terminal correlation can be reduced in value, but it cannot be negative.

5. For a given instantaneous correlation and for given root-mean-squared volatilities, the terminal correlation cannot be higher than the value obtained if the two instantaneous volatilities were constant.

In general, the terminal correlation can be lower than one, or, as we have seen in the limiting case 3, even zero, even if the instantaneous correlation is perfect. Since, as we have seen, what matters for pricing is not the instantaneous correlation, but the terminal correlation, a substantial amount of de-correlation can be effectively obtained by allowing for a time-dependent volatility. This mechanism is particularly effective when the instantaneous correlation is high, and becomes progressively less important for lower and lower values of the instantaneous correlation coefficient. Therefore, as mentioned above, non-constant instantaneous volatilities are likely to play a more important role in the case of same-currency forward rates. As we shall see in Chapters 19, 21 and 22, they

---

[5]Mathematically, this is correct. Financially, however, Merton's conditions about the volatility (see Section 2.4.1) prevent this function from being a possible candidate volatility function.

actually provide an essential ingredient for a coherent simultaneous description of the cap and swaption markets.

5.4 Generalizing the Results

The examples discussed in the previous section have dealt with at most two underlying variables, evolved over at most two steps. However, it is not difficult to extend and generalize the results to the case of n variables, evolved over m price-sensitive events. In particular, if one is dealing with forward rates, there are likely to be exactly as many forward rates in the problem as there are price-sensitive events. In a very common situation encountered in the payoff of path-dependent LIBOR-based derivatives, each of the price-sensitive events is determined by the reset value of one forward rate. Since this setting is particularly common, in what follows I deal with the case of n forward rates, evolved over n price-sensitive events ('look times'). The modifications needed to deal with the case where the number of events is not equal to the number of variables are straightforward.

Consider a collection of n forward rates, f_i, $i = 1, 2, \ldots, n$. For each forward let us make the log-normal assumption:

$$\frac{\mathrm{d} f_i}{f_i} = \mu_i \, \mathrm{d}t + \sigma_i(t) \, \mathrm{d}z_i \tag{5.73}$$

Let us label the times of the price-sensitive events by $t_1, t_2, \ldots, t_n$, and today's time by t_0. Consider then the quantity C_{ij}^k, defined as

$$C_{ij}^k = \int_{t_{k-1}}^{t_k} \sigma_i(u)\sigma_j(u)\rho_{ij}(u) \, \mathrm{d}u, \quad 1 \le k \le n \tag{5.74}$$

Therefore

$$C_{ij}^1 = \int_{t_0}^{t_1} \sigma_i(u)\sigma_j(u)\rho_{ij}(u) \, \mathrm{d}u$$

$$C_{ij}^2 = \int_{t_1}^{t_2} \sigma_i(u)\sigma_j(u)\rho_{ij}(u) \, \mathrm{d}u$$

$$\ldots$$

$$C_{ij}^r = \int_{t_{r-1}}^{t_r} \sigma_i(u)\sigma_j(u)\rho_{ij}(u) \, \mathrm{d}u, \quad r \le n \tag{5.75}$$

Note that if we are dealing with Merton-admissible volatility functions (see Section 2.4.1), the elements of C_{ij}^1 are, in general, all non-zero. For convenience, let us arrange the elements C_{ij}^1 in an $n \times n$ real-symmetric matrix, which we will denote by $\mathbf{C}^1$.

At time t_1 we have assumed that one forward rate, which we will conveniently label f_1, will reset. Therefore, over the next step only $(n-1)$ forward rates will have to be evolved (are still 'alive'). The real-symmetric matrix $\mathbf{C}^2$ will therefore now be of dimension $(n-1) \times (n-1)$. At the last time-step there will be a single element $C_{nn}^n = \int_{t_{n-1}}^{t_n} \sigma_n(u)^2 \, \mathrm{d}u$, giving rise to a degenerate 1×1 matrix $\mathbf{C}^n$. This succession of time-dependent matrices of decreasing size, $\mathbf{C}^1, \mathbf{C}^2, \ldots, \mathbf{C}^n$, fully describes the stochastic evolution of the n forward rates. By generalizing what we saw in the previous section, this succession of matrices is all that is needed for the stochastic part of the Monte Carlo simulation of the problem. As noted above, other techniques, perhaps even closed-form solutions, might be able to reduce the computational burden, but, whatever numerical or analytical approach is chosen, the relevant quantities, i.e. the matrices $\mathbf{C}^k$, do not change.

If one indeed wanted to solve the problem by a series of long jumps in a Monte Carlo framework, one would be faced with the problem of generalizing Equations (5.43) and (5.44), i.e. with the task of expressing the dynamics of k correlated variables in terms of k independent Brownian increments. The general solution to this problem is known as the Cholesky decomposition (see, for example, Kreyszig (1993)). The algorithm is both fast and simple to implement. Alternatively, one could orthogonalize each covariance matrix, and work with the resulting eigenvalues and (now orthogonal) eigenvectors.

Let us gain a deeper understanding of the structure of these matrices. To this effect, let us define new matrices of constant size ($n \times n$) by adding zero values corresponding to the forward rates that have reset, and arrange the elements as follows:

$$
\begin{bmatrix}
C_{11}^1 & C_{21}^1 & \cdots & C_{n1}^1 \\
C_{11}^2 & C_{21}^2 & \cdots & C_{n1}^2 \\
\cdots & \cdots & \cdots & \cdots \\
C_{11}^n & C_{21}^n & \cdots & C_{n1}^n
\end{bmatrix}
\tag{5.76}
$$

$$
\begin{bmatrix}
0 & 0 & \cdots & 0 \\
0 & C_{22}^2 & \cdots & C_{n2}^2 \\
\cdots & \cdots & \cdots & \cdots \\
0 & C_{22}^n & \cdots & C_{n2}^n
\end{bmatrix}
\tag{5.77}
$$

$$
\begin{bmatrix}
0 & 0 & \cdots & 0 \\
0 & 0 & \cdots & 0 \\
\cdots & \cdots & \cdots & \cdots \\
0 & 0 & \cdots & C_{nn}^n
\end{bmatrix}
\tag{5.78}
$$

If we call all the matrices framed with zeros $\mathbf{C}^{\prime r}$, we can form the ($n \times n$) matrix $\mathbf{C}_{ADD}^j$ simply by adding the first j $\mathbf{C}'$ matrices, element by element. If we do so, the (ij)th element of the kth $\mathbf{C}_{ADD}^k$ matrix is given by

$$
\mathbf{C}_{ADD\,ij}^k
$$

$$
= \int_{t_0}^{t_1} \sigma_i(u)\sigma_j(u)\rho_{ij}(u)\mathrm{d}u
$$

$$
+ \int_{t_1}^{t_2} \sigma_i(u)\sigma_j(u)\rho_{ij}(u)\mathrm{d}u
$$

$$
+ \ldots +
$$

$$
+ \int_{t_{k-1}}^{t_k} \sigma_i(u)\sigma_j(u)\rho_{ij}(u)\mathrm{d}u
\tag{5.79}
$$

Therefore the (i, j)th element of the $\mathbf{C}^k_{ADD}$ matrix contains the total terminal covariance from time t_0 to time t_k between variables i and j. In particular, if $i = j = k$, then the element of the $\mathbf{C}^k_{ADDkk}$ matrix simply gives the total variance of the kth forward rate. In this case, and only in this case, it can be directly accessed from the market price of the caplet on the kth forward rate. In general, even in a perfect Black world, the trader must assign $O(n^3)$ covariance elements, and has direct access from the market prices of caplets to only $O(n)$ values. The prices of swaptions do add some information, but, as discussed more precisely in Chapter 19 (see in particular Sections 19.4 and 19.5), not enough to pin down uniquely the $O(n^3)$ quantities that describe the evolution of the forward rates.

On the other hand, as we have argued, all that matters in option pricing (for discrete-look securities) are the elements of these covariance matrices. One might therefore be tempted to dispense altogether with the a priori specification of a 'model', i.e. of a black box that fills in the elements in the matrices, and to estimate, either econometrically or on the basis of trading views, the necessary (time-dependent) volatilities and correlations. It would be tempting to 'define a model' by directly assigning the elements of n covariances. However, the size of the problem and the disproportion between the directly-market-accessible quantities and the number of unknowns is such that, unless this assignment was carried out in a highly structured way, one could virtually rest assured that inconsistencies would be introduced into the overall dynamics. The 'highly structured' procedure for assigning the covariance elements is, however, nothing more than a model in disguise, or, more correctly, a modern specification of an interest-rate model. These are the topics that we will investigate at greater length in Part III of this book.

5.5   Moving Ahead

The first five chapters (Part I) of this book have dealt with the most important definitions and concepts regarding variances, volatilities and correlations in what has so far been assumed to be fundamentally a Black world, i.e. a world of geometrically diffusing underlying assets and rates, complete and frictionless markets, and volatilities at most time-dependent. The 'real' world is, (un)fortunately, considerably more complex. This new dimension of complexity, subsumed under the blanket term of 'volatility smiles', is dealt with in the next twelve chapters, which constitute the body of Part II.

Part II

Smiles – Equity and FX

Before presenting the analysis of several different approaches that have been proposed to account for smiles, here is a bird's eye view of Part II.

1. First (Chapter 6) a financial motivation is given for the deviations from the Black-and-Scholes formula that can give rise to smiles (Smile Tales 1 and 2).

2. The conceptual foundations are laid. These are: (i) a departure from a deterministic root-mean-squared volatility; (ii) the distinction between real and risk-adjusted model parameters (volatilities, jump frequencies, etc.); (iii) the degree of recoverability of real-world parameters from option prices; (iv) a shift in emphasis from models that allow or fail to allow perfect replication towards hedging strategies that produce a narrower or more dispersed distribution of hedging errors. This is also mainly (but not exclusively) done in Chapter 6.

3. Empirical facts about smiles are presented. This is done in Chapter 7.

4. A brief, qualitative survey of the main modelling approaches to capture smiles is presented in Chapter 8.

5. In order to 'get started', I discuss how to obtain from the quoted market prices a smooth input volatility surface. This is done in Chapter 9.

6. The behaviour of the quadratic variation is discussed again, and it is presented as the transition link from the Black-and-Scholes to the smiley world. This topic is dealt with in Chapter 10.

7. Several process-based models are discussed in detail in Chapters 11 and 12 (local-volatility diffusions), Chapter 13 (stochastic-volatility diffusions), Chapter 14 (jump–diffusions) and Chapter 15 (variance–gamma processes).

8. I discuss how, and to what extent, it is possible to move smile surfaces in an arbitrage-free manner without modelling the underlying. This is the topic of Chapter 17.

Chapter 6

Pricing Options in the Presence of Smiles

6.1 Plan of the Chapter

In this chapter I first define what a smile is and introduce the associated concept of implied volatility (Section 6.2). Understanding clearly what information this latter quantity does and does not convey is absolutely crucial in order to use it correctly. I therefore spend some considerable time in showing that some intuitively appealing and apparently commonsensical ways to use this quantity are conceptually flawed and in practice dangerous (Section 6.3).

I then move on to discussing why it is so much easier (but so much less useful) to obtain the dependence of the smile on the strike and on maturity time than on the underlying and on calendar time; and why being able to do the latter is ultimately equivalent to having a full knowledge of the underlying process. I also explain carefully why the two deceptively similar derivatives, $\frac{\partial \widehat{\sigma}}{\partial S}$ and $\frac{\partial \widehat{\sigma}}{\partial K}$ (where $\widehat{\sigma}$ is the implied volatility, S is the underlying and K is the strike) convey fundamentally different information (Section 6.4). I will show in Chapter 12 (Section 12.3 in particular) that knowledge of the '*easy-to-determine*' dependence of the implied volatility on the strike and on the maturity can specify uniquely the '*difficult*' dependence on the underlying and on calendar time. This is important, because I will equate this to knowledge of the full process. This is however only true if the *type* of process is a priori assumed to be a local or a fully stochastic-volatility diffusion.

By this point in the chapter the reader should have accepted the fact that how the smile changes when the underlying (not the strike) changes is 'where the action is' in derivatives pricing. I therefore move on to present two 'tales' that exemplify two limiting cases for this dependence of the smile on the underlying. These tales (Sections 6.5 and 6.6) will give a first introduction to terms ('floating' and 'sticky' smiles) that will be more precisely discussed in Chapter 17.

The final section of the chapter (Section 6.7) deals with a rather different topic, and, were it not for its brevity, it could have been the subject of a self-standing chapter. It still 'belongs' in this introductory chapter because it discusses some important concepts regarding the calibration of models to market smiles. More precisely, I show if and when the statistical analysis of real-world quantities can provide information about the process of the underlying. For its relevance to calibration, this section should be linked with the discussion in Section 1.4 ('The Calibration Debate'), and with those chapters (13 and 14) that deal with many-parameter models.

6.2   Background and Definition of the Smile

The formula that Black and Scholes presented in their (1973) paper offered an easily computable expression to evaluate the 'fair' value of an option, given four easily observable market inputs (the price of the underlying, the strike price, the time to expiry and the funding – riskless – rate to option expiry) and a quasi-observable quantity (the volatility of the underlying). The conditions under which the formula is obtained are very restrictive, and in practice certainly violated. Yet the formula has been immensely popular. I have tried to explain in Part I that part of the reason for its popularity is its robustness *vis-à-vis* a misspecification of the volatility. I will show in Part II (see Chapters 13 and 14 in particular) that this feature remains valid even when the process is not a deterministic–volatility diffusion.

If one takes into account the robustness, the intuitional appeal and the ease of implementation of the model one can begin to understand how a 'virtuous circle' was being established in the early 1980s: on the one hand, the formula became the industry standard for plain-vanilla over-the-counter (OTC) options; on the other, it acquired the status of a benchmark against which all more complicated models had to be calibrated for the relevant limiting cases (some of the modern yield curve models still boast recovery of the Black prices for caps and swaptions as one of their most desirable features). This process of calibration at the same time enforced that hedges in plain-vanilla options of complex exotic derivatives would be transacted at the Black prices, thereby closing the 'circle of mutual support' described in Chapter 1.

Despite the apparent circularity of the reasoning, traders have always been well aware of the shortcomings of the Black model, and have been quoting prices that substantially deviated from the Black-and-Scholes formula, at least since 1987. The same traders, however, have been so reluctant to abandon the simplicity and intuitional appeal of the Black-and-Scholes formula that they have preferred to account for all its imperfections and inadequacies by means of a skilful 'doctoring' of the only relatively opaque parameter, ie, the volatility of the underlying.

This is perhaps where the luck of the model played a significant part by turning this possible weakness into a strength: had several inputs been similarly opaque, or, at the other extreme, had all the inputs been totally transparent and unquestionable, there would have been no easy way for traders to express their prices by adjusting a single number, the 'implied' Black volatility.

For these reasons it has become established market practice to quote the price of plain-vanilla options using this volatility 'metric'. This practice is followed in the equity, in the FX and in the interest-rate area.[1] The market chooses to retain the simplicity and

---

[1] A similar situation developed in the early years of tranched-credit-derivatives pricing. The early models assumed a Gaussian copula among the reference assets. Also, the same correlation coefficient was employed between any pair of reference assets. More sophisticated pricing practices soon developed, and traders now

convenience of a Black-like quote by assigning different implied volatilities for options with identical underlying and expiration, but different strikes. The dependence on the strike of the implied volatility for options of the same maturity is referred to in what follows as 'the smile'. Terms such as 'smirk', 'frown', etc. are sometimes used in the literature, but I will refer to all these different shapes of the implied-volatility curve as 'smiles'. When the collection of smiles for different maturities is considered, I will often speak of the smile surface.

It is essential to stress from the beginning that this practice is purely a short-cut to quote a price, and does not directly imply anything about the process of the underlying (or about an 'equivalent' or 'compensated' process). Furthermore, the direct link between the implied volatility and the root-mean-squared volatility is lost if the smile curve is not flat. Once we recognize that the assumptions of the Black-and-Scholes world are so strongly violated that we have to introduce a strike dependence on the implied volatility, the latter quantity simply becomes *the wrong number to put in the wrong formula to get the right price of plain-vanilla options*.

To make the point clear, the next section will deal with two simple but important case studies, i.e. the delta and vega hedging in the presence of smiles of a plain-vanilla option and of a cash-or-nothing (European digital) option.

6.3 Hedging with a Compensated Process: Plain-Vanilla and Binary Options

6.3.1 Delta- and Vega-Hedging a Plain-Vanilla Option

The first case we want to examine is the following. Let us assume that a, say, 30-delta option[2] has an implied volatility of 24% and that the at-the-money implied volatility is, say, 20%. By definition this would mean that the price of the out-of-the-money option is obtained by using an input volatility of 24% in the Black formula, and, similarly that a 20% volatility must be used to obtain the price for the 50-delta option. We do not know what 'true' process gave rise to this deviation from a flat implied volatility curve, and therefore decide to hedge using the simple and robust Black formula. We have to decide, however, which input volatility to use to calculate the hedge ratio. Do the market quotes about Black implied volatilities tell us anything about what percentage volatility should be more appropriate in order to evaluate the Black delta of the 30-delta option? In other words, would our hedge be more accurate if we tried to compensate for the inadequacies of the Black formula by using the Black delta formula with a 24% volatility, instead of 20%?

---

make use of more realistic copulae (e.g. the Student copula), and assign a richer correlation structure between the reference assets than a single number. There is, however, a one-to-one correspondence between the price of a tranched credit derivative and the output of a single input of a Gaussian copula model. Therefore, the practice has emerged to communicate prices by quoting *the* Gaussian–copula correlation, even if traders now agree that this model is inadequate.

[2]A note on terminology. The expression 'a 30-delta option' means the following. Consider the implied volatility associated with the particular strike of that option. Use this implied volatility in the (now incorrect) Black delta formula, $\mathcal{N}(h_1)$. The resulting number, which is between 0 and 1, multiplied by 100, gives the market quote for the delta of that option. If we are in the presence of a smile, the Black formula does not apply, and the procedure *is therefore nothing but a way to quote a strike after taking a reasonable normalization with respect to the degree of at-the-moneyness*.

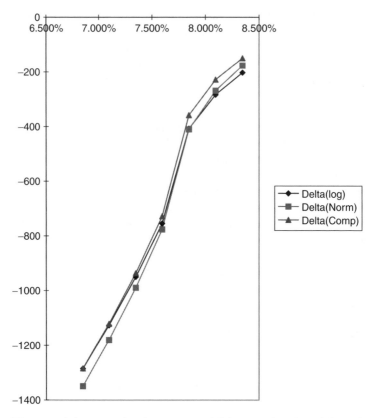

Figure 6.1   The normal, log-normal and compensated deltas as a function of the option strike (see the text for a discussion).

The approach is tempting. Unfortunately, in the presence of smiles the implied volatility quote does not directly tell us anything about the process of the underlying. In particular, it does not follow that the Black delta evaluated with the higher volatility should provide a 'better' hedge for the out-of-the-money option than the hedge carried out on the basis of the at-the-money volatility.

This point is illustrated in Figures 6.1 and 6.2, and in Table 6.1. In obtaining these values I have assumed that the true distribution for the forward rate, f, was normal rather than log-normal, and, from its absolute volatility, σ_{abs}, obtained the percentage (log-normal) volatility, σ_{log}, that produces the same at-the-money price. I discuss in Chapter 16 that this percentage volatility is accurately, although not exactly, given by $\sigma_{abs} = \sigma_{log} f$. The caplet prices were then calculated for several strikes. For an at-the-money strike the normal and log-normal prices virtually coincided, but, away from the at-the-money strike, discrepancies were obviously found between the prices obtained using the two different distributional assumptions.

Since in this example I have assumed that the true underlying process is known, I also know what the correct hedge ratio should be. I can therefore ask the question: If I used the implied smiley volatility with the log-normal Black formula, would I obtain better hedge ratios than if I used the at-the-money volatility? Or, to phrase the question

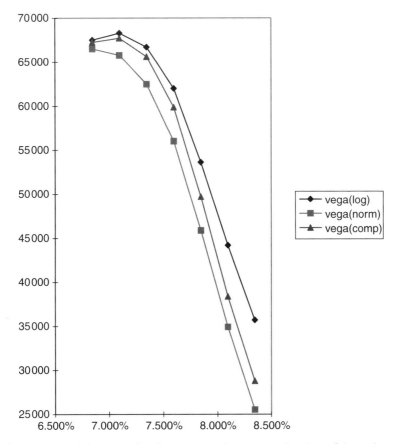

Figure 6.2 The normal, log-normal and compensated vegas as a function of the option strike (see the text for a discussion).

Table 6.1 The delta (in futures contracts) and the vega (in $) for a caplet with the strikes in the left-hand column (Strike). The columns Delta(Norm) and Vega(Norm) indicate the delta and vega under the assumption that the forward rate was normally distributed. The columns Delta(log) and Vega(log) report the same quantities under the assumption of log-normality. The columns Delta(Comp) and Vega(Comp) give the delta and vega obtained using the 'compensated' log-normal volatility. See the text for a discussion.

Strike	Delta(log)	Delta(Norm)	Delta(Comp)	Vega(log)	Vega(Norm)	Vega(Comp)
6.846%	−1,285	−1,349	−1,285	67,511	66,511	67,263
7.096%	−1,127	−1,181	−1,122	68,299	65,786	67,721
7.346%	−950	−990	−936	66,715	62,500	65,625
7.596%	−755	−776	−728	62,013	56,018	59,886
7.846%	−407	−410	−358	53,640	45,873	49,721
8.096%	−283	−269	−228	44,193	34,932	38,379
8.346%	−202	−176	−149	35,712	25,524	28,805

differently: Can the information about the true process contained in the smiley implied volatilities be profitably used to estimate the delta simply by using this implied volatility in the Black formula?

In order to answer these questions I proceed as follows. First, the 'true' (i.e. given our assumptions, the normal) deltas and vegas were calculated for a variety of strikes. These true risk statistics are shown in the columns Delta(Norm) and Vega(Norm), respectively. The same quantities were then calculated using the Black formula for the delta and vega with the same percentage volatility as determined by the relationship $\sigma_{abs} = \sigma_{log} f$ as input. (We know that this volatility will reproduce the correct at-the-money prices.) The hedge ratios so obtained are shown in the columns Delta(log) and Vega(log). Finally, the delta and vega statistics were calculated using the Black formula and a 'compensated' volatility equal to the implied smiley volatility that produces the away-from-the-money prices. These are shown in columns Delta(Comp) and Vega(Comp).

We can now ask: When used in conjunction with the (incorrect) Black formula, do these strike-dependent 'compensated' volatilities provide a better approximation of the true (normal) deltas and vegas than the single value given by the at-the-money log-normal volatility? As one can see from Figures 6.1 and 6.2 and from Table 6.1, the answer is in general 'no': a small improvement in the vega has, in fact, to be counterbalanced by a similarly small deterioration of the approximation in the case of the delta. The fact that the delta turned out to be slightly worse and the vega slightly better was, of course, just due to the specific choice of the strike and of the smile-generating process (a normal, rather than log-normal diffusion). In general, however, the trader will simply observe a smile, and will not be able to tell by which process it has been generated. Therefore, the implied smiley volatilities can only be reliably used for the purpose of obtaining prices.

6.3.2   Pricing a European Digital Option

A second example can make the same point even more clearly. Let us consider a European cash-or-nothing binary option. This option pays $1 if the underlying ends above the strike of $100 at expiry, and zero otherwise. Since there is only one 'look time', this option is also called a European digital. Let us also assume again that the true process for the underlying is a normal diffusion.

The payoff of this cash-or-nothing option can be approximated, in the absence of transaction costs and bid–offer spreads, with arbitrary precision by means of a simple call spread: in the limit as ϵ goes to zero, the strategy of buying a call at $100 − \epsilon$ and selling a call at $100 (both with a notional of $\frac{1}{\epsilon}$) would approximate the required payoff as closely as we may wish. See Chapter 17 for a more detailed discussion. Therefore the analytic price of the European digital, *PV(ED)*, is obtained as the limit as ϵ goes to zero of the price of the two call spreads:

$$PV(ED) = \mathcal{N}(h_2) = \lim_{\epsilon \to 0} \frac{1}{\epsilon} [Call(K - \epsilon) - Call(K)] \qquad (6.1)$$

In a Black-and-Scholes world and in the absence of market frictions, the cost of setting up this strategy converges to the well-known term $\mathcal{N}(h_2)$, with

$$h_2 = \frac{\ln \dfrac{S}{K} - \dfrac{1}{2}\sigma^2 t}{\sigma \sqrt{t}} \qquad (6.2)$$

and

S = stock price
K = strike
σ = volatility
t = time to expiry.

If there are no smiles, the formula is totally unambiguous, since there is one and only one volatility, σ, for a given maturity. In the presence of smiles, however, the problem changes. It is tempting to use the analytic digital formula, i.e. $\mathcal{N}(h_2)$, with the quoted implied volatility for the strike equal to the barrier, K. Alternatively, we could use the limit of a tight call spread, with each call price obtained using the appropriate implied volatility in the Black formula. This requires some care, because, when calculating the value of the two calls, which have different strikes, their implied volatility is different. This difference does tend to zero with ϵ, but the notionals, $\frac{1}{\epsilon}$, diverge towards infinity, amplifying the effect of any small difference. Fortunately, the combined result of the two effects is to provide in the limit a finite value for the replicating strategy.[3] However, in the presence of smiles, this limit of the infinitely tight call spread does not converge to the value given by the $\mathcal{N}(h_2)$ formula, with the term h_2 calculated using the smiley implied volatility corresponding to the strike level.

We therefore seem to be faced with two plausible ways of pricing the cash-or-nothing option: either by using the formula $\mathcal{N}(h_2)$, with the smiley implied volatility corresponding to the barrier; or by using the limit of the infinitely tight call spread, with each component call valued using the appropriate implied volatility. The two methodologies, however, in general give different answers. Which one gives the theoretically correct price?

In order to answer this question, recall that we defined an implied volatility as 'the wrong number to put in the wrong formula to get the right price *of plain-vanilla options*'. The question 'Which of these two prices should one believe?' therefore has an unequivocal answer: the price is given by limit of the call spread that is constructed on the basis of the prices of plain-vanilla options.[4] Once again, the implied volatility, when used outside its correct domain of applicability, does not convey any information about an 'equivalent' or 'compensated' process.

6.4 Hedge Ratios for Plain-Vanilla Options in the Presence of Smiles

Section 6.2 showed that special care must be used when employing the Black implied volatility function in the presence of smiles. In particular, I stressed that it can be safely used only for the purpose of obtaining a price – as its definition implies – but that other uses, such as the calculation of a delta or a vega via the use of the Black formula, are in general unwarranted.

If, however, we forget for a moment how the Black formula was originally obtained, and what the links between this formula and the volatility of the underlying are, we could

---

[3]This can be proven by expanding the term $\mathcal{N}(h_2)$ in the vicinity of K.

[4]In reality, of course, one would not be able to deal at the quote prices for a 'market-size' transaction in the large (let alone infinite) notionals required. None the less, the call–spread procedure is still valid in order to obtain the theoretical 'mid' price of the European digital.

regard the market practice of quoting a plain-vanilla option price in the presence of smiles as made up of three components:

1. an a priori agreement of an 'arbitrary formula', which is a function of several inputs;

2. an agreement on the procedure needed in order to obtain from the market or from the product specification all the inputs but one (i.e. today's stock price, the funding rate to maturity, the strike, the time to maturity plus an extra input);

3. the price quote, expressed in terms of the remaining unobservable input.

If we look at price-making in this light, no specific interpretation in terms of more fundamental quantities is in general warranted for this last input, despite its being called 'volatility'. This interpretation of the price-making process is obviously somewhat strained: even in the presence of smiles, the Black formula, for all its imperfections, is clearly not an arbitrary formula; and the implied volatility, despite the fact that it is not 'truly' a time-dependent volatility, is in some imprecise way 'similar' to its well-defined cousin that applies when the process for the underlying is a pure diffusion driven by a time-dependent volatility. However, this way of looking at implied volatilities and at the Black formula provides a useful way of looking at option pricing. This can be seen as follows.[5]

From the definitions given, we can always write in a purely formal way the price, *Opt*, of an option as

$$Opt = Black(S, K, r, T; \sigma_{\text{impl}}) \qquad (6.3)$$

where *Opt* is the price of a plain-vanilla call or put, S, K, T and r are the stock price, the strike, the time to expiry and the short rate, respectively; σ_{impl} is the price-generating number chosen by the trader to make a price; and *Black* is the agreed-upon function to obtain a quoted price from this last input.

6.4.1   The Relationship Between the True Call Price Functional and the Black Formula

When dealing with a non-flat implied-volatility surface it is essential to draw a clear distinction between the true price functional that gives the value of a call as a function of the state variables, and the market-reference Black pricing formula. In the presence of smiles, in this section I regard the latter simply as a convenient agreed-upon way of quoting a price. To make the discussion concrete, I will assume that the underlying is a stock price, and the associated option is a call. Nothing material turns on this choice.

In what follows I will analyse the problem of a trader who observes with infinite accuracy[6] a smiley implied volatility surface. The trader is agnostic as to what the true process for the underlying might be, and simply expects that the true call pricing functional

---

[5]The remainder of this section has been adapted from Section 11.2 of Rebonato (2002).

[6]When I say that the trader knows the smile surface with 'infinite' accuracy I mean that she has carried out an interpolation/extrapolation of the smile surface in such a way that she can associate a unique and certain implied volatility to a continuum of strikes, and to all the maturities of interest. How to obtain these smooth input volatility surfaces is described in Chapter 9.

will depend on

- today's value of the stock price,

- the residual time to maturity,

- the strike of the option,

- a discount factor (numeraire),

- an unknown set of parameters describing the 'true' dynamics (such as diffusion coefficients, jump amplitudes, etc.), and, possibly,

- the past history of the relevant stochastic quantities.

The parameters describing the process of the underlying (volatility, jump frequency, jump amplitude, etc.) can, in turn, themselves be stochastic. However, they are all, obviously, strike-independent. The unknown 'true' parameters and the full history up to time t will be symbolically denoted by $\{\alpha_t\}$ and $\{\mathcal{F}_t\}$, respectively.

The Black formula, on the other hand, used to translate contemporaneous observed market prices for different strikes and maturities into a set of implied volatility numbers, depends in the presence of smiles on

- today's value of the stock price,

- the residual time to maturity,

- a discount factor (numeraire),

- the strike of the option and

- a single *strike-dependent* parameter (the implied volatility).

I will denote the stock price in the problem as S and the volatility of the diffusion part of its unknown true process as σ. I do not assume, however, that the true process is just a complex diffusion, and the symbol $\{\alpha_t\}$ collectively denotes all the other parameters (e.g. jump frequencies, jump amplitude ratios) that might characterize the true process. The symbol K, as elsewhere, has been reserved for the strike of the call, and I will denote the true functional by $C(S_t, t, T, K, \{\alpha_t\}, \{\mathcal{F}_t\}, \sigma)$, and the Black formula by $Black(S_t, T - t, K, \sigma_{\text{impl}}(t, T, S, K))$.

6.4.2 Calculating the Delta Using the Black Formula and the Implied Volatility

The trader is aware that, given the existence of a non-flat implied volatility curve, she does not inhabit a Black world, and that, in particular, the Black implied volatility, σ_{impl}, is not linked in any simple way to the volatility, σ, of the true process – more specifically, she knows that is not equal to its root mean square: the implied volatility is just 'the wrong number to put in the wrong (Black) formula to get the right call price'. Therefore, as of 'today' (time 0), by the very definition of implied volatility, the trader can only write

$$C(S_0, 0, T, K, \{\alpha_0\}, \{\mathcal{F}_0\}, \sigma) = Black(S, T - 0, K, \sigma_{\text{impl}}(0, T, S, K)) \qquad (6.4)$$

(Since, for simplicity, I will always deal in the following example with a single expiry time, T, as seen from today, I will lighten the notation by writing $\sigma_{\text{impl}}(0, T, S, K) = \sigma_{\text{impl}}(S, K)$.)

The trader would then like to be able to calculate the delta, i.e. to compute

$$\Delta = \frac{\partial C(S, 0, T, K, \{\alpha_0\}, \{\mathcal{F}_0\}, \sigma)}{\partial S} \tag{6.5}$$

The task appears difficult because the trader does not know the true functional. Today, however, thanks to (6.4), she can always write,

$$\Delta = \frac{\partial Black(S, T, K, \sigma_{\text{impl}}(S, K))}{\partial S} \tag{6.6}$$

which, because of the dependence of the implied volatility on S, she knows to be given by

$$\Delta = \mathcal{N}(h_1) + \frac{\partial Black(S, T, K, \sigma_{\text{impl}}(S, K))}{\partial \sigma_{\text{impl}}(S, K)} \frac{\partial \sigma_{\text{impl}}(S, K)}{\partial S}$$

$$= \mathcal{N}(h_1) + BlackVega(S, T, K, \sigma_{\text{impl}}(S, K)) \frac{\partial \sigma_{\text{impl}}(S, K)}{\partial S} \tag{6.7}$$

In Equation (6.7) the quantity *BlackVega* is the derivative of the Black function with respect to the implied volatility, $\mathcal{N}(.)$ denotes the cumulative normal distribution, and h_1 is the usual argument of $\mathcal{N}(.)$ in the Black formula calculated with the implied volatility. From Equation (6.7) it is clear that the only difficulty in calculating the delta is associated with the term $\frac{\partial \sigma_{\text{impl}}(S, K)}{\partial S}$. How can the trader estimate this quantity?

6.4.3   Dependence of Implied Volatilities on the Strike and the Underlying

From today's plain-vanilla option market the trader can, at least in principle, observe a continuous series of implied volatilities as a function of the call and put strikes, or, more precisely, she can observe a series of contemporaneous call prices for different strikes given today's stock price, S_0. The trader, by inversion of the Black's formula, then knows how to convert these prices into implied volatilities. In other words, for a given S_0, she observes the variation of the function $\sigma_{\text{impl}}(S, K)$ along the K dimension, $\sigma_{\text{impl}}(S_0, K)$. However, she cannot say anything, just from this market information, about how this function varies, if at all, when S changes. For the sake of concreteness, let us assume that the trader observes that, as a function of K, the quantity $\sigma_{\text{impl}}(S_0, K)$ increases as K decreases (for a fixed S_0). In order to make some progress, the trader decides to make a few assumptions about the 'true' process, namely that it is a diffusion, that the true process volatility – which bears no direct relationship to the implied volatility – is of the form $\sigma(S)$, and that this true volatility function decreases when S (not K!) increases, i.e.

$$\frac{\mathrm{d}S}{S} = \sigma(S)\,\mathrm{d}z \tag{6.8}$$

$$\frac{\partial \sigma(S)}{\partial S} < 0 \tag{6.9}$$

(The drift has been ignored for simplicity.) The question faced by the trader is: How can she compute the delta, $\frac{\partial C(S,0,T,K,\{\alpha_0\},\{\mathcal{F}_0\},\sigma)}{\partial S}$? Naturally enough, given her imperfect knowledge of the process, she would like to make as much use as possible of the information embedded in the quoted market price of options. In particular, she would like to use the expression

$$\Delta = \mathcal{N}(h_1) + BlackVega(S,T,K,\sigma_{\text{impl}}(S,K))\frac{\partial \sigma_{\text{impl}}(S,K)}{\partial S}$$

This approach might be promising even if the true process (6.8) were known, because it might be difficult to calculate its derivative with respect to S analytically. The market-given plot of $\sigma_{\text{impl}}(S_0,K)$, however, only gives the trader information about how the implied volatility changes as a function of the strike, K, not of the underlying, S. In order to calculate the delta the trader must therefore make some much stronger assumptions about the true process. If the trader assumed, for instance, that the implied volatility were of the form $\sigma_{\text{impl}}(S,K) = \sigma_{\text{impl}}(S-K)$, then we she could easily switch from $\frac{\partial}{\partial S}$ to $\frac{\partial}{\partial K}$, and could read the information she needed directly off today's market function $\sigma_{\text{impl}}(S_0,K)$. Alternatively, if the trader knew that the implied volatility function was of the form $\sigma_{\text{impl}} = \sigma_{\text{impl}}(\ln S/K)$, the change in implied volatility as a function of S could be read off today's chart for the change of σ_{impl} as a function of K. For a process of the general form (6.8), however, she cannot know a priori whether the implied volatility function will indeed turn out to be of the form, say, $\sigma_{\text{impl}}(S-K)$, i.e. whether the prices implied by the true process (6.8) would actually give rise to an implied volatility that only depends on the difference $(S-K)$. In general, therefore, the trader will have to add to her information set some views about the behaviour of the implied volatility function along the S dimension.

In order to make some progress, the trader decides to test the hypothesis that the true process volatility should be of the form $\sigma = g(S)$, for some particular function g that gives $\frac{\partial \sigma(S)}{\partial S} < 0$. The dependence of the volatility on the underlying might be very complex, and perhaps only available following an algorithmic route (see, for instance, the local-volatility models described in Chapters 11 and 12). If this is the case, how can the trader go about finding the dependence of the implied volatility on the underlying (i.e. ultimately, the delta)? She could conceptually attempt to answer this question by proceeding as follows. She could begin by running a Monte Carlo simulation of the process (6.8) starting with $S_0 + \delta S$ and $\sigma(S_0 + \delta S)$ using for the initial process volatility. By averaging over discounted expectations, she could then calculate the prices of several calls for different strikes, and convert these prices into an implied volatility function, $\sigma_{\text{impl}}(S_0 + \delta S, K)$. She could then repeat the exercise with today's price for the underlying shifted down by the same amount, i.e. she could re-run the Monte Carlo simulation with a starting point equal to $S_0 - \delta S$ (and volatility $\sigma(S_0 + \delta S)$), calculate the prices for the same set of strikes and convert them into a new function, $\sigma_{\text{impl}}(S_0 - \delta S, K)$. Now, for each strike K, she would finally be in a position to compute the term $\frac{\partial \sigma_{\text{impl}}(S)}{\partial S}$ by approximating it as

$$\frac{\partial \sigma_{\text{impl}}(S,K)}{\partial S} \simeq \frac{\sigma_{\text{impl}}(S_0 + \delta S, K) - \sigma_{\text{impl}}(S_0 - \delta S, K)}{2\delta S} \tag{6.10}$$

As we shall see in Chapters 23 and 24, if the true process volatility does display a decreasing behaviour in S (see Equation (6.8) and the assumption above) the implied volatility curve will indeed display a monotonically decreasing shape in K. The important point, however, is that the true process volatility was *assumed* to be a decreasing function of the underlying, S, and that the implied volatility was *found* to be a decreasing function of the strike, K. A priori, i.e. before doing the price calculations outlined above, one could not have immediately concluded that a decreasing true volatility with S would give rise to a decreasing implied volatility with K (although some good financial intuition could have suggested that this might have been the case).

From this thought experiment one can draw a first conclusion: in general, even if the trader knew perfectly today's implied volatility curve as a function of the strike K for the current stock price, S_0, she could not in general and in a model-neutral way determine the delta. There is only one alternative to specifying the process for the underlying, as the trader had to do in order to run the Gedanken Monte Carlo simulation described above: the trader could try to make some assumptions directly about the dependence of the smile surface on the underlying, such as, for instance, $\sigma_{impl}(S, K) = \sigma_{impl}(S - K)$ or $\sigma_{impl}(S, K) = \sigma_{impl}(\ln(S) - \ln(K))$, or, more generally, $\sigma_{impl}(S, K) = \sigma_{impl}(h(S) - g(S))$, where $h(.)$ is some function.

Are these assumptions reasonable? The question can be rephrased as: How do call prices across strikes (i.e. the implied volatility curve) change in the real world when S changes? Clearly, the question is difficult because, when the trader observes a market change in S, and she simultaneously observes a change in the call price, she cannot be sure that the true (and possibly stochastic) volatility function might not have changed as well at the same time. However, if it is reasonable to invoke a sort of 'adiabatic approximation', i.e. to say that the volatility should change more slowly than the price, the trader can attempt to answer the question empirically. Indeed, this is the type of analysis undertaken in the interest-rate case in Chapter 23.

Useful as this information might be, one must be very careful in assigning a priori the behaviour of the implied volatility as a function of the underlying. Chapter 17 discusses in detail if, when and to what extent this exercise can be carried out.

6.4.4   Floating and Sticky Smiles and What They Imply about Changes in Option Prices

We have reached the conclusion that the evaluation of the delta is equivalent to a statement as to how the implied volatility changes as a function of the stock price. If, for instance, the assumption $\sigma_{impl}(S, K) = \sigma_{impl}(S - K)$ were true, then, as S moves to $S + \delta S$, the trader would observe that the price of the call with strike $K + \delta S$ would now be recoverable by inputting the same implied volatility in the Black formula. If the assumption $\sigma_{impl}(S, K) = \sigma_{impl}(\ln S - \ln K) = \sigma_{impl}(\ln S/K)$ were true, then the trader would observe that, as S moves to $(1 + \delta)S$, the call price with strike $K(1 + \delta)$ would be recoverable by inputting in the Black formula the same implied volatility and strike $K(1 + \delta)$; etc. In Chapter 17, I call this behaviour the (absolute or relative, respectively) floating smile. Recall, however, that the Black formula is homogeneous of degree one in S and K, i.e. if both S and K are multiplied by the same constant $(1 + \delta)$, the call price is simply multiplied by $(1 + \delta)$. Therefore, if the smile were, for instance, relatively floating, when both the underlying and the strike move from S and K to $S(1 + \delta)$ and $K(1 + \delta)$, respectively, the ratio of the stock price to the strike would not change, the (relatively floating) implied volatility would be the same, and the price of a call would simply be multiplied by $(1 + \delta)$. Once again, it is only by observing how real call prices change when the underlying changes that one can deduce the dependence on S of the implied volatility, and, therefore, calculate the correct delta.

This scaling ('floating') behaviour of the option price as a function of the underlying appears very 'natural'. The most different type of behaviour is probably the following. Let us suppose that, when $S = S_0$, the true process gives rise to the price $Black(S_0, K, \sigma_{\text{impl}}(S_0, K))$ for a K-strike call. Let us also suppose that, when the underlying instantaneously moves to $S_0 + \delta S$, the price of the same-(K)-strike call is given by $Black(S_0 + \delta S, K, \sigma_{\text{impl}}(S_0, K))$. When prices behave this way the underlying process is said to give rise to a sticky smile. Note carefully that for a fixed strike K the implied volatility $\sigma_{\text{impl}}(S_0, K)$ used to calculate the price when S moved from S_0 to $S_0 + \delta S$ has not changed to $\sigma_{\text{impl}}(S_0 + \delta S, K)$ (although the call price is now obviously different). If this is the case, then the implied volatility is independent of S, one can write $\sigma_{\text{impl}}(S, K) = \sigma_{\text{impl}}(K)$,

$$\frac{\partial \sigma_{\text{impl}}(S, K)}{\partial S} = 0 \tag{6.11}$$

and in evaluating the delta

$$\Delta = \mathcal{N}(h_1) + BlackVega(S, K, \sigma_{\text{impl}}(S, K)) \frac{\partial \sigma_{\text{impl}}(S, K)}{\partial S} \tag{6.12}$$

the last term disappears and the trader recovers the simple Black expression (with the implied volatility as input):

$$\Delta_{Black} = \mathcal{N}(h_1) \tag{6.13}$$

Summarizing: if a smile were truly sticky, a K-strike option would always have the same implied volatility irrespective of where the underlying moved, i.e. irrespective of the degree of in-the-moneyness of the option itself. If a smile were perfectly floating, the implied volatility would always remain the same for the same degree of (log-) in-the-moneyness, and the price of same-delta options would be exactly proportional to the underlying. Perfectly floating and perfectly sticky constitute two extreme cases of smiles. A given process will in general produce a behaviour intermediate between the two. It is impossible to deduce just by inspection of the smile curve as a function of K for a given S_0 whether the smile is sticky, floating or intermediate in nature. Indeed, one can prove that an infinity of processes is compatible with any (admissible) set of market call prices today (no matter how finely spaced in expiry and/or strike). See, for example, Britten-Jones and Neuberger (1998). More fundamentally, smiles can be of an altogether more complex nature, i.e. they can be stochastic. This means that knowledge of the future realization of the underlying and of the sticky or floating character of the smile does not tell us what the future smile will be like. Stochastic smiles are dealt with in Chapter 17. Today's smile just gives us a snapshot but what we would actually need is a (short) movie.

Exercise 1 *Assume that the true process is given by a normal diffusion, i.e. in Equation (6.8), assume $\sigma(S) = \frac{\sigma_0}{S}$. Calculate, using the appropriate closed-form expression for normal diffusions, a set of call prices for different strikes starting from a given S_0. Repeat the exercise for $S_0 + \delta S$ and $S_0 - \delta S$. Obtain $\sigma_{\text{impl}}(S_0, K)$, $\sigma_{\text{impl}}(S_0 + \delta S, K)$ and $\sigma_{\text{impl}}(S_0 - \delta S, K)$. Calculate the derivatives $\frac{\partial \sigma_{\text{impl}}(S, K)}{\partial S}$ and $\frac{\partial \sigma_{\text{impl}}(S, K)}{\partial K}$. Comment on their relative magnitude,* *and compare with the relative magnitude of the same derivatives in the log-normal (Black) case. What can you conclude about the degree of 'stickiness' of the normal-diffusion smile?*

We have reached the conclusion that a good starting point towards choosing an appropriate process and evaluating the delta (and, by extension of the reasoning, the other derivatives) of a call option can be profitably split into two components:

1. An empirical part, which addresses the question: What is the functional dependence of the implied volatility on S and K, $\sigma_{\text{impl}}(S, K)$? The answer to this question can only be obtained by observing price *changes* (not just prices). See, for instance, the analysis in Chapter 23. The observation of these price changes should, in theory, be separated by small time intervals (to avoid the possibility that the true process volatility might change, at the same time polluting the price picture).

2. A modelling part: once the function $\sigma_{\text{impl}}(S, K)$ has been determined, one can either determine the delta directly using formula (6.7); or one can fit a model that simultaneously produces today's prices with S_0 (a relatively easy task) and the prices that give rise to the function $\sigma_{\text{impl}}(S, K)$ (a much more difficult task).

In theory, if we 'just' want to price and hedge plain-vanilla options, the two approaches are equivalent. The second route in point 2 above is however more appealing because, if one can think in terms of a model, one's intuition is significantly enhanced, and we can understand *why*, say, the delta displays a certain dependence on the underlying. If the model allows for closed-form solutions, then the deltas, gammas, vegas, etc. can be obtained easily and quickly, without having to contend with numerical problems which, especially for gammas, can often be burdensome. More generally, once a model is specified one can do a lot more than just calculating the risk statistics, and the evaluation of complex derivatives becomes possible.

On the other hand, the desirability of a model is often assessed on the basis of its ability to reproduce an evolution of the smile surface (as a function of time and of the underlying) congruous with the trader's intuition. It is therefore also tempting to try to assign directly how the smile surface is deformed when the underlying moves, and as time goes by. Appealing as this approach might be, it is prone to risk of arbitrage. Why this is the case is explained in Chapter 17.

In the discussion above I have made reference to 'sticky' and 'floating' smiles, and I have pointed out that the associated behaviours of the smile surface are at the opposite ends of the spectrum of the possible evolution patterns of the smile as a function of the underlying. In order to gain some financial intuition about these important, albeit stylized, modes of deformation, I present a couple of 'smile tales' in the following sections.

6.5   Smile Tale 1: 'Sticky' Smiles

An option trader considers entering a strategy consisting of a long and a short position in plain-vanilla options on forward rates spanning different portions of the same steep yield curve. The early-expiring forward rates trade at around 3%, and the long end of the curve has forward rates in the 6% area. The trader wants to delta-hedge dynamically her option positions through time, and 'trade the gamma', much as discussed in Chapter 4. In other words, she hopes that the realized volatility will be greater than the implied volatility. If this is the case, since she is going to be long gamma, every time she re-hedges she will be selling when prices rise and buying when prices fall. She hopes that the cumulative effect of these re-hedging transactions will more than compensate her for the premium she has paid up-front.

The two options that the trader is considering buying trade at the same implied volatility. She observes that, when the yield curve moves, the forward rates in the high portion of the curve move by more basis points than the forward rates in the low-maturity portion. Given the posited shape of the yield curve, this is to be expected, since, in a Black world, the *absolute* one-standard-deviation move of any forward rate should be

$$\sigma_T(t) f(t, T, T + \tau) \qquad (6.14)$$

where $\sigma_T(t)$ is the percentage volatility at time t of the forward rate, $f(t, T, T + \tau)$, expiring at time T and spanning the period $[T \ T + \tau]$. Since the percentage volatility for the two options is the same, the long-maturity forward (at 6%) should move, on average, roughly twice as much as the front-end-maturity forward rate (at 3%).

The trader, however, observes that the basis point moves of the two forward rates do not quite scale in the two-to-one ratio predicted by their implied percentage volatilities. The 3% forward rate moves on average more than half as much as the 6% forward. After running a regression, she concludes that the 'low' forward rate moves, approximately, by 75% as much.

Therefore the trader forms the belief that, *ceteris paribus*, as the level of a particular forward rate increases, its percentage volatility tends to be reduced. Similarly, when forward rates fall, their percentage volatility seems to increase. In other words, perhaps the trader subscribes to a world view according to which

$$df = \mu_f \, dt + f^\beta \sigma(t) \, dz_t \qquad (6.15)$$

with $\beta < 1$. If the trader's view were that the curve moved strictly in parallel, then $\beta = 0$. Note that, in the expression above, the term $\sigma(t)$ has remained purely a function of time.

This particular assumption about the link between the percentage volatility and the level of the underlying rates is referred to as the constant elasticity of variance (CEV) framework, and will be discussed in Chapter 24. More generally, these distributional assumptions can be generalized as

$$df = \mu_f \, dt + \sigma(f_t, t) \, dz_t \qquad (6.16)$$

Models consistent with the dynamics (6.16) are called 'local-volatility models'. The trader in our story is aware of all these models, but likes to think in terms of Black implied volatilities. Also, her back-office system does not incorporate the CEV model, let alone the more sophisticated local-volatility approaches, and can only price Black options. The trader knows that a process such as

$$df = \mu_f \, dt + f^\beta \sigma(t) \, dz_t \qquad (6.17)$$

will give rise to a price distribution different from the log-normal, and prices different from the Black prices for non-at-the-money options. Therefore she adjusts her prices to reflect these beliefs and quotes different implied volatilities for options with the same

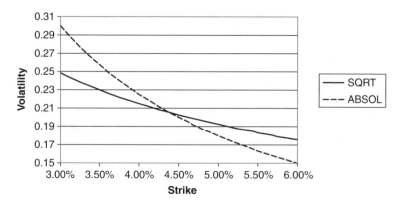

Figure 6.3   The smiles quoted by a trader who believed in a CEV model for interest rates, with $\beta = \frac{1}{2}$ or $\beta = 0$.

expiry but different strikes. If one plots the implied volatility against the strike one would probably obtain a curve of the shape shown in Figure 6.3. Despite appearances, this is called a smile.

The most important feature of Smile Tale 1 is that the trader in the story believes in a deviation from the log-normal behaviour for the forward rates that is *a function of the absolute level of the rates themselves*. Furthermore, if rates tomorrow were to move, say, up, the trader in our story would still use the same graph to read the implied volatility of a same-strike option. In other words, her beliefs about the relative movement (in basis points per day) of a 3% forward rate with respect to the movement of a 6% forward rate will not be different according to whether rates 'today' have moved up or down. Her implied-volatility-vs-strike curve would therefore not move with the level of rates. This property is often referred to in the market as a 'sticky' smile. It is important to point out that it is a property of implied, not instantaneous, volatilities.

6.6   Smile Tale 2: 'Floating' Smiles

A fund manager is heavily invested in equities and believes that, strategically, such an equity-heavy asset allocation is desirable for the near-to-medium term future. She is however afraid of the possibility of a market crash, and, as insurance, decides to buy out-of-the-money puts on the index. Since many of her colleagues are in a similar position, and all share the same fears, they are all buying insurance protection, and by so doing bid up the prices of out-of-the-money puts.

Arbitrageurs operating as traders for the investment bank Short Term Capital scour the earth for arbitrage opportunities; in particular for mis-priced options. They cannot fail to notice that, due to the systematic bidding up of the fund manager, out-of-the-money puts trade four vegas above the at-the-money options. If the universe indeed behaved as postulated by the Black model, for a given maturity there can only be one volatility for the underlying process, irrespective of the strike we might choose to transact. Therefore there would seem to be a killing to be made by selling the out-of-the-money puts and buying as a vega hedge the cheap at-the-money options.

Senior management of Short Term Capital, however, are alerted by Risk Management of this trade idea, and begin to ask some probing questions, such as: What would happen if the sudden market crash the fund managers are seeking insurance against did happen?

The Head of Research is brought into the discussion, and she points out that, in that event, even neglecting the drying up of liquidity, one of the fundamental requisites of the Black strategy, i.e. the ability to carry out a continuous re-hedging strategy, would fail. More ominously, given the proposed strategy of the traders, if a crash occurred, the arbitrageurs would always lose out: since over a price gap re-hedging is impossible, the delta-hedged out-of-the-money short calls would always lose more money than what is made by the at-the-money long options. A risk-averse Risk Management is therefore confronted with a portfolio not only with a finite variance (because continuous re-hedging cannot take place during a gap), but also, and more worryingly, whose returns are skewed to the left.

There is much to-ing and fro-ing between the Head of Trading, Senior Management, the Head of Research and Risk Management. As this goes on, the fund managers continue to buy protection and the out-of-the-money puts now trade at six vegas above the at-the-money options.

The trading opportunity is becoming more and more enticing. The point comes when the out-of-the-money puts are so expensive that (even) Risk Management acknowledge that it is worth the risk to short them. What triggered the decision? Once Short Term Capital recognizes that the conditions for a perfect arbitrage do not exist, what tilts the balance is a trade-off between the risk of being 'caught out' by a crash and the enticement of extracting six vegas from the strategy if the crash does not occur. Despite the conventional wisdom that option prices do not depend on the investor's aversion to risk, the decision to trade, at least in this story, has reflected the bank's appetite for risk. Since the riskless portfolio cannot be put in place in the presence of jumps of unknown amplitude, it is no longer true that option pricing is independent of risk preferences. A market price for jump risk enters the valuation of the option. The mathematics are a bit more involved than in the straightforward Black-and-Scholes case, and will be discussed in Chapter 14, but the intuition is simple: whenever effective hedging is not possible, risk aversion makes the buyer of the option 'see' a less positive expected return on the underlying. In the presence of unhedgeable price gaps, this means 'seeing' the jumps as more frequent and more 'to the left' than in the real world.

6.6.1 Relevance of the Smile Story for Floating Smiles

While all of this trading activity has been going on the equity index has been moving all over the place: from 6000 it went to 4500 and back up to 7500. In this story, fund managers always face the problem of protecting their portfolios from the market level where they are. At any point in time they buy puts that are out-of-the-money with respect to the *then-current* at-the-money level. They do not get sentimentally attached to puts struck at 5000 (quite useful when the index used to be around 6000, but in-the-money when the index is at 4500, and providing rather cold comfort when it is at 7000). The bidding up of the prices of puts (and hence of their implied volatility) tends to take place around a certain degree of out-of-the-moneyness, which, in turn, migrates with spot. *This is the essence of a floating smile.* The fund manager will not use, when the index is at 7000, the same implied-volatility-vs-strike curve that prevailed when she bought the puts when the index was at 5000. And once again, the floating nature of the smile is a feature of the *implied* volatilities, not of the *instantaneous* ones.

Another way of characterizing this assumed behaviour of the fund managers is to postulate that they always seek protection by buying similarly out-of-the-money puts. For this reason, this picture of the world is sometimes referred to as the 'sticky delta' model. In order to avoid confusion, I will not use this terminology in the rest of the book.

The purpose of these two 'smile stories' is to show that plausible but radically different explanations can be found for the same phenomenon, i.e. for the fact that the implied volatilities of options of the same maturity but different strikes are not the same, and that the resulting smile is 'tilted to the left'. Reality, needless to say, can be considerably more subtle and complicated: regimes of sticky and floating smiles, for instance, are not as neatly separated as the two stylized stories above seem to indicate. One important conclusion that can be drawn even from these very simple stories, however, is that it is important to distinguish as clearly as possible the following questions:

- What financial mechanisms can give rise to smiles?

- What mathematical models can reproduce smiles?

- How can a model be calibrated to market prices in a way that is consistent with the underlying *financial* picture of the trading world?

The last question has raised the topic of calibration, i.e. of the process by means of which the free parameters of a model are chosen so as to yield the desired outputs (e.g. prices today, future smile surfaces). In the case of equity or FX options this problem is relatively simple when, for each expiry, the implied volatility is just a constant across strikes. But it appears with a vengeance in the presence of smiles. One of the problems with the complex calibration procedures required to deal with smiles is that the global fit to the market prices is typically obtained by varying a very large number of parameters. The optimization is almost always strongly non-linear, and many competing minima of similar numerical quality often exist. (See, for example, the discussion in Section 13.7.) How can the trader ensure that the calibration has been carried out in a 'sensible' manner? How can one choose among very different solutions of virtually identical numerical quality? Before leaving this introductory chapter it is therefore useful to explore in some detail one important aspect of the calibration process that has a direct bearing on the choice of the best parameter set.

6.7   When Does Risk Aversion Make a Difference?

In the following chapters we will often find that the option pricing formulae contain a combination of real-world quantities (mean-reversion speeds, jump amplitudes, etc.) and risk-aversion parameters ('market prices of risk'). These two sets of quantities are often combined in such a way that is impossible to disentangle one from the other. Since this feature is common to virtually all the pricing approaches described in the following chapters, its discussion is presented below.

6.7.1   Motivation

In Part II (see Chapters 13 and 14 in particular) I will show that, via the measure transformation required to arrive at the market prices of options, risk aversion can change some real-world parameters, such as, for instance, the frequency of downward jumps, or their amplitude. This motivates the (generally true) claim that, in moving from the real world to the risk-adjusted world, measure changes alter the values of drift-related terms. This is clearly true in the derivation of the Black-and-Scholes formula, where the real-world drift of the stock does not enter the valuation, and it is only the riskless rate that matters. Similarly, in the last sections of Chapter 2 I indicated that, given the diffusive equation for an asset or rate, changing measure changes the drift, but leaves the diffusive part unaltered.

Similar considerations also apply to the stochastic-volatility or the jump–diffusion case. As shown in detail in Chapter 13, in fact, if the stochastic volatility is assumed to be mean-reverting, the move from the real-world measure to the pricing measure will alter both the mean-reversion speed and the mean-reversion level. However, it will leave the volatility of the volatility unaltered. Similarly, if we believe that the true process is a jump–diffusion, the discussion in Chapter 14 will show that it is the risk-adjusted, and not the real-world, jump frequency and jump amplitude ratio that will affect the prices of options.

The questions I am addressing in the remainder of this chapter are therefore the following. Suppose that we have chosen to estimate the (risk-adjusted) parameters of a model from the observed market prices of options. Given the existence of a measure transformation in moving from the real to the risk-adjusted world, have we really lost all ability to comment on the reasonableness of the implied parameters by comparing them with their statistical (real-world) estimates? If, for instance, the implied jump frequency obtained by fitting a jump–diffusion model to market prices turned out to be 10 times as large as the statistically estimated one, should we just shrug our shoulders? What if the implied frequency were *half* the statistical one? Can the measure transformation really 'do anything' to the real-world process? Are there situations when, even in the presence of risk-averse agents, risk aversion does not change the value of 'implied' (i.e. risk-adjusted) parameters from their real-world values?

The answers to these questions will be that the scrambling is often less unconstrained than it is often assumed, and that informative constraints on the measure-induced parameter change can sometimes be imposed on the basis of an underlying financial model and of the market dynamics. If the problem is looked at from a purely mathematical point of view, in fact, all the quantities mentioned above (reversion speed, reversion level, jump frequency, jump amplitude ratio, etc.) can in general change in very complex and arbitrary ways, and often it can be very difficult to say something even about the sign of the change. If, however, one complements the mathematical analysis with a simple financial model of the market dynamics and of the nature of risk aversion, it is often possible to say something more precise about the origin, the approximate magnitude and the sign of the drift transformations. I will present two instances of such an analysis in the context of stochastic-volatility models (see Section 13.2.3) and of two-regime stochastic volatility (see Section 27.4.2, subsection 'Eigenvalues and Eigenvectors'). Indeed, for the quantities above to differ when moving from the real-world to the risk-adjusted measure some conditions about the net supply and demand for options have to be satisfied. Both these aspects are explored below.

6.7.2 The Importance of an Assessment of Risk Aversion for Model Building

This aspect of model building is often neglected, and when the trader has estimated a set of 'implied parameters', the reaction is typically to throw one's hand up in surrender, and, no matter how 'implausible' these fitted parameters are, to state that 'nothing can be inferred from a comparison between the real-world and the risk-adjusted quantities'. In reality, many diagnostic tests can, and should, be carried out, because ultimately the risk adjustments to the real-world parameters should stem from a plausible financial model of how investors behave. It is true that one should probably not expect a quantitative match between the risk-adjusted quantities estimated from traded option prices and those obtained from the real world after adjustment for risk aversion. Yet, at least a qualitative or order-of-magnitude congruence should be recovered. This is not different from the debate centred around the equity premium puzzle (see, for example, Cornell (1999) or Dimson (2002) for a good discussion): the fact that the equity risk premium that can be estimated from the growth rate of equities and on the basis of reasonable assumptions about risk aversion does not seem to tally with reality has not simply been accepted with a shrug and by blithely saying that 'the equity growth rate changes because of risk aversion, and therefore it cannot be compared with the statistically observed one'. In reality, the dissonance between the 'measured' and theoretically estimated equity premia has spawned an immense literature that has questioned virtually all the assumptions underlying the economic models of investors' behaviour and the statistical analysis of the data.

One might retort that, despite all the books and articles written on the subject, we appear to be none the wiser about the origin of the equity risk premium. This might well be true, to some extent, but I believe that a statement of this type, translated to the field of option modelling, is simply a 'cop out'. If, in order to fit the market data with a jump–diffusion process we require a risk-adjusted jump frequency and a jump amplitude such that the stock market, in the pricing measure, is expected to fall by 80% five times a month, we can invoke the mysterious ways of measure transformations, and proceed to price and hedge options on the basis of the model thus calibrated. Alternatively, and more palatably, we can observe that, given plausible real-world estimates of the frequency and magnitude of equity market crashes, the degree of risk aversion implied by these estimated parameters would point to such a risk-averse representative investor that she would probably never to get out of bed in the morning (let alone hold common stock). If, instead of surrendering in the face of the complexity of the measure transformation we pursued the type of analysis I suggest below, we would be led to explore alternative models for the stock dynamics that might give a more congruous simultaneous picture of investor behaviour and option prices. This line of analysis has been thoughtfully carried out, for instance, in Bliss and Panigirtzoglou (2004). The results of these studies are also discussed later on (see Chapter 14).

Why do we care if the model is not correctly specified or properly calibrated, as long as it 'prices the market' today? Because, as I have argued in Chapter 1, recovering today's prices of the hedging options is not enough, and the cost of future re-hedging transactions will greatly affect the profitability of a trade. When markets are not complete and perfect replication is not possible, the success of a (partial) hedging strategy will depend both on having specified a correct model, and on having calibrated it correctly.

6.7.3   The Principle of Absolute Continuity

Some features of the measure transformation can be of help in carrying out the analysis discussed above. In moving between measures, in fact, the change in measure is constrained by the principle of absolute continuity. The principle ultimately goes back to the equivalence of the real-world measure and of any pricing measure (i.e. to the requirement that events impossible in one measure should remain impossible in any other related measure). This means that if jumps in the underlying are impossible in the real-world measure, they should be impossible in *any* pricing measure; if the volatility (or the jump frequency, or the jump amplitude ratio) in one measure is deterministic, so will they have to be in any other measure; if the volatility does not display jumps in one pricing measure it cannot do so in the objective one; switching measure can alter the transition frequencies of a Markov-chain process, but not the Markov-chain nature of the process; a reducible Markov chain cannot become an irreducible one; etc.

As I have said, the origin of these constraints is the requirement that all measures used for pricing should be equivalent (share the same null set). If, say, downward price jumps are observed in the real world, risk aversion can make a trader 'perceive' their probability of occurrence higher than is statistically observed. However, if we all agree that jumps *never* occur, the trader will not be able to seek compensation for a risk that does not exist. Equivalent measures can be wildly different, but they all agree on which events are possible and impossible.

6.7.4 The Effect of Supply and Demand

I mentioned above that excess supply and demand can affect the sign of the transformation of some parameters. This statement can appear surprising, because it is generally thought that supply-and-demand considerations should have no part in determining the prices of options, which can be arrived at in the canonical Black-and-Scholes treatment purely using no-arbitrage arguments. These arguments, however, only hold exactly true if the market can be considered to be complete and the parameters of the underlying process purely deterministic. (See also the discussion in Section 6.7.9 'The EMH Again'.)

I show below by means of a simple example that, in a Black-and-Scholes world with differing views among risk-averse traders about volatility:

- if the supply and demand for options is balanced and the market clears, the implied volatility that can be extracted from the price of the options *will not reflect any risk aversion (market price of risk), even if the individual traders are risk averse.* Furthermore, the risk-adjusted volatility coincides with the market expectation of the real-world volatility;

- if the supply and demand for options are unbalanced, for the market to clear the volatility level that can be extracted from the market prices will no longer coincide with the average of the market expectations;

- the greater the demand (supply) for options, the higher (lower) the level of the risk-adjusted volatility will be with respect to the average of the real-world expected volatility.

6.7.5 A Stylized Example: First Version

In order to derive the results mentioned above, I will have to make the assumption that the traders in the market are risk averse, and base their decision on the maximization of some expected, discounted utility function. The only essential feature of this utility function is that it should be concave (negative second derivative). The choice of the utility function is commented upon in the next subsection, but the same qualitative conclusions would have been reached if I had used, say, a logarithmic utility function instead of the power law that I have chosen. In other words, for the example below to be relevant, the results must be independent of the particular functional form for the utility function. For simplicity, I also choose a one-period setting: the traders enter their positions today, and can consume only at option expiry. After option expiry they retire.

Comments on the Choice of the Utility Function

Utility functions that depend on wealth, such as the one I will use below, are 'vacuous'. As Cochrane (2001) points out, unlike Uncle Scrooge very few of us gain intrinsic pleasure from bathing in gold coins held in a vault. In reality, agents maximize expected consumption, not just wealth, and one should consider how the payoff from a certain strategy co-varies with other sources of wealth. Also, investors can draw down their wealth over their lifetime, and a multi-period setting is more appropriate. However, if we limit ourselves to a single period, if we assume that investors do not have any other source of income, and that they are 'forced' to consume all their wealth at the end of the period, the problem is greatly simplified, and the basic intuition is not materially changed.

A more serious criticism would be that the whole concept of the utility function might be flawed. See, for instance, the critique of the usefulness of the 'classical' concept of the utility function by the behaviourist school (e.g. Kahneman and Tversky (2000)). While, on this matter, the jury is still out, I think it constitutes a useful conceptual framework within which to analyse at a qualitative level many important situations. I have expressed my views about models in Section 1.1.1, and, from this point of view, it is irrelevant to discuss whether utility theory is 'true' or 'false'; it is simply a model of reality (in this case, investor behaviour) with a given range of useful applicability. I think that the example presented below is within these limits.

As for the choice of the particular utility function, its only relevant feature for the discussion to follow is its negative convexity, at least over the range of wealth of interest. For simplicity I have therefore chosen

$$U(W) = (W + a)^\alpha \qquad (6.18)$$

with $a = -45\,000$ and $\alpha = 0.125$. (for $W > 45\,000$). I will call the offset quantity a the 'displacement coefficient'. The resulting utility function as a function of wealth is shown in Figure 6.4.

The Assumptions

In this first example I shall consider two traders who have different subjective views about the future outcome of volatility. More specifically, let us assume that both traders believe that the true process for the underlying is a pure diffusion with deterministic volatility, but they do not agree about the future realized value of this volatility. They are both planning to enter a position in an at-the-money plain-vanilla option (say, a call), expiring in one year's time. After doing the trade, they will enter in a delta-hedging strategy, where the appropriate amount of stock is dictated by the Black-and-Scholes formula with the

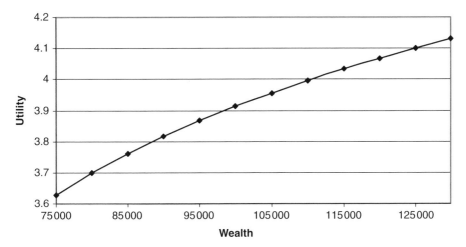

Figure 6.4 The utility function used in the example.

volatility input they believe appropriate. Roughly speaking, the profit or loss made during the life of the option will be equal to the difference between the Black-and-Scholes call prices with the true future realized volatility and with the volatility assumed for hedging (markets are assumed to be perfect, trading continuous, etc.). If the reader is not happy with this statement, she should re-read Chapter 4.

Since, apart from the disagreement about the realized value of the realized volatility, both traders agree in their belief that they inhabit a Black-and-Scholes world, *the* quantity about which they express their views is the root-mean-squared volatility to option expiry. There is no prior market in volatility. Given their beliefs, both traders will not hedge the vega of their positions, but will 'trade the gamma', and they are essentially making a market in implied volatilities. See again the discussion in Section 4.3 of Chapter 4. For the purpose of the following discussion it is therefore both reasonable and expedient to assume that their final wealth will be simply proportional to the difference between the realized and the assumed implied volatility over the life of the option.

As mentioned above (and again purely for the sake of simplicity), I will assume a finite-horizon model: both traders have a certain wealth at time t_0, buy or sell an option, as they see fit, dynamically re-hedge it during its life, and do not enter any other option trades until the expiry of the option. They have no other sources of income and they do not consume before option expiry.

Both traders are risk averse. They hold subjective views about the expected future value of the (root-mean-squared) volatility to expiry, but they are not sure about its outcome. Each trader therefore associates a subjective real-world probability to each possible future value of the volatility. The resulting probability density will be called the real-world subjective probability functions for Traders 1 and 2.

The Market-Clearing Process

The first trader believes that the realized root-mean-squared volatility will have a value centred around 19.00%, and that its realizations are normally distributed around this value with an (absolute) standard error of 5.00%. The second trader believes that the realized root-mean-squared volatility will have a value centred around 21.00%, and that its realizations are normally distributed around this value with an (absolute) standard error of 5.00%. Both traders will only enter a trade if the change in their discounted expected utility from the trade is positive. Before entering the trade the utility, U, for Trader 1 as a function of his initial wealth, $W_{0,1}$, is

$$U_1 = U(W_{0,1}) \tag{6.19}$$

with a similar expression for Trader 2. For simplicity and to lighten notation, I will begin by assuming that the initial wealth for both traders is the same, and therefore

$$W_{0,1} = W_{0,2} = W_0 \tag{6.20}$$

Ignoring discounting, the expectation of the change in utility for trader 1, ΔU_1, will be given by

$$\Delta U_1 = E_{Q_1}[U_1(W_{1,1})] - U_1(W_0) = \int U_1(W_{1,1})\phi_{Q_1}(W_{1,1})\,dW_{1,1} - U(W_0) \tag{6.21}$$

where E_{Q_1} denotes expectation with respect to the subjective probability measure, Q_1, of Trader 1, $\phi_{Q_1}(W_{1,1})$ is Trader 1's subjective probability density of wealth, and $U_1(W_{1,1})$ is the utility as a function of the wealth of Trader 1 at time 1. A similar expression holds for Trader 2. A necessary condition for either trader to enter a transaction is that ΔU_i should be positive. Thanks to the assumptions made above about the nature of the trade, the final wealth will be a function of the difference between the assumed and the realized root-mean-squared volatility to option expiry. If we denote by $\widehat{\sigma}_T$ the root-mean-squared volatility over the life of the option, we can write

$$W_{1,1} = f_1(\widehat{\sigma}_T) \tag{6.22}$$

Therefore

$$E_{Q_1}[U_1(W_{1,1})] = \int U_1(W_{1,1})\phi_{Q_1}(W_{1,1})\,dW_{1,1} = \int U_1(f_1(\widehat{\sigma}_T))\Psi_{Q_1}\left[f_1(\widehat{\sigma}_T)\right]d\sigma_T \tag{6.23}$$

where now Ψ_{Q_1} is Trader 1's subjective probability density for the realized root-mean-squared volatility. Finally, given the traders' Gaussian assumption about the distribution of the volatility the expression above can be rewritten as

$$E_{Q_1}[U(W_{1,1})] = \int U_1(W_{1,1})\phi_{Q_1}(W_{1,1})\,dW_{1,1} = \int U_1(f_1(\widehat{\sigma}_T))\Psi_{Q_1}\left[f_1(\widehat{\sigma}_T)\right]d\sigma_T$$

$$= \int U_1(f_1(g(z)))\Psi_{Q_1}(f_1(g(z)))\,dz \tag{6.24}$$

In this expression $g(z)$ is the Gaussian probability density of the volatility with expectation $\mu_1 = 19.00\%$ and standard deviation $v_1 = 5\%$ for Trader 1. The same expression (with the appropriate indices) applies to Trader 2.

For concreteness, I have assumed that the initial wealth of both traders, W_0, was $\$100\,000$, and that the size of the trade was such as to produce $\$2000$ for every percentage point difference between the expected and the realized volatility. So, if the realized volatility turned out to be exactly 19.00% Trader 1 would make no gain or no loss, and Trader 2 would lose $\$4000 = \$2000 * 100 * (19.00\% - 21.00\%)$.

Given our assumptions about the nature of the payoff, the volatility trade has a payoff linear in the realized volatility, σ_T, of the type

$$W_T = k(\sigma_T - \sigma_0) \tag{6.25}$$

The first trader will enter the volatility transaction provided that the strike, σ_0, is sufficiently different from his central view $\mu_1 = 19.00\%$. What is 'sufficient' in this context depends on his risk aversion. With the assumptions made we can write the expected utility for Trader 1 as

$$E_{Q_1}[U_1(W_{1,1})] = E_{Q_1}[U_1(W_0 + W_T)] = E_{Q_1}[U_1(W_0 + k(\sigma_T - \sigma_0))]$$

$$= \frac{1}{\sqrt{2\pi}} \int_{-\infty}^{+\infty} [W_0 + k(\mu_1 + v_1 z - \sigma_0) + a]^\alpha \exp[-\tfrac{1}{2}z^2]\,dz \tag{6.26}$$

where $k = \$2000$ per percentage point in volatility. For the particular values chosen for the utility function and the probability distribution Trader 1 will have a non-negative change in expected utility (and will therefore enter the trade) as long as the strike σ_0 is above (and including) 19.40%, or below approximately 18.60% (clearly, he will be happy to take a long position in volatility for strikes *below* 18.60% and a short position for strikes *above* 19.40%). The converse is true for Trader 2: she will be happy to go long volatility for strikes below and including 20.60%, and to go short volatility for strikes above 21.40%. The changes in expected utility for both traders are shown in Figures 6.5 and 6.6 and in Table 6.2.

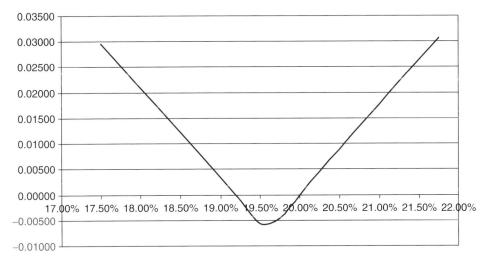

Figure 6.5 Change in expected utility (Trader 1).

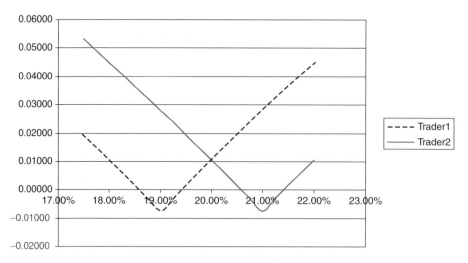

Figure 6.6   Change in expected utility (both traders).

Table 6.2   Change in expected utility (both traders).

Strike	Trader1	Trader2
17.50%	0.01938	0.05318
17.75%	0.01501	0.04906
18.00%	0.01059	0.04492
18.25%	0.00615	0.04075
18.50%	0.00166	0.03654
18.75%	−0.00286	0.03230
19.00%	−0.00742	0.02803
19.25%	−0.00287	0.02372
19.50%	0.00166	0.01938
19.75%	0.00614	0.01500
20.00%	0.01059	0.01059
20.25%	0.01500	0.00614
20.50%	0.01938	0.00166
20.75%	0.02372	−0.00287
21.00%	0.02803	−0.00743
21.25%	0.03230	−0.00287
21.50%	0.03654	0.00166
21.75%	0.04074	0.00614
22.00%	0.04492	0.01059

Conclusions from the First Version of the Example

How can we read Table 6.2? First of all, note that, because of the convexity in their utility functions, neither trader would willingly enter a transaction simply because the strike is 'on the right side' of the expectation: Table 6.2 shows a negative change in expected utility for a strike of, say, 21.25% for Trader 2 even if her expectation is 21.00%.

The second observation is that both traders would be happy to be 'long' volatility for a strike such as, say, 18.00%. Similarly, they would both be happy to take the same side of the trade for a strike of, say, 21.75%: both these strikes are sufficiently far away from their expectations that, even after applying to the possible payoffs the convex weights coming from their utility functions, they would still see such trades as 'good bets'. Unfortunately, at these strikes they would both like to take the same side of the trade. Therefore no trade would take place, and the market would not clear. There is a range of strikes, however, between 19.40% and 20.60%, where, even after adjusting for their risk aversion, the two traders would like to take *opposite* sides of the same transaction. Actually, in the allowed range, there is a particular value for the strike such that the sum of the expected utilities for the two traders is maximum. See Figure 6.7 and Table 6.3.

In our simple example there is no reason why the trade should occur exactly at this strike, but, if it did, the observed market strike would be exactly at 20.00%, i.e. at the average between the subjective expectations of Trader 1 and Trader 2. Furthermore, 20.00% is the middle point of the range of possible strikes. In this sense, *the market-implied volatility level does give an unbiased estimate of the 'market expectation'.* If we believe in markets as efficient processors of information, 'implying' the volatility from the prices of options *is*, in our example, a worthwhile exercise. Furthermore, even if the individual traders are risk averse, the 'market consensus' that we can extract from the option prices has turned out to be unpolluted by attitudes to risk. Looking at this example in more detail, we can also say that, as

- the difference in opinion about the expectation of the volatility (i.e. the difference between μ_1 and μ_2) becomes smaller,

- the uncertainty about the realization of the volatility (v) increases, and

- the risk aversion increases

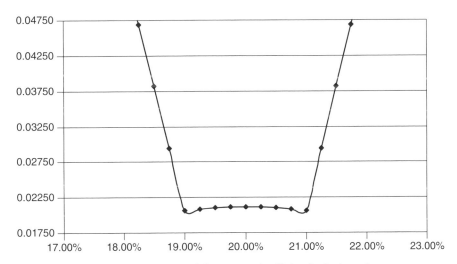

Figure 6.7 The sum of the expected utilities for both traders.

Table 6.3 The expected utilities for Traders 1 and 2.

Strike	Trader1	Trader2
17.50%	0.01938	0.14616
17.75%	0.01501	0.13470
18.00%	0.01059	0.12314
18.25%	0.00615	0.11149
18.50%	0.00166	0.09973
18.75%	−0.00286	0.08787
19.00%	−0.00742	0.07590
19.25%	−0.00287	0.06383
19.50%	0.00166	0.05164
19.75%	0.00614	0.03934
20.00%	0.01059	0.02692
20.25%	0.01500	0.01439
20.50%	0.01938	0.00173
20.75%	0.02372	−0.01105
21.00%	0.02803	−0.02395
21.25%	0.03230	−0.01105
21.50%	0.03654	0.00173
21.75%	0.04074	0.01439
22.00%	0.04492	0.02692

the range of strikes over which the two traders would be willing to take opposite sides of the same trade narrows. If the risk aversion increases equally in the two traders, the range will narrow symmetrically (eventually down to a point) around the central 'market estimate' (20%).

Let us remember, however, that this result has been obtained assuming identical initial wealth, identical standard deviations in the volatility expectations and identical utility functions. It is interesting to see what happens as we relax some of these assumptions.

6.7.6   A Stylized Example: Second Version

We want to relax the assumption now that the utility function is the same for both traders. We leave unchanged the initial wealth for Trader 2, but we assume that her exponent α (see Equation (6.18)) is now 0.2, and that the displacement coefficient a (see Equation (6.18)) is now given by −\$54 000. Otherwise the expectations of the two traders are as before, and the reasoning proceeds exactly along the same lines (see Figure 6.8).

We want to find whether there still exists a range of strikes such that a trade will take place. We find that Trader 1 will buy volatility for strikes smaller than approximately 18.600% and willingly sell it for strikes above 19.408%. As for Trader 2, she will buy and sell volatility for strikes below 20.532% and above 21.467%, respectively. There still is a non-zero range of strikes (between 19.408% and 20.532%) over which the expected utility of both traders will be enhanced by taking the opposite sides of the same transaction. See Figure 6.9. However, the middle point of the range of possible strikes now no longer

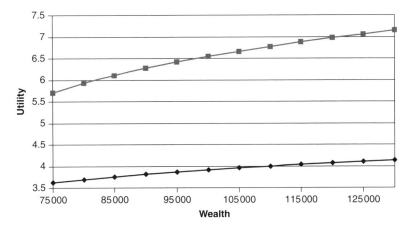

Figure 6.8 The two utility functions.

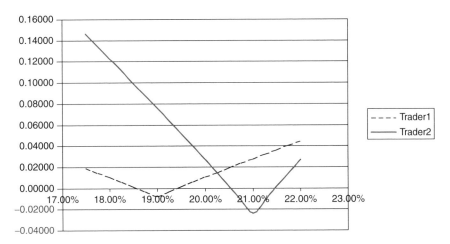

Figure 6.9 Change in expected utility for the two traders with different utility functions.

exactly coincides with the average of the expectations (19.97% instead of 20.00%). More dramatically, if we look at the strike that maximizes the sum of the expected utilities for both traders, instead of being in the middle, it is now at one extreme of the admissible range (i.e. at 19.408%). See Figure 6.10.

Conclusions from the Second Version of the Example

The conclusion that we can draw from this example is that if the risk aversions of the two players are not identical, the strike where the market will clear no longer gives a direct indication as to the market consensus level of volatility. Just by altering one of the assumptions of our initial example, the market has ceased to be an efficient information-processing machine. To be more precise, it is still efficient in its processing, but it now conveys joint information about the expectations of the two traders and their aversion to risk.

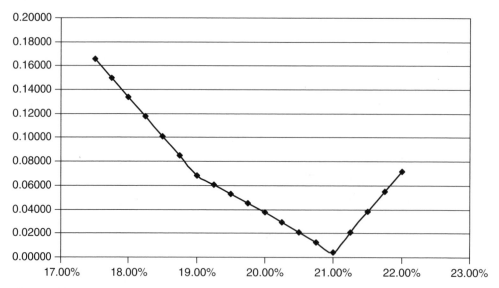

Figure 6.10   Sum of the expected utilities for two traders with different utility functions.

6.7.7   A Stylized Example: Third Version

We go back to the case where both traders have exactly the same risk aversion (the displacement coefficient *a* has been changed for this example to −$10 000 for both traders), but we now assume that a third trader comes along, who shares the same risk aversion and the same views as the second. By what we have seen above, the second and third traders will never trade between themselves, and, therefore, if they trade at all, they will only do so with Trader 1. Over which range of strikes will the transaction take place? Note that, even if the individual transactions with Trader 3 and with Trader 2 look exactly as enticing, if Trader 1 were to deal simultaneously with *both* counterparties, his book would be twice as large (see Figure 6.11). Given the convexity of his utility function, even if his views about the realization of the volatility have not changed, he will now only be ready to trade over a different range of strikes.

Traders 2 and 3 will see their expected utilities increase for strikes below 20.754% and above 21.246%. Trader 1 will be happy to deal for strikes below 18.494% and above 19.506%. Trades between Traders 2 and 3 on one side and Trader 1 on the other will therefore take place in the range 19.506% and 20.754%. Also in this third case the middle point of this range is no longer 20.00% (but 20.13%) and the maximum of the expected utilities (see Figure 6.12) is asymmetrically placed. Note that neither the middle of the range, nor the maximum of the sum of the expected utilities coincides with any obvious average of expectations (i.e. an expectation taken with weights given either by the number of players or by the money backing each trade).

6.7.8   Overall Conclusions

What have we tried to model with the second and third cases? By changing the risk aversion of one of the players I have tried to model a situation where one of the players

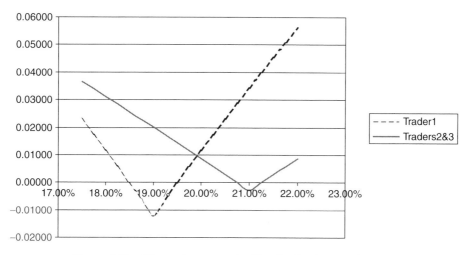

Figure 6.11 Change in expected utility for the three-trader case.

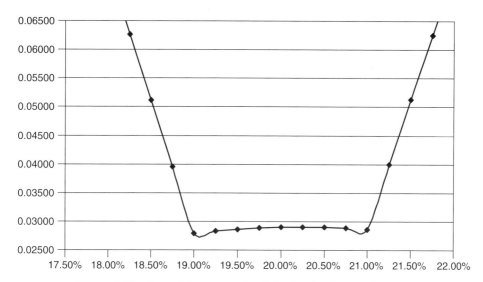

Figure 6.12 Sum of the expected utilities for the three-trader case.

might be subject to a set of incentives different from the other. If, instead of dealing with a pseudo-stochastic-volatility case we had tried to model aversion to downward jumps, this situation could arise if, say, fund managers heavily invested in equities were particularly afraid of market crashes, or of underperforming a market index, and were compensated accordingly. Hedge fund managers, on the other hand, who might take the opposite side of the trade, could have different (strongly performance-based) incentives.

By allowing an extra player in case 3 I have tried to account for an excess of option supply or demand. According to the EMH, excess supply always creates (thanks to pseudo-arbitrageurs) enough demand to absorb it, and vice versa. I discuss this point in the following section, but in my example I have not allowed for a twin of Trader 1 to appear to soak up the extra demand for options. When an excess of demand or supply occurs, but pseudo-arbitrageurs cannot fully operate in the market (and the other conditions about the initial wealth and utility functions apply), the equilibrium strike will be all the way at the boundary of the admissible range. More importantly, *it will neither be equal to anybody's expectation of the volatility, nor to any risk-aversion-independent average.* A statement like 'the market expectation of the volatility is X%' would in this case therefore be unwarranted.

It is just as important to observe the *direction* of the change of the equilibrium strike away from the econometrically obtainable one. In the third example, for instance, the extra size of the positions for Trader 1 (coupled with the convexity of his utility function) would create a situation where he would have to be enticed by strikes farther away from his central expectation than would have been the case in the smaller-size trade situation. Similarly, one can check that a greater risk aversion for one player will also require a strike farther away from his expectation.

Why is the third case relevant in practice? Because, as I have argued in Chapter 1, option products are successful and trade in volume when there is a consistent supply or demand for the optionality from outside the community of the professional traders (i.e. if there are *bona fide* customers). These external counterparties, however, tend to be consistently 'the same way around': liability managers desire interest-rate protection (and therefore create an unbalanced demand for caps); investors and issuers desire attractive investment or funding rates (creating a supply for swaption optionality); retail investors like equity principal-protected instruments (thereby bidding up the prices for equity volatility); fund managers would like to have portfolio insurance (and systematically demand put protection); US mortgage Agencies (Fannie Mae and Freddie Mac) want to hedge their pre-payment risk by paying the fixed swap rate and buying swaption volatility; etc. In other words, the net customer demand is far from balanced, professional traders cannot act as simple volatility brokers, and the example in case 3 can therefore be very relevant.

Clearly, the three cases above are not the only ones worth examining: for instance, the 'wealth' of one of the players might come in part from sources other than the direct outcome of the trader. A fund manager, for instance, often gets a compensation proportional to the total amount of the funds invested – therefore he has to do 'well enough' to keep the investors with the fund, and significant underperformance with respect to his peers can be more detrimental that absolute losses. Or, to give another example, the manager of the investment fund of an insurance company, who typically is not directly compensated on the basis of the mark-to-market P&L of her trades, might be afraid that a fall in equities below a certain level might trigger insolvency limits for the company, and the need to raise more capital, possibly at times of financial turmoil. In such a situation she could face the risk of curtailment of bonus, job loss, reputational damage, etc. Actually, when these extra sources of wealth become very important (i.e. when one party 'has to' hedge), transaction can easily take place at actuarially unfair levels.

Summarizing: the main conclusions of these sections are as follows:

1. in general, identifying the market-implied value of a quantity (say, the volatility) with the market consensus is unwarranted;

2. however, if the agents in the market have similar wealth and aversion to the relevant sources of risk, the risk-adjusted quantities will differ appreciably from the average of the real-world expectations only if there exists a systematic imbalance of supply or demand;

3. whenever one suspects that such an imbalance might occur, one should also try to check, whenever possible, that the *direction* of this bias is consistent with the underlying financial model used to explain the market dynamics.

These criteria are simple and robust (i.e. very weakly, if at all, dependent on the detailed specification of the utility function). They can therefore provide useful guidance in the case of complex calibrations. If we are prepared to say something stronger at least about the *type* of utility function, the bounds for the acceptable values for the calibrated parameters can become much tighter. Examples of such tight bounds are presented in Chapter 14.

6.7.9 The EMH Again

The main conclusion drawn from the discussion above is that risk-adjusted quantities such as jump amplitudes, jump frequencies, reversion levels of the volatility, etc can differ significantly from the corresponding real-world expectations formed by the market participants only if there exists an excess of supply or demand for certain types of options (at least if traders share the same utility function, and have similar initial wealths).

I have mentioned above, however, that according to the EMH, supply or demand *per se* should not affect prices. If, say, extra supply were to move prices away from fundamentals, pseudo-arbitrageurs would be enticed to move in and make a profit. If this is the case, after the trades have taken place, the risk-adjusted values for quantities such as, say, the jump frequency, should have the same value as their real-world expectations. In other words, if the insurance seekers were to bid up the prices of out-of-the-money puts beyond what is warranted by the nature of the true process for the underlying, the EMH prescribes that the pseudo-arbitrageurs should come into action selling the same options and causing the risk-adjusted jump frequency to come down. The ease with which short positions can be entered in the derivatives market (via puts, forward contract or selling futures) should facilitate this process.

For the reasons discussed in Section 1.2 and in the second Smile Tale (Section 6.6), I think that this view is often not realistic. In a nutshell, my objection rests on the fact that the correcting trades of the pseudo-arbitrageurs, *even if their knowledge is correct*, are not risk-free, nor are they guaranteed to bring about the expected profits instantaneously. If this is the case, a combination of agency-relationship effects and institutional constraints can severely hinder the actions of the pseudo-arbitrageurs, and supply and demand *can* affect option prices – and consequently drive a wedge between the risk-adjusted and the real-world quantities discussed above.

Chapter 7

Empirical Facts About Smiles

7.1 What is this Chapter About?

In this chapter I look at the interest-rate, equity and FX option markets, and present some fundamental empirical facts about smiles that should always be kept in mind when assessing the outputs (prices, densities, transition probabilities, etc.) produced by the various models discussed in what follows. As mentioned in the preface, it is not the purpose of this book to provide a statistical or econometric study of option markets. Therefore sometimes these 'empirical' facts are presented without the qualifications and caveats that would be required if a careful discussion of the estimation procedures were presented. In a sense, they represent the statistical results about which I believe a broad consensus could be obtained, if all the econometric is were dotted and the statistical ts crossed. Also, I have presented a selective rather than systematic review of the empirical work.

Finally, in this chapter I have tried to present the empirical information in as 'neutral' (as opposed to 'theory-laden') a manner as possible. I intend to provide an explanation for these empirical features and discuss their relevance for the choice of modelling approach in the following chapters as the various models are introduced.

7.1.1 'Fundamental' and 'Derived' Analyses

It is important to point out the existence of at least two possible strands of empirical analysis, which I will call 'fundamental' and 'derived'. (See also the related discussion in Chapter 1 between the fundamental and applied approaches to option pricing in general, and the discussion of model re-calibration in particular.) In the fundamental analysis, it is recognized that the values of options and other derivative contracts are ultimately derived from the dynamics of the underlying assets, and therefore the focus is on the dynamical properties of the latter. The approach is of great interest to the plain-vanilla trader, for whom the underlying asset is the main hedging instrument. Studies such as Cont's (2001) or Ait-Sahalia's (2002), to name a couple, fall into this category.

The derived approach is of greater interest to the complex-derivatives trader, for whom not only the underlying asset, but also other plain-vanilla options constitute the set of hedging instruments. The dynamics of option prices (or, more commonly, of the implied

volatilities) therefore become as, if not more, important than the process for the underlying. Therefore for the complex-derivatives trader mis-specification of the dynamics of
the underlying asset is often considered to be a 'second-order effect'. This is because,
typically, the complex trader will engage in substantial vega and/or gamma hedging of the
complex product using plain-vanilla options. Once a suitable hedge has been put in place,
it is often found that the delta exposure of the complex instrument and of the plain-vanilla
hedging options to a large extent cancel out. When this is the case, the *net* dependence
of the whole portfolio on moves of the underlying (the delta) can be relatively modest,
and consistent errors in the estimation of the delta exposure of the complex product and
of the plain-vanilla hedging options can compensate each other. Needless to say, for this
to happen it is necessary that the same model be used for pricing both sets of options.
In particular, if the chosen model failed to recover to an acceptable accuracy the prices
of the options used for hedging, and the trader therefore used a different model to price
them and to estimate their sensitivity to changes in the underlying, she would deny herself
some of the benefits from the cancellation of errors mentioned above.

The discussion in Chapter 1 (and in particular Sections 1.3 and 1.4) can be profitably
revisited at this point.

7.1.2   A Methodological Caveat

The rationale for studying carefully the cross-sectional features and the dynamic behaviour
of smile surfaces stems from the underlying assumption that the same process that
describes the dynamics of the underlying is also responsible for the evolution and properties of the option prices that make up the smile surfaces. In other words, if one holds
this (logically-consistent) view, plain-vanilla options are truly *derivative* securities, and
their behaviour is fully determined once the process of the underlying is assigned.

The assumption is, at the same time, obvious from the theoretical point of view, and
extremely surprising to anyone who has worked in, or just visited, a trading room. It
implies that, as soon as information arrives, individual plain-vanilla option traders adjust
their quotes for all the maturities and expires in such a way that the market will clear
by creating a smile surface that is fully consistent with the (unknown) dynamics of the
underlying. The possibility of such a 'magical' price adjustment happening should not
be dismissed out of hand simply by observing how an individual trader alters her quote,
because it is the collective actions of many traders that will ultimately determine the new
equilibrium smile.[1] Indeed, there are numerous unexpected examples, from game theory
to optimal resource allocation, where many atomically 'wrong' inputs produce remarkably
efficient collective strategies or results. None the less, the faith in the ability of the market
to process information in such an almost supernaturally efficient manner should not be
underestimated. As I have pointed out in Chapter 1, whenever the reader is faced with
such appeals to the efficiency of markets, she should always ask herself: How easy would
it be for the pseudo-arbitrageurs to correct possible mistakes? I believe that quite a few
five-dollar notes *do* lie on the pavement, but unfortunately they tend to fall into cracks
where they are difficult to spot and from where it is even more difficult to retrieve them.

---

[1] Similarly, the observation that rich uncle Rupert's behaviour is irrational when it comes to investments is
not, *per se*, sufficient reason to claim that asset prices are influenced by the action of irrational investors, and
that the rational-investor paradigm of classical finance is flawed. See the discussion in Section 1.2.

From the practical point of view, I shall regard the ability of a model to reproduce the observed changes in the plain-vanilla option prices (the smile surface) as a desirable feature first and foremost because of the practice of vega hedging and re-hedging that I have discussed in Chapter 1. If this fitting feature then happens to be capable of accounting for important empirical properties of the underlying I will consider this, as an additional intellectually pleasing feature of the model, and possibly as a corroborative indication of its validity. For this reason the emphasis of this chapter is on the empirical properties of the smile surfaces, rather than of the underlying.

7.2 Market Information About Smiles

7.2.1 Direct Static Information

The smile surface at time t, σ_t^{impl}, is the function, $\mathcal{R}^2 \to \mathcal{R}$, that associates to a strike, K, and a maturity, T, the Black implied volatility prevailing at time t:[2]

$$\sigma_t^{\text{impl}} = \sigma_t^{\text{impl}}(K, T) \tag{7.1}$$

Static information about the smile surface can be obtained by observing its behaviour for a fixed maturity as a function of strike, or its dependence on the time to expiry for a fixed strike (term structure of smiles). In principle, a better set of co-ordinates than the strike could be the degree of in-the-moneyness. Defining this is, however, not always straightforward. For all maturities, in fact, the location of the at-the-money (forward) is unambiguous, since it simply depends on a cash-and-carry-arbitrage type of argument. However, choosing a robust metric to identify degrees of moneyness when the Black formula does not apply is not trivial. For a fixed maturity, a common choice is to select points with the same degree of Black out-of-the-moneyness, i.e. points for which the ratio $\ln \frac{K}{S}$ has the same value. This is a reasonable and useful choice, but it should be stressed that it is not model-independent. Similarly, when comparing points of the surface with a similar degree of out-of-the-moneyness across maturities, it can be useful (see Carr and Wu (2003b)) to use the quantity h, defined by

$$h = \frac{\ln \frac{K}{S}}{\sigma \sqrt{T}} \tag{7.2}$$

where σ is some measure of the volatility level of the whole surface. See the discussion in Chapter 17 about this point.

Further information about the smiles surface can be conveyed by a comparison of at-the-money (ATM) volatilities, straddles and risk reversals for each maturity. More precisely, the risk-reversal statistics, $RR(t, T)$, for a given maturity is defined as the

---

[2]In Part I, which dealt with deterministic-volatility diffusions (no smiles), one could readily identify the root-mean-squared volatility, $\widehat{\sigma}$, with the implied volatility, σ_{impl}. This is, in general, no longer warranted when one deals with smiles and it is important to distinguish carefully between the two concepts.

difference between the 25-delta implied volatility for calls and puts of the same maturity:

$$RR(t, T) = \sigma_{\text{impl}}(t, K_{25\Delta p}, T) - \sigma_{\text{impl}}(t, K_{25\Delta c}, T) \tag{7.3}$$

where $K_{25\Delta p}$ ($K_{25\Delta c}$) is the strike that gives a 25-delta to the put (call). The straddle,[3] $ST(t, T)$, is calculated as

$$ST(t, T) = \sigma_{\text{impl}}(t, K_{25\Delta p}, T) + \sigma_{\text{impl}}(t, K_{25\Delta c}, T) - 2\sigma_{\text{impl}}(t, K_{\text{ATM}}, T) \tag{7.4}$$

where $\sigma_{\text{impl}}(t, K_{\text{ATM}}, T)$ is the at-the-money implied volatility. From the definitions one can see that the risk reversal gives an indication about the asymmetry of the smile for a given maturity, while the straddle gives information about its average curvature around the ATM level.

Important static information is conveyed by the analysis of the behaviour of the straddle and of the risk reversal as a function of maturity (i.e. how quickly the smile decays, and how asymmetric it remains) for a fixed time t_0. This information can provide useful indications regarding the process that can generate such a behaviour.

7.2.2   Semi-Static Information

I explained in Section 6.4 why the analysis of how the smile surface changes, for a given strike or for a given degree of moneyness, as the underlying moves, is very important. I call such information 'semi-static' because, of course, in order to observe a change in the smile as the price of the underlying changes, time must elapse (giving rise to theta decay) and the volatility (if stochastic) might change. However, the focus in this analysis is on the change due to the move in the price, not to the passage of time; in other words, one would like to be able to estimate from the observed changes in option prices the quantity

$$\left. \frac{\partial \sigma_{\text{impl}}(t, K, T)}{\partial S} \right|_{t=t_0} \tag{7.5}$$

I have discussed in Section 6.4 that the quantity in (7.5) is arguably one of the most important quantities with which the model prediction should be compared. A large number of models can in fact produce a similar (and, these days, very good) fit to static data. The requirement to match the quantity in expression (7.5) is, however, a much taller order. Unfortunately, an empirical estimation of this quantity is very difficult to obtain.

A smile surface that exactly follows ('floats with') the underlying is often referred to as a *floating* smile. A smile surface that does not move when the underlying changes is said to be *sticky*. Sticky and floating smiles were introduced in a qualitative manner in Chapter 6 with Smile Tales 1 and 2. They are dealt with in detail in Chapter 17.

7.2.3   Direct Dynamic Information

Dynamic information is obtained by collecting time series of the above reference volatilities (or of other quantities representative of the smile surface) and by analysing their time

---

[3] My terminology here is not universally accepted. Very often the straddle is simply the strategy made up of an ATM call and an ATM put.

behaviour. When time series of many implied volatilities are available, it has become common, at least in the equity and interest-rate area, to perform a principal component analysis (PCA) of their absolute or relative changes. See, for example, Alexander (2000) or Rebonato and Joshi (2002). Analysis of the serial autocorrelation of the resulting principal components is also useful.

At a simpler, but possibly more fundamental, level it is extremely important to analyse to what extent the qualitative shape of a smile surface remains unchanged over time, whether it 'oscillates' between a small number of patterns, or whether its shape evolves continuously over time assuming ever different shapes. This is important because different models, even after recovering exactly today's surface, all predict different evolutions for its shape over time. Some, in particular, predict a fundamentally self-similar (time-homogeneous) evolution, while others imply a radical change in shape. I will therefore argue in what follows that the empirical information about the real-world[4] evolution of the smile surface constitutes a powerful tool in assessing the desirability of a model.

7.2.4 Indirect Information

A variety of techniques have been proposed in the literature in order to produce a smooth interpolation between, and extrapolation beyond, the reference implied volatilities (i.e. the volatilities associated with a given triplet of ATM, risk reversal and straddle). This topic is dealt with in some detail in Chapter 9. Once such a smooth surface has been obtained, I show in Chapter 12 that one can obtain, via double differentiation of the call price with respect to the strike,[5] today's risk-neutral probability density function:

$$\phi(t_0, S_0, S_t, t) = \exp[r(t - t_0)] \left. \frac{\partial^2 C}{\partial K^2} \right|_{K = S_t} \tag{7.6}$$

(In Equation (7.6), $\phi(t_0, S_0, S_t, t)$ is the time-t_0 probability density that the stock price will reach value S_t at time t, given that it is at S_0 today (t_0).) This probability density can then be compared with a log-normal one with the same first and second moments, and the *excess* skewness and kurtosis can be estimated. More generally, the whole shape of the density function can be analysed, with special attention paid to the possibility that it might be bimodal. If this were the case, then the market could be expecting either one of two sharply different outcomes (say, either a base-rate hike or a cut) or, more commonly, the possibility that a large jump (devaluation of a currency, equity market crash) might occur. It must always be remembered, however, that these probability densities are risk-adjusted ones.

This type of information is very interesting, but it should always be used with care because it can be very sensitive to the procedure used to obtain the smooth surface.

---

[4]The evolution of the smile surface in the real world has a direct bearing on the choice of model only if we assume that the volatilities of (and correlations among) the state variables are deterministic (non-stochastic). If this is not the case, a change in the drifts of the stochastic processes related to the volatilities (i.e. a change of measure) takes place. When this is the case, a direct comparison between real-world and risk-adjusted quantities is unwarranted. Techniques still exist, however, to extract information about the real-world evolution and compare it with the output of a model (see, for example, Rebonato and Joshi (2002) and Chapter 27).

[5]In practice, other, related, numerical techniques can be more stable. See the discussion in Section 12.3.

In particular, different fitting procedures that produce a similarly good recovery of the observed market prices (or of the implied volatilities) can produce very different probability densities. This is not surprising, because the density is obtained by double differentiation of the prices (see Equation (7.6)).

7.3 Equities

7.3.1 Basic Facts

The most salient empirical features of equity smiles are the following.

Fact 1: Smiles have greatly increased in magnitude (virtually, they have appeared) after the 1987 equity market crash. See, for example, Rubinstein (1994), Jackwerth and Rubinstein (1996), and Ait-Sahalia and Lo (1998) for studies on the S&P500.

Fact 2: The magnitude of the smile as a function of a fixed money strike tends to decrease for increasing option expiries: short maturities display pronounced smiles, and distant maturities give rise to shallow smiles. What constitutes a 'short' or a 'long' maturity, can, of course, change over time.

Fact 3: The magnitude of the smile as a function of the degree of out-of-the-moneyness (as expressed by the delta) is much more constant across different option expiries.

Fact 4: The smile is much more pronounced going from the ATM level towards out-of-the-money puts than in the opposite direction. Going towards out-of-the-money calls the smile either becomes less steep, or is monotonically decreasing, or, sometimes, it is even absent.

Fact 5: The asymmetry in the smile tends to increase during periods of market turbulence.

Figure 7.1 displays both the flattening of the smile for increasing maturities (Fact 2), and its virtual disappearance for strikes towards the direction of out-of-the-money calls (Fact 4).

Despite the fact that, in this chapter, I will tend to keep the 'facts' as separate as possible from their explanation, it should be pointed out that the observed asymmetry of the smile is associated with a (negative) skewness in the risk-neutral density, and that the positive convexity of the smile is due to (or, at least, can be easily explained in terms of) the leptokurtic nature of the density. However, under the conditions for its applicability, the Central Limit Theorem implies that the return distribution should converge to normality as the expiry increases. Therefore, in the long-expiry limit, if smiles reflect option prices consistently arrived at from a process for the underlying with independent and identically distributed increments, then all smiles should become flat. This observation should be revisited when discussing the 'subtler' effects below.

7.3.2 Subtler Effects

Negative Correlation between Changes in the Implied Volatility and the Level of the Underlying

Derman (1999) has noted a strong negative correlation between the level of the 3-month ATM implied volatility and the level of the index for the S&P500 during the period September 1997 to November 1998. I have extended the observation by estimating the

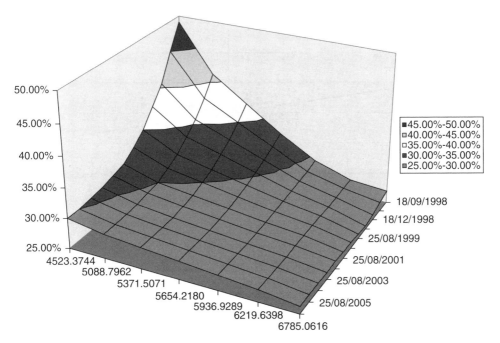

Legend:
- ■45.00%-50.00%
- □40.00%-45.00%
- □35.00%-40.00%
- ■30.00%-35.00%
- ■25.00%-30.00%

Figure 7.1 The smile surface for FTSE option as observed on 18 August 1998. Notice that the smile is very pronounced for short maturities, and becomes shallower and shallower as the time to expiry increases.

strength of the correlation between changes in the implied volatility and in the level of the index for the FTSE, the S&P500 and the STOXX50 indices for several maturities during the period 4-Feb-2000/31-May-2001.[6] The main results are as follows. For the S&P index, the correlation is negative but rather weak, and becomes progressively weaker as the option expiry increases: 35%, 34%, 30%, 28%, 10% for 1-month, 3-month, 6-month, 1-year and 5-year options, respectively. See Figures 7.2–7.6.

Assuming a quadratic relationship between changes in the index and changes in the implied volatility does not substantially improve the quality of the fit. See Figures 7.7 and 7.8.

The picture is somewhat different for the FTSE index, in that the degree of linear correlation is stronger, and does not appear to decay as rapidly (or at all) as a function of the option expiry. The values obtained were: 57%, 64%, 66%, 62% and 42% for 1-month, 3-month, 6-month, 1-year and 5-year options, respectively. See Figures 7.9–7.13.

The data relating to the STOXX50 index present a picture very similar to the FTSE case: the correlation coefficients were found to be 60%, 63%, 63%, 57% and 42% for 1-month, 3-month, 6-month, 1-year and 5-year options, respectively. See Figures 7.14–7.18.

Finally, are changes in the skew or convexity linked to changes in the underlying? At least if one looks at the S&P index, this does not appear to be the case, even for the shortest maturities. See Figure 7.19 (for the skew) and Figure 7.20 (for the convexity).

---

[6]It is a pleasure to thank Dr S. Mahal for useful calculations.

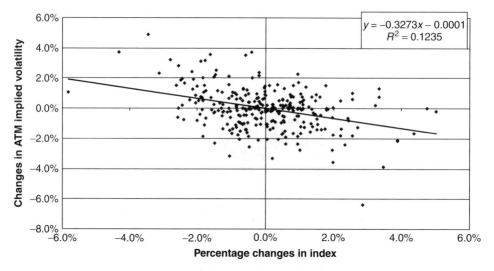

Figure 7.2   S&P 1-month changes in the implied ATM volatility vs changes in the index.

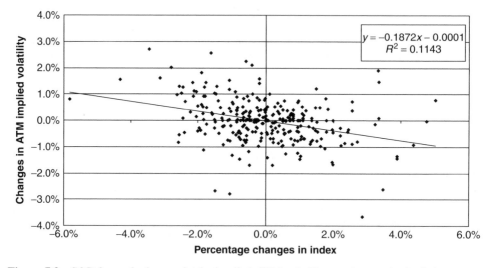

Figure 7.3   S&P 3-month changes in the implied ATM volatility vs changes in the index.

Movements of Call Prices and the Underlying in Opposite Directions

Baskshi *et al.* (2000) examined the S&P500 index option market in 1994 (for a total of
3.8 million observations!) and found that in a substantial number of cases (between 7%
and 17%) call prices and the underlying move in opposite directions. Furthermore, call
and put prices moved in the same direction 17.1% of the times (when sampled once every
three hours). Irrespective of whether the price of the underlying asset goes up or down,
it is more likely for call and put prices to go down together than to go up together.

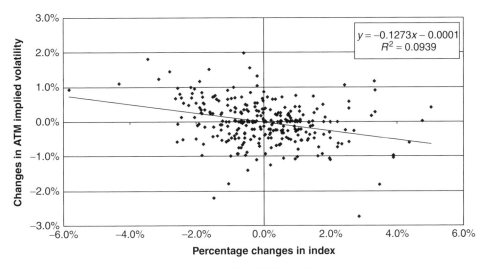

Figure 7.4 S&P 6-month changes in the implied ATM volatility vs changes in the index.

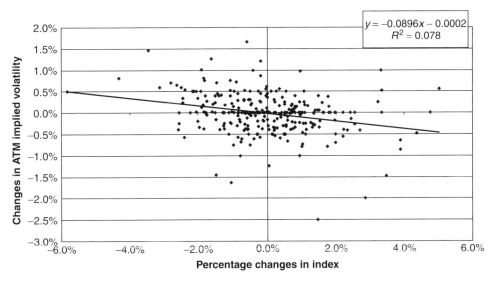

Figure 7.5 S&P 1-year changes in the implied ATM volatility vs changes in the index.

Level, Skew and Convexity as a Function of Maturity

Samuel (2002) examines several equity markets, and from the smile surface and the associated prices constructs for each maturity the cumulative risk-neutral distribution of price changes. He then identifies, again for each maturity, three values of the strike (K_-, K_0 and K_+) such that 0.25, 0.50 and 0.75 of the cumulative distribution lies to their left. Given these three strikes, he reads from the market smile surface the associated implied volatilities (σ_0, σ_+ and σ_-). He introduces a 'volatility' (level), σ_0, a 'skew', χ, and a

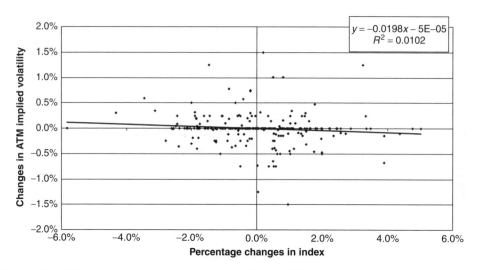

Figure 7.6   S&P 5-year changes in the implied ATM volatility vs changes in the index.

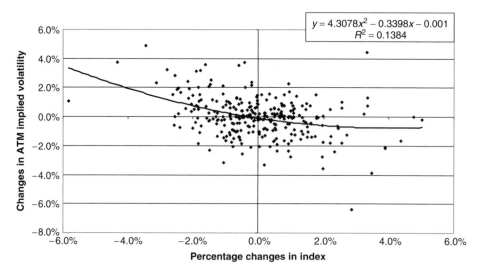

Figure 7.7   Quadratic fit to S&P 1-month changes in the implied ATM volatility vs changes in the index.

'convexity', ω, measure defined as follows:

$$\chi = \frac{\sigma_+ - \sigma_-}{\sigma_0} \tag{7.7}$$

$$\omega = \frac{\sigma_+ + \sigma_- - 2\sigma_0}{\sigma_0} \tag{7.8}$$

These quantities and the procedures to obtain them are discussed in more detail in Chapter 17. Samuel (2002) then plots these three quantities as a function of option

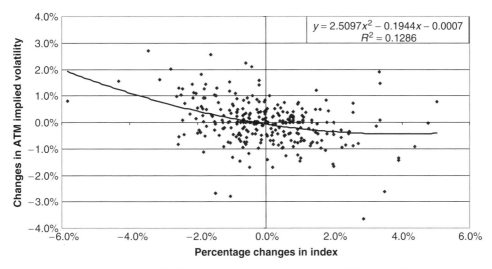

Figure 7.8 Quadratic fit to S&P 3-month changes in the implied ATM volatility vs changes in the index.

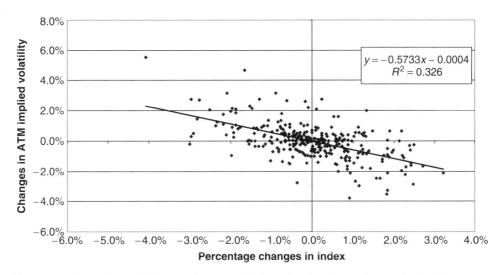

Figure 7.9 FTSE 1-month changes in the implied ATM volatility vs changes in the index.

expiry for several business days and for the FTSE and EUROSTOXX indices.[7] See Figures 7.21–7.26.

These graphs suggest the following:

1. As far as the level is concerned, in 'normal' market conditions the 'central' level remains approximately constant, or increases gently as the option expiry increases; in 'exceptional' market conditions, the 'central' level of short-dated options becomes

---
[7]It is a pleasure to thank Dr David Samuel for useful discussions, and for allowing the use of Figures 7.21–7.26.

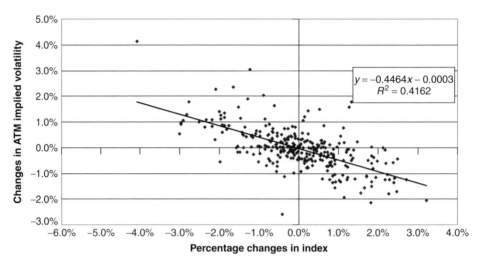

Figure 7.10   FTSE 3-month changes in the implied ATM volatility vs changes in the index.

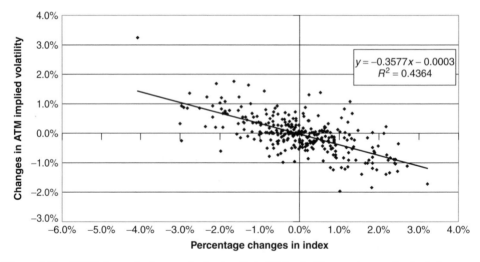

Figure 7.11   FTSE 6-month changes in the implied ATM volatility vs changes in the index.

much higher than for longer-dated expiries (note that the uppermost curve corresponds to a business day in the immediate aftermath of 11 September 2001).

2. The skew parameter increases very sharply with decreasing maturity (the more so during 'exceptional' periods), and remains monotonically increasing for all maturities.

3. The convexity parameter also increases for long maturities; at the short end of the maturity spectrum, however, its precise behaviour depends on the particular market.

4. The shapes of neither the skew nor the convexity curve seem to change as dramatically as the level curve in correspondence with exceptional events.

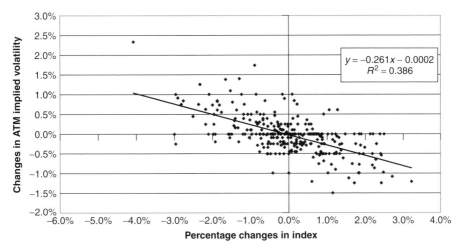

Figure 7.12 FTSE 1-year changes in the implied ATM volatility vs changes in the index.

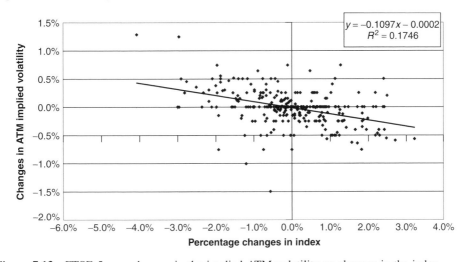

Figure 7.13 FTSE 5-year changes in the implied ATM volatility vs changes in the index.

Persistence of the Smirk as a Function of At-the-Moneyness

Carr and Wu (2003a) document a surprising pattern of the smile asymmetry (the 'smirk', Fact 4) for the S&P500 index. In order to understand their finding, let us define first a 'plausible' measure of moneyness, h, given by the logarithm of the ratio of the strike, K, over the forward, F, normalized by the square root of the time to expiry, T, times some measure of the average volatility of the index[8], σ:

$$h = \frac{\ln \frac{F}{K}}{\sigma \sqrt{T}} \qquad (7.9)$$

---

[8]The average index volatility level can, for instance, be obtained as the average of all the implied volatility quotes.

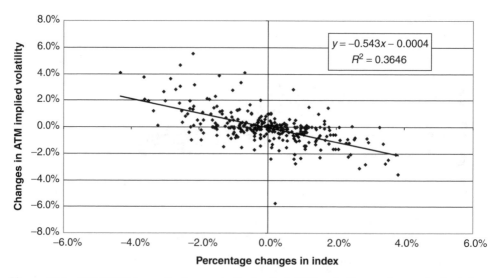

Figure 7.14   STOXX50 1-month changes in the implied ATM volatility vs changes in the index.

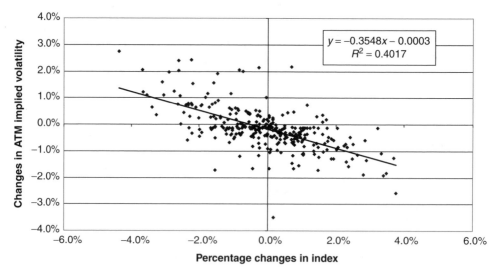

Figure 7.15   STOXX50 3-month changes in the implied ATM volatility vs changes in the index.

This definition of moneyness (which, incidentally corresponds to the average of the h_1 and h_2 terms in the Black formula) is intuitively appealing (roughly speaking, σ is the number of standard deviations that the log strike is away from the log forward price in a Black world), and has been shown (see Backus *et al.* (1997)) to allow a natural link between the slope and curvature of a smile and the skewness and kurtosis of the associated risk-neutral distribution.

When the implied volatility smile (smirk) is plotted out against this plausible measure of moneyness, it fails to flatten out, at least for maturities as long as two years.

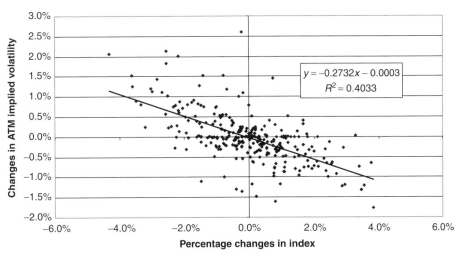

Figure 7.16 STOXX50 6-month changes in the implied ATM volatility vs changes in the index.

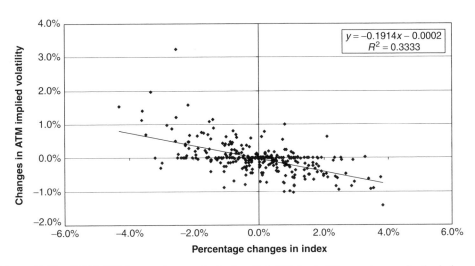

Figure 7.17 STOXX50 1-year changes in the implied ATM volatility vs changes in the index.

The finding is noteworthy because, as I remarked above, the flattening of the smile as the expiry increases should be model-independent and is ultimately a consequence of the Central Limit Theorem (CLT). In particular, the CLT also implies (Carr and Wu (2003a)) that the smile asymmetry should disappear for long enough maturities. The empirical finding reported by Carr and Wu is puzzling. If option prices are indeed consistent with an underlying well-specified process, the persistence of the smile would indicate either that a two-year horizon is not long enough, or that the increments are not serially independent. If this were the case, one would be led to conclude that the observed option prices (as reflected in the implied volatilities) are not compatible with a stock price driven by an independent-increment (Levy) stochastic process.

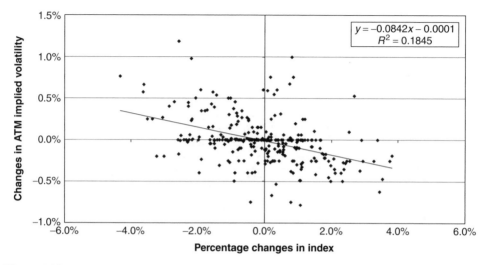

Figure 7.18   STOXX50 5-year changes in the implied ATM volatility vs changes in the index.

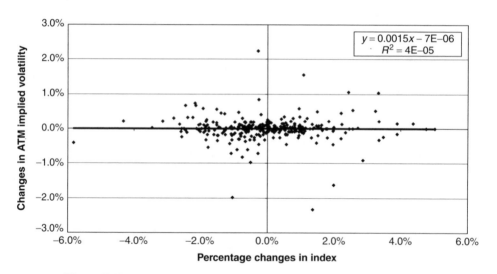

Figure 7.19   S&P 1-month changes in the skew vs changes in the index.

Asymptotic Behaviour of Prices of Out-of-the-Money Options

As the strike of an option progressively moves towards the out-of-the-money region all models for the underlying naturally predict that the option price should go to zero. However, if one looks at options of shorter and shorter maturities, it can be shown (Carr and Wu (2003b)) that these prices converge to zero with a speed that depends on whether the process is purely continuous, purely discontinuous, or a combination of both. This is intuitively understandable. Consider out-of-the-money options for a very short expiry. If the process for the underlying is purely continuous (no jumps), the likelihood of reaching the in-the-money region is very small. On the other hand, if jumps are allowed, there is

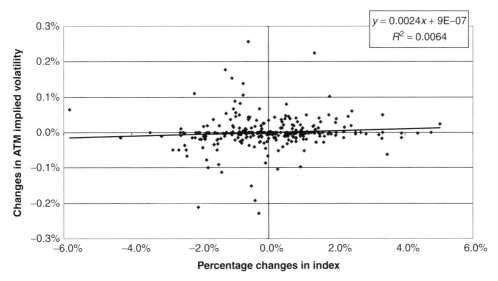

Figure 7.20   S&P 1-month changes in the convexity vs changes in the index.

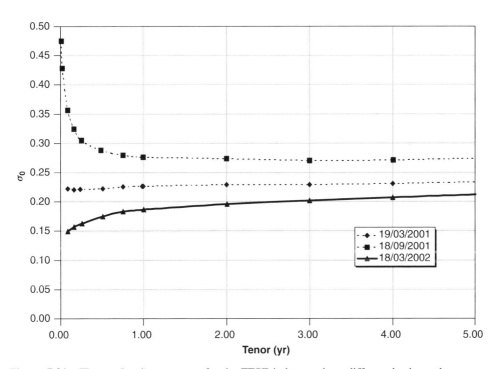

Figure 7.21   The σ_0 (level) parameter for the FTSE index on three different business days.

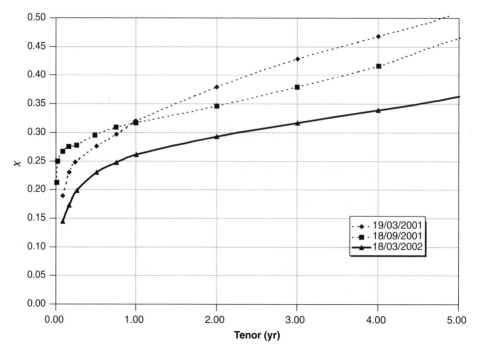

Figure 7.22   The χ (skew) parameter for the FTSE index on three different business days.

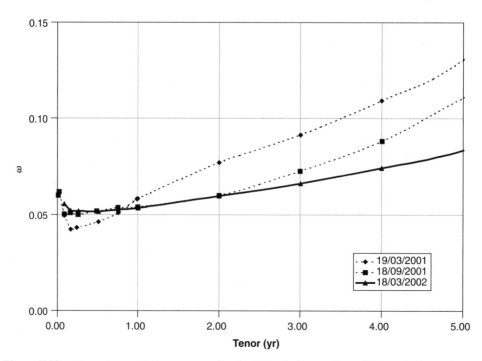

Figure 7.23   The ω (convexity) parameter for the FTSE index on three different business days.

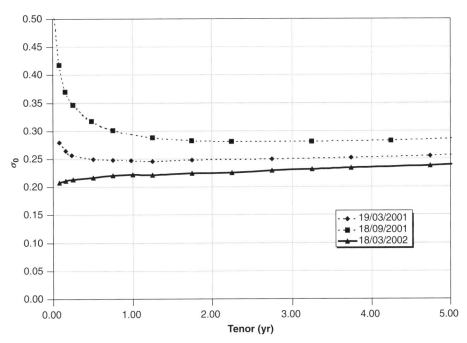

Figure 7.24   The σ_0 (level) parameter for the EUROSTOXX index on three different business days.

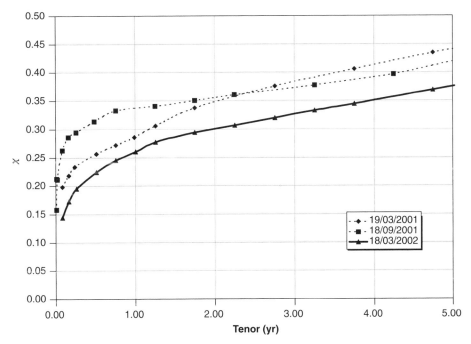

Figure 7.25   The χ (skew) parameter for the EUROSTOXX index on three different business days.

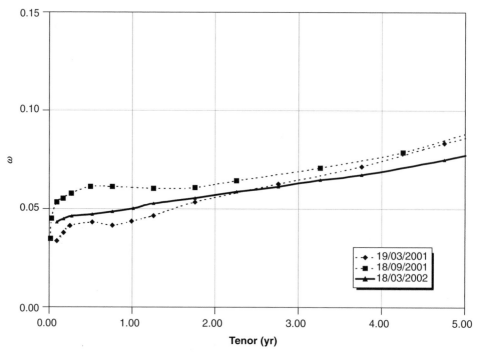

Figure 7.26   The ω (convexity) parameter for the EUROSTOXX index on three different business days.

some finite probability that the out-of-the-money region will be reached even for very short expiries. Indeed, Carr and Wu (2003b) show that the speed of convergence to zero as a function of the option expiry can give information about the continuous or otherwise nature of the underlying process. The conclusion they reach is that both a continuous and a discontinuous component are needed for the S&P index in order to account for the observed option prices.

Could Carr and Wu (2003b) not have looked directly at the paths of the S&P in order to ascertain whether jumps are present? Things are not so simple, because the discretely sampled paths from the three types of process can look very similar unless the sampling frequency is very high.[9] At such high frequencies, market microstructure effects (see, for example, O'Hara (1995)) begin to appear. These observations will be revisited in Chapters 12 and 14.

Floating vs Sticky Behaviour of the Smile Surface

The floating or sticky behaviour of the smile surface is linked to how the smile surface changes when the underlying changes. Saying whether a smile is sticky or floating means asking how it will change when the underlying moves. In the equity case a partial answer to this question is suggested by Figure 7.27. In this figure I display, after normalization, the smile curve for the same option expiry observed in the market on two different dates,

---

[9]Unless, of course, one happens to be sampling one of the extremely rare periods such as October 1987.

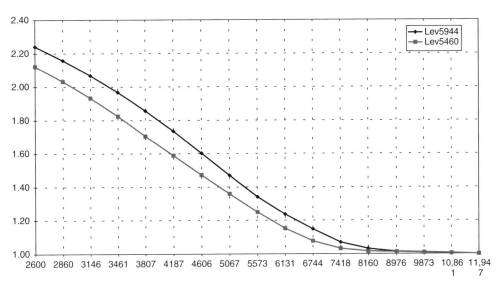

Figure 7.27 The normalized smiles on two trading days (11-Jul-98 and 13-Aug-98) for the FTSE index and expiry of 1 year. The spot levels of the index were 5944 and 5460, respectively. The normalization was obtained by dividing each volatility by the deep-in-the-money-call asymptotic volatility in order to disentangle effects arising from overall changes in levels of the volatility curve from the smile itself. Note that the two normalized smile curves are shifted by approximately 500 points, which roughly corresponds to the difference in the spot level of the index. In other words, in this example the smile floats and is not sticky.

approximately one month apart. Between these two dates the index level (FTSE) had changed significantly. The normalization disentangles the effect due to the change in smile due to the change in level of the underlying from the overall change in volatility level. It was achieved by dividing each quoted volatility by the asymptotic flat volatility corresponding to deep-in-the-money calls (i.e. by expressing every implied volatility as a percentage of the ATM volatility prevailing on the two dates). If the smile surface were sticky, after normalization the two normalized curves should approximately be on top of each other. For a floating smile, the smile curve would migrate with the ATM level. The spot index levels on the two trading dates considered differed by approximately 500 points. This is also the x-axis shift in the two normalized curves. In other words, Figure 7.27 suggests that the change in the smile should be more floating than sticky, at least at the time (the period of market turbulence of 1998), for the change in the underlying (10%, or 500 points) and over the time period (1 month) considered. These qualifications are important, because it should not be assumed that changes in the smile surface over shorter periods of time, under different market regimes and/or for smaller moves in the underlying should necessarily follow the same pattern.

Compelling as this 'one-day evidence' might appear to be, the topic of the dependence of the implied volatility on the underlying is far from settled. Derman (1999), for instance, distinguishes three market regimes ('range-bound', 'trending' and 'jumpy'), and associates to each a different behaviour of the function $\sigma_{\text{impl}}(K, T; S)$ as the underlying changes. More precisely, from the observation of the S&P500 index option market,

Derman heuristically associates the following dependence on S to the implied volatility:

$$\sigma_{\text{impl}}^{\text{range}}(K, T; S) = a - b(T)(K - S_0) \tag{7.10}$$

$$\sigma_{\text{impl}}^{\text{trending}}(K, T; S) = a - b(T)(K - S) \tag{7.11}$$

$$\sigma_{\text{impl}}^{\text{jumpy}}(K, T; S) = a - b(T)(K + S) + 2b(T)S_0 \tag{7.12}$$

where the superscripts 'range', 'trending' and 'jumpy' refer to the corresponding regimes, and S_0 denotes today's value of the spot. The description is suggestive, but empirical tests are not easy to carry out in practice, since recognizing whether we are currently in a range-bound, trending or jumpy period is not simple. Furthermore, Equations (7.10)–(7.12) only predict a linear dependence on the strike. This can constitute a good approximation during certain periods (see, for example, the volatility curve in Alexander (2001) in Figure 2.7), but is certainly inadequate at other points in time (see, for example, Ait-Sahalia (2002, Figure 8), which refers to the same index for a later date).

Principal Components Analysis

The principal components of changes in equity-implied volatilities have been studied by Alexander (2001), Cont and da Fonseca (2002a, 2002b), and Cont *et al* (2002) among others. Their main findings are as follows.

- A small number of principal components (two or three) are sufficient to account for a very high proportion of the observed variability (contrast this observation with the case of swaption-implied volatility matrices, discussed in Chapter 26).

- The usual interpretation of changes in the (log-) level, slope and curvature can be attributed to the first eigenvectors.

- The eigenvectors exhibit high positive autocorrelation and mean reversion over a time-scale close to a month (the same high and positive autocorrelation is displayed by the implied volatilities themselves).

- The autocorrelation structures of the principal components is well approximated by an AR(1)/Ornstein–Uhlenbeck (mean-reverting) process.

7.4   Interest Rates

7.4.1   Basic Facts

Fact 1: Before, approximately, 1994, interest-rate smiles used to be fundamentally flat across strikes.

Fact 2: The earliest and most pronounced smiles in interest rates began to be observed in JPY around 1994, when interest rates became substantially lower than in all other major currencies. As this happened, short-maturity caplet-implied percentage volatilities became much higher then in all other markets.

Fact 3: Between 1994 and 1998 the smile surfaces of interest-rate options in other currencies took the lead from JPY and became somewhat (although not as markedly) sloped.

Fact 4: In this initial period, the shape of the smile used to be monotonically decreasing from low to high strikes. See Figure 7.28. This changed dramatically after the autumn of 1998 (i.e. in the aftermath of the Russia/LTCM crisis).

Fact 5: The magnitude of the smile does not systematically decrease with increasing option maturity; very often it does not appear to decrease at all. See Figure 7.28.

Fact 6: It was common market practice, in the run-up to the Euro conversion date (1 January 1999), to quote the volatilities of caplets of relatively less liquid currencies expected to enter the EMU (such as ITL or ESP) by working out the absolute basis point equivalent with the most liquid currencies (DEM or FRF). Therefore, if a trader observed a DEM forward rate for a given maturity to trade at, say, 4.00% with a volatility of 12%, and was asked for a quote in the volatility of the same-maturity forward rate in ITL trading at, say, 5.5%, she would make a first guess of its volatility as a solution of the equation $f_{DEM}\,\sigma_{DEM} \simeq f_{ITL}\sigma_{ITL}$, i.e.

$$\sigma_{ITL} \simeq \frac{f_{DEM}}{f_{ITL}}\sigma_{DEM} \qquad (7.13)$$

This observation seems to indicate that interest-rate traders, as in our Smile Story 1, subscribed, at least during that period, to a normal (rather than log-normal) view of the distributional properties of forward rates. See Chapter 23 in Part IV of this book for a further discussion.

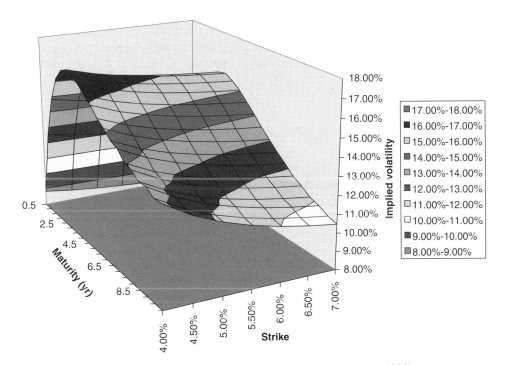

Figure 7.28   The caplet smile surface for DEM (11 May 1998).

7.4.2   Subtler Effects

Swaption-Implied Volatility Surfaces – Dynamic Behaviour

A detailed analysis of the dynamics of the swaption matrix is reported in Chapter 26 and
in Rebonato and Joshi (2002). The most salient features are the following.

Time series of selected ATM swaption-implied volatilities curves are shown in
Figures 7.29–7.31 for the USD. It is interesting to point out that these series appear
to display a rather complex behaviour: during 1998, for instance, there is a strong *upward*
change in the 1×3 swaption series, associated with a large *downward* move in the 10×10
swaption volatility during October 1998. Such a change would therefore produce a change
in the shape, and not just in the level, of the swaption matrix. This situation can be contrasted with the DEM/EUR case, reported in Chapter 26, where large sudden moves are
also present, but appear directionally more correlated. These changes are therefore more
likely to produce a level translation of the swaption matrix, rather than a change in overall
shape.

USD Data   Looking first at the USD data, two main patterns can be recognized. In order
to characterize these patterns, it is useful to consider cross-sections of the swaption matrix
along the expiry axis. So, the first curve obtained from this cross-sectional cut will be
associated with the options of different expiries into the shortest-maturity swap. This curve
will therefore be very similar to a caplet term structure of volatilities. The second curve
then displays options of different expiries into the second-shortest swap; etc. The 'normal'
pattern, displayed in Figure 7.29, prevails when all or most of the curves display a humped
shape. The second pattern ('excited') is instead associated with a monotonically decaying
behaviour, especially for the first curves. See Figure 7.30. Sometimes a 'mixed' case
is observed (see Figure 7.31) where both humped and monotonically decreasing cross-
sectional curves coexist in the same surface. In the case of the USD data the transition
from the normal to the excited state is typically very sudden (sometimes as rapid as two
or three days).

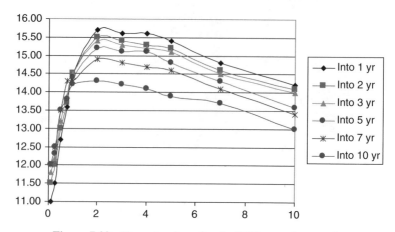

Figure 7.29   Normal pattern for the USD swaption matrix.

EUR/DEM Data The DEM/EUR data collected during the same period display a simpler, but qualitatively similar, set of patterns. The main difference is that no 'mixed cases' were observed during this period for the EUR/DEM. The hump, when present, tended to be shallower than in the USD case. The transition from the normal to the excited state appears to take longer in the case of EUR/DEM than in the case of USD (several days to two to three weeks).

Common Features The shape patterns observed in the matrices were described as 'normal' or 'excited' because the transition from the normal to the excited state is often associated with large movements in the yield curve. The events of 1998 (Russia default, LTCM crisis, etc.) provide typical examples of this behaviour. During more stable periods the humped (normal) pattern is generally observed to prevail.

For future modelling (see Chapter 27), it is important to point out that qualitatively similar patterns are revisited time and time again after a transition. So, after spending a considerable amount of time in a normal state, a swaption matrix tends to return to an excited state similar in shape to previously visited excited states. From this excited state the swaption matrix tends to revert to a normal state similar in shape to the original

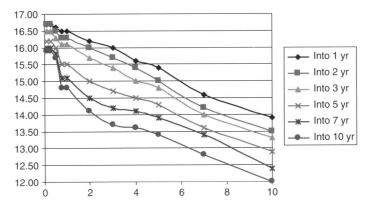

Figure 7.30 Excited pattern for the USD swaption matrix.

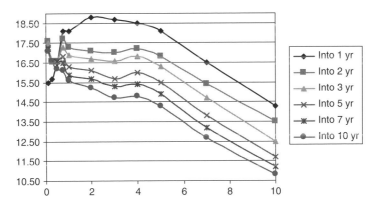

Figure 7.31 Mixed pattern for the USD swaption matrix.

one. Especially in the USD case, the swaption matrix therefore appears to 'oscillate' with random periodicity between a very small number of possible fundamental shapes.

This feature is important, because this picture is not compatible either with an implied volatility matrix 'diffusing' over time, nor with the existence of simple jumps and discontinuities (if a simple jump process were invoked, it would be difficult to explain how the matrix could jump back to an earlier state).

Further features of the swaption-implied volatility matrix (such as the eigenvalues and eigenvectors associated with the time series of their changes) are reported and discussed in Chapters 23, 26 and 27.

Swaption-Implied Volatility Surfaces – Dependence on the Swap Rate Level

If one plots the ATM implied volatilities of different swaptions against the level of the corresponding forward swap rate, a clear functional dependence becomes evident. Indeed, the large increase in the (percentage) implied volatility of swap rates observed towards the end of 2002 can be explained to a large extent by the concomitant strong decrease in rates. In other words, *percentage* volatilities were strongly increasing, but *absolute* volatilities much less so. Over the period 1998–2002, for instance, the maximum level of the 1×1 ATM swaption-implied percentage volatility is about six times the minimum; while the quantity $\sigma_{\text{impl}} SR^{\beta}$ (with σ_{impl} the percentage implied volatility, SR the swap rate, and β an exponent equal to 1.37) varies between approximately 150 and 300.

The same point is illustrated in Figure 7.32 where I have rebased at 1 both the percentage and the absolute volatilities at the beginning of the period. Looking at Figure 7.32, it is clear that the time series of percentage and rescaled volatilities sometimes tell a very different story as to whether a particular period is associated with great rate volatility or not. These features are discussed in greater detail in Chapter 23.

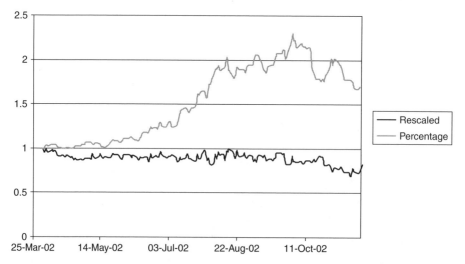

Figure 7.32 The percentage (upper curve) and absolute (lower curve) implied volatility of the 1×1 swap rate in 2002. Both volatilities have been rebased to 1 at the beginning of the period. Looking at the two curves one would draw very different conclusions about the degree of variability of the volatility during this period.

7.5 FX Rates

7.5.1 Basic Facts

Fact 1: In the FX option market the shape of the smile, at least for mature-market/mature-market currency pairs, is much more variable than in the equity or interest-rate case. The smile can frequently change skewness over time (from smile to the left to smile to the right); it can become approximately flat, increase or even reverse its convexity; it can turn into a smirk; etc. The shape of the smile is often synthetically described by means of two related quotes: the 25-delta risk reversal and the 25-delta strangle, which are quoted as the difference between the implied volatilities of the two options underlying the strategies. So, if the risk reversal is positive, the out-of-the-money call is more expensive than the out-of-the-money put. A quote of, say, 2% would indicate that the implied volatility of the call is 2% above the implied volatility of the put. The strangle is instead quoted as the average of the two out-of-the-money implied volatilities minus the ATM volatility. A positive quote for the strangle indicates that out-of-the-money options are relatively more 'expensive' (in implied volatility terms) than ATM options. Roughly speaking, the risk reversal and strangle quotes therefore give indications about the curvature and the slope (second and first derivatives) of the smile curve, respectively. An analysis of the quotes for 25-delta risk reversals over extended periods shows wide variations both in magnitude and in sign; 25-delta strangles, on the other hand, tend to trade around variable, but mainly positive, values. See Cooper and Talbot (1999) for some empirical data regarding the USD/JPY exchange rate.

    Fact 2: The shape of the smile for mature-market/emerging-market currency pairs displays an equity-like smile in the direction of emerging-market-currency put/ \$call.

7.5.2 Subtler Effects

Correlation Between Changes in Level and Changes in Skewness

Bates (1996) uses a parametric (jump–diffusion) fit to USD/JPY and USD/DEM data (2024 days for DEM and 1191 days for JPY), and calculates the first four moments of the fitted distributions. Using this data and a Bayesian-statistical approach, Johnson (2001) finds a significant positive correlation between the trend of the underlying and the third moment (skewness) of the risk-neutral rate distribution. According to these findings, as a currency rallies for an extended period of time, the price distribution becomes more skewed (in the direction of the rallying currency).

    Along similar lines, Campa *et al.* (1998) also document a strong positive correlation between skewness in the risk-neutral probability densities and the spot FX rate for five currencies. The methodology they employ consists of extracting the probability densities implied by the market data using a variety of methods, and the results they obtain are independent of the precise choice of the delta level (e.g. 25-delta).

    Cooper and Talbot (1999) also analyse changes in risk reversals and spot for USD/JPY during the turbulent period of 1998. In their chart B a strong positive correlation between a positive risk reversal and the strengthening of the currency is observed. On the basis of the empirical evidence in Campa *et al.* (1998) and in Bates (1996), Johnson (2001) concludes that there truly is a consistent relationship between trends and time-varying third moments, which deserves to be included in the list of stylized characteristics of currency returns.

I report similar data in Figures 7.33–7.36. More precisely, Figures 7.33–7.36 show scatter plots of daily changes of the underlying rate against changes in the risk reversal. It

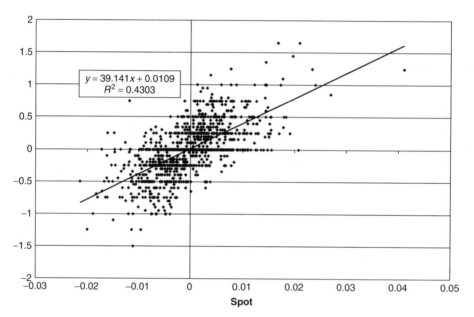

Figure 7.33   USD/EUR percentage daily changes in spot vs 1w RR (31-7-96/1-5-01).

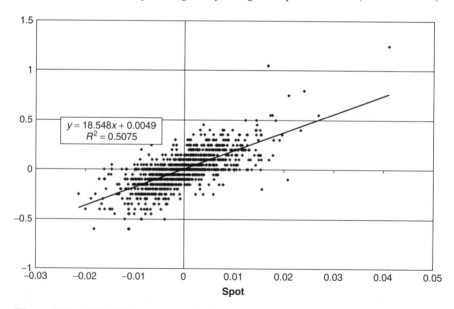

Figure 7.34   USD/EUR percentage daily changes in spot vs 1m RR (31-7-96/1-5-01).

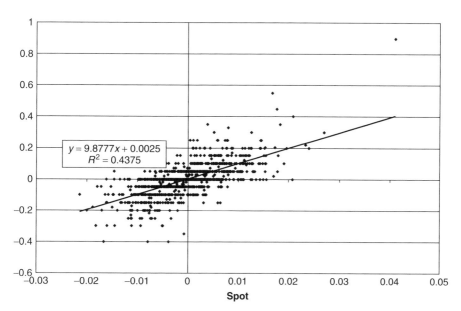

Figure 7.35 USD/EUR percentage daily changes in spot vs 3m RR (31-7-96/1-5-01).

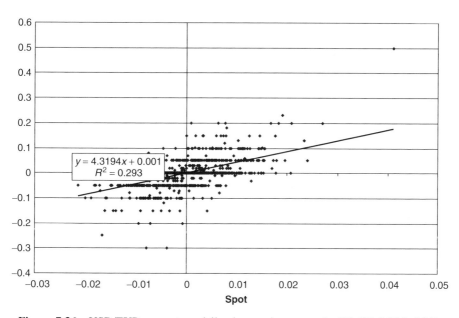

Figure 7.36 USD/EUR percentage daily changes in spot vs 1y RR (31-7-96/1-5-01).

is clear that the effect decreases sharply as the maturity of the option increases. It is also interesting to point out that when weekly changes in the underlying rate and in the risk reversal are considered, the effect virtually disappears. See Figure 7.37 and 7.38. Going back to daily changes, a similar message is conveyed by Figures 7.39–7.42 for USD/GBP and Figures 7.43–7.46 for USD/YEN.

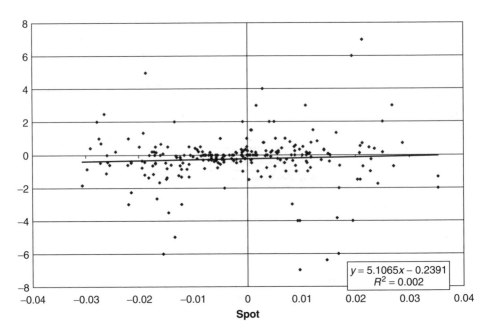

Figure 7.37   USD/EUR percentage weekly changes in spot vs 1w RR (31-7-96/1-5-01).

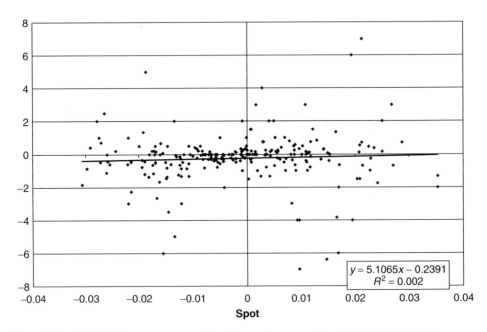

Figure 7.38   USD/EUR percentage weekly changes in spot vs 3m RR (31-7-96/1-5-01).

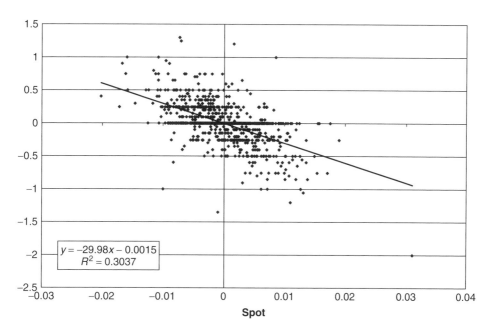

Figure 7.39 USD/GBP percentage daily changes in spot vs 1w RR (31-7-96/1-5-01).

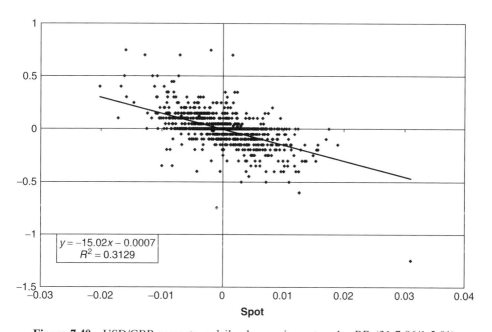

Figure 7.40 USD/GBP percentage daily changes in spot vs 1m RR (31-7-96/1-5-01).

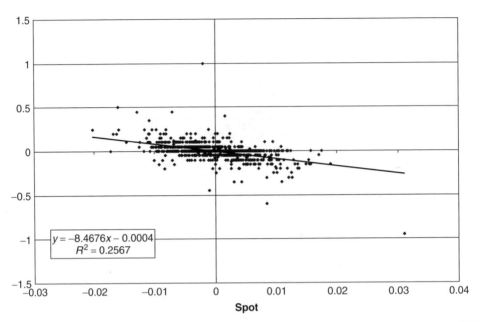

Figure 7.41 USD/GBP percentage daily changes in spot vs 3m RR (31-7-96/1-5-01).

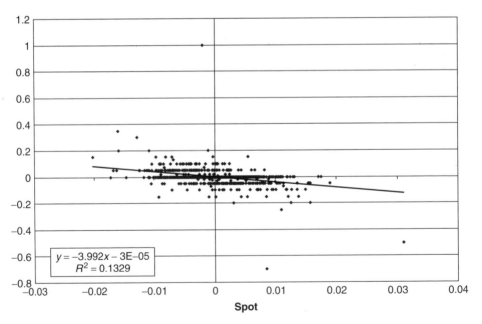

Figure 7.42 USD/GBP percentage daily changes in spot vs 1y RR (31-7-96/1-5-01).

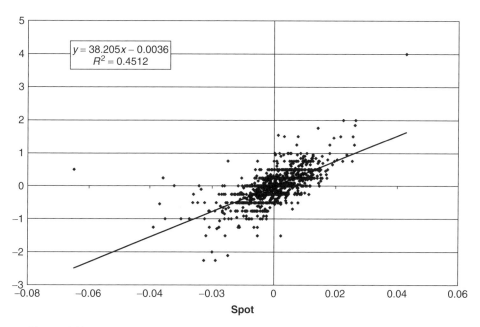

Figure 7.43 USD/YEN percentage daily changes in spot vs 1w RR (31-7-96/1-5-01).

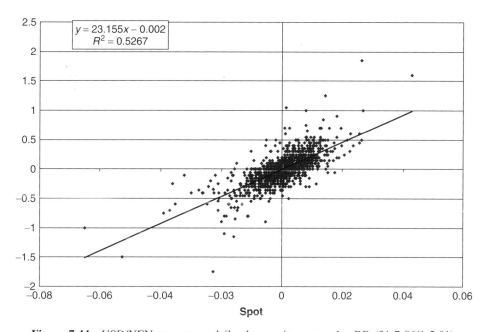

Figure 7.44 USD/YEN percentage daily changes in spot vs 1m RR (31-7-96/1-5-01).

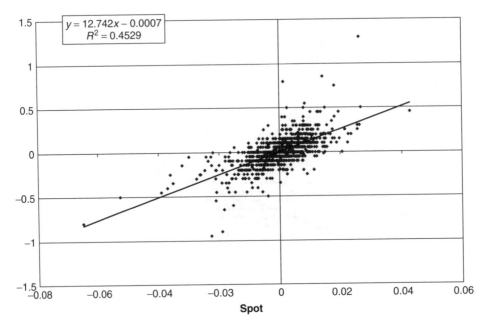

Figure 7.45   USD/YEN percentage daily changes in spot vs 3m RR (31-7-96/1-5-01).

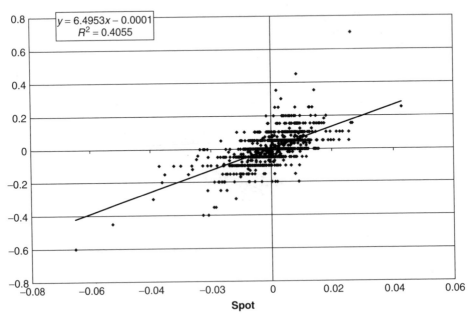

Figure 7.46   USD/YEN percentage daily changes in spot vs 1y RR (31-7-96/1-5-01).

7.6 Conclusions

What conclusions can we draw from this body of empirical evidence? As I said, many of the subtler effects will be discussed in the chapters devoted to the individual models. However, some very 'high-level' messages should already have become apparent. Let me review a few.

- To begin with, the dependence of the smile surface on the strike and on the underlying is so different, and complex, for the different markets, that it would be extremely surprising if a single financial mechanism (stochastic volatility, jumps, etc.) were capable of accounting for this diversity of behaviours. Therefore in what follows I will place great importance on choosing a financially justifiable model for a given market (or market subsection).

- At least in the case of equities, neither pure (deterministic- or stochastic-volatility) diffusions, nor pure discontinuous (jump) processes appear to be enough to account, *by themselves*, for the observed asymptotic behaviour of out-of-the-money options. Therefore, much as I will treat most of the models in isolation, I advocate that more than one smile-producing mechanism should be used. This is true both in the interest-rate and in the equity/FX worlds.

- The observation of the frequent movement in opposite directions of call prices and of the underlying (at least over a three-hour period) cautions against assuming that the observed market prices of options should necessarily be obtainable from a coherent model capable of explaining, at the same time, the behaviour of the underlying and of the associated derivatives. For this reason in Chapter 17 I will discuss if, and to what extent, the evolution of the smile can be assigned without reference to a generating process for the underlying.

Chapter 8

General Features of Smile-Modelling Approaches

In Chapter 7 I briefly reviewed some of the most salient empirical facts about smiles. We can now begin to look in general terms at the classes of models that have been proposed to account for these empirical facts. As in the case of the empirical facts, at this stage the description is kept rather summary, and is meant to give a bird's eye view of the topic. The assumptions underlying the various models and their implications for pricing are treated in detail in the following chapters.

8.1 Fully-Stochastic-Volatility Models

Fully-stochastic-volatility models posit a dynamics of the underlying given by

$$dS = \mu_S(S, V, t)\, dt + \sigma_S(S, V, T)\, dz_t \tag{8.1}$$

$$dV = \mu_V(S, V, t)\, dt + \sigma_V(S, V, t)\, dw_t \tag{8.2}$$

$$V = \sigma^2 \tag{8.3}$$

$$E[dw\, dz] = \rho\, dt \tag{8.4}$$

The term 'fully stochastic' is introduced to differentiate these models from the stochastic-volatility models (discussed below) where the stochasticity only arises because of the functional dependence of the volatility on the underlying. In the more general fully-stochastic case a second source of uncertainty (typically, a second Brownian motion) affects the evolution of the stock price.

Without including options in the set of fundamental trading instruments, markets are not, in general, complete when the volatility is fully stochastic. If the trader can hedge only with the underlying, perfect replication of an option payoff is not possible. Therefore pricing by no-arbitrage alone will not in general give a unique price, unless one can introduce exogenously the market price of risk, or, more generally, the investor's utility function. This is not a route that is commonly followed in practical option pricing.

As for the promise of completion of the market by adding another traded option to the universe of hedging instruments, I discuss in Section 13.2 that this is only true if the *whole process*, and not just today's price, of the hedging option is assumed to be known. This is a tall order.

It is easy to understand at a qualitative level why fully-stochastic-volatility models give rise to a smile. Let us consider, for simplicity, the case when the increments of the Brownian motion that shocks the volatility are uncorrelated with the Brownian increments for the underlying. If this is case, the call option price is simply given by the integral over the density of the root-mean-squared volatilities of the Black-and-Scholes prices associated with each volatility path (this was first shown by Hull and White (1987)):

$$Call_{StVol} = \int Call_{BS}(\widehat{\sigma})\phi(\widehat{\sigma})\, d\widehat{\sigma} \qquad (8.5)$$

In this equation $Call_{StVol}$ is the price of a call as given by an independent-stochastic-volatility model, $Call_{BS}(\widehat{\sigma})$ is the price of a Black-and-Scholes call with root-mean-squared volatility $\widehat{\sigma}$ and $\phi(\widehat{\sigma})$ is the terminal probability density of the root-mean-squared volatilities. So, each realization to expiry T of the volatility process will give rise to a particular root-mean-squared volatility. Contingent on a particular volatility path having being realized, we are back exactly to a Black-and-Scholes world, with the associated root-mean-squared volatility.

To see how smiles come about, consider now the population of volatility paths generated by the chosen volatility process, and recall that at the money the Black-and-Scholes formula is virtually exactly linear in the root-mean-squared volatility, but ceases to be so away from the at-the-money level. See Section 25.5 for a detailed discussion of this point. Therefore, at the money the effect of a high volatility path will be almost exactly cancelled by the associated, 'mirror-image', equi-probability low-volatility path. Away from the at-the-money level, however, the average of Black-and-Scholes option prices obtained with a higher- and lower-than-average root-mean-squared volatility will be higher than the option price evaluated with the average volatility. The smile effect with stochastic-volatility models is therefore a direct consequence of the convexity of the Black-and-Scholes formula.

This observation helps to explain the most salient qualitative features of fully-stochastic-volatility models. Since the convexity of the smile stems from the convexity of the Black-and-Scholes formula, in general the effect will be more pronounced when there is a high probability of finding widely dispersed values of the root-mean-squared volatility. With Brownian-diffusion-based stochastic-volatility models, however, today's volatility can only continuously diffuse away from its initial value. Therefore, for 'reasonable choices' of the coefficients,[1] fully-stochastic-volatility models tend to produce rather shallow smiles for short maturities. In reality, as the 'empirical' facts reported above remind us, one observes the opposite. Many studies (see, for example, Das and Sundaram (1997), Jorion (1988) and Bates (1996)) confirm this observation. It should be pointed out, however that, if the stochastic-volatility process is given a mean-reverting form (in the risk-neutral measure), a combination of high volatility of volatility and high reversion speed can produce pronounced smiles at the short end of the maturity spectrum (see Fouque *et al.* (2000), and the discussion in Chapter 13).

---

[1] What is 'reasonable' is not so obvious: the usual distinction between the risk-adjusted and the real world applies.

Jump–diffusion models, introduced below, might overcome this problem, but, by themselves, they have their own shortcomings. Probably a combined jump–diffusion plus fully-stochastic-volatility model could provide a more satisfactory combined description of market observed option prices. Such a model (Das and Sundaram (1997))

> would (...) be able to generate adequate kurtosis at short maturities (via the jump component) and at moderate maturities (through the stochastic volatility component). Unfortunately, such as choice would not be a parsimonious one.

Finally, note that Equations (8.1) to (8.4) above represent a fairly general approach to fully-stochastic-volatility modelling. Even these equations, however, should not be regarded as *the* most general stochastic-volatility model. A very interesting approach is, for instance, presented by Naik (1993), where the volatility is assumed to undergo a jump process. A variation on this theme is presented in the chapter devoted to a two-regime, stochastic-volatility model (Chapter 27).

8.2 Local-Volatility (Restricted-Stochastic-Volatility) Models

Local-volatility models describe the stochastic evolution of the underlying state variable by means of a volatility term that is a deterministic function of the stochastic underlying stock prices. So, at time t_0 the user does not know what volatility will prevail at a future time t, since the future realization of the underlying is not known. Contingent on the knowledge of the realization of the process for the underlying at an arbitrary future time, however, the volatility is uniquely determined. Owing to the very special type of stochasticity which is allowed for by these models, I often refer to them in what follows as 'restricted-stochastic-volatility models'. 'Local-volatility' models is another common name, which I use for brevity when the distinction from the *bona fide* stochastic-volatility models is not important, or when the context does not give rise to ambiguity. Within the framework provided by this specification, the dynamics of the underlying are therefore given by

$$dS_t = r S_t \, dt + \sigma(S_t, t) \, dz \tag{8.6}$$

The first observation is that the market is still complete, since the (stochastic) volatility functionally depends on the underlying S. Following the procedure described in Chapter 2, one can therefore always set up an exactly replicating portfolio with the underlying security and the 'bond', and risk-neutral valuation will give rise to a unique option price. Furthermore, I will show in Chapter 11 that, given an arbitrary exogenous set of current admissible[2] market prices, it is always possible to recover them by specifying a suitable local-volatility function $\sigma(S, t)$. Therefore local-volatility models would appear to enjoy several very desirable features, i.e.

- the ability to recover exactly the prices of an exogenous set of admissible option prices;

---

[2] See Chapter 17 for a definition of admissibility.

- the promise to create a replicating portfolio that will reproduce exactly the terminal payoff of any complex option; because of this, the approach also offers

- the ability to provide a unique arbitrage-free price for complex options.

Not surprisingly, these models have enjoyed large popularity. Despite, or perhaps because of, these features, I will argue in the following chapters that such faith in the power of local-volatility models is probably misplaced. Let me give a first glimpse of why I have these reservations.

I will show in Chapter 12 that, from a set of *exogenous* market option prices for several expiries, one can derive the underlying marginal (unconditional) risk-neutral price distributions of the underlying at the same horizons. Let us assume that these price distributions have been distilled from market options prices that had been generated by, say, a general (i.e. a random-jump-size) Poisson process. I will also show in Chapter 14 that unique pricing by no-arbitrage and perfect replication of a payoff at expiry are no longer possible in this setting. None the less, let us imagine that from these observed market prices a trader, who did not know that the true process was a jump–diffusion, derived the marginal terminal distribution. This exercise is model independent, and can be achieved in theory perfectly even without any knowledge of the true process that generated the prices. See Chapter 9. Thanks to the flexibility of the local-volatility model, the trader will be able to reproduce these marginal densities via a suitably complex diffusive behaviour, i.e. by imputing from the market prices a suitably complex function $\sigma(S, t)$.

Emboldened by this 'success', and lured by the promise of perfect replicability, the trader might then try to set up the replicating portfolio required by the local-volatility process. Since all of today's prices have been correctly recovered, can she hope that this portfolio will be the correct one? Certainly not. We know, in fact, that, unbeknownst to the trader, the prices had been generated by a random-amplitude jump–diffusion process that admits *no* exactly replicating portfolio. The 'replicating' portfolio suggested by the local-volatility model would therefore certainly be incorrect.

This conclusion is quite obvious if the underlying jump process were such that the jump amplitude is random. This is because we would be trying to set up a perfectly replicating hedge in a situation when one cannot be created, owing to the market incompleteness. Can we perhaps hope that, if the prices used by the trader to calibrate her local-volatility model had been generated by a process that does allow the completion of the market, the resulting hedging strategy would be correct? Unfortunately, one can easily show that the conclusion reached above regarding the incorrectness of the hedge remains valid even if the 'true' distribution had been generated by a process that does in principle allow perfect payoff replication (perhaps by adding a suitable number of options to the hedging instruments). This would be the case, for instance, if a (series of) Poisson jump(s) of known amplitudes were overlaid on top of a deterministic-volatility diffusion.

Summarizing: the fact that we can invoke risk neutrality for valuation purposes does not imply that any modelling approach that produces the same final price distributions and is consistent with risk neutrality will give equivalent results. Or, stated more simply, recovery of today's plain-vanilla option prices is a necessary but not sufficient condition for acceptance of a model. Once gain, it is essential to convince oneself that the *financial* mechanism responsible for the smile can be accounted for by the model.

Finally, it is instructive to look at the price produced by a local-volatility model as follows. Consider a European option, with final maturity T. In order to simplify notation, let us assume that the number of paths that can be followed by the stock can be arbitrarily large, but finite. Select a particular path, say, the ith, of the stock price from time t_0 to time T, and denote this path by $\xi_{0,T}^i$. Along the path the volatility is deterministic and perfectly known. Let $\widehat{\sigma}(\xi_{0,T}^i)$ be the root-mean-squared volatility associated with this path, and $Call_{BS}(\widehat{\sigma}(\xi_{0,T}^i))$ the relative Black-and-Scholes call price. Then the value of a call in the local-volatility setting, $Call_{LV}$, is simply given by

$$Call_{LV} = \sum_i BS(\widehat{\sigma}(\xi_{0,T}^i))\pi(\xi_{0,T}^i) \qquad (8.7)$$

where $\pi(\xi_{0,T}^i)$ is the probability of the ith path. The expression is not particularly useful for practical computations, but it is conceptually useful both to understand the qualitative features of the smile produced by local-volatility models (see Section 12.6) and for the discussion at the end of this chapter.

8.3 Jump–Diffusion Models

8.3.1 Discrete Amplitude

In this model, on top of a Brownian diffusion, the stock price is affected by jumps (i.e. discontinuous moves whose magnitudes do not scale with time – see Section 2.4.1) that occur at random times, but are assumed to be of known amplitude(s). The reason for treating separately jump processes with a finite number of possible jump amplitudes is that, in this case, the market can in principle be completed by adding as many hedging options as possible jump amplitudes to the set of hedging instruments. See Section 14.3. This possibility appears to be appealing, because even when only a few jump amplitudes are possible, the approach can already reproduce many of the qualitative features of the prices of smiley plain-vanilla options observed in the FX and equity markets. In particular, it can give rise to pronounced smiles for short maturities and shallower smiles for long maturities. Furthermore, if the possible jump amplitudes are chosen 'judiciously', as few as three or four can produce option prices similar to those obtained by a random-amplitude jump–diffusion process (while still allowing, at least in principle, completion of the market). Let me note in passing that, if the market could really be completed, the ability to price options by invoking riskless replication would be a mixed blessing: if one thought, for instance, that Smile Tale 2 was the correct origin for the smile, one would not be accounting for the financial mechanism that was assumed to be responsible for the smile itself, i.e. the inability to hedge perfectly across a jump and, consequently, a non-zero aversion to jump risk. However, I will argue in Chapter 14 that, exactly as in the stochastic-volatility case, for the market to be completed the trader must assume knowledge not just of today's prices of the hedging options, but also their prices in all possible future states of the world (i.e. their full joint processes must be known). See the detailed discussion in Chapters 13 and 14.

8.3.2   Continuum of Jump Amplitudes

When the possible amplitude ratios of the jumps can assume a continuum of values one can no longer set up a replicating portfolio with a possibly large but finite number of securities (stock plus hedging options). Obtaining a unique price using a risk-neutral valuation is therefore no longer possible, even in principle.

One should be careful, however, with too 'mechanistic' a transition from complete to incomplete markets, and with the accompanying introduction of the market price of risk in the pricing formula. Formally, if the underlying S can jump to, say, $10\,000\,000\,000$ possible states and a trader had $1\,000\,000\,002$ securities (the stock, the 'bond' and $10\,000\,000\,000$ options) at her disposal to hedge with (and knew their full processes), she should be indifferent to jump risk, perfect replication would be possible, and invoking absence of arbitrage would give rise to a unique price about which all traders would have to agree. If, on the other hand, the same trader were faced with a process with an infinite number of possible jump amplitudes, then her risk aversion should be reflected in the price; an infinity of prices would be consistent with absence of arbitrage. In reality, if the trader could include in her set of hedging securities $10\,000\,000\,000$ options, the prices of the these options would not be 'explained' by the model, but would have to be exogenously 'given'. See the discussion in Section 14.5. The model might therefore well account for all these prices, but, since we can observe them in the market, it is adding precious little extra information. The only contribution by the model would come from the pricing of the $10\,000\,000\,001$st option. But, if we truly knew the process for $10\,000\,000\,000$ options, would not any reasonable interpolating procedure provide pretty much the same answer, irrespective of whether the true process can jump to an infinity of values, or only to $10\,000\,000\,000$ (well chosen) values? What would be the explanatory power of the model? The reader should contrast this situation with the Black-and-Scholes case, where the trader can obtain (admittedly 'slightly' wrong) prices for all strikes and maturities with a single number – the implied volatility.

There are several unexpected similarities between jump–diffusion models and stochastic-volatility models. One of the most striking is that, if the jump amplitudes are log-normally distributed, the price of a call option, $Call_{JD}$, is simply given by the integral of Black-and-Scholes prices, each associated to a particular realization of jumps, and weighed by the probability of occurrence of these jumps. Formally,

$$Call_{JD} = \int Call_{BS}(S(Y))\phi(Y)\,dY \qquad (8.8)$$

where Y and $\phi(Y)$ symbolically indicate the 'jump history' and the associated probability density (see Section 14.6 for a precise explanation). Even if the jump amplitude ratio is symmetric, the process still gives rise to a smile. The smile-producing mechanism is again the non-linearity of the Black-and-Scholes function in the realized 'volatility'. There is, however, an important difference: owing to the discontinuous nature of the process, and to the fact that the size of the jump does not scale with the size of the time-step, jump–diffusion processes give a much higher probability of 'large' moves of the underlying for short times after 'today'. Therefore the non-linearity of the Black-and-Scholes formula is allowed to 'kick in' much earlier, and the smile can be steeper at shorter maturities.

8.4 Variance–Gamma Models

The fundamental idea in the case of the variance–gamma approach is to dispense altogether with a continuous Brownian component and describe the process for the underlying purely in terms of discontinuous jumps. The frequency of arrival of these jumps depends on their magnitude: small jumps occur frequently, and large ones rarely. This set-up is meant to describe the uneven rate of arrival of economic information (with 'run-of-the-mill' innovations arriving almost continuously, and large surprises occurring rarely). In this model, it is therefore the flow of 'economic time' that becomes a random quantity.

The process is discontinuous everywhere, and therefore its statistical properties are quite different from the properties of diffusions. In particular, its first variation (infinite in the diffusive case) is finite. None the less, also in the case of the variance–gamma model one can show that, contingent on a particular random time-length having being drawn, the call price is given by the integral of Black-and-Scholes prices, each associated to a particular realization of economic time, and weighed by its probability of occurrence. More precisely, contingent on a particular value for the 'time' g having being realized, the corresponding conditional option price, $Call_{BS}(g)$, is simply a Black price. The unconditional call price, $Call_{VG}(S_t, K)$, is therefore obtained by integrating numerically over the density for g:

$$Call_{VG}(S_t, K) = \int_0^\infty Call_{BS}(g)\phi(g)\,\mathrm{d}g = \int_0^\infty Call_{BS}(g)\frac{g^{\frac{t}{\nu}-1}\exp(-\frac{g}{\nu})}{\nu^{\frac{t}{\nu}}\Gamma(\frac{t}{\nu})}\,\mathrm{d}g \qquad (8.9)$$

See Chapter 15 for a full discussion.

8.5 Mixing Processes

Not surprisingly, the models briefly described above need not be, and have not been, used in isolation. The jump–diffusion approach, for instance, has been overlaid with a local-volatility component (Andersen and Andreasen (1999)). The idea, in this case, is that the jump–diffusion description is 'almost right', and that the local-volatility addition should only be used as a 'correction term' to get an exact fit to market data.

A similar approach is taken by Britten-Jones and Neuberger (1998), who show how an exogenous set of option prices can be recovered by using a local-volatility component superimposed onto any member of a wide class of (Markovian) stochastic volatility processes. Derman and Kani (1998) allow for a more general (i.e. in general, non-Markovian) volatility process; their procedure is however computationally much more complex.

Jump–diffusions and stochastic volatilities have been combined (for instance, by Duffie *et al.* (2000) for affine processes). Similarly, the variance–gamma model (which is a pure jump model) has been combined with a stochastic-volatility component. While Madan *et al.* (1998) argue that adding a deterministic diffusive component to their variance–gamma process is unnecessary, combining stochastic volatility with discontinuous innovations certainly has a considerable intuitive appeal. On the one hand, even a casual observation of the size of moves of market prices suggests that the existence of jumps is very plausible, and the variance–gamma model, with its in-built link between the size and the frequency of the jumps, has an evident appeal. On the other hand, it is difficult to argue that the variability of the underlying is such that the future smile should be uniquely determined by the future realization of the underlying (as the variance–gamma model implies). This would suggest that there is room for a stochastic-volatility component in the variance–gamma world.

More generally, joining a stochastic diffusive component with jumps (of whatever origin) can fix two often-observed problems: stochastic-volatility models produce appreciable smiles for intermediate maturities, but have difficulties in producing the sharp smiles for short maturities often observed in the market. Jump–diffusion processes, on the other hand, do produce sharp smiles at the short end of the expiry spectrum, but these tend to decay too rapidly. A combination of the two approaches would therefore seem to give the best of both worlds: sharp, short-maturity smiles that persist over intermediate maturities. However, once various correlations, reversion speeds, reversion levels, jump amplitudes, jump variances, etc. have been introduced, the trader is sometimes left with a staggering number of process parameters. If the implied approach is followed, these coefficients immediately become fitting parameters, to be determined by means of very non-linear minimizations. As a result, competing minima of similar numerical quality, but radically different financial interpretation, easily occur. More generally, the models cease to be parsimonious, and it might be difficult to judge whether a good fit to market data indicates a well-specified modelling approach, or is simply the result of the flexibility of the chosen set of parameter functions. I therefore recommend that when such 'rich' models are used, as many financial constraints on the parameter ranges should be used as possible (see the discussion in Section 6.6, and the detailed examples in Sections 13.7 and 14.5.3). The robustness of the implied solution should also be tested against, for instance, small changes in the inputs (see Chapter 9).

8.5.1 A Pragmatic Approach to Mixing Models

Finally, this section about a mixture of models can be profitably closed with the following observation. A trader often finds herself between the rock of fitting exactly to the market prices of the hedging options and the hard place of using a financially-well-justified model. If today's prices are not recovered, the hedging costs predicted by the model will not match the real costs; if the model is financially unsatisfactory, a similar mismatch will occur for the future vega re-hedging costs. Unfortunately, very often financially 'good' models produce acceptable but not exact fits to the market prices of the plain-vanilla options. On the other hand, models, such as local-volatility diffusions, that do recover the market smile by construction are not financially very convincing (see the discussion in Chapter 12).

This state of affairs is encountered not only in FX/equity options, but also in the case of interest-rate derivatives. I show in Part III of this book, in fact, that a set of financially-desirable, time-homogeneous, instantaneous-volatility functions can get the market prices of caplets 'almost' right, but that the 'residual' is often too large too ignore. On the other hand, a choice does exist for the instantaneous-volatility functions that ensure that all the caplets are perfectly priced (again, by construction). This choice, however, is financially very unsatisfactory (see the discussion in Section 21.2). What can one do?

In the case of interest rates I propose the 'fix' of combining the desirable and the undesirable components of the volatility function, *and of optimizing the coefficients of the 'good' component in such a way that the residual 'bad' component should be as small as possible.* I show in Chapter 21 that this can be done in a very simple and effective way. The same approach can be taken in the FX/equity world. One can combine the (financially-dubious) local-volatility model with either jump–diffusions or stochastic-volatility or variance–gamma processes. One can then choose the parameters of the latter ('good') process in such a way that the magnitude of the residual undesirable 'fix' should be as small as possible. The results by Britten-Jones and Neuberger (1998) for stochastic-volatility processes and by Andersen and Brotherton-Ratcliffe (1998) for jump–diffusions can be of great assistance in this task.

8.6 Other Approaches

The modelling approaches briefly described above (and more fully in the following chapters) are by no means the only ones that have been introduced in the literature in order to account for the existence of smiles. Some of the omitted models (such as the Amin (1993) model) are very interesting and would deserve careful attention. My intention, however, has not been to provide an 'encyclopaedia of smile-producing models', but to provide the reader with the analytical tools to assess on her own the suitability of a modelling approach for the financial problem at hand. The following chapters should therefore be seen in this light.

Two more approaches, however, deserve a mention at this stage: the quadratic-variation-based model of Britten-Jones and Neuberger (1996) (see Chapter 10); and the approach based on the direct modelling of the evolution of the smile surface, presented in Chapter 17.

8.6.1 Tight Bounds with Known Quadratic Variation

Britten-Jones and Neuberger (1996) show that, if the quadratic variation of a process is exactly known and if the process of the underlying is everywhere continuous one can obtain a unique price that coincides, not surprisingly, with the Black-and-Scholes one with the associated root-mean-squared volatility. More interestingly, however, if jumps of maximum magnitude d are allowed, the arbitrage-free price is shown to lie between an upper and a lower value. The width of this band is a function of d, and it 'contains' the Black-and-Scholes price. The approach is interesting because it does not require a direct specification of the process of the underlying, yet it provides an optimal hedging strategy that naturally 'nests' the Black hedge ratio. Furthermore, for reasonable sizes of the maximum jump d, the bands are usefully tight. As for the 'jumps', they could be true discontinuities in the stock price process, or could be due to transaction costs, finite re-hedging frequency, etc.

The generality of the approach, and the apparent weakness of the assumptions, would seem to make it very powerful. However, I will show that the requirement of a deterministic and known quadratic variation is less innocuous than it might at first appear. The approach is therefore discussed in considerable detail not only because it is intrinsically interesting and 'elegant', but also because it sheds light on the role of quadratic variation in the pricing of options in the presence of smiles.

8.6.2   Assigning Directly the Evolution of the Smile Surface

As for the second 'unorthodox' approach, it is based on the idea that it might be possible to specify directly the dynamics of the smile surface, rather than obtain it from the future prices implied by a process-based model for the underlying. The justification for this approach is that, in reality, a trader more frequently assesses the quality of a model on the basis of its ability to produce believable future smile surfaces, rather than on the basis of the statistical properties of the implied dynamics for the underlying. See the discussion in Chapter 1 about model re-calibration and vega re-hedging. Therefore a direct modelling of the evolution of the smile surface would appear to afford a more direct translation of the trader's intuition than a process-based approach.

Appealing as this way of thinking might be, the task is made difficult by the fact that moving a future smile surface means moving a number of future inter-related prices (the future conditional option prices). Doing so without incurring the risk of model-independent arbitrage will turn out not to be an easy task. None the less, the analysis of the conditions required to create admissible and 'compatible' future smile surfaces will be both illuminating and useful in practice.[3]

Another by-product of this approach is that, if future smile surfaces are allowed to be stochastic, it is possible to show that two situations can arise: either these future smile surfaces depend on the realization of the underlying (indeed, most process-based models produce a smile surface of this type); or the future smile surfaces are independent of the future realization of the stock price. In this latter case one can always find (see Section 17.7.2) an equivalent *deterministic* future smile that gives rise to exactly the same prices. Therefore, a process-based model with stochastic coefficients (e.g. stochastic volatility, stochastic jump frequency) only provides something that could not be given by an equivalent, deterministic-smile model to the extent that it creates a correlation between future smiles and future realizations of the underlying. This subtle but important point is discussed in detail in Chapter 17.

8.7   The Importance of the Quadratic Variation (Take 2)

All classifications are imperfect, and always fail to capture some important features of reality. None the less, I believe that analysing smile-producing models on the basis of the nature of the stochasticity of the quadratic variation they give rise to is one of the most profitable ways to look at them. Let me try to explain why.

The link between the stochastic quadratic variation (root-mean-squared volatility) and option pricing was made evident by the similarity of the formal expressions for the call prices provided by the different models briefly discussed in this chapter: they all boiled down to an integral of Black-and-Scholes prices, where each price was evaluated contingent on a particular realization of the chosen stochastic variable, and weighed by its probability of occurrence. Furthermore, each of the 'orthodox' models presented above produced a distribution of quadratic variations (and hence of root-mean-squared volatilities) by option expiry. See the discussion in Sections 10.5.4–10.5.6. Therefore, with some careful 'adjustments' discussed in the relevant chapters, one can consider

---

[3]I explain the concept of (Kolmogorov) compatibility in Chapter 17. At this stage compatibility can be understood in terms of congruence of the current market prices and the future smiles.

the 'smiley' price simply as a weighted average of Black-and-Scholes prices over the distribution of the realized quadratic variations.

When option pricing is looked at in this light, many aspects nicely fall conceptually into place. We all agree in fact that in a Black-and-Scholes world no smiles are allowed. But what *exactly* is the common distinguishing feature that characterizes the Black-and-Scholes approach on one side and all the other models that gives rise to smiles on the other? The Black-and-Scholes approach is associated with perfect payoff replicability, unique pricing by no-arbitrage and market completeness. Important as these features are, the existence of smiles does not appear to be logically linked to the impossibility of achieving unique pricing by no-arbitrage, because local-volatility models, for instance, certainly allow unique pricing, but can produce very complex smiles. Lack of market completeness, or the inability to replicate perfectly an option payoff (which are simply equivalent ways of saying that a unique price cannot be arrived at by invoking absence of arbitrage), cannot be the 'culprit' either: see, again, local-volatility models, and, with the caveats above, stochastic-volatility and some jump–diffusion models. However, when we look at the behaviour of the quadratic variation (*of the log-process!*) we seem to have put our finger on the right spot. In a Black-and-Scholes world the quadratic variation is deterministic and exactly known, and this can only happen if the process is a diffusion with a deterministic volatility. A deterministic-volatility diffusion is the only case when 'lucky paths' do not exist. All the other (non-flat) smile structures appear to be simply reflections of the different ways in which the quadratic volatility can be made stochastic, and of the non-linearity of the Black-and-Scholes function in the associated root-mean-squared volatility. If, for instance, the non-linearity can be brought into play only gradually (as is the case with stochastic volatility models), the smile will 'naturally'[4] be shallow at the short end of the maturity spectrum and increase with time to expiry. If, on the other hand, we allow the non-linearity to be brought into play by jumps that can occur instantaneously, then the smile can be much steeper early on.

More generally, we have seen in Chapter 4 that even when the volatility is deterministic, and the process therefore inhabits a Black-and-Scholes world, a finite re-hedging frequency produces stochasticity in the realized quadratic variation. This stochasticity was shown to be closely linked to the magnitude of the slippages between the payoffs of the target option and of the replicating portfolio. For realistic re-hedging frequencies (and even in the absence of transaction costs!) the width of the distribution of the slippages turned out to be far from negligible compared with the option price. From this perspective, the degree of stochasticity in the realized quadratic variation produced by, say, stochastic-volatility or variance–gamma models may well be greater, but is not qualitatively different from what we observed in the deterministic-volatility, finite-re-hedging case. If the stochasticity in the quadratic variation stems from *any* reason other than a perfect functional dependence of the volatility on the underlying (as in the restricted-stochastic-volatility case), exact replication, and unique pricing by no-arbitrage, will not be possible.

If we look at the option pricing problem in this light, the ability to replicate, and its corollary of unique pricing by no-arbitrage, should be assessed on a *continuum*, rather

---

[4]The adverb 'naturally' refers to the case where the volatility of the volatility and the reversion speed are not particularly high. When this is the case, sudden bursts of volatility can occur, and this can to some extent give rise to sudden large volatility changes and, therefore, indirectly, to a significant sampling of the convexity of the Black-and-Scholes formula.

than on a black-and-white, digital basis. Because of the limitations imposed by a finite re-hedging frequency, whatever the 'true' underlying process, perfect replication is always impossible. On the other hand, reducing substantially the variability of the terminal payoff of the 'naked' option by means of some (imperfect, and possibly non-unique) hedging strategy is almost always possible. The lack of uniqueness of no-arbitrage prices when replication is imperfect stems from the fact that, whenever the dispersion of slippages is non-zero, risk aversion plays a role in the price making. However, the tighter the distribution of slippages, the narrower the range of prices that a 'reasonable' aversion to risk can produce. 'Unique' pricing by no-arbitrage becomes the limiting case of 'tight' pricing by no-arbitrage.

Total absence of smiles therefore appears to be associated with the very special and very idealized case of a fully deterministic quadratic variation *for the log process* of the underlying. Much as this view might appear convincing and illuminating, the case of the Britten-Jones and Neuberger (1996) model introduces a word of caution. Here we have a model that does produce smiles, but incorporates from the start a deterministic (and perfectly known) quadratic variation. On the other hand, we seem to have made a convincing identification between stochastic quadratic variations and smiles. Do we have to throw away this way of looking at option prices? Perhaps not. There is in fact something rather unique about the Britten-Jones and Neuberger (1996) model. To understand the nature of its peculiarity we will turn our attention to it in the second to next chapter.

Chapter 9

The Input Data: Fitting an Exogenous Smile Surface

9.1 What is This Chapter About?

Whatever model we might want to use, we will have to calibrate it. In order to do so using the implied approach, we need a set of market inputs. These might be just a set of raw option prices (possibly converted into implied volatilities); or we might choose to apply to the prices some degree of pre-processing designed to turn a relatively small number of market observables into a smooth, differentiable surface of implied volatilities as a function of strike and time to expiry.

I discuss in this chapter when it is better to keep the directly observable implied volatilities undoctored, and when the 'pre-processing' stage is advisable. When the latter option is chosen, I discuss the merits and drawbacks associated with fitting to prices, to implied volatilities or to the associated price densities. I will argue that the first approach is the least desirable, and that fitting the densities to the prices has many positive features.

I do not present a systematic literature survey (the field has become enormous), but I do discuss a few approaches as representative examples of the various types of fitting to illustrate their strengths and weaknesses. I do not even cover all the possible classes of fitting approaches: more exoteric approaches exist (such as minimum entropy) that I just mention in passing. None the less, the most salient general features of the fitting problem should become apparent even from the simplified account I provide.

9.2 Analytic Expressions for Calls vs Process Specification

In many (most) situations it is advisable to create a smooth surface of implied volatilities or prices. Whichever route is chosen, the trader will always have to convert a combination of parameters describing (directly or indirectly) the model smile surface to market option prices. For instance, if one decided to use the mixture-of-normals approach, one would posit that the log-price density for a given expiry should be expressed as a combination of Gaussian densities, each characterized by two parameters. In order to decide whether the right combination of parameters has been chosen, a link must be established between the parameters of these densities and the associated model option prices, which can be compared with the market values.

Whenever it is possible to do so, one should clearly use closed-form expressions to go from the densities to the prices of the observable plain-vanilla calls and puts. Very often these closed-form expressions look very 'Black-and-Scholes-like', and it is tempting to assume that one is dealing with a 'model' in the same sense as, indeed, the Black-and-Scholes case. However, it is important to point out that the availability of a closed-form expression for a call in terms of, say, the moments of a distribution and today's value of the spot is in general not the same as specifying a 'model' (i.e. a process for the underlying). The reason is that being able to integrate analytically the payoff of a European option over its terminal probability density simply means that we know how to evaluate in closed form the *unconditional* price distributions for the various expiry *as of today*. Specifying a process, on the other hand, means being able to assign not just the unconditional distributions today, but also all the future conditional ones. After all, different models that fit equally well today's prices will, in general, prescribe different prices for complex products that depend on future conditional densities. This important distinction is looked at again from a different angle in Section 9.11.

9.3   Direct Use of Market Prices: Pros and Cons

Some models can be implemented by using directly market prices as the inputs to which the model parameters can be fitted. This is theoretically a 'cleaner' approach, in that it is the least data polluting, but it can sometimes be rather dangerous. To understand why this is the case, recall that many (sometimes most) of the parameters of a model refer to the risk-adjusted world, not to real-world measures. Therefore a drift transformation intervenes in the measure change. In practice this means that, say, mean reversion levels, jump frequencies, jump amplitudes, reversion speeds, etc. are not the same as the ones that can be estimated in the real world, but incorporate a risk adjustment. It is often said that these risk-adjusted quantities 'bear no relationship' to their real-world twins, but, as I have discussed in Section 6.7, this statement is often a bit too strong. In general, however, we have little or no indication from statistical analysis of real-world data as to what constitutes a 'realistic' set of values for these risk-adjusted quantities. Since we cannot estimate statistically the input parameters, the approach that is often taken is to attempt to recover the market prices of options by changing the model's (risk-adjusted) parameters until a 'best' fit is obtained. This approach is similar to deriving an 'implied volatility' when using the Black model and a market price. In theory, if the model has n parameters, *and it is correctly specified*, the prices of any set of n options would uniquely determine the parameters' values. In reality, we never expect a model to be fully 'correct', and therefore we use more option prices than parameters, and simply try to achieve a best fit. The fit is typically achieved by a strongly non-linear minimization procedure in an n-dimensional space that can – and, in general, will – have several competing local minima. If the model with which we are trying to reproduce the observed prices has few parameters, the fit is likely to be poor, but probably rather 'robust', in the sense that small changes in the input prices will not change the 'winning' minimum. The most popular pricing models, however, can have a very large number of parameters, and it is often found that several competing minima exist, of very similar 'depth', but associated with very different combinations of parameters. Jump–diffusion models, for instance, can often find a multi-modal solution which is marginally better than a unimodal one, but which would lose out for small variations in the input prices. Since market prices are invariably noisy, the possibility of tilting the balance between two competing minima by a slightly inaccurate input price is a real one. It is therefore safer to work with a globally smooth surface, and to impose the recovery of many 'synthetic' prices, rather than using the observable prices directly.[1]

For some approaches (such as the Derman and Kani) following the direct route totally is in practice almost impossible (the fitting methodology becomes a noise amplifier). More generally, whether one should use directly raw market prices or smoothed 'synthetic' prices depends on whether the chosen fitting procedure is stable under small perturbations of the input quantities.

Despite these caveats, there is a class of option traders who should not use too much pre-processing in dealing with market prices. Unlike complex-derivatives traders, in fact, plain-vanilla traders should be careful not to create overly 'smooth' price surfaces, because a model's inability to price certain options exactly might convey important relative-value information.

9.4 Statement of the Problem

The problem we have qualitatively discussed so far can be more precisely described as follows. Let us assume that we can observe a set of traded market prices, C_K^T, for several strikes, K, and maturities, T. We might, but need not, assume that these prices are known with no 'experimental error'. To be more precise, let us call the strikes and the expiries where we can observe the market prices K_i^j and T_j, respectively, with $j = 1, 2, \ldots, n$, and $i = 1, 2, \ldots, m_j$. Note that K_i^j is the ith strike for the jth maturity, and we have allowed for the possibility that the number of 'visible' strikes might be different for different expiries – hence the dependence on j of the upper limit, m_j.

Let f be a function $\mathcal{R}^2 \to \mathcal{R}^1$ parameterized by M coefficients, c_m, $m = 1, 2, \ldots, M$, that enables us to associate a 'synthetic' option price to an arbitrary pair (strike, maturity). So, the function f returns a price even when (K, T) is not necessarily equal to (K_i^j, T_j). Since there is a one-to-one correspondence between prices and implied volatilities, the function could just as well return not a price, but the implied volatility corresponding to (K, T).

We might then impose two requirements:

1. We might require the function f to be such that the observable market prices are exactly recovered: $f(K_i^j, T_j) = C_{K_i^j}^{T_j}$.

2. Or we might require that the function f be such that some distance, d, between the synthetic and real prices should be minimized. In this case the task is to choose the

---

[1]Using a smooth input smile surface is not enough to ensure a sensible calibration. I discuss at length in this book that the financial reasonableness of the solution must also be considered. See, for example, the discussion in Section 13.7.

set of coefficients $\{c\}$ such that

$$d\left(\widehat{C}^{T_j}_{K^j_i}, C^{T_j}_{K^j_i}\right) \tag{9.1}$$

is minimized. The distance d is often chosen to be the sum of the squared differences between the synthetic $(\widehat{C}^{T_j}_{K^j_i})$ and the market $(C^{T_j}_{K^j_i})$ prices:

$$d\left(\widehat{C}^{T_j}_{K^j_i}, C^{T_j}_{K^j_i}\right) = \sum \left| \widehat{C}^{T_j}_{K^j_i} - C^{T_j}_{K^j_i} \right|^2 \tag{9.2}$$

Stated this way, the problem appears well-posed and totally unambiguous. There are subtler considerations, however, that are best dealt with by examining specific approaches. This is undertaken below.

9.5   Fitting Prices

This line of attack is arguably the most direct: we start from a series of observed market prices and attempt to create a smooth function of the price as the strike varies for each available expiry, T. As a representative example of this class of techniques I will examine in some detail Shimko's approach (1994), which works as follows.

First a cubic-spline fit is carried out through the n liquid (i.e. directly and perfectly observable) market option prices for a range of strikes with a given expiry, T.[2] These prices can be denoted by $C_i, i = 1, 2, \ldots, n$. We will show in what follows that the risk-neutral density of the price evaluated at K, $\phi_T(S)|_K$, is given, modulo discounting, by the second derivative of the call price, C, with respect to the strike (Dupire (1993)):[3]

$$C(K, T) = \exp{-rT} \int_0^\infty \phi_T(x)\,(x - K)^+ \, dx \tag{9.3}$$

$$\rightarrow \phi_T(S)|_K = \exp{rT} \frac{\partial^2 C(K, T)}{\partial K^2} \tag{9.4}$$

For the moment let us accept this result as a given. From Equation (9.4) it is clear that, given the choice for the basis functions (third-order polynomials), the second derivative of the cubic spline fit is a linear function of the strikes, K. This therefore produces a piecewise-linear density function defined by $n + 2$ pairs of strikes and density ordinates.

---

[2]For a review of cubic splines, see, for example, Press et al. (1992), or Kreyszig (1993).

[3]For clarity of exposition in what follows I will assume zero interest rates. If this were not the case there would be a discount factor in Equations (9.3) and (9.4):

$$C(K, T) = \exp[-rT] \int_0^\infty (x - K)^+ \, dx$$

$$\rightarrow \phi_T(S)|_K = \exp[rT] \frac{\partial^2 C(K, T)}{\partial K^2}$$

To see how the procedure works in more detail, recall that we have assumed that we have exact knowledge of the prices, C_i. By saying that we have *exact* knowledge, I mean that we assume that no liquidity effects, bid–offer spread, or other source of noise affect these prices. Given this exact knowledge, we want to recover these prices with no error, and we therefore place the nodes of the splines in correspondence with the n prices, C_i. Note that, by construction, the procedure I am describing is not designed to tell us whether any of these reference prices are 'implausible' or 'unlikely'. This should be contrasted with the output from global-fitting strategies such as the ones described in Sections 9.9–9.12.

What remains to be determined are the densities, and the values of the strike for which the densities can be taken to be zero. These can be obtained as follows. Denote by P_i the probability density that the price should be between K_{i-1} and K_i:

$$P_i = P(K_{i-1} \leq K < K_i) \tag{9.5}$$

Given the choice of cubic splines as the basic function, this probability is linked to the piecewise density function by

$$P_i = \tfrac{1}{2} \left[\phi_T(K_{i-1}) + \phi_T(K_i) \right] (K_i - K_{i-1}), \quad i = 1, 2, \ldots, n \tag{9.6}$$

where, to lighten notation, I have denoted by $\phi_T(K_i)$ the quantity $\phi_T(S)|_{K_i}$. In particular, recalling that K_0 is the strike for which the density goes to zero, P_1 is given by

$$P_1 = P(K < K_1) = \tfrac{1}{2}(K_1 - K_0)[\phi_T(K_0) + \phi_T(K_1)]$$
$$= \tfrac{1}{2}(K_1 - K_0)[0 + \phi_T(K_1)] \tag{9.7}$$

Therefore

$$K_0 = K_1 - \frac{2P_1}{\phi_T(K_1)} \tag{9.8}$$

Similar reasoning applies to the other strike for which the density goes to zero, K_{n+1}, and a swift calculation gives

$$K_{n+1} = K_n + \frac{2P_{n+1}}{\phi_T(K_n)} \tag{9.9}$$

The only quantity on the RHS of Equation (9.9) that we do not know is P_{n+1}. But this can be obtained by imposing normalization of the probabilities:

$$P_{n+1} = P(K > K_n) = 1 - \sum_{i=1}^{n} P_i \tag{9.10}$$

This formally solves the problem.

Apparently, nothing could be simpler. Is this the way to approach the problem? Apart from the usual and well-documented reservations about using splines in general, there are more fundamental concerns. First of all, our input quantities are prices. We are therefore going to mix and use on the same footing quantities of very different magnitudes (out-of-the-money and in-the-money options). A simple change of variables (e.g. working in terms of implied volatilities) would remove this problem without 'polluting' the market data by any smoothing.

More fundamentally, the procedure presented in this section assumes that certain quantities (the reference prices C_i) are known with infinite precision. It does not address the question of whether a much more 'desirable' solution could be obtained if a few of the reference prices were modified even by a very small amount. Therefore there is no possibility of a trade-off between the quality of the global fit and a small variation in the input prices. How can we know whether a solution is 'desirable'? There is no a priori answer, but, for instance, a multi-modal or highly irregular output density should give cause for concern.

9.6   Fitting Transformed Prices

One of the drawbacks of any direct fitting to prices is that out-of-the-money options have smaller prices than at-the-money ones. A fitting procedure that gave equal weight to all prices would be likely to obtain a better fit at the money[4] than in the wings. Yet much of the trading action, especially when it comes to equity derivatives, is concentrated in relatively low-delta options. One way to address this problem is by working with implied volatilities. Another possibility is to rescale the price by using their logarithms. More precisely, if, in keeping with the notation above, $C_{K_{ij}}^{T_j}$ and $\widehat{C}_{K_{ij}}^{T_j}$ are the call market and model prices for maturity T_j and for the ith strike at this maturity, respectively, then we can define w_{ij} or $\widehat{w}_{ij}$ as

$$w_{ij} = \ln C_{K_{ij}}^{T_j} \tag{9.11}$$

$$\widehat{w}_{ij} = \ln \widehat{C}_{K_{ij}}^{T_j} \tag{9.12}$$

This formulation is interesting because it can be shown that minimizing the χ^2 quantity

$$\chi^2 = \frac{1}{N} \sum \left(\ln C_{K_{ij}}^{T_j} - \ln \widehat{C}_{K_{ij}}^{T_j} \right)^2 \tag{9.13}$$

is equivalent to carrying out a maximum likelihood estimation after assuming that the multiplicative errors, ϵ_{ij}, implicitly defined by

$$w_{ij} = \widehat{w}_{ij} \exp(\eta \epsilon_{ij} - \tfrac{1}{2}\eta^2) \tag{9.14}$$

are normally distributed with zero mean and unit variance. The multiplicative formulation ensures that the prices remain positive, while allowing for arbitrarily large errors. The approach is described in Jacquier and Jarrow (1995), Madan et al. (1998) and Elliot et al. (1995).

---

[4]When working with prices it is important to switch from puts to calls as the strike increases so as to work always with out-of-the-money options. Otherwise the uninteresting, and model-independent, intrinsic value dominates more and more for the more interesting options.

9.7 Fitting the Implied Volatilities

Another possibility is to work directly with implied volatilities. Ait-Sahalia (2002) models the S&P smile with third-order polynomials. Since the procedure is quite similar to fitting to prices, it is not discussed in any detail and the reader is referred to the original reference to appreciate the (excellent) numerical quality of the approach.

9.7.1 The Problem with Fitting the Implied Volatilities

If the fit to the implied volatilities is so good and so simple, what else can we want? The main drawback of fitting to implied volatilities is the great sensitivity of the associated price density function to the details of the fitting to implied volatilities. To see why this is the case consider the case illustrated in Figures 9.1 and 9.2.

Two different fitting techniques have been used in order to obtain a global fit to the implied volatilities associated with a set of prices. Both procedures have been successful in the sense that the errors in the fitting have turned out to be minimal, and certainly well within the bid–offer spread. The resulting curves are shown in Figure 9.1, and are so similar that, within the resolution of the figure, they appear to be totally superimposed. The largest difference between the two volatility functions was less than 2 basis points. In short, there would be nothing to make a trader prefer one fit over the other. Let us look, however, at the associated densities. These can be obtained by converting both sets of implied volatilities into Black prices for a continuum of strikes, and by using Equation (9.4). The result of this exercise is shown in Figure 9.2. Despite the similarity of the input volatilities, the densities are now very different, especially on the left side. One density has even become bimodal, and with a very sharp peak. I would challenge any reader to have predicted that by visual inspection of the two volatility curves! Does it matter? Yes, as I discuss below.

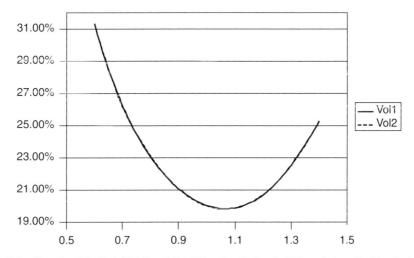

Figure 9.1 Two fits (labelled 'Vol1' and 'Vol2') to implied volatilities of virtually identical numerical quality. The two curves are so close to each other that they are virtually indistinguishable.

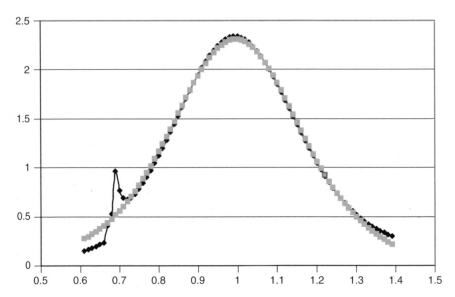

Figure 9.2   The price densities obtained from the optically-identical implied volatilities of Figure 9.1. Note the wild differences in the left tail of the densities.

9.8   Fitting the Risk-Neutral Density Function – General

In the remainder of the chapter I present in some detail two approaches for fitting directly the risk-neutral price density to a set of market prices. I will deal with this topic in some considerable detail because I find the density-function-based approaches the most useful and robust. Ultimately this is because option prices are obtained by *integrating* over a price density, and, as we know, integration is a smoothing operation. Densities, on the other hand, are obtained by double differentiation of call prices, and taking derivatives amplifies noise and irregularities. Therefore, if we obtain a smooth density function we can rest assured that the associated prices and implied volatilities will also be smooth. The converse, however, is not necessarily true, as I have shown above. Should we care if today's prices are well recovered, and well behaved? I argue below that the complex derivatives trader should indeed care.

The two fitting procedures discussed in the following take two different approaches. The first (mixture of normals) expands the unknown 'true' log-price density using Gaussian densities as the basis set of choice. Even if they do not constitute a complete set, we can reasonably expect that complex shapes can be recovered as long as we use a sufficiently large number of basis functions. In principle, other basis functions could have been used. However, the choice of Gaussian densities for the log-price distribution lends itself to easy integration over the terminal payoff of a call, and yields as a result a linear combination of Black-and-Scholes prices.

The second approach relies on a particular class of four-parameter density functions being sufficiently flexible to account for most price densities encountered in market practice. It is more parsimonious and computationally simpler, for instance, when it comes to ensuring the normalization or forward-pricing condition. However, if a given fit were found wanting, there would be no systematic way to improve upon it (while, with the mixture-of-normals approach, we can always add a few more basis functions).

9.8.1 Does It Matter if the Price Density Is Not Smooth?

Should one worry at all if the underlying risk-neutral price distribution is not smooth and 'nice looking', as long as the prices of plain-vanilla calls and puts are correctly recovered? There are at least two reasons why obtaining a smooth and 'plausible' price density function is important. The first is that, for those plain-vanilla options that have been used as inputs in the construction of the price density function, any reasonable procedure that goes back from the distribution itself to the prices is virtually guaranteed to produce good prices. This is, however, no longer guaranteed to be the case even for other plain-vanilla options with the same expiry but different strikes. This can happen if a small number of implied volatilities are used as input to the procedure (in some markets, the at-the-money volatility, the risk reversal and the straddle are the only totally 'uncontaminated' price information available).

This is however not always the case. After all, in the case discussed in Section 9.7.1 a very high number of implied volatilities were used to construct the price density function, and, as shown in Figure 9.1, the maximum price discrepancy was everywhere less than two hundredths of a vega. There is, however, a more fundamental reason for requiring smoothness of the density function. A smooth price density is important because there is a link between the unconditional (marginal) price densities obtained from the quoted prices today, and the conditional densities that will prevail in the future. The nature of this link is a very important and rather involved topic that will be discussed in detail in Chapter 17. At this stage, it is enough to say that the future conditional densities that 'link' the unconditional densities obtainable today describe the probabilities of transition from one future state to another. What any model based on a description of the process of the underlying provides is exactly a systematic way of constructing these probabilities of transition between states in an arbitrage-free manner. So, process-based, arbitrage-free models can be seen as machines that construct the conditional transition probabilities that link the unconditional (marginal) densities.

If one looks at the problem in this manner, it is easy to see the root of the problem: an 'implausible' time-T marginal density such as the one depicted in Figure 9.2 is very likely to imply a correspondingly 'strained' behaviour for the process-generated transition probabilities associated with states ending, at time T, in the neighbourhood of $S_T = 10$. Suppose, in fact, that the price density for an earlier maturity, $T - \Delta t$, turns out to be smooth and unimodal for all values of S. Let us also suppose that a trader attempts to fit the various series of call prices (one series for each maturity) associated with these price densities using, say, a jump–diffusion process. What she would almost certainly find is that the jump frequency and the jump amplitude ratio implied by the fitting procedure will have to change dramatically (and perhaps to become state dependent) in order to fit the prices implied by the bimodal distribution; the more so, the more the trader was successful in recovering close-to-exactly the input prices. This need not have been the case, however, if she had worked with the smooth price density obtained using the 'optically indistinguishable' implied volatility curve labelled 'Vol2' in Figure 9.1.

Does this matter for pricing? It does not for recovering *today's* prices of plain-vanilla options that solely depend on the integration of *today's* unconditional densities. The value of complex products, however, will in general depend on future conditional densities: for instance, for a multi-look trigger swap, on a trigger level being breached, *given that it had not been breached before*; or, for a knock-in cap, on the spot price being above a strike, *given that it was above or below a certain level before*; or, for an average-rate option, on a certain realization of the spot price at time *t*, *given that a particular sequence of prices had been realized*; etc. In a way, a dependence on future conditional densities can be taken as the best definition of a complex product.

For these reasons I advocate direct fitting of the density function as the safest route to obtaining a reliable input to a pricing model. Before looking in some detail at the tools at one's disposal to obtain a good density fit, it is useful to see how prior information about the target density could be included in the process.

9.8.2   Using Prior Information (Minimum Entropy)

It is often the case that the trader might have some prior information (perhaps derived from statistical analysis, or perhaps from market knowledge or from trading views) about the desirable features of the price density. Since, as I discuss in Section 11.8, extracting a volatility surface from a set of prices is akin to an inverse problem, making use of this information can be seen as a regularization technique. In other words, incorporating available statistical information or stylized facts about the market (such as those, for instance, reported in Chapter 7) can make the fitting process less ill-posed.

One way to incorporate this information in the fitting procedure is by means of the so-called minimum-entropy techniques (see, for example, Avellaneda (1998)). In the context of smile-surface fitting, the problem can be defined as follows. To lighten notation, let us simply denote by C_j, $j = 1, 2, \ldots, n$, the n exogenous market prices of plain-vanilla options. Ignoring discounting, these are given by

$$C_j = \int f_j(S_T)\varphi(S_T)\, dS_T \tag{9.15}$$

where, for the case, say, of calls, the function $f_j(S_T)$ is given by

$$f_j(S_T) = \max\left[S_T - K_j\right]^+ \tag{9.16}$$

The density $\varphi(S_T)$ to be estimated could be chosen so as to minimize the functional, H,

$$H(\varphi|\varphi_0) = \int \varphi\left[\ln \varphi - \ln \varphi_0\right] dS_T = \int \varphi \ln \frac{\varphi}{\varphi_0}\, dS_T \tag{9.17}$$

where $\varphi_0(S_T)$ is a prior density function. This prior density reflects our knowledge of (or prejudices about) what constitutes a desirable risk-neutral density (e.g. its being skewed to the left, or unimodal, or leptokurtic). The quantity $H(\varphi|\varphi_0)$, known as the relative entropy of φ from φ_0, expresses the 'distance' in log space between the prior density, φ_0, and the optimal density φ. It can be shown that, if there exists a probability density $\varphi(S_T)$ such that condition (9.15) is satisfied and the relative entropy is finite, the solution can be found in terms of n Lagrange multipliers. Optimizing over the multipliers is equivalent (see Avellaneda (1998)) to minimizing

$$\ln Z(\lambda_1, \lambda_2, \ldots, \lambda_n) - \sum_j \lambda_j C_j \tag{9.18}$$

where the function $Z(.)$ is given by

$$Z(\lambda_1, \lambda_2, \ldots, \lambda_n) = \int f_j(S_T)\varphi_0(S_T) \exp\left(\sum_j \lambda_j f_j(S_T)\right) dS_T$$

$$= \int \max\left[S_T - K_j\right]^+ \varphi_0(S_T) \exp\left(\sum_j \lambda_j \max\left[S_T - K_j\right]^+\right) dS_T \tag{9.19}$$

The optimal probability function $\varphi(S_T)$ given our prior, φ_0, is given by

$$\varphi(S_T) = \varphi_0(S_T)\frac{\exp\left(\sum_j \lambda_j f_j(S_T)\right)}{Z(\lambda_1, \lambda_2, \ldots, \lambda_n)} = \varphi_0(S_T)\frac{\exp\left(\sum_j \lambda_j \max\left[S_T - K_j\right]^+\right)}{Z(\lambda_1, \lambda_2, \ldots, \lambda_n)} \tag{9.20}$$

This expression shows that the prior density $\varphi_0(S_T)$ is locally 'deformed' by the factor $\exp\left(\sum_j \lambda_j f_j(S_T)\right)$, and that the quantity $Z(\lambda_1, \lambda_2, \ldots, \lambda_n)$ in the denominator plays the role of a normalization factor which ensures that

$$\int \varphi(S_T)\, dS_T = 1 \tag{9.21}$$

Equation (9.20) also shows that the prior density function is not modified for any value of S_T lower than the lowest strike, K_j.

The approach is very appealing, but, as usual, the devil is in the implementation details. If Equation (9.20) is used naively, it is not uncommon to find densities that display multi-modal or 'spiky' behaviour. There are ways around these problems, but the literature has become too vast and specialized to review in this context. The minimum-entropy approach can be revisited in the context of Kolmogorov-compatible densities, discussed in Chapter 17. The fitting methods presented below do not make use of any prior, but could be modified to incorporate such information.

9.9   Fitting the Risk-Neutral Density Function: Mixture of Normals

One appealing approach[5] to finding the risk-neutral density, $\Phi(S_T)$, of the (log-) price for a given time horizon, T, is to express it as a linear combination of normal densities,

---

[5] I would like to thank Ms Maria Teresa Cardoso for her help with the numerical work presented in the sections devoted to the mixture-of-normals methodology. This section has been adapted from Rebonato and Cardoso (2004).

$\varphi(\mu_i, \sigma_i^2)$:

$$\Phi(\ln S_T) = \sum_i w_i \varphi(\mu_i, \sigma_i^2) \qquad (9.22)$$

with

$$\varphi(\mu_i, \sigma_i^2) = \mathcal{N}(\mu_i, \sigma_i^2; S_0) \qquad (9.23)$$

and with the normalization condition

$$\sum_i w_i = 1 \qquad (9.24)$$

(This is the approach followed, for instance, by Alexander (2001).) The mean and the variance of the mixture, μ_ϕ and σ_ϕ^2, are related to the means and variances of the original normal distribution by the relationships

$$\mu_\phi = \sum_i w_i \mu_i \qquad (9.25)$$

and

$$\sigma_\phi^2 = \sum_i w_i \sigma_i^2 + \left[\sum_i w_i \mu_i^2 - \left(\sum_i w_i \mu_i \right)^2 \right] \qquad (9.26)$$

Note carefully that, since one is fitting risk-neutral densities, the first moment is not a free-fitting parameter, but must recover the forward condition, i.e. the expectation in the risk-neutral measure of the 'stock' price must equal its forward value. Very often this condition has been enforced in the literature (see, for example, Alexander (2001)), by requiring that all the μ_i should be identical and equal to the risk-neutral drift. This is, however, unnecessarily restrictive, because it forces the distribution of log prices to display no skew. Negative skewness is an important and well-established feature of most risk-neutral densities. I show below how this feature can be naturally incorporated into the method we propose.

Since one of the most common features of empirical distributions is their leptokurtosis, it is also useful to give (see Alexander (2001)) an expression for the excess kurtosis for a mixture of normals. In the case when all the μ_i terms are equal one obtains:

$$\kappa_\phi = 3 \left[\frac{\sum_i w_i \sigma_i^4}{\left(\sum_i w_i \sigma_i^2 \right)^2} - 1 \right] \qquad (9.27)$$

From Equation (9.27) it is clear that the density of a non-degenerate mixture of normals (with the same means!) will always have a positive excess kurtosis (i.e. will be more leptokurtic than a normal density). This is because, for any non-degenerate case,

$$\sum_i w_i \sigma_i^4 > \left(\sum_i w_i \sigma_i^2 \right)^2 \qquad (9.28)$$

As discussed, however, we do *not* want to use normals with the same means, so the result is generally more complex. How can the interesting problem be tackled?

If one wants to use a mixture of normals to fit an empirical price density there are two main routes:

1. One can estimate the first four moments of the empirical distribution of the logarithms of the price density, select two normals as the 'basis set' and fit the four moments exactly. With the fitted mixture-of-normals distribution the prices for the calls, C_K^T, can be determined and compared with the market values. The procedure is very straightforward, but the overall fit is unlikely to be very good.

2. One can determine the optimal weights $\{w\}$ by means of a least-squares fit to the option prices after converting the density into call prices. This procedure is made easy by the fact that I show below that the option price C_K^T is simply given by a linear combination with the same weights $\{w\}$ of Black-and-Scholes formulae.

As mentioned above, however, if all the normal densities in the mixture are 'centred' (in log space) around the forward value, one is automatically guaranteed to recover the no-arbitrage forward pricing condition, but the resulting pricing density will display no skewness. This is at odds with empirical findings (see, for example, Chapter 15). Skewness can be easily obtained by allowing the different constituent Gaussian densities to be centred around different location coefficients, μ_i. By so doing, however, some care must be given to recovering the first moment of the density exactly, since this is linked to the no-arbitrage cash-and-carry forward condition. Furthermore, if the weights are left unconstrained (apart from Equation (9.24)), there is no guarantee that the resulting density will be everywhere positive. The following section shows how both these problems can be overcome.

9.9.1 Ensuring the Normalization and Forward Constraints

Denote by S_i the price of the stock at time T_i: $S(T_i) = S_i$. If we denote by $\Phi(S_i)$ its risk-neutral probability density, we want to write

$$\Phi(S_i) = \sum_k w_k^i \varphi(S_k^i) \tag{9.29}$$

where

$$\varphi(S_k^i) = \mathcal{LN}(\mu_{ik}, \sigma_{ik}^2; S_0) \tag{9.30}$$

and $\mathcal{LN}(\mu_{ik}, \sigma_{ik}^2; S_0)$ denotes a log-normal density with

$$E(S_k^i) = S_0 \exp(\mu_{ik} T_i) \tag{9.31}$$

$$\mathrm{var}(S_k^i) = \left[S_0 \exp(\mu_{ik} T_i)\right]^2 \left[\exp\left(\sigma_{ik}^2 T_i\right) - 1\right] \tag{9.32}$$

By this expression, the risk-neutral[6] density for the stock price is expressed as a sum of log-normal densities, and therefore the resulting stock price density is *not* log normal.

In order to ensure that the density is everywhere positive, we require that all the weights should be positive. This can be achieved by imposing

$$w_k^i = \left(\alpha_k^i\right)^2 \tag{9.33}$$

The normalization condition, which requires that

$$\sum_k w_k^i = 1 \tag{9.34}$$

therefore becomes

$$\sum_k \left(\alpha_k^i\right)^2 = 1 \tag{9.35}$$

This condition can always be satisfied by requiring that the coefficients α_k^i should be the polar co-ordinates of a unit-radius hypersphere. Therefore we can write

$$\alpha_k^i = f(\theta_1^i, \theta_2^i, \dots, \theta_{n-1}^i) \tag{9.36}$$

For instance, for $n = 2$ one simply has

$$\alpha_1^i = \sin(\theta_1^i) \tag{9.37}$$

$$\alpha_2^i = \cos(\theta_1^i) \tag{9.38}$$

This is certainly acceptable, because, for *any* angle θ_1^i,

$$\sin(\theta_1^i)^2 + \cos(\theta_1^i)^2 = \left(\alpha_1^i\right)^2 + \left(\alpha_2^i\right)^2 = 1 \tag{9.39}$$

and Equation (9.35) is satisfied. This decomposition of the weights into angular components is explained in detail in Section 20.3 of Chapter 20, to which the reader is referred for details. I just provide the explicit expression of the coefficients as a function of the angles for ease of reference:

$$\alpha_k^i = \cos\theta_k^i \prod_{j=1}^{k-1} \sin\theta_j^i, \quad k = 1, 2, \dots, m-1 \tag{9.40}$$

$$\alpha_k^i = \prod_{j=1}^{k-1} \sin\theta_j^i, \quad k = m \tag{9.41}$$

---

[6]To lighten the prose, the qualifier 'risk-neutral' is often omitted in what follows where there is no risk of ambiguity.

Why are we expressing the coefficients α_k^i in terms of 'angles'? The reason for doing so is that we will want to optimize the model density over the weights w_k^i in an unconstrained manner, while automatically resting assured that the resulting linear combination is a possible density. This will be the case only if (9.35) is always satisfied. In general, i.e. if one tried to optimize directly over the weights w_k^i, one would have to carry out a heavily constrained numerical search: not only would every weight w_k^i have to be greater than zero but smaller than one, but also every partial sum over the weights would have to be strictly positive[7] and less than one. The procedure suggested above automatically ensures that this will always be the case, and therefore allows one to optimize by carrying out an *unconstrained* optimization over the angle(s) θ.

Apart form the requirements in Equation (9.35), there is at least one more constraint. The no-arbitrage forward condition

$$E_0[S_i(T)] = \int \Phi(S_i = \widetilde{S}_i | S_0 = \widehat{S}) \widetilde{S}_i \, d\widetilde{S}_i = S_0 \exp(rT_i) \tag{9.42}$$

must in fact always be satisfied exactly under penalty of arbitrage.[8] This could be trivially achieved by imposing

$$\mu_{ik} = r \quad \text{for any } k \tag{9.43}$$

This, however, would give rise to densities with kurtosis but no skew. (Indeed, this is the approach suggested by Alexander (2001).) To obtain skew, we want to allow the various basis functions to be centred around different locations in $\ln S$-space, but we want to do so while retaining the forward-pricing condition. This can be achieved as follows. From the relationships above we can write

$$E_0[S_i] = E\left[\sum_k w_k^i S_i^k\right] = \sum_k w_k^i E\left[S_i^k\right] = S_0 \exp(rT_i) \tag{9.44}$$

Recalling that

$$E\left[S_k^i\right] = S_0 \exp(\mu_{ik}T_i) \tag{9.45}$$

we find that

$$\exp(rT_i) = \sum_k w_k^i \exp(\mu_{ik}T_i) \tag{9.46}$$

The summation over the number of basis functions, k, can be split into the first term, and the sum, $\sum'$, over the remaining terms:

$$\exp(rT_i) = w_1^i \exp(\mu_{i1}T_i) + \sum_k{}' w_k^i \exp(\mu_{ik}T_i)$$

---

[7] If, in the real-world measure, we assume that all positive values of the underlying are possible, the density cannot go to zero under any *equivalent* measure.

[8] As usual, I denote by r either the short rate or the difference between the short rate and the dividend yield or the difference between the domestic and the foreign short rates, according to whether one is dealing with the case of a non-dividend paying asset, of a dividend stock or of an FX rate, respectively.

which can be solved for μ_{i1}:

$$\exp(\mu_{i1}T_i) = \frac{\exp(rT_i) - \sum_k' w_k^i \exp(\mu_{ik}T_i)}{w_1^i} \rightarrow$$

$$\mu_{i1} = \frac{\ln\left[\dfrac{\exp(rT_i) - \sum_k' w_k^i \exp(\mu_{ik}T_i)}{w_1^i}\right]}{T_i} \tag{9.47}$$

In other words, if, for any maturity T_i, we choose the first location coefficient according to the expression above, we can always rest assured that the forward condition will be automatically satisfied. Note, however, that, a priori, there is no guarantee that the argument of the logarithm will always be positive. In practice, I have never found this to be a problem.

So, for any set of angles $\{\theta\}$, for any set of σ_{ik}, $k = 1, 2, \ldots, n$, and for any set of μ_{ik}, $k = 2, 3, \ldots, n$, the forward and the normalization conditions will always be satisfied if μ_1^i is chosen to be given by Equation (9.47). In what follows I will always assume that this choice has been made.

9.9.2   The Fitting Procedure

Let $Call_{K_j}^{T_i}(\text{mod})$ be the model value of the call expiring at time T_i for strike K_j, and $Call_{K_j}^{T_i}(\text{mkt})$ the corresponding market prices. The quantity $Call_{K_j}^{T_i}(\text{mod})$ is given by

$$Call_{K_j}^{T_i}(\text{mod}) = \sum_{k=1,n} \alpha_k^i(\theta)^2 \int \varphi(S_i^k) G(S_i^k, K_j)\, dS_i^k \tag{9.48}$$

where $G(S_i, K_j)$ is the payoff function:

$$G(S_i^k, K_j) = \left[S_i^k - K_j\right]^+ \tag{9.49}$$

and $\varphi(S_i^k)$ is the log-normal density:

$$\varphi(S_i^k) = \frac{1}{S_i^k \sigma_{ik}\sqrt{2\pi T_i}} \exp\left[-\frac{1}{2}\left(\frac{\ln\left(\dfrac{S_i^k}{S_0 \exp(\mu_{ik}T_i)}\right) + \frac{1}{2}\sigma_{ik}^2 T_i}{\sigma_{ik}T_i}\right)^2\right] \tag{9.50}$$

Note that each term under the integral sign is simply equal to the value of a Black-and-Scholes call when the 'riskless rate' is equal to μ_{ik} and the volatility is equal to σ_{ik}. Therefore one can write:

$$Call_{K_j}^{T_i}(\text{mod}) = \sum_{k=1,n} \alpha_k^i(\theta)^2 Call_{BS}(\mu_{ik}, K_j, T_i, \sigma_{ik}) \tag{9.51}$$

where μ_{i1} is fixed from the previous forward relationship. Equation (9.51) lends itself to a simple interpretation: for any given strike, K_j, the model price is expressed as a linear combination of Black-and-Scholes prices, with the same strike, time to maturity and volatility, but with the riskless rate equal to μ_{ik} and volatility equal to σ_{ik}.

Now define χ^2 as

$$\chi^2 = \sum \left[Call_{K_j}^{T_i}(\text{mod}) - Call_{K_j}^{T_i}(\text{mkt}) \right]^2 \tag{9.52}$$

Then, in order to obtain the optimal fit to the observed set of market prices we simply have to carry out an *unconstrained* minimization of χ^2 over the $(n-1)$ angles $\{\theta\}$, the n volatilities σ_{ik}, $k = 1, 2, \ldots, n$, the $(n-1)$ location coefficients μ_{ik}, $k = 2, 3, \ldots, n$, and with μ_{1i} given by (9.47). Therefore, for each expiry I have at my disposal $3n - 2$ coefficients. (For $n = 1$, I simply have one coefficient, i.e. one volatility. For $n = 2$ I have four coefficients, i.e. two volatilities, one weight (i.e. one angle θ), and one location coefficient; etc.)

9.10 Numerical Results

9.10.1 Description of the Numerical Tests

In this section I explore how well the mixture-of-normals method works in practice. I do so by looking both at theoretical densities and at market prices. The theoretical densities are obtained from three important models that will be discussed in the following, i.e. the jump–diffusion, the stochastic-volatility and the variance–gamma. I have sometimes used rather 'extreme' choices of parameters in order to test the robustness and flexibility of the approach.

Finally, for simplicity I assume a non-dividend-paying stock (interest rate at 5%) with spot price of $100, and I look at maturities of 0.5, 1, 2 and 4 years. Longer maturities, because of the Central Limit Theorem, would actually produce an easier test. All the optimized coefficients are reported in Tables 9.1–9.3. As for the market prices, they were obtained from the GBP caplet market in March 2003.

9.10.2 Fitting to Theoretical Prices: Stochastic-Volatility Density

The simplest test is probably that of a stochastic-volatility process for the underlying. This is because we know that in this case the process for the logarithm of the price directly generates a risk-neutral density which is made up of a mixture of normals.[9] A mean-reverting process of the type described in Chapter 13 was chosen for the volatility, with an initial value of the volatility equal to the reversion level (12.13%). The volatility of the volatility was given a very high value (100%) to 'stress' the test. We assumed no correlation between the Brownian shocks affecting the underlying and the volatility.

The smiles produced by these parameters are shown in Figure 9.3. The theoretical density, the fitted density and the log-normal density matched to the first two moments

---

[9]Each normal density component would have as variance the square of the root-mean-squared volatility encountered along each volatility path.

Table 9.1 The means, standard deviations and weights obtained for the fits to the jump–diffusion, stochastic-volatility and variance–gamma models discussed in the text using a mixture of three log-normals. The chi-squared statistics are also displayed.

		Jump–diffusion			
	Maturity (years)	0.5	1	2	4
Log-normal 1	Mean	119.13	143.49	119.30	237.47
	Standard dev.	9.98	16.29	36.58	79.90
	λ_1	0.6058	0.3216	0.5077	0.1485
Log-normal 2	Mean	83.75	101.51	184.90	126.95
	Standard dev.	6.73	13.09	35.24	56.98
	λ_2	0.2732	0.2798	0.1357	0.5200
Log-normal 3	mean	61.84	76.71	69.72	62.92
	standard dev.	14.22	26.65	31.77	38.49
	λ_3	0.1210	0.3986	0.3566	0.3315
χ^2		1.11E-08	3.28E-06	8.62E-06	7.25E-07

	Model	Variance–gamma			
	Maturity (years)	0.5	1	2	4
Log-normal 1	mean	106.26	111.40	106.20	137.65
	standard dev.	6.21	10.15	19.40	29.99
	λ_1	0.4501	0.3809	0.5418	0.4449
Log-normal 2	mean	100.43	102.61	120.37	112.16
	standard dev.	9.83	13.52	17.14	27.73
	λ_2	0.4933	0.5500	0.3809	0.4505
Log-normal 3	mean	91.18	90.55	92.23	99.19
	standard dev.	12.89	15.86	21.43	31.07
	λ_3	0.0566	0.0691	0.0773	0.1047
χ^2		6.14E-07	1.61E-07	1.26E-07	9.94E-08

	Model	Stochastic-volatility			
	Maturity (years)	0.5	1	2	4
Log-normal 1	mean	102.53	105.12	110.52	122.17
	standard dev.	5.36	8.70	32.65	30.48
	λ_1	0.4484	0.3479	0.5208	0.2385
Log-normal 2	mean	102.52	105.12	110.51	122.12
	standard dev.	30.07	49.27	86.66	61.96
	λ_2	0.1309	0.1741	0.2046	0.5489
Log-normal 3	mean	102.54	105.14	110.51	122.16
	standard dev.	12.82	19.41	15.44	172.26
	λ_3	0.4206	0.4780	0.2745	0.2126
χ^2		1.99E-07	4.95E-08	1.89E-08	1.16E-08

Table 9.2 χ^2 statistics and maximum error for the mixtures described in Table 9.1.

		Market data				
	Maturity (years)	0.5	1	2	4	8
f_0		0.0346	0.0357	0.0407	0.0487	0.0530
Log-normal 1	Mean	0.0385	0.0324	0.0739	0.0501	0.0547
	Standard dev.	0.0234	0.0206	0.0448	0.0319	0.0350
	λ_1	0.0224	0.3659	0.0131	0.8750	0.8482
Log-normal 2	Mean	0.0346	0.0151	0.0418	0.0562	0.0831
	Standard dev.	0.0211	0.0164	0.0264	0.0577	0.0930
	λ_2	0.9290	0.0030	0.9104	0.0503	0.0363
Log-normal 3	Mean	0.0220	0.0327	0.0146	0.0122	0.0071
	Standard dev.	0.0133	0.0199	0.0089	0.0074	0.0043
	λ_3	0.0057	0.2669	0.0720	0.0626	0.0920
Log-normal 4	Mean	0.0220	0.0415	0.1390	0.0992	0.1233
	Standard dev.	0.0214	0.0254	0.0843	0.0602	0.0770
	λ_4	0.0430	0.3642	0.0045	0.0121	0.0235
χ^2		4.31E-06	7.17E-05	5.32E-05	1.29E-05	1.16E-05

Table 9.3   Same as Table 9.1 for the market data used (GBP caplet implied volatilities, March 2003). The χ^2 statistics are also displayed.

Model		Jump–diffusion			
	Maturity (years)	0.5	1	2	4
Log-normal 1	Mean	119.16	142.15	197.34	212.96
	Standard dev.	10.22	17.12	35.65	92.37
	λ_1	0.6037	0.3593	0.1356	0.3107
Log-normal 2	Mean	83.79	70.09	107.19	84.30
	Standard dev.	6.75	6.69	34.92	32.00
	λ_2	0.2587	0.0903	0.4490	0.2979
Log-normal 3	Mean	68.09	99.64	66.43	47.07
	Standard dev.	15.95	12.14	33.59	28.76
	λ_3	0.1120	0.3381	0.3084	0.2486
Log-normal 4	Mean	50.64	66.10	141.52	134.15
	Standard dev.	12.65	24.09	21.67	40.33
	λ_4	0.0256	0.2123	0.1070	0.1428
χ^2		1.42E-08	1.10E-08	6.41E-07	1.07E-07

are shown in Figure 9.4. The match is excellent everywhere even with just three basis functions. The resulting fit to the smile is shown in Figure 9.5 for the shortest maturity.

It is interesting to point out that we found that, after optimization, the three basis distributions in the mixture turned out to have the same (risk-neutral) mean even if they were not required to be so centred. This is consistent with the assumption of the underlying following a stochastic-volatility process, which automatically produces a mixture

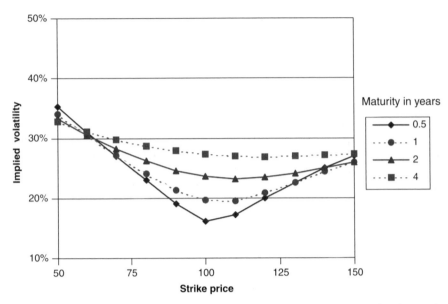

Figure 9.3   The smiles produced by the parameters discussed in the text in the stochastic-volatility case.

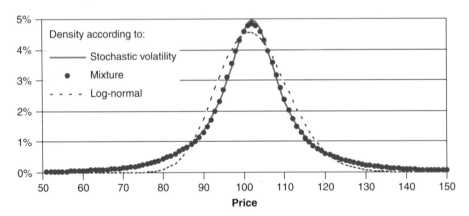

Figure 9.4   The theoretical density, the fitted density and the moment-matched log-normal density in the stochastic-volatility case.

of identically centred distributions. This results in a non-skewed density (see Figure 9.4). On the other hand, the resulting distribution has positive kurtosis, correctly reproduced by the fitting procedure.

9.10.3   Fitting to Theoretical Prices: Variance–Gamma Density

For this model, we consider the whole set of parameters estimated by Madan *et al.* (1998) for the risk-neutral density of the S&P: $\sigma = 12.13\%$, $\nu = 16.86\%$ and $\theta = -0.1436$. Madan *et al.* (1998) show that, in the risk-neutral world, the hypothesis of zero

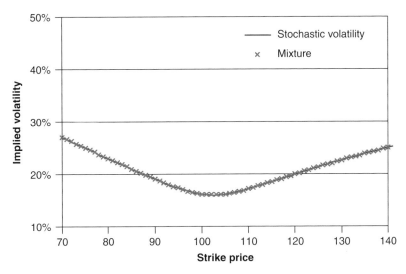

Figure 9.5   The fit to the 0.5-year stochastic-volatility smile obtained using three log-normals.

skewness can be rejected. Their risk-neutral density will therefore provide the first test for our method when the underlying distribution is skewed. The smile produced by the variance–gamma process is shown in Figure 9.6 for different option expiries. Figure 9.7 displays the fit to the two-year density obtained with just three basis functions, together with a moment-matched log-normal fit. Figure 9.8 displays the fit to the one-year smile.

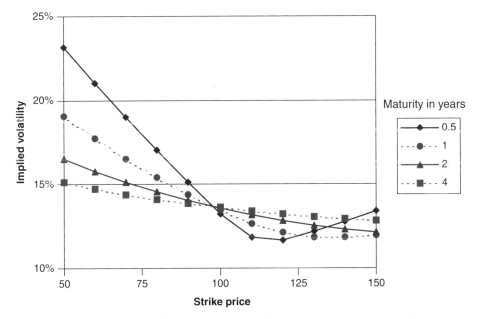

Figure 9.6   The smiles produced by the parameters discussed in the text in the variance–gamma case.

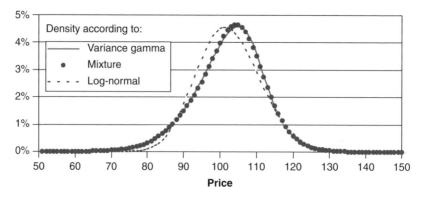

Figure 9.7   The theoretical density, the fitted density and the moment-matched log-normal density in the variance–gamma case.

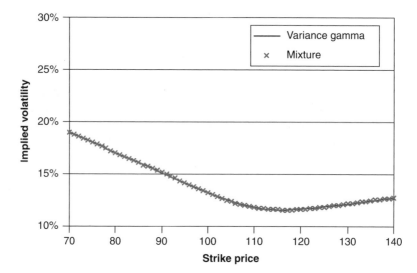

Figure 9.8   The fit to the 0.5-year variance–gamma smile obtained using three log-normals.

It is clear from the figure that the model prices are everywhere well recovered within bid–offer spread.[10]

9.10.4   Fitting to Theoretical Prices: Jump–Diffusion Density

The last theoretical smile I consider is the 'stress case' of a log-normal jump–diffusion process with parameters chosen so as to produce a multi-modal risk-neutral density for some maturities. Under what circumstances a jump–diffusion process can give rise to multi-modal densities, and what this implies for the associated smiles is discussed in Chapter 14. The model parameters used were one jump per year for the jump frequency, and an expectation and volatility of the jump amplitude ratios of 0.7 and 1%, respectively.

---

[10]The bid–offer spread was assumed to be half a vega (50 basis points in volatility).

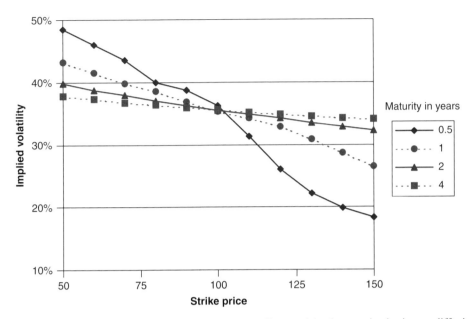

Figure 9.9 The smiles produced by the parameters discussed in the text in the jump–diffusion case.

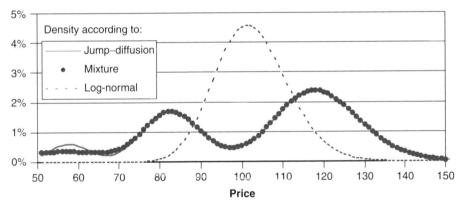

Figure 9.10 The theoretical density, the fitted density and the moment-matched log-normal density in the jump–diffusion case (three log-normals). Note the relatively poor recovery of the theoretical density in the far left tail.

The volatility of the diffusive part was taken to be constant at 12.13%. The resulting smiles are shown in Figure 9.9.

The theoretical density (expiry 0.5 years) is shown in Figure 9.10 with a thin continuous line. The same figure also shows for comparison a moment-matched log-normal density. Given the multi-modal character of the true density, the log-normal fit in this case is close to meaningless. The line with markers then shows the risk-neutral density obtained with a mixture of three log-normals. It is clear that, even for such a difficult-to-match theoretical

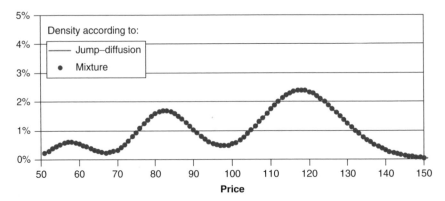

Figure 9.11   The theoretical density, the fitted density and the moment-matched log-normal density in the jump–diffusion case (five log-normals). The density is now well recovered everywhere.

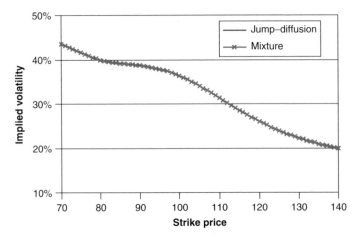

Figure 9.12   The fit to the 0.5-year jump–diffusion smile obtained using three log-normals.

risk-neutral density, a very good agreement is obtained almost everywhere (i.e. with the exception of the very-low-strike region) with as few as three log-normals. Figure 9.11 shows that the fit to the risk-neutral density becomes virtually perfect everywhere with five basis functions. The resulting theoretical and fitted smiles for expiry 0.5 years (the most challenging one) are shown in Figure 9.12. One can observe that everywhere the target and fitted implied volatilities coincide to well within the bid–offer spread. The largest discrepancy was found to be seven basis points in volatility (in these units one vega would be 100 basis points).

9.10.5   Fitting to Market Prices

In order to test the method with real market prices we looked at the smile curves for caplet implied volatilities (GBP, March 2003) for different expiries. See Figure 9.13. Again, the shortest maturity provided the most challenging test. In Figures 9.14–9.18 I

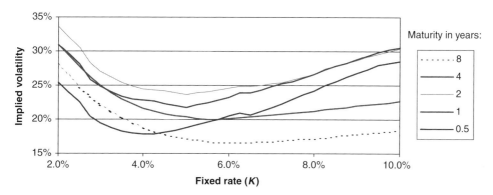

Figure 9.13 The market caplet smiles for several maturities (GBP, March 2003).

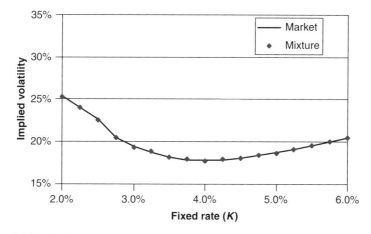

Figure 9.14 The fit to the market data using four log-normals for expiry of 0.5 year.

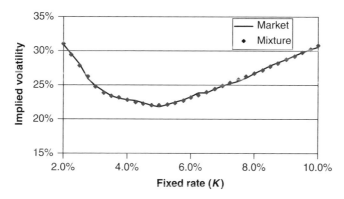

Figure 9.15 The fit to the market data using four log-normals for expiry of 1 year.

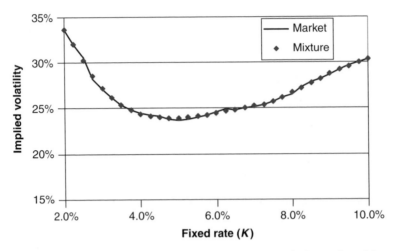

Figure 9.16 The fit to the market data using four log-normals for expiry of 2 years.

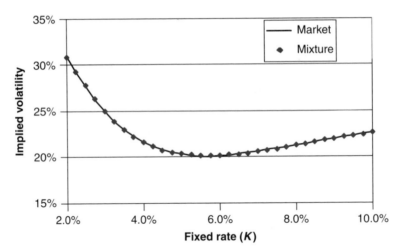

Figure 9.17 The fit to the market data using four log-normals for expiry of 4 years.

show the fits obtained for all the maturities (0.5, 1, 2, 4 and 8 years). Also in this case, the fit is virtually perfect everywhere with four log-normal basis functions.

On the basis of these results, one can conclude that the mixture-of-normals approach provides a simple and robust method to fit even very complex price patterns. The fact that the model price is expressed as a linear combination of Black-and-Scholes prices makes it very easy to calculate the derivative $\frac{\partial C}{\partial S}$. It also makes it very tempting to interpret this derivative as the 'delta' statistic, i.e. as the amount of stock that will allow one to hedge (instantaneously) against movements in the underlying, and to replicate a payoff by expiry. This interpretation is however unwarranted, as I discuss below.

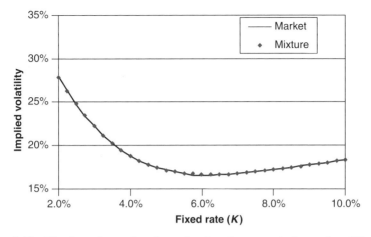

Figure 9.18   The fit to the market data using four log-normals for expiry of 8 years.

9.11   Is the Term $\frac{\partial C}{\partial S}$ Really a Delta?

When one uses a fitting procedure such as the mixture-of-normals approach, or the generalized beta method presented below, one expresses the marginal (unconditional) price densities in terms of one or more basis functions: Gaussian densities in one case, or generalized beta functions in the other. In all these cases the terminal densities display a parametric dependence on the value of the 'stock' price today, S_0. Since the plain-vanilla option prices (denoted by C for brevity in this section) are obtainable as integrals over these probability densities, also these prices will display a parametric dependence on the initial value of the stock. It is therefore possible to evaluate the quantity $\frac{\partial C}{\partial S}$. Furthermore, in the mixture-of-normals case just presented or with the generalized beta approach discussed below one can do so analytically. If one wanted, one could also evaluate $\frac{\partial^2 C}{\partial S^2}$, $\frac{\partial C}{\partial t}$, etc. This has led to the statement, often found in the literature, that these closed-form expressions for the price, the 'delta', the 'gamma', etc. of the plain-vanilla option constitute an alternative pricing model, different from, but on a conceptual par with, say, the Black-and-Scholes model. Some authors speak of 'pricing' and 'hedging' with the mixture-of-normals approach. This is not correct.[11]

To understand why this is the case recall that in the Black-and-Scholes world the quantity $\frac{\partial C}{\partial S}$ plays not just the role of the derivative of the call price with respect to the stock price today, but also of the amount of stock we have to hold in order to be first-order neutral to the stock price movements. So, in the Black-and-Scholes world we *posit* a process for the underlying, and we *obtain* that, if this process is correct, we can create a riskless portfolio by holding $\frac{\partial C}{\partial S}$ amount of stock. By following this delta-neutral

---

[11]I have been guilty of this looseness of language (and thought!) myself in the article Mirfendereski and Rebonato (2001). To avoid misunderstandings, today I would choose a different title.

strategy to expiry we can replicate the terminal payoff. It is the replication property that allows us to identify the fair price of the option with the price of the replicating portfolio.

This is in general not true for the same quantity $\frac{\partial C}{\partial S}$ when seen in the context of the fitting procedures presented in this chapter. If we want, we can still call the terms $\frac{\partial C}{\partial S}$, $\frac{\partial^2 C}{\partial S^2}$, $\frac{\partial C}{\partial t}$, 'delta', 'gamma', 'theta', etc., but their financial interpretation in terms of a self-financing dynamic trading strategy is not warranted (and, without entering a nominalistic discussion, for this reason I tend to avoid the terms 'delta', 'gamma' and 'theta' in the fitting context).

Is this distinction really important? Yes it is, but its significance sometimes fails to be appreciated. In order to understand the argument clearly, let us consider the following example.

Suppose that the true process for the underlying is a stochastic volatility process of the form

$$dS_t = S_t r\, dt + S_t \sigma_t\, dz_t \tag{9.53}$$

$$d\sigma_t = \mu_\sigma\, dt + v\, dw_t \tag{9.54}$$

This process is discussed in Chapter 13. We observe the prices at one particular horizon, but we do not know the true generating process. Erroneously, we believe that the process has been generated by a local-volatility process, of the form

$$dS_t = S_t r\, dt + \sigma(S_t, t)\, dz_t \tag{9.55}$$

This process is described in Chapters 11 and 12. One of its features is that the function $\sigma(S_t, t)$ can be chosen so as to recover exactly an arbitrary (admissible) set of exogenous option prices. Therefore we will certainly succeed in finding a function $\sigma(S_t, t)$ that produces the observed smile curve. Since the only source of uncertainty in the volatility process comes from the stock price itself, the approach lends itself to perfect replication, and to unique pricing by no-arbitrage. See Chapter 2. Our (erroneously but perfectly) fitted local-volatility model will now produce a certain dependence of the option price on the initial value of the stock, $\frac{\partial C}{\partial S}$. Furthermore, given the nature of the process we have assumed, we erroneously interpret this quantity as the right amount of stock to hold to be 'delta neutral', and, after continuous readjustments, to replicate the option payoff by its expiry.

Alternatively, we could have followed a different procedure: given the same option prices, we could have carried out a fit to the implied price density using a mixture-of-normals approach. If the process for the volatility and the process for the underlying are uncorrelated, I show in Chapter 13 that, as long as we use a sufficiently high number of Gaussian basis functions, also in this case we can obtain an arbitrarily close fit to the observed market prices. And, sure enough, we can again compute the quantity $\frac{\partial C}{\partial S}$, but this, in general, will not be the same as the quantity $\frac{\partial C}{\partial S}$ calculated using the local-volatility assumption.

Now, which is the 'correct' delta, the term $\frac{\partial C}{\partial S}$ calculated from the local-volatility construction, or the similar term calculated by differentiating the integral over the mixture of normals with respect to S_0, and which can also be formally written as $\frac{\partial C}{\partial S}$? Not surprisingly, since the true underlying process is a fully stochastic-volatility process, both 'delta' terms are wrong. More fundamentally, the *financial* interpretation we have given to them is also wrong. In both cases, in fact, we have interpreted them as the amount of stock needed in order to hedge locally the price movements of the underlying, and to obtain, after continuous readjustments, a perfect option payoff replication by option expiry. In reality I will show that, in the case of a stochastic-volatility process, perfect payoff replication using just the stock is impossible, and therefore the delta amounts $\frac{\partial C}{\partial S}$, implicitly derived by assuming unique pricing by no-arbitrage, must certainly be wrong.

In short: the ability to recover option prices exactly using a mixture-of-normals approach is no guarantee that the right process has been 'discovered'. If we are pricing anything but European options, *conditional*, and not just *marginal*, densities are important. A fit to today's prices (implied volatilities, risk-neutral densities) is compatible with a variety (actually, as we will see in Chapter 17, with an infinity) of compatible conditional densities. Every model calibrated to the current market prices can be seen as a different prescription for creating these conditional densities, given that the same marginal densities are all recovered.

In general, i.e. when dealing with true process specification, we must always ask ourselves if the process generating these prices is financially plausible and desirable. However, when we use a fitting approach (mixture-of-normals, generalized-beta, etc.) we have no idea of what the generating process for the underlying is, so we cannot even begin to address the question: Have we chosen the right *pricing* approach? We can also calculate all the derivatives we want of the option price, perhaps even analytically, and, if we like Greek words, we can call them 'deltas', 'gammas' and 'thetas'. However, in the absence of a process, and hence of a financially-justifiable construction, we are not authorized in using them as 'true' deltas, gammas, thetas, etc. A fit is *not* a model. For an interesting development of these views, see Piterbarg (2003).

9.12 Fitting the Risk-Neutral Density Function: The Generalized-Beta Approach

Mirfendereski and Rebonato (2001)[12] have proposed another approach to obtain a fit to the risk-neutral density of a (spot or forward) quantity X. The fitting is done by assuming that the distribution belongs to a particular four-parameter functional family (described below) which encompasses the log-normal distribution as a special case. The idea behind the approach is to produce terminal densities which are guaranteed to be well behaved and, at the same time, sufficiently flexible to account for observed market prices convincingly. The advantage with respect to the mixture-of-normals method described above is that the approach, while also very flexible, is more parsimonious, since only three (or even two) parameters are allowed per maturity. The main drawback is that it is less able than the mixture-of-normals method to recover very complex implied-density functions. Whether this is always desirable is, of course, a different matter.[13]

---

[12]The rest of this chapter has been adapted from Mirfendereski and Rebonato (2001). See footnote 11 about the title of the article.

[13]It can be argued that a more flexible model that recovers plain-vanilla prices close to perfectly is more useful for a complex-derivatives trader, who is a price-taker as far as the plain-vanilla options are concerned. A more parsimonious model, on the other hand, that identifies option prices difficult to reconcile with a sufficiently flexible family of density functions can be more useful to a plain-vanilla trader.

The approach will be shown to be of simple practical implementation because, for each expiry, the best combination of parameters that give rise to an optimal (in a sense to be described) match to market call and put prices can be found using a very efficient and rapid mixed numerical–analytical procedure. This is in turn possible because closed-form solutions are presented below not only for call and put prices consistent with this distribution, but also for the cumulative distribution arising from the chosen density. Thanks to these analytic solutions, the search procedure needed to calibrate the model to market prices can be very fast.

The approach presented in this section enjoys several interesting and desirable features: to begin with, since the distribution function is directly modelled, the resulting density is ensured to assume a well-behaved and 'plausible' shape. Since, as noted above, very small changes in implied volatilities (input prices) can give rise to radically different distributions, it conversely follows that an approach starting directly from the distribution can fit a great variety of market prices with little loss of precision.

We seek to minimize χ^2 defined as

$$\chi^2 = \sum_{j=1,n} w_{C_j} [C^{\text{market}}(K_j, T) - C^{\text{model}}(K_j, T; \theta)]^2$$
$$+ w_{P_j} [P^{\text{market}}(K_j, T) - P^{\text{model}}(K_j, T; \theta)]^2 \qquad (9.56)$$

where n is the number of options for which reliable market prices can be observed, the weights w_{C_j} and w_{P_j} may be chosen to specify liquidity or other quality criteria, $C^{\text{market}}(K_j, T)$ and $P^{\text{market}}(K_j, T)$ are the observed market call and put prices, respectively, for a given time to expiry T, $C^{\text{model}}(K_j, T; \theta)$ and $P^{\text{model}}(K_j, T; \theta)$ are given by

$$C^{\text{model}}(K_j, T; \theta) = \int_0^\infty (x - K_j)^+ \varphi_T^{fit}(x; \theta) \, dx$$
$$\qquad\qquad (9.57)$$
$$P^{\text{model}}(K_j, T; \theta) = \int_0^\infty (K_j - x)^+ \varphi_T^{fit}(x; \theta) \, dx$$

and $\varphi^{fit}(x; \theta)$ is the fitted risk-neutral density function. The notation $C^{\text{model}}(K_j, T; \theta)$, $P^{\text{model}}(K_j, T; \theta)$ emphasizes the call and put price dependence on the parameters θ of the distribution.

Keeping in mind the need for flexibility, generality and analytical tractability, I have chosen as the fitting density function a four-parameter family of probability distributions, namely the generalized-beta functions of the second kind (GB2 in what follows) (see Cummins et al., (1990)). The choice is motivated by the fact that

- the GB2 density can assume a wide variety of different shapes;

- it can easily accommodate 'fat tails' (which result in the commonly observed implied volatility smiles observed in the market);

- it degenerates into a log-normal distribution when using certain combinations of the four parameters, thus allowing a convenient, consistent, and smooth transition to 'flat volatility' models; and

- it affords analytic solutions that make the calibration process both practical and efficient.

The GB2 distribution, φ, is defined as follows:

$$\varphi(x) = \frac{|a| x^{ap-1}}{b^{ap} B(p, q) \left[1 + (\frac{x}{b})^a \right]^{p+q}} \tag{9.58}$$

where a, b, p, and q are the four parameters, and $B(p, q)$ is the beta function, defined in terms of the gamma function as

$$B(p, q) = \frac{\Gamma(p)\Gamma(p)}{\Gamma(p+q)} \tag{9.59}$$

For future use, the hth moment of the GB2 distribution can be derived and expressed as follows:

$$E_{\text{GB2}}[X^h] = \frac{b^h B \left(p + \dfrac{h}{a}, q - \dfrac{h}{a} \right)}{B(p, q)} \tag{9.60}$$

Volatility smiles can be interpreted as deviations from the log-normal (LN in what follows) density of the underlying risk-neutral density.

In order to gain a qualitative feel for the shape of the GB2 distribution, and to allow a 'standardized' comparison with the log-normal distribution, a simple transformation of variables is now introduced. Using the following transformation from variable x to variable y,

$$y = \frac{\ln x - \alpha}{\beta}, \quad \text{i.e. } x = \exp(\beta y + \alpha) \tag{9.61}$$

the log-normal density, $\varphi_X(x)$, is transformed into a standard normal density, $\varphi_Y(y) = \mathcal{N}(0, 1)$ (see, for example, Benjamin and Cornell (1970)):

$$\varphi_Y(y) = \left| \frac{dx}{dy} \right| \varphi_X(x)$$

$$= \beta x \varphi_X(x) = \beta \exp(\beta y + \alpha) \varphi_X(\exp(\beta y + \alpha)) \tag{9.62}$$

$$\varphi_{\text{LN}}(x) = \frac{1}{x \beta \sqrt{2\pi}} \exp\left[-\frac{1}{2} \left(\frac{\ln x - \alpha}{\beta} \right)^2 \right], \quad 0 \le x \tag{9.63}$$

$$\varphi_{\text{Normal}}(y) = \left| \frac{dx}{dy} \right| \varphi_{\text{LN}}(\exp(\beta y + \alpha))$$

$$= \frac{1}{\sqrt{2\pi}} \exp\left[-\frac{1}{2} y^2 \right], \quad -\infty \le y \le \infty \tag{9.64}$$

This same transformation can be applied to any fitted risk-neutral density, and the deviation of the resulting plot from normality can give a direct visual indication of such features as skewness or kurtosis. In particular, for the GB2 distribution one obtains

$$\varphi_{GB2}(y) = \left| \frac{dx}{dy} \right| \varphi_{GB2}(\exp(\beta y + \alpha))$$

$$= |\beta \exp(\beta y + \alpha)| \varphi_{GB2}(\exp(\beta y + \alpha); a, b, p, q), \quad -\infty \le y \le \infty \quad (9.65)$$

In this section I focus on the GB2 distribution and the results are therefore plotted and compared with a standard normal plot, as shown in Figure 9.19.

The cluster of normalized fitted GB2 curves displayed in Figure 9.19 were obtained using the set of parameters estimated by fitting the density functions to a series of GBP caplet prices of maturities ranging from 6 months to 10 years (see Section 9.12.2 for numerical details). The plot shows that, despite the difference in maturities, the different smiley distributions, once normalized, display a strong qualitative similarity across maturities, and therefore clearly appear to belong to the same 'family'.

9.12.1   Derivation of Analytic Formulae

In this section we derive closed-form expressions for call and put prices, both in terms of the most general GB2 distribution, and in the case where certain restrictions on the values of the parameters are imposed.

As mentioned above, one of the desirable features of the approach presented here is that the pricing formulae can be expressed in a Black-like form. In order to highlight these similarities, we begin by recalling that the first two moments of a log-normal (LN) distribution,

$$\varphi_{LN}(x) = \frac{1}{x\beta\sqrt{2\pi}} \exp\left[-\frac{1}{2} \left(\frac{\ln x - \alpha}{\beta} \right)^2 \right], \quad 0 \le x \quad (9.66)$$

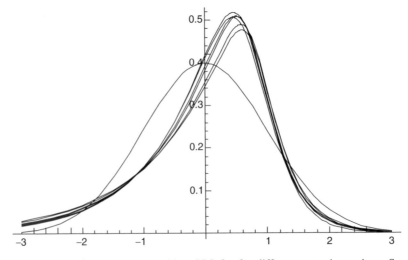

Figure 9.19   Standardized LN and matching GB2 fits for different maturity options. See the text for details.

defined in terms of the parameters α and β, are given by

$$E[X] = \exp\left[\frac{\alpha + \beta^2}{2}\right] \tag{9.67}$$

$$E\left[X^2\right] = \exp\left[2\alpha + 2\beta^2\right]$$

If, for simplicity, we set interest rates to zero, the call and put option prices are given by

$$Call_{LN}(K) = \int_{-\infty}^{+\infty} [x - K]^+ \, \varphi_{LN}(x) \, dx \tag{9.68}$$

$$Put_{LN}(K) = \int_{-\infty}^{+\infty} [K - x]^+ \, \varphi_{LN}(x) \, dx \tag{9.69}$$

The call and put price integrals can then be solved to yield the price in terms of the strike, K, and the two LN parameters:

$$Call_{LN}(K, T) = \exp\left[\frac{\alpha + \beta^2}{2}\right] \mathcal{N}\left(\frac{\alpha + \beta^2 - \ln K}{\beta}\right) - K\mathcal{N}\left(\frac{\alpha - \ln K}{\beta}\right) \tag{9.70}$$

$$Put_{LN}(K, T) = \exp\left[\frac{\alpha + \beta^2}{2}\right] \mathcal{N}\left(-\frac{\alpha - \ln K}{\beta}\right) - K\mathcal{N}\left(-\frac{\alpha + \beta^2 - \ln K}{\beta}\right) \tag{9.71}$$

Expressions (9.70) and (9.71) do not have the usual Black appearance. However, noting that

$$\alpha = \ln F - \frac{\sigma^2 T}{2} \tag{9.72}$$

$$\beta = \sigma\sqrt{T} \tag{9.73}$$

where F is the forward price, T is the time to expiry, and σ is the volatility, and substituting into (9.70) and (9.71), the familiar form of the Black call and put option pricing formulae is obtained:

$$Call_{LN}(K, T) = F\mathcal{N}\left(\frac{\ln\dfrac{F}{K} + \dfrac{\sigma^2 T}{2}}{\sigma\sqrt{T}}\right) - K\mathcal{N}\left(\frac{\ln\dfrac{F}{K} - \dfrac{\sigma^2 T}{2}}{\sigma\sqrt{T}}\right) \tag{9.74}$$

$$Put_{LN}(K, T) = K\mathcal{N}\left(\frac{\ln\dfrac{F}{K} - \dfrac{\sigma^2 T}{2}}{\sigma\sqrt{T}}\right) - F\mathcal{N}\left(\frac{\ln\dfrac{F}{K} + \dfrac{\sigma^2 T}{2}}{\sigma\sqrt{T}}\right) \tag{9.75}$$

Remarkably similar results can be obtained for the call and put using the GB2 distribution. Again, the call and put option prices can be defined by the following integrals:

$$Call_{GB2}(K) = \int_{-\infty}^{+\infty} [x - K]^+ \, \varphi_{GB2}(x) \, dx \tag{9.76}$$

$$Put_{GB2}(K) = \int_{-\infty}^{+\infty} [K - x]^+ \, \varphi_{GB2}(x) \, dx \tag{9.77}$$

which can be solved in absolute generality to yield the call and put price in terms of the strike, K, and the four GB2 distribution parameters,

$$Call_{GB2}(K) = \frac{K \left(\dfrac{b}{K}\right)^{aq} F_1^2 \left[q - \dfrac{1}{a}, p + q; 1 + q - \dfrac{1}{a}; -\left(\dfrac{b}{K}\right)^a\right]}{\left(q - \dfrac{1}{a}\right) B(p, q)}$$

$$- \frac{K \left(\dfrac{b}{K}\right)^{aq} F_1^2 \left[q, p + q; 1 + q - \dfrac{1}{a}; -\left(\dfrac{b}{K}\right)^a\right]}{q B(p, q)} \tag{9.78}$$

$$Put_{GB2}(K) = \frac{K \left(\dfrac{K}{b}\right)^{aq} F_1^2 \left[p, p + q; 1 + p; -\left(\dfrac{K}{b}\right)^a\right]}{p B(p, q)}$$

$$- \frac{K \left(\dfrac{K}{b}\right)^{aq} F_1^2 \left[p + \dfrac{1}{a}, p + q; 1 + p + \dfrac{1}{a}; -\left(\dfrac{K}{b}\right)^a\right]}{\left(p + \dfrac{1}{a}\right) B(p, q)} \tag{9.79}$$

where now $F_1^2 [a, b, c; x]$ is the hypergeometric function, defined as

$$F_1^2 [a, b, c; x] = \frac{\Gamma(c)}{\Gamma(a)\Gamma(b)} \sum_{n=0}^{\infty} \frac{\Gamma(a + n)\Gamma(b + n)}{\Gamma(c + n)} \frac{x^n}{n!} \tag{9.80}$$

and the other symbols have the usual meaning.

The results obtained so far can be rendered more transparent and easy to use by noting that (again for zero interest rates)

$$F = E_{GB2}[X] = \frac{bB\left(p + \dfrac{1}{a}, q - \dfrac{1}{a}\right)}{B(p, q)} \tag{9.81}$$

This being the case, we can then substitute $b = F/\lambda$, where

$$\lambda = \frac{B\left(p + \dfrac{1}{a}, q - \dfrac{1}{a}\right)}{B(p, q)} \tag{9.82}$$

to obtain the following call and put price equations in terms of the strike K, forward F, and three of the four GB2 distribution parameters, a, p and q:

$$
\begin{aligned}
Call_{GB2} = F\, & \frac{\left[\lambda\dfrac{F}{K}\right]^{a\left(q-\frac{1}{a}\right)} F_1^2\left[q-\dfrac{1}{a}, p+q; 1+q-\dfrac{1}{a}; -\lambda^a\left(\dfrac{F}{K}\right)^a\right]}{\left(q-\dfrac{1}{a}\right) B\left(p+\dfrac{1}{a}, q-\dfrac{1}{a}\right)} \\
& - K\, \frac{\left[\lambda\dfrac{F}{K}\right]^{aq} F_1^2\left[q, p+q; 1+q; -\lambda^a\left(\dfrac{F}{K}\right)^a\right]}{q\, B(p,q)}
\end{aligned}
\tag{9.83}
$$

$$
\begin{aligned}
Put_{GB2} = K\, & \frac{\left[\dfrac{K}{F\lambda}\right]^{ap} F_1^2\left[p, p+q; 1+p; -\left(\dfrac{K}{F\lambda}\right)^a\right]}{p\, B(p,q)} \\
& - F\, \frac{\left(\dfrac{K}{F\lambda}\right)^{a\left(p+\frac{1}{a}\right)} F_1^2\left[p+\dfrac{1}{a}, p+q; 1+p+\dfrac{1}{a}; -\left(\dfrac{K}{F\lambda}\right)^a\right]}{q\, B\left(p+\dfrac{1}{a}, q-\dfrac{1}{a}\right)}
\end{aligned}
\tag{9.84}
$$

Note that one of the parameters has been eliminated by imposing the no-arbitrage forward condition.

Although these expressions appear somewhat more unwieldy than (9.78) and (9.79), they are already beginning to be in the familiar Black form, involving as they do a weighted sum of F and K. Unfortunately, unlike the log-normal case, we cannot directly eliminate a second distribution parameter by introducing the volatility, σ. One can however determine an 'equivalent' volatility of the new distribution by imposing that not only the first, but also the second moment of the LN and GB2 distributions should be identical, i.e. that

$$
\exp\left[\frac{\alpha+\beta^2}{2}\right] = b\,\frac{B\left(p+\dfrac{1}{a}, q-\dfrac{1}{a}\right)}{B(p,q)}
\tag{9.85}
$$

$$
\exp\left[2\alpha+2\beta^2\right] = b^2\,\frac{B\left(p+\dfrac{2}{a}, q-\dfrac{2}{a}\right)}{B(p,q)}
\tag{9.86}
$$

Solving for α and β then gives:

$$
\alpha = 2\ln\left[b\,\frac{B\left(p+\dfrac{1}{a}, q-\dfrac{1}{a}\right)}{B(p,q)}\right] - \frac{1}{2}\ln\left[b^2\,\frac{B\left(p+\dfrac{2}{a}, q-\dfrac{2}{a}\right)}{B(p,q)}\right]
\tag{9.87}
$$

$$\beta^2 = -2\ln\left[b\frac{B\left(p+\dfrac{1}{a},q-\dfrac{1}{a}\right)}{B(p,q)}\right] + \ln\left[b^2\frac{B\left(p+\dfrac{2}{a},q-\dfrac{2}{a}\right)}{B(p,q)}\right] \tag{9.88}$$

$$\beta = \sigma_{eq}\sqrt{T} \rightarrow \sigma_{eq} = \sqrt{\frac{1}{T}\ln\left[\frac{B(p,q)B\left(p+\dfrac{2}{a},q-\dfrac{2}{a}\right)}{\left(B\left(p+\dfrac{1}{a},q-\dfrac{1}{a}\right)\right)^2}\right]} \tag{9.89}$$

In the above expressions the second moment of the LN distribution is chosen to be derived from the at-the-money volatility.

We have shown how to determine the 'equivalent' volatility, σ_{eq}, in terms of the GB2 distribution parameters, a, p and q. Note that, since this equivalent volatility is determined by the market (e.g. by the at-the-money implied volatility), we only have two remaining free GB2 distribution parameters, i.e. p and q. I should stress that there is no a priori reason why the second moments of the two distributions should be exactly matched, and that, by so doing, one is restricting the flexibility of the GB2 distribution. Whether the procedure thus modified still retains sufficient flexibility to match to a satisfactory degree market prices is an empirical issue that will be addressed later in the chapter.

Armed with this result, we are now in a position to simplify further the analytic expression for the GB2 call and put price formulae (Equations (9.83) and (9.84)) by recasting the expressions in terms of the incomplete beta function, $\mathcal{I}_z(p,q)$ (see, for example, Abramowitz and Stegun (1964)). The latter is defined as follows

$$\mathcal{I}_z(p,q) = \frac{B_z(p,q)}{B(p,q)} \tag{9.90}$$

where

$$B_z(p,q) = \frac{z^p}{p}F_1^2(p,1-q,1+p;z) \tag{9.91}$$

and, as before, $F_1^2(a,b,c;z)$ is the hypergeometric function. Making use of the following relation for the hypergeometric function (Abramowitz and Stegun (1964, Equation 15.3.4))

$$F_1^2(a,b,c;z) = \frac{1}{(1-z)^a}F_1^2\left(a,c-b,c;\frac{z}{z-1}\right) \tag{9.92}$$

and performing some algebraic acrobatics, we finally obtain the following simplified expressions for the GB2 call and put prices:

$$Call_{GB2} = F\mathcal{I}_z\left(q-\frac{1}{a},p+\frac{1}{a}\right) - K\mathcal{I}_z(q,p) \tag{9.93}$$

$$Put_{GB2} = K\mathcal{I}_{1-z}(q,p) - F\mathcal{I}_{1-z}\left(p+\frac{1}{a},q-\frac{1}{a}\right) \tag{9.94}$$

where z is defined as

$$z = \frac{\left(\dfrac{\lambda F}{K}\right)^{a}}{1 + \left(\dfrac{\lambda F}{K}\right)^{a}} \tag{9.95}$$

This simplified call and put price analytic expressions are now really very similar to the familiar Black(-and-Scholes) option pricing formulae re-derived earlier, and, like the Black-and-Scholes expression, allow simple, robust, and efficient evaluation of vanilla options. In place of the cumulative normal, $\mathcal{N}(.)$, we now have the incomplete beta function, $\mathcal{I}_z(p, q)$, which, like $\mathcal{N}(.)$, also takes on values between 0 and 1. Just as in the case of $\mathcal{N}(.)$ tabulations, standardized plots of $\mathcal{I}_z(p, q)$ exist for different pairs, (p, q) (e.g. see Figure 9.20). Numerical approximation of $\mathcal{I}_z(p, q)$ is also straightforward and efficient numerical routines are available in the literature (see, for example, Press *et al.* (1992, § 6.4)).

Sample plots of the call and put price formulae are shown in Figures 9.21 and 9.22, together with a graph, Figure 9.23, displaying put–call parity.

As mentioned earlier, the GB2 distribution 'degenerates' into a LN distribution when using certain combinations of the four parameters a, b, p and q. For those cases, the GB2 call and put price formulae become identical to the Black option pricing formulae, i.e. the Black pricing formulae are a special 'constant-volatility-across-strikes' case of the more general GB2 formulae. More precisely, by enforcing the relations (9.89) and (9.81), one can first ensure equal first and second moments for the GB2 and corresponding LN distributions. This leaves two free parameters. As p and q become 'large' the resultant GB2 distribution uniformly converges to a log-normal distribution, thereby ensuring that our option pricing formulae approach the Black formulae.

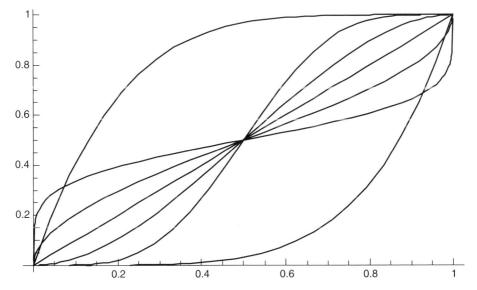

Figure 9.20 The distribution function $\mathcal{I}_z(p, q)$ vs z for different (p, q) pairs.

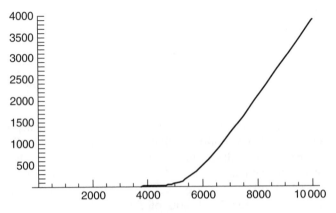

Figure 9.21　GB2 call prices.

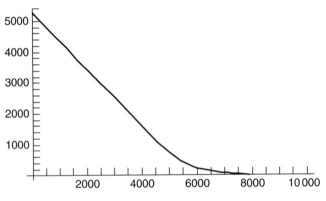

Figure 9.22　GB2 put prices.

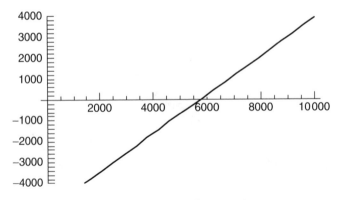

Figure 9.23　GB2 call–put parity.

It is not difficult to obtain closed-form expressions for the 'delta', 'gamma', etc. Explicit differentiation in fact gives

$$\Delta_{\text{Call}} = \mathcal{I}_z \left(q - \frac{1}{a}, p + \frac{1}{a} \right) \tag{9.96}$$

$$\Delta_{\text{Put}} = \mathcal{I}_{1-z} \left(p + \frac{1}{a}, q - \frac{1}{a} \right) = \mathcal{I}_z \left(q - \frac{1}{a}, p + \frac{1}{a} \right) = \Delta_{\text{Call}} - 1 \tag{9.97}$$

$$\Gamma_{\text{Call}} = \Gamma_{\text{Put}} = \frac{a \left(\dfrac{\lambda F}{K} \right)^{aq-1} \lambda}{F B(p,q) \left[1 + \left(\dfrac{\lambda F}{K} \right)^{a} \right]^{p+q}} \tag{9.98}$$

Note that (9.98) is similar in functional form to the GB2 density itself. Comparing the above GB2 'pseudo-Greeks' with the Black deltas and gammas,

$$\Delta_{\text{Call}} = \mathcal{N}(h_1) \tag{9.99}$$

$$\Delta_{\text{Put}} = -\mathcal{N}(-h_1) = \Delta_{\text{Call}} - 1 \tag{9.100}$$

$$\Gamma_{\text{Call}} = \Gamma_{\text{Put}} = \frac{\mathcal{N}'(h_1)}{F \sigma \sqrt{T}} \tag{9.101}$$

one can readily note fundamental similarities. Much as these results seem appealing, the reservations expressed in Section 9.11 regarding the interpretation of these terms as 'true' gamma and delta statistics must always be kept in mind.

9.12.2 Results and Applications

In this section the GB2 function is fitted to the prices of plain-vanilla options from two different markets.

Interest-Rate Results

The first part of the empirical analysis was carried out by looking at all the caplet prices implied from quoted broker cap prices for different strikes and maturities on several days. The results obtained for a particular date (8 July 1998) for DEM are reported in what follows as representative of all the days investigated. The equation used for the forward price of a caplet is as derived in Section 9.3:

$$Call = F \mathcal{I}_z \left(q - \frac{1}{a}, p + \frac{1}{a} \right) - K \mathcal{I}_z(q, p) \tag{9.102}$$

where $\mathcal{I}_z$ is the incomplete beta function, z is as in Equation (3.24), λ is given by

$$\lambda = \frac{B(p,q)}{B \left(p + \dfrac{1}{a}, q - \dfrac{1}{a} \right)} \tag{9.103}$$

Table 9.4 Caplet prices derived from market caplet prices (DEM–May 1998).

Maturity (years)	Strike (%)															
	4.0	4.2	4.4	4.6	4.8	5.0	5.2	5.4	5.6	5.8	6.0	6.2	6.4	6.6	6.8	7.0
1.0	0.0046	0.0032	0.0022	0.0014	0.0008	0.0005	0.0003	0.0001	0.0001	0.0000	0.0000	0.0000	0.0000	0.0000	0.0000	0.0000
1.5	0.0072	0.0057	0.0045	0.0034	0.0025	0.0018	0.0013	0.0009	0.0006	0.0004	0.0003	0.0002	0.0001	0.0001	0.0000	0.0000
2.0	0.0090	0.0076	0.0063	0.0051	0.0041	0.0033	0.0026	0.0020	0.0015	0.0011	0.0008	0.0006	0.0004	0.0003	0.0002	0.0002
2.5	0.0109	0.0094	0.0080	0.0068	0.0057	0.0048	0.0039	0.0032	0.0026	0.0020	0.0016	0.0013	0.0010	0.0008	0.0006	0.0004
3.0	0.0114	0.0100	0.0087	0.0075	0.0064	0.0054	0.0045	0.0038	0.0031	0.0026	0.0021	0.0017	0.0014	0.0011	0.0009	0.0007
3.5	0.0135	0.0120	0.0106	0.0093	0.0081	0.0070	0.0061	0.0052	0.0044	0.0037	0.0031	0.0026	0.0021	0.0018	0.0014	0.0012
4.0	0.0135	0.0120	0.0106	0.0093	0.0082	0.0071	0.0061	0.0052	0.0044	0.0038	0.0032	0.0026	0.0022	0.0018	0.0015	0.0012
4.5	0.0151	0.0135	0.0121	0.0107	0.0095	0.0083	0.0072	0.0063	0.0054	0.0046	0.0039	0.0033	0.0028	0.0024	0.0020	0.0016
5.0	0.0154	0.0138	0.0124	0.0110	0.0097	0.0085	0.0075	0.0065	0.0056	0.0048	0.0041	0.0035	0.0029	0.0025	0.0021	0.0017
5.5	0.0169	0.0153	0.0138	0.0124	0.0110	0.0098	0.0086	0.0076	0.0066	0.0058	0.0050	0.0043	0.0037	0.0031	0.0027	0.0022
6.0	0.0167	0.0151	0.0136	0.0122	0.0109	0.0097	0.0086	0.0075	0.0066	0.0057	0.0050	0.0043	0.0037	0.0031	0.0027	0.0023
6.5	0.0183	0.0167	0.0152	0.0137	0.0124	0.0111	0.0099	0.0088	0.0078	0.0068	0.0060	0.0052	0.0045	0.0039	0.0034	0.0029
7.0	0.0182	0.0166	0.0151	0.0136	0.0123	0.0110	0.0099	0.0088	0.0078	0.0068	0.0060	0.0053	0.0046	0.0040	0.0034	0.0030
7.5	0.0197	0.0181	0.0165	0.0150	0.0136	0.0123	0.0111	0.0100	0.0089	0.0079	0.0070	0.0062	0.0054	0.0048	0.0042	0.0036
8.0	0.0184	0.0168	0.0153	0.0139	0.0126	0.0113	0.0101	0.0091	0.0080	0.0071	0.0063	0.0055	0.0048	0.0042	0.0037	0.0032
8.5	0.0198	0.0182	0.0166	0.0152	0.0138	0.0125	0.0113	0.0101	0.0091	0.0081	0.0072	0.0063	0.0056	0.0049	0.0043	0.0038
9.0	0.0191	0.0175	0.0160	0.0145	0.0132	0.0119	0.0107	0.0096	0.0086	0.0076	0.0068	0.0060	0.0052	0.0046	0.0040	0.0035
9.5	0.0199	0.0183	0.0168	0.0153	0.0140	0.0126	0.0114	0.0103	0.0092	0.0082	0.0073	0.0065	0.0057	0.0051	0.0044	0.0039

Table 9.5 The fitted caplet prices. Cells shaded in grey indicate discrepancies at least as large as one basis point.

Maturity (years)	Strike (%)															
	4.0	4.2	4.4	4.6	4.8	5.0	5.2	5.4	5.6	5.8	6.0	6.2	6.4	6.6	6.8	7.0
1.0	0.0046	0.0032	0.0022	0.0014	0.0008	0.0005	0.0003	0.0001	0.0001	0.0000	0.0000	0.0000	0.0000	0.0000	0.0000	0.0000
1.5	0.0072	0.0057	0.0045	0.0034	0.0025	0.0018	0.0013	0.0009	0.0006	0.0004	0.0003	0.0002	0.0001	0.0001	0.0000	0.0000
2.0	0.0090	0.0076	0.0063	0.0051	0.0041	0.0033	0.0026	0.0020	0.0015	0.0011	0.0008	0.0006	0.0004	0.0003	0.0002	0.0002
2.5	0.0109	0.0094	0.0080	0.0068	0.0057	0.0048	0.0039	0.0032	0.0026	0.0020	0.0016	0.0013	0.0010	0.0008	0.0006	0.0004
3.0	0.0114	0.0100	0.0087	0.0075	0.0064	0.0054	0.0045	0.0038	0.0031	0.0026	0.0021	0.0017	0.0014	0.0011	0.0009	0.0007
3.5	0.0135	0.0120	0.0106	0.0093	0.0081	0.0070	0.0061	0.0052	0.0044	0.0037	0.0031	0.0026	0.0021	0.0018	0.0014	0.0012
4.0	0.0135	0.0120	0.0106	0.0093	0.0082	0.0071	0.0061	0.0052	0.0044	0.0038	0.0032	0.0026	0.0022	0.0018	0.0015	0.0012
4.5	0.0151	0.0135	0.0121	0.0107	0.0095	0.0083	0.0072	0.0063	0.0054	0.0046	0.0039	0.0033	0.0028	0.0024	0.0020	0.0016
5.0	0.0154	0.0138	0.0124	0.0110	0.0097	0.0085	0.0075	0.0065	0.0056	0.0048	0.0041	0.0035	0.0029	0.0025	0.0021	0.0017
5.5	0.0169	0.0153	0.0138	0.0124	0.0110	0.0098	0.0086	0.0076	0.0066	0.0058	0.0050	0.0043	0.0037	0.0031	0.0027	0.0022
6.0	0.0167	0.0151	0.0136	0.0122	0.0109	0.0097	0.0086	0.0075	0.0066	0.0057	0.0050	0.0043	0.0037	0.0031	0.0027	0.0023
6.5	0.0183	0.0167	0.0152	0.0137	0.0124	0.0111	0.0099	0.0088	0.0078	0.0068	0.0060	0.0052	0.0045	0.0039	0.0034	0.0029
7.0	0.0182	0.0166	0.0151	0.0136	0.0123	0.0110	0.0099	0.0088	0.0078	0.0068	0.0060	0.0053	0.0046	0.0040	0.0034	0.0030
7.5	0.0197	0.0181	0.0165	0.0150	0.0137	0.0123	0.0111	0.0100	0.0089	0.0079	0.0070	0.0062	0.0054	0.0048	0.0042	0.0036
8.0	0.0184	0.0168	0.0153	0.0139	0.0126	0.0113	0.0101	0.0091	0.0080	0.0071	0.0063	0.0055	0.0048	0.0042	0.0037	0.0032
8.5	0.0198	0.0182	0.0166	0.0152	0.0138	0.0125	0.0113	0.0101	0.0090	0.0081	0.0072	0.0063	0.0056	0.0049	0.0043	0.0038
9.0	0.0190	0.0175	0.0160	0.0145	0.0132	0.0119	0.0107	0.0096	0.0086	0.0076	0.0068	0.0060	0.0053	0.0046	0.0040	0.0035
9.5	0.0199	0.0183	0.0168	0.0153	0.0139	0.0126	0.0114	0.0103	0.0092	0.0082	0.0073	0.0065	0.0058	0.0051	0.0045	0.0039

Table 9.6 Best-fit GB2 parameters.

Maturity(y)	a	b	p	q
1.0	5.618	0.04960	2.923	5.756
1.5	3.436	0.06232	3.666	10.01
2.0	2.889	0.07355	3.216	10.85
2.5	2.651	0.08371	2.892	11.22
3.0	2.489	0.09166	2.614	11.49
3.5	2.438	0.09959	2.479	11.51
4.0	2.474	0.09763	2.345	10.64
4.5	2.457	0.10155	2.338	10.63
5.0	2.459	0.10216	2.33	10.63
5.5	2.540	0.10186	2.132	9.351
6.0	2.503	0.10358	2.078	9.423
6.5	2.587	0.10265	1.907	8.178
7.0	2.580	0.10293	1.854	8.029
7.5	2.684	0.10101	1.706	6.901
8.0	2.658	0.0991	1.698	6.893
8.5	2.636	0.10224	1.692	6.887
9.0	2.620	0.10117	1.687	6.883
9.5	2.608	0.10316	1.683	6.879

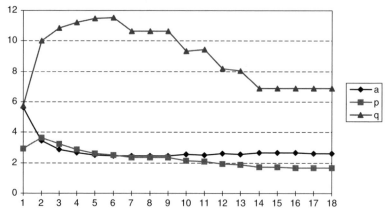

Figure 9.24 Plot of best-fit GB2 parameters.

Table 9.7 The FTSE implied volatilities used as input data. Spot = 5843.32 (29 May 1998).

Maturity	Forward	Disc.	5700	5750	5800	5850	5900	5950	6000	6050
Sep-98	5915.50	0.98	0.2530	0.2493	0.2456	0.2420	0.2385	0.2351	0.2318	0.2286
Dec-98	6000.11	0.96	0.2522	0.2495	0.2469	0.2442	0.2415	0.2387	0.2360	0.2334
Mar-99	6079.46	0.95	0.2528	0.2505	0.2482	0.2458	0.2434	0.2409	0.2385	0.2361
Jun-99	6128.55	0.93	0.2535	0.2515	0.2494	0.2472	0.2450	0.2427	0.2405	0.2384
Sep-99	6195.65	0.91	0.2539	0.2519	0.2499	0.2479	0.2458	0.2436	0.2415	0.2395
Dec-99	6269.07	0.90	0.2543	0.2524	0.2505	0.2485	0.2465	0.2445	0.2425	0.2406
Mar-00	6341.98	0.88	0.2546	0.2528	0.2510	0.2491	0.2473	0.2454	0.2435	0.2417
Jun-00	6383.58	0.87	0.2550	0.2533	0.2515	0.2498	0.2480	0.2463	0.2445	0.2428

and where $B(p, q)$, as above, is the beta function. After discounting, the above pricing equation was used to value caplets with different strikes, and to find the optimal values of a, p and q that minimize the sum of the square errors between the cap prices obtainable using the above equation and the prices observed in the market for different maturities. As many sets of distinct distribution parameters were used in the search as the number of cap maturities.

The results are reported in Tables 9.4 and 9.5, which show the market and fitted caplet prices, respectively. The excellent quality of the fit is apparent. In particular, it is worthwhile pointing out that all caplets, except those whose corresponding cell in the table is shaded in grey, were fitted to within one basis point. The parameters that lead to the best fit are shown in Table 9.6 and in Figure 9.24.

As one can notice, there is a reasonably smooth variation of these parameters (especially a and p) across maturities. This would be of great help if one had to 'guess' a price for a caplet of expiry intermediate between two optimization dates.

Equity Results

As a second test, a fit to the prices of calls on the FTSE100 index in the summer of 1998 was carried out. The market data comprised the forward index value and the implied volatility for different strike prices and for maturities that range from three months to two years. The implied volatilities and the prices for the FTSE100 are shown in Tables 9.7 and 9.8, respectively.

The implied volatilities given for the different contracts were converted to prices using the Black model, and these prices were then used to determine the GB2 distribution that best fitted them. The model prices thus obtained and the associated squared errors per maturity are given in Table 9.9. Again, the agreement is observed to be excellent.

9.12.3   What Does This Approach Offer?

I have presented a parametric approach to modelling plain-vanilla option prices in the presence of smiles. A GB2 distribution was chosen to describe the risk-neutral price distribution, and its parameters were obtained so as to minimize the sum of the squared deviations from the model and market option prices (see Equation (9.56)).

Table 9.8   The market option prices for the data in Table 9.7.

Maturity	5700	5750	5800	5850	5900	5950	6000	6050
Sep-98	418.81	385.79	354.00	323.51	294.41	266.76	240.62	216.06
Dec-98	586.56	553.83	521.93	490.86	460.62	431.28	402.89	375.54
Mar-99	727.12	694.31	662.15	630.57	599.56	569.19	539.56	510.77
Jun-99	837.32	804.79	772.79	741.21	710.02	679.35	649.34	620.15
Sep-99	950.32	917.58	885.27	853.33	821.71	790.54	759.96	730.09
Dec-99	1061.2	1028.2	995.70	963.43	931.46	899.90	868.85	838.46
Mar-00	1167.8	1134.7	1101.9	1069.4	1037.2	1005.4	974.12	943.36
Jun-00	1250.2	1217.3	1184.7	1152.3	1120.3	1088.6	1057.4	1026.7

Table 9.9   The model option prices for the set of data in Table 9.8.

Maturity	5700	5750	5800	5850	5900	5950	6000	6050	Sq Error
Sep-98	418.56	385.71	354.07	323.69	294.62	266.91	240.62	215.77	0.258
Dec-98	586.74	553.87	521.86	490.73	460.51	431.24	402.94	375.64	0.080
Mar-99	727.42	694.38	662.01	630.34	599.37	569.13	539.65	510.94	0.240
Jun-99	837.66	804.85	772.601	740.92	709.84	679.35	649.49	620.26	0.313
Sep-99	950.59	917.61	885.11	853.10	821.58	790.58	760.10	730.14	0.196
Dec-99	1061.4	1028.2	995.55	963.25	931.39	899.98	869.02	838.51	0.130
Mar-00	1167.9	1134.6	1101.8	1069.3	1037.2	1005.6	974.33	943.46	0.111
Jun-00	1250.2	1217.2	1184.5	1152.2	1120.3	1088.8	1057.6	1026.8	0.101

Analytic call and put price formulae were derived for the case of zero-interest rates which can be expressed in such a way as to display a Black-like appearance. The delta and gamma statistics were also expressed in terms of simple closed-form equations, which also turned out to bear a strong formal resemblance to the corresponding Black-like formulae. Put–call parity is preserved, as well as the identity of the 'gamma' of a call and a put.

By virtue of these closed-form solutions the minimization needed to determine the parameters of the GB2 distribution can be accomplished in a very efficient manner. Also, the optimized parameters display a smooth behaviour as a function of option maturity, thereby allowing a simple and smooth interpolation between values estimated for nearby maturities.

As the parameters p and q become 'large' the distribution uniformly converges to the log-normal distribution, which can therefore be considered a special case of the more general approach presented here.

The approach is therefore similar in spirit to the mixture-of-normals method, but is more parsimoniously specified. This allows a simpler, more robust and quicker optimization, at the expense of fitting precision.

Chapter 10

Quadratic Variation and Smiles

10.1 Why This Approach Is Interesting

In Chapter 4 I showed that the quadratic variation is *the* central quantity when pricing options in a Black(-and-Scholes) world. I also argued in the final section of Chapter 8 that almost all modelling approaches that give rise to smiley implied volatility surfaces achieve this goal by making the quadratic variation over a finite period a stochastic quantity. To the best of my knowledge, there is only one approach, presented in this chapter, that achieves the task of creating a non-flat smile surface while retaining (actually, imposing) a deterministic quadratic variation. Understanding how this model achieves this task is rewarding not only for its intrinsic interest, but for the light it sheds on the role of 'lucky paths' when discontinuous price moves are allowed, and for the implications this has for hedging. The discussion in this chapter therefore constitutes a useful preparation for understanding hedging in the presence of more general jump–diffusion processes.

10.2 The BJN Framework for Bounding Option Prices

In 1996 Britten-Jones and Neuberger (1996) (BJN in what follows) introduced a very interesting way of looking at option pricing. Their approach highlights in a very clear way the special role (and the limitations) of the quadratic variation in option pricing, and provides a natural link with the treatment of jump–diffusions, stochastic-volatility and local-volatility models, and with the variance–gamma approach discussed in the following chapters.

Their approach is somewhat unconventional in that, by using the concept of a dominating strategy (see, for example, Pliska (1997)), it allows the determination not of *the* price, but of the upper and lower rational bounds for the price of a contingent claim in a variety of situations where obtaining a unique price via risk-neutral valuation is not possible or appropriate. BJN describe a unified approach to deal with no-arbitrage pricing in complete and incomplete markets, and with the problem of option pricing when only discrete, as opposed to continuous, re-hedging is possible; and, *en passant*, they provide

293

an alternative way of looking at the hedging paradox of Crouhy and Galai (1995) which was first examined in Section 4.9.

Obtaining bounds for option prices is by no means a novel idea, since it can be traced all the way back to Merton's (1973) paper on rational option pricing. The difference between the approach by BJN and the majority of the solutions that have been proposed in the literature is that the BJN bounds are usefully tight, and their width has a continuous dependence on a parameter of their model. As this parameter goes to zero, the Black-and-Scholes solution, which is nested within the BJN set of solutions, is recovered.

In their approach, BJN do not require a priori knowledge of whether the underlying process is a diffusion, a jump–diffusion or a pure jump process, nor do they require the volatility component to be deterministic. They do require, however, that the quadratic variation of the process over a finite time interval should be exactly known. This would appear a weak requirement. It is, after all, always implicitly enforced when we deal with a deterministic-volatility diffusion, and the BJN approach would seem to allow for a lot more. I will show that, as we try to extend the BJN results away from the diffusive context, this apparently innocuous requirement is the Achilles' heel of the approach. Indeed, because of this assumption, despite its apparent appeal, the practical applications and the scope for extensions of the BJN methodology are rather limited. I have none the less devoted some considerable space to it, because appreciating its limitations will help us in understanding and putting in context the more traditional approaches introduced in order to account for smiles. At a very fundamental level, in fact, if one wants to account for smiles I shall argue:

- that in order to extend significantly the realism and domain of applicability of the BJN approach the quadratic variation should be made stochastic;

- that this is exactly what 'traditional' modelling approaches (jump–diffusion, fully-stochastic- and local-volatility models, the variance–gamma model, etc.) achieve;

- that these traditional models can be characterized by the different ways in which this stochasticity in quadratic variation can be achieved (e.g. by retaining or abandoning the assumption of continuity in the paths of the underlying). Each of these choices will have important implications, for instance regarding market completeness and the possibility of achieving perfect portfolio replication;

- that there is another fundamental characterization of stochastic processes for the underlying, depending on whether they produce future smiles that are independent of, or correlated with, the future level of the 'stock' price.

10.3   The BJN Approach – Theoretical Development

10.3.1   Assumptions and Definitions

Let $S(0)$ be the price today of asset S (a 'stock'). We assume that there exists a forward market in the asset S. The forward price for delivery of the stock at time t will be denoted by S_t. A European contingent claim, V, is a security whose payoff at time t only depends on the realization of S at t, i.e. $V = V(S_t)$. For the sake of simplicity I will often omit the adjective 'European' in what follows, but this restriction on the type of contingent claim is essential, and should always be kept in mind.

Permissible Price Sequences

Let π be a price sequence, i.e. an ordered collection of prices, S_i, with $0 \leq i \leq N$. The integer N is assumed to be finite, although as large as one may wish. Therefore a general price sequence is described by

$$\pi = \{S_0, S_1, S_2, \ldots, S_N\} \tag{10.1}$$

The price sequence π is said to be *permissible* if and only if

Condition 1 $S_0 = S(0)$.

Condition 2 $|\ln S_{j+1} - \ln S_j| \leq d, 0 \leq j < N$.

Condition 3 $\sum_{j=0,N-1}(\ln S_{j+1} - \ln S_j)^2 = v$.

The first of the three conditions simply requires that, for a price sequence to be permissible, its first value should be equal to the price of the underlying asset today. We will not lose too much sleep about this.

The second condition prescribes that the jump in the log of the stock price between any two steps should never exceed an arbitrarily large but finite quantity, d. If the underlying 'true' process were a pure diffusion, this condition would not unduly restrict the properties of a permissible price sequence, since 'jump' size, d, would scale with the square root of the time-step, which can be taken as small as desired. If the underlying 'true' process, however, contains discontinuous jumps, perhaps originating from Poisson events, then Condition 2 does pose a significant restriction, and the onus will be on the user to check that the solution to the pricing problem does not significantly depend on the quantity d. See the discussion in Section 10.4 about this point. Note that the treatment presented above does not make any a priori distinction based on the underlying diffusive or jump nature of the stock process. 'True' jumps, finite re-hedging intervals, and, with some caveats, even transaction costs can all be treated on the same footing.

As far as the third condition is concerned, it is easy to recognize the LHS as the sample quadratic variation generated by the price sequence. We therefore require that this sample quadratic variation should be known to be exactly v. If the stock process were a diffusion, then Condition 3 would be the discrete-time equivalent of requiring that the time integral of the square of the instantaneous volatility, $\sigma(u)$, should equal a known quantity, $\widehat{\sigma}^2 t$:

$$\int_0^t \sigma(u)^2 \, du = \widehat{\sigma}^2 t \tag{10.2}$$

Since we know from Chapter 4 that, as far as option pricing for diffusive price process is concerned, the quantity that matters is just $\widehat{\sigma}^2 t$, for this particular case Condition 3 is no more and no less restrictive than requiring a deterministic volatility. The setting presented here is, however, more general, because it encompasses both the finite-re-hedging-interval case, and the mixed jump–diffusion situation. By imposing Condition 3 we are assuming that we know a priori the 'total magnitude' of the moves over the finite re-hedging periods, including the jump events. We will return to this point towards the end of this chapter.

Permissible price sequences are denoted by the symbol P. Since the permissibility depends on the asset, S, because of Condition 1, on the maximum jump size, d, by virtue of Condition 2, and on the quadratic variation,[1] v, because of Condition 3 they are denoted by $P(S, d, v)$.

Residual Volatilities

Having defined a permissible price sequence, one can introduce the concept of residual volatilities,[2] $v_i, 0 \leq i \leq N$, defined, for each step i, to satisfy

Condition 4 $v_0 = v$.

Condition 5 $v_i = v_{i-1} - (\ln S_{i+1} - \ln S_i)^2$.

Condition 5 shows that every price move 'uses up' a random fraction of the total quadratic variation. Despite the fact that the initial quadratic variation (residual volatility) is depleted at a random rate, it is all *exactly* used up by option expiry. From Conditions 4 and 5 above one can deduce

Condition 6 $v_i = v_0 - \sum_{k=0,i-1} (\ln S_{k+1} - \ln S_k)^2$.

Therefore the quantity v_i conveys information about how much of the total variance we still have 'available to use' at time-step i.

Trading Strategy

Finally we introduce a *trading strategy*, H, which specifies the number of forward contracts held at time-step i. We will allow the strategy to depend, in a manner so far unspecified, on the stock price and on the residual volatility at time-step i. Therefore,

$$H = H(S_i, v_i) \tag{10.3}$$

As long as we focus our attention purely on a European option, V, we are in a position to consider the strategy consisting of

- selling the contingent claim at time 0 for an amount of cash equal to V_0;

- paying out to the buyer of V the payoff (if any) of the contingent claim at time T;

- accumulating the profits and losses arising from the strategy H (which we will call the 'hedging profits').

---

[1] Sometimes I will refer to v as the total variance. We know that this is not strictly correct, but, since we will be dealing with driftless forward prices, we do not have to worry too much about the possible differences between the two concepts.

[2] The term 'residual volatility' is the one chosen by BJN. It is somewhat misleading, since the quantities v_i are actually variances (residual quadratic variations) rather than volatilities, but the terminology has been retained for ease of reference to BJN's original work.

To simplify notation in what follows we will assume zero interest rates. Therefore the profits from the overall strategy are given by

$$V_0 - V(S_T) + \sum_{j=0,N-1} H(S_j, v_j)(S_{j+1} - S_j) \tag{10.4}$$

Among all the admissible strategies H, we call an *arbitrage strategy* any strategy H such that, for all permissible paths (i.e. for all permissible price sequences)

$$V_0 - V(S_T) + \sum_{j=0,N-1} H(S_j, v_j)(S_{j+1} - S_j) \geq 0 \tag{10.5}$$

where the inequality is strict for at least one path. If this condition were satisfied, the seller of the option would certainly receive at least as much, and sometimes more, money up-front (V_0) than what she has to pay at the end, $V(S_T)$, plus the costs that the strategy entails, i.e. $\sum_{j=0,N-1} H(S_j, v_j)(S_{j+1} - S_j)$.

10.3.2   Establishing Bounds

Let us now choose an arbitrary trading strategy, say H_1. That is, let us choose an arbitrary rule that will tell us the position in forward contracts that we propose to hold as a hedge against the European option. This rule will be a deterministic function of all the possible values of the residual volatility and stock price. Note that, at this stage, we do not know whether this rule will indeed serve as an effective hedge, and we might want to alter it in the future. For the moment it is just a rule that takes as inputs the stock price and the residual volatility, and returns the amount of forward contracts that we should hold.

Since we do not want to allow arbitrage strategies, it follows that the price for V that we obtain today, V_0, cannot be larger than the maximum cost incurred in paying the final payoff of the claim, and accumulating the hedging profits or losses for the chosen strategy. The maximum (supremum) is therefore over all the permissible paths, π:

$$V_0 \leq \sup_{\pi \in P(S,v,d)} \left\{ V(S_T) - \sum_{i=0,N-1} H(S_i, v_i)(S_{i+1} - S_i) \right\} \tag{10.6}$$

Our choice of trading strategy has so far been completely arbitrary. We want, however, Equation (10.6) to hold for *all* trading strategies; that is, even if one found a second trading strategy, say H_2, such that the right-hand-side of Equation (10.6) were always lower than if we had followed strategy H_1, the inequality (10.6) would still have to be fulfilled. In general, therefore, the price we receive from the sale of the option today must be no greater than even the lowest (infimum) possible realization of the quantity $\{V(S_T) - \sum_{i=0,N-1} H(S_i, v_i)(S_{i+1} - S_i)\}$ over all the possible trading strategies. Therefore

$$V_0 \leq \inf_H \left\{ \sup_{\pi \in P(S,v,d)} \left\{ V(S_T) - \sum_{i=0,N-1} H(S_i, v_i)(S_{i+1} - S_i) \right\} \right\} \tag{10.7}$$

Equations (10.6) and (10.7) define the minimum upper bound for the price today of the contingent claim in two steps: first, *for a given strategy*, we determine the price that is certain to cover the total payout for every possible admissible path; then, we vary the strategies H in order to reduce the total pay-out (i.e. the pay-out arising from the final payment and the re-hedging costs) as much as possible, resting assured that the price V_0 will have to be lower also than this value.

Finally, we define this minimum upper bound as

$$V(S, v) = \inf_{H} \left\{ \sup_{\pi \in P(S,v,d)} \left\{ V(S_T) - \sum_{i=0,N-1} H(S_i, v_i)(S_{i+1} - S_i) \right\} \right\} \qquad (10.8)$$

Clearly, we could have reversed the sign in the argument, and we could have obtained a similar expression for the maximum lower bound. Given the complete symmetry of the two approaches, only the case of the minimum upper bound is developed in what follows.

The minimum (infimum) upper bound in Equation (10.8) could in principle be found by a search over paths and strategies. Whilst conceptually correct, this approach is computationally impracticable, because it requires a search over all possible paths *and* hedging strategies. In order to circumvent this difficulty, BJN recast the same problem in a different form.

10.3.3   Recasting the Problem

In order to make the problem more tractable, note that, since the current price of the asset, S, and the total variance, v, determine both the permissible price sequences, P, and the trading strategies, H, the function $V(S, v)$ defined above provides the minimum upper bound as a function of S and v. More precisely, V is a function with a domain given by all the possible values of S and v. At a future point in time, i.e. as the price evolution unravels, the function itself will not change, only the arguments in its domain will. Therefore the minimum upper bound in state i can be written as $V(S_i, v_i)$. When the problem is looked at in this manner, there is no special meaning attached to the initial and final times; in particular, one can focus on any two 'consecutive' steps, and write

$$V(S_i, v_i) = \inf_{h} \left\{ \sup_{z_i} \{ V(S_{i+1}, v_{i+1}) - h(S_i, v_i)(S_{i+1} - S_i) \} \right\} \qquad (10.9)$$

Note that, in moving from Equation (10.8) to Equation (10.9) several small but important changes have taken place. The supremum is no longer taken over paths, but over realizations of S and v at the next step: for a given (S_i, v_i) we simply have a finite number of possible terminal destinations (S_{i+1}, v_{i+1}) to keep track of, instead of a multitude of connecting paths. Also, the sum over time-steps has disappeared, since we are now dealing with a single time-step (at a time). Finally, the term $V(S_{i+1})$ no longer indicates the terminal pay-out, but simply the value of the minimum upper bound itself at the next time-step.

Let us now implicitly define a variable z_i by the relationship:

$$S_{i+1} = S_i \exp(z_i) \qquad (10.10)$$

From Condition 4 above we can write

$$v_{i+1} = v_i - z_i^2 \tag{10.11}$$

Therefore Equation (10.9) can be rewritten as

$$V(S_i, v_i) = \inf_h \left\{ \sup_{z_i} \{ V(S_{i+1}, v_{i+1}) - h(S_i, v_i)(S_{i+1} - S_i) \} \right\}$$

$$= \inf_h \left\{ \sup_{z_i} \{ V(S_i \exp(z_i), v_i - z_i^2) - h S_i [\exp(z_i) - 1] \} \right\} \tag{10.12}$$

as long as the quantity z_i^2 does not exceed either v_i (otherwise the residual volatility v_{i+1} could not be positive), or d^2 (so as not to violate the condition on the maximum jump size).

Since we are now speaking of two consecutive 'time' slices, and the supremum simply has to be searched over all admissible values of z_i, the setting begins to look more like a traditional dynamic-programming problem (i.e. a usual tree- or lattice-based backward-induction methodology). There still remains, however, the infimum over the trading strategies that makes the problem non-standard. This last hurdle is dealt with by BJN as described below.

10.3.4 Finding the Optimal Hedge

Let us assume that the optimal hedge, $\widehat{h}$, i.e. the hedge that minimizes the quantity

$$\sup_{z_i} \{ V(S_i \exp z_i, v_i - z_i^2) - h S_i (\exp(z_i) - 1) \} \tag{10.13}$$

has somehow been found. Since we have defined $V(S_i, v_i)$ as an *upper* bound (albeit the minimum) one can rest assured that

$$V(S_i, v_i) \geq V(S_i \exp z_i, v_i - z_i^2) - \widehat{h} S_i (\exp z_i - 1) \tag{10.14}$$

The amount by which the upper bound $V(S_i, v_i)$ is greater than the right-hand-side is a function, f, of the permissible value for z_i. We can therefore formally write:

$$f(z_i) = V(S_i, v_i) - V(S_i \exp z_i, v_i - z_i^2) + \widehat{h} S_i (\exp z_i - 1) \tag{10.15}$$

Let us examine some properties of the function f.

Property 1: $f(0) = 0$. This is obvious from the definition, and can be verified by direct substitution in Equation (10.15).

Property 2: $f(z) \geq 0$. This property follows from the definition (10.15) and Equation (10.14).

Property 3: $\frac{\partial f}{\partial z}|_{z=0} = 0$. This follows from Properties 1 and 2: if the function f is equal to zero at the origin, and greater or equal to zero for positive or negative values of z, as long as arbitrarily small in magnitude (Property 2), then the derivative of f with respect to z_i in the neighbourhood of $z_i = 0$ must be equal to 0.

This derivative $\frac{\partial f}{\partial z}$ is easily calculated:

$$\frac{\partial f}{\partial z_i} = -\frac{\partial V}{\partial (S_i \exp z_i)} S_i \exp z_i + 2z_i \frac{\partial V}{\partial z_i} + \widehat{h} S_i \exp z_i \qquad (10.16)$$

Evaluating this quantity at $z = 0$, and equating it to zero because of Property 3, gives

$$\left. \frac{\partial f}{\partial z_i} \right|_{z_i=0} = -\frac{\partial V}{\partial S_i} S_i + \widehat{h} S_i = S_i \left(\widehat{h} - \frac{\partial V}{\partial S_i} \right) = 0 \qquad (10.17)$$

and therefore

$$\widehat{h} = \frac{\partial V}{\partial S_i}, \qquad z_i^2 \leq \min(v_i, d^2) \qquad (10.18)$$

Equation (10.18) therefore determines the optimal strategy. Note that, if all the Black conditions are met, the usual expression for the Black delta holding of forward contracts is recovered. The optimal strategy, however, holds also in all the more general cases where the BJN method is applicable.

As a last step we can substitute the optimal strategy we have just determined in the expression for the minimum upper bound. When we do so we obtain:

$$V(S_i, v_i) = \sup_{z_i} \{ V(S_i \exp(z_i), v_i - z_i^2) + \widehat{h} S_i (\exp(z_i) - 1) \}$$

$$= \sup_{z_i} \left\{ V(S_i \exp(z_i), v_i - z_i^2) - \frac{\partial V}{\partial S_i} S_i (\exp(z_i) - 1) \right\} \qquad (10.19)$$

subject to the constraint on z in Equation (10.18), and with the boundary (initial) condition

$$V(S_i, 0) = V(S_i) \qquad (10.20)$$

Condition (10.20) will be examined in greater detail in the next section. In the meantime Equation (10.19) expresses the solution of the min-max problem in terms of a search over the admissible values of z. In the expression we have obtained there appears the (unknown) derivative of the minimum upper bound function with respect to the forward price. The set-up is therefore quite similar to the usual Black environment, where initial and boundary conditions allow the solution of a second-order parabolic partial differential equation. It is therefore not surprising that a numerical technique very similar to a binomial tree (and of which the binomial tree is a limiting case) can provide a numerical solution to the problem. How this is accomplished in practice is shown in the next section.

10.4   The BJN Approach: Numerical Implementation

In this section we analyse the implementation of the approach proposed by Britten-Jones and Neuberger in detail, with a view to highlighting both the practical aspects of their construction, and the conceptual implications of their procedure.

Let us consider the case of a four-month call option with the underlying, S, at \$100 today, and a strike of \$100 as well. As a first introduction to the methodology, we will build in a slightly different way a 'traditional' binomial tree, i.e. we will discretize a continuous-time diffusion in one of the many and, in the limit, equivalent discrete ways this can be done. No jumps will be allowed in the first part of the exercise. Then we will implement the BJN procedure in order to deal with the case when jumps are indeed present, but leave all the other numerical features of the problem unchanged. For the sake of simplicity I will continue to assume zero interest rates.

10.4.1 Building a 'Traditional' Tree

As for the first part of the construction (i.e. the setting up of the 'traditional tree'), one normally builds binomial trees by specifying a time-step, Δt, and a, possibly time-dependent, volatility, σ. If the two states after the jump, S_{up} and S_{down}, are linked to their parent state, S_0, by the relationships

$$S_{up} = S_0 \exp(\sigma \sqrt{\Delta t}) \tag{10.21}$$

and

$$S_{down} = S_0 \exp(-\sigma \sqrt{\Delta t}) \tag{10.22}$$

the usual moment-matching condition then requires that the stock price can jump to the 'up' or the 'down' states with the well-known probabilities given by Cox *et al.* (1979). We will follow instead a different procedure: in keeping with BJN's approach, we choose to map onto the x-axis, instead of the time variable, a different quantity, i.e. the residual volatility, $v = j(\sigma \sqrt{\Delta t})^2$, with j a positive integer to be discussed below.

10.4.2 Building a BJN Tree for a Deterministic Diffusion

A moment's thought suggests that the choice above is a very 'natural' transformation, since, at least in the diffusive context, option pricing does not 'know' about volatility and time separately: in the Black equation the time variable always appears in conjunction with the volatility, in the form $\sigma \sqrt{t}$, or as its square. Introducing the new variable v in the context of a diffusive process is a natural and beneficial numerical device that makes time flow faster or more slowly according to whether the (non-constant) volatility is higher or lower, in such a way that the new 'volatility-adjusted time' flows at an even pace. See Figure 10.1 and its caption for the numerical details.

Once we have reached the last step of the tree (which coincides with the option expiry) all the volatility has, by Condition 3, certainly and exactly been fully 'used up'. Therefore in every state of the world the value of the option, V, is simply equal to the payoff condition for the corresponding value of the underlying. At each step in the tree and for each possible state, BJN denote the value of the option with the notation $V(S_i, v_i)$, in order to emphasize that it depends both on the level of the underlying and on the residual volatility.

It is worthwhile analysing the meaning of this notation in some further detail. Recall that one of the crucial assumptions of the model is that we avail ourselves of the exact

	4	3	2	1	0
4					128.786
3				120.8931	
2			113.4839		113.4839
1		106.5288		106.5288	
0	100		100		100
−1		93.87129		93.87129	
−2			88.1182		88.1182
−3				82.71769	
−4					77.64817

Figure 10.1 The (S_i, v_i) grid: the grid was built by requiring that the various quantities S_i should be given by $S_i = S_0 \exp(i\delta)$, with $4 \leq \delta \leq -4$, and that the values of the residual volatility, v_i, should be obtainable as $v_j = j\delta^2$, with $j \geq 0$. At maturity $j = 0$.

knowledge of how much total 'volatility' (quadratic variation) will be used up by option expiry, but we do not assume to know how this volatility will actually unfold during the option life. Note that the BJN assumption therefore entails a milder requirement than assuming to know the instantaneous volatility function, $\sigma(t)$, at every time-step. For a purely diffusive process, it is exactly equivalent to requiring that we know either $\widehat{\sigma}(T)$, or $\int_0^T \sigma(u)^2 \, du$, with the two quantities linked by the (by-now-familiar) relationship

$$\widehat{\sigma}(T)^2 T = \int_0^T \sigma(u)^2 \, du \qquad (10.23)$$

The same is not true, however, if the process is a mixed jump–diffusion one, or if we relinquish the continuous-trading assumption, which is the relevant setting for the BJN model. Furthermore, if we no longer impose that we can trade continuously, we lose the ability to distinguish between 'true' jumps (i.e. events originating from the discontinuous nature of the process) and 'pseudo' jumps simply induced by our finite trading frequency. Since, however, we assume that the total volatility, v, is known, we also know at all points in our price/residual-volatility tree how much variance (originating from jumps, finite re-hedging, etc.) we happen to have left. Therefore we can truly and correctly write $V = V(S_i, v_i)$. In particular, the terminal payoff condition can be written in BJN's notation as $V(S_i, 0) = V(S_i)$, where $V(S)$ is the payoff function at maturity. For a four-step tree construction these values can be read, as usual, in the last column in the grid (which we will refrain from calling 'the last time slice'), as displayed in Figure 10.2.

In general, the BJN discretization of a simple diffusion on a computational tree can therefore be built by

- choosing an arbitrary step size, δ;
- placing the values along the y-axis (which give the possible levels of the stock price) at $S_i = S_0 \exp(i\delta)$, with i a positive or negative index;
- allowing for the residual volatility, v_j, the values $j\delta^2$, with j a non-negative integer;
- forcing the stock price at a generic (i, j) point to be linked only to the two possible states $(i + 1, j - 1)$ and $(i - 1, j - 1)$.

	4	3	2	1	0
4					28.78604
3				20.89312	
2			13.48394		13.48394
1		8.159418		6.528839	
0	4.740256		3.161224		0
−1		1.530645		0	
−2			0		0
−3				0	
−4					0

Figure 10.2 The payoff function, $V(S_i, 0) = V(S_i)$, for the 100-strike call is given in the last column. The other values are the discounted option values evaluated as described in the text.

Note that, in the last step of the construction, the second index decreases in moving from one step to the following, because so does the residual volatility. Since, for the moment, we are simply building the BJN lattice in order to discretize a diffusive process, no further conditions are required, and one can easily check by explicit calculation that the same tree would have been obtained by requiring, for instance, the time-step, Δt, to be 0.1 years, and the volatility to be 20.00%, or any other of the infinity of possible combinations giving rise to a $\sigma\sqrt{\Delta t}$ of 0.063246. We are not committing ourselves to any of these choices, however.

We now step backwards one residual-volatility step, and we therefore place ourselves in any of these possible states which have in common the fact that only an amount δ^2 of the total variance is still available to be used. These states are all labelled by $j = 1$. The value of $V(S_i, 1)$ is obtained as a linear combination of the values $V(S_{i+1}, 0)$ and $V(S_{i-1}, 0)$. The weights in this linear combination, p and $(1 - p)$, can be easily obtained by imposing that

$$pS_{i+1,j-1} + (1 - p)S_{i-1,j-1} = S_{i,j} \tag{10.24}$$

(Remember that we are working with forward prices, and therefore no discounting is required.) A simple calculation therefore gives

$$p = \frac{1 - \exp(-\delta)}{\exp(\delta) - \exp(-\delta)} \tag{10.25}$$

which, for the example in Figures 10.1 and 10.2 above happens to give $p = 0.484194$. While this is correct, in order to build an algorithm that can be generalized to the case when jumps are present, we choose to follow a different procedure to 'bring back' the option value. First of all we construct the straight line through the two points $V(S_{i+1}, 0)$ and $V(S_{i-1}, 0)$ using the two relationships:

$$V_{i+1,j-1} = a + bS_{i+1,j-1} \tag{10.26}$$

$$V_{i-1,j-1} = a + bS_{i-1,j-1} \tag{10.27}$$

This 2×2 linear system uniquely determines the values a and b. We then make use of the 'slope' and 'intercept' thus obtained to determine $V(i, j)$ as

$$V_{i,j} = a + bS_{i,j} \tag{10.28}$$

Although cumbersome, one can check that the values obtained using this algorithm are exactly the same as the values that would be obtained by means of the relationship:

$$V_{i,j} = pV_{i+1,j-1} + (1 - p)V_{i-1,j-1} \tag{10.29}$$

with p given by Equation (10.25).

We can now repeat the procedure and travel all the way back to the root. By doing this we obtain for the purely diffusive, deterministic-volatility case the option value of 4.740256 shown in Figure 10.2.

10.4.3   Building a BJN Tree for a General Process

We can now extend this procedure to the case of a mixed jump–diffusion process. In order to account for the possibility of jumps, the tree construction remains the same, but we modify the possible destination nodes from a given parent node. More precisely, we require that, from node (i, j) the reachable points should be $(i + n, j - n^2)$, with n a positive or negative (but not zero) integer.

Some further constraints have to be placed on n, besides its being strictly positive or negative. Looking back to Conditions 2 and 3 of Section 10.3, we do not want a move to be so large that the residual volatility from a given node, v_i, is exceeded; nor do we want the maximum allowable (log) jump to be greater than d. These two conditions taken together require that

$$n^2 \leq \{j, d^2\} \tag{10.30}$$

Therefore, assuming for the moment that we do not have to worry about the d condition, from the node, say, $(-1, 3)$ (with $S_{-1,3} = 93.8713$), the values highlighted in bold in Figure 10.3 are reachable. If either state $(2, 0)$ ($S = 113.484$) or state $(-4, 0)$ ($S = 77.6482$) had been reached from $(-1, 3)$, then all the residual volatility available from

	4	3	2	1	0
4					128.786
3				120.8931	
2			113.4839		113.484
1		106.5288		106.529	
0	100		100		100
−1		93.8713		93.87129	
−2			88.1182		88.1182
−3				82.7177	
−4					77.6482

Figure 10.3   The states reachable from state $(-1, 3)$ are highlighted in bold. It is assumed that $d \geq 3$.

the parent state would have been used and, by construction, the stock price would not be allowed to move any more.

Exercise 1 *When this happens, does the process satisfy the Merton admissibility conditions discussed in Section 2.4 in Chapter 2?*

The flexibility afforded by the choice of the variable v on the x-axis is now apparent: had we built a traditional tree with time on the horizontal axis, we would be forced to move to several possible states on the same time slice, thereby making the recombining-binomial-tree geometry impossible.

Note that, in so far as the last two steps are concerned, the possible values of the option are exactly the same as in the simple binomial case: in the case of the last step simply because, irrespective of which node we might have arrived from, there is no volatility left, and we must therefore simply have the terminal payoff condition:

$$V(S_i, 0) = V(S_i) \tag{10.31}$$

As far as the second-to-last step is concerned, everything must also look exactly the same as in the simple binomial tree, because, on any node $(., 1)$ we only have, by construction, one unit of volatility to play with without violating the total-quadratic-variation condition. We might have arrived at a node $(k, 1)$ directly from the root (if such big jumps had been allowed by the d constraint), but, given that we have only one volatility unit left, we can only move either to node $(k + 1, 0)$ or $(k - 1, 0)$. Once again, the convenience of the seemingly awkward set-up to deal with the case of jumps is clearly becoming apparent.

Note also that it becomes meaningless to distinguish in this context between 'true' jumps, or the case where the trader went on holiday and stopped re-hedging her positions for a couple of weeks: what matters are only the allowable values at re-hedge time.

The procedure truly becomes different from the simple diffusive case when we move to the third-to-last step and beyond. At any of the nodes corresponding to these steps there now are a multiplicity of possible arrival points, and, even if we wanted, we could not calculate the option value as a linear combination of its values at the destination nodes. It is at this point that the optimal hedging strategy determined in the previous section comes into play. To see how this can be accomplished, let us look closely at the expression

$$V(S_i, v_i) = \sup_{z_i}\{V(S_i \exp(z_i), v_i - z_i^2) - \widehat{h}S_i(\exp(z_i) - 1)\}$$

$$= \sup_{z_i}\left\{V(S_i \exp(z_i), v_i - z_i^2) - \frac{\partial V}{\partial S_i}S_i(\exp(z_i) - 1)\right\} \tag{10.32}$$

If we are working our way back from the final expiry to today, $V(S_i, v_i)$ is the new value for the option that we have to determine, and $V(S_i \exp(z_i), v_i - z_i^2)$ are option values that have already been calculated. We are holding a hedging amount of forward contract $\widehat{h}$ (with $\widehat{h} = \frac{\partial V}{\partial S_i}$), and, therefore, the change in value of our portfolio will be linear in the stock price. Finally, we know that the stock price in the state where we have to determine the option value is equal to S_i. Let us move inside the sup{.} operator and consider an arbitrary (known) 'later' value $V(S_i \exp(z_i), v_i - z_i^2)$. From Equation (10.19) we know that, if we have chosen the 'correct' z_i, (i.e. the z_i for which the expression in curly brackets is a maximum), then the new (unknown) value, $V(S_i, v_i)$, is linked to the 'later' (known) value, $V(S_i \exp(z_i), v_i - z_i^2)$, by a linear relationship:

$$V(S_i, v_i) = V(S_i \exp(z_i), v_i - z_i^2) - \widehat{h} S_i (\exp(z_i) - 1)$$

$$= V(S_i \exp(z_i), v_i - z_i^2) - \frac{\partial V}{\partial S_i} S_i (\exp(z_i) - 1) \qquad (10.33)$$

What we do not know in this expression is the slope $\widehat{h}$, i.e. the amount of forward contract (or, more simply, of stock, since we are working with zero interest rates) to hold. We *do* know, however, that $V(S_i, v_i)$ must be an upper bound. Therefore, for any possible value of the arrival $S_i \exp(z_i)$, its value must be worth at least as much as any of the known reachable values $V(S_i \exp(z_i), v_i - z_i^2)$. In addition, it must be a *lower* upper bound, and therefore, putting both constraints together, we deduce that the straight line that we must determine is the one that has the lowest possible value at S_i, and such that all the points on it lie at or above the accessible option values $V(S_i \exp(z_i), v_i - z_i^2)$. This line defines what BJN call the 'convex hull'. Figure 10.4 illustrates graphically the construction. The slope of the straight line ($\frac{\partial V}{\partial S}$) gives the required hedging ratio.

After this construction has been carried out at each node for a given 'variance step' one can move backwards following the same procedure all the way to root, where the required minimum upper bound will be obtained. Despite the somewhat unusual construction, the algorithm can actually be coded in a very fast and efficient way. The following section presents the computational results obtained following this procedure.

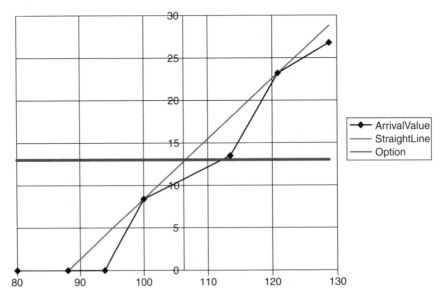

Figure 10.4   The construction of the convex hull straight line: the stock price at the node (S_i, v_i) where the option value has to be evaluated is 106.21. The diamonds labelled 'Arrival Value' indicate the values of the option at the reachable nodes $V(S_i \exp(z_i), v_i - z_i^2)$. The straight line is the lowest line at $S_i = 106$ such that all the reachable points lie on or below the line itself. The value of the option (13.00) is then given by the value of the straight line corresponding to $S_i = 106.21$.

10.4.4   Computational Results

The case study analysed below is that of a plain-vanilla two-month call option, with the underlying at $100. If no jumps are allowed, and the volatility of the underlying is taken to be equal to 20%, the relative Black price is $3.2564. Figure 10.5 shows the convergence (as a function of the number of steps) of the procedure presented above for the degenerate case when jumps are not allowed (i.e. when the convex hull is constructed trivially using two points only).

Similarly, Figure 10.6 shows the convergence results when jumps are indeed allowed. Despite the fact that the convergence is somewhat slower, one can notice that no particularly challenging numerical problems seem to be encountered.

The option values for different starting levels of the stock price, $S(0)$, are reported in Figure 10.7 for the case of 124 steps. It is interesting to note that:

- the jump cases give rise to option prices that are always as least as large as, and most of the time larger than, the option prices obtained without jumps;

- larger maximum possible jumps give rise to option prices that are always as least as large as, and most of the time larger than, the option prices obtained with smaller jumps;

- the increase in option value associated with larger and larger maximum jump sizes seems to become increasingly smaller in moving from the no-jump case to 3%, 5% and 6% maximum relative jump size. This is quite important, given the comments made above regarding Condition 2 for a price sequence to be permissible.

From the prices presented in Figure 10.7 it is possible to obtain the implied volatilities that, 'plugged into' the Black formula, would give the required prices. It is clear from the graph, and indeed, by construction, that the implied volatilities obtainable from the jump

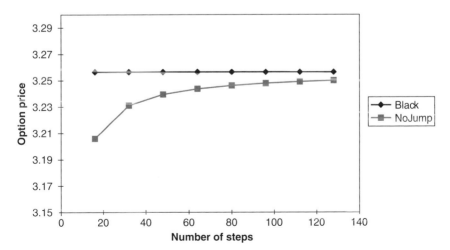

Figure 10.5   The convergence of the BJN procedure as a function of the number of steps for the degenerate no-jump case. Trade details: strike 100, spot 100, interest rates $= 0$, maturity $=$ 2 months, volatility $= 20\%$ (jumps 3%, 5%, 6%). The Black option value is $3.2564.

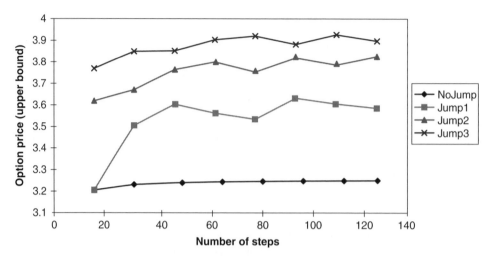

Figure 10.6   The convergence of the BJN procedure as a function of the number of steps for the jump case. Trade details: strike 100, spot 100, interest rates = 0, maturity = 2 months, volatility = 20%, jumps 3% (Jump1), 5% (Jump2), 6% (Jump3). The Black option value is $3.2564.

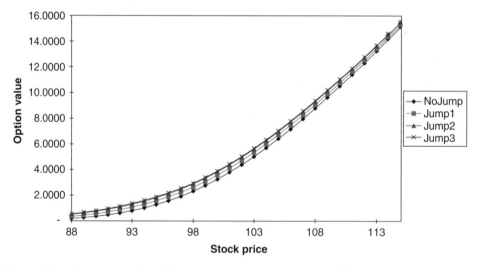

Figure 10.7   Option values for different jump sizes as a function of different starting levels of the stock price, $S(0)$ (124 steps).

prices must be higher than the corresponding no-jump quantities. What is not a priori obvious from Figure 10.7, however, is whether this increase in volatility varies across strikes, or simply amounts to a rigid upward shift across strikes of the no-jump volatility. In order to explore whether the BJN model gives rise to a smile effect, the prices obtained for different strikes for the case study above have been converted to the corresponding implied volatilities and plotted, as shown in Figure 10.8, for the maximum jump sizes of 3%, 5%, 7% and 9%.

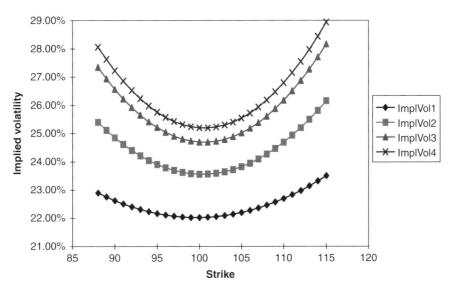

Figure 10.8 The implied volatilities obtained for the case study above and jumps of 3% (ImplVol1), 5% (ImplVol2), 7% (ImplVol3) and 9%(ImplVol4) (128 steps).

Three features are of interest:

1. The increase in implied volatility is not constant across strikes, i.e. the introduction of jumps has indeed given rise to smiles.

2. The increase in this smile is much greater in going from a maximum jump size of 3% to 5% than from 5% to 7%, and similarly for the move from 7% to 9%.

3. The steepness of the smile (i.e. the slope of the implied volatility curve as a function of strike) increases significantly in moving from 3% to 5%, much less from 5% to 7% and almost not at all from 7% to 9%. Also in these respects, therefore, it seems fair to say that, reassuringly, the model seems to depend less and less on the rather arbitrary value d as the maximum jump size increases.

It is also interesting to observe the behaviour of the smile, and of its steepness in particular, as one varies the final maturity of the option. To this effect the calculations were carried out for maturities from 0.25 month to 2 months at regular intervals of 0.25 month, and the results are shown in Figure 10.9. As is apparent, the smile becomes flatter and flatter as the maturity increases, in good qualitative accord with what is observed in the FX and equity markets. The left part of Figure 10.9 could also be profitably compared with the left part of Figure 7.1 in Chapter 7, which shows a market smile surface for the FTSE index: the qualitative similarity is quite apparent.

10.4.5 Creating Asymmetric Smiles

Clearly, given the symmetric nature of the jump (at least in log space) the resulting smile is also similarly symmetric; this feature is approximately displayed (on average) by FX smiles, but certainly not by equities smiles. It is possible, however, to introduce into the

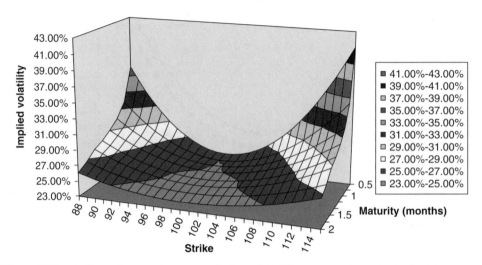

Figure 10.9 Smile surface for the case study but with different maturities obtained with a maximum jump of 6% (64 and 128 time-steps).

numerical procedure an asymmetric maximum jump size in the hope that this might give rise to a skewed smile. More precisely, one can replace the condition

$$n^2 \leq \{j, d^2\} \tag{10.34}$$

with the two conditions

$$n_{\text{up}}^2 \leq \{j, d_{\text{up}}^2\} \tag{10.35}$$

and

$$n_{\text{down}}^2 \leq \{j, d_{\text{down}}^2\} \tag{10.36}$$

which, in turn, imply that

$$|\ln S_{j+1} - \ln S_j| \leq d_{\text{up}}, \qquad \text{if } S_{j+1} > S_j \tag{10.37}$$

$$|\ln S_{j+1} - \ln S_j| \leq d_{\text{down}}, \qquad \text{if } S_{j+1} < S_j \tag{10.38}$$

With this minor modification, the same procedure described above can be followed, and the corresponding implied volatilities obtained for a variety of maturities. Some typical results are shown in Figures 10.10 and 10.11, where, in the 'up' jump, possible values were collected from all reachable states up to 5 steps ahead, but the 'down' jump was constrained to reach no further than 1, 2, 3, 4 or 5 steps. These different cases are denoted as the $(1, 5)$, $(2, 5)$, $(3, 5)$, $(4, 5)$ and $(5, 5)$ case, respectively.

Once again it should be noted, by comparing the two figures, that the smile becomes shallower as the maturity increases from 0.25 month to 2 months; but, more interestingly, the shape of the smile is now markedly asymmetric, and whether the slope, in moving

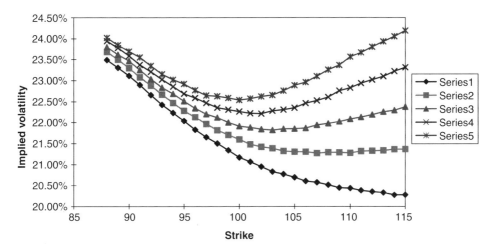

Figure 10.10 The smile surface obtained for several different possible combinations of up and down jumps, from (1,5) (Series1) to the symmetric case of (5,5) (Series5). The option maturity was 2 months and all the other inputs were as per the case study.

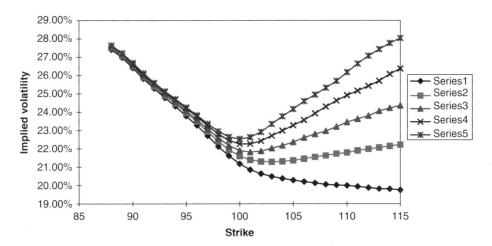

Figure 10.11 The smile surface obtained for several different possible combinations of up and down jumps, from (1,5) (Series1) to the symmetric case of (5,5) (Series5). The option maturity was 0.25 month and all the other inputs were as per the case study.

from at-the-money to in-the-money calls, is positive or negative depends on the number of allowable down steps. Looked at in this light, the results indicate that the asymmetric BJN jump model could also convincingly describe the situation encountered in the case of the FX smile, whose steepness and shape changes frequently over time.

10.4.6 Summary of the Results

Summarizing: the numerical implementation of the BJN approach has shown that

- the method has good convergence properties;

- the dependence on the arbitrary maximum jump size, d, becomes smaller and smaller as d increases;

- the approach naturally gives rise to smiley implied volatilities;

- the slope of the implied volatility curve depends less and less on the maximum jump size as the latter increases, and decreases with increasing maturity, as observed in the FX and equity markets;

- the resulting smile obtainable from the standard BJN approach is approximately symmetric;

- this smile can be turned into an asymmetric smile by imposing a different maximum size for the up and the down jumps; after carrying out this modification, there exist combinations of maximum up and down jumps that give rise to asymmetric smiles;

- with asymmetric smiles, the slope of the smile curve moving from at-the-money calls to in-the-money calls can be positive or negative, depending on the choice of d_{up} and d_{down}.

10.5   Discussion of the Results

The results reported above indicate that the approach proposed by BJN (although not explicitly created for this purpose) could account in a simple way for both symmetric- and asymmetric-type smiles. Given the nature of the mechanism responsible for the smile, the BJN approach would produce the type of smile previously described as 'floating'. There are several interesting points worth noting. These are discussed below.

10.5.1   Resolution of the Crouhy–Galai Paradox

An interesting by-product of the discussion so far is that the Crouhy-and-Galai (1995) paradox mentioned in Section 4.9 is automatically resolved. The dependence of the optimal hedging strategy on both the instantaneous and the residual average volatility occurs, and becomes increasingly noticeable, when the binomial tree becomes coarser and coarser. But a 'jump' can be distinguished from a Brownian increment in a discrete binomial setting only by making the spacing become smaller and smaller and by tracking the different scaling properties of the Poisson jumps and Brownian increments with the magnitude of the time-step. If the tree is of fixed time-step, and, more importantly, if it is coarse, there is little meaning in distinguishing between the movement induced by the current instantaneous volatility and a 'true' jump.

10.5.2   The Difference Between Diffusions and Jump–Diffusion Processes: the Sample Quadratic Variation

The BJN approach provides an interesting financial description of the origin of smiles in equities and FX, and allows the incorporation in its formalism of a variety of practically important features, such as finite re-hedging and market incompleteness. If implemented in the 'asymmetric-jump' version it could not only explain the qualitative features of the observed equity smile, but also its essentially floating nature. Despite these positive features the approach suffers from a subtle but deep-seated limitation. This stems from the requirement that the quadratic variation over the chosen time horizon should be known exactly at the start. As mentioned above, this is admittedly no stronger a condition than requiring that the constant (or deterministic) volatility of a Brownian diffusion should be known a priori. This condition, however, is normally enforced in a purely diffusive setting, and, in this case, as long as sufficiently frequent trading is allowed and the volatility is deterministic and exactly known, there is no such thing as a 'lucky' path (see the discussion in Sections 4.3 and 4.4 of Chapter 4): over a finite period of time, if the volatility generating the evolution of the process is known a priori, we can rest assured that the difference between the quantity $\sum_{j=0,N-1}(\ln S_{j+1} - \ln S_j)^2$ and the integral $\int_0^T \sigma(u)^2 \, du$, can be made as small as desired. The important point is that, if one can sample a diffusion with ever increasing frequency over no matter how small a finite interval, in the limit *every single path* possesses exactly the statistical properties of the parent distribution.

As for the requirement, again in the purely diffusive case, that the volatility should be exactly known a priori it is less taxing than it might prima facie appear, given the possibility to enter a vega hedging strategy that can neutralize the trader to first order against changes in the overall level of the volatility, i.e. in the realized sample quadratic variation.

So, if we were happy to limit ourselves to a diffusive setting, the requirement on the quadratic variation would not be onerous at all. However, the approach is designed to deal with apparently much more complex processes. Is the fixed-and-known-quadratic-variation requirement truly compatible with a situation where 'real' jumps are present?

If jumps can occur, the situation changes radically because, given a *finite* trading horizon, the experienced quadratic variation will in general depend on how many jumps (if any) have occurred before option expiry. Increasing the trading frequency does not help in this respect, nor does the perfect knowledge of the deterministic volatility. Therefore, irrespective of the trading frequency, 'lucky' and 'unlucky' paths now *do* exist.

Since we do not know a priori how many jumps will occur over a finite time interval, for the condition on the total quadratic variation to hold one has to assume that the 'diffusive' volatility out to maturity will be higher if no jumps occur, and correspondingly lower if one or more do take place, and in such a perfect way that $\sum_{j=0,N-1}(\ln S_{j+1} - \ln S_j)^2 = v^2$ in all cases. This requirement on the diffusive volatility can be 'non-physical' because, in order to assume the correct value, the volatility prevailing, say, tomorrow would have to 'know' whether a jump will occur five minutes before the option expiry.

The second problem with the BJN approach is that it is difficult to extend the computational approach to the case of non-plain-vanilla options: we emphasized at the very beginning the assumption of the existence of a market in forwards. In the different states sampled by the tree, in fact, one finds the value of the same forward contract, not of the spot price. Note that there is no discounting from one step to the next: indeed, not only does a parent node 'communicate' with states with possibly different values of the residual volatility, v_i; but, even when two connected states have the same residual volatility, this does not mean that the corresponding events have taken place at the same time. Therefore, if one used a spot rather than a forward process, one would not know how to discount value from connected nodes. It is therefore far from obvious how to extend the algorithmic approach to cases where several price-sensitive events occur, or where compound options have to be evaluated.

10.5.3   How Can One Make the Approach More Realistic?

Have we therefore 'wasted our time' looking at the BJN approach? Not at all. In passing, we have revisited the Crouhy–Galai paradox, and understood its origin more deeply. We have also seen how transaction costs and finite trading frequency can be accommodated in a simple and coherent framework. Interesting as these results might be, the most fruitful contribution of the analysis presented in this chapter is however much deeper.

On the one hand we have seen again how fundamental the quadratic variation is to option pricing. For any given maximum jump size, d, nothing else is required in order to arrive at much tighter bounds than can be obtained simply by invoking rational option pricing. As the time-step goes to zero, if the underlying process is a deterministic diffusion, the 'jump' size can be made arbitrarily small (this, indeed, is the essence of a diffusion), and therefore the upper and lower bounds converge to the same value (the Black price).

We have also identified the main conceptual limitation of the approach in its attempt to deal with jumps and *simultaneously* to prescribe a known quadratic variation. However, this observation also shows us how the problem could be overcome. Recall that, given d, knowledge of the quadratic variation is all that is required in order to determine the bounds. In order to overcome the problems arising from the assumed perfect knowledge of the quadratic variation along each path, we could conceptually repeat the same calculations presented above for a *distribution* of possible quadratic variations. The problem we would have to tackle is how to specify the distribution of these quadratic variations. Prima facie, this line of attack does not seem to be very promising, but, in reality, this is exactly what all the modelling approaches that depart from the deterministic–volatility–diffusion paradigm offer. Jump–diffusions, stochastic-volatility models, gamma–variance processes, local-volatility (Derman-and-Kani/Dupire) diffusions, etc. all make the quadratic variation over a finite interval a stochastic quantity. They differ in the way they produce, explicitly or implicitly, the distribution of the quadratic variation. It is instructive to look at these models in this light.

10.5.4   The Link with Stochastic-Volatility Models

Stochastic-volatility models give rise to a distribution of quadratic variations because we do not know a priori which values the volatility will achieve along each path. Let us assume for the moment that the process for the volatility and the process for the underlying are uncorrelated. If this is the case, how would one calculate the value of a call option using the BJN approach? Conceptually one could proceed as follows. One could first run a simulation for the volatility process. To each realization of the volatility one could associate a quadratic variation. Contingent on this quadratic variation having been realized, the path of the underlying stock price is now a pure diffusion. Therefore, as the step size goes to zero, in the BJN approach the maximum 'jump' size, d, goes to zero, and the upper and lower bounds converge to the same value. But we know from the results in the first part of this chapter that this value is simply the Black-and-Scholes price obtained with the root-mean-squared volatility associated with the quadratic variation along that particular path. In order to obtain the option price if the stochasticity in the quadratic variation is due to stochastic volatility, one would therefore simply have to average all these Black-and-Scholes prices over the (risk-neutral) distribution of the quadratic variations. We have already suggested in Chapter 8, and will see in more detail in Chapter 13, that this is exactly the Hull-and-White formula (an integral of Black-and-Scholes prices over the risk-neutral volatility density), at least as long as the stock and volatility processes are independent.

Looking at the problem from this angle, if the process is a stochastic-volatility diffusion do we obtain a unique arbitrage-free price? Or, equivalently, can we hedge perfectly using only the underlying? The situation seems promising because we have an average of infinitely tight bounds (i.e. an average of prices). However, the weights in this average are, in general, not uniquely determined by the stock price sequence. Therefore, unless we know these weights exogenously (how?), there will be not one, but infinitely many, prices.

10.5.5 The Link with Local-Volatility Models

Local-volatility models, which assume a diffusive coefficient of the form $\sigma(S_t, t)$, also produce a stochastic quadratic variation, because one cannot know a priori which path the stock price will follow, and each future stock price realization will produce a different future instantaneous (local) volatility. However, let us choose a sequence of stock prices. Contingent upon this sequence having been realized, the volatility path (and the associated quadratic variation) are known. Furthermore, in the BJN approach we can allow the step size to go zero, and, since we are dealing with a diffusion, with it the jump size, d, can be made to approach zero as well. As in the stochastic-volatility case the upper and lower bounds will converge, on a path-by-path basis, to a single value, namely the Black-and-Scholes price associated with that particular quadratic variation. The overall price for, say, a call, will however be different, because the weight given to the different paths in the averaging over quadratic variations is now different.

Can one hedge perfectly? Is there a unique no-arbitrage price for an option? The answer is 'yes' to both questions, because the 'weight' in the average is now a unique functional of the stock path, and we can therefore in principle 'hedge against' the uncertainty in the realization of the quadratic variation simply using the underlying. In practice, there are much simpler ways to arrive at the option price, but the fact that, in theory, we could associate a probability with the quadratic variation purely based on the price sequence is enough to guarantee that the average of BJN prices will give *the* unique, no-arbitrage price.

10.5.6 The Link with Jump–Diffusion Models

As we discussed above, the possible occurrence of jumps makes the quadratic variation stochastic. Much as in the stochastic-volatility and in the local-volatility models, the jump frequency and the distribution of jump amplitude ratios will produce a different quadratic variation at the end of each path realization.

For the sake of simplicity, let us assume that the stock process undergoes a diffusion superimposed with a jump with a single, fixed and known jump amplitude ratio. If this is the case, there will be a distribution of possible quadratic variations, one corresponding to no jumps, one to a single jump, one to two jumps, ..., one to N jumps having occurred.

It is not difficult to accept that, since we are dealing with a single jump amplitude, this risk-neutral distribution will be a function of the risk-adjusted jump frequency. (See Chapter 14.) If we can associate a (risk-neutral) probability to each of these occurrences we seem to be in a situation similar to the stochastic-volatility case.

However, we are no longer dealing with a diffusion, and, as the time-step in the BJN lattice is made smaller and smaller the maximum jump size, d, cannot be reduced to zero. Therefore the BJN approach will produce *a series of* upper and lower bounds (not a series of prices), each pair associated with a particular quadratic variation. It is not immediately obvious how all these upper and lower bounds can be combined to produce overall bounds, but what is clear is that now the BJN approach will not produce a single price, even if the risk-adjusted distribution of the quadratic variations were exogenously given.

What is the reason for the difference? Unlike the fully-stochastic-volatility or local-volatility cases, even if we know the quadratic variation associated with a given path, because of the possibility of a jump occurring at random times we do not know how to hedge exactly using just the underlying stock. If we attempted replication using just the stock, we might achieve good hedging on average, but not on a path-by-path basis. For this reason, on the one hand perfect replication is not possible, and on the other we are left with bounds, and not with a single price.

What about these bounds? We have seen in this chapter that the separation between the upper and lower bound is a function of the maximum jump size. If we have a finite, non-zero jump frequency there will be a very low but non-zero probability that N jumps will occur, no matter how large one might choose N. The bounds therefore become wider and wider, and recede to the rational-investor (Merton) bounds (the minimum upper bound for a call is just the stock price). In other words, in this case, unless we want to limit the maximum number of jumps (and hence d) the BJN approach would probably not produce particularly tight bounds.

10.6   Conclusions (or, Limitations of Quadratic Variation)

The discussion in the previous section has highlighted that the stochastic nature of the quadratic variation is what characterizes all the 'traditional' models that produce non-flat-across-strikes volatility surfaces. We have also seen, however, that knowing the distribution of the quadratic variation does not tell the whole story. Whether the stochasticity in the quadratic variation occurs because of discontinuous jumps, or by making the diffusion coefficient stochastic, or because of a functional dependence on the price sequence is an important extra piece of information in the specification of a model, which will have deep consequences for the completeness or otherwise of the market. These features will be discussed in Chapters 12, 13 and 14. Is this all there is to smile-producing models? Not quite.

There is another important dimension in the characterization of a model that we have not explored yet: contingent on the stock price having achieved at a future time a given level, are the different (conditional) future realizations of the smile surface just as likely to occur, or is there a correlation between future conditional smiles and future stock price levels (or, more generally, with the whole price sequence)? The question has a fundamental importance, because I will show that, if future smile surfaces were exactly independent of the future level of the stock price, a suitably chosen deterministic-future-smile setting would produce the same prices. We shall look at this question in Chapter 13, and in more detail in Chapter 17.

Admittedly, this way of looking at models can appear unusual: traditional approaches are normally presented in terms of the realism of the underlying assumptions for the evolution of the underlying, analytical tractability, ease of practical implementation, etc. Indeed, I will examine several modelling approaches following this traditional blueprint in the following chapters. This type of model-by-model analysis, however, tends to obscure the fact that, for all their apparent diversity, different models share some very fundamental common features. I believe, therefore, that examining a model through the looking-glass provided by the analysis outlined above can provide a powerful conceptual insight into the structure of a given modelling approach, about some qualitative features of its associated smiles, about what financial features it can naturally account for, and about its possible intrinsic limitations.

Chapter 11

Local-Volatility Models:
the Derman-and-Kani Approach

In the final section of the previous chapter I mentioned that stochastic-volatility and jump–diffusion models are among the most commonly used to model and account for smiles. In the next three chapters I will analyse in some detail the features of stochastic-volatility models. I will focus first on an important subclass, i.e. on the so-called 'restricted-volatility' or local-volatility models, and examine in detail one of their most popular numerical implementations (the Derman-and-Kani/Dupire method).[1] See Chapters 11 and 12. I will then move on to more general stochastic-volatility approaches (Chapter 13). The next two chapters will introduce a discontinuous component to the process (Chapter 14 for jump–diffusion and Chapter 16 for variance–gamma processes).

11.1 General Considerations on Stochastic-Volatility Models

If we require that the process for the underlying should be everywhere continuous, we are basically left with variations on the diffusion theme, i.e. with a description of the stochastic evolution of the price process of the form

$$dS_t = \mu(S_t, t)\, dt + \sigma(S_t, t)\, dz_t \tag{11.1}$$

In Equation (11.1), S_t indicates the value of the price or rate at time t, $\mu(S_t, t)\, dt$ its drift (in the risk-adjusted or in the real world, as appropriate) and $\sigma(S_t, t)$ its volatility.

As far as the volatility term, $\sigma(S_t, t)$, is concerned, there are several modelling alternatives. In order of increasing complexity, the volatility can be described by a deterministic function of time, by a deterministic function of time and of the underlying stock price, or by a stochastic process driven by a variable other than the stock price. This process for

---

[1]Numerical work carried out by Dr James Pfeffer is gratefully acknowledged.

the volatility, in turn, can be of a continuous nature, or discontinuous (see Naik (1993) for an interesting discussion).

If one does not allow for the possibility of jumps in the volatility, a natural description of its time evolution can be given by a process of the form

$$d\sigma(S_t, t) = \mu_\sigma(S, \sigma, t)\, dt + v(S, \sigma, t)\, dw_t \tag{11.2}$$

In Equation (11.2) $\mu_\sigma(S, \sigma, t)$ and $v(S, \sigma, t)$ denote the drift and the volatility of the diffusion coefficient σ, and the Brownian processes $z(t)$ and $w(t)$ are correlated in such a way that

$$E[dz_t\, dw_t] = \rho\, dt \tag{11.3}$$

Once again, in order to keep the notation as simple as possible, we have assumed that a single Brownian shock, $dw(t)$, affects the volatility; the extension to the multi-factor case does not present conceptual difficulties (but does have an impact on the number of instruments needed to complete the market).

Note that, in general, there can be two distinct sources of stochastic behaviour for the volatility σ: the first stems from the functional dependence of σ on the underlying S, which itself is a stochastic quantity. The second is due to the fact that the volatility is allowed to be shocked by a second Brownian motion, $w(t)$, only imperfectly correlated, if at all, with $dz(t)$, as shown in Equation (11.3). Models displaying stochasticity in the volatility originating both from the functional dependence on S and from a separate (possibly Brownian) process will be referred to in what follows as 'fully-stochastic-volatility models'. Models for which the volatility is stochastic only because of their dependence on the underlying will be described as 'restricted-stochastic-volatility models'. The distinction is important, because, as discussed in Chapter 13, a risk-neutral valuation cannot in general be used to obtain a unique option price for fully-stochastic-volatility models, while it can do so in the restricted-stochastic-volatility case. (Since 'restricted-volatility models' is quite a mouthful, when there is no possibility of ambiguity in what follows I will often refer to them as 'local-volatility models'.) The 'restricted' setting is probably the most general set-up that goes beyond the case of a purely deterministic (time-dependent) volatility, and still allows unique pricing by risk-neutral valuation without introducing other hedging instruments apart from the underlying itself (i.e. other options). Therefore with a local-volatility diffusion the risk-neutral evolution for the stock price is given by

$$dS_t = r_t\, dt + \sigma(S_t, t)\, dz_t \tag{11.4}$$

It is important to point out that, while stochastic, the volatility implied by Equation (11.4) displays a perfect functional dependence on the (random) realization of the underlying. In other words, at a given future point in time, the value of the volatility is uniquely determined by the value attained at that point in time by the stock price (or rate) S. One should therefore not forget that the model described by Equation (11.4), while richer than a purely-deterministic-volatility approach, still contains very strong restrictions about the possible values that can be assumed by the volatility.

11.2 Special Cases of Restricted-Stochastic-Volatility Models

Despite the fact that the assumptions behind the stochastic process for the underlying S described by Equation (11.4) are already very strong, further simplifications are sometimes made. The first level of simplification is to assume that the function $\sigma(S_t, t)$ should be separable, i.e. of the form

$$\sigma(S_t, t) = f(S_t)s(t) \tag{11.5}$$

A further simplification is possible if the function $f(s)$ is assumed to be a simple power law:

$$f(S) = S^\beta \tag{11.6}$$

and in this case

$$dS_t = r_t S_t \, dt + S_t^\beta s(t) \, dz_t \tag{11.7}$$

The reason behind introducing these two simplifications are different: with the first approach (Equation (11.5)), one is motivated by the financial desire to disentangle in a transparent way the dependence of the volatility on time from the dependence on the underlying. The motivation for the second approximation (Equation (11.6)) is partly financial and partly computational. From the computational point of view, for $\beta = 0$, $\frac{1}{2}$ or 1 simple explicit closed-form solutions exist. More complex general solutions in terms of modified Bessel functions are also available for an arbitrary coefficient β (see, for example, Reiner (1998)), although these entail infinite sums of gamma functions. Despite its more restrictive nature, decomposition (11.7) does have some financial justification. Indeed, in what follows we will discuss several important cases where this specification might actually provide a plausible description of financial reality. For the moment, however, we will retain the degree of generality afforded by Equation (11.4). For future reference, it is useful to keep in mind that the class of models described by Equation (11.7) is often referred to as constant-elasticity-of-variance (CEV) models.

11.3 The Dupire, Rubinstein and Derman-and-Kani Approaches

Dupire (1993, 1994), Rubinstein (1994) and Derman and Kani (1998) (DK in what follows) (see also Derman *et al.* (1996)) provide tree-based algorithms to extract the function $\sigma(S_t, t)$ from today's quoted prices of a series of plain-vanilla options of different strikes and maturities, under the assumption that the process for the stock price, S, is described by Equation (11.4). Despite the differences in the numerical implementations, the three approaches share the same conceptual foundations. I will therefore deal in detail with what is probably the most common of the three approaches, i.e. the DK, leaving the extension to the other cases as the proverbial exercise for the reader.

Strictly speaking, Rubinstein's, Dupire's and DK's constructions 'only' require that the user should provide the prices of options for the discrete maturities and strikes that correspond to the nodes of their computational lattices. Since, however, in order to obtain results of acceptable numerical quality a very fine space–time mesh is needed, in what follows I will always assume that a continuous price (or implied-volatility) function vs maturity and strike has already been obtained by some numerical means. This task is far from trivial (see Chapter 9), but I will assume that it has been carried out to the trader's satisfaction.

It is also important to point out that Rubinstein's, Dupire's and DK's approaches provide, at the same time, a 'pricing engine' (the calibrated tree), and the local-volatility surface (i.e. the function $\sigma(S_t, t)$). These two 'pricing ingredients', however, are conceptually completely distinct, and an efficient pricing methodology need not provide the most accurate tool to extract the local volatility (or vice versa). I will argue in what follows that this is indeed the case, and that a different procedure to the one proposed by DK can provide a more efficient pricing mechanism once the function $\sigma(S_t, t)$ has been obtained. See Chapter 12. Before attempting to de-couple the extraction of the local-volatility function from the pricing engine, however, the DK procedure will be analysed in detail.

Since their approach depends more fundamentally than the 'usual' bi- or trinomial tree construction on the Green's function formalism, this topic is examined in the following section in the discrete-time, discrete-space framework best suited to the DK approach.

11.4   Green's Functions (Arrow–Debreu Prices) in the DK Construction

Let us place ourselves in a universe where trading only takes place at discrete time intervals, and where only a finite number of states at each possible time-step are reachable. We impose no restrictions on the trading frequency and the number of states, other than that they both have to be finite. As for the characterization of a state at a given time, we will assume that it is fully and uniquely defined by the realization of the price at that point in time. Therefore, speaking of state (j, k) (with the first index referring to the time slice and the second to the state) is exactly equivalent to speaking of the stock price having attained value S_k a time t_j.

Given this set of prices and times, let us construct a recombining trinomial lattice with nodes located corresponding to the trading times and to the possible prices. See Figures 11.1 and 11.2 below. We will also assume that we have already obtained the set of all the probabilities connecting each parent node at time j with its three 'offsprings' at time $j + 1$. The construction of recombining trees is greatly facilitated by the so-called Green's functions (also sometimes referred to as Arrow–Debreu prices). Their use in the context of tree construction and calibration was pioneered by Jamshidian (1991) for interest-rate models. Given their importance, their main properties are reviewed below.

11.4.1   Definition and Main Properties of Arrow–Debreu Prices

Let us make the assumption that a future (time-t) state of the world is fully characterized by the time-t realization of the stock price. We are therefore dealing with a system described by a single Markovian state variable. Let us identify one such future state of the world on a lattice by two indices, the first labelling time and the second the price level. Given a state k and a time j, the Arrow–Debreu price, $G(j, k)$, is then defined to be the price today of a security that pays \$1 if state k is reached at time j, and 0 otherwise.[2] Given two such state–time pairs, (j, k) and (r, s), the Arrow–Debreu price, $G(j, k, r, s)$, $j > r$, is defined to be the price at time r and in state s of a security that pays \$1 if state k is reached at time j, and 0 otherwise. So, in general, an Arrow–Debreu price should have as argument four sets of quantities: two times, and the collections of state variables required to identify the 'initial' and 'final' states. Since we are assuming that a future state is perfectly represented by the realization of the stock price, these state variables collapse to being just the stock price itself.

It is easy to see how to evaluate the price today of a security with a single pay-off time, and with the payoff itself purely dependent on the realization of the stock price. Let us assume that the security in question pays out at time j the amounts $D^k = D(S_j^k), k = 1, 2, \ldots, n$, if the underlying is in state k at time j. If this is the case, by the definition of the Arrow–Debreu price one can write the value of the j-maturity security at an earlier time r contingent on the then-prevailing state of the world (stock price) being s, $PV_j(r, s)$, as

$$PV_j(r, s) = \sum_k D(S_j^k) G(j, k, r, s) \tag{11.8}$$

In particular, if we are interested in the present value today of the payoff, the expression simplifies to

$$PV_j(0) = \sum_k D(S_j^k) G(j, k, 0, 0) = \sum_k D(S_j^k) G(j, k) \tag{11.9}$$

Arrow–Debreu prices are fundamental in asset pricing, because their existence is directly linked to market completeness. Since a market is said to be complete if there exists a security or combination of securities that can provide a certain payoff in each possible future state of the world, and since perfect payoff replication and unique pricing by no-arbitrage are only possible in a complete market, one can see that exact payoff replication and preference-free pricing are both directly linked to the existence of Arrow–Debreu prices.[3]

Furthermore, since their payoffs are unitary, Arrow–Debreu prices can be easily related (*modulo* discounting) to the (risk-adjusted!) probability of reaching state (j, k). If one deals with time-0 Arrow–Debreu prices, $G(j, k, 0, 0)$, these probabilities are unconditional. If the full set of Arrow–Debreu prices, $G(j, k, r, s)$, are known, then also all the conditional probabilities can be obtained. Since a process for the underlying is fully specified by assigning all the unconditional and conditional probabilities, the set of prices $G(j, k, r, s)$ characterize the stochastic evolution of the underlying. When looked at in this light, Arrow–Debreu prices are often referred to as state price densities. See, for example, Cochrane (2001).

From a practical point of view, if we knew the values the Arrow–Debreu prices $G(j, k)$ for all j and k we could immediately evaluate the prices of calls and puts with strikes

---

[2] Arrow–Debreu prices give the 'response' of the 'system' to a 'unit input': by analogy with their counterparts in physics they are therefore also known as 'Green's functions'.

[3] At least as long as the state of the world if fully characterized by the price of a traded quantity.

k expiring at times j. Constructing Arrow–Debreu prices by brute force, however, is no simpler than evaluating the discounted expectations of call or put payoffs. Fortunately, given the very special nature of the payoffs associated with Arrow–Debreu prices, there is a systematic way to 'update' their values at time $j + 1$ if their values at time j are known. How to do this is shown in the next section.

11.4.2   Efficient Computation of Arrow–Debreu Prices

Given a trinomial lattice and an associated set of probabilities we can easily construct a tree of Arrow–Debreu prices. To begin with, by definition $G(0, 0) = \$1$. The Arrow–Debreu prices of securities paying \$1 in any of the nodes at the first time-step are almost as straightforward to determine, as shown in Figure 11.1, where deterministic and constant interest rates have, for simplicity, been assumed: they are given by the discounted probabilities of reaching each of the three nodes at time-step 1. Note in passing that the discounting rate r in Figure 11.1 is actually the difference between the riskless one-period borrowing/lending rate and the (constant) dividend yield in the case of equities, or the difference between the domestic and foreign rate in the case of FX rates.

The construction is slightly more complex for the second time-step, and is shown in Figure 11.2.

To see how the construction is modified in moving from the first to the second time-step, let us now place \$1 at, say, the central node at time-step 2 (i.e. the node reached after a 'down' jump followed by an 'up' jump, or by an 'up' jump and a 'down' jump, or after two 'mid' jumps). Let us call this node the (mid-mid, 2) node, and let us calculate $G(\text{mid-mid}, 2)$. See Figure 11.2. By putting \$1 at node (mid-mid, 2) one obtains a non-zero value at the roots of the upper, the middle and the bottom trinomial subtree originating at time 1. (These first trinomial subtrees are simply made up of the three branches originating from the top, mid and bottom node at time-step 1.) The contribution, for instance, to the node of the uppermost subtree (the one originating from the state 'up') is given by

$$[\$0 * p(\text{up}, \text{up})$$

$$+ \$0 * p(\text{up}, \text{mid})$$

$$+ \$1 * p(\text{up}, \text{down})] * \exp[-r\,\Delta t] \qquad (11.10)$$

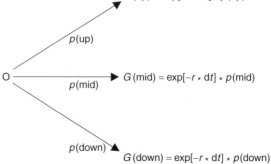

Figure 11.1   The Arrow–Debreu prices for the three states reached at time 1 from the root.

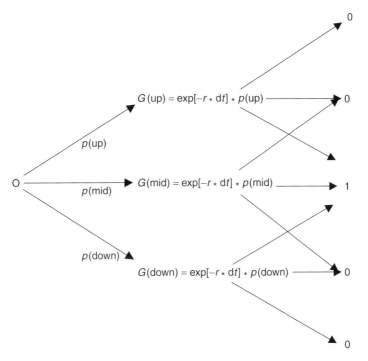

Figure 11.2 Construction of the price of an Arrow–Debreu security paying $1 if the central state at time-step 2 is reached, and $0 otherwise.

This is the value at tree node (up, 1) of $1 placed at node (mid-mid, 2). Similarly, $1 placed in the central node at time 2 will contribute to the central and bottom subtrees as well. We can compute in a similar way the value of $1 placed at (mid-mid, 2) at tree node (mid, 1) and the value of $1 placed at (mid-mid, 2) at tree node (down, 1).

Let us call the three contributions to the three subtrees originating from placing $1 at state (mid-mid, 2) X, Y and Z. Therefore

$$X = [\$0 * p(\text{up, up})$$
$$+ \$0 * p(\text{up, mid})$$
$$+ \$1 * p(\text{up, down})] * \exp[-r\Delta t] \qquad (11.11)$$
$$Y = [\$0 * p(\text{mid, up})$$
$$+ \$1 * p(\text{mid, mid})$$
$$+ \$0 * p(\text{mid, down})] * \exp[-r\Delta t] \qquad (11.12)$$
$$Z = [\$1 * p(\text{down, up})$$
$$+ \$0 * p(\text{down, mid})$$
$$+ \$0 * p(\text{down, down})] * \exp[-r\Delta t] \qquad (11.13)$$

The Arrow–Debreu prices $G(\text{up}, 1)$, $G(\text{mid}, 1)$ and $G(\text{down}, 1)$, however, by definition give the value of a unit payment in states 'up', 'mid' and 'down' at time 1, respectively. Therefore, again given the definition of Arrow–Debreu prices, $G(\text{mid-mid}, 2)$ is equal to

$$G(\text{mid-mid}, 2) = X * G(\text{up}, 1) + Y * G(\text{mid}, 1) + Z * G(\text{down}, 1) \qquad (11.14)$$

The same procedure can be followed for the other nodes at time 2, or, for that matter, for later time-steps. The construction just presented can therefore be generalized, and one can draw the following conclusions:

Conclusion 1 *Once the Arrow–Debreu prices out to time n are known, one can construct all the Arrow–Debreu prices at time $n + 1$ with $O(n)$ operations (in a recombining tree). One does not have to traverse the tree all the way back to the origin again.*

Conclusion 2 *Since there are n time steps, and since obtaining the Arrow–Debreu prices from a given time slice takes $O(n)$ operations, the construction of the whole tree of Arrow–Debreu prices requires $O(n^2)$ computations. A 'naïve' construction whereby each payment is discounted all the way back to the root would require $O(n^3)$ operations. This would soon render the computational cost prohibitive.*

Conclusion 3 *The Arrow–Debreu prices can be used to obtain the value of any security at the origin (i.e. today), provided that the values of this security in all states of the world for which Arrow–Debreu prices are available are known. This property is central to the DK construction.*

It is important to keep in mind that assuming the existence of Arrow–Debreu prices is tantamount to assuming the absence of arbitrage *and* market completeness, and hence risk-neutral pricing (see, for example, Duffie (1996) for a thorough treatment, or Rebonato (1998a) for a relatively short but self-contained discussion). One still has to ask oneself the fundamental question: Are these assumptions actually appropriate to describe the financial problem at hand, or are they leaving out some essential 'ingredients' that would account for the smile shape? This issue is very important, and will be discussed at length later in the chapter.

Finally, note also that the tree recombines. This is computationally expedient, since it avoids the exponential explosion of the number of nodes. This feature is not, however, without its drawbacks, since it greatly reduces the flexibility in the possible values reached by a parent node. This, in turn, is closely linked to the stability of explicit finite differences methods – to which trinomial trees are closely related – and to the failure to obtain positive 'probabilities' emanating from some of the nodes. These two related aspects will also be discussed below.

11.5 The Derman-and-Kani Tree Construction

In order to reproduce exactly the market prices of today's plain-vanilla options, Derman and Kani (1998) recommend a computational procedure based on a trinomial tree. The possible values attainable by the 'stock' price at the different levels and time-steps are arbitrarily pre-chosen. Recombination is ensured by the geometry of the tree. The construction is, in this respect, similar to the explicit finite differences technique: at each node the user has to determine the three emanating probabilities connecting a parent node with its three 'offsprings'. The fundamental difference is that finite differences approaches attempt to find a solution to a partial differential equation (PDE) – typically linear and parabolic for option pricing applications without transaction costs – given the drift and the volatility at each time–space node. In other words, the procedure is akin to a local moment matching, and in the discretization of the various time and space derivatives the local volatility is assumed to be known. Explicit finite differences methods are only conditionally stable, but it is possible and relatively easy to check a priori (i.e. once a given space–time discretization has been chosen) whether a stability violation will be encountered at any of the nodes (see, for example, Ames (1977) and Wilmott (1998)). In the case of the DK construction, however, the local volatilities are a by-product of the algorithm, and, therefore, it is not possible to check beforehand whether any of the nodes will give rise to negative probabilities.

Note carefully that, in discrete-time financial theory (see, for example, Pliska (1997)), absence of arbitrage is linked to the positivity of all the discrete pseudo-probabilities. It is important to stress that the possibility of encountering negative probabilities in the DK algorithmic construction need not entail that the underlying price system produced by a continuous-time, local-volatility process is not arbitrage-free, and might simply reflect the financial arbitrariness of the chosen grid points. In other words, a different length of the time-step, a different positioning of the nodes or a different choice of 'arrival' points could either give rise to or eliminate negative probabilities, without any of the actually traded prices being affected.

11.5.1   Building the First Step

To see how the DK construction is carried out in practice, let us start from the first node (see Figure 11.3).

Three probabilities ($p(\text{up})$, $p(\text{mid})$ and $p(\text{down})$) have to be determined. The usual normalization condition provides the first equation between them:

Equation 1: $p(\text{up}) + p(\text{mid}) + p(\text{down}) = 1$.

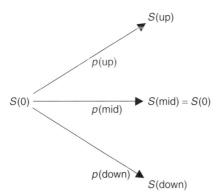

Figure 11.3   The first step of the DK construction, with the stock prices at time 1 denoted by $S(\text{up})$, $S(\text{mid})$ and $S(\text{down})$, and the probabilities connecting today's stock price, $S(0)$, with the three possible values at time 1 denoted by $p(\text{up})$, $p(\text{mid})$ and $p(\text{down})$.

The first moment of S (i.e. the expectation) given its value today is also easily obtainable: a simple no-arbitrage argument shows that it must be equal to the one-period forward value of the stock price given its price today. More generally, when the construction is carried out from a node other than the origin, the first moment-matching condition equates the expectation with the one-period forward price as seen from the parent state:

Equation 2: $S(\text{up})p(\text{up}) + S(\text{mid})p(\text{mid}) + S(\text{down})p(\text{down}) = S(0)\exp[r\Delta t]$.

Note again that, as mentioned earlier, in the Equation 2 above the quantity r denotes the difference between the deterministic short rate and the dividend yield for an equity stock case, or the difference between domestic and foreign rates in the FX case. If the local volatility were known we could at this point simply carry out the usual moment-matching exercise using any of the well-established techniques (see, for example, Nelson and Ramaswamy (1990) or Boyle *et al.* (1994)). In our case, however, we do not have access to the local variance, and this is where DK's method is different from the more traditional approaches.

In order to see how the problem can be overcome, recall that we assumed that the prices of plain-vanilla calls and puts of all strikes and maturities were known. Therefore we know the prices of all calls and puts expiring at time-step, say, 1. In particular, we know, for instance, the price of the call with strike equal to $S(\text{mid})$ (Figure 11.4).

The payoffs of this option in the different states of the world at expiry (i.e. in states 'up', 'down' and mid') are given by:

in state (down) $= 0$
in state (mid) $= 0$
in state (up) $= [S(\text{up}) - S(\text{mid})]$

The Arrow–Debreu price at the origin is, trivially, given by $G(0,0) = 1$. Therefore the model value today of the chosen option, $Opt(\text{mod})$, is equal to

$$Opt(\text{mod}) = \exp[-r\Delta t]$$

$$*\{p(\text{down})*0 + p(\text{mid})*0 + p(\text{up})*[S(\text{up}) - S(\text{mid})]\}G(0,0)$$

$$= p(\text{up})[S(\text{up}) - S(\text{mid})]\exp[-r\Delta t] \tag{11.15}$$

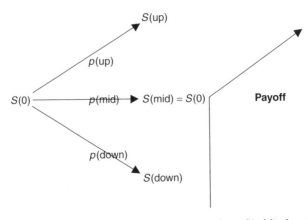

Figure 11.4 The payoff of a call option with strike equal to $S(\text{mid})$ drawn next to the tree construction for the first step.

By imposing that the model and the market prices should be the same,

$$Opt(\text{mod}) = Opt(\text{market}) \tag{11.16}$$

one obtains one equation in one unknown, $p(\text{up})$:

Equation 3: $p(\text{up}) = \dfrac{Opt(\text{market}) \exp[r\,\Delta t]}{[S(\text{up}) - S(\text{mid})]G(0, 0)}.$

This formally closes the set of equations for time-step 1.

A few important numerical comments should be made about the quantity $Opt(\text{market})$. We have assumed in the treatment above that the model value of the option was set equal to the true observed market price of the relative option. This would however introduce an unwanted numerical loss of information, whose origin can be easily understood by noting that at the first time-step we are, after all, evaluating an expectation (which should in principle require integrating from the strike to $+\infty$) using only three sample points. As shown later on, this numerical 'noise' does not disappear or average out for later time-steps, but would give rise, if left 'untreated', to persistent increasing distortions of the local volatility function. DK therefore prefer to set the model price given by the equation above equal not to the true market price, but to the model price obtained with a 'traditional' trinomial tree. More precisely, the quantity $Opt(\text{market})$ above is obtained by pricing the relevant option using a 'traditional' trinomial tree built using no smile, the same state space and a constant volatility equal to the implied volatility of the relevant option. This procedure (similar in spirit to a contravariate technique) attempts to 'purge' out of the DK smiley tree construction the numerical errors originating from the coarseness of the discrete tree. Such errors can therefore be expected to be encountered also in the construction of a 'traditional' trinomial tree. Note, however, that, unlike the DK tree, the latter is built starting from the assumed knowledge of the volatilities. It is therefore not a priori obvious that numerical errors in the constructions of the two trees will be strongly correlated (which is the necessary condition for a contravariate approach to work effectively). As shown in Sections 11.6 and 11.7, this does turn out to be the case, and the procedure proves essential to obtaining numerically acceptable results.

11.5.2 Adding Further Steps

For later time-steps the idea is the same, although there is a slight complication owing to the fact that, as shown below, the model price will be a function not only of one unknown probability, but also of other (already determined) probabilities. It is at this stage that the Arrow–Debreu prices are made use of. More precisely, the algorithm is as follows.

- Consider the first time slice for which probabilities have to be determined.

- Choose as many options expiring at this time slice as the number of nodes minus 2.

- Start from the topmost subtree of the time slice, made up of three branches.

- Choose the first option to be a call and place the strike of the first option exactly at the second node from the top.

- Since, across the whole time slice, only one node has a payoff different from zero (this is the reason why a call with this particular strike was chosen), this will determine the discounted value of the payoff at the parent node in the previous time slice as a function of a single probability.

- Multiply this discounted payoff by the Arrow–Debreu price of the parent node to obtain the model option price today.

- Equating this quantity with the 'market' price of the first out-of-the-money option gives one equation in one unknown.

- Together with the forward-price condition and the probability-normalization condition this equation uniquely determines the three probabilities emanating from the parent node in the previous time slice.

- Move to the second subtree from the top, and add one (call) option with a strike positioned at the middle node of this subtree.

- This option also introduces non-zero payoffs for the subtree above the one being considered, but only adds one unknown probability.

- Multiply the probability-weighted discounted payoffs originating from this option by the appropriate Arrow–Debreu prices at the previous time slice (which have already been determined); in so doing only one new probability is introduced.

- Obtain the model option price, equate it with the 'market' option value and solve for the unknown probability.

- Repeat the same for all the nodes along the time slice.

- Move to the next time slice.

As one can appreciate from the description above, the procedure is conceptually very easy. The only slightly cumbersome aspect is the fact that, as mentioned above, when one moves from the topmost node downwards, the model price becomes a function not only of one unknown probability, but also of one or more of the already determined probabilities for the same time slice. Simple algebraic manipulations give rise to the expressions reported in Derman and Kani (1998) (the symbols have been modified to conform with the notation used above):

$$p_i = \frac{\exp[r\Delta t]C(S_{i+1}, t_{n+1}) - \sum_{j=i+1,2n} G_j(F_j - S_{i+1})}{G_i(S_{i+2} - S_{i+1})} \tag{11.17}$$

$$q_i = \frac{F_i - p_i(S_{i+2} - S_{i+1}) - S_{i+1}}{S_i - S_{i+1}} \tag{11.18}$$

when calls are used, and

$$p_i = \frac{\exp[r\Delta t]P(S_{i+1}, t_{n+1}) + \sum_{j=i+1,2n} G_j(F_j - S_{i+1})}{G_i(S_{i+1} - S_i)} \tag{11.19}$$

$$q_i = \frac{F_i - p_i(S_{i+1} - S_i) - S_{i+1}}{S_i - S_{i+1}} \tag{11.20}$$

when puts are used. In the expressions above, S_{i+2}, S_{i+1} and S_i correspond to $S(\text{up})$, $S(\text{mid})$ and $S(\text{down})$, respectively, in the previous figures; F_i denotes the forward price;

p_i is the 'up' probability emanating from node i at time n; q_i is the 'down' probability emanating from node i at time n; $C(.)$ and $P(.)$ indicate the prices of calls or puts, respectively; and $G(.)$, as before, are the Arrow–Debreu prices.

Despite the fact that, in principle, either a call or a put could be used in the procedure, for practical purposes it is useful to switch option type across the mid point for each time slice so that at-the-money or out-of-the-money options are always used (calls in the top part of the tree and puts in the lower part). If that were not the case one would end up using very deeply-in-the-money options, where the important (time-value-of-money, volatility-related) information is 'swamped' by the uninteresting intrinsic value. Since a long position in a forward contract struck at K plus a long position in a put, also struck at K, is equivalent to a long position in a K-strike call, the simultaneous correct recovery of the forward price and of the out-of-the-money option ensures, by call–put parity, that the in-the-money option will also be automatically correctly priced.

The exposition shows that the method is conceptually simple and elegant, and would appear quite easy to implement. In practice, however, one often encounters serious numerical problems. The main ones are discussed in the following section.

11.6 Numerical Aspects of the Implementation of the DK Construction

The previous section described the general idea behind the DK construction. Its practical implementation, however, can be fraught with difficulties, many of which stem from the fact that the price–time grid is chosen in an 'arbitrary' fashion, i.e. without prior knowledge of the local volatility. This state of affairs gives rise to the numerical problems discussed below. Fixing the first two requires altering the geometry of the tree, whilst the third is partly mitigated by the use of a 'contravariate' parallel tree.

11.6.1 Problem 1: Forward Price Greater Than S(up) or Smaller Than S(down)

This is the case depicted in Figure 11.5. When the forward price is greater than S(up) or lower than S(down) no linear combination of S(up), S(down) and S(mid) with positive

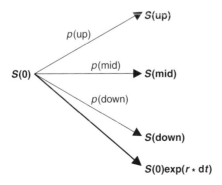

Figure 11.5 The case when the forward price is not 'contained' between S(up) and S(down).

weights can be equal to $S_0 \exp(r \Delta t)$. This is one of the well-known stability problems encountered in the case of the explicit finite differences technique (see Ames (1977)): the method becomes unstable whenever the expectation is greater than the node above $S(\text{up})$ or the node below $S(\text{down})$ at the following time-step. Note that, as mentioned earlier, financially this would imply a possibility of arbitrage; this is, however, only true if the arbitrarily chosen values $S(\text{up})$, $S(\text{down})$ and $S(\text{mid})$ truly were the only possible states reachable from the parent node. In the context of the DK construction, the negative probabilities simply indicate that, given the one-period rate r, the three stock prices at the following time-step do not constitute a suitable discretization of the underlying continuous-time process. Since, as mentioned above, the choice of the grid points is arbitrary, no special financial meaning can be associated to this violation. Finally, note that it is relatively easy to check whether this condition is met at any point in the tree before actually carrying out the construction.

11.6.2   Problem 2: Local Volatility Greater Than $\frac{1}{2}|S(\text{up}) - S(\text{down})|$

The maximum conditional variance that can be calculated from the three values $S(\text{up})$, $S(\text{mid})$ and $S(\text{down})$ is obtained when $p(\text{up}) = p(\text{down}) = \frac{1}{2}$, and $p(\text{mid}) = 0$. It is easy to understand why this should be the case: if there is any probability weight to the middle node this, by necessity, would reduce the overall dispersion, and therefore the variance. Similarly, if the probability of reaching either $S(\text{up})$ or $S(\text{down})$ were greater than $\frac{1}{2}$, one would also have a greater concentration of mass at either node, and therefore, again, a smaller dispersion. Therefore no greater variance can be obtained than for the degenerate case of zero middle probability, and 'up' and 'down' probabilities equal to $\frac{1}{2}$. But, when this is the case, one can easily check that the conditional sample standard deviation is simply given by $\frac{1}{2}|S(\text{up}) - S(\text{down})|$. If this maximum standard deviation 'supported by' the tree construction is not large enough to accommodate the local volatility necessary to price the corresponding option correctly, then at least one of the probabilities must become negative. The result of this is the same as before, i.e. an instability of the associated explicit finite differences scheme. Note carefully again, however, that, unlike the situation with the usual discretizations of PDEs, the local volatilities in the DK construction are not known a priori. Therefore, unlike the case of Problem 1, before building the tree it is not easy to check if the explicit finite differences stability criterion is met. The probability violation on the forward condition can be easily fixed using, for example, non-symmetric or 'abnormal' branching, as first suggested by Hull and White (1990b) in the interest-rate context. Fixing the variance violation is more cumbersome.

11.6.3   Problem 3: Arbitrariness of the Choice of the Strike

The choice of the strike described above gives rise to an algorithm that is motivated by computational rather than financial considerations. In particular, if we want to place strikes exactly on tree nodes, the algorithm described above (with its 'mirror image', whereby one starts from the bottom of the tree) allows us to solve explicitly for one probability at a time. Any other positioning of the same number of strikes would in general require solving a series of 3×3 linear systems.

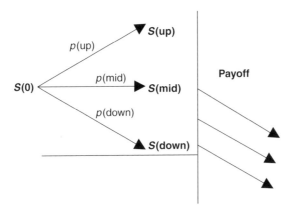

Figure 11.6 The trinomial tree, with different possible values for the strike, still giving rise to a single equation in a single unknown.

It is also possible, however, to retain the simplicity of a one-unknown–one-equation problem by placing the strike not exactly at the middle node, but at any (more out-of-the-money) position located for a put between the middle and the down node. See Figure 11.6. This simple observation gives further insight into the role played by the replacement of the true market prices with the corresponding model value obtained using the 'traditional' trinomial tree. Consider, in fact, the effect of moving the strike progressively more out-of-the-money without crossing the next node. The payoff would change linearly, and multiplication of this discounted payoff by the same Arrow–Debreu price at the parent node would give a purely linear variation in the model option price. We know, however, that, in reality, a 'true' (i.e. Black) one-period option is not a linear function of the strike. If one fitted a model price to the corresponding true call or put market price (as opposed to the 'control' market price) one would pollute the estimation of the local volatility simply because of the numerical failure of the 'naïve' algorithm to capture the correct convexity. Therefore, if one used the 'naïve' Derman-and-Kani approach with, say, a flat (no smile) volatility surface, and one moved the position of the strikes as described above, and shown in Figure 11.6, one would obtain a non-flat local volatility. This numerical effect becomes smaller and smaller as the number of time-steps increases. If, however, the DK model is implemented in this naïve manner (which the authors do not recommend), the speed of convergence can be empirically observed to be very slow.

We have already briefly seen how this problem can be solved. Let us look at the solution in more detail. For each option, one can construct in parallel a trinomial tree with exactly the same geometry, i.e. number of nodes and choice of possible states, but with a deterministic volatility. By analogy with Monte Carlo techniques, this is called the 'contravariate' tree. If an option is considered in isolation, there always is at least one deterministic-volatility function that prices it exactly (e.g. the constant volatility equal to the implied volatility). The price of the 'shadow' market option obtained with the contravariate tree would therefore in theory converge to the true market price. For a finite tree, however, the shadow price will in general display a certain deviation from the true market price. If one then uses the local-volatility trinomial tree as described above but equates the model price that it produces with the pseudo-market price obtained using the contravariate (deterministic-volatility) trinomial tree, the convexity effect almost completely disappears (see the tests below), showing the effectiveness of the recommended procedure.

Summarizing the discussion so far, I have presented in this section some of the fundamental technical features of the implementation of the DK approach. The reader is referred to DK's paper (1998 and references therein) for worked-out numerical examples of the construction, which are therefore not repeated here. Instead, in what follows I present some detailed and specific tests of the implementation of the DK approach in different input regimes (e.g. flat or time-dependent implied volatilities, simple linear smiles, etc.), with a view to assessing the flexibility and robustness of the model in realistic pricing conditions.

11.7   Implementation Results

11.7.1   Benchmarking 1: The No-Smile Case

The first test to which the DK method can be put is the pricing of options in the absence of any smiles or time dependence for the implied volatility function, with and without the fitting to the 'control' market prices (as described previously). With these inputs the derived local volatilities can only be everywhere flat, and equal to the implied volatility. For the purpose of this test, the DK construction was carried out both by fitting to the prices produced by a traditional (i.e. constant-volatility) reference trinomial lattice as explained above, and by fitting directly to the 'true' market prices.

Figure 11.7 shows the local volatility that would be obtained if, instead of using the 'reference tree', one naively fitted to the true market prices. To begin with, the resulting

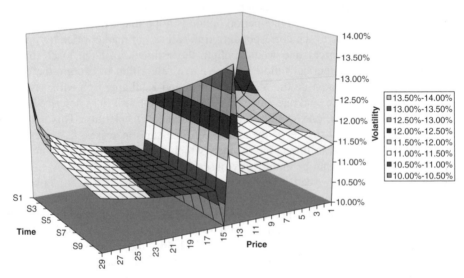

Figure 11.7   This local volatility has been obtained with time-independent volatility and no smile and fitting to the true (Black) market prices rather than the proxy trinomial market prices, as explained in the text. The solution should be a flat local volatility everywhere. The figure displays the last 10 time slices of the tree, as explained in Figure 11.10. (Numerical details: interest rate 5.00%, dividend rate 0.00%, volatility 11.00%, spot 6104.236, number of time-steps 24, time to expiry 1 year.)

local-volatility surface is far from flat on the 'wings'. But, more noticeably, it also displays a large 'jump' in the central section; this corresponds to the switch from calls to puts. Note carefully that the magnitude of this effect does not die away for later and later time-steps, but actually increases in magnitude. No such effect is present when the option prices are obtained using the contravariate technique recommended by DK, i.e. when the prices produced by a flat-volatility trinomial tree are used instead of the true market price. Looking at the poor quality of the results obtained even in this simplest of tests using the 'naïve' procedure, one can conclude that fitting to the proxy trinomial tree option prices, rather than to actual observed market prices, is a must, rather than a nice-to-have feature, in order to obtain reasonable local-volatility surfaces. All the tests in the following will therefore only deal with trees constructed using the recommended procedure.

11.7.2 Benchmarking 2: The Time-Dependent-Volatility Case

The next test is to explore how well the DK approach copes with an input implied volatility surface that displays pure time dependence. See Figure 11.8. As we have seen in Chapter 3, if the implied volatility only depends on the time to maturity, one can always price the market options by means of a time-dependent instantaneous volatility, which does not depend on the price of the stock. Note also that this solution is unique.

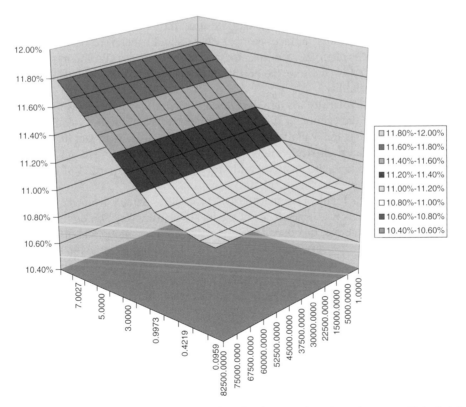

Figure 11.8 The input implied volatility surface for the pure time-dependent case. Note that the points on the maturity axis are not on a linear scale, and therefore the gradient of the implied volatility function vs expiry is monotonically decreasing.

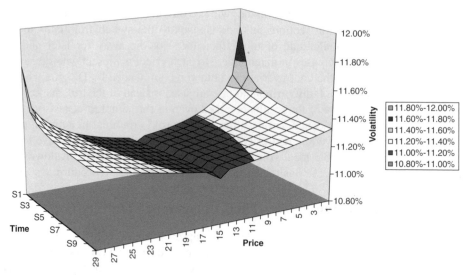

Figure 11.9   The resulting local volatility obtainable from the input implied volatility surface shown in Figure 11.8. The height of the rectangle in Figure 11.10 is 29 steps.

If the DK procedure worked perfectly, and we used the prices from a purely maturity-dependent implied volatility surface as input, there should therefore be no dependence at all on the stock level in the resulting local volatility surface. Furthermore, the time dependence recovered by the tree should match the one admissible time dependence for the instantaneous volatility.

The input implied volatility fed into the DK construction as a test displayed a very mild (and decreasing, see the caption of Figure 11.8) gradient of the implied volatility function as a function of expiry: the overall increase in implied volatility is in fact little more than 1% over 9 years. The numerical results for the local volatility surface are displayed in Figure 11.9, which shows the local volatility for the rectangular portion of the trinomial tree schematically shown in Figure 11.10.

It is apparent from Figure 11.9 that the DK procedure extracts from the input option prices a clear (and spurious) dependence of the local volatility function on the stock price. From the discussion above, this dependence must be a purely numerical artefact. This is not very worrisome at the very edges of the picture (which, as discussed in the caption to Figure 11.10, have very low probabilities of occurrence), but more so in the middle and intermediate regions. For the very 'mild' input implied volatility surface chosen, the effect appears rather small, but, for more pronounced (and more realistic) time dependencies it quickly becomes significantly greater.

11.7.3   Benchmarking 3: Purely Strike-Dependent Implied Volatility

The 'twin' test to which the DK methodology can be subjected consists of giving as input the option prices obtained from a purely strike-dependent implied volatility surface, as displayed in Figure 11.11. Note that, once again, in order to obtain numerically stable results, a very 'mild' smile surface (less than 0.50% in volatility from 0 to 90 delta) was used as input. The corresponding local volatility is shown in Figure 11.12. The

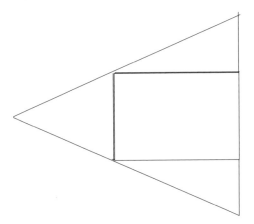

Figure 11.10 The triangle indicates the boundaries of the trinomial tree. The local volatility in the area inside the rectangle is then shown in Figures 11.7, 11.9, 11.12, 11.14 and 11.16. Note that values of the local volatilities close to the top and bottom of the left-hand vertical side of the rectangle have a much lower probability of occurrence than values towards the centre, or than values along the top or bottom horizontal sides towards the right-hand part of the rectangle.

surface obtained is qualitatively very similar to the purely time-dependent case. Once, again, the 'whiskers' at the top and bottom left edges of the rectangle are neither very meaningful, nor particularly worrisome. Comparing this surface with the local-volatility surface obtained with a purely time-dependent implied volatility, the user would be rather hard-pressed in deciding which has been produced by which (apart, perhaps, from a small change in convexity between the two curves). Since we know that, for the purely time-dependent case, any price dependence is a pure artefact, and we find a dependence of the local volatility on the stock price of similar magnitude in the pure stock-dependence case, we can legitimately wonder how much of the resulting structure is 'signal' and how much numerical 'noise'. The way to answer this question, of course, would be to repeat the tests after increasing the dependence of the input implied volatilities on time to maturity and/or strike. It is not easy to do so, however, without encountering serious numerical problems. DK do recommend (cumbersome and not sure-proof) ways around these problems, but, rather than pursuing this avenue, in the next chapter we will present a more efficient way to obtain the local-volatility surface.

11.7.4 Benchmarking 4: Strike-and-Maturity-Dependent Implied Volatility

Finally, the tests reported in Figures 11.13–11.18 deal with the case where the implied volatility surface depends on both strike and maturity, either for a milder (Figures 11.13 and 11.14) or a more pronounced case (Figures 11.15–11.17). For Figures 11.13 and 11.14 the qualitative shape is, once again, quite similar, and the only noteworthy feature seems to be a change in the convexity of the resulting local volatility in going from the purely time-dependent implied volatility input (convex), to the smile-dependent case (roughly flat) to the mixed time-dependent/smiley case (concave). It is far from certain whether anything meaningful should be read into this behaviour, since, as we pointed out,

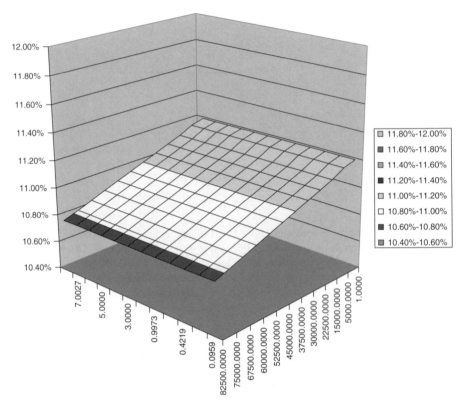

Figure 11.11   The input implied volatility surface for the pure smile case. Note that the points on the strike axis are on a linear scale, apart from the last two. Therefore the gradient of the implied volatility function vs strike is constant in the region of interest, and monotonically decreasing below a strike of 1500. Given the at-the-money value for the strike, equal to 6104, the gradient can be considered, for all intents and purposes, flat.

we know that at least in one case the effect is a pure artefact. In order to explore whether this trend in convexity is systematic the results for the more pronounced mixed input case of Figure 11.15 are shown in Figures 11.16 and 11.17. These refer to the areas depicted in the two rectangles in Figure 11.18.

Note the change in convexity and the increase in the magnitude of the central 'trough' in moving from shorter to longer times (i.e. from the small to the large rectangle). This latter effect, which is certainly a numerical artefact, for long maturities becomes of the same approximate magnitude as the gradient in the input volatility curve.

11.7.5   Conclusions

From these empirical observations it seems fair to conclude that the DK construction is conceptually simple and appealing, but that, at the very least, requires a 'delicate' numerical implementation. As the authors themselves indicate (see, for example, DK (1998)) there are indeed ways to try to fix these problems. These 'solutions' however are far from straightforward and cannot be guaranteed to work in all realistic pricing environments. Overall, the picture has been so clouded by numerical difficulties that we

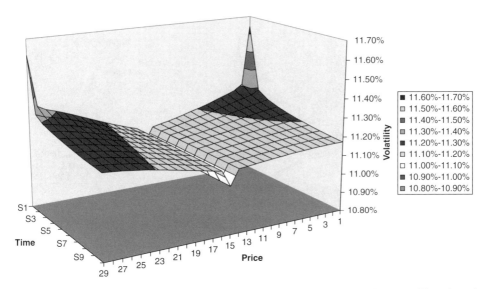

Figure 11.12 The local volatility surface obtained from the input implied volatility given in Figure 11.11. The area displayed is again shown by the rectangle in Figure 11.10.

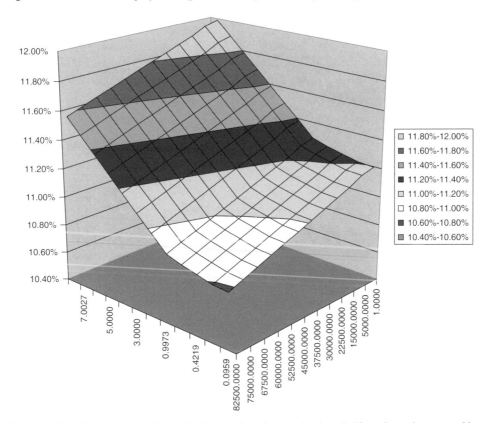

Figure 11.13 The input implied volatility surface for a mixed smile/time-dependent case. Note that the points on neither axes are on a linear scale, and therefore the gradient of the implied volatility function vs both strike and maturity is monotonically decreasing.

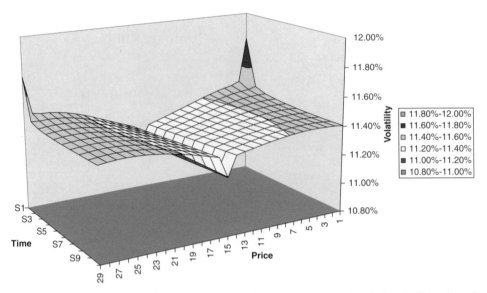

Figure 11.14   The local volatility surface obtained from the input implied volatility given in Figure 11.13. The area displayed is again shown by the rectangle in Figure 11.10.

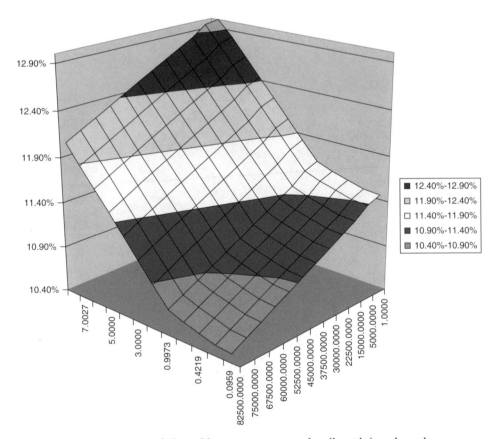

Figure 11.15   As Figure 11.13, but with a more pronounced smile and time dependence.

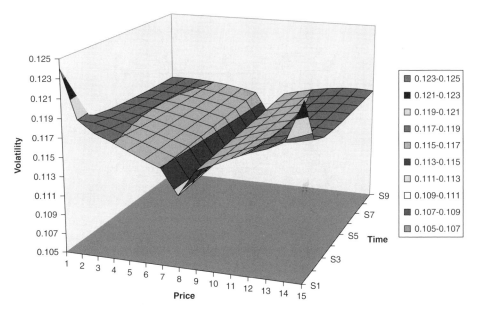

Figure 11.16 The local volatility surface obtained from the input implied volatility given in Figure 11.15. The area displayed is shown by the small rectangle in Figure 11.18.

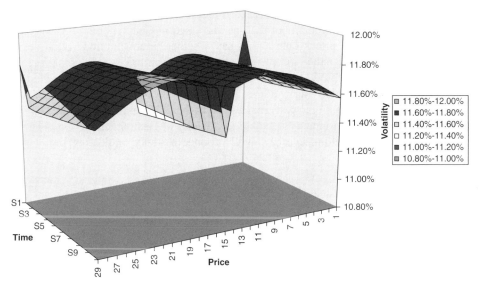

Figure 11.17 The local volatility surface obtained from the input implied volatility given in Figure 11.15. The area displayed is shown by the large rectangle in Figure 11.18.

have not even begun to assess to what extent the local-volatility approach could provide, if implemented in a numerical stable way, a viable and convincing explanation of the financial mechanisms responsible for smiles in different markets. In particular, we have not been able to test whether the future smile surface implied by a local-volatility model is sticky, floating or other in nature. The difficulty of disentangling numerical noise from

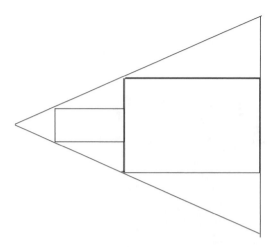

Figure 11.18   The two areas of the trinomial tree shown in Figures 11.16 and 11.17.

the financial signal has stood in the way of such an analysis. A completely different line of approach is therefore presented in the next chapter. The method that I will present can produce results of sufficient numerical quality that an assessment of the financial content of the restricted-stochastic-volatility approach finally becomes possible.

Finally, it is important to remember that, as discussed in Chapters 6 and 8, simply by looking at today's option prices one cannot say whether future implied volatilities are sticky or floating in nature, since the current observed option prices are compatible with both pictures of reality. Observation in the real world of changes in implied volatilities after movements of the underlying would in principle allow one to discriminate between the two 'world pictures'. But how can one check whether a given local volatility function or, more generally, a given model gives rise to a sticky or floating smile? One can only tell whether a given modelling approach will produce a sticky or floating future smile surface by

- positioning oneself at a series of future time–price states;

- evaluating model prices from these new time–price origins;

- obtaining the future conditional implied volatilities; and

- comparing them with today's observable market smile surface.

Once again, the degree of numerical noise present in the DK approach advises against undertaking this type of analysis using the DK tree. The issue of the nature of the smile implied by the DK local-volatility process is however fundamental and will therefore be dealt with in detail in the conceptually identical, but numerically superior, approach presented in the next chapter. Before embarking on this task, however, it is useful to discuss why the simple procedure proposed by Derman and Kani, and Dupire, is intrinsically prone to numerical instabilities. This topic is addressed in the following section.

11.8 Estimating Instantaneous Volatilities from Prices as an Inverse Problem

In physics and applied mathematics two problems are often described as 'direct' and 'inverse', or inverse to each other. See, for example, Engl (1993). Typically, if one wants to predict the future evolution of a process or physical system given its present state and a knowledge of the parameters that describe its dynamics, the problem is said to be 'direct'. The associated 'inverse' problem consists of imputing the parameters of the process from its future evolution (e.g. from a set of future marginal densities). Loosely speaking, direct problems deal with finding the effects of known causes, and inverse problems are often concerned with identifying causes from observed effects. For example, determining the heat distribution at a future time given initial conditions and the diffusion coefficients is a direct problem, while deducing the diffusion parameters from a future heat distribution constitutes the associated inverse problem. In a financial context, the most obvious application of these concepts is in the estimation of the instantaneous volatility given a set of prices for plain-vanilla instruments and an assumed process for the underlying.

One salient feature of inverse problems is that very often they do not satisfy the conditions for being 'well-posed'.[4] In particular, either the uniqueness or the continuous dependence of the solution on the input data often fail to be satisfied. Traders who have tried to fit the local-volatility models of Dupire (1994), Derman and Kani (1998) and Derman *et al.* (1996) to market data will be familiar with these problems.

There are well-established ways to tackle this problem, which can be broadly described under the umbrella term of 'regularization', and of which Tikhonov's approach is one of the most common. When the 'physical' qualitative nature of the solution is not known a priori, a common feature of these techniques is to reduce or constrain its high-frequency components, and there exists a copious literature in this area (see again Engl (1993)).

An alternative, and, when applicable, more powerful approach to regularization is to require that the solution should belong to a class of functions identified on the basis of the modeller's understanding of the financial or physical characteristics of the problem. This is, for instance, the approach taken in the interest-rate arena by Rebonato (2002) in his choice of the instantaneous volatility functions of forward rates.

In the equity case, a possible regularization might be obtained by making use of the empirical information about the dependence of the implied volatility on the underlying. See, for example, Derman (1999), Alexander (2001) and the discussion in Chapter 7. The task is not trivial, because market data provide information about *implied* volatilities, while what we need is a functional dependence for the *local* volatility. 'Inspired guesses', however, are not difficult to come by, and indeed Alexander (2001) offers one such possible dependence by arguing that the local volatility should be of the form

$$\sigma(S, t) = b^i(t)S + c(t) \tag{11.21}$$

---

[4]A problem is said to be well-posed if

- for all admissible input data, a solution exists;
- for all admissible input data the solution is unique; and
- if there is continuous dependence of the solution on the input data.

This is the so-called 'Hadamard definition'. See Engl (1993).

where the coefficient $b^i(t)$ (with i = range-bound, trending or jumpy), jumps between three different levels:

$$b^i(t) = 0, \quad \text{if} \quad i = \text{range-bound} \tag{11.22}$$

$$b^i(t) = -b_0, \quad \text{if} \quad i = \text{trending} \tag{11.23}$$

$$b^i(t) = b_0, \quad \text{if} \quad i = \text{jumpy} \tag{11.24}$$

(with b_0 a constant) according to the prevailing regime, as discussed in Chapter 7. Apart from the reservations about the analysis expressed in the same chapter, one should note that the local volatility now becomes non-Markovian, since by itself knowledge of the current value of the volatility does not tell us whether we are in a range-bound, trendy or jumpy regime (such information is contained in the history up to today).

In order to keep the modelling simple, one could abandon the rather complex regime-dependent specification of the coefficient $b(t)$, and simply posit a power-law dependence of the local volatility on the underlying (of which the equation above is clearly a particular case). However, in this case a simple change of variables can provide a much simpler solution, while retaining a Black-like setting (and closed-form expressions for calls and puts): this can be obtained, for instance, using a displaced-diffusion setting (where $S + a$ is assumed to be log-normally distributed – see Chapter 16); or by moving to a CEV approach, where the absolute volatility is assumed to be of the form

$$\sigma(S, t) = S^\beta \sigma(t) \tag{11.25}$$

Summarizing:

1. Without some regularization it is difficult to obtain numerically robust results from the DK procedure.

2. If the regularization is done without recourse to financial information (i.e. by trimming the high-frequency components) the data are allowed to 'speak for themselves'. (Whether what they 'say' makes sense or not, depends of course on whether the model is correctly specified or not.)

3. If the regularization is carried out making use of financial information, the approach often leads to some imperfect[5] but very simple solutions – so simple, in fact, that totally different avenues (e.g. starting from displaced diffusions or CEV models) can provide a much more effective solution to the numerical problem.

These observations do not rule out the possibility that, if the data were allowed to 'speak for themselves' and a suitable regularization procedure were employed, the current market data might give useful information about the dependence of the local volatility on the underlying more complex than what is allowed by a power law. This is a priori plausible because, after all, any non-monotonic dependence of the volatility on the underlying cannot be captured by a power law as in (11.25). In the next Chapter I will therefore look in detail at the dynamic behaviour of smile surfaces when the local volatility is derived from a particular market-information-independent regularization procedure.

---

[5]By 'imperfect' I mean that the market prices for the plain-vanilla options might be imperfectly recovered.

Chapter 12

Extracting the Local Volatility from Option Prices

12.1 Introduction

We have seen in the previous chapter that the Derman-and-Kani tree offers a conceptually elegant solution to the problem of pricing options in the presence of restricted-stochastic-volatility smiles, and of obtaining the local-volatility surface. I have also argued that, in the computational form in which it is normally presented, it is prone to numerical difficulties and gives rise to very 'noisy' estimates of the local volatility surface. I showed that part of the problem stems from the very fact that we do not know a priori the second (local) moment of the variable whose process is to be mapped onto the tree. This makes it difficult to check whether the (a priori arbitrary) choice of the computational grid will, in the end, turn out to be appropriate to handle the problem at hand. In addition I pointed out that, even for mildly time-dependent volatilities, or for shallow smiles, the algorithm can easily fail to find a feasible solution, or tends to produce rather implausible shapes for the local volatility surface. More generally, I discussed the concept of inverse problems, and argued that recovering a local-volatility surface from quoted prices is indeed one instance of this problem. In the absence of a regularization procedure, attempts at 'brute-force' solutions of inverse problems tend to lead to the type of noisy outcomes that we saw in the previous chapter.

Derman and Kani recommend a wealth of numerical 'tricks' to circumvent some of the problems (see, for instance, the references in Derman and Kani (1998)). However, these remedies are either cumbersome or not very effective. See, for example, Barle and Cakici (1995). This is probably because ultimately they fail to address the issue of the regularization of an inverse problem alluded to above. Therefore, unless we tackle this problem, there is little hope for substantial improvements.

345

12.1.1   A Possible Regularization Strategy

One possible regularization technique is proposed in this chapter.[1] It is not based on frequency trimming of the local volatility 'signal', or on a financially-motivated assumption for the functional form of the local-volatility function. Instead, it relies on the idea of using as input a 'deeply' smooth[2] implied volatility surface, and of calculating the local volatility directly from a numerical estimate of the derivatives in the Fokker–Planck equation (see Equation (12.5) below). The smooth surface can be obtained using any of the techniques based on the modelling of the risk-neutral densities described in Chapter 9.

This technique provides a simple and useful alternative to the construction of a tree such as Derman and Kani's. I will argue in fact that, for the specific purpose of extracting the future volatility of the underlying process, it is numerically faster, much more stable and better-behaved than the trinomial tree methodology. Furthermore, if properly implemented, this technique is virtually guaranteed to fail only if 'true' arbitrage opportunities exist among the input prices. In this context, it is essential to note the qualifier 'true', which indicates that the arbitrage violations are not an artefact of the numerical procedure, but really indicate the presence of an arbitrage possibility in the market prices – see the discussions in Section 11.6 about this point.

12.1.2   Shortcomings

It is important to point out two possible shortcomings of the proposed procedure.

First of all, unlike the Derman-and-Kani procedure, it does not automatically provide a pricing engine, and the information about the local volatility must therefore be coupled with a separate valuation algorithm. Direct availability of the local volatility makes Monte Carlo an obvious choice for the latter. Other techniques could, however, be employed, such as the explicit or implicit finite differences schemes (implemented, this time, in the 'traditional' way, i.e. starting from the knowledge of, rather than obtaining as a by-product, the state-dependent variances). In particular, the explicit finite differences method can be particularly well-suited to the task of calculating options by backward induction, given its ability to cope in a robust manner with the case when the coefficients are either time- or state-dependent (see Wilmott (1998)). Irrespective of the method chosen, the important point is that the approach presented below conceptually de-couples the two distinct aspects of option pricing in the presence of smiles, i.e. (i) the extraction from the market prices of the underlying process, and (ii) the evaluation of the necessary expectations from the resulting distributions.

The second, and potentially more serious, shortcoming is that the proper functioning of the approach hinges on the input implied volatility surface being sufficiently smooth. This is often not a problem; indeed, the quality of a simple cubic fit to a market smile ($R^2 = 0.99$ for S&P500, March 2001) leads Ait-Sahalia (2002) to wonder whether 'some degree of self-fulfilling prophecies' might be 'at play here'. However, this cannot be guaranteed always to be the case. If the static fit to the market prices were poor, one

---

[1]Other approaches are possible which do not make explicit use of any regularization. See, for example, Andersen and Brotherton-Ratcliffe (1998).

[2]By 'deeply smooth' I mean an implied volatility function that is not just smooth in itself, but is obtained from a set of risk-neutral densities which are themselves smooth. The reason for this requirement will become apparent when we look at Equation (12.9).

might argue that some important piece of information has been left out of the picture, and that the overall results might be compromised by this. The analysis of the flexibility of the mixture-of-log-normals approach presented in Chapter 9 suggests that this will rarely be the case. In my experience, I have very rarely found this to be a serious problem.

12.2   The Modelling Framework

The set of assumptions necessary in order to implement the method presented below coincides with the assumptions underlying the Derman-and-Kani approach. They are briefly reported in what follows in a concise form not only for clarity and for ease of reference, but also from a slightly different angle, i.e. from the point of view of the conceptual links between local and implied volatilities. These assumptions are as follows:

Assumption 1 *The process for the underlying stock is of the form*

$$\frac{dS_t}{S_t} = \mu(S_t, t)\, dt + \sigma(S_t, t)\, dz(t) \tag{12.1}$$

Note that the time-t value of the instantaneous volatility term $\sigma(S_t, t)$ has been allowed to depend at most on time, and on the realization of the underlying process at that particular point in time. As mentioned in the previous chapter, the function $\sigma(S_t, t)$ is a deterministic function of a stochastic quantity (S_t) and time. A few comments are in order.

To begin with, the process (12.1) for the underlying cannot depend in any way on the strike at which we might have chosen to transact our option: the same process for the underlying must be used to price options with different strikes, and cannot therefore contain any strike-specific information. An implied volatility, on the other hand, can depend on strike, because it is just a short-hand way to quote a price. It might be useful to recall again the definition of implied volatility given in Chapter 6 as 'the wrong number to put in the wrong formula to obtain the right price'. With the procedure presented in this section, we are therefore trying to find the strike-independent local volatilities that can reproduce the market-implied strike-dependent implied volatilities. There is nothing magic in the process: as we have already pointed out, strike-dependent implied volatilities are not true volatilities. See also the comments below.

The second observation is that in Equation (12.1) there is one single source of risk, hedgeable by trading in the underlying stock, S. As pointed out in Section 8.1, this implies that, according to the model, the market is complete, and that, therefore, a risk-neutral valuation will yield a unique price for an option on S. Whether this is the case in reality is, of course, a different matter.

Another way to look at this is to recognize that there is a perfect functional relationship between the future level of the stock price and the value of the future local volatility. At a given point in time, if the value of S is known, then the volatility is perfectly known as well. It is a special (limiting) case of the stochastic volatility class. See again the discussion at the beginning of Section 8.1. To make progress towards the estimation of the local volatility surface (if we assume this process to hold) we must impose some requirements on the market implied volatilities.

Assumption 2 *We assume to know today the prices of plain-vanilla options for a continuum of strikes and maturities. These prices are quoted in terms of implied Black volatilities,* $\widehat{\sigma}(K, T)$.

Assumption 3 *We assume that the function* $\widehat{\sigma}(K, T)$ *is at least twice-differentiable in strike and once-differentiable in maturity.*

In reality we only know option prices at discrete maturities and strikes. For computational purposes we must therefore create a smooth and differentiable surface expressing the implied volatility as a function of strike and maturity. For reasons that will become apparent later on, this implied volatility surface is required to be smooth enough to allow for continuous derivatives of the call price function with respect to the strike up to second order, and with respect to maturity up to first order, included. Note that, despite the fact that we suggested the use of a 'smooth' price function in order to carry out the Derman-and-Kani tree construction, the implied volatility surface was nowhere required to display the continuity of derivatives required in this case. We shall prove below (see Equation (12.9)) that, if the implied volatility surface is not sufficiently smooth and differentiable, discontinuities must occur in the local volatility. Since the approach presented in this chapter and the Derman-and-Kani model are conceptually totally equivalent, the observation that the Derman-and-Kani approach neither requires nor 'knows about' the continuity of these derivatives sheds some interesting light on the origin of the numerically unsatisfactory results we observed in the previous chapter.

Recall again that implied volatilities are simply a short-hand notation to quote a price. Since, for the process described by Equation (12.1), the Black formula in general no longer provides a solution of the fundamental partial differential equation (PDE) (Equation (12.3)) shown below with the call–put boundary conditions, we can no longer impose a simple link between the implied volatility and the root-mean-squared volatility of the process. Therefore

$$\widehat{\sigma}(0, T)^2 T \neq \int_0^T \sigma(S_u, u)^2 \mathrm{d}u \tag{12.2}$$

In other words, if the process is of the form (12.1), implied Black volatilities are not volatilities at all (neither instantaneous nor average).

It is important to point out that time-homogeneity can be a property of implied volatilities and of local volatilities, but stickiness or floatiness of the smile can only be properties of the implied Black volatilities, not of the instantaneous (local) volatilities. It is a priori impossible to tell, from inspection of the local volatility function, whether the resulting future smile will be, for instance, floating or sticky. The only sure-proof way to determine the nature of the future smile is

1. to obtain, by whatever method, the local-volatility surface consistent with today's observed market prices;

2. to calculate future plain-vanilla option prices using the local-volatility surface thus estimated;

3. to obtain the implied Black volatility from these prices;

4. to observe whether the resulting future implied volatility surface displays or lacks any of the features we might deem desirable (time-homogeneity, stickiness, forward propagation, etc.).

The calculation of future option prices can be accomplished in many ways: for instance, by constructing a computational tree, and by using a node in the future as the new 'root' to compute the option prices; or, perhaps, by using a Monte Carlo simulation started at a future point in time, τ, for an arbitrary value of the underlying, S_τ, and with a volatility function given by $\sigma(S_t, t), t \geq \tau$. Note that, from each node in the tree, or from each possible future value of the stock, S_τ, there originates a full implied volatility structure. It is these implied volatility surfaces that can then be compared across times to maturity and across strike levels to determine, for instance, whether they are time-homogeneous and/or sticky or floating.

12.3 A Computational Method

12.3.1 Backward Induction

Having clarified these points, I present an alternative method to extract the local-volatility surface. Let us denote the set of plain-vanilla options (calls) by $C_{K,T}(t, S)$. This symbol denotes the price of a call

- evaluated at time t

- when the stock price at time t has value S

- when the strike is K and

- when the maturity of the option is T.

Since a risk-neutral valuation is still possible, we know that, even if the Black-and-Scholes formula may no longer apply, the call price still satisfies the fundamental Black-and-Scholes PDE:

$$\left[\frac{\partial}{\partial t} + (r - d)S\frac{\partial}{\partial S} + \frac{1}{2}\sigma_{S,t}^2 S^2 \frac{\partial^2}{\partial S^2} - r \right] C_{K,T}(t, S) = 0 \qquad (12.3)$$

where d is the dividend yield, $\sigma_{S,t}$ is the state-and-time-dependent volatility, $C_{K,T}(t, S)$ indicates the value at time t of a K-strike, T-expiry call when the underlying has value S, and all the other symbols have the usual meaning. Equation (12.3) is known as the backward (Kolmogorov) equation, since it tells us how the option price propagates backwards in time. In order to use this equation one needs to know the distribution of option prices at a given future time. Typically the user will know this price distribution at expiry (the 'initial' condition). This choice is no coincidence: even if we disagree about the model for the underlying, we must all agree about the option price at maturity (i.e. its terminal payoff). Therefore, choosing as the future point in time, T, the option expiry has the advantage of providing an unambiguous and model-independent choice for the value of the option itself. If, however, one knew the prices of the option $C_{K,T}(t, S)$

at a generic time $\tau < T$, one could still work one's way backwards to today's price using Equation (12.3). This equation therefore constitutes the natural starting point for the discretization of those approaches that rely on backwards induction (i.e. tree-based or finite-differences-based methodologies).

If we knew the values of the derivatives in Equation (12.3) we could combine this knowledge with the observation of today's option prices, $C_{K,T}(t, S)$, and solve for the only unknown, i.e. the local volatility. The problem with Equation (12.3), however, is that we do not know a priori an analytic solution of the PDE for the option price $C_{K,T}(t, S)$ that we can differentiate (we only know that the Black-and-Scholes equation does not hold in this case, and that the usual delta, gamma and theta derivatives are therefore inappropriate). We could be tempted to circumvent the problem by making use of our knowledge of the implied volatility function to obtain prices, and differentiate the latter. Unfortunately this would require evaluating the first and second derivatives of the call function with respect to the stock price, and the first derivative with respect to time. As we discussed in Section 6.3 in the context of the evaluation of the delta of a plain-vanilla option, these derivatives can be carried out only if we assume to know how the implied volatility varies as a function of S and t, i.e. if $\frac{\partial \widehat{\sigma}}{\partial S}$ and $\frac{\partial \widehat{\sigma}}{\partial t}$ were known. This, in turn, is tantamount to assuming knowledge about the sticky or floating (or other) nature of the smile, about the degree of time-homogeneity (if any) of the implied volatility function, and, more generally, about the precise form of the process for the underlying.

12.3.2   Forward Equations

These problems can be by-passed thanks to the existence of a dual equation, known as the forward (Fokker–Planck) equation:

$$\left[\frac{\partial}{\partial T} + (r - d)K \frac{\partial}{\partial K} - \frac{1}{2}\sigma_{K,T}^2 K^2 \frac{\partial^2}{\partial K^2} + d \right] C_{K,T}(0, S) = 0 \qquad (12.4)$$

A derivation of Equation (12.4) can be found in Derman and Kani (1998) or in Andersen and Brotherton-Ratcliffe (1998). Note how, in moving from the Kolmogorov to the Fokker–Planck equation, inside the operator the time to maturity, T, has replaced the calendar time, t, and the strike, K, has replaced the stock level, S. The Fokker–Planck equation describes how a price propagates forward in time. Typically this equation is used when one knows the distribution density at an earlier time, and one wants to discover how this density spreads out as time progresses, given the drift and volatility of the process. Again, we could choose any time $\tau < T$ as our starting point. However, for a generic choice of τ there would be no unambiguous, model-independent agreement about the risk-neutral density. In complete analogy to the case of the Kolmogorov equation, there is, however, a special time τ at which everyone must agree about the price distribution, namely today, where the risk-neutral density collapses to a δ-function centred at today's price.

The important feature to note in Equation (12.4) is that the derivatives of the unknown call function are now to be evaluated with respect to *strike* and *time to maturity*. Furthermore, even if we do not know the 'true' call functional as a function of S, σ and t, we *do* know a 'black-box' function (the Black function itself) that can produce the (by definition) correct option prices as a function of strike, time to maturity and *implied volatility*. As we shall see immediately below, this is all we need in order to be able to extract the local volatility function.

The two Equations (12.3) and (12.4) above hold for any τ, $0 \leq \tau \leq T$. In particular, therefore, they apply to $t = 0$ (today). In this case the Fokker–Planck equation becomes

$$\left[\frac{\partial}{\partial T} + (r - d)K \frac{\partial}{\partial K} - \frac{1}{2}\sigma_{K,T}^2 K^2 \frac{\partial^2}{\partial K^2} + d \right] C_{K,T}(t, S) = 0 \qquad (12.5)$$

From the discussion above, we have assumed knowledge of the prices of options of all strikes and maturities via the implied volatility surface. In other words, we know the quantity $C_{K,T}(0, S)$ as a function of K and T. This constitutes the fundamental advantage of using the Fokker–Planck rather than the Kolmogorov equations: the process-dependent derivatives $\frac{\partial \widehat{\sigma}}{\partial S}$ and $\frac{\partial \widehat{\sigma}}{\partial t}$ disappear and the derivatives $\frac{\partial \widehat{\sigma}}{\partial K}$ and $\frac{\partial \widehat{\sigma}}{\partial T}$ take their place. This is important, because these derivatives can be directly 'read' from today's smile surface (perhaps smoothly interpolated, as discussed in Chapter 9).

Note that the existence of the dual (Fokker–Planck) equation is saying something very deep: *dynamic* information about the dependence of call prices on the underlying and on calendar time is linked to *static* properties of how call prices vary as a function of strike and maturity. Of course, such a powerful link does not come 'for free', and can only be established if indeed the dynamics of the stock price are of the form (12.1).

Given the knowledge of today's prices we can evaluate (numerically, but very accurately) the derivatives

$$\frac{\partial C_{K,T}}{\partial K}$$

$$= \frac{C_{K+\Delta K,T}(\widehat{\sigma}_T(0, K + \Delta K)) - C_{K,T}(\widehat{\sigma}_T(0, K))}{\Delta K} \qquad (12.6)$$

$$\frac{\partial^2 C_{K,T}}{\partial K^2}$$

$$= \frac{C_{K+\Delta K,T}(\widehat{\sigma}_T(0, K + \Delta K)) + C_{K-\Delta K,T}(\widehat{\sigma}_T(0, K - \Delta K)) - 2C_{K,T}(\widehat{\sigma}_T(0, K))}{\Delta K^2} \qquad (12.7)$$

$$\frac{\partial C_{K,T}}{\partial T}$$

$$= \frac{C_{K,T+\Delta T}(\widehat{\sigma}_{T+\Delta T}(0, K)) - C_{K,T}(\widehat{\sigma}_T(0, K))}{\Delta T} \qquad (12.8)$$

(In expressions (12.6)–(12.8) $\widehat{\sigma}_T(0, K)$ denotes the market-implied volatility at time 0 of the option expiring at time T and with strike K.) Note that, in evaluating the derivatives above, one cannot simply use the closed-form Black derivatives because the derivatives of the pricing functional are not given by the corresponding Black-derived formulae with the implied Black volatility as an input. Therefore, in evaluating the derivatives (12.6)–(12.8) one must do so numerically and, when taking the numerical derivatives with respect to the strike one must change in the Black formula not only the strike itself, but also the implied volatility, $\widehat{\sigma}_K$ (which is a function of the strike).[3]

Once these derivatives have been obtained, one can go back to Equation (12.5) and solve for the only unknown, $\sigma_{K,T}^2$, to obtain:

$$\sigma_{K,T}^2 = 2\frac{\dfrac{\partial C_{K,T}(0,\,S)}{\partial T} + (r-d)K\dfrac{\partial C_{K,T}(0,\,S)}{\partial K} + dC_{K,T}(0,\,S)}{\dfrac{\partial^2 C_{K,T}(0,\,S)}{\partial K^2}K^2} \tag{12.9}$$

Given today's prices of the plain-vanilla options, this is the local volatility that will prevail at time T ($t=T$) when the future stock price is equal to K ($S_t = K$).[4]

By means of Equation (12.9) we have therefore solved the problem of determining the local volatility without constructing a tree. We shall explicitly show below that, although conceptually equivalent to the Derman-and-Kani approach, the method presented here allows the estimation of much smoother local volatility functions. Part of the reason for the increased efficiency in the numerical estimation of the local volatility with the approach described by Equation (12.9) is that one is not imposing the recombination of a computational tree, which is always a burdensome numerical constraint (see also Section 9.5). Furthermore, the awkward and time-consuming ancillary constraint of constructing a contravariate 'traditional' trinomial tree (see the discussion in Section 5.4) is no longer necessary if one uses Equations (12.6)–(12.9) to determine the volatility surface. The results are therefore not only much simpler to obtain, but also faster to compute and more accurate. They are shown in the following sections for some simple cases.

12.3.3 Why Are We Doing Things This Way?

In the approach presented above I have taken the incorrect Black function with the incorrect volatility (the implied volatility) to obtain the (correct) derivatives of the call price with respect to strike and expiry. The procedure worked because we recognized that the 'pseudo-volatility' input to the Black formula had a strike and maturity dependence, and explicitly accounted for its contribution.

We could have followed a different route (see, for example, Britten-Jones and Neuberger (1998)). Instead of making use of a wrong formula (the Black formula) and of a correction term (the dependence of the implied volatility on K and T) we could have

---

[3] Alternatively, one can of course write, for instance,

$$\frac{\partial C_{K,T}}{\partial K} = \frac{\partial Black_{K,T}(\widehat{\sigma}_K)}{\partial K} = \frac{dBlack_{K,T}(\widehat{\sigma}_K)}{dK} + \frac{\partial Black_{K,T}(\widehat{\sigma}_K)}{\partial \widehat{\sigma}_K}\frac{\partial \widehat{\sigma}_K}{\partial K}$$

where the term $\frac{\partial Black_{K,T}(\widehat{\sigma}_K)}{\partial \widehat{\sigma}_K}$ is the vega Black-and-Scholes term, for which there *is* an analytic expression. However, in general the term $\frac{\partial \widehat{\sigma}_K}{\partial K}$ still has to be evaluated numerically.

[4] For Equation (12.9) to make sense the RHS must be positive. How can we be sure that we will not find an imaginary local volatility? This is guaranteed by no-arbitrage considerations. The denominator is proportional (via a positive quantity, K^2) to the risk-neutral price density. In the absence of arbitrage, this must be positive. The positivity of the numerator can then be guaranteed (see Andersen and Brotherton-Ratcliffe (1998)) by portfolio dominance arguments.

used (ignoring discounting) the general definition of the value of a call as the expectation of its terminal payoff in the pricing measure, Q:[5]

$$C_{K,T}(0, S) = E_Q[(S_T - K)^+] \tag{12.10}$$

By so doing, a term such as, for instance, $\frac{\partial C_{K,T}(0,S)}{\partial T}$ would become

$$\frac{\partial C_{K,T}(0, S)}{\partial T} = \frac{\partial E_Q[(S_T + dS_T - K)^+ - (S_T - K)^+]}{\partial T} \tag{12.11}$$

The problem in applying in a naïve way Ito's lemma to the function $E_Q[(S_T - K)^+]$ is that the function is non-differentiable at the strike K. There are ways around this problem, and one can show (see, for example, Chung and Williams (1990)) that one can write

$$d(S_T - K)^+ = 1_{S_T \geq K} \, dS_T + \tfrac{1}{2}\delta(S_T - K)(dS_T)^2 \tag{12.12}$$

where 1_A denotes the indicator function that has the value 1 if the condition A is true, and zero otherwise, and δ is the Dirac distribution. The disadvantage of this approach is that the required level of mathematical sophistication is somewhat higher, and the differential expression (12.12) must be understood in the sense of distributions. Following this route, however, would *not* be an unnecessary complication. The simpler method that I have proposed above does arrive at the particular result we want to obtain (the local volatility) more simply and, for our purposes, correctly. However, the richer treatment that starts from Equation (12.12) provides additional information about quantities directly related to the true process. Assume, in fact, that the underlying process is a *continuous* semi-martingale (i.e. for our purposes, a possibly very complex diffusion), and that $\sigma(.,t)$ is *any* stochastic-volatility function (i.e. not necessarily a local-volatility function). Then, after setting interest rates and dividend yields to zero for notational simplicity, one can show that:

1. The conditional expectation of the square of the volatility function is given by

$$E[\sigma(.,t)^2 | S_t = K] = \frac{2\dfrac{\partial C_{K,T}(0, S)}{\partial T}}{K^2 \dfrac{\partial^2 C_{K,T}(0, S)}{\partial K^2}} \tag{12.13}$$

2. The conditional expectation of the square of the volatility function is given by

$$E[\sigma(.,t)^2] = 2 \int_0^\infty \frac{1}{K^2} \frac{\partial C_{K,T}(0, S)}{\partial T} \, dK \tag{12.14}$$

---

[5] Indeed, the existence of such a pricing measure for all options is equivalent to the absence of arbitrage among the options.

3. The expected squared volatility over some finite period $[T_1 \ T_2]$ is given by

$$\mathrm{E}\left[\int_{T_1}^{T_2} \sigma(.,t)^2\right] = 2\int_0^\infty \frac{C(T_2,K)-C(T_1,K)}{K^2}\,dK \qquad (12.15)$$

So, by using the 'correct' expression for the value of a call one is able to obtain, under the diffusive assumption, information about quadratic-variation-related properties of the process *as implied by the market prices*. I do not pursue this topic here, but an excellent treatment is to be found in the paper by Britten-Jones and Neuberger (1998), which I strongly recommend for interest and clarity.

12.3.4   Related Approaches

Going back to Equation (12.9), it is very transparent and appears to solve in a very straightforward way the problem of determining the local volatility implied by a set of option market prices. Sometimes, however, it can be numerically delicate because of the density-related term, $\frac{\partial^2 C_{K,T}(0,S)}{\partial K^2}$, in the denominator. For values of the stock price very far away from the at-the-money level this quantity becomes very small, and the local volatility therefore remains finite and well-behaved only if the numerator approaches zero at the 'right' speed. Fortunately, it is possible to recast Equation (12.9) in terms of implied volatilities, $\widehat{\sigma}_{K,T}(0,S) = \widehat{\sigma}_{K,T}$, and their derivatives. The advantage is that, in this case, neither the implied volatilities nor their derivatives go to zero in the denominator. See, for example, Andersen and Brotherton-Ratcliffe (1998) and Wilmott (1998):

$$\sigma_{K,T}^2 = 2\frac{\dfrac{\partial\widehat{\sigma}_{K,T}}{\partial T} + \dfrac{\widehat{\sigma}_{K,T}}{T} + 2K(r-d)\dfrac{\partial\widehat{\sigma}_{K,T}}{\partial K}}{K^2\left[\dfrac{\partial^2\widehat{\sigma}_{K,T}}{\partial K^2} - h_1\sqrt{T}\left(\dfrac{\partial\widehat{\sigma}_{K,T}}{\partial K}\right)^2 + \dfrac{1}{\widehat{\sigma}_{K,T}}\left(\dfrac{1}{K\sqrt{T}} + h_1\dfrac{\partial\widehat{\sigma}_{K,T}}{\partial K}\right)^2\right]} \qquad (12.16)$$

with

$$h_1 = \frac{\ln\dfrac{S}{K} + (r-d)T + \dfrac{1}{2}\widehat{\sigma}_{K,T}^2 T}{\widehat{\sigma}_{K,T}\sqrt{T}} \qquad (12.17)$$

Wilmott makes an important point: while the procedure cast in terms of implied volatilities rather than call prices is numerically better-behaved, small differences in the input smile surface can produce a big difference in the estimated local volatility. This comes as little surprise after the discussion presented at the beginning of this chapter about non-regularized inverse problems. The same reservations obviously also apply to the methodology presented above: the results will only be as good as the input prices or implied volatilities. The discussion at the beginning of Chapter 9, which stressed the importance of a good fit to the exogenous smile surface, can be revisited in this context (see, in particular, Section 9.8).

More generally, the advantages discussed in the same chapter of using methods such as the mixture of log-normals or the generalized-beta approach, explicitly constructed to produce smooth and plausible densities, become even more apparent in the light of Equation (12.9), where the denominator is, after all, just proportional to the unconditional density targeted by these approaches. Any irregularity or discontinuity in this function will therefore directly impact the local volatility. The price to be paid if one uses price–density-based fitting methodologies is that the fit to the market prices can sometimes not be excellent, especially if one uses a method (such as the generalized-beta) with a small number of parameters. We have seen, however, that by using a mixture of (log-) normals excellent price recovery is obtained for the price densities produced by a variety of models, even under 'stress' conditions.

Finally, I have mentioned in Section 8.5 that the local-volatility approach is sometimes used in conjunction with a jump–diffusion process in order to fit plain-vanilla option prices exactly in a financially desirable way. Andersen and Andreasen (1999) show that Equation (12.9) can be extended to handle this case, and suggest numerical techniques that can be used for this purpose.

12.4 Computational Results

In what follows I will use Equation (12.9) directly, rather than making use of the equivalent Equation (12.16) in terms of implied volatilities. If I had used real market data instead of stylized model implied-volatility surfaces, the second route would have proved easier to follow. All the qualitative considerations that follow, however, would not have changed.

As a test of the procedure, one can first of all check that, if the implied volatilities are obtained from a time-constant, no-smile implied volatility function, the resulting local volatilities are constant in time and 'space'. This 'entry-level' test, it will be recalled, was successfully passed also by the Derman-and-Kani approach, but only after 'purging' the numerical errors by fitting to the 'proxy' market prices (see Figure 11.7 in Section 11.6). For this simple test, instead, the approach proposed in this chapter immediately gives virtually perfect results without any need for an ancillary construction.

Moving away from the trivial (no-smile, constant-volatility) case, the Derman-and-Kani technique was shown to begin to produce considerable numerical noise for the case of a no-smile, time-dependent implied volatility surface. In this case, the correct resulting local volatilities must be constant across the 'space' (i.e. stock price) direction, and must show (see Chapter 3) the time dependence implied by

$$\widehat{\sigma}(0, t_2)^2 t_2 - \widehat{\sigma}(0, t_1)^2 t_1 = \int_{t_1}^{t_2} \sigma(u)^2 \, du \qquad (12.18)$$

(Note that, in Equation (12.18), the dependence of σ on S has been dropped because we are now in a no-smile situation.) We have seen that if one attempts to recover these relationships with acceptable precision using the traditional Derman-and-Kani procedure, one already encounters rather awkward numerical problems even if the implied volatility only depends on maturity. This case is shown again for convenience in Figure 12.1.

No similar numerical problems are encountered when adopting the procedure described in this section, even when the maturity dependence of the implied volatilities is much stronger than could be dealt with by the Derman-and-Kani approach. As one can appreciate

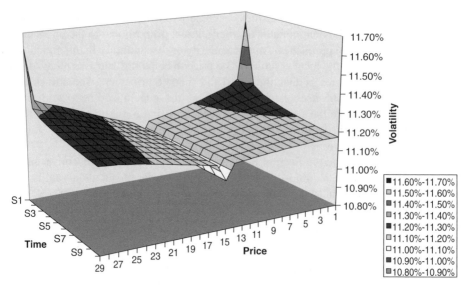

Figure 12.1   The local-volatility surface obtained using the Derman-and-Kani procedure when the implied volatility is purely time-dependent. See the caption to Figure 11.8 for a description of the surface.

from Figure 12.2, which displays the results for the same purely time-dependent, implied-volatility case, the numerical quality of the solution is much higher, despite the fact that the same switch from calls to puts is used in moving across the at-the-money level. In comparing the two figures one should also note that, in order to avoid numerical problems, in the Derman-and-Kani case the maturity dependence of the inputs had to be much more limited (see the captions of Figures 11.8 and 11.11).

12.4.1   Are We Looking at the Same Problem?

Prima facie the two surfaces shown in Figures 12.1 and 12.2 look so qualitatively different that one might wonder whether, given the same market inputs, the surface produced by the Derman-and-Kani procedure would indeed converge to the same smile surface obtained using Equations (12.6)–(12.9). In other words, apart from numerical noise, can one be sure of the uniqueness of the local volatility surface once the prices of the plain vanilla options and the drifts (riskless rate and dividend yield) are given? To answer this question, recall (see Appendix I for a proof) that the second derivative of a call price with respect to the strike is equal to the price probability density, Φ:

$$\frac{\partial^2 C_{K,T}(0, S_0)}{\partial K^2} = \Phi(S_t = K) \tag{12.19}$$

Remember also that we have assumed to know the prices of all the plain-vanilla options (i.e. for options of any maturity and any strike). As a consequence, we know all the unconditional densities. Once the drift has been specified (by no-arbitrage),[6] and if one

---

[6]If the drift is not specified, the uniqueness can no longer be guaranteed. See Dupire (1993) for an interesting example.

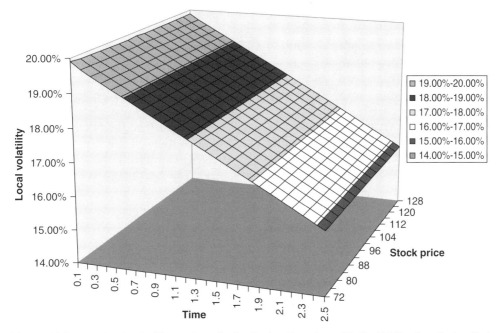

Figure 12.2 The local-volatility surface obtained using Equations (12.6)–(12.9) when the implied volatility is purely time-dependent. See the caption to Figure 11.11 for a description of the surface.

accepts that the process for the underlying is described by Equation (12.1), the solution to this problem is unique, i.e. there is only one process and one time- and state-dependent volatility function that will produce all the densities. Therefore if we find a solution, we can rest assured that it is *the* solution. Therefore the Derman-and-Kani tree and this approach are indeed conceptually exactly equivalent.

If the input prices are 'deeply smooth', by means of Equation (12.9) we can find a smooth and numerically stable local volatility function. We can therefore rest assured that whatever features we examine these will be intrinsic to the local volatility surface itself, and not the accidental by-product of a poor numerical technique. On the strength of this reliable information, in the next sections I will try to develop a qualitative understanding of how several input-implied volatilities relate to the corresponding local volatility surfaces. This task is undertaken below for several common, albeit somewhat stylized, shapes of the smile.

12.5 The Link Between Implied and Local-Volatility Surfaces

In order to gain some intuition about the link between the implied and the local-volatility surfaces, this section begins by showing what local-volatility function a given type of implied volatility surface produces. This section will focus on describing the most salient features of the results. A qualitative explanation of the reasons for the observed behaviours will be given in Section 12.6. In the meantime, several 'pointers' are interspersed with the results presented below as a reminder that a particular feature or behaviour will be referred to in the following discussion section.

The shapes of the implied volatility surfaces examined below are rather stylized, and are not supposed to reflect precisely any particular market on any given date. Rather, they attempt to display the salient features of specific market smiles (e.g. the 'equity smile', the 'FX smile' or the 'interest-rates smile'). Given this choice, some of the smile features are introduced in a piecemeal fashion (e.g. the maturity and strike dependence are sometimes introduced separately) in order better to illustrate the influence of both variables on the resulting local-volatility function. As a result of this choice, the input implied-volatility surfaces are not meant to be particularly realistic (or even asymptotically financially compatible with the absence of arbitrage). This important issue is addressed in Section 12.8.

12.5.1   Symmetric ('FX') Smiles

The class of financial markets that this type of smile is meant to mimic consists, for instance, of the FX options where both underlying FX rates are currencies of 'mature' economies (the shape of the $/Emerging-Market-Currency smile is much more similar to the equity case). In reality (see Chapter 7) the most salient feature of the FX smile is not so much its symmetry, but the fact that the volatilities of out-of-the-money calls do not systematically trade at a premium or a discount with respect to the same-delta out-of-the-money puts. So, despite the fact that the risk reversal can be very variable, as a first approximation and after averaging over sufficiently long periods, one can say that the smile is roughly symmetric for calls and puts. The first case we want to examine therefore is that of an implied volatility surface displaying a symmetric constant quadratic smile and with no time dependence, as shown in Figure 12.3.

The associated local volatility surface is shown in Figure 12.4. The first important feature to point out is that, despite the fact that we started from a symmetric implied

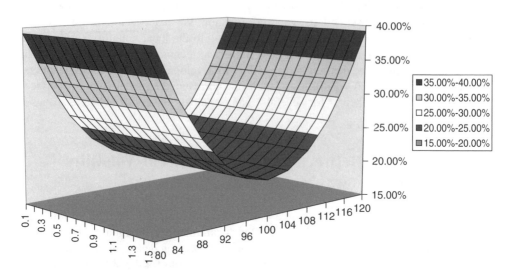

Figure 12.3   A time-constant quadratic implied volatility surface.

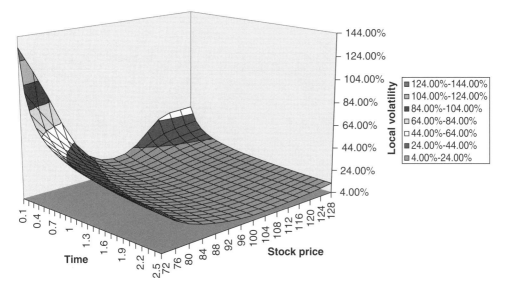

Figure 12.4 The local-volatility function obtainable using Equations (12.6)–(12.9) and the implied volatility function shown in Figure 12.3 as input.

volatility surface, the resulting local-volatility surface is strongly tilted in the direction of the low stock prices. In other words, according to the model described by Equation (12.1), future high realizations of the stock price will be associated with a decreasing volatility, and vice versa. It is tempting to quote at this point Fisher Black's words:

> I have believed for a long time that stock returns are related to volatility changes. When stocks go up, volatilities seem to go down; and when stocks go down, volatilities seem to go up.

We will return to this point later on. For the moment note that the local volatility for short calendar times (i.e. close to today) and very high or very low values of the underlying tends to be much higher than any of the implied volatilities. The qualitative reason for this effect is explained in the next section. In the meantime it is instructive to compare the implied and local volatility functions for different 'times'. See Figures 12.5–12.7. Note that special care must be exercised in making the comparison: the x-axis represents the stock price for the local-volatility function, and the strike for the implied volatility; on the y-axis one can read the implied volatility in one case, and the local volatility in the other; and as for the 'time', it is calendar time for the local-volatility curve, but maturity for the implied volatility. Despite the fact that we seem to be comparing the proverbial apples and oranges, we will show later on that looking at the two lines together can be helpful in developing some intuition about the link between the two surfaces.

We can now introduce time dependence on top of the smile effect, as shown by the implied volatility surface depicted in Figure 12.8. We retain symmetry in the strike dependence. The resulting local volatility is shown in Figure 12.9. Note that the same feature of very high local volatilities for low and high values of the underlying is still present at short times, but that it dies off much more quickly with time. The convexity of the local volatility, always positive in the case of a time-independent symmetric implied

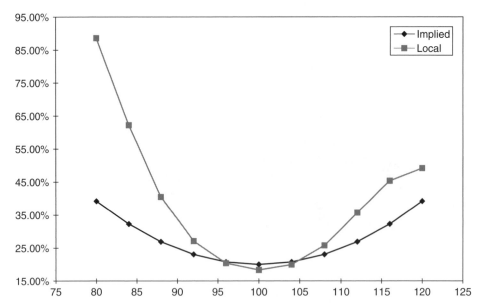

Figure 12.5   The implied and local volatility functions for 'time' = 0.1 years. See the text for the meaning of 'time'.

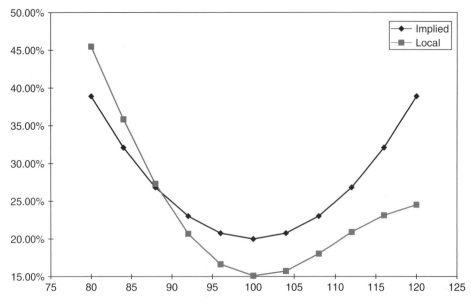

Figure 12.6   Same as Figure 12.5 for 'time' = 0.4 year.

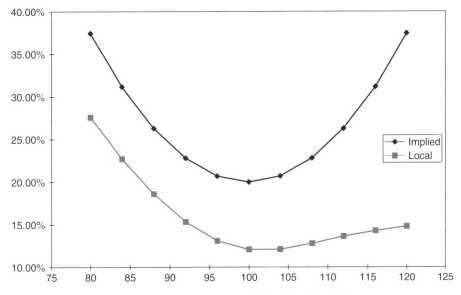

Figure 12.7   Same as Figure 12.5 for 'time' = 1.0 year.

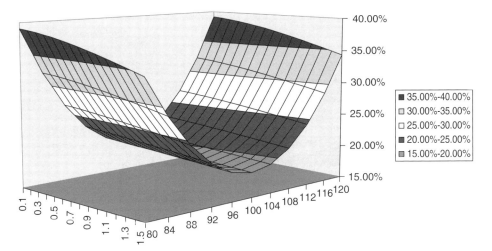

Figure 12.8   A time-decaying, constant-quadratic-smile implied volatility surface.

volatility surface, appears to change sign for distant future times ($t > 2.5$ years) and very low stock levels; otherwise the surface appears to become asymptotically flat. See the discussion in the following section.

12.5.2   Asymmetric ('Equity') Smiles

The second shape for the implied volatility surface we are going to examine is the half-parabolic smile shown in Figure 12.10. This stylized shape is supposed to capture the most salient qualitative feature of equity smiles, or of smiles found in the FX option

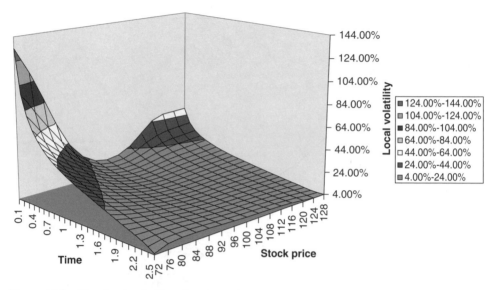

Figure 12.9 The local-volatility function obtainable using Equations (12.6)–(12.9) and the implied volatility function shown in Figure 12.8 as input.

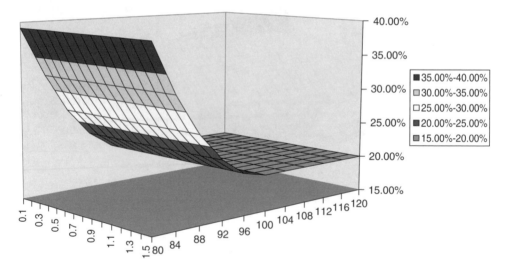

Figure 12.10 A time-constant half-parabolic-smile implied volatility surface.

market for the $ vs Emerging Market Currencies (in this case the high volatility is on the side of $ Call/Emerging-Market-Currency Put). The corresponding local volatility surface is displayed in Figure 12.11, together with the time cross sections for 0.1, 0.4 and 1 year (Figures 12.12–12.14).

The most interesting feature of these curves is the fact that, despite the monotonically increasing implied volatility smile for strikes towards the in-the-money puts direction, the resulting local volatility function displays a very clear minimum in moving from

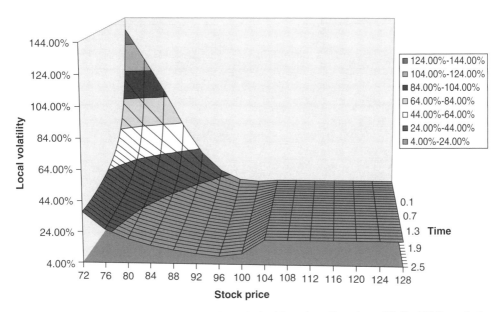

Figure 12.11   The local volatility function obtainable using Equations (12.6)–(12.9) and the implied volatility function shown in Figure 12.10 as input.

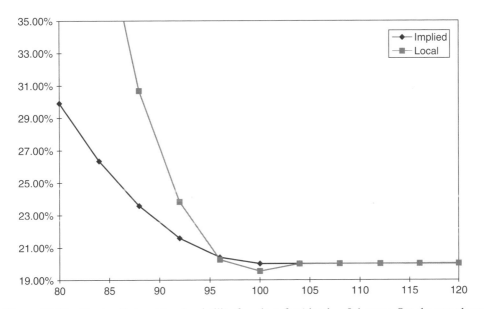

Figure 12.12   The implied and local-volatility functions for 'time' = 0.1 years. See the text about the meaning of 'time'.

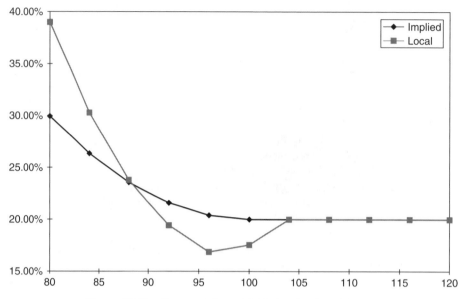

Figure 12.13   Same as Figure 12.12 for 'time' = 0.4 year.

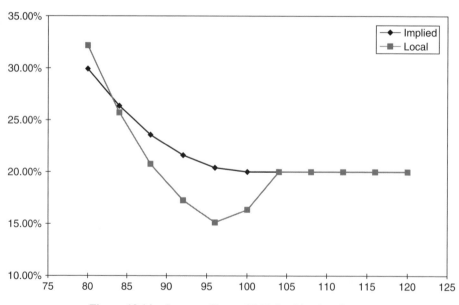

Figure 12.14   Same as Figure 12.12 for 'time' = 1 year.

high stock prices to low stock prices. This minimum, it will be argued later on, is not a numerical artefact, and becomes relatively more and more pronounced as time goes on (see Figures 12.11–12.14, where the usual caveat about the meaning of 'time' applies).

Introducing a time dependence into the implied volatility as shown in Figure 12.15 produces the local volatility surface displayed in Figure 12.16.

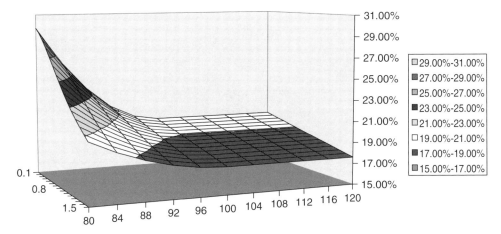

Figure 12.15 A time-decaying half-parabolic-smile implied volatility surface.

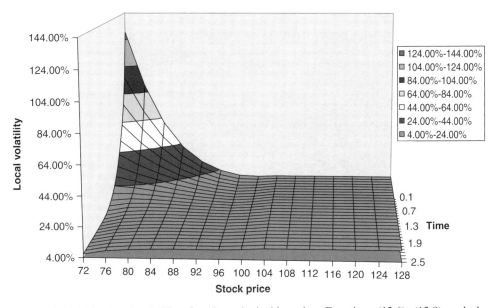

Figure 12.16 The local-volatility function obtainable using Equations (12.6)–(12.9) and the implied volatility function shown in Figure 12.15 as input.

The most salient features are

- the change in convexity for long times and low stock levels;

- the overall asymptotic flattening of the local volatility surface; and

- the fact that the minimum in the local-volatility function for a given time as a function of the stock price is less pronounced, but still present (see Figure 12.17).

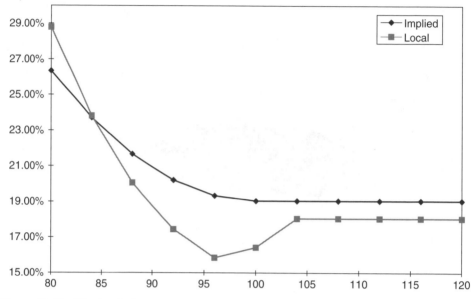

Figure 12.17   The implied and local-volatility functions for 'time' = 0.4 year. See the text for the meaning of 'time'.

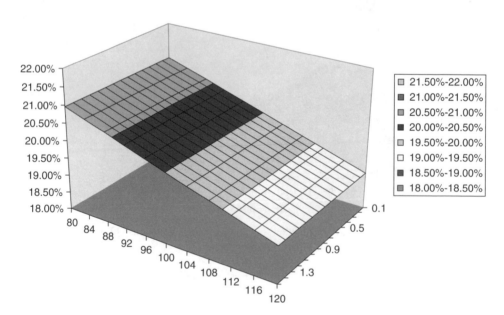

Figure 12.18   A time-constant monotonic-smile implied volatility surface.

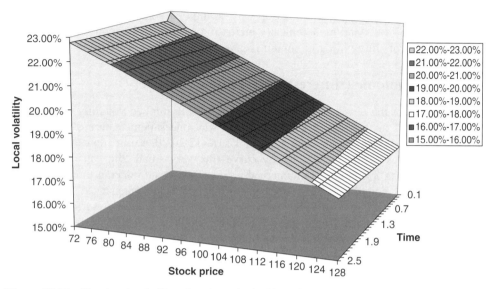

Figure 12.19 The local-volatility function obtainable using Equations (12.6)–(12.9) and the implied volatility function shown in Figure 12.18 as input.

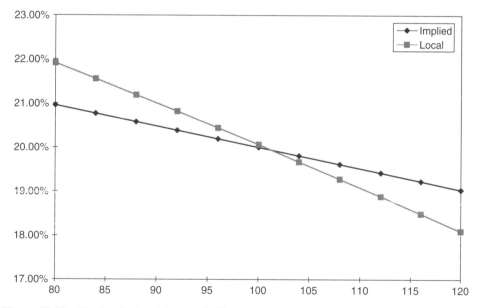

Figure 12.20 The implied and local-volatility functions for 'time' = 0.4 year. See the text for the meaning of 'time'.

A qualitative explanation of the reason why an implied volatility surface which is flat for in-the-money calls and monotonically increasing for out-of-the-money calls can give rise to a local volatility with a minimum is given in the following section.

12.5.3   Monotonic ('Interest-Rate') Smile Surface

Finally, I present the case of a monotonically decreasing implied volatility surface. This surface is meant to describe in an approximate way one salient feature of interest-rate smiles. As clearly noticeable from Figures 12.18–12.20, there are now no significant structural features in the local volatility curve (the very small 'blip' in the top right-hand corner of the 3-d graph is a numerical artefact). Also, introducing time-dependence into the implied volatility surface does not bring about any unexpected features. The only noteworthy feature is that the steepness of the local volatility surface (vs stock price) is more pronounced than the slope of the implied volatility surface (vs maturity). See Figure 12.20. We will try to understand also this behaviour in the following section.

12.6   Gaining an Intuitive Understanding

In this section we want to gain an intuitive understanding of the links between the implied and local-volatility surfaces presented in the previous section. In the reasoning presented below, to account for the various features reported above we will follow a common line of thought. Namely:

- we will imagine that we are performing a Gedanken Monte Carlo simulation of the evolution of the underlying using the local volatilities obtained from the various implied volatility surfaces analysed above;

- we will look at plain-vanilla options with particular strikes and maturities;

- we will try to determine which paths are most likely to be significantly sampled and to provide a large payoff for these options in the Monte Carlo simulation.

Note that, *along a particular path*, the local volatility is no longer a stochastic quantity, and can be thought of as a purely time-dependent volatility, with the time dependence implied by the values of the stock along the chosen path. In other words, *along each point of this path* we can write

$$\sigma(S_t, t) = \sigma'(t) \tag{12.20}$$

If, for a plain-vanilla option with a particular strike or maturity, it was indeed the case that a few similar paths made the largest contributions to the Monte Carlo average, it would be tempting to surmise that the implied volatility for this plain-vanilla option should still be linked to the instantaneous time-dependent volatility by the usual relationship

$$\int_0^t \sigma'(u)^2 \, du = \widehat{\sigma}^2 t \tag{12.21}$$

where the integrand in the equation above is the time-dependent volatility along the 'important' path.

In general this will of course not be exactly true: to begin with, for any final realization of the stock price, and hence of the payoff, the Monte Carlo simulation of our thought experiment will produce a series of paths that will sample the local volatilities encountered from the starting point to the final point. Furthermore, if one truly knew *the* path followed by the underlying, it is not clear what meaning (if any) one can associate with the concept of volatility. I will make the case below, however, that for some special plain-vanilla options one can concentrate on one or a few 'important paths'; if this is the case, making use of Equations (12.20) and (12.21) along these paths can provide a useful tool to understand the shape of the resulting local volatility surface.

The crux of the arguments that I shall use in explaining the shape of the local volatility for symmetric and equity-like smiles is the following. For sufficiently short option expiries it is the *almost-straight paths* in the in-the-money direction (i.e. beyond the strike) that contribute most significantly to the payoff. Intuitively, this is easy to see: let us run a 'mental' Monte Carlo simulation. If the expiry of the option is short and the path begins to wander too much in the out-of-the-money direction, the chances of it 'turning around' so as to end up significantly in-the-money by expiry are low.[7] The more a strike is out-of-the-money, the less 'forgiving' the payoff can be to paths starting in the wrong direction. Conversely, for at-the-money strikes a path can start off in the out-of-the-money direction, and still have a reasonable chance of producing a significant payoff contribution by expiry. Why are these considerations useful? Because, whenever we can talk of relatively easy-to-identify 'important' paths, we can associate with these paths an almost deterministic instantaneous volatility. In these cases a (conditional) implied volatility can therefore be 'guesstimated' using Equation (12.21), and we can therefore hope to be able to establish a correspondence between the two volatilities (local and implied).

These observations will guide us in the analysis below.

12.6.1 Symmetric Smiles

Let us start by examining the case of a symmetric, quadratic smile. In order to understand the qualitative features displayed in Figures 12.3–12.9, we will focus our attention on one particular, and relatively short, maturity, say a month. For the sake of simplicity we will also ignore interest rates; therefore the at-the-money-spot and at-the-money-forward levels coincide, and both have the same value ($S_0 = K_{\text{ATM}}$).

The implied volatility function is assumed to be parabolic as a function of strike, i.e. to be of the form:

$$\sigma_{\text{impl}}(0, T) = a(K - S_0)^2 \tag{12.22}$$

We have pointed out in the previous section that the local volatility for a small but finite t (i.e. close to today)

- will approximately display the same qualitative shape as the implied volatility (see Figure 12.5);

---

[7]Of course, in a Monte Carlo simulation all realized paths have the same probability of occurrence, $(1/n)$, and it is just the *density* of the paths that changes. The short-hand expressions used in this section should be understood in this sense.

- will be lower for $S_t = K_{\text{ATM}}$ than the implied volatility for maturity t and strike $K = S_0$ (see Figure 12.5);

- will be higher for $S_t \gg K_{\text{ATM}}$ or for $S_t \ll K_{\text{ATM}}$ than the implied volatility for maturity t and strike K_{ATM} (see Figures 12.5 and 12.6);

- for a fixed strike $K > K_{\text{ATM}}$ or $K < K_{\text{ATM}}$ will diverge as t approaches zero (see Figure 12.5).

How can we explain this behaviour? Let us look at out-of-the-money puts first. Since the smile is parabolic, the implied volatility of the more out-of-the-money (K_2-strike) put will be higher than the more in-the-money (K_1-strike) implied volatility:

$$\sigma_{\text{impl}}(K_2) > \sigma_{\text{impl}}(K_1) \quad \text{for } K_2 < K_1 \tag{12.23}$$

Consider a path that has given an important payoff contribution to the K_1-strike put. Given our assumptions about the important paths, the average of the local volatility along this important path is not too different from the implied volatility, $\widehat{\sigma}(K_1)$:

$$\int_0^t \sigma'(u)^2 \, \mathrm{d}u = \widehat{\sigma}^2(K_1) t \tag{12.24}$$

The same considerations apply to the important contributing paths for the K_2-strike put, and its average too must be not-too-dissimilar from its own implied volatility, $\widehat{\sigma}(K_2) > \widehat{\sigma}(K_1)$. However, for a path to produce the appropriate average volatility for the more out-of-the-money option, $\widehat{\sigma}(K_2)$, the local volatility encountered *beyond* K_1 must be sufficiently higher than the local volatility *up to* K_1 to provide the correct 'balance of variance'. Therefore the local volatility for very low values of S must be higher than the implied volatilities for the corresponding strikes.

Mutatis mutandis, the same reasoning clearly applies to out-of-the-money calls as well. These observations therefore explain why, for sufficiently out-of-the-money options, the local volatility (as a function of S) will be higher than the corresponding implied volatility (as function of K). They also explain why, as the option expiry becomes shorter and shorter, the local volatility for values of $S \gg S_0$ or $S \ll S_0$ must tend to infinity.

What about at-the-money options? I argued above that, for these options, not only straight paths, but also somewhat tortuous paths can make a significant contribution. By what we have seen, however, as the stock wanders away from the origin in either direction, its local volatility begins to rise. In order to produce an average volatility along the path close to the desired (low) at-the-money implied volatility, the local volatility around the origin must therefore assume *lower* values than $\sigma_{\text{impl}}(K_{\text{ATM}})$.

Taken together these observations provide a qualitative explanation for the shape of the local-volatility surface for parabolic implied volatilities.

12.6.2   Asymmetric Smiles: One-Sided Parabola

Matters change when we move from a symmetric smile to a one-sided parabolic smile (see Figures 12.10–12.17). To begin with, it is easy to see that if we are sufficiently deeply in the high-stock-price region, all the volatilities (implied and local) have to be flat, and equal to $\sigma_{\text{impl}}(K_{\text{ATM}})$. Once we have moved deeply enough into the flat-implied-volatility region, in fact, the local volatility no longer depends on the underlying level and we are back in familiar Black territory.

Also, in the case of out-of-the-money puts and for very short maturities the same reasoning presented above still applies: the 'important' paths are the same, and it does not matter (much) what happens to the paths that begin to wander from the origin towards high stock levels, since they are unlikely to provide much payoff anyhow. The same reasoning does not apply however to out-of-the-money puts of longer maturities. Why is this the case?

Let us begin by looking at options with strikes close to the at-the-money level. We have seen earlier that mildly wandering paths can be important for at-the-money calls and puts. On the out-of-the-money-call side the local volatility experienced by the stock is roughly flat, and close to the at-the-money implied volatility, $\sigma_{\text{impl}}(K_{\text{ATM}})$. On the out-of-the-money-put side, however, the local volatility will have to be increasing for sufficiently out-of-the-money strikes. Therefore, in order to produce the correct average, $\sigma_{\text{impl}}(K_{\text{ATM}})$, the local volatility in the immediate vicinity of the at-the-money strike will have to be *lower* than either the local volatility encountered to the 'right' or to the 'left'. A minimum develops again, this time with a pronounced asymmetry.

This observation is important not just for the insight it gives about the origin of this local minimum, but also, and actually more, because it casts light on the possible future shape of the implied volatility function. In the equity smile case, given the resulting local volatility surface obtained, not even the qualitative shape of today's implied volatility surface will be obtained again in the future unless the stock price happened to be close to today's at-the-money level in the future. We have, in fact, seen that the local minimum in the local volatility is necessary to account, at the same time, for the implied volatilities of both puts and calls. But this local minimum is only encountered (see Figures 12.11 and 12.16) close to today's at-the-money level. If the future stock price, for instance, were to be in the flat local-volatility area, the future implied volatility would also have to be approximately flat. Therefore, we can indeed fit the prices today of plain-vanilla calls and puts implied by a volatility surface with a shape similar to the one in Figure 12.10 using a model for the stock dynamics described by Equation (12.1). However, by so doing we are implying that, in general, the future implied volatility surface will look qualitatively different from what it looks like today. As I discuss in Chapter 1, because of vega re-hedging and model re-calibration, this has profound effects on the future re-hedging costs for non-plain-vanilla options, and therefore on their prices.

Revisiting the Results by Carr and Wu (2003b)

Recall that I mentioned in Section 7.3.2 the results by Carr and Wu (2003b) regarding the continuous or discontinuous nature of the process for the S&P. By examining as a function of time to expiry how quickly the prices of options go to zero they concluded that the process followed by the S&P index displayed both a continuous and a discontinuous component. We have just found, however, that an (admittedly very stylized) 'equity-like' smile can be accounted for by a local-volatility diffusion (a purely continuous process). How can we reconcile these statements?

What we just found is actually perfectly consistent with the result by Carr and Wu. Indeed, we were able to account for short-maturity, out-of-the-money prices, with a local-volatility model, but, for a fixed degree of out-of-the-moneyness, we could only do this by requiring that the local volatility should go to infinity as the expiry goes to zero. In other words, we are 'fixing' the intrinsic inability of diffusions to give a significant probability to 'large' moves after a 'short' period of time by making the local volatility become larger and larger as t (not T!) goes to zero and S (not K!) moves away from the initial at-the-money level. This, however, is clearly unsatisfactory: pushing the local volatility towards infinity forces a continuous process to 'mimic' a discontinuous one in a rather pathological way.

The problems with this approach, however, run deeper: suppose that, day after day, the smile surface remains approximately unchanged. By what we saw in Chapter 7, at least over a short period of time, this is not too far from the truth. By re-calibrating the local-volatility model to the option prices, we will find, day after day, a similar shape for the local volatility, but shifted forward in time. Therefore, every day the prediction of what the local volatility should have done as a function of spot fails to come true.

Let us look at this feature of local-volatility models more precisely. Suppose that on 1 January (time t_0) the stock price is at \$100 and we find that the local volatilities necessary to account for the options struck at \$100 and \$105 and expiring on 1 February (time T) are 20% and 60% for the stock price at \$100 and at \$105, respectively. Furthermore, in order to account for the observed price of the option expiring on 2 January (time t_1) we find the local volatilities at time t_1 for the same values of spot at 20% and 400%:

$$\sigma(S = 100, t = T) = 20\% \tag{12.25}$$

$$\sigma(S = 105, t = T) = 60\% \tag{12.26}$$

$$\sigma(S = 100, t = t_1) = 20\% \tag{12.27}$$

$$\sigma(S = 105, t = t_1) = 400\% \tag{12.28}$$

Suppose now that the true process is a jump–diffusion. A jump occurs at time t_0 and brings the stock price to \$105. However, the smile we observe as a function of residual maturity has hardly changed. If the local-volatility model had been correct, the volatility at time t_1 should now be around 400%. Instead, by fitting to the roughly unchanged smile, we still find it to be around 20%. The prediction made about the local volatility on 1 January turned out to be wrong, but on 2 January we make a prediction about the future local volatility exactly on the same (wrong) basis. Much like the unrepentant sinner mentioned in Section 1.3, every day we discover that yesterday's predictions were wrong, we re-calibrate our model and price options as if the new calibration will remain unchanged until the end of time, we observe a new price move, rediscover that the new calibration was wrong again, and we re-enter the cycle. As I argue throughout this book, this is a very unsatisfactory (and dangerous) way to price and hedge options.

12.6.3   Asymmetric Smiles: Monotonically Decaying

We can finally analyse in a qualitative way the final case, i.e. the monotonically-decreasing implied volatility surface shown in Figure 12.18. The important thing to note is that the local-volatility curve now looks virtually like a replica of itself at any future point in time and for any level of the underlying. In particular, it qualitatively looks, from any future time–price node, almost exactly like the local volatility seen from the origin today. The latter, however, prices today's market options correctly (by construction). Therefore, by and large, one can expect that the future smile surface will be reasonably time-homogeneous.

Note that, if one looks carefully at Figure 12.19, one can see that the iso-local-volatility lines do not run exactly parallel to the time axis (as the iso-implied-volatility lines do in Figure 12.18). This is probably due to the log-normal nature of the underlying process; the effect, however, seems to be rather small. Unlike the case of the one-sided implied volatility surface, it therefore appears that using the model described by Equation (12.1) for the monotonic-smile case can give rise to a roughly self-replicating future implied volatility surface. In other words, in the case of interest-rate options, we do not have to believe that the world tomorrow will be qualitatively different from today's world (at least as long as plain-vanilla options are concerned) in order to use Equation (12.1) in a logically self-consistent manner. This observation also ties in well with the 'Smile Tale 1' presented in Section 6.4 of Chapter 6. In practical terms, the actual future re-hedging costs that we will encounter during the course of the option will be similar to what our model has 'assumed' in coming up with the cost of the option itself.

As a concluding remark to this section, it is important to point out again that some of the local volatilities used for illustrative purposes in the discussion so far were neither very realistic, nor would they have been arbitrage-free if extrapolated to longer maturities. We highlight in the Section 12.8 those conditions on the implied volatility surface that, irrespective of the model, must be satisfied in order to avoid arbitrage. These conditions will also be of great relevance in the context of the discussion in Chapter 17.

12.7 What Local-Volatility Models Imply about Sticky and Floating Smiles

I have argued above that, in general, the only way in order to ascertain the sticky, floating (or otherwise) nature of the smiles produced by a local-volatility model is

- to place oneself at a future point in the tree, (τ, S'_τ);

- to calculate the desired plain-vanilla option future prices emanating from this point;

- to translate the prices into implied volatilities;

- to repeat the procedure from a different node at the same time slice (τ, S''_τ); and, finally,

- to compare the implied volatilities thus obtained, $\sigma(\tau, S'_\tau, K, T)$ and $\sigma(\tau, S''_\tau, K, T)$, $T > \tau$, and observe how they change as a function of S.

While this is always true in general, there are special cases when some useful short-cuts can be taken. Hagan *et al.* (1999, 2002) show in fact an interesting result when the local volatility function is purely of the form

$$\sigma(S_t, t) = \sigma(S_t) \tag{12.29}$$

$$dS_t = S_t \sigma(S_t) dz_t \tag{12.30}$$

By using singular perturbation methods they show that the implied volatility function today, $\widehat{\sigma}(S_0, K)$, is linked to the local volatility by an expression of the form

$$\widehat{\sigma}(S_0, K) = \sigma(\tfrac{1}{2}[S_0 + K]) \left\{ 1 + \frac{\sigma''(\tfrac{1}{2}[S_0 + K])}{24\sigma(\tfrac{1}{2}[S_0 + K])}(S - K)^2 \right\} \tag{12.31}$$

where

$$\sigma''(S_t) = \frac{d^2\sigma(S_t)}{dS_t^2} \tag{12.32}$$

Hagan *et al.* (1999, 2002) point out that the first term inside the curly brackets is by far the dominant one, typically accounting for approximately 99% of the total implied volatility. Therefore the expression for the implied volatility is very closely given by

$$\widehat{\sigma}(S_0, K) \simeq \sigma(\tfrac{1}{2}[S_0 + K]) \tag{12.33}$$

and, in order to understand the qualitative link between local and implied volatilities, I will ignore the higher-order terms in (12.31), and simply use Equation (12.33).

Following Hagan *et al.* (1999, 2002), let us take today's option market (as expressed by the implied volatilities $\widehat{\sigma}(S_0, K) = \widehat{\sigma}_0(K)$) as a given. Finding a local-volatility function that fits (produces) this set of exogenous market prices means finding a local volatility that satisfies

$$\widehat{\sigma}_0(S_0, K) = \sigma(\tfrac{1}{2}[S_0 + K]) \tag{12.34}$$

Evaluating the implied volatility function at a strike equal to $2S - S_0$ gives

$$\widehat{\sigma}_0(S_0, K = 2S - S_0) = \sigma(\tfrac{1}{2}[S_0 + 2S - S_0]) = \sigma(S) \tag{12.35}$$

Reading this formula from right to left, (12.35) says that, to leading order, the value of the local volatility function at point S required to price the market must be equal to the value of the market implied volatility corresponding to the option with strike equal to $K = 2S - S_0$.

Suppose now that, instantaneously, the current value of the spot changes (say, increases) from S_0 to S_0':

$$S_0' = S_0 + \Delta S_0, \quad \Delta S_0 > 0 \tag{12.36}$$

Since the local-volatility function is unaffected by this change, using Equation (12.33) we can both calculate the values of the new implied volatility curve and, at the same time, relate them to the implied volatility curve before the move:

$$\widehat{\sigma}_0(S_0 + \Delta S_0, K) = \sigma(\tfrac{1}{2}[S_0 + \Delta S_0 + K]) = \widehat{\sigma}_0(S_0, K + \Delta S_0) \tag{12.37}$$

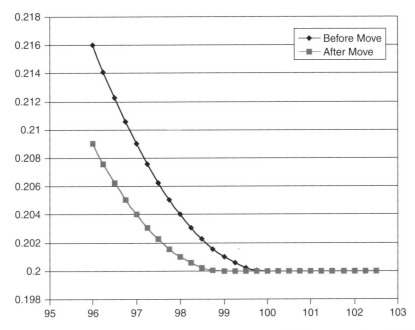

Figure 12.21 The move in the implied volatility as the underlying moves from $100 (curve labelled 'Before Move') to $101 ('After Move').

This means that, as the underlying increases, the implied volatility curve moves to the left, and vice versa. This is shown in Figure 12.21, where it was assumed that the spot price instantaneously moved from $S_0 = 100$ to $S_0' = 101$ (i.e. $\Delta S_0 = +1$).

This behaviour leads Hagan *et al.* (2002) to conclude that a local-volatility approach is poorly suited to describe the observed market dynamics:

> ... This is opposite to typical market behaviour, in which smile and skew move in the *same* direction as the underlying... (emphasis in the original).

In other words, Hagan *et al.* (2002) fully endorse a floating-smile view of the world, for which I have great sympathy in the equity and FX worlds. However, the same conclusions might not be valid when it comes to interest rates. See, in this respect, the discussion in Chapter 7, and in Part IV of this book (Chapters 18 and 24 in particular).

12.8 No-Arbitrage Conditions on the Current Implied Volatility Smile Surface

12.8.1 Constraints on the Implied Volatility Surface

In this section we explore some simple no-arbitrage constraints on the implied volatility surface by looking at it as a function of strike and maturity. The purpose of the analysis is to show the implications these constraints bear for the resulting local-volatility functions. No-arbitrage constraints on implied volatility functions are treated in detail in Chapter 17.

In the remainder of this chapter I discuss the implications of these observations for local-volatility functions.

Smiles can raise the relative value of out-of-the-money options with respect to at-the-money options. This increase, however, can never produce a price for a given option greater than the price of a more in-the-money option with the same expiry on the same underlying. If the condition fails, there exists the possibility for an obvious arbitrage. With this first caveat in mind, let us examine an implied volatility smile surface which might, prima facie, appear plausible. See Table 12.1.

Note that the at-the-money volatilities display a time dependence, but the smile's increase (quadratic) is the same across maturities, i.e. the implied volatility is of the form

$$\widehat{\sigma}(T) = \widehat{\sigma}_{\mathrm{ATM}}(T) + a(K - S_0)^2 \tag{12.38}$$

where K is the strike, $\widehat{\sigma}_{\mathrm{ATM}}(T)$ is a function of time to expiry, T, only, a is a constant, and S_0 is the value of spot today.

Let us compute the prices for calls and puts that this surface implies. (For simplicity we will assume zero interest rates. This will not affect our conclusions because we will compare, in the first instance, options with different strikes and the same expiry). See Table 12.2.

In the right columns of the call price matrix and in the left columns of the put price matrix we find clear violations of the price condition, i.e. prices for out-of-the-money options greater than prices of more in-the-money options with the same expiry. One might be tempted to suggest that the reason for this possible arbitrage is simply that we have allowed the smile to grow too sharply. If one wanted to retain the quadratic behaviour of the smile with strike, one could try to reduce the constant a. This is shown in Table 12.3. One can then check the call and put prices obtainable with the new model implied volatility surface. See Table 12.4.

Despite the fact that the smile is now much less pronounced, the no-arbitrage-violation areas (highlighted in bold in Table 12.4) have receded to the long-maturity part of the matrix, but have not disappeared. From this simple example, one can therefore conclude that decreasing uniformly the constant a would not provide a long-term solution: by increasing the maturity the (relative) effect of a fixed difference in implied volatility becomes progressively greater. Therefore, given a fixed difference in implied volatilities, one can always find a maturity long enough for the out-of-the-money option to be worth more than a more in-the-money option, i.e. for the price violation to appear. We have therefore reached the conclusion that, in order to avoid a model-independent arbitrage, the smile steepness must decrease with increasing maturity. More precisely, it must decrease with maturity quickly enough to (more than) compensate for the increase in relative value due to the increase in maturity.

Keeping this first result in mind, one can try to model a better implied volatility surface by imposing that the quadratic proportionality coefficient should decay with time suitably fast. A possible description of the functional form for the implied volatility function embodying these desiderata could therefore be

$$\widehat{\sigma}(T) = \widehat{\sigma}_{\mathrm{ATM}}(T) + a_T(K - S_0)^2 \tag{12.39}$$

$$a_T = a_0 \exp(-\beta T) \tag{12.40}$$

Table 12.1 A model implied volatility surface, with linear time dependence and quadratic smile, as described by Equation (12.38).

Maturity	Strike										
	80	84	88	92	96	100	104	108	112	116	120
0.1	39.00%	32.09%	26.71%	22.87%	20.57%	19.80%	20.57%	22.87%	26.71%	32.09%	39.00%
0.2	38.80%	31.89%	26.51%	22.67%	20.37%	19.60%	20.37%	22.67%	26.51%	31.89%	38.80%
0.3	38.60%	31.69%	26.31%	22.47%	20.17%	19.40%	20.17%	22.47%	26.31%	31.69%	38.60%
0.4	38.40%	31.49%	26.11%	22.27%	19.97%	19.20%	19.97%	22.27%	26.11%	31.49%	38.40%
0.5	38.20%	31.29%	25.91%	22.07%	19.77%	19.00%	19.77%	22.07%	25.91%	31.29%	38.20%
0.6	38.00%	31.09%	25.71%	21.87%	19.57%	18.80%	19.57%	21.87%	25.71%	31.09%	38.00%
0.7	37.80%	30.89%	25.51%	21.67%	19.37%	18.60%	19.37%	21.67%	25.51%	30.89%	37.80%
0.8	37.60%	30.69%	25.31%	21.47%	19.17%	18.40%	19.17%	21.47%	25.31%	30.69%	37.60%
0.9	37.40%	30.49%	25.11%	21.27%	18.97%	18.20%	18.97%	21.27%	25.11%	30.49%	37.40%
1	37.20%	30.29%	24.91%	21.07%	18.77%	18.00%	18.77%	21.07%	24.91%	30.29%	37.20%
1.1	37.00%	30.09%	24.71%	20.87%	18.57%	17.80%	18.57%	20.87%	24.71%	30.09%	37.00%
1.2	36.80%	29.89%	24.51%	20.67%	18.37%	17.60%	18.37%	20.67%	24.51%	29.89%	36.80%
1.3	36.60%	29.69%	24.31%	20.47%	18.17%	17.40%	18.17%	20.47%	24.31%	29.69%	36.60%
1.4	36.40%	29.49%	24.11%	20.27%	17.97%	17.20%	17.97%	20.27%	24.11%	29.49%	36.40%
1.5	36.20%	29.29%	23.91%	20.07%	17.77%	17.00%	17.77%	20.07%	23.91%	29.29%	36.20%

Table 12.2 (a) Call prices and (b) put prices obtained for the implied volatilities and maturities in Table 12.1.

(a) Call prices

20.15359	16.1625	12.22511	8.428199	5.027136	2.497504	1.113025	0.553261	0.372045	0.348219	0.415336
20.72602	16.6987	12.79582	9.122796	5.911334	3.495777	2.043285	1.359627	1.1351	1.18145	1.433003
21.41095	17.31071	13.38818	9.750357	6.607665	4.237108	2.772675	2.068109	1.87499	2.032182	2.482435
22.09785	17.9111	13.94505	10.30585	7.189319	4.841454	3.380865	2.68082	2.551039	2.828318	3.470462
22.75789	18.48016	14.45964	10.80146	7.691275	5.355787	3.905217	3.237781	3.166085	3.563603	4.387404
23.3839	19.01449	14.93433	11.2478	8.133259	5.804449	4.366643	3.730883	3.727883	4.242811	5.238148
23.97536	19.51527	15.37311	11.65292	8.527693	6.202045	4.778255	4.177233	4.243675	4.872217	6.02986
24.53393	19.98488	15.77986	12.0229	8.883007	6.558188	5.148932	4.584064	4.719461	5.457608	6.769315
25.0619	20.42591	16.15798	12.36242	9.205249	6.879618	5.48503	4.956838	5.160103	6.003931	7.462371
25.5616	20.8408	16.51038	12.67514	9.498937	7.171291	5.79129	5.299795	5.569551	6.515338	8.113971
26.03523	21.23174	16.83951	12.96402	9.767556	7.436984	6.071369	5.616298	5.951044	6.995306	8.728276
26.48481	21.60067	17.14743	13.23145	10.01387	7.679657	6.328159	5.90907	6.307272	7.446766	9.308797
26.91211	21.94928	17.43594	13.4794	10.24011	7.901688	6.564001	6.180351	6.640486	7.872205	9.85852
27.31874	22.27909	17.70655	13.70955	10.44812	8.105022	6.780821	6.432013	6.952601	8.273749	10.38001
27.70612	22.5914	17.96058	13.9233	10.63944	8.291275	6.980229	6.665642	7.245253	8.653235	10.87546

(b) Put prices

0.153588	0.1625	0.225111	0.428199	1.027136	2.497504	5.113025	8.553261	12.37205	16.34822	20.41534
0.726019	0.6987	0.795824	1.122796	1.911334	3.495777	6.043285	9.359627	13.1351	17.18145	21.433
1.410945	1.31071	1.388181	1.750357	2.607665	4.237108	6.772675	10.06811	13.87499	18.03218	22.48244
2.097855	1.911099	1.945053	2.305846	3.189319	4.841454	7.380865	10.68808	14.55104	18.82832	23.47046
2.757894	2.480156	2.45964	2.80146	3.691275	5.355787	7.905217	11.23778	15.16608	19.5636	24.3874
3.383896	3.014493	2.934328	3.247802	4.133259	5.804449	8.366643	11.73088	15.72788	20.24281	25.23815
3.975357	3.51527	3.373106	3.652921	4.527693	6.202045	8.778255	12.17723	16.24368	20.87222	26.02986
4.533933	3.984881	3.779858	4.0229	4.883007	6.558406	9.148932	12.58406	16.71946	21.45761	26.76931
5.0619	4.425912	4.157985	4.362417	5.205249	6.879618	9.48503	12.95684	17.1601	22.00393	27.46237
5.5616	4.840801	4.510384	4.675144	5.498937	7.171291	9.79129	13.2998	17.56955	22.51534	28.11397
6.035235	5.23174	4.839506	4.964022	5.767556	7.436984	10.07137	13.6163	17.95104	22.99531	28.72828
6.484807	5.600666	5.147432	5.231446	6.013869	7.679657	10.32816	13.90907	18.30727	23.44677	29.3088
6.91211	5.949283	5.435937	5.479401	6.240111	7.901688	10.564	14.18035	18.64049	23.8722	29.85852
7.318741	6.279087	5.706546	5.70955	6.448122	8.105022	10.78082	14.43201	18.9526	24.27375	30.38001
7.706121	6.591396	5.960581	5.923305	6.639441	8.291275	10.98023	14.66564	19.24525	24.65324	30.87546

Table 12.3 A similar implied volatility surface, but with a less steep smile. Note that the increase in volatility as one moves out of the money remains the same across maturities.

Maturity						Strike					
	80	84	88	92	96	100	104	108	112	116	120
0.1	32.60%	27.99%	24.41%	21.85%	20.31%	19.80%	20.31%	21.85%	24.41%	27.99%	32.60%
0.2	32.40%	27.79%	24.21%	21.65%	20.11%	19.60%	20.11%	21.65%	24.21%	27.79%	32.40%
0.3	32.20%	27.59%	24.01%	21.45%	19.91%	19.40%	19.91%	21.45%	24.01%	27.59%	32.20%
0.4	32.00%	27.39%	23.81%	21.25%	19.71%	19.20%	19.71%	21.25%	23.81%	27.39%	32.00%
0.5	31.80%	27.19%	23.61%	21.05%	19.51%	19.00%	19.51%	21.05%	23.61%	27.19%	31.80%
0.6	31.60%	26.99%	23.41%	20.85%	19.31%	18.80%	19.31%	20.85%	23.41%	26.99%	31.60%
0.7	31.40%	26.79%	23.21%	20.65%	19.11%	18.60%	19.11%	20.65%	23.21%	26.79%	31.40%
0.8	31.20%	26.59%	23.01%	20.45%	18.91%	18.40%	18.91%	20.45%	23.01%	26.59%	31.20%
0.9	31.00%	26.39%	22.81%	20.25%	18.71%	18.20%	18.71%	20.25%	22.81%	26.39%	31.00%
1	30.80%	26.19%	22.61%	20.05%	18.51%	18.00%	18.51%	20.05%	22.61%	26.19%	30.80%
1.1	30.60%	25.99%	22.41%	19.85%	18.31%	17.80%	18.31%	19.85%	22.41%	25.99%	30.60%
1.2	30.40%	25.79%	22.21%	19.65%	18.11%	17.60%	18.11%	19.65%	22.21%	25.79%	30.40%
1.3	30.20%	25.59%	22.01%	19.45%	17.91%	17.40%	17.91%	19.45%	22.01%	25.59%	30.20%
1.4	30.00%	25.39%	21.81%	19.25%	17.71%	17.20%	17.71%	19.25%	21.81%	25.39%	30.00%
1.5	29.80%	25.19%	21.61%	19.05%	17.51%	17.00%	17.51%	19.05%	21.61%	25.19%	29.80%

Table 12.4 (a) Call prices and (b) put prices obtained for the implied volatilities and maturities in Table 12.3. The areas for which arbitrage violations are encountered have been highlighted in bold.

(a) Call prices

20.04976	16.07463	12.14714	8.366428	5.001227	2.497504	1.085642	0.479076	0.257109	0.18436	0.174246
20.34583	16.41456	12.59201	8.999966	5.870952	3.495777	2.000924	1.21938	0.871653	**0.759082**	**0.787743**
20.77089	16.85222	13.08196	9.581903	6.556597	4.237108	2.719237	1.878981	1.496166	**1.400492**	**1.505028**
21.23171	17.30368	13.5536	10.10009	7.129412	4.841454	3.318258	2.459003	2.077269	**2.022682**	**2.216094**
21.69335	17.74298	13.99461	10.56359	7.623673	5.355787	3.834621	2.974282	2.610603	**2.607937**	**2.894044**
22.14235	18.16188	14.40404	10.98141	8.058757	5.804449	4.288879	3.436778	3.099965	**3.154174**	**3.533095**
22.57353	18.55821	14.78381	11.36067	8.446883	6.202045	4.693938	3.855342	3.550218	**3.663405**	**4.133673**
22.98519	18.93207	15.13643	11.70685	8.796356	6.558188	5.058543	4.236574	3.965825	**4.138607**	**4.698079**
23.37715	19.2844	15.46436	12.02422	9.113132	6.879618	5.388958	4.58551	4.350592	**4.58278**	**5.229053**
23.74992	19.61642	15.7698	12.31616	9.401666	7.171291	5.68986	4.906082	4.707715	**4.998669**	**5.729281**
24.10432	19.92943	16.05469	12.5854	9.665397	7.436984	5.964856	5.201424	5.039871	**5.388703**	**6.201231**
24.44126	20.22466	16.32072	12.83419	9.907051	7.679657	6.216801	5.474085	5.349315	**5.755004**	**6.647114**
24.76167	20.50324	16.56935	13.06436	10.12883	7.901688	6.448005	5.726168	5.637964	**6.099424**	**7.068892**
25.06643	20.76623	16.80187	13.27747	10.33256	8.105022	6.660369	5.959437	5.90746	**6.423582**	**7.468298**
25.35641	21.01457	17.01939	13.47486	10.51976	8.291275	6.855485	6.175386	6.159218	**6.728898**	**7.846871**

(b) Put prices

0.049764	0.074629	0.147139	0.366428	1.001227	2.497504	5.085642	8.479076	12.25711	16.18436	20.17425
0.34583	0.414564	0.592007	0.999966	1.870952	3.495777	6.000924	9.21938	12.87165	16.75908	20.78774
0.770893	0.852216	1.081964	1.581903	2.556597	4.237108	6.719237	9.878981	13.49617	17.40049	21.50503
1.231713	1.303677	1.553601	2.100087	3.129412	4.841454	7.318258	10.459	14.07727	18.02268	22.21609
1.693351	1.742978	1.994605	2.563591	3.623673	5.355787	7.834621	10.97428	14.6106	18.60794	22.89404
2.142348	2.161879	2.404037	2.981414	4.058757	5.804449	8.288879	11.43678	15.09996	19.15417	23.53309
2.573528	2.55821	2.783808	3.36067	4.446883	6.202045	8.693938	11.85534	15.55022	19.66341	24.13367
2.985185	2.932068	3.136431	3.706847	4.796356	6.558188	9.058543	12.23657	15.96582	20.13861	24.69808
3.377147	3.284395	3.464357	4.024217	5.113132	6.879618	9.388958	12.58551	16.35059	20.58278	25.22905
3.749924	3.616424	3.769796	4.316163	5.401666	7.171291	9.68986	12.90608	16.70772	20.99867	25.72928
4.104325	3.929435	4.054688	4.58541	5.665397	7.436984	9.964856	13.20142	17.03987	21.3887	26.20123
4.441263	4.224659	4.320718	4.83419	5.907051	7.679657	10.2168	13.47408	17.34932	21.755	26.64711
4.761666	4.503242	4.569353	5.064357	6.128834	7.901688	10.448	13.72617	17.63796	22.09942	27.06889
5.066432	4.76623	4.801869	5.277472	6.332561	8.105022	10.66037	13.95944	17.90746	22.42358	27.4683
5.356409	5.014574	5.019386	5.474862	6.519755	8.291275	10.85548	14.17539	18.15922	22.7289	27.84687

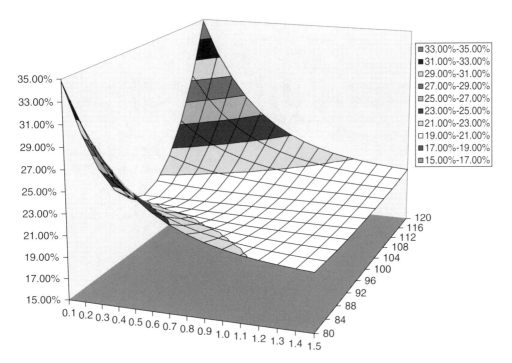

Figure 12.22 The implied volatility surface obtained with an exponentially decaying coefficient a.

The surface thus obtained is shown in Figure 12.22. One can immediately check that the call and put prices now behave correctly (see Table 12.5).

12.8.2 Consequences for Local Volatilities

The functional forms presented above for the smile and for the decay constant are not supposed to show a particularly realistic fit to observed market data. Given their very 'clean' form, however, it is possible to analyse the qualitative behaviour they imply for future option prices. In particular, it is instructive to examine the local volatility surfaces obtainable using the method described in the previous sections using 'good' and 'bad' implied volatility inputs. Figure 12.23, in particular, shows the local volatility surface obtained with the first implied volatility matrix (Table 12.1), which we know to admit arbitrage.

The first observation is that the resulting ('unacceptable') local volatility surface has lost the symmetry of the parent implied volatility function (remember that we started from a quadratic smile); this is due to the log-normal distribution of the underlying price process. The surface appears to be slightly decreasing over time, and, by inspection, could produce a smiley implied volatility surface in the future. Whether this implied volatility surface will be floating, sticky, or otherwise is impossible to say without carrying out the calculations described in the previous section. What one *can* say from the shape of the local-volatility surface is that, whatever the nature of the future smile, it will be less pronounced in the future.

Table 12.5 (a) Call prices and (b) put prices obtained for the implied volatilities and maturities in Figure 12.22.

(a) Call prices

20.08135	16.10519	12.17933	8.399864	5.030646	2.522723	1.116734	0.519318	0.305243	0.243777	0.241211
20.34262	16.42079	12.61146	9.038564	5.931145	3.567072	2.064063	1.263524	0.897095	0.768666	0.7661
20.59696	16.73952	13.03479	9.609231	6.654806	4.368023	2.821996	1.909706	1.437193	1.240191	1.221937
20.80984	17.02387	13.41846	10.115	7.274327	5.042917	3.469695	2.475628	1.912129	1.640314	1.56705
20.98875	17.27769	13.7677	10.57167	7.82424	5.637212	4.044056	2.983245	2.337143	1.987539	1.846825
21.14518	17.50971	14.09085	10.99143	8.323785	6.174226	4.565484	3.447842	2.726063	2.299079	2.085784
21.28842	17.72735	14.39477	11.38282	8.784872	6.667814	5.046564	3.879754	3.088932	2.587367	2.30086
21.42503	17.93602	14.68446	11.75185	9.215428	7.127005	5.495645	4.286079	3.432721	2.860852	2.503182
21.55938	18.13942	14.96345	12.10278	9.621009	7.558071	5.918574	4.67181	3.762207	3.125114	2.69987
21.69426	18.33995	15.23416	12.4387	10.00567	7.965579	6.319609	5.040528	4.080653	3.383756	2.895349
21.83136	18.53913	15.49826	12.76189	10.37246	8.352978	6.701955	5.39486	4.390283	3.639034	3.092239
21.9716	18.73785	15.75686	13.07404	10.72374	8.722949	7.068091	5.736774	4.692613	3.892294	3.291966
22.11539	18.93655	16.01073	13.37648	11.06139	9.077621	7.419977	6.067769	4.988673	4.144279	3.495167
22.26278	19.1354	16.26036	13.67022	11.38692	9.418724	7.759193	6.389012	5.279164	4.395333	3.701971
22.41361	19.33438	16.50609	13.95606	11.70155	9.747683	8.087034	6.701431	5.564567	4.645548	3.912188

(b) Put prices

0.081354	0.105188	0.179332	0.399864	1.030646	2.522723	5.116734	8.519318	12.30524	16.24378	20.25386
0.342624	0.420791	0.61146	1.038564	1.931145	3.567072	6.064063	9.263524	12.8971	16.76867	20.78191
0.596956	0.739524	1.034794	1.609231	2.654806	4.368023	6.821996	9.909706	13.43719	17.24019	21.22194
0.809843	1.023868	1.418464	2.115001	3.274327	5.042917	7.469695	10.47563	13.91213	17.64031	21.56705
0.988747	1.277689	1.767696	2.571674	3.82424	5.637212	8.044056	10.98325	14.33714	17.98754	21.84683
1.145182	1.50971	2.090846	2.991427	4.323785	6.174226	8.565484	11.44784	14.72606	18.29908	22.08578
1.288424	1.727354	2.394765	3.382818	4.784872	6.667814	9.046564	11.87975	15.08893	18.58737	22.30086
1.42503	1.936025	2.684459	3.751846	5.215428	7.127005	9.495645	12.28608	15.43272	18.86085	22.50318
1.559375	2.139417	2.963447	4.102777	5.621009	7.558071	9.918574	12.67181	15.76221	19.12511	22.69987
1.694256	2.339949	3.234159	4.438699	6.005667	7.965579	10.31961	13.04053	16.08065	19.38376	22.89535
1.831357	2.539134	3.498255	4.761886	6.372457	8.352978	10.70195	13.39486	16.39028	19.63903	23.09224
1.971602	2.737851	3.756861	5.074044	6.723743	8.722949	11.06809	13.73677	16.69261	19.89229	23.29197
2.115393	2.93655	4.010728	5.376482	7.061393	9.077621	11.41998	14.06777	16.98867	20.14428	23.49517
2.262785	3.1354	4.260361	5.670216	7.386916	9.418724	11.75919	14.38901	17.27916	20.39533	23.70197
2.413611	3.334382	4.506088	5.956058	7.701549	9.747683	12.08703	14.70143	17.56457	20.64555	23.91219

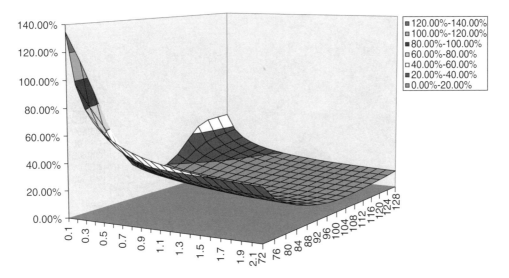

Figure 12.23   The local volatility surface obtained using the 'unacceptable' implied volatilities in Table 12.1.

We can then repeat the calculations described in the first sections of this chapter in order to obtain the local-volatility surface using an 'acceptable' implied volatility surfaces. Two such surfaces (obtained with different decay coefficients β) are shown in Figures 12.24 and 12.25. The results displayed in Figure 12.24, in particular, were obtained with the 'acceptable' implied volatility surface of Figure 12.22.

One can immediately notice that, at the short-time end of the curve, the qualitative behaviour is quite similar to the one obtained for the 'unacceptable' input implied volatility surfaces. Comparing Figures 12.24 and 12.25 one can also notice that, for long times, there remains a very modest but noticeable dependence on time (increasing in Figure 12.24 and decreasing in Figure 12.25). Furthermore, the surface is more symmetric across the strike direction. The most important feature revealed by comparing these two figures, however, is that the dependence of the local volatility on the stock price has all but disappeared for maturities beyond a few years. Therefore the local-volatility surfaces obtained from parabolic implied volatilities that have been rendered 'acceptable' by introducing a decaying smile can produce no smiles in the future!

This observation is very important. Since this analysis has been carried out using some very 'clean' parabolic implied volatility surfaces as inputs, one can easily point to the following conclusions:

1. in order to have non-arbitrageable prices, i.e. in order to avoid higher prices for more out-of-the-money options and, therefore, arbitrage, the implied-volatility smile surface must display a decreasing degree of 'smileyness' as a function of maturity;

2. if one introduces a flattening smile surface, as required by point 1 above, the future local volatilities that can be extracted from it tend to lose their price dependence: they only (and very mildly) depend on time;

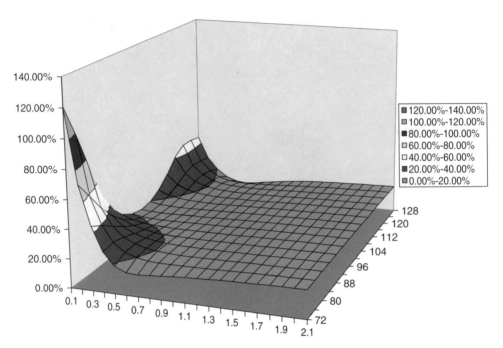

Figure 12.24   A local volatility surface obtained using the 'acceptable' implied volatilities in Figure 12.22.

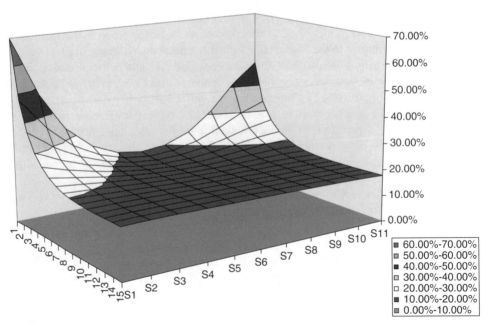

Figure 12.25   Another local volatility surface obtained using an implied volatility surface of the same type as in Figure 12.24, but with a higher decay constant, β.

3. as a consequence, these local volatility surfaces cannot produce future implied smile surfaces with any structure (or, rather, they seem to be only able to produce flat ones);

4. this state of affairs implies that today's smile surface is not only non-time-homogeneous, but is destined to disappear!

Admittedly, the results reported above have been obtained with a particular behaviour of smile flattening (decaying exponential vs maturity, as shown in Equation (12.40)). Also, the smile for the shortest maturity was arbitrarily (albeit plausibly) chosen. Therefore, strictly speaking, the conclusions reached above are not general, even for purely parabolic implied volatility surfaces. It is none the less difficult to see how different patterns consistent with the required decay of the smile surface could produce results that are qualitatively truly different.

These observations, and conclusion 4 in particular, have profound implications for the users of market-calibrated models based on a specification of the volatility surface purely as a deterministic function of time and of the underlying. Note that no assumption was made in obtaining the local volatility functions from the implied volatility surface other than assuming that

$$\sigma = \sigma(S_t, t) \qquad (12.41)$$

Therefore, traders who use local-volatility models when the market implied volatility displays a symmetric smile imply future re-hedging costs (as predicted by the model) that are likely to be materially different from those that will be encountered during the life of the option. I have discussed in Chapter 1 why I think that this is very undesirable. This topic is explored in detail in Chapter 17 by focusing on a particular option instrument (the continuous double barrier). In that chapter I will draw from the analysis of the results some general conclusions about option pricing in the presence of smiles.

12.9 Empirical Performance

Before closing the chapter, it is interesting to report the results of empirical work carried out by Dumas *et al.* (1998) on the hedging performance of the Derman-and-Kani, Dupire (1994) and Rubinstein (1994) approaches. These researchers examined the predictive and hedging performance of these restricted-stochastic-volatility models in the case of equity (S&P500) options in the period June 1988–December 1993. They used the simple Black-and-Scholes (1973) model as a benchmark strategy against which the performance of the more complex approaches could be assessed. The latter was used with an implied volatility input which was smoothed across strikes and maturities. Despite the fact that Dumas *et al.* come from a very different angle, they reach very similar conclusions to the ones expressed above, in so far as equity options are concerned, regarding the hedging performance of the Derman-and-Kani approach. In particular, the study mentioned above reaches the following conclusions:

- the more parsimonious Black-and-Scholes model works best in-sample, at least on the basis of the information criterion mentioned in their paper;

- the prediction errors obtainable from restricted-stochastic-volatility models are larger, compared with the Black-and-Scholes case, when the extracted local-volatility function is used to value options one week later;

- the hedge ratios determined by the Black-and-Scholes model appear more reliable than the corresponding quantities obtained using the more complex restricted-stochastic-volatility models.

On the basis of their study, Dumas *et al.* conclude that 'simpler is better'. The observations presented in earlier parts of this section, although arrived at by following a very different line of reasoning, concur with this conclusion, with the proviso, however, that 'simpler' might well be 'better', but even this 'better' might sometimes not be good enough. The next chapters will present approaches that do produce a more convincing pricing and hedging performance than the Black-and-Scholes model.

I am not aware of empirical studies similar to the one conducted by Dumas *et al.* for FX or interest rates. On the basis of the results of the tests reported and discussed in Sections 12.3–12.5, I would be surprised if very different conclusions were reached for FX options. In the interest-rate area, however, the restricted-stochastic-volatility approach might provide a more realistic, and useful, pricing tool. This is discussed in Parts III and IV of this book.

12.10   Appendix I: Proof that $\frac{\partial^2 Call(S_t,K,T,t)}{\partial K^2} = \phi(S_T)|_K$

Let

- $Call(S_t, k, T, t)$ be the time-t price of a call on stock S with strike K and maturity T;

- $\phi(S_T)|_K$ be the probability (density) that the stock price S at time T, S_T, should be in the range $[K \ \ K + dK]$, contingent on its value at time t being S_t.

Ignoring discounting, and given any terminal price distribution we can write for the time-t price of a call:

$$Call(S_t, K, T, t) = \int_0^\infty (S_T - K)^+ \phi(S_T)\, dS_T \tag{12.42}$$

where $(a - b)^+ = \max(a - b, 0)$. In order to evaluate the first derivative of the function *Call* with respect to the strike we can first re-write Equation (12.42) as

$$Call(S_t, K, T, t) = \int_K^\infty (S_T - K)\phi(S_T)\, dS_T$$

and then make use of the result

$$\frac{\partial}{\partial x} \int_0^x f(t, x)\, dt = f(t, t) + \int_0^x \frac{\partial f(t, x)}{\partial x}\, dt \tag{12.43}$$

This gives

$$
\begin{aligned}
\frac{\partial Call(S_t, K, T, t)}{\partial K} &= \frac{\partial}{\partial K} \int_K^\infty (S_T - K)\phi(S_T)\, dS_T \\
&= -\frac{\partial}{\partial K} \int_\infty^K (S_T - K)\phi(S_T) dS_T \\
&= -(K - K) - \int_\infty^K \frac{\partial[(S_T - K)\phi(S_T)]}{\partial K} dS_T = \int_\infty^K \phi(S_T) dS_T
\end{aligned}
$$

$$(12.44)$$

Differentiating again with respect to K finally gives

$$
\frac{\partial^2 Call(S_t, K, T, t)}{\partial K^2} = \phi(K) \tag{12.45}
$$

where use has been made of the fundamental theorem of calculus: $\frac{\partial}{\partial x} \int_0^x f(t)dt = f(x)$.

Chapter 13

Stochastic-Volatility Processes

13.1 Plan of the Chapter

The restricted-stochastic-volatility models presented in the previous chapter are typically used by practitioners (whether wisely or not is a different matter) for equity and FX problems. In their CEV incarnation, they also appear in the interest-rate arena. This is discussed in Part IV of this book. In this chapter we want to look at a more general modelling approach, while still trying to explain the observed deviation from the Black-and-Scholes prices in terms of stochastic volatility. The financial motivation for pursuing this avenue is the empirical observation that the volatility of financial time series appears to be non-constant, and its variability difficult to explain by means of a deterministic function of time, or of time and stock price. For a review of empirical studies, see, for example, Campbell *et al.* (1997), or, more recently, Fouque *et al.* (2000).

13.2 Portfolio Replication in the Presence of Stochastic Volatility

13.2.1 Attempting to Extend the Portfolio Replication Argument

The Portfolio-Replication Argument: Stochastic Volatility Hedged with Stock Only

Let us see how the replication argument presented in Chapter 2 has to be modified when the volatility is stochastic. Strictly speaking, the title of this section is now inaccurate because, as we shall see, an option payoff cannot actually be replicated even in the absence of frictions just by trading in the underlying. The treatment parallels, however, the deterministic-volatility case, where replication *is* possible, and therefore I will still talk of 'portfolio replication'.

We start by making some assumptions about the nature of the call price functional. We will assume that it is separable, i.e. that it depends in a separable way on the discounting and on the other state variables, and that these state variables are the stock price, S_t, and

389

the volatility, σ_t. Ignoring discounting, we therefore write

$$C_t = C(S_t, \sigma_t, t) \tag{13.1}$$

Employing the same notation used in Chapter 2, the fundamental constitutive SDEs now become:[1]

$$dS_t = \mu_S S_t\, dt + \sigma_t S_t\, dz_t \tag{13.4}$$

$$d\sigma_t = \sigma_t \mu_\sigma\, dt + \sigma_t v_t\, dw_t \tag{13.5}$$

$$dB_t = B_t r_t\, dt \tag{13.6}$$

$$E[dw_t\, dz_t] = \rho \tag{13.7}$$

Using Ito's lemma, we obtain for dC_t:

$$dC_t = C_t \mu_C\, dt + C_t \sigma_C\, dZ_t \tag{13.8}$$

or, more transparently,

$$dC_t = C_t \mu_C\, dt + C_t \sigma_{CS}\, dz_t + C_t \sigma_{C\sigma}\, dw_t \tag{13.9}$$

with

$$C_t \mu_C = \frac{\partial C}{\partial t} + \frac{\partial C}{\partial S}\mu_S S_t + \frac{\partial C}{\partial \sigma}\mu_\sigma \sigma_t$$

$$+ \frac{1}{2}\left[\frac{\partial^2 C}{\partial S^2}\sigma_t^2 S_t^2 + 2\frac{\partial^2 C}{\partial S \partial \sigma}\rho \sigma_t S_t v_t \sigma_t + \frac{\partial^2 C}{\partial \sigma^2}v_t^2 \sigma_t^2\right] \tag{13.10}$$

$$C\sigma_{CS} = \frac{\partial C}{\partial S}\sigma S \tag{13.11}$$

$$C\sigma_{C\sigma} = \frac{\partial C}{\partial \sigma}v\sigma \tag{13.12}$$

$$C_t \sigma_C = \sqrt{\left[\frac{\partial C}{\partial S}\sigma_t S_t\right]^2 + \left[\frac{\partial C}{\partial \sigma}v_t \sigma_t\right]^2 + 2\rho\frac{\partial C}{\partial S}\sigma_t S_t \frac{\partial C}{\partial \sigma}v_t \sigma_t} \tag{13.13}$$

So, σ_{CS} and $\sigma_{C\sigma}$ are the percentage responsiveness of the call price to the Brownian shocks that affect the stock price (dz) and the volatility (dw), respectively.

Exercise 1 *Derive Equation (13.13) by evaluating* $var[dC_t] = E[dC_t^2]$ *and making use of* $E[dw_t\, dz_t] = \rho$.

---

[1]A similar description can be achieved by prescribing a dynamics for the square of the volatility:

$$dS_t = \mu_S S_t\, dt + \sqrt{V} S_t\, dz_t \tag{13.2}$$

$$dV = V_t \mu_V\, dt + V_t v_t\, dw_t \tag{13.3}$$

The details of the results are clearly different, but the reasoning proceeds along similar lines.

Note in passing that, by Equation (13.8), we are not saying that the price of a call should be log-normally distributed, but just a strictly positive semi-martingale, which can always be expressed in the form (13.8).

Taking the deterministic-volatility case treated in Chapter 2 as a blueprint, let us build a portfolio made up of α units of the stock S, β units of the riskless bond B, and one unit of the option C:

$$\Pi_t = \alpha S_t + \beta \, dB_t + C_t \tag{13.14}$$

The evolution of the portfolio will now be

$$
\begin{aligned}
d\Pi_t &= \alpha \, dS_t + \beta B_t r_t \, dt + dC_t \\
&= \alpha\{\mu_S S_t \, dt + \sigma_t S_t \, dz_t\} + \beta B_t r_t \, dt + C_t \mu_C \, dt + C_t \sigma_{CS} \, dz_t + C_t \sigma_{C\sigma} \, dw_t \\
&= \alpha\{\mu_S S_t \, dt + \sigma_t S_t \, dz_t\} + \beta B_t r_t \, dt \\
&\quad + \left[\frac{\partial C}{\partial t} + \frac{\partial C}{\partial S}\mu_S S_t + \frac{\partial C}{\partial \sigma}\mu_\sigma \sigma_t \right. \\
&\quad \left. + \frac{1}{2}\left(\frac{\partial^2 C}{\partial S^2}\sigma_t^2 S_t^2 + 2\frac{\partial^2 C}{\partial S \partial \sigma}\rho\sigma_t S_t v_t \sigma_t + \frac{\partial^2 C}{\partial \sigma^2}v_t^2 \sigma_t^2 \right) \right] dt \\
&\quad + \frac{\partial C}{\partial S}\sigma_t S_t \, dz_t + \frac{\partial C}{\partial \sigma}v_t \sigma_t \, dw_t
\end{aligned}
\tag{13.15}
$$

Re-grouping terms as in the deterministic case gives

$$
\begin{aligned}
d\Pi_t &= \{\alpha\mu_S S_t + \beta B_t r_t\} \, dt \\
&\quad + \left[\frac{\partial C}{\partial t} + \frac{\partial C}{\partial S}\mu_S S_t + \frac{\partial C}{\partial \sigma}\mu_\sigma \sigma_t \right. \\
&\quad \left. + \frac{1}{2}\left(\frac{\partial^2 C}{\partial S^2}\sigma_t^2 S_t^2 + 2\frac{\partial^2 C}{\partial S \partial \sigma}\rho\sigma_t S_t v_t \sigma_t + \frac{\partial^2 C}{\partial \sigma^2}v_t^2 \sigma_t^2 \right) \right] dt \\
&\quad + \left[\alpha\sigma_t S_t + \frac{\partial C}{\partial S}\sigma_t S_t \right] dz_t \\
&\quad + \frac{\partial C}{\partial \sigma}v_t \sigma_t \, dw_t
\end{aligned}
\tag{13.16}
$$

Why is there an asymmetry in the terms in dz and dw? Because we are holding α units of stock, but no 'unit of volatility' (volatility is not a traded asset). It is clear by the way Equation (13.16) has been written that it is possible to neutralize the uncertainty associated with the Brownian motion dz_t by choosing a suitable amount of stock, α. There are, however, no traded instruments left to hedge against the uncertainty in the portfolio value stemming from the term dw_t. We need to introduce another traded asset into our portfolio capable of neutralizing the uncertainty coming from the stochastic nature of volatility. As noted above, however, unlike the stock, volatility is not directly traded in the market. The strategy must therefore be more indirect: we must find another asset that depends on volatility and try to hedge with that.

The Portfolio-Replication Argument: Stochastic Volatility Hedged with the Stock and an Option

The argument is similar to the one in the sub-section above, but now we allow for another traded option, h_t, to be included, alongside the stock and the bond, to our basket of hedging instruments. The equations between (13.8) and (13.13) therefore apply again with C replaced by h, and will not be repeated for the sake of brevity. Also, the same assumptions are made about the dependence of the new option:

$$h_t = h(S_t, \sigma_t, t) \tag{13.17}$$

The portfolio now becomes

$$\Pi_t = \alpha S_t + \beta B_t + \gamma h_t + C_t \tag{13.18}$$

and its evolution will be given by

$$
\begin{aligned}
d\Pi_t &= \alpha\, dS_t + \beta\, dB_t + \gamma\, dh_t + dC_t \\
&= \alpha\{\mu_S S_t\, dt + \sigma_t S_t\, dz_t\} + \beta B_t r_t\, dt \\
&\quad + \gamma\{\mu_h h_t\, dt + h_t \sigma_{hS}\, dz_t + h_t \sigma_{h\sigma}\, dw_t\} \\
&\quad + C_t \mu_C\, dt + C_t \sigma_{CS} S\, dz_t + C_t \sigma_{C\sigma} \sigma\, dw_t
\end{aligned} \tag{13.19}
$$

Substituting and re-grouping terms gives:

$$
\begin{aligned}
d\Pi_t &= \alpha \mu_S S_t\, dt + \beta B_t r_t\, dt \\
&\quad + \gamma \left[\frac{\partial h}{\partial t} + \frac{\partial h}{\partial S} \mu_S S_t + \frac{\partial h}{\partial \sigma} \mu_\sigma \sigma_t \right. \\
&\qquad \left. + \frac{1}{2}\left(\frac{\partial^2 h}{\partial S^2} \sigma_t^2 S_t^2 + 2\frac{\partial^2 h}{\partial S \partial \sigma} \rho \sigma_t S_t v_t \sigma_t + \frac{\partial^2 h}{\partial \sigma^2} v_t^2 \sigma_t^2 \right) \right] dt \\
&\quad + \left[\frac{\partial C}{\partial t} + \frac{\partial C}{\partial S} \mu_S S_t + \frac{\partial C}{\partial \sigma} \mu_\sigma \sigma_t \right] dt \\
&\quad + \frac{1}{2}\left(\frac{\partial^2 C}{\partial S^2} \sigma_t^2 S_t^2 + 2\frac{\partial^2 C}{\partial S \partial \sigma} \rho \sigma_t S_t v_t \sigma_t + \frac{\partial^2 C}{\partial \sigma^2} v_t^2 \sigma_t^2 \right) dt \\
&\quad + \left[\alpha + \gamma \frac{\partial h}{\partial S} + \frac{\partial C}{\partial S} \right] \sigma_t S_t\, dz_t + \left[\gamma \frac{\partial h}{\partial \sigma} + \frac{\partial C}{\partial \sigma} \right] v_t \sigma_t\, dw_t
\end{aligned} \tag{13.20}
$$

In order to neutralize the uncertainty from dw_t the term in brackets in the last line of Equation (13.20) must be zero. To ensure this, we must choose

$$\gamma = -\frac{\dfrac{\partial C}{\partial \sigma}}{\dfrac{\partial h}{\partial \sigma}} \tag{13.21}$$

Not surprisingly, the 'hedge ratio' for the volatility risk is simply equal to the ratio of the volatility responsiveness of the hedging option h to the volatility responsiveness of the option C. Once this value for γ is substituted everywhere into Equation (13.20) one can solve for the value of α that neutralizes the uncertainty coming from dz_t. This gives

$$\alpha = -\frac{\partial C}{\partial S} - \gamma \frac{\partial h}{\partial S} = -\frac{\partial C}{\partial S} + \frac{\frac{\partial C}{\partial \sigma}}{\frac{\partial h}{\partial \sigma}} \frac{\partial h}{\partial S} \tag{13.22}$$

Finally, we want to impose that the portfolio today should have zero cost. This produces for the amount β of the bond (borrowing/lending):

$$\beta = \frac{-\alpha S - \gamma h - C}{B} = \frac{\left[\frac{\partial C}{\partial S} - \frac{\frac{\partial C}{\partial \sigma}}{\frac{\partial h}{\partial \sigma}} \frac{\partial h}{\partial S} \right] S + \frac{\frac{\partial C}{\partial \sigma}}{\frac{\partial h}{\partial \sigma}} h - C}{B} \tag{13.23}$$

Exercise 2 *Derive Equation (13.23).*

Exercise 3 *If one could write $\frac{\frac{\partial C}{\partial \sigma}}{\frac{\partial h}{\partial \sigma}} = \frac{\partial C}{\partial h}$ what would the implications be for the term α, and for the composition of the resulting portfolio? Where does the difference between $\frac{\frac{\partial C}{\partial \sigma}}{\frac{\partial h}{\partial \sigma}}$ and $\frac{\partial C}{\partial h}$ come from? (Hint: there would be no difference if the derivatives were total instead of partial.) Comment on the financial implications.*

This set of equations would appear to have formally solved the problem of preference-free pricing (portfolio replication) of an option C in the presence of stochastic volatility. Matters, however, are not quite so simple: unique pricing by no arbitrage (as can be obtained if we can replicate perfectly) is only possible if we know *the full process*, not just today's price, for the hedging option h. If we knew the value of the hedging option, h, in all future states of the world (that is to say, for all possible combinations of S_t and σ_t) then we could compute all the required derivatives, such as $\frac{\partial^2 h}{\partial S^2}$, $\frac{\partial^2 h}{\partial S \partial \sigma}$, $\frac{\partial^2 h}{\partial \sigma^2}$, etc. But in reality we only know the price today, h_0, of the hedging option, not its process. This important point is discussed at greater length in a similar context in Chapter 14, Section 14.3. Therefore we cannot obtain a preference-free solution quite in the same way as we were able to do in the deterministic-volatility case. None the less we can still arrive at a PDE (or, rather, at an infinity of PDEs) governing the behaviour of the price of a call by reasoning as follows.

The PDE in the Stochastic-Volatility Case

In order to simplify notation, let me define the operators $\mathcal{BS}[f]$ and $\mathcal{A}[f]$:

$$\mathcal{BS}[f] = \frac{\partial f}{\partial t} + \frac{\partial f}{\partial S} \mu_S S_t + \frac{\partial f}{\partial \sigma} \mu_\sigma \sigma_t + \frac{1}{2} \mathcal{A}[f] \tag{13.24}$$

with

$$\mathcal{A}[f] = \left[\frac{\partial^2 f}{\partial S^2} \sigma_t^2 S_t^2 + 2 \frac{\partial^2 f}{\partial S \partial \sigma} \rho \sigma_t S_t v_t \sigma_t + \frac{\partial^2 f}{\partial \sigma^2} v_t^2 \sigma_t^2 \right] \tag{13.25}$$

Then Equation (13.20) can be rewritten more concisely as follows:

$$d\Pi_t = \alpha \mu_S S_t \, dt + \beta B_t r_t \, dt$$
$$+ \gamma BS[h] \, dt + BS[C] dt$$
$$+ \left[\alpha + \gamma \frac{\partial h}{\partial S} + \frac{\partial C}{\partial S} \right] \sigma_t S_t \, dz_t$$
$$+ \left[\gamma \frac{\partial h}{\partial \sigma} + \frac{\partial C}{\partial \sigma} \right] v_t \sigma_t \, dw_t \tag{13.26}$$

Substituting the expressions derived above for α, β and γ into Equation (13.26), and after some algebraic manipulations, one obtains:

$$\left[\frac{\partial h}{\partial \sigma} \right]^{-1} \left[\frac{1}{2} \mathcal{A}(h) + \left(\frac{\partial h}{\partial S} S - h \right) r + \frac{\partial h}{\partial t} \right]$$
$$= \left[\frac{\partial C}{\partial \sigma} \right]^{-1} \left[\frac{1}{2} \mathcal{A}(C) + \left(\frac{\partial C}{\partial S} S - C \right) r + \frac{\partial C}{\partial t} \right] \tag{13.27}$$

Note that the real-world drifts both of the stock price and of the volatility have disappeared.

Exercise 4 *Substitute the expressions obtained above for α and γ into Equation (13.20) and show that, indeed, neither the real-world drift of the stock, μ_S, nor the real-world drift of the volatility, μ_σ appear in the resulting expression.*

There is a non-surprising symmetry in Equation (13.27): we can regard it as the equation obtained by hedging option C with the stock and option h. We would have obtained exactly the same equation, however, if we had taken the complementary view, and attempted to hedge option h using option C (and the stock). More interestingly, Equation (13.27) shows the absence of any cross dependencies on either side of the equation: the LHS only depends on h, S and t, and the RHS is purely a function of C, S and t. Remember, though, that we did not impose any constraints on option h, apart that its payoff at time T should depend only on S_T. In particular, it could have had any strike, K, and any maturity, T. For Equation (13.27) to be valid for any K and T both sides of the equation must therefore be independent of any option-specific feature (such as its strike or maturity). We can therefore require that either side of the equation should be equal to some function of the state variables, S_t, σ_t and t, but not of K or T. Therefore:

$$\left[\frac{\partial C}{\partial \sigma} \right]^{-1} \left[\frac{1}{2} \mathcal{A}(C) + \left(\frac{\partial C}{\partial S} S - C \right) r + \frac{\partial C}{\partial t} \right] = -g(S, \sigma, t) \tag{13.28}$$

or

$$\left[\frac{1}{2}\mathcal{A}(C) + \left(\frac{\partial C}{\partial S} S - C \right) r + \frac{\partial C}{\partial t} \right] = -g(S, \sigma, t) \frac{\partial C}{\partial \sigma} \qquad (13.29)$$

(The negative sign in front of the function g is purely for convenience: see later.) This is the PDE satisfied by the option price when the volatility is stochastic. More precisely, Equation (13.29) gives a whole family of PDEs (one for any choice of the function $g(S, \sigma, t)$). Which is the 'right choice' for this function? If we are 'just' interested in obtaining a non-arbitrageable set of option prices compatible with the underlying following some stochastic-volatility process, then *any* choice for g describes a possible arbitrage-free trading universe in which volatility is stochastic. Perhaps one particular choice for g will also recover exactly today's market prices. If this were the case we would have found at least *a* world in which today's prices match the observed prices and follow a stochastic-volatility diffusion. This does not automatically mean that the true process is indeed a stochastic-volatility diffusion, but, at least, we would have some corroborative evidence that this might be the case.

Let us look at the matter more closely. Given a set of options $C_i, i = 1, 2, \ldots, N$, for a given g Equation (13.29) has to be satisfied by all of the option prices simultaneously. Assume that the market prices of these options are given exogenously, and that the function $g(.)$ is parameterized by a set of coefficients, $\{\alpha\}, k = 1, 2, \ldots, n$. If the market prices were perfectly consistent with a stochastic-volatility model, and if the chosen parametric function $g(.)$ was sufficiently flexible, we could find the set of coefficients, $\{\widehat{\alpha}_k\}$, such that the solutions to the N PDEs (13.29) with the appropriate initial and boundary conditions yielded exactly the market prices.

This, in general, will not be possible. Logically, this failure to match all the prices exactly (or even within their bid–offer spreads) might arise either because we have not guessed the correct functional form for the function $g(.)$, or, more likely, because the underlying process generating the prices is not exactly a stochastic-volatility diffusion. Since, in real life, there will always be some differences between the model and market prices, in practical situations a best fit will be carried out over the parameters of the phenomenological function g, and it will be up to the trader to decide whether the discrepancies are such that the model should be accepted or rejected. Note that it is not just the magnitude of the discrepancies between the model and market prices that matter, but also the 'structure' of the errors. If the larger discrepancies were predominantly found, for instance, for short maturities, or for out-of-the-money puts, rather than randomly scattered across strikes and expiries, this could provide useful indications as to the overall appropriateness of the model.

If we leave the function g totally general (i.e. price-, volatility- and time-dependent), it is not difficult to obtain excellent fits to market prices. A model that can account for anything that is thrown at it, however, has very little explanatory power. Therefore we might want to restrict the flexibility of the function g, but, at the moment, we have very little guidance as to how this can be accomplished in a financially justifiable manner. This problem is tackled in the next section by associating a financial interpretation to the quantity g.

13.2.2   The Market Price of Volatility Risk

If one combines Equation (13.29) with the expression (derived from Ito's lemma) for the drift of C (Equation (13.10)), one easily obtains:

$$\frac{\partial C}{\partial t} + \frac{1}{2}\mathcal{A}(C) = C\mu_C - \frac{\partial C}{\partial S}S_t\,(\mu_S - r) - \frac{\partial C}{\partial \sigma}\sigma_t\,(\mu_\sigma - g) \qquad (13.30)$$

Using Equation (13.29) one can then write

$$C(\mu_C - r) = \frac{\partial C}{\partial S}S_t\,(\mu_S - r) + \frac{\partial C}{\partial \sigma}\sigma_t\,(\mu_\sigma - g)$$

Recall, however, that

$$\frac{C_t\sigma_{CS}}{\sigma_t} = \frac{\partial C}{\partial S}S_t \qquad (13.31)$$

$$\frac{C_t\sigma_{C\sigma}}{v} = \frac{\partial C}{\partial \sigma}\sigma_t \qquad (13.32)$$

Therefore one can write, after dividing through by σ_C,

$$\frac{\mu_C - r}{\sigma_C} = \frac{\sigma_{CS}}{\sigma_C}\frac{\mu_S - r}{\sigma} + \frac{\sigma_{C\sigma}}{\sigma_C}\frac{\mu_\sigma - \lambda_\sigma}{v} \qquad (13.33)$$

where I have defined

$$g \equiv \lambda_\sigma(S, \sigma, t)\sigma \qquad (13.34)$$

How should we interpret Equation (13.33)? First of all, note that, as the volatility becomes less and less stochastic, the term $\sigma_{C\sigma}$ tends to zero and we are back to the market-price-of-risk result obtained in Chapter 2 in the deterministic-volatility-diffusion case:

$$\sigma_{CS} = \sigma_C \qquad (13.35)$$

$$\sigma_{Cv} = 0 \qquad (13.36)$$

and, therefore,

$$\frac{\mu_C - r}{\sigma_C} = \frac{\mu_S - r}{\sigma} \qquad (13.37)$$

In order to understand Equation (13.33) in the more general (and interesting) case when the volatility *is* stochastic, note that it can be rewritten as

$$\mu_C = r + \sigma_{CS}\frac{\mu_S - r}{\sigma} + \sigma_{C\sigma}\frac{\mu_\sigma - \lambda_\sigma}{v} \qquad (13.38)$$

This expression decomposes the real-world percentage return from the call into three components:

- the riskless return, r, i.e. the drift that the call, the stock and any asset should have in a risk-neutral world;

- the excess return from the stock over the riskless rate due to risk aversion ($\mu_S - r$) per unit 'stock price risk' (σ), times the responsiveness of the call price to the Brownian shocks affecting the stock (σ_{CS});

- the difference between the drift of the volatility process in the real and risk-neutral worlds ($\mu_\sigma - \lambda_\sigma$) per unit 'volatility risk' (v), times the responsiveness of the call price to the Brownian shocks affecting the volatility ($\sigma_{C\sigma}$).

As in the deterministic-volatility case (see Section 2.2.3 in Chapter 2), to arrive at this result we have not invoked the validity of the CAP or of any other asset-pricing model, nor have we specified any form for the investor's utility function. The only requirements have been the diffusive behaviour for the stock and the volatility, the ability (thanks to this) to create a riskless replicating portfolio, and the absence of arbitrage opportunities.

How are we to interpret Equation (13.38)? The analogous result obtained in the deterministic-volatility-diffusion case, i.e.

$$\mu_C = r + \lambda(S, t)\frac{\mu_S - r}{\sigma} \tag{13.39}$$

was easy to understand, because we can think of the riskless rate, r, as a direct market observable (say, the return on short-dated Treasury bills). But what are we to make of the function λ_σ? To understand this, let us move to the pricing measure. Recall that if we can hedge with a bond, the stock and another option the portfolio can be made riskless. Therefore, for pricing purposes, the return from any asset can be set equal to the riskless rate, r:

$$\mu_C = \mu_S = r \tag{13.40}$$

and Equation (13.33) becomes

$$\mu_\sigma = \lambda_\sigma \tag{13.41}$$

This implies that, for pricing purposes, if perfect replication is possible *the drift of the volatility process in the real and in the risk-adjusted worlds must coincide*. From this it also follows that, if we assume that we can perfectly hedge with the stock and an option, and pursue an 'implied' route to determining the function g (i.e. if we determine g by matching the market prices) we lose all information about how risk preferences alter the drift of the volatility process.

How are the functions μ_σ and λ_σ related? We can answer this question by looking at these results from a different angle. We know that, if perfect hedging with the stock and an option is allowed, the risk from both sources of uncertainty (stock price uncertainty and volatility uncertainty) can be simultaneously removed. If this is the case, for pricing purposes the return from *any* asset, and therefore, in particular, from the call C, must be equal to the riskless rate of return. We have seen (Equation (13.38)) that this implies

$$\sigma_{C\sigma}\frac{\mu_\sigma - \lambda_\sigma}{v} = 0 \quad \rightarrow \quad \mu_\sigma = \lambda_\sigma \tag{13.42}$$

The quantity λ_σ therefore is interpreted as the drift of the volatility process that would be observed if investors were risk-neutral. If the model were correctly specified (i.e. if market prices were indeed produced by a stochastic-volatility diffusion of the assumed type, and the correct functional dependence of λ_σ on the state variables had been guessed) the function λ_σ, as implied by a fit to option market prices, would provide the drift that the volatility process would have in a world where investors did not require any compensation for bearing volatility risk. Looking at the problem in this light we can see a deeper link with the deterministic-volatility case. In Equation (13.39) instead of regarding the riskless rate, r, as the return on the Treasury bills, let us look at it in a more abstract and general way as the return from any asset that would be required by risk-neutral investors. Then we can see a very pleasing symmetry in the two terms on the RHS of Equation (13.38).

These results are interesting. Let us not forget, however, that they have been obtained under the restrictive assumption of perfect replicability of the option payoff in the presence of stochastic volatility. Recall that this required *the full process* of the hedging option, h, to be known today (i.e. the possible values of h not just today, but in all possible future states of the world). This information in reality is not available to the trader. Therefore risk aversion can, to some extent, affect the quantity λ_σ, which will no longer be exactly equal to the volatility drift that risk-neutral investors would 'see'. In this more general and realistic setting of imperfect payoff replication, the question of how the financial plausibility of the market-implied function λ_σ can be assessed remains open. This is looked at in the following section.

13.2.3   Assessing the Financial Plausibility of λ_σ

One of the stated objectives in undertaking the analysis presented above was to gain some intuition about the financially desirable features of the function λ_σ. In other words, if we pursue the implied route, can we say something about the reasonableness of the risk-adjusted volatility drift so distilled? The question can be addressed as follows.

Let us assume that we have managed to estimate the real-world drift of the volatility process (or at least some of its most salient features, such as, for instance, whether or not it is mean-reverting). In principle this should give us some guidance. If the stochastic-volatility approach is well-specified, in fact, we might want to ask ourselves what changes a plausible pattern of risk aversion should make to the real-world volatility drift. If we were dealing with a jump–diffusion process, it would be relatively easy to guess the nature of the transformation brought about by risk aversion: as shown in Chapter 14, risk-averse investors will see negative jumps occurring more frequently and more downward than in the real world. With a stochastic-volatility model, however, it is not intuitively obvious to guess in what 'direction' the real-world drift of the volatility should be altered to account for risk aversion. It has even been argued (Hull and White (1987), see also the discussion in Campbell *et al.* (1997)) that the price of volatility risk is hardly priced in the option market.[2] Lewis (2000) presents a detailed discussion of when and to what extent risk aversion does change the volatility drift. The (interesting and formally correct) results he obtains rely in a rather opaque way on a number of common, but not for this reason necessarily very robust, assumptions, such as the existence of a representative investor, a particular investment horizon and specific functional forms for the volatility process and for the utility function. Ultimately, and unlike the jump–diffusion case, I do not find these results intuitively compelling, and I wonder whether market prices are indeed altered because of risk aversion from what they would be in a hypothetical risk-neutral universe

---

[2]Wiggins (1987) argues that the risk premium associated with stochastic volatility is zero if the investor has a logarithmic utility function and the underlying asset is the market portfolio.

as these findings suggest. It is therefore tempting to argue that, in the stochastic-volatility case, one can say little more than that the risk-adjusted drift should not be 'too dissimilar' from the real-world one. I think that this statement is probably too weak, and deal with this topic in the next section. In the meantime, there are immediate constraints that can be imposed on the function λ_σ. For instance, if we want the recovery of the market prices to be financially motivated, and not just a fitting exercise, it is plausible to ask that the pricing function g (and hence λ_σ) should be time independent. Doing otherwise would mean that we believe that the aversion to volatility risk will change in the future in a deterministic (i.e. *fully predictable*) manner. This is logically possible, but difficult to justify on financial grounds.[3] Also, availing oneself of the possible dependence of the function g on S and σ should only be done if a financial rationale can be found.

Recall that, in principle, the function λ_σ could even be stochastic. Much as I think that a convincing case can be made for a stochastic λ_σ, such a modelling approach would be quite difficult in practice. On the other hand, assuming a deterministic dependence on time is computationally easy, but, as discussed above, of dubious financial meaning. Therefore, the requirement that λ_σ should not be parameterized using time-dependent coefficients seems to me an appealing starting point. In what follows I will therefore advocate that the parameters $\{\alpha\}$ that describe the function g should be time independent, thereby enforcing a time-homogeneous character to the resulting smile surfaces.

Parameter Hedging vs Replication Hedging

Can we say something more precise about the link between the real-world and the risk-adjusted drift of the volatility? In order to answer this question, I will make use of the result obtained in Section 6.7 of Chapter 6 that, for risk aversion to alter the risk-neutral value of some financial quantity, there must be a net imbalance of supply and demand for some options. See, in particular, Sections 6.7.4 and 6.7.5. With this caveat in mind, let us look at the actions of a complex-derivatives trader, who will always try to hedge the uncertainty about the volatility process by using option(s) as her hedging instruments. This will obviously be the case if the volatility is stochastic, but, as we have seen in Chapter 4, also if it is deterministic, but not perfectly known to the trader. Even if perfect replication is not possible, the trader can still engage in what I call 'parameter hedging', i.e. she will calculate, perhaps very approximately, the sensitivities of the instrument to be hedged and of the hedging option to 'volatility risk' (see Section 13.6.2), and arrive at a volatility hedge ratio. It is important to stress that this hedging strategy is, in general, not a self-financing trading strategy, and therefore the goal of the trader is not to obtain a perfect replication of the terminal payoff, but to reduce the dispersion of the slippages as much as possible.

Despite the practice being theoretically 'disreputable', this is what is in reality always carried out in trading practice. Given an option payoff and a process for the underlying, in theoretical terms the market is either complete or incomplete, and perfect replication is either possible or impossible. If possible, 'true' hedging is the (unique) strategy that ensures the replication of the payoff. This dichotomous distinction is only valid in theory, however. Even if the underlying follows exactly the Black-and-Scholes script, trading

---

[3]Making the degree of risk aversion to stochastic volatility time dependent in general produces time-dependent smile surfaces, i.e. future smile surfaces that do not look like today's. I argue at length in this book that, unless this is financially motivated, such a feature is undesirable.

restrictions, bid–offer spreads and ignorance of the true volatility make perfect replication impossible.[4] Irrespective of whether perfect replication is theoretically possible or not, however, *some* degree of hedging is always possible: the variability of the payoff from the naked option can always be significantly reduced by engaging in a reasonable hedging strategy. One such strategy can be based on the approximate 'hedge ratio' approach alluded to above, and discussed in Section 13.6.2. In practice, this is achieved by choosing a plausible model, parameterized by a number of coefficients, and determining the sensitivity of the price, as predicted by this model, to changes in the parameters. I call this imperfect-hedging approach 'parameter hedging'. Needless to say, this will not be a self-financing trading strategy. Note also that we do not even require that the model chosen by the trader should be the 'correct' one. We have already seen something similar in Section 4.5.3 of Chapter 4, where we examined the performance of a trader who successfully 'defended' by means of an incorrect gamma-trading strategy the consistently wrong Black price of a call obtained with an incorrect volatility.

Implications for the Function λ_σ

Where does this leave us with the assessment of the financial plausibility of the quantity λ_σ implied by option market prices? Can we guess how aversion to volatility risk will affect this function?

To begin with, it is reasonable to assume that traders will engage in the type of parameter hedging just described. If this is the case, they will typically hedge one option with another with some different characteristics (e.g. with a different strike and/or maturity – see the tests in Section 13.6 below). If the complex trader wants to exact a reasonable profit from her transaction, typically there will be a substantial amount of 'basis risk', i.e. a significant mismatch between the characteristics of the option to be hedged and of the hedging option(s). In the case, for instance, of the principal-protected retail equity products described in Chapter 1, the mismatch would typically be in option maturities: the trader would sell to the retail investor long-dated (say, five-year) volatility, and hedge herself by buying in the market the much-shorter-dated (say, under-one-year) liquid volatility. If the volatility were stochastic, but the volatilities of different-maturity options changed by almost identical amounts, parameter hedging would be both simple and effective. What the trader fears are different changes in the implied volatilities of the hedged and hedging options, and, in particular, changes poorly predicted by her vega hedge ratio. The crucial questions for a trader are therefore: 'How will a shock to the instantaneous stock volatility propagate down the implied volatility curve?' and 'How persistent will such a volatility shock be?'.

These questions cannot be answered without specifying precise dynamics for the process of the volatility. A pure driftless diffusion for the volatility, for instance, would imply a long 'memory' for a given shock, and therefore a close-to-parallel propagation of the shock down the maturity axis. A strongly-mean-reverting process, on the other hand, would imply that changes in the implied volatilities of short-dated options should be much more pronounced than changes in long-dated options. In general, any specification of the process for the volatility will give rise to different vega hedge ratios to be

---

[4]In the language of Chapter 4, even if the underlying follows a geometric diffusion with deterministic volatility, market imperfections will make the realized quadratic variation at option expiry a stochastic quantity.

used in parameter hedging. In particular, if a mean-reverting process for the volatility were chosen, I would be tempted to argue that the 'volatility risk' can be understood as follows. Consider again the hedging behaviour of a complex trader who has sold (perhaps to retail customers) long-dated options, and has to hedge herself using short-dated options. As I argued above, her hedging programme is made more difficult if there is a marked difference in changes in implied volatilities down the maturity spectrum. If this is the case, the trader will 'fear' a strong mean reversion of the volatility, which would make changes in the implied volatility of short-dated options very different from the changes in implied volatility of longer-dated ones. If this reasoning is correct, the reversion speed in the pricing measure should be higher than in the real world.

When the problem is looked at in this light, in addition to the theoretical desiderata presented in the sections above, good requirements for the function λ_σ would be that

- it should produce time-homogeneous smile surfaces (thereby predicting realistic future re-hedging costs – see the discussion in Sections 1.1.4 and 1.3.2 of Chapter 1), and that

- it should provide 'useful' hedge ratios (thereby providing at least partial insulation from volatility risk). This can be achieved if the changes in the implied volatility at different maturities predicted by the model resemble the corresponding changes observed in the market.

In the light of these considerations, the next section explores the characteristics of one class of process for the volatility that has the potential to fulfil these desiderata, namely mean-reverting volatility processes.

13.3 Mean-Reverting Stochastic Volatility

The treatment of the drift of the volatility process has so far has been very general. In order to obtain more concrete results we have to say something precise about the functional form of the drift. How should we do that?

Answering the question is not easy, both for technical and for conceptual reasons. The technical reason is that the volatility is not directly observable, and that some estimation procedure (moving window, exponential decay, GARCH-type estimate, etc.) must be chosen in order to distill it from the time series for the underlying. As usual, technical problems can be challenging, but ultimately not insurmountable. Let us therefore assume that we have estimated to our satisfaction the real-world dynamics of the volatility. There still remains, however, a conceptual problem. This stems from the fact that, unless we want to prescribe a precise functional form for the market price of risk as a function of its state variables, what is required for pricing purposes is the behaviour of the instantaneous volatility in the risk-neutral measure, not in the real-world measure where the statistical estimation has been carried out. Therefore a drift transformation intervenes between the two measures, which 'scrambles' whatever information we might have gathered about the real-world drift of the volatility.

So, for instance, the fact that, in the real world, volatility is observed not too wander to very high or very low levels in a random-walk-like fashion, but to revert to some long-term level, is intrinsically interesting, but does not tell us anything *directly* about how the drift in the adjusted measure should behave. Of course, one could always posit that in the pricing measure the drift should have a particular functional form (for instance, should be a constant, or a deterministic function of time), but, apart from analytical tractability, there would be little a priori justification for doing so.

I take a different approach, and, in keeping with my ideas as to how models should be used (see Chapter 1), I investigate to what extent a given mean-reverting process for the risk-adjusted volatility can account for a number of observable static and dynamic properties. The static properties are the call prices today, and the dynamic ones are the future prices of options with different maturities and/or degrees of at-the-moneyness, i.e. the evolution of the smile and the vega hedge ratios discussed above. If these properties are satisfactorily accounted for, I will have reason to believe that the risk-adjusted dynamics I have chosen may provide a useful pricing tool. This, however, will not commit me to subscribe to any view about the real-world process for the volatility or about the nature of the measure transformation.

Following a common approach (see, for example, Fouque *et al.* (2000)), I choose to pursue this programme by describing the instantaneous volatility, σ_t, as some positive function of a 'latent variable', Y_t, and require that this function should have a mean-reverting behaviour. This naturally brings us to Ornstein–Uhlenbeck processes, which are therefore briefly reviewed below.

13.3.1   The Ornstein–Uhlenbeck Process

Description

Let us require that the process for the latent variable, Y_t, should be of the form

$$dY_t = k_Y (m_Y - Y_t) \, dt + v_Y \, dw_t \tag{13.43}$$

In Equation (13.43), k_Y, if positive, is called the reversion speed of Y, m_Y its reversion level, $v_Y(Y)$ its volatility and dw_t the increment of a standard Brownian motion. If k_Y were negative the process would be said to be mean-fleeing rather than mean-reverting. I will always consider k_Y positive in what follows. If $v_Y(Y)$ is a constant, v, such a process is known as an Ornstein–Uhlenbeck diffusion. If at time t the value of Y_t happens to be above (below) its reversion level there is a deterministic pull downwards (upwards) towards it. Superimposed on this deterministic behaviour there are the random shocks provided by dw_t.

Features

Ornstein–Uhlenbeck processes are conditionally Gaussian. This means that not only are all the unconditional (marginal) distributions today Gaussian, but so also are all the future conditional distributions. See, for example, Nielsen (1999). These processes enjoy a number of important properties (see, for example, Fouque *et al.* (2000), Nielsen (1999), Gardiner (1985), etc.) that make them popular for financial modelling. For our purposes the most salient ones are:

1. given an initial condition, Y_0, the realization of the process at a later time t is given by

$$Y_t = m_Y + (Y_0 - m_Y) \exp[-k_Y t] + v \int_0^t \exp[-k_Y (t - s) \, ds] \tag{13.44}$$

2. from Property 1 it follows that the distribution of Y_t is Gaussian with

$$Y_t \sim \mathcal{N}\left(m_Y + (Y_0 - m_Y)\exp[-k_Y t], \frac{v^2}{2k_Y t}[1 - \exp(-2k_Y t)]\right) \qquad (13.45)$$

3. as t goes to infinity, the distribution of Y_t does not depend on Y_0, and is given by $Y_t \, \mathcal{N}\left(m_Y, \frac{v^2}{2k_Y}\right)$.

Note from Property 2 that the distribution of Y_t only depends on the product $k_Y t$, and not on k_Y or t separately. Therefore, *as far as the distribution is concerned*, allowing the time t to become large is the same as imposing a high mean reversion.

From Property 3 one can see that the variance of the limit (i.e. of the invariant) distribution only depends on the ratio of the instantaneous variance of Y to its reversion speed. This is intuitively plausible: a high volatility, v, tends to disperse the realizations of Y, but a high reversion speed 'contains' them around the reversion level, m_Y. As a consequence, *for a given horizon*, t, there is some function of these two quantities such that the two effects exactly compensate each other. Indeed, when the chosen time t is finite, one can always find a particular combination of v and k_Y such that the variance of the marginal distribution, V_t, is unchanged. This can be achieved by expressing v as a function of k_Y as

$$v = \sqrt{\frac{2V_t k_Y}{1 - \exp(-2k_Y t)}} \qquad (13.46)$$

These values of the diffusion coefficient v as a function of the reversion speed, however, will give the same unconditional variance, V_t, only at the chosen horizon t. It will not be possible to determine a ratio (or any other function) of v and k_Y such that the variance will be the same for all horizons t. This feature is important in understanding the possible shapes of the smile surface, and is discussed next.

13.3.2 The Functional Form Chosen in This Chapter

Several choices have been made for the variable Y: see, for example, Hull and White (1987), Wiggins (1987), Scott (1987), Stein and Stein (1991) and Heston (1993). The latter is probably the most widely used because it lends itself to a closed-form solution. In the remainder of this chapter I will assume the following functional form for the joint risk-neutral dynamics of the stock price and its volatility:

$$dS_t = r_t S_t \, dt + \sigma_t S_t \, dz_t \qquad (13.47)$$

$$d\sigma_t = RVS(RVL - \sigma_t)\, dt + v\sigma_t \, dw_t \qquad (13.48)$$

$$E[dz_t \, dw_t] = \rho \qquad (13.49)$$

Very often in this chapter I will work with $\rho = 0$. Several variations on this theme are possible, but the qualitative behaviour discussed below remains similar. This choice means that I have established a very simple correspondence between the latent variable introduced above and the instantaneous volatility: $Y_t = \sigma_t$. As for term $v_Y(Y)$, I have chosen it to

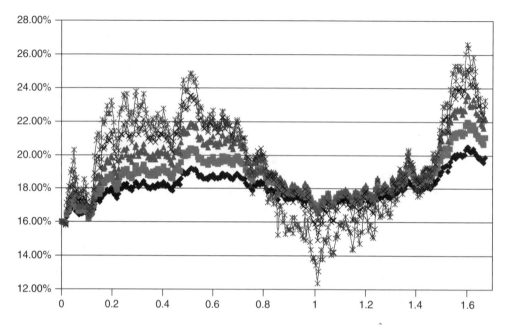

Figure 13.1   A few sample paths of the volatility process. The ratio $\frac{v^2}{2k}$ was kept constant at 0.0025, and the reversion speed was doubled in each series from 0.1 (corresponding to the series with least variability) to 1.6 (most-varying series). All the volatility paths were shocked by the same Brownian increments, dw_t.

be proportional to the volatility itself, i.e. of the form $v\sigma_t$. This ensures positivity of the volatility at all times, but makes the process not of the classic Ornstein–Uhlenbeck form. None the less it is still possible to find an expression for the realization of the process after a finite time. See, for example, Brigo and Mercurio (2001). These choices are by no means unique, and one can create a more complex dependence by positing

$$\sigma_t = \psi(Y_t) \qquad (13.50)$$

for some function ψ. ($\psi(Y) = \sqrt{Y}$ is, for instance, a popular choice, in which case Y is interpreted as the instantaneous variance of the stock process.) A few sample paths of the volatility and of the stock price processes are shown in Figures 13.1 and 13.2.

13.3.3   The High-Reversion-Speed, High-Volatility Regime

Consider a situation when the volatility of the volatility process is high, but the reversion speed is also high. The consequence of such a combination will be a dynamics for the stock price displaying high and sudden bursts of volatility, which quickly reverts to the normal level. If this is the case, it is plausible to surmise that, over a sufficiently long period of time, the realized quadratic variation will not be very different for different volatility paths. Because of the high reversion speed, the probability that the volatility might wander off to very high or very low values, which would strongly affect the quadratic variation, is very low. One would therefore expect that, for long maturities, the price obtained with this

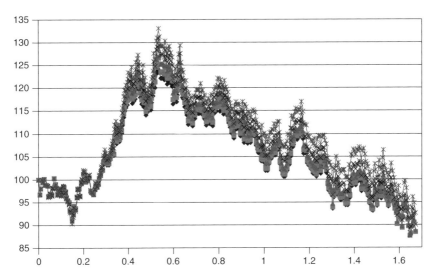

Figure 13.2 A few sample paths of the stock processes corresponding to the volatility paths in Figure 13.1. All the stock price paths were shocked by the same Brownian increment, dz_t. Note how it takes a considerably longer time for the stock paths than for the volatility paths to diverge significantly: after a quarter of a year the volatilities are already dispersed over a range from 18.2% to 23.5%, while over the same period the stock prices are still between 97.76 and 97.98. The stock path that reaches the topmost value is the one associated with the most variable volatility path.

high-reversion-speed, high-volatility regime should not be very different from what could be obtained using an appropriate deterministic quadratic variation. As a consequence, long-maturity smiles should be almost deterministic-volatility-like, i.e. flat.

The same considerations, however, do not apply to very short maturities. Over a short period of time, whether we experience a volatility burst or not is a random event, and the high reversion speed might not 'have the time' to bring down the volatility to its normal level. Therefore at short maturities more pronounced, and almost jump–diffusion-like, smiles can be expected.

These qualitative observations are important. They suggest that, if the volatility process does indeed display a high reversion speed and high volatility, many of the objections that are raised against stochastic-volatility models (i.e. their inability to produce steep and quickly decaying smiles) can be overcome *without introducing difficult-to-justify time-dependent parameters*. A thorough treatment of stochastic volatility models in this regime is given in Fouque *et al.* (2000).

13.4 Qualitative Features of Stochastic-Volatility Smiles

This section explores the smile shapes (as a function of strike and of option maturity) that a stochastic-volatility process can produce 'naturally'. This analysis is important for two related reasons:

1. given a market smile surface, we might want to gauge at a qualitative level if 'sensible' combinations of the process parameters can convincingly account for it;

2. if we have decided that a stochastic-volatility description is appropriate, from the observation of the market smile surface we might want to choose an initial desirable combination of parameters to begin the χ^2 search of a locally optimal solution. I explain elsewhere (see Section 13.7) why a theoretically superior global optimal solution might not be necessarily desirable.

13.4.1   The Smile as a Function of the Risk-Neutral Parameters

Analysing the qualitative features of the smiles produced by stochastic-volatility processes is rather complex, because there is a subtle interplay between the different parameters (the reversion level, RVL, the reversion speed, RVS, and the volatility of the volatility, v) that characterize the process. For the sake of simplicity, I will mainly analyse the case when there is no correlation between the process for the stock price and the process for the volatility. If we work using a log-normal diffusion for the stock price this assumption is certainly poor. It might not be so unsatisfactory, however, if we use displaced diffusions (see Chapter 16), or a CEV process. See also the discussion in Part IV. At a qualitative level, very often the main effect of introducing a negative correlation is simply to 'tilt' the model smiles in the direction observed in the market.

I start with the case when the current instantaneous volatility is at its reversion level: in Equation (13.48), $\sigma(0) = RVL = 20.00\%$; as for the volatility of the volatility, unless otherwise stated I use below $v = 10\%$. I first analyse the behaviour of the smile as a function of the reversion speed. See Figures 13.3–13.5. For maturities up to two years the at-the-money volatility is seen to increase for all reversion speeds, but less so the higher the reversion speed. The most noteworthy feature is that, as the reversion speed increases, the smile becomes steeper for short expiries, and flatter for long maturities. This is in agreement with the qualitative discussion presented above.

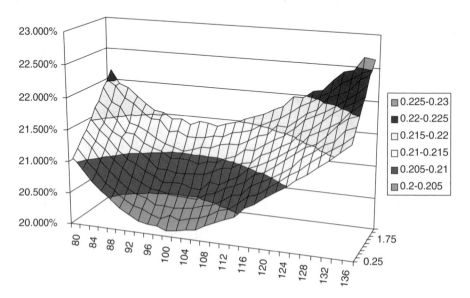

Figure 13.3   The shape of the smile produced when $S(0) = 100$, $\sigma(0) = 20.00\%$, $RVL = 20\%$, $RVS = 0$, $v = 0.1$ and $\rho = 0$ for maturities out to 1 year.

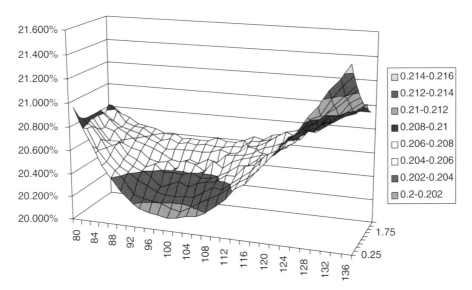

Figure 13.4 The shape of the smile produced when $S(0) = 100$, $\sigma(0) = 20.00\%$, $RVL = 20\%$, $RVS = 1$, $v = 0.1$ and $\rho = 0$ for maturities out to 1 year.

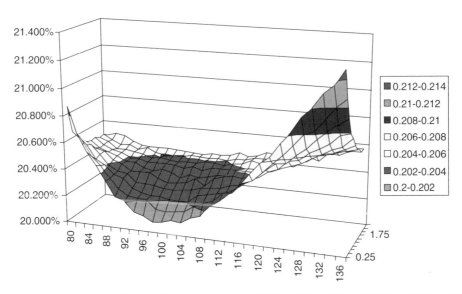

Figure 13.5 The shape of the smile produced when $S(0) = 100$, $\sigma(0) = 20.00\%$, $RVL = 20\%$, $RVS = 2$, $v = 0.1$ and $\rho = 0$ for maturities out to 1 year.

The next three figures (Figures 13.6–13.8) show the effect of an increasing reversion speed when the volatility of the volatility is half as large as in the previous case. Despite the qualitative similarity, the smile is now much less pronounced, both at the short end and at the long end.

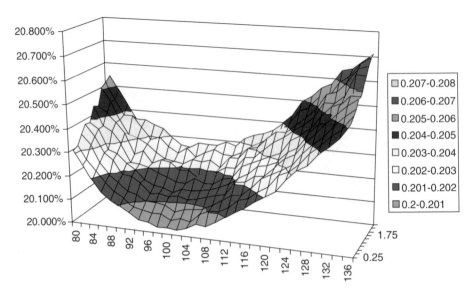

Figure 13.6   The shape of the smile produced when $S(0) = 100$, $\sigma(0) = 20.00\%$, $RVL = 20\%$, $RVS = 0$, $v = 0.05$ and $\rho = 0$ for maturities out to 1 year.

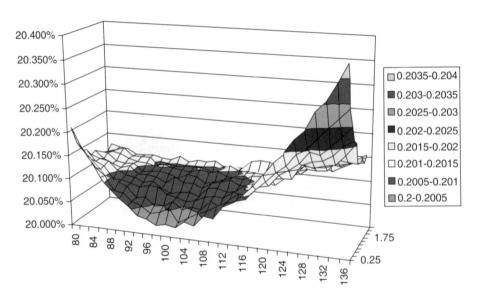

Figure 13.7   The shape of the smile produced when $S(0) = 100$, $\sigma(0) = 20.00\%$, $RVL = 20\%$, $RVS = 1$, $v = 0.05$ and $\rho = 0$ for maturities out to 1 year.

Figures 13.9–13.11 display the effect of having a reversion level (still at 20%) way below today's value of the volatility (assumed to be 28.00%). This might occur if the volatility were currently experiencing a 'burst'. If the reversion speed is zero, clearly there is no effect, but for non-zero reversion rates the 'smiley' shape of the implied-volatility curve is totally overcome by a decline in the level of the smile.

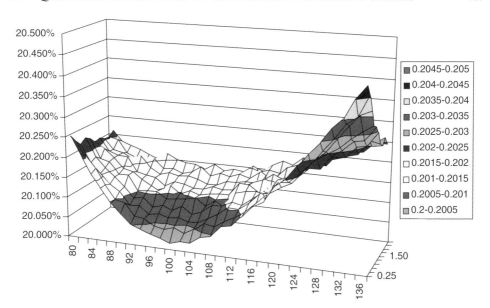

Figure 13.8 The shape of the smile produced when $S(0) = 100$, $\sigma(0) = 20.00\%$, $RVL = 20\%$, $RVS = 2$, $v = 0.05$ and $\rho = 0$ for maturities out to 1 year.

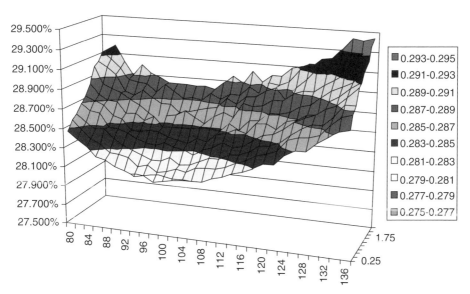

Figure 13.9 The shape of the smile produced when $S(0) = 100$, $\sigma(0) = 28.00\%$, $RVL = 20\%$, $RVS = 0$, $v = 0.1$ and $\rho = 0$ for maturities out to 1 year.

As these figures show, the effect is very dramatic. However, the initial volatility ($\sigma(0) = 28.00\%$) was chosen to be way above the reversion level. Would we obtain a similar smile behaviour if the volatility were only mildly above the reversion level? In order to analyse this situation the next three figures (Figures 13.12–13.14) refer to the

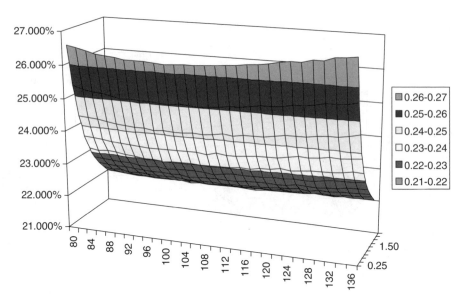

Figure 13.10   The shape of the smile produced when $S(0) = 100$, $\sigma(0) = 28.00\%$, $RVL = 20\%$, $RVS = 1$, $v = 0.1$ and $\rho = 0$ for maturities out to 1 year.

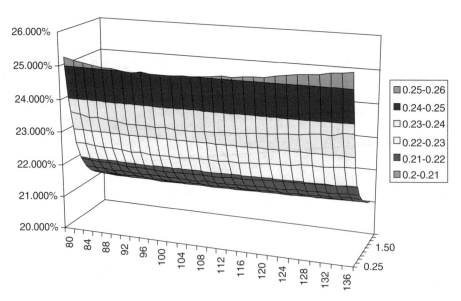

Figure 13.11   The shape of the smile produced when $S(0) = 100$, $\sigma(0) = 28.00\%$, $RVL = 20\%$, $RVS = 2$, $v = 0.1$ and $\rho = 0$ for maturities out to 1 year.

same set-up, but now the current volatility (at 22.50%) is only a few percentage points above its long-term level. The zero-mean-reversion case presents no surprises, but when a non-zero reversion speed is introduced, we see a more complex behaviour, as longer-dated out-of-the-money implied volatilities tend to increase because of the stochastic nature of

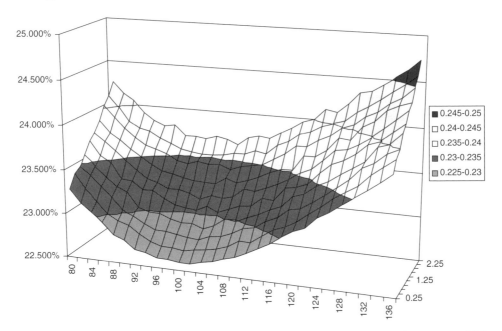

Figure 13.12   The shape of the smile produced when $S(0) = 100$, $\sigma(0) = 22.50\%$, $RVL = 20\%$, $RVS = 0$, $v = 0.1$ and $\rho = 0$ for maturities out to 1 year.

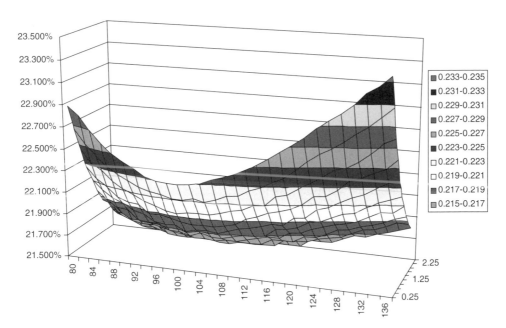

Figure 13.13   The shape of the smile produced when $S(0) = 100$, $\sigma(0) = 22.50\%$, $RVL = 20\%$, $RVS = 1$, $v = 0.1$ and $\rho = 0$ for maturities out to 1 year.

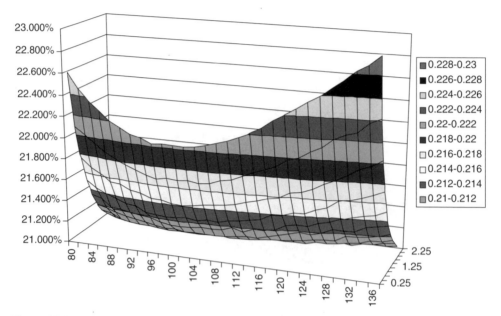

Figure 13.14   The shape of the smile produced when $S(0) = 100$, $\sigma(0) = 22.50\%$, $RVL = 20\%$, $RVS = 2$, $v = 0.1$ and $\rho = 0$ for maturities out to 1 year.

the volatility, but tend to decrease because of the deterministic drift to the lower reversion level. Note that, with zero reversion speed, the volatility 'does not know' that it is above the level RVL, and therefore does not revert to it. Therefore the smile is *increasing* for longer maturities, as already observed. On the other hand, for a reversion speed of $RVS = 1$, the smile *decreases* towards the reversion level as the option expiry increases. Therefore there must be a reversion speed, $0 < RVS < 1$, such that the implied volatility for at-the-money options is approximately flat as a function of expiry. Observing such a behaviour in the market data should therefore not be automatically taken as an indication that a stochastic-volatility description is inappropriate.

If today's volatility is below (at 17.50%) the long-term reversion level, the qualitative behaviour is somewhat different. See Figures 13.15–13.17. The zero-reversion-speed case produces the same overall smile shape and increase in at-the-money volatility given by the stochastic nature of the volatility. As the reversion speed increases, however, at-the-money volatilities are strongly pulled up by the deterministic term, and the smile becomes extremely flat for longer maturities.

A complementary way to look at these results is to analyse the risk-neutral volatility densities as a function of the option expiry with and without reversion speed. These are shown in Figures 13.18–13.20. It is apparent from Figure 13.19 that the probability density of the volatility virtually stops 'dispersing' after a certain time. The differences for the one-year expiry are shown in Figure 13.20.

Needless to say, if the parameters of the stochastic-volatility process are made time dependent the behaviour of the smile can become very complex. Also, further combinations of parameters could be explored. Even the relatively simple analysis presented in this section is however useful in order to understand what market smile shapes a stochastic-volatility process can 'naturally' recover. Furthermore, the analysis of the case

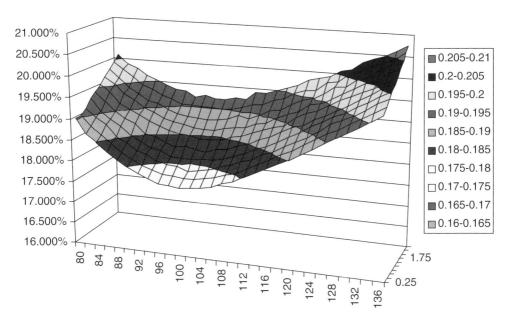

Figure 13.15 The shape of the smile produced when $S(0) = 100$, $\sigma(0) = 17.50\%$, $RVL = 20\%$, $RVS = 0$, $v = 0.1$ and $\rho = 0$ for maturities out to 1 year.

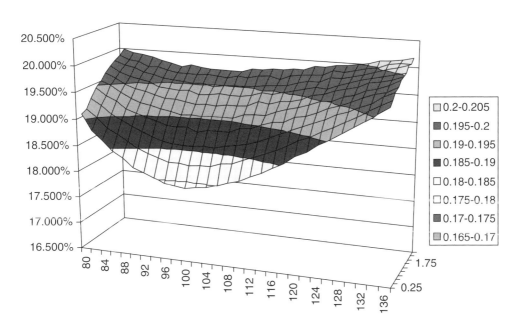

Figure 13.16 The shape of the smile produced when $S(0) = 100$, $\sigma(0) = 17.50\%$, $RVL = 20\%$, $RVS = 1$, $v = 0.1$ and $\rho = 0$ for maturities out to 1 year.

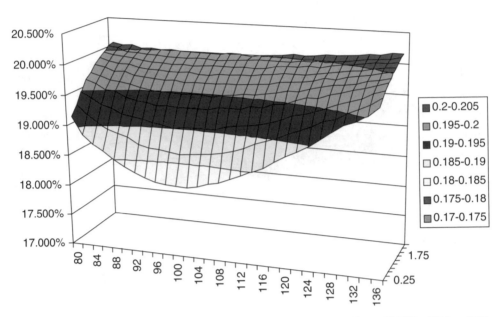

Figure 13.17   The shape of the smile produced when $S(0) = 100$, $\sigma(0) = 17.50\%$, $RVL = 20\%$, $RVS = 2$, $v = 0.1$ and $\rho = 0$ for maturities out to 1 year.

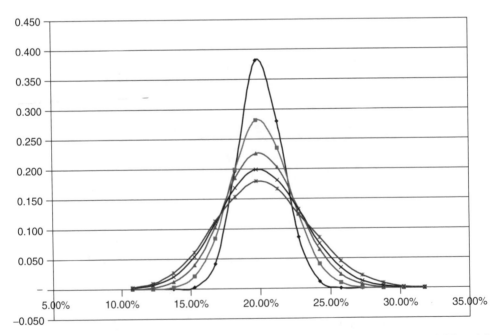

Figure 13.18   The risk-neutral volatility densities for option expiries ranging from 0.25 to 1.5 years with $S(0) = 100$, $\sigma(0) = 20.0\%$, $RVL = 20\%$, $v = 0.05$, $\rho = 0$ and no reversion speed.

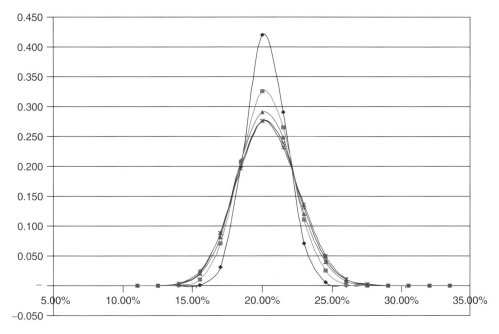

Figure 13.19 As Figure 13.18, but with a reversion speed of 1. Notice how, for this high reversion speed, the densities virtually stop dispersing after a relatively short time.

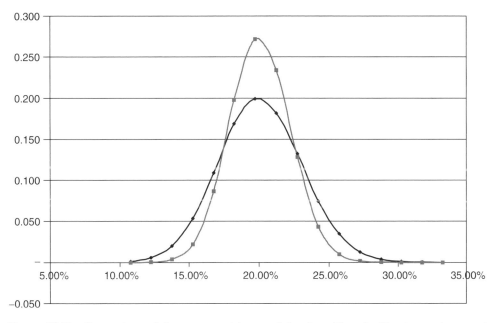

Figure 13.20 Comparison of the one-year risk-neutral density with and without reversion speed (the other parameters are the same as in Figures 13.18 and 13.19).

of a current volatility below or above its reversion level is very important in understanding the shape of conditional future smiles. This aspect is explored in the next section.

13.5   The Relation Between Future Smiles and Future Stock Price Levels

Let us assume[5] that the joint processes for the stock price and its volatility are given by Equations (13.48) and (13.47). For simplicity, I assume that the volatility starts 'today' from a value equal to its reversion level. Let us run a Gedanken Monte Carlo experiment, follow the stock price evolution out to one year, and observe its realized value. Let us repeat the procedure over and over again. Conditional on each of these future stock price values having been realized, let us calculate the future smile surface in each of these states of the world.

Recall that the parameters of the volatility process are time independent, and that we have posited zero correlation between the increments of the process for the stock price and the volatility. Do we expect the future conditional smile surfaces to be identical to each other, or to display a dependence on the realization of the stock price? Do we expect them to be similar to today's smile surface?

In order to answer these questions I display in Figure 13.21 the average conditional at-the-money volatility in six months' time as a function of the future realization of the stock

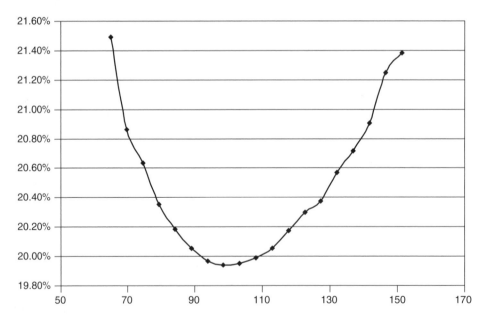

Figure 13.21   The average conditional expectation of the at-the-money volatility in six months' time as a function of the future realization of the stock price (today's value of the stock was $100, and zero interest rates were assumed). See the text for further details.

---

[5]I wish to thank Dr Mark Joshi and Dr Chris Hunter for useful discussions on the topics covered in this section and the following sections.

price (today's value of the stock was $100, and zero interest rates were assumed). Note carefully that I have to speak of an *average* future at-the-money volatility: the future stock price in fact is not a sufficient statistic to identify the future state of the world (whose full characterization would require also a specification of the future realized volatility). Therefore I must 'summarize' the distribution of future smiles using some descriptive statistics, and I have chosen for this purpose the average of the at-the-money six-month volatility.

Figure 13.21 shows that if the stock price is very high or very low the future six-month at-the-money volatility is much higher than the future at-the-money volatility obtained when the future stock price realization is close to the starting level ($100). Also, the shape of the future conditional smile is different in the large-move case, or in the little-change case. If the stock price move has been small, the average smile tends to be of the type described in Figures 13.15–13.17, which corresponded to the case of a current volatility below the long-term level. If the stock price move has been large, the average smile is more similar to the cases shown in Figures 13.12–13.14, which corresponded to the case when the current volatility is above the long-term level.

I give below an intuitive explanation for this behaviour. In the context of the present discussion, what matters is that, *even if we assumed zero correlation between the instantaneous increments in the stock price and the volatility*, there is a clear dependence of the level and shape of the future smile on the realization of the stock price. This observation is of intrinsic interest because, as discussed in Chapter 1, the price of an option should reflect the cost of the future vega-re-hedging trades, which, in turn, clearly depend on the future conditional smile surfaces. Therefore a stochastic-volatility process is saying something very specific about these re-hedging costs as a function of the future realizations of the stock price. The relevance of this is general, but can be fully appreciated in the case of a forward-starting call spread option, which depends to first order on the future realization of the smile surface. See again the discussion in Chapter 3.

More generally, the empirical findings mentioned above indicate that, if one were to assume (or to observe) that future smile surfaces are stochastic but independent of the future stock level, one is implicitly saying that they have *not* been generated by a stochastic-volatility process. The importance of this will become clear in Chapter 17. For the moment, one can regard a stochastic-volatility model as a prescription for producing future smiles that produce well-identifiable patterns of dependence on the future realization of the stock price. It is up to the trader to decide, on the basis of her financial 'picture of the world' and of the available empirical data, whether this description is convincing or not.

13.5.1   An Intuitive Explanation

How can we gain an intuitive understanding of the very clear and very strong dependence of the future conditional smiles on the future realization of the stock price? Consider the case when the future stock price is very high or very low. Although by no means certain, it is very likely that, along the path that led to these 'extreme' realizations of the stock price, the volatility should have been high. Therefore, conditional on the stock price being at, say, $20 or $200 after one year, it is more likely than not that the one-year volatility should be higher than the level it started from. So, to begin with, the future volatility over the next six months is likely to be rather high, which explains the high future at-the-money volatility. Furthermore, since the spot volatility at one year is likely to be above the long-term reversion level, the future conditional smile surface is likely to display a behaviour similar to that displayed in Figures 13.13 and 13.14.

The opposite reasoning applies if we observe the stock price in one year's time to be close to the starting point ($100). Conditional on this occurrence, the future spot volatility is likely to be rather low, and the future at-the-money volatility is consequently likely to be correspondingly lower. Note that the effect is less strong: if the stock price assumes extreme values, it almost 'must' have had a high volatility, at least at some point during its life. If the stock price ends close to where it started, it might have had a low-volatility path, but it might also have had wild but approximately self-cancelling swings up and down, which would require a high realized volatility to have a decent probability of occurrence. If the future conditional volatility is indeed low, it will be below its reversion level, and therefore the future smile will be more likely to be of the form shown in Figures 13.16 and 13.17.

After this qualitative discussion, the reader should think very deeply again about the pricing of a forward-starting call (spread) option.

13.6 Portfolio Replication in Practice: The Stochastic-Volatility Case

We have established that perfect replication will not be possible by hedging with the stock only. We have also seen, however, that hedging by assuming that the underlying process is a diffusion with deterministic volatility often performs better than one might expect. For instance, I pointed out that for European options the distribution of the 'slippages' between the payoffs of the imperfectly-replicating portfolio and of the option strongly depends on the terminal distribution of realized quadratic variations, and on how this quantity compares with the implicit quadratic variation used for the hedging. We also saw that a stochastic quadratic variation is obtained even if the volatility is deterministic, whenever the re-hedging frequency is finite (lucky paths begin to matter, the more so the coarser the re-hedging interval).

If the hedging problem is looked at from this perspective, it matters relatively little whether the terminal distribution of quadratic variations is generated by a finite re-hedging frequency or, perhaps, by a stochastic-volatility process. I referred to the ability of a Black-and-Scholes-based hedging strategy to deliver acceptable replication results for a relatively wide range of distributions of quadratic variations as the 'robustness' of the Black-and-Scholes model. See Section 4.6 in Chapter 4. In this spirit, I examine in detail in the sections below the performance of a naïve Black-and-Scholes-based hedging strategy when the true process is a diffusion with stochastic volatility. I will engage in an unashamedly simple case of parameter hedging. Other hedging strategies might be more effective, but it is useful to obtain a benchmark case.

13.6.1 The Hedging Methodology

In order to carry out the tests referred to above, I place myself in the same computational framework described in Chapter 4. So, my goal is to replicate as best as possible the payoff of a call option at expiry. I assign an arbitrary real-world drift to the stock price and to the volatility, and an approximate hedging strategy (based on the Black-and-Scholes formula) in order to rebalance at each time-step the holdings of cash and stock in the replicating portfolio. At option expiry I will check the differences (slippages) between the payoffs of the option and the replicating portfolio. The cost of the option will then be related to the set-up cost of the (now-imperfectly-) replicating portfolio.

Note carefully that I did not say that the price of the option should be *equal to* the set-up cost of the replicating portfolio. This is because, even in the continuous limit, replication will no longer be perfect, the trading strategy will not be self-financing and we are therefore fully in parameter-hedging territory. I will assume, in fact, that the trader either does not know the nature of the true stochastic-volatility process, or, if she does, cannot estimate its parameters. She knows exactly, however, the *average* quadratic variation produced by the true process over the life of the option. She will therefore estimate, and try to 'defend' via a dynamic hedging strategy, not the true, and unknown, value of the option, but the value obtained using the Black-and-Scholes formula with a constant volatility given by the root-mean-square of the known average quadratic variation. The delta (and, as we shall see later on, the vega) amounts of stock and hedging option will also be obtained using the Black-and-Scholes formula with the same input volatility. We will therefore analyse the distribution of the outcomes *given that this particular strategy has been put in place*.

This last statement is very important. When perfect replication is no longer possible, unique pricing by no-arbitrage is unwarranted and the risk aversion of the trader becomes important. The variability of the returns from the naked (unhedged) option is irrelevant. When the volatility is stochastic, perfect replication might be impossible, but *some* hedging certainly can be attempted. Looking at the situation from a CAPM angle, even if the trader assumed that the true process of the underlying is unknown, she can only expect compensation for the undiversifiable part of the return volatility. See also Cochrane's (2001) statement in Section 1.5 of Chapter 1.

The hedging strategy that I analyse below is certainly not unique, nor necessarily the best one. However, whatever reduction in the volatility of returns of the naked European option it provides constitutes a good starting point in assessing the appropriate risk–return trade-off.

For the actual numerical experiments, I have used a mean-reverting stochastic volatility of the form

$$d\sigma_t = RVS(RVL - \sigma_t)\,dt + v\sigma_t\,dw_t \tag{13.51}$$

but, for the purpose of the following discussion, the precise functional form does not really matter. In the spirit of the approach described in Chapter 4, the parameters RVS and RVL are assumed to be the real-world (and not the risk-adjusted) ones. This is because I am not attempting to value the option using a risk-neutral simulation of the stock price, but to see to what extent the set-up cost of the replicating portfolio is sufficient to cover the liability from the sold European call.

As mentioned above, the trader does not know the true nature of the process of the underlying, but attempts to hedge a call option purely on the basis of her knowledge of the average realized quadratic variation. In the trader's eyes the option is therefore worth what the Black-and-Scholes formula predicts with the associated average root-mean-squared volatility used as an input. She will attempt to protect the value of the option so calculated either by using only the stock, or with the stock and another option. In either case she will have to decide how to translate the hedge ratios obtained in

Section 13.2 above into Black-and-Scholes-related quantities. How exactly this is done is explained in the next section.

13.6.2   A Numerical Example

The Set-Up

In this section I present the results obtained using the methodology outlined above using two sets of parameters. In both cases the maturity of the option to be hedged was chosen to be one year, and the strike to be at-the-money-spot (stock price at the start, S_0, equal to 100, strike also equal to 100, constant rate, r, of 5%). I then set the parameters of the volatility process for the normal and 'stressed' case as follows:

Normal case: volatility today $(\sigma_0) = 17\%$, reversion level $(RVL) = 17\%$, reversion speed $(RVS) = 0.4$, the percentage volatility of the volatility $(v) = 32\%$, and average root-mean-squared volatility $= 17\%$.

Stressed case: volatility today $(\sigma_0) = 34\%$, reversion level $(RVL) = 34\%$, reversion speed $(RVS) = 0.6$, the percentage volatility of the volatility $(v) = 64\%$, and average root-mean-squared volatility $= 37\%$.

The parameters chosen for the stressed case are rather extreme: the volatility of the volatility, in particular, is very high. This is shown in a typical path of the volatility, displayed in Figure 13.22. To give another idea of the degree of variability in the terminal stock price introduced by this choice of parameters, there is a 1% probability that, in the

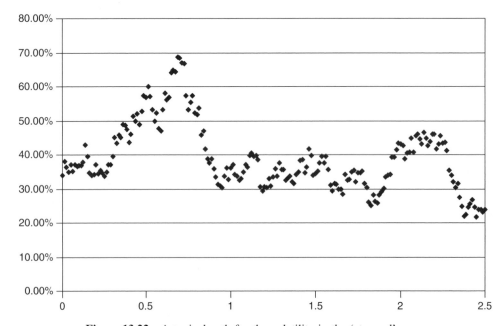

Figure 13.22   A typical path for the volatility in the 'stressed' case.

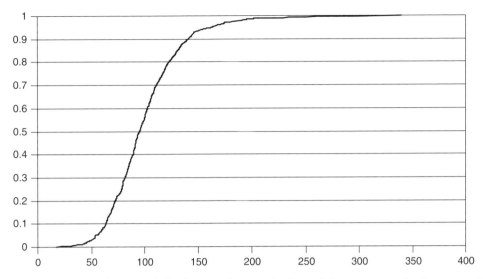

Figure 13.23 The risk-neutral distribution of terminal values of the stock price for the 'stressed' parameters discussed in the text.

real world, the stock price would be lower than $40 or higher than $210 at the end of one year. The 5th and 95th percentiles are $53.5 and $162.0, respectively. See Figure 13.23.

The average root-mean-squared volatilities, obtained computationally using a much higher number of paths, turned out to be 17.00% and 37.00% for the normal and stressed cases, respectively.

For the purpose of comparison, the cost of the (imperfectly) replicating portfolio obtained by using as input to the Black formula the average root-mean-squared volatilities above turned out to be $9.33 and $16.03, for the normal and stressed cases, respectively.

Two hedging strategies were employed, one based on the stock only, and the other based on the stock and another hedging option. This second option, h, was also chosen to be approximately at-the-money, but to have a maturity of two years. With the first (stock-only) hedging strategy the amount of stock to hold was assumed to be given by the Black-and-Scholes formula for the delta with the average root-mean-squared volatility used as input. With the second hedging strategy the amount of stock to hold, α, and of the second option, γ, were chosen to be given by (see Equations (13.21) and (13.22)):

$$\gamma(\widehat{\sigma}) = -\frac{\dfrac{\partial C(\widehat{\sigma})}{\partial \widehat{\sigma}}}{\dfrac{\partial h(\widehat{\sigma})}{\partial \widehat{\sigma}}} \tag{13.52}$$

$$\alpha(\widehat{\sigma}) = -\frac{\partial C(\widehat{\sigma})}{\partial S} + \frac{\dfrac{\partial C(\widehat{\sigma})}{\partial \widehat{\sigma}}}{\dfrac{\partial h(\widehat{\sigma})}{\partial \widehat{\sigma}}} \frac{\partial h}{\partial S} \tag{13.53}$$

where the expression $(\widehat{\sigma})$ indicates that the relevant quantity has been evaluated using the average root-mean-squared volatility. From Equation (13.22) one can see that evaluating the correct amount of hedging option would require knowing the derivatives of the options prices with respect to the *instantaneous* volatility. In my example, however, the trader does not have this information, and will therefore approximate these quantities by the derivatives of the option prices with respect to the input constant volatility, $\widehat{\sigma}$:

$$\frac{\partial C(\sigma)}{\partial \sigma} \simeq \frac{\partial C(\widehat{\sigma})}{\partial \widehat{\sigma}} \tag{13.54}$$

$$\frac{\partial h(\sigma)}{\partial \sigma} \simeq \frac{\partial h(\widehat{\sigma})}{\partial \widehat{\sigma}} \tag{13.55}$$

On the basis of the trader's limited information, these hedging ratios are therefore simply linked to the Black-and-Scholes deltas and vegas of the options, $\Delta_{BS}^C(\widehat{\sigma})$, $\kappa_{BS}^C(\widehat{\sigma})$, and $\Delta_{BS}^h(\widehat{\sigma})$, $\kappa_{BS}^h(\widehat{\sigma})$:

$$\gamma(\widehat{\sigma}) = -\frac{\kappa_{BS}^C(\widehat{\sigma})}{\kappa_{BS}^h(\widehat{\sigma})} \tag{13.56}$$

$$\alpha(\widehat{\sigma}) = -\Delta_{BS}^C(\widehat{\sigma}) + \frac{\kappa_{BS}^C(\widehat{\sigma})}{\kappa_{BS}^h(\widehat{\sigma})}\Delta_{BS}^h(\widehat{\sigma}) \tag{13.57}$$

During the course of each simulated path, the trader will have to buy and sell different amounts $\gamma(\widehat{\sigma})$ of the hedging option, h. I assume for simplicity that the 'market' prices for these transactions are given by the Black formula with the root-mean-squared volatility $\widehat{\sigma}$.

Another important issue to examine is the robustness of the two approximate hedging strategies to a mis-specification of the average root-mean-squared volatility. I therefore also present below the results obtained in the normal case if the trader uses a constant 'wrong' volatility of 14% to hedge the option C.

Finally, in the computer experiment I used 2048 paths of a 'smart' Monte Carlo, with a variable number of steps to the final maturity, as discussed below.

Presentation of the Results

The results are summarized in tabular form in Tables 13.1–13.3. The first two tables refer to the normal case, hedged with the correct volatility (Table 13.1) and with the wrong volatility (Table 13.2). The third table refers to the stressed case. In all the tables, the first column reports the number of time-steps used in the simulation. This is useful because there are two possible causes for the failure to replicate perfectly, namely the finiteness of the step size, and the fact that we know the process very imperfectly. Therefore we would like to know how much of the slippage is attributable to the finite re-hedging interval, and how much to the stochastic nature of the volatility.

The second column reports the average of the slippage, i.e. of the terminal difference between the payoff of the option and of the replicating portfolio[6] when both the stock and another option are used to construct the hedging portfolio. The third column reports the standard deviation of the same quantity. The fourth and fifth columns report the average and standard deviations of the slippages when only the stock is used for hedging.

---

[6]The portfolio is, of course, only imperfectly replicating, but, for the sake of brevity, in what follows it will be referred to as the replicating portfolio *tout court*.

Table 13.1 Descriptive statistics of the simulation for the normal case.

Nsteps	Avg(P-O)	StDev(P-O)	Avg(PSmpl-O)	StDev(PSmpl-O)	StDev(Opt)	Corr(Port)	Corr(Smpl)
10	0.277	2.052	0.134	3.4497	9.5857	−0.560	−0.5312
20	0.183	1.593	0.124	2.6904	10.2076	−0.691	−0.5282
40	0.030	1.372	−0.079	2.1141	10.6658	−0.720	−0.6556
80	0.033	1.260	0.012	1.7711	9.7861	−0.775	−0.7177
160	−0.037	1.131	−0.122	1.6403	10.4761	−0.844	−0.8004
320	−0.019	1.017	−0.014	1.4536	10.2164	−0.848	−0.8380
440	−0.017	1.062	−0.036	1.4208	10.3277	−0.851	−0.8457

Table 13.2 Descriptive statistics of the simulation for the normal case hedged with the wrong volatility.

Nsteps	Avg(P-O)	StDev(P-O)	Avg(PSmpl-O)	StDev(PSmpl-O)	StDev(Opt)	Corr(Port)	Corr(Smpl)
10	−0.741	2.364	−1.457	4.2358	11.3162	−0.564	−0.5435
20	−0.931	1.935	−1.382	2.9572	10.7930	−0.642	−0.5862
40	−0.875	1.630	−1.403	2.5173	10.4782	−0.632	−0.5810
80	−0.835	1.290	−1.289	1.9172	10.0363	−0.714	−0.7051
160	−0.956	1.246	−1.390	1.7740	10.7595	−0.670	−0.6793
320	−0.832	1.181	−1.193	1.5944	9.7409	−0.766	−0.7952
440	−0.916	1.101	−1.329	1.4385	9.4907	−0.703	−0.7125

Table 13.3 Descriptive statistics of the simulation for the stressed case.

Nsteps	Avg(P-O)	StDev(P-O)	Avg(PSmpl-O)	StDev(PSmpl-O)	StDev(Opt)	Corr(Port)	Corr(Smpl)
10	0.564	5.389	0.355	9.6787	24.3004	−0.641	−0.6012
20	0.201	5.034	0.173	8.5176	23.4735	−0.733	−0.6719
40	0.157	4.179	−0.017	6.3224	23.3644	−0.718	−0.7008
80	0.069	4.018	−0.094	6.5687	26.1707	−0.835	−0.7487
160	−0.393	4.782	−0.691	6.3623	31.2616	−0.820	−0.8449
320	−0.082	3.879	−0.104	5.1761	20.4399	−0.843	−0.8500
440	0.143	3.768	0.205	4.9430	28.4196	−0.849	−0.8487

The next column reports the standard deviation of the naked option. Note that we are not making any use of the average of the option payoffs for purposes of comparison with the set-up cost of the replicating portfolio, or to impute a fair option price. This is because the evolution has been carried out in the real, and not in the risk-neutral, measure. This quantity is therefore not reported in the tables. The standard deviation of the option payoff is instead important because, together with the standard deviation of the slippages, it will give an idea of the reduction in the uncertainty of outcomes in moving from the naked option to the imperfectly hedged option.

Finally, the last two columns report the correlation between the realized quadratic deviation and the slippage between the payoff of the option and of the replicating portfolios, both when stock and option (column 7), or just the stock (column 8), are used for hedging.

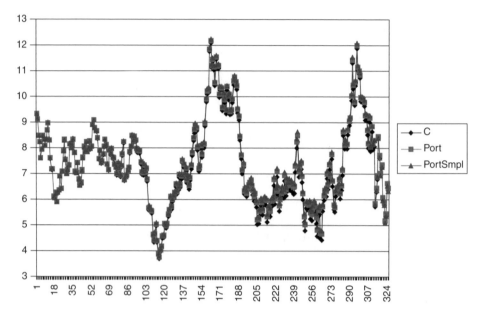

Figure 13.24   The outcome of a typical simulation path.

The outcome of a typical simulation path is shown in Figure 13.24. It is interesting to note that the realized values of the option (as assessed by the trader), of the stock-only portfolio and of the stock-and-option portfolio are 'optically' virtually indistinguishable. At a qualitative level, both hedging strategies, however imperfect, would therefore appear to be surprisingly effective.

Discussion of the Results

Starting from the non-stressed ('normal') case hedged with the correct average volatility, the first observation is that both the stock-only and the stock-and-option strategies achieve a reduction in the standard deviation of the terminal payoff with respect to the naked option by an order of magnitude, at least when the re-hedging frequency is greater than once a week. If the trader cares not just about the standard deviation, but about the fatness of the tails as well, she will have even more reason to prefer the hedged strategies, since the kurtoses of the naked option, of the stock-hedged and of the stock-and-option strategies are 4.75, 2.50 and 3.75, respectively. See Figures 13.25–13.28. (Interestingly, the tails appear to be fatter when the stock and the option are used for hedging, than when just the stock is used.)

Using both the stock and an option in order to hedge reduces the standard deviation by a factor of 1.35 with respect to the stock-only case: the improvement is therefore significant, but not dramatic. It is of course very difficult to generalize: these results have been obtained using the same strike, and a mismatch of one year for the two options. Varying the strike and the maturity of the hedging option can produce a variety of results.

The correlation between the realized root-mean-squared volatility and the slippage is very high (and very similar for the two hedging strategies). See the scatter plot in

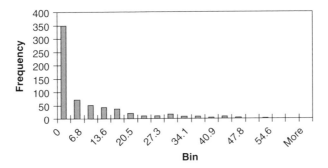

Figure 13.25 Histogram of realized payoff for the option only (normal case).

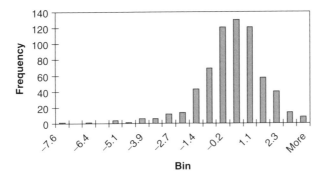

Figure 13.26 Histogram of realized payoff for the option hedged with the stock only (normal case, hedging with correct volatility).

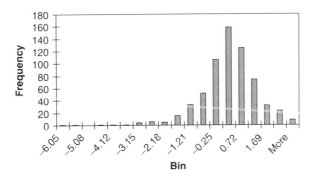

Figure 13.27 Histogram of realized payoff for the option hedged with the stock and another option (normal case, hedging with correct volatility).

Figure 13.29. Therefore, also in this case the realized quadratic variations have a very high explanatory power in accounting for the slippages.

Finally, note that, despite the fact that two hedging strategies have different distributions of outcomes, they both appear to be on average unbiased: within numerical noise the expectation of the payoff from the portfolio is zero.

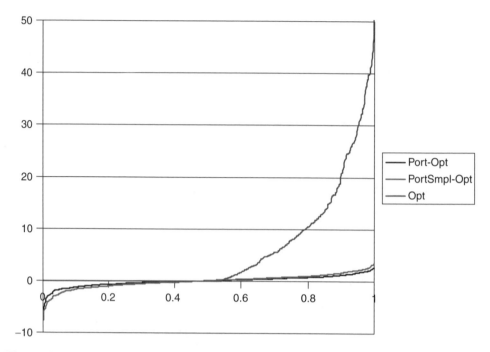

Figure 13.28   The distribution of outcomes for the three cases shown in Figures 13.25–13.27.

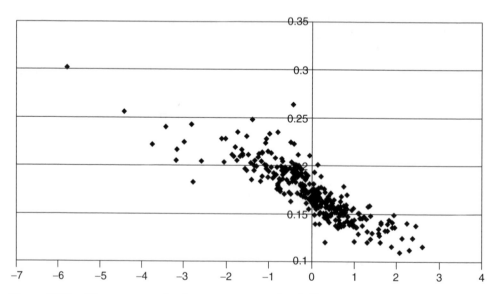

Figure 13.29   Slippages vs realized root-mean-squared volatility (normal case, hedging with the correct volatility).

What happens if the trader had used a wrong volatility to hedge (14% instead of 17%)? The first observation is that now the expectation of the slippages is non-zero, as one would expect, and that it is closer to zero in the case of the stock-and-option hedging. This is not surprising, since part of the error in the volatility specification is cancelled out by the volatility error made in choosing the amount of hedging option. Interestingly, the standard deviation of the slippages, using both just the stock or using the stock and an option, is barely different from the correct-volatility case explored above, and so is their ratio. Not surprisingly, the realized quadratic variation now explains a significantly smaller fraction of the slippages (approximately 70%); it is still, however, the dominant factor.

How robust are these results? The stressed case mentioned above provides an answer to this question. The reduction in standard deviation from the naked portfolio to either of the hedged portfolios is still approximately one order of magnitude, but it is not as pronounced. (I am still assuming that the trader knows the correct average quadratic variation.) Also, in this case the realized quadratic variation has a very high explanatory power, at least when the re-hedging frequency is sufficiently high.

Summarizing: I have shown in this section a simple example of parameter hedging, and discussed to what extent this strategy can reduce the uncertainty of returns that would be experienced if the trader held a naked option. The success (or otherwise) of the strategy depended on the ability of the approximate vega hedge ratios to predict the changes in prices of the two options in the strategy as the volatility changed. The hedge ratios in turn are a function of the type of process chosen for the volatility, and of the parameterization of this process. In particular, locating the reversion level above, below or at the current level of the volatility will have a strong impact on the future model-predicted smile surface, and hence on the hedge ratios and on the degree of success of the parameter hedging strategy. For this reason the calibration issue is discussed in some detail below in a real market case.

Exercise 5 *Here we assume that the trader (somehow) knew exactly the average quadratic variation. How could you make use of the results in Section 12.3.3 to obtain a useful 'market estimate' of this quantity?*

Exercise 6 *Repeat the procedure described above, but without assuming that during the course of the each simulation the trader finds the market prices of the option, h, at the Black prices with the root-mean-squared volatility, $\hat{\sigma}$. Assume instead that the market prices of the option, h, are given by a stochastic-volatility pricing formula. Note carefully that the reversion speed and the reversion level in the pricing formula and in the simulation should not be the same.*

13.7 Actual Fitting to Market Data

In this section I present the results of different fits to market data. The market smile, shown in Table 13.4, refers to Citigroup stock during October 2003. The model used was a combined stochastic-volatility, jump–diffusion model. We have not discussed the features of the smile produced by jumps, but we will focus in the discussion below on the stochastic-volatility part of the fit.

Two different fits were carried out: the first by allowing all the parameters to find the 'best' possible values (the 'unconstrained' set); the second using a simple constraint, as

Table 13.4 The market smile for Citigroup stock during October 2003.

Market	mkt 0.085	mkt 0.252	mkt 0.504	mkt 0.750	mkt 1.002	mkt 1.254	mkt 1.503	mkt 1.749	mkt 2.001	mkt 2.253
21.0	66.30%	52.30%	46.40%	43.86%	43.14%	42.88%	42.48%	41.76%	41.18%	40.71%
23.2	62.71%	49.97%	44.57%	42.30%	41.70%	41.50%	41.16%	40.52%	39.99%	39.57%
25.4	57.88%	46.83%	42.13%	40.22%	39.76%	39.65%	39.39%	38.84%	38.40%	38.03%
27.6	53.37%	43.89%	39.88%	38.31%	37.98%	37.95%	37.77%	37.30%	36.93%	36.63%
29.8	49.12%	41.11%	37.80%	36.54%	36.34%	36.37%	36.26%	35.88%	35.58%	35.33%
32.0	45.02%	38.47%	35.86%	34.90%	34.81%	34.91%	34.87%	34.57%	34.33%	34.13%
34.2	41.03%	35.96%	34.05%	33.37%	33.39%	33.56%	33.58%	33.35%	33.17%	33.02%
36.4	37.06%	33.59%	32.35%	31.94%	32.06%	32.30%	32.38%	32.22%	32.09%	32.00%
38.6	33.09%	31.36%	30.77%	30.60%	30.83%	31.13%	31.27%	31.17%	31.10%	31.05%
40.8	29.26%	29.33%	29.29%	29.35%	29.68%	30.04%	30.24%	30.21%	30.18%	30.17%
43.0	26.00%	27.56%	27.90%	28.18%	28.61%	29.04%	29.30%	29.32%	29.34%	29.36%
45.2	24.16%	26.13%	26.62%	27.10%	27.63%	28.13%	28.44%	28.51%	28.57%	28.62%
47.4	24.02%	25.12%	25.45%	26.10%	26.73%	27.30%	27.66%	27.77%	27.87%	27.95%
49.6	23.85%	24.55%	24.38%	25.18%	25.91%	26.55%	26.97%	27.11%	27.24%	27.35%
51.8	23.52%	24.27%	23.44%	24.35%	25.18%	25.89%	26.36%	26.53%	26.68%	26.81%
54.0	23.49%	23.99%	22.61%	23.61%	24.53%	25.32%	25.83%	26.03%	26.19%	26.34%
56.2	23.49%	23.54%	21.89%	22.95%	23.97%	24.83%	25.38%	25.59%	25.77%	25.93%
58.4	23.49%	23.47%	21.26%	22.36%	23.49%	24.42%	25.01%	25.23%	25.42%	25.58%
60.6	23.49%	23.46%	20.77%	21.85%	23.07%	24.07%	24.71%	24.93%	25.12%	25.28%
62.8	23.49%	23.46%	20.77%	21.38%	22.70%	23.78%	24.45%	24.67%	24.86%	25.04%
65.0	23.49%	23.46%	20.77%	20.96%	22.36%	23.52%	24.24%	24.47%	24.66%	24.83%

Table 13.5 The parameters obtained for the unconstrained and the constrained fits to the market smile.

	Best unconstrained fit	Best constrained fit	Constrained above	Constrained below
JDS_InitialVol	24.206%	24.358%	26.568%	25.566%
JDSV_VolVariance	46.1%	47.6%	48.2%	50.0%
JDSV_ReversionLevel	19.052%	24.358%	26.568%	25.566%
JDSV_ReversionSpeed	20.992%	16.185%	16.148%	17.855%
JDSV_Correlation	−0.55	−0.56	−0.56	−0.68
JDSV_JumpMean	0.70	0.71	0.67	0.92
JDSV_JumpSigma	8.02%	8.00%	10.58%	0.10%
JDSV_JumpLambda	0.193	0.191	0.208	0.103

discussed below (the 'constrained' set). See Table 13.5. In both cases time-independent parameters were used, thereby ensuring that the future will look (in a statistical sense) like today. The two sets of parameters were used to produce simultaneous fits to the whole available market smile surface, which covered expiries from approximately one month to two years.

Starting from the unconstrained results, the first observation is that the quality of the fit is very good. See Figures 13.30–13.35 and Table 13.6. Furthermore, with one possible exception, discussed below, all the optimized parameters turned out to be very 'plausible': the volatility was of the order of 25%; a negative correlation ($\sim -55\%$) was found between the increments of the underlying and of the volatility, in agreement with the empirical findings discussed in Chapter 7; the correlation was not so high (say, greater than 95%) as to make the approach effectively one-factor; the jump frequency was approximately one jump every five years; and the expected risk-adjusted magnitude of the jump corresponded to a price fall by 30%. All these values should be looked at

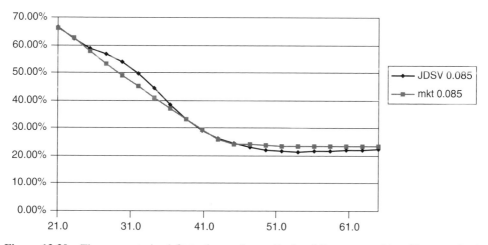

Figure 13.30 The unconstrained fit to the market smile for different maturities. The maturity is in the figure legend.

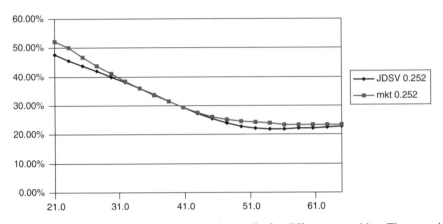

Figure 13.31   The unconstrained fit to the market smile for different maturities. The maturity is in the figure legend.

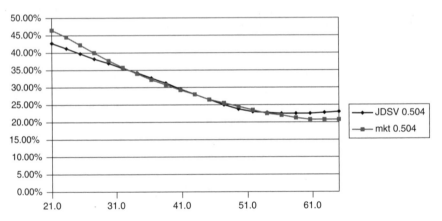

Figure 13.32   The unconstrained fit to the market smile for different maturities. The maturity is in the figure legend.

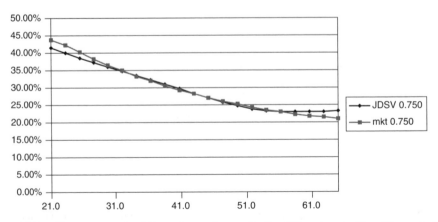

Figure 13.33   The unconstrained fit to the market smile for different maturities. The maturity is in the figure legend.

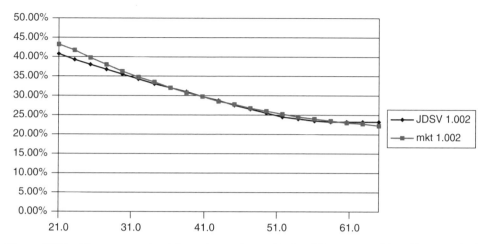

Figure 13.34 The unconstrained fit to the market smile for different maturities. The maturity is in the figure legend.

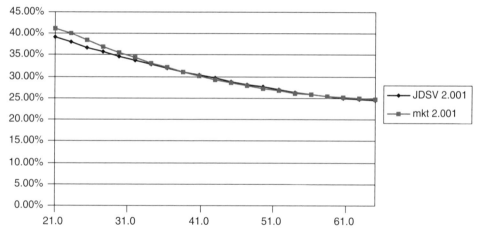

Figure 13.35 The unconstrained fit to the market smile for different maturities. The maturity is in the figure legend.

carefully in the light of the discussion presented in Section 6.7 of Chapter 6, and appear to pass the 'sanity checks' recommended there. Only one result is slightly puzzling: the current value of the instantaneous stochastic volatility (∼21%) is not at its long-term level (∼19%). At the time of the fitting there was no market or company-specific news that might indicate that the current volatility should be at an 'unusual' level. We know, however, from the discussion in Sections 13.4 and 13.5 that if the current volatility is above or below its long-term level the current smile will change significantly. In other words, the fit implies that today's smile is 'special', and will change in the near future. We have also discussed the implications this feature has on future re-hedging costs (see Chapter 1) and on the vega hedge ratios used in parameter hedging. Is this difference between the current and the long-term volatility level an essential feature of the fit? Are

Table 13.6 The unconstrained fit to the whole market smile surface.

JDSV	JDSV 0.085	JDSV 0.252	JDSV 0.504	JDSV 0.750	JDSV 1.002	JDSV 1.254	JDSV 1.503	JDSV 1.749	JDSV 2.001
21.0	66.42%	47.74%	42.80%	41.43%	40.67%	40.16%	39.77%	39.47%	39.22%
23.2	62.14%	45.70%	41.25%	39.96%	39.25%	38.77%	38.42%	38.15%	37.94%
25.4	58.95%	43.75%	39.75%	38.57%	37.91%	37.47%	37.16%	36.93%	36.76%
27.6	56.58%	41.89%	38.29%	37.22%	36.63%	36.24%	35.97%	35.79%	35.67%
29.8	53.75%	40.04%	36.88%	35.92%	35.40%	35.06%	34.85%	34.72%	34.64%
32.0	49.71%	38.11%	35.51%	34.68%	34.22%	33.95%	33.79%	33.70%	33.67%
34.2	44.40%	36.02%	34.14%	33.47%	33.09%	32.88%	32.78%	32.74%	32.76%
36.4	38.47%	33.81%	32.70%	32.26%	32.00%	31.87%	31.82%	31.84%	31.90%
38.6	33.10%	31.56%	31.19%	31.01%	30.91%	30.88%	30.91%	30.98%	31.09%
40.8	29.12%	29.36%	29.59%	29.70%	29.80%	29.90%	30.02%	30.17%	30.33%
43.0	26.35%	27.30%	27.97%	28.35%	28.66%	28.92%	29.15%	29.38%	29.60%
45.2	24.36%	25.45%	26.38%	27.01%	27.51%	27.93%	28.29%	28.61%	28.90%
47.4	22.94%	23.93%	24.96%	25.74%	26.40%	26.96%	27.44%	27.85%	28.23%
49.6	22.05%	22.88%	23.84%	24.65%	25.40%	26.06%	26.63%	27.13%	27.57%
51.8	21.61%	22.28%	23.10%	23.83%	24.56%	25.25%	25.88%	26.44%	26.95%
54.0	21.47%	22.02%	22.69%	23.30%	23.94%	24.60%	25.23%	25.82%	26.37%
56.2	21.53%	21.98%	22.52%	23.01%	23.54%	24.11%	24.71%	25.29%	25.85%
58.4	21.69%	22.07%	22.52%	22.90%	23.31%	23.79%	24.31%	24.85%	25.40%
60.6	21.92%	22.24%	22.61%	22.91%	23.23%	23.61%	24.04%	24.52%	25.03%
62.8	22.18%	22.45%	22.76%	23.00%	23.24%	23.53%	23.88%	24.29%	24.74%
65.0	22.46%	22.70%	22.96%	23.14%	23.32%	23.54%	23.81%	24.14%	24.53%

the prices truly 'trying to tell us something', or could we find a fit that does not display this characteristic, and yet is of similar numerical quality? More fundamentally, is the model well specified?

To answer these questions, a second fit was carried out by forcing the current level of the volatility to coincide with its long-term level. The search for the optimal parameters was started from different initial points. The results are shown in the same Table 13.5, in Figures 13.36–13.41 and in Table 13.7. The interesting observation is that the quality of the fit barely changed. Even more encouraging, the other fitting parameters have changed by very small amounts, and convey the same overall financial 'picture'. This suggests that the parameterization is stable with respect to small changes in the fitting procedure, giving credence to the hypothesis that the model is indeed well specified. In

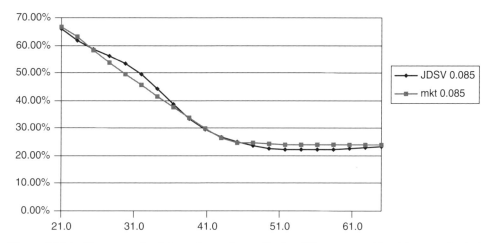

Figure 13.36   The constrained fit to the market smile for different maturities. The maturity is in the figure legend.

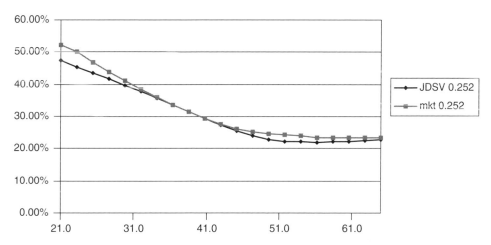

Figure 13.37   The constrained fit to the market smile for different maturities. The maturity is in the figure legend.

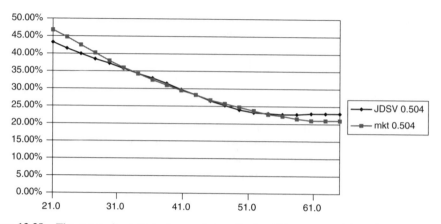

Figure 13.38   The constrained fit to the market smile for different maturities. The maturity is in the figure legend.

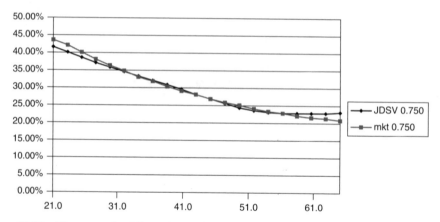

Figure 13.39   The constrained fit to the market smile for different maturities. The maturity is in the figure legend.

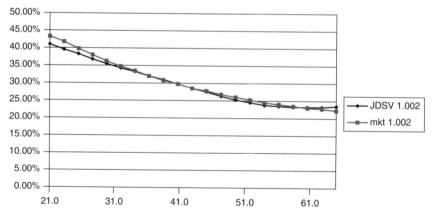

Figure 13.40   The constrained fit to the market smile for different maturities. The maturity is in the figure legend.

Table 13.7 The constrained fit to the whole market smile surface.

JDSV	JDSV 0.085	JDSV 0.252	JDSV 0.504	JDSV 0.750	JDSV 1.002	JDSV 1.254	JDSV 1.503	JDSV 1.749	JDSV 2.001
21.0	65.50%	47.35%	42.88%	41.67%	40.99%	40.52%	40.16%	39.88%	39.66%
23.2	61.35%	45.35%	41.31%	40.16%	39.52%	39.08%	38.75%	38.51%	38.32%
25.4	58.11%	43.42%	39.79%	38.73%	38.13%	37.72%	37.43%	37.23%	37.08%
27.6	55.66%	41.57%	38.31%	37.34%	36.80%	36.44%	36.20%	36.03%	35.93%
29.8	52.85%	39.74%	36.88%	36.01%	35.52%	35.22%	35.02%	34.91%	34.85%
32.0	48.94%	37.85%	35.49%	34.72%	34.30%	34.05%	33.91%	33.85%	33.83%
34.2	43.83%	35.84%	34.10%	33.48%	33.13%	32.94%	32.86%	32.84%	32.88%
36.4	38.13%	33.71%	32.67%	32.24%	32.00%	31.89%	31.86%	31.90%	31.98%
38.6	32.99%	31.52%	31.15%	30.98%	30.88%	30.87%	30.91%	31.00%	31.13%
40.8	29.15%	29.36%	29.56%	29.65%	29.75%	29.86%	29.99%	30.15%	30.34%
43.0	26.42%	27.31%	27.92%	28.29%	28.58%	28.85%	29.10%	29.34%	29.58%
45.2	24.42%	25.44%	26.32%	26.92%	27.42%	27.84%	28.21%	28.54%	28.86%
47.4	22.98%	23.92%	24.89%	25.64%	26.30%	26.86%	27.35%	27.77%	28.16%
49.6	22.09%	22.87%	23.78%	24.56%	25.29%	25.94%	26.52%	27.03%	27.49%
51.8	21.66%	22.29%	23.06%	23.76%	24.46%	25.14%	25.77%	26.34%	26.86%
54.0	21.54%	22.06%	22.68%	23.25%	23.87%	24.50%	25.13%	25.72%	26.28%
56.2	21.61%	22.04%	22.55%	23.00%	23.49%	24.04%	24.62%	25.19%	25.76%
58.4	21.79%	22.15%	22.57%	22.92%	23.31%	23.75%	24.25%	24.77%	25.32%
60.6	22.03%	22.34%	22.69%	22.96%	23.25%	23.60%	24.01%	24.47%	24.96%
62.8	22.31%	22.57%	22.86%	23.08%	23.30%	23.56%	23.88%	24.26%	24.70%
65.0	22.60%	22.83%	22.87%	23.25%	23.41%	23.60%	23.84%	24.15%	24.52%

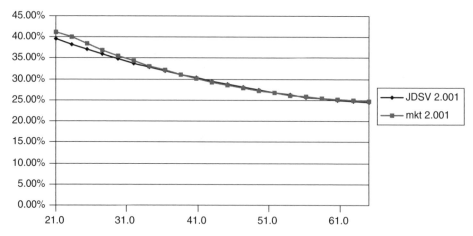

Figure 13.41 The constrained fit to the market smile for different maturities. The maturity is in the figure legend.

short, the new fit is almost as good, but now it does not imply that there is anything 'special' about today, and does not produce, in particular, any strong change in the current shape of the smile surface. If we believe that 'today' is in no way 'special', the constrained results therefore give an example not just of a good fit, but of a successful and financially well-motivated fitting procedure. Recalling the discussion in Chapter 1 about model re-calibration and vega re-hedging, I would prefer to price and hedge using the constrained rather than the unconstrained solution.

13.8 Conclusions

In this chapter we have looked in some detail at stochastic-volatility models. To begin with, I have discussed the qualitative features of the smile surfaces they produce. We have compared the empirical findings reported in Chapter 7 and the model results presented in Section 13.4, and we have found that with 'typical' parameters these model smiles are somewhat at odds with the market smiles: in particular, it is difficult to obtain sufficiently steep smiles for short maturities. This does not agree with empirical findings in the equity and FX arenas. This shortcoming could be overcome if one gave a time dependence to the parameters that characterize the process. This, however, has the unpleasant consequence of creating non-time-homogeneous smile surfaces: the future looks different from the future.

A more appealing way to bring about a better agreement with typical option prices while preserving time homogeneity is to parameterize the stochastic-volatility models using a high reversion speed and a high volatility of volatility. By so doing, steep smiles for short maturities can be obtained more 'naturally'. It should be kept in mind, however, that the volatility of the volatility is not a 'free parameter', because it remains unchanged in moving across measures. So, a good, time-homogeneous fit with a volatility of the volatility coefficient greatly at odds with the corresponding statistical quantity should be regarded with suspicion. Fouque *et al.* (2000) provide a wealth of useful techniques to estimate the parameters of a high-volatility, high-reversion speed volatility process, *if* the process is indeed of this nature.

Moving to the qualitative features of the implied volatility surface, we have found that the future smile (which is stochastic, i.e. not fully determined by the future realization of the stock price) can display predictable shape changes if the volatility happens to be well above or well below its long-term reversion level. This type of time-inhomogeneity is a structural feature of the model, and not the artefact of a numerical fitting procedure to a mis-specified model. Whether the trader finds convincing or at least plausible the model predictions of the short-term evolution of the smile when the volatility is, say, unusually high is a different matter, but at least the predicted dynamics does have a well-defined financial rationale in this case.

These observations become particularly relevant if we want to analyse the behaviour of future smiles as a function of the future realization of the stock price. In particular, we found that there is a clear relationship between the future shape of the smile and the future value attained by the stock price. Also, the future likely evolution of the smile surface could be to a large extent explained by the realization of the future stock price. We provided an intuitive explanation of why this should be the case. These observations will be revisited in the Chapter 17, which is devoted to the direct modelling of the dynamics of the smile surface.

The last part of this chapter was devoted to a discussion of the practical (parameter) hedging of a call option when the true process is a stochastic-volatility diffusion, but the trader 'lives' in a Black-and-Scholes world. We found that, if the trader knows exactly the *average* quadratic variation (which is now a stochastic quantity), the hedging based on reasonably chosen, Black-based hedge ratios is remarkably good. This is true not only if another option is used for hedging, but even if just the stock is used. The picture changes somewhat if the trader guesses the wrong average quadratic variation. When this happens, hedging with another option, i.e. vega hedging, becomes much more important. These results should be compared with those presented at the end of Chapter 14, devoted to jump–diffusion processes.

Finally, the chapter concluded with a careful discussion of desirable and undesirable fits to market data.

Chapter 14

Jump–Diffusion Processes

14.1 Introduction

Let us remind ourselves of the most important empirical features of equity smiles:

1. The overall qualitative shape of the equity smile has been relatively constant over many years, at least since 1987. A well-defined smile appeared rather suddenly in the immediate aftermath of the 1987 crash.

2. The shape of the smile, especially for equity indices, is strongly asymmetric, with implied volatilities for out-of-the-money puts considerably higher than for out-of-the-money calls. The risk-neutral density is therefore strongly skewed to the left.

3. The equity smile is more pronounced for short maturities and shallower for longer maturities.

4. In the equity case a convincing case can be made that the smile should be floating (see the discussion in Section 7.3.2 of Chapter 7). It is therefore reasonable to require that the chosen model should generate a future smile surface which approximately maintains its shape as a function of the future level of at-the-moneyness.

Given these financial desiderata, which modelling approaches can account for them in a satisfactory way? Let us examine in this light the models examined so far.

- We have seen in the previous chapter that when fully stochastic-volatility models are parameterized with constant coefficients, they often produce shallow smiles for short maturities, and more pronounced smiles at the long end of the maturity spectrum. This feature is therefore in conflict with the third empirical feature mentioned above. There are at least two common ways to overcome this feature. The first is to parameterize the process using strongly time-dependent coefficients. For instance, the volatility of the volatility and/or the reversion speed of the volatility can be made to display a dependence on calendar time. These choices, however, imply a time-inhomogeneous future behaviour for the smile surface. (See, for example, Das and Sundaram (1997) for an empirical study). In other words, when we use

439

fully stochastic-volatility models thus parameterized we are implicitly subscribing to the view that the shape of the future smile will change significantly in the future. This would be in disagreement with the first empirical feature above. Alternatively, one can use a high (but constant) volatility of volatility coupled with a strong (but constant) reversion speed. This possibility can be appealing, but, for this approach to be justified, the dynamics of the volatility of the underlying should display the characteristics discussed in Fouque *et al.* (2000)[1].

- Fully stochastic-volatility models *can* produce an asymmetric smile, and therefore a skewed risk-neutral density, by introducing a negative instantaneous correlation between the increments of the volatility and of the underlying. When the asymmetry is very pronounced, however (as is often observed to be the case in equities), the required correlation would have to be very high. When this is the case a fully stochastic-volatility model becomes more and more similar to a one-factor model, of the restricted-volatility (CEV) family. In other words, the stochasticity arising from the second factor (the volatility shock) becomes less and less important as an *independent* source of randomness as the correlation coefficient increases.

- The local-volatility modelling approach successfully recovers (by construction) any admissible set of market prices for plain-vanilla equities or FX options. Therefore it can certainly recover a skewed and steep smile. As we have seen in Chapter 12, however, for typically observed shapes of the implied volatility surface local-volatility approaches fail to reproduce a self-similar future smile. The future is therefore predicted to look qualitatively different from the present. Again, this is in conflict with the third empirical feature above. The resulting lack of time homogeneity is, in my opinion, fundamentally unsatisfactory.

These shortcomings point to the fact that something appears to be missing in a purely diffusive description. Further evidence that an important component is still missing comes from the work by Carr and Wu (2003b) mentioned in Chapter 7. Recall in fact that they looked at the speed with which out-of-the-money prices of S&P options go to zero as a function of the option expiry, and concluded that both a continuous and a discontinuous component was present in the dynamics of the index. Their study indicates the direction in which we may want to extend the modelling presented so far.

In this chapter a richer process for the underlying that combines both continuous and discontinuous innovations is introduced. I will show that it can account at least qualitatively for many of the empirical observations highlighted above, including the persistence of the floating nature of the smile. In particular, for some natural choices about the nature of the jumps, jump–diffusion models can produce floating smiles of an approximately time-homogeneous nature. Furthermore, they 'naturally' give rise (as shown below) to pronounced smiles for short maturities, that flatten for longer times to expiry. See, in this respect, the observations at the end of Section 12.6.2.

These observations by themselves would make the analysis of jump–diffusion models interesting. There are further important financial reasons, however, to believe that

---

[1] In a stochastic-volatility model where the volatility is of the mean-reverting type the reversion speed and the reversion level are in general (Girsanov-) transformed in moving between the objective and the pricing measures. The volatility of the volatility remains however unchanged. Therefore the validity of the approach advocated by Fouque *et al.* (2000) is predicated upon the actual occurrence of a high volatility of volatility in the empirical time series. This approach is discussed in some detail in Chapter 12.

introducing jumps should capture important features of the equity smiles. Being able to identify these financial reasons is very important. It is one of the main messages of this book, in fact, that the ability of a mathematical model to reproduce certain static empirical features (such as today's prices) is *per se* a weak reason to recommend its endorsement. In the case of jump–diffusions, however, a plausible financial 'story' can be formulated that appears to capture some important features of the shape of the equity smile curve. This is presented below.

14.2 The Financial Model: Smile Tale 2 Revisited

The financial model presented in this section formalizes and makes more precise the 'Smile Tale 2' presented in Section 6.6 of Chapter 6. We had assumed in this tale that there existed a first set of economic agents (pension funds, institutional investors, mutual funds, etc. collectively referred to in what follows as 'the fund players') who are natural holders of equities. One of the main sources of risk to which they are exposed is the possibility of large downward movements in the equity indices in which they are (or, 'have to be') invested. For this reason they are buyers of insurance, typically in the form of out-of-the-money equity puts, and, by so doing, they bid up the prices of these options.

There is another set of economic agents (e.g. relative-value traders working for hedge funds or for the proprietary desks of other financial institutions). These are just the 'pseudo-arbitrageurs' (or, more simply, 'arbitrageurs' for brevity) discussed in Chapter 1 in the context of the efficient-market hypothesis. The task of bringing back the value of assets (and of options in particular) towards fundamentals is their responsibility. They have no preferential habitat in term of option strikes. If the dynamics of the underlying were exactly diffusive, and the trading universe exactly of the Black type, these players would face very little risk and would naturally exert a pull towards re-equilibration of the option prices by selling the 'expensive' out-of-the-money options ('expensive' because their prices had been bid up away from fundamentals by the insurance-seeking fund players), and vega-hedging themselves by buying 'cheap' at-the-money options. If the process of the underlying index were truly a log-normal Brownian diffusion, the arbitrageurs would therefore 'safely' reap a riskless profit at the expense of the fund players, and therefore the smiley shape of the strike/implied volatility function could not persist in equilibrium.

In the real world, however, there exist rare but large jumps. When these rare events occur the continuous-time re-hedging that is necessary for the arbitrageurs to capture the 'extra value' between the at-the-money and the out-of-the-money implied volatilities can no longer take place. By itself, this fact will create a variance of returns for the arbitrageurs. If the latter are risk averse, and perceive the variance of their portfolio returns as their 'risk', they will demand extra compensation for assuming the jump risk. Therefore, even if the upward and downward jumps are just as likely, the arbitrageurs will not move into action until the smile is steep enough (i.e. until the difference between the out-of-the-money and the at-the-money implied volatilities is large enough).

If downward jumps are more likely than upward jumps, however, their occurrence has farther-reaching consequences than just increasing the variance of the slippages: if the arbitrageur has hedged herself assuming a Brownian diffusion, when a downward jump occurs she will always make a loss. To see why this must be the case let us consider her strategy in greater detail. The arbitrageur observes a smile curve which is roughly flat for values of the strike above the at-the-money level, and which rises monotonically for strikes below the at-the-money level. For instance, the 'market' smile the trader observes could be of the form shown in Figure 12.10. If she believes that she inhabits a Black-and-Scholes world, it is natural for her to enter the following transactions (see Table 14.1 and Figure 14.1):

Table 14.1 Two sub-portfolios, before (left box) and after (right box) the jump. For each of the two boxes, the first column refers to the sub-portfolio with the out-of-the-money option, and the second to the sub-portfolio with the at-the-money option. The stock price before the jump is at 100 and the residual maturity 1 year; the two strikes are at 100 at 80. The amount of cash before the jump makes each sub-portfolio worth zero. A 'Ratio' amount of portfolio 2 makes the Total Portfolio vega and gamma neutral. When the jump occurs, the stock price moves from 100 to 80.

Strike	80.0000	100.0000	80.0000	100.0000
Price	6.3725	21.1859	6.3725	21.1859
Delta	−0.4602	−0.8451	−0.1120	−0.4602
Gamma	0.0248	0.0149	0.0248	0.0149
Vega	31.7562	19.0534	19.0534	39.6953
Cash	−43.1862	−88.7954	**−12.3906**	**−53.9828**
Port	0.0000	−0.0000	2.9456	4.0169
Ratio	1.6667		**0.4800**	
TotalPort	−0.0000		−1.0175	

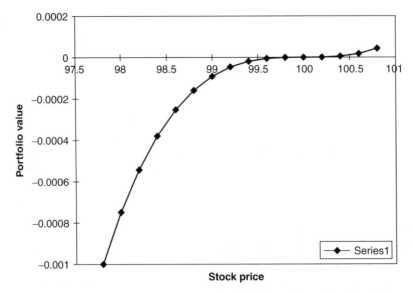

Figure 14.1 The P&L of the total portfolio described in Table 14.1 as a function of the post-jump value of the stock. Note how the total portfolio is gamma neutral at the origin.

- she sells an out-of-the-money put;

- she constructs a zero-cost, delta-neutral replicating portfolio to cancel the delta exposure of the out-of-the-money put;

- she neutralizes the vega exposure of the out-of-the-money put by buying an amount of at-the-money put with the same vega;

- she eliminates the residual delta exposure introduced by the last transaction by dealing in an appropriate (delta) amount of stock and by borrowing or lending cash.

Note that, for the moment, the delta and vega transactions carried out by the arbitrageur are those suggested by the standard Black formula used with the at-the-money volatility. This is consistent with an arbitrageur who does not 'believe in jumps' and considers the higher implied volatilities purely a result of the desire for insurance of the fund players. Also, we have, rather arbitrarily, assumed that the arbitrageur is trying to obtain the 'biggest bang for the buck', i.e. that she has chosen to hedge herself by buying the option which has, at the same time, the maximum difference in implied volatility and is closest in strike to the chosen out-of-the-money put. Given the assumed shape of the equity smile curve she observes, the option chosen as a 'buy' is therefore the at-the-money option. This assumption is not necessary, and the choice of option strikes will be discussed later in the chapter.

If the trader has correctly guessed the volatility of the purely time-dependent diffusive component of the process, the overall hedged portfolio will make exactly no gains and no losses until the first jump. (I have assumed continuous, frictionless trading. See Section 14.11 and Figure 14.33 in particular for a more realistic treatment.) When the first jump occurs the total portfolio (options plus hedges) will no longer have an overall zero value, and, as shown above, over a downward jump the overall portfolio will always make a loss. This is because the portfolio made up of the out-of-the-money put, which the arbitrageur has shorted, and of the accompanying delta amount of stock will increase in absolute value by more than the associated at-the-money put and its delta hedges. The effect of a particular downward jump on a portfolio that has been kept balanced as explained above at all times before the jump event is shown in Table 14.1. The portfolio P&L over jumps of different amplitude (upward and downward) is shown in Figure 14.1.

Let me stress again that, even if we had assumed that in the real world the likelihood of occurrence of upward jumps is the same as the probability of downward jumps, the presence of jumps, of whichever sign, will introduce a finite variance to the terminal value of the portfolio. If the arbitrageur is risk averse, and perceives risk in terms of portfolio variance, she will therefore demand some compensation for this form of risk even if the expected jump amplitude ratio were one (or, up to a point, even if it were positive). If, in addition, jumps are more likely to be downwards, the arbitrageur will demand additional compensation. The total 'expected' jump amplitude will therefore be made up of an 'actuarial' component, plus another part as compensation for the uncertainty introduced by the existence of jumps *of any sign*.

It is important to point out that in the model we have outlined the true process of the underlying equity index is mixed diffusive–jump in nature. The jumps, in particular, are of random amplitude, and, as discussed below, the market is incomplete with respect to their occurrence. In this setting a risk-neutral valuation will therefore fail to provide a unique option price, and the result will depend to some extent on the arbitrageurs' appetite for risk. This feature obviously is computationally unpleasant, but, in a way, it is one of the central features employed in this chapter in order to explain and account for the stylized facts that characterize equity smiles. Because of its importance, the topic of market completeness in the presence of jumps is discussed in the next section.

14.3   Hedging and Replicability in the Presence of Jumps: First Considerations

Several pricing models, starting from Merton's (1990), have superimposed a discontinuous (jump) component to a diffusion. The treatments that can be found in the literature differ in the degree of hedging allowed, and in the nature of the jump process (log-normally- or otherwise-distributed jumps, a finite or an infinite number of possible jump amplitudes, etc.). It is therefore important to state clearly the nature of the jumps and the trading universe of 'fundamental securities' assumed to exist at the trader's disposal for hedging purposes. More precisely, if the process of the underlying is a jump–diffusion with a *continuous* jump amplitude three situations can arise.

1. In the first case, the hedging of an option with anything but the underlying stock (or index) is disallowed. The market is incomplete, and for a general path realization the trader cannot expect to replicate the final payoff of a plain-vanilla option even if she could trade without friction in continuous time.

2. The second pricing framework allows hedging of an option (e.g. out-of-the-money puts) with one or more other options (e.g. the at-the-money calls/puts). In other words, the second approach recognizes that *some* degree of hedging is possible, and is likely to be entered into by the market participants, but that also in this case the resulting portfolio will not exactly replicate the terminal payoff of the plain-vanilla option. The market is still incomplete, but, with a judicious choice of the hedging instrument, the variance of returns from the overall portfolio (option to hedge plus imperfectly hedging options) can be significantly reduced.

3. In the third case it is assumed that the trader can include an *infinite* number of options in her trading strategy. In this case a perfect hedge against the infinite number of possible realizations of the jump amplitude would seem to be possible, and the market would appear completable. See, however, the caveat in Section 14.3.1.

If the jump–diffusion process is such that only a *finite number* of possible jump amplitudes are possible, then, depending on the degree of hedging possible, the following situations can arise.

1. If the hedging of an option with anything but the underlying stock (or index) is disallowed, then the market is still incomplete. Therefore, once again, for a general path realization the trader cannot expect to replicate the final payoff of a plain-vanilla option.

2. If as many hedging options as possible jump amplitudes are allowed, then it is in theory possible to complete the market, and to set up an exactly replicating portfolio. Since the number of possible amplitudes has been assumed to be finite,

the completion of the market only requires a finite number of plain-vanilla options. Also in this case, however, see the reservations I raise in Section 14.3.1.

The second statement is certainly correct and would appear to be quite powerful. This is because, as I show in Section 14.7, a continuous-amplitude jump process can often be closely approximated by a similar process with a finite (and sometimes rather small) number of possible jump amplitude ratios. It would therefore seem that one could efficiently 'approximate' a continuous-amplitude jump process with a process with only a finite number of possible jump amplitude ratios. One could then invoke the completeness of the latter setting to impute 'almost' unique pricing by no arbitrage also in the more general case. Unfortunately, this approach is less useful than it might appear. I show in the next section, in fact, that, in order to determine the holdings of the hedging options required to create a riskless portfolio one must know not only their prices today, but also their prices in all possible future states of the world.

14.3.1 What Is Really Required To Complete the Market?

I show analytically in Section 14.5 to what extent it is possible to hedge a contingent claim when the process for the underlying is a mixed jump–diffusion. It is useful, however, to gain an intuitive understanding of the nature of the problem by looking at a very simple discrete-time setting. This case study will also be of help in understanding the origin and limitations of statements such as:

> If only a finite number of jump amplitudes are possible, then the market can be completed by introducing among the set of hedging instruments as many plain-vanilla calls as possible jump amplitudes.

Completion of the market, in this context, means that, in the absence of frictions, an arbitrary payoff could be exactly replicated via a self-financing trading strategy that only involves the underlying, a bond and as many plain-vanilla options as possible jump amplitudes. If this is the case, we know from Chapter 2 that we can arrive at a *unique*, preference-independent price by invoking no arbitrage.

Let us consider a one-period problem.[2] I extend the replication construction presented in Chapter 2 to incorporate the possibility of jumps. For simplicity we will assume that only one jump amplitude is possible, and therefore the underlying can move either to an 'up' or a 'down' diffusive state, or to a 'jump' state.[3] We know the values of the stock today and in all the three possible states that can be reached tomorrow, but we do not claim to know the probabilities of reaching them. Similarly, we know the values today and in all these possible future states of the world of a bond, B, and of the (call) option, O_1, of strike K_1 that we want to use for hedging purposes. To ensure unambiguous (i.e. model-independent) knowledge of the value of the option O_1 in all the possible future states, we impose that its expiry should take place in one period's time. In this case the value

---

[2] I wish to thank Mark Joshi for pointing out to me this very clear example.

[3] How do we know that the up and down states are associated with the diffusive part, and the third state with the jump component? The only way to tell is to examine how the value of the stock changes in the various states as we change the length of the time-step, Δt. The diffusive steps will scale as $\sqrt{\Delta t}$, while the magnitude of the jump will remain unchanged as the time-step is reduced. See Section 2.4.1 in Chapter 2.

after the time-step of the hedging option will simply be equal to its payoff:

$$\text{Payoff}(O_1) = \max[S_j - K_1, 0], \qquad j = \text{up, down, jump} \qquad (14.1)$$

We also know the values that the option, O_2, that we want to price will attain in all the possible future states of the world. This is because we assume that it also is an option expiring in one period's time. Therefore it is, say, a call with a different strike, K_2:

$$\text{Payoff}(O_2) = \max[S_j - K_2, 0], \qquad j = \text{up, down, jump} \qquad (14.2)$$

See Figure 14.2.

We want to construct a portfolio made up of the stock, the bond and the hedging option with weights α, β and γ, respectively, such that, in all states of the world, it will have the same value as the option to be hedged. As we discussed in Chapter 2, the problem of finding the 'fair' price of the option O_2 today is therefore solved by determining weights α, β and γ such that

$$\alpha S_{\text{up}} + \beta B_{\text{up}} + \gamma O_{1,\text{up}} = O_{2,\text{up}} \qquad (14.3)$$

$$\alpha S_{\text{down}} + \beta B_{\text{down}} + \gamma O_{1,\text{down}} = O_{2,\text{down}} \qquad (14.4)$$

$$\alpha S_{\text{jump}} + \beta B_{\text{jump}} + \gamma O_{1,\text{jump}} = O_{2,\text{jump}} \qquad (14.5)$$

This gives rise to a 3×3 system of linear equations. Subject to some obvious constraints on the known terms, this system admits a unique solution $\{\widehat{\alpha}, \widehat{\beta}, \widehat{\gamma}\}$. Absence of arbitrage

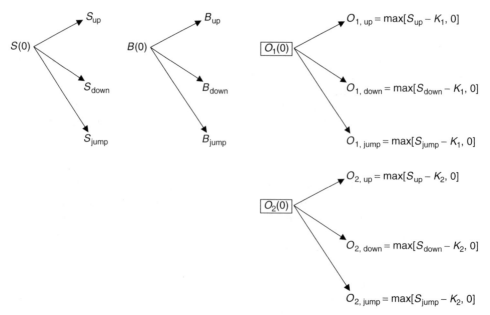

Figure 14.2 The values of the stock, the bond, the hedging option and the option to be hedged today and after one time-step.

then requires that the fair price today of the option O_2, i.e. the quantity that we were looking for, should be equal to

$$O_2(0) = \widehat{\alpha}S(0) + \widehat{\beta}B(0) + \widehat{\gamma}O_1(0) \tag{14.6}$$

As long as we deal with a one-period option to be hedged with one-period options of different strikes, it is easy to see how this reasoning can be extended to more complex cases where two, three, $\ldots$, n, possible jump amplitudes exist: we would simply have to add as many hedging options to our portfolio. For n possible jump amplitudes we would have to solve an $(n + 2) \times (n + 2)$ linear system to find the weights as above.

Why is this setting interesting? Because I show below that the price of most options priced assumed a finite number of jump amplitudes and quickly converges to the price that would obtain with a continuum of possible jump amplitudes, provided that the moments of the continuous and discrete jump distributions are matched. This would be very important. It would mean that, if 'only' n jump amplitudes were possible, and we could hedge with as many plain-vanilla options, we would always have to agree about the price of any other option, and our risk preferences would play no role in determining the price. To the extent that a relatively small number of 'well-chosen' jump amplitudes produce a stock price distribution very similar to the one produced by the continuous case, one would conclude that in pricing complex options risk preferences would likely play a very limited role even in the more general case (i.e. even in the case of random jump amplitudes).

This statement, formally correct, needs a strong qualification. The origin of the problem can be seen as follows. Let us extend our analysis to a two-period trading horizon. For graphical clarity Figure 14.3 shows only the upper branch of the two-period bushy tree, but similar branches can also be imagined emanating from the 'down' and 'jump' states.

Let us try to repeat the same reasoning presented above for this upper branch. Once again we will try to hedge a two-period option (O_2) with the stock, the bond and another option, O_1, that now however expires in two periods' time. The system of equations for this upper branch now reads:

$$\alpha S_{\text{up,up}} + \beta B_{\text{up,up}} + \gamma O_{1,\text{up,up}} = O_{2,\text{up,up}} \tag{14.7}$$

$$\alpha S_{\text{up,down}} + \beta B_{\text{up,down}} + \gamma O_{1,\text{up,down}} = O_{2,\text{up,down}} \tag{14.8}$$

$$\alpha S_{\text{up,jump}} + \beta B_{\text{up,jump}} + \gamma O_{1,\text{up,jump}} = O_{2,\text{up,jump}} \tag{14.9}$$

In order to avoid arbitrage, one must impose that the value of this replicating portfolio should equal the price of the option to price in the 'up' state at time 1.

There is a formal similarity with the one-step problem discussed above, but the value of the replicating portfolio now contains $O_{1,\text{up}}$. This is the price of the hedging option 1 in the future if state 'up' prevails. Unlike $O_1(0)$, the quantity $O_{1,\text{up}}$, which is the future conditional price of option 1 in the 'up' state, is not known from today's market prices. The same reasoning clearly applies to the other nodes (not shown in the figure): $O_{1,\text{down}}$ and $O_{1,\text{jump}}$ are also not known from today's market prices. Therefore, in order to price option O_2 by replication, one should know not just the price of the hedging option today, $O_1(0)$, but also its value *in all the future possible states of the world*.

Why are we troubled by this requirement? Have we not availed ourselves of similar information when we have assumed to know the possible values of the stock price in all

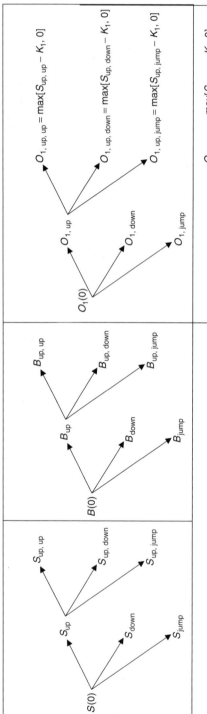
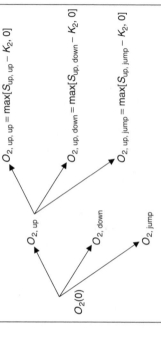

Figure 14.3 The values of the stock, the bond, the hedging option and the option to be hedged today and after one time-step for all the reachable states, and after two time-steps for the states emanating from the upper node at time 1.

the future states of the world? Not really: recall that we have not specified the probabilities of these states being reached, and therefore by assigning future possible stock values we are basically simply defining the space spanned by the price movements. Furthermore, in the simple setting presented in Chapter 2, specifying the state of the world is ultimately fully equivalent to assigning the realization of the stock price.[4] Now we are assigning to the same state the simultaneous prices of two assets (the underlying stock and the hedging option). Clearly, we will not be able to do so without creating possibilities of arbitrage unless we assume some quite detailed knowledge about the joint evolutions of the stock and of the hedging option. But this is just the information typically provided as the output of a calibrated model. (See, however, also the discussion in Chapter 17.) Therefore, the deceptively simple extension of the canonical binomial construction presented in Chapter 2 to the case of three possible branching states actually brings us into completely different, and far more complex, territory.

Exercise 1 *Following the reasoning just presented, build a suitable tree to explain why also in the case of a fully stochastic-volatility model knowledge of the process of the hedging option is required to price derivatives in a unique preference-free manner.*

Generalizing: not just knowledge of the prices of as many hedging options as possible jump amplitudes is required, but also *of their full process*. This, however, is a strongly model-dependent piece of information, and, unlike the situation encountered in the one-period setting, two traders might disagree about the future price of the hedging options, and, therefore, ultimately about the price of the option O_2 today. Unless the very strong assumption is made that we know the prices of the hedging options in all possible future states, even in the presence of a finite number of possible jump amplitudes the option market therefore remains incomplete, and perfect replication is not possible.

14.4 Analytic Description of Jump–Diffusions

14.4.1 The Stock Price Dynamics

Since jump processes are less widely used than Brownian diffusions in financial applications, I briefly describe them in this section. See also Merton (1990) for one of the earliest (and clearest) descriptions of jump processes in the context of option pricing. In this chapter I largely follow Merton's approach and notation. Many of the applications of mixed jump–diffusion processes are in the credit derivatives area. The literature is immense, but one interesting paper dealing with the necessary change in measure when jumps are possible is Schoenbucher (1996). In the interest-rate area, a detailed discussion of the change of measure can be found in Glasserman and Kou (2000) and Glasserman and Merener (2001).

We will assume that the stock behaviour is described in the real ('econometric') world by a mixed jump–diffusion process of the form[5]

$$\frac{dS(t)}{S(t)} = (\mu - \lambda k)\, dt + \sigma(t)\, dz(t) + dq \tag{14.10}$$

---

[4]In other words, the stock price process is an adapted process. See Chapter 5.

[5]For ease of reference, in this chapter I have tried to use, as much as possible, the same notation as in Merton (1990). Some of the symbols, however, have been changed in order to keep consistency with the notation employed elsewhere in this book.

In Equation (14.10) above, $S(t)$ denotes the stock price, μ its drift in the real world, $\sigma(t)$ its percentage volatility,[6] $dz(t)$ is the increment of a standard Brownian motion and dq is the increment of a Poisson process. As for the latter, λ is the mean number of events (jumps) per unit time in the real world. If $Y - 1$ is the percentage change in the stock price before and after the jump, one can define

$$k = E[Y - 1] \qquad (14.11)$$

to be the expected size of the percentage jump amplitude. Note that, by this definition, if we want the stock price to remain strictly positive at all times, so must the quantity Y: $Y = 1$ corresponds to no jump, $Y = 0$ represents a jump of negative amplitude equal to the stock price at the time of the jump, and any value of Y greater than 1 gives an 'upward' jump. These observations suggest some of the desirable distributional properties of the random quantity Y, discussed below. Finally, in the standard treatment the increments of the Brownian and Poisson processes are assumed to be independent.

The intuitive interpretation of Equation (14.10) is that the stock price follows a diffusive behaviour, characterized by a time-dependent percentage volatility, $\sigma(t)$, on top of which discontinuous jumps, of random magnitude and sign, are superimposed with a known deterministic frequency, λ. The stock price path is therefore continuous (but nowhere differentiable) between jumps, and discontinuous when a jump occurs. If a jump does not occur, the process for the stock price has the usual diffusive form

$$\frac{dS(t)}{S(t)} = (\mu - \lambda k)\, dt + \sigma(t)\, dz(t) \qquad (14.12)$$

If the jump takes place, the stock price instantaneously changes from S to SY, and the overall percentage change in the stock price (due both to the diffusive and to the jump components) is given by

$$\frac{dS(t)}{S(t)} = (\mu - \lambda k)\, dt + \sigma(t)\, dz(t) + (Y - 1) \qquad (14.13)$$

The Counting Process and the Compensator

Let $n(t)$ be the number of jumps from time 0 to time t. This quantity is called a 'counting process'.[7] The process $n(t)$, $\mathcal{R} \to \mathcal{I}$, takes on integer values, starts at zero, $n(0) = 0$, and increases by one every time there is a jump. If the jump process is Poisson in nature, one can directly obtain from the defining properties of Poisson processes (see, for example,

---

[6]The percentage volatility at time t is therefore the square root of the instantaneous variance contingent on no jump events occurring at time t.

[7]A note on terminology: the arrival time, τ, of a jump is a stopping time. A collection of stopping times is called a *point process*: $\{\tau_1, \tau_2, \ldots, \tau_k\}$. Despite the name, this is not a process that, loosely speaking, should be a random variable indexed by time. A point process can be turned into a 'real' process first by defining an *indicator process*, $N(t)$, for each stopping time:

$$N(t) = \mathbf{1}_{\{\tau \le t\}} \qquad (14.14)$$

Ross (1997)) that, if λ is the frequency (intensity) of the jumps, the probability of k jumps having occurred out to time t is given by

$$P[n(t) = \widehat{n}] = \exp[-\lambda t]\frac{(\lambda t)^{\widehat{n}}}{\widehat{n}!} \tag{14.16}$$

This expression will be made use of when calculating the pricing formula for calls in the jump–diffusion case.

In order to obtain the expected value of the increment, $dn(t)$, of the counting process, recall that, for a Poisson process, the occurrence of a jump is independent of the occurrence of previous jumps, and that the probability of two simultaneous jumps is zero. Let us then assume that, out to time τ, j jumps have occurred. Then, over the next small time interval, dt, one extra jump will occur with probability $\lambda\,dt$, and no jumps will occur with probability $1 - \lambda\,dt$. The change in the counting process will therefore be 1 with probability $\lambda\,dt$ and 0 with probability $1 - \lambda\,dt$. Therefore

$$\mathrm{E}[dn(t)] = 1 * \lambda\,dt + 0 * (1 - \lambda\,dt) = \lambda\,dt \tag{14.17}$$

If the jump frequency is constant, the expected number of jumps from time 0 to time t is therefore given by

$$\mathrm{E}[n(t)] = \lambda t \tag{14.18}$$

It is important to observe that, from Equations (14.12) and (14.18), it follows that the instantaneous expected return from the stock is μ: during 'normal' times (no jumps), the stock deterministically grows at a rate $\mu - \lambda k$; occasionally jumps occur, altering its expected growth rate by the expectation of the jump amplitude ratio, k, times the probability of occurrence of the jump, $\lambda\,dt$. For this reason one sometimes introduces a compensated counting process, $M(t)$, defined by

$$dM(t) = dn(t) - \lambda\,dt \tag{14.19}$$

Given the definitions above the expectation of $dM(t)$ is, by construction, zero:

$$\mathrm{E}[dM(t)] = \mathrm{E}[dn(t) - \lambda\,dt] = \mathrm{E}[dn(t)] - \lambda\,dt = \lambda\,dt - \lambda\,dt = 0 \tag{14.20}$$

It is easy to check that the process $M(t)$ satisfies the conditions for being a martingale. The process $M(t)$ is called the *compensated* counting process because it is constructed so as to ensure that on average it exactly 'compensates' for the increase in the number of jumps accumulated in $n(t)$. See Figure 14.4.

Then one can create the sum of the indicator processes associated with each stopping time in the set $\{\tau_1, \tau_2, \ldots, \tau_k\}$:

$$n(t) = \sum_{i=1,k} \mathbf{1}_{\{\tau_i \leq t\}} \tag{14.15}$$

This quantity is called the *counting process*. See Schoenbucher (2003) for a simple and clear introduction.

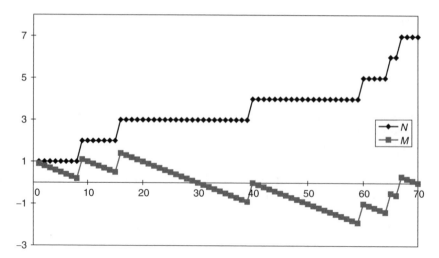

Figure 14.4   A realization of a counting process $n(t)$ and its associated compensated process $M(t)$. Note that the expectation of $M(t)$ is zero, whilst the expectation of $n(t)$ grows with time (at the rate λ).

Closed-Form Expression for the Realization of the Stock Price

If the volatility, σ, the jump frequency, λ, the expectation of the jump amplitude ratio, k, and the instantaneous drift, μ, are all constant, it is possible to write a closed-form expression for the realization of the stock price after a finite time t, given its value, $S(0)$, at time t_0 as

$$S(t) = S(0) \exp\left[(\mu - \tfrac{1}{2}\sigma^2 - \lambda k)t + \sigma Z(t)\right] Y(n) \tag{14.21}$$

In Equation (14.21) the first part of the RHS has the same expression as in the diffusive case, and therefore

$$Z(t) = \int_0^t \mathrm{d}z(s) \tag{14.22}$$

The interesting term is the multiplicative factor $Y(n)$. The argument n denotes different realizations of the counting process, i.e. the number of jumps that have occurred between time 0 and time t. $Y(n)$ is therefore given by

$$Y(0) = 1$$

$$Y(1) = Y_1$$

$$Y(2) = Y_1 Y_2$$

$$\cdots$$

$$Y(n) = \prod_{j=1,n} Y_j \tag{14.23}$$

In Equation (14.23), Y_k is the kth realization of the jump amplitude ratio, the various $Y(i)$ are independently and identically distributed, and the variable n has a Poisson distribution with intensity λ. It is important to point out that *when* the jumps occur between time 0 and time t is irrelevant for the time-t value of the stock price, and that only the total number of jumps matters. This is because we are dealing with a *geometric* diffusion, and the jumps have been chosen to be multiplicative rather than, say, additive.[8]

In some cases these assumptions can be relaxed without adding much complexity to the solution. For instance, the modification of this formula is straightforward if

- the instantaneous drift is not constant; in this case it would have to be replaced by the average growth rate, $\widehat{\mu} = \frac{1}{t} \int_0^t \mu(s)\, ds$;

- the average jump frequency is not constant; in this case it would have to be replaced by the average jump frequency, $\widehat{\lambda} = \frac{1}{t} \int_0^t \lambda(s)\, ds$;

- the volatility is not constant; in this case it would have to be replaced by its root mean squared value, $\widehat{\sigma}$, $\widehat{\sigma}^2 = \frac{1}{t} \int_0^t \sigma^2(s)\, ds$.

The only requirements so far for the random variables Y is that they should be non-negative and independently and identically distributed. If, in addition, these variables are required to have a log-normal distribution, then it is easy to show (see Merton (1990)) that the ratio of the stock price after time t, $S(t)$, to the stock price today, $S(0)$, is also log-normally distributed. This property will be used below to derive a pricing formula. In order to do so we first have to present an extension of Ito's lemma to deal with jumps. This is shown in the next section. Before doing so, however, let me point out that we still have not said anything about the drift of the stock, μ, and, in particular, we are not at this stage invoking a risk-neutral evolution for the stock price.

Extending Ito's Lemma

Let us assume that the price of a derivative on the stock, C, can be written as a twice-differentiable function of the stock price, S: $C = C(S, t)$. How can we write the stochastic differential equation (SDE) for C when the dynamics for the underlying are mixed jump–diffusive in nature? If the nature of the process is such that over any finite interval there is a finite number of jumps, the result is very simple (for a proof in a very general setting, i.e. when the process for S is a semi-martingale with a finite number of jumps, see Jacod and Shiryaev (1988)). The required SDE for C will contain a familiar diffusive Ito-like component, and a new contribution arising from the jump events. More precisely, given Equation (14.10), we can write

$$\frac{dC}{C} = (\mu_C - \lambda k_C)\, dt + \sigma_C\, dz(t) + dq_C \tag{14.24}$$

$$\mu_C = \frac{(\mu - \lambda k)S \dfrac{\partial C}{\partial S} + \dfrac{1}{2}\sigma^2 S^2 \dfrac{\partial^2 C}{\partial S^2} + \dfrac{\partial C}{\partial t} + \lambda E_t[C(SY, t) - C(S, t)]}{C(S, t)} \tag{14.25}$$

---

[8]With a geometric Brownian motion it is the logarithm of the random variable that follows a Brownian diffusion. If one had chosen the same process for the stock itself, rather than its logarithm, then the same property would apply for additive jumps.

$$\sigma_C = \frac{\frac{\partial C}{\partial S} S \sigma}{C(S, t)} \qquad (14.26)$$

$$k_C = E_t[Y_C - 1] \qquad (14.27)$$

where $[Y_C - 1]$ is the percentage change in the option price before and after the jump, and k_C is therefore the expectation of the percentage change in the option price. As for the Poisson increment for the option price, dq_C, it is perfectly functionally dependent on the Poisson process for the stock price, dq, i.e. the option price changes discontinuously if and only if the stock price does too. The important thing to note is that jumps simply provide an extra 'intuitive' additive term; in particular, there is no equivalent of the cross-variation terms brought about by the transition from standard to stochastic calculus.

In Equations (14.24) and (14.25) the diffusive terms are familiar. The 'new' terms can be understood as follows. Let us look at Equation (14.25) first. Recall that SY is the value of the stock price after a jump. The quantity $C(SY, t) - C(S, t)$ is therefore the difference in the price of the function (the call) before and after the jump. The term $\lambda E_t[C(SY, t) - C(S, t)]$ is then equal to the expectation at time t (i.e. immediately before the possible jump) of the change in value of the call because of the jump itself, times the jump probability per unit time, λ. It is therefore plausible to expect (see Merton (1990) for a proof) that the deterministic term (in dt) in Equation (14.25) should contain, in addition to the deterministic contribution to the expectation (the usual term $(\mu - \lambda k) S \frac{\partial C}{\partial S} + \frac{1}{2}\sigma^2 S^2 \frac{\partial^2 C}{\partial S^2} + \frac{\partial C}{\partial t}$), a contribution given by $\lambda E_t[C(SY, t) - C(S, t)]$. As for the term $\lambda k S$, it is the expected change in the stock price across jumps. If we multiply this quantity by how much the call price changes as the stock price changes, $\frac{\partial C}{\partial S}$, we can see that the term $-\lambda k S \frac{\partial C}{\partial S}$ 'compensates' for the average trend imparted to the option price by the presence of jumps.

It is important to point out that the combined term $\lambda E_t[C(SY, t) - C(S, t)] - \lambda k S \frac{\partial C}{\partial S}$ gives a non-zero contribution because of the non-linearity (in S) of the call function C. Let us suppose for a moment that, modulo a proportionality constant, $C(S) = S$. If that were the case we would have

$$E_t[C(SY, t) - C(S, t)] = E_t[S_t Y - S_t] = S_t E_t[Y - 1] = S_t k \qquad (14.28)$$

$$\frac{\partial C}{\partial S} = 1 \qquad (14.29)$$

and therefore

$$\lambda E_t[C(SY, t) - C(S, t)] - \lambda k S \frac{\partial C}{\partial S} = 0 \qquad (14.30)$$

This observation should be kept in mind when studying the case of products with linear payoffs (treated in Section 14.5.1).

The PDE: Formal Solution

Let us assume for the moment that one knew the percentage return to be expected both from the stock and from the option, μ and μ_C, to be, say, $\widehat{\mu}$ and $\widehat{\mu}_C$, respectively.

These requirements are extremely strong, and are not necessary in the standard (i.e. purely diffusive) Black-and-Scholes setting. Under some conditions we will be able to avoid assuming that we know what these quantities are. For the moment, however, let us keep the treatment as general as possible. Under these assumptions, one can rewrite Equation (14.25) as[9]

$$(\widehat{\mu} - \lambda k)S\frac{\partial C}{\partial S} + \frac{1}{2}\sigma^2 S^2\frac{\partial^2 C}{\partial S^2} + \frac{\partial C}{\partial t} + \lambda E_t[C(SY) - C(S)] - \widehat{\mu}_C C = 0 \qquad (14.31)$$

Coupled with the appropriate boundary and initial conditions for the derivatives contract, e.g. in the case of a call,

$$C(S, T) = \max[S - K, 0] \qquad (14.32)$$

Equation (14.31) provides a formal solution to the call pricing problem. The adjective 'formal' highlights not so much the technical difficulties in solving what has now become a differential-difference equation, but the fact that its solution requires exogenous knowledge of the drift of the stock and of the call.

Can one get around this problem? Is it possible to invoke similar arguments to those invoked in the diffusive case, and express the call pricing formula as a function of the riskless rate? Recall that, when the stock follows a pure diffusion, the 'disappearance' of the real-world drift stems from the ability to construct a perfectly hedging (replicating) portfolio. In order to explore whether a similar solution can be arrived at in the jump–diffusion case it is therefore necessary to look in detail at hedging in the presence of discontinuous jumps.

14.5 Hedging with Jump–Diffusion Processes

14.5.1 Hedging with a Bond and the Underlying Only

The expressions just derived give us an idea of how, and to what extent, a hedging strategy can be attempted. Following the same reasoning employed in Chapter 13, let us in fact create a portfolio, Π, made up of α units of stock, β units of bond and one call:

$$\Pi_t = \alpha S_t + \beta B_t + C_t \qquad (14.33)$$

The evolution of Π will be given by

$$\begin{aligned}
d\Pi_t &= \alpha \, dS_t + \beta B_t r_t \, dt + dC_t \\
&= \alpha\{(\mu - \lambda k)S \, dt + \sigma S \, dz(t) + S \, dq\} + \beta B_t r_t \, dt \\
&\quad + (\mu_C - \lambda k_C) \, dt + \frac{\partial C}{\partial S} S\sigma \, dz_t + C \, dq_C \qquad (14.34)
\end{aligned}$$

---

[9]This formula differs from the equivalent expression in Merton (1990) because I work in calendar time, while Merton switches to time to maturity.

where use has been made of Equations (14.25) and (14.26). Regrouping terms gives

$$d\Pi_t = \{\alpha(\mu - \lambda k)S_t + \beta B_t r_t + (\mu_C - \lambda k_C)C_t\}\, dt$$
$$+ S\left[\alpha\sigma + \frac{\partial C}{\partial S}\sigma\right] dz_t$$
$$+ \alpha S\, dq + C\, dq_C \tag{14.35}$$

Note that

$$S dq = S(Y - 1) \tag{14.36}$$
$$C\, dq_C = C(Y_C - 1) \tag{14.37}$$

Recall also that CY_C is the value of the call immediately after a jump in the stock price has taken place:

$$CY_C = C(YS) \tag{14.38}$$

and

$$dq_C = CY_C - C = C(YS) - C(S) \tag{14.39}$$

Therefore Equation (14.35) can be rewritten as

$$d\Pi_t = \{\alpha(\mu - \lambda k)S_t + \beta B_t r_t + (\mu_C - \lambda k_C)C_t\}\, dt$$
$$+ S\left[\alpha + \frac{\partial C}{\partial S}\right]\sigma\, dz_t$$
$$+ \alpha(SY - S) + C(SY) - C(S) \tag{14.40}$$

There are two sources of uncertainty in Equation (14.40), one associated with the term in dz_t and one with the realization of the jump amplitude ratio, Y. It is therefore clear that by hedging just with a bond and the stock it will not be possible to protect the portfolio simultaneously against the uncertainty stemming from the Brownian diffusion *and* against the discontinuous innovations: we only have one quantity to play with (the amount of stock, α) and two independent stochastic terms to neutralize (the diffusive term in dz_t and the jump term). With the treatment followed in the stochastic-volatility case in mind, however, we might hope that adding to the hedging portfolio a (different) plain-vanilla option might allow completion of the market, perfect replication of the terminal payoff and, as a consequence, risk-neutral valuation. Matters, unfortunately, are not that simple. In addition to the caveats pointed out in the case of stochastic-volatility processes,[10] hedging is in fact intrinsically more complex in the presence of jump processes. This is because even if we introduce another option into the set of hedging instruments perfect replication will be possible only in a very special case. This situation is examined below.

---

[10]I.e. that the full process, not just the price today, of the hedging option must be exogenously known.

Hedging with a Bond and the Underlying Only: the Case of Linear Products

Before dealing with the case of hedging the derivative C with the stock, a bond and another option, it is worthwhile pausing and considering the special case when the derivative instrument C, instead of being an option, is a product whose value displays a linear dependence on the underlying, S. Essentially one is therefore dealing with the case of a forward contract. In order to avoid confusion with the rest of the treatment, in this section the value of the contingent claim when the latter is a forward contract will be denoted by F. The last line in Equation (14.40) therefore reads

$$\alpha(SY - S) + F(SY) - F(S) = \alpha S(Y - 1) + F(S)(Y - 1) \tag{14.41}$$

where the right-hand side follows because of the assumed linearity of the product. In this special case it is therefore sufficient to choose α equal to

$$\alpha = -\frac{F(S)}{S} \tag{14.42}$$

for the uncertainty stemming from the jump component to be neutralized for any possible value of the jump amplitude, Y. Looking at the second line of (14.40), it is then an easy step to show that this hedge ratio automatically takes care of the diffusive component as well. For this particular type of instrument a risk-neutral valuation is still applicable, and, therefore, the equilibrium strike of a forward contract is simply given by the forward price of the stock.

  A posteriori, i.e. after we have obtained the result, this is not surprising, because, after all, the cash-and-carry arbitrage that underpins the no-arbitrage derivation of the equilibrium forward price relies on a *static* (buy-and-hold) replicating strategy that will therefore be valid whatever the true process for the underlying might be.

14.5.2 Hedging with a Bond, a Second Option and the Underlying

Let us return to the hedging problem in the case of a more general contingent claim, C. The approach is by now familiar: we build a portfolio made up of one call to be replicated, α units of stock, β units of bond and γ units of a second ('hedging') option, h. Our goal is to make the evolution of the portfolio purely deterministic. If we succeed, we can choose the amount of the discount bond such that the portfolio value today should be exactly zero. Under penalty of arbitrage a zero-value deterministic portfolio will have to show zero growth. If we managed to make the portfolio deterministic, this last condition would then provide a partial differential equation obeyed by the option price that, unlike Equation (14.31), will not contain real-world risk preferences (embedded in the drift terms μ_C and μ). Let us see if, and to what extent, we can carry out this programme.

  Taking the approach followed in Chapter 13 as a guide we begin by forming a portfolio Π as follows:

$$\Pi_t = \alpha S_t + \beta B_t + \gamma h_t + C_t \tag{14.43}$$

Its evolution will be given by

$$d\Pi_t = \alpha\{(\mu - \lambda k)S_t\,dt + \sigma(t)S_t\,dz(t) + S_t\,dq\}$$

$$+ \beta B_t r_t\,dt$$

$$+ \gamma\left[(\mu_h - \lambda k_h)h_t\,dt + \sigma_h(t)h_t\,dz(t) + h_t\,dq_h\right]$$

$$+ (\mu_C - \lambda k_C)C_t\,dt + \sigma_C(t)C_t\,dz(t) + C_t\,dq_C \qquad (14.44)$$

where the terms k_h and dq_h have their usual meanings. Note that the symbols k, k_C, k_h, dq, dq_C and dq_h refer to asset-specific quantities, but the jump frequency is the same for all the instruments: because of the perfect functional dependence of the jumps, when a jump occurs, it affects all the prices in the economy, albeit to different extents.

Re-grouping terms now gives

$$d\Pi_t = \{\alpha(\mu - \lambda k)S_t + \beta B_t r_t + \gamma(\mu_h - \lambda k_h)h_t + (\mu_C - \lambda k_C)C_t\}\,dt$$

$$+ S\sigma\left[\alpha + \gamma\frac{\partial h}{\partial S} + \frac{\partial C}{\partial S}\right]dz_t$$

$$+ \alpha S\,dq + \gamma h\,dq_h + C\,dq_C \qquad (14.45)$$

In order for the term associated with the Brownian diffusion to be identically zero the amount of stock, α, must be equal to

$$\alpha = -\frac{\partial C}{\partial S} - \gamma\frac{\partial h}{\partial S} \qquad (14.46)$$

Substituting this expression into the last line of Equation (14.45) (i.e. into the line that contains the perfectly functionally correlated jumps dq, dq_C and dq_h) one obtains

$$\alpha S\,dq + C\,dq_C + \gamma h\,dq_h = C\,dq_C + \gamma h\,dq_h - \frac{\partial C}{\partial S}S\,dq - \gamma\frac{\partial h}{\partial S}S\,dq \qquad (14.47)$$

Recall, however, that

$$C\,dq_C = C(Y_C - 1) = C(YS) - C(S) \qquad (14.48)$$

and similarly for $S\,dq$ and $h\,dq_h$. Therefore one can write Equation (14.47) as

$$C(Y_C - 1) + \gamma h(Y_h - 1) - S(Y - 1)\left[\frac{\partial C}{\partial S} + \gamma\frac{\partial h}{\partial S}\right]$$

$$= C(YS) - C(S) + \gamma\left[h(YS) - h(S) - (SY - S)\frac{\partial h}{\partial S}\right] - (SY - S)\frac{\partial C}{\partial S} \qquad (14.49)$$

By analogy with the stochastic-diffusion treatment (see Section 13.2.1 in particular), one would now be tempted to try to choose the amount γ in such a way that the last line should be identically equal to zero:

$$\gamma = -\frac{(SY - S)\dfrac{\partial C}{\partial S} - [C(YS) - C(S)]}{(SY - S)\dfrac{\partial h}{\partial S} - [h(YS) - h(S)]} \tag{14.50}$$

Before attempting to do so, it is useful for future developments to discuss the term γ in more detail.

Interpretation of the γ Term

The term γ lends itself to simple but useful manipulation. Equation (14.50) can in fact be rewritten as

$$\gamma = -\frac{(SY - S)\dfrac{\partial C}{\partial S} - [C(YS) - C(S)]}{(SY - S)\dfrac{\partial h}{\partial S} - [h(YS) - h(S)]} = -\frac{\dfrac{\partial C}{\partial S} - \dfrac{C(YS) - C(S)}{SY - S}}{\dfrac{\partial h}{\partial S} - \dfrac{h(YS) - h(S)}{SY - S}} \tag{14.51}$$

and it can be given the following interpretation: the numerator $\frac{\partial C}{\partial S} - \frac{C(YS)-C(S)}{SY-S}$ is the difference between

- the ratio of the change in the price of the call C to the change in the underlying due to the diffusive component, $\frac{\partial C}{\partial S}$, i.e. the 'usual' Black delta term, minus
- the ratio of the change in the price of the call C to the change in the underlying due to the jump component, $\frac{C(YS)-C(S)}{SY-S}$.

A similar interpretation holds for the term $\frac{\partial h}{\partial S} - \frac{h(YS)-h(S)}{SY-S}$ in the denominator. The notation can be simplified by denoting these quantities by the symbols

$$\widehat{\Delta}_C \equiv \frac{\partial C}{\partial S} - \frac{C(YS) - C(S)}{SY - S} \tag{14.52}$$

$$\widehat{\Delta}_h \equiv \frac{\partial h}{\partial S} - \frac{h(YS) - h(S)}{SY - S} \tag{14.53}$$

Then one can write

$$\gamma = -\frac{\dfrac{\partial C}{\partial S} - \dfrac{C(YS) - C(S)}{SY - S}}{\dfrac{\partial h}{\partial S} - \dfrac{h(YS) - h(S)}{SY - S}} = -\frac{\widehat{\Delta}_C}{\widehat{\Delta}_h} \tag{14.54}$$

It is interesting to compare this quantity with the similar quantity obtained in the Chapter 13. See, in particular, subsection 'The Portfolio-Replication Argument: Stochastic Volatility Hedged with the Stock and an Option' in Section 13.2.1.

Impossibility of Perfect Hedging with a Random Jump Amplitude

Let us return to the hedging argument. In the expression above the 'hedging amount' of option, O_1, depends on Y. The quantity Y, however, is a random variable. Contingent on a particular value of this quantity being realized (i.e. if we knew its magnitude and sign before the jump), it would be possible to choose a value for γ such that the change in the value of the option h due to the jump could perfectly compensate for the jump component in the option C. It is clear from the same expression, however, that no single value of γ can ensure that, *for any possible realization of the random variable Y*, the amount γ of option h would be just right to ensure that the change in the value of the rest of the portfolio due to the jump would be exactly compensated by the change in h, also due to the jump. Perfect replication is therefore impossible.

This same observation, however, provides an indication of what is required for the replication. This is explored in the next section.

14.5.3   The Case of a Single Possible Jump Amplitude

Replication

One situation when replication could be attempted would be if Y, instead of being a random variable with infinitely many possible realizations, could only assume a single value, say Y_0. If this were the case Equation (14.50) would become

$$\gamma_0 = -\frac{\dfrac{\partial C}{\partial S} - \dfrac{C(Y_0 S) - C(S)}{S Y_0 - S}}{\dfrac{\partial h}{\partial S} - \dfrac{h(Y_0 S) - h(S)}{S Y_0 - S}} \equiv -\frac{\widehat{\Delta}_0 C}{\widehat{\Delta}_0 h} \tag{14.55}$$

The crucial difference with Equation (14.54) is that the jump amplitude is now known (Y_0), and therefore it *is* possible to choose a value γ_0 that will neutralize the effect of the jump. Substitution into Equation (14.45) of the expressions obtained for α and γ_0 therefore gives

$$d\Pi_t = \left\{ \left[-\frac{\partial C}{\partial S} + \frac{\widehat{\Delta}_0 C}{\widehat{\Delta}_0 h} \frac{\partial h}{\partial S} \right] (\mu - \lambda k) S_t \right.$$
$$+ \beta B_t r_t +$$
$$- \frac{\widehat{\Delta}_0 C}{\widehat{\Delta}_0 h} (\mu_h - \lambda k_h) h$$
$$\left. + (\mu_C - \lambda k_C) C \right\} dt \tag{14.56}$$

Note that the stochastic terms no longer appear in the evolution of the portfolio, which is therefore purely deterministic.

Exercise 2 *Check that the terms in dz and in dq in Equation (14.56) do indeed disappear, making the portfolio purely deterministic.*

Let us now choose the value for β that would give zero initial value to the portfolio:

$$\beta = \frac{-\alpha S - \gamma_0 h - C}{B}$$

$$= \frac{\left(\dfrac{\partial C}{\partial S} - \dfrac{\widehat{\Delta}_0 C}{\widehat{\Delta}_0 h}\dfrac{\partial h}{\partial S}\right) S + \dfrac{\widehat{\Delta}_0 C}{\widehat{\Delta}_0 h} h - C}{B} \tag{14.57}$$

The last step is now to impose that the portfolio, being purely deterministic and having zero value today, should have a growth rate of zero:

$$d\Pi = 0$$

$$= \left[-\frac{\partial C}{\partial S} + \frac{\widehat{\Delta}_0 C}{\widehat{\Delta}_0 h}\frac{\partial h}{\partial S} \right] dS$$

$$+ \frac{\left(\dfrac{\partial C}{\partial S} - \dfrac{\widehat{\Delta}_0 C}{\widehat{\Delta}_0 h}\dfrac{\partial h}{\partial S}\right) S + \dfrac{\widehat{\Delta}_0 C}{\widehat{\Delta}_0 h} h - C}{B} \, dB +$$

$$- \frac{\widehat{\Delta}_0 C}{\widehat{\Delta}_0 h} \, dh$$

$$+ \, dC \tag{14.58}$$

which can be rewritten as

$$\left[-\frac{\partial C}{\partial S} + \frac{\widehat{\Delta}_0 C}{\widehat{\Delta}_0 h}\frac{\partial h}{\partial S} \right](\mu - \lambda k)S$$

$$+ \left[\left(\frac{\partial C}{\partial S} - \frac{\widehat{\Delta}_0 C}{\widehat{\Delta}_0 h}\frac{\partial h}{\partial S} \right) S + \frac{\widehat{\Delta}_0 C}{\widehat{\Delta}_0 h} h - C \right] r +$$

$$- \frac{\widehat{\Delta}_0 C}{\widehat{\Delta}_0 h} [(\mu_h - \lambda k_h)h]$$

$$+ (\mu_C - \lambda k_C)C = 0 \tag{14.59}$$

Rearranging the terms that contain the short rate r gives

$$\left[-\frac{\partial C}{\partial S} + \frac{\widehat{\Delta}_0 C}{\widehat{\Delta}_0 h}\frac{\partial h}{\partial S} \right](\mu - r - \lambda k)S$$

$$+ \left[-\frac{\widehat{\Delta}_0 C}{\widehat{\Delta}_0 h} h(\mu_h - r - \lambda k_h) \right]$$

$$+ (\mu_C - r - \lambda k_C)C = 0 \tag{14.60}$$

Equation (14.60) appears to contain both the drift of the stock, μ, and the drift of the two options, μ_h and μ_C. That this is fortunately not the case can be seen by using the definitions of k_h and k_C, and substituting in Equation (14.60) the expressions derived above (using the extended version of Ito's lemma in Equation (14.25)) for μ_h and μ_C. Let us start from the expression for the latter in the particular case when there is only one possible jump amplitude ratio:

$$C\mu_C = (\mu - \lambda k)S\frac{\partial C}{\partial S} + \frac{1}{2}\sigma^2 S^2 \frac{\partial^2 C}{\partial S^2} + \frac{\partial C}{\partial t} + \lambda E_t[C(SY_0) - C(S)] \qquad (14.61)$$

Given the special nature of the jump process, this general expression can be greatly simplified. To begin with the last term, since there is only one possible jump amplitude ratio the expectation is now trivial, and the term is now simply equal to

$$\lambda E_t[C(SY_0) - C(S)] = \lambda[C(SY_0) - C(S)] \qquad (14.62)$$

As for the term k_C, it is given by

$$k_C = E_t[Y_C - 1] \qquad (14.63)$$

where Y_C is the percentage change in the value of option C when the stock jumps. Therefore

$$C(S)k_C = E_t[C(SY_0) - C(S)] = [C(SY_0) - C(S)] \qquad (14.64)$$

So the drift term becomes

$$C\mu_C = (\mu - \lambda k)S\frac{\partial C}{\partial S} + \frac{1}{2}\sigma^2 S^2 \frac{\partial^2 C}{\partial S^2} + \frac{\partial C}{\partial t} + C\lambda k_C \qquad (14.65)$$

and therefore the quantity $C(\mu_C - \lambda k_C)$ in Equations (14.24) and (14.60) can be written as

$$C(\mu_C - \lambda k_C) = (\mu - \lambda k)S\frac{\partial C}{\partial S} + \frac{1}{2}\sigma^2 S^2 \frac{\partial^2 C}{\partial S^2} + \frac{\partial C}{\partial t} \qquad (14.66)$$

The same obviously applies to the option h:

$$h(\mu_h - \lambda k_h) = (\mu - \lambda k)S\frac{\partial h}{\partial S} + \frac{1}{2}\sigma^2 S^2 \frac{\partial^2 h}{\partial S^2} + \frac{\partial h}{\partial t} \qquad (14.67)$$

Note that in the Equations (14.66) and (14.67) neither the drifts of the two options, nor the expectation of their percentage change after the jump, appear on the RHS. Substitution of these equations into Equation (14.60) and regrouping terms therefore gives

$$rS\frac{\partial C}{\partial S} + \frac{1}{2}\sigma^2 S^2 \frac{\partial^2 C}{\partial S^2} + \frac{\partial C}{\partial t} - Cr$$
$$= \frac{\widehat{\Delta}_{0C}}{\widehat{\Delta}_{0h}}\left(rS\frac{\partial h}{\partial S} + \frac{1}{2}\sigma^2 S^2 \frac{\partial^2 h}{\partial S^2} + \frac{\partial h}{\partial t} - hr\right) \qquad (14.68)$$

There are several important features to point out in this equation. First of all, *all* the real-world drifts (i.e. not just the drifts of the options) have now disappeared. Second, in analogy with the stochastic-volatility case, the price processes of the stock and of both the options (C and h) appear in the PDE. Therefore, in order to be able to find, say, the value of C, one must know the value of h not just today, but in all possible future states of the world. We had already reached this conclusion in the stochastic-volatility case and using the qualitative argument presented in Section 14.3.1 of this chapter, but we can now see more quantitatively how the result comes about. The similarity with the stochastic-volatility case however runs deeper, and is explored below.

The Separation of the PDE

Further insight can be gained by manipulating the PDE just obtained for the single-jump-amplitude case. The treatment mirrors what we did in the stochastic-volatility case. If the PDE (14.68) could be written as a LHS that is purely a function of S and C (and time), and a RHS that is only a function of h, S (and time) then both sides would have to be equal to a function of, at most, S and t. To this effect, in order to simplify notation define first

$$BS(C) = rS\frac{\partial C}{\partial S} + \frac{1}{2}\sigma^2 S^2\frac{\partial^2 C}{\partial S^2} + \frac{\partial C}{\partial t} - rC \tag{14.69}$$

with a similar expression holding for $BS(h)$:

$$BS(h) = rS\frac{\partial h}{\partial S} + \frac{1}{2}\sigma^2 S^2\frac{\partial^2 h}{\partial S^2} + \frac{\partial h}{\partial t} - rh \tag{14.70}$$

Then rearrangement of the terms in Equation (14.68) gives

$$\frac{BS(C)}{\widehat{\Delta_0}C} = \frac{BS(h)}{\widehat{\Delta_0}h} \tag{14.71}$$

For this to be true for any possible pair of options C and h, neither side can depend on any specific feature of the two options, and has to be equal to the same function, g', of, at most, S and t. It is important to point out, however, that, just as in the stochastic-volatility case, nothing requires this function to be deterministic. One can therefore write

$$\frac{BS(C)}{\widehat{\Delta_0}C} = \frac{BS(C)}{\dfrac{\partial C}{\partial S} - \dfrac{C(Y_0 S) - C(S)}{SY_0 - S}} = g'(S, t) \tag{14.72}$$

Expanding expression (14.72) gives

$$rS\frac{\partial C}{\partial S} + \frac{1}{2}\sigma^2 S^2\frac{\partial^2 C}{\partial S^2} + \frac{\partial C}{\partial t} - rC = g'(S, t)\left[\frac{\partial C}{\partial S} - \frac{C(Y_0 S) - C(S)}{SY_0 - S}\right] \tag{14.73}$$

In passing, we can pause for a moment and compare this equation with the corresponding relationship (13.29) obtained in the stochastic-volatility case and reported below after minor rearrangements for ease of reference:

$$rS\frac{\partial C}{\partial S} + \frac{1}{2}\sigma^2 S^2\frac{\partial^2 C}{\partial S^2} + \frac{\partial C}{\partial t} - rC = g'(S,t)\left[\frac{\partial C}{\partial S}\right] \tag{14.74}$$

The similarities are striking: the only difference is the presence of the extra term, $\frac{C(Y_0 S)-C(S)}{SY_0 - S}$, due to the presence of the jump.

Going back to Equation (14.73), it can be rewritten as

$$\frac{\partial C}{\partial S}S[r - gk] + \frac{1}{2}\sigma^2 S^2\frac{\partial^2 C}{\partial S^2} + \frac{\partial C}{\partial t} + g[C(Y_0 S) - C(S)] = rC \tag{14.75}$$

with

$$g \equiv \frac{g'}{Sk} \tag{14.76}$$

Equations (14.75) and (14.76) are very important. To begin with, compare the PDE just obtained with Equation (14.31). The first observation is that neither the drift of the stock nor the drift of the option enter the governing PDE. Furthermore, comparing term by term Equation (14.75) with Equation (14.25) one can interpret it as the equation governing the price of an option C if

- in the real world the instantaneous growth rate changed from μ to r for all assets;
- the same expectation for the percentage jump amplitude, k, prevailed as in the real world; and
- the real-world jump frequency changed from λ to g.

Therefore, if only a single jump amplitude is possible, for the purpose of valuing derivative contracts we can assume that all options (and the underlying stock price) grow at the same riskless rate, r, and display a jump frequency g.

Let us pause briefly to examine these results. We have obtained that, if a single jump amplitude is possible and we know the full process for the hedging option, perfect hedging is now possible. In this very special setting (i.e. a single jump amplitude and knowledge of the full process of the hedging option), the value of the portfolio has therefore been protected not only against the Brownian source of uncertainty, but also against the possibility of jumps. Even if we were extremely averse to *undiversified* jump risk, we could not expect to be compensated for this source of uncertainty because, in our setting, we have perfectly hedged it away. If this setting were correct, the prices of options could not incorporate any information about risk aversion. If this were the case, Smile Tale 2, which identified the steepness of the smile at short maturities with aversion to jump risk, would not be correct.

Note also that, *for a single jump amplitude*, knowledge of the real-world value of the jump amplitude ratio k *is* relevant for pricing purposes. Recall, in fact, that k is linked to the expectation of the magnitude of the jump amplitude. In the case of a single possible jump amplitude, $kS = SY_0 - S$. In moving between measures, we can change the probability of various *possible* events, but, by the principle of absolute continuity (see Section 6.7.3 in Chapter 6), we cannot change the *nature* of a process, i.e. we cannot make impossible events possible, and vice versa. Therefore, if in the real world the only possible jump amplitude is Y_0, then it will have to be so in the risk-neutral world too. In all measures, the distribution of jump amplitudes is just a Dirac-δ distribution centred at Y_0. Note that, if we had as few as two possible jump amplitudes, their locations would still be unchanged in moving across measures, but their expectation, and therefore k, *would* in general change as a function of risk aversion.

14.5.4 Moving to a Continuum of Jump Amplitudes

I will not attempt to repeat the (imperfect) replication argument for the case of a *continuum* of possible jump amplitude ratios. If we allowed for more and more (but still finitely many) jump amplitude ratios, we could extend the argument above by adding more and more hedging options (as long as we are, more and more heroically, happy to assume knowledge of their full process).

With some degree of hand-waving, we should not be surprised by the statement that, as all these jump amplitude ratios merge into a continuous distribution, both the expectation of the jump amplitude ratios and the jump frequency are affected by the change in measure. Risk-averse investors, who cannot perfectly hedge, will 'see' jumps to be more downwards than in reality, and to occur more frequently. The situation becomes somewhat reminiscent of what happens to reversion levels and reversion speeds when an Ornstein–Uhlenbeck (mean-reverting) process is transformed from the real-world measure to the pricing measure. Think, for instance, of the CIR term-structure model, or of mean-reverting stochastic-volatility processes. In both these cases, knowledge of the real-world reversion level and/or reversion speed is, by itself, of no assistance in calibrating the model.

A corollary of the result about the number of options required to hedge in the case of n possible jump amplitudes is that we need an (uncountable) number of options to hedge in the case of a continuous distribution of jump amplitudes. If looked at in this light, hedging the uncertainty associated with the 'full' jump–diffusion process would seem a hopeless task. Some comfort can however be drawn from the fact that the overall dynamics and the prices obtained with a relatively small number of (well-chosen) jump amplitudes is not too different from what was obtained when an infinitely many possible jump amplitudes is possible. One might therefore hope that hedging with a correspondingly small number of plain-vanilla options might provide a useful strategy even if the true process was a 'full' jump–diffusion.

The requirement that we should know the full process for the 'small number' of hedging options still appears formidable. We can, however, take a more pragmatic approach and explore the extent to which approximate hedging with a small number of options can be effective in reducing the uncertainty in the payoffs of a complex product *even if the true parameters of the process are not known* (as long as the jump–diffusion nature of the process has been correctly guessed). This angle is explored later on in Sections 14.7 and 14.11.

14.5.5 Determining the Function g Using the Implied Approach

In principle, the calibration of a jump–diffusion pricing model could be carried out by estimating the real-world frequency and the real-world distribution of jumps and by accounting explicitly for the aversion to jump risk on the basis, say, of an assumed utility function. If we tried to follow this route we would be attempting two very difficult tasks (the statistical estimation of the parameters of a rare event, and the distillation of the pattern of risk aversion) when the two components are in reality not needed separately. See the discussion about the 'naïve replication' approach in Section 2.3.2 of Chapter 2. Furthermore, investors could only be expected to be averse to risk that they cannot diversify (hedge) away. So, what matters for pricing is not the *total* variability of the option returns, but the *residual* variability once a chosen imperfect hedge has been put in place. Unlike the Black-and-Scholes case, however, there is now no unique best hedging strategy. Therefore, if we wanted to follow the 'fundamental' approach, we would not only have to estimate the real-world parameters of the process and the aversion to jump risk of the 'representative' investor,[11] but also determine an a priori unknown hedging strategy to whose 'slippages' the risk aversion could then be applied.

Not surprisingly, for derivatives-pricing purposes the 'implied' route is almost univer-sally followed in practice: the *risk-adjusted* parameters of the model are varied so as to recover as best as possible[12] the observed market prices. If we take this view, we will not expect that all the option prices visible in the market will be exactly recovered by the implied procedure. Instead, we will attempt to assess whether it is at all possible to determine a 'plausible' function g, such that the observed market prices are satisfactorily accounted for.

What do we mean by 'plausible'? The function g can, in principle, be quite flexible (and, as mentioned above, could even be stochastic). Just by making this function purely time-dependent the quality of the fit can often be substantially improved. It is essential to keep in mind, however, that every choice we make about the functional dependence of g on its state variables has direct consequences for the evolution of the smile surface. A time-decaying implied jump frequency, for instance, would imply that future smiles will not be as steep as they are today. This poses no mathematical problems, but does raise an important financial question as to the desirability of the model. Suppose, in fact, that we have managed to obtain an acceptable fit with a constant risk-adjusted frequency. This would ensure, among other features, time homogeneity (as a function of residual maturity) of the smile surface. This means, that, when we evolve the stock price according to our model, perhaps using a Monte Carlo simulation, it will implicitly create future states of the world (smile surfaces and option prices) similar to what we observe today. The future hedging costs it will imply will therefore be similar to the hedging costs incurred in buying same-maturity options today. We are perfectly entitled to believe that this should not be the case, and that the future will look materially different from the present. This view, however, should be dictated by our financial or economic analysis, and should not be passively and implicitly accepted simply because it produces a better fit to the current market prices. See, in this respect, the discussion in Chapter 1 about market efficiency and the informational content of option prices.

As I have said, if we place ourselves in a setting where perfect replication is not possible, the risk-adjusted jump frequency need no longer be the same as the real-world

---

[11]Even speaking of a 'representative' investor is not as straightforward as it seems – I do not enter the topic here, and use the term in a rather hand-waving manner.

[12]Recovery 'as best as possible' of the market prices does not mean that the parameters should be varied in a totally unconstrained way. Certain solutions, i.e. certain sets of coefficients, might give a (slightly) better fit, but might suggest a financially implausible dynamics. See the discussion in Section 13.7.

one. Unfortunately, by itself this observation says nothing about whether this risk-adjusted frequency should be higher or lower than the real-world (econometric) one. If we believe in a particular financial 'story' as to the origin of the smile, however, the sign of the difference between the real-world and the risk-adjusted frequency becomes well defined. If Smile Tale 2 that opened this chapter was correct, for instance, the market dynamics between arbitrageurs and fund managers should produce a risk-adjusted jump frequency *higher than* (and not simply different from) the econometric one. Similarly, in the presence of a continuum of possible jump amplitudes the expectation of the percentage jump amplitude, k, would change in moving between measures. For Smile Tale 2 to be correct, however, one would expect to find the risk-adjusted expected jump to be not just different, but more 'to the left' than the real-world one. In other words, risk-averse traders 'see' more severe and/or more frequent jumps.

Can we say something more precise? Can we establish more binding constraints about the risk-adjusted jump frequencies and the risk-adjusted distribution of jump amplitude ratios? This topic is explored in the following section.

The Link Between the Real-World and the Risk-Adjusted Jump Frequency

Despite the fact that our analysis started from the real world, we ultimately presented a procedure, based on the 'implication' of the risk-adjusted jump frequency from observed option prices, that completely circumvented the need to estimate the econometric jump intensity. If one had confidence that the chosen jump–diffusion approach is indeed the correct one, this is a very desirable feature, since the statistical estimation of the parameters of rare events is clearly difficult, and so is the a priori estimation of risk aversion. However, in reality we do not even know whether our guess of a jump–diffusion for the process driving the underlying was the appropriate one. After calibrating the model, is it possible to say something about the reasonableness of the chosen model and of the best-fit parameters (in particular, of the risk-adjusted jump frequency and of the average jump amplitude ratio)? Lewis (2002) presents a nice argument that addresses this question indirectly. He starts by positing that investors maximize their expected utility, U, of wealth, W, and that the utility function has the simple form

$$U(W) = W^\gamma \tag{14.77}$$

It is easy to see that the exponent γ is related to the investor's risk aversion: γ equal to 1 clearly corresponds to risk indifference, while a γ smaller than one produces a concave utility function and will therefore describe the behaviour of risk-averse investors. Furthermore, in order to stress that the jump amplitude, Y, should be a positive quantity, Lewis writes it as

$$Y \equiv e^x \tag{14.78}$$

Let $p(x)$ be the probability density of the real-world jump amplitudes. Under these assumptions, it can be shown that a risk-averse investor would price options as if she were risk neutral, but the jump frequency was changed from λ to λ_γ, with

$$\lambda_\gamma = \lambda \int p(x) e^{(\gamma-1)x} \, dx \tag{14.79}$$

and the density of the jump amplitude ratio was transformed from $p(x)$ to $q(x)$:

$$q(x) = \frac{p(x)e^{(\gamma-1)x}}{\displaystyle\int p(x)e^{(\gamma-1)x}\,\mathrm{d}x} \tag{14.80}$$

Equations (14.79) and (14.80) establish a link (via the parameter γ) between the degree of risk aversion on the one hand, and how much the jump frequency can increase and how much the density of jump amplitude ratios can migrate to the left on the other. Figure 14.5 shows the real-world density of possible jump amplitude ratios, and the risk-adjusted densities obtained for different values of the risk-aversion exponent, γ. Figure 14.6 shows the ratio of the real-world jump frequency, λ, to the risk-adjusted frequency, λ_γ, again for different values of γ.

The first observation that can be drawn from these figures, and from the equations that generated them, is that, reassuringly enough, for a value of the exponent γ that corresponds to risk aversion, the risk-adjusted frequency, λ_γ, will be *higher* than the real-world frequency, λ; and that the risk-adjusted density of possible jump amplitude ratios, $q(x)$, is shifted to the *left* of the econometric density, $p(x)$.

What further use can be made of these results? From the risk-adjusted jump frequency and from some order-of-magnitude estimates of the real-world jump intensity and jump amplitude expectation (say, a jump every five years with an expected loss of 25%) one can impute the constant risk-aversion coefficient, and see whether the implied pattern of risk aversion looks plausible. Alternatively, starting from a plausible risk-aversion coefficient, one can try to impute from market prices the real-world jump frequency and

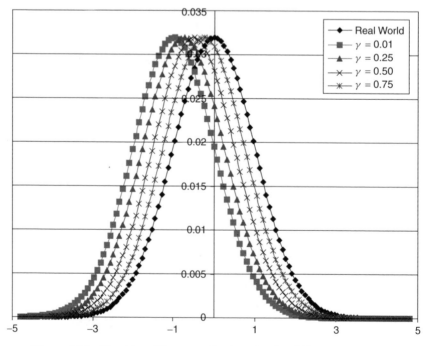

Figure 14.5   Densities of jump amplitude ratios for different values of γ.

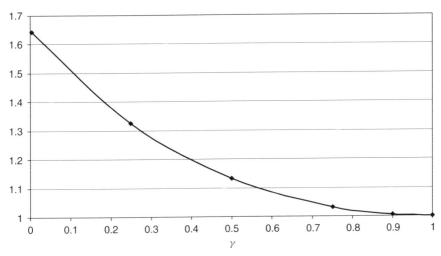

Figure 14.6 Ratio of the real-world jump frequency to the risk-adjusted jump frequency for different values of γ.

the expectation of the jump amplitude ratio. These values can then be compared with the real-world ones to check whether the overall 'story' is believable. A third, and perhaps most useful, approach is bounding the risk-adjusted values of the jump frequency and of the expectation of the jump amplitude ratio. This can be achieved by estimating bounds for the same quantities in the real-world measure, and by obtaining the possible range of the corresponding risk-adjusted values using the limiting values ($\gamma = 1$ and $\gamma = 0$) for the chosen utility function. The bounds so obtained could provide some indication of the reasonableness of a set of fitted parameters, or help in choosing between different competing minima of similar quality (see the discussion in Section 13.7).

All of these estimates are very difficult, and the agreement should not be expected to be much better than an order-of-magnitude level. None the less, if, for instance, the optimal γ obtained by the fitting procedure implied a risk-loving rather than a risk-averse investor, the validity of the whole approach would be put in doubt. Similar considerations would apply if the expectation of the jump amplitude implied an 'up' rather than a 'down' average jump. This is of some use, but more stringent constraints can be obtained. Note from the figures above, in fact, that for a positive γ the risk-adjusted jump frequency can at most be approximately 1.7 times larger than the real-world one. On the other hand, Figure 14.6 shows that, if the real-world jumps were equally likely to be up or down and of symmetric magnitude, and the real-world parameters as above, risk aversion (as described by the chosen utility function) can make the investor 'expect' a downward jump as large as 40%.

This type of qualitative analysis can be very useful, because, in the presence of a large number of parameters, blind optimizations are notoriously prone to producing results of similar numerical quality, but with very different sets of 'optimal' coefficients. Should we prefer a fit with a risk-adjusted jump frequency 10 times larger than the statistical one and an expectation of the jump amplitude ratio close to what was observed in real life, or a similar-quality fit with a much lower jump frequency and a more downward bias to the jumps? The results presented above can help in deciding between the two alternatives.

This type of analysis is also useful when the inputs are noisy (as will often be the case for the informationally important out-of-the-money options). The approach by Lewis (2002) can therefore be used in order to create a 'grid' of acceptable ranges for some of the optimization parameters. In other words, this approach can therefore be used as a useful 'regularization' strategy to produce a stable and plausible set of results.

14.5.6   Comparison with the Stochastic-Volatility Case (Again)

There are strong similarities but also important differences when the results above are compared with the stochastic-volatility case.

To start with the similarities, in both cases we attempted to hedge the source of 'extra' uncertainty with an another option (I am referring for simplicity to the single-amplitude-ratio case). This led, not surprisingly, to the disappearance from the equations of the real-world growth rates, and to a separation of the governing PDEs into blocks that only depended on one set of variables at a time.

The most important difference is the fundamentally greater complexity of a 'full' jump–diffusion compared with a stochastic-volatility process. In this latter case, as long as we assume that we know the process of a single option, or, alternatively, that we have reliably determined the homonymous (deterministic) function g of Chapter 13, we can produce perfect replication of the terminal payoff of a second option. Risk-neutral valuation is therefore valid. In order to obtain the same result for a jump–diffusion process we have to require a single possible jump amplitude. With a continuum of possible jump amplitudes one needs infinitely many plain-vanilla options that span a whole new dimension of uncertainty.

This should not be surprising. With full jump–diffusion processes we are dealing with a compound stochastic process: one source of randomness comes from the counting process, whose realizations tell us when the jump occurs; the second source comes from the draw of the jump amplitude ratio, given that a jump event has happened. This extra dimension will be directly reflected in the pricing formula (see below), that is made up of a sum over the possible number of jumps (weighted by their probability of occurrence) and an integral over the possible jump amplitudes.

Finally, recall that, when we are dealing with deterministic-volatility diffusions, 'lucky paths' in the sense of Chapter 4 do not exist. This is no longer true when dealing with jumps: over a finite time interval, the jump either occurs or it does not. The nature of the stochasticity in the sample quadratic variation is discussed later in this chapter.

So far the treatment has been very general. In order to obtain practical pricing formulae we have to specialize the process considerably. Recall that, if the distribution of possible jump–amplitude ratios is log-normal, we observed above that *when* the jump(s) occur(s) does not matter for the realization of the stock price after a finite time (see Equation (14.21)). This simplification will be very useful in arriving at a pricing formula. This is discussed in the following section.

14.6   The Pricing Formula for Log-Normal Amplitude Ratios

In order to arrive, at least in one important case, at a valuation formula for the value of a call option when the underlying follows a mixed jump–diffusion process, it is useful to define the quantity X_n as follows. First of all let

$$X_0 = 1 \tag{14.81}$$

As for the distribution of X_n after a finite time T, let us require that it should have the same distribution as the n-times repeated product of the quantity Y, i.e. of the amplitude ratio for a single jump. If this is the case one can show (Merton (1990)) that the price of a call option, C, of strike K, expressed as a function of time and of the current stock price, S_0, is given by

$$C(S_0, t) = \sum_{n=0}^{\infty} \frac{\exp(-\lambda\tau)(\lambda\tau)^n}{n!} E_n[\mathcal{CBS}(\widehat{S}_n, \tau, K, \sigma, r)] \tag{14.82}$$

where

$$\widehat{S}_n = S_0 X_n \exp(-\lambda k \tau) \tag{14.83}$$

$E_n[.]$ is the expectation operator over the distribution of X_n, and $\mathcal{CBS}(\widehat{S}, \tau, K, \sigma, r)$ is the Black-and-Scholes price of a call of strike K, when the volatility is σ, the short rate is r, and the expiry of the option (in years) is τ.

Equation (14.82) is easy to interpret: given a (risk-adjusted) jump frequency λ, the term $\frac{\exp(-\lambda\tau)(\lambda\tau)^n}{n!}$ gives the probability of n events (jumps) occurring over a period τ. As for the term $\widehat{S}$, it is the compensated value of the stock price, given that it started from S_0 at time 0, and experienced n jumps. The pricing formula is therefore a weighted average of an infinite series of Black-and-Scholes call prices, the first one calculated with the quantity $S_0 \exp(-\lambda k \tau)$ playing the role of the initial stock value, the second with $S_0 X_1 \exp(-\lambda k \tau)$, etc.

If the random quantities X_n are allowed to have arbitrary distributions, this is as far as one can go in terms of getting a semi-closed-form expression for the call price: in practice, one would have to carry out numerically an expectation over the distribution of the X_n, as indicated by term $E_n[.]$.

If, however, one is prepared to make the assumption that Y should have a log-normal distribution, the product X will also be log-normally distributed and the expression can be substantially simplified. Let us denote by δ the percentage volatility of Y, and by γ[13] the quantity

$$\gamma = \ln(1 + k) \tag{14.84}$$

If this is the case, the probability densities for the random variables X_n are known analytically, and are given by log-normal distributions with variance

$$\text{var}[X_n] = n\delta^2 \tag{14.85}$$

and expectation

$$E_n[X_n] = \exp(n\gamma) \tag{14.86}$$

---

[13]Needless to say, this γ bears no relationship to the exponent of the utility function discussed in Section 14.5.5.

Under the log-normal assumption for Y, the expression for the K-strike, τ-maturity call price therefore becomes (see Merton (1990))

$$C(S_0, t) = \sum_{n=0}^{\infty} \frac{\exp(-\lambda'\tau)(\lambda'\tau)^n}{n!} CBS(S_0, \tau, K, s_n, r_n) \tag{14.87}$$

with

$$\lambda' = \lambda(1 + k) \tag{14.88}$$

$$s_n^2 = \sigma^2 + \frac{\text{var}[X_n]}{\tau} = \sigma^2 + \frac{n\delta^2}{\tau} \tag{14.89}$$

$$r_n = r - \lambda k + \frac{\ln E_n[X_n]}{\tau} = r - \lambda k + \frac{n\gamma}{\tau} \tag{14.90}$$

and $CBS(S_0, \tau, K, s_n, r_n)$ denotes the Black-and-Scholes formula with stock price S_0, time to expiry τ, strike K, volatility s_n and riskless rate r_n. Together with Equations (14.85) and (14.86), Equations (14.89) and (14.90) show that the quantities s_n^2 and r_n can be interpreted as the variance and growth rate of the stock per unit time if n jumps have taken place.

Note that, since we have assumed that the variance of the jump ratio, δ^2, should be deterministic, the 'effective' variance should in principle be estimated from real-world data (i.e. from the diffusive volatility, σ, and from the standard deviation of the jump amplitude ratio, δ). The 'effective' growth rate, however, contains a combination of real-world and risk-adjusted world quantities, and even in principle cannot therefore be estimated directly from a statistical analysis of the stock price dynamics. In practice, however, estimation of the real-world variance of the jump amplitude ratio, δ^2, is very arduous, because rare events are, well, rare, and because it is difficult, given an observed change in the market price to identify and separate the diffusive and jump components. Since real price moves do not occur with a 'jump' or 'diffusion' label attached to them, if we observe a 'largish' price move can we easily say whether this was due to a 'large' Brownian shock or to a 'small' jump? The estimation of the real-world quantity δ is therefore typically carried out jointly with the estimation of the risk-adjusted parameters (λ and k) by means of a cross-sectional analysis of observed market prices. As usual, it is always important to ensure that the value of δ obtained following this procedure should at least lie within 'plausible' bands.

14.7   The Pricing Formula in the Finite-Amplitude-Ratio Case

We have seen in the previous sections that a continuous-amplitude jump–diffusion process for the underlying does not allow exact replication of the payoff of a derivative contract even if the trader could hedge with an arbitrarily large, but finite, number of plain-vanilla options. We have also seen that, if the number of possible jump amplitudes is finite, such a dynamic replication is in principle possible, as long as the trader can complete the market by adding to the universe of hedging instruments as many plain-vanilla options as possible jump amplitudes (and assumes knowledge of their processes). This, as discussed, is a tall order. Apart from rather theoretical hedging considerations, however, analysing in some detail the option prices produced when only a few possible jump amplitude ratios are possible is instructive. This is not just because of the intuitive insight into more general features of option pricing in the presence of jumps (such as some features of the risk-neutral density and of the smile surface discussed below). The main interest in looking at the case of a finite (and small) number of jump amplitudes is that in practice we will try to hedge a complex product with a small number of plain-vanilla options. Our hope will be that, even if we do not know exactly the parameters of the process (i.e. the full process for the hedging options) we can still arrive at an approximate but effective hedging strategy, at least if we have correctly guessed the discontinuous nature of the process for the underlying and some of its main features. See Section 14.11. Such an approximate procedure would be more easily justifiable if a jump–diffusion process with a small number of possible jump amplitudes could be shown to be in some sense 'close' or 'similar' to a continuous-jump amplitude process. This could occur, for instance, if it gave rise to marginal and conditional price densities not too different from what is produced by the 'full' jump–diffusion process. Despite the fact that the log-normal-amplitude formula is computationally easier to use, this section therefore tackles the case when only a finite number of jump amplitudes are possible.

Let us consider, on the one hand, a jump–diffusion process for the underlying with a log-normal jump amplitude ratio for the Poisson component. Let μ_A and σ_A denote the expectation and standard deviation of the jump amplitude ratio, respectively. On the other hand, let us consider a jump–diffusion process with discrete jump amplitude ratios, $A_1, A_2, \ldots, A_n$. Let us also assume that the latter are chosen so as to ensure that the first few moments of the discrete and continuous log-normal jump amplitude coincide. In other words, if, for instance, we want to impose matching of the first two moments only, let

$$\mu_A = \frac{1}{n} \sum_{j=1,n} A_j = \langle A \rangle \tag{14.91}$$

$$\sigma_A^2 = \frac{1}{n} \sum_{j=1,n} [A_j - \langle A \rangle]^2 \tag{14.92}$$

The following related questions then arise:

- How different are the prices of plain-vanilla and exotic options produced by the continuous and discrete jump amplitude models, respectively, for a relatively small number of possible discrete jump amplitude ratios?

- How quickly does the price of an option and the price distribution for the underlying converge as a function of the number of possible discrete jump amplitude ratios, if relationships (14.91) and (14.92) above are satisfied?

In the following section I show that the prices of plain-vanilla options converge quickly as a function of the number of possible jump amplitude ratios when the first moments of the discrete jump amplitude ratio distribution are kept constant.

14.7.1   The Structure of the Pricing Formula for Discrete Jump Amplitude Ratios

If the distribution of the jump amplitude ratio is not log-normal, the price of a call, $C(S_0, t)$, is given by Equation (14.82), which is repeated below for ease of reference:

$$C(S_0, t) = \sum_{n=0}^{\infty} \frac{\exp(-\lambda\tau)(\lambda\tau)^n}{n!} E_n[CBS(\widehat{S}_n, \tau, K, \sigma, r)] \tag{14.93}$$

Recall that X_n is a random variable equal to the product of the n random variables that describe the jump amplitude ratios. More precisely

$$X_n = Y_1 Y_2 \dots Y_n \tag{14.94}$$

and Y_j is implicitly defined by

$$S_{\text{after}} = S_{\text{before}} Y_j \tag{14.95}$$

As for the quantity X_0, it is given by $X_0 = 1$.

Expressions (14.82) and (14.94) clearly show why in the discrete-amplitude case the evaluation of the call price can soon become cumbersome. Let us assume that there are, say, three distinct possible jump amplitude ratios. The very first term in the summation corresponds to the case where no jumps have taken place ($X_0 = 1$). The second term corresponds to the case where a single jump has taken place. If we know that the probabilities for the three jump amplitudes Y_1, Y_2 and Y_3 are given by p_1, p_2 and p_3, respectively, then the expectation in the second term ($n = 1$) in the summation in Equation (14.82) becomes

$$E_1[CBS(\widehat{S}_1, \tau, K, \sigma, r)]$$

$$= p_1 CBS(SY_1 \exp(-\lambda\tau), \tau, K, \sigma, r)$$

$$+ p_2 CBS(SY_2 \exp(-\lambda\tau), \tau, K, \sigma, r)$$

$$+ p_3 CBS(SY_3 \exp(-\lambda\tau), \tau, K, \sigma, r) \tag{14.96}$$

The third term ($n = 2$) corresponds to the case when two jumps have occurred between time 0 and time T. The corresponding expression for the expectation is now more complicated, since the following distinct products of jump amplitude ratios and probabilities might have occurred:

$$X_{11}^2 = Y_1 Y_1 \text{ with probability } p_1 p_1 \tag{14.97}$$

$$X_{22}^2 = Y_2 Y_2 \text{ with probability } p_2 p_2 \tag{14.98}$$

$$X_{33}^2 = Y_3 Y_3 \text{ with probability } p_3 p_3 \tag{14.99}$$

$$X_{12}^2 = Y_1 Y_2 \text{ or } Y_2 Y_1 \text{ with probability } p_1 p_2 + p_2 p_1 \tag{14.100}$$

$$X_{13}^2 = Y_1Y_3 \text{ or } Y_1Y_3 \text{ with probability } p_1p_3 + p_3p_1 \qquad (14.101)$$

$$X_{23}^2 = Y_2Y_3 \text{ or } Y_3Y_2 \text{ with probability } p_2p_3 + p_3p_2 \qquad (14.102)$$

Note again that, since we are dealing with amplitude *ratios*, the order of the jumps does not matter: a proportional jump of amplitude Y_j followed by another of amplitude Y_k produces the same effect on the stock price as a jump Y_k followed by a jump Y_j. It is for this reason that only the product X_n, which does not depend on the order of jumps, enters the final expression.

It is easy to see that the combinatorial problem, although conceptually simple, soon becomes computationally very heavy, the more so the higher the term in the summation, and the larger the possible number of distinct amplitude ratios.

14.7.2 Matching the Moments

Let us look more carefully at how the first two moments of the densities in the cases of a log-normal and of a two-amplitude-ratio jump process are matched. Let us denote the density in the discrete case by $\Phi(.)$. Then, for two possible equiprobable jump amplitudes the discrete density is given by

$$\Phi(Y) = \tfrac{1}{2}[\delta(Y - Y_1) + \delta(Y - Y_2)] \qquad (14.103)$$

where, in the expression above, the symbol δ denotes the Dirac-δ distribution. If that is the case the expectation of Y is given by

$$E[Y] = \int Y\Phi(Y)\,dY = \tfrac{1}{2}\int Y[\delta(Y - Y_1) + \delta(Y - Y_2)]\,dy$$

$$= \tfrac{1}{2}[Y_1 + Y_2] \qquad (14.104)$$

But from the definitions above $k = E[Y - 1]$ and therefore

$$k + 1 = E[Y] = \tfrac{1}{2}[Y_1 + Y_2] \rightarrow k = \tfrac{1}{2}[Y_1 + Y_2] - 1 \qquad (14.105)$$

If, without loss of generality, we then assume that $Y_2 > Y_1$ and we impose the matching of the second moments of the continuous (log-normal) and discrete distributions, we can write

$$\delta^2 = \text{var}[\ln(Y)] = \tfrac{1}{4}[\ln Y_2 - \ln Y_1]^2 \rightarrow \tfrac{1}{2}\ln\left[\frac{Y_1}{Y_2}\right] = \delta \qquad (14.106)$$

Equations (14.105) and (14.106) therefore ensure that a discrete jump-amplitude-ratio distribution with identical probabilities and possible values Y_1 and Y_2 as above generates the same moments as a log-normal jump ratio distribution with parameters k and δ.[14] Using these results we can now compare the option valuations resulting from the two approaches.

---

[14]We have solved the moment-matching problem by imposing the probabilities and solving for the amplitudes. Clearly, the approach whereby one amplitude was chosen arbitrarily, and the second amplitude and one probability solved for, could have been employed as well.

14.7.3 Numerical Results

In order to establish a benchmark case for the calculations, a call option with one year to expiry, and a stock price today of $100 was chosen. Interest rates were assumed to be constant at 0% and the volatility of the diffusive part of the stock price process was also taken to be constant at 16%. Ignoring the jump component, the Black-and-Scholes price for the at-the-money option is 6.3763. One can then begin to analyse the case of log-normal jump amplitude ratios.

The Case of Log-Normal Jump Amplitude Ratios

From the relationships established in the previous section one can see that a value of $k = 0$ corresponds to the case of possible percentage jump amplitudes being symmetrically positioned with respect to the level of the stock before the jump. In other words, the (risk-adjusted) probability of a jump that increases the stock price by $X\%$ is the same as the probability of a jump reducing the price by the same percentage amount. A jump variance parameter δ of 10% approximately corresponds to the jump amplitude ratios being in a one-standard-deviation range of 0.9–1.1.

As a first check, if the amplitude location coefficient is 0 ('symmetrical' percentage jumps), and as the jump variance (δ^2) tends to zero the jump–diffusion formula must tend to the Black-and-Scholes expression with the same diffusion coefficient. In this case all the Black-and-Scholes terms in summation (14.82) have exactly the same value; the individual weights, i.e. the quantities $\frac{\exp(-\lambda\tau)(\lambda\tau)^n}{n!}$, are all different, but they add up to one. Therefore the jump–diffusion call price coincides, as it should, with the Black-and-Scholes value of 6.3763. See Table 14.2.

The same value is again recovered for arbitrary but finite k and δ, in the limit as the frequency λ tends to zero. In this case, in fact, the Black-and-Scholes-like terms in the summation do assume different values, but only the weight of the first (no-jump) term is appreciably different from zero. See Table 14.3. In general, i.e. when k, δ and λ assume arbitrary non-zero values and the jump frequency affects the weights in the summation, the variance and location parameters k and δ determine the magnitude of the Black-and-Scholes-like terms.

For a case with plausible parameters ($\lambda = 0.5, k = 1, \delta = 0.1$), the magnitude of the different contributing terms are shown in Table 14.4. Note that, even with a jump frequency corresponding to one jump every two years, and a jump amplitude ratio in a one-standard-deviation range of 10%, the call price for the chosen maturity (one year) is virtually fully converged after the first five terms.

Discrete Number of Jump Amplitude Ratios: Analysis of Prices

If only a discrete number of possible jump amplitude ratios are allowed, the following limiting case can be analysed. To begin with, if a single jump amplitude ratio is allowed, the same price must be obtained with the log-normal jump amplitude ratio distribution as its variance δ^2 tends to zero. Furthermore, the matching must be term by term: in other words, for all values of n, after adjusting the frequency and the volatility in the log-normal case, and the price in the discrete case, the products of the different weights

Table 14.2   The columns 'Index' and 'AdjVol' contain the number of jumps and the quantity $\sqrt{\sigma^2 + \frac{Index*\delta^2}{\tau}}$, respectively. The column 'AdjRate' contains the quantity $r - \lambda k + Index\frac{\gamma}{\tau}$. The prices were calculated with $\sigma = 16.00\%$, $r = 0\%$, $S_0 = 100$, Strike $= 100$, $k = 0$, and $\delta = 0.000001$.

Index	AdjVol	AdjRate	Poisson	BSTerm	Price
0	0.1600	0.0000	0.77880	6.3763	4.9659
1	0.1600	0.0000	0.19470	6.3763	6.2073
2	0.1600	0.0000	0.02434	6.3763	6.3625
3	0.1600	0.0000	0.00203	6.3763	6.3754
4	0.1600	0.0000	0.00013	6.3763	6.3762
5	0.1600	0.0000	0.00001	6.3763	6.3763
6	0.1600	0.0000	0.00000	6.3763	6.3763
7	0.1600	0.0000	0.00000	6.3763	6.3763
8	0.1600	0.0000	0.00000	6.3763	6.3763
9	0.1600	0.0000	0.00000	6.3763	6.3763
10	0.1600	0.0000	0.00000	6.3763	6.3763
11	0.1600	0.0000	0.00000	6.3763	6.3763
12	0.1600	0.0000	0.00000	6.3763	6.3763
13	0.1600	0.0000	0.00000	6.3763	6.3763
14	0.1600	0.0000	0.00000	6.3763	6.3763
15	0.1600	0.0000	0.00000	6.3763	6.3763
16	0.1600	0.0000	0.00000	6.3763	6.3763

Table 14.3   As Table 14.2, but with $\lambda = 0.00001$, $\delta = 0.1$, and $k = 0.1$. See the text for a discussion.

Index	AdjVol	AdjRate	Poisson	BSTerm	Price
0	0.1600	0.0000	1.00000	6.3763	6.3763
1	0.1887	0.0953	0.00000	12.6128	6.3763
2	0.2135	0.1906	0.00000	19.3245	6.3763
3	0.2358	0.2859	0.00000	25.9806	6.3763
4	0.2561	0.3812	0.00000	32.3317	6.3763
5	0.2750	0.4766	0.00000	38.2705	6.3763
6	0.2926	0.5719	0.00000	43.7615	6.3763
7	0.3092	0.6672	0.00000	48.8050	6.3763
8	0.3250	0.7625	0.00000	53.4194	6.3763
9	0.3400	0.8578	0.00000	57.6311	6.3763
10	0.3544	0.9531	0.00000	61.4695	6.3763
11	0.3682	1.0484	0.00000	64.9645	6.3763
12	0.3816	1.1437	0.00000	68.1451	6.3763
13	0.3945	1.2390	0.00000	71.0384	6.3763
14	0.4069	1.3343	0.00000	73.6697	6.3763
15	0.4190	1.4297	0.00000	76.0625	6.3763
16	0.4308	1.5250	0.00000	78.2381	6.3763

Table 14.4   As Table 14.2, but with $\lambda = 0.5$, $k = 1$ and $\delta = 0.1$. See the text for a discussion.

Index	AdjVol	AdjRate	Poisson	BSTerm	Price
0	0.1600	−0.0500	0.57695	4.2922	2.4764
1	0.1887	0.0453	0.31732	9.7748	5.5781
2	0.2135	0.1406	0.08726	16.1576	6.9881
3	0.2358	0.2359	0.01600	22.7528	7.3521
4	0.2561	0.3312	0.00220	29.1934	7.4163
5	0.2750	0.4266	0.00024	35.2989	7.4249
6	0.2926	0.5219	0.00002	40.9910	7.4258
7	0.3092	0.6172	0.00000	46.2462	7.4259
8	0.3250	0.7125	0.00000	51.0698	7.4259
9	0.3400	0.8078	0.00000	55.4815	7.4259
10	0.3544	0.9031	0.00000	59.5073	7.4259
11	0.3682	0.9984	0.00000	63.1761	7.4259
12	0.3816	1.0937	0.00000	66.5165	7.4259
13	0.3945	1.1890	0.00000	69.5562	7.4259
14	0.4069	1.2843	0.00000	72.3213	7.4259
15	0.4190	1.3797	0.00000	74.8361	7.4259
16	0.4308	1.4750	0.00000	77.1229	7.4259

and Black-and-Scholes terms must be identical:

$$\frac{\exp(-\lambda'\tau)(\lambda'\tau)^n}{n!} CBS(S_0, \tau, K, s_n, r_n) = \frac{\exp(-\lambda\tau)(\lambda\tau)^n}{n!} E_n[CBS(\widehat{S}_n, \tau, K, \sigma, r)]$$

(14.107)

Tables 14.5 and 14.6 show that this is indeed the case.

The case of two distinct jump amplitude ratios matched to the first two moments of the corresponding log-normal distribution is particularly interesting. For $k = -0.1$, $\lambda = 0.5$ and $\delta = 0.1$ the resulting equiprobable amplitude ratios are 0.810299 and 0.989701. Note that, since the location parameter k is negative, the jump amplitude ratios are biased towards 'down' jumps. In fact, given the chosen value for jump amplitude volatility δ, both the 'up' and the 'down' jumps are likely to bring the stock price below its pre-jump level.

Tables 14.7 and 14.8 show the components of the price for the log-normal and the equivalent discrete amplitude cases, respectively. For the one-jump-amplitude discrete case (Table 14.8), the column with the quantity X reports the possible values of the product of the percentage jump amplitudes when $0, 1, 2, \ldots, 7$ jumps have occurred. Note that the price (6.9852) is noticeably different from the log-normal-amplitude case (7.4213).

Table 14.9 illustrates the case when two jump amplitudes are possible. If only one jump has occurred the possible products are, trivially, either $X_1 = 0.810299$ or $X_2 = 0.989701$ (see part (a)). If two jumps have occurred, the product Y can be given by $X_1^2 = 0.656584$, $X_2^2 = 0.979508$ or $X_1 X_2 = 0.81954$, occurring with probabilities 0.25, 0.25 and 0.5, respectively, as shown in part (b). These probabilities, in general, are given for higher

Table 14.5   The components of the call price for the single-jump-amplitude and log-normal cases. The parameters are as in Table 14.2 (i.e. vanishing variance of jump amplitude), but with $\lambda = 0.5$ and $k = 0.1$.

Index	AdjVol	AdjRate	Poisson	BSTerm	Price
0	0.1600	−0.0500	0.57695	4.2922	2.4764
1	0.1600	0.0453	0.31732	8.6978	5.2364
2	0.1600	0.1406	0.08726	14.6717	6.5167
3	0.1600	0.2359	0.01600	21.4569	6.8599
4	0.1600	0.3312	0.00220	28.2917	6.9222
5	0.1600	0.4266	0.00024	34.7396	6.9306
6	0.1600	0.5219	0.00002	40.6603	6.9315
7	0.1600	0.6172	0.00000	46.0533	6.9316
8	0.1600	0.7125	0.00000	50.9574	6.9316
9	0.1600	0.8078	0.00000	55.4158	6.9316
10	0.1600	0.9031	0.00000	59.4689	6.9316
11	0.1600	0.9984	0.00000	63.1536	6.9316
12	0.1600	1.0937	0.00000	66.5033	6.9316
13	0.1600	1.1890	0.00000	69.5484	6.9316
14	0.1600	1.2843	0.00000	72.3167	6.9316
15	0.1600	1.3797	0.00000	74.8334	6.9316
16	0.1600	1.4750	0.00000	77.1213	6.9316

Table 14.6   As Table 14.5 for the equivalent discrete-amplitude case. Note that the price matching is term by term.

Index	Poisson	X	AdjS	BSterm	Price
0	0.60653	1.00000	95.12294	4.083	2.47637
1	0.30327	1.10000	104.63524	9.101	5.23636
2	0.07582	1.21000	115.09876	16.887	6.51667
3	0.01264	1.33100	126.60864	27.166	6.85995
4	0.00158	1.46410	139.26950	39.402	6.92218
5	0.00016	1.61051	153.19645	53.220	6.93059
6	0.00001	1.77156	168.51610	68.519	6.93149
7	0.00000	1.94872	185.36770	85.368	6.93157
8	0.00000	2.14359	203.90448	103.904	6.93158
9	0.00000	2.35795	224.29492	124.295	6.93158
10	0.00000	2.59374	246.72441	146.724	6.93158
11	0.00000	2.85312	271.39686	171.397	6.93158
12	0.00000	3.13843	298.53654	198.537	6.93158
13	0.00000	3.45227	328.39020	228.390	6.93158
14	0.00000	3.79750	361.22922	261.229	6.93158
15	0.00000	4.17725	397.35214	297.352	6.93158
16	0.00000	4.59497	437.08735	337.087	6.93158

Table 14.7   The components of the call price for the log-normal case ($k = -0.1$, $\lambda = 0.5$ and $\delta = 0.1$).

Index	AdjVol	AdjRate	Poisson	BSTerm	Price
0	0.1600	0.0500	0.63763	8.9599	5.7131
1	0.1887	−0.0554	0.28693	5.2132	7.2089
2	0.2135	−0.1607	0.06456	3.0115	7.4033
3	0.2358	−0.2661	0.00968	1.7387	7.4202
4	0.2561	−0.3714	0.00109	1.0055	7.4213
5	0.2750	−0.4768	0.00010	0.5829	7.4213
6	0.2926	−0.5822	0.00001	0.3387	7.4213
7	0.3092	−0.6875	0.00000	0.1973	7.4213
8	0.3250	−0.7929	0.00000	0.1152	7.4213
9	0.3400	−0.8982	0.00000	0.0674	7.4213
10	0.3544	−1.0036	0.00000	0.0395	7.4213
11	0.3682	−1.1090	0.00000	0.0232	7.4213
12	0.3816	−1.2143	0.00000	0.0136	7.4213
13	0.3945	−1.3197	0.00000	0.0080	7.4213
14	0.4069	−1.4250	0.00000	0.0047	7.4213
15	0.4190	−1.5304	0.00000	0.0028	7.4213
16	0.4308	−1.6358	0.00000	0.0016	7.4213

Table 14.8   The components of the call price for the equivalent one-discrete-jump-amplitude case.

Index	Poisson	X	AdjS	BSterm	Price
0	0.60653	1.00000	105.12711	9.419	5.71308
1	0.30327	0.90000	94.61440	3.879	6.88933
2	0.07582	0.81000	85.15296	1.217	6.98161
3	0.01264	0.72900	76.63766	0.280	6.98514
4	0.00158	0.65610	68.97390	0.046	6.98521
5	0.00016	0.59049	62.07651	0.005	6.98521
6	0.00001	0.53144	55.86886	0.000	6.98521
7	0.00000	0.47830	50.28197	0.000	6.98521
8	0.00000	0.43047	45.25377	0.000	6.98521
9	0.00000	0.38742	40.72840	0.000	6.98521
10	0.00000	0.34868	36.65556	0.000	6.98521
11	0.00000	0.31381	32.99000	0.000	6.98521
12	0.00000	0.28243	29.69100	0.000	6.98521
13	0.00000	0.25419	26.72190	0.000	6.98521
14	0.00000	0.22877	24.04971	−	6.98521
15	0.00000	0.20589	21.64474	−	6.98521
16	0.00000	0.18530	19.48027	−	6.98521

Table 14.9 The components of the call price for the case of two equivalent discrete jump amplitudes. See the text for details.

(a)

Index	Poisson	X							
0	0.606531	1							
1	0.303265	0.810299	0.989701						
2	0.075816	0.656584	0.801954	0.979508					
3	0.012636	0.532029	0.649822	0.793695	0.969421				
4	0.00158	0.431103	0.52655	0.64313	0.78552	0.959437			
5	0.000158	0.349322	0.426663	0.521127	0.636506	0.77431	0.949556		
6	1.32E-05	0.283055	0.345724	0.422269	0.51576	0.629951	0.769424	0.939776	
7	9.4E-07	0.229359	0.28014	0.342164	0.41792	0.510449	0.623463	0.7615	0.930098

(b) Probabilities

1							
0.5	0.5						
0.25	0.5	0.25					
0.125	0.375	0.375	0.125				
0.0625	0.25	0.375	0.25	0.0625			
0.03125	0.15625	0.3125	0.3125	0.15625	0.03125		
0.015625	0.09375	0.234375	0.3125	0.234375	0.09375	0.015625	
0.007813	0.054688	0.164063	0.273438	0.273438	0.164063	0.054688	0.007813

(continued overleaf)

Table 14.9 (*continued*)

(c) AdjSpot

105.1271	0	0	0	0	0	0	0
85.18437	104.0444	0	0	0	0	0	0
69.02479	84.30707	102.9729	0	0	0	0	0
55.93071	68.31392	83.43881	101.9124	0	0	0	0
45.32059	55.35469	67.61037	82.57949	100.8628	0	0	0
36.72322	44.85384	54.7846	66.91406	81.72902	99.82405	0	0
29.75678	36.34501	44.3919	54.22039	66.22493	80.88731	98.79598	0
24.11188	29.45032	35.9707	43.93471	53.66198	65.54289	80.05427	97.7785

(d) BSTerm

								Price
9.41928	0	0	0	0	0	0	0	5.7131
1.222699	8.725674	0	0	0	0	0	0	7.2216
0.046194	1.073596	8.065417	0	0	0	0	0	7.4160
0.000409	0.037919	0.9398	7.438401	0	0	0	0	7.4324
7.6E-07	0.000312	0.031016	0.820144	6.84441	0	0	0	7.4334
2.78E-10	5.35E-07	0.000237	0.025279	0.713495	6.28309	0	0	7.4335
2.19E-14	1.81E-10	3.75E-07	0.000179	0.02053	0.618764	5.753999	0	7.4335
0	6.66E-15	1.17E-10	2.62E-07	0.000135	0.016613	0.534908	5.256609	7.4335

number of jump occurrences by the binomial coefficients. Part (c) then gives the value of the factor $\exp(-\lambda kT)$ times the value of the stock price today multiplied by the appropriate product of jump amplitude ratios. Part (d) provides the Black-and-Scholes formula calculated with the adjusted spot after the jump. Note that the price (7.4335) is now very close to the log-normal-amplitude case (7.4213).

Several interesting features should be pointed out. First of all, despite the fact that the jumps are always 'downwards' the price of a call is higher than the Black-and-Scholes price obtained with the same diffusion coefficient and no jump. This is due to the combined effect of the compensator that enters the drift (the forward price has to be a martingale irrespective of the process), and the increase in volatility due to the jump component. Note also that, owing to call/put parity, and given the chosen zero interest rates, the value of the put is identical to the call for the at-the-money strike despite the downward nature of the jump. Therefore, irrespective of the value for k (i.e. irrespective of whether up or down jumps are assumed to be more likely) the value of both calls and puts is always higher than the corresponding Black-and-Scholes value with the same diffusion coefficient.

The data in Tables 14.5–14.9 were obtained for a strike equal to today's value of spot. Table 14.10 confirms that the prices are very similar for the given choice of parameters even with only two possible jump amplitude ratios over a wide range of strikes.

Table 14.10 Call prices for zero, one, or two discrete jump amplitudes compared with the log-normal-amplitude case over a wide range of strikes. The parameters used were $k = -0.1$, $\lambda = 0.5$, $\delta = 0.1$, $r = 0$, $\sigma = 0.16$ and $S_0 = 100$.

Strike	No Jump	SingleAmpl	TwoAmpl	Log-Normal	Diff
90	12.32117	12.85403	13.33986	13.31970	−0.02017
91	11.61446	12.16474	12.65450	12.63419	−0.02031
92	10.93181	11.49752	11.98936	11.96914	−0.02022
93	10.27373	10.85278	11.34488	11.32498	−0.0199
94	9.64065	10.23084	10.72140	10.70204	−0.01936
95	9.03286	9.63192	10.11923	10.10062	−0.0186
96	8.45056	9.05617	9.53858	9.52093	−0.01765
97	7.89383	8.50368	8.97963	8.96312	−0.01651
98	7.36265	7.97443	8.44246	8.42726	−0.0152
99	6.85688	7.46833	7.92709	7.91336	−0.01373
100	6.37629	6.98521	7.43348	7.42134	−0.01214
101	5.92052	6.52483	6.96151	6.95106	−0.01045
102	5.48918	6.08688	6.51101	6.50233	−0.00868
103	5.08179	5.67100	6.08174	6.07488	−0.00686
104	4.69778	5.27674	5.67339	5.66839	−0.005
105	4.33650	4.90361	5.28559	5.28247	−0.00313
106	3.99727	4.55108	4.91794	4.91667	−0.00127
107	3.67934	4.21855	4.56997	4.57054	0.000563
108	3.38195	3.90544	4.24121	4.24355	0.002341
109	3.10428	3.61108	3.93110	3.93515	0.004053
110	2.84549	3.33481	3.63907	3.64475	0.005686

Note also that the call prices for different strikes are not systematically higher either for continuous or discrete jump amplitude ratios. Whether the call price from the two-jump- or the log-normal-jump-amplitude-ratio case turns out to be larger for a given strike depends on the details of the differences in the densities produced by the two processes. It is therefore instructive to look in detail at the differences in the (risk-neutral) probability densities obtained with continuous and discrete jump amplitude ratios, and the similar difference between the pure diffusion case (same diffusion coefficient) and the two different jump processes. These differences are shown in Figure 14.7.

In order to illustrate the qualitative features more clearly, the 'symmetric' ($k = 0$) case is analysed first. Let us consider the cases when no, one or two jumps occur. The first observation is that the differences between the density for the no-jump case and the density when one or two jumps have occurred are an order of magnitude larger than the differences in densities between the one- and the two-jump case. It is therefore not surprising that the prices of calls in the presence of jumps of whatever nature (i.e. continuous or discrete) should be quite similar, and significantly different when compared with the pure-diffusion case.

Figure 14.7 also displays additional interesting qualitative features: first of all, the presence of jumps causes the density to decrease around the at-the-money spot level. Since, in this case, the jumps are symmetrically positioned around the diffusive path, the out-of-the-money density (corresponding to levels associated with the occurrence of jump events) is correspondingly increased. This is ultimately the mechanism giving rise to the jump–diffusion smile.

These effects are illustrated particularly clearly if the magnitude of the diffusive component is reduced with respect to the jump part of the process, by moving the volatility from 16% to 1%. See Figure 14.8. In this case one can readily observe the reduction in density away from the at-the-money level. Having reduced the volatility let us compare the continuous- and the discrete-jump-amplitude-ratio cases. For log-normally-distributed jumps the density is 'spread' out over a wide range, with significant tails reaching values

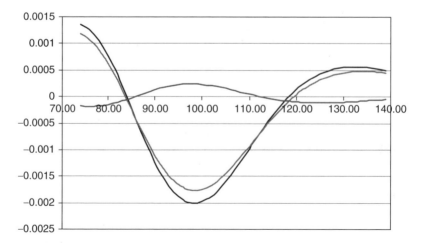

Figure 14.7   Density differences: log-normal vs two-amplitude jump process (bottom line on the left); pure diffusion vs log-normal (middle line on the left); pure diffusion vs two-amplitude jump (top line on the left); parameters: $r = 0$, $\sigma = 0.16$, $k = 0$, $\delta = 0.1$ ($Amp_1 = 0.9$, $Amp_2 = 1.1$).

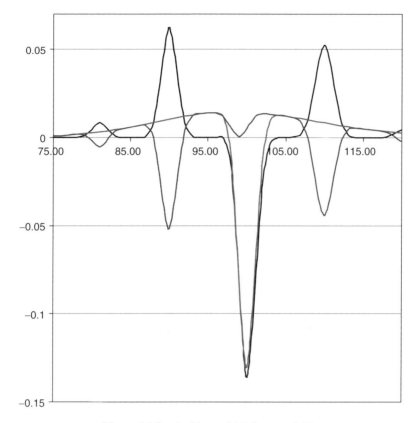

Figure 14.8 As Figure 14.7 for $\sigma = 0.01$.

as low as 70 or 120. Comparing this density with the density produced by the two-jump-amplitude case, one can notice the significant difference corresponding to the up or down jump ($k = 0$) around the (approximate) levels 110 and 91, and the 'harmonics' (two-jump events) around 121 and 82. The finite widths in the density differences between the continuous and two-amplitude cases visible around the levels 121, 110, 91 and 82 would shrink to zero if the diffusive component were to disappear altogether. The call prices corresponding to this low-volatility case are shown in Table 14.11.

The effects displayed in Figure 14.8 are helpful in understanding at a qualitative level the effect of discrete or continuous jump amplitude ratios on the terminal stock price density. The combination of parameters depicted in Figure 14.7 gives much more relative importance to the diffusive and the jump components.

14.8 The Link Between the Price Density and the Smile Shape

Jump–diffusion processes do produce non-flat smile surfaces. However, the precise shape of the smile and, in particular, its convexity depends on a rather subtle interaction between the various parameters that characterize the process. I intend to show that there is a link

Table 14.11   As Table 14.10, but with $\sigma = 0.01$.

Strike	No Jump	SingleAmpl	TwoAmpl	Log-Normal	Diff
90	10.00000	10.00000	10.25977	10.39552	0.135751
91	9.00000	9.00000	9.38992	9.47249	0.082574
92	8.00000	8.00000	8.55810	8.56067	0.00257
93	7.00000	7.00000	7.73485	7.66085	−0.074
94	6.00000	6.00000	6.91231	6.77377	−0.13854
95	5.00000	5.00000	6.08979	5.90005	−0.18975
96	4.00000	4.00000	5.26729	5.04020	−0.22709
97	3.00032	3.00032	4.44527	4.19481	−0.25046
98	2.00796	2.00796	3.63028	3.36838	−0.2619
99	1.08211	1.08211	2.86500	2.59693	−0.26807
100	0.39894	0.39894	2.26117	1.98730	−0.27387
101	0.08452	0.08452	1.89016	1.61578	−0.27438
102	0.00904	0.00904	1.66658	1.40337	−0.26321
103	0.00045	0.00045	1.48387	1.24534	−0.23854
104	0.00001	0.00001	1.30612	1.10555	−0.20057
105	0.00000	0.00000	1.12863	0.97875	−0.14988
106	0.00000	0.00000	0.95116	0.86404	−0.08713
107	0.00000	0.00000	0.77392	0.76071	−0.01321
108	0.00000	0.00000	0.59915	0.66802	0.068867
109	0.00000	0.00000	0.43833	0.58523	0.146891
110	0.00000	0.00000	0.31615	0.51155	0.195398

between the convexity of the smile and the uni- or multi-modal nature of the associated risk-neutral price density.[15]

The first observation is that a jump–diffusion process can, but need not, produce a bi- or multi-modal density. Intuitively this can be understood as follows. Recall, that, in the case of a log-normal jump amplitude, the call price is given by a weighted average of several Black-and-Scholes prices (see Equation (14.87)), with each term corresponding to a different number of jumps. Each of these terms will be calculated with a different growth rate, which depends on the number of jumps that have occurred (see Equation (14.90)). To every term one can associate a partial price density. As the initial delta distribution for the stock price evolves over time, these different partial contributions to the total density will therefore evolve in S_t space at different growth rates. The longer the time to expiry, the farther apart the central first moments of these partial distribution will move. *By itself* this feature tends to give rise to a multi-modal distribution, and this multi-modality would become more and more pronounced as time goes by. There exist, however, other features of the process that can counteract this.

To begin with, the higher the variance of the jump amplitude ratio, the more diffuse (less sharply localized) each density contribution will be. If several density contributions are very spread out, they will begin to overlap, and therefore reduce, or altogether negate, the multi-modality. Similarly, if the jump frequency is very high, for short times the partial

---

[15]It is a pleasure to thank Dr Dherminder Kainth for pointing out to me the features of jump–diffusion processes discussed in this section.

contributions to the overall densities become more important, and this tends to produce more multi-modal densities. However, if enough time is allowed to pass, the partial densities will ultimately begin to overlap to a significant extent, restoring a unimodal density. Finally, the higher the diffusive component (which never produces a multi-modal density), the less pronounced the contribution to the total density from the jumps, and the less likely is it to be multi-modal. Summarizing:

- a small variance in the jump amplitude ratio will tend to produce a multi-modal density;

- a high jump frequency will tend to produce a multi-modal density for short time horizons, and a unimodal one for long time horizons;

- a high diffusive component (i.e. a high volatility) will tend to produce a unimodal density;

- a long time horizon has two competing effects: it allows the growth terms (Equation (14.90)) to separate the density components; but it also facilitates the 'smearing' of the density contributions.

Why is the uni- or multi-modality of the price density important? Because one can observe that unimodal densities tend to be associated with *convex* smile surfaces (i.e. surfaces that qualitatively look like the market-observed ones); whereas multi-modal densities tend to be associated with *concave* smile curves (which are unlike what is normally observed in the market). This is shown in Figures 14.9–14.22. Starting from an expected jump amplitude ratio of 0.85 and a jump volatility of 20% with a frequency of 0.4 jumps/year (a set of plausible parameters), one obtains over a time horizon of half a year the unimodal density in Figure 14.9; the associated 'normal' smile is shown in Figure 14.10.

If the expectation of the jump amplitude ratio is now decreased to 0.70 (implying a downward jump of expected size 30%), and the other parameters are kept the same, the density is beginning to be deformed towards bimodality. See Figure 14.11. The smile

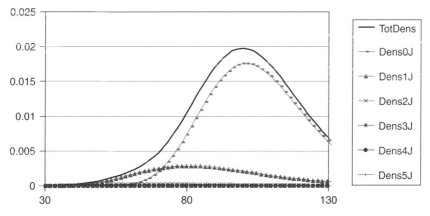

Figure 14.9 The densities produced by no jumps, one jump, two jumps, ..., five jumps with $Stock_0 = 100$, $\sigma = 25\%$, $r = 5.00\%$, $JumpAmpl = 0.85$, $JumpVol = 20.0\%$, $\lambda = 0.4$ and $T = 0.5$.

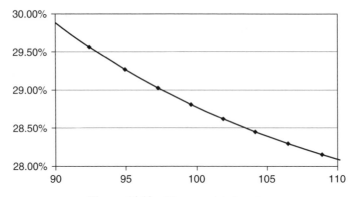

Figure 14.10   The associated smile.

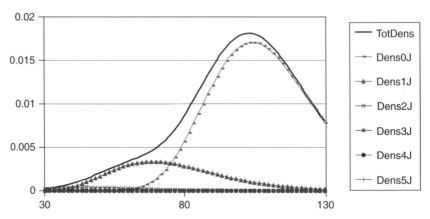

Figure 14.11   The densities produced by no jumps, one jump, two jumps, ..., five jumps with $Stock_0 = 100$, $\sigma = 25\%$, $r = 5.00\%$, $JumpAmpl = 0.70$, $JumpVol = 20.0\%$, $\lambda = 0.4$ and $T = 0.5$.

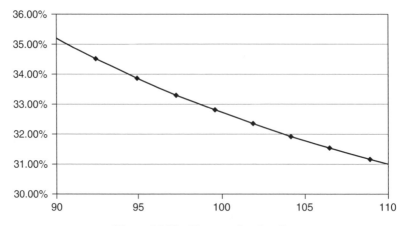

Figure 14.12   The associated smile.

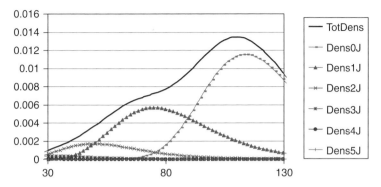

Figure 14.13   The densities produced by no jumps, one jump, two jumps, ..., five jumps with $Stock_0 = 100$, $\sigma = 25\%$, $r = 5.00\%$, $JumpAmpl = 0.70$, $JumpVol = 20.0\%$, $\lambda = 1.0$ and $T = 0.5$.

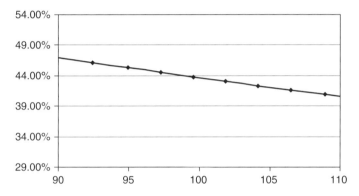

Figure 14.14   The associated smile.

(Figure 14.12) has moved to a higher level (there is more 'variance' produced by the larger jumps), and it is less convex.

If we increase the jump frequency to one jump per year, the one-jump and two-jump components of the total density have become more important (see Figure 14.13), and the overall price has therefore moved even further towards bimodality. The associated smile is at an even higher level, and is now virtually linear as a function of strike, as shown in Figure 14.14.

The transition towards a bimodal density continues by reducing the volatility of the jump amplitude ratios from 20% to 1% (see Figures 14.15 and 14.16). Finally, if the diffusive volatility is reduced from 25% to 12.5% the discrete peaks from the jumps become the dominant feature of the density, which is now multi-modal (see Figure 14.17). The associated smile now has a negative convexity, as shown in Figure 14.18. The feature becomes more pronounced as the diffusive volatility is reduced further to 10%. See Figures 14.19 and 14.20.

Finally Figures 14.21–14.24 show that, *for short maturities*, even a low diffusive volatility fails to give rise to a multi-modal density, and the smile therefore remains convex if the jump amplitude ratio is centred around 1. This is true at short time horizons irrespective of whether the volatility of the jump amplitude ratio is low (Figures 14.21

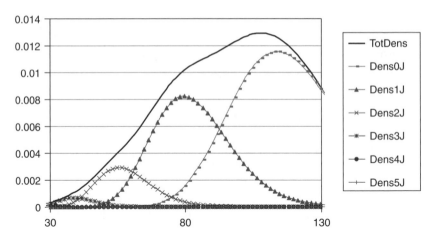

Figure 14.15   The densities produced by no jumps, one jump, two jumps, ..., five jumps with $Stock_0 = 100$, $\sigma = 25\%$, $r = 5.00\%$, $JumpAmpl = 0.70$, $JumpVol = 1.0\%$, $\lambda = 1.0$ and $T = 0.5$.

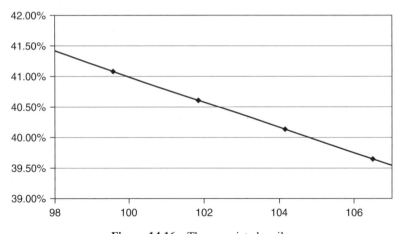

Figure 14.16   The associated smile.

and 14.22) or high (Figures 14.23 and 14.24). However, this need not be the case for longer maturities in the case of low volatility of the jump amplitude ratio, because the locations of the partial densities will grow farther and farther apart (because of the term (14.90)). Whether uni- or multi-modality will prevail will therefore depend on a subtle and difficult-to-predict interplay between the competing factors outlined above.

Again, why is this important? If we believe that a convex smile is a well-established market feature that should be reproduced *at all maturities* by a reasonable model, there exists a range of jump–diffusion parameters outside which this feature is no longer guaranteed. If the parameters are determined by a numerical search routine guided by the requirement that the prices for a series of (possibly short-dated) options should be recovered as well as possible, the resulting solution might lie outside the desirable range.

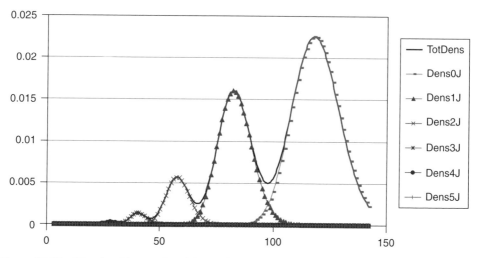

Figure 14.17   The densities produced by no jumps, one jump, two jumps, ..., five jumps with $Stock_0 = 100$, $\sigma = 12.5\%$, $r = 5.00\%$, $JumpAmpl = 0.70$, $JumpVol = 1.0\%$, $\lambda = 1.0$ and $T = 0.5$.

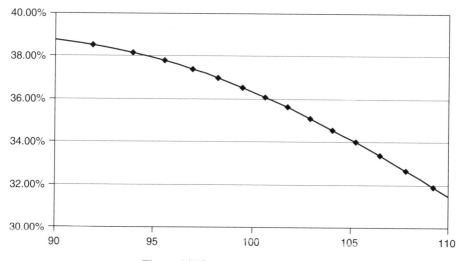

Figure 14.18   The associated smile.

This feature is not a mathematical curiosity, and is actually often encountered in practice when 'brute-force' optimization searches are carried out. These considerations can provide further guidance in the calibration of a jump–diffusion model to market data.

14.8.1   A Qualitative Explanation

Can we reach a qualitative understanding as to why this change in convexity occurs? Let us start from a purely geometric-diffusive process (with deterministic volatility). For any given maturity the resulting smile will be flat, and, in log space, the associated density a

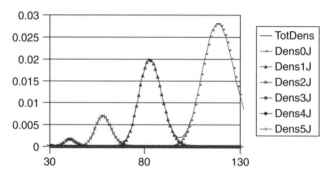

Figure 14.19 The densities produced by no jumps, one jump, two jumps, ..., five jumps with $Stock_0 = 100$, $\sigma = 10.0\%$, $r = 5.00\%$, $JumpAmpl = 0.70$, $JumpVol = 1.0\%$, $\lambda = 1.0$ and $T = 0.5$.

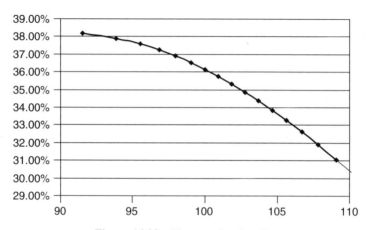

Figure 14.20   The associated smile.

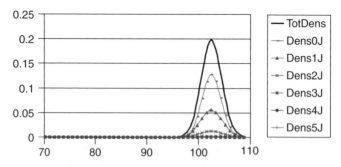

Figure 14.21 The densities produced by no jumps, one jump, two jumps, ..., five jumps with $Stock_0 = 100$, $\sigma = 2.5\%$, $r = 5.00\%$, $JumpAmpl = 1.0$, $JumpVol = 1.0\%$, $\lambda = 1$ and $T = 0.5$. Note that even a very low *JumpVol* does not produce concave smiles.

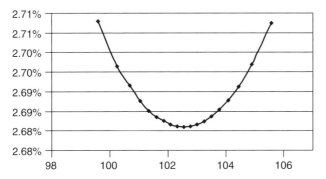

Figure 14.22 The associated smile.

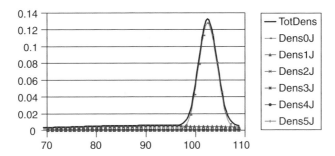

Figure 14.23 The densities produced by no jumps, one jump, two jumps, ..., five jumps with $Stock_0 = 100$, $\sigma = 2.5\%$, $r = 5.00\%$, $JumpAmpl = 1.0$, $JumpVol = 25.0\%$, $\lambda = 1$ and $T = 0.5$.

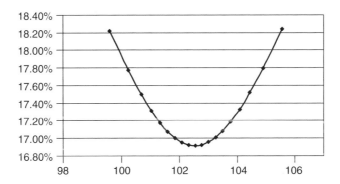

Figure 14.24 The associated smile.

Gaussian. As we begin to introduce jumps, but retain the unimodality of the density, we are effectively fattening the tails by removing probability mass from the centre. (Remember that the density must integrate to one no matter how we shuffle the probability mass around.) This will therefore give relatively more value to out-of-the-money options, and the associated implied volatility will be higher than for at-the-money options. Because of this, the smile displays a positive convexity. If we create a bimodal density (say, by using a small jump frequency) the localized probability mass is still partly 'taken away' from the centre, but now also from the outer portions of the tail. Therefore a very-out-of-the-money option will still be more valuable than in the absence of jumps, but can be less so than before we partially depleted the tail density to 'fatten' the intermediate peak. The final result is that the associated implied volatility will be less high for the very-out-of-the-money option than it was in the unimodal case. This can give rise to a change in convexity of the smile.

14.9   Qualitative Features of Jump–Diffusion Smiles

This section explores the smile shapes (as a function of strike and of option maturity) that a jump–diffusion process can produce 'naturally'. This analysis is important for two related reasons:

1. given a market smile surface, we might want to gauge at a qualitative level if 'sensible' combinations of the process parameters can convincingly account for it;

2. if we have decided that a jump–diffusion description is appropriate, from the observation of the market smile surface we might want to choose an initial desirable combination of parameters to begin the χ^2 search of a locally optimal solution. I have already explained elsewhere (see Section 13.7) why a theoretically superior global optimal solution might not be desirable.

14.9.1   The Smile as a Function of the Risk-Neutral Parameters

In order to gain a deeper understanding of the types of smile surfaces a jump–diffusion approach can produce 'naturally', I display below the results obtained with a variety of parameters.

The first observation is about the effect of the centring of the proportional jump amplitudes. Figures 14.25 and 14.26 display the smile as a function of fixed delta and fixed strike for a symmetric smile, and Figures 14.27 and 14.28 do the same for a jump amplitude of 0.85 (the percentage volatility of the jump amplitude was 20% in both cases). Note that, in fixed-strike space, the 0.85 jump amplitude smile does not appear to be particularly asymmetric, at least for short maturities, and it is only in delta space that the 'smirk' becomes clearly apparent. In both cases the most remarkable feature is the speed with which the smile flattens out (as a function of option expiry).

With the parameters chosen, in order to recover a more asymmetric (equity-like) smile, it is necessary to decrease the jump amplitude ratio to 0.65 (see Figures 14.29 and 14.30), but the price to pay for this is that, by so doing, short-expiry out-of-money calls have now acquired a rising implied volatility. Whether this is desirable or not depends on the equity market being considered, and, for a given market, on the specific period. Note also that, in order to obtain this feature, the expected size of the 'market crash' is now 35%, and a crash of such magnitude arrives (in the risk-adjusted world) once every 10 years. So, the jump frequency might be close to the statistical value, but the required jump amplitude appears to incorporate a substantial risk adjustment.

What would happen if we increased the jump frequency? We look at this by reverting to a jump amplitude of 0.85, but increasing the jump amplitude to once every two years.

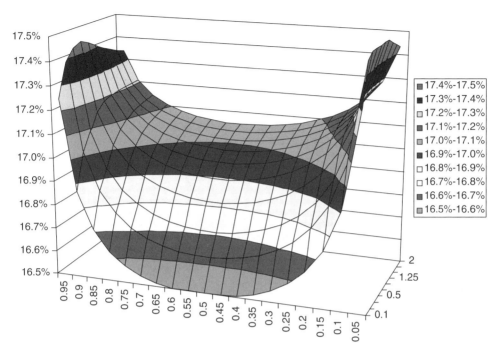

Figure 14.25 Jump–diffusion smile for a fixed delta ($S_0 = 100$, $r = 0$, $\sigma = 0.16$, $T = 0$, $\lambda = 0.1$, *JumpAmpl* $= 1.00$, *JumpVol* $= 20\%$).

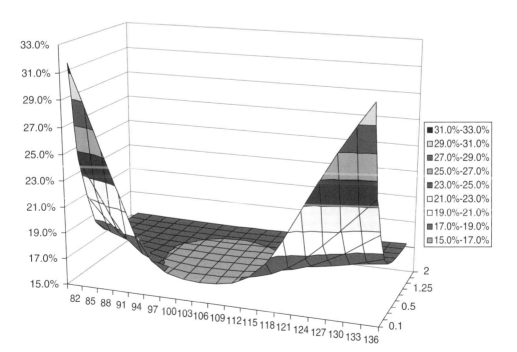

Figure 14.26 Same as Figure 14.25 for a fixed strike.

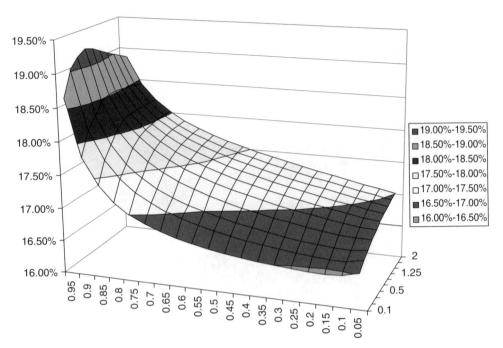

Figure 14.27   Jump–diffusion smile for a fixed delta ($S_0 = 100$, $r = 0$, $\sigma = 0.16$, $T = 0$, $\lambda = 0.1$, *JumpAmpl* $= 0.85$, *JumpVol* $= 20\%$).

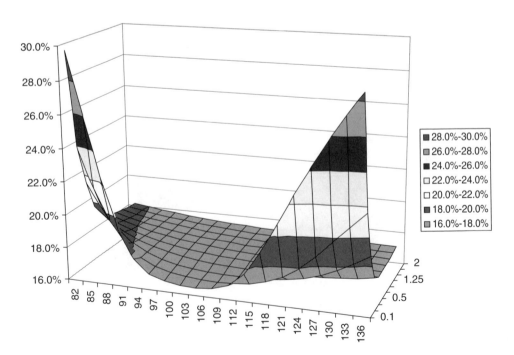

Figure 14.28   Same as Figure 14.27 for a fixed strike.

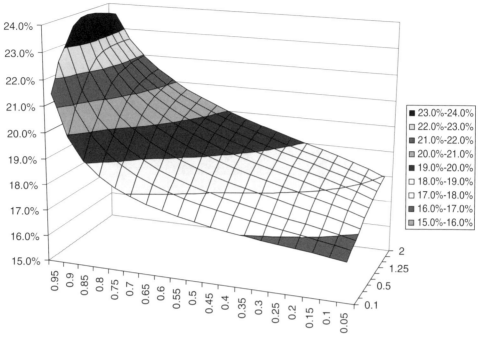

Figure 14.29 Jump–diffusion smile for a fixed delta ($S_0 = 100$, $r = 0$, $\sigma = 0.16$, $T = 0$, $\lambda = 0.1$, *JumpAmpl* = 0.65, *JumpVol* = 20%).

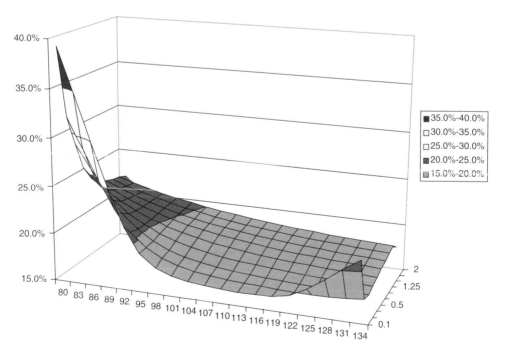

Figure 14.30 Same as Figure 14.29 for a fixed strike.

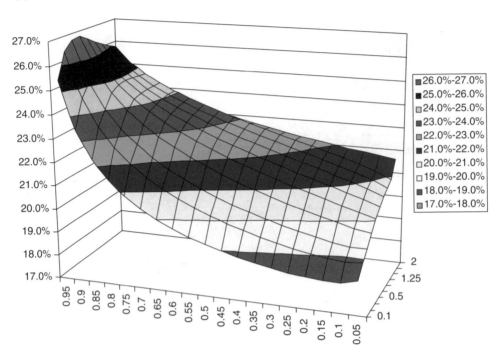

Figure 14.31   Jump–diffusion smile for a fixed delta ($S_0 = 100$, $r = 0$, $\sigma = 0.16$, $T = 0$, $\lambda = 0.5$, *JumpAmpl* $= 0.85$, *JumpVol* $= 20\%$).

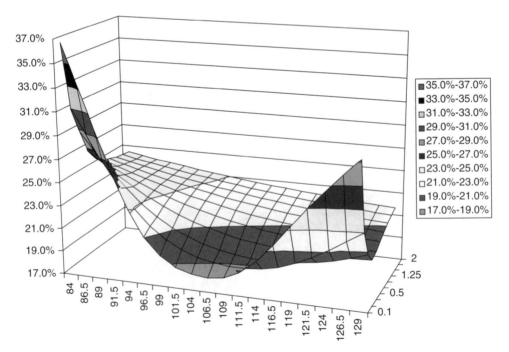

Figure 14.32   Same as Figure 14.31 for a fixed strike.

See Figures 14.31 and 14.32. The main effect is an overall increase in the level of the implied volatilities. Also, the smile at the short end becomes steeper, both as a function of the stock price and of the delta. This is not surprising: more jumps produce more overall 'variance' and fatten the tails. Furthermore, the smile remains more downward sloping as a function of fixed strike for the longer expiries. Also, in delta space the smile becomes more downward sloping.

14.9.2 Comparison with Stochastic-Volatility Smiles

It is interesting to compare these observations with the case of stochastic-volatility smiles. The most noticeable features are the speed of the flattening of the smiles (as a function of option expiry) produced by the jump–diffusions, and the difficulty encountered by stochastic-volatility models to give steep smiles at the short end of the maturity spectrum. The shallower stochastic-volatility smiles, however, are more persistent (see, for example, Figures 13.3–13.7 in Chapter 13). Also, we saw in the case of stochastic-volatility smiles that the positioning of the current volatility with respect to the long-term reversion level had a strong effect on the qualitative shape of the smile. If the current volatility level is significantly different from its long-term reversion level, the smile will change shape dramatically over a relatively short time period. There is, however, no equivalent of such a reversion level in the jump–diffusion model, and therefore the future smiles it produces are more self-similar. Much as I prefer, *in general*, self-similar smiles, this might not be the case in this instance: if we have experienced a jump, or if the volatility has been shocked to unusually high or low levels, there might well be financially justifiable transition periods back to 'normality'. In this transition period the smile surface might be significantly different from the 'normal' one.

Finally, jump–diffusion smiles are deterministic: contingent on a future realization of the stock price being obtained, there is one and only one future (conditional) smile associated with it. Therefore, with jump–diffusion processes there is no dependence of the future smile on the realized value of the underlying,[16] which was an important feature of stochastic-volatility models. Whether this is good or bad depends on the market and the views of the trader. In this context (at least) two important questions arise: 'Is it possible to identify some regularities in the smiles and the movements of the underlying?'; and, if so, 'Are the links observed in practice at least qualitatively similar to those predicted by the model?'. I would invite the reader to think again about the case of the pricing of a forward-starting call (spread) option.

The last part of this chapter deals with hedging jump–diffusion processes in practice. In particular, I will address the case when the trader does not know the true process, and therefore puts in place an approximate hedging strategy. In order to appreciate the results, it is important to remind ourselves of what is meant by slippages, and of which slippages are relevant for pricing when hedging is imperfect. This topic is dealt with in the next section.

---

[16]This feature is a direct consequence of the memory-less character of Poisson processes.

14.10   Jump–Diffusion Processes and Market Completeness Revisited

It is well known that investors' risk aversion cannot be recovered from (and does not influence) the prices of traded options if the underlying process is a pure diffusion with deterministic coefficients: Black's formula is independent of (i.e. is valid for) any pattern of risk aversion. Unfortunately, given the vast predominance, in the option literature if not in reality, of diffusions, as opposed to jump processes, we sometimes become very lazy in distinguishing between risk neutrality, absence of arbitrage, absence of risk aversion, etc. I clarify in this section some of these important concepts, because they will be useful in analysing the results of the hedging experiments described below.

Recall that, if the process for the underlying is a diffusion and all the usual perfect-market assumptions are met, we do not need risk-neutral investors for the Black-and-Scholes formula to apply. Whatever their risk aversion, it will not enter their appraisal of the value of a (plain-vanilla) option because they can build a perfectly replicating portfolio and the variance of returns of the option plus the hedging portfolio can be made exactly zero. (For brevity, I will call the option plus the hedging portfolio the 'total portfolio'). In other words, in the expression derived in Chapter 2 for the market price of risk

$$\mu = r + \lambda\sigma \tag{14.108}$$

(where μ is the drift, i.e. in this context the expected return from the total portfolio, r the riskless rate, σ the volatility of the portfolio and λ the market price of risk), it is not λ that goes to zero, but the volatility of the *total* portfolio.

Whenever one is dealing with a diffusion and one constructs a tree, or performs a Monte Carlo simulation, to price a given option, one should therefore always have, in the back of one's mind, a 'parallel' tree or simulation in which the accompanying replicating hedging instruments are evolved. Strictly speaking, it is only the combined portfolio that will have zero variance, but one routinely takes an implicit 'mental short-cut', that can be reconstructed as follows:

- we dispense with the construction of the 'parallel' tree altogether;

- we recognize that the variance of return of the option by itself is anything but zero;

- we obtain the correct result by 'pretending' that the risk aversion of the investor (rather than the variance of the overall portfolio) is zero;

- we therefore discount the *uncertain* cashflows from the option considered in isolation at the riskless rate.

In other words, when we apply the expression $\mu = r + \lambda\sigma$ to the total portfolio, we 'cheat', and put λ rather than σ equal to zero. The advantage that we reap is that we can now dispense altogether with the parallel tree built 'in the back of our minds' and containing the perfect hedges.

When, however, a perfect hedge cannot be put in place, perhaps because of the existence of a jump component in the process, this convenient sleight of hand is no longer possible. The variance of the portfolio returns (the 'slippages' of Chapter 2) now becomes crucial,[17] together with the risk aversion of the investor. Valuing the option by itself (without the partial hedging strategy we have chosen) no longer makes sense, since the perfect hedging portfolio 'somewhere in the back of our minds' no longer exists. Similarly, simply looking at the variance of returns obtained by holding the 'naked' option does not make a lot of sense either, because *some* hedging, albeit imperfect, is certainly possible, and better than none. (See the results in Section 14.11 and Cochrane's (2001) quote that closes Section 1.5.) At the same time, since there is no such thing as *the* perfect hedging strategy, there is no single correct hedging portfolio. We have therefore reached the first conclusion, namely that the trader will obtain one overall variance of return for every imperfect hedge she might dream up. The financial subtleties, however, are not over yet.

Since we have been 'spoiled' by the familiar Brownian processes with perfect hedges, we have become accustomed to identifying absence of arbitrage with the existence of a unique price for the option. This is, however, a special case that applies only when a perfectly replicating strategy can be put together, and the returns from the total portfolio (i.e. the one made up of the option and of the parallel perfect hedging strategy 'in the back of our minds') can therefore be made purely deterministic. In general, however, given a set of possible prices for the securities traded in the market in different states of the world, three different cases can arise (see Pliska (1997) for a very clear discussion):

1. a pricing measure exists and is unique;

2. there are infinitely many pricing probability measures;

3. there are no pricing measures.

Case 1 applies when markets are complete, but case 2 is true if not every contingent claim is replicable (i.e. when markets are not complete). Arbitrage, however, should not be allowed to exist not only in the restrictive case 1, but also in case 2. If the problem is looked at in this manner, obtaining a unique price from a no-arbitrage argument, as is possible in case 1, is the exception rather than the rule, and the lack of uniqueness of option prices in the case of incomplete markets is very fundamental.

How can we observe in an incomplete market a single quoted price for an option, if that is the case? Because, out of the infinitely many possible pricing measures that could coexist in an incomplete market, 'the market' chooses a single one. The pricing measure is chosen among the infinitely many possible by the process of market clearing. This, incidentally, is the meaning of Bjork's (1998) often repeated quote: 'Who chooses the measure? The market!'

This observation has an interesting corollary. If option payoffs can be perfectly replicated, option prices contain no information about risk aversion. To the extent, however, that perfect replication is impossible, *some* information about risk aversion can be recovered from the observed market prices of options. Whether, to what extent, and under what conditions the investors' risk aversion can be recovered in practice, by itself or in conjunction with other statistically accessible quantities, from observations of option prices in incomplete markets is a complex topic. We can however make some qualitative observations. Let us assume for a moment that we have found an 'implied' methodology

---

[17]Actually, it is not just the variance that matters, unless one wants to impose some additional and strong conditions on the investor's utility function, but the full distribution of returns from the total portfolio.

by means of which, from the prices of plain-vanilla options, we manage to gain access to the investors' risk aversion (see, however, the discussion at the end of this section). Note in passing that, even if we could gain access to this jump risk aversion, what we could obtain from the market prices of options would only be related to the 'average' utility function of the market agents. For all its intrinsic interest, this quantity would not tell the individual trader how an equity option should be priced given *her* risk aversion (which will, in general, be different from the market's). To use Bjork's words again, in incomplete markets, the market itself, not the trader, chooses the pricing measure.

Let us none the less make for the moment another heroic assumption: let us suppose that the trader will adopt as her own the distilled market's risk aversion. Even in this case she would still have to evaluate at least the (non-zero) variance of return from the option and her chosen hedging strategy. As discussed, the relevant quantity for her is not the variance of returns from the (exotic) option in isolation, but the variance of returns from the option itself plus its proposed hedging strategy. As for the latter, not only can there be no such thing as a perfectly replicating strategy (by the very definition of market incompleteness); but there is not even an a priori general agreement about (or knowledge of) the 'best' hedging strategy. As mentioned above, the resulting overall variance of returns of the combined (exotic option + hedging strategy) portfolio, would therefore depend on the particular hedge chosen by the trader.

Looking at the problem in this light, the trader would seem to arrive at a price not only by taking into account her risk aversion, but also by carrying out a portfolio-variance-minimizing search over all the possible hedging strategies that can be put together using the instruments traded in the economy. This is less surprising than it might at first sound if one thinks of the pricing behaviour of an exotic trader who is faced with a new complex product; who begins to experiment with some tentative hedging strategies and quotes some rather 'defensive' prices; and who refines and becomes progressively more confident about her hedging strategy, and consequently 'tightens her price'.

The degree of portfolio variability (i.e. the distribution of slippages) that the trader can expect when employing a very simple hedging strategy and the underlying process is a jump–diffusion, is analysed in the following section where I bring to the forefront the imperfectly replicating portfolio that can safely lie in the deterministic-volatility case in 'the back of our minds'. The results should therefore be analysed in the light of the discussion of this section, and of the 'robustness' of the Black-and-Scholes pricing approach already examined in Chapters 4 and 13.

14.11   Portfolio Replication in Practice: The Jump–Diffusion Case

The treatment mirrors what we did in the stochastic-volatility case: the real-world (jump–diffusive) evolution of the stock price is simulated and an imperfectly replicating portfolio is constructed and rebalanced in parallel. At expiry (time T) we examine the slippages, defined in Chapter 4, between the terminal option payoff and the time-T value of the portfolio. The reader might want to re-read Section 13.6 and the observations made there about the non-self-financing nature of the trading strategy.

Once again, it is assumed that the trader does not know the true nature of the process of the underlying, but attempts to parameter-hedge an option purely on the basis of her knowledge of the average realized quadratic variation (including the jumps) and of the expectation of the jump amplitude ratio, Y_0:

$$\langle Y \rangle = Y_0 \tag{14.109}$$

The trader will recognize the value of the option as if it were given by the Black-and-Scholes formula with the associated average square root volatility as input. She will then attempt to protect the value of the option so calculated either by using only the stock, or by using the stock and another option. In either case she will have to decide how to translate into Black-and-Scholes-related quantities the hedge ratios obtained in Section 14.5 above. The next section explains how this can be done.

14.11.1 A Numerical Example

The Set-Up

I present in this section the results obtained when the initial stock price is \$100 and the option maturity is one year. To each path there will in general correspond a different realized root-mean-squared volatility, $\hat{\sigma}$, due both to the diffusive component (the same for each path as the trading frequency approaches infinity) and to the jumps. For the case study analysed below, the *average* root-mean-squared volatility, obtained computationally using a very large number of paths, turned out to be 17.10%. I assume that the trader knows this quantity exactly. For the purpose of future comparison, the cost of the (imperfectly) replicating portfolio obtained by using as input to the Black formula the average root-mean-squared volatilities above turned out to be \$9.37.

As mentioned, I will employ two hedging strategies, one based on the stock only, and the other based on the stock and another hedging option. This second option, h, will also be chosen to be approximately at-the-money, but to have a maturity of two years. With the first (stock-only) hedging strategy the amount of stock to hold will be assumed to be given by the Black-and-Scholes formula for the delta with the (perfectly known) average root-mean-squared volatility used as input.

For the second hedging strategy we have to choose a 'vega' amount of option to hold. We know that, even if the trader knew the true process and its parameters, no hedging strategy based on the stock and one option could provide an exact hedging. Recall that this is because in Equation (14.111) the quantity YS is stochastic (there is no single jump amplitude ratio). None the less, one can hope that an acceptable hedging might be achieved by 'pretending' that a single jump amplitude ratio existed, and that it was equal to its expectation. If this were the case the hedge ratios for the amounts to hold of the stock, α, and of the second option, γ, would be given by (see Equations (14.110) and (14.111) and (14.87)):

$$\alpha = -\frac{\partial C}{\partial S} - \gamma \frac{\partial h}{\partial S} \tag{14.110}$$

$$\gamma = -\frac{\dfrac{\partial C}{\partial S} - \dfrac{C(Y_0 S) - C(S)}{S Y_0 - S}}{\dfrac{\partial h}{\partial S} - \dfrac{h(Y_0 S) - h(S)}{S Y_0 - S}} \tag{14.111}$$

Evaluating the correct amount of hedging option would require knowing the correct derivatives of the two options prices with respect to the stock ($\frac{\partial C}{\partial S}$ and $\frac{\partial h}{\partial S}$). The trader, however, does not know these quantities, and therefore decides to approximate them with the derivatives of the Black-and-Scholes option prices with respect to the stock using as input the root-mean-squared volatility, $\widehat{\sigma}$. Note that this latter quantity *also incorporates the contributions from the jumps*:

$$\frac{\partial C(\sigma)}{\partial S} \simeq \frac{\partial C(\widehat{\sigma})}{\partial S} \tag{14.112}$$

$$\frac{\partial h(\sigma)}{\partial S} \simeq \frac{\partial h(\widehat{\sigma})}{\partial S} \tag{14.113}$$

As for the terms

$$C(Y_0 S) - C(S) \tag{14.114}$$

and

$$h(Y_0 S) - h(S) \tag{14.115}$$

the trader will simply use the Black-and-Scholes formula evaluated at S_t and at $S_t Y_0$, again with volatility $\widehat{\sigma}$, and with the appropriate strikes and maturities. During the course of each simulated path, the trader will have to buy and sell different amounts $\gamma(\widehat{\sigma})$ of the hedging option, h. I assume for simplicity that the 'market' prices for these transactions are given by the Black formula with the root-mean-squared volatility $\widehat{\sigma}$.

Overall the strategy is rather crude and could certainly be refined. It is however interesting to study how even this simple strategy will perform. This is presented below.

Exercise 3 *What would you do if the expectation of the jump amplitude ratio was $\langle Y \rangle = Y_0 = 1$?*

Exercise 4 *We assume that the trader (somehow) knew exactly the average quadratic variation. How could you make use of the results in Section 12.3.3 to obtain a theoretically incorrect (why?) but useful 'market estimate' of this quantity?*

Exercise 5 *Repeat the procedure described above, but without assuming that during the course of each simulation the trader finds the market prices of the option h at the Black prices with the root-mean-squared volatility $\widehat{\sigma}$. Assume instead that the market prices of the option h are given by the jump–diffusion formula presented above (see Section 14.6). Note carefully that the jump frequency and jump amplitude ratio in the pricing formula and in the simulation should not be the same.*

14.11.2   Results

In the computer experiments reported in this section I used 2048 paths of a 'smart' Monte Carlo, with a variable number of steps to the final maturity, as discussed below.

Looking at the results, the first observation is that 'optically' a hedging portfolio made up of a bond and the stock only will perform either very well (see Figure 14.33), or very

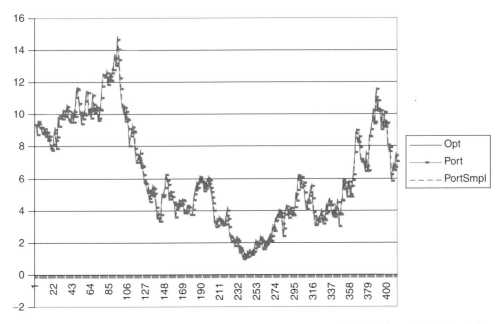

Figure 14.33   The behaviour of the call to be hedged (curve labelled 'Opt') and of the hedging portfolios when no jump occurs to the expiry of the first option (Mat_1). The hedging portfolio with the stock only is labelled 'PortSimpl', and the portfolio with the stock and an option is labelled 'Port'. The simulation parameters were $S_0 = 100$, $Strike_1 = 100$, $\sigma = 17.00\%$, $\nu = 0.2$, $RevLev = 100$, $RevSpeed = 0.2$, $Mat_1 = 1$, $r = 5\%$, $JAmpl = 0.90$, $JVol = 0.1$, $\lambda = 0.40$, $Mat_2 = 2$, $Strike_1 = 100$ and $Nsteps = 440$.

poorly (see Figure 14.34), according to whether a jump has occurred or not during the life of the option. The good performance of the stock-and-bond-only hedge in the absence of jumps is remarkable, given the number of crude approximations made in arriving at the hedge parameters (above all, the association of the average root-mean-squared volatility with the Black constant volatility). It is even more remarkable if one considers that, when no jumps occur, the estimate of the root-mean-squared volatility used to determine the Black hedging ratios is not only crude, but also biased. The trader in fact knows the correct *average* quadratic deviation of the process, but this average is over all the paths, i.e. the paths with no jumps and the fewer paths when jumps do occur. The average quadratic variation is therefore associated with neither type of path in isolation, and when jumps do not occur the realized quadratic will almost certainly be lower than what was assumed in setting up the hedges.

The same two figures display the performance of the hedging portfolio when vega hedging is undertaken. (Recall that, in order to vega-hedge, an option with the same strike but double maturity has been chosen.) When no jumps occur along the path the hedging performance is again optically almost perfect, but not significantly better than what was obtained using a stock-and-bond-only hedge. The difference in performance with and without vega hedging changes radically when a jump does occur (see Figure 14.34). Visually the quality of the tracking of the call value is remarkable, especially if we consider how simplistically the vega amount of stock had been calculated. See Equations (14.112)–(14.115). The first

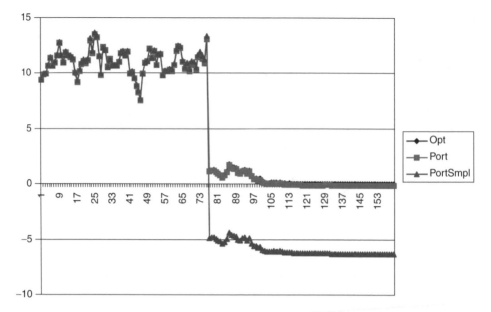

Figure 14.34   Same as Figure 14.33 when a jump does occur.

Table 14.12   Summary information of the hedging tests. See the text for a detailed explanation.

Nsteps	Avg(P-O)	StDev (P-O)	Avg (PSmpl-O)	StDev (PSmpl-O)	StDev(Opt)	Corr(Port)	Corr(Smpl)
10	0.072	1.184	−0.853	4.2202	9.4094	0.0946	−0.6518
20	0.014	0.957	−0.674	3.1938	9.1206	0.1291	−0.6516
40	0.054	0.573	−0.703	2.7375	9.1651	0.3285	−0.7390
80	0.054	0.525	−0.808	2.6074	9.7038	0.3182	−0.7472
160	0.075	0.826	−0.771	2.1738	8.3864	0.1816	−0.8266
320	0.018	0.553	−0.727	1.9762	10.1018	0.0245	−0.8278
440	0.036	0.686	−0.847	2.2092	9.6713	0.1267	−0.8533
440	0.059	0.482	−0.717	2.1002	8.8426	0.3196	−0.8145
440	0.063	0.548	−0.769	2.0189	9.5102	0.2374	−0.8219

qualitative conclusion is therefore that, even if the trader does not know the nature of the true process, let alone its exact parameters, but does know the average quadratic variation, an acceptable replication along the path can still be achieved by means of an approximate vega hedging.

Let us look at the quality of the hedging performance more quantitatively. Table 14.12 reports a wealth of information regarding the hedging simulations conducted as described in the previous section. The various columns display (starting from the left-most):

- Column 1: the number of re-hedging steps along the life of the option (one year).

- Column 2: the average of the differences (slippages) between the values at expiry of the replicating vega-hedged portfolio and of the option to be hedged. Note that this average does not appear to depend on the number of steps, and that it is a rather small, but consistently positive, number.

- Column 3: the standard deviation of the quantity whose average is reported in column 2. Note that the standard deviation decreases when the hedging frequency is increased from 20 times a year to approximately 80 times a year, but then appears to have reached an asymptotic value: we cannot reduce it any more, no matter how finely we re-hedge.

- Column 4: the average of the differences between the values at expiry of the replicating delta-hedged portfolio and of the option to be hedged. Unlike the vega-hedged case, the bias is now large (and strongly negative), and approximately independent of the re-hedging frequency.

- Column 5: the standard deviation of the quantity whose average is reported in column 4. The dispersion of the results is much greater than for the vega-hedged case. It also soon ceases to improve as a function of the re-hedging frequency.

- Column 6: the standard deviation of the payoffs from the naked (unhedged) option. This is reported in order to give an idea of the degree of replication brought about by the vega- and delta-hedging strategies. It is apparent that vega hedging reduces the slippages by up to a factor of 20, but delta hedging only by a factor of about 4. This result should be compared with the findings in the stochastic-volatility case (where introducing an option for hedging purposes was less effective in reducing the standard deviation).

- Column 7: the correlation between the deviation of the realized quadratic variation from its average level and the slippages in the case of the vega-hedged portfolio. If one engages in vega hedging it appears that the explanatory power of the realized quadratic variation to account for the (much smaller) slippages is rather poor. In other words, if we vega-hedge, the effectiveness of our strategy is no longer strongly dependent on the realized quadratic variation. Also in this case the results are different from the stochastic-volatility case. See Figure 14.35, which shows that in most of the cases the approximate vega hedging is successful in producing very small slippages for a variety of realized quadratic variations, but occasionally fails rather dramatically. This tends to occur when the underlying stock experiences a jump that brings the option to be hedged very close to the strike when there is little time to expiry (very high gamma).

- Column 8: the correlation between the deviation of the realized quadratic variation from its average level and the slippages in the case of the stock-only-hedged portfolio. The correlation is now very high, and becomes higher as the hedging frequency is increased. Whether we manage to replicate well or not now *does* depend on the random realized quadratic variation. Looking at Figure 14.36, one can recognize a high density of relatively small (and positive) slippages, and a low density of very large (and very negative) slippages, associated with low realized quadratic variation (no jumps) and high realized quadratic variation (jumps), respectively.

Finally, Figure 14.37 displays the histogram of the realized root-mean-squared volatilities. The very fat right tail is a direct consequence of the existence of jumps, and explains,

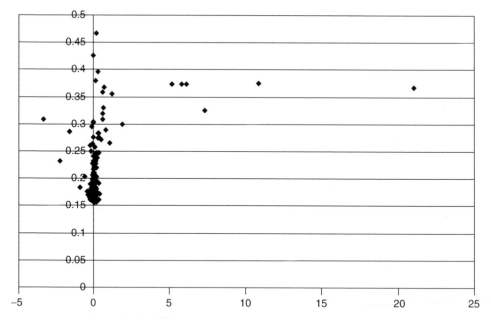

Figure 14.35   Realized root-mean-squared volatility vs slippages (vega hedging).

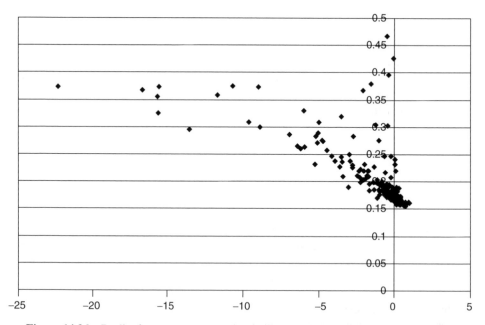

Figure 14.36   Realized root-mean-squared volatility vs slippages (stock-only hedging).

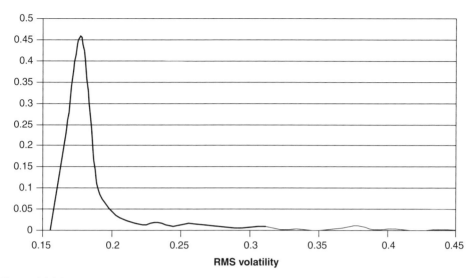

Figure 14.37 Histogram of the realized root-mean-squared volatilities obtained during the course of the simulation.

on the one hand, the existence of a pronounced smile, and on the other, the origin of the very large slippages in the delta-hedged case.

14.11.3 Conclusions

These results can be profitably compared with the stochastic-volatility case. In that case we found that, *if we assumed that we knew the average quadratic deviation*, for reasonable values of the volatility of the volatility and of the reversion speed of the volatility, vega hedging was producing a noticeable, but not dramatic, improvement. Again, it is difficult to generalize, but the magnitude of the improvement brought about by using a second option was comparable with what obtained in the deterministic-volatility case if the volatility is imperfectly known. When it comes to jump–diffusions, however, the situation changes and vega hedging becomes crucial. This is a direct consequence of the discontinuous nature of the paths. In the presence of jumps, being correctly delta hedged 'on average' is no longer adequate. Also, in our computer experiment we chose to hedge with a same-strike, different-maturity option. This was probably a good choice, because jumps produce the largest slippages when they suddenly bring an option close to at-the-money, thereby increasing its gamma. If the two options have a similar strike, they are more likely to experience a similar change in gamma.

Finally, it must be stressed that we are fully in parameter-hedging territory: the strategy cannot be guaranteed to be self-financing and, even if we put in place the 'cleverest' hedge, there will in general be some slippage at the end of any given path. Therefore the quantity to monitor is the distribution of the slippages (its variance, its tails, etc.) and only on the basis of this analysis will the trader be able to make a price. As I have argued throughout this book, however, while this situation is *theoretically* different from the deterministic-volatility (or, to some extent, the stochastic-volatility) case, *in practice* the existence of a finite-variance distribution of slippages is the norm and not the exception. Cochrane's (2001) remarks at the end of Chapter 1 are particularly valid also in this context.

Chapter 15

Variance–Gamma

15.1 Who Can Make Best Use of the Variance–Gamma Approach?

In Chapter 1 I drew a distinction between models that attempt to reproduce as accurately as possible the evolution of the future smile surface, and models that focus on recovering the dynamics of the underlying. In a 'perfect world' there should be no difference between the two sets of models: if the market is perfectly efficient in distilling the statistical properties of the process for the underlying into prices of plain-vanilla options, the model that best accounts for the properties of the underlying will also give rise to the best description of the present and future smiles (i.e. of the present and future prices of plain-vanilla options).

I also argued in Chapter 1 that in the real world the possibility should be at least entertained that the dynamics of the underlying and the price-making mechanism for the plain-vanilla options might be imperfectly coupled. If this was correct, the prices quoted by traders might not be compatible with any process displaying the properties that we expect of a reasonable description of the underlying (e.g. time homogeneity, smooth dependence of the option prices on the strike, perhaps, but not necessarily, unimodal risk-neutral price density, etc.).

I stated clearly in Chapter 1 what my views are: on the basis of the historical evolution of pricing practice (e.g. the sudden appearance of certain types of smiles) and of the difficulty of enforcing the pseudo-arbitrage that could make the option market more efficient, I strongly endorse the second ('imperfect') view of the world. The joint practices of vega re-hedging and model re-calibration together produce a logically inconsistent, but empirically very robust, approach to pricing *complex* derivatives (i.e. derivatives that take not only the stock process, but also the plain-vanilla options, as their underlyings). Simplifying greatly, one can reconstruct the practice of complex-derivatives trading as follows: the vega hedge is put in place on the trade date at the current market prices for hedging the complex option. Because of this the model should recover correctly the prices of these hedging instruments, hence the emphasis on the price recovery of the current plain-vanilla options. If the hedging instrument has been 'intelligently' chosen, the net residual deltas from the complex instrument and from the hedging portfolio will largely cancel out. If static replication is possible, the future prices of options would be irrelevant, and the dynamics both of the underlying and of the smile surface are irrelevant. Static replication (see Chapter 17) is however the exception rather than the rule, and, in general, future vega re-hedging will have to be carried out.[1] The more the trader has to vega re-hedge, the more she will become concerned about *future* option prices and stock price dynamics. Therefore I have argued that, given models that produce similar good-quality fits to today's plain-vanilla option prices, the approach should be chosen that gives rise to the most appealing evolution for the smile surface.

From the discussion above it follows that, if a choice has to be made, I endorse the view that the model should be chosen that best predicts the future evolution of the smile surfaces because it is likely to be the model that most efficiently incorporates in *today*'s price the cost of *future* vega re-hedging. If it also produces a convincing explanation of the dynamics of the underlying, this should be seen as an important added bonus (that reduces the degree of logical inconsistency in the approach), but not as the deciding factor in choosing a model.

Even if my views (and the logical inconsistencies they imply) are accepted for the pricing of complex derivatives, there is no denying that this approach is of little use to the plain-vanilla trader, who ultimately will want to engage in the type of gamma trading described in Chapter 4. Ultimately, the plain-vanilla trader will 'buy' volatility when she believes it to be cheap, and sell it when expensive.[2] If the trader were to vega hedge herself she would be writing away the very trading opportunity she set out to capture in the first place. Plain-vanilla traders are therefore most exposed to mis-specifications in the dynamics of the underlying, and should be more interested than complex traders in a model that provided a satisfactory description of the stochastic process for the underlying.[3] Much as the Black formula, with the market implied volatility, provides, by definition, the correct price, the delta (and the gamma and the vega, etc.) it produces is in general different from the delta (and the gamma and the vega, etc.) that the true model would give.

The variance–gamma approach presented in this chapter provides a very convincing description of the dynamics of the underlying. In particular, as I discuss in Section 15.3, a comparison of the empirical properties of the S&P dynamics with the predictions of the variance–gamma model reveals several very appealing features. For this reason it should be of great interest to the plain-vanilla traders.

The approach is financially motivated by the concept of 'trading time'. This concept is mathematically translated into a stochastic time change. Furthermore, the approach deserves careful attention because it dispenses altogether with a continuous component in the process for the underlying (no Brownian component), yet produces *time-homogeneous* fits to current option prices of similar quality to those obtained using stochastic-volatility

---

[1] A note on terminology: sometimes the term 'static replication' is used in the literature to denote strategies whereby a set of 'replicating' options are bought or sold at time t_0, and possibly unwound at a future point in time if a certain event occurs. I do not refer to these strategies as *static* replication, because the possibility that some option positions might have to be unwound before their expiry exposes the trader to uncertainty about the future smile. See the discussion in Chapter 17. I reserve the term 'static replication' to those (very few) cases where the initial replicating options are left to expire in or out of the money.

[2] This picture of the activity of a plain-vanilla trader is very simplistic: very often she will also be engaged in relative-value trades, where different portions of the smile surface are traded against each other. With some important caveats, the general considerations, however, remain valid.

[3] There are problems with marking-to-market and marking-to-model if the back- and front-office models are substantially different (for instance: when is the profit booked, when is the trader delta neutral, when is the trader breaking her limits?).

and/or jump–diffusion approaches. This at least suggests that what has always been regarded, since Bachelier onwards, as the 'natural' starting point for the modelling of a price process (possibly to be enriched but not to be abandoned), is perhaps just a convenient modelling tool, rather than an essential feature of a desirable modelling approach.

15.2 The Variance–Gamma Process

15.2.1 Definition

Following Madan *et al.* (1998), one can start from a standard, unit-variance, driftless Brownian motion, $B(t)$:

$$B(t) = W(t) \tag{15.1}$$

The first way to make this process more 'interesting' is to add a deterministic drift term, θ:

$$B(t; \theta) = \theta t + W(t) \tag{15.2}$$

So far the description, if not the notation, is wholly familiar. At this point, however, the stochastic term can be modified by allowing for a time change, i.e. by specifying a law that describes how the flow of time is altered. The simplest way is to prescribe a deterministic time change, via a constant (or purely time-dependent) volatility, σ. In this case the time-changed Brownian motion becomes

$$B(t; \theta, \sigma) = \theta t + \sigma W(t) \tag{15.3}$$

If this is done, we are still on very familiar ground, i.e. simply in a deterministic-volatility setting. Alternatively, one can prescribe that the time change should be stochastic, with a prescribed distribution. What we would like to be able to achieve is for the flow of time to accelerate or slow down in the future in a random fashion. Making time flow stochastic can be appealing, but, however complex this time flow might be, we must require that the clock should never 'tick back': our uncertainty about the future must always increase, albeit not necessarily at a constant or at a deterministic rate. This can be achieved as follows. If one requires that the Brownian motion should be evaluated at a time given by a gamma process, γ, with unit mean rate and variance ν:

$$\gamma = \gamma(t; 1, \nu) \tag{15.4}$$

one obtains a new process, X, defined by

$$X(t; \theta, \sigma, \nu) = B(\gamma(t; 1, \nu); \theta, \sigma) = \theta \gamma(t; 1, \nu) + \sigma W(\gamma(t; 1, \nu)) \tag{15.5}$$

This new process is called 'variance–gamma'. Note carefully that the 'stochastic time' enters both next to the drift θ and in the stochastic term. Requiring a unit mean rate for γ reflects the requirement that the 'average' flow of time is undisturbed: as the variance ν goes to zero, the adjusted time γ flows exactly as the clock time t.

15.2.2   Properties of the Gamma Process

The gamma process that enters the definition of the variance–gamma process has the following properties:

1. The process is infinitely divisible, with independent and identically distributed increments over non-overlapping intervals of identical length.

2. Consider a gamma process, γ, with mean rate μ and variance rate ν. The increment, g, of this gamma process over a finite interval, h,

$$g_h = \gamma(t + h; \mu, \nu) - \gamma(t; \mu, \nu) \tag{15.6}$$

has a distribution $f_h(g)$ given by

$$f_h(g) = \left(\frac{\mu}{\nu}\right)^{\frac{\mu^2 h}{\nu}} \frac{g^{\frac{\mu^2 h}{\nu} - 1} \exp\left(-\frac{\mu}{\nu} g\right)}{\Gamma\left(\frac{\mu^2 h}{\nu}\right)} \tag{15.7}$$

In this expression $\Gamma(.)$ denotes the gamma function.

3. Over time the gamma process undergoes discrete increments. The frequency of arrival of these increments depends on their size. Small increments have very high probability of occurrence. Large increments occur rarely. More quantitatively, the rate of arrival, k_γ, as a function of the jump size, x, is given by

$$k_\gamma(x) = \frac{\mu^2 \exp\left(-\frac{\mu}{\nu} x\right)}{\nu x}, \quad x > 0 \tag{15.8}$$

$$k_\gamma(x) = 0, \quad x < 0 \tag{15.9}$$

See Figure 15.1. We can therefore regard $k_\gamma(x)$ as a spectral frequency density. The integral of this spectral frequency density between jump size x_a and jump size x_b gives the rate of arrival of jumps in this size range. Integrating Equation (15.8) over all jump sizes produces a diverging result, indicating that the arrival rate is infinite. The process is none the less 'well behaved' (non-explosive), because the size of the jump decreases with the frequency. To simulate a gamma process one therefore truncates the spectral frequency density (15.8) below a jump size of magnitude ϵ.

15.2.3   Properties of the Variance–Gamma Process

From the construction above, *conditional on a particular realization of the time change g having occurred*, the density, ϕ, of the variance–gamma process, X, is clearly normal, and is given by

$$\phi(g)\,\mathrm{d}g = \frac{1}{\sigma\sqrt{2\pi g}} \exp\left[-\frac{(X - \theta g)^2}{2\sigma^2 g}\right] \mathrm{d}g \tag{15.10}$$

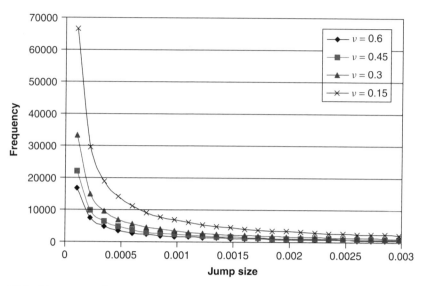

Figure 15.1   Frequency of arrival as a function of jump size for a gamma process ($\mu = 1$), for different variance rates.

Using Equation (15.7) with $\mu = 1$ one can then integrate (15.10) over all the time changes, g, to obtain for the unconditional density, $f_{X(t)}$,

$$
\begin{aligned}
f_{X(t)}(X) &= \int_0^\infty \phi(g) f_h(g)\, dg \\
&= \int_0^\infty \frac{1}{\sigma\sqrt{2\pi g}} \exp\left[-\frac{(X - \theta g)^2}{2\sigma^2 g}\right] f_h(g)\, dg \\
&= \int_0^\infty \frac{1}{\sigma\sqrt{2\pi g}} \exp\left[-\frac{(X - \theta g)^2}{2\sigma^2 g}\right] \frac{g^{\frac{t}{\nu}-1} \exp\left(-\frac{g}{\nu}\right)}{\nu^{\frac{t}{\nu}} \Gamma\left(\frac{h}{\nu}\right)}\, dg
\end{aligned}
\tag{15.11}
$$

The property of increasing arrival rate of jumps with decreasing jump size is inherited by the variance–gamma process from the gamma process. The rate of arrival, k_X, as a function of the jump size is in fact given by

$$
k_X(x) = \frac{\exp\dfrac{\theta x}{\sigma^2}}{\nu|x|} \exp\left(-\frac{\sqrt{\dfrac{2}{\nu} + \left(\dfrac{\theta}{\sigma}\right)^2}}{\sigma}|x|\right)
\tag{15.12}
$$

This density is shown in Figure 15.2 for three values of θ. This parameter controls the symmetry of the jumps: for $\theta < 0$ same-magnitude negative jumps are more likely than positive jumps, and vice versa for $\theta > 0$. The case $\theta = 0$ corresponds to a symmetric

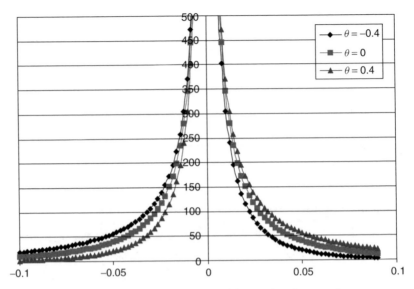

Figure 15.2 Frequency of arrival as a function of jump size for a variance–gamma process ($\sigma = 0.2$, $v = 0.25$), for different values of theta ($\theta = -0, 4, 0, 0.4$).

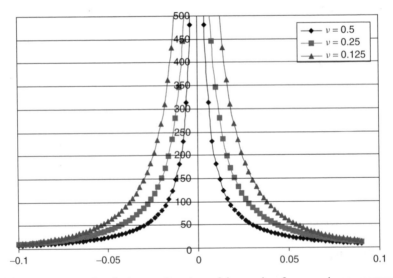

Figure 15.3 Frequency of arrival as a function of jump size for a variance–gamma process ($\sigma = 0.2$, $\theta = 0$), for different values of v ($v = 0.5, 0.250, 0.125$).

jump density. The ability to introduce a dependence of the arrival frequency on the sign of a given jump gives rise to skewed distributions, and to tilted smile curves.

As for the dependence of $k_X(x)$ on the variance rate v, the higher this quantity, the greater the likelihood of large-size jumps. This produces higher kurtosis for the associated density, higher tail probabilities, and more pronounced, but symmetric, smiles. See Figure 15.3.

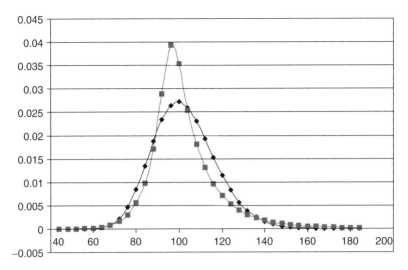

Figure 15.4 Risk-neutral densities obtained with a geometric Brownian motion (diamonds) and a variance–gamma process ($\theta = 0.1$, $\nu = 0.5$) with the same volatility ($\sigma = 20.0\%$). Time $= 0.5$ year, initial stock price $= \$100$.

Taken together, the parameters θ and ν therefore have the ability to give rise to asymmetric and leptokurtic distributions, and, therefore to 'smirky' smiles.

Finally, for the purpose of the statistical analysis presented later on, it is useful to give the expression, derived in Madan *et al.* (1998), for the density, h, of the logarithm of the stock price, $z \equiv \ln(\frac{S_t}{S_0})$:

$$h(z) = \frac{2 \exp\left(\dfrac{\theta x}{\sigma^2}\right)}{\nu^{\frac{t}{\nu}} \sqrt{2\pi}\, \sigma \Gamma\left(\dfrac{t}{\nu}\right)} \left(\frac{x^2}{\dfrac{2\sigma^2}{\nu + \theta^2}}\right)^{\frac{t}{2\nu} - \frac{1}{4}} \mathcal{K}_{\frac{t}{\nu} - \frac{1}{2}}\left(\frac{1}{\sigma^2}\sqrt{x^2 \frac{2\sigma^2}{\nu + \theta^2}}\right) \quad (15.13)$$

where $\mathcal{K}(.)$ is the modified Bessel function of the second kind, and

$$x = z - mt - \frac{t}{\nu} \ln\left(1 - \theta\nu - \frac{1}{2}\sigma^2\nu\right) \quad (15.14)$$

A typical density is shown in Figure 15.4.

15.2.4 Motivation for Variance–Gamma Modelling

The financial motivation behind modelling time as a random variable is that it is plausible and appealing to argue that 'economic' time does not flow with uniform speed, but is affected by the uneven arrival rate of unpredictable news. Given the unpredictable nature of the frequency of arrival of the individual pieces of information it is natural to associate a distribution to the length of an 'economic time' unit interval. By a suitable scaling via the deterministic time change, the 'normal speed of time' can be given a conventional value of one. Larger or smaller realizations for the economic length of the time interval would therefore correspond to more 'excited' or 'quieter' trading periods.

Furthermore, it is reasonable to assume that small pieces of news arrive frequently, while 'large surprises' should be rare. This is borne out by the distribution of jump sizes (see Figures 15.1 and 15.2). It is exactly because we are allowing for more and more frequent arrivals of pieces of information (jumps) as their magnitude decreases that we can dispense with a continuous Brownian component: all increments are discontinuous (jumps), but the more frequent ones are very small jumps (perhaps down to tick-size moves).

Finally, as mentioned above, whatever distribution we might want to give to the length of the economic time interval, we must ensure that, as physical time increases, economic time must also increase (possibly at a lower, but never at a negative, rate: 'surprises' can never disappear).

15.2.5 Properties of the Stock Process

In moving from the Black-and-Scholes universe to the new setting, the dynamics of the stock price is simply obtained by replacing the Brownian motion with a variance–gamma process. One must distinguish carefully, however, between the stock price evolution in the statistical (real) world, and in the risk-neutral world. Let us denote by m the mean rate of return of the stock under the objective measure, and by r the riskless rate. Then the evolution of the stock price in the real and risk-neutral worlds, respectively, are given by

$$S_t = S_0 \exp[mt + X(t; \sigma_{rw}, \nu_{rw}, \theta_{rw}) + \omega_{rw}t] \tag{15.15}$$

and

$$S_t = S_0 \exp[rt + X(t; \sigma_{rn}, \nu_{rn}, \theta_{rn}) + \omega_{rn}t] \tag{15.16}$$

where the subscripts 'rw' and 'rn' denote the real-world and the risk-neutral measures. The terms ω_{rw} and ω_{rn} ensure that the expectation of the stock price return should be equal to the statistical or risk-neutral return, respectively. Therefore, they play the same role as the compensator introduced for jump–diffusion processes. More precisely, in the real world one must require that

$$E_0[S_t] = S_0 \exp(mt) = E_0[S_0 \exp((m + \omega_{rw})t + X_{rw})]$$

$$= S_0 \exp((m + \omega_{rw})t \ E_0[X_{rw}] \tag{15.17}$$

$$\rightarrow E_0[X_{rw}] = \exp(-\omega_{rw}t) \tag{15.18}$$

Similarly, in the risk-neutral world one obtains (see Madan *et al.* (1998))

$$E_0[X_{rn}] = \exp(-\omega_{rn}t) \tag{15.19}$$

Explicitly:

$$\omega_{rw} = \frac{1}{\nu_{rw}} \ln\left[1 - \theta_{rw}\nu_{rw} - \frac{1}{2}\sigma_{rw}^2\nu_{rw}\right] \tag{15.20}$$

and

$$\omega_{\text{rn}} = \frac{1}{v_{\text{rn}}} \ln\left[1 - \theta_{\text{rn}} v_{\text{rn}} - \frac{1}{2}\sigma_{\text{rn}}^2 v_{\text{rn}}\right] \tag{15.21}$$

Note that, unlike the purely diffusive case, where the volatility is invariant under the Girsanov measure transformation, no process parameter remains unchanged in moving from the objective to the risk-neutral measure.

15.2.6   Option Pricing

Brute Force

The brute-force approach to obtaining the price of a call option is computationally ineffi-cient, but conceptually very transparent. It also provides the conceptual route to arriving at the more sophisticated pricing formulae presented below. It is obtained by recognizing that, contingent on a particular value of g (the 'informationally-adjusted' length of the unit time interval) having been realized, the quantity $X(t)$ is normally distributed, with mean θg and variance $\sigma^2 g$. This being the case, the probability of X being in the range $[X\ X + dX]$, $\psi(X_t, g)\,dX$, conditional on the realization g, is given by

$$\psi(X_t, g)\,dX = \frac{1}{\sigma\sqrt{2\pi g}} \exp\left(-\frac{[X - \theta g]^2}{2\sigma^2 g}\right) dX \tag{15.22}$$

As for the probability of the 'time' g lying in the interval $[g\ g + dg]$, $\phi(g)$, it is given by (see Equation (15.7))

$$\phi(g, t, v) = \frac{g^{\frac{t}{v}-1} \exp\left(-\frac{g}{v}\right)}{v^{\frac{t}{v}} \Gamma\left(\frac{t}{v}\right)} \tag{15.23}$$

with $\Gamma(.)$ the gamma function. So, the *unconditional* probability density of X being in the range $[X\ X + dX]$, $f(X_t, g)dX$, is obtained by integrating $\psi(X_t, g)$ over the density for g, (15.23), and is given by

$$f(X_t, g) = \int_0^\infty \psi(X_t, g)\phi(g, t, v)\,dg$$

$$= \int_0^\infty \frac{1}{\sigma\sqrt{2\pi g}} \exp\left(-\frac{[X - \theta g]^2}{2\sigma^2 g}\right) \frac{g^{\frac{t}{v}-1} \exp\left(-\frac{g}{v}\right)}{v^{\frac{t}{v}} \Gamma\left(\frac{t}{v}\right)} \,dg \tag{15.24}$$

Consider a European option. Its payoff at time t is given by *Payoff*(S_t). The realization of the stock price at time t is given by

$$S_t = S_0 \exp[rt + X(t; \sigma_{\text{rn}}, v_{\text{rn}}, \theta_{\text{rn}}) + \omega_{\text{rn}}t] \tag{15.25}$$

and, dropping the subscripts 'rn', the payoff is therefore

$$Payoff(S_t) = Payoff(S_0 \exp[rt + X(t; \sigma, \nu, \theta) + \omega t]) \tag{15.26}$$

which has the same probability of occurrence as $X(t; \sigma, \nu, \theta)$. The price, P, of the variance–gamma European option is therefore obtained by integrating the terminal payoff over the distribution of g:

$$P = \int_0^\infty Payoff(S_t) \frac{1}{\sigma\sqrt{2\pi g}} \exp\left(-\frac{[X - \theta g]^2}{2\sigma^2 g}\right) \frac{g^{\frac{t}{\nu}-1} \exp\left(-\frac{g}{\nu}\right)}{\nu^{\frac{t}{\nu}} \Gamma\left(\frac{t}{\nu}\right)} \, dg$$

$$= \int_0^\infty Payoff(S_0 \exp[rt + X(t) + \omega t]) \frac{1}{\sigma\sqrt{2\pi g}}$$

$$\times \exp\left(-\frac{[X - \theta g]^2}{2\sigma^2 g}\right) \frac{g^{\frac{t}{\nu}-1} \exp\left(-\frac{g}{\nu}\right)}{\nu^{\frac{t}{\nu}} \Gamma\left(\frac{t}{\nu}\right)} \, dg \tag{15.27}$$

with $X(t) = X(t; \sigma, \nu, \theta)$. So, for instance, for a European call option struck at K, $Call(S_t, K)$, one obtains:

$$Call(S_t, K)$$

$$= \int_0^\infty (S_0 \exp[rt + X(t) + \omega t] - K)^+ \frac{1}{\sigma\sqrt{2\pi g}}$$

$$\times \exp\left(-\frac{[X - \theta g]^2}{2\sigma^2 g}\right) \frac{g^{\frac{t}{\nu}-1} \exp\left(-\frac{g}{\nu}\right)}{\nu^{\frac{t}{\nu}} \Gamma\left(\frac{t}{\nu}\right)} \, dg \tag{15.28}$$

which, in the brute-force approach, can be easily integrated numerically.

Semi-Brute Force

The next step towards obtaining a semi-analytic expression for the call option price is to recognize that, again contingent on a particular value for the 'time' g having been realized, the corresponding conditional option price, $Call(g)$, is simply a Black price. More precisely, if one defines

$$\zeta \equiv -\frac{\theta}{\sigma^2} \tag{15.29}$$

$$s = \frac{\sigma}{\sqrt{1 + \left(\frac{\theta}{\sigma}\right)^2 \frac{\nu}{2}}} \tag{15.30}$$

$$\alpha = \zeta s \tag{15.31}$$

the conditional price, $Call(g)$, is given by

$$Call(g) = S_0 \left(1 - \frac{v(\alpha + s)^2}{2}\right)^{\frac{t}{v}} \exp\left(\frac{g(\alpha + s)^2}{2}\right) \mathcal{N}\left(\frac{d}{\sqrt{g}} + (\alpha + s)\sqrt{g}\right)$$

$$- K\exp(-rt)\left(1 - \frac{v\alpha^2}{2}\right)^{\frac{t}{v}} \exp\left(\frac{g\alpha^2}{2}\right) \mathcal{N}\left(\frac{d}{\sqrt{g}} + \alpha\sqrt{g}\right) \qquad (15.32)$$

with

$$d = \frac{1}{s}\left[\ln\frac{S_0}{K} + \left(r + \frac{1}{v}\ln\left[\frac{1 - \frac{v(\alpha + s)^2}{2}}{1 - \frac{v\alpha^2}{2}}\right]\right)t\right]$$

The unconditional call price, $Call(S_t, K)$, is therefore obtained by integrating numerically over the density for g:

$$Call(S_t, K) = \int_0^\infty Call(g) \frac{g^{\frac{t}{v} - 1}\exp\left(-\frac{g}{v}\right)}{v^{\frac{t}{v}}\Gamma\left(\frac{t}{v}\right)} \, dg \qquad (15.33)$$

Mutatis mutandis, there is an obvious similarity between this result and the pricing formulae we obtained for jump–diffusion and stochastic-volatility processes (at least in the case of zero correlation).

Semi-Analytic Solution Using Special Functions

Equation (15.33) is already usable for practical pricing purposes. One can however do even better. First, the option price can be expressed semi-analytically in terms of modified Bessel functions of the second kind and of the degenerate hypergeometric function (two variables). This is achieved again by conditioning on a particular random time g, and recognizing, as in the 'brute-force' approach above, that, once this conditioning is done, the distribution of the logarithm of the stock price is normal. The call option price is then obtained by integrating with respect to the gamma density. More precisely, the call pricing formula has a familiar Black-like structure (see Madan *et al.* (1998) for a derivation):

$$C(S_0, K, T, r) = S_0 \Psi\left(d\sqrt{\frac{1 - c_1}{v}}, (\alpha + s)\sqrt{\frac{v}{1 - c_1}}, \frac{T}{v}\right)$$

$$- K\exp(-rT)\Psi\left(d\sqrt{\frac{1 - c_2}{v}}, \alpha s\sqrt{\frac{v}{1 - c_2}}, \frac{T}{v}\right) \qquad (15.34)$$

with r the (constant) short rate, K the strike and T the time to option expiry. (See Madan *et al.* (1998) for a description of the symbols, and a precise definition of the distribution $\Psi(.).$)

15.3   Statistical Properties of the Price Distribution

I mentioned in the introductory section that one of the most appealing features of the variance–gamma approach (at least for a plain-vanilla trader) is the fact that it recovers well the statistical properties of equity indices. More precisely, Madan *et al.* (1998) use transaction prices for S&P futures and for the associated options over the period January 1992 to September 1994. The closing prices for the S&P index over the same period were also available. By analysing these data Madan *et al.* reached the following conclusions.

15.3.1   The Real-World (Statistical) Distribution

In order to answer the question as to whether the variance–gamma distribution can adequately describe the observed log returns, the following 'horse race' was set up: three competing distributions were considered, the log-normal one, the symmetric variance–gamma (obtained by setting $\theta = 0$), and the full variance–gamma distribution described above. The parameters of the distribution were then fitted using a maximum-likelihood estimation procedure to the available data (closing prices). Expression (15.13) was used for the variance–gamma distribution (in the nested symmetric case the parameter θ was kept fixed at 0).

The mean return was found to lie in the range between 5.69% (log-normal case) and 5.91% (full variance–gamma case). Also the fitted standard deviation turned out to be similar, ranging from 11.71% (symmetric variance–gamma case) to 11.91% (log-normal case).

Moving to the third moment, the skew parameter θ was found to be insignificantly different from 0 when the full variance–gamma distribution was used. As for the excess kurtosis, both the symmetric and the full variance–gamma distribution gave a (significant) daily excess kurtosis of 0.002.

After this fitting is done, which distribution best fits the empirical (real-world) distribution of returns? A chi-squared test strongly rejected the log-normal distribution in favour of the symmetric variance–gamma one ($\chi^2 = 83.94$). It is important to note, however, that, *when the statistical distribution of returns is used*, no improvement is observed in moving from the symmetric to the full variance–gamma case: at least over the period of observation, the return distribution is fat tailed, but not asymmetric (in log space).

15.3.2   The Risk-Neutral Distribution

The picture changes radically when we move from the real-world to the risk-neutral distributions. These are obtained by a least-squares fit to the observed option prices (see Madan *et al.* (1998) for a detailed discussion of the procedure).

The estimates of the second moment are not dramatically different: the full variance–gamma distribution gives 11.48%, the symmetric variance–gamma distribution 13.01% and the log-normal distribution 12.13%.

However, the kurtosis estimate for the symmetric and full variance–gamma cases are substantially higher (0.1861 and 0.1686) than what was found using real-world returns. Furthermore, the skew parameter is now significantly different from zero, and negative: $\theta = -0.1436$. This negative skewness, and a significant excess kurtosis, would be expected in the presence of risk aversion (see the discussion in Madan *et al.* (1998) for

the simple case of a one-period economy with HARA utility and marginal utility given
by $(1 + e^x)^{-1}$).

As for the horse race in the risk-neutral world, the log-normal (Black-and-Scholes)
model is rejected in 30.8% of the cases when pitted against the symmetric variance–gamma model, but 91.6% of the time when compared with the full variance–gamma
model. Also, the full (asymmetric) variance–gamma model is preferred to the symmetric
model 91.6% of the time.

Therefore, in moving from the real to the risk-neutral world, the Black-and-Scholes
approach becomes more attractive than the symmetric variance–gamma model; however, the full variance–gamma model, which was statistically indistinguishable from its
symmetric version in the real world, now becomes the clear winner.

15.4   Features of the Smile

The shape of the smile surface obtained with the parameters estimated by Madan *et al.*
is shown in Figures 15.5–15.12.

The following features are worthwhile noting. The smile produced by the variance–gamma model displays characteristics rather similar to jump–diffusion smiles. This
is not surprising, given the discontinuous nature of the process. Plotted as a function of
strike, the smile is steep at the short end, and flattens out for longer maturities. This
ability to produce steep smiles for short maturities is important, and is not shared by
stochastic-volatility models (unless one uses high volatility of volatility and high mean

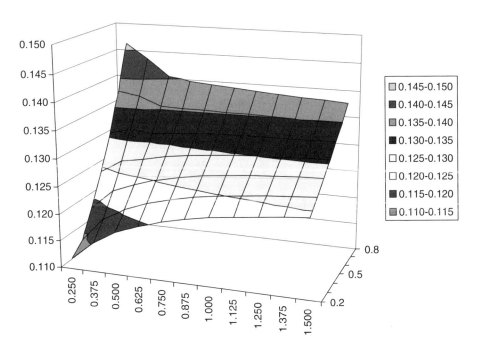

Figure 15.5 Smile as a function of delta (0.2–0.8) for expiries from 0.25 to 1.5 years (Madan
et al. parameters).

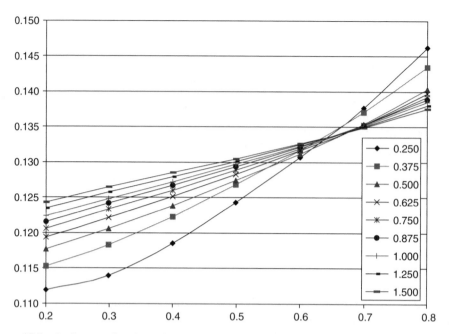

Figure 15.6   Smile as a function of delta (0.2–0.8) for expiries from 0.25 to 1.5 years (Madan *et al*. parameters). Cross-section of the surface.

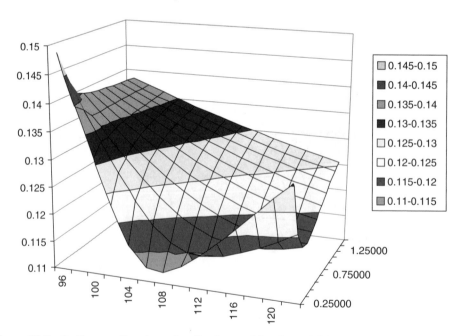

Figure 15.7   Smile as a function of strike for expiries from 0.25 to 1.5 years (Madan *et al*. parameters).

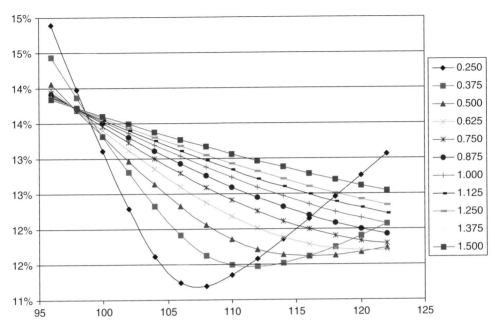

Figure 15.8 Smile as a function of strike for expiries from 0.25 to 1.5 years (Madan *et al.* parameters). Cross-section of the surface.

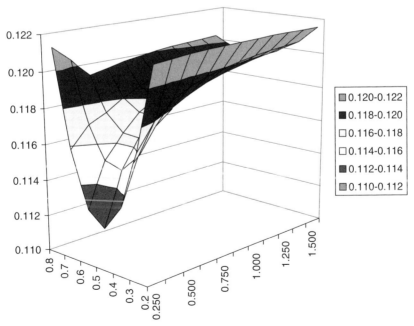

Figure 15.9 Smile as a function of delta (0.2–0.8) for expiries from 0.25 to 1.5 years (Madan *et al.* parameters for the symmetric variance–gamma model $-\theta = 0.0$).

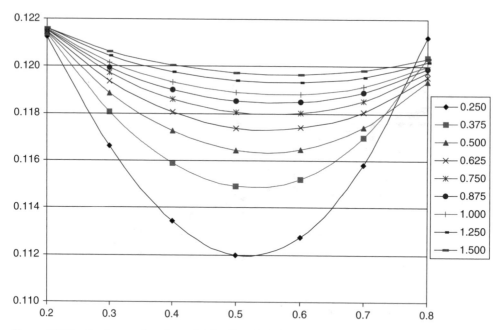

Figure 15.10   Smile as a function of delta (0.2–0.8) for expiries from 0.25 to 1.5 years (Madan *et al.* parameters for the symmetric variance–gamma model $-\theta = 0.0$). Cross-section of the surface.

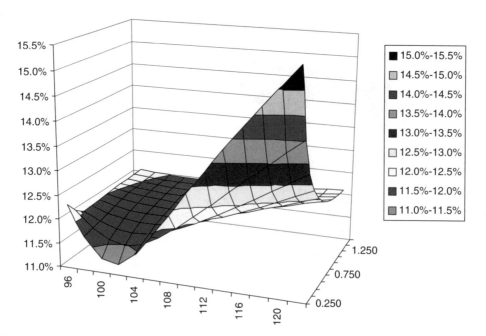

Figure 15.11   Smile as a function of strike for expiries from 0.25 to 1.5 years (Madan *et al.* parameters for the symmetric variance–gamma model $-\theta = 0.0$).

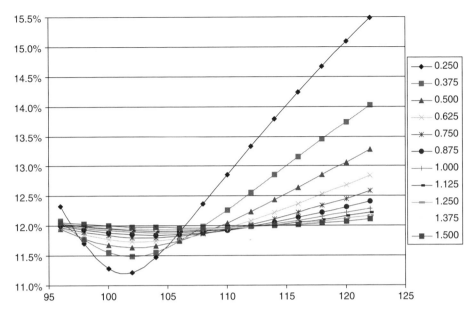

Figure 15.12 Smile as a function of strike for expiries from 0.25 to 1.5 years (Madan *et al.* parameters for the symmetric variance–gamma model $-\theta = 0.0$). Cross-section of the surface.

reversion). If the real-world parameters are used, the smile is approximately symmetric both in delta space and in strike space. This is not in agreement with market data.

If the risk-neutral parameters are used, the plots of the smile, both as a function of strike and as a function of delta, display a marked asymmetry, which persists for long maturities. For short maturities the smile is monotonically decreasing for all maturities as a function of delta, but has a 'hockey-stick' shape as a function of strike. Even when the smile hooks its way back up towards out-of-the-money calls, it remains markedly asymmetric.

The flattening of the smile, in both the symmetric and the asymmetric cases for increasing maturities, is due to the assumption of independence of the increments and to the Central Limit Theorem, so it is neither surprising nor peculiar to the variance–gamma process. See, however, the discussion in Section 7.3.2 of Chapter 7 (in particular, the subsection 'Persistence of the Smirk as a Function of At-the-Moneyness').

In both the symmetric and the asymmetric cases, the level of the at-the-money volatility increases as a function of maturities, *even if all the process parameters are time independent*. This observation is important: if one only looked at at-the-money volatilities, and naively tried to impute a time dependence of the volatility assuming a pure diffusive process (as suggested, for instance, in Chapter 3 in the absence of smiles), one would conclude that the volatility would have to be time dependent, and increasing. The analysis of the properties of the variance–gamma process, however, shows that this need not be the case.

15.5 Conclusions

The variance–gamma process enjoys many positive features, especially for the plain-vanilla trader. Its description of financial reality is simple and convincing, and, at least in the equity case, well corroborated by empirical evidence. It is unlikely that the model tells 'the full story' (and it was probably not designed to do so). It must be recalled, for instance, that the future smiles it implies are perfectly deterministic, i.e. contingent upon a future realization of the stock price there is one and only one possible smile associated with it. I consider this feature (incidentally also shared by jump–diffusion processes) at best an expedient approximation to market reality.

From the perspective of a complex-derivatives trader, it is unlikely that just a handful of (time-independent) parameters will suffice to reproduce exactly the observed market prices. On the other hand, if the trader could 'live with' the initial mis-pricing of the plain-vanilla options needed for the day-one hedging, the evolution of the smile surface predicted by the model (the second important desideratum for a complex trader) is likely to be plausible and appealing, at least in an 'average' sense (see the comment above regarding the deterministic nature of the future smile surfaces).

Chapter 16

Displaced Diffusions and Generalizations

16.1 Introduction

Displaced diffusion is a very simple variation on the geometric diffusion theme that, to my knowledge, was first introduced by Rubinstein (1983). The distinguishing feature of a displaced-diffusion process is the requirement that the quantity $S_t + a$, rather than S_t, should follow a geometric Brownian process:

$$\frac{\mathrm{d}(S_t + a)}{S_t + a} = \mu_a \, \mathrm{d}t + \sigma_a \, \mathrm{d}z_t \tag{16.1}$$

In Equation (16.1) μ_a and σ_a are the percentage drift and volatility of the quantity $S_t + a$ and the constant a (normally chosen to be positive for reasons that will become clear below) is called the displacement coefficient. As for the quantity S, it can be interpreted to be a forward or spot stock price, an index level, an FX rate or an interest rate.

Displaced diffusions are useful because they combine extreme simplicity with an interesting link to constant-elasticity-of-variance (CEV) processes. This link will be explored in detail in Chapter 24. The reasoning will be that, while CEV processes have more appealing theoretical properties (see below), displaced diffusions can often be 'made to resemble' CEV diffusions very closely while retaining the analytical simplicity of a log-normal setting. See Marris (1999). Despite the fact that this is, in my opinion, possibly their greatest appeal, in this chapter I will consider displaced-diffusion processes in their own rights.

The main drawback of displaced diffusions is that it is only the quantity $S + a$, rather than S, that is guaranteed to be positive. Therefore, if a is positive, S can assume values between $-a$ and $+\infty$. Since we typically would like the quantities we model (equity prices, rates, etc.) to be strictly positive, this constitutes an obvious drawback. By the same token, however, a displaced-diffusion approach can be particularly suitable for modelling inflation, especially in environments when disinflation is a real possibility. I do not pursue this angle in this book.

I will use displaced diffusions extensively in the chapter devoted to stochastic-volatility extensions of the LIBOR market model (Chapter 20). I insert a discussion of their properties at this point, however, because they constitute a natural complement to the jump–diffusion, stochastic-volatility or Kolmogorov approaches.

16.2   Gaining Intuition

16.2.1   First Formulation

In order to get an intuitive feel for the properties of displaced diffusions, let us start from a description of the dynamics of the forward 'stock price', S, under its own terminal measure as a mixture of a normal and a log-normal responsiveness to the same Brownian shock, dz_t:

$$dS_t = \sigma_{\text{abs}}\, dz_t + S_t \sigma_{\text{log}}\, dz_t \qquad (16.2)$$

The reason for working in terms of a forward rather than a spot price is that, because of the absence of the drift term, the treatment is going to be somewhat simpler. Equation (16.2) can be rewritten as

$$dS_t = \sigma_{\text{log}}\left(S_t + \frac{\sigma_{\text{abs}}}{\sigma_{\text{log}}}\right) dz_t \qquad (16.3)$$

Since, for any constant a, $dS = d(S+a)$, Equation (16.3) can be written as

$$dS_t = d\left(S_t + \frac{\sigma_{\text{abs}}}{\sigma_{\text{log}}}\right) = \sigma_{\text{log}}\left(S_t + \frac{\sigma_{\text{abs}}}{\sigma_{\text{log}}}\right) dz_t \qquad (16.4)$$

and therefore

$$\frac{d\left(S_t + \frac{\sigma_{\text{abs}}}{\sigma_{\text{log}}}\right)}{\left(S_t + \frac{\sigma_{\text{abs}}}{\sigma_{\text{log}}}\right)} = \sigma_{\text{log}}\, dz_t \qquad (16.5)$$

Comparing Equations (16.5) and (16.1) (with $\mu_a = 0$), it is clear that they have exactly the same form, provided that we equate

$$\frac{\sigma_{\text{abs}}}{\sigma_{\text{log}}} = a \qquad (16.6)$$

and

$$\sigma_{\text{log}} = \sigma_a \qquad (16.7)$$

Therefore a displaced diffusion with displacement coefficient a can be seen as a process whereby the underlying has two distinct types of responsiveness to the same Brownian motion, one proportional to the level of the underlying (via the coefficient σ_{log}) and one absolute (via the coefficient σ_{abs}), and where the displacement coefficient is given by the ratio of the two sensitivities to the Brownian shock. Equation (16.6) also shows that the process will tend to a purely log-normal process as the coefficient a goes to zero, and to a normal diffusion as a goes toward infinity.

Exercise 1 *How are the results of this section to be modified if the underlying S has a non-zero drift? [Hint: Recall that, under the pricing measure, the drift of the underlying is fully determined by no-arbitrage arguments.]*

16.2.2 Second Formulation

Another simple manipulation of Equation (16.1) can be useful in the context of the discussion of the link between displaced diffusions and CEV processes (see Chapter 24). See Marris (1999). Let us write (ignoring the drift again)

$$dS_t = \left[\gamma S_t + (1 - \gamma)S_0\right]\sigma_\gamma \, dz_t \tag{16.8}$$

Note that, despite the fact that the term in square brackets looks like a weighted average, the term $(1 - \gamma)S_0$ is actually just a constant, say ξ. Clearly, if γ is zero we are in the normal-diffusion case, with $\sigma_{abs} = S_0\sigma_\gamma$. For any other value of γ, one can write

$$dS_t = \left[S_t + \frac{\xi}{\gamma}\right]\gamma\sigma_\gamma \, dz_t \tag{16.9}$$

and, looking back at Equation (16.1), one can readily make the identification

$$S_t + a = S_t + \frac{\xi}{\gamma} \rightarrow \frac{\xi}{\gamma} = \frac{(1 - \gamma)S_0}{\gamma} = a \tag{16.10}$$

$$\sigma_a(t) = \gamma\sigma_\gamma \tag{16.11}$$

This second formulation might seem less transparent than the first one, but it will provide a clear link between the displaced diffusion and the CEV process, as discussed in Chapter 24.

16.3 Evolving the Underlying with Displaced Diffusions

Because of the log-normal character of the process for $(S_t + a)$, it is very easy to obtain a closed-form expression for the underlying at a later time T. The realization of S_T, given its value S_t at time t, is in fact given by

$$S_T = (S_t + a)\left[\exp \int_t^T \mu_a(u) \, du - \tfrac{1}{2}\sigma_a^2(u) \, du + \sigma_a(u) \, dz_u\right] - a \tag{16.12}$$

or, equivalently, in terms of γ and σ_γ

$$S_T = \frac{S_t}{\gamma}\left[\exp \int_t^T \mu_a(u) \, du - \tfrac{1}{2}\gamma^2\sigma_\gamma^2(u) \, du + \gamma\sigma_\gamma(u) \, dz_u - 1\right] \tag{16.13}$$

Note that expressions (16.12) and (16.13) are truly closed-form solutions only if the drifts are purely a function of time. Once the no-arbitrage requirements are imposed this will, in general, no longer be case. There are, however, well-established numerical techniques to deal with this problem: see, for example, Kloeden and Platen (1992), Hunter *et al.* (2001) and Rebonato (2002).

16.4 Option Prices with Displaced Diffusions

Call option prices are particularly easy to obtain. The reasoning goes as follows. Let us denote the price of a T-expiry, K-strike caplet today (time t_0) when the underlying process is a displaced diffusion with displacement coefficient a by $Caplet_a(t_0, T, K)$. This price is given by the discounted expectation of the terminal payoff under the terminal measure, Q:

$$Caplet_a(t_0, T, K) = \mathrm{E}_{t_0}^Q\left[(S_T - K)^+\right] P(t_0, T) \tag{16.14}$$

where $\mathrm{E}_{t_0}^Q$ denotes the expectation at time t_0 under Q, and $P(t_0, T)$ is the time-t_0 value of the discount bond maturing at time T. By adding and subtracting the displacement coefficient under the expectation sign, Equation (16.14) can be written as

$$\mathrm{E}_{t_0}^Q\left[(S_T - K)^+\right] B(t_0, T) = \mathrm{E}_{t_0}^Q\left[((S_T + a) - (K + a))^+\right] P(t_0, T) \tag{16.15}$$

If we denote by Ψ_a the Q-probability density of $S_T + a$, the RHS of Equation (16.15) can be rewritten as

$$\mathrm{E}_{t_0}^Q\left[((S_T + a) - (K + a))^+\right]$$
$$= \int_{K+a}^\infty (S_T + a)\Psi_a \, \mathrm{d}(S_T + a) - (K + a) \int_{K+a}^\infty \Psi_a \, \mathrm{d}(S_T + a) \tag{16.16}$$

We know, however, that, because of (16.1), the distribution of the logarithm of $(S_T + a)$ is normal. Therefore one can write

$$\int_{K+a}^\infty (S_T + a)\Psi_a \, \mathrm{d}(S_T + a) - (K + a) \int_{K+a}^\infty \Psi_a \, \mathrm{d}(S_T + a)$$
$$= (S_0 + a)\mathcal{N}(h_1^a) - (K + a)\mathcal{N}(h_2^a) \tag{16.17}$$

with

$$h_1^a = \frac{\ln \frac{S_0 + a}{K + a} + \frac{1}{2}v_a^2}{v_a} \tag{16.18}$$

$$h_2^a = \frac{\ln \frac{S_0 + a}{K + a} - \frac{1}{2}v_a^2}{v_a} \tag{16.19}$$

with $\mathcal{N}(.)$ denoting the cumulative normal distribution and with

$$v_a^2 = \int_{t_0}^{T} \sigma_a^2(u)\, du \qquad (16.20)$$

Putting the pieces together we have

$$Call_a(S_0, T, K, \sigma_a) = \left[(S_0 + a)\mathcal{N}(h_1^a) - (K + a)\mathcal{N}(h_2^a)\right] P(t_0, T) \qquad (16.21)$$

Therefore, the price of a call when the process follows a displaced diffusion is simply given by the Black formula, evaluated with the new 'stock price' given by $S_{t_0} + a$, with a strike equal to $K + a$, and with a volatility equal to $\frac{v_a}{\sqrt{T}}$. The only quantity that is not obviously obtainable from the market price is the volatility v_a (or σ_a) to be used in Equation (16.21). This topic is addressed in the next section.

16.5 Matching At-The-Money Prices with Displaced Diffusions

16.5.1 A First Approximation

Suppose that the underlying forward rate or stock price follows a geometric (non-displaced) diffusion with percentage volatility, $\sigma_{\log}$. For a generic strike, K, and a given expiry, T, this process will produce the Black call price, $Black(S_0, K, T, \sigma_{\log})$. (Note that S_0 denotes the *forward* price today.) We can ask the following question: if the process were instead a diffusion of the type (16.1), what volatility σ_a would produce the same call price for the strike K? For simplicity I am going to assume that both $\sigma_{\log}$ and σ_a are constant; the extension to the time-dependent case is straightforward. To keep the notation simple I am also going to ignore discounting. Since we know analytically the price for a K-strike call when the process is a displaced diffusion (see (16.21) above) we have to find the displaced volatility σ_a such that the at-the-money log-normal and displaced-diffusion prices are the same:

$$(S_0 + a)\mathcal{N}(h_1^a) - (K + a)\mathcal{N}(h_2^a) = S_0\mathcal{N}(h_1) - K\mathcal{N}(h_2)$$

$$= (S_0 + a)\mathcal{N}\left(\frac{\ln\dfrac{S_0 + a}{K + a} + \dfrac{1}{2}\sigma_a^2 T}{\sigma_a \sqrt{T}}\right) - (K + a)\mathcal{N}\left(\frac{\ln\dfrac{S_0 + a}{K + a} - \dfrac{1}{2}\sigma_a^2 T}{\sigma_a \sqrt{T}}\right)$$

$$= S_0\mathcal{N}\left(\frac{\ln\dfrac{S_0}{K} + \dfrac{1}{2}\sigma_{\log}^2 T}{\sigma_{\log} \sqrt{T}}\right) - K\mathcal{N}\left(\frac{\ln\dfrac{S_0}{K} - \dfrac{1}{2}\sigma_{\log}^2 T}{\sigma_{\log} \sqrt{T}}\right) \qquad (16.22)$$

Not surprisingly, for a generic strike the (approximate) answer is rather cumbersome (see Marris (1999)). However, if the strike K corresponds to the at-the-money level, K_{ATM}, there exists a very simple but often sufficiently accurate approximation. If one sets

$$\sigma_a = \frac{S_0}{S_0 + a}\sigma_{\log} \tag{16.23}$$

one obtains

$$(S_0 + a)\mathcal{N}\left(\frac{\ln\dfrac{S_0 + a}{K_{ATM} + a} + \dfrac{1}{2}\left(\dfrac{S_0}{S_0 + a}\sigma_{\log}\right)^2 T}{\dfrac{S_0}{S_0 + a}\sigma_{\log}\sqrt{T}}\right)$$

$$-(K_{ATM} + a)\mathcal{N}\left(\frac{\ln\dfrac{S_0 + a}{K_{ATM} + a} - \dfrac{1}{2}\left(\dfrac{S_0}{S_0 + a}\sigma_{\log}\right)^2 T}{\dfrac{S_0}{S_0 + a}\sigma_{\log}\sqrt{T}}\right)$$

$$\simeq S_0\mathcal{N}\left(\frac{\ln\dfrac{S_0}{K_{ATM}} + \dfrac{1}{2}\sigma_{\log}^2 T}{\sigma_{\log}\sqrt{T}}\right) - K_{ATM}\mathcal{N}\left(\frac{\ln\dfrac{S_0}{K_{ATM}} - \dfrac{1}{2}\sigma_{\log}^2 T}{\sigma_{\log}\sqrt{T}}\right) \tag{16.24}$$

In other words, if one uses the volatility $\sigma_a = \frac{S_0}{S_0 + a}\sigma_{\log}$, the at-the-money price will be recovered to a high degree of accuracy. This property is very useful in the calibration of a displaced diffusion model, as is shown in Chapter 25. In Chapter 24, I will also show that the approximate result 16.23 can be easily extended to the case of CEV diffusions. The following sections show the accuracy of the simple approximation for displaced diffusions, and how to improve upon it.

16.5.2 Numerical Results with the Simple Approximation

The quality of the naïve approximation is shown in Tables 16.1–16.8. It is acceptable for short maturities, but begins to be noticeably imprecise for five years or more (with a percentage volatility of 20%). So, this approximation could be used with confidence for, say, short-dated equity options, but should be treated with more care in the case of long maturities. I show below how this first-order approximation can be improved.

16.5.3 Refining the Approximation

In order to obtain a more accurate approximation for the at-the-money prices we can reason as follows.[1] Let us start from the Black formula for a 'standard' (i.e. non-displaced) diffusion, and define $\sigma_{\log} = \sigma_0$. Again ignoring discounting, let us write for the at-the-money call price ($K = S_0$):

$$Black(S_0, S_0, \sigma_0, T) = S_0\left[\mathcal{N}(h_1) - \mathcal{N}(h_2)\right] \tag{16.25}$$

---

[1] I wish to thank Mark Joshi for useful discussions.

Table 16.1 Prices obtained using the naïve approximation for $S_0 = \$100$, at-the-money volatility $\sigma = 20\%$, and option expiry one year. The various columns display the results for values of the displacement coefficient ranging from 0 (exact log-normal case, in italics) to 104.

Option expiry = 1	0	8	16	24	32	40	48	56	64	72	80	88	96	104
76	*24.677*	24.708	24.735	24.759	24.780	24.799	24.816	24.831	24.845	24.857	24.869	24.879	24.889	24.898
80	*21.186*	21.221	21.251	21.278	21.301	21.322	21.340	21.357	21.372	21.386	21.398	21.409	21.420	21.429
84	*17.932*	17.968	17.998	18.025	18.048	18.069	18.087	18.103	18.118	18.132	18.144	18.155	18.165	18.175
88	*14.960*	14.991	15.018	15.042	15.062	15.081	15.097	15.111	15.124	15.136	15.147	15.157	15.166	15.174
92	*12.299*	12.323	12.344	12.362	12.377	12.391	12.403	12.414	12.424	12.432	12.440	12.448	12.455	12.461
96	*9.968*	9.981	9.993	10.003	10.011	10.019	10.026	10.032	10.037	10.042	10.047	10.051	10.054	10.058
100	***7.966***	**7.967**	**7.969**	**7.970**	**7.971**	**7.972**	**7.973**	**7.973**	**7.974**	**7.974**	**7.975**	**7.975**	**7.975**	**7.976**
104	*6.280*	6.271	6.262	6.255	6.248	6.242	6.237	6.232	6.228	6.224	6.220	6.217	6.214	6.211
108	*4.888*	4.868	4.851	4.836	4.823	4.811	4.801	4.791	4.783	4.775	4.768	4.761	4.755	4.749
112	*3.758*	3.730	3.707	3.686	3.668	3.651	3.637	3.624	3.612	3.601	3.591	3.582	3.574	3.566
116	*2.856*	2.823	2.795	2.771	2.749	2.729	2.712	2.697	2.683	2.670	2.658	2.648	2.638	2.629
120	*2.147*	2.112	2.082	2.055	2.032	2.011	1.992	1.976	1.961	1.947	1.935	1.923	1.913	1.903
124	*1.598*	1.563	1.532	1.505	1.482	1.461	1.442	1.426	1.411	1.397	1.385	1.373	1.363	1.354

Table 16.2 Implied volatilities obtained using the naïve approximation for $S_0 =\$100$, at-the-money volatility $\sigma = 20\%$, and option expiry one year. The various columns display the results for values of the displacement coefficient ranging from 0 (exact log-normal case, in italics) to 104.

Option expiry = 1	0	8	16	24	32	40	48	56	64	72	80	88	96	104
76	20.00%	20.23%	20.43%	20.61%	20.74%	20.87%	20.98%	21.09%	21.18%	21.26%	21.34%	21.41%	21.47%	21.53%
80	20.00%	20.18%	20.34%	20.48%	20.60%	20.70%	20.79%	20.87%	20.95%	21.02%	21.08%	21.13%	21.19%	21.23%
84	20.00%	20.14%	20.26%	20.37%	20.46%	20.55%	20.62%	20.68%	20.74%	20.79%	20.84%	20.88%	20.92%	20.96%
88	20.00%	20.10%	20.19%	20.27%	20.34%	20.40%	20.45%	20.50%	20.54%	20.58%	20.62%	20.65%	20.68%	20.71%
92	20.00%	20.07%	20.13%	20.18%	20.22%	20.26%	20.30%	20.33%	20.36%	20.38%	20.40%	20.43%	20.44%	20.46%
96	20.00%	20.04%	20.07%	20.09%	20.11%	20.13%	20.15%	20.17%	20.18%	20.20%	20.21%	20.22%	20.23%	20.24%
100	**20.00%**	**20.00%**	**20.01%**	**20.01%**	**20.01%**	**20.02%**	**20.02%**	**20.02%**	**20.02%**	**20.02%**	**20.02%**	**20.02%**	**20.02%**	**20.03%**
104	20.00%	19.98%	19.95%	19.94%	19.92%	19.91%	19.89%	19.88%	19.87%	19.86%	19.85%	19.84%	19.83%	19.83%
108	20.00%	19.95%	19.90%	19.87%	19.83%	19.80%	19.77%	19.75%	19.73%	19.71%	19.69%	19.67%	19.65%	19.64%
112	20.00%	19.92%	19.86%	19.80%	19.75%	19.70%	19.66%	19.62%	19.59%	19.56%	19.53%	19.51%	19.48%	19.46%
116	20.00%	19.90%	19.81%	19.74%	19.67%	19.61%	19.55%	19.51%	19.46%	19.42%	19.39%	19.35%	19.32%	19.29%
120	20.00%	19.88%	19.77%	19.68%	19.59%	19.52%	19.45%	19.39%	19.34%	19.29%	19.25%	19.21%	19.17%	19.13%
124	20.00%	19.86%	19.73%	19.62%	19.52%	19.44%	19.36%	19.29%	19.23%	19.17%	19.12%	19.07%	19.02%	18.98%

Table 16.3 Prices obtained using the naïve approximation for $S_0 = \$100$, at-the-money volatility $\sigma = 20\%$, and option expiry two years. The various columns display the results for values of the displacement coefficient ranging from 0 (exact log-normal case, in italics) to 104.

Option expiry = 2	0	8	16	24	32	40	48	56	64	72	80	88	96	104
76	*26.160*	26.231	26.293	26.346	26.393	26.435	26.472	26.506	26.536	26.563	26.588	26.611	26.632	26.651
80	*23.083*	23.152	23.211	23.263	23.308	23.348	23.384	23.416	23.445	23.471	23.494	23.516	23.536	23.554
84	*20.234*	20.296	20.350	20.396	20.437	20.472	20.504	20.533	20.558	20.582	20.603	20.622	20.639	20.656
88	*17.624*	17.676	17.720	17.758	17.792	17.821	17.847	17.870	17.891	17.910	17.928	17.943	17.958	17.971
92	*15.259*	15.296	15.329	15.356	15.381	15.402	15.421	15.438	15.453	15.466	15.479	15.490	15.500	15.510
96	*13.135*	13.157	13.176	13.192	13.205	13.217	13.228	13.238	13.246	13.254	13.260	13.267	13.272	13.278
100	***11.246***	**11.252**	**11.256**	**11.259**	**11.262**	**11.265**	**11.267**	**11.268**	**11.270**	**11.271**	**11.272**	**11.273**	**11.274**	**11.275**
104	*9.581*	9.570	9.560	9.551	9.543	9.536	9.530	9.524	9.518	9.513	9.508	9.504	9.500	9.497
108	*8.123*	8.097	8.075	8.054	8.036	8.020	8.006	7.993	7.981	7.970	7.960	7.951	7.942	7.935
112	*6.858*	6.819	6.784	6.754	6.727	6.704	6.682	6.663	6.645	6.629	6.614	6.601	6.589	6.577
116	*5.766*	5.716	5.672	5.634	5.600	5.569	5.542	5.517	5.495	5.475	5.456	5.439	5.424	5.409
120	*4.831*	4.772	4.720	4.675	4.636	4.600	4.569	4.540	4.514	4.490	4.469	4.449	4.431	4.414
124	*4.033*	3.968	3.911	3.862	3.818	3.779	3.744	3.713	3.684	3.659	3.635	3.614	3.594	3.575

Table 16.4 Implied volatilities obtained using the naïve approximation for $S_0 =\$100$, at-the-money volatility $\sigma = 20\%$, and option expiry two years. The various columns display the results for values of the displacement coefficient ranging from 0 (exact log-normal case, in italics) to 104.

Option expiry = 2	0	8	16	24	32	40	48	56	64	72	80	88	96	104
76	20.00%	20.23%	20.44%	20.61%	20.76%	20.89%	21.01%	21.11%	21.21%	21.29%	21.37%	21.44%	21.50%	21.56%
80	20.00%	20.19%	20.35%	20.49%	20.62%	20.72%	20.81%	20.90%	20.97%	21.04%	21.11%	21.16%	21.22%	21.26%
84	20.00%	20.15%	20.27%	20.38%	20.48%	20.56%	20.64%	20.71%	20.76%	20.82%	20.86%	20.91%	20.95%	20.99%
88	20.00%	20.11%	20.20%	20.28%	20.35%	20.42%	20.47%	20.52%	20.56%	20.60%	20.64%	20.67%	20.70%	20.73%
92	20.00%	20.07%	20.14%	20.19%	20.24%	20.28%	20.32%	20.35%	20.38%	20.40%	20.43%	20.45%	20.47%	20.49%
96	20.00%	20.04%	20.07%	20.10%	20.13%	20.15%	20.17%	20.19%	20.20%	20.22%	20.23%	20.24%	20.25%	20.26%
100	**20.00%**	**20.01%**	**20.02%**	**20.02%**	**20.03%**	**20.03%**	**20.04%**	**20.04%**	**20.04%**	**20.04%**	**20.05%**	**20.05%**	**20.05%**	**20.05%**
104	20.00%	19.98%	19.96%	19.95%	19.93%	19.92%	19.91%	19.90%	19.89%	19.88%	19.87%	19.86%	19.86%	19.85%
108	20.00%	19.95%	19.91%	19.88%	19.84%	19.82%	19.79%	19.77%	19.75%	19.73%	19.71%	19.69%	19.68%	19.66%
112	20.00%	19.93%	19.87%	19.81%	19.76%	19.72%	19.68%	19.64%	19.61%	19.58%	19.55%	19.53%	19.51%	19.49%
116	20.00%	19.90%	19.82%	19.75%	19.68%	19.62%	19.57%	19.52%	19.48%	19.44%	19.41%	19.37%	19.34%	19.32%
120	20.00%	19.88%	19.78%	19.69%	19.61%	19.53%	19.47%	19.41%	19.36%	19.31%	19.27%	19.23%	19.19%	19.16%
124	20.00%	19.86%	19.74%	19.63%	19.53%	19.45%	19.37%	19.31%	19.24%	19.19%	19.13%	19.09%	19.04%	19.00%

Table 16.5 Prices obtained using the naïve approximation for $S_0 = \$100$, at-the-money volatility $\sigma = 20\%$, and option expiry five years. The various columns display the results for values of the displacement coefficient ranging from 0 (exact log-normal case, in italics) to 104.

Option expiry = 5	0	8	16	24	32	40	48	56	64	72	80	88	96	104
76	*30.345*	30.502	30.637	30.754	30.856	30.946	31.026	31.097	31.161	31.218	31.271	31.319	31.363	31.403
80	*27.825*	27.966	28.086	28.190	28.281	28.361	28.431	28.494	28.551	28.602	28.649	28.691	28.730	28.765
84	*25.476*	25.597	25.699	25.788	25.865	25.933	25.993	26.047	26.095	26.138	26.177	26.213	26.246	26.276
88	*23.295*	23.392	23.475	23.546	23.608	23.663	23.711	23.754	23.792	23.826	23.858	23.886	23.912	23.936
92	*21.275*	21.348	21.409	21.462	21.508	21.547	21.583	21.614	21.641	21.666	21.689	21.709	21.728	21.745
96	*19.411*	19.458	19.497	19.530	19.559	19.583	19.605	19.624	19.641	19.656	19.669	19.681	19.693	19.703
100	***17.694***	**17.715**	**17.731**	**17.745**	**17.756**	**17.766**	**17.774**	**17.780**	**17.786**	**17.791**	**17.795**	**17.799**	**17.803**	**17.806**
104	*16.116*	16.111	16.106	16.100	16.095	16.089	16.083	16.078	16.073	16.068	16.063	16.059	16.054	16.050
108	*14.669*	14.640	14.613	14.589	14.567	14.547	14.528	14.511	14.495	14.481	14.467	14.455	14.443	14.432
112	*13.344*	13.292	13.245	13.203	13.166	13.132	13.101	13.073	13.047	13.024	13.002	12.982	12.963	12.946
116	*12.132*	12.059	11.994	11.936	11.885	11.838	11.796	11.758	11.723	11.691	11.661	11.634	11.609	11.586
120	*11.027*	10.934	10.852	10.780	10.715	10.657	10.605	10.557	10.514	10.474	10.438	10.404	10.373	10.345
124	*10.018*	9.908	9.812	9.726	9.650	9.582	9.520	9.464	9.414	9.367	9.325	9.286	9.250	9.216

Table 16.6 Implied volatilities obtained using the naïve approximation for $S_0 = \$100$, at-the-money volatility $\sigma = 20\%$, and option expiry five years. The various columns display the results for values of the displacement coefficient ranging from 0 (exact log-normal case, in italics) to 104.

Option expiry = 5	0	8	16	24	32	40	48	56	64	72	80	88	96	104
76	20.00%	20.25%	20.47%	20.65%	20.81%	20.95%	21.07%	21.19%	21.29%	21.38%	21.46%	21.53%	21.60%	21.66%
80	20.00%	20.21%	20.38%	20.53%	20.66%	20.78%	20.88%	20.97%	21.05%	21.13%	21.19%	21.25%	21.31%	21.36%
84	20.00%	20.16%	20.30%	20.42%	20.53%	20.62%	20.70%	20.77%	20.84%	20.90%	20.95%	21.00%	21.04%	21.08%
88	20.00%	20.12%	20.23%	20.32%	20.40%	20.47%	20.53%	20.59%	20.63%	20.68%	20.72%	20.75%	20.79%	20.82%
92	20.00%	20.09%	20.16%	20.23%	20.28%	20.33%	20.37%	20.41%	20.45%	20.48%	20.50%	20.53%	20.55%	20.57%
96	20.00%	20.06%	20.10%	20.14%	20.17%	20.20%	20.23%	20.25%	20.27%	20.29%	20.30%	20.32%	20.33%	20.34%
100	**20.00%**	**20.02%**	**20.04%**	**20.06%**	**20.07%**	**20.08%**	**20.09%**	**20.10%**	**20.11%**	**20.11%**	**20.12%**	**20.12%**	**20.13%**	**20.13%**
104	20.00%	19.99%	19.99%	19.98%	19.98%	19.97%	19.96%	19.96%	19.95%	19.95%	19.94%	19.94%	19.93%	19.93%
108	20.00%	19.97%	19.94%	19.91%	19.89%	19.86%	19.84%	19.82%	19.81%	19.79%	19.77%	19.76%	19.75%	19.73%
112	20.00%	19.94%	19.89%	19.84%	19.80%	19.76%	19.73%	19.70%	19.67%	19.64%	19.62%	19.59%	19.57%	19.55%
116	20.00%	19.92%	19.84%	19.78%	19.72%	19.67%	19.62%	19.58%	19.54%	19.50%	19.47%	19.44%	19.41%	19.38%
120	20.00%	19.89%	19.80%	19.72%	19.64%	19.58%	19.52%	19.46%	19.42%	19.37%	19.33%	19.29%	19.25%	19.22%
124	20.00%	19.87%	19.76%	19.66%	19.57%	19.49%	19.42%	19.36%	19.30%	19.24%	19.19%	19.15%	19.11%	19.07%

Table 16.7 Prices obtained using the naïve approximation for $S_0 = \$100$, at-the-money volatility $\sigma = 20\%$, and option expiry 10 years. The various columns display the results for values of the displacement coefficient ranging from 0 (exact log-normal case, in italics) to 104.

Option expiry = 10	0	8	16	24	32	40	48	56	64	72	80	88	96	104
76	*35.782*	36.048	36.274	36.469	36.639	36.788	36.919	37.036	37.141	37.236	37.322	37.400	37.471	37.536
80	*33.659*	33.894	34.094	34.265	34.414	34.545	34.660	34.763	34.855	34.937	35.012	35.080	35.142	35.198
84	*31.663*	31.864	32.035	32.182	32.308	32.419	32.517	32.604	32.681	32.751	32.814	32.871	32.923	32.971
88	*29.787*	29.953	30.093	30.213	30.317	30.407	30.487	30.557	30.620	30.676	30.727	30.773	30.814	30.852
92	*28.024*	28.155	28.264	28.357	28.437	28.506	28.566	28.620	28.667	28.709	28.747	28.782	28.813	28.841
96	*26.370*	26.464	26.542	26.608	26.663	26.711	26.752	26.788	26.820	26.848	26.873	26.896	26.916	26.935
100	*24.817*	**24.875**	**24.922**	**24.960**	**24.992**	**25.018**	**25.041**	**25.060**	**25.076**	**25.090**	**25.102**	**25.113**	**25.122**	**25.131**
104	*23.360*	23.383	23.400	23.411	23.419	23.424	23.428	23.430	23.431	23.431	23.430	23.429	23.428	23.426
108	*21.994*	21.983	21.969	21.955	21.940	21.924	21.909	21.895	21.881	21.867	21.854	21.842	21.830	21.819
112	*20.713*	20.669	20.627	20.587	20.549	20.514	20.481	20.451	20.422	20.396	20.371	20.347	20.325	20.305
116	*19.511*	19.436	19.366	19.302	19.244	19.190	19.140	19.094	19.051	19.012	18.976	18.942	18.910	18.880
120	*18.384*	18.279	18.184	18.097	18.018	17.946	17.880	17.820	17.764	17.713	17.666	17.622	17.581	17.542
124	*17.328*	17.194	17.075	16.967	16.869	16.780	16.699	16.625	16.557	16.495	16.437	16.383	16.334	16.288

Table 16.8 Implied volatilities obtained using the naïve approximation for $S_0 = \$100$, at-the-money volatility $\sigma = 20\%$, and option expiry 10 years. The various columns display the results for values of the displacement coefficient ranging from 0 (exact log-normal case, in italics) to 104.

Option expiry = 10	0	8	16	24	32	40	48	56	64	72	80	88	96	104
76	20.00%	20.28%	20.52%	20.72%	20.90%	21.06%	21.19%	21.32%	21.43%	21.52%	21.61%	21.69%	21.77%	21.84%
80	20.00%	20.23%	20.43%	20.60%	20.75%	20.88%	20.99%	21.09%	21.19%	21.27%	21.34%	21.41%	21.47%	21.53%
84	20.00%	20.19%	20.35%	20.49%	20.61%	20.71%	20.81%	20.89%	20.96%	21.03%	21.09%	21.14%	21.19%	21.24%
88	20.00%	20.15%	20.28%	20.39%	20.48%	20.56%	20.63%	20.70%	20.76%	20.81%	20.85%	20.89%	20.93%	20.97%
92	20.00%	20.11%	20.21%	20.29%	20.36%	20.42%	20.48%	20.52%	20.56%	20.60%	20.63%	20.66%	20.69%	20.72%
96	20.00%	20.08%	20.15%	20.20%	20.25%	20.29%	20.33%	20.36%	20.38%	20.41%	20.43%	20.45%	20.47%	20.48%
100	**20.00%**	**20.05%**	**20.09%**	**20.12%**	**20.15%**	**20.17%**	**20.19%**	**20.20%**	**20.22%**	**20.23%**	**20.24%**	**20.25%**	**20.25%**	**20.26%**
104	20.00%	20.02%	20.03%	20.04%	20.05%	20.05%	20.06%	20.06%	20.06%	20.06%	20.06%	20.06%	20.06%	20.05%
108	20.00%	19.99%	19.98%	19.97%	19.96%	19.94%	19.93%	19.92%	19.91%	19.90%	19.89%	19.88%	19.87%	19.86%
112	20.00%	19.96%	19.93%	19.90%	19.87%	19.84%	19.81%	19.79%	19.77%	19.75%	19.73%	19.71%	19.69%	19.67%
116	20.00%	19.94%	19.88%	19.83%	19.79%	19.74%	19.70%	19.67%	19.63%	19.60%	19.57%	19.55%	19.52%	19.50%
120	20.00%	19.92%	19.84%	19.77%	19.71%	19.65%	19.60%	19.55%	19.51%	19.47%	19.43%	19.40%	19.36%	19.33%
124	20.00%	19.89%	19.80%	19.71%	19.64%	19.57%	19.50%	19.44%	19.39%	19.34%	19.29%	19.25%	19.21%	19.18%

Recalling that, for our choice of strike,

$$h_1 = \frac{\ln\dfrac{K}{S_0} + \dfrac{1}{2}\sigma_0^2}{\sigma_0\sqrt{T}} = \frac{\ln\dfrac{S_0}{S_0} + \dfrac{1}{2}\sigma_0^2}{\sigma_0\sqrt{T}} = \frac{1}{2}\sigma_0\sqrt{T} \qquad (16.26)$$

and

$$h_2 = \frac{\ln\dfrac{K}{S_0} - \dfrac{1}{2}\sigma_0^2}{\sigma_0\sqrt{T}} = \frac{\ln\dfrac{S_0}{S_0} - \dfrac{1}{2}\sigma_0^2}{\sigma_0\sqrt{T}} = -\frac{1}{2}\sigma_0\sqrt{T} \qquad (16.27)$$

one can write

$$\mathcal{N}(h_1) = \mathcal{N}(0 + \tfrac{1}{2}\sigma_0\sqrt{T}) \qquad (16.28)$$

$$\mathcal{N}(h_2) = \mathcal{N}(0 - \tfrac{1}{2}\sigma_0\sqrt{T}) \qquad (16.29)$$

Let us define $\Delta x = \tfrac{1}{2}\sigma_0\sqrt{T}$. Then we can expand the function $\mathcal{N}(.)$ around 0:

$$\mathcal{N}(0 + \tfrac{1}{2}\sigma_0\sqrt{T}) \simeq \mathcal{N}(0) + \left.\frac{d\mathcal{N}}{dx}\right|_0 \Delta x + \frac{1}{2}\left.\frac{d^2\mathcal{N}}{dx^2}\right|_0 \Delta x^2 + \frac{1}{6}\left.\frac{d^3\mathcal{N}}{dx^3}\right|_0 \Delta x^3 + \ldots \quad (16.30)$$

Evaluating the derivatives of the cumulative normal distribution[2] at 0 gives

$$\left.\frac{d\mathcal{N}}{dx}\right|_0 = \frac{1}{\sqrt{2\pi}} \qquad (16.31)$$

$$\left.\frac{d^2\mathcal{N}}{dx^2}\right|_0 = 0 \qquad (16.32)$$

$$\left.\frac{d^3\mathcal{N}}{dx^3}\right|_0 = -\frac{1}{\sqrt{2\pi}} \qquad (16.33)$$

So, the expression for the at-the-money call price can be written

$$Call(S_0, T, S_0, \sigma_0) = Black(S_0, S_0, \sigma_0, T) \simeq \frac{1}{\sqrt{2\pi}} S_0 [2\Delta x - \tfrac{1}{3}\Delta x^3] \qquad (16.34)$$

If we had been dealing with the at-the-money price for a displaced diffusion, we know from Equation (16.21) that the at-the-money call price would have just been given by the Black formula evaluated with an initial value for the forward of $S_0 + a$ and a strike

---

[2]In order to evaluate the derivatives, recall that the cumulative normal distribution is given by

$$\mathcal{N}(x) = \frac{1}{\sqrt{2\pi}} \int_{-\infty}^{x} \exp\left(-\frac{1}{2}u^2\right) du$$

also of $S_0 + a$. Therefore, if we define $\Delta x_a = \frac{1}{2}\sigma_a\sqrt{T}$ the same reasoning used above tells us that the displaced-diffusion, at-the-money call price, $Call_a(S_0, T, S_0, \sigma_a)$, will be given by

$$Call_a(S_0, T, S_0, \sigma_a)$$

$$= Black(S_0 + a, S_0 + a, \sigma_0, T) \simeq \frac{1}{\sqrt{2\pi}}(S_0 + a)[2\Delta x_a - \frac{1}{3}\Delta x_a^3] \qquad (16.35)$$

If we want the same at-the-money call prices in the log-normal and displaced-diffusion cases, Equations (16.34) and (16.35) should be set equal to each other:

$$\frac{1}{\sqrt{2\pi}}S_0\left[2\Delta x - \frac{1}{3}\Delta x^3\right] = \frac{1}{\sqrt{2\pi}}(S_0 + a)\left[2\Delta x_a - \frac{1}{3}\Delta x_a^3\right] \qquad (16.36)$$

After inserting the definitions for Δx and Δx_a, one obtains:

$$\sigma_0\frac{S_0}{S_0 + a}\left(1 - \frac{1}{24}\sigma_0^2 T\right) = \sigma_a\left(1 - \frac{1}{24}\sigma_a^2 T\right) \qquad (16.37)$$

Note, first of all, that, if we ignore the higher-order terms, the expression reduces to the naïve approximation

$$\sigma_a = \frac{S_0}{S_0 + a}\sigma_0 \qquad (16.38)$$

To get a (much) more accurate approximation, one can either solve a cubic equation, or simply approximate the small term σ_a^2 inside the square brackets on the RHS using the naïve approximation presented in the previous section, i.e. $\sigma_a^2 = \left(\frac{S_0}{S_0+a}\sigma_0\right)^2$:

$$\sigma_0\frac{S_0}{S_0 + a}\left(1 - \frac{1}{24}\sigma_0^2 T\right) = \sigma_a\left[1 - \frac{1}{24}\left(\frac{S_0}{S_0 + a}\sigma_0\right)^2 T\right] \qquad (16.39)$$

By so doing, one obtains:

$$\sigma_a \simeq \frac{\sigma_0\dfrac{S_0}{S_0 + a}\left(1 - \dfrac{1}{24}\sigma_0^2 T\right)}{1 - \dfrac{1}{24}\left(\dfrac{S_0}{S_0 + a}\sigma_0\right)^2 T} \qquad (16.40)$$

Let us see how good this approximation is.

16.5.4   Numerical Results with the Refined Approximation

The excellent quality of the refined approximation is shown in Tables 16.9–16.16. Note that the match in implied volatility is essentially perfect even for a 10-year option expiry, despite the fact that Equation (16.40), instead of the more precise Equation (16.37), has been used in obtaining the call prices.

Table 16.9 Prices obtained using the more precise approximation for $S_0 = \$100$, at-the-money volatility $\sigma = 20\%$, and option expiry one year. The various columns display the results for values of the displacement coefficient ranging from 0 (exact log-normal case, in italics) to 104.

Option expiry = 1	0	8	16	24	32	40	48	56	64	72	80	88	96	104
76	*24.677*	24.708	24.734	24.757	24.778	24.797	24.813	24.828	24.841	24.854	24.865	24.875	24.885	24.894
80	*21.186*	21.220	21.250	21.276	21.298	21.319	21.337	21.353	21.368	21.381	21.393	21.404	21.415	21.424
84	*17.932*	17.966	17.996	18.022	18.044	18.064	18.082	18.098	18.113	18.126	18.138	18.149	18.159	18.168
88	*14.960*	14.990	15.016	15.038	15.058	15.076	15.091	15.105	15.118	15.129	15.140	15.149	15.158	15.166
92	*12.299*	12.322	12.341	12.357	12.372	12.385	12.396	12.407	12.416	12.425	12.432	12.439	12.446	12.452
96	*9.968*	9.979	9.990	9.998	10.006	10.013	10.019	10.024	10.029	10.034	10.038	10.042	10.045	10.048
100	***7.966***	**7.966**	**7.966**	**7.966**	**7.966**	**7.966**	**7.966**	**7.966**	**7.966**	**7.966**	**7.966**	**7.966**	**7.966**	**7.966**
104	*6.280*	6.269	6.259	6.250	6.243	6.236	6.230	6.225	6.220	6.215	6.211	6.208	6.204	6.201
108	*4.888*	4.866	4.848	4.832	4.818	4.805	4.794	4.784	4.775	4.766	4.759	4.752	4.746	4.740
112	*3.758*	3.729	3.704	3.682	3.663	3.646	3.630	3.617	3.604	3.593	3.583	3.574	3.565	3.557
116	*2.856*	2.822	2.792	2.767	2.744	2.724	2.707	2.691	2.676	2.663	2.651	2.640	2.630	2.621
120	*2.147*	2.111	2.079	2.052	2.028	2.006	1.987	1.970	1.955	1.941	1.928	1.917	1.906	1.896
124	*1.598*	1.561	1.530	1.502	1.478	1.457	1.438	1.421	1.406	1.392	1.380	1.368	1.358	1.348

Table 16.10 Implied volatilities obtained using the more precise approximation for $S_0 =\$100$, at-the-money volatility $\sigma = 20\%$, and option expiry one year. The various columns display the results for values of the displacement coefficient ranging from 0 (exact log-normal case, in italics) to 104.

Option expiry = 1	0	8	16	24	32	40	48	56	64	72	80	88	96	104
76	20.00%	20.23%	20.42%	20.59%	20.72%	20.85%	20.96%	21.07%	21.16%	21.24%	21.31%	21.38%	21.44%	21.50%
80	20.00%	20.18%	20.33%	20.47%	20.59%	20.68%	20.77%	20.85%	20.93%	20.99%	21.05%	21.11%	21.16%	21.21%
84	20.00%	20.14%	20.26%	20.36%	20.45%	20.53%	20.60%	20.66%	20.72%	20.77%	20.81%	20.86%	20.90%	20.93%
88	20.00%	20.10%	20.18%	20.26%	20.32%	20.38%	20.43%	20.48%	20.52%	20.56%	20.59%	20.62%	20.65%	20.68%
92	20.00%	20.06%	20.12%	20.17%	20.21%	20.25%	20.28%	20.31%	20.33%	20.36%	20.38%	20.40%	20.42%	20.44%
96	20.00%	20.03%	20.06%	20.08%	20.10%	20.12%	20.13%	20.15%	20.16%	20.17%	20.18%	20.19%	20.20%	20.21%
100	**20.00%**	**20.00%**	**20.00%**	**20.00%**	**20.00%**	**20.00%**	**20.00%**	**20.00%**	**20.00%**	**20.00%**	**20.00%**	**20.00%**	**20.00%**	**20.00%**
104	20.00%	19.97%	19.95%	19.92%	19.91%	19.89%	19.87%	19.86%	19.85%	19.84%	19.83%	19.82%	19.81%	19.80%
108	20.00%	19.94%	19.90%	19.85%	19.82%	19.78%	19.76%	19.73%	19.71%	19.68%	19.66%	19.65%	19.63%	19.61%
112	20.00%	19.92%	19.85%	19.79%	19.73%	19.69%	19.64%	19.60%	19.57%	19.54%	19.51%	19.48%	19.46%	19.44%
116	20.00%	19.89%	19.80%	19.72%	19.65%	19.59%	19.54%	19.49%	19.44%	19.40%	19.36%	19.33%	19.30%	19.27%
120	20.00%	19.87%	19.76%	19.66%	19.58%	19.50%	19.44%	19.38%	19.32%	19.27%	19.22%	19.18%	19.14%	19.11%
124	20.00%	19.85%	19.72%	19.61%	19.51%	19.42%	19.34%	19.27%	19.21%	19.15%	19.09%	19.04%	19.00%	18.96%

Table 16.11 Prices obtained using the more precise approximation for $S_0 = \$100$, at-the-money volatility $\sigma = 20\%$, and option expiry two years. The various columns display the results for values of the displacement coefficient ranging from 0 (exact log-normal case, in italics) to 104.

Option expiry = 2	0	8	16	24	32	40	48	56	64	72	80	88	96	104
76	*26.160*	26.231	26.293	26.346	26.393	26.435	26.472	26.506	26.536	26.563	26.588	26.611	26.632	26.651
80	*23.083*	23.152	23.211	23.263	23.308	23.348	23.384	23.416	23.445	23.471	23.494	23.516	23.536	23.554
84	*20.234*	20.296	20.350	20.396	20.437	20.472	20.504	20.533	20.558	20.582	20.603	20.622	20.639	20.656
88	*17.624*	17.676	17.720	17.758	17.792	17.821	17.847	17.870	17.891	17.910	17.928	17.943	17.958	17.971
92	*15.259*	15.296	15.329	15.356	15.381	15.402	15.421	15.438	15.453	15.466	15.479	15.490	15.500	15.510
96	*13.135*	13.157	13.176	13.192	13.205	13.217	13.228	13.238	13.246	13.254	13.260	13.267	13.272	13.278
100	***11.246***	**11.252**	**11.256**	**11.259**	**11.262**	**11.265**	**11.267**	**11.268**	**11.270**	**11.271**	**11.272**	**11.273**	**11.274**	**11.275**
104	*9.581*	9.570	9.560	9.551	9.543	9.536	9.530	9.524	9.518	9.513	9.508	9.504	9.500	9.497
108	*8.123*	8.097	8.075	8.054	8.036	8.020	8.006	7.993	7.981	7.970	7.960	7.951	7.942	7.935
112	*6.858*	6.819	6.784	6.754	6.727	6.704	6.682	6.663	6.645	6.629	6.614	6.601	6.589	6.577
116	*5.766*	5.716	5.672	5.634	5.600	5.569	5.542	5.517	5.495	5.475	5.456	5.439	5.424	5.409
120	*4.831*	4.772	4.720	4.675	4.636	4.600	4.569	4.540	4.514	4.490	4.469	4.449	4.431	4.414
124	*4.033*	3.968	3.911	3.862	3.818	3.779	3.744	3.713	3.684	3.659	3.635	3.614	3.594	3.575

Table 16.12 Implied volatilities obtained using the more precise approximation for $S_0 = \$100$, at-the-money volatility $\sigma = 20\%$, and option expiry two years. The various columns display the results for values of the displacement coefficient ranging from 0 (exact log-normal case, in italics) to 104.

Option expiry = 2	0	8	16	24	32	40	48	56	64	72	80	88	96	104
76	20.00%	20.22%	20.42%	20.59%	20.73%	20.85%	20.97%	21.07%	21.16%	21.24%	21.32%	21.39%	21.45%	21.51%
80	20.00%	20.18%	20.33%	20.47%	20.59%	20.68%	20.78%	20.86%	20.93%	21.00%	21.06%	21.11%	21.16%	21.21%
84	20.00%	20.14%	20.26%	20.36%	20.45%	20.53%	20.60%	20.66%	20.72%	20.77%	20.82%	20.86%	20.90%	20.93%
88	20.00%	20.10%	20.18%	20.26%	20.32%	20.38%	20.43%	20.48%	20.52%	20.56%	20.59%	20.62%	20.65%	20.68%
92	20.00%	20.06%	20.12%	20.17%	20.21%	20.25%	20.28%	20.31%	20.34%	20.36%	20.38%	20.40%	20.42%	20.44%
96	20.00%	20.03%	20.06%	20.08%	20.10%	20.12%	20.13%	20.15%	20.16%	20.17%	20.18%	20.19%	20.20%	20.21%
100	**20.00%**	**20.00%**	**20.00%**	**20.00%**	**20.00%**	**20.00%**	**20.00%**	**20.00%**	**20.00%**	**20.00%**	**20.00%**	**20.00%**	**20.00%**	**20.00%**
104	20.00%	19.94%	19.95%	19.92%	19.91%	19.89%	19.87%	19.86%	19.85%	19.84%	19.83%	19.82%	19.81%	19.80%
108	20.00%	19.94%	19.90%	19.85%	19.82%	19.78%	19.75%	19.73%	19.70%	19.68%	19.66%	19.64%	19.63%	19.61%
112	20.00%	19.92%	19.85%	19.79%	19.73%	19.68%	19.64%	19.60%	19.57%	19.54%	19.51%	19.48%	19.46%	19.44%
116	20.00%	19.89%	19.80%	19.72%	19.65%	19.59%	19.54%	19.49%	19.44%	19.40%	19.36%	19.33%	19.30%	19.27%
120	20.00%	19.87%	19.76%	19.66%	19.58%	19.50%	19.43%	19.37%	19.32%	19.27%	19.22%	19.18%	19.14%	19.11%
124	20.00%	19.85%	19.72%	19.61%	19.51%	19.42%	19.34%	19.27%	19.20%	19.14%	19.09%	19.04%	19.00%	18.95%

Table 16.13 Prices obtained using the more precise approximation for $S_0 = \$100$, at-the-money volatility $\sigma = 20\%$, and option expiry five years. The various columns display the results for values of the displacement coefficient ranging from 0 (exact log-normal case, in italics) to 104.

Option expiry = 5	0	8	16	24	32	40	48	56	64	72	80	88	96	104
76	*30.345*	30.487	30.609	30.715	30.808	30.891	30.964	31.029	31.088	31.142	31.190	31.235	31.276	31.313
80	*27.825*	27.949	28.056	28.148	28.229	28.301	28.365	28.422	28.474	28.520	28.563	28.601	28.637	28.670
84	*25.476*	25.579	25.667	25.743	25.811	25.870	25.923	25.970	26.013	26.051	26.086	26.118	26.148	26.175
88	*23.295*	23.373	23.441	23.500	23.551	23.596	23.637	23.673	23.706	23.736	23.763	23.787	23.810	23.831
92	*21.275*	21.328	21.374	21.413	21.448	21.479	21.506	21.530	21.552	21.572	21.591	21.607	21.623	21.637
96	*19.411*	19.437	19.460	19.480	19.497	19.512	19.526	19.538	19.549	19.559	19.569	19.577	19.585	19.592
100	***17.694***	**17.694**	**17.694**	**17.694**	**17.694**	**17.693**	**17.693**	**17.693**	**17.693**	**17.693**	**17.693**	**17.693**	**17.693**	**17.693**
104	*16.116*	16.090	16.068	16.048	16.031	16.016	16.002	15.990	15.979	15.969	15.960	15.952	15.944	15.937
108	*14.669*	14.618	14.575	14.537	14.503	14.474	14.447	14.423	14.402	14.382	14.364	14.348	14.333	14.319
112	*13.344*	13.270	13.207	13.151	13.103	13.059	13.021	12.986	12.955	12.926	12.900	12.876	12.854	12.834
116	*12.132*	12.038	11.956	11.885	11.822	11.766	11.716	11.671	11.631	11.594	11.561	11.530	11.502	11.476
120	*11.027*	10.913	10.815	10.729	10.653	10.586	10.526	10.473	10.424	10.380	10.339	10.302	10.268	10.237
124	*10.018*	9.888	9.775	9.676	9.590	9.513	9.444	9.382	9.326	9.275	9.229	9.187	9.148	9.112

Table 16.14 Implied volatilities obtained using the more precise approximation for $S_0 = \$100$, at-the-money volatility $\sigma = 20\%$, and option expiry five years. The various columns display the results for values of the displacement coefficient ranging from 0 (exact log-normal case, in italics) to 104.

Option expiry = 5	0	8	16	24	32	40	48	56	64	72	80	88	96	104
76	20.00%	20.23%	20.42%	20.59%	20.74%	20.86%	20.98%	21.08%	21.17%	21.26%	21.33%	21.40%	21.47%	21.52%
80	20.00%	20.18%	20.34%	20.47%	20.59%	20.69%	20.79%	20.87%	20.94%	21.01%	21.07%	21.12%	21.18%	21.22%
84	20.00%	20.14%	20.26%	20.36%	20.45%	20.53%	20.60%	20.67%	20.73%	20.78%	20.83%	20.87%	20.91%	20.95%
88	20.00%	20.10%	20.19%	20.26%	20.33%	20.39%	20.44%	20.48%	20.52%	20.56%	20.60%	20.63%	20.66%	20.68%
92	20.00%	20.06%	20.12%	20.17%	20.21%	20.25%	20.28%	20.31%	20.34%	20.36%	20.38%	20.40%	20.42%	20.44%
96	20.00%	20.03%	20.06%	20.08%	20.10%	20.12%	20.14%	20.15%	20.16%	20.18%	20.19%	20.20%	20.20%	20.21%
100	**20.00%**	**20.00%**	**20.00%**	**20.00%**	**20.00%**	**20.00%**	**20.00%**	**20.00%**	**20.00%**	**20.00%**	**20.00%**	**20.00%**	**20.00%**	**20.00%**
104	20.00%	19.97%	19.95%	19.92%	19.90%	19.89%	19.87%	19.86%	19.85%	19.83%	19.82%	19.81%	19.81%	19.80%
108	20.00%	19.94%	19.89%	19.85%	19.81%	19.78%	19.75%	19.72%	19.70%	19.68%	19.66%	19.64%	19.62%	19.61%
112	20.00%	19.92%	19.85%	19.78%	19.73%	19.68%	19.64%	19.60%	19.56%	19.53%	19.50%	19.48%	19.45%	19.43%
116	20.00%	19.89%	19.80%	19.72%	19.65%	19.59%	19.53%	19.48%	19.43%	19.39%	19.36%	19.32%	19.29%	19.26%
120	20.00%	19.87%	19.76%	19.66%	19.57%	19.50%	19.43%	19.37%	19.31%	19.26%	19.21%	19.17%	19.13%	19.10%
124	20.00%	19.85%	19.72%	19.60%	19.50%	19.41%	19.33%	19.26%	19.19%	19.14%	19.08%	19.03%	18.99%	18.94%

Table 16.15 Prices obtained using the more precise approximation for $S_0 = \$100$, at-the-money volatility $\sigma = 20\%$, and option expiry 10 years. The various columns display the results for values of the displacement coefficient ranging from 0 (exact log-normal case, in italics) to 104.

Option expiry = 10	0	8	16	24	32	40	48	56	64	72	80	88	96	104
76	*35.782*	36.001	36.188	36.351	36.493	36.619	36.730	36.830	36.920	37.001	37.075	37.143	37.205	37.262
80	*33.659*	33.845	34.004	34.141	34.262	34.368	34.463	34.547	34.624	34.693	34.755	34.813	34.865	34.914
84	*31.663*	31.812	31.941	32.052	32.149	32.236	32.312	32.381	32.442	32.498	32.549	32.595	32.638	32.677
88	*29.787*	29.899	29.996	30.079	30.153	30.218	30.275	30.327	30.373	30.416	30.454	30.489	30.521	30.551
92	*28.024*	28.099	28.163	28.219	28.268	28.311	28.349	28.384	28.415	28.443	28.468	28.492	28.513	28.533
96	*26.370*	26.407	26.439	26.466	26.490	26.512	26.531	26.548	26.563	26.577	26.589	26.601	26.612	26.621
100	**24.817**	**24.817**	**24.817**	**24.817**	**24.816**	**24.816**	**24.815**	**24.815**	**24.815**	**24.815**	**24.814**	**24.814**	**24.814**	**24.814**
104	*23.360*	23.324	23.293	23.265	23.241	23.219	23.200	23.183	23.167	23.153	23.140	23.128	23.117	23.107
108	*21.994*	21.923	21.861	21.807	21.760	21.718	21.680	21.646	21.615	21.588	21.562	21.539	21.518	21.498
112	*20.713*	20.608	20.518	20.438	20.369	20.307	20.251	20.201	20.156	20.116	20.078	20.044	20.013	19.984
116	*19.511*	19.375	19.257	19.154	19.063	18.982	18.910	18.845	18.786	18.733	18.684	18.640	18.599	18.561
120	*18.384*	18.218	18.074	17.949	17.838	17.739	17.651	17.572	17.500	17.435	17.376	17.321	17.271	17.225
124	*17.328*	17.134	16.966	16.819	16.689	16.574	16.471	16.378	16.295	16.219	16.149	16.086	16.027	15.974

Table 16.16 Implied volatilities obtained using the more precise approximation for $S_0 = \$100$, at-the-money volatility $\sigma = 20\%$, and option expiry 10 years. The various columns display the results for values of the displacement coefficient ranging from 0 (exact log-normal case, in italics) to 104.

Option expiry = 10	0	8	16	24	32	40	48	56	64	72	80	88	96	104
76	20.00%	20.23%	20.43%	20.60%	20.75%	20.88%	21.00%	21.10%	21.20%	21.28%	21.36%	21.43%	21.49%	21.55%
80	20.00%	20.18%	20.34%	20.48%	20.60%	20.70%	20.80%	20.88%	20.96%	21.02%	21.09%	21.14%	21.20%	21.24%
84	20.00%	20.14%	20.26%	20.37%	20.46%	20.54%	20.61%	20.68%	20.74%	20.79%	20.84%	20.88%	20.92%	20.96%
88	20.00%	20.10%	20.19%	20.27%	20.33%	20.39%	20.44%	20.49%	20.53%	20.57%	20.61%	20.64%	20.67%	20.69%
92	20.00%	20.07%	20.12%	20.17%	20.21%	20.25%	20.28%	20.32%	20.34%	20.37%	20.39%	20.41%	20.43%	20.45%
96	20.00%	20.03%	20.06%	20.08%	20.10%	20.12%	20.14%	20.15%	20.16%	20.18%	20.19%	20.20%	20.21%	20.21%
100	**20.00%**	**20.00%**	**20.00%**	**20.00%**	**20.00%**	**20.00%**	**20.00%**	**20.00%**	**20.00%**	**20.00%**	**20.00%**	**20.00%**	**20.00%**	**20.00%**
104	20.00%	19.97%	19.94%	19.92%	19.90%	19.88%	19.87%	19.85%	19.84%	19.83%	19.82%	19.81%	19.80%	19.79%
108	20.00%	19.94%	19.89%	19.85%	19.81%	19.78%	19.75%	19.72%	19.69%	19.67%	19.65%	19.63%	19.62%	19.60%
112	20.00%	19.92%	19.84%	19.78%	19.72%	19.67%	19.63%	19.59%	19.55%	19.52%	19.49%	19.46%	19.44%	19.42%
116	20.00%	19.89%	19.80%	19.72%	19.64%	19.58%	19.52%	19.47%	19.42%	19.38%	19.34%	19.31%	19.27%	19.24%
120	20.00%	19.87%	19.75%	19.65%	19.57%	19.49%	19.42%	19.36%	19.30%	19.25%	19.20%	19.16%	19.12%	19.08%
124	20.00%	19.85%	19.71%	19.60%	19.49%	19.40%	19.32%	19.25%	19.18%	19.12%	19.07%	19.02%	18.97%	18.93%

16.6   The Smile Produced by Displaced Diffusions

The smiles produced by displaced diffusions have a natural downward-sloping bias. This is easy to understand. We have seen that increasing the displacement coefficient, a, from 0 to higher and higher values makes the resulting distribution become more and more Gaussian-like. However, normal diffusions are more skewed to the left than log-normal ones, hence the smile naturally rises towards the out-of-the-money puts. See Figures 16.1–16.3.

This is important, because the risk-neutral (if not the objective-measure[3]) price density displays a pronounced left skew both in interest rates (see Part IV) and in equities. As usual, we should ask ourselves whether we really believe that, financially, this is due to the fact that some quantity $S+a$, rather than S, is log-normally distributed. At face value, this is perhaps rather difficult to justify. However, as I discuss in Part IV, a displaced diffusion can be considered a simple proxy for a CEV process. If we make this mental identification, the financial question to ask is whether we believe that moves in the underlying less-then-proportional to its level better describe the market we are looking at than geometric moves. I will make the point in Part IV that a convincing case for this can be made in the case of interest rates, at least in the pricing measure.

16.6.1   How Quickly is the Normal-Diffusion Limit Approached?

We know that, as the displacement coefficient a goes to infinity, the displaced diffusion process asymptotically approaches a normal diffusion. A relevant question is: how big

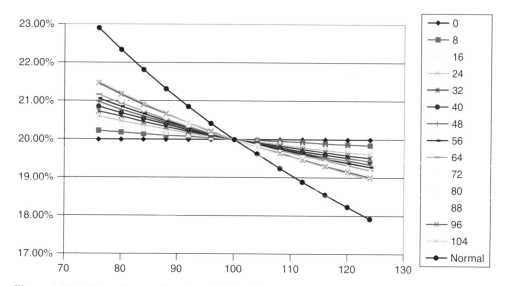

Figure 16.1   The smile as a function of strike for several values of the displacement coefficient for option expiry $T = 1$ year. The normal case, corresponding to a displacement coefficient $a = \infty$, is also shown.

---

[3]Analysing S&P data, Madan *et al.* find no evidence of a left skew in the objective measure, but a pronounced skew in the risk-neutral distribution. See the discussion in Chapter 15.

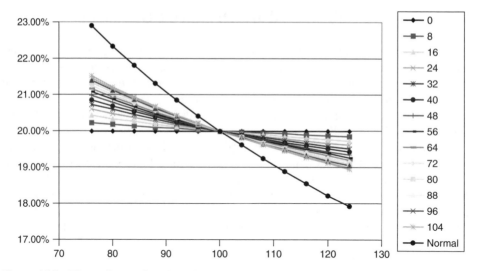

Figure 16.2 The smile as a function of strike for several values of the displacement coefficient for option expiry $T = 2$ years. The normal case, corresponding to a displacement coefficient $a = \infty$, is also shown.

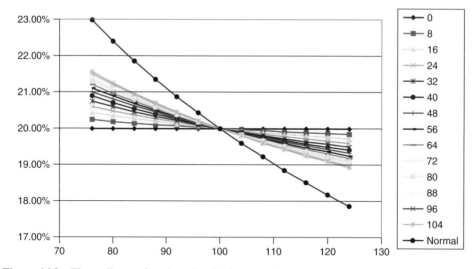

Figure 16.3 The smile as a function of strike for several values of the displacement coefficient for option expiry $T = 10$ years. The normal case, corresponding to a displacement coefficient $a = \infty$, is also shown.

must the displacement coefficient become for the normal limit to be effectively reached (i.e. for option prices to be essentially indistinguishable from the prices obtained using the normal assumption)?

In order to answer this question we must first obtain the 'equivalent' volatility of the normal-diffusion process. This can be arrived at following a very similar line of reasoning to the one employed above. We have already established that, at-the-money, a log-normal call option price can be very well approximated as

$$Call(S_0, T, K = S_0, \sigma_0) = Black(S_0, S_0, \sigma_0, T) \simeq \frac{1}{\sqrt{2\pi}} S_0[2\Delta x - \tfrac{1}{3}\Delta x^3] \quad (16.41)$$

with

$$\Delta x = \tfrac{1}{2}\sigma_0 \sqrt{T} \quad (16.42)$$

The exact expression for a normal-diffusion call option price, $Call_{abs}$ (see, for example, Haug (1998)) is

$$Call_{abs}(S_0, T, K, \sigma_0) = (S_0 - K)N(x) + \frac{1}{\sqrt{2\pi}}\sigma_{abs}\sqrt{T}\exp[-\tfrac{1}{2}x^2] \quad (16.43)$$

with

$$x = \frac{S_0 - K}{\sigma_{abs}\sqrt{T}} \quad (16.44)$$

At-the-money, this gives

$$Call_{abs}(S_0, T, K = S_0, \sigma_0) = \frac{1}{\sqrt{2\pi}}\sigma_{abs}\sqrt{T} \quad (16.45)$$

In order to find the value of the absolute volatility that (approximately) produces the same at-the-money call price as the Black formula with percentage volatility σ_0, we can simply retain terms linear in Δx, in which case we obtain

$$\frac{1}{\sqrt{2\pi}}\sigma_{abs}\sqrt{T} \simeq \frac{1}{\sqrt{2\pi}}S_0\,[2\Delta x] = \frac{1}{\sqrt{2\pi}}S_0\sigma_0\sqrt{T} \quad (16.46)$$

and therefore

$$\sigma_{abs} \simeq S_0\sigma_0$$

Alternatively, if we can retain terms up to Δx^3 we obtain

$$\frac{1}{\sqrt{2\pi}}\sigma_{abs}\sqrt{T} \simeq \frac{1}{\sqrt{2\pi}}S_0[2\Delta x - \tfrac{1}{3}\Delta x^3] \quad (16.47)$$

and therefore

$$\sigma_{abs} \simeq S_0\sigma_0\left(1 - \frac{1}{24}\sigma_0^2 T\right) \quad (16.48)$$

The reader can verify that Equation (16.48) is spectacularly accurate. Using this expression in conjunction with Equation (16.37) one can match the at-the-money price virtually exactly, and explore how quickly the displaced-diffusion prices approach the normal prices as the displacement coefficient, a, increases. The results are shown in Figures 16.4–16.6.

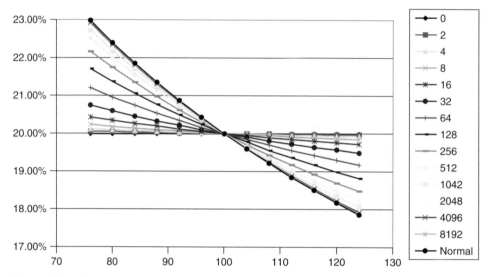

Figure 16.4 The speed of the approach to the normal limit when the underlying has starting value of the order of 100, for option expiry $T = 1$ years. Note how, using Equation (16.48), the at-the-money prices are all virtually the same.

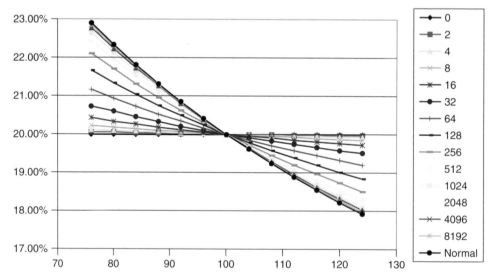

Figure 16.5 The speed of the approach to the normal limit when the underlying has starting value of the order of 100, for option expiry $T = 2$ years. Note how, using Equation (16.48), the at-the-money prices are all virtually the same.

One has to be careful in analysing these results because the same scaling properties that hold with a log-normal diffusion (e.g. if the forward price doubles, the at-the-money log-normal call price also doubles) no longer apply in the displaced-diffusion case. However, by repeating the experiment for values of the underlying ranging from 0.05 (an

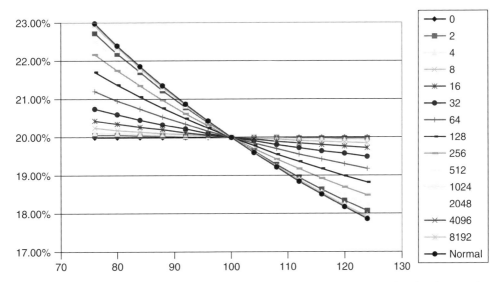

Figure 16.6 The speed of the approach to the normal limit when the underlying has starting value of the order of 100, for option expiry $T = 10$ years. Note how, using Equation (16.48), the at-the-money prices are all virtually the same.

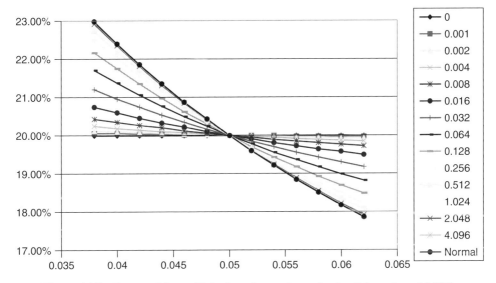

Figure 16.7 Same as Figure 16.6 when the starting value is of the order of 5.00%.

'interest-rate' case) to 100 (an 'FX-' or 'stock-price' case) one can see that, in order for the prices to be very similar (less than half a vega difference in implied volatility for most strikes), the displacement coefficient should be several times as large as the level of the 'stock' today, S_0. See Figure 16.7 and Tables 16.17 and 16.18.

Table 16.17 The prices for different values of the displacement coefficients (in the columns, ranging from 0 to 409.6%) and for different strikes (in the rows, ranging from 3.8% to 6.2%) in the interest-rate case (option expiry = 10 years, initial value of the forward rate = 5.00%). Note how, using Equation (16.48), the at-the-money prices are all virtually the same. The last column displays the results for the normal case.

	0	0.001	0.002	0.004	0.008	0.016	0.032	0.064	0.128	0.256	0.512	1.024	2.048	4.096	Normal
0.038	0.0179	0.0179	0.0179	0.0180	0.0181	0.0182	0.0185	0.0187	0.0189	0.0191	0.0192	0.0193	0.0193	0.0193	0.0193
0.04	0.0168	0.0169	0.0169	0.0169	0.0170	0.0171	0.0173	0.0175	0.0177	0.0178	0.0179	0.0180	0.0180	0.0180	0.0180
0.042	0.0158	0.0159	0.0159	0.0159	0.0160	0.0161	0.0162	0.0164	0.0165	0.0167	0.0167	0.0168	0.0168	0.0168	0.0168
0.044	0.0149	0.0149	0.0149	0.0149	0.0150	0.0151	0.0152	0.0153	0.0154	0.0155	0.0156	0.0156	0.0156	0.0156	0.0156
0.046	0.0140	0.0140	0.0140	0.0140	0.0141	0.0141	0.0142	0.0143	0.0144	0.0144	0.0145	0.0145	0.0145	0.0145	0.0145
0.048	0.0132	0.0132	0.0132	0.0132	0.0132	0.0132	0.0133	0.0133	0.0134	0.0134	0.0134	0.0134	0.0134	0.0134	0.0134
0.05	**0.0124**	**0.0124**	**0.0124**	**0.0124**	**0.0124**	**0.0124**	**0.0124**	**0.0124**	**0.0124**	**0.0124**	**0.0124**	**0.0124**	**0.0124**	**0.0124**	**0.0124**
0.052	0.0117	0.0117	0.0117	0.0117	0.0116	0.0116	0.0116	0.0115	0.0115	0.0115	0.0115	0.0114	0.0114	0.0114	0.0114
0.054	0.0110	0.0110	0.0110	0.0110	0.0109	0.0109	0.0108	0.0107	0.0106	0.0106	0.0106	0.0105	0.0105	0.0105	0.0105
0.056	0.0104	0.0103	0.0103	0.0103	0.0103	0.0102	0.0101	0.0100	0.0098	0.0098	0.0097	0.0097	0.0097	0.0096	0.0096
0.058	0.0098	0.0097	0.0097	0.0097	0.0096	0.0095	0.0094	0.0092	0.0091	0.0090	0.0089	0.0089	0.0088	0.0088	0.0088
0.06	0.0092	0.0092	0.0091	0.0091	0.0090	0.0089	0.0088	0.0086	0.0084	0.0082	0.0081	0.0081	0.0081	0.0081	0.0080
0.062	0.0087	0.0086	0.0086	0.0086	0.0085	0.0083	0.0081	0.0079	0.0077	0.0075	0.0074	0.0074	0.0074	0.0073	0.0073

Table 16.18 The implied volatilities for different values of the displacement coefficients (in the columns, ranging from 0 to 409.6%) and for different strikes (in the rows, ranging from 3.8% to 6.2%) in the interest-rate case (option expiry = 10 years, initial value of the forward rate = 5.00%). Note how, using Equation (16.48), the at-the-money prices are all virtually the same. The last column displays the results for the normal case.

	0	0.001	0.002	0.004	0.008	0.016	0.032	0.064	0.128	0.256	0.512	1.024	2.048	4.096	Normal
0.038	20.00%	20.06%	20.12%	20.23%	20.43%	20.75%	21.20%	21.70%	22.17%	22.51%	22.73%	22.85%	22.92%	22.95%	22.98%
0.04	20.00%	20.05%	20.10%	20.18%	20.34%	20.60%	20.96%	21.37%	21.74%	22.02%	22.19%	22.29%	22.35%	22.37%	22.40%
0.042	20.00%	20.04%	20.07%	20.14%	20.26%	20.46%	20.74%	21.05%	21.34%	21.56%	21.69%	21.77%	21.81%	21.83%	21.86%
0.044	20.00%	20.03%	20.05%	20.10%	20.19%	20.33%	20.53%	20.76%	20.97%	21.13%	21.23%	21.28%	21.31%	21.33%	21.35%
0.046	20.00%	20.02%	20.03%	20.07%	20.12%	20.21%	20.34%	20.49%	20.63%	20.73%	20.79%	20.83%	20.85%	20.86%	20.87%
0.048	20.00%	20.01%	20.02%	20.03%	20.06%	20.10%	20.16%	20.24%	20.30%	20.35%	20.38%	20.40%	20.41%	20.41%	20.42%
0.05	**20.00%**	**19.99%**	**20.00%**	**20.00%**	**20.00%**	**20.00%**	**20.00%**	**20.00%**	**20.00%**	**20.00%**	**20.00%**	**19.99%**	**19.99%**	**19.99%**	**19.99%**
0.052	20.00%	19.99%	19.98%	19.97%	19.94%	19.90%	19.84%	19.77%	19.71%	19.66%	19.63%	19.61%	19.60%	19.60%	19.59%
0.054	20.00%	19.98%	19.97%	19.94%	19.89%	19.81%	19.69%	19.56%	19.43%	19.34%	19.28%	19.25%	19.23%	19.22%	19.21%
0.056	20.00%	19.98%	19.96%	19.92%	19.84%	19.72%	19.55%	19.36%	19.17%	19.04%	18.95%	18.90%	18.88%	18.86%	18.85%
0.058	20.00%	19.97%	19.94%	19.89%	19.80%	19.64%	19.42%	19.17%	18.93%	18.75%	18.64%	18.57%	18.54%	18.52%	18.50%
0.06	20.00%	19.97%	19.93%	19.87%	19.75%	19.57%	19.30%	18.99%	18.70%	18.48%	18.34%	18.26%	18.22%	18.20%	18.17%
0.062	20.00%	19.96%	19.92%	19.85%	19.71%	19.49%	19.18%	18.82%	18.47%	18.22%	18.06%	17.96%	17.91%	17.89%	17.86%

16.7   Extension to Other Processes

It is clear that the treatment presented in this chapter can be easily applied to more general contexts: there is nothing stopping us, for instance, from assuming that the volatility of $S + a$ should be stochastic. Indeed, this is the approach followed in Part IV of this book. The appeal of this is as follows. Let us assume that we believe that a large part of the smile shape for interest rates derives from the deviation from proportionality with the level of the move size. If this were the case, a *log-normal* volatility would continuously change simply in response to the changes in level of the underlying rates, and a CEV description (perhaps proxied by a displaced diffusion) could be more appropriate. We might also believe that, after accounting for these volatility increments strongly correlated with the moves in the underlying, there remains a significant degree of variability in the volatility. Rather than using a log-normal stochastic volatility, which would then have to be very highly correlated with the diffusive process describing the underlying, one can use a CEV/displaced-diffusion process instead with an independent stochastic process to describe the uncorrelated residual variability. This is indeed one of the approaches suggested in Chapter 24 and used in Chapter 23 in the case of interest rates.

In theory one could couple a displaced-diffusion approach with a local-volatility (restricted-stochastic-volatility) description for the underlying. I am however sceptical about this approach: as I have explained in Chapter 12, if we can give a good financial a priori justification for expecting at least a certain type of dependence of the volatility on the underlying, we can be justified in embedding this prior into our calibration of the model to the market data. This is, for instance, what one can do with the CEV/displaced-diffusion approach. In more general cases, however, letting the market 'speak for itself', and imply from option prices the parameters of a displaced-local-volatility process might not be so wise. To begin with, the procedure would place a reliance (in my opinion difficult to justify) on the option market's informational efficiency; it is also fraught with the technical difficulties associated with inverse problems (see the discussion in Section 12.1 of Chapter 12). The resulting displaced-local-volatility surface would be likely to be numerically difficult to obtain, and to justify financially.

Could one couple a displaced diffusion with log-normal jumps? By so doing we would be positing a process of the type

$$\frac{d(S_t + a)}{S_t + a} = (\mu - \lambda k_a)\, dt + \sigma_a(t)\, dz(t) + dq_a \tag{16.49}$$

Now $Y_a - 1$ is the percentage change in the quantity $S + a$ before and after the jump, and one can define

$$k_a = E[Y_a - 1] \tag{16.50}$$

to be the expected size of the percentage jump amplitude of $S + a$. So, if a jump does occur, $S + a$ instantaneously changes from $S + a$ to $(S + a)Y_a$, and the overall percentage change in the stock price (due both to the diffusive and to the jump components) is given by

$$\frac{d(S_t + a)}{S_t + a} = (\mu - \lambda k_a)\, dt + \sigma_a(t)\, dz(t) + (Y_a - 1) \tag{16.51}$$

To a large extent we can still make use of the formulae obtained in the log-normal jump case. We can, for instance, apply the same reasoning followed above in arriving at the price of a call:

$$E_{t_0}^Q \left[(S_T - K)^+ \right] = E_{t_0}^Q \left[((S_T + a) - (K + a))^+ \right]$$

$$= \int_{K+a}^{\infty} (S_T + a) \Psi_a' \, d(S_T + a)$$

$$- (K + a) \int_{K+a}^{\infty} \Psi_a' \, d(S_T + a) \qquad (16.52)$$

We now note that $(S_T + a)$ has the jump–diffusion distribution Ψ_a' implied by Equation (16.49), rather than the log-normal diffusion distribution Ψ_a that we assumed above. With this proviso, the same derivation that led to a semi-analytical formula for the price of a call in the 'simple' jump–diffusion case (see Section 14.6 of Chapter 14) can then be followed in the displaced-diffusion case. One will simply have to keep in mind that all the model parameters now refer to $S + a$ rather than S: the volatility of the jump amplitude ratio, for instance, will now be the volatility of the jumps in $S + a$ instead of S, etc. And, of course, negative values of S can be reached after a jump.

Chapter 17

No-Arbitrage Restrictions on the Dynamics of Smile Surfaces

The topics covered in this chapter are very important, because I introduce a different (non-process based) way of looking at derivatives pricing. In order to motivate the treatment I present a couple of case studies. These examples will suggest that it would be desirable to specify directly the dynamics of the future smile surface, without having to go through the tortuous route of specifying a process for the underlying first. This approach departs from the route taken by the more common models, which start from the specification of a process for the underlying. Unfortunately, this requires introducing quite a lot of new notation and terminology, and requires careful (but sometimes tedious) definition of such intuitive concepts as 'floating smiles', 'forward-propagated smiles', etc.

Specifying directly the evolution of the smile surface would appear to fit in well with the pricing philosophy discussed in Chapter 1: the exotic trader, I argued there, should be more concerned with predicting with reasonable accuracy her future re-hedging costs (i.e. with predicting the future smile surface) than with specifying a 'good' process for the underlying. It would seem natural to do so by specifying directly how the smile should evolve over time. However, I will show in this chapter that achieving this without exposing oneself to the risk of being arbitraged is not easy. In a nutshell, understanding why this is the case is not difficult: assigning a future smile surface means specifying a multitude of future option prices. These prices, however, are not independent, since they 'share' the same underlying (so, for instance, a given call cannot be worth more than a same-maturity, more-out-of-the-money call). Indeed, the ability to create a linear combination of assets that dominates another asset (or portfolio of assets) is what arbitrage is all about. If future prices (smiles) are 'moved around' without some strong constraints, it should come as no surprise that such dominating portfolios might end up being inadvertently created.

In order to develop some intuition for a rather unconventional approach, in what follows I present a couple of examples that explain what the 'trader's dream' is, and why it is so difficult to realize.

17.1   A Worked-Out Example: Pricing Continuous Double Barriers

Continuous double barriers (also known as continuous knock-outs, one-touch barriers or, sometimes, boxes) are instruments that pay $1 at maturity unless a reference rate (often a spot FX rate) touches or breaches two pre-set barriers at any (trading) time throughout the life of the option. If either barrier is touched or breached no payment takes place. Clearly, for the value at any point in time of the continuous double barrier to be non-zero, the current value of the reference rate must be greater than the lower barrier and smaller than the higher barrier.

It is not difficult to write the PDE that must be satisfied by the price of the option; what is more complicated is finding a solution that matches the initial and boundary conditions. One is greatly assisted in the search for a solution by a uniqueness theorem often invoked in the PDE arena, which, broadly speaking, states that, if we find *a* solution to the PDE satisfying both the boundary and initial conditions, we can rest assured that it will be *the* solution.

Analytic semi-closed-form equations do exist in the literature for the double-barrier problem, which enjoy different degrees of generality (non-constant interest rates, non-constant volatilities, etc. For a compendium of useful formulae see Haug (1998)). In this section I describe a general semi-analytic method to obtain the solution by constructing an approximating series of portfolios satisfying with arbitrary precision both the initial conditions, and an increasing discrete subset of the continuous boundary conditions. The technique, known as 'portfolio replication' is not new. I will present it, however, from a slightly unconventional angle. I should also clarify that, despite the fact that the algorithm will be presented in terms of a trading strategy, it should only be regarded as a means towards obtaining a very general and intuitively transparent pricing solution, rather than as an actually implementable trading strategy.

Despite the apparent simplicity of the approach, the static portfolio replication strategy actually involves some rather subtle points in option pricing. In order to appreciate their implications I begin by introducing below a simple paradox.

17.1.1   Money For Nothing: A Degenerate Hedging Strategy for a Call Option

The paradox referred to above is the following. Let us assume, for the sake of simplicity, that:

1. there are no market frictions (trading can be continuous, no bid–offer spreads, etc.);

2. all the assumptions underpinning the Black-and-Scholes derivation (log-normal process for the underlying, constant – or at most deterministic – volatility, etc.) are exactly met in the real world. In particular, recall that under the Brownian-diffusion assumption the process for the underlying is continuous;

3. we have zero interest rates (this assumption is only made for the sake of simplicity, and the restriction is easy to remove).

Under these assumptions the strategy that gives rise to an apparent paradox is to sell an at-the-money European call option for any price the buyer is prepared to pay (no matter how small), and then engage in a costless self-financing trading strategy that will enable the seller to meet her terminal obligations no matter what the final realization of the underlying turns out to be, and keep the premium. More precisely, the idea is as follows. Without loss of generality, assume that the stock price today is $100. Borrow $100 today. Sell a European call option with strike $100 and maturity T. Accept any premium the buyer is prepared to pay, no matter how small, as long as strictly positive. Then engage in the following hedging strategy.

- If the stock price at any point in time is above or at $100, hold one stock. When the stock trades for $100, the option seller – party A in what follows – can always convert her $100 in cash into $100 worth of stock at no cost. In particular she can do so today.

- If the stock price goes below $100 at any point in time party A sells the stock exactly at $100, i.e. A converts her wealth from stock to cash (her wealth is therefore still $100).

- If the stock price comes back above $100 party A will buy back the stock exactly at $100, thereby converting her cash wealth into a stock holding that is worth exactly the same (therefore incurring no profit and no loss).

- Party A should continue with the same (self-financing) strategy until maturity.

- At option maturity, if the stock price ends below zero, the option is out-of-the-money, party A must be holding $100 in cash, with which she can pay back her debt. Party A keeps the premium.

- If the option ends in-the-money, party A delivers the stock and receives the strike ($100). With the cash from the strike, A repays the debt. Party A keeps the premium.

(Incidentally, note that this strategy corresponds to carrying out a Black delta-hedging strategy by using zero volatility in the formula: the delta amount of stock is therefore equal to 0 or 1.) Have we discovered a money machine?

After a moment's thought, it is easy to see that the flaw in the argument lies in the assumption that party A will be able to decide what to do when the stock price is exactly at $100. Suppose in fact that, as the price *rises towards* $100, the trader decided to go long the stock at $100. The price process might however fail to cross the strike and retrace its steps. In this case the trader would have to sell the too-hastily-bought stock for a price lower than $100. To avoid this, party A could try to trade infinitesimally close to $100, but *before* the strike is crossed. But, if the trader 'jumped the gun' she would have no guarantee that the path would not reverse, forcing her again to a costly unwinding. Similarly, if party A, to be on the safe side, waited until the barrier is crossed, she will have to pay more than $100. I will call this the 'perforation' effect. Exactly at $100, the price could go either way, and the trader therefore does not know what to do. With hindsight, even the initial description of the set-up, with the stock price exactly at $100, was a bit of a sleight-of-hand, and the hedging strategy ambiguous: should the trader hold the stock, or be fully invested in cash?

Owing to the finite 'perforation' effect, party A will always make a loss: she will only be able to sell 'a bit' below $100 and to buy 'a bit' above $100. The magnitude of these losses will depend on the volatility of the underlying (which the strategy decided to ignore).

The total amount of these losses will depend on the particular realization, but the strategy (even in the absence of transaction costs) will no longer be self-financing, and will therefore give rise to a finite variance of portfolio returns by time T. In addition, the cumulative losses will never be smaller than 0 (the latter value occurring only for those paths that start at $100 and never go below their starting value).

Party A might be tempted to try to rescue her strategy by proposing to trade more and more frequently, thereby reducing each perforation cost, which one can expect to be proportional to $\sigma\sqrt{\Delta t}$. However, also this attempt to rescue the money-spinning scheme would not work, because each individual loss might well be lower, but there will be proportionally more potential crossings of the re-hedging boundary, and one can show that the net effect will be the same. This observation will be important in the following discussion of the static replication of the double-barrier problem.

Table 17.1 displays the Black value for an option with maturities and volatilities as displayed in the two left-hand columns, and the average of the costs incurred over the life of the option in the column labelled *PerfCost*. The corresponding exact Black price, and the ratio between the two values are given in the columns *Black* and *Ratio*, respectively.

17.1.2 Static Replication of a Continuous Double Barrier

Having established these results, we can now tackle the problem of the static replication, by means of plain-vanilla options, of the continuous double barrier. For the sake of concreteness we will consider the case of a continuous double barrier with upper and lower boundaries at $100 and $110.

If neither of these values is touched by the reference price throughout the life of the option, the buyer of the knock-out receives $1 at the end of year 1. For this she pays today a premium, strictly less than $1. For the sake of simplicity we ignore interest rates. For the problem to make sense, today's value of the reference price must be strictly more

Table 17.1 The Black values (column *Black*) of options with maturities and volatilities as displayed in the left-hand columns (column *Vol* and *Mat*), the average of the perforation costs incurred over the life of the option (column *PerfCost*), and the ratio between the two (column *Ratio*).

Vol	Mat	Black	PerfCost	Ratio
20.00%	1	7.9656	6.2534	1.2738
20.00%	0.75	6.9013	5.0576	1.3645
20.00%	0.5	5.6372	4.0183	1.4029
20.00%	0.25	3.9878	3.0562	1.3048
20.00%	0.125	2.8204	2.1746	1.2969
5.00%	0.25	0.9973	0.7382	1.3511
40.00%	0.25	7.9656	5.4182	1.4702
40.00%	0.25	7.9656	5.5688	1.4304

than $100 and less than $110. We assume no transaction costs, no bid–offer spreads, and the ability to deal in arbitrarily large sizes.

As mentioned earlier, we will attempt to construct a replicating portfolio that satisfies the boundary and initial conditions to within an arbitrary degree of accuracy. We will then invoke the uniqueness theorem to claim that, if we have found *a* solution that satisfies the aforementioned conditions, then it must be *the* solution. In addition we will show that the replicating portfolio built using the procedure described below will need no re-balancing until expiry of the option, or breach of either barrier. For this reason, the construction is sometimes referred to as the 'static-replicating-portfolio' strategy. However, I will not make use of this term, which I reserve for those instruments for which a replicating portfolio can always be left in place until expiry of the option, irrespective of the path of the underlying. Let us look at the procedure in detail.

The first step is the matching of the terminal[1] conditions at the final expiry (time T). The true profile (see Figure 17.1) displays two discontinuities, at $100 and at $110, where the payoff profile jumps from $0 to $1 and vice versa. This terminal payoff can be approximated by purchasing today a T-maturity call struck at $100 - \epsilon$, selling a T-maturity call struck at $100, selling another T-maturity call struck at $110, and finally purchasing a T-maturity call struck at $110 + \epsilon$. See Figure 17.1.

The notional of each call option is simply equal to $1/\epsilon$. As ϵ goes to zero the profile of the call spread approximates as closely as we may wish the discontinuous terminal payoff of the knock-out option, and the notionals become larger and larger. At time t the set-up cost of this portfolio, Π_1, will depend on the prevailing spot value of the underlying reference price, and on the maturity of the options. We will denote this dependence using the notation $\Pi_1(t, T | S_t = \widehat{S_t}; \epsilon)$, where the parametric dependence on the call spread

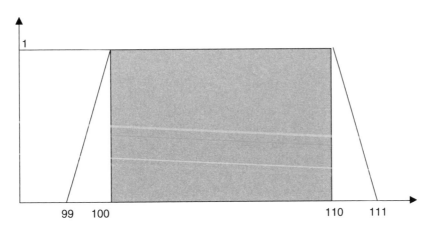

Figure 17.1   The true initial (i.e. expiry) condition of a unit double-barrier option (shaded area), and the approximating payoff with a width ϵ of 1. The approximating payoff is obtained by purchasing a call struck at $99, selling a call at $100, selling a call at $110 and purchasing a call at $111. The notional for all these calls is equal to $1/\epsilon$. The two axes in the figure are not drawn to scale.

---

[1] In PDE language this condition is typically referred to as the 'initial' condition. *Pace* PDE enthusiasts, I will use the more financially transparent term 'terminal' instead.

width, ϵ, has been explicitly included to emphasize the fact that the value of the portfolio does depend on ϵ.

Let us now consider an arbitrarily small time interval Δt, and let us place ourselves at the boundary levels, \$100 and \$110, Δt years before expiry (i.e. at time $T - \Delta t$). We can evaluate the values of the four T-maturity options contingent on our being at \$100 and \$110 at time $T - \Delta t$, i.e. we can evaluate $\Pi_1(T - \Delta t, T | S_{T-\Delta t} = 100; \epsilon)$ and $\Pi_1(T - \Delta t, T | S_{T-\Delta t} = 110; \epsilon)$. The only assumption required for the evaluation of these quantities is that the future volatility of the underlying should be known today. This is certainly the case if the volatility is assumed to be a deterministic function of time. But this is also the case if we assume, for instance, that the future volatility is a known function of the absolute future level of the underlying price, as it is for local-volatility models. We will discuss this point at greater length later in the chapter.

For the moment I should point out that the value at time $T - \Delta t$ of the four-option portfolio set up to satisfy the terminal condition is not equal to zero either at \$100 or at \$110, i.e.

$$\Pi_1(T - \Delta t, T | S_{T-\Delta t} = 100; \epsilon) \neq 0 \tag{17.1}$$

and

$$\Pi_1(T - \Delta t, T | S_{T-\Delta t} = 110; \epsilon) \neq 0 \tag{17.2}$$

The boundary conditions at time $T - \Delta t$, which would require the value of the replicating portfolio to be equal to 0, are therefore not met. How can we fix this? Let us denote the values of the four-option portfolio at \$100 and \$110 by a and b:

$$\Pi_1(T - \Delta t, T | S_{T-\Delta t} = 100; \epsilon) = a \neq 0 \tag{17.3}$$

and

$$\Pi_1(T - \Delta t, T | S_{T-\Delta t} = 110; \epsilon) = b \neq 0 \tag{17.4}$$

To satisfy the boundary conditions at time $T - \Delta t$ we need to add to the portfolio of four options built thus far a suitable position in two plain-vanilla options whose discounted values at \$100 and \$110 should be exactly equal to $-a$ and $-b$, respectively. At the same time these two options should be chosen in such a way as not to 'spoil' the terminal condition at time T.

It is easy to see that it is possible to fulfil both conditions by choosing an out-of-the-money call expiring at time T and struck at \$110, and an out-of-the-money put, also maturing at time T, and struck at \$100. The payoffs of these two options are exactly zero inside the range [\$100 \$110] and at the boundary values; the initial conditions are therefore still satisfied. If we denote by α and β the unknown holdings of call and put, with (hopefully) obvious notation, we will then impose that

$$\alpha Call(S_{T-\Delta t} = 100, K = 110, T - \Delta t, T)$$
$$+ \beta Put(S_{T-\Delta t} = 100, K = 100, T - \Delta t, T) = -a \tag{17.5}$$

and

$$\alpha Call(S_{T-\Delta t} = 110, K = 110, T - \Delta t, T)$$

$$+\beta Put(S_{T-\Delta t} = 110, K = 100, T - \Delta t, T) = -b \qquad (17.6)$$

This set of two linear equations in two unknowns, α and β, constitutes a 2×2 linear system that will yield as a solution the amounts of out-of-the-money call and put to sell. We will denote the value at time $T - \Delta t$ of the portfolio of six options, now satisfying both the terminal conditions and the boundary conditions, at time $T - \Delta t$ and when the stock price is equal to $\widehat{S}$, by $\Pi_2(T - \Delta t, T | S_{T-\Delta t} = \widehat{S}; \epsilon)$. In particular, note that, by construction, we now have

$$\Pi_2(T - \Delta t, T | S_{T-\Delta t} = 100; \epsilon) = 0 \qquad (17.7)$$

and

$$\Pi_2(T - \Delta t, T | S_{T-\Delta t} = 110; \epsilon) = 0 \qquad (17.8)$$

The procedure should now be clear: we move one further step Δt away from the terminal maturity and we evaluate the values of the six-option portfolio at time $T - 2\Delta t$ conditional on the underlying being at both barriers: $\Pi_2(T - 2\Delta t, T | S_{T-2\Delta t} = 100; \epsilon)$ and $\Pi_2(T - 2\Delta t, T | S_{T-2\Delta t} = 110; \epsilon)$. Neither of these two values will be equal to zero, but we will find that

$$\Pi_2(T - 2\Delta t, T | S_{T-2\Delta t} = 100; \epsilon) = c \neq 0 \qquad (17.9)$$

and

$$\Pi_2(T - 2\Delta t, T | S_{T-2\Delta t} = 110; \epsilon) = d \neq 0 \qquad (17.10)$$

From the previous reasoning, we should now look for two additional out-of-the-money options (a call struck at \$110 and a put struck at \$100) so as to match the boundary conditions at time $T - 2\Delta t$. We must make sure, however, that these new options will not spoil the construction up to this point. A moment's thought suggests that their expiration will have to be at time $T - \Delta t$, and their strikes at \$100 (for the put) and at \$110 (for the call), so that the boundary conditions at time $T - \Delta t$, which were already taken care of, are not affected. Once again, we will find a 2×2 system, given by

$$\gamma Call(S_{T-2\Delta t} = 100, K = 110, T - 2\Delta t, T - \Delta t)$$

$$+\delta Put(S_{T-2\Delta t} = 100, K = 100, T - 2\Delta t, T - \Delta t) = -c \qquad (17.11)$$

and

$$\gamma Call(S_{T-2\Delta t} = 110, K = 110, T - 2\Delta t, T - \Delta t)$$

$$+\delta Put(S_{T-2\Delta t} = 110, K = 100, T - 2\Delta t, T - \Delta t) = -d \qquad (17.12)$$

whose solutions will give the required amounts of out-of-the-money call and put, γ and δ.

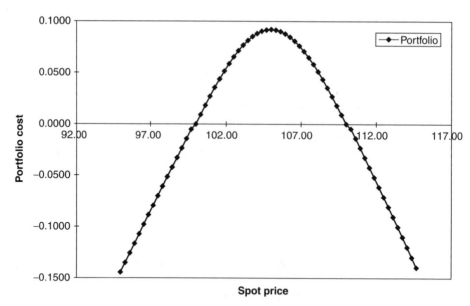

Figure 17.2   The cost of the replicating portfolio as a function of today's spot price. Note that the solution to the double-barrier problem only makes sense (and can therefore be meaningfully read) within the 100/110 band. The value of the replicating portfolio, however, is given by the dotted line for any value of the underlying, inside, at, or outside the barrier.

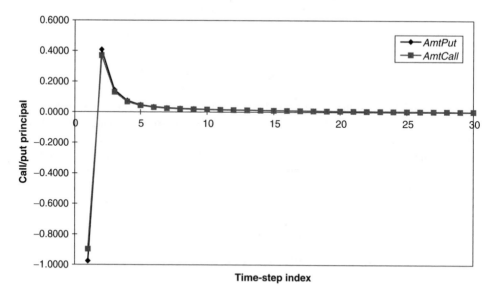

Figure 17.3   The amount of calls (*AmtCall*) and puts (*AmtPut*) necessary to replicate the payoff of the $100/$110 double-barrier problem with 30 steps between today and option expiry. The step number is on the *x*-axis. Step number 1 corresponds to the time slice Δt years before expiry.

We can repeat this procedure all the way to the origin. Altogether, $4 + 2(n - 1)$ plain-vanilla options will be required to carry out the portfolio strategy (the integer n is the number of time-steps, i.e. $T/\Delta t$). Let us indicate the final portfolio by $\Pi(\Delta t, \epsilon)$, where only the parametric dependence on the call spread width, ϵ, and on the chosen time-step, Δt, has been retained.

What we have constructed is a portfolio of options that matches at the discrete times $i\Delta t$, $i = 0, 1, 2, \ldots, n$, the boundary conditions of the double barrier, and which super-replicates the terminal (expiry) condition. It is plausible to surmise (and it can be proven that this is indeed the case) that the present value of the double barrier, $PV(Double\text{-}Barrier)$, will be given by

$$PV(DoubleBarrier) = \lim_{\epsilon \to 0, n \to \infty} \Pi(\Delta t, \epsilon) \qquad (17.13)$$

With this method for finding the present value of a continuous double knock-out option the solution is expressed in terms of an infinite series of closed-form expressions (the Black prices of calls and puts). The series does not converge particularly rapidly, nor are the individual computations (i.e. the evaluations of the Black formulae) extremely fast. The main strength of the static-portfolio replication technique lies in its flexibility, since it can be applied not only to the case of deterministic time-dependent volatilities, but whenever the user can assume that the future implied volatility of an option of a given maturity can be known (or 'guessed') today. In particular, if the trader believed the smile to be floating or sticky, she could be tempted to embed this belief in the construction of the replicating portfolio.

In the next section I show that this way of looking at the portfolio-replication problem has taken us right to the heart of the problem of how a future smile can be assigned, and why it is unavoidable to do so. In particular, I will analyse in detail what costs will be incurred if the portfolio has to be unwound. When we tackle this topic, the previous discussion of the paradox about the trading strategy consisting of selling an option and keeping the premium at no cost will prove useful. In addition, we will have to reconcile our strategy with the current market prices of the full series of plain-vanilla options with maturities at all the various time-steps. In other words, we will have to ask the fundamental question: what beliefs about the values of future option prices (i.e. the future smile) are compatible with today's plain-vanilla option prices? These topics are dealt with in the rest of this chapter. In the meantime Figures 17.2 and 17.3 show the price of the replicating portfolio (and therefore the option value), and the necessary amounts of calls and puts for the $100/$110 double-barrier problem.

17.2 Analysis of the Cost of Unwinding

The portfolio built using the procedure described above will certainly produce the required payoff if the underlying stock price ends up anywhere between $100 and $110 without having ever touched either boundary throughout the life of the option. But what happens if the stock price breaches either barrier before expiry? The trader who put in place the static strategy made up of a very large number of calls and puts will have to unwind all the unexpired options as soon as the barrier is touched. By looking at Figure 17.2 one can immediately see, in fact, that, outside and away from either barrier, the value of the plain-vanilla portfolio and the value of the double barrier rapidly diverge.

In this context, the discussion of the finite perforation cost becomes very useful: once again, the trader in reality will not be able to 'catch' the stock price exactly at $100 (or $110), but will incur a cost due to the finite difference between the actual transaction price and the theoretical unwinding level. As in the money-for-nothing paradox explored above, by making the trading interval smaller and smaller, the perforation cost (which, as we argued in Chapter 2, should depend for a diffusive process on $\sqrt{\Delta t}$) can be made arbitrarily small. Unlike the previous example, however, increasing the trading frequency does not expose the trader to more and more potential crossings of the barrier level (and, therefore, to more and more small losses). With a continuous-double-barrier case, once either trigger level is touched, the option is dead, the finite perforation cost is incurred only once and can therefore be truly reduced (in our frictionless world) without having to pay any price.

There still remains, however, one problem. When determining the amounts of calls and puts (displayed in Figure 17.3) necessary to meet the boundary conditions at any of the intermediate times, we had to calculate the discounted value of the later payoffs *contingent on the future stock price being at either barrier*. The volatility that entered this calculation was therefore the future implied volatility for the stock price at the chosen intermediate time and at the appropriate barrier. If the volatility were truly perfectly deterministic (and perfectly known to the trader), the market in plain-vanilla options would not only give us information about the implied future volatility (see Chapter 3), but would also provide the trader with the instruments to 'lock-in' this future volatility. In a deterministic-volatility world, therefore, giving a series of spot option prices for different maturities is equivalent to providing a series of future option prices starting on all the intermediate expiries.

In the presence of smiles, however, the problem is much more complex. In order to tackle the problem in the presence of smiles, the trader could take either of two different routes: the first one (model-based) would be

1. to start from an assumption for the dynamics for the underlying; for the sake of concreteness, let us assume that the trader has chosen a local-volatility process, such as the one described by Equation (8.6) of Chapter 8;

2. to determine, using the prices of traded plain-vanilla options, the local volatility surface $\sigma(S_t, t)$;

3. to place herself at either boundary at the appropriate future point in time;

4. to evaluate the future discounted values of the payoffs (i.e. the future option prices) by using the chosen numerical method (e.g. a trinomial tree if the Derman-and-Kani construction had been used to extract the local volatilities, or, perhaps, a Monte Carlo procedure);

5. to solve the 2×2 system on the basis of these future option values in order to determine the required amounts of calls and puts.

Note that, given the assumption in point 1 above, recovering the future option values obtained from a given chosen model is as essential in order to prevent arbitrage as the recovery of today's prices of plain-vanilla options. In other words, if the model were correct, assuming any other value for the future values of the plain-vanilla options would be an arbitrage violation no less severe than using a non-market price for a spot-starting plain-vanilla option. The only difference between the present and future prices, in this respect, is that different models will predict different (model-dependent) future values for future option prices, but all (perfectly calibrated) models must accept the same current set of option prices on immediate penalty of arbitrage. Therefore the arbitrage violation incurred by assuming future option prices not identical to the ones predicted by the model is model-contingent, whilst failure to recover spot option prices is a model-independent arbitrage violation.

The second (theoretically more dubious, but intuitively appealing) strategy would be the following.

1. The trader could make an assumption about the nature of the smile (e.g. sticky, floating, forward-propagated, etc.) and about its degree of time homogeneity. This assumption could be made on the basis of statistical information, trading views, or a combination of the two.

2. Given this assumption, the trader could then calculate the future value of the discounted payoffs by enforcing directly the sticky or floating assumption about the smile and using the Black formula with the appropriate future implied volatility as an input. In particular, if the trader assumed the smile to be floating, she would translate today's smile surface to either barrier. Depending on the barrier, the future options would therefore have either today's at-the-money implied volatility, or the volatility corresponding to today's option with a strike out-of-the-money by an amount of dollars equal to the width of the barrier. Alternatively, if the trader had assumed a sticky smile, the relevant volatilities would simply correspond to today's volatilities for the upper and lower barrier levels. Note that assuming to know the future smile surface greatly simplifies the task of producing the future option prices: since a smiley volatility is 'the wrong number to put in the wrong formula to get the right price', we do not need a complex pricing model, and, by virtue of the very definition of smile, the Black formula can be directly employed to calculate call prices.

3. From the values thus calculated, the trader would then have to solve the 2×2 systems described above and determine the amounts of calls and puts to match the boundary condition.

It must be stressed again that, if one believed in a particular model description of the dynamics of the underlying, the second procedure would, in general, be theoretically incorrect (prone to arbitrage), because the assumed future prices would not be consistent with the underlying financial model and with today's market prices. This requirement, however, should be taken with a pinch of salt. I have argued, for instance, that a process description such as the one provided by Equation (8.6) for equity or FX products leaves a lot to be desired. Yet, the prices it produces are, *within the local-volatility model*, arbitrage-free. So, the local-volatility model might well protect the trader from arbitrage, but only if the true process is indeed a local-volatility diffusion, and the trader has correctly estimated the local-volatility surface. As a consequence, feeling overly constrained by the model output should probably not be considered an imperative (or, sometimes, perhaps even desirable).

One could therefore be tempted to approach the pricing problem from a different angle. Since, after all, the desirability of a given model is assessed on the basis of its ability to recover today's prices and to produce a plausible future evolution of the smile surface, why not dispense with the model step entirely and directly specify the evolution of the smile surface? Perhaps we can find some clearly identifiable statistical features of the smile dynamics that could guide us as to how this smile dynamics could be specified. See, in this respect, Section 17.3 below, suggestively called 'The Trader's Dream'. Unfortunately, I will show that matters are not that simple. For the moment, the example presented above makes perfectly clear the link about the future re-hedging costs, the option value and the underlying assumptions about the smile type. To give an idea of the impact of different assumptions about future smiles, Table 17.2 shows the portfolio replication option prices obtained with a constant (no smile) volatility (column *Const*), a sticky smile (column *Fixed*), a floating smile (column *Float*), for a constant or a time-dependent volatility.

Going back to the general pricing philosophy behind this example, one could object that, if the trader were to follow the second approach, she would, in a sense, assume to know the answer beforehand, since she would be imposing the future implied volatility surface, rather than obtaining it from the no-arbitrage dynamics of a model. I take a different view: the acceptance of a model ultimately depends on its ability to reproduce qualitative features of the smile that the trader feels confident with. I have argued at length in this book that the at-least-approximate reproduction of today's smile surface could be one such qualitative feature. When looked at in this light the model-based and the replication approaches would appear to be not so different after all.

Probably a more constructive approach is to recognize that different plain-vanilla-option strategies will be needed to hedge different exotic products: if the hedging strategy were truly static in nature, as might be the case, for instance, for a single-look European digital option, then today's option prices would be all that matters. If, on the other hand, substantial future re-hedging is required, then recovering future option prices becomes essential, and therefore the trader will want to ensure that the smile predictions of a given

Table 17.2 The double-barrier option prices calculated using the portfolio replication technique with a constant volatility (column *Const*), a sticky smile (column *Fixed*), a floating smile (column *Float*) and flat or time-dependent volatility.

ATMVol	Flat volatility			Time-dependent volatility	
	Const	*Fixed*	*Float*	*Fixed*	*Float*
10%	0.0061	0.0068	0.0074	0.0065	0.0069
9%	0.0167	0.0173	0.0178	0.0173	0.0178
8%	0.0411	0.0414	0.0416	0.0420	0.0424
7%	0.0914	0.0911	0.0908	0.0926	0.0929
6%	0.1834	0.1820	0.1812	0.1849	0.1848
5%	0.3312	0.3283	0.3269	0.3327	0.3323
4%	0.5374	0.5329	0.5315	0.5388	0.5382

model are reasonable, and/or to correct and supplement these predictions with exogenous (and, possibly, theoretically incompatible) information.

It is also useful to revisit at this point the example of an option with a forward-setting strike, analysed in the case of purely time-dependent volatilities in Section 3.8 of Chapter 3. I argued in that context that, in order to hedge the volatility exposure arising from the option, the trader had to 'lock-in' the future portion of the volatility between the time of the strike reset and the option maturity. I also pointed out how a plausible hedging strategy would have to display, before the reset of the strike, an appreciable sensitivity to volatility (to match the vega exposure), but no delta and no gamma. I proposed a long and a short position in wide, symmetric strangles to fulfil, at least approximately, these combined requirements. Finally, I noted that, as the strike-resetting time was approached, the chosen strangles ceased to produce a flat profile, needed to give no delta and no gamma, for smaller and smaller movements of the underlying from the original at-the-money position. During the life of the option the strikes would therefore have to be adjusted; the closer to the time of the strike reset, the more frequently these readjustments are likely to take place. All these readjustments expose the trader to the *future* price of options. The trader will therefore have to take into account in her price-making the future implied volatility of options with different degrees of in- and out-of-the-moneyness and different maturities. As a consequence, future option prices (i.e. future implied volatility surfaces), might well turn out to have as great an impact as the spot option prices on today's cost of the hedging strategy (and therefore on the value of the forward-resetting option).

17.3 The Trader's Dream

One of the more interesting approaches to giving a direct specification of the future smile dynamics is probably Samuel's (2002) methodology. His reasoning goes as follows. First of all the trader will need a smooth fitted implied volatility surface. Any of the methods presented in Chapter 9 would do, although a parametric approach is probably desirable. For a given maturity the smile is symbolically shown in the top left-hand corner of Figure 17.4 (reproduced with thanks from Samuel (2002)). From the smile surface (i.e. from a collection of current prices) one can distill an implied risk-neutral probability density, ϕ_T. Ignoring discounting, this can be done using Equation (9.4) in Chapter 9[2]:

$$\phi_T = \frac{\partial^2 C}{\partial K^2} \qquad (17.14)$$

This step is represented pictorially by the top right-hand quadrant in Figure 17.4. Given this density, one can determine the values of the strike, K, that correspond to the 25th, 50th and 75th percentiles of the density. See the bottom right-hand corner of Figure 17.4. Let these three values of the strike be denoted by K_-, K_0, and K_+. At this point one can determine the coordinates K_-, K_0, and K_+ on the x-axis of the implied volatility plot, and directly read the corresponding values of the implied volatility, σ_-, σ_0 and σ_+.

---

[2]For simplicity, in this chapter I will assume zero interest rates. Therefore there is no discounting factor in Equation (17.14).

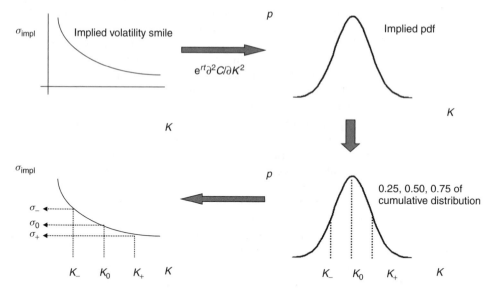

Figure 17.4 A pictorial representation of the procedure used by Samuel (2002) to obtain the quantities σ_0^T, χ^T and ω^T. (David Samuel is kindly thanked for allowing the reproduction of Figures 17.4–17.12 in this chapter.)

These three values can be combined to give rise to a measure of the volatility 'level', σ_0, of the skew:

$$\chi = \frac{\sigma_+ - \sigma_-}{\sigma_0} \tag{17.15}$$

and of the convexity:

$$\omega = \frac{\sigma_+ + \sigma_- - 2\sigma_0}{\sigma_0} \tag{17.16}$$

These three quantities (σ_0, χ and ω), similar in nature to the at-the-money volatility, the risk-reversal and the straddle discussed in Chapter 9, characterize the smile at a given maturity: σ_0^T, χ^T, ω^T. See Figure 17.5.[3]

Their behaviour as a function of option maturity, T, and their time-serial properties can then be studied. Figure 17.6, for instance, shows the behaviour of the level parameter, σ_0^T, on three dates for the FTSE. Two of the dates (19-Mar-2001 and 18-Mar-2002) are simply spaced one year apart, and display a 'normal' behaviour. The third date, however, corresponds to a week after the events of 11 September 2001 (18-Sep-2001) and displays a clearly different behaviour. Figures 17.7 and 17.8 show the same type of plot for the skew and convexity parameters. It is interesting to observe that the same patterns are observed, on the same days, for the EuroStoxx (see Figures 17.9–17.11). Note, for instance, how the skew curve moves considerably lower than the 'normal' curves on the 18-Sep-2001.

---

[3]Figures 17.5–17.12 have already been produced in Chapter 7. They are reproduced here for ease of reference.

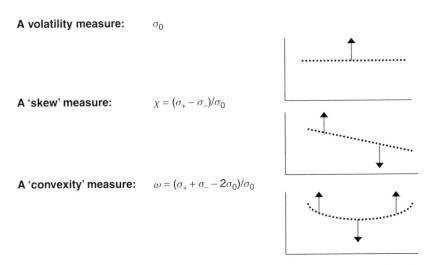

A volatility measure: σ_0

A 'skew' measure: $\chi = (\sigma_+ - \sigma_-)/\sigma_0$

A 'convexity' measure: $\omega = (\sigma_+ + \sigma_- - 2\sigma_0)/\sigma_0$

Figure 17.5   The modes of deformation of the smile described by the quantities σ_0^T, χ^T and ω^T.

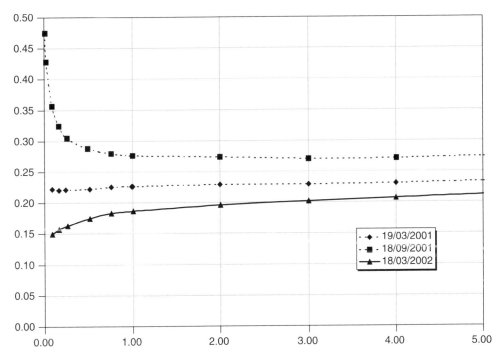

Figure 17.6   The level parameter σ_0^T as a function of the option expiry (x-axis) for the FTSE100 index on three trading dates. See the text for details.

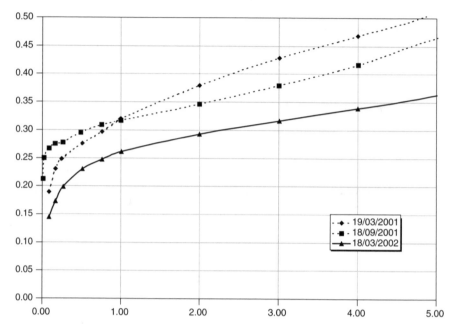

Figure 17.7 The skew parameter χ^T as a function of the option expiry (x-axis) for the FTSE100 index on three trading dates. Note that the underlying density is that of the price, not of the logarithm of the price. Therefore, in a Black-and-Scholes world the price distribution would be log-normal and skewed to the right. A price-density skew tending toward zero therefore implies a log-density strongly negatively skewed. See the text for further details.

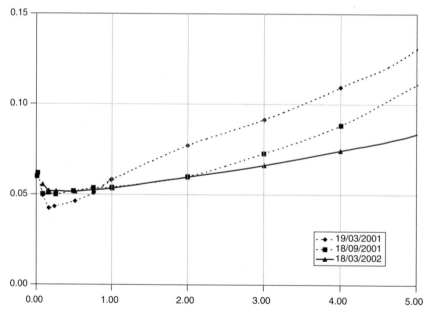

Figure 17.8 The convexity parameter ω^T as a function of the option expiry (x-axis) for the FTSE100 index on three trading dates. See the text for details.

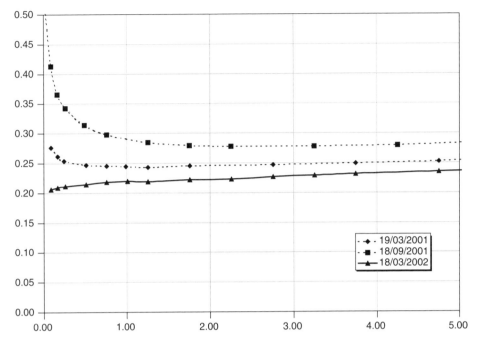

Figure 17.9   The level parameter σ_0^T as a function of the option expiry (x-axis) for the EuroStoxx index on three trading dates. See the text for details.

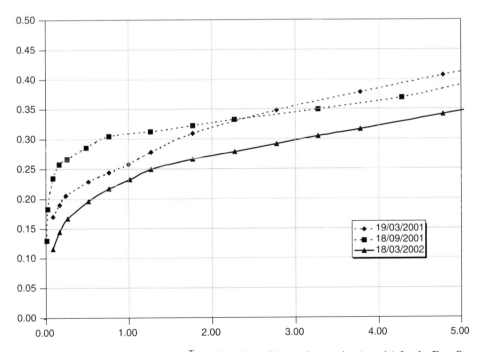

Figure 17.10   The skew parameter χ^T as a function of the option expiry (x-axis) for the EuroStoxx index on three trading dates. See the text for details.

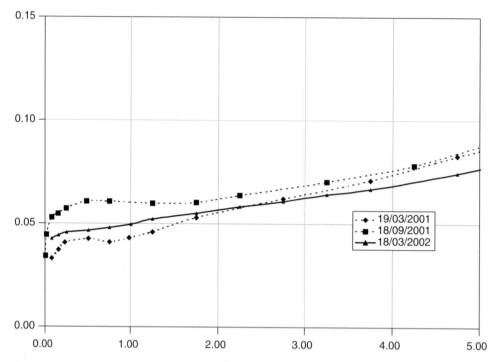

Figure 17.11   The convexity parameter ω^T as a function of the option expiry (*x*-axis) for the EuroStoxx index on three trading dates. See the text for details.

Samuel (2002) calls these recognizable patterns the 'finger prints' of the smile surfaces of the various markets.

Samuel (2002) also makes a comparison with the evolution of the skew curve implied by a local-volatility model: see Figure 17.12. The original market skew curve (dotted line), which is recovered by construction by the local-volatility model, evolves deterministically to a much lower level one year forward in the 'tree'. Therefore, the local-volatility model implicitly assumes that, in one year's time, the trader will encounter with certainty the type of skew curve that is associated with 'exceptional' events. I fully concur with Samuel in finding this behaviour undesirable, especially if one is pricing products such as forward-starting options.

The way out of this impasse proposed by Samuel is to assume that it might be possible to assign directly the dynamics of the parameters σ_0^T, χ^T and ω^T, which are in spirit akin to the principal components of the smile surface. The nature of this dynamics might be suggested by a careful analysis of their statistical properties. The approach is clearly appealing and would dispense altogether with the specification of the process for the underlying. For this reason, I call it 'the trader's dream'. I show in the remainder of this chapter that, unfortunately, unless some very strong constraints are put in place, this dream can easily turn into a nightmare. Understanding why this is the case will bring about an interesting and powerful insight into option pricing.

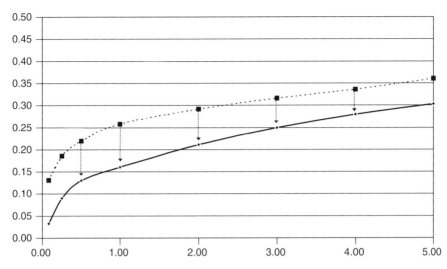

Figure 17.12 The evolution over one year of the skew parameter as a function of option expiry (the skew curve) implied by a local-volatility model. Note how the curve has migrated downwards.

17.4 Plan of the Remainder of the Chapter

I present[4] below some results regarding the model-independent, arbitrage-free specification of future volatility smiles. The specification of an arbitrage-free dynamics for the smile surface is not a novel idea; see, for example, Schoenbucher (1996). The crucial difference between his approach and the one presented here, however, is that Schoenbucher posits a particular (stochastic-volatility) process for the underlying and derives, *given this process*, the arbitrage-free dynamics for the implied volatility surface. In this work we do not assume the process for the underlying to be known. Our results are therefore weaker, but more general.

A concept that traders are familiar with is the distinction between 'sticky' or 'floating'[5] smiles. Also, traders often speak and think in terms of 'forward-propagated' smiles. These concepts have been criticized as being rough rules of thumb, without theoretical foundations (see, for example, Derman (1999)). I show that they can be made precise and defined in such a way that they reflect traders' usage and intuition. I therefore provide a precise definition of a floating smile, I show under what conditions today's prices allow for the existence of such a floating smile surface and I highlight the implicit assumptions a trader makes when speaking, for instance, of a floating or of a forward-propagated smile. I also show that, if it exists, the future floating smile surface consistent with today's price is unique, and can, in principle, be obtained by Fourier transform.

---

[4]Many of the ideas presented in the rest of this chapter originated from a talk given by Eric Reiner. Although the conclusions I reach are different, the conceptual debt is evident. I also benefited from discussions with Chris Hunter, Peter Jaeckel and, above all, Mark Joshi, whom I would like to thank.

[5]The term 'sticky-delta' is often used to describe floating smiles. The discussion below shows why, and in what circumstances, this two terms can be used interchangeably.

An unexpected by-product of the analysis presented below is that, under relatively mild conditions, even if the future smiles are stochastic, as long as they are independent of the future realization of the underlying, there exists a single future *deterministic* floating smile such that options would have exactly the same price if they were valued under the stochastic regime or in this equivalent deterministic-smile setting.

I conclude the chapter by presenting some computational results showing to what extent popular processes satisfy the independence condition mentioned above. In particular, I show that if the underlying true process were a jump–diffusion with stochastic intensity and/or jump amplitude and/or variance of amplitude, the future smile surfaces display a very mild dependence on the future realization of the underlying. I conclude that, in the case of this process, introducing stochasticity to the jump component 'buys' the trader very little on top of the results given by the much simpler equivalent deterministic setting. Therefore, the replication strategy proposed below can be applied in an approximate but accurate way also if the underlying process were a jump–diffusion with stochastic jump amplitude and frequency. I also find that, if the true process were, instead, a stochastic-volatility diffusion there would be an appreciable correlation between future smile surfaces and future realizations of the underlying, and that therefore stochastic-volatility processes do not produce prices that could be obtained from a set of equivalent future smile surfaces.

17.5 Conditions of No-Arbitrage for the Stochastic Evolution of Future Smile Surfaces

17.5.1 Description of the Market

Condition 1 (Perfect Market) *We place ourselves in an economy with a perfect, friction-less market, where traders incur no bid–offer spreads, short sales of calls and puts are allowed in arbitrarily large (but finite) sizes, no taxes are levied, etc.*

Condition 2 (Traded Instruments) *In this perfect-market economy, an underlying 'stock' and plain-vanilla calls of all maturities and strikes are traded. The strikes span a continuum of values, but, for the sake of simplicity, the maturities of the plain-vanilla calls and puts belong to a set $[T_i]$, $i = 0, 1, 2, \ldots, N$, with N arbitrarily large but finite. T_0 represents today. Also for the sake of simplicity, we will assume deterministic interest rates, and therefore N deterministic bonds, B_i, $i = 1, 2, \ldots, N$, also trade. Finally, trading also takes place in complex products of contractual maturity $T_k \in [T_i]$, i.e. in instruments whose payoffs may depend on the history of the underlying up to and including time T_k.*

Condition 3 (Probability Space) *We place ourselves in a filtered probability space $(\Omega, \mathcal{F}_t, Q)$. The state space that we require contains all the present and possible future realizations of the underlying and of the prices of plain-vanilla calls at times $[T_i]$. $\mathcal{F}_t$ is the natural filtration generated by the prices of all the plain-vanilla calls and of the underlying on the arbitrarily large but finite number, $N + 1$, of dates $[T_i]$.*

By availing ourselves of the knowledge of the filtration $\mathcal{F}_t$ we require that we can know, at each of the discrete points in time, what smile surfaces and which values of the underlying have occurred, and which have not. As for the probability measure Q, it is characterized by the following condition:

Condition 4 (Pricing Condition) *If we denote by $C(K, t, T_j)$ the price at time t of a K-strike call of maturity T_j, and by S_{T_j} the value of the stock at time T_j, then we require that a measure Q should exist, satisfying*

$$E_Q[(S_{T_j} - K)^+ | \mathcal{F}_t] B_j^t = C(K, t, T_j) \quad \text{for any } K, T_j$$

It is important to point out that we do not assume that this measure is unique or that it will remain constant over time. In particular, we allow for the possibility that the measure might change stochastically.

Condition 5 (Price Information) *The prices are known today of plain-vanilla calls and puts for an arbitrarily large, but finite, number of expiries, and for a continuum of strikes. They are denoted by $Call_0(S_0, K, T_j)$, $Put_0(S_0, K, T_j)$ with $j = 1, 2, \ldots, N$.*

To lighten notation, in what follows the dependence of the maturities on the indices is often omitted. In practice the market only provides a finite (and often rather small) number of actual price quotes for calls and puts for different strikes and maturities. It is assumed that a sufficiently smooth interpolation/extrapolation between and beyond these points has been adopted by the trader, so that the resulting smile surface should give rise to twice-strike-differentiable implied unconditional densities. In practice, this point is not trivial, but I have dealt with this topic in Chapter 9, and therefore I do not pursue this line of enquiry here.

Definition 1 (Admissible Smile Surface) *A smile surface such that conditions (17.17)–(17.22) are satisfied is called **admissible**:*

$$\frac{\partial Call(t, T, S_t, T)}{\partial K} < 0 \tag{17.17}$$

$$\frac{\partial^2 Call(t, T, S_t, T)}{\partial K^2} > 0 \tag{17.18}$$

$$\frac{\partial Call(t, T, S_t, T)}{\partial T} > 0 \tag{17.19}$$

$$\frac{\partial Put(t, T, S_0, T)}{\partial K} > 0 \tag{17.20}$$

$$Call(t, T, S_t, T)|_{K=0} = S_t \tag{17.21}$$

$$\lim_{K \to \infty} Call(t, T, S_t, K) = 0 \tag{17.22}$$

Condition 6 (Admissibility) *We will always assume that today's smile surface is admissible.*

Admissible smile surfaces prevent the possibility that, for instance, more-out-of-the-money calls should be worth more than more-in-the-money calls ($\frac{\partial Call(t,T,S_t,T)}{\partial K} < 0$); or require a strictly positive price density.

Exercise 1 *Show what kind of arbitrage strategy you could build if the condition $\frac{\partial^2 Call(t,T,S_t,T)}{\partial K^2} > 0$ were violated (Hint: Think butterflies.)*

For today's smile surface, the admissibility conditions are necessary and sufficient in order to rule out the possibility of *static* strategies *constructed today* that can be arbitraged.[6] When the smile surface in question is in the future, however, we will show that the admissibility conditions are necessary, but not sufficient for absence of model-independent arbitrage.

17.5.2   The Building Blocks

Definition 2 (Current Smile Surface) *Let the implied volatility today,* $\sigma_{impl}(t_0, T, K, S_0)$, *be the function of strike and maturity that produces the number which, input in the Black-and-Scholes formula,* $BS(.)$, *for any strike and expiry and with today's value of the underlying, gives today's market price for the corresponding call:*

$$\sigma_{impl}(0) = \sigma_{impl}(t_0, T, K, S_0) : Call_0(S_0, K, T)$$

$$= BS(S_0, K, T, \sigma_{impl}(t_0, T, K, S_0)), \quad \forall K, T \tag{17.23}$$

The quantity $\sigma_{impl}(t_0, T, K, S_0)$ *as a function of* T *and* K *is also referred to as the* ***current smile surface***.

In what follows the derivatives of the $BS(.)$ function with respect to the strike will be required. Unlike the derivatives of the function $BS(.)$ with respect to the underlying, which require information about how the smile surface changes when the stock price changes, and therefore depend on the true process of the underlying, the derivatives with respect to the strikes do not require such knowledge and can be simply observed from the (smoothly interpolated) market prices today. These derivatives are therefore independent of the true process. See the discussion in Section 6.3 of Chapter 6.

Note in passing that one could write $\sigma_{impl} = \sigma_{impl}(t, T, K, S)$, concentrate on the dependence of the implied volatility function on S, posit a process for S (e.g. a stochastic-volatility diffusion) and derive the dynamics of the implied volatility function using Ito's lemma. This is the route followed by Schoenbucher (1996). Since we want to avoid speaking about the process for the stock, and we do not want to be constrained by the choice of a particular process, we do not pursue this route.

Needless to say, the use of the implied volatility quantity in conjunction with the Black-and-Scholes formula should not be taken as a market endorsement of the process posited by the Black-and-Scholes model. Rather, an implied volatility is a conventional, market-agreed-upon way of quoting a price; it is simply 'the wrong number to put in the wrong formula to get the right price'.

Definition 3 (State of the World) *Let a* ***state of the world at time*** t, X_t, *be described by the value of the underlying plus the associated values of calls for all possible strikes and expiries:*

$$X_t = \{S_t \cup Call_t(S_t, K, t, T), \quad \forall K, T\} \tag{17.24}$$

---

[6]An example of such a static strategy, for instance, would be the purchase of a call of strike K_1, and the sale for a higher price of a same-maturity call of strike K_2, with $K_2 > K_1$. The strategy is static because it does not require readjustment until expiry of both options.

The values of the corresponding puts are derived from call/put parity.[7] Puts are therefore not explicitly analysed below, but a symmetric treatment in terms of puts rather than calls could be presented.

Definition 4 (Future Conditional Smile Surface) *Given a state of the world X_t, the* ***future (time-t) conditional implied volatility,*** *$\sigma_{\text{impl}}(t, T, K, X_t)$, is the function of strike and maturity that, for any $Call_t \in X_t$, and for any strike and expiry, produces the number which, input into the Black-and-Scholes formula, $BS(.)$, with the associated future value S_t of the underlying, gives the prices for the corresponding call in the state of the world X_t:*

$$\sigma_{\text{impl}}(t) = \sigma_{\text{impl}}(t, T, K, X_t) : Call_t(S_t, K, t, T)$$
$$= BS(S_t, K, T, \sigma_{\text{impl}}(t, T, K, S_t)), \quad \forall K, T \qquad (17.25)$$

The quantity $\sigma_{\text{impl}}(t, T, K, X_t)$ as a function of T and K is also referred to as the ***future (time-t) conditional smile surface***.

Definition 4 establishes a one-to-one correspondence between a future call price for a given strike and maturity and its associated implied volatility, $\sigma_{\text{impl}}(t, T, K, S_t)$. Therefore, the state of the world at time t can be equivalently described by specifying the value at time t of the underlying and the associated future (time-t) conditional implied volatility surface.

If one knew what the true process for the underlying is, requiring that the future conditional smile surface should depend on the underlying and on all the call prices could be replaced by the condition that the implied volatility surface should depend on S_t, on the type of process, and on whatever additional stochastic processes (if any) (e.g. stochastic volatilities) define the process for the underlying. Definition 4 is, however, more general, because it does not require knowledge of the true process and of its parameters.

17.6   Deterministic Smile Surfaces

17.6.1   Equivalent Descriptions of a State of the World

The definitions presented so far have been expressed in terms of smile surfaces. For many applications it is useful to establish a correspondence between smile surface and state (or price) densities. This can be accomplished by recalling the following well-known result: the current risk-neutral price density for time T, $f_0(S_T)$, i.e. the risk-neutral (unconditional) probability density that the underlying will have value S_T at time T, given that state X_0 prevails today, is given by (see, for example, Breeden and Litzenberger

---

[7]Strictly speaking, the stock price can be seen as a call struck at zero. Therefore specifying the values of *all* calls *and* of the underlying could be seen as redundant. Since, however, the stock price also enters the Black formula, which gives the price of calls, as one of its arguments, I prefer, for the sake of clarity, to overspecify slightly the definition of the state of the world. To avoid inconsistencies, a purist might want to add the condition that, for any implied volatility and maturity, $Call_t(S_t, K = 0, t, T) = S_t$.

(1978) or Dupire (1994))

$$f_0(S_T) = \exp r(T - t_0)\frac{\partial^2 Call_0(S_0, K, t_0, T)}{\partial K^2}$$

$$= \exp r(T - t_0)\frac{\partial^2 BS(S_0, K, t_0, T, \sigma_{impl}(t_0, T, K, S_0))}{\partial K^2} \qquad (17.26)$$

As Breeden and Litzenberger point out, virtually no assumptions have to be made regarding the stochastic process for the underlying in order to arrive at Equation (17.26), and individual preferences and beliefs are not restricted in any way. The only (extremely mild) requirement necessary to obtain Equation (17.26) is that call prices should be obtainable as discounted expectations, under *some* measure, of the terminal payoff. This is why we required condition 4 to hold, and it is no more onerous than requiring absence of arbitrage.

Note that, even if all the unconditional densities obtained using Equation (17.26) were known exactly (for a continuum of times T) this would not determine uniquely the underlying process, which would only be unambiguously specified if all the *conditional* densities were provided as well. See, for example, Baxter and Rennie (1996).

Definition 5 (Future Conditional Risk-Neutral Price Density) *The future   (time-t) conditional risk-neutral price density, $f_t(S_T|X_t)$, is defined to be*

$$f_t(S_T|X_t) = \exp(r\tau)\frac{\partial^2 Call_t(S_t, K, t, T; X_t)}{\partial K^2} =$$

$$= \exp(r\tau)\frac{\partial^2 BS(S_t, K, t, T, \sigma_{impl}(t, T, K, X_t))}{\partial K^2} \qquad (17.27)$$

i.e. it is the risk-neutral probability density that the underlying will have value S_T at time T given that state X_t prevails at time t ($\tau = T - t, T > t$).

Definition 6 (Future Conditional Risk-Neutral State Density) *The future   (time$-t$) conditional risk-neutral state density, $\Phi_t(X_T|X_t)$, is defined to be the risk-neutral probability density that the world will be in state X_T at time T given that state X_t prevails at time t.*

Therefore the state of the world at time t can be equivalently described in terms of

(i) *the value at time t of the underlying plus the values of all the calls:*

$$X_t = \{S(t) \cup Call_t(S_t, K, t, T), \quad \forall K, T\} \qquad (17.28)$$

(ii) *the value at time t of the underlying and the associated future (time-t) S_t-conditional implied volatility surface:*

$$X_t = \{S_t \cup \sigma_{impl}(t, T, K, S_t), \quad \forall K, T\} \qquad (17.29)$$

(iii) *the value at time t of the underlying and the associated future (time-t) S_t-conditional risk-neutral density:*

$$X_t = \{S_t \cup f_t(S_T | S_t)\}, \quad \forall T \tag{17.30}$$

From the properties of the conditional expectations the following relationship must hold between present and future risk-neutral state densities:

$$\Phi_0(X_{T_2}) = \int \Phi_0(X_{T_1}) \Phi_{T_1}(X_{T_2} | X_{T_1}) \, dX_{T_1} \tag{17.31}$$

Equation (17.31), which poses restrictions on the future conditional state densities, is very general, but not very easy to use in practice, since it conditions the expectation on the full state of the world (i.e. on a future realization of the stock price and of *all* the associated calls). It would be helpful to express condition (17.31) in a more manageable form by conditioning only on the realization of the stock price. We explore below under what circumstances this is possible and meaningful – this will lead us directly to the concept of a floating smile.

Definition 7 (Deterministic Smile Surface) *Given an admissible smile surface today (time t_0) a **future, time-t conditional smile surface** is said to be **deterministic** if the future smile surface can be expressed at time t_0 as a deterministic function of time, maturity, strike and the realization of the stock price at time t, S_t.*

This need not, in general, be the case. Stochastic-volatility processes, for instance, do not produce future deterministic smile surfaces: since at a future point in time there can be an infinite number of possible volatilities, there can be no function of time, maturity, strike and the realization of the stock price at time t, S_t, that unambiguously identifies the future smile. Examples of processes that *do* generate deterministic smile surfaces are:

- geometric-diffusion (Black-and-Scholes) process with constant and time-dependent volatilities;
- jump–diffusions with constant or time-dependent coefficients;
- displaced diffusions (Rubinstein (1983)) and their generalizations such as displaced jump-diffusions;
- the Derman–Kani restricted-stochastic-(local-) volatility model;
- the variance–gamma process.

17.6.2 Consequences of Deterministic Smile Surfaces

If the future smile surface is deterministic, given the knowledge of the future value of S_t the prices of all future calls are also known. Recall, however, that we have defined the state of the world to be uniquely identified by the joint values of the stock price and of all the calls prices. Therefore, if the smile is deterministic the state of the world X_t is fully determined by S_t, and the (conditional and unconditional) price and state densities coincide:

$$\Phi(X_t) = f(S_t) \tag{17.32}$$

$$\Phi(X_T | X_t) = f(S_T | S_t) \tag{17.33}$$

Deterministic smile surfaces are important because they allow us to work with the much simpler *price* densities rather than the state densities. For any current price density, $f_0(S_0)$, and conditional deterministic price density, $f_t(S_T | S_t)$, it is always true that

$$f_0(S_{T_2}) = \int f_0(S_{T_1}) f_{T_1}(S_{T_2} | S_{T_1}) \, dS_{T_1} \tag{17.34}$$

Using Equation (17.26) and ignoring discounting to lighten notation, one can therefore write:

$$f_0(S_{T_2}) = \left. \frac{\partial^2 BS(S_0, K, t_0, T_2, \sigma(t_0, T_2, S_0, K))}{\partial K^2} \right|_{K=S_{T_2}} \tag{17.35}$$

$$f_0(S_{T_1}) = \left. \frac{\partial^2 BS(S_0, K, t_0, T_1, \sigma(t_0, T_1, S_0, K))}{\partial K^2} \right|_{K=S_{T_1}} \tag{17.36}$$

$$f_{T_1}(S_{T_2} | S_{T_1}) = \left. \frac{\partial^2 BS(S_t, K, T_1, T_2, \sigma(T_1, T_2, S_{T_1}, K))}{\partial K^2} \right|_{K=S_{T_1}} \tag{17.37}$$

Note carefully that in Equations (17.35) and (17.36) only derivatives with respect to the strike (not the stock price!) appear. These derivatives can therefore be evaluated in a model-independent way simply given today's call prices for the two maturities T_1 and T_2. The associated densities are therefore market-given. The same, however, does not apply to the conditional density in Equation (17.37).

17.6.3   Kolmogorov-Compatible Deterministic Smile Surfaces

In order to lighten the notation further, let us define the operator

$$\frac{\partial^2 BS}{\partial K^2}[.] \equiv \Theta[. \,] \tag{17.38}$$

Then Equation (17.37) can be rewritten as

$$\Theta\left[S_0, K, t_0, T_2, \sigma(t_0, T_2, S_0, K)\right] \tag{17.39}$$

$$= \int \Theta[S_0, K, t_0, T_1, \sigma(t_0, T_1, S_0, K)] \Theta\left[S_t, K, T_1, T_2, \sigma(T_1, T_2, S_{T_1}, K)\right] dS_{T_1}$$

with $\Theta(S_0, K, t_0, T_1, \sigma(t_0, T_1, S_0, K))$ and $\Theta(S_0, K, t_0, T_2, \sigma(t_0, T_2, S_0, K))$ market-given, and $\Theta(S_t, K, T_1, T_2, \sigma(T_1, T_2, S_{T_1}, K))$ is to be determined so as to satisfy Equation (17.39). Given the definition of a deterministic smile, there is a one-to-one correspondence between the quantity $\Theta[S_t, K, T_1, T_2, \sigma(T_1, T_2, S_{T_1}, K)]$ and future conditional deterministic densities (conditional future smile surfaces). There are in general infinitely many solutions $\Theta[S_t, K, T_1, T_2, \sigma(T_1, T_2, S_{T_1}, K)]$ such that Equation (17.39) is satisfied. Therefore, even if we require the smile surface to be deterministic, there still exist infinitely many future smile surfaces compatible with today's prices of calls and puts.

Definition 8 (Kolmogorov Compatibility) *Any future deterministic conditional density or smile surface such that Equation (17.39) is satisfied is called a* **Kolmogorov-compatible density***.*

Proposition 1 *Given a current admissible smile surface, if all the future deterministic smile surfaces for times $T_1, T_2, \ldots, T_n$ are Kolmogorov-compatible no model-independent strategy revised on the same set of dates can generate arbitrage profits.*

A proof of the proposition can be arrived at by recalling that a necessary and sufficient condition for absence of arbitrage is the existence of at least one measure under which the expectation of the future discounted cashflows equals today's prices.

17.6.4 Conditions for the Uniqueness of Kolmogorov-Compatible Densities

The equations obtained up to this point determine the links between the present and the future densities that must be satisfied by deterministic smile surfaces in order to avoid model-independent arbitrage. One extra condition is required in order to ensure uniqueness of the resulting conditional density. This condition is often implicitly assigned by popular process-based models, and is derived below.

Condition 7 (Distance Condition) *Let us assume that a Kolmogorov-compatible conditional probability density is of the form*

$$f(S_T|S_t) = f'(P(S_T) - P(S_t)) \tag{17.40}$$

for some functions $f'(.)$ and $P(.)$. If this is the case, the probability density is said to satisfy the **distance condition***.*

Equation (17.40) requires that the transition probability of the stock price at two different times should only depend on the distance between (some function of) the starting and arrival points (whence the name 'Distance Condition'). If the function $P(S) = S$, one recovers a normal diffusion for the underlying. If $P(S) = \ln(S)$, one recovers a log-normal diffusion. If $P(S) = \ln(S + \alpha)$, we are in a log-normal displaced-diffusion case; etc.

As of today, the current price density can always be written as some function f'_0 of $P(S_0)$. If the smile is deterministic, we also know that Equation (17.39) must be satisfied. If, in addition, the Condition 7 is satisfied, the current risk-neutral density for the function P of the underlying for time T_2, f', can be written as

$$h_0(S_{T_2}) = \int f_0(S_{T_1}) g(S_{T_2} - S_{T_1}) \, dS_{T_1} \tag{17.41}$$

where we have set $f_0(S_{T_1}) = f_0'(P_{T_1})$, $h_0(S_{T_2}) = f_0'(P_{T_2})$ and $g(S_{T_2} - S_{T_1}) = f_{T_1}'(P_{T_2} - P_{T_1})$. Recall now the definition of the convolution of two functions: given $f(x)$ and $g(x)$, their convolution, $h(x)$, is given by

$$h(x) \equiv f * g \equiv \int f(s)g(x - s)\,ds \qquad (17.42)$$

From this definition it is easy to see that Equation (17.41) has the form of a convolution, which can be denoted symbolically as

$$\int f_0(S_{T_1})g(S_{T_2} - S_{T_1})\,dS_{T_1} = f_0 * g \qquad (17.43)$$

Why is this relevant? Because there is a theorem in Fourier analysis that states that convolution in the direct space corresponds to a simple multiplication in Fourier space. More precisely, if we denote by $\mathcal{F}(f)$, $\mathcal{F}(g)$ and $\mathcal{F}(h)$, respectively, the Fourier transforms of f, g and h we have

$$\text{if } h(x) = \int f(s)g(x - s)\,ds \text{ then } \mathcal{F}(h) = \mathcal{F}(f)\mathcal{F}(g) \qquad (17.44)$$

This is useful, because Equation (17.44) shows that, given the market densities $f_0(S_{T_1})$ and $h_0(S_{T_2})$, we can try to obtain the Fourier transform of the unknown future density $g(S_{T_2} - S_{T_1})$ simply by taking the ratio of $\mathcal{F}(h)$ to $\mathcal{F}(f)$. The uniqueness of Fourier transforms and of their inverses then allows us to say that, if it exists, there is a unique future deterministic time-T_1 conditional density (smile surface) for expiry at time T_2 compatible with today's state of the world. If we denote by $\mathcal{F}^{-1}$ the inverse Fourier transform operator, this unique future density is given by

$$f_{T_1}'(P_{T_2} - P_{T_1}) = \mathcal{F}^{-1}\left[\frac{\mathcal{F}[f_0'(P_{T_2})]}{\mathcal{F}[f_0'(P_{T_1})]}\right] \qquad (17.45)$$

Therefore, under Condition 7, the future, conditional risk-neutral density, and, therefore, the future conditional smile surface, can be uniquely obtained from the market-given risk-neutral densities.[8] We have seen that, if the smile is deterministic and Condition 7 is satisfied, if a future density exists, it is unique. It follows that, under the same conditions, *there exists a unique Kolmogorov-compatible future density*.

Let me summarize the results so far. For the future price density to be uniquely determined by today's prices, the first requirement is that the future smile surface should be a deterministic function of the future stock price. In other words, we must be dealing with a deterministic smile. By itself this condition guarantees that there will be infinitely many future densities compatible with today's prices (today's smile, today's risk-neutral densities). If we want uniqueness, this is not enough. We must also require that there should be some function, P, of the stock price such that all densities can be written as a function of the 'starting' and 'arrival' values of this function. This requirement is satisfied

---

[8]For Equation (17.45) to describe a density, the further requirement that it should be strictly positive must be imposed.

in the most trivial case by geometric diffusions (the Black-and-Scholes model), where the probability density is purely a function of the difference $\ln S_{T_2} - \ln S_{T1}$.

Given a set of exogenous market prices, we will in general fail to find an admissible solution to Equation (17.45). In other words, market prices tend to reject the hypothesis that future densities only depend on the distance between (some function of) the values of the underlying at the two different times, T_1 and T_2. However, the result just obtained can still be useful. If we believe that Condition 7 is reasonable, we can make use of it in the context of the minimum-entropy technique described in Chapter 9. We can, in other words, use as our prior the intuitively appealing condition that the future density should only depend on the 'starting' and 'arrival' values of the function P. We can then use this prior to find the Kolmogorov-compatible density that is 'closest' to our prior.

17.6.5 Floating Smiles

The requirements necessary to obtain a unique Kolmogorov-compatible future density appear to be rather restrictive. However, they do not constrain in any way the future function, g, apart from requiring that is should satisfy Condition 7. In particular, we have not said anything about self-similarity (in some reasonable metric) of future densities. However, one of the potentially desirable conditions for a smile function is that it should be self-similar when its arguments S_t and t undergo certain transformations. I want to explore this angle in this section. In particular, we can ask the following questions:

- What will the smile surface look like when the underlying changes?

- What will the smile surface look like when we move forward in time?

The answer to the first question leads to the concept of floating or sticky smiles. The second question is related to the existence or otherwise of an arbitrage-free forward-propagated smile. To make these concepts precise, in the deterministic case first, we proceed as follows.

The smile surface today, i.e. for a fixed S_0, can always be trivially written as some function, $\widehat{\sigma}(.)$, of $\ln[K/S_0] \equiv y_0$:

$$\sigma_{\text{impl}}(t_0, T, K, S_0) = \widehat{\sigma}(t_0, T, \ln[K/S_0]) = \widehat{\sigma}(t_0, T, y_0) \qquad (17.46)$$

This observation, *per se*, contains no information, but is useful in establishing the following conditions, which are central to the treatment to follow.

Condition 8 (Stock Homogeneity) *If the time-t smile surface is deterministic and of the form*

$$\sigma_{\text{impl}}(t, T, K, S_t) = \widehat{\sigma}(t, T, y_t) \qquad (17.47)$$

*with $y_t \equiv \ln[K/S_t]$ and $\widehat{\sigma}$ the same function that describes the current smile surface, then it is said to be **stock-homogeneous**.*

Definition 9 (Floating Smile) *A future deterministic smile surface such that Condition 8 is satisfied for all t is called a **floating smile surface**.*

Since the definition of a floating smile surface requires that Condition 8 should hold for any t, it must be true also for an instantaneous change in the stock price. This condition therefore directly relates to the translation properties (in log space) of the smile surface with the stock price. However, we do not know yet whether, and under what conditions, such a floating surface can exist without allowing arbitrage. This would certainly be the case if the deterministic floating smile surfaces had been produced by an arbitrage-free process, but we have not based our treatment on the specification of a particular process, and we must, therefore, follow some other route. In our language, the condition necessary for the existence of a deterministic floating smile is the following.

Let us assume that Conditions 7 and 8 are satisfied. If the conditional probability density is of the form $f(S_T | S_t) = \xi(\ln S_T - \ln S_t)$, i.e. if the function $P(.)$ above is given by $P \equiv \ln(S)$ (and f' is therefore the probability density for $\ln[S_t]$), then the corresponding future smile surface is floating.

The definition of a floating smile gives a privileged role to the Black-and-Scholes co-ordinates. In particular, for fixed t and T, all pairs $\{K, S_t\}$ such that their ratio is a constant, produce the same value for y_t. Therefore, if the smile surface is floating, all such pairs $\{K, S_t\}$ give rise to the same implied volatility, and to a set of call prices simply proportional to S_t (given the homogeneity properties of the Black-and-Scholes formula).

As defined, the floating smile singles out a set of (log-normal) co-ordinates as privileged, but still does not tell us anything about the invariance properties of the smile. These can be obtained as follows.

Definition 10 (Forward-Propagated Smile) *A floating smile surface such that the function that gives the implied volatility as a function of residual maturity and strike is **independent of calendar time** is said to be forward-propagated.*

There is no guarantee, in general, that a forward-propagated smile will be Kolmogorov-compatible (i.e. that today's prices admit a forward-propagated smile without allowing model-independent arbitrage opportunities). If the trader felt that forward propagation was a desirable property, she could try to find the future condition densities (smile surfaces) that are Kolmogorov-compatible, and that are 'closest' – given some suitably defined distance – to forward-propagated densities (smile surfaces). Again, the minimum-entropy approach referred to in Section 9.8.2 could be used, with a forward-propagated smile as the prior.

Let us take stock again of the results so far. We have established more and more restrictive conditions on the smile surface. These conditions have allowed us to translate more and more demanding desiderata on the (unknown) underlying process. Since in this chapter we do not pursue a process-based approach, we have translated these requirements into conditions on the smile surface or the associated densities. More precisely we have defined the following.

- **Deterministic smile**: there exists some function of maturity T, strike K and time t such that, conditional on the future stock price being known, the future smile surface is known today exactly. While in some ways already restrictive (stochastic-volatility processes do not fall into this category), this is the mildest requirement. Formally, it states that the smile surface can be written as a four-argument function, $\mathcal{R}^4 \rightarrow \mathcal{R}^1$

$$\widehat{\sigma}_{\text{det}} = \widehat{\sigma}_{\text{det}}(t, T, K, S_t) \tag{17.48}$$

- **Floating smile**: there exists some function today of time t, maturity T and of the ratio $y_t = K/S_t$ in terms of which one can express today all the future smile surfaces. Therefore the function is now of the type $\mathcal{R}^3 \to \mathcal{R}^1$, and we are restricting the type of dependence of the smile surface to the form:

$$\widehat{\sigma}_{\text{float}} = \widehat{\sigma}_{\text{float}} \left(t, T, \frac{K}{S_t} \right) \tag{17.49}$$

- **Forward-propagated smile**: there exists some function today of residual maturity $\tau = T - t$ and of the ratio $y_t = K/S_t$ in terms of which one can express today all the future smile surfaces. The function is now $\mathcal{R}^2 \to \mathcal{R}^1$, because

$$\widehat{\sigma}_{\text{fwd}} = \widehat{\sigma}_{\text{fwd}} \left(T - t, \frac{K}{S_t} \right)$$

So, deterministic, floating and forward-propagating smiles impose progressively more burdensome requirements: deterministic smiles simply require that, given the future stock price, the future smile should be uniquely determined. No restrictions are imposed, however, on the values of future options of different strikes and/or residual maturities. Floating smiles add the requirement that the future smile should be uniquely known once the ratio $y_t = K/S_t$ is known. The transformation from the ratio $y_t = K/S_t$ to the implied volatility allowed by floating smiles, however, can display an explicit dependence on calendar time. If smiles are 'just' floating, future smiles do not have to look like today's smile. Forward-propagated smiles add the requirement that all option prices should only depend on the residual time to maturity. Smiles therefore become homogeneous both in 'stock–space' and in 'time'.

17.7 Stochastic Smiles

So far we have dealt with deterministic smiles. This forced us to exclude from our analysis all underlying processes that give rise to future smiles that depend on the realization of stochastic quantities other than the stock price. I will try in this section to extend the domain of applicability of the present approach. I will do so by describing today's smile as a function of a number of parameters, $\{\alpha\}$, and by assigning a stochastic behaviour to these parameters. This is done as follows.

Definition 11 (Filtrations) *Denote by $\Im_\alpha$ the natural filtration generated by the stochastic evolution of the processes $\{\alpha\}$. Denote by $\Im_S$ the natural filtration generated by the stochastic evolution of the process S. Denote by $\Im_{S,\alpha}$ the natural filtration generated by the stochastic evolution of the processes S and $\{\alpha\}$. We assume that we are given a probability space $(\Omega, P, \Im_{S,\alpha})$ that satisfies the 'usual conditions'.*

With the above definition we are simply saying that we allow ourselves knowledge at time t of the evolution of the stock price and of the random variables $\{\alpha\}$. Our expectations can therefore be conditioned on the realization of all these quantities.

Condition 9 (Stochasticity) *Let us impose that the future (time-t) conditional implied volatility function, $\sigma_{\text{impl}}(t, T, K, S_t)$, should be a stochastic quantity, whose values depend on the realization of a discrete set of random variables $\{\alpha_t\}$.*

Condition 10 (Discreteness) *Let us assume that the random variables $\{\alpha\}$ that determine the realization of the future implied volatility surface (the future conditional density) can assume an arbitrarily large but finite number of values. Let $\{\pi_{ij}^t\}$ denote the probability of the ith realization of the jth parameter α at time t.*

Condition 10 is simply introduced to keep the notation simple. It could be removed with little effort. Note in passing that the approach is superficially similar to that described in Chapter 25. See also Joshi and Rebonato (2003) in their stochastic-volatility extension of the LIBOR market model. The important difference is that I assume in this chapter that the parameters describing the *implied* volatility surface are stochastic. In Chapter 25, on the other hand, I assume that the parameters of the *instantaneous* volatility are stochastic. This apparently minor difference ensures automatically that all the resulting future smile surfaces are Kolmogorov-compatible, and arbitrage-free.

Condition 11 (Independence) *Let us assume that the future smile surface can be written as $\sigma_{\text{impl}}^t = \sigma(t, T, y_t; \{\alpha_t\})$ and that the values of these random variables $\{\alpha\}$ at time t should be independent of $y(t)$:*

$$\text{Prob}(\alpha_t | y_t) = \text{Prob}(\alpha_t) \rightarrow \text{Prob}(\alpha_t, y_t) = \text{Prob}(\alpha_t)\text{Prob}(y_t) \qquad (17.50)$$

Let us look at these conditions in some detail. As for Condition 9, the random variables $\{\alpha\}$ could be very different in nature. They could, for instance, be the second, third, fourth, ..., moments of a future probability density; they could be the future market prices of at-the-money volatilities, straddles and risk reversals; they could be the coefficients of a parametrically-fitted density (see, for example, Samuel's 'fingerprints' (2002) or many of the approaches described in Chapter 9). All these interpretations are possible, as long as the random variables, however chosen, are independent of y_t. Whether, and to what extent, it is realistic and appropriate to make, say, the third moment or the skew independent of the underlying is clearly an empirical question. Similar assumptions are however also embedded, often in a less transparent way, in process-based modelling approaches, and our conditions at least force the trader to specify clearly her modelling assumptions in the 'language' that she prefers.

The most demanding condition is that the processes for the parameters $\{\alpha\}$ should be independent of the process from the underlying. It is not even obvious, at this stage, if such a requirement is exactly compatible with any underlying process. I will show below that there are processes for which this assumption is at least a close approximation. When this is the case, an interesting result about the existence of an equivalent deterministic smile will follow.

17.7.1   Stochastic Floating Smiles

Definition 12 (Stochastic Floating Smile) *Let us assume that a smile surface satisfies Conditions 9 and 11, and let $\varphi(\alpha_1^t, \alpha_2^t, \ldots, \alpha_n^t)$ denote the joint probability of occurrence of $\{\alpha_1^t, \alpha_2^t, \ldots, \alpha_n^t\}$ at time t. Then, if it is possible to choose a measure Q such that the* *time-τ expectation of $\widehat{\sigma}$ over the stochastic variables $\{\alpha\}$ at time t $(t > \tau)$ is equal to its time-τ value*

$$E_Q[\widehat{\sigma}_{\alpha_t}(t, T, y_t)]$$

$$= \int_{\alpha_t} \widehat{\sigma}(t, T, y_t)\varphi(\alpha_1, \alpha_2, \ldots, \alpha_n) \, d\alpha_1, \, d\alpha_2, \ldots, \, d\alpha_n = \widehat{\sigma}_{\alpha_0}(\tau, T, y_\tau) \qquad (17.51)$$

*then a future implied volatility function generated by the processes $\{\alpha\}$ is said to produce a **floating stochastic-volatility surface**.*[9]

17.7.2 Introducing Equivalent Deterministic Smile Surfaces

If no arbitrage is to be allowed, a probability measure must always exist such that the relative price of a call today (time T_0) is given by the weighted expectation of the relative call price at a later time t. Usually this condition is employed by choosing the 'future time' to be the option expiry, in which case the call price is simply equal to the option payoff. This, however, need not be the case, and any intermediate time t, $T_0 < t < T$, can be used.

Let us assume that we are dealing with a stochastic smile surface such that Conditions 9 to 11 are satisfied. Then, if the numeraire is chosen to be the (deterministic) discount bond maturing at time T, $Z(0, T)$, one can write, for $t \leq T$,

$$\frac{Call_0(S_0, T)}{Z(0, t)} = Z(t, T)E_P[Call_t|\Im_{S,\alpha_0}]$$

$$= Z(t, T) \sum \pi_i \int Call_t(S_t, T, X_i(t)) f_0(S_t) \, dS_t$$

$$= Z(t, T) \sum \pi_i \int BS(S_t, t, T, \sigma_{\text{impl}}(t, T, S_t, K; X_i(t))) f_0(S_t) \, dS_t$$

$$= Z(t, T) \sum \pi_i \int BS(S_t, t, T, \widehat{\sigma}_{\alpha_i}(t, T, y_t)) f_0(S_t) \, dS_t$$

$$= Z(t, T) \sum \pi_i \int \left[\int (S_T - K)^+ f_t(S_T|S_t)_i \, dS_T \right] f_0(S_t) \, dS_t \qquad (17.52)$$

where π_i is the probability of the ith realization of the multiplet $\{\alpha\}$. Note carefully that the quantity y_t depends on the strike, K.

It is worthwhile commenting briefly on this derivation. In the first line the price of a call today is expressed *not* as the discounted expectation of the terminal payoff, but as the discounted expectation of the future (time-t) call prices. It is for this reason that, despite the fact that the option expiry is at time T, the discounting on the RHS 'connects' two future times, T and t. The second line expresses this expectation as a weighted sum over the discrete probabilities π_i. The future call prices, in turn, can be considered as

---

[9]Traders tend to use the terms 'floating' and 'sticky-delta' interchangeably. Indeed, it is easy to show that the definition of a floating smile we provide produces, in the special case of a deterministic future smile surface, the same value for the delta for any fixed value of y_t, and hence the 'sticky-delta' condition. Therefore, our definition of a floating smile is consistent with and generalizes the market intuition of a 'sticky-delta' smile.

the result of the application of the Black-and-Scholes formula with the appropriate future volatility (lines 3 and 4). Finally, the last line expresses each Black-and-Scholes price as a discounted expectation of the terminal payoff.

Proposition 2 *If the smile is floating, the price of a call today in the presence of a floating stochastic smile is identical to the price that would be obtained with the single deterministic stock-homogeneous (floating) future smile associated with the average conditional density* $\overline{f_t}(S_T|S_t)$. *Such a smile is called the* **equivalent deterministic future smile**.

Proof. From Equation (17.52), after interchanging the order of integration one obtains:

$$Call_0(S_0, T)/Z(0, T)$$

$$= \sum \pi_i \int \left[\int (S_T - K)^+ f_t(S_T|S_t)_i \, dS_T \right] f_0(S_t) \, dS_t$$

$$= \int \left[\sum \pi_i \int (S_T - K)^+ f_t(S_T|S_t)_i \, dS_T \right] f_0(S_t) \, dS_t$$

$$= \int \left[\int (S_T - K)^+ \sum \pi_i f_t(S_T|S_t)_i \, dS_T \right] f_0(S_t) \, dS_t$$

$$= \int \left[\int (S_T - K)^+ \overline{f_t}(S_T|S_t) \, dS_T \right] f_0(S_t) \, dS_t$$

$$= \int BS(S_t, t, T, \overline{\sigma}(t, T, y_t)) f_0(S_t) \, dS_t \qquad (17.53)$$

where $\overline{f_t}(S_T|S_t)$ is the average conditional density, given by

$$\overline{f_t} = \sum \pi_i f_t(S_T|S_t)_i \qquad (17.54)$$

and $\overline{\sigma}(t, T, y_t)$ is the associated deterministic floating smile (implied volatility). ∎

In going from the second to the third line the order of the sum over π_i and of the integration over dS_t is inverted. Similarly, in the fourth line there is an inversion of the sum over π_i and of the integration over dS_T. The inner kernel of the fourth line is then recognized as defining an average density. The final result is therefore that for any stochastic future floating smile there always corresponds a *deterministic* floating future smile that produces identical prices for all calls and puts. This deterministic smile is the equivalent deterministic future smile.

17.7.3   Implications of the Existence of an Equivalent Deterministic Smile Surface

A variety of processes have been proposed in order to describe the stock-price dynamics. Each of these processes gives rise to a set of future smile surfaces. In some cases these smile surfaces are deterministic, in others stochastic. From the results derived above, however, we can conclude that sometimes this stochasticity can be 'wasted'. A stock-price process that gives rise to a stochastic smile surface can in fact produce option prices different from the prices obtainable from an equivalent deterministic future smile *only if it produces stochastic future smiles which are not independent of the future realization of the stock price.* Therefore the ability to create a future stochastic smile surface correlated with a future realization of the stock price is the only feature of a model that can provide anything more complex than a deterministic-smile setting.

Very often, the complexity of today's observed smile surface is taken as an indication that a model that produces stochastic future smiles must be employed in order to account for today's observed prices. This might well be the case, but only if the probability of occurrence of future smiles is not independent of the future stock-price realization.

17.7.4 Extension to Displaced Diffusions

Empirical observations indicate that there exists a negative correlation between the future level of smile surfaces and of stock prices. This would seem to invalidate one of the crucial conditions of the approach outlined above. As long as the dependence is relatively simple, however, the approach can sometimes be rescued by a simple change of variables. One possible way to do this is to recast the distance condition in terms of a function other than $\ln(S_t)$. Another attractive route is to employ the approximate but accurate equivalence between CEV process and displaced-diffusion processes (Marris (1999), Rubinstein (1983)). This can be achieved as follows.

Definition 13 *Define the present or future a-displaced implied volatility, σ_{impl}^a, as the quantity that, input into the Black-and-Scholes formula with $(S + a)$ as spot and $(K + a)$ as strike, produces the value of a call with spot equal to S and strike equal to K. Also, define*

$$y_t^a \equiv \ln\left[\frac{K + a}{S_t + a}\right] \tag{17.55}$$

Mutatis mutandis, all the treatments presented above can be recast in terms of the new quantity, y_t^a. Clearly, the distance condition is now expressed in terms of the function $\ln(S_t + a)$.

17.8 The Strength of the Assumptions

For the approach presented above to be valid the most important condition is the independence of the future stock price and of the future smile surface. 'Innocuous' as this requirement might seem, it is not so easy to think of realistic processes that fulfil this condition. For instance, we have already seen in Chapter 13, Section 13.5, one example of violation of the independence in the case of stochastic-volatility processes. We observed there that, contingent on a very high or a very low realization of the stock price at a future time t, the conditional future smile was likely to be higher than today's smile. I gave in that context a qualitative explanation for the finding.

This is, however, not always the case. Let us consider, for instance, jump–diffusion processes. In order to obtain stochastic smiles one could make either the jump frequency or the jump amplitude, or both, stochastic. When this is done, a dependence between future smiles and future stock prices is still found. Empirically, however, one observes this dependence to be weak. This suggests that perhaps relatively little is 'bought' by making these two quantities stochastic, since an equivalent deterministic smile would produce very similar answers. It is important to stress that what matters is not the dispersion of the future smiles, but the correlation of the latter (or lack thereof) with the future stock prices.

17.9   Limitations and Conclusions

In a way, this chapter could have been titled 'The Revenge of the Process-Based Model': despite the fact that we started from an attempt to dispense with the specification of the dynamics of the underlying, we discovered that, without this guidance, the pitfalls of model-independent arbitrage are very difficult to avoid. Should one therefore 'throw away' the trader's dream, and revert to one of the traditional approaches? Or, are we perhaps paying too much attention to the requirement of no arbitrage?

Starting from the second questions, it is important to stress again that traditional, i.e. process-based, models are only arbitrage-free if the dynamics they posit are indeed correct. In practice, this means that they guarantee the impossibility for someone else to make money at our expense *only if the assumed process for the underlying is correct, and its parameters exactly known*. So, the 'arbitrage-free' label has become the *sine-qua-non* badge of acceptability of a model, but, as with so many labels, it is often forgotten how little it actually guarantees in practice. For instance, a constant-volatility model, a jump–diffusion model and a local-volatility model can all be constructed to be arbitrage-free, yet they all predict very different present and future option prices, and the trader who knew which one was the 'true' model could make unlimited profits at the expense of the users of the other (arbitrage-free) models. Even more starkly, diffusion and jump models do not even agree about which events are possible and which impossible (i.e. they do not share the same null set), let alone assign the same pseudo-probabilities to the different states of the world.

Furthermore, as discussed in Chapter 1, arbitrages are in practice sometimes difficult to find, often hard to implement, and rarely truly riskless. Therefore the threat that, by using a model that is not arbitrage-free, one might unwittingly become a money-generating machine for a competitor trader is often considerably emptier than it might appear at first sight.

Does this mean that the notion of freedom of arbitrage is useless? Certainly not. Logical clarity and self-consistency at least in an idealized world are very powerful conceptual crutches, and a solid practical guide: even if real surfaces are not frictionless, Newtonian mechanics, which predicts that a ball will roll forever on the perfect table, is a better tool than Aristotelian mechanics, which, in apparent agreement with observation, claims that the ball will stop unless a force is continuously applied to it. Claiming that, since real balls do stop unless an engine keeps on propelling them, we could just as well use Aristotelian dynamics is not a useful suggestion, and I would not like to climb on a plane designed by such a 'realist' engineer.

However, well-defined theoretical concepts are there to help us in thinking correctly, but should not become a strait-jacket: *pace* Galileo, a stone and a feather will *not* fall at the same speed when dropped from the top of the tower of Pisa, unless one managed to encase it in a vacuum tube. A trader entering a contract for differences on the arrival time on the ground of the stone and the feather would be well advised not to bet too much on the 'arbitrage-free' result of a zero difference.

Moving away from metaphors, if I had to make a price on, say, a forward-starting option I would probably rather make use of a robust, even if theoretically arbitrageable, model that produced palatable future smile surfaces than of an arbitrage-free model that predicted totally unacceptable smiles. The comfort provided by the assurance that nobody can make money at my expense (*if the posited dynamics for the underlying is correct*) could easily only last as long as the first important re-hedging time.

Clearly, if a trader could find a process-based approach that priced the current market *and* produced desirable future smile surfaces, I would wholeheartedly recommend making use of such a model. Indeed, the philosophy of this book is to regard the process for the underlying as little more than a mechanism to produce desirable and arbitrage-free present and future smile surfaces. Finding such a model, unfortunately, is very difficult, and might not even be possible if option prices were made by traders in an 'inconsistent' manner (as discussed in Chapter 1, this possibility should not be ruled out off-hand). This is, after all, the reason why this book runs to over 800 pages. For this reason, I recommend, for instance, that even today's prices should be accurately, but perhaps not perfectly, recovered, despite the fact that this is the theoretical arbitrage *par excellence*. This is particularly true if the price for achieving today's perfect fit is a poor future smile surface. The example of local-volatility models springs to mind. More generally, a compromise must in general be struck between what intuition and historical (statistical) information suggest to be a sound approach, and the recommendations of a theoretically sound model. Logical inconsistencies riddle the practice of option pricing and hedging at every turn, and, as discussed in Chapter 1, lie not at its periphery but at its very core.

Part III

Interest Rates – Deterministic Volatilities

Chapter 18

Mean Reversion in Interest-Rate Models

18.1 Introduction and Plan of the Chapter

This chapter looks at the role of mean reversion in the context of interest-rate models. In dealing with this topic I will draw a sharp distinction between mean reversion in the real and in the risk-adjusted worlds. In this sense the discussion to be found in this chapter is a natural continuation of the arguments presented in Chapter 4, with which it shares several common points, but from which it also differs in important ways. More precisely, I will argue that:

1. much as in the equity/FX case, the nature of the drift of interest-rate *asset(s)* in the real (econometric) measure (i.e. in the real world) is irrelevant to interest-rate option pricing;

2. unlike the equity/FX case, however, in specifying the risk-adjusted dynamics of the (*non-traded*) spot rate the drift can, to some extent, be assigned by the user without necessarily violating the requirement of no-arbitrage. In particular, if one so wished, a mean-reverting risk-neutral drift could be imparted to the short rate;

3. the effect of this mean-reverting component is to make it possible, at least for suitable choices of the parameters, for a short-rate-based interest-rate model to price correctly market instruments such as caplets and, at the same time, to produce an approximately time-homogeneous evolution of the term structure of volatilities;

4. when it comes to forward-rate-based interest-rate models, this freedom to specify their (mean-reverting or otherwise) drift in the risk-neutral world is lost again. This is because forward rates, unlike the short rate, are first cousins of *traded* instruments (FRAs and swaps), and they must therefore ultimately reflect, more or less directly, the martingale condition.

In the second part of this chapter I will discuss a somewhat 'pathological' case of mean reversion, i.e. the mean reversion encountered in the case of the BDT model. *En route*, an

603

often-mentioned paradox encountered in the algorithmic construction of the BDT model will be resolved. These results are intrinsically interesting. The main purpose of this part of the chapter, however, is not to highlight the shortcomings of the BDT approach, but to stress the close link between mean reversion and the evolution of the volatility of the short rate. This observation will then be extended to more general, but still short-rate-based, modelling approaches, and it will be shown how the shortcomings of the BDT approach can be avoided.

The analysis of interest-rate models based on the evolution of the short rate will not be pursued beyond this chapter, and the remaining part of the book will deal with the forward-rate-based LIBOR market model approach. While, in principle, one could still think in terms of mean reversion also in the forward-rate context, I will show in Chapters 19 and 21 that one can express the same concepts using a different language, more directly related to market observables (e.g. by making reference to the time homogeneity of the term structure of volatilities.)

18.2   Why Mean Reversion Matters in the Case of Interest-Rate Models

Before tackling these issues in detail it is useful to give a first explanation of the reason why mean reversion matters at all in the case of short-rate-based interest-rate models. If it seems puzzling to question something so apparently 'obvious', remember that we have shown in Chapters 2 and 4 that the real-world mean reversion, even if present, would be totally irrelevant for the fair pricing of options; and that it could not enter, under penalty of arbitrage, the dynamics of stock prices or the FX rate in the risk-neutral (pricing) measure. Mean reversion in the risk-neutral evolution of the short rate can, however, to some extent be specified by the model user, and does have a profound impact on the evolution of observable quantities, such as the term structure of volatilities. How is this possible? The short (and somewhat cryptic) answer to the puzzle is that the short rate is not a traded asset. A more transparent explanation runs along the following lines.

Let the dynamics of the whole yield curve be governed by the evolution of the short rate. In this single-factor world let P be the price of a generic interest-rate-dependent instrument. One often chooses P to be the price of a bond, but, in a single-factor framework, it could be anything as long as it is a *traded* asset. Since we are assuming that the dynamics of the yield curve is driven by the short rate, the price of this asset will be a function of the short rate itself (and of time). We can therefore formally write $P = P(r, t)$. Let us now assume that the risk-adjusted process for the short rate is indeed mean-reverting:

$$\mathrm{d}r_t = \alpha(k - r)\,\mathrm{d}t + \sigma_r\,\mathrm{d}z_t \tag{18.1}$$

where k is the reversion level and α the reversion speed of the short rate. Since we would like P to be strictly positive, we can write for its dynamics:[1]

$$\frac{\mathrm{d}P}{P} = \mu_P\,\mathrm{d}t + \sigma_P(P, t)\,\mathrm{d}z \tag{18.2}$$

---

[1]Note that, by allowing the volatility $\sigma_P(P, t)$ to depend on P as well as t, we are not assuming that the asset price P should be log-normally distributed.

Intuitively, we might expect that the mean-reverting nature of the mean-reverting risk-neutral dynamics for r should affect the drift of P. This is because we expect the drift of P to be linked to the drift of r by an Ito term of the form $\mu_P P = \frac{\partial P}{\partial r} \mu_r$. We have learnt in Chapter 4 that the drift (if it contains the variable P) can affect the total variance of the asset, and therefore it appears reasonable to expect that the total variance of P should be affected by the mean-reverting dynamics for r. But we also know from Chapter 4 that what matters for pricing options on assets is the *volatility* (i.e. the term $\sigma_P(P, t)$), not the *variance*, of the underlying. What is not obvious, therefore, is whether and how the drift of the underlying factor (the short rate) can alter the volatility of the traded instrument P. If it did not, it would have no effect on option pricing.

In order to see more clearly into this matter, let us use Ito's lemma in order to calculate explicitly the drift, μ_P, and the volatility, σ_P, of the asset P, which appear in the SDE (18.2). The calculation is straightforward, and, beginning with the drift, gives

$$P\mu_P = \frac{\partial P}{\partial t} + \frac{\partial P}{\partial r}\mu_r + \frac{1}{2}\frac{\partial^2 P}{\partial r^2}\sigma_r^2 \tag{18.3}$$

with

$$\mu_r = \alpha(k - r) \tag{18.4}$$

However, since P denotes the price of a traded asset, we also know that its risk-neutral drift must be equal to the riskless rate itself:

$$\mu_P P = rP \tag{18.5}$$

Therefore, combining the above two equations, one can write:

$$\frac{\partial P}{\partial t} + \frac{\partial P}{\partial r}\mu_r + \frac{1}{2}\frac{\partial^2 P}{\partial r^2}\sigma_r^2 = rP \tag{18.6}$$

Solving for $\frac{\partial P}{\partial r}$ gives

$$\frac{\partial P}{\partial r} = \frac{rP - \frac{1}{2}\frac{\partial^2 P}{\partial r^2}\sigma_r^2 - \frac{\partial P}{\partial t}}{\mu_r}$$

$$= \frac{rP - \frac{1}{2}\frac{\partial^2 P}{\partial r^2}\sigma_r^2 - \frac{\partial P}{\partial t}}{\alpha(k - r)} \tag{18.7}$$

We also know, however, that the term $\frac{\partial P}{\partial r}$ appears in the contribution Ito's lemma gives for the stochastic part, σ_P, of the process of $P(r, t)$:

$$P\sigma_P = \frac{\partial P}{\partial r}\sigma_r \tag{18.8}$$

Therefore, combining the equation obtained above for the derivative $\frac{\partial P}{\partial r}$ with expression (18.7), one obtains for the volatility of P:

$$\sigma_P P = \frac{rP - \dfrac{1}{2}\dfrac{\partial^2 P}{\partial r^2}\sigma_r^2 - \dfrac{\partial P}{\partial t}}{\alpha(k - r)}\sigma_r \qquad (18.9)$$

This expression does not tell the full story, because the terms $\frac{\partial^2 P}{\partial r^2}$ and $\frac{\partial P}{\partial t}$ might, and in fact do, contain a dependence on α and k as well (see the next section), but already shows that the drift of r (and, in particular, its mean reversion) will affect the *volatility* of P, not its risk-neutral drift (which is beyond the modeller's control, given the requirement of no arbitrage). The effect of assigning (in the risk-neutral world) a particular drift to the short rate – which we can do, because the short rate is not a traded asset – is therefore to modify the component of the process for the traded asset P that affects the prices of options, i.e. its volatility. If we were to value an option on P, in fact, this mean-reversion-dependent volatility σ_P could clearly have a significant impact on the pricing. As a consequence, assigning a mean-reverting behaviour to the risk-neutral drift of the driving variable, r, directly and strongly affects the very quantity (i.e. the volatility, as opposed to the variance) that matters for option pricing.

18.2.1 What Does This Mean for Forward-Rate Volatilities?

The result obtained above shows that the mean-reversion parameters affect the volatility of the bond prices in some way. However, it is not very transparent what this effect is. Even if we managed to obtain a more transparent expression for the volatility of P, it is rather difficult to think in terms of the volatility of discount bond prices, since these always go to zero with the residual maturity of the bond, and all 'the action' is therefore contained in how quickly this bond price volatility approaches zero.[2] A more transparent quantity would be the volatility of the forward rates implied by a short-rate process of the form (18.1). In order to see what these volatilities look like, it is necessary to remind ourselves of the expression for the bond price, $P(t, T)$, as a function of α and k:

$$P(t, T) = A(\tau)\exp\left[-B(\tau)r_t\right] \qquad (18.10)$$

with

$$B(\tau) = \frac{1}{k}\left[1 - \exp\left(-\alpha\tau\right)\right] \qquad (18.11)$$

$$A(\tau) = \exp\left[\left(k - \frac{\sigma_r^2}{2\alpha^2}\right)(B(\tau) - \tau) - \left(\frac{\sigma_r^2}{4\alpha}B(\tau)^2\right)\right] \qquad (18.12)$$

$$\tau = T - t \qquad (18.13)$$

It is not difficult to obtain this result, but the derivation would require an unnecessary detour at this point. We can take the result on faith, and the interested reader can study

---

[2]For a very similar reason, one quotes *yields* of discount bonds, and not their prices, and implied volatilities instead of option prices.

the derivation in Vasicek (1977). In passing, note that the bond price does not depend on t, the calendar time, and on T, its maturity, separately. This is a consequence of the fact that we are working with a process with time-independent parameters (α, k and σ_r). The particularly simple shape of the forward-rate term structure of volatilities that I obtain below is due to this (after all, financially rather appealing) assumption. While the picture could be enriched by adding time dependence to some or all of the process parameters, the conclusions would not change materially.

Using these expressions, the percentage volatility of the bond price, σ_P, can be calculated from Equation (18.9), or directly from Equation (18.10), and one obtains

$$\sigma_P = -B(t, T)\sigma_r \tag{18.14}$$

Exercise 1 *Using Equation (18.10) evaluate the derivatives in Equation (18.9), and check that the result (18.14) is indeed obtained. Explain why one should not worry about the case when $r = k$.*

Forward rates are linked to bond prices by the relationship

$$f(t, T) = -\frac{\partial \ln P(t, T)}{\partial T} \tag{18.15}$$

Using Ito's lemma, after tedious but simple algebra one can obtain the volatility for the forward rate when the process for the short rate is mean reverting. Rather than displaying the expression for the forward-rate volatility as a function of expiry, which is rather involved and by inspection not very informative, Figure 18.1 shows the volatility of forward rates as a function of their expiries (i.e. the term structure of volatilities) for different values of the reversion speed of the short-rate process.

Exercise 2 *Obtain the expression for the volatility of the forward rate explicitly, making use of Ito's lemma and of the definition of the forward rate as (minus) the logarithmic derivative of the bond price with respect to maturity. Note: think about how to handle the derivative $\frac{\partial}{\partial T}$ when applying Ito's lemma.*

The important observation is that a constant short-rate volatility produces a term structure of volatilities for the forward rates that decays with their residual expiry. Therefore the introduction of a mean-reverting process for the short rate in the risk-neutral world should not be seen as motivated by a desire to mimic mean-reverting properties that might have been observed in the real world, but *as a mechanism to produce a decaying volatility for forward rates of different maturities*. The importance and financial desirability of this feature will be discussed in the context of the LIBOR market model. In the meantime, we can note that the caplet market, which normally does display a term structure of volatilities that decays for expiry greater than one or two years, is at least broadly consistent with this picture.

As a final comment, it is interesting to observe that the mechanism to produce this financially desirable effect (i.e. the decaying term structure of volatilities) is rather indirect, and that it is not particularly easy to 'modulate' the dependence of the forward-rate volatility on their expiry using the reversion speed and reversion-level parameters. This is one of the advantages of the LIBOR market model presented in the next chapters.

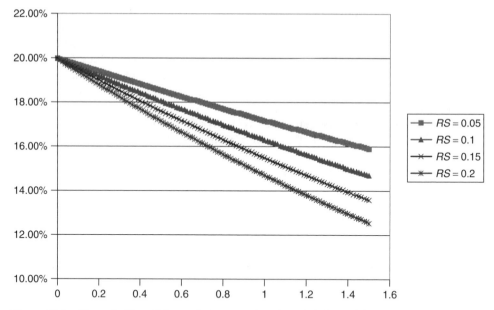

Figure 18.1   The volatility of forward rates as a function of their expiries (i.e. the term structure of volatilities) for different values of the reversion speed (labelled RS in the figure) of the short-rate process ($r(0) = 5.00\%$, $\sigma_r = 0.01$, reversion level $k = 0.05$).

18.3   A Common Fallacy Regarding Mean Reversion

The following argument has a ring of plausibility:

> We know that, in the real world, interest rates of developed economies do not diffuse as time goes by to very high or very low levels. We do not expect rates in USD, for instance, to be more than, say, 80%, no matter how long a time horizon we consider. In this respect, over long time horizons, rate processes do not behave like simple Brownian diffusions. Our uncertainty about the future level of rates grows rather quickly over a period of time of a few years, but, beyond that our 'uncertainty fan' grows less than linearly, and ultimately, a, say, two-standard-deviation range of future values for rates stops growing in size. Mean reversion in the real world is a good mechanism to produce this behaviour. If mean reversion is present, the variance of forward rates does not increase linearly with time (as would happen if all forward rates had the same constant volatility and followed a simple diffusion), but is 'pulled in' and contained within some reasonable bands. If one ignored this real-world effect, one would price caplets far too expensively. In other words, if one did not understand that the real-world mean reversion causes the term structure of volatilities to decay with option expiry, and priced caplets with an implied volatility that did not decay with expiry, one would be paying too much. This is because long-dated out-of-the-money caplets would buy protection against the realization of rates that, thanks to mean reversion, are exceedingly unlikely to succeed. So, the reason why the implied volatility of caplets declines is that there is mean reversion in the real world.

This line of reasoning is appealing. It is also incorrect. In a diffusive, perfect-replication framework, the drift of forward rates in the real world is totally irrelevant, and, when it comes to pricing, it is the *risk-neutral* drift, and not the *real-world* drift that matters. In making an argument based on the unconditional variance of forward rates in the real world as a justification for the declining implied volatilities of caplets, one is confusing variance with quadratic variation: the first is of interest for actuarial (insurance-like) pricing, the latter for pricing when perfect payoff replication is possible. By saying that, because of mean reversion in the real world, we would be 'paying for insurance that we do not need', we are taking an actuarial (buy-and-hold) view, which is *not* the methodology used in arriving at option prices when perfect payoff replication is possible. See, in this respect, the nice discussion in Chapter 1 of Baxter and Rennie (1996).

Mean reversion in the risk-neutral world *does* matter, and caplet prices *do* display a decreasing implied volatility, but not (directly) because of the existence of mean reversion in the real world; rather, because mean reversion provides a good financial mechanism to produce decaying term structures of volatilities of forward rates. I present the argument as to why this should be the case in the next chapters.

Another way to look at the matter is the following. Suppose that, by a statistical analysis based on 30 years' worth of hourly data, I have established beyond doubt that the real-world process for the evolution of the price of IBM shares is a diffusion with a constant volatility, and with a mean-reverting drift. Would you make use of this information to change the riskless drift in the Black-and-Scholes formula (which, given our statistical analysis, is certainly incorrect)? Would you use anything but the constant volatility to calculate the Black-and-Scholes price and delta? Would you argue that out-of-the-money IBM calls, whose Black-and-Scholes prices do not take into account the mean-reversion-affected unconditional variance, are too expensive because they 'buy us protection for outcomes that will not occur'? If you have answered 'yes' to any of these questions, you should definitely re-read Chapter 4.

Somewhat surprisingly, while most traders would agree that 'discovering' the mean-reverting nature of the real-world price dynamics for IBM shares should not affect our Black-and-Scholes pricing methodology, they fail to draw the same conclusion in the case of interest rates, despite the fact that the drifts appearing in the evolution of forward rates are evidently derived via a no-arbitrage argument ultimately similar to the Black-and-Scholes reasoning (see, for example, Vasicek (1977) or Heath *et al.* (1987, 1989)).

18.3.1 The Grain of Truth in the Fallacy

Having destroyed the argument based on the real-world mean reversion of rates, it is appropriate to step back a moment and put things into perspective. We have concluded that the 'good' reason for having mean reversion in the risk-neutral world is that we want to produce a decaying term structure of volatilities for the forward rates. One could check that, indeed, this is what we observe in the market, take it as a 'fact of nature' and move on to the next problem.

A more inquisitive mind, however, could ask a different question: *Why* do forward rates display (possibly after a certain maturity) a decaying term structure of volatilities? Broadly speaking, I believe that an explanation can be found along the following lines. Nominal rates are the sum of real rates plus inflation. Let us make the first heroic assumption that real rates are, at least approximately, constant. Then the variability in nominal rates would be almost exclusively due to the variability in inflation. The monetary authorities of developed economies, however, implicitly or explicitly target an inflation level, and they do so by changing rates at the short end. By so doing they change the expectations of future inflation. When a central bank raises rates at the short end, it signals that it wants to control inflation, and the inflation expectation further down the curve is reduced. This is a mean-reverting mechanism of sorts. And, if I were to make a guess about the future level of inflation in five or 10 years' time, my best guess would probably be the centre of the current inflation target band. Therefore, given our assumptions about real rates, the volatility *today* of forward rates expiring in five or 10 years' time should be less than the volatility of forward rates expiring in three to six months. So, in this picture, mean reversion in the real world does make a come-back through the back door. Note, however, that invoking mean reversion in the real world for an indirect explanation of the market-observed decaying term structure of volatilities hinges on accepting the 'story' that I have just presented. Observing, on the other hand, that the effect of mean reversion in the risk-adjusted world is to produce a decaying term structure of volatilities, and that this squares with market observations, is a fact that may, but need not, be explained by additional 'stories'.

Mean reversion is a delicate subject that gives rise to many mistakes in option pricing, especially in the interest-rate world. For this reason, the following sections will explore in greater depth this interplay between mean reversion in the risk-neutral world and the evolution of quantities that directly affect option pricing.

18.4   The BDT Mean-Reversion Paradox

Of the several one-factor models used for pricing interest rate options, the Black, Derman and Toy (BDT) (Black *et al.* (1990)) is one of the best known, and sometimes is still used, at least for the evaluation of compound (Bermudan-like) swaptions. Despite its conceptual and practical shortcomings, in what follows we will discuss some features of the BDT model for the insight this analysis can bring to the topic of mean reversion.[3]

The BDT approach enjoys several appealing features, such as the capability to price exactly an arbitrary set of received market discount bonds; the log-normal distribution of the short rate, which makes calibration to (Black) caplets prices particularly straightforward; and, last but not least, ease of implementation.

The first feature (exact pricing of the yield curve) is shared by a variety of no-arbitrage models, such as the Ho-and-Lee (1986) or the Hull-and-White (1990a). The second (log-normal distribution of rates) is also shared by the Black-and-Karasinski (1991) model (which, unlike the BDT model, displays 'true' mean reversion). Only the BDT approach, however, allows log-normal rates and calibration to caplet prices (in the absence of smile effects) that can be accomplished almost by inspection. From a practical point of view, it is probably only because of this feature that the model is still used by some houses in real-life pricing applications that require backward induction, rather than making use of conceptually superior, but more cumbersome to calibrate, short-rate-based approaches such as the Black and Karasinski.

This ease of calibration to caplet prices is, at the same time, the strongest point and, indirectly, the greatest shortcoming of the BDT model. It directly stems from the inflexible specification of the reversion speed, which, as shown below, is completely determined by the future behaviour of the short-rate volatility. In this section I therefore intend to

---

[3]Sections 18.4–18.6 have been adapted from Rebonato and Kazziha (1997).

highlight the close connection between the ease of calibration to caplet prices and the particular link between the reversion speed and the logarithmic derivative of the short rate volatility.

Let us start by considering a deterministic-volatility Brownian diffusion for the logarithm of the short rate of the form

$$d \ln r(t) = \mu_r(t)\, dt + \sigma_r(t)\, dz(t) \tag{18.16}$$

with $\mu_r(t)$ a *deterministic* drift, $dz(t)$ the increment of a Brownian process and $\sigma_r(t)$ the instantaneous percentage volatility of the short rate. We have seen in Chapter 4 that, if the drift is deterministic, the unconditional variance of the variable r out to time T is simply given by

$$\text{var}(\ln r_T) = \int_0^T \sigma_r(u)^2\, du \tag{18.17}$$

We have also pointed out that if the drift is not purely deterministic, but contains the (stochastic) state variable, the unconditional variance is no longer simply linked to the time integral of the square of the instantaneous volatility. In particular, for a mean-reverting process of the form

$$d \ln r(t) = [\theta_t + k\,(\psi_t - \ln r_t)]\, dt + \sigma_r(t)\, dz(t) \tag{18.18}$$

(with reversion speed k, reversion level $\psi(t)$, and θ_t a deterministic drift component) the unconditional variance will, in general, depend on the reversion speed.

It is well known from the literature (see, for example, Hull and White (1990a), Rebonato and Kazziha (1997), Rebonato (1998a)) that the continuous-time equivalent of the BDT model can be written as

$$d \ln r(t) = \left[\theta_t - f'\,(\psi(t) - \ln r_t)\right] dt + \sigma_r(t)\, dz(t) \tag{18.19}$$

with

$$f'(t) = \frac{\partial \ln \sigma_r(t)}{\partial t}$$

and both θ_t and $\sigma_r(t)$ deterministic functions of time. From Equation (18.19) one can formally see that it is only in the presence of a time-decaying short rate volatility $\left(\frac{\partial \ln \sigma_r(t)}{\partial t} < 0\right)$ that the resulting reversion speed $(-f')$ is positive and the model displays mean reversion. (See Section 18.7 for a more intuitive illustration of this observation.) Equation (18.19) can be rewritten as a diffusion of the general form

$$d \ln r(t) = [a_t\,(b_t - \ln r_t)]\, dt + \sigma_r(t)\, dz(t) \tag{18.20}$$

where a_t, b_t and $\sigma_r(t)$ are deterministic functions of time. The SDE (18.20) can easily be solved, and the variance calculated, giving

$$\text{var}[\ln r(T)] = \exp\left[-2 \int_0^T a(s)\, ds\right] \int_0^T \sigma(t)^2 \exp\left[2 \int_0^t a(s)\, ds\right] dt \tag{18.21}$$

Note that, by Equation (18.21), the variance of the logarithm of the short rate depends on the reversion speed. This, however, seems to create a paradox. We will show below, in fact, that the following three 'facts' are true:

Fact 1: The unconditional variance of the short rate in the BDT model does *not* depend on the instantaneous volatility from time 0 to time $T - \Delta t$ (as one would have been led to expect from Equation (18.17)).

Fact 2: The unconditional variance does *not* depend on the reversion speed $-f'$ (as one might have surmised from Equation (18.19)).

Fact 3: One can show (see below) that

$$\text{var}\,[\ln r(N\Delta t)] = N\Delta t \sigma^2(N\Delta t) \qquad (18.22)$$

where $\sigma^2(N\Delta t)$ is the square of the instantaneous short rate volatility at time $T = N\Delta t$. Therefore the total unconditional variance of the short rate from time 0 to time T only depends on the value of the instantaneous volatility at time T.

How can these apparently contradictory facts be reconciled? How can it be, in other words, that the total variance of the short rate depends neither on the full integral of the (square of the) short rate nor on the reversion speed?

It is important to stress that Equation (18.22) is crucial for calibration purposes: given that the arbitrage-free drift of the forward rates in the Black pricing measure is zero (and therefore certainly does not contain the forward rate itself), the market Black implied volatilities $(\widehat{\sigma}(T))$ provide direct information about the unconditional variance of the relevant forward rates (spot rates at expiry). From the quoted implied Black volatilities of caplets of different expiries the user can almost exactly obtain their exact BDT price by assigning a time-dependent short rate volatility matching the implied Black volatilities. In other words, if one sets

$$\sigma(N\Delta t) = \widehat{\sigma}(T), \quad N\Delta t = T \qquad (18.23)$$

one can rest assured that, for practical purposes, the caplet will be priced almost exactly.

It is well known amongst practitioners that this is the case. What is not generally appreciated is *how* this can be, because the equations above would suggest that in general both the instantaneous short rate volatility from time 0 to time T and the reversion speed $-f'$ should affect the unconditional variance from time 0 to time T. I will therefore begin to show that Fact 3 is true, i.e. that the 'empirically known' result mentioned above regarding the unconditional variance is indeed correct.

18.5   The Unconditional Variance of the Short Rate in BDT – the Discrete Case

A calibrated BDT lattice is fully described (see the original paper by Black *et al.* (1990) for a detailed description of the procedure)

- by a vector $r = \{r_{i0}\}$, $i = 0, k$, whose elements are the lowest values of the short rate at time-step i;

- by a vector $\sigma = \{\sigma_i\}$, $i = 0, k$, whose elements are the volatilities of the short rate from time-step i to time-step $i + 1$.

This is all that is needed to characterize the BDT model. Every rate r_{ij}, in fact, can be obtained as

$$r_{ij} = r_{i0} \exp\left[2\sigma_i j \sqrt{\Delta t}\right] \qquad (18.24)$$

(Δt, as usual, is the time-step in years). Let us now define (see Figure 18.2) k random variables $y_1, y_2, \ldots, y_k$ by

$$y_k = 1 \quad \text{if an up move occurs at time } (k-1)\Delta t \qquad (18.25)$$

$$y_k = 0 \quad \text{if a down move occurs at time } (k-1)\Delta t \qquad (18.26)$$

For instance, for the path highlighted in Figure 18.2, $y_1 = 0$, $y_2 = 1$, $y_3 = 0$ and $y_4 = 0$. Let us also assume, as is true in the BDT case, that the variables y_j are independent and that the probability $P[y_k = 1] = P[y_k = 0] = \frac{1}{2}$. Let us now define the variable

$$X_k = \sum_{j=1,k} y_j \qquad (18.27)$$

X_k therefore gives the 'level' of the short rate at time $k\Delta t$, and the value of the short rate at time $k\Delta t$ in the state labelled by X_k is given by

$$r_{k,X_k} = r_{k0} \exp[2\sigma_i X_k \sqrt{\Delta t}] \qquad (18.28)$$

To lighten notation let us define $r_{k,X_0} = r_{k0}$. The next task is then to evaluate the expectation, $E[\ln r_{k,X_k}]$, and the variance, $\mathrm{var}[\ln r_{k,X_k}]$, of the logarithm of this quantity. To do

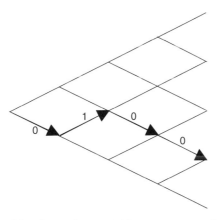

Figure 18.2   Values assumed by the random variables y_1, y_2, y_3 and y_4 for the down-up-down-down path highlighted.

this, we observe that the distribution of X_k is simply given by the Bernoulli (binomial) distribution

$$P[X_k = j] = \frac{C_k^j}{2^k} \tag{18.29}$$

with

$$C_k^j = \frac{k!}{(k-j)!j!} \tag{18.30}$$

Therefore

$$P[r_{k,X_k} = r_{k0}\exp[2\sigma_k j\sqrt{\Delta t}] = P[X_k = j] = \frac{C_k^j}{2^k} \tag{18.31}$$

We can now evaluate $E[\ln r_{k,X_k}]$ (abbreviated as $E[\ln r_k]$):

$$E[\ln r_k] = \sum_{j=0,k} (\tfrac{1}{2})^k C_k^j (\ln r_k + 2\sigma_k j\sqrt{\Delta t})$$

$$= \ln r_k^k (\tfrac{1}{2})^k 2^k + (\tfrac{1}{2})^k 2\sigma_k \sqrt{\Delta t} \sum_{j=0,k} j C_k^j \tag{18.32}$$

In arriving at Equation (18.32) use has been made of the fact that

$$\sum_{j=0,k} C_k^j = 2^k \tag{18.33}$$

Given, however, the definition of C_k^j, it is also true that

$$jC_k^j = kC_{k-1}^{j-1} \tag{18.34}$$

Therefore, after substituting (18.34) into Equation (18.32) one obtains:

$$E[\ln r_k] = \ln r_k + k\sigma_k\sqrt{\Delta t} \tag{18.35}$$

In order to calculate the variance

$$\text{var}[\ln r_k] = E[(\ln r_k)^2] - (E[\ln r_k])^2 \tag{18.36}$$

we will also need the term $E[(\ln r_k)^2]$. This can be evaluated as follows:

$$E[(\ln r_k)^2] = \sum_{j=0,k} \left(\tfrac{1}{2}\right)^k C_k^j \left(\ln r_k + 2\sigma_k\sqrt{\Delta t}\,j\right)^2$$

$$= (\ln r_k)^2 + 2k\sigma_k\sqrt{\Delta t}\ln r_k + 4\sigma_k^2\Delta t \sum_{j=1,k} j^2 C_k^j \tag{18.37}$$

But the term inside the summation sign is simply equal to

$$j^2 C_k^j = k(k-1)C_{k-2}^{j-2} + kC_{k-1}^{j-1} \qquad (18.38)$$

and therefore the last summation adds up to

$$\sum_{j=1,k} j^2 C_k^j = k(k-1)2^{k-2} + k2^{k-1} \qquad (18.39)$$

Putting the pieces together the unconditional variance is given by

$$
\begin{aligned}
\text{var}[\ln r_k] &= \text{E}[(\ln r_k)^2] - (\text{E}[\ln r_k])^2 \\
&= (\ln r_k)^2 + 2k\sigma_k \ln r_k \sqrt{\Delta t} + \sigma_k^2 \Delta t k(k+1) - (\ln r_k + k\sigma_k \sqrt{\Delta t})^2 \\
&= \sigma_k^2 k \Delta t \qquad (18.40)
\end{aligned}
$$

Equation (18.40) therefore shows that Fact 3 is indeed true: despite the fact that the continuous-time limit of the model displays both mean reversion and a non-constant short rate volatility, the unconditional variance of the logarithm of the short rate in the BDT model only depends on the final instantaneous volatility of the short rate (i.e. on the volatility at time $T = n\Delta t$). Expression (18.40) therefore formally validates the 'empirical' procedure, well known among practitioners, to calibrate to caplet market prices. Table 18.1 shows the results of calibrating the BDT tree using the Black implied volatilities as direct input to Equation (18.40).

Note, however, that Fact 3 has been proven to be true, but the paradox is still unexplained. To find an answer, let us move to Fact 2.

Table 18.1 Caplet prices per unit principal and at-the-money strikes for the GBP sterling curve of expiries reported on the left-hand column, as evaluated using the Black model (column Black), and the BDT model calibrated as described in the text (column BDT).

Expiry	Black	BDT
01-Nov-95		
31-Jan-96	0.000443	0.000431
01-May-96	0.000773	0.000757
31-Jul-96	0.001148	0.001133
31-Oct-96	0.001559	0.001548
30-Jan-97	0.002002	0.001994
01-May-97	0.002422	0.002416
01-Aug-97	0.002746	0.002742
31-Oct-97	0.003024	0.003020
30-Jan-98	0.003265	0.003263
02-May-98	0.003471	0.003471
01-Aug-98	0.003449	0.003452
31-Oct-98	0.003406	0.003411

18.6   The Unconditional Variance of the Short Rate in BDT – the Continuous-Time Equivalent

The above derivation has shown that, in discrete time, the unconditional variance of the short rate is indeed given by expression (18.40) and therefore only depends on the instantaneous value of the short rate at time T. What is still not apparent, however, is why the reversion speed and/or the instantaneous short rate volatility from time 0 to time $T - \Delta t$ do not appear in the equation.

To see why this is the case it is more profitable to work in the continuous-time equivalent of the BDT model (Equation (18.19)), and to consider again the general expression for the variance of a mean-reverting diffusion:

$$\mathrm{d}\ln r_t = [a(t)(b(t) - \ln r_t)]\,\mathrm{d}t + \sigma(t)\,\mathrm{d}z(t) \tag{18.41}$$

I show in Appendix I that its variance is given by

$$\mathrm{var}[\ln r_T] = \exp\left[-2\int_0^T a(s)\,\mathrm{d}s\right]\int_0^T \sigma(t)^2\exp\left[2\int_0^t a(s)\,\mathrm{d}s\right]\mathrm{d}t \tag{18.42}$$

As Equation (18.42) shows, the unconditional variance of the logarithm of the short rate out to time T does indeed depend in general both on the reversion speed and on the values of the instantaneous volatility $\sigma(t)$ from time 0 to time T. This result is completely general, but, if one specializes it to the case of the BDT model, $a(t) = -f'$ and $f(t) = \ln\sigma(t)$. By direct substitution the unconditional variance of the log of the short rate out to time T therefore becomes

$$\mathrm{var}[\ln r(T)] = \exp[2f(T) - f(0)]\int_0^T \sigma(t)^2\exp[-2(f_t - f_0)]\,\mathrm{d}t$$

$$= \exp[2f(T)]\int_0^T \sigma(t)^2\exp[-2f_t]\,\mathrm{d}t \tag{18.43}$$

Making use of the fact that $f(t) = \ln\sigma(t)$ in Equation (18.43), one can immediately verify that, in the BDT case, the unconditional variance is indeed simply given by

$$\mathrm{var}\,[\ln\sigma_T] = \sigma_T^2\int_0^T \mathrm{d}u = \sigma_T^2 T \tag{18.44}$$

We have therefore reached an interesting conclusion. Take any mean-reverting process for which the reversion speed is exactly equal to the negative of the logarithmic derivative of the instantaneous volatility with respect to time (i.e. $a(t) = -\frac{\partial\ln\sigma(t)}{\partial t}$). For such a process neither the reversion speed nor the past instantaneous volatility affect the unconditional variance, which only depends on the instantaneous short rate volatility at the final time.

This observation fully explains the BDT paradox, and sheds light on the reason why a more satisfactory model like the Black and Karasinski (which displays 'true' mean reversion) is considerably more difficult to calibrate. The reader might however still be puzzled as to 'what went wrong' from the algorithmic point of view: by the end of the

BDT construction one has used all the degrees of freedom at one's disposal and all of today's market inputs (bond and caplet prices) have been correctly recovered. How could one have done anything differently and still retained a log-normal distribution for the short rate? We address this question in the next section.

18.7 Mean Reversion in Short-Rate Lattices: Recombining vs Bushy Trees

In order to understand what 'went wrong', let us look at the 'algorithmic' origin of the result just obtained. More precisely, let us consider the BDT construction over two time-steps in the cases of a steeply decreasing and a steeply increasing short rate volatility function. Figures 18.3–18.6 represent the first two steps of a non-recombining ('bushy') tree and of a BDT tree with the same time-dependent volatility, and with the same probabilities ($\frac{1}{2}$) for both jumps. On the y-axis one can read the logarithm of the short rate. Given that an 'up' state is linked to its corresponding 'down' state by the relationship

$$r_{\text{up}} = r_{\text{down}} \exp\left[2\sigma_t \sqrt{\Delta t}\right] \tag{18.45}$$

and that the volatility can depend on the time-step, but not on the state, all the 'up' and 'down' logarithms have the same separation (in log space) at a given time-step. Therefore, both in the bushy tree and in the BDT tree, the y-axis distance between any two states originating from the same node is given by $2\sigma_t \sqrt{\Delta t}$. It is important to point out that in both trees the construction must recover not only the total unconditional variance from the origin, but also the conditional variance from each node.

From the two couples of corresponding figures (i.e. from Figures 18.3 and 18.4 and Figures 18.5 and 18.6) one can immediately appreciate that, in the bushy case, any drift could have been assigned to the short rate, and the construction would still have been possible. Looking at Figure 18.4, however, which refers to the case of sharply decreasing volatility in the BDT construction, one can see that the only way to ensure that at each node the condition $r_{\text{up}} = r_{\text{down}} \exp\left[2\sigma_t \sqrt{\Delta t}\right]$ is fulfilled and that the tree recombines is to push the two 'up' nodes (labelled up/up and up/down in the figures) towards the two 'down' nodes (labelled down/down and down/up) in Figure 18.4. Similarly, looking at Figure 18.5 one can see that, if the volatility of the short rate is increasing, the 'up' nodes must be moved up even farther, and the 'down' nodes moved farther down.

Note that all the nodes can be moved up or down by the same amount (i.e. by adding a purely time-dependent drift) without affecting the feasibility of the construction, as can be appreciated by comparing Figures 18.6 and 18.7. Indeed, this is the 'device' used to recover the exogenous bond prices exactly. The nodes cannot be moved in a state-dependent way, however, without compromising the BDT recombining construction.

It is clear from the figures that the moving down of the 'up' nodes and up of the 'down' nodes shown in Figure 18.4 therefore introduces a mean-reverting component to the process for the short rate. Similarly, the pushing apart of the nodes shown in Figure 18.6, necessary to ensure recombination, introduces a mean-fleeing component. In the BDT case the requirement of recombination therefore strongly limits the possible drifts, over and above the drift imposed by recombination, that can be specified by

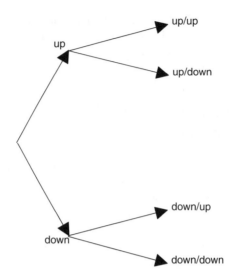

Figure 18.3   A bushy-tree construction for the case of decreasing volatility.

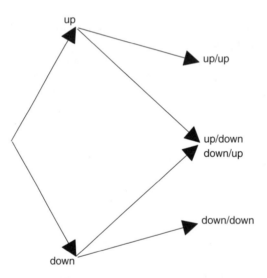

Figure 18.4   The corresponding BDT construction for the same decreasing volatility.

the user. In particular, this 'extra' drift can at most be time dependent (the term $\mu(t)$ in Equation (18.16), algorithmically accounted for by the construction in Figure 18.7), and, therefore, cannot introduce 'true' mean reversion (since this would require the state variable, r).

   From these considerations one can see from yet another angle why a mean reversion (of sorts) can only occur with the BDT algorithm if the volatility is time dependent (and, more specifically, decaying). Note that the negative aspects introduced by the procedure are more insidious than the usual limitations of one-factor or low-dimensionality models: the binomial recombining-lattice geometry introduces an inextricable link between its

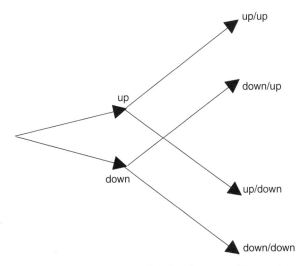

Figure 18.5 A bushy-tree construction for the case of increasing volatility.

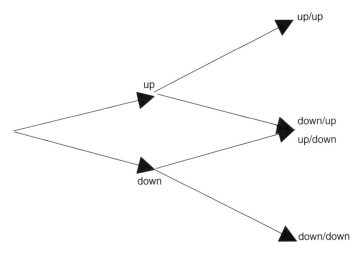

Figure 18.6 The corresponding BDT construction for the same increasing volatility.

reversion speed and the (logarithmic) derivative of the short rate volatility. The time-decaying volatility needed in the BDT model in order to 'contain' an excessive dispersion of rates does succeed in obtaining an unconditional distribution of rates consistent with the one implied by the cap market. However, in the absence of mean reversion, this can only be obtained by means of a lower and lower future volatility. The future term structure of volatilities predicted by the BDT model is therefore radically different from the term structure of volatilities observed today, and in the future will become lower and lower and flatter and flatter. The future vega re-hedging costs predicted by the BDT model are therefore unlikely to be encountered in real life. Furthermore, day after day the model will have to be re-calibrated to account for a future implied volatility surface

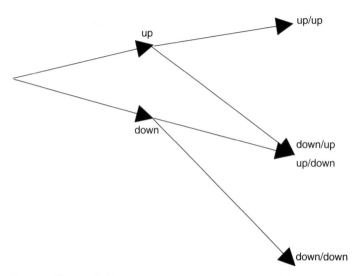

Figure 18.7   Same as Figure 18.6 but with a purely time-dependent (negative) drift (the term $\theta(t)$ in Equation (18.18)).

that systematically fails to come true. Given the discussion in Sections 1.1.4 and 1.3.2 of Chapter 1, these are highly undesirable features.

18.8   Extension to More General Interest-Rate Models

The previous section highlighted that the limitations of the BDT model directly stem from the algorithmic prescription for its construction and from the binomial choice for the geometry of the tree in particular. This, however, need not be the case. For instance, a procedure based on a three-branching (trinomial) lattice could be used. The construction and the calibration become more cumbersome, but a very significant advantage is reaped. In computational terms, this can be seen as gaining one degree of freedom (e.g. one extra probability, or the location of the third node); in financial and economic terms, as the ability to specify a 'true' (i.e. volatility-independent) mean reversion.

As we saw in the equity/FX case, mean reversion in the real world has no direct bearing on option pricing, since the transformation from the real-world to the pricing measure effects a drift transformation that 'scrambles' the real-world dynamics. In the interest-rate case, however, one is typically evolving non-traded quantities. No-arbitrage considerations therefore do not directly dictate that these non-traded state variables should have a drift equal to the riskless rate. When one is dealing with interest rates, one is therefore at liberty to start with very general functional forms for the specification of the drift of the (non-traded) short rate in the risk-neutral world. As we saw in Section 18.2, this will then affect the volatility of the traded asset prices. In particular, this specification could incorporate a mean-reverting feature. Despite the fact, however, that one can introduce a mean-reverting term into the risk-neutral dynamics of the short rate, it is not a priori obvious why it should be advantageous to do so.

In qualitative terms, the explanation goes as follows. If part of the burden to avoid 'excessive' dispersion of the rates is shouldered by a mean-reverting term (rather than by a time-decaying volatility, as in the BDT case), then the volatility can be constant, or mildly varying, and the market prices of caplets can still be recovered by the model. This observation, however, raises another question: why should we want to require that the volatility of the short rate be constant, or mildly varying? Or, more generally: since our information about the real-world mean reversion does not imply anything about the drift of the risk-adjusted dynamics, how does one 'guess' the nature of the risk-adjusted mean reversion?

The key to a satisfactory answer to both questions lies in the observation that the transformation from the real-world to the pricing measure affects (via Girsanov's theorem) the drift but not the volatility of the stochastic quantities of interest. Therefore, in a deterministic-volatility setting, our calibrated model will imply that whatever future volatility structure we are left with in the pricing measure after recovering the caplet market prices, this will be the same as the one that we should expect in the real world. Because of this, whatever property we calculate in the risk-adjusted world, *as long as purely related to and derived from the measure-invariant volatilities*, can be directly compared with the corresponding real-world quantity.[4] One such quantity is the evolution of the term structure of volatilities. On the basis of the empirical observations mentioned in Chapter 7, we may believe that term structures of volatilities by and large preserve their shape over time. If this is the case, one possible (and useful) criterion to choose an appropriate mean-reverting dynamics for the driving factors (the short rate or the forward rates) could therefore be the following: choose the parameters of the risk-adjusted mean-reverting process in such a way that the volatility functions needed to price the market-traded options produce (reasonably) time-homogeneous evolutions for the term structure of volatilities. In other words, make sure that the future trading universe looks acceptably similar to the universe we observe today.

The ultimate justification for this possible criterion is the empirical observation that term structures of volatilities remain approximately self-similar over time (see, in this regard, the discussion in Chapter 19). Therefore, unless we have specific views to the contrary, it is reasonable to assume that they will (at least approximately) retain their structural features also in the future. Needless to say, if the trader thought that the future will not be like the past, she should use a model that reflects, in the evolution of the relevant volatilities, this particular belief. This issue is tackled in Chapter 19, where I argue that one of the main reasons why the modern (LIBOR market model) approach is so much preferable to the 'traditional' (short-rate-based) framework is because the former gives the trader a direct way of controlling the evolution of those quantities (such as the term structure of volatilities) that have a direct impact on future re-hedging costs.

It is worthwhile pointing out that imposing time homogeneity for some financial quantities can have wider applicability than the purely interest-rate case. Similar conclusions can be drawn, in fact, in the case of the implied volatility smile. I have stressed in the

---

[4]Note that this is not true if we believed that the correct dynamics of the yield curve should be expressed in terms of a stochastic-volatility diffusion. Indeed, some of the techniques presented in Part IV of this book deal with the question of how this comparison across measures should be carried out when the volatility is assumed to be stochastic.

equity/FX case that reproducing today's smile is only a (relatively small) part of the over-all task of a model. As I discuss in Chapter 1, just as important is the model's prediction of the future smile.

Note also that, if enough liquid instruments were traded in the market, and exactly priced by a model, so as to capture not only the prices embedded in today's smile or in today's cap volatility term structure, but also of the evolution of these quantities, then the trader's job would truly be one of pure arbitrage. In the case of interest-rate options I will argue in Chapter 19 that the missing liquid instruments are serial options. In the equity/FX world, forward-setting options of the type discussed in Section 3.8 of Chapter 3 would be required in addition to plain-vanilla calls and puts. If that were the case, the exotic trader's task would be considerably simpler (or, perhaps, her job would disappear): she would not have to worry whether the market is 'implying' an unreasonable future evolution for the smile or for the term structure of caplet volatility. She could simply engage in the transactions suggested by her model (calibrated to all the products), virtually resting assured that she could 'lock-in' any price discrepancy. 'True' model arbitrages, are, however, exceedingly rare, and, as the name suggests, they will only prove to be true arbitrages if the world indeed evolves as the model predicts.[5] So, ultimately, the justification for having to specify correctly the future evolution of smile surfaces or term structures of volatilities comes down to the intrinsic incompleteness of option markets.

In the light of this discussion, one can leave the short-rate models with the observation that, apart from all their other shortcomings, they provide the user with a rather blunt instrument when it comes to making the model produce a pre-chosen future evolution for the term structure of volatilities. Some models, as we have seen, just cannot accomplish this goal. Others (like the Black-and-Karasinski or the Hull-and-White) have the potential to deliver this result, but offer a very indirect way of producing the desired effect. I have always felt that driving the term structure of volatilities from the short-rate end is like pushing, rather than pulling, a rope. The next chapters will show how, by means of a LIBOR-market-model-type of approach, one can establish a more constructive interaction with a rope.

18.9   Appendix I: Evaluation of the Variance of the Logarithm of the Instantaneous Short Rate

From Equation (18.41) one can write

$$d \ln r(t) + a(t) \ln r(t) = a(t)b(t)\, dt + \sigma(t)\, dz(t) \qquad (18.46)$$

This implies that

$$\exp\left[-\int_0^t a(s)\, ds\right] d\left[\ln r(t) \exp\left[\int_0^t a(s)\, ds\right]\right]$$
$$= a(t)b(t)\, dt + \sigma(t)\, dz(t) \qquad (18.47)$$

---

[5]This should be contrasted with the model-independent arbitrages discussed in Chapter 17.

But the quantity $\ln r(T) \exp\left[\int_0^T a(s)\,ds\right]$ can be written as

$$\ln r(T)\left[\int_0^T a(s)\,ds\right] = \ln r(0) + \int_0^T a(t)b(t)\exp\left[\int_0^t a(s)\,ds\right]dt$$

$$+ \int_0^T \sigma(t)\exp\left[\int_0^t a(s)\,ds\right]dz(t) \qquad (18.48)$$

and, therefore

$$\ln r(T) = \exp\left[-\int_0^T a(s)\,ds\right]\ln r(0)$$

$$+ \exp\left[-\int_0^T a(s)\,ds\right]\int_0^T a(t)b(t)\exp\left[-\int_0^t a(s)\,ds\right]dt$$

$$+ \exp\left[-\int_0^T a(s)\,ds\right]\int_0^T \sigma(t)\exp\left[\int_0^t a(s)\,ds\right]dz(t)$$

Remembering that, for any deterministic function $f(t)$,

$$\text{var}\left[\int_0^t f(u)\,dz(u)\right] = \int_0^t f(s)^2\,dt \qquad (18.49)$$

it then follows that

$$\text{var}[\ln r(T)] = E[(\ln r(T))^2] - (E[\ln r(T)])^2$$

$$= \exp\left[-2\int_0^T a(s)\,ds\right]\int_0^T \sigma(t)^2 \exp\left[2\int_0^t a(s)\,ds\right]dt \qquad (18.50)$$

Chapter 19

Volatility and Correlation in the LIBOR Market Model

19.1 Introduction

Until the mid-1990s no clear consensus had emerged among practitioners or academics as to the 'favourite' or most widely used interest-rate model.[1] Trade-offs always had to be made between ease of calibration (or, more often than not, lack thereof), availability of closed-form solutions, realism of the distributional assumptions, etc. The common feature of almost all these earlier models was that the yield curve was assumed to be driven by the unobservable short rate (plus, sometimes, another equally unobservable variable, such as the yield of the consol, or the variance of the short rate). In all cases, the trader had to perform, explicitly or implicitly, a transformation between the input values of the unobservable state variables, and those quantities, such as the term structure of implied volatilities of forward or swap rates, that she could observe in the market. The model, in this respect, acted as the black box that transformed what the user could input (e.g. the volatility of the short rate) into what the user would have liked to be able to input (e.g. caplet or swap volatilities).

The Heath–Jarrow–Morton (1989) (HJM in what follows) approach radically changed the set of driving state variables by focusing attention on the infinite number of (instantaneous) forward rates that describe the yield curve. These instantaneous forward rates were still, strictly speaking, unobservable, but they were somewhat closer to what the user had direct access to (i.e. discrete-tenor forward LIBOR rates).

In its original form, however, the HJM model is hardly more user-friendly, when it comes to calibration to market data, than traditional short-rate-based models. A number of papers appeared in these early years proposing more or less cumbersome methodologies to specify the volatility functions in such a way that cap prices could be approximately recovered. Furthermore, the fact that no non-exploding solutions exist for log-normally

---

[1] I have surveyed the evolution of interest-rate models in Rebonato (2004).

distributed instantaneous forward rates[2] did not make matters any simpler. Practitioners decided to avert their eyes from the problem, and pretend that it did not exist; academics proposed several partial and, one has to say, highly artificial solutions.

The LIBOR market model approach (LMM in what follows), pioneered by Brace *et al.* (1995), Jamshidian (1997), Musiela and Rutkowski (1997), Rutkowski (1998) and others, radically changed the situation. Now direct market observables (i.e. LIBOR–forward or swap–rates and their volatilities) became the building blocks of the new methodology, earning the new approach the title of 'the market model'. The LMM formalism quickly proved to be ideally suited for discrete-look, path-dependent derivatives products in a multi-factor framework. Acceptance of the LMM approach was facilitated by the fact that it shared with the HJM model one fundamental insight, which had by then become familiar among practitioners, namely that the no-arbitrage conditions describing the deterministic part of the evolution of forward rates could be expressed purely in terms of their correlations and volatilities. As a result, the research emphasis became focused on the correct specification of the time-dependent instantaneous volatility of the underlying state variables, i.e. the discrete LIBOR rates.

At the same time, it became progressively clear that in order to achieve de-correlation among forward rates introducing a non-flat volatility for the forward rates could provide a more important and often more realistic mechanism than invoking a large number of driving factors (see the discussion in Chapter 5). In other words, the attention gradually shifted from the *instantaneous* to the *terminal* correlation amongst rates. In a nutshell, the simultaneous specification of these time-dependent volatilities and correlations became not one of the problems, but *the* problem, in the specification of the LMM model.

Calibrating the LMM model simply to caplet or to European swaption prices (if the forward-rate-based or the swap-rate-based implementation is chosen, respectively) is very simple indeed, and, as shown below, can be accomplished exactly in an infinity of ways. The fact that so many possible solutions exist creates however a problem: each specification of the time-dependent volatilities will give rise to a different degree of terminal correlation amongst the forward rates, and to a different evolution of the term structure of volatilities. The question therefore arises as to whether it is in some way possible to choose among these exact (or quasi-exact) calibrations to caplet prices so that other desirable properties are recovered. This is one of the questions addressed in this chapter.

19.2 Specifying the Forward-Rate Dynamics in the LIBOR Market Model

19.2.1 First Formulation: Each Forward Rate in Isolation

In order to see how the forward rates that describe the yield curve can be evolved in an arbitrage-free way one can proceed as follows. Let us assume first that, perhaps on the basis of the discussion presented in the following chapters, the functional dependence on calendar time, t, and on the forward-rate expiry, T_i, of the instantaneous volatility, σ_i, of

---

[2]'Explosion' in this context means that a log-normally-distributed instantaneous forward rate will reach infinity in a finite time with probability one.

the ith forward rate has been chosen:

$$\sigma_i = \sigma(t, T_i) \qquad (19.1)$$

Similarly, we will also assume that the trader has chosen a correlation function, ρ:

$$\rho_{ij} = \rho(t, T_i, T_j) \qquad (19.2)$$

These two important topics are dealt with in Chapters 21 and 22. Let then $\widehat{\sigma}(T_i)$ (or, sometimes, more briefly, just $\widehat{\sigma}_i$) be the implied Black volatility of the forward rate of maturity T_i, $f_i(T_i)$ (often abbreviated in what follows as f_i). Since we are, for the moment, ignoring the possibility of smiles, the instantaneous and the implied Black volatilities are linked by the relationship

$$\widehat{\sigma}_i^2 T_i = \int_0^{T_i} \sigma(u, T_i)^2 \, \mathrm{d}u \qquad (19.3)$$

If Equation (19.3) is satisfied, the Black price of the ith caplet is exactly recovered. Condition (19.3) is therefore referred to in what follows as the caplet-pricing condition.

If we consider one forward rate at a time and impose that its process should be an arbitrage-free diffusion with deterministic volatility, its evolution can be most simply described by a SDE of the form

$$\frac{\mathrm{d}f_i}{f_i} = \mu_i(\{f\}, t) \, \mathrm{d}t + \sigma_i \, \mathrm{d}w_i \qquad (19.4)$$

where the drift term $\mu_i(\{f\}, t)$ is derived by invoking absence of arbitrage. The formal solution of Equation (19.4) (see Chapter 5), given today's value, $f_i(0)$, for the forward rate, is given by

$$f_i(t) = f_i(0) \exp\left[\int_0^t \left(\mu_i(\{f_u\}, u) - \tfrac{1}{2}\sigma(u, T_i)^2\right) \mathrm{d}u\right] \exp\left[\int_0^t \sigma(u, T_i) \, \mathrm{d}w_u\right] \qquad (19.5)$$

As mentioned, in the equation above the drift $\mu_i(\{f_u\}, u)$ reflects the no-arbitrage condition, and is, in general, a function of the instantaneous volatilities of the forward rates, of the correlation amongst them, and of the forward rates themselves. Once the volatility and correlation functions have been specified, these drifts are therefore uniquely determined. The expression for the drift depends on the chosen numeraire. Obtaining it would at this point entail a rather long detour. The interested reader could see, for example, Jamshidian (1997), or Rebonato (2002) for a simpler derivation. Since this book is about volatility and correlation, for our purposes the most important feature of these drifts is that they are purely a function of forward-rate volatilities and correlations. Once these functions are chosen, the drifts follow automatically, and therefore they are no longer explicitly dealt with in this chapter. In a way, despite the fact that so much emphasis is often devoted to obtaining expressions for the no-arbitrage drifts, the 'real action' with the LMM lies in the choice of the input volatility and correlation functions.

For future reference, if n forward rates describe the yield curve, Equation 19.4 can be written in matrix form as:

$$\frac{d\mathbf{f}}{\mathbf{f}} = \boldsymbol{\mu}(\mathbf{f}, t)\, dt + \mathbf{S}\, d\mathbf{w} \tag{19.6}$$

where the vector $\frac{d\mathbf{f}}{\mathbf{f}}$ is to be understood in a component-wise fashion (i.e. its first, second, ..., nth elements are $\frac{df_1}{f_1}$, $\frac{df_2}{f_2}$, ..., $\frac{df_n}{f_n}$), and the $[n \times n]$ matrix $\mathbf{S}$ is a time-dependent diagonal matrix whose iith element is given by the instantaneous volatility of the ith forward rate:

$$\mathbf{S} = \begin{bmatrix} \sigma_1 & \cdots & \cdots & 0 \\ 0 & \sigma_2 & 0 & 0 \\ \cdots & \cdots & \cdots & \cdots \\ 0 & 0 & \cdots & \sigma_n \end{bmatrix} \tag{19.7}$$

An exogenous correlation structure between forward rates can be recovered by requiring that

$$\rho\, dt = d\mathbf{w}\, d\mathbf{w}^{\mathrm{T}} \tag{19.8}$$

where ρ is the desired $[n \times n]$ correlation matrix.

Equations (19.4)–(19.8) give a perfectly adequate description of the LMM forward-rate dynamics if as many factors as forward rates are retained, but provide no obvious indication as to how the dimensionality of the problem can be reduced. This problem can be addressed as follows.

19.2.2   Second Formulation: The Covariance Matrix

Let us now assume that only m independent Brownian shocks (factors) describe the evolution of the forward rates. Let us rewrite Equation (19.6) as

$$\frac{d\mathbf{f}}{\mathbf{f}} = \boldsymbol{\mu}(\mathbf{f}, t)\, dt + \boldsymbol{\sigma}\, d\mathbf{z} \tag{19.9}$$

where now $d\mathbf{z}$ is an $[m \times 1]$ vector whose elements are the increments of m orthogonal Brownian motions:

$$d\mathbf{z}\, d\mathbf{z}^{\mathrm{T}} = \mathbf{I}\, dt \tag{19.10}$$

$\mathbf{I}$ is the identity matrix:

$$\mathbf{I} = \begin{bmatrix} 1 & 0 & \cdots & 0 \\ 0 & 1 & \cdots & 0 \\ \cdots & \cdots & 1 & \cdots \\ 0 & 0 & \cdots & 1 \end{bmatrix} \tag{19.11}$$

and the (j, k)th element of the $[n \times m]$ matrix $\boldsymbol{\sigma}$,

$$
\boldsymbol{\sigma} = \begin{bmatrix}
\sigma_{11} & \sigma_{12} & \cdots & \sigma_{1m} \\
\sigma_{21} & \sigma_{21} & \cdots & \sigma_{2m} \\
\cdots & \cdots & \cdots & \cdots \\
\sigma_{n1} & \sigma_{n2} & \cdots & \sigma_{nm}
\end{bmatrix}
\tag{19.12}
$$

contains the responsiveness of the jth forward rate to a random shock from the kth factor. So, for instance, if the first factor had been chosen to represent shocks to the level of the yield curve, the column vector

$$
\begin{bmatrix}
\sigma_{11} \\
\sigma_{21} \\
\cdots \\
\sigma_{n1}
\end{bmatrix}
\tag{19.13}
$$

would give the responsiveness of the first, second, $\ldots$, nth forward rate to a level change; if the second factor represented shocks to the slope of the yield curve, the column vector

$$
\begin{bmatrix}
\sigma_{12} \\
\sigma_{22} \\
\cdots \\
\sigma_{n2}
\end{bmatrix}
\tag{19.14}
$$

would give the responsiveness of the first, second, $\ldots$, nth forward rate to a slope change; etc.

We have seen in Chapter 5 that the covariance matrix between the forward rates is the crucial quantity that determines the stochastic part of their evolution. I have shown in Rebonato (2002) that the same covariance matrix elements also constitute the most important component of the deterministic part of the forward-rate evolution. The formulation presented in this section is therefore particularly useful, because it can be shown by straightforward matrix multiplication that the covariance matrix, $\boldsymbol{\Sigma}$, between the forward rates is given by

$$
\boldsymbol{\Sigma} = \boldsymbol{\sigma}\boldsymbol{\sigma}^{\mathrm{T}}
\tag{19.15}
$$

Exercise 1 *Obtain Equation (19.15) by remembering that* $\mathrm{covar}\left[\frac{\mathrm{d}f_j}{f_j}, \frac{\mathrm{d}f_k}{f_k}\right] = \mathrm{E}\left[\frac{\mathrm{d}f_j}{f_j}\frac{\mathrm{d}f_k}{f_k}\right]$, *and explicitly calculating the terms* $\frac{\mathrm{d}f_j}{\mathrm{d}f_j}\frac{\mathrm{d}f_k}{\mathrm{d}f_k}$ *using Ito's rules:* $\mathrm{d}t\,\mathrm{d}t = 0$, $\mathrm{d}z_j\,\mathrm{d}t = 0$ *and* $\mathrm{d}z_j\,\mathrm{d}z_k = \delta_{jk}$.

Another useful feature of the formulation (19.9) is that the caplet-pricing condition (19.3) can be automatically satisfied (and, for $m > 1$, in infinitely many ways) as long as

$$
\sum_{k=1,m} \sigma_{jk}^2 = \sigma_j^2
\tag{19.16}
$$

Exercise 2 *Prove Equation (19.16).*

19.2.3   Third Formulation: Separating the Correlation from the Volatility Term

The second formulation just presented does not distinguish between volatility and corre-lation information, because it directly uses the forward-rate covariance elements. I discuss in Rebonato (2002) why it may be desirable to model separately the volatility component (about which some almost-direct[3] information can be obtained from the market prices of caplets), and the correlation component, which I believe can be more profitably described on the basis of statistical information.[4] This can be accomplished as follows.

Let us start from Equation (19.9), which can be rewritten term-by-term as

$$\frac{df_i}{f_i} = \mu_i(\{f\}, t)\, dt + \sum_{k=1,m} \sigma_{ik}\, dz_k \tag{19.17}$$

and multiply and divide each loading σ_{ik} by the volatility, σ_i, of the ith forward rate:

$$\frac{df_i}{f_i} = \mu_i(\{f\}, t)\, dt + \sigma_i \sum_{k=1,m} \frac{\sigma_{ik}}{\sigma_i}\, dz_k \tag{19.18}$$

Making use of the caplet-pricing condition (19.16), this can be rewritten as

$$\frac{df_i}{f_i} = \mu_i(\{f\}, t)\, dt + \sigma_i \sum_{k=1,m} \frac{\sigma_{ik}}{\sqrt{\sum_{k=1,m} \sigma_{ik}^2}}\, dz_k \tag{19.19}$$

If now we define the quantity b_{ik} as

$$b_{ik} \equiv \frac{\sigma_{ik}}{\sqrt{\sum_{k=1,m} \sigma_{ik}^2}} \tag{19.20}$$

Equation (19.19) can be rewritten in a more compact way as

$$\frac{df_i}{f_i} = \mu_i(\{f\}, t)\, dt + \sigma_i \sum_{k=1,m} b_{ik}\, dz_k \tag{19.21}$$

Expression (19.21) is very useful because, if we denote by **b** the $[n \times m]$ matrix of elements b_{jk}, it can be readily shown that

$$\mathbf{b}\mathbf{b}^{\mathsf{T}} = \rho \tag{19.22}$$

---

[3]The information is 'almost' direct because from the market prices of caplets we only have information about the root-mean-squared instantaneous volatility. See the discussion in Sections 19.4 and 19.5.

[4]Swaption prices do contain some information about the correlation function. However, I have argued in Rebonato (2002) and Rebonato (2004) why it might not be a good idea to make use of this 'implied' information. See also de Jong *et al.* (1999). It must be said, however, that my views are not universally accepted (see, for example, Alexander (2003) and Schoenbucher (2003)). The topic is also discussed at length in Section 1.4 of Chapter 1.

Exercise 3 *Prove Equation (19.22). (Hint: Look at the treatment for the two-factor case discussed in the next chapter.)*

Finally, if the root mean square of the chosen instantaneous volatility is equal to the Black volatility, the caplet-pricing condition

$$\sum_{k=1,m} \sigma_{jk}^2 = \sigma_j^2 \tag{19.23}$$

simply becomes

$$\sum_{k=1,m} b_{jk}^2 = 1 \tag{19.24}$$

But Equation (19.24) is certainly always satisfied as long as we have constructed the coefficients $\{b_{ik}\}$ using Equation (19.20). We have therefore achieved the desired task of decomposing the stochastic dynamics for the forward rates in terms of coefficients, σ_i, purely dependent on their volatilities, and coefficients, **b**, which solely depend on the correlation structure. I will show in the next chapters how this decomposition can be profitably made use of in the calibration of the LMM. Before moving on to this task, it is useful to highlight the links between the treatment presented so far and the result of the Principal Component Analysis (PCA) of the correlation matrix. This is undertaken in the next section.

19.3   Link with the Principal Component Analysis

The formulations presented above allow for a transparent link with the results of the PCA. If as many factors as forwards rates are retained, one particular set of loadings, say, $\{\widehat{b}_{ik}\}$, is linked in fact to the eigenvectors, $\{a_{ik}\}$, and eigenvalues, λ_k, of the correlation matrix by the relationship

$$\widehat{b}_{ik} = a_{ik}\sqrt{\lambda_k} \tag{19.25}$$

For this particular choice, in addition to the constraint (19.24), also the orthogonality relationships

$$\sum_{i=1,n} b_{ik}b_{ij} = \delta_{jk} \tag{19.26}$$

will be satisfied. (Note carefully that the sum is now over forward rates, not over the independent Brownian motions.) If we are using a full-factor version of the LMM, there is no special merit in this particular rotation of the axes, apart, perhaps, from being able to use the intuition afforded by the well-known interpretation of the PCA eigenvectors as level, slope, curvature, etc. However, if we had to use fewer factors than forward rates, it is important that the modes of deformation retained should capture as much as possible of the variability across forward rates. Clearly, if one simply 'threw away' the eigenvectors of order higher than m (where m is the number of retained factors), the caplet pricing condition would no longer be satisfied. What is required therefore is a reallocation of the overall variance from higher-frequency modes of deformation to the retained factors. In what follows I will present a technique to carry out this reallocation in an 'optimal' way (where 'optimal' means 'in such a way that an exogenous correlation matrix can best be recovered').

The three formulations presented so far provide an 'empty receptacle' into which the volatilities and correlation functions can be 'poured'. We have not said anything yet as to how these functions might be chosen. This is the topic of the next three chapters. In order to put this treatment into context, and to provide some intuition, I conclude this chapter with two case studies that

- highlight the link between the *current* term structure of volatilities and the *future* instantaneous volatilities;

- show (again) the difference between instantaneous and terminal correlation;

- display the intrinsic incompleteness of the caplet and swaption markets.

19.4   Worked-Out Example 1: Caplets and a Two-Period Swaption

Let us consider the case of two forward rates, f_1 and f_2, and the swap rate SR_{12} expiring at the same time as the first forward rate and maturing at the same time as the second: $f_1 = f_1(t, T_1, T_2)$, $f_2 = f_2(t, T_2, T_3)$, $SR_{12} = SR_{12}(t, T_1, T_3)$. See Figure 19.1. The underlying swap rate, SR_{12} (SR in what follows), can be written as a linear combination of the two forward rates:

$$SR_{12} = SR = w_1 f_1 + w_2 f_2 \qquad (19.27)$$

with w_1 and w_2 the weights given in Chapter 20, Equation (20.32), or derived, for example, in Rebonato (2002).

Let us consider a discrete trading horizon made up of two dates only (the reset dates of the caplets), and, for the sake of simplicity, let us constrain all quantities, such as volatilities or correlations, to be piecewise constant over each of the two possible 'time-steps'. Let us further assume that the two caplets associated with the forward rates f_1

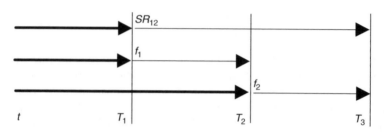

Figure 19.1   The reset and expiry times of the two forward rates, f_1 and f_2, and of the swap rate SR_{12}. The thick arrows indicate where the relative rate expires. The thin arrow shows the period covered by that rate; the arrow ends at maturity time.

and f_2 trade in the market with implied Black volatilities, $\widehat{\sigma}_1$ and $\widehat{\sigma}_2$, of 20%, and that the two rates display an instantaneous correlation ρ. Finally, let the swaption spanned by these two forward rates (i.e. the option to enter at time T_1 a two-period swap starting at time T_1 and maturing at time T_3) have a market implied (Black) volatility, $\widehat{\sigma}_{SR}$, of 18%.

We want to allow for the possibility that the second forward rate might assume a different instantaneous volatility from time T_1 to time T_2. To do this, I will assign two volatilities for the second forward rate, the first prevailing from time T_0 to time T_1:

$$\sigma_{2,1} \equiv \sigma(t, T_2), \quad T_0 \le t \le T_1 \tag{19.28}$$

and the second from time T_1 to time T_2:

$$\sigma_{2,2} \equiv \sigma(t, T_2), \quad T_1 < t \le T_2 \tag{19.29}$$

For symmetry of notation, I shall also denote the volatility of the first forward rate over the first time interval by $\sigma_{1,1}$; however, the fuller notation is in this case redundant, because there is only one period before the expiry of the first forward rate, and we have assumed the volatilities to be piecewise constant.

I will show in the next chapter (see also Jaeckel and Rebonato (2003) and references therein) that one can write a reasonably accurate approximation for the volatility of the swaption, σ_{SR}, from time T_0 to its expiry (time T_1) in terms of the volatility of and the correlation between the underlying forward rates as

$$
\begin{aligned}
\sigma_{SR}^2 SR^2 \\
= w_1^2 f_1^2 \sigma_{1,1}^2 + w_2^2 f_2^2 \sigma_{2,1}^2 + w_1 w_2 f_1 f_2 \sigma_{1,1} \sigma_{2,1} \rho
\end{aligned}
\tag{19.30}
$$

See Section 20.5 of Chapter 20 for a discussion of the approximations required to obtain Equation (19.30). Note carefully that in Equation (19.30) there appears the instantaneous volatility of the second forward rate only from time T_0 to time T_1.

Let us now require that both caplets and the swaption should be simultaneously exactly priced. As for the first caplet, no choice is left but to ensure that its unconditional variance should indeed be equal to the value implied by the Black market volatility. This uniquely determines $\sigma_{1,1}$ via the relationship

$$\widehat{\sigma}_1^2 (T_1 - T_0) = \int_{T_0}^{T_1} \sigma_{1,1}^2 \, du = \sigma_{1,1}^2 (T_1 - T_0) \to \widehat{\sigma}_1 = \sigma_{1,1} \tag{19.31}$$

This relationship establishes one term in the RHS of Equation (19.30). Remember, however, that we do want the swaption volatility to be recovered in a way compatible with the value $\sigma_{1,1}$ which has already been fixed, and we also require the caplet expiring at time T_2 to be correctly priced. The pricing of the second caplet will require that

$$\widehat{\sigma}_2^2 (T_2 - T_0) = \int_{T_0}^{T_2} \sigma_2^2 \, du = \sigma_{2,1}^2 (T_1 - T_0) + \sigma_{2,2}^2 (T_2 - T_1) \tag{19.32}$$

The quantities still at our disposal in order to achieve these tasks are therefore the instantaneous volatility of the second forward rate from time T_0 to time T_1, $\sigma_{2,1}$, its volatility from time T_1 to time T_2, $\sigma_{2,2}$, and the correlation between the two forwards from time T_0 to time T_1, ρ. Looking at Equation (19.30), however, one can readily see that there are infinitely many solutions. One can obtain $\sigma_{SR}^2 T_1 = (18\%)^2 T_1$, for instance, by accepting a constant volatility for the second forward rate ($\sigma_{2,1} = \sigma_{2,2} = 20\%$) and imposing a lower-than-one correlation (case (a)); or perhaps by having a perfect correlation between the forward rates and a volatility for the second forward rate from time T_1 to time T_2, $\sigma_{2,2}$, lower than 20% (case (b)); or in many other ways. Let us explore more carefully what each choice entails.

If the first route is chosen, i.e. if one chooses $\rho < 1$, one can find a solution even with flat (20%) instantaneous volatilities for the second forward rate. In the second case ($\rho = 1$), on the other hand, finding a solution requires a two-step procedure. First, one must decrease,[5] from its average level, the instantaneous volatility of the second forward rate from T_0 to T_1 so as to recover the volatility of the swap rate:

$$\sigma_{SR}^2 SR^2 = \left(w_1 f_1 \sigma_{1,1} + w_2 f_2 \sigma_{2,1} \right)^2 \quad \rightarrow$$

$$\sigma_{2,1} = \frac{\sigma_{SR} SR - w_1 f_1 \sigma_{1,1}}{w_2 f_2} \tag{19.33}$$

Having done that, one must consistently increase the volatility during the second period above its average value in such a way that the second caplet is correctly priced:

$$\widehat{\sigma}_2^2 (T_2 - T_0) = \sigma_{2,1}^2 (T_1 - T_0) + \sigma_{2,2}^2 (T_2 - T_1) \quad \rightarrow$$

$$\sigma_{2,2}^2 = \frac{\widehat{\sigma}_2^2 (T_2 - T_0) - \sigma_{2,1}^2 (T_1 - T_0)}{T_2 - T_1} \tag{19.34}$$

In between these two extreme cases (i.e. perfect instantaneous correlation or flat constant volatility for the second forward rate throughout its life) there obviously exist infinitely many intermediate possible solutions.

This example allows one to draw two important conclusions:

1. an imperfect correlation is strictly necessary in order to account for lower-than-weighted-average swaption volatilities only if the instantaneous volatilities of forward rates are assumed to be constant throughout the life of the forward rate itself;

2. if a convincing explanation of the observed market volatility of swaptions requires significantly non-constant, time-dependent instantaneous volatilities of the underlying forward rates, there are important implications about the evolution over time of the term structure of volatilities.

Let us look at the second point in more detail. Note that, for the simple example just considered, at time T_0 the term structure of volatilities (i.e. the function that gives the average volatilities of forward rates of different maturities) was flat (at 20%) for both forwards. This term structure of volatilities remains unchanged for case (a); in case (b),

---

[5]In order to say with certainty that the volatility will have to be decreased one would have to know the exact values of w_1, w_2, f_1 and f_2. However, in practice, most reasonable values for these quantities give rise to a lower level of the volatility of the second forward rate from time T_0 to time T_1.

however, the term structure at time T_1 has to be different (higher) for the 'front' forward (the only one still 'alive' in this simple example) to attain its correct total variance, i.e. to price the time-2 caplet correctly.

This observation allows us to draw a more general conclusion: any choice of the apportioning of the volatility of the second forward rate throughout its life will uniquely determine the evolution of the term structure of volatilities. If we choose as our criterion for a 'good' time dependence of the volatility of the forward rates the time homogeneity of the resulting term structure of volatilities, we might obtain one result. If we require that market swaption prices should be recovered as well as possible (for a given correlation function), we might obtain a different one. Luckily, I discuss in Rebonato (2002) that the 'solutions' for the time dependence of the forward-rate volatility functions arrived at via these two conceptually very different routes, while by no means identical, do display a reassuring degree of internal coherence.

A second important example can further illustrate the importance of the time dependence of the volatility of each forward rate, namely the case of serial options presented below.

19.5 Worked-Out Example 2: Serial Options

Let us consider the case of an option expiring at time T_1, whose payoff depends on the value at time T_1 of the forward rate $f(t, T_2, T_3)$, spanning the period $[T_2 T_3]$. Such an option is sometimes called a 'serial option'. See Figure 19.2. Note that the expiry time of the option (T_1) is before the reset time of the forward rate (T_2), i.e. $T_2 > T_1$. Therefore at time T_1 the forward rate that determines the payoff has not yet reset. In order to determine the option payoff, the buyer and the seller of the option have to obtain a number of market quotes of the forward rate and 'distill' from these a value for $f(T_1, T_2, T_3)$.

Recall that via the market price of a caplet expiring at time T_2 one obtains information about the total variance of the forward rate $f(t, T_2, T_3)$ from the trade date ('today') to the forward expiry (T_2), i.e. the value of the integral

$$\int_0^{T_2} \sigma_{T_2}(u)^2 \, du \tag{19.35}$$

where $\sigma_{T_2}(u)$ indicates the instantaneous volatility at time u of the forward rate expiring at time T_2. In order to price the serial option one would need the value of the integral

$$\int_0^{T_1} \sigma_{T_2}(u)^2 \, du \tag{19.36}$$

Figure 19.2 The important event times for a serial option: the thick arrow indicates the period spanned by the forward rate, i.e. the period $[T_2 T_3]$; the option expiry (at time T_1) is indicated by the thin arrow.

Unfortunately, there is no plain-vanilla instrument whose value directly depends on this quantity. The price of the caplet expiring at time T_1, in fact, does give information about

$$\int_0^{T_1} \sigma_{T_1}(u)^2 \, du \qquad (19.37)$$

but, as discussed in Section 3.5 of Chapter 3, this is the variance of a different instrument, which has no direct bearing on the value of Equation (19.35) above.

What if the expiry of the serial option coincided with the expiry of a two-period swaption, spanning the forward rates $f(t, T_1, T_2)$ and $f(t, T_2, T_3)$, i.e. the forward rates that reset at times T_1 and T_2? (To lighten notation I will, in what follows, sometimes refer to these forward rates as f_1 and f_2, respectively.) Could the combined information from the two caplets and this swaption be enough to determine the variance of $f(t, T_2, T_3)$ from today to the serial option expiry? Unfortunately this is not the case. This can be seen as follows. If one knew the correlation between f_1 and f_2 from time t_0 to time T_1, then, equating the implied volatility of the swaption with the expression given in the previous worked-out example involving the volatilities of the two forward rates, one would obtain:

$$\sigma_{SR_{1,2}}(T_1)^2 SR_{1,2}^2 T_1$$
$$\simeq w_1^2 f_1^2 \sigma_1(T_1)^2 T_1 + w_2^2 f_2^2 \sigma_2(T_1)^2 T_1^2 + 2 f_1 f_2 w_1 \sigma_1(T_1) T_1 w_2 \sigma_2(T_1) T_1 \rho \qquad (19.38)$$

If we knew the correlation, the only unknown would be the quantity $\sigma_2(T_1)$, which could therefore be extracted from the price of the swaption and of the T_1-expiry caplet. This quantity would then permit the unambiguous pricing of the serial option described above. Unfortunately, the whole construction is predicated on the correlation between the two forwards being known with certainty. In reality, for any choice of the (time-dependent) quantity ρ there corresponds a different possible choice for $\sigma_2(T_1)$. The value of serial options cannot therefore be uniquely determined by no-arbitrage arguments from the prices of the liquid plain-vanilla instruments. It is easy to show that introducing more caplets or swaptions would not help.

Similar considerations can be extended to the case of forward-starting swaptions (i.e. swap options that expire before the start of the underlying swap). A moment's reflection shows in fact that serial options are just a particular case of forward-starting swaptions (i.e. one-period forward-starting swaptions).

19.6   Plan of the Work Ahead

In the present chapter I have presented some formulations for the evolution of the forward rates that are useful for recovering exactly the current market prices of caplets. I have stressed that this market information constrains but does not pin down uniquely the coefficients of the model. It would be tempting to make use of additional market information from the traded prices of swaptions. Unfortunately these instruments bring into play an additional unknown quantity, i.e. the instantaneous correlation. If we could observe reliable prices for serial options (and/or forward-starting swaptions) of a great number of maturities and expires we could close the circle, but unfortunately this is not the case.

So, the plan of the work ahead is, in a nutshell, how to choose in a desirable way the time dependence of the volatility functions (i.e. how to choose the functions $\sigma_i(t)$), and how to apportion this time-dependent volatility to the different modes of deformation of the yield curve (i.e. how to choose the coefficients $\{b_{jk}\}$). In a way, stating our goal this way does not say much, because, once these quantities are given, there is absolutely nothing else to a fully specified LIBOR market model. Any choice we might dream up recovers the market prices of the hedging instruments (assumed to be caplets) and corresponds to an arbitrage-free evolution for the forward rates. We want to choose these input quantities, however, in such a way that the caplets are correctly priced, and 'something else' ends up having desirable properties. The 'something else' might be the observed prices of swaptions; or a statistically determined correlation matrix; or the time-homogeneity desideratum that the future, as seen by the model, should look at least approximately like the present. The art of calibrating the LIBOR market model boils down to obtaining this 'something else' in a coherent and financially meaningful way. This is the topic succinctly addressed in the remaining chapters of Part III. A more detailed and in-depth treatment can be found in Rebonato (2002).

Chapter 20

Calibration Strategies for the LIBOR Market Model

20.1 Plan of the Chapter

Three important calibration problems are dealt with in this chapter. The general assumption underlying the treatment presented below is that we have a set of market and/or historical data that we would like our implementation of the LIBOR market model to recover, either exactly or as best we can. This 'target set' need not be today's statistical or market data, because we might want to impose exogenous requirements (trading views) on future prices, as we implicitly do when we require a certain behaviour for the evolution of the term structure of volatilities. This exercise must be undertaken with care, but it is none the less possible: for instance, many (actually, infinitely many) future term structures of volatilities are compatible with today's market prices, as discussed in Section 19.2 of Chapter 19.

The question I address in this chapter therefore is: How can we implement the LIBOR market model in such a way that it is compatible with this target information set?

Note that I am not addressing the conceptually separate question: to what set of current prices (caplets?, all swaptions? co-terminal swaptions?) should I simultaneously try to calibrate the model? I will assume that this choice has been made elsewhere, perhaps on the basis of the discussion in Chapter 1.

A full treatment of the topics in this chapter is to be found in Rebonato (2002).

20.2 The Setting

From a computational point of view, the type of problem for which the LIBOR market model constitutes an ideal tool is the pricing of discrete-look, path-dependent derivatives in a multi-factor framework. The payoff of the derivative product should only depend on a finite number of price-sensitive events, because the LIBOR market model evolves a set of *discrete* LIBOR rates in *continuous* time. Ideally, it should be path dependent, because the forward-rate process implied by the LIBOR market model is in general non-Markovian and therefore does not lend itself to straightforward mapping onto recombining trees. Backward induction is therefore difficult with the LIBOR market model, while a forward-induction (Monte Carlo) evolution is very easy. Finally, the approach can easily be multi-factor because one does not have to (or, rather, cannot) build recombining trees that pay an exponential price in the number of state variables (the so-called 'curse of dimensionality'). The computational burden of carrying out a Monte Carlo simulation, on the other hand, grows in an approximately linear fashion with the number of evolved state variables. Examples of securities that readily lend themselves to pricing using the combined LIBOR market model/Monte Carlo approach are therefore trigger swaps, indexed-principal swaps, knock-out caps, one-way floaters, ratchet caps, discrete-sampling average-rate caps, obligation flexi caps, etc.

We have seen in the previous chapter that, for all these applications, it is very easy to calibrate the LIBOR market model to caplet volatilities. Let us take, in fact, the third formulation of the forward-rate dynamics when m factors shock the yield curve:

$$\frac{\mathrm{d}f_i^t}{f_i^t} = \mu_i(\{f^t\}, t)\,\mathrm{d}t + \sigma_i^t \sum_{k=1,m} b_{ik}^t\,\mathrm{d}z_k \tag{20.1}$$

We have seen that if the square of the chosen instantaneous volatility functions $\sigma_i^t \equiv \sigma(t, T_i)$ properly integrate to

$$\widehat{\sigma}(T_i)^2 T_i = \int_0^{T_i} \sigma(u, T_i)^2\,\mathrm{d}u \tag{20.2}$$

and if

$$\sum_{k=1,m} b_{ik}^2 = 1 \tag{20.3}$$

then all the caplets will be correctly priced. As for the quantities ('loadings') b_{ik}^t, they can be interpreted as the sensitivities at time t of the ith forward rate to the kth shocks. Note that the loadings b_{ik}^t can have a calendar-time dependence, and are specific to each individual forward rate via the first index. They cannot, however, be of the form $b_{ik}(f_i, t)$ and preserve the log-normal distributional feature for the forward rate f_i. Therefore the third formulation truly represents the most general specification of any m-factor model consistent with log-normal forward rates.[1]

20.2.1   A Geometric Construction: The Two-Factor Case

Can one gain some intuitive (or geometric) understanding for condition (20.3)? Let us consider the case when only two factors are allowed to shock the yield curve ($m = 2$). Then, ignoring the drifts, which are irrelevant for the discussion, one can write

$$\frac{\mathrm{d}f_i^t}{f_i^t} = \sigma_i^t \left[b_{i1}^t\,\mathrm{d}z_1 + b_{i2}^t\,\mathrm{d}z_2 \right] \tag{20.4}$$

---

[1]For a given choice of numeraire, the drift of a given forward rate is in general non-zero, and its distribution is therefore not exactly log-normal. The caplet prices, however, are exactly consistent with the Black prices obtained from a log-normal density *in the appropriate terminal measure*. See Rebonato (2002) for a discussion of this subtle point.

and condition (20.3) simply becomes

$$b_{i1}^2 + b_{i2}^2 = 1 \tag{20.5}$$

Equation (20.5) is quite interesting. Recall, in fact, that, for any angle θ, it is always true that

$$\sin^2(\theta) + \cos^2(\theta) = 1 \tag{20.6}$$

Therefore any angle θ, $0 \leq \theta < \pi$, specifies a possible set of coefficients, b_{i1}, b_{i2}, and therefore a possible allocation of the loadings onto the two Brownian motions compatible with the recovery of the caplet prices. How can we choose among this infinity of solutions? One possible way is to look at the correlation function implied by a given choice of θ. What we would like to do is to relate the angles θ to the model-implied correlation function, thereby constraining the infinity of solutions. To calculate the model correlation between forward rate j and forward rate k, ρ_{jk}, we must evaluate

$$\rho_{jk} = \frac{E\left[\dfrac{df_k^t}{f_k^t}\dfrac{df_j^t}{f_j^t}\right]}{\sqrt{E\left[\dfrac{df_j^t}{f_j^t}\dfrac{df_j^t}{f_j^t}\right]E\left[\dfrac{df_k^t}{f_k^t}\dfrac{df_k^t}{f_k^t}\right]}} \tag{20.7}$$

Let us start from the denominator. For the two-factor case, the quantity $E\left[\dfrac{df_k^t}{f_k^t}\dfrac{df_k^t}{f_k^t}\right]$ simply becomes

$$E\left[\frac{df_k^t}{f_k^t}\frac{df_k^t}{f_k^t}\right] = \sigma_k^2\,[b_{k1}\,dz_1 + b_{k2}\,dz_2]\,[b_{k1}\,dz_1 + b_{k2}\,dz_2]$$

$$= \sigma_k^2(b_{k1}^2 + b_{k2}^2)\,dt = \sigma_k^2(\sin^2\theta_k + \cos^2\theta_k)\,dt = \sigma_k^2\,dt \tag{20.8}$$

where use has been made of the fact that we have chosen to work with orthogonal Brownian increments, and therefore

$$E[dz_1\,dz_2] = 0 \tag{20.9}$$

$$E[dz_1\,dz_1] = E[dz_2\,dz_2] = dt \tag{20.10}$$

Similarly,

$$E\left[\frac{df_j^t}{f_j^t}\frac{df_j^t}{f_j^t}\right] = \sigma_j^2(b_{j1}^2 + b_{j2}^2)\,dt = \sigma_j^2(\sin^2\theta_j + \cos^2\theta_j)\,dt = \sigma_j^2\,dt \tag{20.11}$$

Therefore the denominator is just equal to

$$\sqrt{E\left[\frac{df_j^t}{f_j^t}\frac{df_j^t}{f_j^t}\right]E\left[\frac{df_k^t}{f_k^t}\frac{df_k^t}{f_k^t}\right]} = \sigma_k\sigma_j\,dt \tag{20.12}$$

As for the numerator, by again making use of the orthogonality relationships (20.9) and (20.10), one readily computes

$$
E\left[\frac{\mathrm{d}f_k^t}{f_k^t}\frac{\mathrm{d}f_j^t}{f_j^t}\right] = \sigma_k\left[b_{k1}\,\mathrm{d}z_1 + b_{k2}\,\mathrm{d}z_2\right]\sigma_j\left[b_{j1}\,\mathrm{d}z_1 + b_{j2}\,\mathrm{d}z_2\right]
$$

$$
= \sigma_k\left[\sin\theta_k\,\mathrm{d}z_1 + \cos\theta_k\,\mathrm{d}z_2\right]\sigma_j\left[\sin\theta_j\,\mathrm{d}z_1 + \cos\theta_j\,\mathrm{d}z_2\right]
$$

$$
= \sigma_k\sigma_j[\sin\theta_k\sin\theta_{j1} + \cos\theta_k\cos\theta_j]\,\mathrm{d}t
$$

$$
= \sigma_k\sigma_j[\cos(\theta_k - \theta_j)]\,\mathrm{d}t \tag{20.13}
$$

Putting all the pieces together we obtain

$$
\rho_{jk} = [\cos(\theta_k - \theta_j)] \tag{20.14}
$$

This equation shows, that, in the two-factor case, the correlation between two forward rates is purely a function of the difference between the 'angles' that we saw were associated with the loadings. So, for any of the infinite choices of angles such that the caplets are correctly priced, there corresponds a particular correlation function. I will show in what follows that this simple observation can provide a useful tool to calibrate the LIBOR market model to a set of caplet prices and to an exogenous correlation matrix.

20.2.2   Generalization to Many Factors

Can we systematically generalize the results just obtained to more than two factors? This can be easily achieved by noting that, when we are dealing with m factors, the caplet-pricing condition (20.3) simply defines the co-ordinates of a point on the surface of a hypersphere of radius 1. Therefore, by recalling the expressions for the polar co-ordinates of a point on the surface of a unit-radius hypersphere, one can immediately generalize to m factors by writing:

$$
b_{ik} = \cos\theta_{ik}\prod_{j=1}^{k-1}\sin\theta_{ij}, \quad k = 1, 2, \ldots, m-1 \tag{20.15}
$$

$$
b_{ik} = \prod_{j=1}^{k-1}\sin\theta_{ij}, \quad k = m \tag{20.16}
$$

At the moment, being able to express the caplet-pricing condition in terms of arbitrary angles might seem to provide little, if any, advantage. We will show later in the chapter that the introduction of these new variables $\{\theta\}$ is actually computationally very useful, since it allows us to cast a constrained-optimization problem in terms of an equivalent unconstrained one.

20.2.3   Re-Introducing the Covariance Matrix

Let us go back to the case when as many factors as forward rates are retained. Let us consider any path-dependent pricing problem such that the expiries and maturities of a set of n forward rates constitutes all the dates when price-sensitive events occur. There is therefore a direct correspondence between the number of price-sensitive events and the number of forward rates necessary to describe a given LIBOR problem. After each of these price-sensitive events takes place, the number of forward rates left in the problem is therefore reduced by one. Let then $h(i)$ be the number of forward rates 'alive' at time-step i. (This coincides with the number of residual price-sensitive events still to be set at time-step i.) As discussed in detail in Sections 5.3 and 5.4 of Chapter 5, what any model (implicitly or explicitly) produces for this type of problem is a series of discrete covariance elements of the type

$$\text{Cov}^i_{jk} = \int_{t_i}^{t_{i+1}} \sigma(u, T_j)\sigma(u, T_k)\rho_{jk}\, du \qquad (20.17)$$

If, at each time-step, the chosen number of factors, m, is equal to the number of forward rates necessary to describe the yield curve, $h(i)$, the problem of finding a formulation of the LIBOR market model perfectly consistent with an arbitrary set of instantaneous volatilities and the correlation matrix is conceptually straightforward. This task can in fact always be exactly accomplished simply by orthogonalizing the time-dependent covariance matrix above and by working with the associated eigenvectors and eigenvalues (Principal Component Analysis). These covariance matrices, obtained from our choice of volatility and correlation functions, can be labelled 'desired' covariances, and should be distinguished from the covariance matrices that we could obtain if we had to use fewer factors than forward rates.

In the context of the present discussion, how the volatilities and correlation might have been chosen (i.e. on the basis of market information, or of statistical analysis, or of a combination of the two) is irrelevant. The important point is that if we work with a full-factor LIBOR market model we have just enough degrees of freedom to recover any exogenous set of covariance elements we might want. Perhaps our choice of covariance elements might be 'poor', in the sense that it will imply an unsatisfactory dynamics for the yield curve (indeed, the greatest danger of the LIBOR market model lies in its flexibility); or perhaps no set of covariance elements will satisfactorily recover the market prices of caplets and swaptions. However, we only have to make 'hard choices' (i.e. we only have to use a parameterization of the LIBOR market model that will fail to recover whatever desired covariance elements we might have chosen to use) if we have to work with fewer factors than forward rates. This will rarely be the case for path-dependent problems, where straightforward Monte Carlo simulations can be used, and using a very large number of factors is a feasible computational proposition. The need to reduce (sometimes drastically) the dimensionality of the problem occurs routinely, however, when the option problem at hand is compound in nature, as is the case for Bermudan swaptions. We therefore tackle in the next sections the problem of how to reduce the dimensionality of a LIBOR implementation in a systematic way. We will see that this problem can be directly linked to the calibration of the LIBOR market model to a correlation function when the number of factors is smaller than the number of forward rates alive.

20.3 Fitting an Exogenous Correlation Function

We have seen that if one retained $m(i) = h(i)$ factors at each time-step there would be just enough degrees of freedom in order to specify any feasible exogenously specified covariance matrix. When such 'liberality' in the number of factors is not affordable, the interesting question is what happens to the model covariance matrices when one is forced to retain only $m(i) < h(i)$ factors at each time-step:

$$[\text{Cov}^i_{jk}]_{\text{mod}} = \int_{t_i}^{t_{i+1}} \sum_{r=1,m_i} \sigma_{jr}(u)\sigma_{rk}(u)\,du \tag{20.18}$$

where use has been made of Equation (19.15).

Suppose that we orthogonalized the desired covariance matrices and simply 'threw away' the eigenvectors and eigenvalues higher than $m < h(i)$. While the 'shape' of the retained eigenvectors would be PCA-like, we would no longer recover, for instance, the caplet prices, since in the caplet-pricing equation

$$\sum_{k=1,h(i)} \sigma^2_{jk} = \sigma^2_j \tag{20.19}$$

we would have thrown away the terms

$$\sum_{k=m,h(i)} \sigma^2_{jk} \tag{20.20}$$

Clearly, the model covariance elements obtained by retaining only $m < h(i)$ factors will be different from the 'desired' ones. For a given exogenous choice of the time-dependent instantaneous volatilities and correlations the calibration problem we are tackling is therefore tantamount to specifying the behaviour of the model time-dependent coefficients $\{b_{jk}\}$ when only $m(i) < h(i)$ factors are retained.

We know that the most general h-factor implementation of a log-normal, forward-rate LIBOR market model is fully specified by the matrix $\{b_{jk}\}$, $j = 1, h(i)$, $k = 1, m(i)$. For future reference we denote by b_r the rth column vector in the matrix B of elements $\{b_{jk}\}$:

$$\begin{bmatrix} b_{1r} \\ b_{2r} \\ \dots \\ b_{h(i)r} \end{bmatrix} \tag{20.21}$$

In general, an arbitrary target ('market' in what follows) correlation function will not be reproducible with $m(i) < h(i)$ orthogonal factors. The trader is therefore faced with the problem of determining the elements of the matrix $\{b_{jk}\}$ in such a way that

1. the sum of the squared coefficients $\{b_{jk}\}$ over factors adds up to one:

$$\sum_{k=1,m} b^2_{jk} = 1 \tag{20.22}$$

   (this will ensure correct pricing of the caplets);

2. the discrepancies between the implied (model) and market correlation matrices are minimized in some precise way to be defined.

We also know, however (see Section 19.3 in Chapter 19), that if we used a full-factor PCA approach the vectors b_r would also be normalized to one

$$\sum_{j=1,h(i)} b_{jk}^2 = 1 \qquad (20.23)$$

and orthogonal to each other

$$b_r b_s = \delta_{rs} = \sum_{j=1,h(i)} b_{jr} b_{js} \qquad (20.24)$$

While not strictly necessary for pricing purposes, it would be 'nice' if our final solution, besides satisfying conditions 1 and 2, were also made to display the orthonormality relationships (20.23) and (20.24), especially if this could be done at little extra cost. We therefore refer to Equations (20.23) and (20.24) as two 'nice-to-have' conditions.

In order to carry out this programme we can proceed as follows. We know that the model correlation matrix is given by

$$[\rho_{jk}]_{\text{mod}} = [bb^{\text{T}}]_{jk} = \sum_{r=1,m} b_{jr} b_{rk}$$

We would like to vary the coefficients b_{rk} in such a way that a suitably defined 'distance' between the target and model correlation matrices is minimized. One such distance could for instance be the usual χ^2 measure:

$$\chi^2 = \sum \left([\rho_{jk}]_{\text{mod}} - [\rho_{jk}]_{\text{market}}\right)^2 = \sum \left(\sum_{r=1,m} b_{jr} b_{rk} - [\rho_{jk}]_{\text{market}}\right)^2 \qquad (20.25)$$

However, optimizing the coefficients $\{b_{jk}\}$ in order to recover as closely as possible an exogenous correlation matrix is a complicated exercise, given the joint constraints imposed about sums over factors (and, possibly, about sums over forward rates).

This is where the expression of the $\{b\}$ coefficients in terms of the polar co-ordinates of the surface of a unit-radius hypersphere becomes very useful. The trader can, in fact, perform an *unconstrained* optimization over the angles to a target correlation surface, resting assured that the unit-radius condition (20.22) will always be automatically satisfied, and therefore the caplets correctly priced. Given its unconstrained nature, the optimization can easily be made quick and efficient for up to, say, 20 or so forward rates. We have therefore achieved the task of pricing the caplets correctly and of recovering as well as possible an exogenous correlation matrix. There is a priori no guarantee that the solution we find by following this procedure will bear any resemblance to the familiar level/slope/curvature interpretation of the first modes of deformation, but, apart from some loss of intuition, this has no 'hard' disadvantages. (See, however, Section 20.4 below.) Is there anything that we can do about the nice-to-have conditions (20.23) and (20.24)?

A result proven in Rebonato (1999a) can be of assistance. In simple terms it states the following. Take a solution B, i.e. a set of vectors b_r, such that conditions 1 and 2 are satisfied. This means that, by altering the angles θ we cannot find a solution such that the 'distance' between the target and the model correlation matrices could be reduced any further. Let us denote this optimal model correlation matrix by $[\widehat{\rho}_{jk}]_{\text{mod}}$. In general, the vectors b_r producing this optimal solution will not satisfy conditions (20.23) and (20.24). Recall, however, that the matrix B has dimensions $(h(i) \times m)$. We can therefore build the square, real, symmetric matrix $A = BB^T$, that will have dimensions $(h(i) \times h(i))$, but rank m. Being square, real and symmetric, it can always be orthogonalized, but, given its rank, only its first m eigenvalues will be different from zero. Therefore, throwing away the eigenvectors higher than m will not entail any loss of information (unlike what would have happened if we had started from the orthogonalization of the desired covariance matrix, and simply discarded some eigenvectors). Let us denote by a_{jk}, $j = 1, 2, \ldots, h(i)$, $k = 1, 2, \ldots, m$, the m non-zero eigenvectors of A. These vectors now satisfy the nice-to-have conditions (20.23) and (20.24). But, now that the original vectors b_r have been scrambled by the matrix orthogonalization procedure, what has happened to the absolutely necessary conditions 1 and 2? It can be shown that the caplet-pricing and matrix-matching properties of the vectors b_r have not been affected at all by the transformation to the vectors a, and we still have

$$\sum_{k=1,m} a_{jk}^2 = 1 \tag{20.26}$$

and, most importantly,

$$\sum_{r=1,m} b_{jr}b_{rk} = \sum_{r=1,m} a_{jr}a_{rk} = [\widehat{\rho}_{jk}]_{\text{mod}} \tag{20.27}$$

The proof of this theorem can be found in Rebonato (1999a). What remains to be seen is how well this method works in practice. This is done in the next section.

20.4 Numerical Results

In this section I set myself the task of fitting simultaneously and exactly to all the market forward-rate volatilities, and of recovering in the best possible way a given ('target' or 'market') correlation matrix by using the procedure described above. All the results reported below refer to the case of a collection of twelve 12-month forward rates.

As we know, any combination of the angles $\{\theta\}$ in Equations (20.15) and (20.16) is, by construction, compatible with the exact recovery of the volatilities of all the individual forward rates. We have also seen that the coefficients $\{b_{jk}\}$ are a function of the angles $\{\theta\}$, and at the same time uniquely determine the correlation surface. The plan is therefore to follow Equation (20.25), and to vary the angles until the χ^2 distance between the target and the model correlation matrices is minimized.

20.4.1 Fitting the Correlation Surface with a Three-Factor Model

Random numbers were first of all chosen for the 2×12 angles θ_{ij}, $i = 1, 2, \ldots, 12$, $j = 1, 2$. The coefficients $\{b_{ij}\}$, $i = 1, 2, \ldots, 12$, $j = 1, 2, 3$, were created using Equations (20.15) and (20.16). Let B be the 12×3 matrix made up by the vectors

b_{ij}. The model correlation matrix was then constructed as $\{\rho_{\text{mod}}\} = BB^{\text{T}}$. The random numbers (θ) were then varied until the sum of the squared discrepancies, χ^2,

$$\chi^2 = \sum [\rho_{\text{mod}}^{ij} - \rho_{\text{market}}^{ij}]^2 \tag{20.28}$$

over the whole matrix was reduced to a minimum. The 'market' (target) correlation function was assumed to be given by the following expression (see the discussion in Chapter 22 regarding this choice of correlation function):

$$\rho_{\text{market}}^{ij} = LongCorr + (1\text{-}LongCorr)\exp\left[-\beta|T_i - T_j|\right] \tag{20.29}$$

$$\beta = d_1 - d_2\max(T_i, T_j) \tag{20.30}$$

and $LongCorr = 0.3$, $d_1 = -0.12$, $d_2 = 0.005$.

When the optimal vectors $\{b_{ij}\}$ were found (see Figure 20.1 and Table 20.1), the resulting 12×12 matrix was orthogonalized, giving rise to new vectors $\{a_{ij}\}$. Given the rank of the BB^{T} matrix, only three of the resulting eigenvalues were different from zero. The vectors $\{b_{ij}\}$ and $\{a_{ij}\}$, the model correlation matrix (BB^{T}), the target correlation matrices, the eigenvectors and the eigenvalues resulting from the orthogonalization are shown in Table 20.2 and in Figures 20.2–20.5.

It is interesting to observe that, despite the fact that no orthogonality constraints were imposed in the optimization, the solution qualitatively turned out to be very similar to what we found using PCA. Indeed, as shown in Figure 20.1, the rotation induced by the orthogonalization was minor.

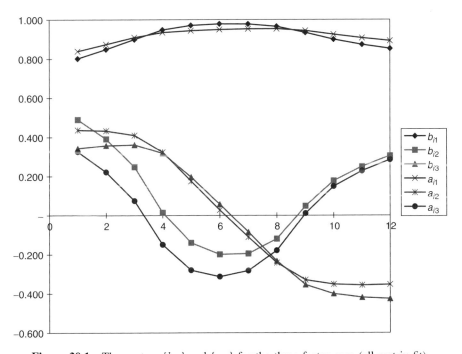

Figure 20.1 The vectors $\{b_{ij}\}$ and $\{a_{ij}\}$ for the three-factor case (all-matrix fit).

Table 20.1 The vectors $\{b_{ij}\}$ and $\{a_{ij}\}$ for the three-vector case (all-matrix fit).

$\{b_{i1}\}$	$\{b_{i2}\}$	$\{b_{i3}\}$	$\{a_{i1}\}$	$\{a_{i2}\}$	$\{a_{i3}\}$
0.802	−0.490	0.342	0.839	0.436	0.33
0.848	−0.391	0.357	0.874	0.432	0.22
0.899	−0.248	0.361	0.909	0.410	0.07
0.948	−0.014	0.318	0.934	0.323	−0.15
0.971	0.140	0.196	0.944	0.175	−0.28
0.978	0.199	0.057	0.949	0.027	−0.31
0.977	0.195	−0.085	0.953	−0.111	−0.28
0.965	0.120	−0.233	0.954	−0.242	−0.18
0.934	−0.048	−0.354	0.944	−0.329	0.01
0.899	−0.177	−0.401	0.924	−0.351	0.15
0.873	−0.250	−0.420	0.906	−0.356	0.23
0.851	−0.305	−0.426	0.891	−0.353	0.28

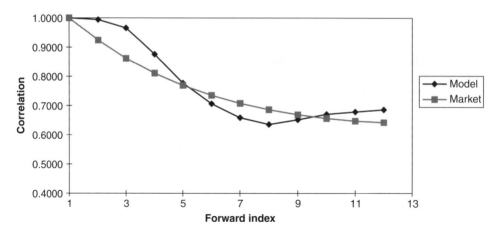

Figure 20.2 The market and model correlations between the first, the third, the fifth and the eighth forward rates and all the other forwards obtained using three factors, and imposing an overall best fit to the whole correlation matrix.

The shortcomings of low-dimensionality models in reproducing correlation functions with positive convexity at the origin are well known (see, for example, Rebonato and Cooper (1995) or Rebonato (2002), where the implications for pricing are discussed at length), and were indeed observed again in this study. Without repeating material presented elsewhere, their results can be summarized as follows. If we use non-time-dependent volatilities, retaining a small number of factors creates too strong a correlation between adjacent forward rates, and too weak a correlation between distant forward rates. If the instantaneous volatilities of the forward rates were constant, the instantaneous correlation would be the only mechanism available to produce terminal correlation. Therefore, the model correlation surface obtained with a small number of factors would systematically misprice swaptions: overall, 'short' swaptions would turn out too 'expensive' because the

Table 20.2 The model and market correlation matrices.

(a) Model correlation matrix

0	1	2	3	4	5	6	7	8	9	10	11
1.0000	0.993951	0.9658	0.8761	0.7771	0.7065	0.6590	0.6358	0.6517	0.6705	0.6787	0.6864
0.9940	1.0000	0.9884	0.9233	0.8388	0.7725	0.7224	0.6891	0.6852	0.6890	0.6885	0.6896
0.9658	0.9884	1.0000	0.9707	0.9089	0.8509	0.7995	0.7541	0.7240	0.7074	0.6949	0.6870
0.8761	0.9233	0.9707	1.0000	0.9805	0.9428	0.8966	0.8395	0.7739	0.7277	0.6976	0.6762
0.7771	0.8388	0.9089	0.9805	1.0000	0.9886	0.9590	0.9079	0.8305	0.7694	0.7297	0.7002
0.7065	0.7725	0.8509	0.9428	0.9886	1.0000	0.9899	0.9547	0.8838	0.8213	0.7796	0.7477
0.6590	0.7224	0.7995	0.8966	0.9590	0.9899	1.0000	0.9862	0.9333	0.8780	0.8393	0.8086
0.6358	0.6891	0.7541	0.8395	0.9079	0.9547	0.9862	1.0000	0.9780	0.9397	0.9098	0.8845
0.6517	0.6852	0.7240	0.7739	0.8305	0.8838	0.9333	0.9780	1.0000	0.9900	0.9756	0.9610
0.6705	0.6890	0.7074	0.7277	0.7694	0.8213	0.8780	0.9397	0.9900	1.0000	0.9968	0.9903
0.6787	0.6885	0.6949	0.6976	0.7297	0.7796	0.8393	0.9098	0.9756	0.9968	1.0000	0.9982
0.6864	0.6896	0.6870	0.6762	0.7002	0.7477	0.8086	0.8845	0.9610	0.9903	0.9982	1.0000

(b) Market correlation matrix

0	1	2	3	4	5	6	7	8	9	10	11
1.0000	0.9240	0.8618	0.8109	0.7692	0.7353	0.7079	0.6861	0.6691	0.6564	0.6476	0.6424
0.9240	1.0000	0.9271	0.8674	0.8186	0.7787	0.7463	0.7203	0.6998	0.6842	0.6728	0.6654
0.8618	0.9271	1.0000	0.9302	0.8731	0.8264	0.7884	0.7576	0.7331	0.7141	0.6998	0.6900
0.8109	0.8674	0.9302	1.0000	0.9334	0.8789	0.8344	0.7982	0.7692	0.7463	0.7288	0.7162
0.7692	0.8186	0.8731	0.9334	1.0000	0.9366	0.8847	0.8424	0.8083	0.7811	0.7599	0.7441
0.7353	0.7787	0.8264	0.8789	0.9366	1.0000	0.9398	0.8906	0.8506	0.8186	0.7933	0.7739
0.7079	0.7463	0.7884	0.8344	0.8847	0.9398	1.0000	0.9430	0.8965	0.8590	0.8290	0.8058
0.6861	0.7203	0.7576	0.7982	0.8424	0.8906	0.9430	1.0000	0.9462	0.9025	0.8674	0.8397
0.6691	0.6998	0.7331	0.7692	0.8083	0.8506	0.8965	0.9462	1.0000	0.9494	0.9086	0.8760
0.6564	0.6842	0.7141	0.7463	0.7811	0.8186	0.8590	0.9025	0.9494	1.0000	0.9527	0.9147
0.6476	0.6728	0.6998	0.7288	0.7599	0.7933	0.8290	0.8674	0.9086	0.9527	1.0000	0.9559
0.6424	0.6654	0.6900	0.7162	0.7441	0.7739	0.8058	0.8397	0.8760	0.9147	0.9559	1.0000

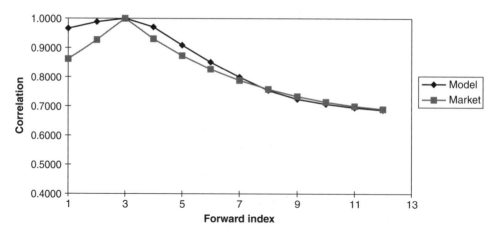

Figure 20.3 The market and model correlations between the first, the third, the fifth and the eighth forward rates and all the other forwards obtained using three factors, and imposing an overall best fit to the whole correlation matrix.

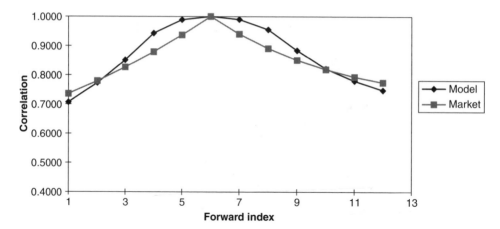

Figure 20.4 The market and model correlations between the first, the third, the fifth and the eighth forward rates and all the other forwards obtained using three factors, and imposing an overall best fit to the whole correlation matrix.

model correlation would be too high, and 'long' swaptions too 'cheap' because the model correlation would be too low. With this proviso in mind, the overall agreement found by using the procedure described above is however good, and shown more clearly by the model correlation surface shown in Figure 20.6.

20.4.2   Fitting the Correlation Surface with a Four-Factor Model

We have seen that, if we use only three factors, there are important systematic[2] discrepancies between the model and the target (market) correlation matrices. How much better could we

---

[2]By 'systematic' I mean that the discrepancies between the model and target correlation matrices are not random, but display an identifiable structure.

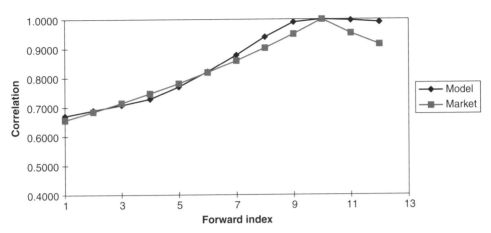

Figure 20.5   The market and model correlations between the first, the third, the fifth and the eighth forward rates and all the other forwards obtained using three factors, and imposing an overall best fit to the whole correlation matrix.

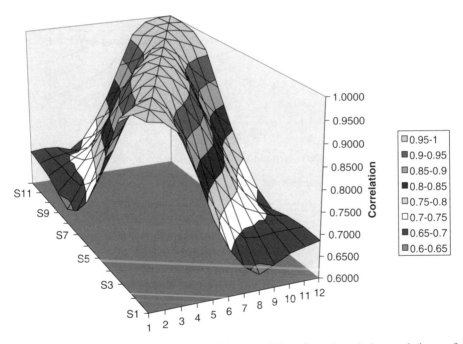

Figure 20.6   The correlation surface obtained by overall best fit to the whole correlation surface with three factors.

do if we used, say, four factors instead? In other words, to what extent is the agreement between the model and target correlation surfaces sensitive to the number of factors?

To answer this question, the same procedure described in the previous section is followed below using four factors instead of three. This is achieved simply by adding a further column of n (12) angles to the set used for the three-factor case. After starting from totally random angles and optimizing again as described above to the whole-matrix quality function, the vectors $\{b_{ij}\}$ and $\{a_{ij}\}$ shown in Figure 20.7 were obtained. Once again, the vectors $\{b_{ij}\}$ thus obtained turned out to bear a close resemblance to the first four eigenvectors usually found with Principal Component Analysis (PCA). In particular, qualitatively it seems that the vectors $\{b_{ij}\}$ and their orthogonalized counterparts $\{a_{ij}\}$ are linked by a phase rather than frequency transformation. This would indicate that the discussion above can be extended to higher dimensions.

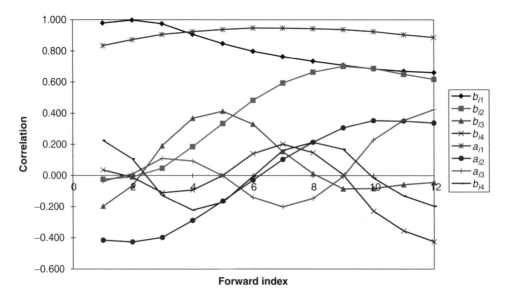

Figure 20.7   The vectors $\{b_{ij}\}$ and $\{a_{ij}\}$ for the four-factor case (all-matrix fit).

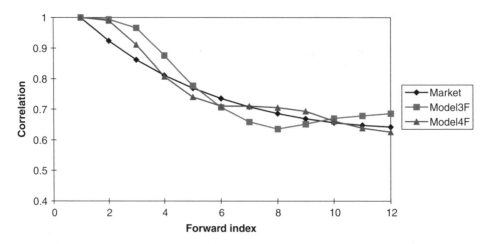

Figure 20.8   Comparison between the market and model correlations between the first, the fifth and the eighth forward rates and all the other forwards obtained using three or four factors (Model3F and Model4F, respectively) and imposing an overall fit to the correlation matrix.

It is interesting to compare the 'improvement' in the fitting of the same columns of the correlation matrix in going from three to four factors. As is apparent from Figures 20.8–20.10, the greatest changes take place for the first series, i.e. for the correlation between the first and second forward rates and all the others. Overall, however, the improvement is rather limited, confirming the findings mentioned above (see also Rebonato and Cooper (1995)) that the convergence to an exponentially decaying target correlation surface is very slow. In particular, the same qualitative features concerning the negative convexity at the origin are still observed.

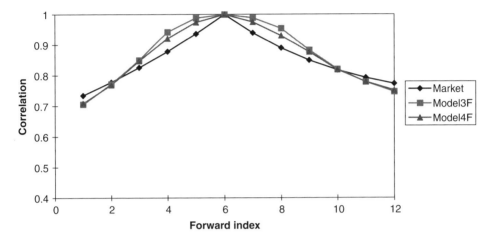

Figure 20.9 Comparison between the market and model correlations between the first, the fifth and the eighth forward rates and all the other forwards obtained using three or four factors (Model3F and Model4F, respectively) and imposing an overall fit to the correlation matrix.

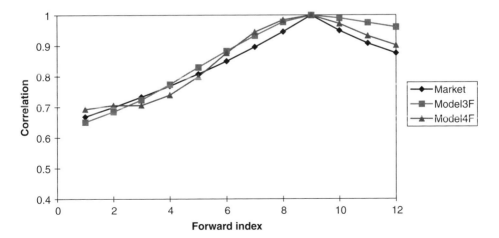

Figure 20.10 Comparison between the market and model correlations between the first, the fifth and the eighth forward rates and all the other forwards obtained using three or four factors (Model3F and Model4F, respectively) and imposing an overall fit to the correlation matrix.

20.4.3   Fitting Portions of the Target Correlation Matrix

The analysis so far has shown the results obtained by using the equally-weighted sum of the squared discrepancies over the whole correlation matrix as the quality (distance) function. One might argue, however, that for pricing certain products specific sub-sections of the correlation matrix might be more important, and that one should therefore try to achieve a closer fit to these particular areas of the correlation matrix. How much better can we do if we 'only' try to recover a portion of the correlation matrix? And, is it desirable to do so? In order to answer these questions, it is instructive to examine in detail the model correlation surfaces obtained by using different distance functions.

Trigger-Swap Targeting

With four factors there are enough degrees of freedom to match exactly up to three columns of the correlation matrix. In particular, the first three columns could be targeted: this choice for the quality function could be motivated by the desire to capture exactly (or as well as possible) the correlation between the first short-maturity LIBOR index rates and the residual co-terminal swap rates in the case of a trigger swap. This would be relevant for pricing a trigger swap, because typically the reset of a three- or six-month forward rate would determine whether a swap comes to life or disappears and the correlation between the index rate and the underlying swap rates is therefore very important. See Rebonato (2002) for a detailed discussion. Achieving the goal of fitting exactly the first few columns of the correlation matrix is indeed possible. However, by doing so one obtains an increasingly unsatisfactory fit (see Figures 20.11–20.14) to the remaining columns of the correlation matrix. This gives rise to a highly unrealistic correlation between later indices and the residual swaps.

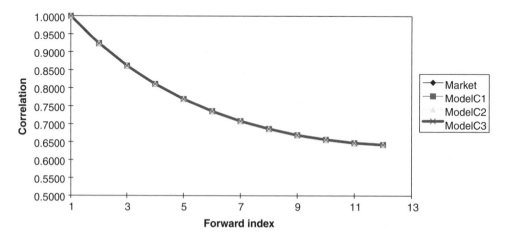

Figure 20.11 Comparison between the market and model correlations between the first, the third, the fifth and the eighth forward rates and all the other forwards obtained using four factors and imposing an exact fit to the first (ModelC1), the first and second (ModelC2), the first, second and third (ModelC3) columns of the correlation matrix.

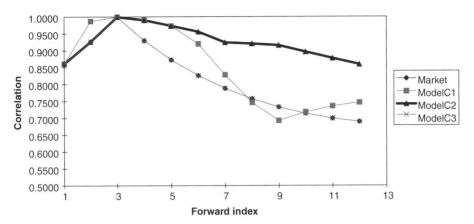

Figure 20.12 Comparison between the market and model correlations between the first, the third, the fifth and the eighth forward rates and all the other forwards obtained using four factors and imposing an exact fit to the first (ModelC1), the first and second (ModelC2), the first, second and third (ModelC3) columns of the correlation matrix.

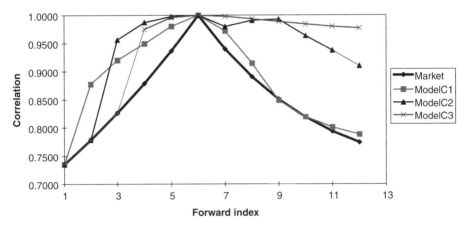

Figure 20.13 Comparison between the market and model correlations between the first, the third, the fifth and the eighth forward rates and all the other forwards obtained using four factors and imposing an exact fit to the first (ModelC1), the first and second (ModelC2), the first, second and third (ModelC3) columns of the correlation matrix.

Bermudan-Swap Targeting

Even more interesting is to explore how the whole correlation matrix behaves when use is made of all the available degrees of freedom (i.e. of all the angles that define the correlation matrix) in order to fit as closely as possible to the elements of the matrix that most directly influence the value of a particular Bermudan swaption (a 9NC2, pronounced '9-non-call-2', was chosen for the example[3]). Since the European swaptions underlying a

---

[3]A 9NC2 Bermudan swaption is a Bermudan swaption with final maturity of 9 years where the optionality cannot be exercised for the first two years.

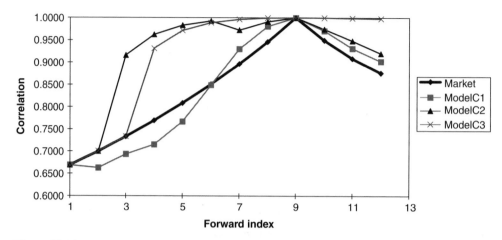

Figure 20.14   Comparison between the market and model correlations between the first, the third, the fifth and the eighth forward rates and all the other forwards obtained using four factors and imposing an exact fit to the first (ModelC1), the first and second (ModelC2), the first, second and third (ModelC3) columns of the correlation matrix.

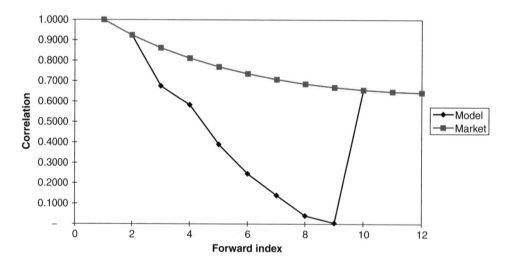

Figure 20.15   Comparison between the market and model correlations between the first, the third, the fifth and the eighth forward rates and all the other forwards obtained using four factors and imposing a best fit to the elements of the correlation matrix that affect the value of a 9NC2 Bermudan swaption.

9NC2 Bermudan swaption are the co-terminal $2 \times 7, 3 \times 6, \ldots, 8 \times 1$ swaptions, an attempt was made to recover as well as possible the target correlation between the forward rates underlying all these swaptions.

Despite the fact that the fit to the desired portion of the correlation surface is successfully achieved (see Figures 20.15–20.17), it is clear that the resulting overall surface is completely unrealistic. See Figure 20.18. In addition, the resulting eigenvectors bear

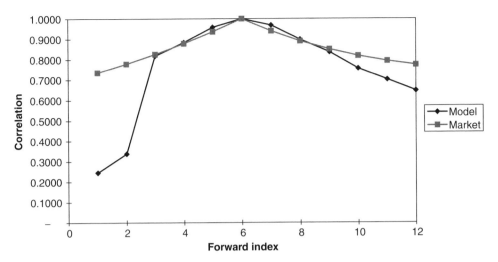

Figure 20.16 Comparison between the market and model correlations between the first, the third, the fifth and the eighth forward rates and all the other forwards obtained using four factors and imposing a best fit to the elements of the correlation matrix that affect the value of a 9NC2 Bermudan swaption.

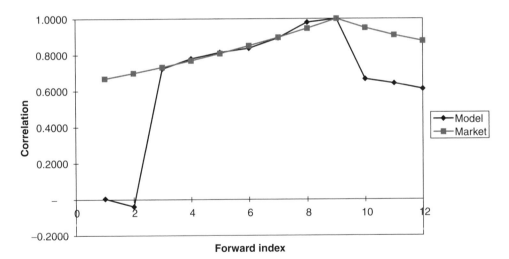

Figure 20.17 Comparison between the market and model correlations between the first, the third, the fifth and the eighth forward rates and all the other forwards obtained using four factors and imposing a best fit to the elements of the correlation matrix that affect the value of a 9NC2 Bermudan swaption.

hardly any resemblance to the familiar results of the PCA. This leaves us without any intuitional insight into the possible interpretation of the most important resulting eigenvectors, such as the fact that they are usually identified with changes in the level, slope, curvature, etc. of the yield curve.

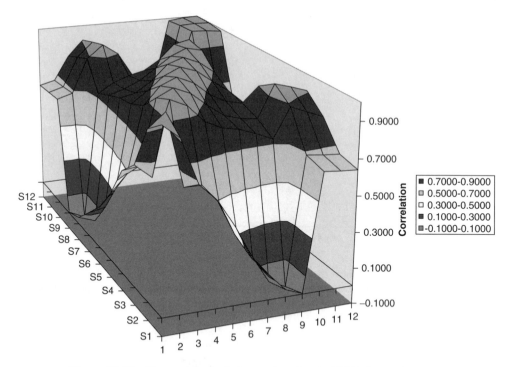

Figure 20.18   The model correlation surface for the 9NC2 Bermudan case.

More generally, the results obtained in the Bermudan-swaption fit caution strongly against using a low-dimensionality forward-rate-based model to price Bermudan swaptions by forcing an exact pricing of a subset of the underlying European swaptions (perhaps the most valuable of the underlying European swaptions).

One-Way-Floater Targeting

Along similar lines, one could use as the quality function the sum of squared errors along the tridiagonals of the model and market correlation matrices. This choice could be seen as an attempt to reflect the importance of the correlation amongst contiguous forward rates in the pricing of instruments of the resettable-cap family (instruments, that is, where a stochastic strike on a given forward rate is determined by the reset of the immediately preceding forward rate). Without going into a detailed analysis, the resulting model correlation matrix (see Figure 20.19) displays, once again, the shortcomings of imposing over-fitting to particular subsections of the correlation surface.

As one can see from Figure 20.19, the effect of achieving an excellent ('too good') recovery of the correlation along the three main diagonals has the effect of imposing an unrealistic de-correlation amongst forward rates farther apart. This pathological correlation matrix, in turn, will produce undesirable tilts and twists in the yield curve. After a sufficiently long 'model time' has elapsed, this will have a strong effect on the evolution of the yield curve, and, therefore, ultimately on the price of the resettable product.

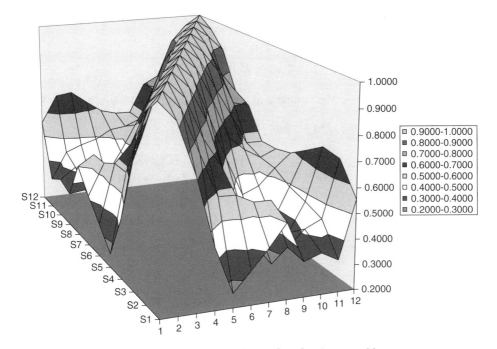

Figure 20.19 The model correlation surface for the resettable-cap case.

20.5 Analytic Expressions to Link Swaption and Caplet Volatilities

20.5.1 What Are We Trying to Achieve?

The most immediate application of the technique presented in this section is the recovery of the swaption prices implied by a set of volatilities and correlations among forward rates. Typically, the volatilities will have been chosen in order to fit the caplet prices, and the trader might want to see what swaption prices these (and the chosen correlation function) imply. Alternatively, one might try to get as good a fit to the whole swaption matrix as possible, while still working in a forward-rate-based version of the LIBOR market model. This might be desirable if the product being valued depends to first order on swaption, rather than caplet, volatilities. The special, and very important, case of the calibration of the LIBOR market model to the set of co-terminal swaptions underlying a Bermudan swaption is treated separately in the next section. Results very similar or equivalent to the ones reported below have been obtained independently by a number of authors. See, for example, Hull and White (2000) or Andersen and Andreasen (2000).

20.5.2 The Set-Up

A swap rate, SR, can be written as a linear combination of forward rates:

$$SR = \sum_{i=1,n} w_i f_i \qquad (20.31)$$

where n is the number of accrual periods in the swap. The weights $\{w\}$ are given by

$$w_i = \frac{P_i(t, T_i + \tau)\tau}{\sum_{k=1,n} P_k(t, T_k + \tau)\tau} \tag{20.32}$$

where $P_i(t, T_i + \tau)$ is the price at time t of a discount bond maturing at time $T_i + \tau$.

Exercise 1 *Prove Equations (20.31) and (20.32).*

Let us assume that the dynamics of the forward rates is given. Using the first formulation in Chapter 19, and ignoring drifts, irrelevant for the discussion, one can write

$$\frac{df_i}{f_i} = \sigma_i \, dw_i \tag{20.33}$$

with

$$E[dw_i \, dw_k] = \rho_{ik} \tag{20.34}$$

Applying Ito's lemma to Equation (20.31) one can write

$$\sigma_{SR}^2 SR^2 = \sum_{j=1,n} \sum_{k=1,n} \frac{\partial SR}{\partial f_j} \frac{\partial SR}{\partial f_k} \sigma_j f_j \sigma_k f_k \rho_{jk} \tag{20.35}$$

or, equivalently,

$$\sigma_{SR} = \frac{\sqrt{\sum_{j=1,n} \sum_{k=1,n} \frac{\partial SR}{\partial f_j} \frac{\partial SR}{\partial f_k} \sigma_j f_j \sigma_k f_k \rho_{jk}}}{\sum_{i=1,n} w_i f_i} \tag{20.36}$$

The derivatives $\frac{\partial SR}{\partial f_j}$ are rather involved, because the weights $\{w\}$ indirectly depend on the forward via their dependence on the discount bonds P. However, Jaeckel and Rebonato (2000) show that, for short-to-medium option expiries and underlying swap lengths, to a very good approximation one can write

$$\frac{\partial SR}{\partial f_j} \simeq w_j \tag{20.37}$$

For longer swaptions, the full derivative can be worked out (see Rebonato (2002) and Jaeckel and Rebonato (2000)). When this is done, w_j would still constitute the leading term, and it can be shown that the additional terms would be non-zero only if the yield curve were non-flat. For this reason the additional (smaller) terms are also referred to as the 'shape corrections'. Let us call the correct derivative w'_j. Then, according to whether one wants to use the simpler or the more accurate expression, Equation (20.36) can be rewritten as

$$\sigma_{SR} = \sqrt{\frac{\sum_{j=1,n} \sum_{k=1,n} w_j w_k \sigma_j f_j \sigma_k f_k \rho_{jk}}{\left(\sum_{i=1,n} w_i f_i\right)^2}} \tag{20.38}$$

or

$$\sigma_{SR} = \sqrt{\frac{\sum_{j=1,n} \sum_{k=1,n} w'_j w'_k \sigma_j f_j \sigma_k f_k \rho_{jk}}{\left(\sum_{i=1,n} w_i f_i\right)^2}} \tag{20.39}$$

respectively. Note that in Equation (20.39) the prime only appears in the numerator. The reason for keeping the square of the swap rate (the denominator) under the square root will become apparent in what follows.

Up to this point expression (20.39) is exact. Note, however, that it implies that, if we start from deterministic volatilities for the forward rates, the volatility of the swap rate will be stochastic, because it will depend on the realization of the future yield curve via the dependence of the swap-rate volatility on the forward rates and on the weights. Recall that our goal is to determine the price for a European swaption implied by a set of volatilities and correlations for the forward rates. If the swaption is to be valued using a Black formula, we would want to integrate the square of its instantaneous volatility from today to the swaption expiry, $T_{\exp}$:

$$\widehat{\sigma}_{SR}^2 T_{\exp} = \int_0^{T_{\exp}} \sigma_{SR}^2(u)\, \mathrm{d}u \tag{20.40}$$

However, looking at the correct expression (20.39) (or, for that matter, at the approximate expression (20.38)) one immediately realizes not only that there is no exact solution, but, more fundamentally, there is no such thing as a single deterministic Black *swap-rate* volatility associated with a set of deterministic Black *forward-rate* volatilities. It is not just that log-normal volatilities for forward rates are distributionally incompatible with log-normal volatilities for swap rates.[4] More fundamentally, deterministic forward-rate volatilities are not compatible with deterministic swap-rate volatilities.

Fortunately, Jaeckel and Rebonato (2003) and Rebonato (2002) prove the following. Let us assume that the terms $\{f\}$, $\{w\}$ and $\{w'\}$ are deterministic and equal to their respective values today. Let us denote by $f_j(0)$ and $w'_j(0)$ the value of the jth forward rate and weight derivative, respectively, as calculated from *today's* yield curve. Then equation (20.39) becomes

$$\sigma_{SR}(t) \simeq \sqrt{\frac{\sum_{j=1,n} \sum_{k=1,n} w'_j(0) w'_k(0) \sigma_j(t) f_j(0) \sigma_k(t) f_k(0) \rho_{jk}(t)}{\left(\sum_{i=1,n} w_i(0) f_i(0)\right)^2}} \tag{20.41}$$

where I have emphasized which quantities retain their time dependence, and which are assumed to be constant ('frozen'). If this approximation is made, when Equation (20.41) is integrated according to Equation (20.40), one can obtain an approximate *deterministic* swap-rate implied volatility. When this volatility is used in conjunction with the Black formula for the European swaption price, the result is extremely close to what would be obtained if the fully consistent swaption prices had been calculated (perhaps using a Monte Carlo simulation) using the correct volatilities (20.39). Jaeckel and Rebonato (2003) and Rebonato (2002) explain the reason for, and the intuition behind, this result. For the purpose of the present discussion it is sufficient to state that the numerical quality

---

[4] I showed in Rebonato (1999b) that the effect of this inconsistency is rather minor.

of the approximation is excellent. See again Rebonato (2002) or Jaeckel and Rebonato (2001, 2003) for numerical results.

Before closing this section a simple manipulation of the expressions obtained so far will prove useful for future applications. Let us consider a set of co-terminal swaps,[5] and define

$$\zeta_r^i \equiv \frac{(w_r^i)' f_r}{\sum_{m=1,n(i)} w_m^i f_m} \tag{20.42}$$

where w_m^i is the mth weight of the ith swap, and $n(i)$ is the number of periods in the ith swap. With this definition Equation (20.41) can be rewritten in a more compact way as

$$\sigma_{SR}(t) \simeq \sum_{j=1,n} \sum_{k=1,n} \zeta_j'(0)\zeta_k'(0)\sigma_j(t)\sigma_k(t)\rho_{jk}(t) \tag{20.43}$$

This expression will be used in the calibration to co-terminal swaptions discussed below.

20.6   Optimal Calibration to Co-Terminal Swaptions

The final calibration topic discussed in the context of the standard (log-normal) LIBOR market model deals with how to achieve a financially desirable simultaneous fit to all the co-terminal European swaptions underlying a given Bermudan swaption. The 'financially desirable' qualifier is important. It is relatively easy to fit all the co-terminal swaptions almost exactly even with a one-factor, short-rate-based model such as the Black, Derman and Toy. However, such a fit would have undesirable implications for the future volatility structure and for the correlation between rates. Therefore what I propose in this section is a method to obtain the market prices of co-terminal swaptions (almost) exactly while recovering, at the same time, some important properties of the forward-rate covariance matrix. Since caplets are secondary but still important instruments in the hedging of Bermudan swaptions, the correct recovery of their current and future prices is also important in arriving at the price of the Bermudan swaption. See, in this context, my comments in Chapter 1 about vega (re)-hedging and model re-calibration.

20.6.1   The Strategy

First of all, let us make a joint log-normal assumption for the forward rates and for the co-terminal swap rates underlying a given Bermudan swaption. See Rebonato (1999c) for a discussion of how mild the pricing inconsistencies of this assumption are. With this assumption of joint log-normality, and using the different formulations presented in Chapter 19, their associated SDEs can be written as follows:

$$\frac{\mathrm{d}f_r}{f_r} = \mu_{f_r}\,\mathrm{d}t + \sigma_r^f\,\mathrm{d}W_{f_r} \tag{20.44}$$

$$\frac{\mathrm{d}f_r}{f_r} = \mu_{f_r}\,\mathrm{d}t + \sum_{m=1,n} \sigma_{rm}^f\,\mathrm{d}z_m \tag{20.45}$$

---

[5]Given a yield curve defined by a finite set of forward rates, co-terminal swaps are swaps that start at the different reset times of the various forward rates and all terminate at the maturity of the last forward rate.

$$\frac{\mathrm{d}f_r}{f_r} = \mu_{f_r}\,\mathrm{d}t + \sigma_r^f \sum_{m=1,n} b_{rm}^f\,\mathrm{d}z_m \tag{20.46}$$

$$\frac{\mathrm{d}\mathbf{f}}{\mathbf{f}} = \boldsymbol{\mu}_f\,\mathrm{d}t + \mathbf{S}^f\boldsymbol{\beta}^f\,\mathrm{d}\mathbf{z} = \boldsymbol{\mu}_f\,\mathrm{d}t + \boldsymbol{\sigma}^f\,\mathrm{d}\mathbf{z} \tag{20.47}$$

for the forward rates. With obvious notation the same formulation of the SDEs for the swap rates can be written as:

$$\frac{\mathrm{d}SR_i}{SR_i} = \mu_{SR_i}\,\mathrm{d}t + \sigma_i^{SR}\,\mathrm{d}W_{SR_i} \tag{20.48}$$

$$\frac{\mathrm{d}SR_i}{SR_i} = \mu_{SR_i}\,\mathrm{d}t + \sum_{m=1,n_i} \sigma_{im}^{SR_i}\,\mathrm{d}z_m \tag{20.49}$$

$$\frac{\mathrm{d}SR_i}{SR_i} = \mu_i^{SR}\,\mathrm{d}t + \sigma_i^{SR} \sum_{r=1,s} b_{ir}^{SR}\,\mathrm{d}z_r \tag{20.50}$$

$$\frac{\mathrm{d}\mathbf{SR}}{\mathbf{SR}} = \boldsymbol{\mu}_{SR}\,\mathrm{d}t + \mathbf{S}^{SR}\boldsymbol{\beta}^{SR}\,\mathrm{d}\mathbf{z} = \boldsymbol{\mu}_{SR}\,\mathrm{d}t + \boldsymbol{\sigma}^{SR}\,\mathrm{d}\mathbf{z} \tag{20.51}$$

Note that the increments $\mathrm{d}W$ are not orthogonal,[6] but the $\mathrm{d}z$ are. Recall (see Section 19.2.1) that $\mathbf{S}^f$ is the $(n \times n)$ diagonal matrix containing on the main diagonal the instantaneous volatility of the different forward rates, σ_r^f, $1 \leq r \leq n$, i.e.

$$\mathbf{S}^f \equiv \begin{bmatrix} \sigma_1^f & 0 & 0 & \cdots & 0 \\ 0 & \sigma_2^f & 0 & \cdots & 0 \\ 0 & 0 & \sigma_3^f & & \\ 0 & 0 & 0 & \cdots & 0 \\ 0 & 0 & 0 & 0 & \sigma_n^f \end{bmatrix} \tag{20.52}$$

A similar interpretation holds for the matrix $\mathbf{S}^{SR}$:

$$\mathbf{S}^{SR} \equiv \begin{bmatrix} \sigma_1^{SR} & 0 & 0 & \cdots & 0 \\ 0 & \sigma_2^{SR} & 0 & \cdots & 0 \\ 0 & 0 & \sigma_3^{SR} & & \\ 0 & 0 & 0 & \cdots & 0 \\ 0 & 0 & 0 & 0 & \sigma_n^{SR} \end{bmatrix} \tag{20.53}$$

Also, I showed in the Chapter 19 that

$$\boldsymbol{\beta}^f(\boldsymbol{\beta}^f)^{\mathrm{T}} = \boldsymbol{\rho}^f \tag{20.54}$$

and, similarly,

$$\boldsymbol{\beta}^{SR}(\boldsymbol{\beta}^{SR})^{\mathrm{T}} = \boldsymbol{\rho}^{SR} \tag{20.55}$$

---

[6]A remark on notation. Elsewhere in the book I have denoted non-orthogonal Brownian increments by $\mathrm{d}w_k$, and orthogonal Brownian increments by $\mathrm{d}z_k$. Here the notation is changed slightly to avoid confusion with the weights w_k, and so the (non-orthogonal) increments $\mathrm{d}w_k$ are written as $\mathrm{d}W_k$.

Finally, note that the forward and the swap rates are affected by the same Brownian shocks, but with different sets of responsiveness. The responsiveness to the orthogonal Brownian shocks are given by $(\sigma_{rm}^f, b_{rm}^f)$ and by $(\sigma_{im}^{SR_i}, b_{ir}^{SR})$ for the forward and the swap rates, respectively. If the volatilities σ_r^f and σ_i^{SR} are chosen to give the correct root-mean-squared volatility for the associated caplets and swaptions, the caplet and co-terminal swaptions are correctly priced if the conditions

$$\sum_{r=1,s} [b_{ir}^f]^2 = 1 \tag{20.56}$$

and

$$\sum_{r=1,s} [b_{ir}^{SR}]^2 = 1 \tag{20.57}$$

hold true, respectively.

We saw in the previous section that a swap rate can be written as a linear combination of forward rates. When applied to the co-terminal swaptions this gives in matrix form:

$$\mathbf{SR} = \mathbf{w} \quad \mathbf{f} \tag{20.58}$$

$$(m \times 1) = (m \times m)(m \times 1) \tag{20.59}$$

where the vector $\mathbf{SR}$ contains the m co-terminal swap rates, the vector $\mathbf{f}$ represents the underlying forward rates (i.e. the forward rates in the longest co-terminal swap), and the $(m \times m)$ matrix $\mathbf{w}$ contains the weights

$$\mathbf{w} = \begin{bmatrix} w_{11} & w_{12} & w_{13} & \cdots & w_{1m} \\ 0 & w_{22} & w_{23} & \cdots & w_{2m} \\ 0 & 0 & w_{33} & \cdots & w_{3m} \\ \cdots & \cdots & \cdots & \cdots & \cdots \\ 0 & 0 & 0 & 0 & 1 \end{bmatrix} \tag{20.60}$$

In the matrix above the element w_{ij} represents the weight of the jth forward rate in the weighted average (Equation (20.58)) that produces the ith co-terminal swap rate. Note that the mth co-terminal swap rate coincides with the mth forward rate. Therefore $w_{mm} = 1$.

We now make the assumption, justified in the previous section, that the weights can be assumed to be constant and 'frozen' at today's value, and therefore write the swap-rate covariance matrix as

$$\mathrm{E}\left[\frac{\mathrm{d}SR_i}{SR_i}\frac{\mathrm{d}SR_j}{SR_j}\right] = \mathrm{E}\left[\frac{\sum_{r=1,n_i} w_{ir}\,\mathrm{d}f_r}{\sum_{r=1,n_i} w_{ir}f_r} \frac{\sum_{r=1,n_j} w_{jr}\,\mathrm{d}f_r}{\sum_{r=1,n_j} w_{jr}f_r}\right]$$

$$= \mathrm{E}\left[\frac{\sum_{r=1,n_i} w_{ir}f_r\sigma_r^f\,\mathrm{d}W_r^f}{\sum_{r=1,n_i} w_{ir}f_r} \frac{\sum_{s=1,n_j} w_{js}f_s\sigma_s^f\,\mathrm{d}W_s^f}{\sum_{s=1,n_j} w_{js}f_s}\right]$$

$$= \frac{\sum_{r=1,n_i} w_{ir}f_r\sigma_r^f \sum_{s=1,n_j} w_{js}f_s\sigma_s^f\rho_{rs}^f}{\sum_{r=1,n_i} w_{ir}f_r \sum_{s=1,n_j} w_{js}f_s}\,\mathrm{d}t \tag{20.61}$$

This expression can be simplified if we use the following definition:

$$\zeta_r^i = \frac{w_{ir} f_r}{\sum_{r=1,n_i} w_{ir} f_r} \tag{20.62}$$

Using these quantities we can in fact re-express more concisely the swap-rate covariance matrix as

$$\text{covar}\left[\frac{\text{d}\mathbf{SR}}{\mathbf{SR}}\right] = \text{E}\left[\frac{\text{d}SR_i}{SR_i} \frac{\text{d}SR_j}{SR_j}\right]$$

$$= \sum_{r=1,n_i} \sum_{s=1,n_j} \zeta_r^i \zeta_s^j \sigma_r^f \sigma_s^f \rho_{rs}^f \tag{20.63}$$

This can be rewritten in matrix form as

$$\text{covar}\left[\frac{\text{d}\mathbf{SR}}{\mathbf{SR}}\right] = \mathbf{Z}\mathbf{S}^f \boldsymbol{\beta}^f (\boldsymbol{\beta}^f)^{\text{T}} (\mathbf{S}^f)^{\text{T}} \mathbf{Z}^{\text{T}} \tag{20.64}$$

where the superscript T indicates the transpose of a matrix, $\mathbf{Z}$ is the $(n \times n)$ matrix containing the weights $\{\boldsymbol{\zeta}\}$, n is the number of co-terminal swaps, and use has been made of relationship (20.54) to express the correlation as a function of the forward-rate coefficients $\boldsymbol{\beta}^f$.

Let us pause for a second. We have managed to express the covariance matrix between the *co-terminal swap rates* totally in terms of *forward-rate-specific* quantities, i.e. the volatilities $\mathbf{S}^f$ and the loadings $\boldsymbol{\beta}^f$. The link between swap rates and forward rates is provided by the weight coefficients contained in ζ_r^i, which we have assumed to be constant (an equal to their values today). The nature of the dependence can be made more explicit by recognizing that

$$\text{covar}\left[\frac{\text{d}\mathbf{f}}{\mathbf{f}}\right] = \mathbf{S}^f \boldsymbol{\beta}^f (\boldsymbol{\beta}^f)^{\text{T}} (\mathbf{S}^f)^{\text{T}} = \boldsymbol{\sigma}^f (\boldsymbol{\sigma}^f)^{\text{T}} \tag{20.65}$$

and therefore

$$\text{covar}\left[\frac{\text{d}\mathbf{SR}}{\mathbf{SR}}\right] = \mathbf{Z}\, \text{covar}\left[\frac{\text{d}\mathbf{f}}{\mathbf{f}}\right] \mathbf{Z}^{\text{T}} = \mathbf{Z}\boldsymbol{\sigma}^f (\boldsymbol{\sigma}^f)^{\text{T}} \mathbf{Z}^{\text{T}} \tag{20.66}$$

and

$$\text{covar}\left[\frac{\text{d}\mathbf{f}}{\mathbf{f}}\right] = \mathbf{Z}^{-1} \boldsymbol{\sigma}^{SR} (\boldsymbol{\sigma}^{SR})^{\text{T}} (\mathbf{Z}^{\text{T}})^{-1} = \mathbf{Z}^{-1} \mathbf{S}^{SR} \boldsymbol{\beta}^{SR} (\boldsymbol{\beta}^{SR})^{\text{T}} (\mathbf{S}^{SR})^{\text{T}} (\mathbf{Z}^{\text{T}})^{-1} \tag{20.67}$$

How can one make use of these relationships in order to calibrate to co-terminal swaption in a financially desirable way? From the discussion above we know that, as long as the sensitivities in $\boldsymbol{\beta}^{SR}$ satisfy the pricing relationship (20.57), and as long as the volatilities in the matrix (20.53) are chosen to give the correct root-mean-squared volatility, all the co-terminal swaptions will be priced exactly. Equation (20.67), however, shows that for any such admissible choice of the volatilities $\mathbf{S}^{SR}$ and of the sensitivities $\boldsymbol{\beta}^{SR}$, there will correspond one and only one covariance matrix among forward rates, and that this can be obtained (thanks to the constant-$\mathbf{Z}$ approximation) purely by means of matrix operations.

We can therefore first use a volatility matrix $\mathbf{S}^{SR}$ that correctly integrates to the required root-mean-squared volatilities of the co-terminal swaptions:

$$\int_0^{T_i} \sigma_i^{SR}(u)^2 \, du = \left(\widehat{\sigma}_i^{SR}\right)^2 T_i \qquad (20.68)$$

Having done that, we can optimize the coefficients $\boldsymbol{\beta}^{SR}$ so as to obtain (using Equation (20.67)) the most desirable covariance matrix *among forward rates*. While we do this optimization, we know that the pricing conditions for the swaptions will not be spoiled, because the coefficients $\boldsymbol{\beta}^{SR}$ affect the correlation, not the volatility, of the swap rates. This is one of the reasons why the decomposition presented in Chapter 19 is so useful.

If we focus just on the diagonal of the forward-rate covariance matrix we will price all the caplets associated with the given set of co-terminal swaptions as well as possible (and, very often, close to perfectly). More generally, we can try to obtain the whole forward-rate covariance matrix as well as possible, contingent on all the co-terminal swaptions being priced correctly. I show in Rebonato (2002) that this second route is actually preferable (and the reader who has followed the discussion in Section 20.4 will not be surprised by the result).

We appear to have one problem left: the coefficients $\boldsymbol{\beta}^{SR}$ which we want to optimize to obtain the best forward-rate covariance matrix possible must be linked by the relationship

$$\sum_{r=1,s} [b_{ir}^{SR}]^2 = 1 \qquad (20.69)$$

if we want to price the co-terminal swaptions correctly. The numerical search would therefore appear to be highly constrained and thus cumbersome. We know already, however, how to tackle this problem, i.e. by making use of the generalized angles introduced in a similar context in Section 20.3. The pricing constraint (20.53) can in fact always be satisfied if one chooses the coefficients $\{\boldsymbol{\beta}^{SR}\}$ to be such that

$$b_{ik}^{SR}(t) = \cos\theta_{ik}(t) \prod_{j=1,k-1} \sin\theta_{ij}(t), \quad k = 1, s-1$$

$$b_{ik}^{SR}(t) = \prod_{j=1,k-1} \sin\theta_{ij}(t), \qquad k = s \qquad (20.70)$$

This last 'trick' solves the problem: given any set of swap-rate volatilities $\mathbf{S}^{SR}$ that satisfy the root-mean-square condition for the co-terminal swaptions, the weights $\boldsymbol{\beta}^{SR}$ fully determine the forward-rate covariance matrix via the matrix relationships (20.67). These weights can be optimized in an unconstrained fashion by expressing them in terms of the polar co-ordinates of the surface of a unit-radius hypersphere. The associated angles can then be varied until the forward-rate covariance matrix becomes as good as possible (given the chosen forward-rate correlation function, the market prices of the co-terminal swaptions, and the chosen swap-rate volatility functions $\mathbf{S}^{SR}$).

The quality of the numerical results is excellent and the reader is referred to Rebonato (2002) for a detailed analysis of numerical results, both in stylized cases and using market data.

Chapter 21

Specifying the Instantaneous Volatility of Forward Rates

21.1 Introduction and Motivation

In the previous chapters I have discussed a few calibration methodologies that allow the recovery of the prices of caplets or swaptions, *given* volatility or correlation functions chosen by the trader so as to satisfy some very mild requirements. For instance, when discussing the calibration to an exogenous correlation matrix, the volatilities of the forward rates were simply required to satisfy the 'norm' condition that

$$\int_0^{T_i} \sigma_i(u)^2 \, \mathrm{d}u = \widehat{\sigma}_{T_i}^2 T_i \tag{21.1}$$

where $\sigma_i(t)$ is the instantaneous volatility of the ith forward rate at time t and $\widehat{\sigma}_{T_i}$ the implied (Black) volatility of the associated caplet. Similarly, when discussing the calibration to co-terminal swaptions, the only requirement on the swap-rate instantaneous volatility was that

$$\int_0^{T_{SR}} \sigma_{SR}(u)^2 \, \mathrm{d}u = \widehat{\sigma}_{T_{SR}}^2 T_{SR} \tag{21.2}$$

where now $\sigma_{SR}(t)$ is the instantaneous volatility of a swap rate at time t and $\widehat{\sigma}_{T_{SR}}$ the implied (Black) volatility of the associated swaption. I have not said anything, however, about how these functions should be chosen. The question is important, because, for instance, neither Equation (21.1) nor Equation (21.2) contains enough information to determine uniquely the instantaneous volatility functions for forward or swap rates, respectively.

As for the 'target' correlation function introduced in Section 20.3 of the previous chapter, I did not mention how this might have been arrived at. Historical estimation clearly provides one possible route. Alternatively, the relationships between forward and swap rate volatilities presented in Section 20.5 allow for a market-implied route. I have discussed elsewhere (see Rebonato (2002)) that estimating the correlation function from the prices of caplets and swaptions is not only technically arduous, but also relies on a strong belief in the congruence of the caplet and swaption markets. See again Rebonato (2002) for a discussion of why these two sister markets might be systematically out of line with each other. Irrespective of whether the reader is convinced by the argument presented there or not, she will probably need a functional form for the correlation function, with free parameters to be optimized either to the historical correlation, or to the market data.

Therefore both for instantaneous volatilities and for instantaneous correlation we are faced with the task of choosing desirable functional forms, parameterized by a handful of coefficients, such that they satisfy not only the 'mild pricing requirements' mentioned above, but that also more general financial desiderata. This is the task undertaken in the present chapter and the next.

21.2   The Link between Instantaneous Volatilities and the Future Term Structure of Volatilities

The first financial desideratum that I will explore is a plausible evolution of the term structure of volatilities. For instance, early versions of the LIBOR market model were often implemented using flat (time-independent) volatility functions for the various forward rates, i.e. volatility functions of the type

$$\sigma(t, T_i) = k_{T_i} \tag{21.3}$$

Unfortunately, as shown below, little can be said in favour of this choice apart from numerical simplicity, since the evolution of the term structure of volatilities it implies is one of the most unrealistic. Therefore, despite the fact that such a volatility function could easily be made to satisfy condition (21.1), it would not qualify as a desirable choice in the sense discussed above.

Recall that the term structure of volatilities at time t is the time-t function that associates an implied (Black) volatility, $\widehat{\sigma}_{t,T}$, to each maturity, T. It is related to the instantaneous volatility, $\sigma_T(u)$, by the relationship

$$\int_t^T \sigma_T(u)^2 \, du = \widehat{\sigma}_{t,T}^2 (T - t) \tag{21.4}$$

What one observes from the market is today's set of Black volatilities (as a function of T):

$$\int_0^T \sigma_T(u)^2 \, du = \widehat{\sigma}_{0,T}^2(T) = \widehat{\sigma}_T^2(T) \tag{21.5}$$

where the lighter notation $\widehat{\sigma}_T^2(T)$ has been introduced to denote $\widehat{\sigma}_{0,T}^2(T)$. One such function for GBP is shown in Figure 21.1.

The most noticeable features of this curve are the steep increase in implied volatilities from the very short maturities up to approximately $1\frac{1}{2}$ years, and the fact that, after this maturity, the implied volatilities are monotonically decreasing (often with an upward

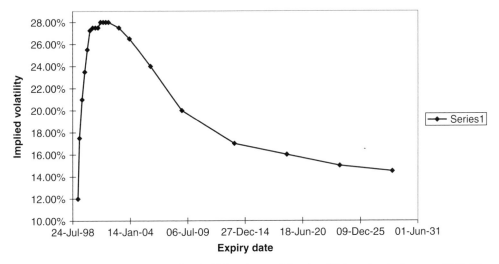

Figure 21.1 The term structure of volatilities observed for the GBP market in January 1999. The dates on the *x*-axis are the expiry dates of six-month caplets.

convexity). See also the discussion in Chapter 7, and Chapter 26 for a more detailed description. The fact that this implied volatility curve has a highly structured shape (and that this shape, as shown later in the chapter, is, at least during 'normal' periods, roughly constant over time) is very important for the choice of the instantaneous volatility function. Let us focus attention on the implied volatilities associated with two specific maturities in Figure 21.1. One can directly read from this graph that, in order to price, say, the 10-year 6-month caplet and the 15-year 6-month caplet one would need root-mean-squared volatilities of approximately 20.00% and 16.00%, respectively. Let us now assume that the trader chooses to describe the instantaneous volatilities of all the forward rates by constants equal to their root-mean-squared volatilities. With this choice the instantaneous volatilities of the two forward rates will always be equal to 20.00% and 16.00% throughout their lives. This choice however implies that, after five years, the implied volatility for the caplet which is today 15 years from expiry, should still be equal to 16%. Today's 10-year implied volatility, however, is, from the same graph, around 20.00%. Therefore the flat-volatility assumption implies a change in today's implied volatility function. Generalizing, it is easy to see from this discussion that the future term structure of volatility implied by a flat-instantaneous-volatility assumption will look like today's implied volatility curve translated in maturity by as many years as one is looking ahead in the future. An example, still from the GBP market, but referring to mid-1998, is shown in Figure 21.2.

The curves in Figure 21.2 were obtained by enforcing the constant-instantaneous-volatility assumption, and display today's term structure of volatilities, and the term structure of volatilities after one, two and four years, as implied by the flat-instantaneous-volatility assumption. The dramatic change in shape in the term structure of volatilities implied by the flat-volatility assumption is clearly apparent from this figure.

Apart from this rather extreme case, the important observation is that *any* choice of instantaneous volatility for the forward rates spanning the yield curve will uniquely determine, via Equation (21.4), the evolution of the term structure. Therefore the frequently raised objection that, given our poor knowledge about the future instantaneous volatility

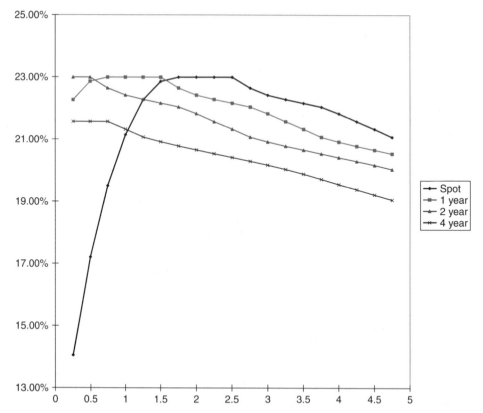

Figure 21.2 The evolution of the term structure of volatilities implied by a flat-instantaneous-volatility assumption over four years. The implied volatility curve in one year's time can be obtained by translating the spot curve by one year to the left along the maturity axis, and similarly for the two- and four-year curves.

of a forward rate, Occam's razor should be extensively used, and the simplest (i.e. the flat) assumption should be enforced does not stand up to scrutiny. Our knowledge might be poor indeed, but the flat-volatility hypothesis is in no way 'neutral', implying as it does a very extreme evolution for the term structure of implied volatilities. An informed opinion can (and should) be formed by a trader about the evolution of tradable quantities such as the term structure of volatilities. Avoiding making a choice about instantaneous volatilities delegates to an opaque black-box model the expression of a view about the future prices of caplets.

All the trading houses who have seriously embraced the LIBOR market model (LMM) framework have therefore had to make choices about the functional form of the instantaneous volatility function. Many of the methods that have been put in place are quite similar in spirit, and all attempt to come to terms with the problem of giving the user a reasonably direct control over the volatility evolution. The approach described below makes no claim to being 'the best', but it is representative of several common and practical implementations, and is both intuitively appealing and easy to use. A very similar parametric form was, to my knowledge, independently introduced by Brace (personal communication, 1997), but several houses were already using similar, or virtually identical, functional choices. A systematic discussion of the pros and cons of several functional forms for the instantaneous volatility function can be found in Rebonato (2002).

21.3 A Functional Form for the Instantaneous Volatility Function

Let us begin by assuming that the instantaneous volatility at time t of the forward rate expiring at time T is given by the expression

$$
\begin{aligned}
\sigma_t^T &= [a + b(T - t)]\exp[-c(T - t)] + d \\
&= [a + b(\tau)]\exp[-c(\tau)] + d, \qquad \tau = T - t
\end{aligned}
\tag{21.6}
$$

The quantity τ therefore represents the residual time to maturity of a particular forward rate. As for the functional form chosen, the presence of a linear term together with a decaying exponential allows for the existence of a hump in the curve, and the asymptotic instantaneous volatility is assumed to tend asymptotically to a finite value, d. A few typical shapes are displayed in Figure 21.3.

The functional form (21.6) has the advantage of being extremely simple, and of affording, at the same time, a transparent interpretation of some of the parameters, or of their combinations. This can be seen as follows. To begin with, in the limit as τ goes to zero, instantaneous and average volatilities tend to coincide, and therefore the relationship

$$
\sigma_t^T = a + d = \lim_{T \to 0} \widehat{\sigma}(T)
\tag{21.7}
$$

(where $\lim_{T \to 0} \widehat{\sigma}(T)$ is the implied Black volatility of a caplet of vanishingly short expiry) gives some indication about the possible range of values for the sum of a and d.

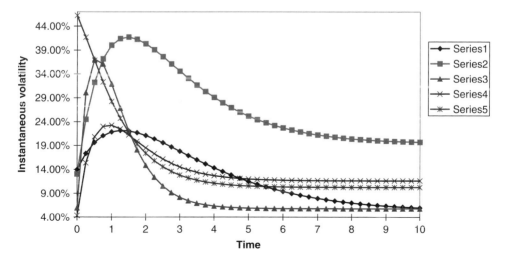

Figure 21.3 A variety of shapes for the instantaneous volatility curve produced by the functional form (21.6).

Furthermore, in the limit as τ goes to infinity, the instantaneous volatility should converge to the implied volatility of the 'very long' expiry caplet:

$$\lim_{T \to \infty} \sigma_t^T = d = \lim_{T \to \infty} \widehat{\sigma}(T) \tag{21.8}$$

Finally, it is easy to show that the maximum of the instantaneous volatility curve occurs for a value of τ, $\widetilde{\tau}$, given by

$$\widetilde{\tau} = \frac{1}{c} - \frac{a}{b} \tag{21.9}$$

If a trader estimated statistically the portion of the life of a future or forward contract that is associated with its highest volatility, this third relationship can provide some additional information about the plausible range of values for the parameters $\{a, b, c, d\}$.

21.3.1   Financial Justification for a Humped Volatility

The last criterion brings us directly to the justification for the humped shape as a possible candidate for the instantaneous volatility curve. Note that the presence of a hump in the term structure of volatility is not, by itself, a direct reason for imposing a similar shape on the instantaneous volatility curve. A humped term structure of volatilities, for instance, could in principle be obtained if all forward rates experienced a different constant instantaneous volatility, and this was equal to the implied volatility; or if all the forward rates displayed the same time-dependent instantaneous volatility and this was to display a maximum for some future time $\widetilde{\tau}$. (Rebonato (2002) explains why these choices are neither realistic nor financially appealing.)

A more compelling financial justification for the existence of a hump in the instantaneous volatility curve comes from the observation of the trading dynamics of different forward and future contracts. At the short end of the maturity spectrum futures contracts are 'pinned' by the imminent setting of short-term deposit rates, which are, in turn, influenced by the actions of the monetary authorities. Central banks tend (or try?) to signal their intentions well ahead of their rate decisions, and therefore, in most cases, surprises at the very short end are rare. In 'normal' periods, i.e. in the absence of surprises from the monetary authorities, the uncertainty and the trading activity in the front futures contracts therefore tend to decline as they approach expiry.

At the opposite end of the maturity spectrum the variation in market expectations about very distant forward rates is mainly driven by changing expectations about long-term inflation. Again, the presumed actions of central banks, which often implicitly or explicitly operate with an inflation target, is important, and, by and large, the best estimate for the level of inflation five or 10 years in the future is the inflation target itself.

Where the greatest uncertainty resides is in the intermediate region between, say, six and 18 months, as tightening or loosening regimes can easily be reversed or continued beyond what was originally anticipated. If this view is correct, this state of affairs would give rise during 'normal' periods to a maximum in the market uncertainty (and, therefore, in the volatility of the forward rates) in the intermediate-maturity region, and the volatility of the long-dated or of the very-short-dated forward rates should not be as pronounced as that of the intermediate-maturity forward rates.

If, on the other hand, there is a lack of market consensus about the short-term actions of the monetary authorities, the uncertainty about the reset values of the cash rates which most directly affect the earliest expiring forward rates (roughly speaking, the front futures contracts) can become very high. If this is the case, the instantaneous volatility should sharply increase at the short end, and the hump would disappear. The functional form of Equation (21.6) easily allows for both regimes.

These qualitative considerations therefore give a rationale for the functional choice (21.6), and the relationships (21.7)–(21.9) between the coefficients and some quasi-observable market quantities can be helpful in estimating a plausible range of values for the free parameters. It must be stressed, however, that these relationships can give a useful indication about the plausible range of values for the coefficients, but should probably not be used to fix three of the four parameters. Not only is the statistical estimation of quantities such as the maximum in the instantaneous volatility function always difficult, but, even if these estimates (based on past history) were truly robust, there would still be no guarantee that the (forward-looking) option market has incorporated them into the prices of the liquid traded options. This observation can be particularly important in periods shortly after a major transition in a financial regime, such as the introduction of the EUR. Past history, in this case, can provide very unsatisfactory or incomplete information. I therefore show below how to bring into play the (forward-looking) information that the caplet and swaption markets can provide.

21.4 Ensuring Correct Caplet Pricing

Given a set of parameters $\{a, b, c, d\}$ one can check, for each forward rate, whether the integral of the square of the instantaneous volatility out to the expiry of the forward rate coincides with the total Black variance, i.e. whether[1]

$$\widehat{\sigma}_T^2 T = \int_T^0 ([a + b(\tau)] \exp[-c(\tau)] + d)^2 \, \mathrm{d}\tau \tag{21.10}$$

In general, a given set of parameters $\{a, b, c, d\}$ will not allow the exact fulfilment of condition (21.10) for more than a handful of forward rates. Therefore, the same set of parameters $\{a, b, c, d\}$ will not recover the Black caplet prices of all the forward rates. In order to achieve the exact recovery of today's term structure of volatilities, one can associate to each forward rate a different scaling factor, k_T, defined as

$$k_T^2 = \frac{\widehat{\sigma}_T^2 T}{\displaystyle\int_T^0 ([a + b(\tau)] \exp[-c(\tau)] + d)^2 \, \mathrm{d}\tau} \tag{21.11}$$

and write for the forward-rate-specific instantaneous volatility function

$$\sigma_t^T = k_T [a + b(T - t)] \exp[-c(T - t)] + d \tag{21.12}$$

By introducing this forward-specific normalization factor the caplet condition is therefore fulfilled by construction everywhere along the curve. In order to illustrate the procedure,

---

[1]In Equation (21.10) the integration is over $\tau = T - t$, and the lower and upper limits of integration are therefore T and 0, respectively.

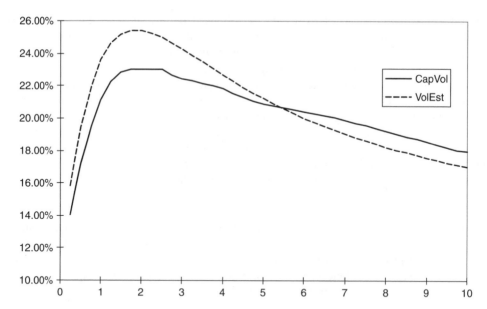

Figure 21.4   A market (GBP 27-Nov-98) implied volatility curve ('CapVol') and the model curve ('VolEst') obtainable from Equation (21.10) with a set of parameters $\{a, b, c, d\}$ chosen to minimize the overall differences between the two curves, before the re-scaling in Equation (21.11) (i.e. with $k_T = 1$ for all T).

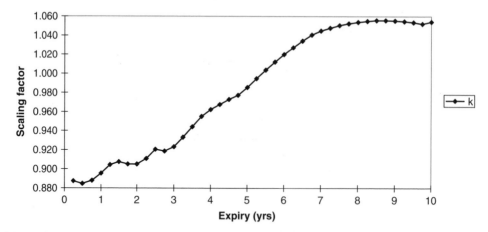

Figure 21.5   The expiry-dependent normalization factor, k_T, obtained using Equation (21.11), necessary to bring about exact pricing of the caplets. Note that the y-axis is rather compressed, spanning as it does the values from approximately 0.9 to 1.05. The variation in the scaling parameter is therefore rather muted.

Figure 21.4 shows a market implied volatility curve ('CapVol') and the model curve ('VolEst') obtainable from Equation (21.10) with a suitable choice of parameters before the normalization (21.11).

Figure 21.5 then shows the expiry-dependent normalization factor, k_T, obtained using Equation (21.11), necessary to bring about exact pricing of the caplets. Analysing a curve like the one in Figure 21.5 is very useful, and explains why the parameterization proposed above can be very effective in controlling the evolution of the term structure of volatilities. In order to understand why, let us consider the case where all the $\{k_T\}$ coefficients were exactly unity. From Equation (21.4) (see Rebonato (2002) for a proof) one can readily see that, if that were the case, the future term structure of volatilities would look (as a function of residual time to maturity) exactly like today's. Therefore looking at the degree of variation of the $\{k_T\}$ values across maturities gives a measure of the degree of time homogeneity of the implied volatility curve. To give a concrete example, Figures 21.6 and 21.7 show the evolution of the term structure of volatilities obtained from the instantaneous volatility curve in Figure 21.4 after normalization.

As one can readily appreciate, despite the fact that the future term structure of volatilities is not identical to today's curve, its qualitative shape is fundamentally preserved. Figures 21.6 and 21.7, in particular, can be profitably compared with the implied volatility surface that would be obtained using the flat-volatility assumption, as displayed in Figures 21.2 and 21.8.

Therefore, a choice of parameters $\{a, b, c, d\}$ such that today's model term structure of volatilities already (i.e. before the normalization factors $\{k_T\}$ are brought into play) bears a strong resemblance to the market implied volatility curve will automatically ensure that the 'correction factors' $\{k_T\}$ will be very close to unity. If this is the case, the term structure of volatilities will be reasonably time stationary. One possible criterion for the choice of the $\{a, b, c, d\}$ coefficients could therefore be the minimization of the discrepancy between the curves labelled 'VolEst' and 'CapVol' in Figure 21.4. The fact that the functional form proposed in Equation (21.6) allows analytic evaluation of the

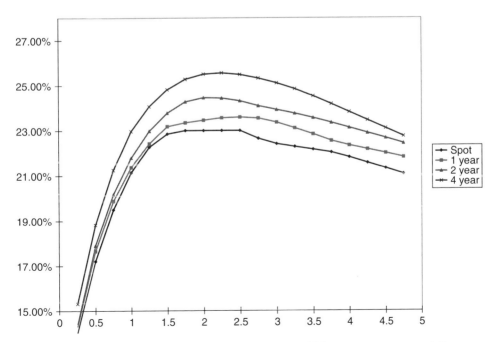

Figure 21.6 The evolution of the term structure of volatilities over one, two and four years obtained from the instantaneous volatility curve in Figure 21.4 after normalization.

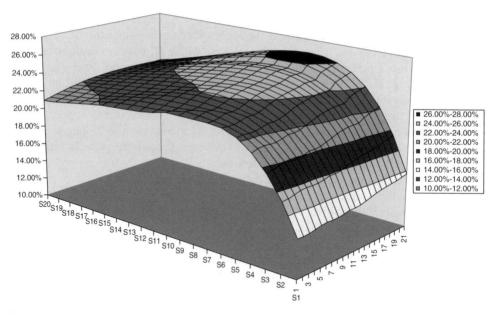

Figure 21.7   The evolution of the term structure of volatilities over a period of 10 years obtained from the instantaneous volatility curve in Figure 21.4 after re-scaling.

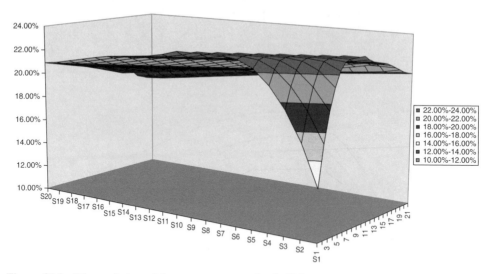

Figure 21.8   The evolution of the term structure of volatilities over a period of 10 years obtained from flat-instantaneous-volatilities curve. See also Figure 21.2.

integral in Equation (21.4) makes the procedure simple and computationally fast (a few seconds on a middle-of-the-range PC).

It is both important and encouraging to observe that the $\{a, b, c, d\}$ coefficients determined in realistic market cases by imposing that the normalization coefficients $\{k_T\}$ should be as close as possible to one (and hence give rise to an approximately time-homogeneous term structure of volatilities) generally imply instantaneous volatilities broadly compatible with the financial 'story' presented in Section 21.3.1.

The next obvious question is: To what extent is it actually possible and desirable to achieve a time homogeneous term structure of volatilities? The question is addressed in the next section by employing a two-pronged approach, i.e. from an empirical and from a market implied perspective.

21.5   Fitting the Instantaneous Volatility Function: Imposing Time Homogeneity of the Term Structure of Volatilities

The question as to whether, or to what extent, term structures of volatilities have indeed been time homogeneous in the past is obviously an empirical one. Whether they will still display this feature in the future, however, adds an essential element of market judgement. Figures 21.9 and 21.10 show a small representative portion of the historical market implied volatility out to a maximum 10-year maturity which has been collected over a period of approximately two years (1996/1997) for GBP and FRF. The examples are somewhat 'ancient' because I want to discuss here market information relating to a period when the smile was simple in shape (basically, monotonically decreasing) and relatively small in magnitude. See Part IV of this book (and Chapters 25 and 27 in particular) for a discussion including smiles.

The two figures are representative of the two main regimes for the evolution of term structures of volatilities, i.e. the 'normal' and 'excited' shapes that I describe and discuss in Chapter 26. When the first regime prevails, the overall structural features (such as, for instance, the steepness of the implied volatility curve close to the origin) tend to be very constant over time. Even much finer features, such as the existence of a plateau between

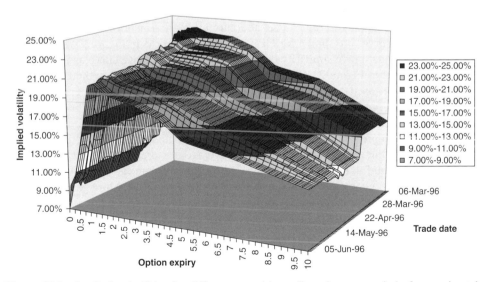

Figure 21.9   Implied volatilities for different maturities collected over a period of approximately three months in 1996 for GBP.

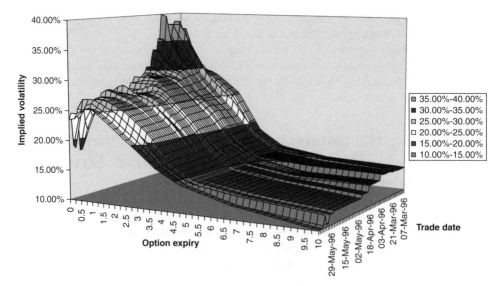

Figure 21.10   Implied volatilities for different maturities collected over a period of approximately three months in 1996 for FRF.

approximately 1.5 and 2.5 years for the GBP data, seem to be preserved, despite the fact that the plateau itself might change level (see Figure 21.9).

As for the second regime, this is associated with periods where the uncertainty about the short end of the yield curve can dramatically increase. As can be appreciated by looking at the far side of Figure 21.10, the change from the humped to the decaying state can occur very abruptly (in a matter of days), and tends to disappear somewhat more slowly (over many days or a few weeks).

If only the first regime existed, a good criterion for the choice of the instantaneous volatility parameters would be to recover in a reasonably time-homogeneous manner the *average* (over trading days), rather than the current, term structure of volatilities. The resulting average curves are shown for GPB and pre-Euro DEM in Figure 21.11. One can readily notice the qualitative similarity between the obtained average curve and the sample of curves presented in Figure 21.10. The motivation for this procedure would be to make the model produce, as its guess for the future term structure of volatilities, something very close to what has been observed in the past. Given the discussion in Section 1.3 of Chapter 1 about future re-hedging costs, this is certainly plausible and desirable.

The same procedure can, of course, be followed by including in the average also the 'unstable' periods, but in this case looking at the average of radically different regimes can be much less meaningful. I discuss in Chapter 27 how this problem can be tackled in a more satisfactory manner (i.e. by introducing a shift in volatility regimes). More generally, if the trader had extra information (or simply different views) about the evolution of the implied volatility curve, she could always choose a set of parameters that embody these views.

This way of looking at the volatility parameterization actually constitutes one of the greatest strengths of the LMM approach: by choosing a particular instantaneous-volatility function, and therefore a future term structure of volatilities, the exotic trader directly expresses a view about the quantities (the instantaneous volatilities of forward rates) that constitute the difficult-to-hedge component of the present value of exotic trades. This state

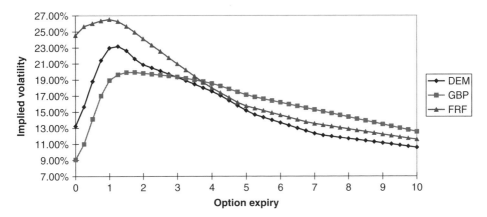

Figure 21.11 The average (over approximately two years of trading dates – 1996, 1997) of the implied volatilities at different maturities observed in the market for GBP, DEM and FRF.

of affairs can be compared with the predicament of a trader who has to use one of the many models that take as input much more opaque quantities, such as the volatility of the all-driving short rate.

Note carefully that roughly parallel shifts in the term structure of volatilities (which can often be adequately captured also by the black-box models) are unlikely to hurt the trader significantly, as long as she has put in place a reasonable vega hedge (see again the discussion in Chapter 1). But, as the discussion in the previous chapter has shown, there are not enough liquid instruments to 'lock-in', with suitable hedges, the contribution to the value of an exotic trade originating from the apportioning of the instantaneous volatility over the option life *given a fixed root-mean-squared volatility*. In other words, the exotic trader will find it most difficult to hedge against changes in the value of an exotic product arising from *changes in the shape (not the level)* of the term structure of volatilities. It is therefore exactly in this latter dimension that the superiority of the LMM approach can be most easily appreciated.

21.6 Is a Time-Homogeneous Solution Always Possible?

A further important comment regarding this proposed approach is that today's term structure of volatilities can sometimes indicate the extent to which the market 'believes' that it can remain unchanged in shape and level over time. More precisely, one can easily show (see, for example, Rebonato (2002) for a proof) that, if the market operates in an arbitrage-free log-normal Black world and the quantity

$$\xi(T) \equiv \widehat{\sigma}_T^2 T \tag{21.13}$$

is not a strictly increasing function of maturity, then the future term structure of volatilities cannot have the same shape and level as today's. In other words, if $\xi(T_1) > \xi(T_2)$, with $T_1 < T_2$, then, even if we changed the functional form of the instantaneous volatility and added as many parameters as we want, we would still not be able to find a normalization vector $\{k_T\}$ exactly equal to 1 for all the forward rates. The converse is also true: if the term structure of volatilities is such that the quantity $\xi(T)$ is strictly increasing in

T, an instantaneous volatility of the form $g(T - t)$ that prices the caplet market exactly can always be found. Such an instantaneous-volatility function would generate an exactly time-homogeneous evolution of the term structure of volatilities. See Rebonato (2002) for a proof.

Summarizing: as discussed in Section 3.6.2 of Chapter 3, the failure of the quantity $\xi(T)$ to be strictly increasing does not imply an arbitrage possibility (even in a perfect Black world). It *does* imply, however, either that the market does not believe in the forward rates being log-normally distributed, or that it believes that the level and/or the shape of the implied volatility curve will change in the future.

Interestingly enough, particularly strong and systematic violations of the condition $\frac{d\xi(T)}{dT} > 0$ were observed in recent years for European currencies in the run-up to the Euro conversion. During this period observation of caplet pricing practice for the less liquid currencies (say, ITL and ESP) and comparison with the same-maturity quotes available for DEM indicated that traders tended to subscribe to a more normal/square-root process for the forward rates, than to a log-normal process. If one couples this observation with the fact that the rates in most currencies were expected to move down towards convergence, one can readily explain why term structures of volatilities with locally decreasing $\xi(T)$ were observed.

21.7   Fitting the Instantaneous Volatility Function: The Information from the Swaption Market

In the first part of this chapter I proposed one possible criterion (i.e. imposing that the vector $\{k_T\}$ should be as constant as possible) in order to choose the functional form and pin down the parameters of the instantaneous volatility function. As mentioned in the first section, however, if one couples this approach with a plausible choice for the instantaneous correlation function, one can bring into play the combined information from the cap and swaption markets. This can be done by making use of the relationship between forward-rate and swap-rate volatilities discussed in Section 20.5 (see Equation (20.41) in particular). These equations provide a convenient link between the swap-rate volatilities implied by a set of chosen instantaneous volatilities and correlations on the one hand, and the corresponding market prices of swaptions on the other.

If we assumed to know with certainty the forward-rate instantaneous volatility functions, and that the cap/swaption markets were perfectly coherent, then the swaption implied volatility matrix would uniquely pin down the unknown correlation function (more precisely, would allow us to determine the covariance elements discussed in Section 5.4 of Chapter 5). Instantaneous volatility functions are, however, not God-given; nor should one automatically assume that the cap and swaption markets should be perfectly 'in line' with each other (see Chapter 1). Therefore a combined approach, where considerations about the time-homogeneity of the term structure of volatilities are analysed together with the resulting model swaption implied volatility matrix, is in practice probably the most profitable.

If this route is taken, the trader would not expect to match the market and model swaption volatility matrices almost perfectly everywhere, but would try to modify the choices of instantaneous volatility and/or correlation whenever the discrepancies showed a particularly strong or systematic bias. Tables 21.1–21.3 and Figures 21.12–21.15 provide some examples of good and obviously poor matches.

Table 21.1 The implied swaption volatilities for GBP observed in the market on 24 November 1998. On the *x*-axis one can read the maturity (in months) of the swap into which the option can be exercised; on the *y*-axis one can read the expiry date.

	12	18	24	30	36	42	48	54	60	66	72	78	84	90	96	102	108
24-May-99	19.95%	20.19%	20.43%	19.95%	19.47%	18.98%	18.50%	18.38%	18.26%	18.20%	18.14%	18.08%	18.02%	17.94%	17.86%	17.78%	17.71%
24-Nov-99	21.97%	21.48%	20.99%	20.50%	19.99%	19.74%	19.48%	19.24%	18.99%	18.74%	18.49%	18.25%	18.00%	17.75%	17.51%	17.26%	17.01%
24-May-00	22.00%	21.50%	21.00%	20.50%	20.00%	19.63%	19.25%	19.00%	18.75%	18.44%	18.13%	17.82%	17.51%	17.24%	16.97%	16.69%	16.43%
24-Nov-00	22.00%	21.50%	21.00%	20.50%	20.00%	19.50%	19.00%	18.76%	18.50%	18.13%	17.76%	17.39%	17.01%	16.72%	16.43%	16.14%	15.84%
24-May-01	21.76%	21.25%	20.76%	20.13%	19.51%	19.01%	18.51%	18.14%	17.77%	17.39%	17.02%	16.64%	16.27%	16.04%	15.81%	15.57%	15.35%
24-Nov-01	21.50%	21.01%	20.50%	19.76%	19.01%	18.51%	18.01%	17.51%	17.01%	16.64%	16.26%	15.89%	15.51%	15.35%	15.18%	15.01%	14.84%
24-May-02	21.50%	20.87%	20.26%	19.50%	18.76%	18.19%	17.63%	17.09%	16.56%	16.20%	15.85%	15.49%	15.13%	14.99%	14.84%	14.69%	14.55%
24-Nov-02	21.50%	20.76%	20.00%	19.26%	18.50%	17.89%	17.26%	16.69%	16.11%	15.77%	15.43%	15.10%	14.76%	14.63%	14.51%	14.38%	14.25%
24-May-03	21.01%	20.26%	19.51%	18.69%	17.89%	17.26%	16.64%	16.12%	15.61%	15.33%	15.06%	14.78%	14.51%	14.38%	14.26%	14.13%	14.01%
24-Nov-03	20.51%	19.76%	19.01%	18.14%	17.26%	16.64%	16.01%	15.56%	15.11%	14.90%	14.68%	14.47%	14.25%	14.13%	14.00%	13.88%	13.75%
24-May-04	20.07%	19.28%	18.51%	17.72%	16.94%	16.35%	15.76%	15.29%	14.83%	14.62%	14.42%	14.21%	14.01%	13.88%	13.75%	13.62%	13.49%
24-Nov-04	19.63%	18.83%	18.01%	17.32%	16.63%	16.07%	15.50%	15.03%	14.55%	14.36%	14.15%	13.96%	13.75%	13.62%	13.49%	13.35%	13.22%
24-May-05	19.20%	18.35%	17.51%	16.91%	16.32%	15.78%	15.26%	14.76%	14.28%	14.09%	13.89%	13.70%	13.51%	13.37%	13.23%	13.09%	12.96%
24-Nov-05	18.76%	17.89%	17.01%	16.51%	16.01%	15.51%	15.00%	14.51%	14.00%	13.82%	13.63%	13.44%	13.25%	13.11%	12.97%	12.83%	12.69%
24-May-06	18.22%	17.44%	16.66%	16.20%	15.74%	15.28%	14.82%	14.36%	13.90%	13.71%	13.52%	13.32%	13.13%	12.97%	12.82%	12.67%	12.52%
24-Nov-06	17.68%	17.00%	16.31%	15.89%	15.47%	15.06%	14.64%	14.22%	13.80%	13.60%	13.40%	13.20%	13.00%	12.84%	12.67%	12.51%	12.35%
24-May-07	17.14%	16.54%	15.96%	15.58%	15.21%	14.83%	14.46%	14.08%	13.70%	13.49%	13.29%	13.08%	12.88%	12.70%	12.53%	12.35%	12.18%
24-Nov-07	16.59%	16.10%	15.61%	15.28%	14.94%	14.61%	14.27%	13.94%	13.60%	13.39%	13.18%	12.97%	12.75%	12.57%	12.38%	12.20%	12.01%
24-May-08	16.05%	15.65%	15.26%	14.96%	14.67%	14.38%	14.09%	13.79%	13.50%	13.28%	13.07%	12.84%	12.63%	12.43%	12.23%	12.04%	11.84%
24-Nov-08	15.51%	15.21%	14.91%	14.66%	14.40%	14.16%	13.90%	13.65%	13.40%	13.18%	12.95%	12.73%	12.50%	12.30%	12.09%	11.88%	11.67%

Table 21.2 The model swaption volatilities for 24 November 1998 obtained using the $\{a, b, c, d\}$ parameters that gave rise to the vector of normalization factors k_T shown in Figure 21.5.

	12	18	24	30	36	42	48	54	60	66	72	78	84	90	96	102	108
24-May-99	19.42%	19.78%	20.06%	19.69%	19.29%	18.87%	18.45%	18.34%	18.22%	18.16%	18.09%	18.03%	17.96%	17.88%	17.80%	17.71%	17.63%
24-Nov-99	21.54%	21.15%	20.74%	20.31%	19.86%	19.62%	19.38%	19.15%	18.91%	18.68%	18.44%	18.21%	17.98%	17.74%	17.51%	17.27%	17.04%
24-May-00	21.69%	21.25%	20.79%	20.33%	19.88%	19.53%	19.18%	18.94%	18.70%	18.41%	18.12%	17.82%	17.53%	17.28%	17.02%	16.76%	16.51%
24-Nov-00	21.70%	21.24%	20.77%	20.32%	19.85%	19.39%	18.93%	18.69%	18.45%	18.11%	17.76%	17.41%	17.06%	16.79%	16.51%	16.24%	15.97%
24-May-01	21.45%	20.98%	20.52%	19.95%	19.38%	18.92%	18.46%	18.11%	17.77%	17.42%	17.07%	16.72%	16.38%	16.15%	15.93%	15.71%	15.49%
24-Nov-01	21.17%	20.72%	20.25%	19.57%	18.89%	18.44%	17.98%	17.52%	17.07%	16.72%	16.37%	16.02%	15.67%	15.51%	15.34%	15.18%	15.01%
24-May-02	21.13%	20.55%	19.98%	19.30%	18.63%	18.11%	17.61%	17.12%	16.63%	16.30%	15.97%	15.63%	15.30%	15.16%	15.01%	14.86%	14.72%
24-Nov-02	21.08%	20.40%	19.72%	19.05%	18.37%	17.81%	17.24%	16.72%	16.19%	15.88%	15.56%	15.25%	14.93%	14.81%	14.68%	14.55%	14.43%
24-May-03	20.60%	19.91%	19.24%	18.51%	17.79%	17.22%	16.66%	16.19%	15.72%	15.46%	15.20%	14.93%	14.68%	14.55%	14.43%	14.30%	14.18%
24-Nov-03	20.11%	19.44%	18.77%	17.99%	17.20%	16.64%	16.07%	15.66%	15.24%	15.04%	14.83%	14.63%	14.42%	14.30%	14.17%	14.05%	13.93%
24-May-04	19.70%	19.00%	18.30%	17.59%	16.89%	16.35%	15.81%	15.39%	14.96%	14.76%	14.57%	14.37%	14.17%	14.04%	13.92%	13.79%	13.66%
24-Nov-04	19.29%	18.56%	17.83%	17.21%	16.58%	16.07%	15.56%	15.12%	14.69%	14.49%	14.30%	14.11%	13.92%	13.79%	13.66%	13.53%	13.40%
24-May-05	18.88%	18.11%	17.36%	16.81%	16.27%	15.78%	15.30%	14.85%	14.41%	14.23%	14.04%	13.86%	13.67%	13.54%	13.41%	13.27%	13.14%
24-Nov-05	18.45%	17.67%	16.88%	16.42%	15.96%	15.50%	15.04%	14.59%	14.14%	13.96%	13.78%	13.60%	13.43%	13.29%	13.15%	13.02%	12.88%
24-May-06	17.94%	17.23%	16.53%	16.10%	15.68%	15.26%	14.85%	14.43%	14.02%	13.83%	13.65%	13.47%	13.29%	13.14%	13.00%	12.85%	12.71%
24-Nov-06	17.43%	16.81%	16.18%	15.80%	15.41%	15.04%	14.65%	14.28%	13.90%	13.71%	13.52%	13.34%	13.15%	13.00%	12.84%	12.69%	12.53%
24-May-07	16.92%	16.37%	15.84%	15.49%	15.15%	14.80%	14.46%	14.12%	13.78%	13.59%	13.40%	13.21%	13.02%	12.85%	12.69%	12.53%	12.37%
24-Nov-07	16.40%	15.95%	15.50%	15.19%	14.89%	14.58%	14.28%	13.98%	13.67%	13.47%	13.28%	13.08%	12.88%	12.71%	12.54%	12.37%	12.20%
24-May-08	15.89%	15.52%	15.16%	14.89%	14.63%	14.36%	14.09%	13.83%	13.56%	13.36%	13.16%	12.95%	12.75%	12.57%	12.39%	12.21%	12.03%
24-Nov-08	15.39%	15.11%	14.83%	14.61%	14.37%	14.14%	13.91%	13.68%	13.45%	13.25%	13.04%	12.83%	12.63%	12.44%	12.24%	12.06%	11.86%

Table 21.3 The difference between the market data and model data in Tables 21.1 and 21.2.

	12	18	24	30	36	42	48	54	60	66	72	78	84	90	96	102	108
24-May-99	0.53%	0.42%	0.37%	0.26%	0.18%	0.11%	0.05%	0.04%	0.03%	0.04%	0.04%	0.05%	0.06%	0.06%	0.07%	0.07%	0.08%
24-Nov-99	0.43%	0.33%	0.25%	0.19%	0.14%	0.12%	0.10%	0.09%	0.08%	0.06%	0.05%	0.04%	0.02%	0.01%	0.00%	-0.02%	-0.03%
24-May-00	0.31%	0.25%	0.21%	0.16%	0.12%	0.09%	0.07%	0.06%	0.05%	0.03%	0.01%	-0.01%	-0.03%	-0.04%	-0.05%	-0.07%	-0.08%
24-Nov-00	0.30%	0.27%	0.23%	0.19%	0.15%	0.11%	0.07%	0.06%	0.05%	0.03%	0.00%	-0.03%	-0.05%	-0.07%	-0.09%	-0.10%	-0.12%
24-May-01	0.31%	0.27%	0.23%	0.18%	0.13%	0.09%	0.05%	0.02%	0.00%	-0.03%	-0.06%	-0.08%	-0.11%	-0.12%	-0.13%	-0.14%	-0.15%
24-Nov-01	0.33%	0.29%	0.26%	0.19%	0.12%	0.08%	0.03%	-0.01%	-0.05%	-0.08%	-0.11%	-0.13%	-0.16%	-0.16%	-0.16%	-0.17%	-0.17%
24-May-02	0.37%	0.32%	0.27%	0.20%	0.13%	0.08%	0.03%	-0.02%	-0.07%	-0.10%	-0.12%	-0.14%	-0.17%	-0.17%	-0.17%	-0.17%	-0.17%
24-Nov-02	0.42%	0.36%	0.29%	0.21%	0.14%	0.08%	0.02%	-0.03%	-0.09%	-0.11%	-0.13%	-0.15%	-0.18%	-0.18%	-0.17%	-0.17%	-0.17%
24-May-03	0.42%	0.34%	0.27%	0.18%	0.10%	0.04%	-0.02%	-0.07%	-0.11%	-0.12%	-0.14%	-0.15%	-0.17%	-0.17%	-0.17%	-0.17%	-0.17%
24-Nov-03	0.39%	0.32%	0.24%	0.15%	0.06%	0.00%	-0.06%	-0.10%	-0.14%	-0.14%	-0.15%	-0.16%	-0.17%	-0.17%	-0.17%	-0.17%	-0.17%
24-May-04	0.37%	0.29%	0.21%	0.13%	0.05%	0.00%	-0.06%	-0.10%	-0.13%	-0.14%	-0.15%	-0.16%	-0.17%	-0.17%	-0.17%	-0.17%	-0.18%
24-Nov-04	0.34%	0.26%	0.18%	0.11%	0.05%	0.00%	-0.05%	-0.09%	-0.13%	-0.14%	-0.15%	-0.16%	-0.17%	-0.17%	-0.17%	-0.18%	-0.18%
24-May-05	0.32%	0.24%	0.15%	0.10%	0.05%	0.00%	-0.04%	-0.09%	-0.13%	-0.14%	-0.15%	-0.16%	-0.17%	-0.17%	-0.18%	-0.18%	-0.19%
24-Nov-05	0.30%	0.22%	0.13%	0.09%	0.05%	0.01%	-0.03%	-0.08%	-0.13%	-0.14%	-0.15%	-0.16%	-0.16%	-0.18%	-0.18%	-0.19%	-0.19%
24-May-06	0.28%	0.20%	0.13%	0.09%	0.06%	0.02%	-0.03%	-0.07%	-0.11%	-0.12%	-0.13%	-0.15%	-0.16%	-0.17%	-0.17%	-0.18%	-0.19%
24-Nov-06	0.25%	0.19%	0.12%	0.09%	0.06%	0.02%	-0.02%	-0.06%	-0.10%	-0.11%	-0.12%	-0.13%	-0.15%	-0.16%	-0.17%	-0.18%	-0.19%
24-May-07	0.22%	0.17%	0.12%	0.09%	0.06%	0.02%	-0.01%	-0.05%	-0.08%	-0.09%	-0.11%	-0.12%	-0.14%	-0.15%	-0.16%	-0.17%	-0.19%
24-Nov-07	0.20%	0.16%	0.11%	0.08%	0.05%	0.02%	-0.01%	-0.04%	-0.07%	-0.08%	-0.10%	-0.12%	-0.13%	-0.14%	-0.16%	-0.17%	-0.19%
24-May-08	0.17%	0.13%	0.09%	0.07%	0.04%	0.02%	-0.01%	-0.03%	-0.06%	-0.08%	-0.09%	-0.11%	-0.13%	-0.14%	-0.16%	-0.17%	-0.19%
24-Nov-08	0.12%	0.10%	0.07%	0.05%	0.03%	0.01%	-0.01%	-0.03%	-0.05%	-0.07%	-0.09%	-0.10%	-0.12%	-0.14%	-0.16%	-0.18%	-0.19%

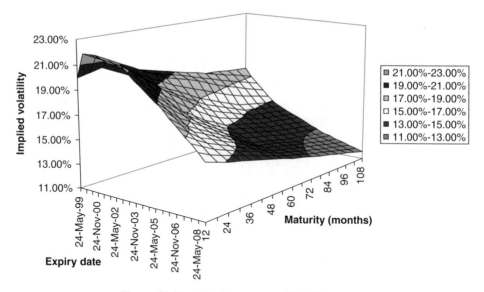

Figure 21.12   The data presented in Table 21.1.

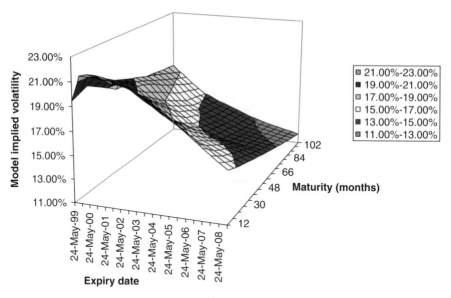

Figure 21.13   The data presented in Table 21.2.

In particular, Figures 21.14 and 21.15 show that the effect of moving from a flat to a time-dependent instantaneous volatility is very noticeable. It is also important to point out that one can empirically observe (see, for example, Rebonato (2002)) that allowing for a time-dependent volatility can have a stronger impact on the resulting swaption volatility matrix than varying (within reasonable limits) the instantaneous correlation. Therefore taking caplet and swaption prices together is a blunt instrument in order to pin down the

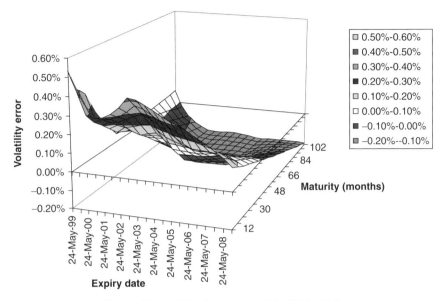

Figure 21.14 The data presented in Table 21.3.

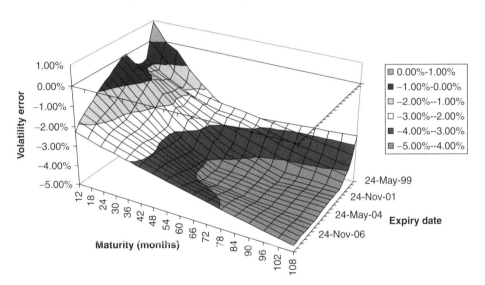

Figure 21.15 The difference between the market and model data obtained using the same correlation function used to produce Table 21.2 and Figure 21.14, but with time-independent volatilities for the forward rates. Note the different scale for the z-axis in Figures 21.14 and 21.15. See the discussion in the text.

correlation function (see also Sidenius (1999) and De Jong *et al.* (1999) who concur about this point). If the trader attempted this implied route to estimating the correlation between forward rates she would not only be faced with the usual problems of having to rely on the market's informational efficiency (see Section 1.4.3 of Chapter 1), but also with the specific problem that the dependence of the correlation on the liquid market instruments is relatively weak. This might prompt the trader to conclude that, if she had to choose between a one-factor model with realistic instantaneous volatilities, and a multi-factor approach with flat instantaneous volatilities, she would probably opt for the former. I would concur with this choice, but, at the same time, this conclusion should not make us conclude that 'correlation hardly matters at all': what appears to be the case for swaptions might not be the case at all for other exotic instruments,[2] and the 'neglected' correlation might turn out to be much more important for the pricing of a particular exotic instrument. The trader should always check, when pricing exotic products, whether the correlation impact is indeed as mild and benign as it appears to be in the case of swaptions.

Finally, the analysis of the model and market implied swaption volatility matrices clearly indicates that the swaption market (at least in all the major currencies) seems to trade strongly at odds with a flat-instantaneous-volatility assumption. See, for instance, Figure 21.14. This observation suggests that the market concurs with the analysis presented in the previous section, and implies a significant dependence of the instantaneous volatility functions on the residual time to maturity.

21.8   Conclusions

In this chapter I have highlighted the link between the (non-directly-observable) time dependence of the instantaneous volatility of forward rates and the evolution of today's (observable) term structure of volatilities. I have argued that this way of looking at option pricing is both powerful and helpful, and constitutes one of the strongest points in favour of the LMM approach.

I then proposed a specific separable functional form for the instantaneous volatility function. I have shown how the range of acceptable parameters characterizing this description can be narrowed down (if not really pinned down uniquely) by the joint requirements of a good fit to the swaption implied volatility function, and of an approximately time-stationary behaviour for the term structure of caplet volatilities. Statistical data can also supply useful indications by giving an idea of the most likely ranges for the various parameters. Furthermore, the functional form for the instantaneous volatility suggested in Section 21.2 has the advantage of allowing for a very transparent link between statistically- and market-accessible quantities, and some of the parameters.

I have also presented market examples from the swaption markets, and I have made the case that (within a range of 'reasonable' values) the instantaneous correlation plays a relatively minor role in determining the implied volatility of a swaption. I have therefore argued that this market does not provide a very accurate tool to discriminate between different possible functional forms or parameterizations for the correlation function. This does not mean, unfortunately, that instantaneous correlation 'does not matter' for any exotic instrument. The topic of how to choose a desirable correlation function is therefore tackled in the next chapter.

---

[2]The examples of flexi caps and of Total Accrual Redemption Notes (TARNs) spring to mind.

Chapter 22

Specifying the Instantaneous Correlation Among Forward Rates

22.1 Why Is Estimating Correlation So Difficult?

When we deal with same-currency interest rates we are in a regime of relatively high correlation among the state variables. This is just the situation where the time dependence of the instantaneous volatility has the strongest impact on terminal de-correlation (see, in this respect, the discussion in Chapter 5). It is easy to see why this is the case. If the instantaneous correlation among a set of variables is already close to zero, there is little further 'scrambling' that can be produced by time-dependent volatilities. However, if the instantaneous correlation is close to one, volatilities 'out of phase' with each other (i.e. one volatility being high when the other is low) can produce a significant decrease in terminal correlation.

So, the precise time behaviour of forward-rate volatilities can be very important in order to understand their terminal de-correlation. Speaking of the time dependence of the volatility *tout court* can however be rather delicate. This is because there are two distinct possible sources of time dependence for the volatility. One arises because the underlying phenomenon is intrinsically not time-homogeneous (the future is different from today). In a world without smiles, this is the informational content that one is tempted to draw from a stock-declining implied volatility. See, in this respect, the discussion in Chapter 3.[1] The second type of time dependence arises because, as time goes by, a certain asset or the associated rate changes its nature; for instance, its residual maturity decreases. This applies to bonds and forward rates. So, we can still have time homogeneity if the volatility depends on calendar time, as long as the dependence is of the form $f(T - t)$.

Why does this matter in the context of the estimation of interest-rate correlation from option prices? Because the terminal correlation, $\widehat{\rho}_{ij}(t, T)$, which, as we saw in Chapter 5,

---

[1] Recall, however, that one should always ask the questions: 'Is the market informationally efficient?' and 'Is it really trying to tell us something about future volatility, or is there a supply-and-demand effect at play?'.

one can more or less directly impute from observed market prices,

$$\widehat{\rho}_{ij}(t, T) = \frac{\int_{t}^{T} \sigma_i(u)\sigma_j(u)\rho_{ij}(u)\,du}{\sqrt{\int_{t}^{T} \sigma_i(u)^2\,du \int_{t}^{T} \sigma_j(u)^2\,du}} \tag{22.1}$$

(with $T \leq \min(T_i, T_j)$) depends both on the time dependence of the volatility and on the instantaneous correlation. Therefore, if we wanted to extract information about the correlation among forward rates from, say, swaption prices, this would only be possible if our assumption about the time dependence of the instantaneous volatility of the forward rates was correct. But, when dealing with same-currency forward and swap rates, we are just in the regime of relatively high *instantaneous* correlation alluded to above. In this regime the nature of the time dependence of the volatility can significantly affect the terminal de-correlation, and relatively small differences in the specification of the instantaneous volatility functions can have a big impact on the 'implied' correlation.

There are also more fundamental problems. Extracting the correlation among forward rates from swaption data implies a great faith in the joint informational efficiency of the caplet and swaption markets. I have expressed my doubts about this in Chapter 1, and therefore I will not repeat the argument here. See, however, Rebonato (2002) for a discussion of the systematic and similar biases observed in the instantaneous volatility curves distilled from caplet and swaption data in several currencies. Similar reservations are also expressed in Fan *et al.* (2003).

In view of the above, my first, and perhaps most important, message in modelling correlation is to keep the treatment simple and transparent. Above all, I believe that the trader should resist the temptation to use the $O(n^2)$ elements of a correlation matrix in order to recover 'at all costs' the market prices of swaptions.

22.2   What Shape Should We Expect for the Correlation Surface?

In a time-homogeneous world, the de-correlation between two forward rates depends on (at least) two quantities: how 'distant' (in expiry times) the two forward rates are; and the expiry of, say, the first of the two.[2] The dependence of the de-correlation on the first quantity is intuitively easy to guess: the farther apart the two forward rates are, the less we should expect them to move 'in step'. The second dependence is not so straightforward to guess a priori. On the one hand, it is reasonable to expect that the de-correlation between two forward rates expiring, say, in nine and 10 years' time should be smaller than the de-correlation between forward rates expiring in one and two years' time (despite the fact that the distance in expiries is the same). It is not obvious, however, whether this dependence of the rate of de-correlation on the expiry of the first forward rate should be monotonic. Should we take as a necessary desideratum for a 'good' model correlation function that the de-correlation between same-distance forward rates should be the stronger the shorter

---

[2]Needless to say, if the future looks different than the past, there would also be a separate dependence on calendar time.

the expiry of the first rate, *irrespective of how short this expiry might be*? Intuitively, this requirement makes sense, and, for instance, Schoenmakers and Coffey (2000) (see below) directly build this requirement into their construction of their correlation surface. The empirical evidence, however, is not so clear. I review in Rebonato (2002) some studies (e.g. Longstaff *et al.* (2000a)) that suggest that imposing this requirement might not be supported by market data. I therefore keep an open mind on the matter at this stage.

22.3 Features of the Simple Exponential Correlation Function

The simplest functional form for a correlation function is possibly the following:

$$\rho_{ij}(t) = \exp[-\beta|T_i - T_j|], \qquad t \leq \min(T_i, T_j) \tag{22.2}$$

with T_i and T_j the expiries of the ith and jth forward rates, and β a positive constant. Note that, at the risk of being pedantic, one should perhaps write

$$\rho_{ij}(t) = \exp\left[-\beta|(T_i - t) - (T_j - t)|\right] \tag{22.3}$$

which obviously is equivalent to (22.2). The full expression (22.3) will come in handy, however, when we deal with more general (non-linear) functions, g, of the residual time to expiry, of the form

$$\rho_{ij}(t) = \exp[-\beta|g(T_i - t) - g(T_j - t)|] \tag{22.4}$$

Equation (22.2) clearly satisfies the requirements of the first type of dependence: the farther apart two forward rates are, the more de-correlated they are. Furthermore, for any positive β one can rest assured that the corresponding matrix ρ will always be an admissible correlation matrix (i.e. a real, symmetric matrix with positive eigenvalues). What expression (22.2) does not handle well is the second desideratum: two forward rates, separated by the same 'distance', $T_i - T_j$, will de-correlate just as much irrespective of whether the first forward rate expires in three months or 30 years. See Figure 22.1.

This financially undesirable feature is directly reflected in the absence of an explicit time dependence in Equation (22.2). The financial blemish, however, has a desirable computational effect: in the LIBOR market model, in fact, the central quantities that drive both the deterministic and the stochastic parts of the evolution are the covariance elements

$$C(i, j, k) = \int_{T_k}^{T_{k+1}} \sigma_i(u)\sigma_j(u)\rho_{ij}(u) \, du \tag{22.5}$$

If the correlation function ρ_{ij} is of the form (22.2), however, the absence of an explicit time dependence allows one to write

$$C(i, j, k) = \rho_{ij} \int_{T_k}^{T_{k+1}} \sigma_i(u)\sigma_j(u) \, du \tag{22.6}$$

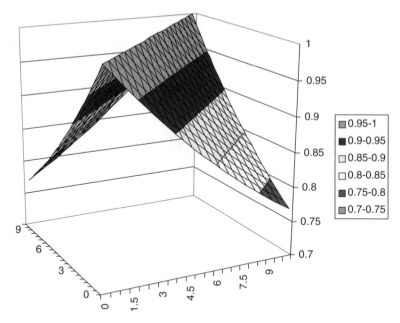

Figure 22.1 The correlation surface in the case of the simple exponential function (Equation (22.2)).

and, with the functional forms for the instantaneous volatility discussed in Chapter 21, the integral (22.6) can be pre-calculated analytically, thereby lightening the computational burden. This advantage is not crucial and, by itself, would not justify the use of a crude correlation function, if this had a seriously negative pricing impact. However, I show later in this chapter that, as long as the 'same degree of de-correlation is, on average, correctly recovered, the details of the shape of the correlation function are relatively unimportant. Therefore, one does not have to pay too high a price for simplicity and ease of computation. Furthermore, Joshi (2001), (unpublished result, quoted in Rebonato (2002)), argues that the functional form (22.2) is more general and less *ad hoc* than one might at first surmise. Joshi in fact shows the following. Take a very simple yield curve described by three forward rates. If

- the correlation function between the forward rates is of the form

$$\rho = \rho(|T_i - T_j|) \tag{22.7}$$

and

- the part of the responsiveness to shocks of forward rate f_1 that is uncorrelated with the responsiveness of f_2 is also uncorrelated with changes in f_3, then the correlation function must be of the form

$$\rho(T_i - T_j) = \exp(-\beta|T_i - T_j|) \tag{22.8}$$

where β is a *constant*. Rebonato (2002) discusses an extension of this simple example.

Finally, a very simple and very useful generalization of the functional form (22.2) can always be used at 'no extra cost': we can easily impose that the asymptotic de-correlation among forward rates should not go asymptotically to zero with increasing 'distance', but to some finite level, *LongCorr*, simply by rewriting Equation (22.2) in the form

$$\rho_{ij}(t) = LongCorr + (1 - LongCorr)\exp[-\beta|T_i - T_j|] \qquad (22.9)$$

Also, in this case the matrix is always real, symmetric and has positive eigenvalues (and therefore it is a possible correlation matrix). This extension is so simple and so useful that in what follows I will implicitly assume that it is always carried out, also for the more complex forms presented below.

22.4 Features of the Modified Exponential Correlation Function

In order to obviate the shortcomings of the simple exponential functional form (22.2) I have suggested elsewhere (Rebonato (1999c)) the simple modification

$$\rho_{ij}(t) = \exp[-\beta_{\min(T_i,T_j)}|T_i - T_j|] \qquad (22.10)$$

with $\beta_{\min(T_i,T_j)}$ no longer a constant, but a function of the expiry of the earliest-expiring forward rate. If the function were chosen to produce a decay constant that became smaller and smaller as the first expiry decreased, the second requirement of a desirable correlation function would be fulfilled automatically. However, as Schoenmakers and Coffey (2000) have correctly pointed out, for an arbitrary function $\beta_{\min(T_i,T_j)}$ it cannot be guaranteed that all the eigenvectors of the associated matrix ρ will be positive (in the first edition of this book I had chosen a polynomial dependence on $\min(T_i, T_j)$ for the function $\beta_{\min(T_i,T_j)}$). When this happens, the resulting matrix ρ may fail to represent a possible correlation matrix.

Fortunately, this problem can be easily fixed, because, if one chooses

$$\beta\min(T_i, T_j) = \beta_0 \exp[-\gamma\min(T_i, T_j)] \qquad (22.11)$$

one can show that the eigenvalues of ρ_{ij}, now defined by

$$\rho_{ij}(t) = \exp\{-\beta_0\exp[-\gamma\min(T_i, T_j)]|T_i - T_j|\} \qquad (22.12)$$

are always all positive. Furthermore, expression (22.12) preserves the computationally desirable feature of not having an explicit dependence on time, t. Therefore, also in this case the correlation function can be 'pulled out' of the covariance integral, making its analytic evaluation possible. The shape of the modified exponential correlation function is displayed in Figure 22.2.

Let us compare the qualitative behaviours of the modified exponential and of the simple exponential correlation functions. To carry out the comparison in a meaningful way, let

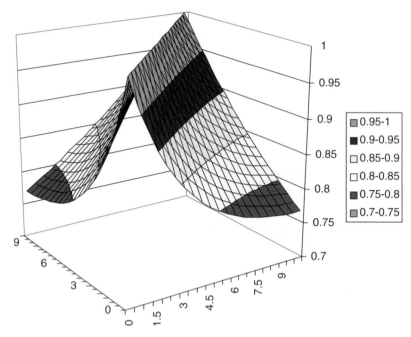

Figure 22.2 The correlation surface in the case of the modified exponential function (Equation (22.12)).

us choose a combination for the decay constants β_0 and γ in such a way that the de-correlation between the forward rate expiring in 10 years' time (the 'last' forward rate) and the forward rate expiring an infinitesimal time, ϵ, after today (the 'first' forward rate) has the same value as in the simple exponential model:

$$\rho_{\epsilon,10} = \exp[-\beta|10 - \epsilon|] = \exp\{-\beta_0 \exp[-\gamma \min(\epsilon, 10)]|\epsilon - 10|\} \qquad (22.13)$$

When this is done, the characterizing features of the modified exponential model are found to be the following.

- The modified exponential model displays a de-correlation between the last forward rate and all the others identical to the one displayed by the simple exponential (this is because of the enforcement of condition (22.13)).

- The de-correlation between the first and the second, third, etc. forward rates produced by the modified exponential model is more pronounced than for the simple model. Since we have required that the de-correlation between the first and the last forward rates should be the same in both cases, this means that the *rate of de-correlation* between the first and later forward rates will decrease significantly as the maturity of the second forward rate increases.

The differences between the simple and the modified exponential correlation surfaces are shown in Figures 22.3 and 22.4.

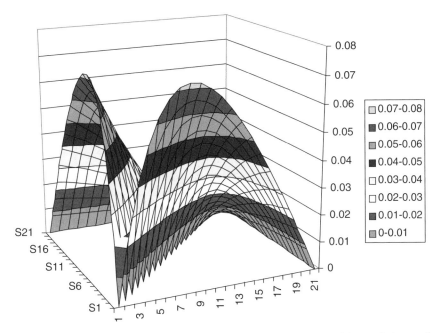

Figure 22.3 Differences between the simple and the modified exponential correlation surfaces.

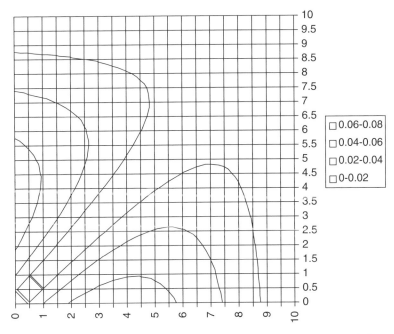

Figure 22.4 Differences between the simple and the modified exponential correlation surfaces.

22.5   Features of the Square-Root Exponential Correlation Function

The third functional form for the correlation function we are going to explore is the following:

$$\rho_{ij}(t) = \exp\left[-\widehat{\beta}|\sqrt{(T_i - t)} - \sqrt{(T_j - t)}|\right] \tag{22.14}$$

The first observation is that when this correlation function appears in the covariance element (22.5) it is no longer possible to take the correlation 'out of the integral'. Depending on the choice of volatility function, it is therefore very likely that no analytic expression can be found for (22.5). So, in order to justify the added complexity we would want some financially – or econometrically – important advantage as a compensation. The shape of the square-root correlation function is shown in Figure 22.5.

In order to understand the behaviour of the square-root model, let us choose again the decay constant $\widehat{\beta}$ in such a way that the de-correlation between the first (front) and the last (10-year) forward rates is the same as in the simple exponential case:

$$\rho_{\epsilon,10} = \exp[-\beta|10 - \epsilon|] = \exp\left[-\widehat{\beta}|\sqrt{(\epsilon - t)} - \sqrt{(10 - t)}|\right], \quad t \le \epsilon \tag{22.15}$$

When this is done the distinguishing features of the square-root model are the following.

1. The de-correlation of the first forward rate with all the others follows a similar pattern as the de-correlation produced by the modified exponential model: a high

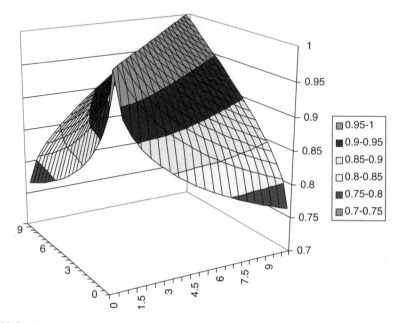

Figure 22.5   The correlation surface in the case of the square-root function (Equation (22.14)).

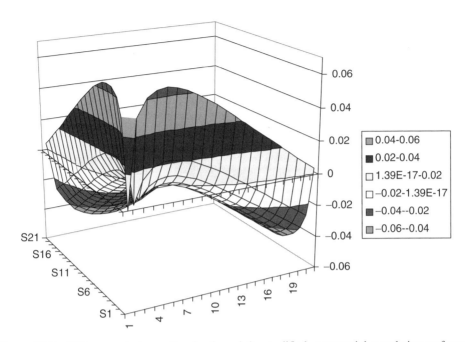

Figure 22.6   Differences between the simple and the modified exponential correlation surfaces.

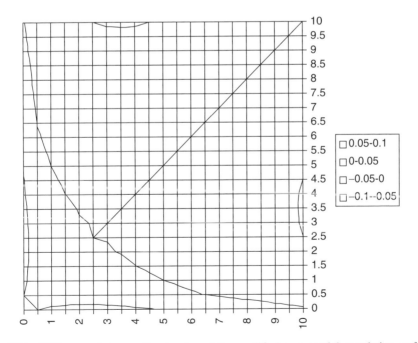

Figure 22.7   Differences between the simple and the modified exponential correlation surfaces.

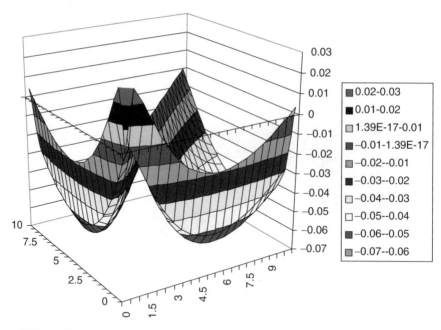

Figure 22.8   Differences between the square-root and the square-root exponential correlation surfaces.

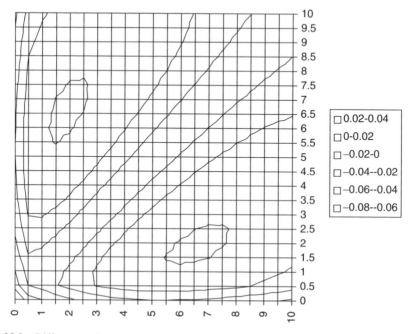

Figure 22.9   Differences between the square-root and the square-root exponential correlation surfaces.

rate of de-correlation between the first and the front forward rates, and a low rate of de-correlation between the first and the last forward rates. In this respect the square-root model 'buys' us relatively little with respect to the modified exponential model.

2. For the square-root model the correlation between the last and the first forward rate is, by construction, the same as in the simple or modified exponential cases (see Equations (22.15) and (22.13)). The correlation between the last and the second forward rate, however, is considerably higher for the square-root approach than what is implied by the simple and modified exponential cases. Similarly for the third, fourth and the other forward rates at the front of the yield curve. In other words, the square-root model says that long-end forwards are more strongly correlated than the other models predict with all the long-dated forward rates, and less so with the front ones. As a result of this, a different concavity is produced for the correlation surface.

The differences between the simple and the square-root correlation surfaces are shown in Figures 22.6 and 22.7; the differences between the square-root and the modified exponential correlation surfaces are shown in Figures 22.8 and 22.9.

22.6 Further Comparisons of Correlation Models

Another way to understand the salient features of the different approaches is to observe that both the square-root and the modified exponential models imply a strong de-correlation between the first and the second, third, etc. forward rates; however, in the square-root model these relatively-early-expiring forward rates quickly become linked to the dynamics of the last forward rates, while in the modified exponential model they remain de-coupled both from the front and from the end. We would therefore expect that, by matching the de-correlation between the first and the last forward rate, the overall correlation between all the forward rates should be greater in the square-root model. In particular, the first eigenvalue should be higher for the square-root correlation than for the simple or modified exponential one. This is indeed found to be the case, and the same feature is shown in a more direct manner in Figures 22.8 and 22.9.

The comparisons carried out in the previous three sections could have been performed differently: for instance, rather than matching the de-correlation between the first and the 10-year forward rate across models, the average degree of correlation could have been matched. The qualitative features described above would not have changed significantly, although the prices of correlation-dependent products in general would. For a given instantaneous volatility function, for instance, swaption prices depend to first order (albeit mildly) on the average de-correlation, rather than on the detail shape of the correlation function (see, for example, De Jong *et al.* (1999) and Rebonato (2002)).

22.7 Features of the Schoenmakers–Coffey Approach

One should mention an interesting approach suggested by Schoenmakers and Coffey, which they call semi-parametric. The reader is referred to Schoenmakers and Coffey (2000) for details and to Rebonato (2002) for a discussion, but the salient features are the following. Given n forward rates, consider a series of coefficients $\{d_i\}$, $i = 1, 2, \ldots, n$, such that

$$d_1 = 1 \tag{22.16}$$

$$d_i > d_j, \qquad \text{for } i > j \tag{22.17}$$

$$\frac{d_i}{d_{i+1}} > \frac{d_j}{d_{j+1}}, \qquad \text{for } j > i \tag{22.18}$$

One can then show that from any such sequence one can construct a possible correlation matrix. Furthermore, these conditions can be used directly to ensure that the de-correlation between same-distance forward rates should decrease with the expiry of the first rate (i.e. that the function $\rho_{i,i+p}$ should be an increasing function of i for a fixed p).

By Equations (22.16) to (22.18) one has obtained a description of an $O(n^2)$ quantity (the correlation matrix) in terms of n numbers. Schoenmakers and Coffey reduce the number of degrees of freedom further by assigning a parametric form to the function d (seen as a function of the index, i). For this reason they call their approach *semi-parametric*. The approach is interesting, and the feature that the function $\rho_{i,i+p}$ should be an increasing function of i for a fixed p is built into (actually, motivates) the model. Much as this assumption appears plausible, recent empirical work has cast some doubts on its validity.

22.8 Does It Make a Difference (and When)?

If one displays a correlation surface graphically, the differences between different approaches can appear striking. However, I have mentioned above some results that suggest that, as long as the average de-correlation produced is the same, the pricing impact is in general rather limited. To understand why this is the case recall that the dynamics of the forward rates can be written in the form

$$\frac{df_i}{f_i} = \mu_i(\{f\}, t)\, dt + \sigma_i \sum_{k=1,m} b_{ik}\, dz_k, \qquad i = 1, 2, \ldots, n \tag{22.19}$$

In Equation (22.19), n is the number of forward rates, $m \le n$ is the number of factors and the $[n \times m]$ matrix $\mathbf{b}$ of elements b_{jk} is linked to the correlation matrix by

$$\mathbf{b}\mathbf{b}^{\mathrm{T}} = \rho \tag{22.20}$$

i.e. it is the pseudo-square root of the correlation matrix. This expression is very useful because it establishes a link between the correlation matrix and the loadings, b_{ik}, of the different orthogonal drivers, dz_k, onto the forward rates. We can try to understand what the different shapes of the correlation matrix imply for these loadings. We will do so by looking at the vectors, b_{ik}, as obtained by orthogonalizing the correlation matrix obtained with different choices of correlation functions. Perhaps we will find that a given correlation shape produces different shapes for the eigenvectors (hence different loadings

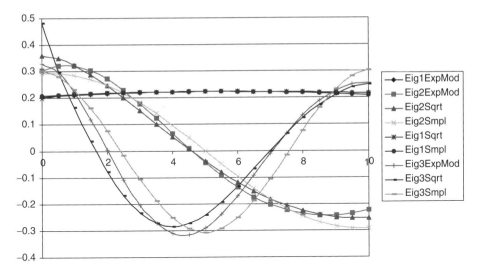

Figure 22.10   The first three eigenvectors for the three correlation models discussed in the text.

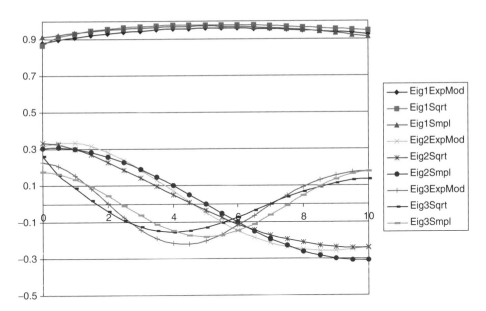

Figure 22.11   The first three eigenvectors multiplied by the square root of the associated eigenvalues for the three correlation models discussed in the text.

onto the forward rates), or that the eigenvalues have different relative magnitudes (and
therefore that different modes of deformation have a different relative importance). This
might give us a more 'financial' insight as to the characteristics of different correlation
functions.

If we are only interested in the relevance of the shape of the correlation function, we
should run this test in such a way that some measure of 'average de-correlation' is kept

Table 22.1   The first three eigenvalues for the three correlation models discussed in the text.

	ModExp	Sqrt	SimpleExp
Eig1	18.56674	19.32929	19.0076561
Eig2	1.103786	0.87525	1.10266989
Eig3	0.479937	0.29536	0.34332555

constant. In order to keep things simple I have imposed again the constraint that, for the different correlation functions discussed below, the de-correlation out to a given fixed maturity should be kept constant.

When a comparison among the eigenvectors and eigenvalues is carried out, one actually finds that, as long as the same de-correlation between the first and the 10-year forward rates is kept constant, the differences among the various modelling approaches are very small, and, by inspection, there is very little to choose between them. See Figures 22.10 and 22.11: some small qualitative differences are beginning to creep in with the third eigenmode (note, for instance, the loading onto the first forward rate), but the associated eigenvalue is between 40 and 60 times smaller than the first. See Table 22.1.

Looking at these figures it comes as little surprise that, in general, different shapes for the correlation matrix, even when visually quite different, should give rise to rather modest pricing effects. Products do exist for which these small differences can produce significantly different prices, but these are the exception rather than the norm. One such rare case is resettable caps, for which the strike of the ith caplet is equal (or, more generally, linked) to the reset of the $(i - 1)$th forward rate. It is easy to see that, in this particular case, the ability of two contiguous forward rates to de-correlate *in the last portions of their lives* can make a significant pricing difference. But, again, this is the exception rather than the rule.

These considerations suggest that the modelling of the correlation function can, and perhaps should, be kept relatively simple. Therefore, in light of the considerations expressed in Section 22.1, I do not recommend using too many fitting parameters for the correlation function, and any of the approaches above, which require two or at most three parameters, are adequate for most applications.

Part IV

Interest Rates – Smiles

Chapter 23

How to Model Interest-Rate Smiles

23.1 What Do We Want to Capture? A Hierarchy of Smile-Producing Mechanisms

In keeping with the philosophy that informs this book, I will start with a discussion of the financial mechanisms that might give rise to smiles in the interest-rate area. The most salient empirical features of interest-rate smiles have been reviewed in Chapter 7. Subtler empirical aspects are discussed in several chapters of Part IV, including this one. By combining these empirical findings with the theoretical properties of different models, I will argue that, in order to account for smiles in a satisfactory manner, one should capture three financially distinct components of the volatility of forward rates:

1. a very strong correlation (almost a functional dependence) between the percentage volatility and the underlying;

2. the tendency of the volatility to switch between regimes;

3. a further diffusive behaviour of the volatility *within each regime*.

More precisely, I will make the point that, because of the strong dependence of the percentage volatility on the level of the underlying rates, it is advisable first to carry out a change of variables that removes this dominant component. Once this simple transformation away from the log-normal description of the forward rates has been carried out, the evolution of the forward rates is (almost) uncorrelated with the dynamics of the volatility.

I will then argue that the switching between well-defined (and financially justifiable) volatility regimes can explain a large part of the observed smiles, even when as few as two 'free parameters' are used in the fitting.

Finally, an additional diffusive behaviour for the volatility of the transformed variables provides the most important residual missing ingredient for a satisfactory description of the stochastic behaviour of the forward-rate volatility.

If this analysis is correct, one can conclude that capturing component 1 is the most important modelling feature, and that 2 might be as, if not more, important than 3. This chapter and the following will deal with part 1 of this programme.

23.2   Are Log-Normal Co-Ordinates the Most Appropriate?

In this chapter I discuss both empirical and theoretical results about swaption implied volatilities (see also Rebonato (2003a)).[1] The theoretical analysis is based on some properties of CEV processes. These are discussed in some detail in the next chapter. For the moment I simply make use of the well-known observation that CEV models of the form

$$\mathrm{d}x = \mu \, \mathrm{d}t + x^{\beta}\sigma_{\beta} \, \mathrm{d}w \qquad (23.1)$$

produce call prices whose implied volatilities display, *as function of strike*, an inverse power-law behaviour. However, it is not obvious what behaviour for the implied volatility *as a function of the underlying* these CEV model predicts. The first (theoretical) question that I address is therefore: what behaviour for the at-the-money implied volatility as a function of an instantaneous change in the underlying *would* be generated by a CEV process for the underlying? I then move to the complementary (empirical) question: given this information about the CEV-induced implied volatility dynamics, *could* the empirically observed behaviour of the implied volatilities as a function of changes in the underlying swap rates be explained by a CEV process?

Let me put the relevance of these questions into perspective. First of all, if the underlying followed a geometric diffusion with constant or time-dependent volatility, inverting same-maturity prices to obtain an implied volatility would always give, by definition, the same value for the implied volatility. Furthermore, if we lived in a log-normal world, as the underlying moves, the price of an at-the-money call would exactly scale as the ratio of the old to the new level of the swap rate. This immediately follows because of the homogeneity of degree one of the Black formula.[2] If we live in a CEV world, this is no longer true. To begin with, the implied volatility as a function of strike is not flat. Therefore, if we assume that the process for the at-the-money forward swap rate is given by an equation such as (23.1), the percentage implied volatility (which is obtained by inverting the now 'inappropriate' Black formula) will in general not remain the same across strikes. In addition, a change in the level of the underlying causes a change in the at-the-money call price that does not scale in a proportional fashion.

With these considerations in mind, the theoretical questions in the first paragraph of this section can be rephrased more precisely as follows:

- if we observe today's at-the-money implied volatility and swap rate to be σ_0^{ATM} and SR_0, respectively, and the process for the swap rate is of the CEV type with an exponent β, can we say that tomorrow's implied volatility, $\sigma_{\mathrm{ATM}}(SR)$, when the

---

[1]Parts of this chapter have been adapted from Rebonato (2003a).

[2]Saying that a function, $f(x)$, is homogeneous of degree one in x means that $f(kx) = kf(x)$, with k a constant. More generally, a function $f(x)$ is said to be homogeneous of degree n in x if $f(kx) = x^n f(x)$.

swap rate has moved to level *SR*, is given by

$$\sigma_{\text{ATM}}(SR) = \sigma_0^{\text{ATM}} \left(\frac{SR}{SR_0} \right)^{\gamma} \tag{23.2}$$

for some exponent γ?

- If this is the case, how are the exponents γ and β related?

As for the empirical questions addressed in this chapter, they can be formulated as follows.

- Is there is a correlation between changes in the level of forward rates and changes in the implied volatility?

- If such a correlation exists, is there a transformation (a change of co-ordinates) that can be applied to the forward rates, such that this correlation disappears?

- Would a log-linear regression between changes in the underlying forward rates and changes in implied volatility be statistically significant in accounting for the empirical data?

- How is the slope from this log-linear regression linked to the exponent that gives zero correlation between the changes in implied volatilities and the power-law-transformed underlying forward rates?

Before tackling these issues, let me define precisely in the next sub-section what I mean by 'appropriate co-ordinates'.

23.2.1 Defining Appropriate Co-ordinates

Ideally, one would like to be able to find some function, f, of the state variable x, such that the volatility of f, σ_f, would not display any dependence on x itself. The transformation from x to $f(x)$ can be seen as a change of co-ordinates. In terms of these transformed co-ordinates, one would like to be able to express the SDE for f in the form

$$df(x) = \sigma_f(t) \, dz \tag{23.3}$$

with $\sigma_f(t)$ a deterministic function of time. In a log-normal (Black) world the function f is clearly

$$f(x) = \ln(x) \tag{23.4}$$

because we know that

$$d \ln x = -\tfrac{1}{2}\sigma_f(t)^2 \, dt + \sigma_f(t) \, dz \tag{23.5}$$

Similarly, if the process for x was a normal diffusion, the function would simply be

$$f(x) = x \tag{23.6}$$

Consider now the case when the function $f(x)$ is $f(x) = x^\xi$. Then

$$\mathrm{d}f = \mathrm{d}(x^\xi) = \xi x^{\xi-1}\,\mathrm{d}x \qquad (23.7)$$

If we want this transformation to be the right change of co-ordinates then it must be the case that

$$\mathrm{d}f(x) = \mathrm{d}(x^\xi) = \sigma_f(t)\,\mathrm{d}z \qquad (23.8)$$

From (23.7) it follows that

$$\xi x^{\xi-1}\,\mathrm{d}x = \sigma_f(t)\,\mathrm{d}z$$

Therefore

$$\mathrm{d}x = \frac{\sigma_f(t)}{\xi}x^{1-\xi}\,\mathrm{d}z \qquad (23.9)$$

and, by setting

$$\frac{\sigma_f(t)}{\xi} = \sigma_\beta \qquad (23.10)$$

$$1 - \xi = \beta \qquad (23.11)$$

one can see that the change of co-ordinates from x to $f(x) = x^\xi$ is appropriate if the process for x was a CEV diffusion with exponent $\beta = 1-\xi$ (at least as long as $\xi < 1$ – see below).

23.3   Description of the Market Data

The market data used for the study presented in this chapter consist of time series of daily at-the-money swaption implied volatilities and of the associated at-the-money forward swap rates. (USD, period 5-Jun-1998/22-Nov-2002 for a total of 1166 days.) The data are particularly significant because they span the turbulent period of the Russia/LTCM crisis. The swaptions and swap rates analysed belonged to the $n \times m$ series,[3] with $n = 1, 3, 5$, and $m = 1, 3, 5, 10$. Figure 23.1 displays the time series of the volatilities. Figure 23.2 shows the time series of one particular swap rate and of the associated percentage swaption volatility (1×1). Figures 23.3–23.14 display the scatter plots of the implied volatilities and of the swap rates for the various available combinations of option expiries and underlying swap lengths.

---

[3] The $n \times m$ swaption is the option to enter in n years' time a swap with m years of residual maturity.

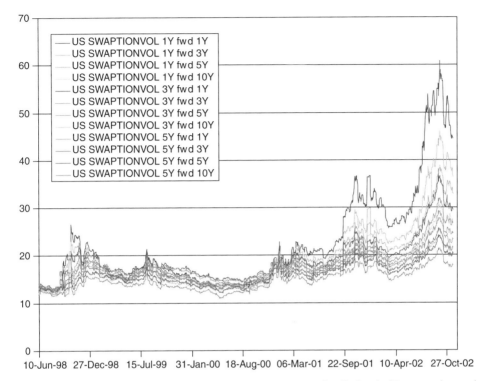

Figure 23.1 Time series of different at-the-money percentage-implied-volatility swaption series (USD market). Note how the shortest-maturity, shortest-expiry (1 × 1) series (top line) reaches 60% in 2002.

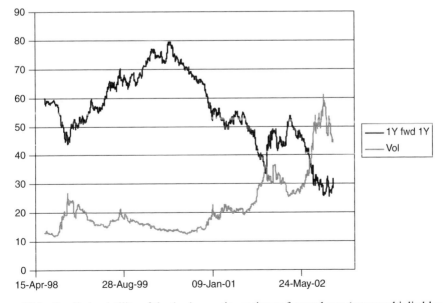

Figure 23.2 Implied volatility of the 1 × 1 swaption series vs forward rate (rates multiplied by 10).

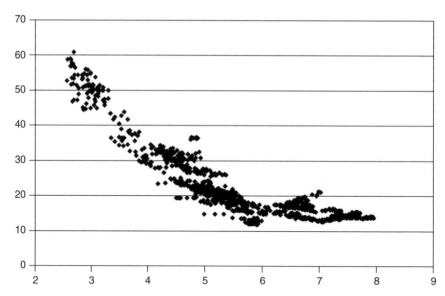

Figure 23.3   Scatter plot of implied volatilities and swap rates (1 × 1 swaption series).

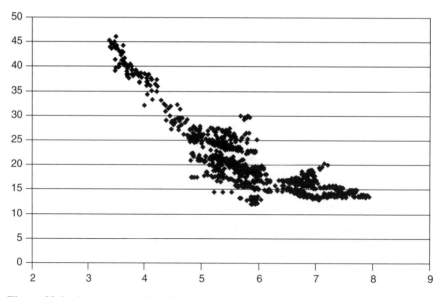

Figure 23.4   Scatter plot of implied volatilities and swap rates (1 × 3 swaption series).

Figures 23.15, 23.16 and 23.17 show again the scatter plots of selected implied volatilities vs the corresponding swap rate levels. The points, however, are now displayed with
a chronological link by joining with a continuous line the realizations corresponding to
consecutive business days. The features displayed by these three graphs are discussed
in more detail at the end of the chapter (Section 23.8) and in Chapter 27. Already at
this stage, however, one can say that the points in the scatter plot appear clustered into

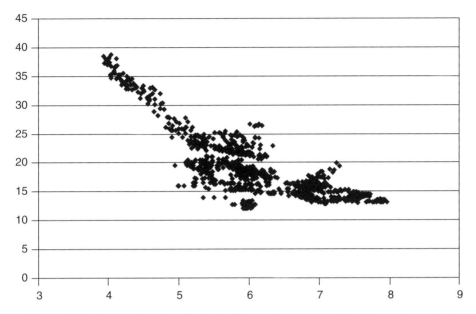

Figure 23.5 Scatter plot of implied volatilities and swap rates (1 × 5 swaption series).

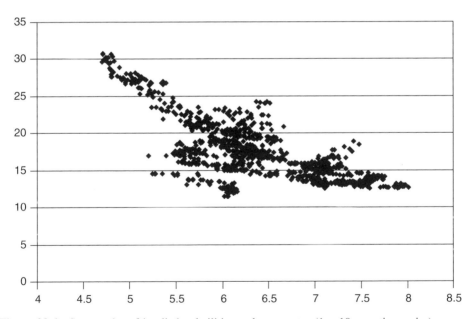

Figure 23.6 Scatter plot of implied volatilities and swap rates (1 × 10 swaption series).

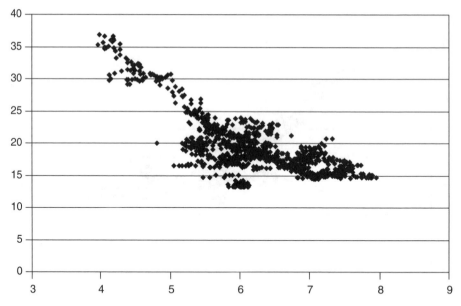

Figure 23.7   Scatter plot of implied volatilities and swap rates (3 × 1 swaption series).

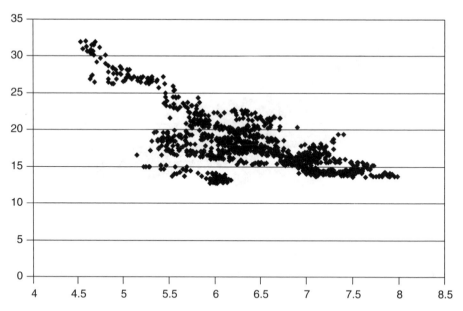

Figure 23.8   Scatter plot of implied volatilities and swap rates (3 × 3 swaption series).

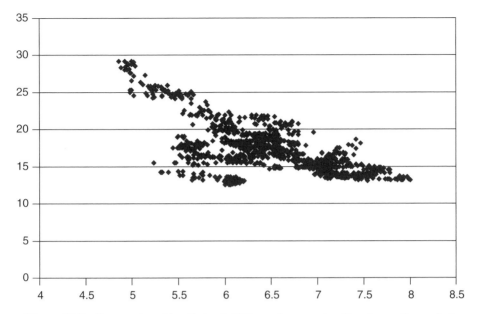

Figure 23.9 Scatter plot of implied volatilities and swap rates (3×5 swaption series).

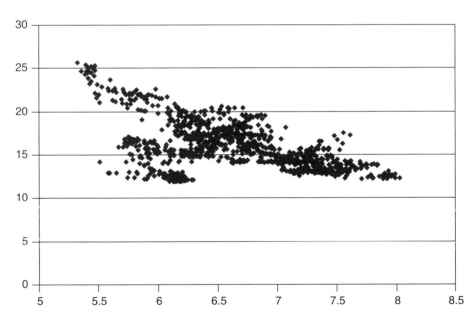

Figure 23.10 Scatter plot of implied volatilities and swap rates (3×10 swaption series).

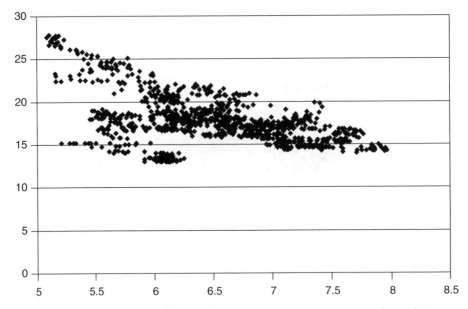

Figure 23.11   Scatter plot of implied volatilities and swap rates (5 × 1 swaption series).

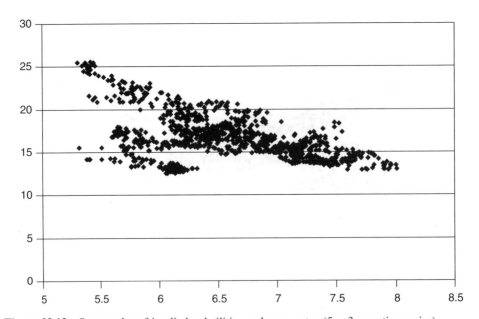

Figure 23.12   Scatter plot of implied volatilities and swap rates (5 × 3 swaption series).

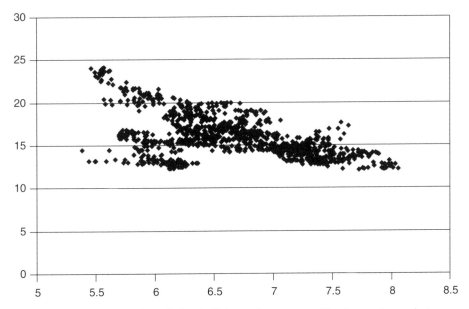

Figure 23.13   Scatter plot of implied volatilities and swap rates (5 × 5 swaption series).

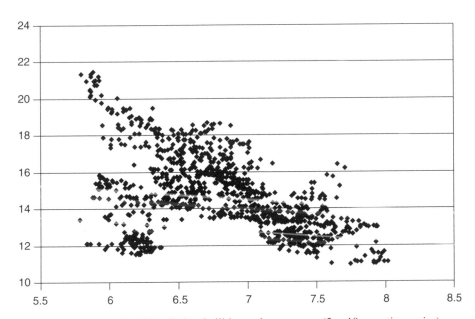

Figure 23.14   Scatter plot of implied volatilities and swap rates (5 × 10 swaption series).

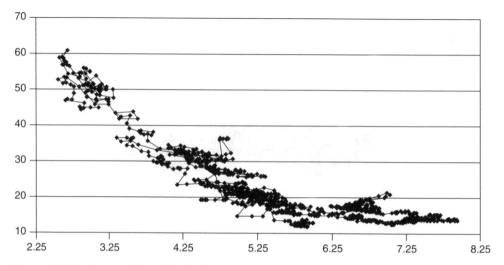

Figure 23.15 Scatter plot of implied volatilities and swap rates (1 × 1 swaption series). The realizations corresponding to consecutive business days are linked by a continuous line.

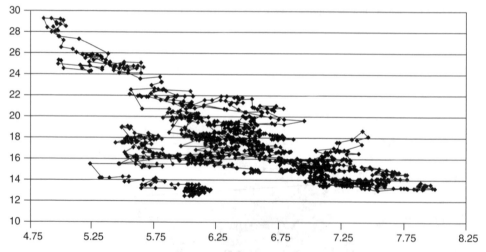

Figure 23.16 Scatter plot of implied volatilities and swap rates (3 × 5 swaption series). The realizations corresponding to consecutive business days are linked by a continuous line.

subdomains within which an inverse power-law behaviour appears to prevail (although, possibly, with a different exponent). Even more interesting is that these clusters appear to be arrived at via a single entry or exit point. This would seem to indicate the existence of distinct implied volatility regimes, with sudden switches between one regime and the other.

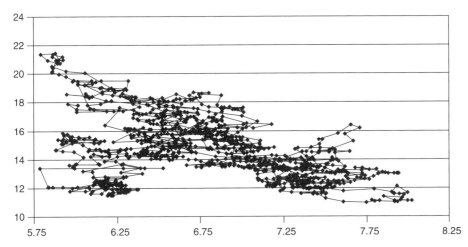

Figure 23.17 Scatter plot of implied volatilities and swap rates (5 × 10 swaption series). The realizations corresponding to consecutive business days are linked by a continuous line.

23.4 Empirical Study I: Transforming the Log-Normal Co-ordinates

From the scatter plots and the time series presented above it is clear that a large part of the variability in the implied volatility can be described by a functional dependence of the implied volatility on the level of the at-the-money swap rate. If one wanted to make use of a stochastic-volatility model for the evolution of the term structure it is therefore essential that a mechanism first be provided capable of producing a similar degree of deterministic dependence of the implied volatilities on the level of yield curve. This is indeed the rationale behind the modelling approach presented in Chapter 25. See also Joshi and Rebonato (2003), Rebonato and Joshi (2002), and Andersen and Andreasen (2000). All these modelling approaches specify the dynamics of the *instantaneous* volatility. The figures presented above refer, however, to *implied* volatilities. One must therefore verify that the implicit conjecture that a similar behaviour will be observed for the implied volatilities is indeed correct. In order to explore this, for each scatter plot the quantity

$$y(\alpha) = \sigma_{\text{impl}} SR^\alpha \tag{23.12}$$

was constructed. When the exponent α is equal to 0, the variable $y(\alpha)$ is simply equal to the percentage volatility. When it is equal to 1 we are dealing with an absolute volatility. Table 23.1 shows the empirical correlation coefficient between the market-quoted percentage implied volatilities ($\alpha = 0$) and the swap rates. More generally, for any choice of α we will find a different degree of correlation between $y(\alpha)$ and SR. The exponent α can therefore be varied until it gives rise to a zero correlation between $y(\alpha)$ and SR. Table 23.2 displays the exponent required to give zero correlation.

This rescaling is intrinsically interesting because it shows that a more 'natural' choice of co-ordinates can radically change one's conclusions about a particular period being 'volatile' or 'quiet'. Let us look, for instance, at the implied volatility for the 1 × 1

Table 23.1   The exponent required to produce a zero correlation between the implied volatilities and the swap rates for the various swaption series. The column on the right displays the average exponent for the 1×, 3×, and 5× series.

1 × 1	*1.37*	1× series	1.41
1 × 3	*1.44*		
1 × 5	*1.45*		
1 × 10	*1.37*		
3 × 1	*1.12*	3× series	1.12
3 × 3	*1.17*		
3 × 5	*1.14*		
3 × 10	*1.06*		
5 × 1	*0.80*	5× series	0.87
5 × 3	*0.88*		
5 × 5	*0.88*		
5 × 10	*0.91*		

Table 23.2   Empirical correlation coefficient between the implied volatilities and the swap rates. The column on the right displays the average exponent for the 1×, 3×, and 5× series.

1 × 1	*−0.86*	1× series	−0.80
1 × 3	*−0.83*		
1 × 5	*−0.79*		
1 × 10	*−0.70*		
3 × 1	*−0.73*	3× series	−0.65
3 × 3	*−0.68*		
3 × 5	*−0.63*		
3 × 10	*−0.54*		
5 × 1	*−0.51*	5× series	−0.51
5 × 3	*−0.53*		
5 × 5	*−0.51*		
5 × 10	*−0.47*		

series during the period leading to October 2002. See Figure 23.1. This figure assumes that the *percentage* volatility is the appropriate quantity to track, and that therefore log-normal co-ordinates are the appropriate ones. On the basis of this assumption, and looking at the time series depicted in Figure 23.1, one would conclude that the period under consideration has witnessed an exceptionally high level of uncertainty in rates (much higher than what was experienced during the Russia crisis). The picture becomes radically different if one changes co-ordinates and looks at the 'rescaled volatility' $y(\alpha) = \sigma_{impl} S^{\alpha}$ (with α chosen as in Table 23.2). See Figure 23.18. The same message is conveyed

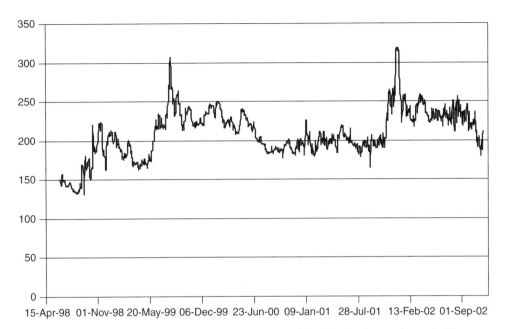

Figure 23.18   Time series of the quantity $y(\alpha) = \sigma_{\text{impl}} S^{\alpha}$ for the 1×1 swaption volatility.

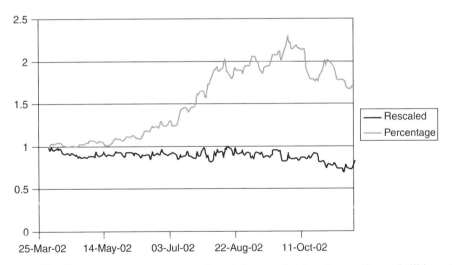

Figure 23.19   The percentage (upper curve) and the rescaled 1×1 swaption volatilities, after rescaling to 1 at the beginning of the period.

with even greater clarity by Figure 23.19, where both the percentage and the rescaled volatilities are shown over the same period, after rebasing each for ease of comparison to the value of 1 at the beginning of the period. The quantity y displays a much more regular behaviour, and actually *declines* over the same period during which the implied volatility reaches unprecedented heights. (During the same period the swap rate attained similarly exceptionally low values – see again Figure 23.2.)

These empirical findings motivate the question of whether, and to what extent, the quantity y, which refers to *implied* volatilities, is related to the *instantaneous* volatility of a CEV process. Answering this question would provide a useful piece of information in the modelling of interest rates. This is accomplished in the next section.

23.5   The Computational Experiments

It might be possible, but it is certainly not straightforward, to answer the question formulated at the end of Section 23.4 by following a semi-analytic route. The difficulty stems from the fact that the concept of implied volatility is totally based on a log-normal co-ordinate system that becomes analytically cumbersome as soon as one leaves the Black setting (the implied volatility simply becomes 'the wrong number to put in the wrong formula to get the right price'). I therefore follow a computational approach.

I start by assuming that the 'true' process for the underlying (the swap rate) is indeed of the form (23.1). For simplicity, I choose to carry out the valuation of a payer swaption (call on the swap rate) in the measure under which the swap rate itself is a martingale. This implies using as numeraire the fixed leg of the annuity of the associated swap. Therefore, ignoring the present-valuing, irrelevant for the discussion, the problem reduces to the evaluation of a K-strike call on the swap rate with payoff, P, given by

$$P = \max[SR_T - K]^+ \tag{23.13}$$

I assume that the swap rate follows a process as in Equation (23.1), and choose several values of the CEV exponent β (say, 1, corresponding to the log-normal case, 0.75 and 0.5, corresponding to the square-root process). To each value of β I associate a different volatility coefficient[4] $\sigma = \sigma_\beta$, chosen so as to give the same price today for the at-the-money call. To do so for an arbitrary strike one would require a numerical inversion of the Black formula (see, for example, Marris, 1999). However, if one is simply working with at-the-money options, an extension of the discussion presented in Chapter 16 suggests that a very good approximation can be obtained by 'guessing' the value of σ_β to be given by

$$\sigma_{\beta'} SR^{\beta'} = \sigma_{\beta''} SR^{\beta''} \tag{23.14}$$

In particular, if, say, $\beta'' = 1$ (corresponding to the log-normal case), and the associated percentage volatility is simply denoted by σ, then Equation (23.14) gives

$$\sigma_\beta = \sigma \frac{SR}{SR^\beta} \tag{23.15}$$

We will check in Section 23.6 that this choice does produce the correct at-the-money price. For the moment we will take this result on faith.

---

[4]To be precise, the quantity σ that appears in Equation (23.1) should be called the deterministic component of the instantaneous volatility (which is given by σS^β). For simplicity, however, I will refer to σ simply as the volatility.

Having chosen the volatility using Equation (23.15), I first calculate the value of at-the-money call options of different maturities using 'today's' value of the swap rate. I then impart various instantaneous changes to its level and recalculate the prices of at-the-money swaptions. Clearly, since the underlying swap rate has moved, the absolute value of the strike is different for each swaption. What remains constant is only their at-the-moneyness. Finally, I convert these prices into implied percentage volatilities, σ_{impl}, and I plot these quantities as a function of the at-the-money swap rate level, SR: $\sigma_{\text{impl}}(SR)$. I stress that the procedure differs from the more usual investigation of the strike dependence of the implied volatility, which is a well known, but, in this context, irrelevant topic.

23.6 The Computational Results

The results of the tests described in Section 23.5 are shown in Figures 23.20 and 23.21 for the exponent β in Equation (23.1) equal to 0.75 and 0.5. I conducted the test using five maturities, ranging from 1 to 5 years. See Tables 23.3 and 23.4. The first five data columns in these tables display the at-the-money implied volatilities when the swap rate is moved. Incidentally, the prices and implied volatilities obtained for the reference level show that Equations (23.14) and (23.15) were highly effective in producing the correct at-the-money call prices.

From these figures qualitatively it appears that, indeed, if the underlying process is a CEV diffusion, the implied volatility changes as a function of the at-the-money volatility as an inverse power law. Furthermore, within numerical error, the same curve is traced by the implied volatilities irrespective of the maturity of the option. The average of these implied volatilities for each swap-rate level is shown in the sixth column of both tables. Finally, the seventh column shows the implied volatility that would be obtained by imposing that the implied volatility should behave as

$$\sigma_{\text{impl}}(SR) = \sigma_{\text{impl}}(SR_0) \left(\frac{SR}{SR_0} \right)^{1-\beta} \tag{23.16}$$

As one can see the fit is virtually perfect. This allows one to conclude that:

1. if the process for the underlying is a β-CEV diffusion, as in Equation (23.1), the associated at-the-money implied volatilities for all maturities also change with the swap rate following an inverse power law; and

2. the exponents β and γ of the CEV process and of the implied volatilities, respectively, are linked by the simple relationship $\gamma = 1 - \beta$. Therefore

$$\sigma_{\text{impl}}(SR) = kSR^{1-\beta} = kSR^{\gamma} \tag{23.17}$$

for a constant k given by

$$k = \frac{\sigma_{\text{impl}}(SR_0)}{(SR_0)^{1-\beta}} \tag{23.18}$$

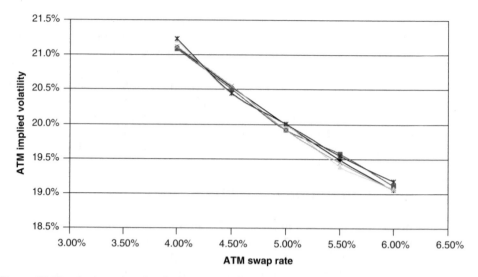

Figure 23.20   At-the-money implied volatilities for different maturities as the swap rate is moved from its initial value for the exponent $\beta = 0.75$.

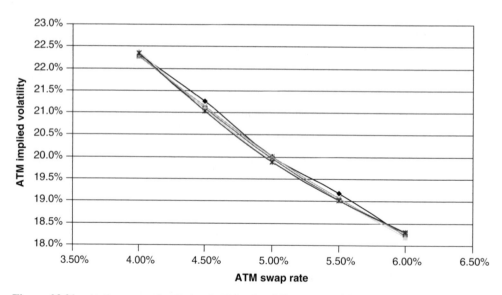

Figure 23.21   At-the-money implied volatilities for different maturities as the swap rate is moved from its initial value for the exponent $\beta = 0.50$.

It is reassuring that, if $\beta = 1$, we are in a log-normal world ($\gamma = 1 - \beta = 0$), and one recovers the independence of the implied volatility from the swap-rate level implied by the homogeneity of degree one of the now-correct Black formula.

So far we have established a link *from* the process *to* the exponent: if the process for the underlying is a CEV diffusion of the type (23.1), then the implied volatility is linked to the level of the at-the-money swap rate by a relationship of the type (23.16). Clearly, the

Table 23.3 At-the-money implied volatilities for different maturities as the swap rate is moved from its initial value for the exponent $\beta = 0.75$. The average of the implied volatilities across maturities is also displayed, together with the theoretical at-the-money implied volatility.

	1	2	3	4	5	Average	Analytic
4.00%	21.1%	21.1%	21.2%	21.1%	21.2%	21.2%	21.1%
4.50%	20.5%	20.5%	20.4%	20.6%	20.4%	20.5%	20.5%
5.00%	20.0%	19.9%	20.0%	19.9%	20.0%	20.0%	20.0%
5.50%	19.5%	19.6%	19.4%	19.4%	19.5%	19.5%	19.5%
6.00%	19.1%	19.1%	19.1%	19.1%	19.2%	19.1%	19.1%

Table 23.4 At-the-money implied volatilities for different maturities as the swap rate is moved from its initial value for the exponent $\beta = 0.50$. The average of the implied volatilities across maturities is also displayed, together with the theoretical at-the-money implied volatility.

	1	2	3	4	5	Average	Analytic
4.00%	22.3%	22.3%	22.4%	22.3%	22.3%	22.3%	22.3%
4.50%	21.3%	21.1%	21.1%	21.2%	21.0%	21.1%	21.0%
5.00%	20.0%	20.0%	19.9%	20.0%	19.9%	20.0%	20.0%
5.50%	19.2%	19.0%	19.0%	19.1%	19.0%	19.1%	19.0%
6.00%	18.2%	18.3%	18.2%	18.2%	18.3%	18.2%	18.2%

reverse need not be true: the relationship between implied volatilities and at-the-money swap rates could be of the type (23.16), and yet the underlying process might not be a CEV diffusion. Can we say something stronger?

23.7 Empirical Study II: The Log-Linear Exponent

In order to examine further the relationship between CEV processes and power-law implied volatilities, let us look again at the transformed variable $y(\alpha)$, defined in Equation (23.12). Recall that the maturity-dependent exponent α had been numerically determined so that the linear correlation coefficient between the variables $\{y\}$ and the at-the-money swap-rate levels $\{SR\}$ would be zero. Clearly, when the variable $y(\alpha)$ is defined as in Equation (23.12), such an exponent can always be found. This does not automatically mean, however, that there is no dependence left between SR and y. The relationship between the variables SR and y could give a value of zero to the coefficient of linear correlation, but could still be such as to display a lot of structure. I therefore undertake a more direct test of the power-law hypothesis. More precisely, I investigate how well a linear relationship between the variables $\ln \sigma_{impl}$ and $x = \ln(kSR^\delta)$ describes the empirical data.[5] If, after taking logs, the linear relationship held exactly one could

---

[5]Because of the proliferation of exponents, the following brief summary should help the reader:

Table 23.5 The zero-correlation exponent α and the (negative of the) slope δ.

Series	ZeroCorr	Slope
1 × 1	1.37	1.40
1 × 3	1.44	1.46
1 × 5	1.45	1.46
1 × 10	1.37	1.39
3 × 1	1.12	1.12
3 × 3	1.17	1.14
3 × 5	1.14	1.09
3 × 10	1.06	0.94
5 × 1	0.80	0.74
5 × 3	0.88	0.82
5 × 5	0.88	0.82
5 × 10	0.91	0.83

write

$$\ln \sigma_{\text{impl}} = \ln k + \delta \ln SR \tag{23.19}$$

If Equation (23.19) were the correct description of the relationship between σ_{impl} and $\ln SR$, then the residuals would have zero correlation with $\ln SR$. How well are the data explained by a relationship like (23.19)? And what is the link between δ and α? The answer is provided by Table 23.5 which shows the zero-correlation exponent α and the (negative of the) slope δ. It is interesting to observe how similar the slopes $\{\delta\}$ turned out to be to the (negative of the) zero-correlation exponents $\{\alpha\}$. Summary results of the regressions for the various swaption series are presented in Table 23.6. Figures 23.22–23.24 show the graphs of $\ln \sigma_{\text{impl}}$ vs $\ln SR$ for a few swaption series.

As Table 23.6 indicates, the explanatory power of the linear relationship becomes increasingly poorer as the expiry of the option increases. However, I discuss in the next section how this might be related to the existence of distinct volatility regimes, each one possibly still of a power-law type. In other words, a plot such as Figure 23.24 suggests that the strong linear relationship might still hold for each temporally connected section of the graph, but that different clusters might have different slopes and/or intercepts. Shifts in the volatility regimes are the topic of Chapters 26 and 27.

- α denotes the *empirical* exponent that gives zero correlation between the quantity $y(\alpha) \equiv \sigma_{\text{impl}} SR^{\alpha}$ and the swap rate, SR;

- β denotes the *theoretical* exponent in the candidate (CEV) model for the evolution of the swap rate;

- γ denotes the exponent that best fits the theoretically obtained behaviour between levels of swap rates and of implied volatilities under the assumption that the swap rate follows a CEV behaviour;

- δ denotes the *empirical* exponent derived from the slope of the log-linear regression of the observed implied volatility against KSR^{δ}.

Table 23.6 Summary of the regression statistics.

	1 × 1	1 × 3	1 × 5	1 × 10	3 × 1	3 × 3	3 × 5	5 × 1	5 × 3	5 × 5	5 × 10
R^2	0.845	0.753	0.667	0.498	0.543	0.465	0.393	0.280	0.265	0.251	0.204
Standard error	0.151	0.150	0.151	0.154	0.138	0.140	0.141	0.141	0.126	0.125	0.125
Observations	1165	1165	1165	1165	1165	1165	1165	1165	1165	1165	1165
Intercept	5.381	5.527	5.524	5.319	4.987	4.972	4.853	4.616	4.342	4.306	4.260
Lower 95%	5.323	5.442	5.417	5.175	4.878	4.842	4.708	4.444	4.194	4.151	4.080
Upper 95%	5.440	5.613	5.631	5.464	5.095	5.102	4.999	4.788	4.490	4.461	4.441
t-statistic	179.752	126.971	101.155	72.322	89.890	75.026	65.578	52.637	57.532	54.623	46.382
Slope	−1.402	−1.465	−1.461	−1.350	−1.130	−1.140	−1.089	−0.985	−0.819	−0.820	−0.828
Lower 95%	−1.436	−1.513	−1.520	−1.428	−1.190	−1.210	−1.167	−1.075	−0.897	−0.902	−0.922
Upper 95%	−1.367	−1.417	−1.401	−1.272	−1.070	−1.070	−1.011	−0.894	−0.740	−0.739	−0.734
t-statistic	−79.726	−59.612	−48.318	−33.964	−37.155	−31.825	−27.463	−21.241	−20.471	−19.740	−17.265

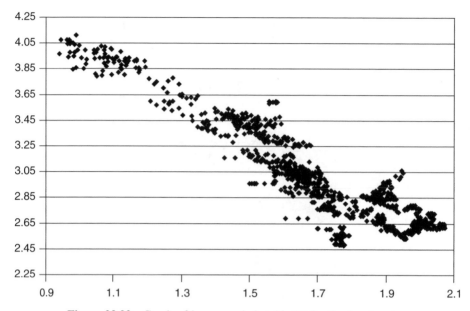

Figure 23.22   Graph of $\ln \sigma_{impl} = \ln k + \delta \ln SR$ for the 1×1 series.

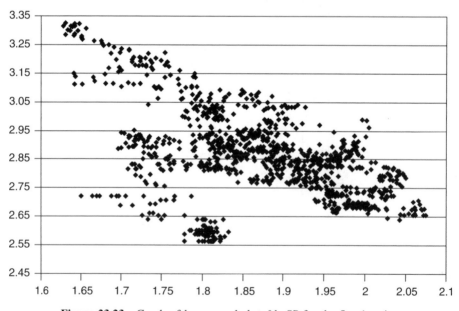

Figure 23.23   Graph of $\ln \sigma_{impl} = \ln k + \delta \ln SR$ for the 5×1 series.

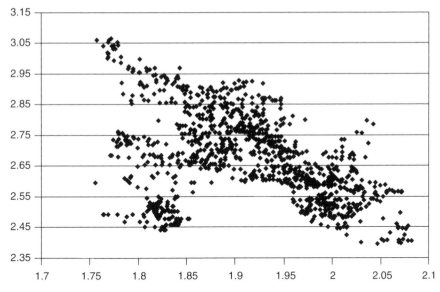

Figure 23.24 Graph of $\ln \sigma_{impl} = \ln k + \delta \ln SR$ for the 5×10 series.

23.8 Combining the Theoretical and Experimental Results

We are finally in a position to put the theoretical results and the empirical data together. We have established that a CEV diffusion produces implied volatilities that follow the law (23.16). The empirical data also indicate that one cannot reject at the 95% confidence level the hypothesis that the implied volatilities and the swap-rate levels should be linked by a power law, and that the exponent δ should assume the values given in Table 23.5. If this behaviour had indeed been generated by a CEV process, the coefficients γ, β and δ should be linked by

$$\gamma = 1 - \beta = \delta \Longrightarrow \beta = 1 - \delta \qquad (23.20)$$

Unfortunately, for most of the swaption series analysed the β-CEV exponent produced by Equation (23.20) turn out to be negative, which is clearly not compatible with a CEV explanation. For those series (mainly the $5\times$ series) where β is positive, and where a CEV diffusion *could* therefore have produced the data, the exponent β is very small (in the range 0.1–0.2), suggesting an almost normal behaviour. These are, however, the same series where the volatility regime switch mentioned above appears more evident. It might therefore be the case that the lower exponent is simply arising from the inappropriateness of a simple linear model.

23.9 Where Do We Go From Here?

The empirical analysis presented in this chapter has shown that a large part of the variability of the at-the-money implied volatility can be accounted for by the variability of the underlying swap rate, and that the dependence is of a power-law type. When this contribution to the variability of the implied volatility is stripped out, there remains (a considerably smaller) degree of variability that can arguably be described by a stochastic-volatility approach (as described in Chapter 25 and in Rebonato and Joshi (2002)). The first conclusion is therefore that it could be a misguided attempt to account for all the variability displayed by swaption *percentage* volatilities in terms of log-normal swap rates with a stochastic volatility. As Figures 23.1, 23.2 and 23.21 clearly show, in fact, a high degree of functional dependence exists between the volatilities and the swap rates, and, as a consequence, a simple transformation of variables can be effective in de-coupling the dynamics of the swap rates and their volatility (once appropriately chosen).

However, when one moves from these qualitative features to the quantitative analysis of the data, it becomes apparent that, if the underlying process was truly of the CEV type, the exponent β derived from Equation (23.20) would have to be *negative* in order to account for the empirical behaviour of the implied volatilities. This is unfortunately not compatible with a CEV description as the sole mechanism for producing the negative slope in the implied volatility plots. One is therefore left with three logical alternatives:

1. the changes in implied volatilities are compatible with a well-specified stochastic process for the underlying, but this is not (exactly, or exclusively) of the CEV type;

2. the changes in implied volatilities are compatible with a well-specified stochastic process for the underlying, this is of the CEV type, but the exponent γ has been mis-estimated in the empirical analysis;

3. the changes in implied volatilities, which are, after all, simply prices quoted by traders, are not derived from a coherent arbitrage-free process for the underlying.

As for the first possibility, it might be the case that the exponent itself is a function of the level of swap rates: for instance, when swap rates are high, they might behave almost log-normally, but when they are low they might approach a more normal behaviour. Alternatively, the true process could be a diffusion (perhaps of the CEV type) but with the coefficient σ in Equation (23.1) now stochastic. An 'extra' negative skew in the implied volatility plot could be generated if this stochastic coefficient followed a diffusion with Brownian increments negatively correlated with the increments of the forward (or swap) rates.

The third possibility is unpalatable from a theoretical point of view, because it should in theory expose the trader who made prices in this manner to the risk of being arbitraged. It should not, however, be discarded a priori if the arbitrage that could punish the inconsistent trader were very difficult to put in place in practice. See again the discussion in Chapter 1.

Finally, visual inspection of the chronologically linked empirical data suggested that a volatility regime switch might be at play. This qualitative finding is in agreement with the empirical results in Rebonato (2002), who has shown the existence of regime switches in the shape of the swaption matrix for USD and EUR/DEM. Work to translate this insight into a coherent modelling framework is presented in Chapter 27. (See also Rebonato and Kainth (2004)).

The most important message from the analysis presented in this chapter is therefore that, while insufficient by itself to account for the observed market behaviour, a CEV process is likely to be very important in accounting for a good part of the observed dependence of implied volatilities on the level of swap rates. If one recalls the discussion presented in Chapter 1 about the importance of 'guessing' correctly the future smile surface (see Sections 1.1–1.3 in particular), it is easy to see why a CEV-based modelling of this part of the volatility dynamics can be so important. For this reason in the next chapter I explore in some detail the properties of the proposed CEV process in the context of the LIBOR market model.

Chapter 24

Constant-Elasticity-of-Variance (CEV) Processes in the Context of the LMM

24.1 Introduction and Financial Motivation

Let me summarize briefly the results obtained in the previous chapter.

1. We have seen that the level of interest rates and the associated implied volatility display a strong inverse relationship.

2. We established that a power law can describe this relationship to a good degree of accuracy.

3. We pointed out that an inverse relationship between the underlying (in this case, interest rates) and *implied* volatilities is obtained if one posits a process for the underlying rates of the type

$$dx = \mu(x, t)\, dt + \sigma_\beta(t) x^\beta\, dz \tag{24.1}$$

4. We established a link between the exponent of the empirical power law and the exponent of the process (24.1).

5. We concluded from the quantitative analysis of the data that, by itself, the process (24.1) cannot fully account for the variation in implied volatilities with the level of rates (the exponent β implied by the empirical data would have to be negative). None the less, it may be a useful starting point for modelling the dynamics of rates.

6. We made the conjecture that a stochastic-volatility term, with a negative correlation between the Brownian increments of the process x and of the volatility, could improve the quality of the modelling. Also, the possibility of a regime shift was suggested – this feature will be discussed in detail in Chapter 27.

729

Apart from the ability to reproduce (a good part of) the observed empirical behaviour, is there any other reason to believe that an equation of the type (24.1) could be useful for the problem at hand? The tell-tale sign that a process of this type might be appropriate would be the empirical observation of an inverse relationship between the level of the underlying and the *instantaneous* volatility. The latter, however, is not a directly observable quantity, and the empirical analysis must therefore be carried out on the basis of some indirect information.

The increase in the *percentage implied* volatility as the underlying increases has, for many years, been part of the accepted traders' lore, both for equities and for interest rates. In the first case, the so-called leverage effect has been invoked to explain the phenomenon: for a fixed level of debt, as the value of the firm's assets declines, so does the share price, but the firm's leverage increases, thereby causing an increase in volatility. As for interest rates, there exists among traders a generalized belief that the impact of a given information shock on rates is not independent of, but is less than proportional to, the level of the rates themselves. Interestingly enough, much as this belief is common, there is little empirical evidence to back it. Indeed, studies by Chan *et al.* (1992) would seem to indicate that, if anything, the dependence should be *super*-linear. If this were correct, there would appear to be a case of inconsistency between the changes in option prices (the smile surface) and the process for the underlying. See, on this point, the discussion in Section 1.1.2 of Chapter 1.

Whatever the true behaviour of the underlying, I have already expressed the view (see Section 1.1.3) that, from the point of view of a complex-derivatives trader, the most important requirement of a model should be its ability to reproduce the changes in the future implied volatility surface. Looking at the problem from this angle, a smile-generating CEV process of the type (24.1) might therefore provide a useful starting point. For this reason in this chapter I look in some detail at CEV processes in the context of the LIBOR market model (LMM).

24.2   Analytical Characterization of CEV Processes

Following Andersen and Andreasen (1998), suppose that we have a (forward) process, x_t, with an SDE of the form

$$\mathrm{d}x_t = \phi(x_t)\sigma(t)\,\mathrm{d}z_t \tag{24.2}$$

and such that $x(0) > 0$ (i.e. such that the value *today* of the forward process is strictly positive). By Equation (24.2) the total volatility of x, i.e. the quantity $\phi(x_t)\sigma(t)$, is assumed to be separable into a purely time-dependent part, $\sigma(t)$, and a stochastic component, $\phi(x_t)$, which is perfectly functionally dependent on the process itself. We would like to impose, for reasons explained below, that, if the forward process were ever to attain zero, its total volatility should collapse to zero. Since the term $\sigma(t)$ is deterministic and purely time-dependent, if we want to achieve this goal we must require that $\phi(0) = 0$.

It is easy enough to write an SDE such as (24.2). However, if we want to make sure that to this SDE there should correspond well-behaved solutions we have to impose some conditions on $\phi(x_t)$. To this effect, let us require that the function ϕ should satisfy the local Lipschitz continuity condition and the linear growth condition. The linear growth condition need not concern us too much, at least for the range of exponents ($0 \le \beta \le 1$)

we are interested in. The local Lipschitz condition, however, *is* of interest to us, and therefore deserves some attention. It requires that, for any $\epsilon > 0$, one can always find a constant, C_ϵ, dependent on ϵ, such that, for x and y positive but smaller than ϵ,

$$|\phi(x) - \phi(y)| \leq C_\epsilon |x - y| \tag{24.3}$$

If both the linear growth condition and the local Lipschitz condition are satisfied, one can show that there always exist well-behaved (non-explosive), path-wise unique solutions for the arbitrage-free SDE (24.2) of the process x. The growth condition ensures that the solution does not explode, and the Lipschitz condition ensures that it is unique. Furthermore, if, as we requested, $x(0) > 0$, the process remains positive at all times. This sounds encouraging. However, the CEV process (Equation (24.1)) we are interested in, i.e. a process where the function $\phi(x_t)$ has the form

$$\phi(x_t) = x(t)^\beta \tag{24.4}$$

will not satisfy the local Lipschitz condition at zero[1] for

$$0 < \beta < 1 \tag{24.5}$$

However, the following properties still hold. Given a process as in (24.1), with $0 < \beta < 1$

1. all it solutions are non-explosive;

2. for $\beta > \frac{1}{2}$ the SDE (24.1) has a *unique* solution;

3. for $\beta = 1$, $x = 0$ is an unattainable barrier (the forward process always remains *strictly* positive);

4. for $0 < \beta < 1$, $x = 0$ is an attainable barrier;

5. for $0 < \beta < \frac{1}{2}$ the solution is not unique, unless one assigns a separate boundary condition for $x = 0$.

If $\frac{1}{2} < \beta < 1$, the uniqueness of the solution (property 2), the attainability of zero (property 3) and the requirement $\phi(0) = 0$ ensure that zero is an absorbing barrier. Property 5, however states that for $0 < \beta < \frac{1}{2}$ the solution is in general not unique. This can be remedied by adding a financial requirement. Let us assume in fact that the forward rate (or the asset price) has reached zero. We know that, for $\beta > 0$, it cannot become negative. Could it perhaps be 'reflected back' into positive territory? Conditional on the price process, x, being at zero, if any positive value was accessible, the associated relative price could not possibly be a martingale; or, in more financial terms, we should certainly buy this asset (for \$0) at the boundary, because in the future it will be worth either zero, or something positive. This is just the definition of an arbitrage. Therefore we

---

[1]This can be seen as follows. Recall first the average value theorem, which states that, given a differentiable function, $\phi(.)$, and two points in its domain, x and y, it is always possible to write $\frac{\phi(x)-\phi(y)}{x-y} = \phi'(\eta)$, for some $\eta \in [x, y]$. Given our choice for the function ϕ, i.e. $\phi(x) = x^\beta$, its derivative, ϕ', is $\phi'(x) = \beta x^{\beta-1}$. Therefore $\phi'(0)$ is not bounded for $0 < \beta < 1$, and the local Lipschitz condition (24.3) cannot be satisfied.

must add the financial requirement that zero should be an *absorbing* barrier: if the rate or price ever reaches it, it must remain there forever.

The solution seems both elegant and 'innocuous'. In reality it can be financially rather unpleasant, especially in those regimes (of very low rates) where simpler proxy approaches (such as the mapping to displaced diffusions, discussed in Chapter 16) become unsatisfactory and one is therefore 'forced' to use bona fide CEV processes. We discuss this in the following section.

24.3   Financial Desirability of CEV Processes

Recall that we have mentioned in Chapter 16 that, when forward rates are not 'too low' (i.e. approximately at or above 5%), and for reasonable market percentage volatilities (i.e. for rates at these levels, of the order of 30%) mapping the CEV process to an equivalent displaced diffusion can be both simple and effective. However, if we are dealing with rates as low as those found in the JPY yield curve in the late 1990s, or in USD in the early 2000s, a typical displacement coefficient of a few percentage points gives much too much weight to negative rates. We also know (see Chapter 23) that when rates are this low, percentage volatilities are very high (when in 2002 USD rates were around 1.00% the associated percentage volatilities were around 60%). Extending the reasoning presented in Section 16.5, and from Chapter 23, we know how to find a volatility σ_β so as to match closely, at-the-money, the market caplet prices. To first order this approximate equivalent volatility is given by

$$\sigma_\beta f^\beta = \sigma f \qquad (24.6)$$

where σ is the percentage volatility. Using this equivalence, we can study the absorbing properties of CEV processes with the levels of rates and volatilities observed in the USD swaption market in the early 2000s. When simple numerical experiments are carried out, the 'exact' CEV process for a forward rate starting at around 1% gives a probability of approximately 50% of it being absorbed at zero over five years. Therefore, in the low-rate, high-volatility regime of interest the choice we made for the behaviour of the process upon reaching the zero barrier is not just an innocuous tinkering at the edges of a probability distribution, but has very important pricing consequences. In other words, by requiring zero to become an absorbing barrier, we have eliminated all possibilities of arbitrage, but are we happy with the financial implications?

The concern is not a 'philosophical' one about 'what truly happens' at zero, but is the very concrete observation that, because of absorption at zero, the density in the strictly positive region becomes progressively depleted. Given a fixed horizon T, as more and more paths reach zero and remain absorbed there forever, the probability density of non-zero terminal values becomes smaller and smaller. The overall density, as time goes by, becomes the sum of an infinitely sharp delta distribution at the origin, plus a diffuse but smaller and smaller distribution for the remaining values of the forward rate. Furthermore, any diffusive path sooner or later will reach the x-axis. Therefore, in the limit as T goes to infinity all the probability mass becomes concentrated at the origin. Given the posited diffusive nature of the forward-rate process, the zero level is therefore not just an absorbing barrier, but actually a 'black hole': every path will eventually fall into it, and none will escape. If you think that this is 'just a mathematical oddity' and that we should not worry about it, consider the following. With the rates and the volatility mentioned above, *and even ignoring discounting*, the price of a European digital call struck at zero (i.e. the price of a contract that pays $1 if rates in five years' time are positive) is about 50 cents! Would you like to sell the European digital at this level?

Are there ways around these problems? As usual, the answer is 'yes', but the 'fixes' do not come for free. One simple solution, suggested by Andersen and Andreasen (1998), is to posit that below a certain very low level rates suddenly become log-normal. More generally, and financially more pleasingly, we could make the CEV exponent level-dependent:

$$dx = \sigma_\beta(t)x^{\beta(x)}\,dz \tag{24.7}$$

with

$$\beta(x) = 1, \quad \text{for } x \le x_{\text{low}} \tag{24.8}$$

$$\beta(x) = 0, \quad \text{for } x \ge x_{\text{high}} \tag{24.9}$$

Both these approaches solve the problem by making the zero barrier inaccessible: in continuous time, as the forward rates become lower and lower their absolute volatility decreases, and this prevents them reaching the origin. This is also the intuition behind positing a behaviour for the forward rate of the type (Joshi, 2003)

$$dx = \frac{x}{1 + ax}\sigma_t\,dz_t \tag{24.10}$$

For a fixed constant a, when x is very low its volatility tends to zero in a log-normal fashion; when it is very high, it tends to σ_t, therefore approaching a normal-diffusion behaviour.

Ways around the problem are therefore not difficult to come by. In general, however, the price to be paid is that even semi-analytic solutions for the caplets prices are no longer available and the calibration phase can therefore become burdensome. More fundamentally, all these solutions, individually reasonable and plausible, imply very different behaviours for the risk-neutral density in the neighbourhood of zero, and therefore very different prices for low-strike receiver swaptions, floorlets and European digitals.

To see this in practice, take, for instance, Andersen and Andreasen's (1998) plausible fix. Let us accept the CEV behaviour for all levels of the forward rate above 0.0000001%, and let us impose that it should switch to a log-normal diffusion below this level. Since a diffusion produces continuous paths, the process will have to go through the regime-switching level, its volatility will promptly change to log-normal, and zero has therefore become an inaccessible barrier. Furthermore, by requiring that the CEV behaviour should prevail for all values of the process above such a ridiculously low level, we might feel that we have barely altered the financial properties of the 'true' CEV process. Therefore, we might feel that such a small 'tinkering' with the process should have a limited effect on the prices of options. Perhaps we might even be tempted to guess that, as the switching level approaches zero from above, we should asymptotically obtain the CEV prices.

This is far from true, no matter how low the transition level. Since zero has become an inaccessible barrier, the density for the altered process no longer displays the Dirac-delta at zero, and therefore the forward price for the five-year European digital discussed above is not 50 cents, but $1! This example simply highlights that the financial implications of all the 'solutions' proposed above should be scrutinized carefully, and, when possible, the model prices should be carefully compared with the corresponding market values.

In what follows I will assume that we are happy to work with an 'unadulterated' CEV process. The numerical techniques described below can be extended without too much difficulty to (some of) the alternative processes proposed above. It is important, however, to separate clearly the numerical effects from the intrinsic properties of the various processes.

24.4 Numerical Problems with CEV Processes

When it comes to implementing a pricing model based on a CEV process, two very different problems have to be tackled: (i) the quick and accurate evaluation of plain-vanilla option prices (this is important in the calibration phase when, typically, the model parameters are varied and the model prices recalculated until a good fit to observed market prices is obtained); and (ii) the evolution forward in time of the yield curve between the price-sensitive events. These, in turn, can be separated by several years (in the interest-rate case the 'very-long-step procedure' that I have described in Rebonato (2002) is most efficiently implemented with a single-step evolution to the final maturity of the deal, which can be 10 years in the future or more).

Let us see how these 'technical' problems can be tackled. Starting from the evaluation of call prices when the underlying follows a CEV process, explicit closed-form solutions obviously exist for β equal to 0 (normal case) and 1 (log-normal case). For other values of the exponent β the call (caplet) price can be expressed in terms of the non-central, chi-squared distribution (see, for example, Hull and White (2000)). 'Naïve' evaluations of this distribution (see, for example, Abramowitz and Stegun (1964)) involve the evaluation of an infinite number of gamma functions. More efficient, but computationally still rather intensive, methods exist (see, for example, Glasserman (2003)).

As for the evolution of the process after a finite time, exact closed-form expressions exist for the log-normal and the normal cases. For an arbitrary exponent, semi-analytic expressions involving the non-central, chi-squared distribution exist for $\frac{1}{2} < \beta < 1$ (see, again, Glasserman (2003)). For $\beta < \frac{1}{2}$ I am not aware of any approximations other than the simple Euler scheme.

Taken together, these 'semi-analytic' solutions do not lend themselves readily to fast numerical implementations, especially for the more interesting case of $\beta < \frac{1}{2}$. On the other hand, if one resorted to a 'brute-force' Monte Carlo evolution of the rates, discussed below, the procedure would become painfully slow. So, just when we 'need' to evolve a bona fide CEV process (i.e. when rates are very low and percentage volatilities very high, making the displaced-diffusion mapping inaccurate) typical step sizes must be made as short as approximately one month. The next section therefore explores how, and to what extent, these problems can be overcome numerically.

24.5 Approximate Numerical Solutions

Numerical solutions useful to price complex (i.e. non-single-horizon) interest-rate derivatives in a CEV setting, fall into three classes:

1. mapping to displaced diffusions;

2. transformation of variables;

3. modifications of the predictor–corrector (Euler) scheme.

I review these approaches in turn below.

24.5.1 Approximate Solutions: Mapping to Displaced Diffusions

The simplest way to deal with the numerical problems highlighted above is to carry out a mapping from the space of CEV processes to the space of displaced diffusions. A priori these two processes might appear to have little in common (besides both being diffusions). This is, however, not the case. Marris (1999) shows an interesting correspondence between the distributions produced by the two processes. Indeed, if the exponent β in Equation (24.1) is taken to be equal to the coefficient[2] γ in Equation (16.8), then the caplet prices, and hence the implied volatilities, produced by the two approaches are extremely similar over a very wide range of strikes. (This was indeed the main reason for introducing in Section 16.2.2 the second formulation of the displaced-diffusion process.) Looking at the problem in this light, a displaced-diffusion process can therefore be regarded as a useful computational proxy for the more desirable CEV process.

Despite the fact that the distributions produced by CEV processes and displaced diffusions share a strong similarity, there always is a range of sufficiently out-of-the-money options for which the approximation becomes unsatisfactory. As discussed above, serious problems are likely to arise in the low-rate, high-percentage-volatility regimes. In these cases the simple displaced-diffusive solution becomes unsatisfactory, and different lines of attack must be taken. These are discussed below.

24.5.2 Approximate Solutions: Transformation of Variables

A different possible route to address the numerical difficulties of evolving CEV processes is the following. Start from the SDE

$$\mathrm{d}f = \mu_f(\{f\})\,\mathrm{d}t + f^\beta \sigma_\beta\,\mathrm{d}w \tag{24.11}$$

and consider a variable y, $y = y(f)$. Then, by Ito's lemma,

$$\mathrm{d}y = \left[\frac{\partial y}{\partial t} + \mu_f(\{f\})\frac{\partial y}{\partial f} + \frac{1}{2}\frac{\partial^2 y}{\partial f^2}f^{2\beta}\sigma_\beta^2\right]\mathrm{d}t + \frac{\partial y}{\partial f}f^\beta\sigma_\beta\,\mathrm{d}w \tag{24.12}$$

---

[2]The coefficient γ mentioned here has nothing to do with the exponent γ in Chapter 23. Apologies for running out of Greek letters.

Therefore, with hopefully self-evident notation,

$$\sigma_y = \frac{\partial y}{\partial f} f^\beta \sigma_\beta \tag{24.13}$$

The numerical problems arising from the presence of the stochastic state variable in the volatility term would disappear if the quantity σ_y were chosen in such a way that its volatility turned out to be purely a function of time (and of the maturity of the jth forward rate):

$$\sigma_y = \sigma_y(t, T) \tag{24.14}$$

An inspired guess suggests that, if we choose

$$y(f) = -\frac{1}{\beta + 1} f^{-\beta+1} \tag{24.15}$$

indeed we will obtain

$$\sigma_y = \frac{\partial y}{\partial f} f^\beta \sigma_\beta = \sigma_\beta \tag{24.16}$$

We can therefore evolve the quantity y, which has a deterministic volatility, and then translate to the forward rate f that we are interested in. Is such a simple change of variables the solution we were looking for? Unfortunately, the problem has not totally disappeared, because the drift term is now more involved, as one can appreciate from Equation (24.12). The Hunter–Jaeckel–Joshi approximation (see Hunter *et al.* (2001)) allows us to deal numerically with state-dependent drifts, but, as the drift becomes more complex, the approximation becomes more stretched.

Whether this approach is more practical and accurate than the predictor–corrector method presented below depends on the level of the volatility and on the number of forward rates to be evolved simultaneously. I therefore present an alternative, and sometimes more effective, method in the next section.

24.5.3   Approximate Solutions: the Predictor–Corrector Method

If the SDE for a quantity S is of the form

$$dS = \mu \, dt + \sigma \, dz \tag{24.17}$$

with μ and σ constants, the exact solution $S(\Delta t)$ given $S(0) = S_0$ is

$$S(\Delta t) = S_0 + \mu \Delta t + \sigma Z \sqrt{\Delta t} \tag{24.18}$$

with

$$Z\sqrt{\Delta t} = \int_0^{\Delta t} dz(s) \simeq \sqrt{\delta t} \sum_{i=1,n} \epsilon_i \tag{24.19}$$

(In the expression above, the '=' sign is to be understood as equality in distributions, and the summation on the last term on the RHS runs over the n sub-intervals of equal length δt into which the finite time-step Δt can be subdivided.) Furthermore, we know that, if we are only interested in the distribution, ϕ, of $S_{\Delta t}$ after time Δt, given its value S_0 today, this is given *exactly* by

$$\phi(S_{\Delta t}|S_0) = \mathcal{N}(S_0 + \mu\Delta t, \sigma^2\Delta t) \tag{24.20}$$

Therefore a possible sample from this distribution is obtained simply by drawing

$$S_{\Delta t}(Z) = S_0 + \mu\Delta t + Z\sigma\sqrt{\Delta t} \tag{24.21}$$

with $Z \in \mathcal{N}(0, 1)$.

These expressions are exact if the drift and the volatility are constant. If the drift and the volatility are purely time dependent, then Equation (24.20) is still valid with $\int \mu(u)\,\mathrm{d}u$ replacing $\mu\Delta t$ and the root-mean-squared volatility replacing σ. If we are dealing with a process of the form (24.1), however, in general both the drift and the volatility will depend on S. One can, of course, still try to use Equations (24.18) and (24.20), perhaps by 'freezing' the state-dependent drift and volatility at their initial values, but these equations now become just an approximation (usually referred to as the Euler scheme). For it to be accurate the time-step must become sufficiently small that the change in the drift and in the volatility due to the change in the underlying over the time-step can be ignored.

When the Euler scheme is used to evolve the yield curve, the resulting small-stepped approach is often referred to as 'brute-force Monte Carlo'. In the limit as the time-step Δt goes to zero, it never fails, but it can seriously slow down a numerical calculation. This is particularly true in the interest-rate area where very long time-steps should be used whenever possible in the course of a simulation. See, on this point, the discussion of the very-long-step procedure discussed in Rebonato (2002).

This problem has been recognized for a long time even in the relatively simple case of the deterministic-volatility LMM, where the no-arbitrage drifts depend, in general, on the forward rates themselves, and the terminal distribution is therefore not exactly log-normal. Hunter *et al.* (2001) (see also Kloeden and Platen (1992)) found a solution to this problem by employing a simple predictor–corrector method in the evaluation of the drift term.

When one moves to a CEV process, however, the state variable enters not only the drift, but also the stochastic coefficient (i.e. the term in $\mathrm{d}z_t$.) What is needed therefore is an extension of the predictor–corrector method to this problem that allows the approximate but accurate evaluation of the realization of a CEV process over a long time interval. The inspiration for the solution presented below is clearly from the work by Hunter *et al.* (2001) and by Kloeden and Platen (1992).[3]

---

[3]Calculations performed by Dr Niemeyer are gratefully acknowledged.

The Information Content of the Quantity $\int_0^T dz(s)$ in CEV Processes

With the deterministic-volatility LMM one deals with the problem of evolving a variable f when the drift is state-dependent, but the volatility is purely time-dependent:

$$\frac{df}{f} = \mu(f, t)\, dt + \sigma_t\, dz_t \tag{24.22}$$

In this section I address the complementary problem, and look for an approximate but accurate solution to the terminal value of a forward rate when the drift is deterministic, but the volatility is state-dependent:

$$df = \mu_f\, dt + \sigma(f_t, t)\, dz_t \tag{24.23}$$

and the dependence of the volatility on the forward rate is of the CEV type:

$$\sigma(f_t, t) = f^\beta \sigma_t \tag{24.24}$$

We know that the correct solution can be formally expressed as

$$f(T) = f(0) + \int_0^T \mu_f(u)\, du + \int_0^T f_u^\beta \sigma_u\, dz_u \tag{24.25}$$

or, if f is strictly positive (as it will be if $\frac{1}{2} < \beta \le 1$),

$$f(T) = f(0) \exp\left[\int_0^T \mu'_f(u)\, du + \int_0^T f_u^{\beta-1} \sigma_u\, dz_u\right] \tag{24.26}$$

for some (now state-dependent) drift μ'. For $\beta = 1$ or $\beta = 0$ (the log-normal and normal case, respectively) we know that the final realization $f(T)$ is purely a function of the quantity Z, with

$$Z\sqrt{T} = \int_0^T dz_u, \qquad \beta = 0, 1 \tag{24.27}$$

In these two cases, and *only* in these two cases, one can therefore write *exactly* $f(T) = f(T, Z)$. These are, however, very special cases. In general (i.e. for arbitrary β), the terminal value $f(T)$ is a function of the whole path $\int_0^T dz_u$, and therefore one can only write

$$f(T) = f\left(T, \int_0^T dz_u\right) \tag{24.28}$$

I have already mentioned that, since no analytic solution is known for the integrals (24.25) and (24.26) for arbitrary β, in order to sample the path sufficiently accurately one would normally have to carry out a short-stepped Monte Carlo simulation. This is exactly the computational bottle-neck of a Monte Carlo implementation of the CEV-extended LMM referred to above. I show below that, by extending the Kloeden and Platen (1992) approximation to the volatility of a CEV process, accurate option pricing of complex products can often be obtained even after evolving the forward rate to its terminal maturity (or to the price-sensitive event) in a single step. Therefore, we can sometimes recover the long-jump procedure which is at the heart of efficient numerical implementations of the LMM even in the presence of a CEV process. To obtain this, we would only require convergence in distribution. Surprisingly, however, the results presented below turn out to have wider applicability. I show in fact that, in the case of the CEV process, the dependence of the terminal value $f(T)$ on information contained in the integral $\int_0^T \mathrm{d}z_u$, *other than the value Z defined by Equation (24.27)*, is often weak. Therefore one can empirically observe that the approximation based on the full Kloeden-and-Platen formula provides not only approximate *weak* convergence (in distribution), but also approximate *path-wise* convergence (in the terminal value). In other words, if we evolved the process for the forward rate using a finely spaced Monte Carlo simulation we would obtain *at the end of each individual path* a realization for $f(T, \int_0^T \mathrm{d}z_u)$ very similar to the realization $f(T, Z)$ obtained using the approximation below coupled with the knowledge of the value Z:

$$f\left(T, \int_0^T \mathrm{d}z_u\right) \simeq f(T, Z) \tag{24.29}$$

if

$$Z\sqrt{T} = \int_0^T \mathrm{d}z_u \tag{24.30}$$

The Approximate Equations

Consider a process $x(t)$ with a SDE given by

$$\mathrm{d}x(t) = \mu(x, t)\,\mathrm{d}t + \sigma(x, t)\,\mathrm{d}z(t) \tag{24.31}$$

Given a finite time-step Δt, and a value $x(t_0)$ for the initial value of the process, the Euler scheme (Taylor scheme of order one) gives the approximation

$$x(t_0 + \Delta t) = x(t_0) + \mu(x_0, t)\Delta t + \sigma(x_0, t)\Delta z(t) \tag{24.32}$$

with $\Delta z(t) = z(t + \Delta t) - z(t)$. Note that the value of the variable x at the *beginning* of the step, x_0, appears in the drift and in the volatility. This is the 'brute-force' approach mentioned above.

Kloeden and Platen (1992) propose that, given the stochastic process, x, at time t_0, $x(t_0)$, with state-dependent drifts and volatilities, $\mu(x_t, t)$ and $\sigma(x_t, t)$, respectively, one can approximate its value at a later time $t_0 + \Delta t$, $x(t_0 + \Delta t)$, as

$$\begin{aligned}
x(t_0 + \Delta t) \simeq x(t_0) &+ \tfrac{1}{2}\left[\mu(x_0, t) + \mu(\widehat{x}, t)\right]\Delta t \\
&+ \tfrac{1}{4}\left[\sigma(\widehat{x}^+, t) + \sigma(\widehat{x}^-, t) + 2\sigma(x_0, t)\right]\Delta z(t) \\
&+ \tfrac{1}{4}\frac{\left[\sigma(\widehat{x}^+, t) - \sigma(\widehat{x}^-, t)\right]\left[\Delta z(t)^2 - \Delta t\right]}{\sqrt{\Delta t}}
\end{aligned} \tag{24.33}$$

where

$$\widehat{x} = x(t_0) + \mu(x_0, t)\Delta t + \sigma(x_0, t)\Delta z(t) \tag{24.34}$$

$$\widehat{x}^+ = x(t_0) + \mu(x_0, t)\Delta t + \sigma(x_0, t)\sqrt{\Delta t} \tag{24.35}$$

$$\widehat{x}^- = x(t_0) + \mu(x_0, t)\Delta t - \sigma(x_0, t)\sqrt{\Delta t} \tag{24.36}$$

Note that the term $\widehat{x}$ is simply equal to the first-order term of the Taylor approximation (Euler scheme), i.e. in the forward-rate context of interest to us, it is equal to the value for $x(t_0 + \Delta t)$ that would be obtained using what Hull and White (2000) call the 'innocuous' approximation.

The Structure of the Approximation

Let us look at Equation (24.36) in more detail. Following Joshi (2003), and letting $\mu = 0$ for the moment, if we define

$$a = \frac{1}{4} \frac{\sigma(\widehat{x}^+, t) - \sigma(\widehat{x}^-, t)}{\sqrt{\Delta t}} \tag{24.37}$$

$$b = \frac{1}{4}\left[\sigma(\widehat{x}^+, t) + \sigma(\widehat{x}^-, t) + 2\sigma(x_0, t)\right] \tag{24.38}$$

$$c = -\frac{1}{4}\left[\sigma(\widehat{x}^+, t) - \sigma(\widehat{x}^-, t)\right]\sqrt{\Delta t} \tag{24.39}$$

one can write

$$x(t_0 + \Delta t) \simeq az^2 + bz + c \tag{24.40}$$

with $z \in \mathcal{N}(0, 1)$. (To lighten notation I have denoted by z the quantity $\Delta z(t)$.) Expression (24.40) shows that the terminal realization of the quantity x is a quadratic function of the random draw z. Let us interpret for the moment the quantity x as the forward rate itself: $x(t) = f(t)$ (see, however, the discussion in the following section). If this is the case, looking at the approximation in this light it is easy to obtain an expression for the density of $x(t_0 + \Delta t)$, $\phi(x(t_0 + \Delta t)) \equiv \phi(f_T)$, $T = t_0 + \Delta t$:

$$\phi(f_T)\,df_T = \Phi(z)\,dz \rightarrow \phi(f_T) = \frac{\Phi(z)}{\left|\frac{df_T}{dz}\right|} \tag{24.41}$$

where

$$\Phi(z) \equiv \mathcal{N}'(0, 1) = \frac{1}{\sqrt{2\pi}}\exp\left[-\frac{1}{2}z^2\right] \tag{24.42}$$

Since

$$\frac{df_T}{dz} = 2az + b \tag{24.43}$$

one obtains

$$\phi(f_T) = \frac{\frac{1}{\sqrt{2\pi}}\exp\left[-\frac{1}{2}z^2\right]}{|2az + b|} = \frac{\frac{1}{\sqrt{2\pi}}\exp\left[-\frac{1}{2}z^2\right]}{|2az + b|} \tag{24.44}$$

When the derivative $|\frac{df_T}{dz}|$ becomes zero the relationship between the random draw and the terminal value of the forward rate ceases to be one-to-one. Let us call $\hat{z}$ the value of z such that $|\frac{df_T}{dz}| = 0$:

$$\hat{z} = -\frac{b}{2a} \tag{24.45}$$

and $\hat{f_T}$ the associated value of f_T:

$$\hat{f}(T) = a\hat{z}^2 + b\hat{z} + c = c - \frac{b^2}{2a} \tag{24.46}$$

with a, b and c (which are functions of Δt) given by Equations (24.37)–(24.39). This implies that no forward rate below $\hat{f_T}$ is ever reached by the approximation, and every value above $\hat{f_T}$ is reached twice. This, however, is not the case for the true CEV process that we are trying to approximate.

How can we get around this? Following Joshi (2003), suppose that we want our approximation to be valid for any random draw between $-\hat{z}$ and $+\hat{z}$. (For instance, we could choose $-\hat{z} = -4$; this would mean that we 'throw away' approximately 0.005% of the total density by ignoring values of z outside this range.) Looking at Equations (24.37)–(24.39), (24.35)–(24.36) and (24.45), and given the exponent β and the initial value of the forward rate, one can relate the critical value $\hat{z}$ to the maximum jump length, $\widehat{\Delta t}$, that can be reached in a single jump without entering the 'forbidden' region.

How binding are these constraints? For $\beta = 0.2$, and the equivalent percentage volatility $\sigma = \sigma_\beta f^{\beta-1} = 40\%$, the maximum jump size is approximately 5 years. Increasing the exponent, however, makes the maximum jump size smaller: for $\beta = 0.4$, 0.6 and 0.8 the maximum jump size becomes approximately 2.2, 1.1 and 0.64 years, respectively. Since, as discussed in Chapter 23, low values of β are probably the most interesting for interest-rate pricing problems, this would seem encouraging. However, the critical value of the jump size that we have determined ensures that we retain a one-to-one correspondence between the draw z and the terminal forward rate, but does not guarantee the accuracy of the solution. For these values of β the approximation becomes more strained for a different reason, i.e. because the absorption at zero of the true CEV process (which the approximation cannot correctly capture) becomes more and more important. We will explore below the range of validity of the approach.

Interpretation of the Quantity x

In the deterministic-volatility LMM it is quite clear that the presence of the state variables in the drift terms produces a relatively minor deviation from log-normality for the forward rates. Therefore it is natural to interpret the quantity x as the logarithm of the forward rates themselves. When we are working with the CEV process, however, this choice is no longer so obvious: for values of β close to 1 the distribution of the forward rates should be closer to log-normal, but as β approaches 0 it might be more natural to interpret x as the forward rate itself, rather than its logarithm. It can therefore be useful to calculate the terminal values of the forward rate using Equations (24.33) and (24.36) above applied both to the forward rate and to its logarithm ($f(T)_{norm}$ and $f(T)_{log}$), and then calculating

$$f(T) \simeq \beta f(T)_{log} + (1 - \beta) f(T)_{norm} \tag{24.47}$$

Clearly, for $\beta = 0$ or $\beta = 1$ we recover the exact solutions (24.25) and (24.26). If the exponent is closer to 1 or to 0, greater weight will be given to the associated solution. I discuss below if and when this approximation is useful.

The Numerical Experiments: Methodology

In order to focus attention on the accuracy of the approximation of the CEV volatility, we place ourselves in the terminal measure of a forward rate, under which measure the no-arbitrage drift is zero. We choose values of β of 0.25, 0.5 and 0.75. Since we want to test the procedure in the regime where the displaced-diffusion approximation is likely to be unsatisfactory, we assume an initial value of the forward rate of 3.00%. We choose a typical market value of its percentage volatility (40%), and translate it into the CEV volatility that gives the same at-the-money call prices. This can be accurately done using the techniques described in Chapter 16 (see also Marris (1999) and Rebonato (2002)). As for the time horizons, I present the results for one-year jumps.

Once these choices are made we perform accurate numerical (Monte Carlo) evaluations of the integral $\int_0^T dz_u$. We use 10 000 paths for the simulation and a time-step of 0.004 years.[4] At the end of each path we calculate the 'exact' value $f(T, \int_0^T dz_u)$. We call the set of values obtained using this short-stepped procedure our 'target'. We also associate with each path thus constructed the quantity Z, defined as in Equation (24.27). We then use Equations (24.33)–(24.36) to obtain an approximate value $f(T, Z)$. We do so either by interpreting the quantity x in Equations (24.33)–(24.36) as the forward rate itself, or its logarithm. The approximate forward rate thus obtained is denoted $f(T)_{\mathrm{norm}}$ or $f(T)_{\mathrm{log}}$, respectively. We explore the distribution of $f(T)$ obtained using the 'exact' simulation, using the predictor–corrector approximation (24.33)–(24.36) and using the simple Euler scheme (Equation (24.18)). Finally, we also look, on a path-by-path basis, at the quantity ξ, defined as

$$\xi_T = f\left(T, \int_0^T dz_u\right) - f(T, \Delta Z) \qquad (24.48)$$

and we analyse its distribution, $\phi = \phi(\xi_T)$.

The Numerical Experiments: Results

In this section we compare the results obtained with $\beta = 0.25$ and $\beta = 0.75$ for the short-stepped solution ('Target'),[5] and the approximate solutions obtained by

- applying the predictor–corrector method to the forward rate ('PC-Normal');

- applying the predictor–corrector method to the logarithm of the forward rate ('PC-Log');

- applying the predictor–corrector method using Equation (24.47) ('Pred-Corr');

---

[4]The help of Mr Bernd Niemeyer with the Monte Carlo simulations presented in this section is gratefully acknowledged.

[5]In order to reduce the numerical noise due to the finite sampling, all the averages and standard deviations were scaled by the percentage error of the average and standard deviation of the Target results. So, the Target average and standard deviation are exact by construction.

- evolving the forward rate in a single step using the Euler approximation ('Normal');

- evolving the logarithm of the forward rate in a single step using the Euler approximation ('Lognormal').

The first observation is that, for the volatilities, the initial values and the horizon times described in the previous section, all the approximations produce excellent averages. The forward pricing condition would therefore be almost exactly recovered in all cases. The standard deviation is also well recovered in all cases, apart from the Lognormal approximation. For the skew and kurtosis, all the predictor–corrector-based approximations outperform the Normal and Lognormal results. Among the PC-based approximations, the mixture of the normal and log-normal approximations (Equation (24.47)) appears to perform best. All these statistics are reported in Table 24.1.

The densities obtained are shown in Figures 24.1–24.3. Note that the normal and lognormal densities are much poorer, the former especially for $\beta = 0.75$, and the latter for $\beta = 0.25$.

In order to explore the pricing impact of the errors, Tables 24.2 and 24.3 present the forward value (i.e. without discounting) of caplets of different strikes. Since the forward condition is well recovered by all the approaches, it is not surprising to find that in-the-money caplets are well priced in all cases. Moving out of the money, all the predictor–corrector approximations outperform the other approaches. Not surprisingly, the PC-Log approximation works slightly better for $\beta = 0.75$, and the PC-Normal approximation for $\beta = 0.25$.

It is also interesting to look at the quality of the path-wise convergence (see Figures 22.4–22.6). In all cases (i.e. for all exponents), the PC approximation produces terminal paths on average more similar to the target ones than the other approximations. For instance, for $\beta = 0.25$, the average absolute error for the Pred-Corr approximation is less than a basis point, but 6 and 17 basis points for the Normal and Lognormal

Table 24.1 Descriptive statistics of the terminal values (initial value $= 0.03$, equivalent percentage volatility $= 40\%$) for the various approximations.

(a) $\beta = 0.75$

	Target	PC-Normal	PC-Log	Pred-Corr	Normal	Lognormal
Average	0.03000	0.03000	0.03000	0.03000	0.03003	0.03000
Standard deviation	0.40000	0.40014	0.39927	0.39948	0.39179	0.40983
Skew	0.89851	0.86360	0.86343	0.86368	0.05365	1.29398
Kurtosis	1.28740	0.97528	1.06919	1.04523	−0.19031	3.04923

(b) $\beta = 0.25$

	Target	PC-Normal	PC-Log	Pred-Corr	Normal	Lognormal
Average	0.03000	0.03001	0.03002	0.03001	0.03002	0.02999
Standard deviation	0.40000	0.39949	0.40097	0.39959	0.39975	0.41866
Skew	0.30736	0.31934	0.19590	0.28142	0.04915	1.28191
Kurtosis	−0.00919	0.06205	−0.60666	−0.15081	−0.17646	3.05426

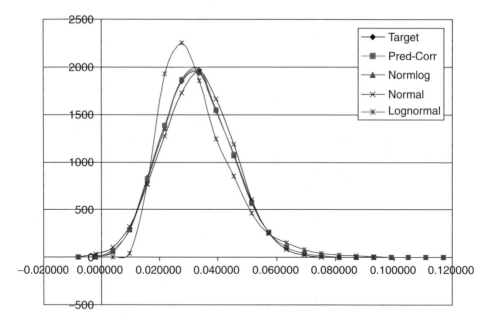

Figure 24.1 The densities obtained using the various approximations ($\beta = 0.25$). In the legend 'Normlog' refers to a linear combination of the 'Normal' and 'Lognormal' results.

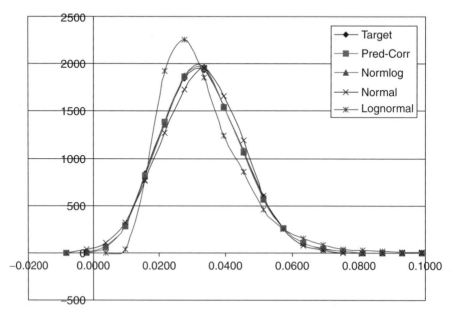

Figure 24.2 The densities obtained using the various approximations ($\beta = 0.50$). In the legend 'Normlog' refers to a linear combination of the 'Normal' and 'Lognormal' results.

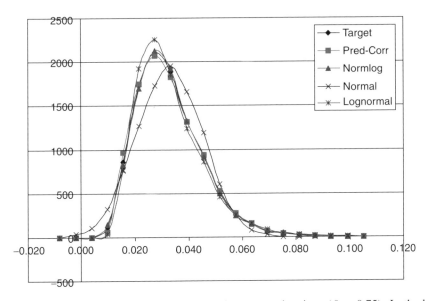

Figure 24.3 The densities obtained using the various approximations ($\beta = 0.75$). In the legend 'Normlog' refers to a linear combination of the 'Normal' and 'Lognormal' results.

Table 24.2 Forward values of caplets of various strikes for the various approximations ($\beta = 0.75$).

	1.50%	2.00%	2.50%	3.00%	3.50%	4.00%	4.50%	5.00%	5.50%	6.00%
Target	0.01518	0.01089	0.00739	0.00476	0.00293	0.00174	0.00099	0.00056	0.00031	0.00017
PC-Normal	0.01515	0.01089	0.00742	0.00480	0.00297	0.00175	0.00099	0.00055	0.00030	0.00016
PC-Log	0.01517	0.01089	0.00739	0.00477	0.00294	0.00174	0.00098	0.00055	0.00030	0.00016
Pred-Corr	0.01517	0.01089	0.00740	0.00478	0.00295	0.00174	0.00099	0.00055	0.00030	0.00016
Normal	0.01557	0.01134	0.00769	0.00479	0.00270	0.00135	0.00060	0.00024	0.00008	0.00002
Lognormal	0.01510	0.01076	0.00729	0.00475	0.00301	0.00188	0.00116	0.00072	0.00045	0.00028

Table 24.3 Forward values of caplets of various strikes for the various approximations ($\beta = 0.25$).

	1.50%	2.00%	2.50%	3.00%	3.50%	4.00%	4.50%	5.00%	5.50%	6.00%
Target	0.01542	0.01118	0.00759	0.00478	0.00277	0.00147	0.00071	0.00032	0.00013	0.00005
PC-Normal	0.01542	0.01118	0.00757	0.00476	0.00276	0.00147	0.00072	0.00033	0.00014	0.00006
PC-Log	0.01542	0.01124	0.00772	0.00494	0.00289	0.00150	0.00066	0.00023	0.00005	0.00000
Pred-Corr	0.01542	0.01119	0.00761	0.00480	0.00279	0.00148	0.00070	0.00030	0.00012	0.00004
Normal	0.01558	0.01135	0.00770	0.00479	0.00270	0.00135	0.00060	0.00024	0.00008	0.00002
Lognormal	0.01511	0.01077	0.00730	0.00475	0.00302	0.00188	0.00116	0.00072	0.00045	0.00028

approximations, respectively. As for the standard deviation of the absolute errors, it is between 1 and 2 basis points for the best and worst PC approximations, but 6 and 20 basis points for the Normal and Lognormal approximations, respectively.

Finally, Figure 24.7 displays the structure of the errors as a function of the terminal value of the target rate, obtained with the Pred-Corr approximation for $\beta = 0.25$. The

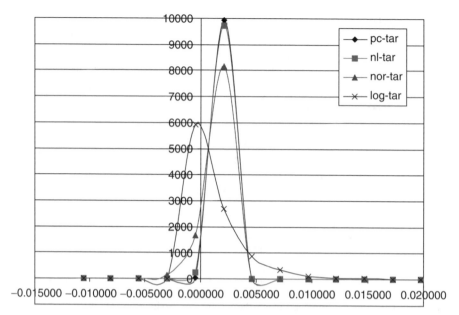

Figure 24.4   The densities of the path-wise errors obtained using the various approximations ($\beta =$ 0.25). In the legend 'nl-tar' refers to the differences between the target and a linear combination of the 'Normal' and 'Lognormal' results.

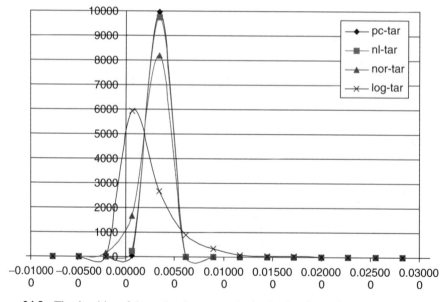

Figure 24.5   The densities of the path-wise errors obtained using the various approximations ($\beta =$ 0.50). In the legend 'nl-tar' refers to the differences between the target and a linear combination of the 'Normal' and 'Lognormal' results.

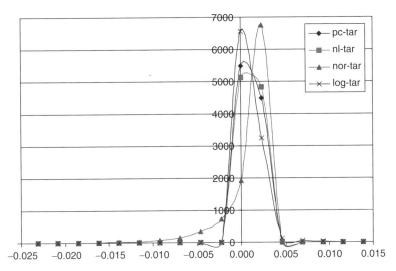

Figure 24.6 The densities of the path-wise errors obtained using the various approximations ($\beta = 0.75$). In the legend 'nl-tar' refers to the differences between the target and a linear combination of the 'Normal' and 'Lognormal' results.

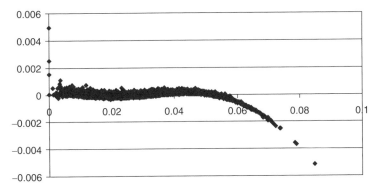

Figure 24.7 The structure of the errors vs the terminal values of the target rates for the Pred-Corr case ($\beta = 0.25$). Terminal values of the rates on the x-axis, and errors on the y-axis.

terminal values of the target rate are shown on the x-axis, and the errors on the y-axis. One can observe a quadratic dependence of the errors for high realizations of the target rate. This is not surprising given the discussion about Equations (24.37)–(24.40).

24.6 Problems with the Predictor–Corrector Approximation for the LMM

Despite the encouraging results shown above, there are two problems that have to be tackled before the predictor–corrector method presented above can be applied in practice to the LMM.

The first problem is the following. So far we have failed to mention the drifts (i.e. we have always implicitly assumed that we were working in the terminal measure). This is perfectly adequate for the pricing of, say, a single caplet, but for this purpose we would not use a Monte Carlo evolution anyhow. For the pricing of a complex derivative, several forward rates will have to be evolved at the same time, and no numeraire will make them all simultaneously driftless. See Rebonato (2002) on this point. Unfortunately, the drifts contain the forward rates themselves. Therefore, when applying the formulae proposed above for a given forward rate, its drift will contain forward rates that might not have been already 'updated' by the predictor–corrector procedure. This would create a problem, because the Hunter *et al.* (1999) formula for the jth forward rate can contain, depending on the choice of numeraire, both the initial and the approximate final values of some or even all the forward rates in the yield curve. It would therefore seem that, in order to obtain an approximate expression for the terminal value of the jth forward rate, the correct terminal values of the other rates would be required. Simply using the initial ('frozen') values of the forward rates in the drift for the jth forward rate would create an inconsistency and, for long jumps, noticeable numerical errors.

This problem can be solved by choosing, as common numeraire for all the forward rates, the discount bond associated with the terminal measure of the *last* forward rate.[6] When this choice is made, the last forward rate is driftless, the treatment above applies to this forward rate with no changes, and therefore we can obtain its (approximate) terminal value. The drift, μ, of the second-, third-, ... , nth-to-last forward rate contains the last, last two, ... , last $n-1$ forward rates only:

$$\mu_{f_i} = -\sigma_i(t) \sum_{k=i+1,j} \frac{\sigma_k(t)\rho_{ik}(t)f_k(t)\tau_k}{1 + f_k(t)\tau_k} \qquad (24.49)$$

Therefore, by updating the last forward rate first, and all the others in descending order, the drift of the current forward rate contains forward rates that have already been correctly evolved, and for which the initial and (approximate) terminal values are therefore available. The formulae above can therefore be applied recursively.

The second problem is that the predictor–corrector method presented above was cast in a single-factor framework. With the LMM, however, we would almost certainly want to work with many factors. The formulae presented above do extend to several factors, but soon become unwieldy and numerically very slow. The solution to this problem is to recast the original LMM problem, expressed, say, in the form

$$\frac{df_i}{f_i} = \mu_i(\{f\}, t)\,dt + \sum_{k=1,m} \sigma_{ik}\,dz_k = \mu_i(\{f\}, t)\,dt + \sigma_i \sum_{k=1,m} b_{ik}\,dz_k \qquad (24.50)$$

(with dz_k the increments of *independent* Brownian motions) in the equivalent form

$$\frac{df_i}{f_i} = \mu_i(\{f\}, t)\,dt + \sigma_i\,dw_k \qquad (24.51)$$

---

[6]Incidentally, this is also the recommended choice for reasons linked to the Hunter *et al.* method. See Rebonato (2002) on this point.

with $\mathrm{d}w_k$ the increments of *correlated* Brownian motions, and

$$\sigma_i^2 = \sum_{k=1,m} \sigma_{ik}^2 \tag{24.52}$$

With this formulation each forward rate is shocked by a single Brownian shock, and the Kloeden and Platen approximations above can therefore be directly applied. The increments $\mathrm{d}w_k$ are now no longer orthogonal to each other (as the $\mathrm{d}z_k$ were), but are chosen in such a way that the original correlation matrix is still recovered:

$$\mathrm{E}\left[\mathrm{d}w_j,\ \mathrm{d}w_k\right] = \rho_{jk} = \left[\mathbf{bb}^\mathrm{T}\right]_{jk} \tag{24.53}$$

This can always be done using a simple modification of the Choleski decomposition (see, for example, Kreyszig (1993)).

Summarizing: by choosing the numeraire carefully, and by using a system of non-orthogonal axes, the predictor–corrector method can be still be applied to many-forward-rates LMM problems.

Chapter 25

Stochastic-Volatility Extensions of the LMM

25.1 Plan of the Chapter

I have shown in Chapter 23 that, if one assumes forward rates to be log-normally distributed in their own terminal measure, there exists a strong dependence between changes in the level of rates and changes in the level of the implied volatility. I have also shown that if we move from a geometric diffusion to a CEV description of the dynamics of the forward rates, most of this correlation disappears.

When this transformation of co-ordinates is carried out, the conclusions that one can draw about the degree of variability in the volatility of forward rates can change dramatically. See Figure 25.1, which I show again for ease of reference. This is particularly true in periods when the level of rates changes (in percentage terms) dramatically, as indeed happened during the months of 2002 displayed in this figure. What I am trying to model in this chapter is therefore the (relatively more limited) variability of the lower curve, not the dramatic changes of the upper one. I intend to model this relatively modest variability using a mean-reverting diffusion process for the volatility of the new state variables in the new co-ordinate system.

Before embarking on this project, though, and looking at the same figure again, one might wonder whether such an apparently small degree of variability is really an essential part of the description of the volatility process. The answer is not straightforward. To begin with, I show in the next chapter that occasionally the rather 'tame' picture conveyed by Figure 25.1 ceases to be valid, and large and sudden changes in the level of volatility do occur. I will argue in the next two chapters, however, that modelling this feature using a Brownian diffusion is very unsatisfactory, and that a two-state regime switch (Markov-chain process), whereby the instantaneous volatility 'oscillates' between two easily identifiable regimes, accounts much better for the empirical evidence. So, even if bursts of volatility do occur, *within each regime* the variability of the volatility might still be rather limited, and the large sudden changes should probably not be described by a diffusive process.

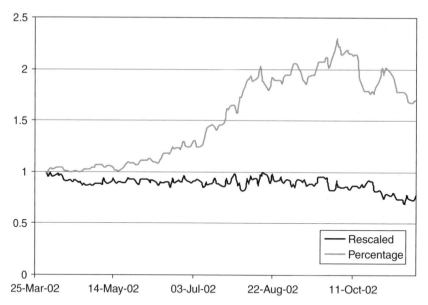

Figure 25.1   Rescaled (lower curve) and percentage (upper curve) volatilities (1×1 swaption series) rebased at 1 on 1-Apr-2002. See Chapter 23 for a discussion.

A description in terms of Brownian processes can, however, still make sense within each regime, and, despite the picture conveyed by Figure 25.1, be rather important. This is because it is the *expectation* of future volatility that matters, coupled with the aversion to volatility risk. Since in the presence of stochastic volatility perfect hedging is no longer possible,[1] a volatility risk premium enters the drift of the volatility process, and the volatility 'distilled' from the traded price need not coincide with the historically observed one. I have discussed the volatility risk premium in Chapter 13.

The shapes of market smile surfaces provide some indirect corroboration of this view. I will show in Chapter 27, in fact, that, after the change of variables discussed above, just positing a two-regime volatility process provides an intriguingly good qualitative description of the observed smile surface. However, it is only after adding a diffusive component to the variability of the volatility that a (time-homogeneous) fit of trading quality can be obtained. It is true that I have made the point throughout this book that the quality of the fit to the current smile surface is, *by itself*, a very poor indicator of the quality of a modelling approach. However, in this case I have systematically built the different components of the volatility description (CEV change of variables, two regimes and diffusive variability) on the basis of a clear financial motivation, and the final agreement between the theoretical and observed smile therefore *can* provide a meaningful corroboration of the overall approach.[2]

---

[1] At least as long as one is hedging purely with the underlying. If one allows for plain-vanilla options to be added to the set of hedging instruments, one would still need to know their full process, not just their prices today. See Chapter 13.

[2] Needless to say, in order to make this statement I still have to rely on some degree of market efficiency, i.e. I must assume that the salient features of the 'true' volatility dynamics are reflected in the option prices.

25.2 What is the Dog and What is the Tail?

Before starting the description of this approach another observation is in order. If, as proposed, a strong correlation (or, indeed a functional dependence) between the forward rates and the level of volatilities is assumed, whenever a large (Brownian) shock to the forward rates occurs a large change in the volatility will take place as well. Furthermore, if the change in the level of rates and volatility is large enough, the modelling approach proposed in the next chapters will suggest that this can give rise to a switch in volatility regime from a normal to an excited state. Typically, the expected lifetime in the excited state turns out to be rather short, and the combined effect of a functional dependence with the forward rates and of the volatility shift is to produce sudden but short-lived bursts in volatility. In this picture, it is therefore the changes in the level of rates that bring about the changes in the volatility.

With GARCH-type processes (for which typically the volatility will be some function of the past *squared* returns in the underlying) the volatility can also change rapidly, and display localized bursts ('clusters'). Furthermore, GARCH processes also display a volatility that is functionally dependent on (the history of) the underlying. And also in the GARCH case the driver of a large change in volatility is the realization of a large return in the underlying. So, in both approaches the 'dog' is the level of rates and the 'tail' is the level of volatilities. However, this need not necessarily be the case. Consider, in fact, the case of a diffusive (or otherwise) process for the volatility which is weakly (or not at all) dependent on the process of the forward rates. Also in this case the magnitudes of the interest-rate and volatility changes are linked: following a volatility 'spike', subsequent moves in forward rates will, on average, be larger than 'usual'. In this description, however, it is a large change in the volatility (the dog) that wags the forward-rate tail. Two questions therefore naturally arise: 'Is a GARCH description ultimately equivalent to the approach described in these chapters?'; and, if not, 'What description is the correct one for the phenomenon at hand?'.

The picture that emerges by assuming an independent process for the volatility can be easily ruled out: a large increase in volatility will in fact increase the probability of a large change in the forward rates *of either sign*. However, we have seen in previous chapters that, apart from the regime switch, large increases in the forward rates are associated with large decreases in the volatility and vice versa. So, empirically there appears to be a link not only between the levels of the two processes, but also between the signs of the changes. An uncorrelated volatility process is therefore not the dog.

A similar argument, however, also shows that a GARCH-type process is unlikely be responsible for the observed behaviour. The increase in volatility produced by a GARCH process in fact depends on the *square* of the past returns, and is therefore sign-insensitive: a large increase in the level of rates can produce an increase in volatility just as effectively as a large fall. This, again, is against the empirical evidence presented in previous chapters.

All of this ties in well with financial intuition: in most situations, the arrival of new information will have a first-order impact on the level of rates; the subsequent increase in uncertainty will *then* cause volatility to increase. On the other hand, it is difficult to think of a financial mechanism that might give rise to a large increase in volatility first, that then feeds into larger-than-normal moves in the yield curve. In a nutshell, in the picture I am presenting, the forward rates are the dog, and the volatility is definitely the tail.

25.3   Displaced Diffusion vs CEV

I have discussed in the previous chapter that, for suitable values of the exponent, the CEV process can prevent forward rates from becoming negative. In this respect is it therefore more desirable, but also more difficult to implement, than the displaced-diffusion approach. However, for computational purposes and for simplicity of exposition I will assume in this chapter that, given a preferred exponent for the CEV process, the equivalent displacement coefficient has been determined, and I will work directly with displaced diffusions. In most cases this should give rise to few problems. When the level of rates is particularly low (at this writing, short-term interest rates in USD stand at 1.00%), the displaced-diffusion solution might become questionable. In these cases, the CEV approach could be used instead, possibly coupled with the numerical techniques described in the previous chapter. In either case, the approach presented in what follows would not change, and only the interpretation of the volatility that assumes a diffusive behaviour does: it would be in one case the volatility of $(f + a)$, and in other the term σ_β in

$$\mathrm{d}f = \mu_f \, \mathrm{d}t + f^\beta \sigma_\beta(t) \, \mathrm{d}z_t \tag{25.1}$$

25.4   The Approach

The method here proposed is discussed at greater length in Joshi and Rebonato (2003) and Rebonato (2002). The reader is therefore referred to these works for more details. The broad outline of the approach is as follows.

In order to extend the standard LIBOR market model (LMM) one can start from its usual deterministic-volatility formulation, with the instantaneous volatility function discussed in Chapter 21:

$$\frac{\mathrm{d}f_T(t)}{f_T(t)} = \mu_{f_T} \, \mathrm{d}t + \sigma(t, T) \, \mathrm{d}z_T(t) \tag{25.2}$$

$$\sigma(t, T) = k_T g(T - t) \tag{25.3}$$

$$g(T - t) = [a + b(T - t)] \exp[-c(T - t)] + d \tag{25.4}$$

where $\sigma(t, T)$ is the instantaneous volatility at time t of the T-maturity forward rate, and k_T is a forward-rate-specific constant needed in order to ensure correct pricing of the associated caplet. Ignoring smiles for the moment, we have seen (Equation (21.11)) that the caplet pricing condition is ensured in the deterministic-volatility setting by imposing that

$$\frac{\widehat{\sigma}(T)^2 T}{\displaystyle\int_0^T g(u, T)^2 \, \mathrm{d}u} = k_T^2 \tag{25.5}$$

The reason for proposing this separable functional form for the instantaneous volatility is that, when the latter is deterministic, this function lends itself very readily to finding the most time-homogeneous evolution of the term structure of volatilities and of the swaption matrix consistent with a given family of parameterized functions $g(T - t)$. As we saw in the Chapter 19, this can be achieved simply by imposing that the idiosyncratic terms, k_T, should be as constant as possible across forward rates. Why do I insist on the time homogeneity of the term structure of volatilities? Because of the link between future re-hedging costs and the future smile surface discussed in Chapter 1. When perfect hedging is not possible, the success of an approximate (parameter-) hedging strategy will be based on how well the model 'knows' about the future re-hedging costs. For a detailed discussion of this point, see also Rebonato (2002) or Brigo and Mercurio (2001).

Once this volatility function has been chosen, the arbitrage-free stochastic differential equation for the evolution of the T_i-expiry forward rate in the Q-measure associated with the chosen numeraire is given by

$$\frac{\mathrm{d}f_{T_i}(t)}{f_{T_i}(t)} = \mu^Q(\{f_{T_j}(t)\}, t)\,\mathrm{d}t + \sigma(t, T_i) \sum_{k=1,m} b_{ik}\,\mathrm{d}z_k^Q(t) \tag{25.6}$$

In this expression $\mathrm{d}z_k^Q$ are orthogonal increments of standard Q-Brownian motions, $\mu^Q(\{f_{T_j}(u)\}, u)$ is the measure-, forward-rate- and time-dependent drift that reflects the conditions of no arbitrage, and the coefficients $\{\mathbf{b}\}$, linked by the caplet-pricing condition $\sum_{k=1,m} b_{ik}^2 = 1$, fully describe the correlation structure given the chosen number, m, of driving factors (see Chapter 19 and Rebonato (1999a, 2002)).

In order to account for smiles, this standard deterministic-volatility formulation can be extended in two ways:

1. by positing a displaced-diffusion evolution of the forward rates according to

$$\frac{\mathrm{d}\left[f_{T_i}(t) + \alpha\right]}{f_{T_i}(t) + \alpha} = \mu_\alpha^Q\left(\{f_{T_j}(t)\}, t\right)\,\mathrm{d}t + \sigma_\alpha(t, T_i) \sum_{k=1,m} b_{ik}\,\mathrm{d}z_k^Q(t) \tag{25.7}$$

and

2. by making the instantaneous volatility non-deterministic via the following stochastic mean-reverting behaviour for the coefficients a, b, c and d, or their logarithm, as appropriate:

$$\mathrm{d}a_t = RS_a(RL_a - a_t)\,\mathrm{d}t + \sigma_a(t)\,\mathrm{d}z_t^a \tag{25.8}$$

$$\mathrm{d}b_t = RS_b(RL_b - b_t)\,\mathrm{d}t + \sigma_b(t)\,\mathrm{d}z_t^b \tag{25.9}$$

$$\mathrm{d}\ln c_t = RS_c(RL_c - \ln c_t)\,\mathrm{d}t + \sigma_c(t)\,\mathrm{d}z_t^c \tag{25.10}$$

$$\mathrm{d}\ln d_t = RS_d(RL_d - \ln d_t)\,\mathrm{d}t + \sigma_d(t)\,\mathrm{d}z_t^d \tag{25.11}$$

Note that in Equation (25.7) both the drifts and the volatilities refer to the quantity $f + a$. Also, in Equations (25.8)–(25.11) all the Brownian increments are uncorrelated with each other and with all the Brownian increments $\mathrm{d}z_k^Q(t)$ and the symbols RS_a, RS_b, RS_c, RS_d,

RL_a, RL_b, RL_c and RL_d denote the reversion speeds and reversion levels, respectively, of the relative coefficients, or of their logarithms, as appropriate.

It is important to comment on the assumption of independence of the increments of the Brownian processes shocking the volatility on the one hand, and the forward rates on the other. This independence is crucial to the practical implementation presented below, and is financially motivated by the change of variables behind a displaced-diffusion or CEV description. Recall, in fact, from Chapter 23 that a CEV exponent close to zero was shown to produce changes in implied volatilities almost independent of changes in the underlying, in good (if not perfect) agreement with empirical observations. In practice this de-coupling of the volatility and interest-rate dynamics is achieved by means of the displacement coefficient α (see Rubinstein (1983) and Marris (1999) for the link with the CEV model), which is introduced to account for the deviation from exact proportionality with the level of the basis point move of the forward rates. It is this feature that produces a monotonically decaying (with strike) component of the smile surface. In addition, the stochastic behaviour of the (coefficients of) the instantaneous volatility is invoked in order to account for the residual variability displayed in Figure 25.1. I show below that this feature can also account for the more recently observed 'hockey-stick' shape of the smile curves.

What is the financial meaning of Equations (25.8)–(25.11)? Given the econometric interpretation that can be given to a, b, c and d (see the discussion in Chapter 21), Equations (25.8)–(25.11) allow the initial slope, the long-term level and the location of the maximum of the instantaneous volatility functions to fluctuate stochastically around some long-term levels. The resulting changes in the instantaneous volatility are shown in Figures 25.2–25.5.

25.5 Implementing and Calibrating the Stochastic-Volatility LMM

One of the most appealing features of the LMM is its ease of calibration to market prices. For the stochastic-volatility extension to remain popular and useful it is necessary to provide similarly practical and financially well motivated calibration procedures. An overview of how this can be accomplished is given in this section. Again, Rebonato (2002) and Joshi and Rebonato (2003) provide more details.

The general strategy that can be followed to calibrate the stochastic-volatility extension of the LMM presented above in an efficient way rests on three simple observations.

1. Given the posited independence between the forward rates and the stochastic volatilities, *conditional on a particular volatility path having been realized*, the problem looks exactly like a standard (deterministic-volatility) LMM problem.

2. The Black formula is, at-the-money, almost exactly linear in the root-mean-square volatility.

3. Joshi and Rebonato (2003) show that surprisingly few volatility paths are sufficient for an accurate sampling of the volatility probability density.

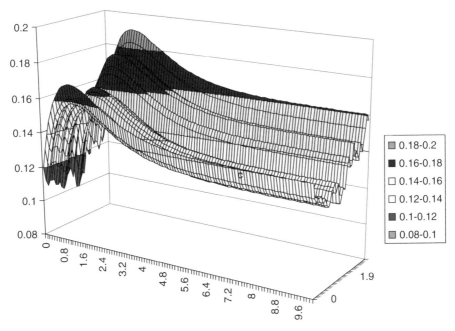

Figure 25.2   The instantaneous volatility curve when $a = -0.02$, $b = 0.1$, $c = 1$, $d(0) = 0.14$, and d is stochastic.

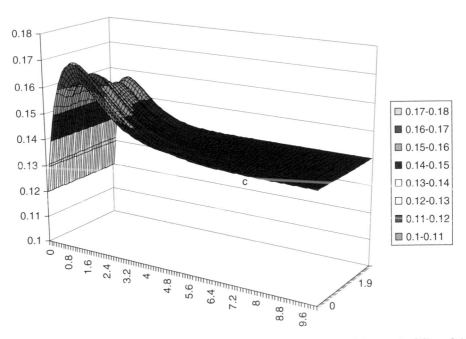

Figure 25.3   The instantaneous volatility curve when $a = -0.02$, $b = 0.1$, $c = 1$, $d(0) = 0.14$, and c is stochastic.

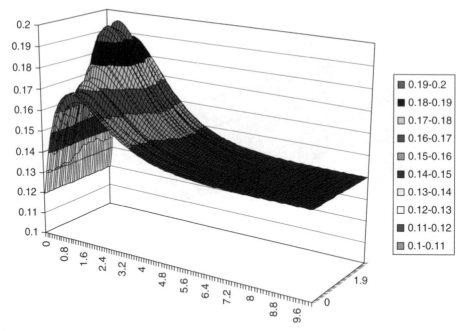

Figure 25.4   The instantaneous volatility curve when $a = -0.02$, $b = 0.1$, $c = 1$, $d(0) = 0.14$, and b is stochastic.

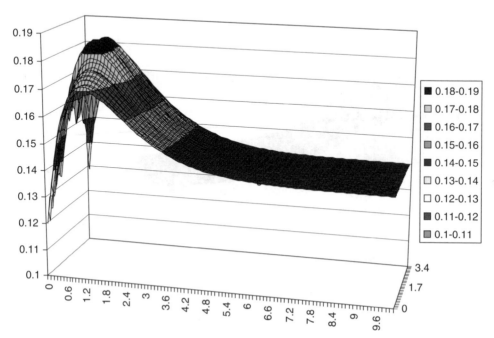

Figure 25.5   The instantaneous volatility curve when $a = -0.02$, $b = 0.1$, $c = 1$, $d(0) = 0.14$, and a is stochastic.

25.5.1 Evolving the Forward Rates

How can we use these results? Let us divide the (sometimes very long) interval over which the forward rates have to be propagated into smaller steps, Δs_l, $l = 1, \ldots, m$, and evolve a, b, c and d over these time segments using Equations (25.8)–(25.11). Let a_l, b_l, c_l and d_l denote the values of the coefficients that prevail in the lth sub-interval. Since these coefficients (or their logarithms) follow a Ornstein–Uhlenbeck process, the evolution of the coefficient over the sub-interval can be done exactly. For each small step one can create a forward-rate marginal covariance matrix for that step, C_l^f. More precisely, the entry of C_l^f for the forward rates expiring at T_j and T_k will be

$$C_l^f(j, k) = G(l, j)G(l, k)\rho_{jk}\Delta s_l \qquad (25.12)$$

with

$$G(l, j) \equiv (a_l + b_l(T_j - s_l)) \exp\left[-c_l(T_j - s_l) + d_l\right] \qquad (25.13)$$

Let us construct a total covariance matrix $\mathbf{C}^f$ by summing C_l^f for $l = 1, \ldots, m$:

$$\mathbf{C}^f(j, k) = \sum_{l=1,m} C_l^f(j, k) \qquad (25.14)$$

One can then calculate a pseudo-square-root,[3] $\mathbf{A}^f$, of $\mathbf{C}^f$ and evolve the forward rates across the typically much longer interval $\Delta T_r = \sum_{l=1,\ldots m} \Delta s_l$ according to

$$\ln f_j(T_{r+1} + \alpha) = \ln f_j(T_r + \alpha) + \mu_j \Delta T_r + \sum_i A_{ij}^f Z_i \qquad (25.15)$$

with Z_i independent standard normal draws. In order to carry out the evolution one will in general have to apply the accurate predictor–corrector approximation presented by Hunter *et al.* (2001) *on a path-by-path basis*. The fundamental advantage of the technique is that only the volatility process need be short-stepped, and, conditional on a particular volatility path having been obtained, the forward rates can still be evolved, as in the standard LMM, using the predictor–corrector methodology and the powerful 'very-long-jump' procedure (see, for example, Rebonato (2002)). Therefore the pricing of complex derivatives in a trading environment becomes a demanding but feasible computational task.

25.5.2 Calibrating to Caplet Prices

The same set-up can be used to calibrate to the caplet surface, to calculate semi-analytically the price of a European swaption, and to calibrate almost exactly and in an optimal way a forward-rate-based stochastic-volatility LMM to the set of co-terminal European swaptions that underlie a given Bermudan swaption. For the sake of brevity only the first case

---

[3]In principle, one could carry out an orthogonalization of the covariance matrix. Evaluation of the pseudo-square root is however computationally more desirable.

is treated below, but the reader is referred to Joshi and Rebonato (2003) and to Rebonato (2002) for a detailed analysis of the other cases.

How can we calibrate the model to caplet prices? I present below a two-part strategy to calibrate the model exactly to the at-the-money prices. One could follow different procedures, perhaps by attempting to get an overall best fit to the whole surface without recovering exactly any one set of market prices. I have chosen to give a 'privileged' status to the at-the-money prices, but, if the trader did not feel this to be important, the second step of the procedure below could be skipped. This would have the advantage of making the resulting solution exactly (instead of approximately) time homogeneous.

Calibrating to Caplet Prices: First Step

Let us focus attention on the diagonal elements, $C_l^f(j, j)$, of the covariance matrix (25.12) constructed above and, to lighten notation, let us call them V_l^j, with

$$C_l^f(j, j) \equiv V_l^j \tag{25.16}$$

If we sum over all the diagonal elements V_l^j, of the marginal covariance matrix to obtain for the jth forward rate we obtain the main diagonal elements of the total covariance matrix, $\mathbf{C}^f(j, j)$:

$$\mathbf{C}^f(j, j) \equiv \mathbf{V}^j = \sum_{l=1,m} V_l^j \tag{25.17}$$

To each set of realizations V_l^j there corresponds a volatility path, and a root-mean-squared volatility. To price the jth caplet conditional on a particular volatility path having been realized, one can therefore compute the root-mean-squared volatility, $\widehat{\sigma}_j$, associated with this path:

$$\widehat{\sigma}_j^2 T = \mathbf{V}^j = \sum_{l=1,m} V_l^j \tag{25.18}$$

and use it in the displaced-diffusion Black formula, $Black(.)$. This will be the caplet price contingent on a particular volatility path having been realized. Adapting results first presented by Hull and White (1987), the price, P_j, of the jth caplet will then be given by

$$P_j = \int Black(\widehat{\sigma}_j)\phi(\widehat{\sigma}_j)\,d\widehat{\sigma}_j \tag{25.19}$$

The density $\phi(.)$ is not known analytically, but it can be sampled very efficiently using low-discrepancy numbers (see observation 3 above). To make the procedure computationally practical, a single evolution to the longest caplet maturity can be carried out. With the forward rates evolved to the terminal horizon all the caplets (i.e. caplets for all strikes and maturities) can be priced at once. An entire caplet surface can therefore be evaluated in under a second using a Pentium II, 200 MHz computer.

By doing so, we can therefore express all the caplet prices as a function of the parameters of the volatility process. As a first step in the procedure, these parameters can be varied so as to minimize the sum of the squared discrepancies between the market and the model caplet prices. Let us denote all these parameters collectively by $\{\alpha\}$, and their optimal set of values by $\{\widetilde{\alpha}\}$. If the trader wanted an overall best fit without necessarily recovering exactly any particular set of caplet prices, nothing else would be required. If exact recovery of the at-the-money caplets were deemed to be desirable, the step below can be undertaken.

Calibrating to Caplet Prices: Second Step

As in the deterministic-volatility case, after the first step the agreement between model and market prices will, in general, not be perfect. In order to match these two quantities exactly at-the-money, one can now invoke the almost exact linearity in volatility for the at-the-money strike of the Black formula (see observation 2 above). Let k_{T_i} be the ratio between the market and the model at-the-money price for the ith caplet. Then, if one multiplies the optimized instantaneous volatility of the ith forward rate by k_{T_i}, along any given path the root-mean-squared volatility will also be multiplied by k_{T_i} and so will be (approximately but extremely accurately) the at-the-money caplet price. This second step can be carried out analytically, and therefore the computational burden is minimal.

Quality of the Fit to Market Caplet Prices

As discussed at length in this book, closeness of fit to a market caplet smile surface should not be *per se* the only, or even the main, test of the reasonableness of a model. It is none the less obviously important to check the quality of the match between model and market prices. Figures 25.6–25.9 show the results obtained for the fit to a market smile caplet surface (GBP 1-Aug-2000). It is important to point out that the fit was obtained using the same parameters for the whole surface (i.e. for all strikes and all maturities). The figures

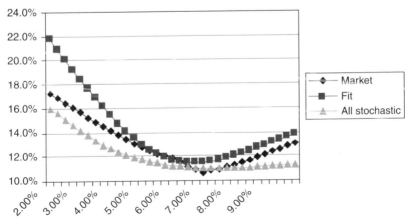

Figure 25.6   Fit to the market caplet smile (GBP 1-Aug-2000) when all the coefficients are allowed to display the stochastic behaviour described in Equations (25.8)–(25.11) (curves labelled 'All stochastic'), or when only the 'level' parameter d is allowed to be stochastic (curves labelled 'Fit'). Maturities from 1 to 8 years.

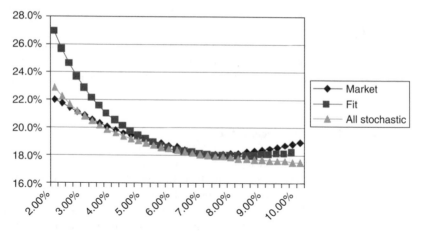

Figure 25.7   Fit to the market caplet smile (GBP 1-Aug-2000) when all the coefficients are allowed to display the stochastic behaviour described in Equations (25.8)–(25.11) (curves labelled 'All stochastic'), or when only the 'level' parameter d is allowed to be stochastic (curves labelled 'Fit'). Maturities from 1 to 8 years.

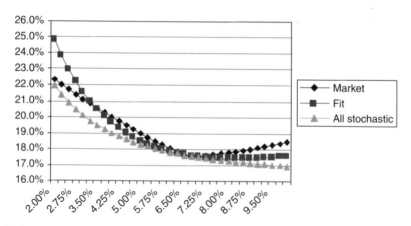

Figure 25.8   Fit to the market caplet smile (GBP 1-Aug-2000) when all the coefficients are allowed to display the stochastic behaviour described in Equations (25.8)–(25.11) (curves labelled 'All stochastic'), or when only the 'level' parameter d is allowed to be stochastic (curves labelled 'Fit'). Maturities from 1 to 8 years.

show the quality of the fit obtained by allowing either all the coefficients or only d to be stochastic. In both cases perfect fit of the at-the-money prices was imposed by using the rescaling factors, k_{T_i}.

With the exception of the shortest maturity, the agreement between the market and the model smile surfaces remains very good in a wide region around the at-the-money strike (at-the-money is perfect by construction because we have followed the two-step procedure outlined above). Allowing for a stochastic behaviour for all the coefficients obviously provides a better overall fit. The quality of the only-d-stochastic fit, however, is not much worse, and only appears to fail noticeably for extremely out-of-the-money

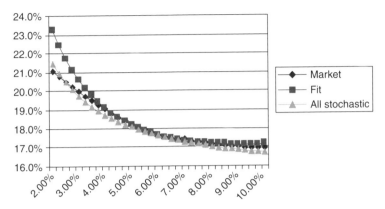

Figure 25.9 Fit to the market caplet smile (GBP 1-Aug-2000) when all the coefficients are allowed to display the stochastic behaviour described in Equations (25.8)–(25.11) (curves labelled 'All stochastic'), or when only the 'level' parameter d is allowed to be stochastic (curves labelled 'Fit'). Maturities from 1 to 8 years.

strikes. For these strikes the reliability of market quotes is questionable in any case. Furthermore, the optimal solutions turned out to be very similar irrespective of whether a restricted (d-only) or general optimization was carried out. This lends some reassurance as to the robustness of the procedure.

Degree of Time Homogeneity of the Solution

Since we have chosen to follow a two-step procedure in order to get a perfect at-the-money fit to the market prices, we have been forced to introduce forward-rate-specific rescaling coefficients, k_{T_i}. From the discussion in Chapter 19 we know that, by so doing, the resulting term structure of volatilities is no longer exactly time homogeneous. For the two-step procedure to make financial sense these coefficients should therefore provide a fine-tuning of an almost correct solution, but should not alter it too strongly. It is therefore very important (and encouraging) to draw attention to the fact that the rescaling coefficients, k_{T_i}, necessary to ensure perfect fit to the at-the-money prices, obtained in the market case discussed were empirically found to be extremely close to unity. See Figure 25.10. Similar results were found for all the market cases examined.

  The importance of this result cannot be stressed strongly enough. By virtue of the fact that the optimized coefficients are such that the scaling factors are approximately independent of the forward rates we can achieve not only a perfect fit to today's at-the-money prices and a very good fit to today's smile surface, but we can also ensure that the future will (statistically) look like the present. If we believe the self-similarity (at least in a statistical sense) of the smile surface to be a robust and persistent market property, this feature is therefore directly linked to obtaining a desirable estimate of the future re-hedging costs. To the extent that a model 'guesses' a substantially correct relationship between future realizations of the yield curve and future smile surfaces it will be able to incorporate this information into the price of exotic products. This is at the root of the market lore about 'gamma-vega'. The ability of the proposed approach to display, at least approximately, this property is possibly its most important feature.

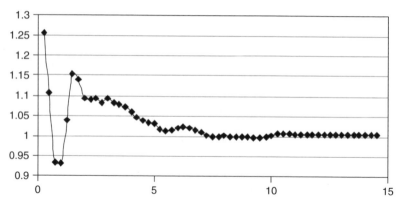

Figure 25.10   The scaling factors k_{T_i} necessary to bring about exact recovery of the at-the-money prices.

25.6   Suggestions and Plan of the Work Ahead

The ability to produce a good fit to a market implied volatility surface is a necessary but by no means sufficient condition for the adequacy of a modelling approach. One would therefore like to have additional, and more powerful, indicators of the suitability of a modelling approach. In particular, given the importance I give to the recovery of the correct future vega re-hedging costs, one might want to compare the real-world and model-predicted evolution of the term structures of volatilities. Unfortunately, naïve comparisons between real-world and risk-adjusted quantities are unwarranted because of the Girsanov transformation of the drift of the volatility process in moving between measures. I therefore address in the next chapter the topic of how, despite this drift transformation, a meaningful comparison can sometimes still be carried out.

Chapter 26

The Dynamics of the Swaption Matrix

26.1 Plan of the Chapter

I discuss in this chapter[1] how empirical data about the evolution of the swaption matrix[2] can provide information that can be used to assess the quality of an interest-rate model. This is important because, as I have argued throughout this book, tests of models based purely on the quality of fits to current market prices tend to be rather weak and uninformative.

Bringing information about the evolution of the swaption matrix into play is, however, not straightforward. When the volatility becomes stochastic one must be very careful in making naïve comparisons about the evolution of the volatilities in the real world and as predicted by a model. This is because the risk-adjusted and the real-world drifts of the volatility process are changed by a Girsanov transformation in moving across measures (see, for example, Lewis (2000)). This is correct, but rather abstract. To see more directly why a naïve comparison might be misleading, consider, for instance, the case of a mean-reverting process for the instantaneous volatility of the forward rates. We have seen (see Chapter 13) that the reversion speed of the volatility can change, because of risk aversion, in moving between the real-world and the risk-neutral measures. Let us suppose for a moment that the (measure-invariant) volatility of the volatility was 'large'. In this situation, if in the risk-adjusted world the reversion speed were to be, say, much higher than in the real world, a time-series analysis of the model-produced implied volatilities would display a 'burstiness' not observed in the real world. This would translate (see Section 13.2.3) into a greater model-implied de-coupling of volatilities of different-expiry forward rates than observed in reality. This could happen even if the stochastic-volatility model were correctly specified. Direct observation of the real-world and model-produced behaviour of implied volatilities could therefore suggest the wrong conclusion.

---

[1]Parts of this chapter have been adapted from Rebonato and Joshi (2002), and Rebonato (2002).

[2]The swaption matrix is the collection of at-the-money volatilities of swaptions of different expiries and different lengths of the underlying swap.

Fortunately, there can be some volatility-related quantities that do remain unchanged in moving from one measure to the other, at least if the process for the volatility is a simple diffusion. I will show below that these quantities can be obtained as a by-product of the orthogonalization of the covariance matrix of the changes in implied volatility. It is important to keep in mind, however, that the measure invariance of these quantities is not universal. In the next chapter I will discuss a model based on volatility-regime switches where the quantities that are invariant in the measure transformation for simple diffusions cease to be so when a Markov-chain process for the volatility is introduced. The methodology I present in this chapter will still provide, however, some useful information.

This chapter looks at swaption, rather than caplet, information. This might appear surprising, because the formulation of the LIBOR market model I present in this book is based on the evolution of forward rates. The reason for this is that brokers' quotes of *cap*, rather than *caplet*, implied volatilities are directly screen-visible.[3] In the presence of smiles, it is not a simple and model-independent task to extract from these quotes the at-the-money volatilities of the underlying caplets. The swaption information is, on the other hand, much 'cleaner', since each screen quote refers to one single at-the-money option. The construction of the swaption implied volatility matrix is therefore a much simpler and unambiguous task, since it requires at most a two-dimensional interpolation/extrapolation exercise. For this reason in the present and in the following chapters I often choose to work with swaption, rather than caplet, implied volatilities.

26.2   Assessing the Quality of a Model

I indicated in the first section that I intend to use swaption-matrix information to assess the quality of a model. What do I mean by that? There are several levels at which the 'validity' or 'reasonableness' of a modelling approach, such as the stochastic-volatility model discussed in the previous chapter, can be assessed. The most demanding test would require a substantial congruence between the relevant marginal and conditional moments of the distributions of the stochastic quantities produced by the model and observed in reality. If this test were rigorously applied, all the modelling approaches (including the standard LIBOR market model) based on a geometric Brownian motion assumption for the underlying (be it an FX or interest-rate or an equity price) would probably be strongly rejected.

A weaker criterion of a model's adequacy and reasonableness is to require that some well-chosen high-level descriptive statistics should compare well across measures. The implicit hope in doing so is that option pricing might depend to first order on these high-level statistics, and only weakly on the finer details. An example of this approach is the comparison the results of PCA obtained using real-world and model-produced data. Indeed, many of the most popular implementations of the deterministic-volatility LIBOR market model are explicitly based on a rescaling and matching of the Brownian drivers to the eigenvalues and eigenvectors obtained from orthogonalization of the real-world

---

[3]The market adopts the following convention in quoting a cap implied volatility: given the strike and the expiry of the cap, the associated implied volatility is the single number that must be input into the Black formulae for all the associated caplets in order to obtain the desired market price for the whole cap by adding up all the resulting caplet prices. Note that this procedure implies a much greater degree of price opaqueness than what is normally entailed by quoting an implied volatility, since, even in the absence of smiles, a *cap* implied volatility is not related in any obvious way to the root-mean-squared volatility of any of the underlying caplets.

correlation or covariance matrices. See, for example, Hull and White (2000), Rebonato (1999) and the discussion in Section 19.3.

It must be stressed that a PCA can be used in two distinct manners. In the first approach it is assumed that the underlying process is indeed a Brownian diffusion. In this case the eigenvectors produced by the orthogonalization of the covariance matrix provide a convenient 'rotation of axes', and the eigenvalues the projections onto these new axes, but the resulting dynamics is statistically fully equivalent to the original one. Very often one will want to use this approach to retain fewer modes of deformation than present in the original dynamics, but, if this culling of the eigenvectors is not carried out, the original and the derived processes are fully equivalent. The same orthogonalization of an empirically obtained covariance matrix can be used even if the underlying process was not a Brownian diffusion. If this is the case, however, even if one employed all the resulting eigenvectors and eigenvalues to simulate the process, one would not obtain a model evolution statistically equivalent to the original dynamics. These eigenvalues and eigenvectors can still be used, however, as complex but high-level informative 'summary statistics' describing the underlying process. When used in this sense, they would be on a conceptual par with, but richer than, such familiar statistics as the mean, the standard deviation, the coefficient of serial correlation, etc. I therefore explore in this chapter not only whether the proposed stochastic instantaneous volatility approach introduced in the previous chapters passes the more stringent test of an overall distributional match; but also whether, and under what circumstances, it can be made to satisfy the weaker criteria of a PCA test, when the PCA is understood in the second sense.

The results reported and discussed in Sections 26.3 and 26.4 are intrinsically interesting. They also have a wider appeal, because the proposed methodology can constitute a useful blueprint for analysing the financial desirability of a wide class of yield-curve models that produce stochastic future swaption matrices.

26.3 The Empirical Analysis

26.3.1 Description of the Data

The data set used consisted of 83 136 data points (57 156 for USD and 25 980 for DEM), corresponding to all the trading dates between 1-Jan-1998 and 1-May-2001 (866 trading days, 3 years and 4 months). In the case of USD for each trading day the following at-the-money implied volatilities were available: 3m, 6m, 9m, 1y, 2y, 3y, 4y, 5y, 7y and 10y into 1y, 2y, 3y, 5y, 7y and 10y. (A remark on notation and terminology: the $a \times b$ European swaption is the swaption expiring in a years', or months', time, as appropriate, to exercise into a b-year swap. So, the 6m × 5y, read '6 months into 5 years', swaption is the option to pay or receive fixed for five years in six months' time.)

In the case of DEM/EUR the following expiries were available: 3m, 6m, 1y, 2y and 3y for exercise into 2y, 3y, 4y, 5y, 7y and 10y swaps. Less than 0.12% of the data was missing, unreliable or corrupted. For these cases, in order to preserve equal time spacings between observations, rather than eliminating the trading day, a bilinear interpolation between the neighbouring cells was carried out. Care was taken to ensure that the interpolation procedure did not alter the final results in any significant way.

The data set is particularly significant because it encompasses both the Russia crisis and the series of unexpected rate cuts carried out by the US Fed in the first months of 2001.

Indeed, non-monotonic implied volatility smiles have appeared in the swaption market after the events associated with the Russia crisis. Despite the fact that in this chapter I do not directly address the smile issue, and restrict my attention to at-the-money volatilities, anecdotal market evidence indicates that it was indeed the occurrence of dramatic changes in the swaption implied volatility matrix during this period that prompted the trading community to revise the shape of quoted volatility surfaces.

Using this data the absolute[4] daily changes in implied volatilities were calculated. The resulting data were organized in a matrix, with the first column containing the changes for the first expiry into the first swap length, the second column containing the changes for the first expiry into the second swap length,..., the sixty-sixth (thirtieth) column containing the changes of the eleventh (fifth) expiry into the sixth swap length for USD (DEM/EUR). In moving across columns, the data therefore naturally present a relatively smooth behaviour as one moves, for a fixed expiry, to swap of increasing length. Then there is a discontinuity as one moves from one expiry to the next. This feature is important in order to understand the structure of the results (e.g. the eigenvectors or the correlation matrix, which cannot be arranged in any two-dimensional array without giving rise to some discontinuities).

Since the data presented are considerably more complex than the more familiar equity or FX implied volatility data, it is worthwhile familiarizing oneself with the data set-up in order better to appreciate the graphs and results presented in what follows. More precisely, since three-dimensional graphs can be dazzling, but are rather difficult to read in detail, I present most of the graphical information by providing on the same graph the implied volatility corresponding to the various expiries on the x-axis, with differently marked curves referring to different swap lengths. The series corresponding to different expiries for a fixed swap length are called the 'into' series. So, the curve corresponding to the implied volatilities of the $3m \times 4y$, $6m \times 4y$, $1y \times 4y$, $2y \times 4y$ and $3y \times 4y$ swaptions will be referred to as the 'into 4y' series.

26.3.2   Results

Qualitative Patterns of the Swaption Matrix

Some of the more salient empirical features of the dynamics of the swaption matrices have been presented in Section 7.4.2 (see also Figures 26.1–26.7). I briefly recall the main results:

1. In all currencies well-identifiable patterns (labelled 'normal' and 'excited') were observed.

2. The transition from one regime to the other (especially from the normal to the excited state) was often rapid (a few days).

3. The fraction of the total time spent in the two regimes was very different for the two states, with most of the time spent in the normal state.

4. Very large changes in implied volatilities are more pronounced for USD than for DEM/EUR.

---

[4]Qualitatively very similar results were obtained by conducting the analysis using percentage, rather than absolute, daily changes.

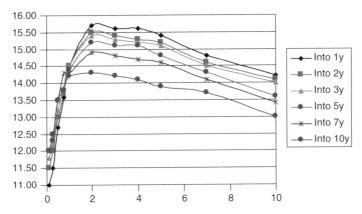

Figure 26.1 Different patterns for the swaption matrix (at-the-money) in the USD market – normal behaviour.

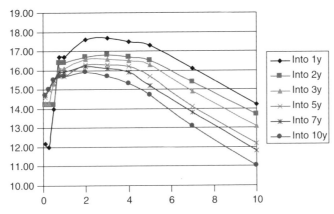

Figure 26.2 Different patterns for the swaption matrix (at-the-money) in the USD market – transitional behaviour.

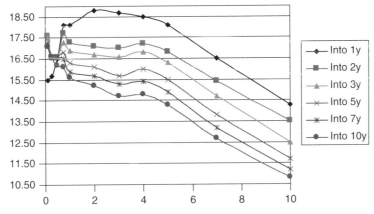

Figure 26.3 Different patterns for the swaption matrix (at-the-money) in the USD market – transitional behaviour.

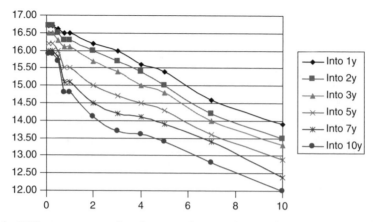

Figure 26.4 Different patterns for the swaption matrix (at-the-money) in the USD market – excited behaviour.

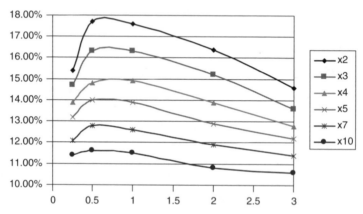

Figure 26.5 Different patterns for the swaption matrix (at-the-money) in the DEM/EUR market – normal behaviour.

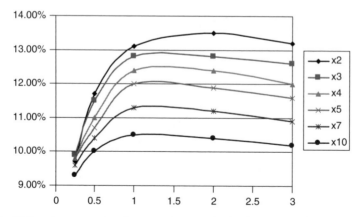

Figure 26.6 Different patterns for the swaption matrix (at-the-money) in the DEM/EUR market – normal behaviour.

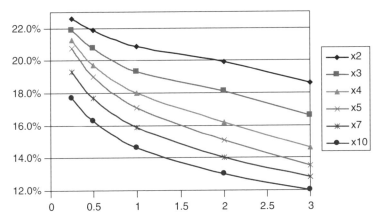

Figure 26.7 Different patterns for the swaption matrix (at-the-money) in the DEM/EUR market – excited behaviour.

Besides being of intrinsic interest, these results are relevant for modelling the stochastic volatility of the forward or swap rates that drive the swaption matrix. Since this latter quantity is in fact given by suitable integrals of the instantaneous volatility, these results suggest that the hypothesis of a purely diffusive behaviour for the instantaneous volatility is strongly rejected.[5] The rejection of the diffusive behaviour for the implied volatility components is not surprising per se. A geometric-diffusion approach has none the less provided a useful first approximation both in the equity and FX worlds and in interest-rate modelling. In this restricted *modus operandi* modellers have accepted the fact that the real-world distributional features of the relevant underlying quantity might be poorly described by a diffusive behaviour, but have none the less retained a Brownian-shock modelling description as long as the shape of the eigenvectors, and the relative magnitude of the eigenvalues, could be matched in the real and risk-adjusted worlds. The results in the following section therefore present PCA data not only for their intrinsic interest, but also in order to explore whether a diffusive-stochastic-volatility LIBOR market model can be justified along these lines.

Correlation and PCA Results

Using the data described above, I constructed the correlation matrix between the (absolute) changes in the implied volatilities. The columns and rows in the matrix were organized as described in Section 26.3.1. Table 26.1 displays a small portion of the USD correlation matrix in order to highlight some of the main features of the whole matrix (similar considerations apply to the DEM/EUR matrix). The 36 elements in the bordered box in the top left-hand corner of the matrix contain the correlation between changes in implied volatilities of the $1y \times 1y$, $1y \times 2y, \ldots, 1y \times 10y$ swaptions. Similarly, the 36 elements in the bordered box in the top right-hand corner of the matrix contain the correlation between changes in implied volatilities for the $2y \times 1y$, $2y \times 2y, \ldots, 2y \times 10y$ swaptions; etc.

---

[5]A series of χ^2 tests to check the hypothesis of whether the sample distribution of any of the empirical implied volatility series could have been drawn from a normal distribution with matching first two moments always gave a probability of less than 10^{-13}.

Table 26.1 A portion of the USD correlation matrix. The 36 elements in the bordered box in the top left-hand corner contain the correlation between changes in implied volatilities of the $1y \times 1y$, $1y \times 2y$, ..., $1y \times 10y$ swaptions. Similarly, the 36 elements in the bordered box in the top right-hand corner of the matrix contain the correlation between changes in implied volatilities for the $2y \times 1y$, $2y \times 2y$, ..., $2y \times 10y$ swaptions.

	1 year into						2 year into					
	1	2	3	5	7	10	1	2	3	5	7	10
1	1	0.7573313	0.70383312	0.70272808	0.6829902	0.66714772	0.84221759	0.72208199	0.67399784	0.66102105	0.6565227	0.61186077
2	0.7573313	1	0.92506863	0.87005919	0.83106392	0.79883191	0.68091232	0.88853052	0.81245114	0.83970274	0.7961068	0.71600212
3	0.70383312	0.92506863	1	0.90081514	0.86441631	0.84816343	0.67311099	0.88370878	0.86123263	0.83457423	0.83785346	0.77343124
5	0.70272808	0.87005919	0.90081514	1	0.90266159	0.87633016	0.65330642	0.87442905	0.85059915	0.87059137	0.83632581	0.81131332
7	0.6829902	0.83106392	0.86441631	0.90266159	1	0.89152726	0.63271429	0.84005688	0.83775257	0.85980908	0.86171228	0.84958077
10	0.66714772	0.79883191	0.84816343	0.87633016	0.89152726	1	0.62925843	0.83917766	0.85590297	0.84799235	0.87911282	0.88349286
1	0.84221759	0.68091232	0.67311099	0.65330642	0.63271429	0.62925843	1	0.72983905	0.67236483	0.66607135	0.64950144	0.58603538
2	0.72208199	0.88853052	0.88370878	0.87442905	0.84005688	0.83917766	0.72983905	1	0.9065737	0.89238509	0.86824658	0.80100429
3	0.67399784	0.81245114	0.86123263	0.85059915	0.83775257	0.85590297	0.67236483	0.9065737	1	0.89298015	0.90110557	0.85150274
5	0.66102105	0.83970274	0.83457423	0.87059137	0.85980908	0.84799235	0.66607135	0.89238509	0.89298015	1	0.92530429	0.84412453
7	0.6565227	0.7961068	0.83785346	0.83632581	0.86171228	0.87911282	0.64950144	0.86824658	0.90110557	0.92530429	1	0.92073865
10	0.61186077	0.71600212	0.77343124	0.81131332	0.84958077	0.88349286	0.58603538	0.80100429	0.85150274	0.84412453	0.92073865	1

There are several interesting features worth noting:

- for a given expiry, the correlation tends to be a convex function of the swap lengths; this feature remains true for all expiries, and in both currencies;

- for a given swap length (i.e. for a given 'into' series), the correlation displays less convexity as a function of swaption expiry than as a function of the underlying swap length;

- given the way the USD matrix has been organized, there are discontinuities with a periodicity of 6 (the number of expiries) both as one moves across columns (from one 'into' series to the next) and as one moves down rows (from one swap length to the next); similar considerations apply to the DEM/EUR matrix;

- the correlation between changes in implied volatilities of very 'distant' swaptions (i.e. swaptions with greatly different expiries and swap lengths) is very low (approximately 20% for USD and 15% for DEM/EUR).

With these preliminary considerations in mind, one can better understand the shape of the overall correlation matrices for the two currencies, reported in Figure 26.8 for the case of the DEM/EUR currency (the qualitative shape of the USD matrix is the same). One can easily recognize the jagged structural features of the correlation matrix due to the transition from one expiry series to the next, or from one swap length series to the next. It is important to point out that this jagged behaviour, clearly displayed in Figure 26.8, is not due to noise, but to the way the two-dimensional data must be organized along a one-dimensional axis. The individual correlation curves inside each of the 6 × 6 boxes in Table 26.1 are indeed remarkably smooth, indicating that prima-facie statistical noise should not be a concern as far as the interpretation of the data is concerned.

With these correlation matrices one can obtain, by orthogonalization of the correlation matrix, the associated eigenvectors and eigenvalues. The results for USD and DEM/EUR are shown in Figures 26.9–26.11.

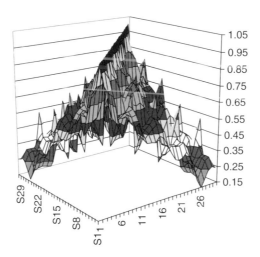

Figure 26.8 The full EUR/DEM correlation matrix.

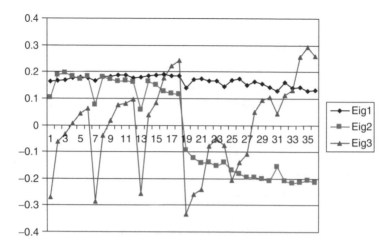

Figure 26.9   The first three eigenvectors of the correlation matrix for USD.

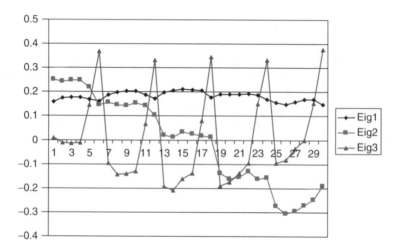

Figure 26.10   The first three eigenvectors of the correlation matrix for DEM/EUR.

The first noteworthy feature is the strong qualitative similarity of the results for the two currencies. The shape of the eigenvectors also lends itself to an interesting interpretation: the first principal component, as usual, displays loadings of similar magnitude across the various swaption implied volatilities, and therefore describes the typical up-and-down rigid shift of the swaption matrix.[6] This first mode of deformation, however, only accounts for less than 60% both in USD and DEM/EUR. The second mode of deformation corresponds to the first three series moving up (down) and the last three series moving down (up). Finally, the third eigenvector mainly picks up movements *within* each series, with, say,

---

[6]The first eigenvector is virtually flat when the *correlation*, as opposed to the *covariance*, matrix is orthogonalized. Therefore the most important mode of deformation is a parallel shift only after scaling by the volatilities. See the discussion later in the section.

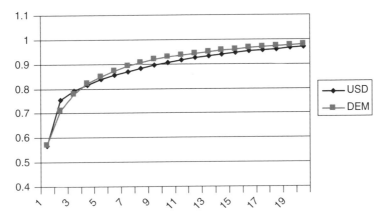

Figure 26.11 The eigenvalues of the correlation matrix for USD and DEM/EUR.

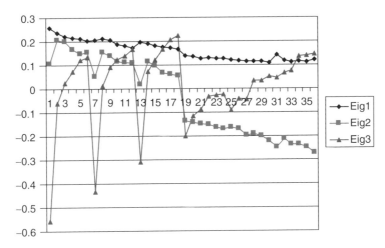

Figure 26.12 The first three eigenvectors of the covariance matrix for USD.

the implied volatility of swaptions into short swap lengths moving up and the volatility of swaptions into long swap lengths moving down.

Finally, it is also worth pointing out the remarkable similarity, in the two currencies, of the explanatory power of an increasing number of eigenvectors, as shown in Figure 26.11. For both USD and for DEM/EUR, it takes approximately 10 eigenvectors to explain 90% of the variability across series of expiries and swap lengths. This result should be contrasted with the findings of PCA on yields or forward rates, where, typically, 90% of the variability is explained by four or fewer eigenvectors (see, for example, Martellini and Priaulet (2001) for a recent survey of results). It must be stressed that the data sample used for this study included two particularly 'excited' periods, i.e. both the Russia crisis and its aftermath, and the aggressive easing by the Fed in early 2001. It would be interesting to see whether data in more 'normal' periods would display the same features.

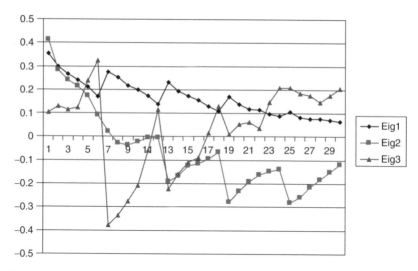

Figure 26.13   The first three eigenvectors of the covariance matrix for DEM/EUR.

Similar, but, at the same time, interestingly different, results were obtained by orthogonalizing the covariance matrix rather than the correlation matrix. See Figures 26.12 and 26.13. The most noteworthy difference is that the loadings onto the various implied volatilities now display a pronounced decaying behaviour as one moves across columns, indicating that the top left-hand corner of the swaption matrix is more volatile than the bottom right-hand corner. This observation, not surprising *per se*, will become very relevant in the discussion of the role of mean reversion in the stochastic-volatility model discussed later in this chapter. Without pre-empting future results, it is worthwhile pointing out that these findings will be shown to be compatible with a mean-reverting process for the instantaneous volatility. Finally, the explanatory power of an increasing number of covariance-matrix eigenvectors was found to be quite similar to what was found by orthogonalizing the correlation matrix.

26.4   Extracting the Model-Implied Principal Components

Up to this point we have established some empirical properties of the swaption matrix. If we looked at these same quantities (e.g. at the eigenvalues and eigenvectors obtained by orthogonalizing the correlation and covariance matrices) as predicted by the model proposed in the previous chapter, how would they compare? More specifically (see also Rebonato and Joshi (2002)), we could ask the following questions.

1. If one uses the stochastic-volatility approach described in Chapter 25, how many principal components are required in order to account for the stochastic evolution of the swaption matrix to a given percentage of explanatory power (fraction of variance explained)?

2. How does the first principal component (the eigenvector) obtained from the orthogonalization of the model covariance matrix compare with the corresponding empirically observed quantity?

3. Does this first principal component change its qualitative behaviour when the volatilities are mean reverting?

4. Did the displacement coefficient have a significant effect on the overall qualitative behaviour of the first principal component?

In order to carry out this investigation, one needs the model covariance and correlation matrices of the changes in implied volatilities. These are not directly available from the model specification, and must therefore be obtained numerically. The algorithm used to carry out this investigation was the following.

- For both currencies, typical values for the parameters a, b, c and d that describe the process were first chosen so as to provide an adequate fit to the relative market prices.

- The coefficients a, b, c and d were then evolved over a time-step of one week using the mean-reverting dynamics described in Chapter 25. See (25.8)–(25.11). Since an Ornstein–Uhlenbeck process for the coefficients (or their logarithms) had been chosen, the evolution of the instantaneous volatilities over these time-steps could be accomplished exactly and analytically.

- Given this joint realization of the instantaneous volatilities, the forward rates were evolved over the same time-step using for their evolution the equations in Chapter 25, which give the volatility experienced by each forward rate.

- After performing this step, all the forward rates were then 'shorter' by one week. The market data, however, refer to constant-maturity swaptions. The yield curve must therefore be 'reset' so that the expiries of the various forward rates remained a constant time away from the new spot time. In other words, constant-maturity forward rates (and hence constant-maturity and constant-expiry swaptions) were repeatedly generated during the course of the simulation.

- Given this state of the world all the required swaptions in the different series and for the different expiries were priced, and their prices translated into implied volatilities. This would give rise to the first sample of the model-implied swaption matrix.

- The procedure would then be repeated over the next time-step thereby generating an artificial time series for the swaption implied volatilities (swaption matrices), for a total of 1000 weeks.

- The changes in this time series over 1000 weeks were finally used to generate a covariance matrix that was then diagonalized.

Note that, for numerical reasons, the time-step was taken to be one week (as opposed to the daily spacing between the real-world data). Even over one week, however, the changes in implied volatilities are mainly driven by the stochastic term: for typical values of the volatility and of the forward rates, and for the chosen time-step, the volatility terms are typically 200 to 500 times larger than the drift term,[7] and therefore the numerical procedure presented above adequately estimates the *instantaneous* covariance matrix.

---

[7]For this order-of-magnitude calculation the forward rate was taken to be 6.00% and the instantaneous volatility 15.00%. A constant correlation of 90% among all the forward rates was also assumed.

Table 26.2   The parameters of the instantaneous volatility process used in the simulation.

Coefficient	Initial value	Volatility	Rev. speed	Rev. level
a	−0.02	10.00%	0.5	−0.02
b	0.108	10.00%	0.3	0.108
$\ln(c)$	0.8	10.00%	0.5	0.8
$\ln(d)$	0.114	10.00%	0.4	0.114

The parameters used for this exercise are given in Table 26.2.

In addition to the instantaneous volatility function, a functional shape for the correlation had to be chosen in order to describe the covariance matrix between the forward rates. In keeping with the discussion in Chapter 22, the simplest choice was made, and the correlation function was taken to be

$$\rho_{ij} = \exp[-\beta|T_i - T_j|] \qquad (26.1)$$

with $\beta = 0.1$. (In the equation above, ρ_{ij} denotes the correlation between the forward rate expiring at time T_i and the forward rate expiring at time T_j.) As discussed in Chapter 22, this correlation function is not particularly sophisticated, and can be criticized on financial grounds. However, I have discussed that the detailed shape of the correlation has a small impact on swaption prices, and I concur with De Jong *et al.* (1999) who state that

> ...although swaption prices do depend on the correlation between interest rates of different maturities, this turns out to be a second order effect; swaption prices are primarily determined by the volatilities of interest rates....

The parameters shown in Table 26.2 were typical of those found in Joshi and Rebonato (2003) by optimizing to the caplet smile surface of EUR and USD using the market data prevailing as of 8 September 2000. They were not chosen to produce a best fit to either swaption matrix, but to provide a qualitatively acceptable description of the swaption implied volatility surface. The qualitative features reported below, and the trends in the eigenvectors, were found to be largely insensitive to the details of the parameterization. What *did* make a big difference was whether the reversion speed was assumed to be zero, or equal to a finite 'reasonable' value (where 'reasonable' means similar to the values found in the fitting to actual market data for different currencies). More about this later in the chapter.

Finally, the displacement coefficient α (see Equation (25.7)) was chosen to be equal to 0.02, in agreement with typical best-fit values obtained for both currencies.

26.4.1   Results

The discussion of the results can profitably be started by presenting the graphs of the first principal component obtained by orthogonalizing the covariance matrix using the methodology described above. In Figures 26.14–26.16, the *x*-axis displays the following swaptions, in the order

$1 \times 1, 2, 3, 5, 7, 10$
$2 \times 1, 2, 3, 5, 7, 10$

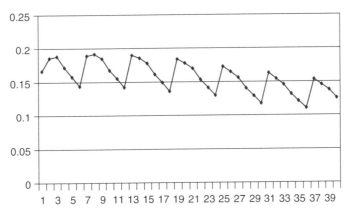

Figure 26.14 The first eigenvector from the orthogonalization of the covariance matrix when the model evolution of the volatility has no mean reversion, and the displacement coefficient of the forward rates is set to 0.

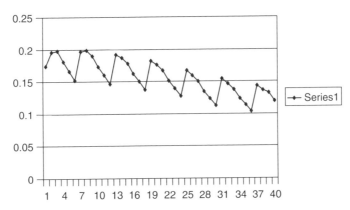

Figure 26.15 The first eigenvector from the orthogonalization of the covariance matrix when the model evolution of the volatility has no mean reversion, and the displacement coefficient of the forward rates is set to a typical market value ($\alpha = 0.02$).

$3 \times 1, 2, 3, 5, 7, 10$
$5 \times 1, 2, 3, 5, 7, 10$
$7 \times 1, 2, 3, 5, 7, 10$
$10 \times 1, 2, 3, 5.$

The first observation from these results, which answers the first of the questions posed in Section 26.3 above, is that, in all cases (i.e. with and without mean reversion and with and without a displacement coefficient), according to the model a very large fraction (approximately 90% for both currencies) of the variability across expiries and swap lengths is explained by the first principal component. This was observed despite the fact that four independent Brownian processes affect the instantaneous volatility process. The finding is not surprising, because the prices of European swaptions are mainly affected by the

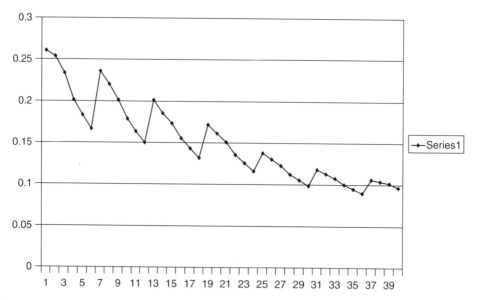

Figure 26.16   The first eigenvector from the orthogonalization of the covariance matrix when the model evolution of the volatility displays mean reversion, and the displacement coefficient of the forward rates is set to a typical market value ($\alpha = 0.02$).

stochastic behaviour of the d coefficient.[8] See Joshi and Rebonato (2003) in this respect. On the other hand, the fraction of the total variability (percentage of variance) explained by the first principal component in the two currencies examined was empirically found to be slightly less than 60%. See Figure 26.11. Therefore the first conclusion is that a significant degree of the real-world complexity is not accounted for by the model proposed in this chapter. This is a priori not surprising. The more relevant question is whether this initial step, albeit incomplete, is in the right direction.

In order to answer this question one can refer again to Figures 26.9, 26.10, 26.12 and 26.13, which display the first principal component as estimated from the empirical data. Two features are noteworthy: first of all the clear periodicity in the values, which corresponds to the transition from one 'into' series to the next. The second important feature is that, when one uses correlation data, the average magnitude of the first eigenvector is roughly constant as one moves from one series to the next. In other words, the first mode of deformation is roughly parallel across the swaption matrix. When the covariance matrix is orthogonalized, however, the first eigenvector displays a noticeable decay as one moves down the series. Since both descriptions must ultimately be equivalent, this means that the variability of the implied volatilities must decay as one moves to later-expiring swaption series. Let us keep this in mind as we examine the model-implied eigenvectors.

---

[8]This observation should not be taken to imply that the stochastic behaviour of the a, b and c parameters 'does not matter': b and c control the location of the 'hump' in the instantaneous volatility curve, which in turn controls the degree of terminal de-correlation between forward rates. Several complex products are sensitive to different extents to this terminal de-correlation, and it would therefore be unwarranted to extrapolate conclusions from plain-vanilla to complex instruments.

The model-obtained eigenvector (obtained from the orthogonalization of the *covariance* matrix) clearly displays the same periodicity as the empirical eigenvectors, irrespective of whether a displacement coefficient and/or a non-zero mean-reversion speed is used. See Figures 26.14–26.16. When no reversion speed and a zero displacement coefficient are used, the first covariance-matrix eigenvector obtained from the model remains roughly constant as one moves down the x-axis. This does not square with the empirical results. To a limited extent, a non-zero, positive displacement coefficient, which indicates a deviation of the forward-rate distributions from log-normality towards normality, produces some degree of decay in the first eigenvector. The effect is however rather limited, and probably due to the fact that both initial yield curves were upward sloping. It is when the reversion speed has a value similar to what was obtained in the fit to the smile surface, however, that the model data display a decay similar to what can be observed from real data. This result is particularly noteworthy, because the reversion speed used in the present study had been independently determined by fitting to smile data, and without any prior knowledge of the shape of the empirical eigenvalues.

Why do we find a better agreement with the empirical data when we introduce mean reversion? Recall that we concluded, by comparing the empirical eigenvectors obtained from the correlation and the covariance matrices, that the variability of the implied volatilities had to decay as one moves to later-expiring swaption series. But mean reversion in the instantaneous volatility is exactly one natural financial mechanism that can give rise to this effect: a burst in the instantaneous volatility will produce a noticeable change in short-expiry implied volatilities (which can be approximately thought of as a time average of the instantaneous volatility), but will have a more muted effect as the expiry of the option increases. See also the discussion in Section 13.2.3 of Chapter 13. Therefore, it appears that the empirical data are consistent with a mean-reverting behaviour for the instantaneous volatility (in the risk-adjusted world!) of the type described in Chapter 25, and as independently calibrated to static cross-sectional data (a single-day volatility surface).[9]

26.5 Discussion, Conclusions and Suggestions for Future Work

On the basis of the findings presented in this chapter, what can one say about the desirability of the stochastic-volatility extension of the LIBOR market model presented in Chapter 25? The empirical and theoretical analyses I have presented up to this point convey a mixed but overall encouraging picture. Certain important features of the real data are not captured: the empirical data presented above, for instance, indicate clearly that the swaption matrix tends to oscillate between well-defined shape patterns, with different, and sometimes quite short, transition periods. Such a behaviour is certainly not compatible with a stochastic-volatility model with constant reversion speed. However, neither is it compatible with a jump–diffusion process (which does not produce, in its standard formulation, stochastic smile surfaces), nor with any of the CEV extensions that

---

[9]In their study, Joshi and Rebonato (2003) carried out optimizations of the volatility coefficients to market smile data for several different trading days. While obviously not identical, the resulting parameters displayed marked stability and robustness.

have been proposed in the literature.[10] In the next chapter I will show that a modelling approach based on a discrete, two-state Markov chain for the instantaneous volatility can provide a better answer to the modelling of these features. I will also show that these regime transitions, far from being a second-order effect, are likely to be very important in accounting for the observed market smiles.

Despite these shortcomings, even in its present form the proposed modelling approach displays several important encouraging features. First, I have shown in this chapter that, after orthogonalizing the model and empirical covariance matrices of the changes in implied volatilities, the qualitative shape of the first eigenvector turned out to bear a close resemblance to the corresponding empirical quantity. In particular, the same periodicity was observed in the real and model data.

Second, the decaying behaviour of the first principal component as a function of increasing expiry, observed in the real data when the covariance matrix is orthogonalized, was found to be naturally recoverable and explainable by the mean-reverting behaviour for the instantaneous volatility. This feature in turn constitutes the most salient characteristic of the stochastic-volatility extension of the LIBOR market model proposed in Chapter 25.

Furthermore, the values for the mean reversion that had been previously and independently obtained using *static* information (i.e. by fitting to the smile surface) turned out to be adequate to explain in a satisfactory way the qualitative features of such *intertemporal* features as the shape of the eigenvectors (obtained from time-series analysis).

It therefore appears fair to say that, despite the obvious shortcomings, the extension of the standard deterministic-volatility LIBOR market model presented in the previous chapter appears to be a useful first step in the right direction. How this model can be enriched further is the topic of the next chapter.

---

[10]Linking the volatility in a deterministic manner to the stochastic forward rates could produce sharp moves in the level of the swaption matrix, if the forward rates displayed a discontinuous behaviour (as in Glasserman and Kou (2000) and Glasserman and Merener (2001)). It is difficult, however, to see how a deterministic functional dependence on the forward rates could give rise to a sudden change in the *shape* of the swaption matrix.

Chapter 27

Stochastic-Volatility Extension of the LMM: Two-Regime Instantaneous Volatility

27.1   The Relevance of the Proposed Approach

One of the recurring messages from this book has been that many approaches provide a fit to current plain-vanilla option prices of similar quality, and that therefore additional criteria must be used in order to choose a 'good' model. I have argued in Chapter 1 that the joint practices of the theoretically inconsistent vega (re-)hedging and of daily re-calibrating the model expose the trader to future realizations of the smile surface (i.e. to the future prices of the re-hedging options). From the perspective of a complex-derivatives trader, an important criterion for the success of a model should therefore be its ability to predict, either in a deterministic or in a stochastic manner, the current and *future* prices of the vega-hedging instruments (i.e. the future smile). The main feature of the modelling approach presented in this chapter is therefore not aimed at obtaining a more accurate recovery of the empirical smile surface today, but a more convincing description of the evolution of the future smile surface. The extension presented below of the stochastic-volatility version of the LIBOR market model (LMM) discussed in the previous chapters should be seen as a description of the smile surface dynamics that, by being more closely aligned with empirical evidence, will provide a better pricing and hedging tool for traders.

27.2   The Proposed Extension

How could one improve upon the approach presented in the previous chapter in such a way as to retain its desirable features and to take into account the empirical evidence discussed above?[1]

---

[1] Points of this chapter have been adapted from Rebonato and Kainth (2004).

The most salient missing features are probably

- the ability to reproduce rapid transitions of the swaption matrix from one 'mode' to another;

- the ability to return, after one such transition has taken place, to a shape similar to the original one;

- the recovery of fatter tails in the distribution of changes of implied volatilities (in agreement with empirical data); and

- a better apportioning of the total variance among the eigenvectors obtained from orthogonalizing the changes in swaption implied volatilities.

A simple and natural way to model these features, while retaining the simplicity and intuition behind the approach described above, is the following. Let us posit the existence of a latent variable, y, that follows a two-state Markov-chain process between two states, x and n, with transition probabilities:

$$\begin{bmatrix} \lambda_{x \to x} & \lambda_{n \to x} \\ \lambda_{x \to n} & \lambda_{n \to n} \end{bmatrix} \tag{27.1}$$

and which can only take the values 1 (if state n prevails) or 0 (if state x prevails). One could then proceed as follows.

1. Choose a simple criterion to determine whether the swaption matrix is currently in the normal or excited state. Looking at the figures in Chapters 7 and 26, one such criterion could be whether the n-year-into-1-year swaption series displays a hump or not. Given today's shape for this curve, we therefore know with certainty which state we are in.

2. Posit the existence of two instantaneous volatility functions for each forward rate. Using the notation introduced in the previous chapters, these can described by the following functional forms:

$$\sigma_i^n(t, T_i) = [a_t^n + b_t^n(T - t)] \exp(-c_t^n(T - t)) + d_t^n \tag{27.2}$$

$$\sigma_i^x(t, T_i) = [a_t^x + b_t^x(T - t)] \exp(-c_t^x(T - t)) + d_t^x \tag{27.3}$$

with different coefficients $\{a^n, b^n, c^n, d^n\}$ and $\{a^x, b^x, c^x, d^x\}$ associated with the normal (superscript n) and excited state (superscript x).

3. At any point in time the instantaneous volatility for forward rate i, $\sigma_i(t, T_i)$, is given by

$$\sigma_i(t, T_i) = y_t \sigma_i^n(t, T_i) + (1 - y_t)\sigma_i^x(t, T_i) \tag{27.4}$$

4. All the coefficients $\{a^n, b^n, c^n, d^n\}$ and $\{a^x, b^x, c^x, d^x\}$ are stochastic, and follow the same Ornstein–Uhlenbeck process described in the stochastic-volatility model presented in Chapter 25. Recall that their processes are all uncorrelated, between themselves and with the forward rates.

5. The transition of the instantaneous volatility from the normal to the excited state occurs with frequency $\lambda_{n \to x}$, and the transition from the excited state to the normal state with frequency $\lambda_{x \to n}$. The latent variable y remains in the excited or normal state with probabilities per unit time, $\lambda_{x \to x}$ and $\lambda_{n \to n}$, respectively. Note that if we tried to 'imply' these frequencies from the prices of traded options, they would all be risk-adjusted and not real-world frequencies.

6. Since the same assumption of independence between the volatility processes and the forward rate processes is enforced, once again along each volatility path the problem is exactly equivalent to the deterministic case, apart from the fact that, at random times, the coefficients would switch from one state to the other.

7. Because of point 6, the evaluation of the variances or covariances along each path proceeds exactly as described in Chapter 25, with possibly different coefficients 'half-way through' some of the paths if a transition has occurred. The evaluation of caplets and European swaptions would be virtually unaltered.

Since the properties of Markov chains, which are a central ingredient of this description, are not as widely known as the properties of, say, Brownian diffusions, they are briefly reviewed in the following section.

27.3 An Aside: Some Simple Properties of Markov Chains

Markov chains are frequently used to model time series that undergo regime changes. (See, for example, Hamilton (1994), Ross (1997) or Gourieroux and Jasiak (2001) for their main properties.) Following Hamilton (1994), let us assume that we have a stochastic process, y, which at each point in time can be in any of N possible discrete states. For simplicity, I will place myself in a discrete-time setting. From one time-step to the next, y can either remain in the prevailing state, or migrate to any of the possible states. The probability of remaining in the prevailing state is denoted by $\lambda_{i \to i}(t)$, or, more simply, $\lambda_{ii}(t)$. The transition probability for the process y to move at time t from state i to state j is denoted by $\lambda_{i \to j}(t)$, or, more simply, $\lambda_{ij}(t)$. Since at every point in time the process must 'do something' (i.e. either undergo a transition or remain in the current state), it must be the case that

$$\lambda_{i1} + \lambda_{i2} + \ldots + \lambda_{iN} = 1 \tag{27.5}$$

It is often convenient to arrange the probabilities in a matrix, known as the transition matrix, Λ:

$$\Lambda = \begin{bmatrix} \lambda_{11} & \lambda_{21} & \ldots & \lambda_{N1} \\ \lambda_{12} & \lambda_{22} & \ldots & \lambda_{N2} \\ \ldots & \ldots & \ldots & \ldots \\ \lambda_{1N} & \lambda_{2N} & \ldots & \lambda_{N1} \end{bmatrix} \tag{27.6}$$

Because of (27.6), each column of the transition matrix Λ adds up to 1. Note in passing the conventional ordering of the indices: since the index of the 'departure' state is first, the element of, say, the first row and second column is denoted by λ_{21}. This convention is not always followed, and to preserve a more matrix-like indexing, in some fields (quantum mechanics in particular) the departure state is sometimes associated with the second index, and the arrival state with the first. To conform to financial notation I retain the 'awkward' matrix notation, but preserve the natural ordering of arrival and departure states.

In general, the transition probabilities could depend on the whole history of y up to time t:

$$P(y_{t+1} = j | y_t = i, y_{t-1} = k, \ldots) = \lambda_{ij}(t) \tag{27.7}$$

If, however, the transition probability only depends on the current state,

$$P(y_{t+1} = j | y_t = i, y_{t-1} = k, \ldots) = P(y_{t+1} = j | y_t = i) = \lambda_{ij}(t) \tag{27.8}$$

the process is said to be a *Markov chain*.

In some contexts, notably in credit default modelling (see, for example, Schoenbucher (1996)), some states might be such that, if they are ever reached, the process remains in that state for ever. If this is the case, these states are called *absorbing*, the Markov chain *reducible*, and the associated transition matrix can be rearranged in such a way that all its non-zero elements are on or above the main diagonal. In the present chapter we will always work with *irreducible* transition matrices, i.e. with processes for which no state is absorbing. Because of Equation (27.6), for a two-state Markov chain to be irreducible it is necessary and sufficient that $\lambda_{ii} < 1, i = 1, 2$.

If we have a discrete number of possible states (as will always be assumed to be the case in this chapter) it is convenient to denote the state at the current time t by a vector, ξ_t, which contains zeros in the unoccupied states, and a 1 in the prevailing state:

$$\xi_t = \begin{bmatrix} 0 \\ \ldots \\ 1 \\ \ldots \\ 0 \end{bmatrix} \tag{27.9}$$

When we are looking at the current time this column vector (whose elements trivially add up to 1) can be regarded as a discrete probability density, with a Dirac-delta distribution localized around the current state. (Of course, since we are dealing with discrete states, we should be dealing with a Kronecker delta, δ_{ij}. Thinking of a delta distribution as the limit of an 'infinitely narrow' Gaussian distribution, however, helps the intuition, and I will retain the continuous description.)

As of today we can be interested in how the expectation of the occupancy of future states of the world will change, i.e. we would like to know how this delta function spreads out over time. It is easy to guess that the transition matrix will 'smear out' today's delta-like density into a more diffuse distribution. More precisely, using the notation introduced above, conditional on the current state occupancy being equal to i, the expectation of the state vector at the next time-step is given by the ith column of the transition matrix:

$$E\left[\xi_{t+1} | y_t = i\right] = \begin{bmatrix} \lambda_{i1} \\ \lambda_{i2} \\ \ldots \\ \lambda_{iN} \end{bmatrix} \tag{27.10}$$

or, equivalently, by

$$E\left[\xi_{t+1}|y_t = i\right] = \Lambda \xi_t \tag{27.11}$$

More generally, it is straightforward to show that the expectation of the occupation state m time-steps from today, ξ_{t+m}, is given by

$$E\left[\xi_{t+m}|y_t = i\right] = \Lambda^m \xi_t \tag{27.12}$$

where the symbol Λ^m denotes the repeated (m times) application of the transition matrix.

These definitions and results can be brought together to produce some interesting results. Assume that a Markov chain is irreducible (i.e. that it contains no absorbing states). Since every column of the transition matrix adds up to unity, it is easy to show (Hamilton (1994)) that unity is always an eigenvalue of the transition matrix. If all the other eigenvalues are inside the unit circle (i.e. have magnitude smaller than 1), then the Markov chain is said to be *ergodic*, and the associated eigenvector, denoted by π, is called the *vector of ergodic probabilities*. It enjoys the properties

$$\Lambda \pi = \pi \tag{27.13}$$

and

$$\lim_{m \to \infty} \Lambda^m = \pi 1^T \tag{27.14}$$

where 1 is an $(N \times 1)$ vector of 1s, and the superscript T denotes matrix transposition. From these properties it follows (see again Hamilton (1994)) that, if the Markov chain is ergodic, the long-run forecast of the occupation vector ξ, i.e. $\lim_{m \to \infty} \xi_{t+m}$, is given by the vector of ergodic probabilities, π, and is independent of the current state. Therefore this vector of ergodic probabilities can be regarded as providing the unconditional expectation of the occupation probability of each state. Finally, an ergodic Markov chain is a (covariance-) stationary process.

27.3.1 The Case of Two-State Markov Chains

The financial modelling approach proposed above allows for two states only, the normal and the excited. In this particularly simple situation the general results and definitions above can be specialized as follows. If the Markov chain is irreducible, the two eigenvalues of the transition matrix, ϵ_1 and ϵ_2, are given by

$$\epsilon_1 = 1 \tag{27.15}$$

and

$$\epsilon_2 = -1 + \lambda_{11} + \lambda_{22} \tag{27.16}$$

The second eigenvalue will be inside the unit circle, and the Markov chain therefore ergodic, provided that $0 < \lambda_{11} + \lambda_{22} < 2$. In this case, the vector of ergodic probabilities is given by

$$\pi = \begin{bmatrix} \dfrac{1 - \lambda_{22}}{2 - \lambda_{11} - \lambda_{22}} \\[2ex] \dfrac{1 - \lambda_{11}}{2 - \lambda_{11} - \lambda_{22}} \end{bmatrix} \qquad (27.17)$$

and the unconditional occupation probability of states 1 and 2, $P\{y = 1\}$ and $P\{y = 2\}$, are given by

$$P\{y = 1\} = \frac{1 - \lambda_{22}}{2 - \lambda_{11} - \lambda_{22}} \qquad (27.18)$$

$$P\{y = 2\} = \frac{1 - \lambda_{11}}{2 - \lambda_{11} - \lambda_{22}} \qquad (27.19)$$

respectively.

It is also interesting to observe that, if $\lambda_{11} + \lambda_{22} > 1$, the process is more likely to remain in the current state than to migrate, and the variable ξ would be positively serially correlated. If $\lambda_{11} + \lambda_{22} < 1$, the process is more likely to migrate from the current state, and the variable ξ would be negatively serially correlated.

27.4   Empirical Tests

27.4.1   Description of the Test Methodology

In order to test the effectiveness of the model extension proposed above one can begin by studying the qualitative behaviour of a two-regime stochastic-volatility LMM by using the two instantaneous volatility functions (normal and excited) depicted in Figure 27.1.

The swaption data described in detail in Chapters 26 and 27 were chosen to carry out the test. The reason for using swaption rather than caplet data is also explained in Chapter 26. Once again we want to create a time series of model-implied swaption matrices so that they can be analysed by PCA, or by other means. The following extension of the algorithm described in Section 26.4 can be used to determine the eigenvalues and eigenvectors of the model implied volatility covariance matrix.

- The parameters of the normal and excited volatility curves were determined so as to be consistent with the financial interpretation of the two volatility states as a normal and an excited state, and to provide a good fit to caplet prices. See the discussion in point 1 below. The parameters so obtained are reported in Table 27.1

- On the basis of the current swaption matrix, the decision was made as to the current value of the latent variable y (0 or 1). In general, deciding in which state a Markov-chain process currently finds itself is not a trivial matter. However, given the discussion in Section 26.3.2, the normal and excited states can be convincingly characterized by the humped or monotonically decaying shape of the 1×1 implied volatility series, respectively. Therefore I choose the shape of these swaption volatilities to decide unambiguously whether today's state for y is 0 or 1.

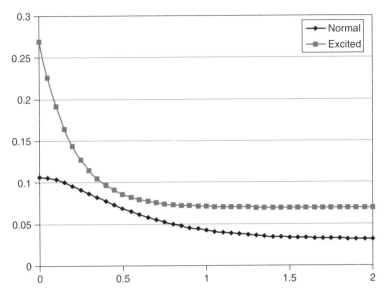

Figure 27.1 The normal and excited instantaneous volatility curves chosen for the study.

Table 27.1 The parameters describing the normal and excited volatility curves.

	Initial value	Volatility of the volatility	Reversion speeds	Reversion levels	Displacement
a_lower	0.08	0.67	0.55	0.08	0.029
b_lower	0.27	0.03	0.35	0.27	
c_lower	3.41	0.77	0.11	3.41	
d_lower	0.03	0.18	0.64	0.03	
a_upper	0.20	0.45	0.33	0.20	0.020
b_upper	0.08	0.01	0.35	0.08	
c_upper	5.34	0.77	0.13	5.34	
d_upper	0.07	0.19	0.63	0.07	

- The $a^{n(x)}$, $b^{n(x)}$, $c^{n(x)}$ and $d^{n(x)}$ coefficients were evolved from today's state over a simulation period of one week.

- Conditional on this evolution of the instantaneous volatilities and on the prevailing value for y, the forward rates were also evolved over the same one-week period.

- Given this state of the world the at-the-money swaptions were priced and their implied volatilities obtained.

- At this point (i.e. one time interval Δt from today) the prevailing value of the latent variable y was updated on the basis of the transition probability using a random draw.

- The procedure was repeated over a large number of time-steps, thereby creating a time series of model implied volatilities for the swaptions.

- These quantities were then analysed (e.g. the covariance matrix of the volatility changes were orthogonalized, the skew and kurtosis analysed, etc.) and compared with the market data.

The following observations are in order.

1. In order to limit the number of degrees of freedom, the $a^{n(x)}$, $b^{n(x)}$, $c^{n(x)}$ and $d^{n(x)}$ coefficients were not treated as fully free-fitting parameters; instead, we started from shapes for the 'normal' and 'excited' instantaneous volatility functions consistent with the financial model discussed above, and locally optimized the parameters around these initial guesses.

2. The test was run by fitting to *caplet* data and then exploring *swaption* data. No best fit to swaption-related quantities was attempted in the choice of $a^{n(x)}$, $b^{n(x)}$, $c^{n(x)}$ and $d^{n(x)}$. The test is therefore quite demanding, in that it requires a satisfactory description of the evolution of swap rates using parameters estimated on the basis of forward-rate information alone.

3. The levels and the shapes of the normal and excited volatility curves refer to the risk-neutral world and not to the real-world measure. The same consideration applies to the frequency of transition from one state to the other. Therefore no immediate conclusions can be drawn from these values. Despite this, I present below an order-of-magnitude comparison of the transition frequency.

4. Fits to caplet prices of very similar (and very good) quality can be obtained with different parameters for the normal and excited coefficients. Therefore recovery of the caplet prices is a poor criterion to choose between different instantaneous volatility curves. I suggest below that an analysis of the kurtosis of the changes in implied volatilities and of the eigenvalues' behaviour can provide better information.

5. Statistical estimates of kurtosis are in general very noisy, and, anyhow, because of point 3 above, cannot be directly compared with the model values. This is because the model kurtosis will depend on the transition probability matrix, and this matrix, once implied from the market prices, is risk adjusted (i.e. pertains to the pricing measure, not the real-world measure). Therefore we did not attempt a fit to the kurtoses for the various swaption series. However, we present below the real and risk-adjusted values for a qualitative comparison.

27.4.2   Results

The Real and Model Path of Implied Volatilities

Assigning a regime switch to the *instantaneous* volatility does not automatically ensure that the *implied* volatility (which was linked to the root-mean-squared integral of the former) will also display a noticeable discontinuity. Since the empirical evidence refers to implied volatilities, it is important to check that the desired effect is indeed produced.

To this effect, Figures 27.2 and 27.3 display time series of the changes in instantaneous and implied volatilities for a 5×5 constant-maturity swaption obtained using the procedure described above and the best-fit parameters in Table 27.1. It is clear that the proposed

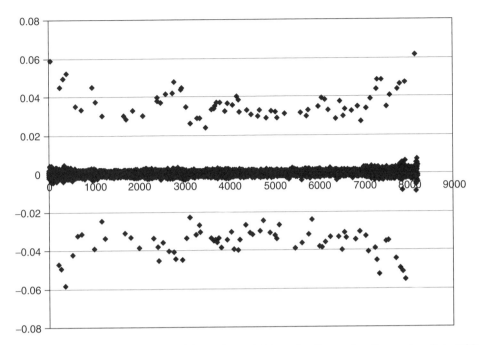

Figure 27.2   The instantaneous volatility path: model data (5×5 swaption time series, fit to USD data).

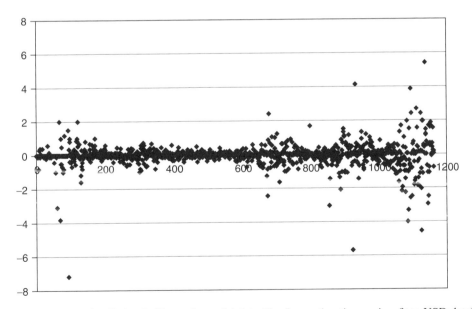

Figure 27.3   The implied volatility path: model data (5×5 swaption time series, fit to USD data).

process does produce regime shifts also in the implied volatility changes, with most changes being 'small', and a relatively smaller fraction of changes very high.

Figures 27.4 and 27.5 display two of the empirical time series of implied volatilities, showing the qualitative similarity between the model and real-world data. Also, in this case the time spent in the normal and excited states in the real and risk-adjusted world cannot be directly compared because of the risk-adjusted nature of the quantities (the level of the volatility curves and the frequency of the jump) that enter the pricing of caplets.

Recovery of the Market Smile Surface

The fit to the market smile surface (USD data Mar2003) is shown in Figure 27.6. It is clearly of very high quality, the more so if we recall that it was obtained by choosing beforehand values of the transition probabilities that would produce acceptable ratios for the eigenvalues obtained by orthogonalizing the implied volatility model covariance matrix. See, in this regard, the discussion below. (Recall that the purely diffusive stochastic-volatility model presented in Chapter 25 loaded more than 90% of the explanatory power onto the first eigenvector.) With these transition probabilities the coefficients for the normal and excited volatility curves were then obtained as described above.

The fit was obtained using the same time-independent coefficients for the whole surface, and therefore the resulting swaption matrix displays a desirable time-homogeneous behaviour.

This fit should be compared with the fit obtainable with a regime switch between purely deterministic volatilities. This important feature is discussed in Section 27.5.

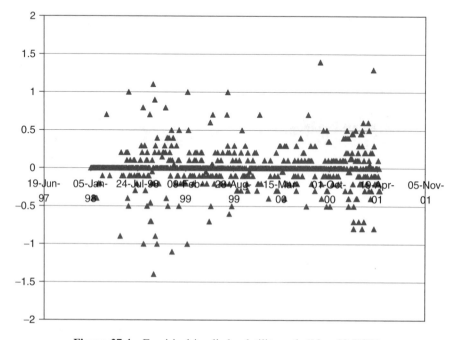

Figure 27.4   Empirical implied volatility path (10×10 USD).

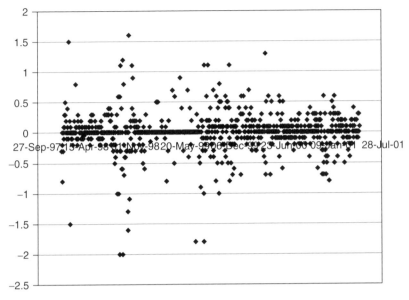

Figure 27.5 Empirical implied volatility path (1×3 EUR).

Kurtosis

Table 27.2 shows the kurtosis of the distribution of the implied volatility changes for the two-regime model. This quantity is displayed for several swaptions series and was obtained using the parameters listed above for the two instantaneous-volatility states and the jump intensities. Note that these values of kurtosis are substantially larger than the kurtosis that would be obtained using a single-regime stochastic-volatility LMM, and much closer to the values estimated using market data. The usual caveats about the change of measure apply.[2] Since the true distribution of the changes in implied volatility is not known a priori it is not possible to associate statistical error bars to the experimental values. However, in order to give an idea of the possible estimation uncertainty Table 27.3 displays the real-world estimates obtained using the first and second halves of the available data.

Skew

No explicit attempt was made to reproduce the skew of the distribution of the change in implied volatilities. None the less Table 27.4 shows good agreement between the model (theoretical) and real-world quantities. The same observations about the statistical error bars and the change of measure hold, and again the estimates obtained using the first and second halves of the data are presented (see Table 27.5).

---

[2] It might seem surprising that also the kurtosis (and the skew) should be measure dependent (they are measure invariant in the purely diffusion approach of Chapter 25). The reason is that *all* the quantities affected by the transition frequency (which is certainly risk-adjusted) change in moving between measures. These quantities are, for instance, the eigenvalues, the kurtosis and the skew.

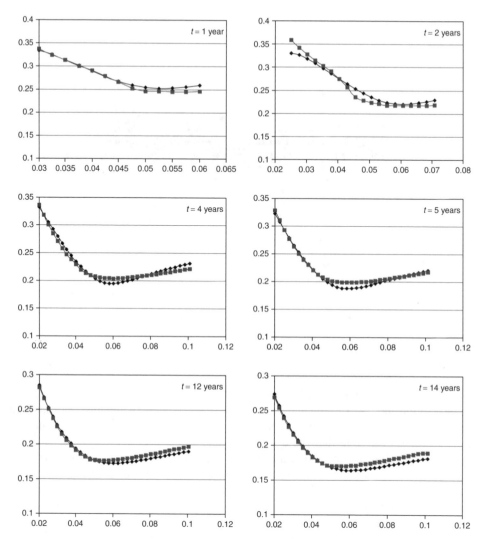

Figure 27.6   The quality of the recovery to the market smile surface. USD data, option expiries from 1 to 14 years.

Table 27.2   Model and empirical kurtosis.

Kurtosis	Real	Model
1 × 2	14.3935	11.43534
1 × 5	10.10832	15.01118
1 × 10	20.11422	17.20576
3 × 3	15.93261	17.2059
3 × 5	11.70314	21.18686

Table 27.3 As for Table 27.2, using the first and second halves of the available data.

Kurtosis	Real	Real(I)	Real(II)	Model
1×2	14.3935	16.09731	4.821323	11.43534
1×5	10.10832	10.27761	2.640147	15.01118
1×10	20.11422	11.99224	28.02998	17.20576
3×3	15.93261	12.06961	4.364113	17.2059
3×5	11.70314	8.457682	3.049932	21.18686

Table 27.4 Model and empirical kurtosis.

Skew	Real	Model
1×2	0.767421	0.202036
1×5	0.529616	0.386044
1×10	0.868207	0.296187
3×3	1.421207	0.352619
3×5	0.443754	0.327331

Table 27.5 As for Table 27.4, using the first and second halves of the available data.

Skew	Real	Real(I)	Real(II)	Model
1×2	0.767421	1.056023	-0.03201	0.202036
1×5	0.529616	0.515964	0.322293	0.386044
1×10	0.868207	1.260718	0.501672	0.296187
3×3	1.421207	1.36261	0.294108	0.352619
3×5	0.443754	0.375826	0.140795	0.327331

Eigenvalues and Eigenvectors Again

I have argued in Chapter 26 (see also Rebonato and Joshi (2002)) that a comparison between the eigenvectors and eigenvalues estimated from real-world data and simulated by the model is a useful tool to assess the quality of a model, and to overcome the difficulties in comparing real-world and risk-adjusted quantities. One of the main conclusions from this type of analysis was that the simple (i.e. purely diffusive) stochastic-volatility model produced a good qualitative shape for the eigenvectors obtained from the orthogonalization of the covariance matrix of the changes in implied volatilities. The relative size of the eigenvalues in the original model, however, was at variance with what was observed in reality. As pointed out in footnote 1, however, this comparison is, strictly speaking, no longer warranted in the presence of a regime change. In order to understand the nature of the transformation brought about by the measure change, one can reason as follows. The eigenvectors decompose the possible changes in the implied volatilities into orthogonal modes of deformation. If all the eigenvectors are retained they provide a possibly more efficient, but otherwise totally equivalent, set of co-ordinates. A change in measure, as usual, can change the probability of different events happening, but cannot make impossible events possible, and vice versa. See the discussion in Section 6.7.3 of Chapter 6. Therefore what risk aversion can change is the relative importance of different modes of deformation, i.e. the relative magnitude of the eigenvalues. If risk-averse traders find it more difficult to hedge their complex-option positions when, say, tilts in the swaption matrix occur, they might assign a greater probability to the second mode of deformation than to the first (the 'parallel' eigenvector). If, however, tilts were 'impossible' in the real-world measure, traders could not 'invent them' and ask for compensation for the undiversifiable risk associated with them. It is therefore plausible that risk aversion should not change the shape of the eigenvectors, but should alter the relative magnitudes of the eigenvalues. Note in passing that, since the relative importance of different modes of deformation can change across measures, a given eigenvector, say the second, in the real world can assume a different index, say the third, in the pricing measure.

Can we say something a bit more precise? Let us look at the problem from a slightly different angle, i.e. by focusing on the transition probability rather than on the eigenmodes. If $\lambda_{n \to x}$ is the risk-adjusted transition probability from the normal to the excited state (similar considerations apply to the probability $\lambda_{x \to n}$) , one can write

$$\lambda_{n \to x} = \lambda_{n \to x}^{\text{rw}} + \Delta \lambda_{n \to x} \qquad (27.20)$$

where $\lambda_{n \to x}^{\text{rw}}$ is the real-world transition probability and $\Delta \lambda_{n \to x}$ is the change in transition probability in switching between measures. We can therefore regard the change in eigenvalues in moving from the purely diffusive state to the Markov-chain description as being due to two distinct contributions, the first coming from the real-world transition probability, and the second from risk aversion. The principle of absolute continuity, however, guarantees that if the real-world process were indeed a two-state Markov chain, so would the risk-adjusted process. See again the discussion in Section 6.6.3. If the effect of risk aversion were to make investors 'imply' a higher transition probability from the normal to the excited state, then the results (e.g. the kurtosis) obtained from the fit to the market data would display an 'overshoot' in moving from the purely diffusive case to the Markov-chain case. In particular, if the kurtosis found in the diffusive-volatility case were too low compared with the empirical data, and the model were correctly specified, the risk-adjusted kurtosis would turn out to be *higher* than the econometric one.

Can we expect $\Delta \lambda_{n \to x}$ to be positive? To answer this question we have to put ourselves in the shoes of a trader who hedges a complex product following a delta and vega strategy, much as described in Chapter 1. We have seen in Chapter 13 that hedging against a simple *level* mis-specification of the volatility by means of vega hedging is relatively easy. It is changes, and especially *sudden* changes, in the shape of the smile surface that tax the hedging ability of the trader. Therefore one can expect that the distribution of slippages[3] should display a greater variance if a regime switch has occurred during the life of the complex option. As a consequence, a risk-averse trader would 'fear' the occurrence of regime switches, and incorporate in her prices a higher (risk-adjusted) frequency of transition. If this is the case the risk-adjusted distribution of volatility changes would

---

[3]Recall that in Chapter 4 we defined 'slippages' as the differences between the payoff of an option, and the payoff of the hedging strategy.

display the characteristics of a higher-than-real-world transition probability. In particular, the risk-adjusted kurtosis would be higher than the statistical one. We test this prediction below.

With these considerations in mind, the changes in the 'synthetic' implied-volatility time series generated as described above were used to generate a covariance matrix. After diagonalization of this matrix, I examine below both the magnitude of the first few eigenvalues and the form of the corresponding eigenvectors. See Figures 27.7 and 27.8. Note how the qualitative shape of the eigenvectors is recovered not only for the first but also for the second and third. Therefore the model singles out as important modes of deformation for the implied-volatility matrix the same modes of deformation found in the real world. Note, however, that the second and third eigenvectors have 'switched' in moving across measures. In the light of the discussion above this is perfectly acceptable.

One of the shortcomings of the diffusive stochastic-volatility modelling discussed in Chapter 25 was the apportioning of the overall variability of the implied volatility changes across the various eigenmodes. Recall that the purely diffusive model was giving far too much weight to the first eigenvalue: if one defines the spectral weights, ϑ, as

$$\vartheta_i = \frac{\lambda_i}{\sum \lambda_k} \tag{27.21}$$

ϑ_1 turned out to be approximately 95%. To what extent does this picture change when we introduce the dynamics proposed in this chapter? If we compute the spectral weights for our two-regime model under the assumption that both jump rates, $\lambda_{x \to n}$ and $\lambda_{n \to x}$, were equal to approximately one jump per year, we would obtain a very similar picture of the dynamics to that obtained within the one-state model, i.e. approximately 95% of the spectral weight would be concentrated in the first mode. However, if we set the jump

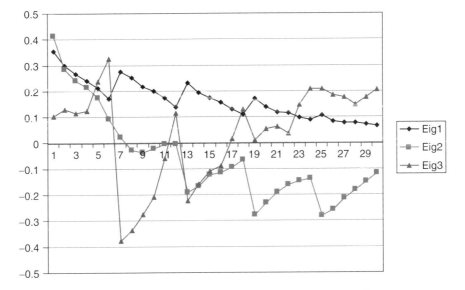

Figure 27.7 The first three eigenvectors: USD, market data.

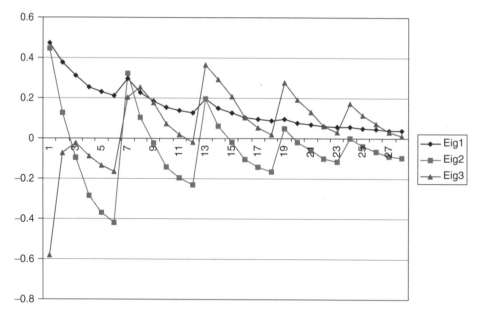

Figure 27.8   The first three model eigenvectors as obtained using the approach described in this chapter.

intensities to values more similar to the real-world jump rates, we find a very different behaviour. The relative magnitude of the real-world jump rates can be approximately estimated from the empirical observations that the majority of time is spent in the unexcited state; that the volatility jumps into the excited state approximately once a year; and that it stays in the excited state for approximately two to three weeks, after which it returns to the unexcited state. This suggests a real-world jump intensity of the order of one jump per year from the normal to the excited state, and an intensity of an order of magnitude larger for the transition from the excited state to the normal state.

If we take this order-of-magnitude estimate in the real world as appropriate for the risk-adjusted frequencies, we get far more promising results: the second eigenvalue now has approximately 12% of the spectral weight, and it takes four eigenvectors to 'explain' more than 99% of the observed variability. This is illustrated in Figures 27.9 and 27.10.

Despite the fact that reality (see Figure 27.9) is still considerably more complex, the new, regime-switching feature brings about a significant improvement.

27.5   How Important Is the Two-Regime Feature?

Whenever a new modelling feature is introduced it is important to ascertain to what extent the better fit to available data is simply obtained by virtue of having more parameters at one's disposal, or because new meaningful features have indeed been introduced. In order to answer this question, an additional very stringent test can be carried out.[4] In order to test the genuine explanatory power of the new approach, one can proceed as

---

[4]Numerical help by Mark Joshi is gratefully acknowledged.

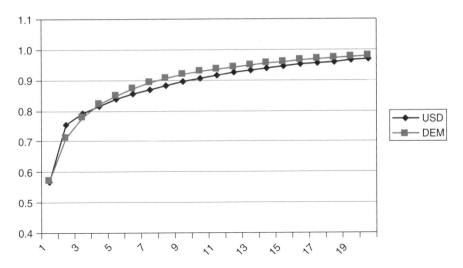

Figure 27.9 The relative magnitude of the empirical eigenvalues.

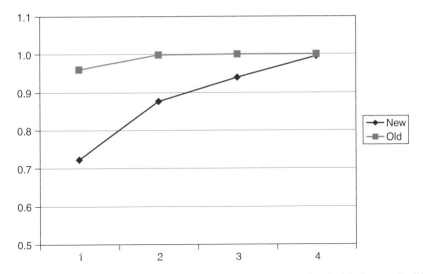

Figure 27.10 Same as Figure 27.9, for the model eigenvalues obtained with the purely diffusive model (curve labelled 'Old'), and with the two-state model (curve labelled 'New').

follows. I first made an a priori choice for the two instantaneous volatility functions, one for the normal state and one for the excited state. Their overall shape was required to be consistent with the financial justification discussed above: a lower-level humped (normal) curve, and a higher-level monotonically decaying (excited) curve. In this new test *each volatility curve was now assumed to be deterministic*, and therefore the stochasticity in the shape of the volatility functions was removed as a mechanism to produce a good fit to the caplet prices. Furthermore, the parameters of these two curves were not fit in any way to current market data, but were chosen to be consistent with the financial model presented above. The only flexibility allowed in the two instantaneous-volatility curves was in their overall levels, controlled by two scaling factors.

These two scaling factors were the first two fitting parameters. The second two fitting parameters were the transition probabilities, $\lambda_{n \to x}$ and $\lambda_{x \to n}$. So, in this more stringent test there are only four parameters (two scaling constants and two transition probabilities) at one's disposal to fit a full smile surface spanning all strikes and maturities from one to 15 years. Also, in order to test the robustness of the results, which should not depend on the details of the two instantaneous-volatility curves as long as one is humped and the other monotonically decaying, various initial plausible guesses were used for the two volatility states.

Some of the combinations of parameters used are shown in Table 27.6, and Figure 27.11 shows the corresponding instantaneous and implied volatilities for the normal and excited states obtained from the parameters in the first column.

The results of this much simplified fit are shown in Figure 27.12. The parameters in the first column in Table 27.6 were used. The fits obtained with the other sets of parameters (also shown in Table 27.6) were of very similar quality, showing that the fit does not depend on the fine features of the chosen volatility functions, but on the overall financial mechanism based on the regime switch.

The fit is clearly far from perfect, but many of the qualitative features of the real-world smile surface are correctly recovered. What is remarkable is the quality of fit given the extremely small number of fitting parameters. This is very interesting, because it indicates that a switch in volatility regimes can be as, if not more, important than a diffusive stochasticity in order to account for the observed market smiles. This observation suggests that, perhaps, an appropriate hierarchy of the financial mechanisms responsible for smiles would rank the link between implied volatilities and the level of the underlying as the most important; the regime switch as the second; and the diffusive variation of the shape of the instantaneous-volatility function as only the third.

Furthermore, it is interesting to note that the relative levels of the normal and excited volatility states obtained via the fit turned out to be consistent with the financial interpretation given to these two quantities: the monotonically decaying (excited) state was higher than the humped (normal) state. Finally, the (risk-adjusted) transition probabilities, $\lambda_{n \to x}$

Table 27.6   The parameters used in the deterministic-volatility test. Three different sets of coefficients were used for the 'excited' instantaneous volatility. The quality of the fit and the scaling factors turned out to be very similar in all cases.

	Case 1	Case 2	Case 3
a_normal	−0.04	−0.04	−0.04
b_normal	0.64	0.64	0.64
c_normal	1.2	1.2	1.2
d_normal	0.14	0.14	0.14
a_excited	0.41	0.41	0.41
b_excited	−0.1	0.1	−0.03
c_excited	1	1.1	0.7
d_excited	0.15	0.15	0.15

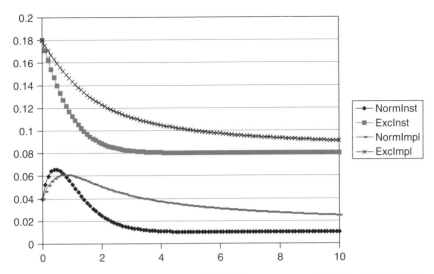

Figure 27.11 The normal and excited deterministic instantaneous volatilities (labelled 'NormInst' and 'ExcInst'), and the associated implied volatilities (labelled 'NormImpl' and 'ExcImpl').

and $\lambda_{x \to n}$, were also naturally found to imply a lower probability of transition from the lower to the excited state than vice versa.

It is important to stress that a better fit could clearly have been obtained, for instance, by optimizing over the parameters that control the shape of the normal and excited volatility curves, but this was not the purpose of the exercise. Actually, Table 27.6 shows that, even by starting from financially plausible but otherwise rather different initial guesses for the volatility curves, fits of similar quality, and with similar scaling and transition parameters, were found. This should be an indication of the robustness of the approach.

One can therefore conclude that, while further modelling flexibility is probably required to obtain an accurate fit to today's smile surface, even by itself the two-regime feature can account for important features of the dynamics of the swaption matrix, and therefore should be taken as an important part of the description of the smile surface.

27.6 Conclusions

In this chapter I have presented a simple two-regime extension of the stochastic-volatility LMM. Its main positive features are the following.

1. It retains the features of fast convergence, simple and efficient pricing of interest-rate derivatives, and fast calibration to the caplet and swaption markets enjoyed by the simple stochastic-volatility model discussed in Chapter 26, and introduced by Rebonato and Joshi (2003) and Joshi and Rebonato (2002).

2. It produces a good-quality fit to the market data in a manner that is financially justifiable. Since this fit is obtained with time-independent parameters, and the forward-rate specific coefficients necessary to ensure perfect pricing of the caplets

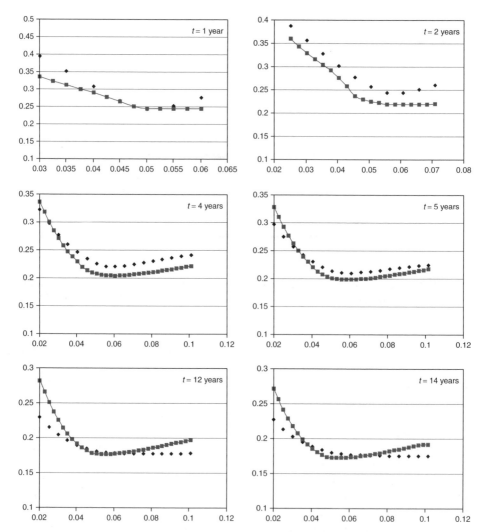

Figure 27.12   The fit to market data obtained using the deterministic-volatility two-regime model. The quality of the fit should be compared with the results displayed in Figure 27.6 (obtained by allowing all the coefficients to be stochastic).

are very close to one, the statistical properties of the volatility surfaces are time stationary, and the future 'looks' (statistically) like the present.

3. The eigenvectors are recovered equally well as with the simple stochastic-volatility model (and are in good agreement with the real world). The relative sizes of the eigenvalues obtained with the jumpy model display a marked improvement: the first model eigenvalue is still too big, but the second is now approximately five times larger than in the purely diffusive case.

4. The risk-adjusted kurtosis and the skew of the distribution of the changes in the implied volatilities show better agreement with the real-world data, and are moved

from the diffusive case in the direction that a positive degree of risk aversion to regime switches would imply.

5. When a simple fit to today's smile surface was attempted starting from two simple deterministic instantaneous-volatility functions, an acceptable fit for the whole surface (all strikes, all maturities) was found even by using as few as four parameters, suggesting that the two-regime feature should be taken as an important part of the description of the smile surface.

Overall, the proposed approach appears to be capable of providing a realistic and practically useful description of the dynamics of forward rates and of their volatilities.

Bibliography

Abramowitz, M. and Stegun, I. A. (1964) *Handbook of Mathematical Functions*, Applied Mathematics Series, Vol. 55. Washington: National Bureau of Standards; reprinted 1968 by Dover Publications, New York.

Ait-Sahalia, Y. (2002) 'Telling from Discrete Data Whether the Underlying Continuous-Time Data is a Diffusion', *Journal of Finance*, **57**, no. 5, October, 2075–2112.

Ait-Sahalia, Y. and Lo, A. (1998) 'Nonparametric Estimation of State–Price Densities Implicit in Financial Asset Prices', *Journal of Finance*, **53**, no. 5, 499–547.

Alexander, C. (2000) 'Principal Component Analysis of Implied Volatility Smiles and Skews', ISMA Centre Discussion Paper in Finance, December.

Alexander, C. (2001) *Market Models – A Guide to Financial Data Analysis*. Chichester: John Wiley & Sons.

Alexander, C. (2003) 'Common Correlation and Calibration of the Log-Normal Forward Rate Model', *Wilmott*, **March**, 68–77.

Ames, W. F. (1977) *Numerical Methods for Partial Differential Equations*. New York: Academic Press.

Amin, K. I. (1993) 'Jump Diffusion Option Valuation in Discrete Time', *Journal of Finance*, **48**, no. 5, 1833–1863.

Andersen, L. and Andreasen, J. (1998) 'Volatility Skews and Extensions of the LIBOR Market Model', Working Paper, GenRe Financial Products, August.

Andersen, L. and Andreasen, J. (1999) 'Jumping Smiles', *Risk*, **12**, no. 11, 65–68.

Andersen, L. and Andreasen, J. (2000) 'Volatility Skews and Extensions of the LIBOR Market Model', *Applied Mathematical Finance*, **7**, March, 1–32.

Andersen, L. and Andreasen, J. (2001) 'Factor Dependence of Bermudan Swaptions: Fact or Fiction?', *Journal of Financial Economics*, **62**, 3–37.

Andersen, L. and Brotherton-Ratcliffe, R. (1998) 'The Equity Option Volatility Smile: An Implicit-Difference Approach', *Journal of Computational Finance*, **1**, no. 2, 5–38.

Avellaneda, M. (1998) 'Minimum-Relative-Entropy Calibration of Asset-Pricing Models', *International Journal of Theoretical and Applied Finance*, **1**, no. 4, 447–472.

Avellaneda, M., Levy, A. and Paras, A. (1995) 'Pricing and Hedging Derivative Securities in Markets with Uncertain Volatilities', *Applied Mathematical Finance*, **2**, no. 2, 73–88.

Backus, D., Foresi, S. and Wu, L. (1997) 'Accounting for Biases in Black and Scholes', Working Paper, New York University.

Bahra, B. (1997) 'Implied Risk-Neutral Probability Density Functions from Option Prices: Theory and Applications', Bank of England Working Paper Series, No. 66.

Barle, S. and Cakici, N. (1995) 'Growing a Smiling Tree', *Risk*, **8**, October, 76–81.

Barone, E., Cuoco, D. and Zautzik, E. (1990). 'The Term Structure of Interest Rates: A Test of the Cox, Ingersoll and Ross Model on Italian Treasury Bonds', Unpublished Working Paper, Research Department, Bank of Italy, March.

Baskshi, G. C., Cao, C. and Chen, Z. (2000) 'Do Call Prices and the Underlying Stock Always Move in the Same Direction?', *Review of Financial Studies*, **13**, 549–584.

Bates, D. S. (1996) 'Dollar Jump Fears, 1984–1992: Distributional Abnormalities Implicit in Currency Futures Option Prices', *Journal of International Money and Finance*, **15**, 65–93.

Baxter, M. and Rennie, A. (1996) *Financial Calculus*. Cambridge: Cambridge University Press.

Benjamin, J. R. and Cornell, C. A. (1970) *Probability, Statistics, and Decision for Civil Engineers*. New York: McGraw-Hill.

Bjork, T. (1998) *Arbitrage Theory in Continuous Time*. Oxford: Oxford University Press.

Black, F. (1976) 'The Pricing of Commodity Contracts', *Journal of Financial Economics*, **3**, 167–179.

Black, F. and Karasinski, P. (1991) 'Bond and Option Pricing When Short Rates Are Lognormal', *Financial Analyst Journal*, **47**, July–August, 52–59.

Black, F. and Scholes, M. (1973) 'The Pricing of Options and Corporate Liabilities', *Journal of Political Economics*, **81**, 637–653.

Black, F., Derman, E. and Toy, W. (1990) 'A One-Factor Model of Interest Rates and its Application to Treasury Bond Options', *Financial Analyst Journal*, **46**, 33–39.

Boyle, P. P. (1977) 'Options: A Monte Carlo Approach', *Journal of Financial Economics*, **4**, 323–338.

Boyle, P. P., Evnine, J. and Gibbs, S. (1994) 'Valuation of Options on Several Underlying Assets', Working Paper, University of Waterloo, Ontario.

Brace, A. and Womersley, S. (2000) 'Exact Fit to Swaption Volatility Using Semidefinite Programming', Working Paper presented a the ICBI Global Derivatives Conference, Paris.

Brace, A., Gatarek, D. and Musiela, M. (1995) 'The Market Model of Interest Rate Dynamics', Working Paper, School of Mathematics, University of New South Wales, Australia.

Breeden, D. T. and Litzenberger, R. H. (1978) 'Prices of State-Contingent Claims Implicit in Option Prices', *Journal of Business*, **51**, 621–651.

Brigo, D. and Mercurio, D. (2001) *Interest Rate Models – Theory and Practice*. Berlin: Springer-Verlag.

Britten-Jones, M. and Neuberger, A. (1996) 'Arbitrage Pricing with Incomplete Markets', *Applied Mathematical Finance*, **3**, 347–363.

Britten-Jones, M. and Neuberger, A. (1998) 'Option Prices, Implied Price Processes and Stochastic Volatility', London Business School Working Paper, available at www.london.edu/ifa

Brown, H., Hobson, D. and Rogers, C. (1998) 'Robust Hedging of Barrier Options', Working Paper, University of Bath.

Campa, J., Chang, M. K. and Reider, R. L. (1998) 'Implied Exchange Rate Distributions: Evidence from the OTC Options Markets', *Journal of International Money and Finance*, **17**, 117–160.

Campbell, J. Y., Lo, A. W. and MacKinlay, A. C. (1997) *The Econometrics of Financial Markets*. Princeton: Princeton University Press.

Carr, P. and Chou, A. (1997) 'Hedging Complex Barrier Options', Working Paper, Morgan Stanley and MIT Computer Science.

Carr, P. and Wu, L. (2003a) 'The Finite Moment Log Stable Process and Option Pricing', *Journal of Finance*, **58**, no. 2, 753–777.

Carr, P. and Wu, L. (2003b) 'What Type of Process Underlies Options? A Simple and Robust Test', *Journal of Finance*, **58**, no. 6, 2581–2610.

Carr, P., Ellis, K. and Gupta, V. (1998) 'Static Hedging of Exotic Options', *Journal of Finance*, **53**, 1165–1191.

Chan, K. C., Karolyi, G. A., Longstaff, F. A. and Sanders, A. B. (1992) 'An Empirical Comparison of Alternative Models of the Short-Term Interest Rate', *Journal of Finance*, **57**, no. 5, 281–312.

Chatfield, C. and Collins, A. J. (1989) *Introduction to Multivariate Analysis*. London: Chapman & Hall.

Chung, K. L. and Williams, R. J. (1990) *Introduction to Stochastic Integration*, 2nd edition. Boston, MA: Birkhauser.

Cochrane, J. H. (2001) *Asset Pricing*. Princeton: Princeton University Press.

Cochrane, J. H. and Saa-Requejo, J. (1998) 'Beyond Arbitrage: "Good-Deal" Asset Price Bounds in Incomplete Markets', Working Paper, Graduate School of Business, University of Chicago.

Cochrane, J. H. and Saa-Requejo, J. (2000) 'Beyond Arbitrage: Good Deal Asset Price Bounds in Incomplete Markets', *Journal of Political Economy*, **108**, 79–119.

Cont, R. (2001), 'Empirical Properties of Asset Returns: Stylized Facts and Statistical Issues', *Quantitative Finance*, **1**, no. 2, 223–236.

Cont, R. and da Fonseca, J. (2002a) 'Deformation of Implied Volatility Surfaces: An Empirical Analysis', Working Paper, Ecole Polytechnique, Centre de Matematiques Appliquees, available at http://www.cmap.polytechnique.fr/ rama/

Cont, R. and da Fonseca, J. (2002b) 'Dynamics of Implied Volatility Surfaces', Working Paper, Ecole Polytechnique, Centre de Matematiques Appliquees, available at http://www.cmap.polytechnique.fr/ rama/

Cont, R., da Fonseca, J. and Durrleman, V. (2002) 'Stochastic Models of Implied Volatility Surfaces', *Economic Notes*, **31**, no. 2.

Cooper, N. and Talbot, J. (1999) 'The Yen/Dollar Exchange Rate in 1998: Views from the Options Markets', *Bank of England Quarterly Bulletin*, **February**, 68–77.

Cornell, B. (1999) *The Equity Premium*. Chichester: John Wiley & Sons.

Cox, J. C., Ross, S. A. and Rubinstein, M. (1979) 'Option Pricing: A Simplified Approach', *Journal of Financial Economics*, **7**, 229–263.

Crouhy, M. and Galai, D. (1995) 'Hedging with a Volatility Term Structure', *The Journal of Derivatives*, **2**, no. 3, 45–52.

Cummins, J. D., Dionne, G. and McDonald, J. B. (1990) 'Application of the GB2 Family of Distributions in Modelling Insurance Loss Processes', *Insurance: Mathematics and Economics*, **9**, 257–272.

Das, S. R. (2002) 'Liquidity Risk Part 3 – Long-Term Capital Management', *Futures and Options World (FOW)*, **February**, 55–62.

Das, S. R. and Sundaram, R. K. (1997) 'Of Smiles and Smirks: A Term-Structure Perspective', Working Paper, Harvard Business School, and Stern School of Business, New York, December.

De Jong, F., Driessen, L. and Pelsser, A. (1999) 'LIBOR and Swap Market Models for the Pricing of Interest-Rate Derivatives: An Empirical Comparison', Working Paper.

Der Kiureghian, A. and Liu, P.-L. (1986) 'Structural Reliability Under Incomplete Probability Information', *ASCE Journal of Engineering Mechanics*, **112**, no. 1, 85–104.

Derman, E. (1999) 'Volatility Regimes', *Risk*, **12**, no. 4, 55–59.

Derman, E. and Kani, I. (1998) 'Stochastic Implied Trees: Arbitrage Pricing with Stochastic Term and Strike Structure of Volatility', *International Journal of Theoretical and Applied Finance*, **1**, no. 1, 61–110.

Derman, E., Ergener, D. and Kani, I. (1994) 'Static Option Replication', Goldman Sachs Quantitative Strategies Research Notes, May.

Derman, E., Kani, I. and Zou, J. (1996) 'The Local Volatility Surface: Unlocking the Information in Index Option Prices', *Financial Analysts Journal*, **July/August**, 25–36.

Dimson, E. (2002) *The Triumph of the Optimist*. Princeton: Princeton University Press.

Dothan, M. U. (1990) *Prices in Financial Markets*. Oxford: Oxford University Press.

Dudenhausen, A., Schloegl, E. and Schloegl, L. (1998) 'Robustness of Gaussian Hedges under Parameter and Model Mis-Specification', Technical Report, Department of Statistics, University of Bonn.

Duffie, D. (1996) *Dynamic Asset Pricing Theory*, 2nd edition. Princeton: Princeton University Press.

Duffie, D., Pan, J. and Singleton, K. (2000) 'Transform Analysis and Asset Pricing for Affine Jump-Diffusions', *Econometrica*, **68**, 1343–1376.

Dumas, B., Fleming, J. and Whaley, R. (1998) 'Implied Volatility Functions: Empirical Tests', *Journal of Finance*, **53**, no. 6, December, 2059–2084.

Dunbar, N. (2000) *Inventing Money*. Chichester: John Wiley & Sons.

Dupire, B. (1993) 'Pricing and Hedging with Smiles', Paribas Capital Markets Swaps and Options Research Team.

Dupire, B. (1994) 'Pricing with a Smile', *Risk*, **7**, 32–39.

El Karoui, N., Jeanblanc-Pique, M. and Shreve, S. E. (1998) 'Robustness of the Black and Scholes Formula', *Mathematical Finance*, **2**, 93–126.

Elliot, R. J., Lahaie, C. H. and Madan, D. B. (1995) *Filtering Derivative Security Valuations from Market Prices*, Proceedings of the Isaac Newton Workshop in Financial Mathematics. Cambridge: Cambridge University Press.

Engl, H. E. (1993) *Regularization Methods for the Stable Solution of Inverse Problems*, Surveys on Mathematics for Industry, Vol. 3. Berlin: Springer-Verlag, pp. 71–143.

Engle, R. F. and Granger, C. (1987) 'Cointegration and Error Correction: Representation, Estimation and Testing', *Econometrica*, **50**, 987–1008.

Fabozzi, F. J. (Ed.) (2001) *The Handbook of Mortgage-Backed Securities*. New York: McGraw-Hill.

Fan, R., Gupta, A. and Ritchken, P. (2003) 'Hedging in the Possible Presence of Unspanned Stochastic Volatility: Evidence from Swaptions Markets', *Journal of Finance*, **58**, no. 5, 2219–2248.

Fouque, J.-P., Papanicolau, G. and Sircar, K. R. (2000) *Derivatives in Financial Markets with Stochastic Volatility*. Cambridge: Cambridge University Press.

Gardiner, C. W. (1985) *Handbook of Stochastic Methods*, 2nd edition. New York: Springer-Verlag.

Geman, H., El Karoui, N. and Rochet, J.-C. (1995) 'Changes of Numeraire, Changes of Probability Measure and Option Pricing', *Journal of Applied Probability*, **32**, 443–458.

Glasserman, P. (2003) *Monte Carlo Methods in Financial Engineering*. New York: Springer-Verlag.

Glasserman, P. and Kou, S. G. (2000) 'The Term Structure of Simple Forward Rates with Jump Risk', Working Paper, Columbia University.

Glasserman, P. and Merener, N. (2001) 'Numerical Solutions of Jump-Diffusion LIBOR Market Models', Working Paper, Columbia University.

Gourieroux, C. and Jasiak, J. (2001) *Financial Econometrics*. Princeton: Princeton University Press.

Granger, C. (1986) 'Developments in the Study of Cointegrated Variables', *Oxford Bulletin of Economics and Statistics*, **3**, 213–228.

Hagan, P. S., Kumar, D., Lesniewski, A. and Woodward, D. (2002) 'Managing Smile Risk', *Wilmott*, **September**, 84–108.

Hagan, P. S., Lesniewski, A. and Woodward, D. (1999) 'Equivalent Black Volatilities', *Applied Mathematical Finance*, **6**, 147–157.

Hamilton, J. D. (1994) *Time Series Analysis*. Princeton: Princeton University Press.

Harrison, J. M. and Kreps, D. (1979) 'Martingales and Arbitrage in Multiperiod Securities Markets', *Journal of Economic Theory*, **20**, 381–408.

Harrison, J. M. and Pliska, S. (1981) 'Martingales and Stochastic Integrals in the Theory of Continuous Trading', *Stochastic Processes and Their Applications*, **11**, 215–260.

Haug, E. G. (1998) *Option Pricing Formulas*. New York: McGraw-Hill.

Hayre, L. (Ed.) (2001) *A Guide to Mortgage-Backed and Asset-Backed Securities*. Chichester: John Wiley & Sons.

Heath, D., Jarrow, R. A. and Morton, A. (1987) 'Bond Pricing and the Term Structure of Interest Rates: A New Methodology', Working Paper, Cornell University.

Heath, D., Jarrow, R. A. and Morton, A. (1989) 'Bond Pricing and the Term Structure of Interest Rates: A New Methodology', Working Paper, revised edition, Cornell University.

Heston, S. (1993) 'A Closed Form Solution for Options with Stochastic Volatility with Applications to Bond and Currency Options', *Review of Financial Studies*, **6**, 77–105.

Ho, T. S. Y. and Lee, S.-B. (1986) 'Term Structure Movements and Pricing Interest Rate Contingent Claims', *Journal of Finance*, **41**, 1011–1028.

Hull, J. (1993) *Options, Futures and Other Derivative Securities*, 2nd edition. Englewood Cliffs: Prentice Hall International Editions.

Hull, J. and White, A. (1987) 'The Pricing of Options on Assets with Stochastic Volatility', *Journal of Finance*, **42**, no. 2, 281–300.

Hull, J. and White, A. (1988) 'The Use of Control Variate Technique in Option Pricing', *Journal of Financial Quantitative Analysis*, **23**, 237–251.

Hull, J. and White, A. (1990a) 'Pricing Interest-Rate Derivative Securities', *Review of Financial Studies*, **3**, 237–251.

Hull, J. and White, A. (1990b) 'Valuing Derivative Securities Using the Explicit Finite Differences Method', *Journal of Financial and Quantitative Analysis*, **25**, 87–100.

Hull, J. and White, A. (1994a) 'Numerical Procedures for Implementing Term Structure Models I: One-Factor Models', *Journal of Derivatives*, **Fall**, 7–16.

Hull, J. and White, A. (1994b) 'Numerical Procedures for Implementing Term Structure Models II: Two-Factor Models', *Journal of Derivatives*, **Winter**, 37–49.

Hull, J. and White, A. (2000) 'Forward Rate Volatilities, Swap Rate Volatilities and the Implementation of LIBOR Market Model', *Journal of Fixed Income*, **10**, no. 2, 46–62.

Hunter, C., Jaeckel, P. and Joshi, M. (2001) 'Drift Approximations in a LIBOR Market Model', accepted for publication in *Risk Magazine*; also QUARC (Quantitative Research Centre) Working Paper, available at www.Rebonato.com

Jackwerth, J. C. (1997) 'Generalized Binomial Trees', *Journal of Derivatives*, **5**, no. 2, 7–17.

Jackwerth, J. C. and Rubinstein, M. (1996) 'Recovering Probability Distributions from Option Prices', *Journal of Finance*, **51**, no. 5, 1611–1631.

Jacod, J. and Shiryaev, A. N. (1988) *Limit Theorems for Stochastic Processes*. Berlin: Springer-Verlag.

Jacquier, E. and Jarrow, R. A. (1995) 'Dynamic Evaluation of Contingent Claim Models: An Analysis of Model Error', Working Paper, Johnson Graduate School of Management, Cornell University, Ithaca, New York.

Jaeckel, P. and Rebonato, R. (2001) 'Valuing American Options in the Presence of User-Defined Smiles and Time-Dependent Volatility: Scenario Analysis, Model Stress and Lower-Bound Pricing Applications', *Journal of Risk*, **4**, no. 1, 35–61.

Jaeckel, P. and Rebonato, R. (2003) 'Linking Caplet and Swaption Volatilities in a LIBOR Market Model Setting', accepted for publication in *Journal of Computational Finance*; also RBoS QUARC (Quantitative Research Centre) Working Paper, available at www.Rebonato.com

Jamshidian, F. (1991) 'Forward Induction and Construction of Yield Curve Diffusion Models', Working Paper, Financial Strategies Group, Merryll Lynch Capital Markets, New York.

Jamshidian, F. (1997) 'LIBOR and Swap Market Models and Measures', *Finance and Stochastics*, **1**, 293–330.

Jeffrey, C. (2003) 'Risk Reversal for Power Swaps', *Risk*, **16**, no. 10, 20–24.

Johnson, T. C. (2001) 'Volatility, Momentum, and Time-Varying Skewness in Foreign Exchange Returns', London Business School Working Paper No. 324, available at www.london.edu/ifa

Jorion, P. (1988) 'On Jump Processes in the Foreign Exchange and in the Stock Markets', *Review of Financial Studies*, **Winter**, 427–445.

Jorion, P. (2000) 'Risk Management Lessons from Long-Term Capital Management', *European Financial Management*, **6**, September, 277-300.

Joshi, M. (2001) 'A Short Note on Exponential Correlation Functions', Working Paper, RBoS, QUARC (Quantitative Research Centre).

Joshi, M. (2003) 'Observations on Applying the Predictor-Corrector to CEV Processes', Working Paper, RBoS, QUARC (Quantitative Research Centre).

Joshi, M. and Rebonato, R. (2003) 'A Displaced-Diffusion Stochastic-Volatility LIBOR Market Model: Motivation, Definition and Implementation', *Quantitative* Finance, **3**, no. 6, 458–469; also Working Paper, Quantitative Finance and QUARC (Quantitative Research Centre), available at www.Rebonato.com

Joshi, M. and Theis, J. (2002) 'Bounding Bermudan Swaptions in a Swap-Rate Market Model', *Quantitative Finance*, **2**, 370–377.

Kahneman, D. and Tversky, A. (Eds) (2000) *Choices, Values and Frames*. Cambridge: Cambridge University Press.

Karatzas, I. and Shreve, S. E. (1991) *Brownian Motion and Stochastic Calculus*. Berlin: Springer-Verlag.

Kloeden, P. E. and Platen, E. (1992) *Numerical Solutions of Stochastic Differential Equations*. Berlin: Springer-Verlag.

Kreyszig, E. (1993) *Advanced Engineering Mathematics*, 7th edition. Chichester: John Wiley & Sons.

Kumar, S. M. and Persaud, A. (2002) 'Pure Contagion and Investors' Shifting Risk Appetite: Analytical Issues and Empirical Evidence', *International Finance*, **5**, 401–426.

Lamberton, D. and Lapeyre, B. (1991) 'Introduction au calcul stochastique appliqué à la finance', *Ecole National des Ponts et Chaussées*, **March**.

Lewis, A. (2000) *Option Valuation Under Stochastic Volatility*. Newport Beach: Finance Press.

Lewis, A. (2002) 'Fear of Jumps', *Wilmott*, **December**, 60–67.

Longstaff, F. A., Santa-Clara, P. and Schwartz, E. S. (2000a) 'Throwing Away a Billion Dollars: The Cost of Sub-Optimal Exercise Strategies in the Swaptions Markets', Working Paper, UCLA, presented at the ICBI Risk Conference, Geneva.

Longstaff, F. A., Santa-Clara, P. and Schwartz, E. S. (2000b) 'The Relative Valuation of Caps and Swaptions: Theory and Empirical Evidence', Working Paper, UCLA, presented at the ICBI Risk Conference, Geneva.

Lyons, T. J. (1995) 'Uncertain Volatility and the Risk-Free Synthesis of Derivatives', *Applied Mathematical Finance*, **2**, 117–133.

Madan, D. B. and Seneta, E. (1990) 'The Variance Gamma (VG) Model for Share Market Returns', *Journal of Business*, **63**, no. 4, 511–524.

Madan, D. B., Carr, P. P. and Chang, E. C. (1998) 'The Variance Gamma Process and Option Pricing', *European Finance Review*, **2**, 7–105.

Mahayni, A. (2003) 'Effectiveness of Hedging Strategies Under Model Misspecification and Trading Restrictions', *International Journal of Theoretical and Applied Finance*, **6**, no. 5, 521–540.

Maltz, A. M. (1997) 'Estimating the Probability Distribution of the Future Exchange Rate from Option Prices', *Journal of Derivatives*, **5**, no. 2, 18–36.

Marris, D. (1999) 'Financial Option Pricing and Skewed Volatility', M. Phil. thesis, Statistical Laboratory, University of Cambridge.

Marris, D. and Lane, A. (2002) 'Efficient HJM Approximations of LIBOR Market Models', Contribution to BSF Conference, Bachelier Institute, University of Texas.

Martellini, L. and Priaulet, P. (2001) *Fixed-Income Securities*. Chichester: John Wiley & Sons.

Merton, R. C. (1973) 'Theory of Rational Option Pricing', *Bell Journal of Economics and Management Science*, **4**, 141–183.

Merton, R. C. (1983) 'On the Mathematics and Economics Assumptions of Continuous-Time Models', in: W. F. Sharpe and P. Cootner (Eds), *Financial Economics: Essays in Honour of Paul Cootner*. Englewood Cliffs: Prentice Hall.

Merton, R. C. (1990) *Continuous-Time Finance*. Oxford: Blackwell.

Mirfendereski, D. and Rebonato, R. (2001) 'Closed-Form Solutions for Option Pricing in the Presence of Volatility Smiles: A Density-Function Approach', *Journal of Risk*, **3**, no. 3, 1–16.

Misina, M. (2003) 'What Does the Risk Appetite Index Measure?', Working Paper 2003-23, Bank of Canada, August.

Musiela, M. and Rutkowski, M. (1997) 'Continuous-Time Term Structure Models: A Forward-Measure Approach', *Finance and Stochastics*, **1**, no. 4, 261–292.

Naik, V. (1993) 'Option Valuation and Hedging Strategies with Jump in the Volatility of Asset Returns', *Journal of Finance*, **48**, no. 5, 1969–1984.

Neftci, S. (1996) *Mathematics of Financial Derivatives*. San Diego: Academic Press.

Nelson, D. B. and Ramaswamy, K. (1990) 'Simple Binomial Approximations in Financial Models', *Review of Financial Studies*, **3**, 393–430.

Nielsen, L. T. (1999) *Pricing and Hedging of Derivatives Securities*. Oxford: Oxford University Press.

O'Hara, M. (1995) *Market Microstructure Theory*. Oxford: Blackwell.

Oksendal, B. (1995) *Stochastic Differential Equations*, 5th edition. Berlin: Springer-Verlag.

Pirkner, C. D., Weigend, A. S. and Zimmerman, H. (1999) 'Extracting Risk-Neutral Densities Using Mixture Binomial Trees', in: *Proceedings of the 1999 IEEE/IAFE/Informs Conference on Computational Intelligence for Financial Engineering*. New York: IEEE, pp. 135–158.

Piterbarg, V. V. (2003) 'Mixture of Models: A Simple Recipe for a... Hangover?', Working Paper, Bank of America.

Pliska, S. R. (1997) *Introduction to Mathematical Finance*. Oxford: Blackwell.

Press, W. H., Teukolsky, S. A., Vetterling, W. T. and Flannery, B. P. (1992) *Numerical Recipes in FORTRAN – The Art of Scientific Computing*, 2nd edition. Cambridge: Cambridge University Press.

Rebonato, R. (1997) 'A Class of Arbitrage-Free Log-Normal-Short-Rate Two-Factor Models', *Applied Mathematical Finance*, **4**, no. 4, 223–236.

Rebonato, R. (1998a) *Interest-Rate Option Models*, 2nd edition. Chichester: John Wiley & Sons.

Rebonato, R. (1998b) 'The Age of Innocence', *Futures and Options World*, **Summer**, 16-20.

Rebonato, R. (1999a) 'On the Simultaneous Calibration of Multifactor Lognormal Interest Rate Models to Black Volatilities and to the Correlation Matrix', *Journal of Computational Finance*, **2**, 5–27.

Rebonato, R. (1999b) 'On the Pricing Implications of the Joint Log-Normality Assumption for the Cap and Swaption Markets', *Journal of Computational Finance*, **3**, 57–76.

Rebonato, R. (1999c) 'Calibrating the BGM Model', *Risk*, **March**, 88–94.

Rebonato, R. (2002) *Modern Pricing of Interest-Rate Derivatives: The LIBOR Market Mode and Beyond*. Princeton: Princeton University Press.

Rebonato, R. (2003a) 'Which Process Gives Rise to the Observed Dependence of Swaption Implied Volatilities on the Underlying?', *International Journal of Theoretical and Applied Finance*, **6**, no. 4, 419–442; and Working Paper, QUARC (Quantitative Research Centre), available at www.rebonato.com

Rebonato, R. (2003b) 'Theory and Practice of Model Risk Management', in: P. Field (Ed.), *Modern Risk Management: A History*. London: Risk Books.

Rebonato, R. (2004) 'Interest-Rate Term-Structure Pricing Models: A Review', *Proceedings of the Royal Society London*, **460**, 1–62.

Rebonato, R. and Cardoso, M. T. (2004) 'Unconstrained Fitting of Non-Central Risk-Neutral Densities Using a Mixture of Normals', submitted to *Journal of Risk*.

Rebonato, R. and Cooper, I. (1995) 'The Limitations of Simple Two-Factor Interest-Rate Models', *Journal of Financial Engineering*, **5**, 1–16.

Rebonato, R. and Joshi, M. (2002) 'A Joint Empirical/Theoretical Investigation of the Modes of Deformation of Swaption Matrices: Implications for the Stochastic-Volatility LIBOR Market Model', *International Journal of Theoretical and Applied Finance*, **5**, no. 7, 667–694; and Working Paper, QUARC (Quantitative Research Centre), available at www.rebonato.com

Rebonato, R. and Kainth, D. (2004) 'A Two-Regime, Stochastic-Volatility Extension of the LIBOR Market Model', accepted for publication in *International Journal of Theoretical and Applied Finance*; and Working Paper, QUARC (Quantitative Research Centre), available at www.rebonato.com

Rebonato, R. and Kazziha, S. (1997) 'Unconditional Variance, Mean Reversion and Short-Rate Volatility in the Calibration of the BDT Model and of Tree-Based Models in General', *Net Exposure*, **2**, November (no page number, electronic journal).

Reiner, E. (1998) 'Understanding Skew and Smile Behaviour in the Context of Jump Processes and Applying These Results to the Pricing and Hedging of Exotic Options', Working Paper presented at the Global Derivatives Conference, Paris, 28 April 1998.

Ross, S. (1976) 'The Arbitrage Pricing Theory of Capital Asset Pricing', *Journal of Economic Theory*, **13**, 341–360.

Ross, S. M. (1997) *Introduction to Probability Models*, 6th edition. San Diego: Academic Press.

Rubinstein, M. (1983) 'Displaced Diffusion Option Pricing', *Journal of Finance*, **38**, no. 3, 213–217.

Rubinstein, M. (1994) 'Implied Binomial Trees', *Journal of Finance*, **69**, no. 3, 771–818.

Rutkowski, M. (1998) 'Dynamics of Spot, Forward and Futures LIBOR Rates', *International Journal of Theoretical and Applied Finance*, **1**, no. 3, 425–445.

Samuel, D. (2002) 'Pricing Forward-staring Options', presented at the Global Derivatives and Risk Management Conference, Barcelona, May.

Schoenbucher, P. J. (1996) 'The Term Structure of Defaultable Bonds', Working (Discussion) Paper B-384, Department of Statistics, Faculty of Economics, University of Bonn, Adenauerallee 24–42, D-53113 Bonn; email: schonbuc@addi.finasto.uni-bonn.de

Schoenbucher, P. J. (2000) 'A Market Model for Stochastic Implied Volatility', Working Paper, Department of Statistics, University of Bonn.

Schoenbucher, P. J. (2003) *Credit Derivatives Pricing Models: Models, Pricing and Implementation*. Chichester: John Wiley & Sons.

Schoenmakers, J. and Coffey, B. (2000) 'Stable Implied Calibration of a Multi-Factor LIBOR Market Model Via a Semi-Parametric Correlation Structure', Working Paper 611, Weierstrass-Institut fuer Angewandte Analysis und Stochastik, Berlin.

Scholes, M. (2000) 'Crises and Risk', *Risk*, **May**, 98-102.

Scott, L. O. (1987) 'Option Prices When the Variance Changes Randomly: Theory, Estimation and an Application', *Journal of Financial and Quantitative Analysis*, **22**, 419–438.

Shefrin, H. (2000) *Beyond Greed and Fear*. Boston, MA: Harvard Business School Press.

Shiller, R. J. (2000) *Irrational Exuberance*. Princeton: Princeton University Press.

Shimko, D. C. (1994) *Finance in Continuous Time*. Miami: Kolb Publishing Company.

Shleifer, A. (2000) *Inefficient Markets – An Introduction to Behavioural Finance*, Clarendon Lectures in Economics. Oxford: Oxford University Press.

Shleifer, A. and Vishny, R. (1997) 'The Limits of Arbitrage', *Journal of Finance*, **52**, 35–55.

Shreve, S. (1997) 'Stochastic Calculus for Derivatives', Course Notes for 1997 Risk Training Course, London.

Shreve, S., Chalasani, P. and Jha, S. (1997) 'Stochastic Calculus and Finance', unpublished lecture notes, Carnegie Mellon University.

Sidenius, J. (1999) 'LIBOR Market Models in Practice', *Journal of Computational Finance*, **3**, 75–99.

Stein, E. and Stein, J. (1991) 'Stock Price Distributions with Stochastic Volatility: An Analytic Approach', *Review of Financial Studies*, **4**, 727–752.

Tilley, J. A. (1993) 'Valuing American Options in a Path Simulation Model', *Transactions of the Society of Actuaries*, **45**, 83–104.

Vasicek, O. (1977) An Equilibrium Characterization of the Term Structure', *Journal of Financial Economics*, **5**, 177–188.

Wiggins, J. B. (1987) 'Option Values Under Stochastic Volatility: Theory and Empirical Estimates', *Journal of Financial Economics*, **19**, 351–372.

Wilmott, P. (1998) *Derivatives*. Chichester: John Wiley & Sons.

Index

9NC2 Bermudan swaptions   655–66
Abramowitz, M.   284, 734
absolute continuity principle   186–7
absolute pricing, concepts   17–18, 29, 178
absorbing states, Markov chains   786–7
across-market comparisons, practices   27–9
adaptness definition, filtration   151–2, 593–4
adiabatic approximation, volatility   178
admissible smile surfaces, concepts   583–4
agency relationships   21–5, 199
Ait-Sahalia, Y.   201, 206, 222, 255, 346
Alexander, C.   19, 27, 143, 205, 222, 260, 263, 343
Ames, W.F.   327, 332
Amin, K.I.   245
amplitude jump-diffusion models   241–2, 257–8, 270–2, 315–16, 443–55, 460–509, 561, 582–99, 797–8
analytic (PDE) approach
   see also partial differential equations
   payoff replication   31–7
anchoring effects   21
Andersen, L.   145, 243, 245, 346, 350–2, 354–5, 659, 715, 730, 733
Andreasen, J.   145, 243, 355, 659, 715, 730, 733
angular components, decomposition of weights   261–3
appropriate discount factors, concepts   21
appropriate pricing measure, payoff replication   57, 64–5, 105–6, 184–7
arbitrage   5–11, 20–7, 31–4, 40–2, 54–6, 70–3, 85–6, 104–5, 180, 182–4, 346, 375–85, 441–9, 501–2, 563–99, 679–80, 731
   Britten-Jones and Neuberger   293–317
   concepts   5–11, 20–7, 563–99, 731
   Efficient Market Hypothesis   10–11, 20–7, 197–9, 441–4, 467
   implied volatility   7, 11–12, 26, 85–6, 346, 375–85, 441–4, 563–99

no-arbitrage conditions   5–6, 18, 31–4, 54–6, 70–1, 76–8, 187, 237–48, 261–3, 276–7, 283–7, 293–317, 323–6, 356–7, 375–85, 419, 441–4, 531–2, 563–99, 626–8, 679–80
   pseudo-arbitrageurs   10–11, 20–1, 24, 197–9, 202, 441–4, 467, 511–12
   supply/demand imbalances   20–6, 187, 197–9, 399–401
   true arbitrage   346, 598, 622
Aristotelian physics   30, 598
Arrow–Debreu prices   322–34
   concepts   322–34
   definition   322–3
   efficient computations   324–6
   main properties   322–4
asymmetric smiles   204–7, 209–35, 260, 267–92, 309–14, 333–8, 358–73, 391, 439–41, 494–9, 515–17, 522–7, 553–61, 575–81, 743–9, 793–801
at-the-money (ATM) options   22–4, 33, 90, 94, 138, 169–72, 182–9, 203–38, 257, 284, 311, 338, 369–85, 402–27, 439–44, 476–85, 493–4, 503–9, 527, 533–66, 573–80, 704–49, 756–82
   displaced diffusions   533–61, 742–9, 756–64, 771
   interest-rate smiles   704–49, 756–801
   swaption matrix   765–82, 788–801
autocorrelation, principal components analysis   205, 222
Avellaneda, M.   103, 258–9
average volatility, concepts   89, 102, 116, 213–14, 370–3, 418–37, 502–9
average-rate options   258, 640

Bachelier   513
back-office models   512
Backus, D.   214
backward induction   54, 299, 346, 349–57, 640

backward (Kolmogorov) equation   246, 349–57,
    530, 588–93
balance-of-variance condition, concepts   85
Barle, S.   345
barrier options   385, 564–75
basis risk, concepts   400–1
basket options   4–5, 18–19, 141
Baskshi, G.C.   208
Bates, D.S.   227
Baxter, M.   58, 60, 83, 150, 586, 609
Bayesian-statistical approach   227
BDT see Black–Derman–Toy model
behavioural finance, concepts   21–2, 44
Bermudan swaptions   22, 610–22, 655–66
Bernoulli distribution   614
Bessel functions   321, 517, 521
bid–offer spreads   16, 32, 102–3, 172–3, 270–2
    out-of-model hedging   16
    perfect payoff replication   32
binary options   169, 172–3
binomial distribution   38–73, 103–4, 135–9,
    300–34, 449, 614–15, 617–22, 640
    bushy binomial trees   53–65, 135–9, 300–17,
        321–2, 449, 617–22
    mean reversion   614–22
BJN see Britten-Jones and Neuberger
Bjork, T.   150–1, 501–2
Black, F.   359, 610, 612
Black and Karasinski model   610, 616–17, 622
Black-and-Scholes model   3–5, 15–32, 81–132,
    143, 151, 164, 168–99, 203–317, 348–87,
    418–44, 471, 476–85, 512, 533–4, 543–4,
    564–6, 584–99, 609, 704–5, 760–1
    see also implied volatility; partial differential
        equations
    advantages   3–5, 28–9, 81–4, 121–2, 127–9,
        168, 385–6, 418
    benchmark status   168, 418
    component parts   168–73
    displaced diffusions   533–4, 543–4, 760–1
    hedging performance   15, 385–6, 418–37,
        502–9, 512, 523, 622
    historical background   3–5, 121, 168
    in-model hedging   15
    misconceptions   101
    out-of-model hedging   15
    quadratic variation   98, 122–7, 143, 245–8,
        293–317
    risk aversion   122–3, 184–99, 419–37,
        500–2
    robustness issues   127–9, 168–9, 418, 422,
        427, 502–9
    smiles   168–99, 203–92, 348–87, 584–99,
        704–5, 760–1
    spot and forward processes   81–4
    true call price functional   174–6

weaknesses   98, 103–4, 168, 173–4, 213–15,
    247–8, 512
wrongness issues   30, 103–4, 121–7, 174–8,
    352–3, 400, 422–37, 718
Black–Derman–Toy (BDT) model   603,
    610–22, 662
    concepts   603, 610–22, 662
    continuous time equivalent   611–17
    critique   610–11
    discrete time case   612–22
    lattices   612–22
    paradox   610–12
    short-rate unconditional variance   612–22
    weaknesses   610–11, 617–20
Bliss   186
bonds
    discount bonds   19–20, 82–4, 610–22
    forward rates   607–8
    hedging   455–65, 502–9
    jump-diffusion models   455–65, 502–9
boundary conditions   34, 300–17, 348, 395,
    564–75
boxes see continuous double barriers
Boyle's approach   105, 328
Brace, A.   626, 670
break-even points, trading the gamma   108–16
Breeden, D.T.   585–6
Brigo, D.   404, 755
Britten-Jones and Neuberger (BJN)   99, 102,
    129, 179, 243–5, 248, 293–317, 352–4
    see also quadratic variation
    case studies   307–17
    computational results   307–17
    concepts   99, 102, 129, 179, 243–5, 248,
        293–317, 352–4
    discussion of the results   312–16
    numerical implementation   300–12
    optimal hedge   299–317
    price bounds   293–317
    problems   298–9, 312–16
    theoretical development   294–300
    tree construction   299–317
Brotherton-Ratcliffe, R.   245, 346, 350–2, 354
Brownian motion   32–7, 67–73, 81–4, 91–9,
    110–14, 120–1, 132, 144–7, 157–8, 163,
    237–43, 267–77, 312–13, 320, 390–2, 397,
    402–5, 441–56, 464, 501, 513–18, 529–65,
    611–12, 628–42, 663–5, 726–30, 748–56,
    766, 771
    displaced diffusions   529–61
    LIBOR market model   628–30, 641–2,
        663–5, 748–56, 766, 771
    variance–gamma process   513–18
brute-force
    Monte Carlo simulation   734, 737–49
    variance–gamma pricing process   519–21

bubbles 10
Buffet, W. 29
building blocks 75–99
bushy binomial trees 53–65, 135–9, 300–17, 321–2, 449, 617–22

Cakici, N. 345
calibration 6–7, 11–27, 168–9, 184–99, 249–92, 321–2, 371, 427–37, 449, 610–22, 626–37, 639–66, 733–4, 736–49, 756–64, 781
    Black–Derman–Toy model 610–22, 662
    concepts 11–27, 168, 184, 249–92, 371, 427–37, 449, 733–49, 756–64, 781
    debate 17–27, 168
    fundamental approach 6–7
    historical/implied calibration contrasts 18–20
    jump-diffusion models 465–70
    LIBOR market model 626–37, 639–66, 733–4, 736–49, 756–64, 781–2
    practices 11–27, 168–9, 427–37, 783
    re-calibrated models 15–18, 246, 371, 436, 511–12, 783
    smiles 168–9, 184–99, 249–92, 427–37, 759–64
calls 104–39, 172–99, 204–9, 238–92, 323–405, 416–44, 471–509, 519–20, 532–61, 564–99, 704–27
    Britten-Jones and Neuberger 301–17, 352–3
    degenerative hedging strategy 564–71
    displaced diffusions 532–61, 735, 742–9
    generalized beta of the second kind 278–92, 354–5
    portfolio-replication 389–401, 418–37, 444–509, 564–99
Campa, J. 227
Campbell, J.Y. 389, 398
Capital Asset Pricing Model (CAPM) 36, 419
caplets 19–29, 155–6, 161, 164, 170–2, 222–4, 244–5, 267, 272–5, 287–92, 532, 608–22, 626–700, 732–49, 759–66, 785, 788–801
    LIBOR market model 626–86, 732–49, 759–66, 785, 788–801
    swaption volatilities 626–66, 680–6, 759–64, 788–801
CAPM see Capital Asset Pricing Model
caps 22–4, 76, 149, 198, 258, 287–92, 397, 626–66, 766
Cardoso, M.T. 259
Carr, P. 213, 215–16, 220, 371–2, 440, 521
cash-and-carry-arbitrage 203, 261
cash-or-nothing (European digital) options 16, 169, 172–3, 574–5, 733–4
Central Banks 672

Central Limit Theorem (CLT) 206, 215, 265–77, 527
CEV see constant elasticity variance
CG see Crouhy-Galai...
Chan, K.C. 730
'chartism' 4
cheap convexity 13
CIR interest-rate model 44, 465
Citigroup 427–9
closed-form solutions
    direct density modelling 245
    jump-diffusion models 452–5
    smiles 179–80, 403–37, 564–99, 734
    stochastic-volatility models 179–80, 403–37, 532
CLT see Central Limit Theorem
co-integration concepts 141, 143–4
co-terminal swaptions 26, 659–66
Cochrane, J.H. 29–30, 188, 323, 419, 509
Coffey, B. 689, 691, 697–700
compensated processes
    concepts 169–73, 451–5, 518–19
    jump–diffusion models 451–5, 518–19
complete markets 9, 17, 19–20, 237–41, 293–317, 323, 326, 444–9, 499–502, 582–3, 752
    jump–diffusion models 20, 237–41, 293–317, 444–9, 499–502
    option pricing framework 293–317, 323, 326, 499–502
complex products 4–6, 8–10, 14–19, 26–7, 28, 83–4, 129, 201–2, 257–8, 313–14, 399–400, 473–85, 502, 511–28, 748–9, 759, 783
computers 11, 766
consensus prices 13–14
constant elasticity variance (CEV) 181–4, 344, 389, 406, 440–1, 529–34, 553, 560, 597, 704–6, 718–27, 729–56, 781–2
    analytic characterization 730–2
    approximations 734–52
    brute-force Monte Carlo 734, 737–49
    displaced diffusions 529–34, 553, 560, 597, 735, 742–9, 752
    drift approximations 734–49
    financial desirability 732–4
    implied volatility 704–6, 718–27, 730–49, 756
    information content 738–42
    LIBOR market model 704–6, 729–49, 754, 756, 781–2
    numerical problems 734
    predictor–corrector method solutions 736–49, 752
    smiles 730–49, 756

constant elasticity variance (CEV) *(continued)*
   transformation-of-variables solutions   735–6,
      752
   unadulterated processes   734
constant volatility
   concepts   90–1, 101, 106–16, 117–21,
      147–8, 285–7, 334, 355–7, 389, 419–37,
      598, 737–9
   trading the gamma   114–16, 117–21
Cont, R.   201, 222
contingent claims   38–73, 101–39, 239–40,
      293–317, 418–37, 444–509, 519–21,
      564–99
   see also payoff replication
   fair values   38, 54–65, 73, 423–4
   multi-period settings   53–6
   valuation approaches   38–73, 106–21
continuous double barriers   385, 564–75
   case studies   564–75
   concepts   385, 564–75
   static replication   566–71
   unwinding costs   570–5
continuous jump amplitudes   444–55, 465–85
continuous time   38, 65–73, 98–9, 103–39,
      276, 294, 319–20, 371–2, 440–509,
      512–13, 611–17, 639–66
   Black–Derman–Toy model   611–17
   discretization strategies   103–39, 302–4, 327,
      350
   hedging errors   103–4
   self-financing continuous-time strategy
      103–4, 276, 419, 445–6, 502–3, 565
contravariate trees, concepts   333–4, 352
convergence   137–8, 302–4, 307–9, 333–4,
      473–85, 738–9, 801
   Britten-Jones and Neuberger   302–4, 307–9
   discretization strategies   137–8, 302–4,
      333–4
   jump amplitude ratios   473–85
convex hull, concepts   306
convexity   13, 44, 188–96, 206, 209–35,
      238–48, 333–4, 337–8, 359–68, 485–509,
      575–81, 668–9
Cooper, I.   144, 648, 653
Cooper, N.   227
copula uses   168–9
Cornell, B.   186
correlation   141–64, 206–22, 227–35, 416–27,
      440, 520–1, 626–700, 760–803
   concepts   141–64, 206–22, 227–35, 416–27,
      440, 520–1, 626–700, 760–82
   covariance   17–18, 29, 87, 158–64, 628–31,
      642–66, 689–700, 760–82, 785–803
   estimation issues   18–19, 27, 642–700
   fitting   686–700, 778–81

forward rates   142–64, 417–27, 626–37,
      641–66, 686–700, 705–27, 760–82
functional forms   686–700, 778–81
generalized results   162–4
imperfectly correlated variables   144–64
importance   4–5, 18, 27, 80–4, 141–64,
      686–700, 778–81
instantaneous correlation   75–6, 141–64,
      626–37, 642–66, 667–700, 778–81
instantaneous volatility   149–50, 626–37,
      680–6, 688–700, 777–81
LIBOR market model   625–700, 760–82
matrix   143–64, 628–37, 642–66, 688–700,
      760–82
model comparisons   686–700, 778–81
modified exponential function   691–7
multi-factor models   144–6, 626–37, 641–66,
      686–700
relative pricing   17–18
Schoenmakers–Coffey approach   697–700
simple exponential function   689–97
square-root exponential function   694–7
swaption matrix   771–81, 784–801
terminal correlation   75–6, 141–64, 626–37,
      648–66, 687–700, 780–1
time-dependent volatility   144–64, 687–700
zero correlation   715–27
counting processes
   concepts   450–3, 470
   jump–diffusion models   450–3, 470
covariance   17–18, 29, 87, 158–64, 628–31,
      642–66, 689–700, 760–82, 785–803
   LIBOR market model   628–31, 642–66,
      689–700, 760–82, 785–803
   matrix   628–37, 642–66, 760–82, 785–803
   relative pricing   17–18, 29
credit derivatives   4, 29, 141, 168–9, 449
credit spreads   4
Crouhy, M.   120, 135–9, 294, 312–14
Crouhy–Galai set-up (CG)   135–9, 294, 312–14
cubic polynomial   6
cubic splines, surface-fitting input data   252–4,
      346
current smile surfaces, concepts   584–5
current volatility, forward quantities   76, 87–9

da Fonseca, J.   222
Das, S.R.   239, 439
De Jong, F.   685, 778
decaying term structure of volatility, forward
      rates   607–12, 788–9
deeply smooth implied volatility surfaces,
      concepts   346, 357–87, 575–81
default frequencies   4–5
default swaps   29
definitions   75–7, 87–9

degenerative hedging strategy   564–71
delta hedging   7, 8–9, 12–17, 77–84, 104–39,
    169–99, 274–7, 419–44, 505–9, 565–6,
    796–8
  critique   8–9, 512
  vega hedging   8–9, 169–73, 182–3, 419
deltas   7–9, 12–17, 77–84, 90–5, 104–39,
    169–204, 227–35, 274–7, 287–92, 350,
    419–44, 486, 494–512, 523–7, 564–71,
    732–3, 786–7, 796–8
DEM market   678–86, 767–81
demand/supply imbalances   20–7, 187–99,
    399–401, 687
densities
  see also risk-neutral. . .
  direct density modelling   245
  future conditional densities   257, 277
  generalized beta of the second kind   275–92,
    354–5
  smiles   206, 209–22, 227–35, 245, 256–92
  state price densities   323
derivatives pricing
  absolute pricing   17–18, 29, 178
  across-markets comparisons   27–9
  approaches   5–8, 30, 95, 129, 168–9, 185–6,
    294, 316–20, 385–6, 389–437, 439–41,
    511–28, 563–99, 621–2, 625–6, 686–700,
    752, 766–7, 778–81, 783–803
  Arrow–Debreu prices   322–34
  background   3–73, 82–3, 141–64, 167–99,
    201–2, 237–41, 262–3, 319–87, 511–28,
    563–99, 639–66, 729–49, 766–7, 795–801
  bounds   293–317
  Britten-Jones and Neuberger   99, 102, 129,
    179, 243–5, 248, 293–317, 352–4
  Derman and Kani model   243, 251, 319–87,
    572–3
  displaced diffusions   532–61, 735, 742,
    754–64, 771
  dynamics   201–2, 563–99
  Efficient Market Hypothesis   8, 9–14, 20–7,
    42–3, 197–9, 202, 441–4, 467, 752
  jump–diffusion models   5, 31–3, 95, 184–5,
    197, 224–41, 257–8, 265–77, 293–319,
    355, 372, 398, 427–509, 513, 521, 523,
    560–1, 582–99, 797–8
  LIBOR market model   19, 28–9, 530, 594,
    604, 607, 621–2, 625–700, 704–5,
    729–803
  model roles   3–30, 402, 439–41, 563–99
  non-process-based models   563–99
  payoff replication   3–5, 28–30, 31–73,
    239–40, 322–3, 389–401, 418–37,
    444–509, 564–99
  performance comparisons   385–437, 502–13,
    523, 621–2, 766–7, 795–801

process-based models   563, 598–9
quadratic variation   8, 31–2, 95–9, 102–3,
    122–9, 143, 245–8, 293–317, 352–4,
    376–85, 404–5, 418–37, 502–9
quality assessments   385–437, 502–13, 523,
    621–2, 766–7, 795–801
real world measure   4, 17–18, 35–6, 41–8,
    50, 59–65, 69, 73, 105–6, 131–9, 184–99,
    262–3, 394–8, 419–37, 441–4, 467–72,
    511–12, 765–6, 790–801
relative pricing   17–18, 33–4, 47–8, 51–3,
    57–65, 69–73, 111, 178, 390–1, 595–6
stochastic-volatility models   5, 17, 20, 31, 32,
    95–9, 153, 237–41, 242–8, 265–77,
    294–441, 449, 456–9, 470, 512–13,
    521, 523, 527, 560, 715–30, 751–66,
    771–803
switching of numeraires   52–3, 58–65, 71–3,
    748–51
two-regime instantaneous volatility   783–803
variance–gamma process   95, 96, 99, 243–4,
    247, 265–77, 511–28, 587
derived analysis, empirical data   201–2
Derman, E.   206, 221–2, 243, 319, 581, 603–4
Derman and Kani (DK) model   243, 251,
    319–87, 572–3, 587
  assumptions   347–9
  concepts   243, 251, 319–45, 347–57, 385–6,
    587
  hedging performance   385–6
  implementation results   334–44, 355–6,
    385–6
  input regimes   334–44
  numerical aspects   331–8, 345–6, 349–57,
    385–6, 572–3
  problems   331–4, 338–44, 345–6, 355–6
  regularization   343–87
  tree construction   326–31, 572–3
deterministic correlation   15, 20
deterministic discounting, concepts   80–5, 91–2
deterministic smiles   585–93, 755–6
deterministic volatility   15, 20, 31–6, 95–9,
    129, 153, 188–99, 203, 245–8, 294–328,
    333–4, 389–405, 418–37, 453–65, 470,
    491–509, 513, 568–75, 585–700, 736–49,
    754–6, 782, 799–801
  equivalent deterministic future smiles   595–9
  interest rates   601–700, 736–49, 754–6, 782,
    799–801
  LIBOR market model   736–49, 754–6, 782,
    799–801
  market price of risk   34–6, 396–405
  out-of-model hedging   15
  portfolio-replication argument   32–6,
    389–401, 418–37, 457–65, 502–9, 568–75,
    582–99

deterministic volatility *(continued)*
   quadratic variation 95–9, 129, 245–8,
    294–317, 404–5
diffusion processes 5–6, 20, 31, 69–70,
   104–39, 143, 176–7, 179–80, 188–9,
   396–401, 418–37, 705–6, 771, 797–8
   displaced diffusions 406, 529–61, 735,
    742–9, 771
   Feynman–Kac theorem 36–7, 56, 73, 105,
    119–21
   jump–diffusion models 312–14
   perfect payoff replication 32–3, 98, 102,
    104–39, 418, 444–5, 455, 460, 500–2
   re-hedging frequencies 122–7, 295–317,
    418–19, 505–9
   shortcomings 440–1, 529, 771, 797–8
digital options 16, 169–73, 247–8, 574–5,
   733–4
dimensionality reduction, LIBOR market model
   640, 643–66
Dimson, E. 186
Dirac distribution 353, 465, 734
direct density modelling, smiles 245
direct dynamic information, smiles 204–5,
   563–99
direct problems, concepts 343–4
direct static information, smiles 203–4, 782
discontinuous components 371–2, 440–509,
   523
discount bonds 19–20, 82–4, 610–22
discount factors, concepts 21–2, 27–8, 80–4
discounted expectations, terminal payoff 36–73,
   105–6, 120–1, 177–8, 329–44, 532–3,
   567–75
discrete time 38, 58, 65, 103–4, 322–3, 348,
   445–9, 513–17, 594, 612–22, 639–66
   Black–Derman–Toy model 612–22
   hedging errors 103–4
discretization strategies
   continuous time 103–39, 302–4, 327, 350
   convergence 137–8, 302–4, 333–4
   problems 121, 139
displaced diffusions 406, 529–61, 587, 589–91,
   597, 732, 735, 742–52, 754–64, 771
   advantages 529–30
   asymptotic aspects 553
   at-the-money options 533–61, 742–9,
    756–64
   concepts 406, 529–61, 597, 732, 735,
    742–9, 754–64
   constant elasticity variance 529–34, 553,
    560, 597, 735, 742–9, 752, 754
   critique 529–30
   equivalent volatility 554–7, 732–3
   extensions 560–1
   formulations 530–1

implied volatility 534–61, 597, 754–64
   LIBOR market model 732, 735, 742–52,
    754–64, 771
   local volatility 560–1
   normal-diffusion limits 553–9
   numerical results 534–59
   option prices 532–61
   refined-approximation results 544–52
   simple-approximation results 534–44
   smiles 553–61, 587, 589–91, 597, 754–64
   stochastic-volatility models 560, 754–64, 771
   underlying 530–2
   weaknesses 529, 771
displacement coefficients, utility functions
   188–99
distance condition, concepts 589–91
dominating strategies 293–317
dotcom mania 10
double differentiation, call prices 205
drift 37, 69–70, 72–3, 81–2, 104–16, 131–4,
   143, 356–7, 394–405, 454–5, 500–2, 513,
   530–2, 604–12, 626–8, 736–49, 765–6
   estimations 3, 17, 131–4, 401–5, 626–8,
    736–49
   functional form 401–5
   mean-reverting real-world drift 131–4, 143,
    400–5, 604–10, 765–6
   predictor–corrector method solutions
    736–49, 759
   real-world situation 131–4, 143, 394–405,
    454–5, 500–2, 604–10, 765–6
Dudenhausen, A. 103
Duffie, D. 243, 326
Dumas, B. 385–6
Dunbar, N. 25
Dupire model 321–2, 342–4, 356, 385–6,
   586

easy-to-determine dependencies, implied
   volatility 167
econometric issues 20–4, 182–4, 441–4, 467,
   517–19, 796
economic agents, concept 182–4, 441–4, 467,
   517–18
economic time, concepts 517–19
effective volatility theory 321–2
Efficient Market Hypothesis (EMH) 8, 9–14,
   20–7, 42–3, 187, 193–4, 197–9, 202,
   441–4, 467, 752
   concepts 8, 9–14, 20–7, 197–9, 202, 441
   critique 9–14, 20–7
   empirical evidence 25–6
   forms 9–10
   parable 12–14
   pseudo-arbitrageurs 10–11, 20–7, 197–9,
    202, 441

regulatory constraints 11, 25, 199
  risk management 11–14, 193–4, 197–9, 441
eigenvalues/eigenvectors, concepts 766–82,
  795–803
El Karoui, N. 103
Elliot, R.J. 254
EMH *see* Efficient Market Hypothesis
empirical data
  see also real world
  derived analyses 201–2
  Derman and Kani model 334–44
  Efficient Market Hypothesis 25–6
  fundamental approach 201–2
  LIBOR market model 626–37, 639–66,
    736–49, 756–64, 781–803
  local volatility 385–6
  models 3–4, 180, 201–35, 238, 265–77,
    287–92, 334–44, 355–68, 385–6, 389,
    416–44, 511–28, 597–8, 626–37, 639–66,
    680–6, 703–27, 736–49, 756–64, 767–803
  smiles 180, 201–35, 238, 265–77, 287–92,
    334–44, 355–68, 385–6, 389, 416–44,
    511–28, 597–8, 702–27, 742–9, 767–803
  swaption matrix 767–81, 784–801
Engl, H.E. 343
Engle, R.F. 143
equal-step random walks 114
equities 6, 26, 76–89, 149–51, 165–99,
    206–22, 227, 235, 244–5, 309–14, 343–4,
    361–73, 389–401, 416–44, 494–9, 522–7,
    553–61, 575–81, 768
  asymmetric smiles 206–7, 209–22, 309–14,
    361–8, 370–3, 391, 439–41, 494–9,
    522–7, 553–61, 575–81
  forward quantities 76–84
  generalized beta of the second kind 291–2
  instantaneous correlation 149–51
  market crash 1987 6, 206, 439
  mean reversion 609
  risk premiums 186, 398, 565, 752
  root-mean-squared volatility 85–6
  smiles 6, 26, 165–99, 206–22, 227, 235,
    244–5, 255, 268–9, 291–2, 309–14,
    361–73, 385–6, 389–401, 416–44, 553–61,
    575–81, 768
  supply/demand imbalances 24–5, 187,
    197–9, 399–401, 687
  symmetric smiles 206–7, 209–22, 309–14,
    358–62, 369–73, 385, 439–41, 494–9,
    522–7, 575–81
  variance–gamma process 512–13, 522–7
equity forward contracts
  see also forward quantities
  concepts 76–84, 87–9, 148–51, 417–27
  hedging 77–84, 417–27

equity indices 4–5, 18–19, 141, 206–22, 255,
    268–9, 371–2, 385–6, 440–4, 512–13,
    522–7, 576–80
  basket options 4–5, 18–19, 141
  FTSE 207, 211–13, 217–18, 221, 290–1,
    576–80
  S&P500 6, 206–11, 216–17, 220–2, 255,
    268–9, 371–2, 385–6, 440, 512, 522–7,
    553
  smiles 206–22, 255, 268–9, 371–2, 385–6,
    440–4, 576–80
  variance–gamma process 512–13, 522–7
equity premium puzzle 186, 752
equivalence of measures, concepts 59–65,
    186–7
equivalent deterministic future smiles, concepts
    595–9
equivalent volatility 283–7, 554–7, 595–6,
    732–3
  displaced diffusions 554–7, 732–3
  generalized beta of the second kind 283–7
ergodic Markov chains, concepts 787
Euler scheme 734, 736–49
  see also predictor–corrector method solutions
Euro 223, 678–86, 767–81
European digital options 16, 169, 172–3,
    574–5, 733–4
European options 16, 57, 80–4, 120–1, 153–5,
    169–73, 277, 294–300, 418, 519–21,
    564–71, 733–4, 759–64, 767–81
European swaptions 19, 22, 626–37, 655–66,
    759–64, 767–81, 785–801
EUROSTOXX 207, 211–15, 219–20, 576–80
exceptional price moves, trading the gamma
    111–13
excited instantaneous volatility curves 788–801
exotic options 22, 258, 385, 473–85, 502,
    564–75, 610–22, 640, 655–86
  see also complex products
expectations
  concepts 36–73, 76, 151, 177–8, 353–4,
    471–2, 532–3, 567–75, 734, 752
  fair prices 38, 56–65, 73, 177–8
  Feynman–Kac theorem 36–7, 56, 73, 105,
    119–21
  'naïve expectation' 41–2, 47–8, 50, 533–52,
    734, 765
  nested expectations 56–65, 73
  payoff replication 36–73, 567–75
  probabilities 56–7, 70–1, 471–85, 532–3
  tiltings 69–70, 184, 406, 796
  tower law 57, 73
explicit finite differences method 326–44, 346

fair values, contingent claims 38, 54–65, 73,
    423–4

Fan, R.   688
Feynman–Kac theorem   36–7, 56, 73, 105,
    119–21
filtration, adaptness definition   151–2, 593–4
financial quantities, implication processes   27
finite differences methods   326–44, 346
finite numbers, jump–diffusion models   444–5,
    472–85, 503–4
floating smiles   7, 178–84, 204, 220–2,
    312–17, 342, 348–50, 373–5, 381, 439–44,
    563, 573–5, 581–99
floating-rate borrowers   22
floorlets   733
Fokker–Planck equation   346, 350–7
foreign exchange (FX)   4–5, 22–9, 85–6,
    143–6, 165–99, 222–35, 244–5, 287–92,
    309–14, 358–62, 369–73, 386, 440–1, 557,
    668–86, 732, 767–81, 791–801
    empirical data   4, 222–6, 227–35, 244–5,
        358–62, 386, 791–801
    forward quantities   76–89, 142–64, 668–86
    implied volatility   22–4, 85–6, 165–99,
        222–6, 227–35, 309–14, 358–62, 369–73,
        440–1, 668–86, 767–81, 791–801
    root-mean-squared volatility   85–6, 790–5
    smiles   165–99, 222–6, 227–35, 244–5,
        287–92, 309–14, 358–62, 369–73, 440–1,
        557, 767–81, 791–801
    supply/demand imbalances   22–4, 687
    symmetric smiles   358–62, 369–73
    yield curves   4–5, 29, 143–6, 225–6, 668–71
forward contracts, concepts   76–84, 300,
    417–27
forward exchange rates, definition   76–7
forward (Fokker–Planck) equation   346, 350–7
forward induction
    see also Monte Carlo. . .
    LIBOR market model   640
forward options *see* forward-setting options
forward prices   19, 76–84, 87–9, 287–92,
    294–317, 331–2, 417–27, 530–4, 556–9
    current volatility   76, 87–9
    definitions   76, 81–2
    Derman and Kani model   331–2
    future volatility   19, 76, 87–9, 417–27
    spot quantities   76–84, 87–9
    volatility   19, 76, 80–4, 87–9, 294–317,
        331–2, 417–27
forward processes, concepts   19, 76, 77–84,
    87–9, 417–27
forward quantities   19, 26, 76–84, 87–9,
    142–64, 287–92, 294–317, 331–2, 417–27,
    530–4, 556–9, 603–764
    definitions   76–7, 81–2
    spot quantities   76–84, 87–9
forward rate agreements (FRAs)   86

forward rates   5, 18–19, 26, 76–7, 80–9,
    142–64, 287–92, 343, 603–66, 667–803
    see also interest rates
    bond prices   607–8
    co-integration concepts   143–4
    concepts   5, 18–19, 76–7, 80–9, 142–3,
        287–92, 603–37, 667–749, 783–803
    constant elasticity variance   529–34, 553,
        560, 704–6, 718–27, 729–49, 754–6,
        781–2
    correlation   142–64, 417–27, 626–37,
        641–66, 686–700, 705–27, 760–82
    current volatility   76, 87–9
    decaying term structure of volatility   607–12,
        788–9
    definitions   76–7, 81–2
    future volatility   19, 76, 87–9, 752
    implied volatility   705–82, 790–801
    instantaneous volatility   26, 81, 89, 148–50,
        343, 603–37, 640–66, 667–700, 754–64,
        771, 777–803
    instantaneous-correlation specification
        686–700, 778–81
    LIBOR market model   626–700, 704–5,
        729–803
    logarithm of the instantaneous short rate
        616–23, 625–6
    mean reversion   603–23, 751–81
    smiles   180–4, 342, 703–803
    spot quantities   76–84, 87–9
    'sticky' smiles   180–4, 342
    two-regime instantaneous volatility   783–803
    zero levels   732–3, 756
forward volatility, meaninglessness   88
forward-forward volatility, meaninglessness   88
forward-propagated smiles   563, 573–5, 581,
    592–9
forward-setting options, hedging   89–95, 575
Fouque, J.-P.   402, 405, 436, 440
four-factor interest-rate models   650–66
Fourier transform   581, 590
framing effects   21
FRAs *see* forward rate agreements
free parameters, fundamental approach   5, 27,
    184
FRF market   677–86
front-office models   512
FTSE   207, 211–13, 217–18, 221, 290–1,
    576–80
fully-stochastic-volatility models   237–9,
    276–7, 320, 439–41
    concepts   237–9, 276–7, 320, 439–41
    definition   320
fund managers   24–5, 183–99, 399–401,
    441–4, 467
    see also institutions; traders

compensation 198, 441–4
  insurance requirements 198, 441–4, 609
  supply/demand imbalances 24–5, 197–9,
    399–401
fundamental approach
  concepts 5–7
  critique 5–7
  empirical data 201–2
  free parameters 5, 27, 184
future conditional densities 257, 277
future surfaces
  equivalent deterministic future smiles 595–9
  evolution 783–803
  future stock prices 416–27, 445–9, 499
  non-process-based models 563–99
  smiles 18, 99, 129, 246, 316–17, 347–9,
    381–5, 399–405, 416–37, 439–41, 445–9,
    499, 511–28, 563–99, 726–7, 730, 755,
    763, 767–81, 783–803
  stochastic evolution 582–99, 767–803
  two-regime instantaneous volatility 783–803
future transactions, vega hedging 15–18, 27,
    246, 417, 431–7, 783
future volatility 19, 76, 87–9, 189–99, 416–27,
    511–28, 563–99, 752
  forward prices 19, 76, 87–9, 417–27
  forward quantities 76, 87–9, 417–27
  forward rate 19, 76, 87–9, 752
  spot quantities 19, 76–84, 87–9
futures contracts 86–7, 672–3
FX *see* foreign exchange

Galai, D. 120, 135–9
Galileo Galilei 598
gamma 12–13, 27, 90–6, 108–21, 180–99,
    202, 243–7, 265–77, 287–92, 442, 512–28,
    734, 763
  properties 513–14
  trading the gamma 108–21, 180–4, 189–99,
    202, 400, 512
  variance–gamma process 95, 96, 99, 243–4,
    247, 265–77, 511–28
GARCH-type estimates 401, 753
Gatarek, D. 626
Gaussian copula 168–9
Gaussian distributions 36, 68, 91, 139, 157,
    170–1, 190–1, 249–50, 256–7, 260–77,
    402–5, 530–61, 734, 742–9, 771, 786–7
GB2 *see* generalized beta of the second kind
GBP market 668–86, 761–4
Gedanken Monte Carlo simulation 160, 178,
    368–73, 416–27
generalized beta of the second kind (GB2)
  applications 287–92, 354–5
  concepts 275–92, 354–5
  definition 279–80

geometric construction, LIBOR market model
    640–2, 751, 766, 771
geometric diffusion, concepts 453–4, 491–4,
    529–34, 587, 751, 771
Girsanov's theorem 38, 69–73, 440, 519, 621,
    765
Glasserman, P. 449, 734, 782
Gourieroux, C. 785
Granger, C. 143
Green's function *see* Arrow–Debreu prices

Hagan, P.S. 373
Hamilton, J.D. 143, 785, 787
HARA utility 523
Haug, E.G. 564
Heath–Jarrow–Morton (HJM) approach 18,
    625–6
hedge-fund models
  see also predictive models; pseudo-arbitrageurs
  concepts 4, 10, 25
  historical background 4
hedge-ratio approach, concepts 399–401,
    422–7
hedging 4–15, 28–9, 77–84, 89–93, 101–39,
    169–99, 237–48, 385–6, 399–401, 418–37,
    444–509, 563–99, 752, 796–8
  see also delta. . .; vega. . .
  behaviour in practice 121–9, 418–37,
    502–9, 783
  Black-and-Scholes model performance
    385–6, 418–37, 502–9, 523
  bonds 455–65, 502–9
  Britten-Jones and Neuberger 99, 102, 129,
    179, 243–5, 248, 293–317
  compensated processes 169–73
  constant volatility 90–1, 101, 106–16,
    117–21, 389, 419–37
  Crouhy–Galai set-up 135–9, 294, 312–14
  degenerative hedging strategy 564–71
  equities 77–84, 385–6
  errors 103–4
  finite re-hedging intervals 122–7, 135–9,
    189–99, 247, 295–317, 418–27
  forward contracts using spot quantities
    77–84, 88–9
  forward-setting strike 89–95, 575
  general framework 102–6
  instantaneous volatility 117–21, 126–7,
    135–9, 184, 401–5, 422–37
  interest rates 79–80, 386
  jump–diffusion models 293–317, 398,
    427–37, 444, 455–509, 797–8
  mean-reverting process 131–4, 143, 400–5
  misconceptions 101
  mortgage-backed securities 28, 198
  optimal hedge 299–317

hedging *(continued)*
  options   80–4, 89–93, 101–39, 169–99,
    201–2, 237–48, 293–317, 389–401,
    418–37, 444–509, 564–99
  parameter hedging   399–401, 418–41, 502–9
  performance comparisons   385–437, 502–13,
    523, 622, 766–7, 795–801
  plain-vanilla options   80–4, 89–93, 101–39,
    169–99, 201–2, 237–48, 293–317, 385–6,
    511–28, 783
  portfolio-replication   389–401, 418–37,
    444–512, 564–99
  quadratic variation   293–317, 418–37, 502–9
  re-hedging strategies   15–18, 108–29, 135–9,
    180–4, 186, 189–99, 203, 246, 247,
    293–317, 371, 385, 401, 417–19, 431–7,
    505–12, 563–99, 662, 755, 763, 783, 796–8
  robustness issues   7–8, 28–9, 103–4, 121–9,
    139, 168–9, 250–1, 265, 344, 418, 422,
    427, 502–12, 599
  root-mean-squared volatility   118–21, 122–9,
    131, 189–99, 419–37, 503–9
  time-dependent volatility   80–4, 101, 116–27,
    399–400
  total variance   88–9, 120–1, 130–1, 135–9,
    296–317, 500–2
  trading the gamma concepts   108–21, 180–4,
    189–99, 202, 400
  trading restrictions   102–4
  uncertainty sources   4–5, 103–4, 193–4,
    237–41, 399–401, 441, 464
  wrong volatility   125–7, 174–8, 347, 352–3,
    400, 422–37
Heston, S.   403
historical calibration, concepts   18–20
HJM *see* Heath–Jarrow–Morton approach
Ho and Lee model   610
Hull, J.   76, 238, 315, 398, 403, 734
Hull and White model   238, 315, 398, 403,
    610–11, 622, 659, 734, 740, 767
Hunter, C.   416, 532, 581, 736–7, 748

IBM   609
imperfectly correlated variables   144–64
implication processes, financial quantities   27
implicit finite differences method   346, 418
implied calibration, concepts   18–20, 26–7
implied correlation, concepts   26–7
implied volatility   7, 18–19, 26, 83–6, 89, 99,
    108–21, 151, 167–235, 249–92, 335–8,
    346–87, 397–401, 439–41, 553–99,
    607–37, 659–86, 703–82, 790–803
  see also smiles
  acceptable prices   381–5
  arbitrage   7, 11–12, 26, 85–6, 346, 375–85,
    441–4, 563–99

concepts   7, 18–19, 26, 83–6, 89, 99,
    108–21, 151, 167–235, 249–92, 335–8,
    346–87, 397–401, 439–41, 553–99,
    607–37, 659–86, 703–82, 790–5
constant elasticity variance   704–6, 718–27,
    730–49, 756, 781–2
deeply smooth surfaces   346, 357–87, 575–81
dependencies   167, 176–8, 201–35, 335–8,
    344, 347–8, 351, 358–87, 703–27
displaced diffusions   534–61, 597, 754–64,
    771
easy-to-determine dependencies   167
foreign exchange   22–4, 85–6, 165–99,
    222–6, 227–35, 309–14, 358–62, 369–73,
    440–1, 668–86, 767–81, 790–801
forward rates   705–82, 790–801
instrumental approach   7
interest rates   703–82, 790–801
inversion   176–7, 258, 718–19, 729–30
local volatility links   5, 177, 181–2, 239–41,
    276–7, 315, 322–44, 357–87
Monte Carlo simulation   368–73, 661
no-arbitrage conditions   375–85, 441–4,
    563–99, 626–8
power-law implied volatility   705, 714,
    719–27
pre-processed inputs   249–92
quoting conventions   766
risk aversion   183–99, 396–401, 441–4,
    500–2, 752, 795–8, 803
root-mean-squared volatility   169, 203, 348,
    669, 756, 790–5
strike dependencies   176–8, 201–35, 335–8,
    347–8, 351, 358–87, 703–27
surface dynamics   7, 18, 99, 129, 169–84,
    202–3, 206–35, 238–317, 333–44, 346–87,
    399–444, 485–517, 522–7, 553–99,
    668–71, 703–803
surface-fitting input data   255–92, 334–44,
    346–87, 575–81, 752, 756–64, 783–803
swaption matrix   765–82, 784–801
swaptions   224–6, 630–1, 704–27, 732–49,
    759–801
time series   204–5, 706–27, 765–6, 797
in-model hedging, concepts   15–17
in-the-money options   179, 216–17, 221, 254,
    311, 331, 362–4, 368, 376–85, 565, 743–9
incomplete markets   9, 17, 293–317, 323, 326,
    444–9, 499–502
independent-increment (Levy) stochastic
    processes   215
indexed principle swaps   640
indicator process, concepts   450–1
indirect information, smiles   205–6
infinite accuracy, smiles   174–5
infinite variance   66

inflation models   529
information costs, Efficient Market Hypothesis
    11, 25
informational efficiency   5–6, 8, 9–14, 20–7,
    42–3, 193–4, 197–9, 202, 441, 560, 687–8,
    752
initial conditions, partial differential equations
    37, 567–71
'innocuous' approximations   740
inputs
    Derman and Kani model   334–44, 355–7
    modelling   5, 15–27, 128–9, 185–6, 249–92,
        307–17, 334–87, 406–17, 427–37, 575–81,
        752, 756–64, 783–803
    smile-surface fitting   249–92, 307–17,
        334–44, 346–87, 406–16, 427–37, 575–81,
        752, 756–64, 783–803
instantaneous correlation   75–6, 141–64,
    626–37, 642–700, 778–81
    see also correlation
    concepts   75–6, 141–64, 626–37, 680–700,
        778–81
    equities   149–51
    estimation issues   687–8
    fitting   686–700, 778–81
    functional forms   686–700, 778–81
    importance   686–700, 778–81
    instantaneous volatility   149–50, 630–1,
        680–6, 688–700, 778–81
    matrix   144–6, 631–7, 642–66, 688–700,
        778–81
    model comparisons   686–700, 778–81
    modified exponential function   691–7
    Schoenmakers–Coffey approach   697–700
    shape variety   688–700, 788–801
    simple exponential function   689–97
    specification   686–700, 778–81
    square-root exponential function   694–7
instantaneous short rate, logarithm variance
    616–23, 625–6
instantaneous volatility   26, 80–9, 99, 102,
    117–27, 131–9, 146–50, 184, 244–5,
    343–87, 401–16, 422–37, 594–5, 612–700,
    715–16, 751–64, 771, 777–803
    average volatility   102
    balance-of-variance condition   85
    caplet-pricing requirements   673–7, 759–64
    concepts   26, 80–9, 99, 102, 117–21, 126–7,
        131, 135–9, 184, 244–5, 343–4, 401–16,
        422, 594–5, 616–37, 640–66, 667–700,
        754–6, 771, 777–803
    estimation problems   343–4, 401–5
    fitting   677–86, 756–64, 783–803
    forward rates   26, 81, 89, 148–50, 343,
        603–37, 640–66, 667–727, 754–64, 771,
        777–803

functional form   671–3, 690–1
future term structure of volatility   668–71
hedging   117–21, 126–7, 135–9, 401–5,
    422–37
humped-volatility financial justification
    672–8, 780, 799–801
instantaneous correlation   149–50, 630–1,
    680–6, 688–700, 778–81
inverse problems   343–5, 560
    regularization   343–87
root-mean-squared volatility   80–9, 118, 131,
    159–61, 422–37, 756, 790–5
shape variety   668–78, 756–64, 777–8, 780,
    788–801
specification   667–86
swaption-market information   680–6,
    688–700, 759–64, 777–81, 783–803
term structure of volatility   668–71, 715–16,
    754–6, 763–4
time-homogeneity   348–50, 385, 401, 436,
    439, 621–2, 677–86, 754–6, 763–4
total variance   135–9
two-regime instantaneous volatility   783–803
two-state Markov chains   782–803
institutions
    see also fund managers
    prices   13–14, 21, 441
    product control functions   13–14
instrumental approach, concepts   5, 7–8
insurance requirements, fund players   198,
    441–4, 609
interest rates   18, 22–4, 27–9, 76–89, 162–4,
    168–9, 222–6, 235, 244–5, 287–92,
    343–4, 362, 366–8, 372–3, 553–61,
    601–803
    see also LIBOR market model
    Black–Derman–Toy model   610–22, 662
    constant elasticity variance   529–34, 553,
        560, 704–6, 718–27, 729–49, 754, 756,
        781–2
    deterministic volatility   601–700, 736–49,
        754–6, 782, 799–801
    generalized beta of the second kind   287–92
    hedging   79–80, 186
    implied volatility   703–82, 790–801
    instantaneous correlation specification
        686–700, 778–81
    instantaneous volatility specification   667–86,
        754–6, 777–803
    log-normal co-ordinates   703–27, 741–2
    mean reversion   131–2, 603–23, 751–81
    monotonic ('Interest-Rate') smiles   222–6,
        335, 338–44, 362, 366–8, 372–3, 442,
        668–9, 800–1
    root-mean-squared volatility   86–7, 665, 737,
        756, 790–5

interest rates *(continued)*
  smiles   168–9, 222–6, 235, 244–5, 287–92,
    334–8, 362, 366–8, 372–3, 553–61,
    621–2, 701–803
  trading dynamics   672–3
  zero interest rates   252–3, 281–2, 292, 297,
    353–4, 416–17, 483, 564–5, 732–4, 756
interest-rate derivative products   7, 18, 19–27,
  76–89, 141, 145, 149–51, 162–4, 198,
  222–6, 235, 244–5, 287–92, 608–22,
  626–37, 639–803
interest-rate forward contracts
  see also forward quantities
  concepts   76–89, 149–51, 162–4, 287–92
interest-rate modelling   18, 19, 27–9, 44–6,
  162–4, 168–9, 530, 594, 603–803
interest-rate options   7, 18, 19–27, 76, 80,
  86–7, 141, 145, 149, 198, 222–6, 235,
  244–5, 287–92, 608–22, 626–37, 639–803
inverse problems, concepts   343–5, 560
inversion, implied volatility   176–7, 258,
  718–19, 729–30
investors
  behavioural finance   21–2, 44
  Efficient Market Hypothesis   8, 9–14, 20–7,
    42–3, 187, 193–4, 197–9, 441
  risk aversion   9–10, 20, 34–6, 44–6, 69–73,
    122–3, 183–99, 396–401, 419–44, 464–70,
    500–2, 518–19, 522–3, 752, 795–8, 803
IOs   28
irreducible Markov chains   786–803
Ito's lemma   33, 67, 82–3, 98, 110, 150, 152–3,
  158, 353, 390, 396, 453–5, 462, 605–7,
  629–30, 735–6

Jackwerth, J.C.   206
Jacod, J.   453
Jacquier, E.   254
Jaeckel, P.   581, 633, 660–2, 736–7, 748
Jamshidian, F.   322, 626–7
Jarrow, R.A.   254
Jasiak, J.   785
Johnson, T.C.   227
Joshi, M.   145, 205, 224, 416, 445, 534, 581,
  594, 690, 715, 733, 736–7, 740–1, 748,
  754, 756, 760, 765, 776, 778, 780–1, 795,
  798, 801
JPY market   732
jump–diffusion models   5, 31–3, 95, 184–5,
  197, 224–41, 257–8, 265–77, 293–319,
  355, 372, 398, 427–509, 513, 521, 523,
  560–1, 582–99, 797–8
  amplitude models   241–2, 257–8, 270–2,
    315–16, 443–55, 460–509, 561, 582–99,
    797–8
  analytical description   445, 449–55

bond hedging   455–65, 502–9
calibration   465–70
closed-form solutions   452–5
compensated processes   451–5, 518–19
complete markets   20, 237–41, 293–317,
  444–9, 499–502
concepts   439–509, 523, 582–99
continuous jump amplitudes   444–55, 465–85
counting processes   450–3, 470
diffusion processes   312–14
finite numbers   444–5, 472–85, 503–4
future smiles   445–9, 499, 582–99
hedging   293–317, 398, 427–37, 444,
  455–509, 797–8
implied frequency   20, 199, 257–8, 372
jump ratios   471–95, 504–9, 561, 797–8
linear products   457
matching the moments   475–85
payoff replication   444–509, 582–99
portfolio replication   444–509, 582–99
pricing formulas   470–509, 513, 521, 582–99
qualitative smile features   494–9
random-amplitude models   241–2, 257–8,
  270–2, 315–16, 443–55, 460–5, 470–509
real-world situation   464–72, 597–8, 797–8
risk-adjusted jump frequency   465–85, 494–9
risk-neutral density   440–4, 456, 473–509
single-possible-jump-amplitude case   460–5,
  472–85, 503
smiles   6, 98–9, 184–5, 197, 224–6, 227–35,
  239–48, 251, 257–8, 265–77, 295–317,
  355, 372, 405, 427, 473, 484–509, 523,
  560–1, 582–99
stochastic-volatility models   242, 243–4,
  312–16, 319, 355, 372, 398, 405, 427–37,
  449, 456, 458–9, 470, 499, 582–99

Kahneman, D.   44, 188
Kainth, D.   486
kappas   169–73
Karatzas, I.   150
Kazziha, S.   610–11
Kloeden, P.E.   532, 737, 739, 749
knock-in caps   258
knock-out caps   640
Kolmogorov equation   246, 259, 349–57, 530,
  588–93
Kou, S.G.   449, 782
Kreyszig, E.   749
Kronecker delta   786–7
kurtosis   206, 214–15, 260–1, 268–9, 424,
  516–17, 522–3, 743, 790–803

Lagrange multipliers   258–9
Lamberton, D.   150
Lapeyre, B.   150

least-squares fit 261

leptokurtic nature, risk-neutral density 206, 214–15, 260–1, 268–9, 424, 516–17, 522–3, 743, 790–803

leverage effect, concepts 730

Lewis, A. 398, 467, 765

LIBOR market model (LMM) 19, 28–9, 162–4, 530, 594, 604, 607, 621–2, 625–700, 704–5, 729–803

  advantages 607–8, 621, 622, 626, 678–9

  Brownian motion 628–30, 641–2, 663–5, 748–56, 766, 771

  calibration 626–37, 639–66, 736–49, 756–64, 781–2

  case studies 632–6

  concepts 607–8, 621, 622, 625–86, 704–5, 729–64, 783–803

  constant elasticity variance 704–6, 729–49, 754, 756, 781–2

  construction 626–37, 639–66, 736–49, 756–64, 783–803

  covariance matrix 628–31, 642–66, 689–700, 760–82, 785–803

  deterministic volatility 736–49, 754–6, 782, 799–801

  dimensionality reduction 640, 643–66

  displaced diffusions 732, 735, 742–52, 754–64, 771

  drift approximations 734–49, 759, 763

  empirical data 626–37, 639–66, 736–49, 756–64, 781–803

  extensions 751–64, 781–2, 783–803

  four-factor model 650–66

  geometric construction 640–2, 751, 766, 771

  Markov chains 640, 751, 766, 782–803

  Monte Carlo simulation 640, 661, 734, 737–49

  numerical results 646–66, 742–9

  optimal calibration 641, 645–6, 662–6, 763

  portion-fitting considerations 654–9, 667–8, 742–9

  predictor–corrector method CEV solutions 736–49, 752, 759

  principal components analysis 631–2, 643–7, 652, 657–8, 766–7, 771–81, 788

  single-factor model 625–40, 736–49

  smiles 730–803

  stochastic-volatility models 530, 751–67, 771–803

  target-fitting considerations 654–9, 667–8, 742–9

  three-factor model 646–51, 653–66

  two-factor geometric construction case 640–2

  two-regime instantaneous volatility 783–803

linear correlation 142–3

'linear evolution' paradigm 14

linear products, jump–diffusion models 457

Lipschitz continuity condition 730–1

liquidity problems, pseudo-arbitrageurs 25

Litzenberger, R.H. 585–6

LMM *see* LIBOR market model

Lo, A. 206

local volatility 5–6, 88, 98, 116–21, 127, 143, 177, 181–2, 239–41, 243–4, 276–7, 315, 319–89, 440–1, 560–1, 572–5, 580–1, 598–9

  see also Derman and Kani model; restricted-stochastic-volatility models

  concepts 5–6, 88, 98, 116–21, 143, 181–2, 239–41, 243–4, 276–7, 315, 319–89, 440, 560–1, 572–5, 580–1, 598–9

  definition 320

  displaced diffusions 560–1

  empirical performance 385–6

  floating/sticky smiles implications 348–50, 373–5, 381, 573–5, 581–99

  implied volatility links 5, 177, 181–2, 239–41, 276–7, 315, 322–44, 357–87

  Monte Carlo simulation 368–73

  no-arbitrage conditions 375–85, 572–5, 599

  regularization 343–87

  surface dynamics 333–44, 346–87, 440–1, 560–1, 572–5, 580–1, 598–9

log-normal distributions 33–4, 92, 120–1, 146–7, 151, 170–2, 181–2, 205, 242, 249, 256–92, 354–5, 391–2, 406–16, 441–4, 453, 470–509, 522–3, 530–61, 644, 662–3, 679–80, 703–27, 734, 741–9

Longstaff, F.A. 145, 689

Los Alamos National Laboratory 11

LTCM 25–6, 223, 225, 706

lucky paths 97–9, 111–14, 117, 121–7, 293–317, 470

Lyons, T.J. 103

Madan, D.B. 243, 254, 268, 513, 517–19, 521–7, 553

Mahayni, A. 103, 104

market efficiency 5–6, 8, 9–14, 20–7, 42–3, 193–4, 197–9, 202, 441, 560, 687, 752

market information, smiles 203–6, 249–92, 687

market practices

  across-markets comparisons 27–9

  modelling 14–17, 27–9, 168–9, 783

market price of risk (MPR)

  concepts 34–6, 42–8, 69–70, 184–99, 396–405, 500–2

  contingent claims 42–8, 69–70

  deterministic volatility 34–6, 396–405

market terms, definitions 75–7, 87–9

market-clearing processes 189–94

Markov chains 187, 243, 322–3, 344, 640, 751,
    766, 782–803
  absorbing states 786–7
  concepts 187, 243, 322–3, 344, 640, 751,
    766, 782–803
  ergodic property 787
  irreducible Markov chains 786–803
  LIBOR market model 640, 751, 766,
    782–803
  simple properties 785–8
  transition matrix 785–803
  two-state Markov chains 782–803
Marris, D. 529, 531, 533, 597, 718, 735, 742,
    756
Martellini, L. 775
martingales 33–4, 52–3, 57–65, 69–73, 98,
    353–4, 391, 453–5
matrices, contingent claims 40–1
maturity, smiles 7, 167, 209–22, 229–35,
    238–9, 242–4, 251–92, 337–8, 347–51,
    427–41, 486–509, 523–7, 576–80,
    761–801
MBSs *see* mortgage-backed securities
mean reversion 73, 101–39, 143–4, 184–5,
    199, 222, 238, 265, 400–16, 419–37,
    439–40, 465–70, 603–23, 751–81
  Black–Derman–Toy model 603, 610–22
  co-integration concepts 143–4
  common fallacies 608–10
  concepts 101, 131–9, 184–5, 222, 400–16,
    419, 465–70, 603–23, 751–81
  equities 609
  forward rates 603–23, 751–81
  general interest-rate models 620–2
  high-reversion speed 404–6, 436, 439–40,
    523, 527, 604–12, 755–6, 765–6, 778
  interest rates 131–2, 603–23, 751–81
  Ornstein–Uhlenbeck process 402–5, 465,
    759, 777, 784–5
  real-world situation 73, 101, 131–9, 143,
    184–5, 199, 400–5, 419, 465–70, 603–23,
    765–6
  risk-adjusted situation 101–39, 184–6,
    400–16, 465–70, 603–23, 765–6
  short-rate lattices 612–22
  stochastic-volatility models 401–16, 419–37,
    440, 465, 751–64, 765–6, 781–2
  total variance 130–1, 135–9
  'true' role 620–2
measure-invariance observations, volatility
    69–73
memory, shocks 400–1, 440, 749, 756
Mercurio, D. 404
Merener, N. 449, 782
Merton, R.C. 65–7, 83, 161–2, 294, 305–6,
    316, 444, 449, 453, 455, 471–2

minimum entropy 249, 258–9
Mirfendereski, D. 275, 277
mixed jump–diffusion processes
  see also jump–diffusion. . .
  analytical description 445, 449–55
  pricing 470–94
  smiles 295–317, 443–509
mixture-of-normals method, risk-neutral density
    259–77, 292, 354–5
modelling
  across-markets comparisons 27–9
  approaches 5–8, 30, 95, 129, 168–9, 185–6,
    294, 316–20, 385–6, 389–437, 439–41,
    511–28, 563–99, 621–2, 625–6, 686–700,
    752, 766–7, 778–81, 783–803
  classifications 95, 293–320, 439–41
  descriptive dimensions 14–15
  different users 14–17
  empirical data 3–4, 25–6, 180, 201–35, 238,
    265–77, 287–92, 334–44, 355–68, 385–6,
    389, 416–44, 511–28, 597–8, 626–37,
    639–66, 680–6, 703–27, 736–49, 756–64,
    767–803
  fashions 6
  foundations 3–30
  inertia features 14, 29
  inputs 5, 15–27, 128–9, 185–6, 249–92,
    307–17, 334–87, 406–17, 427–37, 575–81,
    752, 756–64, 783–803
  interest-rate modelling 18, 19, 27–9, 44–6,
    162–4, 168–9, 530, 594, 603–803
  jump–diffusion models 5, 31–3, 95, 184–5,
    197, 224–41, 257–8, 265–77, 293–319,
    355, 372, 398, 427–509, 513, 521, 523,
    560–1, 582–99, 797–8
  LIBOR market model 19, 28–9, 530, 594,
    604, 607, 621–2, 625–700, 704–5,
    729–803
  market practices 14–17, 27–9, 168–9, 783
  model roles 3–30, 402, 439–41
  non-process-based models 563–99
  performance comparisons 385–437, 502–13,
    523, 621–2, 766–7, 795–801
  prescriptive dimensions 14–15
  process-based models 563–99
  quality assessments 385–437, 502–13, 523,
    621–2, 766–7, 795–801
  risk management 11–14, 132, 441, 796–8
  risk-aversion assessments 185–6, 419–44,
    464–70, 500–2, 522–3, 752, 795–8, 803
  swaption-matrix quality assessments 766–7
  theory and practice 3–30, 168–9, 783
  uncertainty sources 4–5, 103–4, 193–4,
    237–41, 399–401, 441, 464
  wrongness issues 30, 31–2, 102–4, 121–7,
    174–8, 347, 352–3, 400, 422–37, 718

modes of deformation, swaptions   7, 27, 576–7, 796–8
monotonic ('Interest-Rate') smiles   222–6, 335, 338–44, 362, 366–8, 372–3, 442, 668–9, 800–1
Monte Carlo simulation   91–3, 105–6, 145, 146–7, 150–1, 154–60, 163, 177–8, 333, 346, 349, 416–27, 500, 504–5, 572, 640, 643, 661, 734, 737–49
   brute-force Monte Carlo   734, 737–49
   implied/local volatility links   368–73
   LIBOR market model   640, 643, 661, 734, 737–49
mortgage-backed securities (MBSs)   22, 27–9, 198
   see also pass-throughs
MPR *see* market price of risk
multi-factor models   75–6, 143–64, 320, 626–37, 639–66, 686–700, 778–81
   correlation   144–6, 626–37, 641–66, 686–700, 778–81
   yield curves   143–6, 625–37, 640–66
multi-period settings, contingent claims   53–6
Musiela, M.   626

Naik, V.   239
'naïve expectation', concepts   41–2, 47–8, 50, 533–52, 734, 765
Neftci, S.   65, 68, 150
negative probabilities   327
Nelson, D.B.   328
nested expectations, payoff replication   56–65, 73
Newtonian mechanics   30, 598
Nielsen, L.T.   402
Niemeyer, B.   737, 742
no-arbitrage conditions   5–6, 18, 31–4, 54–6, 70–1, 76–8, 187, 237–48, 261–3, 276–7, 283–7, 293–317, 323–6, 356–7, 375–85, 419, 441–4, 531–2, 563–99, 626–8, 679–80
   non-process-based models   563–99
   smiles   375–85, 441–4, 563–99
   stochastic evolution of future smiles   582–99
'no-good-deal' approaches   29–30, 419, 509
non-process-based models, concepts   563–99
non-recombining (bushy) binomial trees   53–65, 135–9, 300–17, 321–2, 449, 617–22
non-symmetric random walks   68
non-visible trades, prices   13–14
normal distributions *see* Gaussian...
normal parameters, stochastic-volatility portfolio replication   420–7
*n*th-to-default swaps   29
numeraires, concepts   52–3, 58–65, 71–3, 83, 748, 751

OAS *see* option-adjusted spread
obligation flexi caps   640
Occam's razor   670
O'Hara, M.   220
Oksendal, B.   37, 150
one-touch barriers *see* continuous double...
one-way floaters   640, 658–9
optimal hedge, Britten-Jones and Neuberger   299–317
option modelling *see* modelling
option replication *see* payoff replication
option-adjusted spread (OAS), concepts   28–9
option-plus-hedge portfolio   4
options   15–17, 80–4, 89–93, 101–39, 169–99, 201–2, 237–48, 293–317, 389–401, 418–37, 444–509, 511–28, 564–99, 783
   see also at-the-money...; in-the-money...; out-of-the-money...
   customer demand   9
   European options   16, 57, 80–4, 120–1, 153–5, 169–73, 277, 294–300, 418, 519–21, 564–71, 733–4, 759–64, 767–81
   exotic options   22, 258, 385, 473–85, 502, 564–75, 610–22, 640, 655–86
   plain-vanilla options   5–6, 80–4, 89–93, 101–39, 169–99, 201–2, 237–48, 285–7, 293–317, 326–87, 440, 445, 471–528, 566–75, 582–99, 783
   time value of money   109–10, 116–19, 331
Ornstein–Uhlenbeck process, concepts   402–5, 465, 759, 777, 784–5
OTC *see* over-the-counter options
out-of-model hedging
   see also vega hedging
   bid–offer spreads   16
   concepts   15–17
out-of-the-money options   90, 93–4, 117, 169–70, 182–3, 203–4, 206, 216–20, 227–35, 254, 330–1, 368, 370–3, 376–85, 439–44, 493–9, 527, 553–9, 568–73, 608–9, 735, 743–9
over-confident investors   21
over-the-counter (OTC) options   22, 168

PACs   28
Panigirtzoglou   186
parameter hedging, concepts   399–400, 418–41, 502–9
Pareto–Levy distribution   66
partial differential equations (PDEs)   31–7, 56, 73, 83, 327–44, 348–57, 393–5, 454–5, 463–5, 564, 567–71
   see also Black-and-Scholes model
   concepts   31–7, 56, 73, 327–44, 348–57, 393–5, 454–5, 463–5, 564, 567–71

partial differential equations (PDEs) *(continued)*
  Feynman–Kac theorem   36–7, 56, 73, 105,
    119–21
  final conditions   37
  initial conditions   37, 567–71
  stochastic-volatility models   393–5
partition concepts, quadratic variation   96–9
pass-throughs   28–9
  see also mortgage-backed securities
path-dependent options, concepts   108, 122–7,
    155–64, 639–66, 739
payoff replication   4–5, 28–30, 31–73, 98,
    101–39, 239–40, 247–8, 276–7, 293–317,
    323, 399–400, 418–37, 444–509, 519–21,
    564–99, 609, 752
  see also contingent claims; perfect payoff...
  appropriate pricing measure   57, 64–5,
    105–6, 184–7
  binomial replication   38–73, 103–4, 135–9,
    300–34, 449, 640
  concepts   3–5, 28–30, 31–73, 102–21,
    239–40, 247–8, 276–7, 322–3, 389–401,
    418–37, 444–512, 519–21, 564–99,
    639–40
  expectations   36–73, 567–75
  Feynman–Kac theorem   36–7, 56, 73, 105,
    119–21
  Girsanov's theorem   38, 69–73, 440, 519,
    621, 765
  importance   31–2
  jump–diffusion models   444–509
  partial differential equations   31–7, 56, 73,
    393–5, 463–5, 567–71
  portfolio-replication argument   32–6, 106–27,
    239–40, 389–401, 418–512, 564–99
  predictive models   4–5, 29
  switching of numeraires   52–3, 58–65, 71–3,
    748–51
  wrongness issues   30, 31–2, 102–4, 121–7,
    347, 352–3, 400, 422–37
PCA *see* principal components analysis
PDEs *see* partial differential equations
perfect information   5–6, 8, 9–14, 29, 582–3,
    687
perfect payoff replication   4–5, 28–73, 98,
    102–39, 239–40, 247–8, 276–7, 323,
    399–400, 418–19, 444–5, 455, 460, 500–2,
    511–12, 609, 752
  concepts   4–5, 28–30, 32–3, 72, 98, 102,
    104–5, 239–40, 247–8, 276–7, 323,
    399–400, 418–19, 444–5, 455, 460, 500–2
  impossibility   400, 418–19, 460, 609, 752
  requirements   32–3, 72, 98, 102, 104–5,
    247–8, 323, 399–400, 418, 460, 500, 609
perforation effects, concepts   565–75
permissible price sequences, concepts   295–6

Pfeffer, J.   319
plain-vanilla options   5–6, 80–4, 89–93,
    101–39, 169–99, 201–2, 237–48, 285–7,
    293–317, 326–87, 440, 445, 471–528,
    566–75, 582–99, 783
  BJN case study   307–17
  Black-and-Scholes model   81–4, 89–93,
    101–32, 143, 168–99, 203–317, 348–87,
    418–37, 471, 476–85, 502–9, 512, 533–4,
    543–4, 584–99
  constant volatility   101, 106–16, 117–21,
    285–7, 334, 355–7, 389, 419
  generalized beta of the second kind   275–92,
    354–5
  hedging   80–4, 89–93, 101–39, 169–99,
    201–2, 237–48, 293–317, 511–28, 783
  mean-reverting processes   131–4, 143,
    400–16
  time-dependent volatility   80–4, 101, 116–21,
    335–6, 355–87
Platen, E.   532, 737, 739, 749
Pliska, S.R.   150, 293, 327, 501
point process, concepts   450–1
Poisson process   68, 240, 295, 450–3, 473,
    477–85
portfolios
  contingent claims   38–73, 106–27, 239–40,
    389–401, 418–509
  jump–diffusion models   444–509
  options   15–16, 27, 38–73, 105–39, 183–4,
    239–40, 389–401, 418–44, 564–99
  replication argument   32–6, 39–41, 45–8,
    106–27, 239–40, 389–401, 418–512,
    564–99
  static portfolio replication   511–12, 564–99
  stochastic-volatility models   389–401,
    418–37, 449, 458–9
POs   28
power-law implied volatility   705, 714, 719–27
power-reverse-dual swaps   4, 18, 24, 29
pre-payment models   27–9
pre-processed inputs, smiles   249–92
predictive models
  see also hedge-fund models
  concepts   4–5
  payoff replication   4–5, 29
predictor–corrector method solutions, LIBOR
    market model   736–49, 752, 759
prescriptive dimensions, modelling   14–15
present values, forward contracts   78–84, 172–3
Priaulet, P.   775
price series, short-term direction   3–4
prices   8–17, 19, 20–7, 42–3, 76–84, 87–9,
    197–9, 202, 249–92, 293–317, 322–34,
    345–87, 416–27, 441–4, 449–55, 532–61,
    582–99, 759–64

see also derivatives pricing; strike; underlying

Arrow–Debreu prices   322–34

bounds   293–317

Efficient Market Hypothesis   8, 9–14, 20–7, 42–3, 197–9, 202, 441

future volatility   19, 76–84, 87–9, 416–27, 511–28, 563–99

institutions   13–14, 21, 441

non-visible trades   13–14

surface-fitting input data   249–92, 346–87, 427–37, 575–81, 752, 756–64, 783–803

transformed-prices concepts   254

pricing engine, concepts   322

pricing *see* derivatives pricing

principal components analysis (PCA)   144, 205, 222, 631–2, 643–7, 652, 657–8, 766–7, 771–81, 788

concepts   144, 205, 222, 631–2, 643–7, 652, 657–8, 766–7, 771–81, 788

correlation   771–81, 788

swaption matrix   766–7, 771–81, 788

principle of absolute continuity   186–7

prior information (minimum entropy), risk-neutral density   249, 258–9

probabilities

contingent claims   38–73

Derman and Kani model   319–44

expectations   56–7, 70, 471–85, 532–3

generalized beta of the second kind   275–92, 354–5

pseudo-probabilities   48–53, 56–65, 69–73, 327

problems, concepts   343–5

process specification, smile-surface fitting   249–92, 351

process-based models, concepts   563, 598–9

product-control functions   13–14

pseudo-arbitrageurs

see also hedge-fund...; relative-value...

concepts   10–11, 20–1, 24, 197–9, 202, 441–4, 467, 511–12

Efficient Market Hypothesis   10–11, 20–7, 197–9, 202, 441

limitations   24–6, 511–12

liquidity problems   25

types   10

pseudo-Greeks   277–87

pseudo-probabilities, concepts   48–53, 56–65, 69–73, 327

pure diffusion model, concepts   5, 188–9, 783–803

put options   20, 22–4, 176, 182–4, 204, 254, 278, 284–92, 323–4, 328–44, 348, 380–5, 439–41, 483–5, 553–9, 568–70, 622

quadratic variation   8, 31–2, 95–9, 102–3, 122–9, 143, 245–8, 293–317, 352–4, 376–85, 404–5, 418–37, 502–9

see also Britten-Jones and Neuberger

Brownian process   97–9

concepts   8, 31–2, 95–9, 102–3, 122–9, 143, 245–8, 293–317, 352–4, 404–5, 418–37, 502–9

definition   95–6

deterministic volatility   95–9, 129, 245–8, 294–317, 404–5

first approach   95–9

hedging   293–317, 418–37, 502–9

importance   98–9, 129, 143, 246–8, 293–317

problems   298–9, 312–16

properties   96–7

robustness issues   8, 31–2, 127–9, 418, 422, 427

root-mean-squared volatility   95–9, 245–8, 293–317, 419–37, 503–9

sample quadratic variation   312–14

slippage concepts   124–9, 247–8, 418–27, 441–4, 499–509

smiles   245–8, 293–317

stochastic-volatility models   99, 102–3, 246–8, 293–317, 352–4, 404–5, 418–37

total variance   130–1, 143, 296–317

variance contrasts   609

qualitative differences, replicability issues   29

quality assessments, models   385–437, 502–13, 523, 621–2, 766–7, 795–801

quantitative differences

replicability issues   29

smiles   205

quanto swaps, power-reverse-dual swaps   18

Radon-Nikodým derivative   61, 63–5, 72–3

Ramaswamy, K.   328

random walks   68, 114, 116–17, 131–2, 401–5, 513–18

see also mean reversion

Brownian motion   32–7, 67–73, 81–4, 91–9, 110–14, 120–1, 132, 144–7, 157–8, 163, 237–43, 267–77, 312–13, 320, 390–2, 397, 402–5, 441–56, 464, 501, 513–18, 529–65, 611–12, 628–42, 663–5, 726–30, 748–56, 766, 771

variance–gamma process   513–18

random-amplitude jump–diffusion models   241–2, 257–8, 270–2, 315–16, 443–55, 460–5, 470–509

ratchet caps   640

re-hedging strategies   15–18, 108–29, 135–9, 180–4, 186, 189–99, 203, 246, 247, 293–317, 371, 385, 401, 417–19, 431–7, 505–12, 563–99, 662, 755, 763, 783, 796–8

re-hedging strategies *(continued)*
  diffusion processes 122–7, 295–317, 505–9
  finite intervals 122–7, 135–9, 189–99, 247,
    295–317, 418–27
  future costs 9, 18, 371, 385, 401, 417, 431,
    563–75, 755, 763
  trading the gamma concepts 108–16, 180–4,
    189–99, 400
real world 4, 17–18, 35–6, 41–8, 50, 69, 73,
    101, 105–6, 131–43, 184–99, 262–3,
    394–405, 419–44, 457–8, 465–72, 511–12,
    518–19, 597–8, 603–23, 765–81, 790–801
  see also empirical data; risk aversion
  drift 131–4, 143, 394–405, 454–5, 500–2,
    604–10, 765–6
  jump–diffusion models 464–72, 597–8,
    797–8
  mean reversion 73, 101, 131–9, 143, 184–5,
    400–5, 419, 465–70, 603–23, 765–6
  pricing measure 4, 17–18, 35–6, 41–8, 50,
    69, 73, 105–6, 131–9, 184–99, 262–3,
    394–405, 419–37, 441–4, 467–72, 511–12,
    518–19, 765–6, 790–801
  smiles 184–99, 205–6, 250–92, 441–4, 467,
    511–12, 518–19, 597–8, 790–801
  spot and forward processes 81–4
  variance 35–6, 41–8, 50, 69, 73, 101–39,
    441–4, 511–12, 518–19, 522–3, 527,
    608–9
  variance–gamma process 511–12, 518–19,
    522–3, 527
recombining binomial trees 53, 59, 322–34,
    617–22, 640
regularization
  concepts 343–87
  possible strategies 346–7
  problems 343–5
  shortcomings 346–7
regulatory constraints 11, 25, 199
Reiner, E. 321, 581
relative pricing 17–18, 33–4, 47–8, 51–3,
    57–65, 69–73, 111, 178, 390–1, 595–6
  advantages 17
  concepts 17–18, 47–8, 51–3, 111, 178,
    595–6
  martingales 33–4, 52–3, 57–65, 69–73,
    390–1
  pseudo-probabilities 51–3, 57–65, 69–73
relative-value traders 10–11, 14–17, 25, 111,
    441, 512
  see also pseudo-arbitrageurs
Rennie, A. 58, 60, 83, 150, 586, 609
replicating-portfolio strategy 32–6, 39–41,
    45–8, 106–27, 239–40, 389–401, 418–512,
    564–99
residual volatility, concepts 244–5, 296–317

restricted-stochastic-volatility models
  see also local volatility
  concepts 239–41, 243–4, 276–7, 315,
    319–89, 440, 560–1
  definition 320
  empirical performance 385–6
  smiles 239–41, 243–4, 276–7, 315, 319–44,
    346–87, 440, 560–1, 572–5, 580–1
  special cases 321
retail investors, supply/demand imbalances
    24–5, 198–9
returns, risk 10–11, 35–6, 42–8, 69–70,
    396–7, 419–20, 441–4, 467, 500–2,
    518–19, 522
Riemann integrals 152
risk
  absolute pricing 17–18, 29
  basis risk 400–1
  market price of risk 34–6, 42–8, 69–70,
    184–99, 396–405, 500–2
  mean reversion 101–39, 184–5, 400–16,
    465, 603–23, 765–6
  returns 10–11, 35–6, 42–8, 69–70, 396–7,
    419–20, 441–4, 467, 500–2, 518–19, 522
  reversals 203–5, 227–35, 576–80
  smiles 183–99, 203–5, 206, 209–22,
    227–41, 245, 250–92, 315, 346–87,
    406–16, 440–1, 485–509, 518–19, 553–9,
    575–81, 586–99, 752, 790–8
  standard deviation 35–6, 42–6, 72, 108,
    111–12, 122–3
  uncertainty sources 4–5, 103–4, 193–4,
    237–41, 399–401, 441, 464
  variance 35–6, 42–6, 101–39, 441–4
risk aversion 9–10, 20, 34–6, 44–6, 69–73,
    122–3, 183–99, 396–401, 419–44,
    464–70, 500–2, 518–19, 522–3, 752,
    795–8, 803
  assessment issues 185–6, 419–44, 464–70,
    500–2, 752, 795–8, 803
  real-world situation 184–99, 396–405,
    419–44, 464–72, 500–2, 518–19, 522–3,
    795–8, 803
  smiles 183–99, 441–4, 467
  stylized examples 187–99, 258
  utility functions 187–99, 397, 466–7, 501,
    522–3
risk management 11–14, 132, 441, 796–8
  concepts 11–12, 132
  Efficient Market Hypothesis 11–14, 193–4,
    197–9, 441
  impacts 11–14, 132
  tensions 12–14, 441
  traders 11–14, 441
risk premiums
  absolute pricing 17–18, 29

equities   186, 398, 565, 752
 puzzle   186, 752
risk reversals, smiles   203–5, 227–35, 576–80
risk-adjusted jump frequency, jump–diffusion
      models   465–85, 494–9
risk-neutral density   81, 104–8, 117–18, 206,
      209–22, 227–35, 239–41, 245, 256–92,
      315, 320, 326, 389–444, 456, 470,
      473–523, 527, 553–9, 586–623, 732–4,
      765–7, 790–8
 forward constraints   261–5
 general background   256–9, 440–1, 518–19
 generalized beta of the second kind   275–92,
      354–5
 jump–diffusion models   440–4, 456,
      473–509
 leptokurtic nature   206, 214–15, 260–1,
      268–9, 424, 516–17, 522–3, 743, 790–803
 mixture-of-normals method   259–77, 292,
      354–5
 multi/uni-modality issues   486–94
 prior information (minimum entropy)   249,
      258–9
 smiles   206, 209–22, 227–35, 245, 256–92,
      315, 346–87, 406–16, 440–1, 485–509,
      518–19, 553–9, 575–81, 586–99, 752,
      790–8
 smoothness issues   257–9, 511, 575–81
 stochastic-volatility models   320, 326,
      389–437, 440–1, 456, 470
 surface-fitting input data   245, 256–92,
      346–87, 406–16, 575–81, 752, 790–8
 variance–gamma process   516–17, 518–23,
      527
 zero levels   733–4
riskless portfolios, payoff replication   33–41,
      69–70, 389–401, 472
robustness issues
 Black-and-Scholes model   127–9, 168–9,
      418, 422, 427, 502–9
 concepts   7–8, 28–9, 103–4, 121–9, 139,
      168–9, 250–1, 265, 344, 418, 422, 427,
      502–12, 599
 hedging   7–8, 28–9, 103–4, 121–9, 139,
      418, 422, 427, 502–12, 599
 quadratic variation   8, 31–2, 127–9, 418,
      422, 427
root-mean-squared volatility
 admissibility   85–9
 balance-of-variance condition   85
 concepts   80–91, 116, 118, 122–9, 131, 155,
      159–61, 189–99, 238, 245–8, 265,
      293–317, 348, 419–37, 503–9, 665, 669,
      737, 756, 790–5
 equity/FX case   85–6
 futures contracts   86–7

hedging   118–21, 122–7, 131, 189–99,
      419–37, 503–9
implied volatility   169, 203, 348, 669, 756,
      790–5
instantaneous volatility   80–9, 118, 131,
      159–61, 422–37, 790–5
quadratic variation   95–9, 245–8, 293–317,
      419–37, 503–9
time-dependent volatility   84–7, 122–7
Ross, S.M.   451, 785
Rubinstein, M.   206, 321–2, 385–6, 529, 587,
      597, 756
Rubinstein model   321–2, 385–6
Russian default   223, 225, 706, 716, 767–8, 775
Rutowski, M.   626

S&P500   6, 206–11, 216–17, 220–2, 255,
      268–9, 371–2, 385–6, 440, 512, 522–7,
      553
same-expiry options, smiles   7
sample quadratic variation   312–14
Samuel, D.   209–10, 211, 575–80, 594
Schoenbucher, P.J.   449, 581, 584, 786
Schoenmakers, J.   689, 691, 697–700
Scholes, M.   25
 see also Black-and-Scholes model
SDEs *see* stochastic differential equations
self-financing continuous-time strategy, hedging
      errors   103–4, 276, 419, 445–6, 502–3,
      565
semi-martingales   33–4, 353–4, 391, 453–5
semi-static information, smiles   204
sequentials   28
serial options   19–20, 89, 622, 635–6
Shimko, D.C.   252
Shiryaev, A.N.   453
Shleifer, A.   9, 10, 25
shocks   400–1, 440, 749, 756
short-rate lattices, mean reversion   612–22
short-rate unconditional variance,
      Black–Derman–Toy model   612–22
short-rate-based interest-rate models   604–23,
      625–6
short-term direction, price series   3–4
Shreve, S.   150
Sidenius, J.   685
skewness, smiles   204–7, 209–22, 227–35, 260,
      267–92, 361–73, 439–41, 515–17, 522–7,
      553–61, 575–81, 726, 743–9, 793–803
slippage concepts   106, 111–13, 121–9, 247–8,
      418–27, 441–4, 499–509, 796–7
smiles   6–7, 18, 26, 93–9, 129, 151, 165–599,
      701–803
 see also future surfaces; implied volatility
 admissible surfaces   583–4

smiles *(continued)*
  amplitude jump–diffusion models   241–2,
    257–8, 270–2, 315–16, 443–5, 561,
    582–99, 797–8
  asymmetric smiles   204–7, 209–35, 260,
    267–92, 309–14, 333–8, 358–73, 391,
    439–41, 494–9, 515–17, 522–7, 553–61,
    575–81, 743–9, 793–801
  calibration   168–9, 184–99, 249–92,
    427–37, 759–64
  case studies   169–73, 187–99, 307–17,
    564–99
  closed-form solutions   179–80, 403–37,
    564–99, 734
  concepts   166, 167–99, 201–35, 237–92,
    333–8, 346–87, 389–441, 522–7, 783–803
  constant elasticity variance   730–49, 756
  continuous double barriers   564–75
  current surfaces   584–5
  definition   168–9
  deterministic smiles   585–93, 755–6
  direct density modelling   245
  direct dynamic information   204–5, 563–99
  direct static information   203–4
  displaced diffusions   553–61, 587, 589–91,
    597, 742–9, 754–64, 771
  empirical data   180, 201–35, 238, 265–77,
    287–92, 334–44, 355–68, 385–6, 389,
    416–44, 511–28, 597–8, 703–27, 742–9,
    767–803
  equities   6, 26, 165–99, 206–22, 227, 235,
    244–5, 255, 268–9, 291–2, 309–14,
    361–73, 385–6, 389–401, 416–44, 553–61,
    575–81, 768
  equivalent deterministic future smiles   595–9
  floating smiles   7, 178–84, 204, 220–2,
    312–17, 342, 348–50, 373–5, 381, 439–44,
    563, 573–5, 581–99
  foreign exchange   165–99, 222–6, 227–35,
    244–5, 287–92, 309–14, 358–62, 369–73,
    440–1, 557, 767–81, 791–801
  forward rates   180–4, 342, 703–803
  forward-propagated smiles   563, 573–5, 581,
    592–9
  fully stochastic-volatility models   237–9,
    276–7, 320, 439–41
  generalized beta of the second kind   275–92,
    354–5
  indirect information   205–6
  infinite accuracy   174–5
  input data   249–92, 307–17, 334–44,
    346–87, 406–16, 427–37, 575–81, 752,
    783–803
  interest rates   168–9, 222–6, 235, 244–5,
    287–92, 334–8, 362, 366–8, 372–3,
    553–61, 621–2, 701–803

jump–diffusion   6, 98–9, 184–5, 197, 224–6,
  227–35, 239–48, 251, 257–8, 265–77,
  295–317, 355, 372, 405, 427, 473,
  484–509, 523, 560–1, 582–99
LIBOR market model   730–803
log-normal co-ordinates   703–27, 741–2
market information   203–6, 249–92, 687
maturity   7, 167, 209–22, 229–35, 238–9,
  242–4, 251–92, 337–8, 347–51, 427–41,
  486–509, 523–7, 576–80, 761–801
mixed jump–diffusion processes   295–317,
  443–509
monotonic ('Interest-Rate') smiles   222–6,
  335, 338–44, 362, 366–8, 372–3, 442,
  668–9, 800–1
no-arbitrage conditions   375–85, 441–4,
  563–99
non-process-based models   563–99
overview   166–8
pre-processed inputs   249–92
quadratic variation   245–8, 293–317
qualitative jump–diffusion features   494–9
qualitative stochastic-volatility features
  405–16, 499
real-world situation   184–99, 205–6, 250–92,
  441–4, 467, 511–12, 518–19, 597–8,
  790–8
restricted-stochastic-volatility models
  239–41, 243–4, 276–7, 315, 319–44,
  346–87, 440, 572–5, 580–1
risk   183–99, 203–5, 206, 209–22, 227–41,
  245, 250–92, 315, 346–87, 406–16, 440–1,
  485–509, 518–19, 553–9, 575–81, 586–99,
  752, 790–8
risk-neutral density   206, 209–22, 227–35,
  245, 256–92, 315, 346–87, 406–16, 440–1,
  485–509, 518–19, 553–9, 575–81, 586–99,
  752, 790–8
same-expiry options   7
semi-static information   204
steepness   6, 7, 18, 98–9, 169–76, 180–4,
  242, 309–10, 405, 436, 439–42, 499,
  507–9, 523–7
sticky smiles   7, 178–84, 204, 220–2, 342,
  348–50, 373–5, 381, 573–5, 581–99
stochastic-volatility models   95, 98, 179–80,
  185, 237–41, 242–8, 265–77, 293–317,
  333–44, 346–87, 389–441, 499, 523, 527,
  560–1, 581–99, 715–16, 751–64, 771–81,
  783–803
surface dynamics   7, 18, 99, 129, 169–84,
  202–3, 206–35, 238–317, 333–44, 346–87,
  399–444, 485–517, 522–7, 553–99,
  703–803

surface-fitting input data   249–92, 307–17,
    334–44, 346–87, 406–16, 427–37, 575–81,
    752, 756–64, 783–803
symmetric smiles   204–7, 209–22, 227–35,
    260, 267–92, 309–14, 333–8, 358–62,
    369–73, 385, 439–41, 494–9, 515–17,
    522–7, 575–81, 743–9, 793–801
tales   180–4, 199, 223, 441–4, 467
transformed-prices concepts   254
unwinding costs   570–5
variance–gamma process   243–4, 247,
    265–77, 511–28, 587
volatility-regime-switching considerations
    703–27, 751, 785–803
smirks   213–16, 517, 527
    see also asymmetric smiles
spot prices, future volatility   19, 76–84, 87–9
spot processes
    Monte Carlo simulation   91, 93
    volatility   19, 76–84, 87–9
spot quantities, forward quantities   76–84, 87–9
spot rates, future volatility   19, 76–84, 87–9
spread options   4, 25–6, 141, 172–3, 417–18
    correlation   141
standard deviation   35–6, 42–8, 72, 108,
    111–12, 122–6, 214–15, 265–77, 422–4,
    473, 476, 505–9, 742–9
state price densities, concepts   323
state probabilities, security-dependent issues   49
static information, smiles   203–4, 782
static portfolio replication, concepts   511–12,
    564–99
Stegun, I.A.   284, 734
sticky smiles   7, 178–84, 204, 220–2, 342,
    348–50, 373–5, 381, 573–5, 581–99
'sticky-delta' smiles, concepts   595
stochastic calculus
    definitions   151–3
    recommended reading   150
stochastic differential equations (SDEs), concepts
    33–4, 81–4, 390–401, 453–5, 605–6,
    611–12, 627–8, 663, 705–6, 730–1,
    736–40, 755
stochastic evolution
    future smiles   582–99, 767–803
    imperfectly correlated variables   146–50
    terminal correlation   151–64, 780–1
stochastic floating smiles, concepts   594–9
stochastic integrals, definitions   151–3
stochastic smiles   593–9
stochastic time, variance–gamma process
    513–28
stochastic-volatility models   5, 17, 20, 31, 32,
    95–9, 153, 237–41, 242–8, 265–77,
    294–441, 449, 456–9, 470, 512–13, 521,
    523, 527, 560, 715–30, 751–66, 771–803

see also fully...; local volatility
closed-form solutions   179–80, 403–37, 532
criticisms   405
displaced diffusions   560, 754–64, 771
future smiles   416–37, 439–41, 499, 581–99,
    767–803
general considerations   319–20, 389–437
hedged with stock and an option   392–5,
    418–19, 449, 459
hedged with stock only   389–92, 418–19, 449
high-volatility regime   404–6, 436, 439–40,
    523, 527, 732–5, 778
jump–diffusion models   242, 243–4, 312–16,
    319, 355, 372, 398, 405, 427–37, 449, 456,
    458–9, 470, 499, 582–99
LIBOR market model   530, 751–67, 771–81,
    783–803
mean reversion   401–16, 419–37, 465,
    751–6, 765–6, 781–2
partial differential equations   393–5
portfolio replication   389–401, 418–37, 449,
    458–9, 582–99
quadratic variation   99, 102–3, 246–8,
    293–317, 352–4, 404–5, 418–37
qualitative smile features   405–16, 499
risk-neutral valuation   320, 326, 389–437,
    440–1, 456, 470, 765–7, 790–8
smiles   95, 98, 179–80, 185, 237–41, 242–8,
    265–77, 293–317, 333–44, 346–87,
    389–441, 499, 523, 527, 560–1, 581–99,
    715–16, 751–64, 771–81, 783–803
two-regime instantaneous volatility   783–803
stock *see* underlying
stopping times, concepts   450–1
STOXX50 207, 211–15, 219–20
straddles   203–5, 576–80
strangles   93–5, 227–35, 575
stressed parameters, stochastic-volatility portfolio
    replication   420–7
strike   89–93, 167–99, 249–92, 319–87, 441,
    470–509, 523–61, 582–99, 703–27, 743–9,
    803
    see also smiles
Student copula   168–9
Sundaram, R.K.   239, 439
super-hedges   103–4
supply/demand imbalances   20–7, 187–99,
    399–401, 687
swap spreads   25–6
swaps   4, 18, 24, 29, 226, 258, 654–86, 704–27
swaption matrix
    concepts   765–82, 784, 788–801
    correlation   771–81, 784–801
    dynamics   765–82
    empirical data   767–81, 784–801

swaption matrix *(continued)*
principal components analysis 766–7, 771–81, 788
quality assessments 766–71
swaptions 7, 18, 19–27, 76, 141, 145, 149, 198, 222, 224–6, 610–22, 626–37, 648–700, 704–27, 759–803
caplet volatilities 626–66, 680–6, 759–64, 788–801
correlation 141, 145, 149, 626–37, 648–66, 687–700, 766–82
implied volatility 224–6, 630–1, 704–27, 732–49, 759–801
instantaneous volatility 667–86, 687–700, 771, 777–81, 783–803
LIBOR market model 626–37, 648–700, 732–49, 759–803
long optionality 22
modes of deformation 7, 27, 576–7, 796–8
switching of numeraires, concepts 52–3, 58–65, 71–3, 748, 751
symmetric smiles 204–7, 209–22, 227–35, 260, 267–92, 309–14, 333–8, 358–62, 369–73, 385, 439–41, 494–9, 515–17, 522–7, 575–81, 743–9, 793–801
synthetic option prices, surface-fitting input data 250–1, 797

Talbot, J. 227
Taylor approximation 740
tensions, risk management 12–14, 441
term structure of volatility 7, 17, 87–9, 120–1, 607–22, 625–6, 632, 639, 667–86, 715–16, 754–6, 763–4
instantaneous volatility 668–71, 715–16, 754–6, 763–4
LIBOR market model 625–6, 632, 639, 667–86, 754–6, 763–4
time-homogeneity imposition 677–86, 754–6, 763–4
terminal correlation 141–64, 626–37, 648–66, 687–700, 780–1
case studies 151–64
concepts 75–6, 141–64, 626, 687–8, 780–1
European options 153–5
importance 145–6, 687–8
joint evolution 151–64
path-dependent options 155–64, 739
properties 161–2
stochastic variable joint evolution 151–64, 780–1
time-dependent volatility 145, 648, 687–8
terminal payoff, discounted expectations 36–73, 105–6, 120–1, 329–44, 532–3, 567–75
Theis, J. 145

theta 109–10, 116–27, 148–9, 204, 276–7, 359–61, 376–85, 516–17, 620
three-dimensional graphs, complexity issues 768
three-factor interest-rate models 646–51, 653–66
Tikhonov's approach 343
tiltings, expectations 69–70, 184, 406, 796
time decay (theta) 109–10, 116–27, 148–9, 204, 359–61, 376–85, 516–17, 620
time series
implied volatility 204–5, 706–27, 765–6, 797
Markov chains 785–7
time to expiry, Black-and-Scholes model 168–99, 350
time value of money, options 109–10, 116–19, 331
time-dependent volatility 37, 80–9, 101, 144–64, 335–6, 355–6, 359–87, 399–400, 439–41, 687–700
correlation 144–64, 687–700
hedging 80–4, 101, 116–27, 399–400
plain-vanilla options 80–4, 101, 116–21, 335–6, 355–87
root-mean-squared volatility 84–7, 122–7
sources 687–8
term structure of volatility 667–86, 754–6, 763–4
terminal correlation 145, 648, 687–8
trading the gamma 116–21, 400
time-homogeneity 348–50, 385, 401, 436, 439, 512–13, 621–2, 677–86, 752, 754–6, 763–4
total variance
concepts 88–9, 120–1, 130–1, 135–9, 296–317, 500–2
hedging 88–9, 120–1, 130–1, 135–9, 296–317, 500–2
instantaneous volatility 135–9
quadratic variation 130–1, 143, 296–317
tower law, concepts 57, 73
traders 10–11, 14–17, 25, 111, 441, 512, 563–99, 796–8
see also fund managers; pseudo-arbitrageurs
relative-value traders 10–11, 14–17, 25, 111, 441, 512
risk aversion 9–10, 20, 34–6, 44–6, 69–73, 122–3, 183–99, 396–401, 419–44, 464–70, 500–2, 518–19, 522–3, 752, 795–8, 803
risk management 11–14, 441, 796–8
'the trader's dream' 580–99
types 14–17, 25, 441, 512
trading the gamma
concepts 108–21, 180–4, 189–99, 202, 400, 512
constant volatility 114–16, 117–21

exceptional price moves 111–13
  time-dependent volatility 116–21, 400
trading restrictions, hedging 102–4
trading time, concepts 512–13
tranched credit derivatives 4, 141, 168–9
transaction costs 102, 125–6, 129, 138, 172–3,
  247, 314, 401, 417, 567
transformed prices, concepts 254
transition matrix, concepts 785–803
trigger swaps 258, 640, 654–6
trinomial trees, local-volatility models 321–44,
  346, 352, 572–3
true arbitrage 346, 598, 622
  see also arbitrage
true call price functional, Black-and-Scholes
  model 174–6
trust issues, pseudo-arbitrageurs 10–11
Tversky, A. 44, 188
two-factor interest-rate models 640–66
two-regime instantaneous volatility
  see also Markov chains
  LIBOR market model extension 783–803
two-state branching procedures
  justification 65–8
  payoff replication 38–73
two-state Markov chains
  see also Markov chains
  concepts 782–803

UK
  GBP market 668–86, 761–4
  supply/demand imbalances 24–5
uncertainty sources, hedging 4–5, 103–4,
  193–4, 237–41, 399–401, 441, 464
underlying 5–8, 76–7, 151–64, 167–99,
  202–35, 249–344, 347–9, 389–509,
  511–12, 518–19, 530–2, 564–99, 703–27,
  753, 765–82, 800–1
unwinding costs, continuous double barriers
  570–5
US, mortgage-backed securities 22, 198
USD market 732, 754, 767–81, 791–801
utility functions
  concepts 187–99, 397, 466–7, 471–2, 501,
  522–3
  displacement coefficients 188–99
utility maximization 44, 187–99, 397

value at risk (VaR) 8, 11, 25
variance 4, 17–18, 35–46, 65–73, 95, 96, 99,
  101–64, 243–4, 247, 260–77, 296–317,
  441, 471–95, 500–2, 512–28, 608–9,
  612–22
  balance-of-variance condition 85

constant elasticity variance 181–4, 344, 389,
  406, 440–1, 529–34, 553, 560, 597, 704–6,
  718–27, 729–56, 781–2
covariance 17–18, 29, 87, 158–64, 628–31,
  642–66, 689–700, 760–82, 785–803
infinite variance 66
jump ratios 471–95, 504–9, 561, 797–8
logarithm of the instantaneous short rate
  616–23, 625–6
logarithm variance 65–8, 616–23, 625–6
quadratic-variation contrasts 609
real-world situation 35–6, 41–8, 50, 69, 73,
  101–39, 143, 441–4, 471–2, 511–12,
  518–19, 522–3, 527, 608–9
risk-adjusted situation 101–39, 471–2
short-rate unconditional Black–Derman–Toy
  variance 612–22
total variance 88–9, 120–1, 130–1, 135–9,
  296–317, 500–2
volatility 82, 85, 243–4
variance–gamma process 95, 96, 99, 243–4,
  247, 265–77, 511–28, 587
  advantages 512–13, 522, 527–8
  brute-force pricing approach 519–21
  concepts 511–28
  critique 512–13, 522, 527–8
  definition 513–14
  jump sizes 514–18
  motivations 517–19
  performance comparisons 523
  properties 514–17
  real-world situation 511–12, 518–19, 522–3,
  527
  risk-neutral density 516–17, 518–23, 527
  semi-analytic solution 520–1, 561
  semi-brute-force pricing approach 520–1,
  561
  smiles 243–4, 247, 265–77, 511–28, 587
  statistical properties of equity indices
  512–13, 522–7
  stock-process properties 518–19
Vasicek interest-rate model 44, 607
vega hedging
  see also out-of-model hedging
  concepts 8–9, 14–18, 27, 90–3, 104,
  169–76, 182–3, 189–99, 202–3, 246, 371,
  400–1, 417, 419, 422–7, 431–7, 442–4,
  503–12, 662, 763, 783, 796–8
  critique 8–9, 662
  delta hedging 8–9, 169–73, 419
  future costs 9, 18, 371, 385, 417, 431–7, 763
  future transactions 15–18, 27, 246, 417,
  431–7, 783
vibrational prices 108–9, 131, 143
  quadratic variation 131, 143
  trading the gamma concepts 108–9

volatilities
 see also implied. . .; instantaneous. . .;
  stochastic. . .; time-dependent. . .
 average volatility 89, 102, 116, 213–14,
  370–3, 418–37, 502–9
 Black-and-Scholes model 168–99
 constant volatility 90–1, 101, 106–16,
  117–21, 147–8, 285–7, 334, 355–7, 389,
  419–37, 598, 737–9
 current volatility 76, 87–9
 deterministic volatility 15, 20, 31, 32–6,
  95–9, 129, 153, 188–99, 203, 245–8,
  294–328, 333–4, 389–405, 418–37,
  453–65, 470, 491–9, 502–9, 513, 568–75,
  585–700, 736–49, 754–6, 782, 799–801
 drift changes 69–70, 72–3, 81–2, 104–16,
  131–4, 143, 356–7, 394–405, 454–5, 513,
  530–2, 605–12, 626–8, 736–49, 765–6
 effective volatility theory 321–2
 estimation issues 18–19, 84, 131–4, 343–4,
  346–87
 forward processes 19, 76, 80–9, 417–27
 forward rates 19, 26, 76, 80–4, 87–9,
  148–50, 162–4, 343, 603–37, 640–66,
  667–803
 future volatility 19, 76, 87–9, 189–99,
  416–27, 511–28, 563–99, 752
 GARCH-type estimates 401, 753
 high-volatility regime 404–6, 436, 439–40,
  523, 527, 732–5, 778
 importance 18–19, 80–4, 125–7, 168–9,
  176–8
 LIBOR market model 625–37, 640–700,
  704–5, 729–803
 local volatility 5–6, 88, 98, 116–21, 127,
  143, 177, 181–2, 239–41, 243–4, 276–7,
  315, 319–89, 440, 560–1, 572–5, 580–1
 measure-invariance observations 69–73
 prices 19, 34–6, 396–401
 regime-switching considerations 703–27,
  751, 785–803

 relative pricing 17–18, 178
 residual volatility concepts 244–5, 296–317
 root-mean-squared volatility 80–91, 116,
  118, 122–9, 131, 155, 159–61, 189–99,
  238, 245–8, 265, 293–317, 419–37, 503–9,
  665, 737, 756, 790–5
 spot processes 19, 76–84
 term structure of volatility 7, 17, 87–9,
  120–1, 607–22, 625–6, 632, 639, 667–86,
  715–16, 754–6, 763–4
 variance 82, 85, 243–4
 wrong volatility 125–7, 174–8, 347, 352–3,
  400, 422–37, 718
 zero levels 732–3, 756
volatility smiles *see* smiles

well-posed problems, concepts 343–4
Wiener process 151–2
Wilmott, P. 327, 346, 354
wrong volatility, hedging 125–7, 174–8, 347,
  352–3, 400, 422–37, 718
Wu, L. 213, 215–16, 220, 371–2, 440

yield curves 4–5, 14, 29, 143–6, 225–6,
  604–5, 610, 625–37, 640–86, 690–1,
  734–49, 763, 767–81
 correlation 143–6, 625–37, 640–66, 690–1
 Euler scheme 734, 736–49
 foreign exchange 4–5, 29, 143–6, 225–6,
  668–71
 models 14, 29, 143–6, 604–5, 610, 625–37,
  640–86, 734, 763, 767–81
 multi-factor models 143–6, 626–37, 640–66
 shape changes 143–6, 225–6, 604–5, 610,
  640–1
yield enhancement, supply/demand imbalances
  22–4

zero interest rates 252–3, 281–2, 292, 297,
  353–4, 416–17, 483, 564–5, 732–4, 756

Index compiled by Terry Halliday of Indexing Specialists, Hove.